36. Beta from a simple linear regression
$$\beta = [(T \times \textstyle\sum XY) - (\sum Y \times \sum X)] / [(T \times \sum X^2) - (\sum X)^2]$$

37. Alpha from a simple linear regression
$$\alpha = [(\textstyle\sum Y)/T] - [\beta \times (\sum X)/T]$$

38. Standard deviation of the random error term from a simple linear regression
$$\sigma_e = \{[\textstyle\sum Y^2 - (\alpha \times \sum Y) - (\beta \times \sum XY)]/[T-2]\}^{1/2}$$

39. Standard error of beta from a simple linear regression
$$\sigma_\beta = \sigma_e / \{\textstyle\sum X^2 - [(\sum X)^2/T]\}^{1/2}$$

40. Standard error of alpha from a simple linear regression
$$\sigma_\alpha = \sigma_e / \{T - [(\textstyle\sum X)^2 / \sum X^2]\}^{1/2}$$

41. Correlation coefficient
$$\rho = [(T \times \textstyle\sum XY) - (\sum Y \times \sum X)] / \{[(T \times \sum Y^2) - (\sum Y)^2] \times [(T \times \sum X^2) - (\sum X)^2]\}^{1/2}$$

42. Beta of the firm
$$\beta_{firm} = \beta_{debt}[(1-\tau)D/V_u] + \beta_{equity}(E/V_u)$$

43. Beta of the firm's equity
$$\beta_{equity} = \beta_{firm} + (\beta_{firm} - \beta_{debt})(D/E)(1-\tau)$$

44. Adjusted historical beta
$$\beta_a = a + b\beta_h$$

45. Capitalization-of-income method of valuation
$$V = \sum_{t=1}^{\infty} [C_t/(1+k)^t]$$

46. Zero-growth DDM
$$V = D_1/k$$

47. Constant-growth DDM
$$V = D_1/(k-g)$$

48. Multiple-growth DDM
$$V = [\sum_{t=1}^{T} D_t/(1+k)^t] + [D_{T+1}/(k-g) \times (1+k)^T]$$

49. "Normal" price-earnings ratio with constant growth
$$V/E_0 = p\{[1 + r(1-p)]/[k - r(1-p)]\}$$

50. Lintner dividend payout model
$$D_t = ap^*E_t + (1-a)D_{t-1}$$

51. Annual earnings as a random walk
$$E_t = E_{t-1} + \epsilon_t$$

52. Quarterly earnings as an autoregressive process
$$QE_t = QE_{t-4} + a(QE_{t-1} - QE_{t-5}) + b + e_t$$

53. Intrinsi
$$IV_C = M$$
$$IV_P = M$$

54. Put-call parity
$$P_P + P_S = P_C + E/e^{RT}$$

55. Black-Scholes formula for the fair value of a call option
$$V_C = N(d_1)P_S - (E/e^{RT})N(d_2)$$
$$d_1 = [\ln(P_S/E) + (R + .5\sigma^2)T]/\sigma\sqrt{T}$$
$$d_2 = [\ln(P_S/E) + (R - .5\sigma^2)T]/\sigma\sqrt{T}$$
$$\quad = d_1 - \sigma\sqrt{T}$$

56. Black-Scholes formula for the fair value of a put option
$$P_P = (E/e^{RT})N(-d_2) - P_S N(-d_1)$$

57. Fair value of a futures contract
$$P_f = P_S + I - B + C$$

58. Fair value of an index futures contract
$$P_f = P_S + RP_S - yP_S$$

59. Investment company's net asset value
$$NAV_t = (MVA_t - LIAB_t)/NSO_t$$

60. Return on an investment company's shares
$$r_t = [(NAV_t - NAV_{t-1}) + I_t + G_t]/NAV_{t-1}$$

61. Risk tolerance (as implied by a choice of a portfolio)
$$\tau = [2(\bar{r}_C - r_f)\sigma_S^2]/(\bar{r}_S - r_f)^2$$

62. Certainty equivalent return
$$u_i = \bar{r}_p - (1/\tau)\sigma_p^2$$

63. Ex post alpha
$$\alpha_p = ar_p - ar_{fp}$$

64. Ex post alpha based on the CAPM
$$\alpha_p = ar_p - [ar_f + (ar_M - ar_f)\beta_p]$$

65. Ex post characteristic line
$$r_p - r_f = \alpha_p + \beta_p(r_M - r_f)$$

66. Reward-to-volatility ratio (Treynor ratio)
$$RVOL_p = (ar_p - ar_f)/\beta_p$$

67. Reward-to-variability ratio (Sharpe ratio)
$$RVAR_p = (ar_p - ar_f)/\sigma_p$$

68. Ex post characteristic curve
$$r_p - r_f = a + b(r_M - r_f) + c[(r_M - r_f)^2]$$

69. Ex post characteristic lines
$$r_p - r_f = a + b(r_M - r_f) + c[D(r_M - r_f)]$$
$$\text{where: } D = 0 \text{ if } r_M > r_f$$
$$\quad\quad\quad D = -1 \text{ if } r_M < r_f$$

70. Return on a foreign investment
$$r_f = r_d + r_c + r_d r_c$$

71. Standard deviation of a foreign investment
$$\sigma_f = (\sigma_d^2 + \sigma_c^2 + 2\rho_{dc}\sigma_d\sigma_c)^{1/2}$$

FIFTH EDITION

INVESTMENTS

WILLIAM F. SHARPE
Stanford University

GORDON J. ALEXANDER
University of Minnesota

JEFFERY V. BAILEY
Richards & Tierney, Inc.

 Prentice Hall, Englewood Cliffs, New Jersey 07632

Library of Congress Cataloging-in-Publication Data

Sharpe, William F.
  Investments / William F. Sharpe, Gordon J. Alexander, Jeffery V. Bailey. — 5th ed.
    p. cm.
  Includes bibliographical references and index.
  ISBN 0-13-103771-4 (alk. paper). — ISBN 0-13-183344-8 (alk. paper)
  1. Investments. 2. Investment analysis. I. Alexander, Gordon J., 1947– . II. Bailey, Jeffery V. III. Title.
  HG4521.S48 1995
  332.63'2—dc20   94-40167
                                                                              CIP

Produced for Prentice Hall Inc. by Visual Education Corporation, Princeton, New Jersey.
Production Supervisor: Amy Davis
In-house Project Liaison: Alana Zdinak
Acquisitions Editor: Leah Jewell
Interior Design: Circa 86
Cover Design: Rosemarie Paccione
Design Director: Linda Fiordilino
Copyediting Supervisor: Margaret P. Roeske
Proofreading Management: William A. Murray
Manufacturing Buyer: Patrice Fraccio
Assistant Editor: Teresa Cohan

Cover Photograph: William Whitehurst, Global Industry
              The Stock Market

©1995 by Prentice Hall, Inc.
A Simon and Schuster Company
Englewood Cliffs, New Jersey 07632

Printed in the United States of America

10 9 8 7 6 5 4 3 2 1

ISBN 0-13-103771-4

Prentice-Hall International (UK) Limited, *London*
Prentice-Hall of Australia Pty. Limited, *Sydney*
Prentice-Hall Canada Inc., *Toronto*
Prentice-Hall Hispanoamericana, S.A., *Mexico*
Prentice-Hall of India Private Limited, *New Delhi*
Prentice-Hall of Japan, Inc. *Tokyo*
Simon & Schuster Asia Pte. Ltd., *Singapore*
Editoria Prentice-Hall do Brasil, Ltda., *Rio de Janeiro*

To Kathy
WFS

To my mother and in memory
of my father
GJA

To Stephen and Megan
JVB

BRIEF CONTENTS

CONTENTS

Contents

Contents

Investment management once seemed a simple process. Well-heeled investors would hold portfolios composed, for the most part, of the stocks and bonds of "blue chip" U.S. industrial companies, as well as U.S. Treasury bonds, notes, and bills. The choices available to less well-off investors were much more limited, confined primarily to passbook savings accounts and U.S. Savings Bonds. If the investment environment can be thought of as an ice cream parlor, then the customers of past decades were offered only chocolate and vanilla.

Mirroring the diversity of modern society, the investment ice cream parlor now makes available a myriad of "flavors" to the investing public. Investors face a dizzying array of choices. The stocks and bonds of large U.S.-based companies and the debt securities of the U.S. Treasury remain the predominant favorites. However, to mention only a few additional choices, investors can now own the stocks of small U.S.-based companies, the stocks and bonds of companies headquartered from London to Auckland, high-yield bonds, collateralized mortgage obligations, floating-rate notes, swaps, puts, calls, and futures contracts. The list is seemingly endless, and it continues to grow. Furthermore, the ability to purchase these securities has become both increasingly less expensive and more convenient with the advent of advanced communications and computer networks, along with the proliferating market for mutual funds that has developed to serve large and small investors alike.

The difficulty of writing a textbook on investing has increased as the investment environment has become more complex. Virtually all types of securities, be they traditional or of recent origin, merit at least some discussion. The challenge to us as textbook writers therefore is daunting. We must enumerate and describe the various securities and markets in a clear and concise manner that appropriately blends theory and practice. However, with the rapid evolution that the investment industry is undergoing, we must also present a discussion of new investment management techniques. Preventing the textbook from reaching encyclopedic proportions thus becomes a difficult project in itself.

The subject matter for this edition of *Investments* has evolved considerably since 1978 when the first edition was published. For example, in the last several years international investing has expanded rapidly, securities such as swaps and mortgage derivatives have become increasingly popular, and investors have placed much more emphasis on investment "styles." Our task has been to keep *Investments* fresh and stimulating and to continue to offer students and instructors the most thorough survey of the investment environment available. We believe that we have accomplished these objectives and hope that you agree.

We designed *Investments* for advanced undergraduate and graduate students. In doing so, we assumed that such students would have been exposed to basic economics, accounting, statistics, and algebra. Furthermore, it is our belief that serious students of investments should receive a balanced presentation of theory and practical information without being burdened by excessive details. A textbook that focuses solely on institutional features leaves students unable to appreciate the subtle and important issues faced by investment professionals.

Some people will wonder how *Investments* compares with the recently published *Fundamentals of Investments* that we have also written. Although both are intended to be comprehensive, they are dissimilar in two significant ways. First, they are organized differently. *Investments* is written in an integrated fashion, whereas *Fundamentals* is more modular in design. Second, *Investments* is somewhat more theoretical and technical than *Fundamentals*.

As any textbook author will attest, a previous work can always be improved—even one that has been in existence as long as this one. Over the years we have received many helpful suggestions from instructors and reviewers regarding ways in which we can make *Investments* better. In each new edition we have tried to enhance the book's breadth and presentation style. In this, the fifth edition, we have implemented the following improvements from the previous edition:

- **More international content.** The globalization of the investment industry is proceeding at a rapid pace. It is imperative that students become familiar with an increasingly diverse set of international investing concepts. Chapter 26 deals directly with international investing. Moreover, throughout the text we have expanded the discussions of international securities and security markets.

- **Expanded coverage of options and futures and the introduction of swaps.** The use of these types of derivative securities has become commonplace among institutional investors. Accordingly, Chapters 20 and 21 have been extended in order to more fully present the basic concepts underlying options and futures. In addition, Chapter 24 contains an introduction to swaps.

- **Updated material.** Where appropriate, we have updated the text to keep students abreast of the latest developments in investments. We have revised tables and graphs to incorporate current information. Furthermore, we have added discussions of recent important academic research.

- **Additional end-of-chapter problems.** We have roughly doubled the number of questions and problems at the end of each chapter.

- **CFA examination questions.** To give students a sense of the knowledge required of certified investment professionals, we have added questions, where appropriate, from recent Chartered Financial Analyst examinations.

- **Answers to selected problems.** Students often wish to know if they are working in the right direction when solving end-of-chapter problems. At the end of the text, we have included answers to selected problems.

- **Redesigned chapter summaries.** To facilitate a quick review of a chapter's highlights, we have rewritten each chapter's summary in an easy-to-read bulleted format.

- **Institutional Issues.** Students typically want to know how the concepts presented in the text are applied in the "real world." In each chapter, we have added a feature entitled Institutional Issues that offers discussions concerning issues that face large institutional investors, such as pension funds and mutual funds.

- **Annotated references.** For those students who are interested in further study of subjects presented in the text, at the end of each chapter we have included an extensive set of references organized by topic.

- **New co-author.** Jeff Bailey, who contributed to the fourth edition, is now a co-author. Jeff, a CFA and a full-time practitioner with a pension fund consulting firm, has brought a wealth of knowledge about how things are done "in the trenches."

Investments contains several teaching aids that we believe instructors will find valuable. The terms highlighted within the text and listed at the end of each chapter help emphasize important concepts. The glossary allows students to quickly reference terms listed earlier in the text, thereby creating a continuity of concepts across chapters. The bulleted summaries permit students to easily identify the essential thoughts developed in each chapter.

We are particularly proud of the Institutional Issues features presented in each chapter. Specifically written for *Investments*, they are designed to give students a sense of how various investment issues and techniques are applied by practitioners. For example, the Chapter 2 feature discusses how institutional investors create market neutral portfolios utilizing short selling. The Chapter 24 feature considers how pension funds go about structuring groups of money managers to achieve specific investment objectives. The Chapter 26 feature describes the controversial issue of whether or not to hedge the currency risk of an international portfolio. Furthermore, Ann Guenther Sherman of the Hong Kong University of Science and Technology has written two Institutional Issues features that deal with investing in Hong Kong and the People's Republic of China, which we view as the ultimate emerging market—particularly after 1997 when Hong Kong becomes part of the PRC. In summary, we believe that the Institutional Issues features will provide both interesting reading for the students and a stimulating source of classroom discussion material.

An extended supplements package also accompanies *Investments*. Included in this package are:

- Instructor's Manual. Solutions to all end-of-chapter problems are presented in a thorough and well-explained fashion. Also, a set of course outlines that are designed to accommodate a variety of teaching approaches is presented.
- Tutorial Software. This software is available at a discount price.
- Test Item File and Prentice Hall DataManager. The Test Item File gives an instructor access to hundreds of exam questions (true/false, multiple choice, and problems) and their solutions. The Prentice Hall DataManager facilitates classroom management with a computer-assisted test design system and an electronic gradebook.
- Disclosure Information Service. Designed to enhance the classroom experience, the Compact D\SEC Academic Edition combines the most recent, detailed information on 100 SEC-filing public companies with advanced search software to produce a fast, easy, real-world teaching tool that resides on your personal computer.

Many people have assisted us in preparing the fifth edition of this book, and we would like to acknowledge them as well of those who helped us with earlier editions. Specifically, we would like to thank Seth Anderson, Ted Aronson, Ann Bailey, Ed Baker, Michael Barclay, Kenneth S. Bartunek, Jeffrey Born, E. Taylor Claggett, James Conley, Thomas Eyssell, Joe Finnerty, Charlie Freund, Ping Hsiao, Robert Jennings, Lee Jones, Steven L. Jones, Douglas R. Kahi, Ed Keon, Jaroslaw Komarynsky, Linda Kramer, K. C. Ma, S. Maheswaren, Linda J. Martin, Carl McGowan, Ronald Melicher, Tom Nohel, Thomas O'Brien, Martha Ortiz, James A. Overdahl, Lynne Pi, Maggie Queen, Sailesh Ramamurtie, Anthony Sanders, Frederick P. Schadler, Jandhyala L. Sharma, Arlene Spiegel, Len Washko, Robert Wolf, Steve Wunsch, Fernando Zapatero, Emilio Zarruk and Ken Zumwalt.

We would like to give a special thank you to the partners at Richards & Tierney—Tommie Huie, Charlie McPike, Ann Posey, Tom Richards, and Dave Tierney—for their considerable patience and support, and to Ann Guenther Sherman for writing the two previously mentioned Institutional Issues features. We are also especially grateful to the people at Visual Education Corporation, particularly Peggy Roeske and Amy Davis, and at Prentice Hall, particularly Leah Jewell, acquisition editor, Teresa Cohan, assistant editor, Susan McLaughlin, marketing manager, and Alana Zdinak, production editor, for their work in preparing the text for publication.

We learned much by writing this book and hope that you will learn much by reading it. Although we have done our best to eliminate errors from the book, experience tells us that perfection is unattainable. Thus we encourage those students and instructors with constructive comments to send them to us.

WFS
GJA
JVB

William F. Sharpe

William F. Sharpe is currently Professor of Finance at the Stanford University Graduate School of Business. Dr. Sharpe has published articles in a number of professional journals, including *Financial Analysts Journal, Journal of Business, Journal of Finance, Journal of Financial and Quantitative Analysis, Journal of Portfolio Management,* and *Management Science.* Dr. Sharpe is past President of the American Finance Association. In 1990 he received the Nobel Prize in Economics. Dr. Sharpe received his A.B., M.A., and Ph.D. degrees in Economics from the University of California at Los Angeles.

Gordon J. Alexander

Gordon J. Alexander is presently the IDS Professor of Finance at the University of Minnesota. Dr. Alexander has published articles in *Financial Management, Journal of Banking and Finance, Journal of Finance, Journal of Financial Economics, Journal of Financial and Quantitative Analysis,* and *Journal of Portfolio Management.* In addition, he has been an Associate Editor of the *Journal of Financial and Quantitative Analysis* and is currently Book Review Editor of the *Journal of Finance.* Dr. Alexander received his Ph.D. in Finance, M.A. in Mathematics, and M.B.A. from the University of Michigan, and his B.S. in Business Administration from the State University of New York at Buffalo.

Jeffery V. Bailey

Jeffery V. Bailey is a Managing Partner of the firm of Richards & Tierney, Inc., a Chicago-based pension fund consulting organization. He was formerly the Assistant Executive Director of the Minnesota State Board of Investment. Mr. Bailey has published articles in *Financial Analysts Journal* and *Journal of Portfolio Management* as well as having contributed articles to the practitioner handbooks *Managing Institutional Assets* and *Pension Fund Investment Management.* Mr. Bailey is a Chartered Financial Analyst. He received his B.A. in Economics from Oakland University and his M.A. in Economics and M.B.A. in Finance from the University of Minnesota.

Introduction

This book is about investing in marketable securities. Accordingly, it focuses on the investment environment and process. The **investment environment** encompasses the kinds of marketable securities that exist and where and how they are bought and sold. The **investment process** is concerned with how an investor should proceed in making decisions about what marketable securities to invest in, how extensive the investments should be, and when the investments should be made. Before discussing the investment environment and process in more detail, the term **investment** will be described.

Investment, in its broadest sense, means the sacrifice of current dollars for future dollars. Two different attributes are generally involved: time and risk. The sacrifice takes place in the present and is certain. The reward comes later, if at all, and the magnitude is generally uncertain. In some cases the element of time predominates (for example, government bonds). In other cases risk is the dominant attribute (for example, call options on common stocks). In yet others, both time and risk are important (for example, shares of common stock).

A distinction is often made between investment and **savings.** Savings is defined as foregone consumption; investment is restricted to "real" investment of the sort that increases national output in the future. While this definition may prove useful in other contexts, it is not especially helpful here. However, it is useful to make a distinction between real and financial investments.

Real investments generally involve some kind of tangible asset, such as land, machinery, or factories. **Financial investments** involve contracts written on pieces of paper, such as common stocks and bonds. In primitive economies most investment is of the real variety, whereas in a modern economy, much investment is of the financial variety. Highly developed institutions for financial investment greatly facilitate real investment. By and large, the two forms of investment are complementary, not competitive.

The financing of an apartment house provides a good example. Apartments are sufficiently tangible ("bricks and mortar") to be considered real investments. But where do the resources come from to pay for the land and the construction of the apartments? Some may come from direct investment. For example, a wealthy doctor who wants to build an apartment house may use some of his or her own money to finance the project. The rest of the resources may be provided by a mortgage. In essence, someone loans money to the doctor, with repayment promised in fixed amounts on a specified schedule over many years. In the typical case the "someone" is not a person, but an institution acting as a financial intermediary. Thus the doctor has made a real investment in the apartment house, and the institution has made a financial investment in the doctor.

For a second example, consider what happens when General Motors finds itself in need of money to pay for plant construction. This real investment may be financed by the sale of new common stock in the **primary market** for securities. The common stock itself represents a financial investment to the purchasers, who may subsequently trade these shares in the **secondary market** (for example, on the New York Stock Exchange). While transactions in the secondary market do not generate money for General Motors, the fact that such a market exists makes the common stock more attractive and thus facilitates real investment. Investors would pay less for new shares of common stock if there were no way to subsequently sell them quickly and inexpensively.

These examples have introduced the three main elements of the investment environment—securities (also known as financial investments or financial assets), security markets (also known as financial markets), and financial intermediaries (also known as financial institutions). They will be discussed in more detail next.

1.1   THE INVESTMENT ENVIRONMENT

1.1.1   Securities

When someone borrows money from a pawnbroker, he or she must leave some item of value as security. Failure to repay the loan (plus interest) means that the pawnbroker can sell the pawned item to recover the amount of the loan (plus interest) and perhaps make a profit. The terms of the agreement are recorded via pawn tickets. When a college student borrows money to buy a car, the lender usually holds formal title to the car until the loan is repaid. In the event of default, the lender can repossess the car and sell it to recover his or her costs. In this case the official certificate of title, issued by the state, serves as the security for the loan.

When someone borrows money for a vacation, he or she may simply sign a piece of paper promising repayment with interest. The loan is unsecured in the sense that there is no collateral, meaning that no specific asset has been promised to the lender in the event of default. In such a situation the lender would have to take the borrower to court to try to recover the amount of the loan. Only a piece of paper called a promissory note stands as evidence of such a loan.

When a firm borrows money, it may or may not offer collateral. For example, some loans may be secured (backed) with specific pieces of property (buildings or equipment). Such loans are recorded by means of mortgage bonds, which indicate the terms of repayment and the particular assets pledged to the lender in the event of default. However, it is much more common for a corporation to simply pledge all of its assets, perhaps with some provision for the manner in which the division will take place in the event of default. Such a promise is known as a debenture bond.

Finally, a firm may promise a right to share in its profits in return for an investor's funds. Nothing is pledged, and no irrevocable promises are made. The firm simply pays whatever its directors deem reasonable from time to time. However, to protect against serious malfeasance, the investor is given the right to participate in the determination of who will be members of the board of directors. The investor's property right is represented by a share of common stock, which can be sold to someone else, who will then be able to exercise that right. The holder of common stock is said to be an *owner* of the corporation and can, in theory, exercise control over its operation through the board of directors.

In general, only a piece of paper represents the investor's rights to certain prospects or property and the conditions under which he or she may exercise those rights. This piece of paper, serving as evidence of property rights, is called a security. It may be transferred to another investor, and with it will go all its rights and conditions. Thus everything from a pawn ticket to a share of GM common stock is a security. Hereafter the term **security** will be used to refer to *a legal representation of the right to receive prospective future benefits under stated conditions.* The primary task of security analysis is to identify mispriced securities by determining these prospective future benefits, the conditions under which they will be received, and the likelihood of such conditions.

By and large the focus here is on securities that may be easily and efficiently transferred from one owner to another. Thus the concern is with common stocks and bonds rather than with pawn tickets, although much of the material in this book applies to all three types of instruments.

Figure 1.1 and Table 1.1 show the year-by-year results obtained from investing in four types of securities over the 68-year period from 1926 through 1993. In each case the percentage change in a hypothetical investor's wealth from the beginning to the end of the year is shown. This amount, known as the **rate of return** (or simply the *return*), is calculated as follows:

$$\text{Return} = \frac{\text{end-of-period wealth} - \text{beginning-of-period wealth}}{\text{beginning-of-period wealth}}. \tag{1.1}$$

In calculating the return on a security, it is assumed that a hypothetical investor purchased one unit of the security (for example, one bond or one share of common stock) at the beginning of the period. The cost of such an investment is the value entered in the denominator of Equation (1.1). Then the value in the numerator is the answer to a simple question—how much better (or worse) off is the investor at the end of the period?

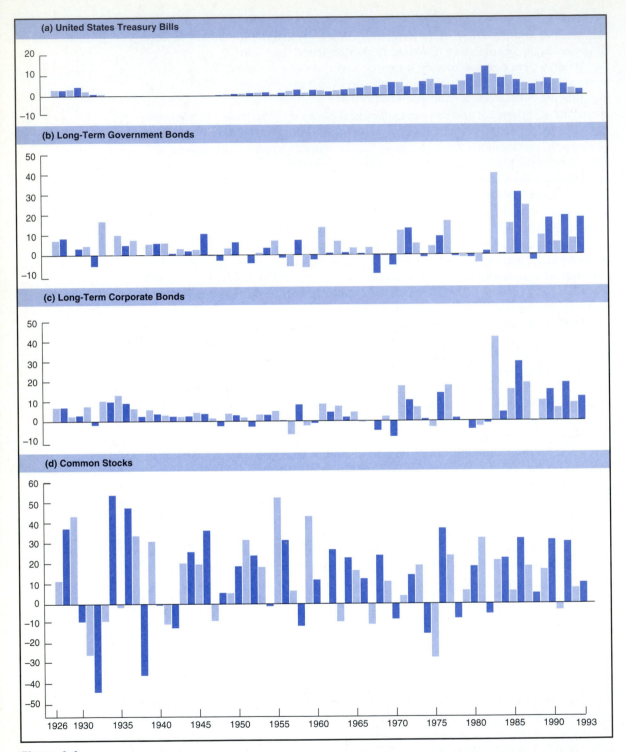

(a) United States Treasury Bills

(b) Long-Term Government Bonds

(c) Long-Term Corporate Bonds

(d) Common Stocks

Figure 1.1

Annual Returns, 1926–1993

Source: *Stocks, Bonds, Bills, and Inflation 1994 Yearbook* (Chicago: Ibbotson Associates, 1994). All rights reserved.

Year	Treasury Bills	Long-Term Government Bonds	Long-Term Corporate Bonds	Common Stocks	Change in CPI
1926	3.27%	7.77%	7.37%	11.62%	−1.49%
1927	3.12	8.93	7.44	37.49	−2.08
1928	3.56	.10	2.84	43.61	−.97
1929	4.75	3.42	3.27	−8.42	.20
1930	2.41	4.66	7.98	−24.90	−6.03
1931	1.07	−5.31	−1.75	−43.34	−9.52
1932	.96	16.84	10.82	−8.19	−10.30
1933	.30	.07	10.38	53.99	.51
1934	.16	10.03	13.84	−1.44	2.03
1935	.17	4.98	9.61	47.67	2.99
1936	.18	7.52	6.74	33.92	1.21
1937	.31	.23	2.75	−35.03	3.10
1938	−.02	5.53	6.13	31.12	−2.78
1939	.02	5.94	3.97	−.41	−.48
1940	.00	6.09	3.39	−9.78	.96
1941	.06	.93	2.73	−11.59	9.72
1942	.27	3.22	2.60	20.34	9.29
1943	.35	2.08	2.83	25.90	3.16
1944	.33	2.81	4.73	19.75	2.11
1945	.33	10.73	4.08	36.44	2.25
1946	.35	−.10	1.72	−8.07	18.16
1947	.50	−2.62	−2.34	5.71	9.01
1948	.81	3.40	4.14	5.50	2.71
1949	1.10	6.45	3.31	18.79	−1.80
1950	1.20	.06	2.12	31.71	5.79
1951	1.49	−3.93	−2.69	24.02	5.87
1952	1.66	1.16	3.52	18.37	.88
1953	1.82	3.64	3.41	−.99	.62
1954	.86	7.19	5.39	52.62	.50
1955	1.57	−1.29	.48	31.56	.37
1956	2.46	−5.59	−6.81	6.56	2.86
1957	3.14	7.46	8.71	−10.78	3.02
1958	1.54	−6.09	−2.22	43.36	1.76
1959	2.95	−2.26	−.97	11.96	1.50
1960	2.66	13.78	9.07	.47	1.48
1961	2.13	.97	4.82	26.89	.67
1962	2.73	6.89	7.95	−8.73	1.22
1963	3.12	1.21	2.19	22.80	1.65
1964	3.54	3.51	4.77	16.48	1.19
1965	3.93	.71	−.46	12.45	1.92
1966	4.76	3.65	.20	−10.06	3.35
1967	4.21	−9.18	−4.85	23.98	3.04
1968	5.21	−.26	2.57	11.06	4.72
1969	6.58	−5.07	−8.09	−7.50	6.11
1970	6.52	12.11	18.37	4.01	5.49
1971	4.39	13.23	11.01	14.31	3.36
1972	3.84	5.69	7.26	18.98	3.41
1973	6.93	−1.11	1.14	−14.66	8.80
1974	8.00	4.35	−3.06	−26.47	12.20
1975	5.80	9.20	14.64	37.20	7.01

1976	5.08%	16.75%	18.65%	23.84%	4.81%
1977	5.12	−.69	1.71	−7.18	6.77
1978	7.18	−1.18	−.07	6.56	9.03
1979	10.38	−1.23	−4.18	18.44	13.31
1980	11.24	−3.85	−2.62	32.42	12.40
1981	14.71	1.86	−.96	−4.91	8.94
1982	10.54	40.36	43.79	21.41	3.87
1983	8.80	.65	4.70	22.51	3.80
1984	9.85	15.48	16.39	6.27	3.95
1985	7.72	30.97	30.90	32.16	3.77
1986	6.16	24.53	19.85	18.47	1.33
1987	5.47	−2.71	−.27	5.23	4.41
1988	6.35	9.67	10.70	16.81	4.42
1989	8.37	18.11	16.23	31.49	4.65
1990	7.81	6.18	6.78	−3.17	6.11
1991	5.60	19.30	19.89	30.55	3.06
1992	3.51	8.05	9.39	7.67	2.90
1993	2.90	18.24	13.19	9.99	2.75
Average return	3.74%	5.36%	5.90%	12.34%	3.25%
Standard deviation	3.32%	8.67%	8.46%	20.44%	4.63%

For example, assume that Widget Corporation's common stock was selling for $40 per share at the beginning of the year and for $45 at the end of the year and paid dividends of $3 per share during the year. The return on Widget for the year would then be calculated as [($45 + $3) − $40]/$40 = .20, or 20%.[1]

Treasury Bills

The first type of security listed in Figure 1.1 involves loaning money on a short-term basis to the U.S. Treasury Department. Such a loan carries little (if any) risk that payment will not be made as promised. Moreover, although the rate of return varies from period to period, at the beginning of any single period it is known with certainty. These investments, called Treasury bills, produced returns ranging from a high of 14.71% per year (in 1981) to a low of virtually zero (actually −.02% in 1938), with an average value of 3.74% during the entire 68-year period.

Long-Term Bonds

The second and third types of securities shown in Figure 1.1 are bonds, and thus also involve loaning money. Each type of bond represents a fairly long-term commitment on the part of the issuer (that is, the borrower) to the investor (that is the lender). This commitment is to make cash payments each year (the coupon amount) up to some point in time (the maturity date) when a single final cash payment (the principal) will also be made. The amount for which such bonds can be bought and sold varies from time to time. Thus, whereas coupon payments are easily predicted, the end-of-period selling price of the security is quite uncertain at the beginning of the period, making it difficult to predict the return in advance.

The second type of security (long-term government bonds) involves approximately 20-year loans to the U.S. Treasury Department and is known as Treasury bonds. The third type of security (long-term corporate bonds) involves 20-year loans to high-quality U.S. corporations and is simply referred to as corporate bonds. To date both types of bonds had their highest annual returns in 1982, reaching 40.36% for government bonds and 43.79% for corporate bonds. However, the lowest annual returns were reached in different years. For government bonds the lowest return occurred in 1967 (-9.18%), whereas the lowest return for corporate bonds was reached in 1969 (-8.09%). Note that on average, government bonds had a higher return than Treasury bills (5.36% > 3.74%), and corporate bonds had a higher return than government bonds (5.90% > 5.36%). Thus, whereas the second and third types of securities have considerable variability, on average they provide somewhat larger returns than Treasury bills.

Common Stocks

The fourth and final type of security is common stocks, which represents a commitment on the part of a corporation to pay periodically whatever its board of directors deems appropriate as a cash dividend. Although the amount of cash dividends to be paid during the next year is subject to some uncertainty, it is relatively predictable. However, the amount for which a stock can be bought or sold varies considerably, making the annual return highly unpredictable. Figure 1.1 shows the return from a portfolio of stocks (currently 500 different firms) selected by Standard & Poor's Corporation to represent the average performance of common stocks. Returns ranged from an exhilarating 53.99% in 1933 to a depressing -43.34% in 1931 and averaged 12.34% per year over the entire period. Such investments can provide substantial returns, being much larger on average than the returns provided by corporate bonds. However, they also have substantial variability as they are much more volatile than either type of long-term bond.

Table 1.1 provides year-by-year annual returns for the four types of securities shown in Figure 1.1. The table also includes the annual percentage change in the Consumer Price Index (CPI) as an indicator of variations in the cost of living. Average annual returns are shown at the bottom of the table. Below these values are the standard deviations of annual returns, which serve as measures of the variability of the returns on the respective securities.[2] Table 1.2 provides average annual returns and standard deviations for securities from the United States, Japan, Germany, and the United Kingdom during the period from 1970 to 1992. The historical record revealed in Figure 1.1, Table 1.1, and Table 1.2 illustrates a general principle: *When sensible investment strategies are compared with one another, risk and return tend to go together.* That is, securities that have higher average returns tend to have greater amounts of risk.

It is important to note that historical variability is not necessarily an indication of prospective risk. The former deals with the record over some past period; the latter has to do with uncertainty about the future. The pattern of returns on Treasury bills provides one example. Although the values have varied from period to period, in any given period the amount to be earned is known in advance and is thus riskless. On the other hand, the annual return on a common stock is very difficult to predict. For such an investment, variability in the past may provide a fairly good measure of the uncertainty surrounding the future return.[3]

To see how difficult it is to predict common stock returns, cover the portion of Table 1.1 from 1941 on, and then try to guess the return in 1941. Having done this, uncover the value for 1941, and try to guess the return for 1942. Proceed in this manner a year at a time, keeping track of your overall predictive accuracy. Unless you are very clever or very lucky, you will conclude that the past pattern of stock returns provides little help in predicting the next year's return. It will later be seen that this apparent randomness in security returns is a characteristic of an **efficient market**—that is, a market where security prices fully reflect information immediately.

Is one of these four types of securities obviously "the best"? No. To oversimplify, the right security or combination of securities depends on the investor's situation and preferences for return relative to his or her distaste for risk. There may be "right" or "wrong" securities for a particular person or purpose. However, it would be surprising indeed to find a security that is clearly wrong for everyone and every purpose. Such situations are simply not present in an efficient market.

1.1.2 Security Markets

Security markets exist in order to bring together buyers and sellers of securities, meaning that they are mechanisms created to facilitate the exchange of financial assets. There are many ways in which security markets can be distinguished. One way has already been mentioned—primary and secondary markets. Here the key distinction is whether or not the securities are being offered for sale by the issuer. Interestingly, the primary market itself can be subdivided into seasoned and unseasoned new issues. A seasoned new issue refers to the offering of an additional amount of an already existing security, whereas an unseasoned new issue involves the initial offering of a security to the public. Unseasoned new issues are often referred to as *initial public offerings*, or *ipo's*.

Another way of distinguishing between security markets considers the life span of financial assets. **Money markets** typically involve financial assets that have life spans of one year or less, whereas **capital markets** typically involve financial assets that have life spans of greater than one year. Thus Treasury bills are traded in a money market, and Treasury bonds are traded in a capital market.

1.1.3 Financial Intermediaries

Financial intermediaries, also known as financial institutions, are organizations that issue financial claims against themselves (meaning that they sell financial assets representing claims on themselves in return for cash) and use the proceeds from this issuance to purchase primarily the financial assets of others. Since financial claims simply represent the right-hand side of the balance sheet for any organization, the key distinction between financial intermediaries and other types of organizations involves what is on the left-hand side of the balance sheet.

For example, a typical commercial bank issues financial claims against itself in the form of debt (such as checking and savings accounts) and equity, but then again so does a typical manufacturing firm. However, looking at the assets held by a commercial bank reveals that most of the bank's money is invested in loans to individuals and corporations as well as in U.S. government securities such as Treasury bills, whereas the typical manufacturing firm has its money invested mostly in land, buildings, machinery, and inventory. Thus the bank has invested primarily in financial assets, whereas the manufacturing firm has invested primarily in real assets. Accordingly, banks are classified as financial intermediaries, and manufacturing firms are not. Other types of financial intermediaries include savings and loan associations, savings banks, credit unions, life insurance companies, mutual funds, and pension funds.

Financial intermediaries provide an indirect method for corporations to acquire funds. As illustrated in Figure 1.2(a), corporations can obtain funds directly from the general public by the use of the primary market, as mentioned earlier. Alternatively, they can obtain funds indirectly from the general public by using financial intermediaries, as shown in Figure 1.2(b). Here the corporation gives a security to the intermediary in return for funds. In turn, the intermediary acquires funds by allowing the general public to maintain such investments as checking and savings accounts with it.

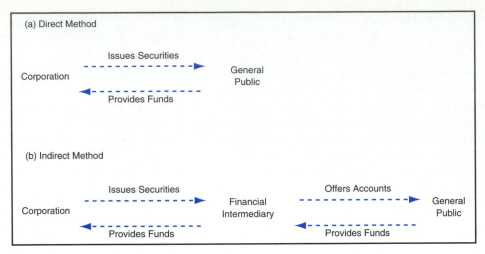

Figure 1.2
Corporate Funds Acquisition

THE INVESTMENT PROCESS

As mentioned previously, the investment process describes how an investor should go about making decisions with regard to what marketable securities to invest in, how extensive the investment should be, and when the investment should be made. A five-step procedure for making these decisions forms the basis of the investment process:

1. Set investment policy.
2. Perform security analysis.
3. Construct a portfolio.
4. Revise the portfolio.
5. Evaluate the performance of the portfolio.

1.2.1 Investment Policy

The initial step, setting **investment policy,** involves determining the investor's objectives and the amount of his or her investable wealth. Because there is a positive relationship between risk and return for sensible investment strategies, it is not appropriate for an investor to say that his or her objective is to "make a lot of money." What is appropriate for an investor in this situation is to state that the objective is to attempt to make a lot of money while recognizing that there is some chance that large losses may be incurred. Investment objectives should be stated in terms of both risk and return.

This step in the investment process concludes with the identification of the potential categories of financial assets for consideration in the ultimate portfolio. This identification will be based on, among other things, the investment

Institutional Investors

The past 30 years have witnessed a concentration of financial power in the hands of a relatively few organizations collectively known as *institutional investors*. The economic and social consequences of this consolidation have been enormous. Because this book is about investing, we will discuss not only the basic concepts, but also how they are applied by, and apply to, these immensely influential organizations.

The term *institutional investors* is used nebulously by practitioners. In a very broad sense, institutional investors are simply financial intermediaries of any type. This definition sets them apart from *retail investors,* who are individuals owning portfolios for which they are the direct beneficiaries.

At times, however, practitioners refer to institutional investors in a more narrow context. For example, when discussing the consequences of increased institutional investor participation in the U.S. common stock market, the focus is primarily on pension funds, mutual funds, insurance companies, and non-pension-fund money invested by bank trust departments. These organizations, in aggregate, own over half the outstanding market value of U.S. corporations.

Unquestionably, the most dynamic institutional investors today are pension funds and mutual funds. Pension funds are a relatively recent phenomenon. General Motors created the first modern U.S. pension fund in 1950. Since then, participation in pension funds has mushroomed, with approximately 40% of the working population enrolled in some type of pension plan today. Pension fund assets, which were only $170 billion in 1970, now total over $3 trillion.

Until the 1970s most U.S. pension funds were invested conservatively in U.S. bonds and common stocks. Since that time these organizations have become the driving force behind many investment industry innovations. They have moved into international stocks and bonds, derivative securities, and various "alternative equity" investments, such as oil and gas, venture capital, and timberland. Furthermore, they have popularized a variety of investment management techniques, such as passive management and market timing.

In terms of sheer growth, mutual funds have been even more impressive than pension funds. As late as 1980, investors had placed only $135 billion in mutual funds. Many investors viewed mutual funds skeptically as speculative investments. The industry still suffered a hangover from the collapse of many "go-go" equity funds in the 1973–1974 recession. Today almost $2 trillion is invested in mutual fund shares.

The financial deregulation of the 1980s led to an explosion of mutual fund products. Mutual fund sponsors expanded their offerings in terms of both types of assets and investment styles. Whereas previously most mutual funds concentrated on investments in U.S. stocks, investors can now own mutual funds investing in foreign stocks, U.S. and foreign bonds, U.S. and foreign short-term fixed-income securities, options, futures, and real estate. Funds may emphasize value or growth stocks, mortgage or Treasury bonds, passive or active management. The variations are seemingly endless and continue to grow. Where once the *Wall Street Journal* could list mutual fund data on half a page, it now devotes over two pages to daily mutual fund activity.

Willie Sutton remarked that he robbed banks because "that's where the money is." Institutional investors command attention because they are now "where the money is." In 1990 institutional investors (narrowly defined) controlled over $6 trillion in assets, the majority invested in common stocks and corporate and government bonds. When the then $40 billion California Public Employees Retirement Fund announced in 1987 its decision to commit 10% of its assets to foreign equities, investment professionals flocked to offer their services. One trade journal called it "a feeding frenzy." By comparison, as the importance of retail investors has declined, the traditional investment services provided to individuals have been reduced in number and increased in price.

The growth in institutional investor portfolios has had a bearing on many of the financial instruments and investment management techniques discussed in this text. Consider the following examples:

SECURITY MARKETS. Institutional investors now dominate security trading. They control over 70% of the daily trading on the New York Stock Exchange

(NYSE). Furthermore, 20 years ago fewer than 25% of NYSE trades involved share amounts over 5,000 shares. Today that figure is over 65%. This growth in large common stock trades has threatened to overwhelm the traditional specialist system. In response, new market mechanisms have been created, including block trading houses and crossing networks (see Chapter 3).

CORPORATE CONTROL. As a consequence of their size, institutional investors collectively own a controlling interest in virtually every large publicly traded U.S. corporation. Only in the last 10 years have institutional investors made a concerted effort to exercise their influence on corporations, but that effort has already had a noticeable impact. Numerous corporate boards have been altered and businesses restructured in response to pressure from institutional investors (see Chapter 17).

FUTURES. Institutional investors have largely avoided commodity futures. However, their involvement with financial futures (which were not even traded 20 years ago) has helped generate effective dollar trading volume in common stock index futures that is frequently larger than the dollar value of trading in the underlying common stocks (see Chapter 21).

INVESTMENT MANAGEMENT. Institutional investors have demanded new types of investment management techniques. For example, by allocating large sums to passive management, they singlehandedly created an industry that now manages over half a trillion dollars (see Chapter 24).

PORTFOLIO PERFORMANCE EVALUATION. Institutional investors have placed considerable emphasis on understanding how well their investments have performed and identifying the sources of those results. This emphasis has led to the development of sophisticated portfolio monitoring and performance analysis systems (see Chapter 25).

QUANTITATIVE TECHNIQUES. Institutional investors have pioneered the application of quantitative security valuation techniques, such as dividend discount models (see Chapter 18). They have explicitly sought to maintain adequate portfolio diversification and to control systematic and unsystematic risk using complex risk models (see Chapters 8, 11, and 24).

FIXED-INCOME SECURITIES. In large part because of the diverse needs of institutional investors, bond trading firms have created an array of complex fixed-income securities. Collateralized mortgage obligations (CMOs), puttable bonds, and floating-rate notes are but a few examples (see Chapter 14).

Given current demographic trends, the growth in assets controlled by institutional investors seems unlikely to abate. For example, as "baby boomers" reach their peak savings years (ages 40–60) over the next two decades, purchases of mutual fund shares and contributions to pension funds will continue to rise. Consequently, the influence of institutional investors on security markets can be expected to increase further in the years ahead.

---

objectives, amount of investable wealth, and tax status of the investor. For example, as shall be seen later, usually it does not make sense for individual investors to purchase preferred stock or for tax-exempt investors (such as pension funds) to invest in tax-exempt securities (such as municipal bonds).

1.2.2 Security Analysis

The second step in the investment process, performing **security analysis,** involves examining a number of individual securities (or groups of securities) within the broad categories of financial assets previously identified. One purpose for conducting such examinations is to identify those securities that currently appear to be mispriced. There are many approaches to security analysis. However, most of these approaches fall into one of two classifications. The first classification is known as **technical analysis;** those who utilize this approach to security analysis are known as technicians or technical analysts. The second classification is known as **fundamental analysis;** those who utilize it are known as fundamentalists or fundamental analysts. In discussing these two approaches to security analysis, the focus at first will be on common stocks. Later they will be discussed in terms of other types of financial assets.

In its simplest form, technical analysis involves the study of stock market prices in an attempt to predict future price movements for the common stock of a particular firm. Initially, past prices are examined in order to identify recurring trends or patterns in price movements. Then more recent stock prices are analyzed in order to identify emerging trends or patterns that are similar to past ones. This matching of emerging trends or patterns with past ones is done in the belief that these trends or patterns repeat themselves. Thus by identifying an emerging trend or pattern, the analyst hopes to predict accurately future price movements for that particular stock.

Fundamental analysis begins with the assertion that the "true" (or "intrinsic") value of any financial asset equals the present value of all cash flows that the owner of the asset expects to receive. Accordingly, the fundamental stock analyst attempts to forecast the timing and size of these cash flows, and then converts them to their equivalent present value by using an appropriate discount rate. More specifically, the analyst must attempt not only to estimate this discount rate but also to forecast the stream of dividends that a particular stock will provide in the future, which is equivalent to forecasting the firm's earnings per share and payout ratios. Furthermore, the discount rate must be estimated. Once the true value of the common stock of a particular firm has been determined, it is compared to the current market price of the common stock in order to see whether or not the stock is fairly priced. Stocks that have a true value less than their current market price are known as overvalued, or overpriced, stocks, whereas those that have a true value greater than their current market price are known as undervalued, or underpriced, stocks. The magnitude of the difference between the true value and the current market price is also important information, because the strength of the analyst's conviction that a given stock is mispriced will depend, in part, on it. Fundamental analysts believe that any notable cases of mispricing will be corrected by the market in the future, meaning that prices of undervalued stocks will show unusual appreciation and prices of overvalued stocks will show unusual depreciation.

1.2.3 Portfolio Construction

The third step in the investment process, **portfolio construction,** involves identifying those specific assets in which to invest, as well as determining the proportions of the investor's wealth to put into each one. Here the issues of selectivity, timing, and diversification need to be addressed by the investor. **Selectivity,** also known as microforecasting, refers to security analysis and thus focuses on forecasting price movements of individual securities. **Timing,** also known as macroforecasting, involves the forecasting of price movements of common stocks in general relative to fixed-income securities, such as corporate bonds. **Diversification** involves constructing the investor's portfolio in such a manner that risk is minimized, subject to certain restrictions.

1.2.4 Portfolio Revision

The fourth step in the investment process, **portfolio revision,** concerns the periodic repetition of the previous three steps. That is, over time the investor may change his or her investment objectives, which, in turn, means that the currently held portfolio may no longer be optimal. Instead, perhaps the investor should form a new portfolio by selling certain securities that are currently held and purchasing certain others that are not currently held. Another motivation for revising a given portfolio is that over time the prices of securities change, meaning that some securities that initially were not attractive may become attractive and others that were attractive at one time may no longer be so. Thus the investor may want to add the former to his or her portfolio, while simultaneously deleting the latter. Such a decision will depend upon, among other things, the size of the transaction costs incurred in making these changes as well as the magnitude of the perceived improvement in the investment outlook for the revised portfolio.

1.2.5 Portfolio Performance Evaluation

The fifth step in the investment process, **portfolio performance evaluation,** involves determining periodically how the portfolio performed, in terms of not only the return earned, but also the risk experienced by the investor. Thus appropriate measures of return and risk as well as relevant standards (or "benchmarks") are needed.

1.3   ASSET OWNERSHIP BY INDIVIDUAL INVESTORS

The *Institutional Issues* section in this chapter discusses the dominance of institutional investors in U.S. security markets. What about individual investors? According to the most recent New York Stock Exchange survey, approximately 51 million individual investors directly owned stock in 1990, implying that roughly one out of every four adults was a stockholder in 1990. Table 1.3 provides some demographics of stockholders from the NYSE survey. It suggests that the average stockholder has an above-average income, has had at least some college education, and is a white-collar worker.

Table 1.4 shows the financial assets and liabilities of U.S. households in 1991. Note that the three largest assets are, in order, pension funds, equities in corporate businesses, and equity in noncorporate businesses. The largest liability by far involves home mortgages. Although some mortgages are held as assets by other individuals (as shown in the table), most are held by financial institutions that obtain them by lending money that was initially provided to them by individuals (reflected in the table by the first two assets listed).

Although the difference between assets and liabilities in Table 1.4 is large, the net worth of households is actually much larger than the indicated $11 tril-

TABLE 1.3
DEMOGRAPHICS OF STOCKHOLDERS OF PUBLIC CORPORATIONS, 1990

Age:	
Under 21	6.8%
21–34	23.0
35–44	24.0
45–64	31.7
65 & over	14.5
	100.0%
Household income:	
Under $15,000	6.3%
$15,000–$24,999	10.2
$25,000–$49,999	44.4
$50,000 & over	39.1
	100.0%
Education:	
3 years high school or less	4.1%
4 years high school	20.0
1–3 years college	28.2
4 years college or more	47.7
	100.0%
Occupation:	
Professional & technical	23.0%
Managers & proprietors	19.0
Clerical & sales	15.5
Craftsmen, foremen, & service workers	13.5
Operatives, farmers, & laborers	2.1
Housewives, retirees, & unemployed adults	26.9
	100.0%

Source: New York Stock Exchange, Inc., *Fact Book: 1992 Data* (1993), p. 71.

lion. This is so because nonfinancial assets, such as cars and household furnishings, have not been taken into consideration.

1.4 THE INVESTMENT INDUSTRY

Government statisticians group a number of related occupations into an industry called "Finance, Insurance, and Real Estate." Table 1.5 shows the number of people employed in such occupations in 1992. As can be seen, the absolute and relative size of the industry has been increasing. In 1992 approximately one out of every 16 nonagricultural workers dealt with investments, broadly defined. Some provide advice (and are thus known as **investment advisors**), some are in sales, some arrange transfers of property or securities from one investor to another, others manage investors' funds (they are known as **professional money managers**), and still others handle the record keeping in this most abstract and paper-oriented of industries.

TABLE 1.4

FINANCIAL ASSETS AND LIABILITIES OF U.S. HOUSEHOLDS, YEAR-END 1992 (IN BILLIONS)

Assets:

Checkable deposits and currency	$ 672
Small time and savings deposits	2,215
Money market fund shares	462
Large time deposits	2
U.S. government securities	650
Tax-exempt obligations	600
Corporate and foreign bonds	131
Mortgages	302
Open-market paper	109
Mutual fund shares	898
Other corporate equities	2,535
Life insurance reserves	434
Pension fund reserves	4,586
Equity in noncorporate business	2,264
Security credit	80
Miscellaneous assets	242
Total financial assets	$16,181

Liabilities:

Mortgages	$ 3,067
Installment consumer credit	741
Other consumer credit	58
Tax-exempt debt	101
Other loans	174
Security credit	57
Trade credit	64
Unpaid life insurance premiums	20
Total liabilities	$ 4,281

Note: The individual numbers for Assets and Liabilities sum to $16,182 and $4,282, respectively; the difference from what is shown is due to rounding.

Source: U.S. Bureau of the Census, *Statistical Abstract of the United States 1993* (Washington, DC), p. 506.

TABLE 1.5

NUMBER OF EMPLOYEES: FINANCE, INSURANCE, AND REAL ESTATE (IN THOUSANDS)

	1960	1970	1980	1992
Financial institutions	934	1,404	2,141	2,561
Security and commodity brokers	114	205	227	438
Insurance carriers	832	1,030	1,224	1,480
Insurance agents, brokers, service	196	288	452	659
Real estate	517	661	981	1,301
Other	76	57	135	233
Total	2,669	3,645	5,160	6,672
Employees in this industry as a percentage of total employees in nonfarm industries	4.92%	5.14%	5.71%	6.15%

Source: U.S. Bureau of the Census, *Statistical Abstract of the United States* (Washington, DC), various issues.

CHAPTER 1

1. Because this book is about investing, it focuses on the investment environment and the investment process.
2. An investment involves the sacrifice of current dollars for future dollars.
3. Investments may be made in real assets or in financial assets (securities) through either primary markets or secondary markets.
4. The primary task of security analysis is to identify mispriced securities by determining the prospective future benefits of owning those securities, the conditions under which those benefits will be received, and the likelihood of such conditions.
5. The rate of return on an investment measures the percentage change in the investor's wealth due to owning the investment.
6. Studies of the historical rates of return on various types of securities demonstrate that common stocks produce relatively high but variable returns. Bonds generate lower returns with less variability. Treasury bills provide the lowest returns with the least variability.
7. In an efficient market, security prices reflect information immediately. Security analysis will not enable investors to earn abnormally high returns.
8. Security markets exist in order to bring together buyers and sellers of securities.
9. Financial intermediaries (financial institutions) are organizations that issue financial claims against themselves and use the proceeds to purchase primarily the financial assets of others.
10. The investment process describes how an investor makes decisions about what securities to invest in, how extensive these investments should be, and when they should be made.
11. The investment process involves five steps: set investment policy, perform security analysis, construct a portfolio, revise the portfolio, and evaluate portfolio performance.
12. Although the investment industry is of modest importance relative to total employment figures, it has a profound impact on everyone's life.

QUESTIONS AND PROBLEMS

1. Why do secondary security markets not generate capital for the issuers of securities traded in those markets?
2. Following the overthrow of communist regimes in Eastern Europe, many of the fledgling democracies placed the development of security markets near the top of their economic agendas. Why do you think that they did so?
3. Colfax Glassworks stock currently sells for $36 per share. One year ago the stock sold for $33. The company recently paid a $3 per share dividend. What was the rate of return for an investor in Colfax stock over the last year?
4. At the beginning of the year, Ray Fisher decided to take $50,000 in savings out of the bank and invest it in a portfolio of stocks and bonds; $20,000 was placed into common stocks and $30,000 into corporate bonds. A year later,

Ray's stock and bond holdings were worth $25,000 and $23,000, respectively. During the year $1,000 in cash dividends was received on the stocks, and $3,000 in coupon payments was received on the bonds. (The stock and bond income was not reinvested in Ray's portfolio.)

   a. What was the return on Ray's stock portfolio during the year?
   b. What was the return on Ray's bond portfolio during the year?
   c. What was the return on Ray's total portfolio during the year?

5. Explain why the rate of return on an investment represents the investor's relative increase in wealth from that investment.

6. Why are Treasury bills considered to be a riskfree investment? In what way do investors bear risk when they own Treasury bills?

7. Why are corporate bonds riskier than U.S. government bonds?

8. In 1951 the Treasury Department and the Federal Reserve System came to an agreement known as the "Accord," whereby the Fed was no longer obligated to peg interest rates on Treasury securities. What were the average returns and standard deviations on Treasury bills for the ten-year periods from 1942 to 1951 and 1952 to 1961? From these data, does it appear that the Fed did indeed stop pegging interest rates?

9. The following table shows the annual returns on a portfolio of small stocks during the 20-year period from 1971 to 1990. What is the average return and standard deviation of this portfolio? How do they compare with the 1971–1990 average return and standard deviation of the common stock portfolio whose annual returns are shown in Table 1.1?

1971: 16.50%	1976: 57.38%	1981: 13.88%	1986: 6.85%
1972: 4.43	1977: 25.48	1982: 28.01	1987: -9.30
1973: -30.90	1978: 23.46	1983: 39.67	1988: 22.87
1974: -19.95	1979: 43.46	1984: -6.67	1989: 10.18
1975: 52.82	1980: 39.88	1985: 24.66	1990: -21.56

10. Does it seem reasonable that higher return securities historically have exhibited higher risk? Why?

11. Give an example, outside of the financial markets, in which you commonly face a trade-off between risk and return.

12. Examining Table 1.1, you can find many years in which Treasury bills produced greater returns than common stocks. How can you reconcile this fact with the statements made in the text, citing a positive relationship between risk and return?

13. Again referring to Table 1.1, in terms of total returns, what was the worst single calendar year for common stock investors? What was the worst year in the 1970s? Compare these two years in terms of return in "constant dollars" (that is, purchasing power). Does this comparison show that the stock market slump of the 1970s was not as disastrous as the "crash" associated with the Great Depression? Explain.

14. Calculate the average annual return on common stocks, government bonds, and Treasury bills during the five decades from the 1930s through the 1980s. Which period was clearly the "decade of the financial asset"?

15. Describe how life insurance companies, mutual funds, and pension plans each act as financial intermediaries.

16. Why does it not make sense to establish an investment objective of "making a lot of money"?
17. What factors might an individual investor take into account in determining his or her investment policy?
18. Distinguish between technical and fundamental security analysis.

E N D N O T E S

[1] In general any cash received during the period is treated as if it were received at the end of the period. However, this treatment typically causes the actual return to be understated. For example, if the dividends on Widget were received at midyear, the investor could have put them in a bank savings account and earned, say, 5% interest on them for the rest of the year. This interest then would have amounted to $.15 $(= .05 \times \$3.00)$, resulting in the annual return being equal to 20.375% $\{= [(\$45 + \$3 + \$.15) - \$40]/\$40 = \$8.15/\$40\}$.

[2] The standard deviation was calculated as being equal to the square root of

$$\sum_{t=1}^{68}(r_t - \bar{r})^2/67,$$

where r_t is the return for year t (so $t=1$ corresponds to 1926, $t=2$ to 1927, and so on) and $\bar{r}$ is the average return over the 68-year period. A larger standard deviation means a greater amount of dispersion in the 68 returns and, hence, indicates more risk.

[3] Studies have found that (1) stocks have not become more volatile recently and (2) stocks have tended to be more volatile during recessions (particularly during the Great Depression of 1929 to 1939).

K E Y   T E R M S

investment environment
investment process
investment
savings
real investments
financial investments
primary market
secondary market
security
rate of return
efficient market
money markets
capital markets

investment policy
security analysis
technical analysis
fundamental analysis
portfolio construction
selectivity
timing
diversification
portfolio revision
portfolio performance evaluation
investment advisors
professional money managers

1. A major source of historical returns on U.S. security markets is contained in either one of the two following publications:

    Roger G. Ibbotson and Rex A. Sinquefield, *Stocks, Bonds, Bills, and Inflation: The Past and the Future* (Charlottesville, VA: Financial Analysts Research Foundation, 1983). Note that the Financial Analysts Research Foundation has since been renamed the Research Foundation of the ICFA. It can be contacted by calling (804) 980-3647.

    Stocks, Bonds, Bills, and Inflation 1994 Yearbook (Chicago: Ibbotson Associates, 1994). This annual yearbook of monthly and annual data can be purchased for $90 by calling (312) 616-1620.

2. Additional historical data on U.S. common stock returns can be found in:

    Jack W. Wilson and Charles P. Jones, "A Comparison of Annual Common Stock Returns: 1871–1925 and 1926–85," *Journal of Business,* 60, no. 2 (April 1987): 239–258.

3. The historical relative returns of U.S. stocks versus bonds are studied in:

    Jeremy J. Siegel, "The Equity Premium: Stock and Bond Returns Since 1802," *Financial Analysts Journal,* 48, no. 1 (January/February 1992): 28–38.

4. Comparable Japanese data for a more limited time period are presented in:

    Yasushi Hamao, "A Standard Data Base for the Analysis of Japanese Security Markets," *Journal of Business,* 64, no. 1 (January 1991): 87–102.

5. Historical data on global bond market returns are presented in:

    Roger G. Ibbotson and Laurence B. Siegel, "The World Bond Market: Market Values, Yields, and Returns," *Journal of Fixed Income,* 1, no. 1 (June 1991): 90–99.

6. The volatility of common stocks is examined in:

    G. William Schwert, "Why Does Stock Market Volatility Change Over Time?" *Journal of Finance,* 44, no. 5 (December 1989): 1115–1153.

    Peter Fortune, "An Assessment of Financial Market Volatility: Bills, Bonds, and Stocks," *New England Economic Review* (November/December 1989): 13–28.

7. For a discussion and analysis of U.S. common stock indices, see:

    G. William Schwert, "Indexes of U.S. Stock Prices from 1802 to 1987," *Journal of Business,* 63, no. 3 (July 1990): 399–426.

CHAPTER 2

Buying and Selling Securities

When a security is sold, many people are likely to be involved. Although it is possible for two investors to trade with each other directly, the usual transaction employs the services provided by brokers, dealers, and markets.

A **broker** acts as an agent for an investor and is compensated via commission. Many individual investors deal with brokers in large retail or "wire" houses —firms with many offices that are connected by private wires with their own headquarters and, through the headquarters, with the major markets. The people in these brokerage firms with prime responsibility for individual investors are termed **account executives** or **registered representatives.**

Institutional investors, such as commercial banks and pension funds, also deal with these large retail brokerage firms, but they typically do so through separate divisions designed to handle their specific trading needs. Institutional investors also conduct business with smaller firms that maintain only one or two offices and specialize in institutional business.

Two other types of brokerage firms are **regional brokerage firms** and **discount brokers.** The former concentrate on transactions within a geographic area, meaning that the securities being traded have a special following in that area of the country. This may be because the issuers of the securities are located in that area. Discount brokers offer "bare-bones" services at low cost—that is, they provide fewer services than "full-service" brokerage firms such as Merrill Lynch and Smith Barney Shearson. Investors who simply want to have their orders executed and do not seek advice can reduce the commissions they pay substantially by using a discount broker.

An account executive's compensation is typically determined largely by the **commissions** paid by his or her customers—an amount that is directly related to the amount of turnover (that is, trading) in an investor's account. This provides some temptation to recommend frequent changes in investors' holdings. Furthermore, since the commission rates on various types of investments differ, there is some temptation to recommend changes in those types of investments with the highest rates. In the long run, account executives who encourage excessive turnover (or "churning") will often lose customers and may even be subjected to lawsuits.[1] Nonetheless, such behavior may be advantageous for them in the short run.

It is a simple matter to open an account with a brokerage firm: Simply appear at (or call) the local office. An account executive will be assigned to you and will help you fill out some forms.[2] After the initial forms have been signed, everything else can be done by mail or telephone. Transactions will be posted to your account as they would to a bank account. For example, you can deposit money, purchase securities using money from the account, and add the proceeds from security sales to the account. Brokers exist (and charge fees) to make security transactions as simple as possible. All that the investor has to do is to provide the broker with what is referred to here as **order specifications.**

In discussing order specifications, it will be assumed that the investors' order involves common stock. In this situation the investor must specify:

1. The name of the firm
2. Whether the order is to buy or sell shares
3. The size of the order
4. How long the order is to be outstanding
5. What type of order is to be used

The last three specifications will be discussed next in more detail.

2.1   ORDER SIZE

When buying or selling common stock, the investor places an order involving either a round lot, an odd lot, or both. Generally, **round lot** means that the order is for 100 shares, or a multiple of 100 shares.[3] **Odd lot** orders generally are for 1 to 99 shares. Orders that are for more than 100 shares but are not a multiple of 100 should be viewed as a mixture of round and odd lots. Thus an order for 259 shares should be viewed as an order for two round lots and an odd lot of 59 shares.

2.2   TIME LIMIT

The investor must specify a time limit on his or her order—that is, the time within which the broker should attempt to fill the order. For **day orders** the broker will attempt to fill the order only during the day in which it was entered. If the order is not filled by the end of the day, it is canceled. If a time limit is not specified by the investor, the broker will treat an order as a day order. Week and month orders expire at the end of the respective calendar week or month during which they were entered, provided that they have not been filled by then.

Open orders, also known as **good-till-canceled** (GTC) **orders,** remain in effect until they are either filled or canceled by the investor. However, during the time period before the order has been filled, the broker may periodically ask the investor to confirm the order. In contrast to GTC orders there are **fill-or-kill orders,** also known as FOK orders. These orders are canceled if the broker is unable to execute them immediately.

Discretionary orders allow the broker to set the specifications for the order. The broker may have virtually complete discretion, in which case he or she decides on all the order specifications, or limited discretion, in which case he or she decides only on the price and timing of the order.

2.3   TYPES OF ORDERS

2.3.1   Market Orders

By far the most common type of order is the **market order.** Here the broker is instructed to buy or sell a stated number of shares immediately. In this situation the broker is obligated to act on a "best-efforts" basis to get the best possible price (as low as possible for a purchase order, as high as possible for a sell order) at the time the order is placed. Consequently, when placing a market order the investor can be fairly certain that the order will be executed while being uncertain of the price. However, there is generally fairly good information available beforehand concerning the likely price at which such an order will be executed. Not surprisingly, market orders are day orders.

2.3.2   Limit Orders

A second type of order is the **limit order.** Here a **limit price** is specified by the investor when the order is placed with the broker. If the order is to purchase shares, then the broker is to execute the order only at a price that is less than or equal to the limit price. If the order is to sell shares, then the broker is to execute the order only at a price that is greater than or equal to the limit price. Thus for limit orders to purchase shares the investor specifies a ceiling on the price, and for limit orders to sell shares the investor specifies a floor on the price. In contrast to a market order, an investor using a limit order cannot be certain that the order will be executed. Hence there is a trade-off between these two types of orders—immediacy of execution with uncertain price versus uncertain execution with bounded price.

For example, assume that the common stock of ABC Corporation is currently selling for $25 a share. An investor placing a limit order to sell 100 shares of

ABC with a limit price of $30 per share and a time limit of one day is not likely to have the order executed, because this price is notably above the current price of $25. Only if today's price becomes much more favorable (meaning in this case that the stock price rises by at least $5 per share) will the limit order be executed.

2.3.3 Stop Orders

Two special kinds of orders are stop orders (also known as stop-loss orders) and stop limit orders. For a **stop order** the investor must specify what is known as a **stop price.** If it is a sell order, the stop price must be below the market price at the time the order is placed. Conversely, if it is a buy order, the stop price must be above the market price at the time the order is placed. If later someone else trades the stock at a price that reaches or passes the stop price, then the stop order becomes, in effect, a market order. Hence a stop order can be viewed as a conditional market order.

Continuing with the ABC Corporation example, a stop sell order at $20 would not be executed until a trade involving others had taken place at a price of $20 or lower. Conversely, a stop buy order at $30 would not be executed until a trade involving others had taken place at a price of $30 or more. If the price did not fall to $20, then the stop sell order would not be executed. Similarly, if the price did not rise to $30, the stop buy order would not be executed. In contrast, a limit order to sell at $20 or a limit order to buy at $30 would be executed immediately, since the current market price is $25.

One potential use of stop orders is to "lock in" paper profits. For example, assume that an investor had purchased ABC stock at $10 per share two years ago, and thus has paper profits of $15 (= $25 − $10) per share. Entering a stop sell order at $20 per share means that the investor will be sure of making roughly $10 (= $20 − $10) per share if the stock falls in price to $20. If instead of falling the stock price rises, then the investor's stop sell order is ignored and the investor's paper profits will increase in size. Thus the stop sell order will provide the investor with a degree of profit protection.[4]

One of the dangers of stop orders is that the actual price at which the order is executed may be some distance from the stop price. This can occur if the stock price moves very rapidly in a given direction. For example, ABC may have an industrial accident that results in a spate of lawsuits and causes the stock price to fall very rapidly to $12 per share. In this situation a stop sell order at $20 may be executed at, say, $16 instead of near the stop price of $20.

2.3.4 Stop Limit Orders

The **stop limit order** is a type of order that is designed to overcome the uncertainty of the execution price associated with a stop order. With a stop limit order the investor specifies not one but two prices—a stop price and a limit price. Once someone else trades the stock at a price that reaches or passes the stop price, then a limit order is created at the limit price. Hence a stop limit order can be viewed as a conditional limit order.

Continuing with the example, the investor could place a stop limit order to sell ABC stock where the stop price is $20 and the limit price is $19. In effect, a limit order to sell ABC stock at a price of $19 or higher would be activated for the investor only if others trade ABC at a price of $20 or less. Conversely, the investor could enter a stop limit order to buy ABC stock where the stop price is $30 and the limit price is $31. This means that a limit order to buy ABC stock at a price of $31 or lower would be activated for the investor only if others trade ABC at a price of $30 or more.

Note that if the stop price is reached, execution is assured for a stop order but not for a stop limit order. Continuing with the ABC example, the industrial accident may cause the stock price to fall to $12 so rapidly that the stop limit order to sell (where the stop price was $20 and the limit price was $19) might not have been executed, whereas the stop order (where the stop price was $20) would have been executed at $16. Hence there is a trade-off between these two types of orders that is very similar to the trade-off between market and limit orders. Once activated, the stop order provides certain execution at an uncertain price whereas a stop limit order provides uncertain execution at a bounded price.

2.4 MARGIN ACCOUNTS

A **cash account** with a brokerage firm is like a regular checking account: Deposits (cash and the proceeds from selling securities) must cover withdrawals (cash and the costs of purchasing securities). A **margin account** is like a checking account that has overdraft privileges: If more money is needed than is in the account, a loan (within limits on its size) is automatically made by the broker.[5]

When opening a margin account with a brokerage firm, an investor must sign a **hypothecation agreement,** also known as a customer's agreement. This agreement grants the brokerage firm the right to pledge the investor's securities as collateral for bank loans, provided that the securities were purchased using a margin account. Most brokerage firms also expect investors to allow them to lend their securities to others who wish to "sell them short," a procedure that will be described later in this chapter.

In order to facilitate either the pledging or the lending of securities, brokerage firms request that securities purchased through a margin account be held in **street name.**[6] This means that the owner of the security, as far as the original issuer is concerned, is the brokerage firm—that is, the registered owner is the brokerage firm. As a result, in the case of common stock the issuer will send all dividends, financial reports, and voting rights to the brokerage firm, not to the investor. The brokerage firm will then act merely as a conduit and simply forward these items to the investor.[7] Accordingly, holding a security in street name will not result in the investor's being treated in a substantively different manner than holding the security in his or her own name.[8]

With a margin account an investor may undertake certain types of transactions that are not allowed with a cash account. These transactions are known as margin purchases and short sales, which will be discussed next.

2.4.1 Margin Purchases

With a cash account an investor who purchases a security must pay the entire cost of the purchase with cash. However, with a margin account the investor must come up with cash for only a percentage of the cost and can borrow the rest from the broker.[9] The amount borrowed from the broker as a result of such a **margin purchase** is referred to as the investor's **debit balance.** The interest charged on loans advanced by a broker for a margin purchase is usually calculated by adding a service charge (for example, 1%) to the broker's **call money rate.** In turn, the call money rate is the rate paid by the broker to the bank that loaned the broker the cash which ultimately went to the investor to pay for part of the purchase.

For example, the bank may loan money to the broker at a rate of 10%, and then the broker may loan this money to the investor at a rate of 11%. Note that the call money rate (10% in this example) can change over time, and with it the interest rate that investors are charged for loans used to finance margin purchases.

The securities purchased by the investor serve as collateral on the loan made by the broker. In turn, the broker uses these securities as collateral on the loan made by the bank. Thus the broker is, in a sense, acting as a financial intermediary in the lending process by facilitating a loan from the bank to the investor.

Initial Margin Requirement

The minimum percentage of the purchase price that must come from the investor's own funds is known as the **initial margin requirement.** Regulations T, U, and G, prescribed in accordance with the Securities Exchange Act of 1934, give the Federal Reserve Board the responsibility for setting this percentage when either common stocks or convertible bonds are being purchased.[10] However, the exchanges where the purchase orders are filled are allowed to set a percentage higher than the one set by the Federal Reserve Board, and brokers are allowed to set it even higher. Thus, hypothetically, the Federal Reserve Board could set the initial margin requirement at 50%, the New York Stock Exchange could then make it 55%, and the broker could ultimately make it 60%. As can be seen in Table 2.1, the initial margin requirement since 1934 as set by the Federal Reserve Board has ranged from 40% to 100%. In 1994 it was 50%.[11]

Consider, as an example, an investor who purchases on margin 100 shares of Widget Corporation for $50 per share. With an initial margin requirement of 60%, the investor must pay the broker $3,000 (= .6 × 100 shares × $50 per share). The remainder of the purchase price, $2,000 [= (1 − .6) × 100 shares × $50 per share], is funded by a loan from the broker to the investor.

Actual Margin

The **actual margin** in the account of an investor who has purchased stocks is calculated as:

$$\text{Actual margin} = \frac{\text{market value of assets} - \text{loan}}{\text{market value of assets}}. \tag{2.1}$$

TABLE 2.1

INITIAL MARGIN REQUIREMENTS OF THE FEDERAL RESERVE BOARD

Period		Initial Margin Requirements		
Beginning Date	**Ending Date**	**Margin Stocks**	**Short Sales**	**Convertible Bonds**
Oct. 1, 1934	Jan. 31, 1936	25–45%	(a)	(b)
Feb. 1, 1936	Mar. 31, 1936	25–55%	(a)	(b)
Apr. 1, 1936	Oct. 31, 1937	55%	(a)	(b)
Nov. 1, 1937	Feb. 4, 1945	40%	50%	(b)
Feb. 5, 1945	Jul. 4, 1945	50%	50%	(b)
Jul. 5, 1945	Jan. 20, 1946	75%	75%	(b)
Jan. 21, 1946	Jan. 31, 1947	100%	100%	(b)
Feb. 1, 1947	Mar. 29, 1949	75%	75%	(b)
Mar. 30, 1949	Jan. 16, 1951	50%	50%	(b)
Jan. 17, 1951	Feb. 19, 1953	75%	75%	(b)
Feb. 20, 1953	Jan. 3, 1955	50%	50%	(b)
Jan. 4, 1955	Apr. 22, 1955	60%	60%	(b)
Apr. 23, 1955	Jan. 15, 1958	70%	70%	(b)
Jan. 16, 1958	Aug. 4, 1958	50%	50%	(b)
Aug. 5, 1958	Oct. 15, 1958	70%	70%	(b)
Oct. 16, 1958	Jul. 27, 1960	90%	90%	(b)
Jul. 28, 1960	Jul. 9, 1962	70%	70%	(b)
Jul. 10, 1962	Nov. 5, 1963	50%	50%	(b)
Nov. 6, 1963	Mar. 10, 1968	70%	70%	(b)
Mar. 11, 1968	Jun. 7, 1968	70%	70%	50%
Jun. 8, 1968	May 5, 1970	80%	80%	60%
May 6, 1970	Dec. 5, 1971	65%	65%	50%
Dec. 6, 1971	Nov. 23, 1972	55%	55%	50%
Nov. 24, 1972	Jan. 2, 1974	65%	65%	50%
Jan. 3, 1974	Present	50%	50%	50%

Actual

^a Requirement was the margin "customarily required" by the broker.
^b Initial margin requirements for convertible bonds were not adopted by the Federal Reserve Board until March 11, 1968.

Source: Federal Reserve Bulletin, various issues.

The daily calculation of the actual margin in an investor's account is known as having the account **marked to the market.** Upon examination of Equation (2.1) it can be seen that at the time of the margin purchase, the actual margin and the initial margin are the same. However, subsequent to the purchase, the actual margin can be either greater than or less than the initial margin.[12] In this example, if Widget stock fell to $25 per share, then the actual margin would drop to 20% [= ($2,500 − $2,000)/$2,500].

Keep in mind that the 100 shares of Widget are being kept as collateral on the loan of $2,000 to the investor. If the price of Widget drops further, the broker may become nervous, because an additional sudden price decline could bring the value of the collateral below the amount of the loan. For example, if the price dropped to $15 per share, the broker would have collateral worth $1,500 [= $15 × 100 shares], whereas the amount of the loan is $2,000. If the investor skipped town, the broker would still have to make good on the bank loan of $2,000, but would have only $1,500 worth of the investor's assets to seize in order to pay off the loan. This means that the broker would have to bear the

$500 difference and hope to track down the investor and recoup this amount at a later date.

Maintenance Margin

To prevent such an occurrence, brokers require that investors keep the actual margin in their accounts at or above a certain percentage. This percentage is known as **maintenance margin.** It is set by the exchanges, not the Federal Reserve Board, with the brokers given the right to set it even higher. As of 1994, the New York Stock Exchange had set this percentage for common stock and convertible bond purchases at 25%.

If an account's actual margin falls below the maintenance margin requirement, the account is said to be **undermargined.** Accordingly, the broker will issue a **margin call,** requesting the investor to either (1) deposit cash or securities into the account, (2) pay off part of the loan, or (3) sell some securities currently held in the account and use the proceeds to pay off part of the loan. Any of these actions will raise the numerator or lower the denominator on the right-hand side of Equation (2.1), thereby increasing the actual margin.[13] If the investor does not act (or cannot be reached), then in accordance with the terms of the account, the broker will sell securities from the account in order to restore the actual margin to (at least) the maintenance margin requirement.

If instead of falling the stock price rises, then the investor can take part of the increase out of the account in the form of cash, because the actual margin in the account will have risen above the initial margin requirement.[14] In this situation the account is said to be **unrestricted** or **overmargined.**

Having discussed the cases where the stock price of the shares purchased on margin either (1) fell to such a degree that the actual margin was below the maintenance margin requirement, meaning that the account was undermargined, or (2) increased, resulting in the actual margin being above the initial margin requirement and the account being unrestricted, there remains one case left to consider. This case involves the situation where the stock price falls, but not by enough to make the actual margin drop below the maintenance margin requirement. That is, the actual margin in the account is below the initial margin requirement but above the maintenance margin requirement. In this situation no action by the investor is necessary. However, the account will be a **restricted account,** meaning that any transaction having the effect of decreasing the actual margin further (such as withdrawing cash) will not be allowed.

Rate of Return

The use of margin purchases allows the investor to engage in **financial leverage.** That is, by using debt to fund part of the purchase price, the investor can increase the expected rate of return of the investment. However, there is a complicating factor in the use of margin, and that is the effect on the risk of the investment.

Consider Widget again. If the investor believes that the stock will rise by $15 per share over the next year, then the expected rate of return on a cash purchase of 100 shares of Widget at $50 per share will be 30% [= ($15 × 100 shares)/($50 × 100 shares) = $1,500/$5,000], assuming that no cash dividends are paid. A margin purchase, on the other hand, would have an expected return of 42.7% {= [($15 × 100 shares) − (.11 × $2,000)]/(.6 × $50 × 100 shares) = $1,280/$3,000}, where the interest rate on margin loans is 11% and the initial margin requirement is 60%. Thus the investor has increased the expected rate of return from 30% to 42.7% by the use of margin.

However, what will happen to the rate of return if the stock falls by $10 per share? In this case the investor who made a cash purchase would have a rate of return equal to −20% [= (−$10 × 100 shares)/$5,000 = −$1,000/$5,000]. The margin purchaser, on the other hand, would have a rate of return equal to −40.7% {= [(−$10 × 100) − (.11 × $2,000)]/$3,000 = −$1,220/$3,000}. Thus the margin purchaser will experience a much larger loss than the cash purchaser for a given dollar decline in the price of the stock.

Margin purchases are usually made in the expectation that the stock price will rise in the near future, meaning that the investor thinks that the stock's current price is too low. If an investor thinks that a given stock is not too low but too high, then the investor may engage in what is known as a short sale, which is discussed next.

2.4.2   Short Sales

An old adage from Wall Street is to "buy low, sell high." Most investors hope to do just that by buying securities first and selling them later.[15] However, with a **short sale** this process is reversed: The investor sells a security first and buys it back later. In this case the old adage about investors' aspirations might be reworded as "sell high, buy low."

Short sales are accomplished by borrowing stock certificates for use in the initial trade, then repaying the loan with certificates obtained in a later trade. Note that the loan here involves certificates, not dollars and cents (although it is true that the certificates at any point in time have a certain monetary value). This means that the borrower must repay the lender by returning certificates, not dollars and cents (although it is true that an equivalent monetary value, determined on the date the loan is repaid, can be remitted instead). It also means that there are no interest payments to be made by the borrower.

Rules Governing Short Sales

Any order for a short sale must be identified as such. The Securities and Exchange Commission has ruled that short sales may not be made when the market price for the security is falling, on the assumption that the short seller could exacerbate the situation, cause a panic, and profit therefrom—an assumption inappropriate for an efficient market with astute, alert traders. The precise rule is that a short sale must be made on an **uptick** (for a price higher than that of the previous trade), or on a **zero-plus tick** (for a price equal to that of the previous trade but higher than that of the last trade at a different price).[16]

Within five business days after a short sale has been made, the short seller's broker must borrow and deliver the appropriate securities to the purchaser. The borrowed securities may come from either (1) the inventory of securities owned by the brokerage firm itself, (2) the inventory of another brokerage firm, (3) the holdings of an institutional investor (such as a pension fund) that is willing to lend its securities, or (4) the inventory of securities held in street name by the brokerage firm for investors who have margin accounts with the firm. The life of the loan is indefinite, meaning that there is no time limit on it.[17] If the lender wants to sell the securities, then the short seller will not have to repay the loan if the brokerage firm can borrow shares elsewhere, thereby transferring the loan from one source to another. However, if the brokerage firm cannot find a place to borrow the shares, then the short seller will have to repay the loan immediately. Interestingly, the identities of the borrower and the lender are known only to the brokerage firm—that is, the lender does not know who the borrower is and the borrower does not know who the lender is.

An Example

An example of a short sale is indicated in Figure 2.1. At the start of the day, Mr. Lane owns 100 shares of *XYZ* Company, which are being held for him in street name by Brock, Inc., his broker. During this particular day, Ms. Smith places an order with her broker at Brock to short sell 100 shares of *XYZ*. (Mr. Lane believes that the price of *XYZ* stock is going to rise in the near future, whereas Ms. Smith believes that it is going to fall.) In this situation Brock takes the 100 shares of *XYZ* that it is holding in street name for Mr. Lane and sells them for Ms. Smith to some other investor, in this case Mr. Jones. At this point *XYZ* will receive notice that the ownership of 100 shares of its stock has changed hands, going from Brock (remember that Mr. Lane held his stock in street name) to Mr. Jones. At some later date Ms. Smith will tell her broker at Brock to purchase 100 shares of *XYZ* (perhaps from Ms. Poole) and use these shares to pay off her debt to Mr. Lane. At this point *XYZ* will receive another notice that the ownership of 100 shares has changed hands, going from Ms. Poole to Brock, restoring Brock to its original position.

Cash Dividends

What happens when *XYZ* declares and subsequently pays a cash dividend to its stockholders? *Before the short sale* Brock would receive a check for cash dividends on 100 shares of stock. After depositing this check in its own account at a bank, Brock would write a check for an identical amount and give it to Mr. Lane. Thus neither Brock nor Mr. Lane has been worse off by having the shares held in street name. *After the short sale*, *XYZ* will see that the owner of those 100 shares is no longer Brock, but is now Mr. Jones. Thus *XYZ* will now mail the dividend check to Mr. Jones, not Brock. However, Mr. Lane will still be expecting his dividend check from Brock. Indeed, if there was a risk that he would not receive it, he would not have agreed to have his securities held in street name. Brock would like to mail him a check for the same amount of dividends that Mr. Jones received from *XYZ*—that is, for the amount of dividends that Mr. Lane would have received from *XYZ* had he held his stock in his own name. If Brock does this, then it will be losing an amount of cash equal to the amount of the dividends

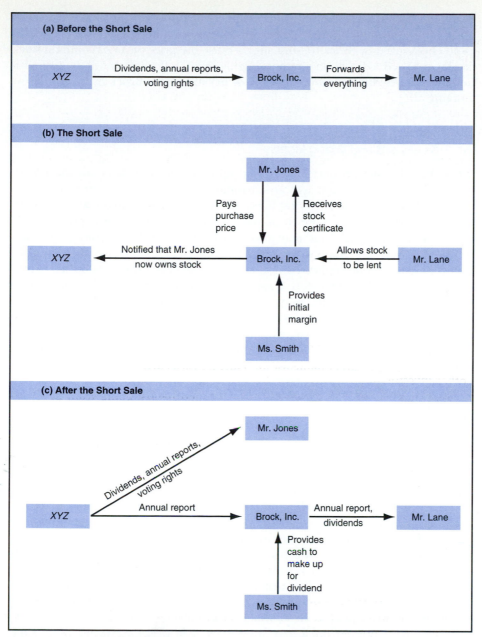

Figure 2.1
Short Selling of Common Stock

paid. In order to avoid incurring this loss, what does Brock do? It makes Ms. Smith, the short seller, give it a check for an equivalent amount.

Consider all the parties involved in the short sale now. Mr. Lane is content because he has received his dividend check from his broker. Brock is content because its net cash outflow is still zero, just as it was before the short sale. Mr. Jones is content because he received his dividend check directly from *XYZ*. What about Ms. Smith? She should not be upset with having to reimburse Brock for the dividend check given by Brock to Mr. Lane, because the price of *XYZ's* common stock can be expected to fall by an amount roughly equal to the amount of the cash dividend, thereby reducing the dollar value of her loan from Brock by an equivalent amount.

Financial Reports and Voting Rights

What about financial reports and voting rights? Before the short sale these were sent to Brock, which then forwarded them to Mr. Lane. After the short sale Brock will no longer be receiving them, so what happens? Financial reports are easily procured by brokerage firms free of charge, so Brock will probably get copies of them from *XYZ* and mail a copy to Mr. Lane. However, voting rights are different. These are limited to the registered stockholders (in this case Mr. Jones) and cannot be replicated in the manner of cash dividends by Ms. Smith, the short seller. Thus when voting rights are issued, the brokerage firm (Brock) will try to find voting rights to give to Mr. Lane if he asks for them. (Perhaps Brock owns shares, or manages a portfolio that owns shares of *XYZ*, and will give the voting rights from these shares to Mr. Lane.) Unless he is insistent, however, there is a chance Mr. Lane will not get his voting rights once his shares have been borrowed and used in a short sale. In all other matters he will be treated just as if he were holding the shares of *XYZ* in his own name.

Initial Margin Requirement

As mentioned previously, a short sale involves a loan. Thus there is a risk that the borrower (in the example, Ms. Smith) will not repay the loan. What would happen in this situation? The brokerage firm would be left without the 100 shares that the short seller, Ms. Smith, owes the firm. Either the brokerage firm, Brock, is going to lose money or else the lender, Mr. Lane, is going to lose money. To prevent this from happening, the cash proceeds from the short sale, paid by Mr. Jones, are not given to the short seller, Ms. Smith. Instead, they are held in her account with Brock until she repays her loan. Will this assure the brokerage firm that the loan will be repaid? No, unfortunately it will not.

In the example assume that the 100 shares of *XYZ* were sold at a price of $100 per share. In this case the proceeds of $10,000 from the short sale are held in Ms. Smith's account, but she is prohibited from withdrawing them until the loan is repaid. Now imagine that at some date after the short sale, *XYZ* stock rises by $20 per share. In this situation Ms. Smith owes Brock 100 shares of *XYZ* with a current market value of $12,000 (= 100 shares × $120 per share), but has only $10,000 in her account. If she skips town, Brock will have collateral of $10,000 (in cash) but a loan of $12,000, resulting in a loss of $2,000. How will Brock protect itself from experiencing losses from short sellers who do not repay their loans? By the use of margin requirements. In this example, Ms. Smith must not only leave the short sale proceeds with her broker, but she must also give her broker initial margin applied to the amount of the short sale.[18] Assuming that the initial margin requirement is 60%, she must give her broker $6,000 (= .6 × $10,000) in cash.

Actual and Maintenance Margin

In this example *XYZ* stock would have to rise in value to a price above $160 per share in order for Brock to be in jeopardy of not being repaid. Thus initial margin provides the brokerage firm with a certain degree of protection. However, this protection is not complete because it is not unheard of for stocks to rise in value by more than 60% [= ($160−$100)/$100]. It is maintenance margin that protects the brokerage firm from losing money in such situations. In order to examine the use of maintenance margin in short sales, the actual margin in a short sale will be defined as:

$$\text{Actual margin} = \frac{\text{market value of assets} - \text{loan}}{\text{loan}}. \qquad (2.2)$$

The numerator in Equation (2.2) is identical to the numerator for calculating actual margin for margin purchases, as shown in Equation (2.1). However, the denominator is different. For short sales it is equal to the current dollar value of the loan, whereas for margin purchases it is equal to the current market value of the assets held in the account.

In this example, if *XYZ* stock rises to $130 per share, the actual margin in Ms. Smith's account will be 23% {= [($100 × 100 shares) × (1 + .6) − ($130 × 100 shares)]/($130 × 100 shares) = $3,000/$13,000}. Assuming that the maintenance margin requirement is 30%, the account is undermargined, thereby causing Ms. Smith to receive a margin call. Just as with margin calls on margin purchases, she will be asked to put up more margin, meaning that she will be asked to add cash or securities to her account.

If instead of rising the stock price falls, then the short seller can take a bit more than the drop in the price out of the account in the form of cash, because in this case the actual margin has risen above the initial margin requirement and the account is thus unrestricted.[19]

Having discussed the cases for short sales where the stock price either (1) fell and the account was thereby unrestricted, or (2) went up to such a degree that the maintenance margin requirement was violated and the account was thereby undermargined, there is one more case left to be considered. This is the case where the stock price goes up but not to such a degree that the maintenance margin requirement is violated. In this case the initial margin requirement has been violated, which means that the account is restricted. Here "restricted" has a meaning similar to its meaning for margin purchases—that is, any transaction that has the effect of further decreasing the actual margin in the account will be prohibited.

An interesting question is: What happens to the cash in the short seller's account? When the loan is repaid, the short seller will have access to the cash. (Actually, the cash is typically used to buy the shares that are needed to repay the loan.) Before the loan is repaid, however, it may be that the short seller can earn interest on the portion of the cash balance that represents margin. (Some brokerage firms will accept certain securities, such as Treasury bills, in lieu of cash for meeting margin requirements.)

In regard to the cash proceeds from the short sale, sometimes the securities may be borrowed only on the payment of a premium by the short seller, meaning that the short seller not only does not earn interest on the cash proceeds but must *pay* a fee for borrowing the shares. In contrast, when large institutional investors short sell stock, they typically negotiate a split with the brokerage firm of the interest earnings on the cash proceeds, thereby *receiving* a fee. However, securities are generally loaned "flat" to small investors—the brokerage firm keeps the cash proceeds from the short sale and enjoys the use of this money, and neither the short seller nor the lender receives any direct compensation. In this case the brokerage firm makes money not only from the commission paid by the short seller, but also on the cash proceeds from the sale. (The brokerage firm may, for example, earn interest by purchasing Treasury bills with these proceeds.)

Rate of Return

The use of short selling results in rates of return to the investor that are of opposite sign to what would be earned if the shares were purchased on margin (assuming that initial margin for the short sale is met by depositing cash and that the short loan is "flat," and ignoring interest on the margin loan). Hence short sales also involve the use of financial leverage.

Consider *XYZ* once again, where Ms. Smith short sold its stock at a price of $100 per share. If she later repays the short loan when the stock is selling for $75 per share and just after *XYZ* has paid a $1 per share cash dividend, then her rate of return would be equal to 40% [= ($100 − $75 − $1)/(.6 × $100) = $24/$60]. In contrast, note that the return for someone who had purchased the stock of *XYZ* on margin would be equal to −40% [= ($75 + $1 − $100)/(.6 × $100) = −$24/$60], whereas the rate of return for someone who had purchased the stock without using margin would be equal to −24% [= ($75 + $1 − $100)/$100 = −$24/$100].

However, if Ms. Smith has incorrectly predicted the future price movement of *XYZ* and it goes up to $120 per share just after paying a $1 per share cash dividend, then her rate of return would be equal to −35% [= ($100 − $120 − $1)/ (.6 × $100) = −$21/$60]. Conversely, if the stock had been purchased on margin, her rate of return would have been equal to 35% [= ($120 + $1 − 100)/ (.6 × $100) = $21/$60]. Without margin, the rate of return on the stock would be equal to 21% [= ($120 + $1 − $100)/$100 = $21/$100].

What happens to these rate of return calculations if interest is earned on both the initial margin and the short proceeds? It increases the rate of return to the short seller. Consider the example where *XYZ* fell to $75, and assume that the short seller earned 5% on the initial margin deposit and 4% on the short proceeds. In this case the return to the short seller would be equal to 51.7% {= [$100 − $75 − $1 + (.05 × .6 × $100) + (.04 × $100)]/(.6 × $100) = $31/$60}, which is notably higher than the 40% previously calculated. Hence financial leverage is even more apparent when either form of interest is paid to the short seller.

Market Neutral Strategies

Institutional investors have traditionally viewed management of common stock portfolios as a one-sided problem: Buy underpriced stocks that are likely to appreciate in value relative to an established benchmark. However, that perspective is rapidly changing as these investors explore investment techniques that involve purchases *and* short sales of stocks so as to systematically control portfolio risk and profit from insights into mispriced securities. These techniques are collectively known as "market neutral" strategies.

The logic underlying market neutral strategies is simple. If on average all securities are fairly priced, then mispricing must be a zero-sum game—underpriced securities must be accompanied by overpriced securities. Therefore if an investor can discover mispriced securities, why should he or she restrict himself or herself to buying the underpriced securities? Why not profit by short selling the overpriced securities as well?

The basic process of implementing market neutral strategies is similarly straightforward. The investor holds a portfolio consisting of three investments: short-term riskfree securities (for example, 90–day Treasury bills), long positions in stocks, and short positions in stocks. The market value of each investment is the same. Furthermore, the long and short stock positions have equal exposures to common causes of stock market variability. (See Chapter 11 for a discussion of factors affecting stock returns.) The resulting portfolio, therefore, is fully hedged against any type of stock market movement.

Why should this hedged portfolio be of interest? After all, it should earn only the riskfree return. The answer lies with the stock selection skills of the market neutral investor. If the investor possesses valuable knowledge of mispriced securities, then he or she will purchase underpriced stocks whose unique circumstances will cause them to increase in value relative to the market. Conversely, he or she will short sell overpriced stocks whose unique circumstances will cause them to decrease in value relative to the market. The net result is that the investor benefits from his or her ability to identify mispriced stocks, without exposure to the vagaries of the stock market.

As a simple example, consider an investor who begins the year with $100 in cash. The investor uses the cash to purchase $100 of stocks. At the same time the investor short sells $100 of stocks. These purchases and short sales have been carefully designed to exhibit no net exposure to any industry or other factor influencing stock market returns. (For example, the investor might form long-short pairs within industries—buy $5 of GM stock and short sell $5 of Ford stock.) At the beginning of the year the investor's portfolio appears as follows:

Long	Short	Cash	Total
$100	− $100	$100	$100

Assume that the investor selects wisely and the long portfolio is worth $110 at year-end, for a 10% return. (By comparison, the stock market's return was 8%.) Furthermore, the short portfolio also has risen in value (but not by as much as the long portfolio or the stock market) to $105 (a 5% return), and the cash holdings have earned $2 in interest (a 2% return). At year-end the investor's portfolio appears as follows:

Long	Short	Cash	Total
$110	− $105	$102	$107

This investor has earned $7 on a $100 portfolio, or a 7% return, without assuming any market risk. The only risk the investor has taken lies in his or her ability to identify mispriced stocks. The return from adroit stock selection is known as "alpha" (see Chapter 25). In fact, the market neutral investor earns a "double alpha" by gaining from insights into both underpriced and overpriced stocks.

Of course, the real world, with its unaccommodating nature, makes the implementation of market neutral strategies much more complex than our simple example implies. Consider the following steps that the market neutral investor must follow:

1. **Establish a margin account.** As the text describes, short selling must be conducted in a margin account. Thus the investor must select a broker to hold the stocks and cash involved in the market neutral strategy.

2. **Make long and short transactions simultaneously.** Long positions must always equal short positions, or the portfolio may be exposed to unintended risks. The New York Stock Exchange's uptick rule (see page 29) and the limited availability of appropriate stocks for short selling complicates this task.

3. **Maintain collateral with the broker.** The stocks from the long positions, cash from the short sales, and a small amount of initial cash (to serve as a liquidity reserve for daily marks to market on the short positions) must be deposited with the broker.

4. **Reimburse for dividends paid and substitute for recalled borrowed stocks.** The investor must compensate the stock lender for any dividends paid on the borrowed stocks. Also, if the borrowed securities are sold by the lender and cannot be replaced, the investor must find appropriate substitutes.

5. **Continuously monitor portfolio positions.** Security price movements will affect the long-short balance in the portfolio. Only careful daily monitoring can prevent the portfolio from moving away from a market neutral stance.

Institutional investors pay special attention to selecting a broker for their market neutral strategies. They invariably choose large, established brokers with impeccable credit ratings. These brokers have the best access to securities for short sales, either through their street name holdings or through security lending networks. Institutional investors also consider the interest income rebates provided by the brokers. Unlike small investors, who typically receive no interest on their short sale proceeds, institutional investors can negotiate to receive anywhere from 75% to 90% of the income earned by the broker on the short sale proceeds.

Any investment organization can implement market neutral strategies. However, investors using quantitative investment processes (for example, dividend discount models—see Chapter 18) are the primary purveyors of this approach. Their processes typically rank a large number of stocks from highly attractive to highly unattractive—a step necessary to develop a diversified collection of long and short opportunities. Moreover these investors' portfolio construction methods usually are very structured, thus facilitating the intricate design and maintenance of offsetting long and short positions.

Some institutional investors extend the market neutral strategies and "equitize" the cash held in their portfolios—that is, they purchase common stock futures contracts (see Chapter 21), effectively creating stock market exposure equal to the value of their cash holdings. Their portfolio returns then become the return on the stock market plus the returns produced by their insights into attractive long and short stocks.

This "equitization" technique opens up a vast range of investment strategies that permit the market neutral investor to "transport" his or her skills to other markets (see Chapter 21). For example, consider a pension fund with an investment policy requiring investment of a portion of its assets in fixed-income securities. It could simply buy a portfolio of bonds to satisfy the policy guidelines. However, suppose that the pension fund had access to skillful market neutral stock managers. The pension fund could use those managers' investment talents, while at the same time purchasing Treasury bond futures contracts to give it the required fixed-income market exposure. Thus the pension fund's investment policy is satisfied and, if the market neutral managers are successful, then the pension fund profits from their skill as well. In essence, the pension fund has "transported" the market neutral stock managers' skills to the bond market.

Market neutral strategies offer no guarantee of success, as they rely on the stock selection abilities of the investor. A poor investor can generate substantial transaction costs (see Chapter 3), while adding no "alpha" to the portfolio. Moreover, if the offsetting long-short positions are constructed inaccurately, the portfolio could experience unpleasant surprises.

Despite these caveats, market neutral strategies represent an intriguing combination of portfolio risk control and security selection. These strategies have been employed on a large scale for only a few years. Nevertheless they are rapidly making their influence felt as institutional investors examine the very essence of how value is added to their portfolios through active management.

2.4.3 Aggregation

An investor with a margin account may purchase several different securities on margin or may short sell several different securities. Alternatively, he or she may purchase some on margin and short sell others. The determination of whether an account is undermargined, restricted, or overmargined depends on the total activity in the account. For example, if one stock is undermargined and another is overmargined, then the overmargined stock can be used to offset the undermargined stock, provided that it is overmargined to a sufficiently large degree. How these multiple transactions are aggregated in one account in order to determine whether the account is undermargined, restricted, or overmargined on any given day will be shown next.

Multiple Margin Purchases

In the case of multiple margin purchases, aggregation is straightforward. The investor's balance sheet is restated by recalculating the market value of all the stocks held using current market prices. Here the "current market price" of any particular security usually means the price at which the last trade was made in the market involving that security on the previous day. Next the total amount of the investor's liabilities is carried over from the previous day because the amounts of the margin loans do not change from day to day. This in turn allows Equation (2.1) to be used to recalculate the actual margin in the account.

Multiple Short Sales

In a similar manner, the actual margin of an investor who has short sold more than one stock can be determined. In this case, however, it is not the assets that are reevaluated every day as the account is marked to the market. Instead, it is the liabilities that are reevaluated based on current market prices, since the short seller's liabilities are shares whose market values are changing every day. Once the dollar values of the liabilities are recalculated, the actual margin in the account can be determined using Equation (2.2).

Both Margin Purchases and Short Sales

The situation where the investor has purchased some stocks, perhaps on margin, and has short sold others is more complicated than either of the situations just described. This is because the equation used to calculate actual margin for margin purchases, Equation (2.1), and the equation used to calculate actual margin for short sales, Equation (2.2), are different. This can be seen by simply noting what is in the denominator in each equation. For margin purchases the market value of the *assets* appears in the denominator. However, for short sales the market value of the *loan* appears in the denominator. If both kinds of transactions are appearing in the same account, neither equation can be used to calculate the overall actual margin in the account. However, the account can be analyzed in terms of the dollar amount of assets that are necessary for the account to meet the maintenance margin requirement. This can be illustrated with an example.

Consider an investor who short sells 100 shares of Widget on July 1 at $50 per share and purchases 100 shares of *XYZ* on margin at $100 per share on July 15. Here the initial and maintenance margin requirements are 60% and 30%, respectively. Furthermore, assume that Widget and *XYZ* are selling for $60 and $80 per share on July 31. In this situation the broker will require the investor to have assets of sufficient value to protect the short sale loan of Widget stock and the margin loan that was used to purchase *XYZ*. In general, the amount required as collateral against a short sale is equal to the current market value of the stock short sold times the quantity of 1 plus the maintenance margin requirement. For the short sale loan of Widget stock, this amounts to $7,800 [= $6,000 × (1 + .3)], where .3 corresponds to the maintenance margin requirement.

The amount required as collateral against a margin purchase is, in general, equal to the dollar value of the margin loan divided by the quantity of 1 minus the maintenance margin requirement. For the cash loan to purchase *XYZ*, this amounts to $5,714 [= $4,000/(1 − .3)].

The total amount required in this example is thus $13,514 (= $7,800 + $5,714). Since the assets in the account are currently worth $16,000, the investor will not receive a margin call. To see whether the account is restricted, the previous calculations are repeated using the initial margin requirement of 60% instead of the maintenance margin requirement of 30%. For the Widget stock loan the amount required for the account to be unrestricted is $9,600 [= $6,000 × (1 + .6)]. The corresponding amount for the *XYZ* margin loan is $10,000 [= $4,000/(1 − .6)]. Summing these amounts gives a total of $19,600 (= $9,600 + $10,000), indicating that this account is restricted.

2.5 SUMMARY

1. Investors typically buy or sell securities through brokers who are compensated for their services with commissions.
2. When transacting in a security, investors must specify the following: the security's name; buy or sell; order size; time limit; and type of order.
3. The four standard types of orders are market, limit, stop, and stop limit.
4. Investors may purchase securities with cash or may borrow from brokerage firms to buy securities on margin.
5. Investors must make down payments on their margin purchases, maintain minimum actual margin levels in their margin accounts, and pay interest on margin loans.
6. If an investor's actual margin falls below the maintenance margin, the investor's account is undermargined. The investor will receive a margin call and must increase the actual margin level in the account.
7. Buying on margin results in financial leverage, thereby magnifying (positively or negatively) the impact of a security's return on the investor's wealth.
8. Short sales involve the sale of securities that are not owned, but rather are borrowed by the sellers. The borrowed securities must ultimately be purchased in the market and returned to the lenders.

9. A short seller must deposit the proceeds of the short sale and initial margin with his or her broker. The short seller must also maintain a minimum actual margin level in his or her margin account or face a margin call.

10. For investors who purchase on margin or short sell several securities, the determination of whether an account is undermargined, restricted, or overmargined depends on the aggregated activity in their accounts.

QUESTIONS AND PROBLEMS

1. Describe the conflict of interest that typically exists in the investment advisory relationship between a brokerage firm and its clients.

2. How many round lots and what odd lot size are in an order for 511 shares?

3. Discuss the advantages and disadvantages to the investor of the following:
   a. Market order
   b. Limit order
   c. Stop order

4. Why are margin account securities held in street name? → liability concerns

5. Lollypop Killefer purchases on margin 200 shares of Landfall Corporation stock at $75 per share. The initial margin requirement is 55%. Prepare Lollypop's balance sheet for this investment at the time of purchase.

6. Buck Ewing opened a margin account at a local brokerage firm. Buck's initial investment was to purchase 200 shares of Woodbury Corporation on margin at $40 per share. Buck borrowed $3,000 from a broker to complete the purchase.
   a. At the time of the purchase, what was the actual margin in Buck's account?
   b. If Woodbury stock subsequently rises in price to $60 per share, what is the actual margin in Buck's account?
   c. If Woodbury stock subsequently falls in price to $35 per share, what is the actual margin in Buck's account?

7. Distinguish between the initial margin requirement and the maintenance margin requirement.

8. Snooker Arnovich buys on margin 1,000 shares of Rockford Systems stock at $60 per share. The initial margin requirement is 50% and the maintenance margin requirement is 30%. If the Rockford stock falls to $50, will Snooker receive a margin call?

9. Avalon Company's stock is currently selling for $15 per share. The initial margin requirement is 60% and the maintenance margin requirement is 35%. Cap Anson buys 100 shares of Avalon stock on margin. To what price must the stock fall for Cap to receive a margin call?

10. Lizzie Arlington has deposited $15,000 in a margin account with a brokerage firm. If the initial margin requirement is 50%, what is the maximum dollar amount of stock that Lizzie can purchase on margin?

11. Explain the purpose of the maintenance margin requirement.

12. Penny Bailey bought on margin 500 shares of South Beloit Inc. at $35 per share. The initial margin requirement is 45% and the annual interest on

margin loans is 12%. Over the next year the stock rises to $40. What is Penny's return on investment?

13. Calculate Buck Ewing's rate of return in parts (b) and (c) of Problem 6 under the assumption that the margin loan was outstanding for one year and carried an interest rate of 10%, and that the prices of $60 and $35 were observed after one year during which the firm did not pay any cash dividends.

14. Ed Delahanty purchased 500 shares of Niagara Corporation stock on margin at the beginning of the year for $30 per share. The initial margin requirement was 55%. Ed paid 13% interest on the margin loan and never faced a margin call. Niagara paid dividends of $1 per share during the year.
    a. At the end of the year, if Ed sold the Niagara stock for $40 per share, what would Ed's rate of return be for the year?
    b. At the end of the year, if Ed sold the Niagara stock for $20 per share, what would Ed's rate of return be for the year?
    c. Recalculate your answers to parts (a) and (b) assuming that Ed made the Niagara stock purchase for cash instead of on margin.

15. Individual investors are sometimes contacted by their brokers and told that they have "unused buying power" in their brokerage accounts. What do the brokers mean by this statement?

16. Beauty Bancroft short sells 500 shares of Rockdale Manufacturing at $25 per share. The initial margin requirement is 50%. Prepare Beauty's balance sheet as of the time of the transaction.

17. Through a margin account, Candy Cummings short sells 200 shares of Madison Inc. stock for $50 per share. The initial margin requirement is 45%.
    a. If Madison stock subsequently rises to $58 per share, what is the actual margin in Candy's account?
    b. If Madison stock subsequently falls to $42 per share, what is the actual margin in Candy's account?

18. Dinty Barbare short sells 500 shares of Naperville Products at $45 per share. The initial margin and maintenance margin requirements are 55% and 35%, respectively. If Naperville stock rises to $50, will Dinty receive a margin call?

19. Sun Prairie Foods stock currently sells for $50 per share. The initial margin requirement is 50% and the maintenance margin requirement is 40%. If Willie Keeler short sells 300 shares of Sun Prairie stock, to what price can the stock rise before Willie receives a margin call?

20. Eddie Gaedel is an inveterate short seller. Is it true that Eddie's potential losses are infinite? Why? Conversely, is it true that the maximum return that Eddie can earn on his investment is 100%? Why?

21. The stock of DeForest Inc. sold at the beginning of the year for $70 per share. At that time Deerfoot Barclay short sold 1,000 shares of the stock. The initial margin requirement was 50%. DeForest stock has risen to $75 at year-end, and Deerfoot faced no margin calls in the interim. Further, the stock paid a $2 dividend at year-end. What was Deerfoot's return on this investment?

22. Calculate Candy Cummings's rate of return in parts (a) and (b) of Problem 17, assuming that the short loan was flat but the initial margin deposit earned interest at a rate of 8%, and that the prices of $58 and $42 were observed after one year during which the firm did not pay any dividends.

23. What aspects of short selling do brokerage houses typically find to be especially profitable?

24. Distinguish between an investor receiving a margin call and having his or her margin account restricted.

25. Pooch Barnhart purchases 100 shares of Batavia Lumber Company stock on margin at $50 per share. Simultaneously, Pooch short sells 200 shares of Geneva Shelter stock at $20 per share. With an initial margin requirement of 60%:
    a. What is the initial equity (in dollars) in Pooch's account?
    b. If Batavia and Geneva rise to $55 and $22 per share, respectively, what is Pooch's equity position (in dollars)?

26. On May 1, Ivy Olson sold short 100 shares of Minnetonka Minerals stock at $25 per share and bought on margin 200 shares of St. Louis Park Company stock for $40 per share. The initial margin requirement was 50%. On June 30, Minnetonka stock sold for $36 per share and St. Louis Park stock sold for $45 per share.
    a. Prepare a balance sheet showing the aggregate financial position on Ivy's margin account as of June 30.
    b. Determine whether Ivy's account is restricted as of June 30.

ENDNOTES

[1] For more on churning, see Seth C. Anderson, Sue L. Visscher, and Donald A. Winslow, "Guidelines for Detecting Churning in an Account," *AAII Journal,* 11, no. 9 (October 1989): 12–14.

[2] For more on opening an account, see Bruce Sanking, "The Brokerage Account Form: Handle with Care," *AAII Journal,* 13, no. 6 (July 1991): 15–16.

[3] Occasionally, a round lot is for less than 100 shares. When this happens, it is usually for stocks that are either high-priced or traded infrequently.

[4] Stop buy orders can be used to lock in paper profits from what are known as short sales, which will be discussed later in this chapter.

[5] There are other types of accounts. Furthermore, an investor may have more than one type of account with a brokerage firm. An interesting new type is the "wrap" account (started in 1980 by E. F. Hutton & Co.) where the broker, for an annual fee, helps the investor select an appropriate professional money manager. See Albert J. Golly, Jr., "The Pros and Cons of Brokerage Wrap Accounts," *AAII Journal,* 15, no. 2 (February 1993): 8–11. See endnote 22.

[6] Investors with cash accounts may voluntarily elect to have their securities held in street name. Reasons offered for doing so include reduced risk of theft and improved record keeping. Typically the brokerage firm will send monthly statements detailing the investor's holdings. See J. Michael Bishop and Henry Sanchez, Jr. "Reading and Understanding Brokerage Account Statements," *AAII Journal,* 14, no. 10 (November 1992): 7–10.

[7] The investor may not receive the voting rights, particularly if the stock has been loaned to a short seller. This situation will be discussed later in this chapter.

[8] The investor whose securities are held in street name may be concerned about what would happen if the brokerage firm were to go bankrupt. If this were to happen, the

Securities Investor Protection Corporation (SIPC), a government-chartered firm that insures investors' accounts against brokerage firm failure, would step in and cover each individual investor's losses up to $500,000. Some brokerage firms have gone further and purchased private insurance in addition to the insurance offered by SIPC. See Henry Sanchez, Jr., "SIPC: What Happens if Your Brokerage Firm Fails," *AAII Journal,* 12, no. 10 (November 1990): 13–16.

[9] With either a cash or a margin account, the investor usually has up to five business days after an order is executed to provide the broker with the necessary cash. Accordingly, the fifth business day after execution is known as the **settlement date**. For margin purchases, the loan value of certain other securities can be used instead of cash as a down payment, in which case these securities must be provided by the settlement date. Sellers of securities must also provide their brokers with their securities by the settlement date. If requested, an investor may be able to get an extension of the settlement date.

[10] Regulation T covers credit extended by brokers and dealers, Regulation U covers credit extended by banks, and Regulation G covers credit extended by anyone other than brokers, dealers, or banks. All common stocks and convertible bonds that are listed on a national securities exchange (for example, the New York Stock Exchange, the American Stock Exchange, or the National Market System of Nasdaq) can be purchased on margin. Furthermore, four times a year the Federal Reserve Board publishes a roster of other securities that can be purchased on margin. The determination of which firms are put on this roster is based on such factors as number of shareholders and firm size.

[11] Initial margin requirements on nonconvertible bonds are set in a similar fashion, except that the Federal Reserve Board is not involved. Typically the investor wishing to purchase nonconvertible bonds on margin will face a much lower initial margin requirement (for example, 10% for purchases of U.S. Treasury securities).

[12] In general at the end of each month the interest on the loan will be calculated and added to the amount of the loan. For ease of exposition, this fact is ignored in the examples given here.

[13] The broker may ask the investor to immediately (in some cases within five business days, in other cases even sooner) bring the actual margin up to a level corresponding to the maintenance margin requirement, or to a level that is even higher, ranging up to the initial margin requirement.

[14] Alternatively, the cash could be used as part of the initial margin requirement on an additional margin purchase by the investor. In fact, if it was large enough, it could be used to meet the entire requirement.

[15] After purchasing a security, an investor is said to have established a *long position* in the security.

[16] The tick rule is not applicable in the over-the-counter market, suggesting that short selling can be done at any time in that market. This market will be discussed in Chapter 3.

[17] The New York Stock Exchange, the American Stock Exchange, and Nasdaq publish monthly lists of the **short interest** in their stocks. (Short interest refers to the number of shares of a given company that have been short sold where, as of a given date, the loan remains outstanding.) To be on the NYSE or AMEX list, either the total short interest must be equal to or greater than 100,000 shares or the change in the short interest from the previous month must be equal to or greater than 50,000 shares. The respective figures for Nasdaq are 50,000 and 25,000.

[18] Table 2.1 presents the initial margin requirement for short sales. Note that it has been set at the same level as for margin purchases of common stocks in the postwar period.

[19] Alternatively, the short seller could short sell a second security and not have to put up all (or perhaps any) of the initial margin.

broker
account executives
registered representatives
regional brokerage firms
discount brokers
commissions
order specifications
round lot
odd lot
day orders
open orders
good-till-canceled orders
fill-or-kill orders
discretionary orders
market order
limit order
limit price
stop order
stop price
stop limit order
cash account

margin account
hypothecation agreement
street name
margin purchase
debit balance
call money rate
initial margin requirement
actual margin
marked to the market
maintenance margin
undermargined
margin call
unrestricted
overmargined
restricted account
financial leverage
short sale
uptick
zero-plus tick
settlement date
short interest

REFERENCES

1. For a discussion of the mechanics of purchasing and selling securities, along with margin purchasing and short selling, see:

DeWitt M. Foster, *The Stockbroker's Manual* (Miami: Pass, 1990). Copies can be obtained by calling (305) 270–2550;

James J. Angel, "An Investor's Guide to Placing Stock Orders," *AAII Journal*, 15, no. 4 (April 1993): 7–10.

2. An interesting discussion of margin requirements and their impact on market volatility is contained in:

David A. Hsieh and Merton H. Miller, "Margin Requirements and Market Volatility," *Journal of Finance*, 45, no. 1 (March 1990): 3–29.

3. A recent study that examines levels and changes in short interest is:

Averil Brent, Dale Morse, and E. Kay Stice, "Short Interest: Explanations and Tests," *Journal of Financial and Quantitative Analysis*, 25, no. 2 (June 1990): 273–289.

4. Market neutral investment strategies are discussed in:

Bruce I. Jacobs and Kenneth L. Levy, "Long/Short Equity Investing," *Journal of Portfolio Management,* 20, no. 1 (Fall 1993): 52–63.

CHAPTER 3

Security Markets

A **security market** can be defined as a mechanism for bringing together buyers and sellers of financial assets in order to facilitate trading. Security markets are **secondary** (as opposed to primary) **markets,** because the financial assets traded on them were issued at some previous point in time. One of their main functions is "price discovery,"—that is, to cause prices to reflect currently available information. The quicker this is done, the more efficiently financial markets will see that capital is allocated to its most productive opportunities.

3.1 CALL AND CONTINUOUS MARKETS

3.1.1 Call Markets

In **call markets,** trading is allowed only at certain specified times. In such a market, when a security is "called," those individuals who are interested in either buying or selling it are physically brought together.[1] Then there may be an explicit auction in which prices are called out until the quantity demanded is as close as possible to the quantity supplied. Alternatively, orders may be left with a clerk, and periodically an official of the exchange sets a price that allows the maximum number of shares from the previously accumulated orders to be traded.

3.1.2 Continuous Markets

In **continuous markets,** trades may occur at any time. Although only investors are needed for such a market to operate, it generally would not be very effective without intermediaries also being present. In a continuous market without intermediaries, an investor who wants to buy or sell a security quickly might have to either spend a great deal of money searching for a good offer or run the risk of accepting a poor one. Because orders from investors arrive more or less randomly, prices in such a market would vary considerably, depending on the flow of buy orders relative to the flow of sell orders. However, anyone willing to take temporary positions in securities could potentially make a profit by ironing out these transitory variations in supply and demand. This is the role of intermediaries known as dealers (also known as market-makers) and specialists. In the pursuit of personal gain, they generally reduce fluctuations in security prices that are unrelated to changes in value and in doing so provide **liquidity** for investors. Here liquidity refers to the ability of investors to convert securities into cash at a price that is similar to the price of the previous trade, assuming that no new information has arrived since the previous trade.

Security markets for common stocks (as well as certain other securities) in the United States typically involve dealers or specialists. The next topic in this chapter involves a detailed description of how these markets function and the role played by dealers and specialists. Whereas the focus is on markets for common stocks, many of the features of such markets are applicable to the markets for other types of financial assets (such as bonds). **Organized exchanges,** which are central physical locations where trading is done under a set of rules and regulations, will be discussed first. Examples of such exchanges for common stocks are the New York Stock Exchange, the American Stock Exchange, and various regional exchanges.

3.2   MAJOR MARKETS IN THE UNITED STATES

3.2.1   New York Stock Exchange

The New York Stock Exchange (NYSE) is a corporation that has 1,366 full members. It has a charter and a set of rules and regulations that govern its operation and the activities of its members. A board of 26 directors that is elected by the membership supervises the exchange. Of the directors, 12 are members and 12 are not; the latter are known as "public directors." The remaining two directors are full-time employees: a chairperson who also functions as the chief executive officer and a vice-chairperson who also functions as president.

In order to become a member, a **seat** (comparable to a membership card) must be purchased from a current member.[2] By holding a seat, the member has the privilege of being able to execute trades using the facilities provided by the exchange. Since most trades of common stocks, in both dollar size and number of shares, take place on the NYSE, this privilege is valuable.[3] Not surprisingly, many brokerage firms are members, meaning that either an officer (if the brokerage firm is a corporation) or a general partner (if the brokerage firm is a partnership) or an employee of the firm is a member. Indeed, many brokerage firms have more than one member. A brokerage firm with one or more NYSE memberships is often referred to as a **member firm** (or member corporation or member organization).

A stock that is available for trading on the NYSE is known as a **listed security.** In order for a company's stock to be listed, the company must apply to the NYSE.

The initial application is usually informal and confidential. If approved, the company then makes a formal application that is announced publicly. Given an earlier approval on the informal application, approval at this stage is almost certain. The general criteria used by the NYSE in approving an application are "(1) the degree of national interest in the company; (2) its relative position and stability in the industry; and (3) whether it is engaged in an expanding industry, with prospects of at least maintaining its relative position."[4] Companies that are approved for listing must agree to pay a nominal annual fee and provide certain information to the public. After listing, if trading interest in a security declines substantially, it may be **delisted** by the exchange, meaning that it is no longer available for trading on the NYSE. (Delistings also occur when a listed company is acquired by another company or is merged into another company.) At other times there may be a **trading halt,** meaning that there is a temporary suspension of trading in that security. Trading halts typically are issued for a given stock when trading in it is roiled due to rumors or a recently made news announcement (such as a rumor of a takeover attempt or an announcement of unexpected low quarterly earnings). The opening of trading can be delayed for similar reasons or if a large imbalance in orders has accumulated since the previous close.

Panels (a) and (b) of Table 3.1 show the specific criteria that are used by the NYSE to determine whether to list or delist a stock. Companies may apply for listing on more than one exchange, and under certain conditions an exchange may set up "unlisted trading privileges" for transactions in a stock already listed on another exchange.

An interesting example of securities that are listed on two exchanges (dually listed) involves certain foreign companies that are listed on a major exchange in their home country as well as on a U.S. exchange. In some cases the stock itself is traded in the United States. (Most dually listed Canadian stocks are traded in this manner.) In other cases, what is traded in the United States is not the foreign company's stock but what is known as **American Depository Receipts** (ADRs). ADRs are financial assets that are issued by U.S. banks and represent indirect ownership of a certain number of shares of a specific foreign company that are held on deposit in a foreign bank. The U.S. bank that has created the ADRs sees to it that the U.S. investor receives, in U.S. dollars, all cash dividends that the company pays. In addition, anything else that is received by the bank, such as financial reports, is forwarded to the investor. In return for providing these services, the bank charges a small fee. This fee is paid for by the company if the ADR is *sponsored;* if the ADR is *unsponsored,* then the investor must pay the fee. (Typically this is done by the bank keeping part of the dividend that it receives from the company and passing the remainder on to the investor.)[5]

The NYSE listing requirements for foreign stocks are shown in panel (c) of Table 3.1. Such stocks are evaluated on a worldwide basis. If difficulties are encountered in determining the number of round-lot stockholders, then the firm must attest to the depth and liquidity of its shares. In comparison with U.S. stocks, the listing requirements for foreign stocks are more rigorous. For example, U.S. firms must have net tangible assets of at least $18,000,000 whereas for foreign firms these assets must amount to at least $100,000,000.

TABLE 3.1
NEW YORK STOCK EXCHANGE CRITERIA FOR LISTING AND DELISTING A SECURITY

(a) Initial Listing Requirements of the NYSE[a]

1. Either (a) the pretax income for the most recent year must be at least $2,500,000 and the pretax income over each of the preceding two years must be at least $2,000,000 or (b) the pretax income over the most recent three years must be at least $6,500,000 in total with a minimum of $4,500,000 in the most recent year.
2. Net tangible assets must be worth at least $18,000,000.
3. There must be a least 1,100,000 shares outstanding that are publicly held, and these shares must have an aggregate market value of at least $18,000,000 (this amount is subject to periodic adjustment based on market conditions).
4. There must be either (a) at least 2,000 stockholders who each own a minimum of 100 shares or (b) at least 2,200 stockholders with the monthly trading volume averaging at least 100,000 shares over the most recent six months.

(b) NYSE Conditions for Delisting a Security[b]

1. The number of stockholders that each own at least 100 shares falls below 1,200.
2. The number of shares that are publicly held falls below 600,000.
3. The aggregate market value of publicly held shares falls below $5,000,000 (this amount is subject to periodic adjustment based on market conditions).

(c) NYSE Alternative Listing Requirements for Foreign Companies

1. The cumulative pretax income for the most recent three years must be at least $100,000,000, with a minimum of $25,000,000 in each one of these years.
2. Net tangible assets must be worth at least $100,000,000.
3. There must be at least 2,500,000 shares outstanding that are publicly held, and these shares must have an aggregate market value of at least $100,000,000.
4. There must be at least 5,000 shareholders who each own a minimum of 100 shares.

[a]Generally, all these requirements must be met for initial listing.
[b]Normally a security will be considered for delisting if any one of these conditions occur. However, under certain circumstances a security may be delisted even though none of the conditions occur.

Source: Adapted from *Fact Book: 1992 Data*, New York Stock Exchange, 1993.

New York Stock Exchange Members

Members in the NYSE fall into one of four categories, depending on the type of trading activity in which they engage. These categories are commission brokers, floor brokers, floor traders, and specialists. Of the 1,366 members of the NYSE, roughly 700 are commission brokers, 400 are specialists, 225 are floor brokers, and 41 are floor traders. The trading activities of members in these categories are as follows:

1. **Commission brokers.** These members take orders that the public has placed with brokerage firms and see to it that they are executed on the exchange. The brokerage firms that they work for are paid commissions by the customers for their services.

2. **Floor brokers,** also known as two-dollar brokers. These members assist commission brokers when there are too many orders flowing into the market for the commission brokers to handle alone. For their assistance, they receive part of the commission paid by the customer. (Sometimes both floor brokers, as defined here, and commission brokers are lumped together and called floor brokers.)

3. **Floor traders.** These members trade solely for themselves and are prohibited by exchange rules from handling public orders. They hope to make money by taking advantage of perceived trading imbalances that result in temporary mispricings, thereby allowing them to "buy low and sell high." These members are also known as registered competitive market-makers, competitive traders, or registered traders.

4. **Specialists.** These members perform two roles. First, any limit order that the commission broker cannot execute immediately because the current market price is not at or better than the specified limit price will be left with the specialist for possible execution in the future. If this order is subsequently executed, the specialist is paid part of the customer's commission. The specialist keeps these orders in what is known as the **limit order book** (or specialist's book). Stop and stop limit orders are also left with the specialist, who then enters them in the same book. In this capacity the specialist is acting as a broker (that is, agent) for the customer's broker and can be thought of as a "broker's broker."

Second, the specialist acts as a **dealer** in certain stocks (in particular, for the same stocks in which he or she acts as a broker). This means that the specialist buys and sells certain stocks for his or her own account and is allowed to seek a profit in doing so. However, in acting as a dealer, the specialist is required by the NYSE to maintain a "fair and orderly market" in those stocks in which he or she is registered as a specialist. Thus the NYSE expects the specialist to buy or sell shares from his or her own account when there is a temporary imbalance between the number of buy and sell orders. (In doing so, specialists are allowed to short sell their assigned stocks.) Even though the NYSE monitors the trading activities of the specialists, this requirement is so ill-defined that it is difficult, if not impossible, to enforce.

As might be inferred from the preceding discussion, specialists are at the center of the trading activity on the NYSE. Each stock that is listed on the NYSE currently has one specialist assigned to it.[6] (In a few instances in the past, two or more specialists were assigned to the same stock.) There are over 2,000 common stocks listed on the NYSE and only 400 specialists. This suggests that each specialist is assigned more than one stock, and indeed this is the case.

All orders involving a given stock must be taken physically to a **trading post,** a spot on the floor of the NYSE where the specialist for that stock stands at all times during the hours the NYSE is open.[7] It is here that an order is either executed or left with the specialist.

Placing a Market Order

The operation of the New York Stock Exchange is best described by an example. Mr. B asks his broker for the current price of General Motors shares. The broker punches a few buttons on a televisionlike quotation machine and finds that the current **bid** and **asked prices** on the NYSE are as favorable as the prices available on any other market, being equal to 61 and 61¼, respectively. In addition, the quotation machine indicates that these bid and asked prices are good for orders of at least 100 and 500 shares, respectively. This means that the NYSE specialist is willing to buy at least 100 shares of GM at a price of $61 (the bid price) and is willing to sell at least 500 shares of GM at $61.25 (the asked price).[8] After being given this information, Mr. B instructs his broker to "buy 300 at market," meaning that he wishes to place a market order with his broker for 300 shares of GM.

At this point the broker transmits the order to his or her firm's New York headquarters, where the order is subsequently relayed to the brokerage firm's "booth" on the side of the exchange floor. Upon receiving the order, the firm's commission broker goes to the trading post for GM.

The existence of a standing order to buy at 61 means that no one else is prepared to sell at a lower price, and the existence of a standing order to sell at 61¼ means that no higher price need be paid. This leaves only the spread between the two prices for possible negotiation. If Mr. B is lucky, another broker (for example, one with a market order to sell 300 shares for Ms. S) will "take" the order at a price "between the quotes" (here, at 61⅛). Information will be exchanged between the two brokers and the sale made. Figure 3.1 illustrates the procedure used to fill Mr. B's order.

If the gap between the quoted bid and asked prices is wide enough, an auction may occur among various commission brokers, with sales made at one or more prices between the specialist's quoted values. This auction is known as a **double** (or two-way) **auction,** since both buyers and sellers are participating in the bidding process.

What if no response came forth from the floor when Mr. B's order arrived? In such a case the specialist would "take the other side," selling 300 shares to Mr. B's broker at a price of $61.25 per share. The actual seller might be the specialist or another investor whose limit order is being executed by the specialist.

If the bid-ask spread on a stock is no larger than the standard unit in which prices are quoted (typically ⅛ of a point, or 12.5 cents, on the NYSE), market orders are generally executed directly by the specialist. This is because there is no spread for possible negotiation. In the previous example, if the specialist had quoted bid and asked prices of 61 and 61⅛, then there is no incentive for Mr. B's commission broker to try to obtain a better price for the purchase order than 61⅛, since any seller could obtain a price of 61 from the specialist. That is, to entice someone other than the specialist to sell GM to Mr. B, his commission broker would have to offer a better price than 61, since this is the price the seller could obtain from the specialist. Given that the next highest price is 61⅛, and that the specialist is willing to sell at that price, Mr. B's commission broker will deal with the specialist rather than the "crowd."

Placing a Limit Order

So far the discussion has been concerned with what would happen to a market order that was placed by Mr. B. What if Mr. B placed a limit order instead of a market order? There are two situations that can occur with a limit order. First, the limit price may be within the bid and asked prices of the specialist. Second, the limit price may be outside these prices.

In the first situation, where the specialist is quoting prices of 61 and 61¼, assume that Mr. B has placed a limit order with his broker to buy 300 shares of GM at a price of 61⅛ or better. When this order is carried to the trading post, it is

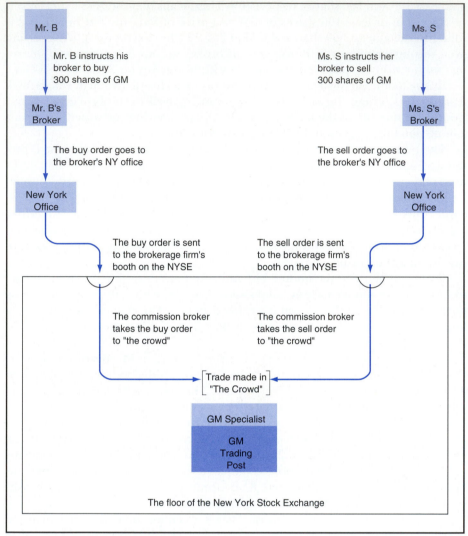

Figure 3.1

Order Flow for an NYSE-Listed Security

possible that it will be executed by the commission broker for the limit price of 61⅛, since someone in the "crowd" may be willing to take the other side of the transaction. After all, anyone with a sell order can transact with the specialist at the specialist's price of 61. To these people, the limit price of 61⅛ looks more attractive, since it represents a higher selling price to them. Thus they would prefer doing business with Mr. B's commission broker rather than with the specialist.

In the second situation, assume that Mr. B has placed a limit order to buy 300 shares of GM with a limit price of 60. When this order is carried to the trading post, the commission broker will not even attempt to fill it, because the limit price is outside the specialist's current bid and asked prices. That is, because anyone with a sell order can deal with the specialist at a price of 61, there is no chance that anyone will want to sell to Mr. B for the lower limit price of 60. Thus the order will be given to the specialist to be entered in the specialist's book for possible execution in the future. Limit orders in the book are executed in order of price. For example, all purchase orders with limit prices of 60½ will be executed (if at all) before Mr. B's order is executed. If there are several limit orders in the book at the same price, they are executed in order of arrival (that is, first in first out).

It may not be possible to fill an entire order at a single price. For example, a broker with a market order to buy 500 shares might obtain 300 shares at 61⅛ and have to pay 61¼ for the remaining 200. Similarly, a limit order to buy 500 shares at 61⅛ or better might result in the purchase of 300 shares at 61⅛ and the entry of a limit order in the specialist's book for the other 200 shares.

Large and Small Orders

The NYSE has developed special procedures to handle both routine small orders and exceptionally large orders. In 1976 the NYSE developed an electronic system known as Designated Order Turnaround (or DOT) to handle small orders, defined at that time as market orders involving 199 or fewer shares and limit orders involving 100 or fewer shares. Subsequent developments led to DOT being replaced by a procedure known as the **Super Designated Order Turnaround** system (or SuperDOT), which now accepts market orders involving 30,999 or fewer shares and limit orders involving 99,999 or fewer shares. In order to use Super-DOT, the member firm must be a participating subscriber. With this system, the New York office of the customer's brokerage firm can send the customer's order directly to the specialist, whereupon it will be exposed to the crowd and executed immediately (if possible), with a confirmation of the execution sent to the brokerage firm. Although SuperDOT usually sends relatively small market orders directly to the specialist for execution, it has been programmed to send certain other orders directly to the firm's floor brokers for execution.[9] In deciding where to send the order, SuperDOT looks at such things as order size and type of order. (For example, market orders and limit orders where the limit price is far from the current quotes of the specialist would be sent directly to the specialist. Each member firm sets the parameters that it wants SuperDOT to use in making such decisions.)

SuperDOT has greatly facilitated the execution of "basket" trades (a form of "program trading"), where a member firm submits orders in a number of securities all at once. Before SuperDOT, brokers from member firms would carry trade tickets with preprinted amounts that were to be used if the firm suddenly launched a basket trade. These tickets had to be brought by hand to the appropriate trading posts for execution. With SuperDOT, all trades in a basket can be sent simultaneously to the various trading posts on the floor for immediate execution.

Exceptionally large orders, which are known as **blocks,** are generally defined as orders involving at least 10,000 shares or $200,000, whichever is smaller. Typically, these orders are placed by institutional customers and may be handled in a variety of ways. One way of handling a block order is to take it directly to the specialist and negotiate a price for it. However, if the block is large enough, it is quite likely that the specialist will lower the bid price (for sell orders) or raise the asked price (for buy orders) by a substantial amount. This will occur because specialists are prohibited by the exchange from soliciting offsetting orders from the public and, thus, do not know how easily they can obtain an offsetting order. Even with these disadvantages, this procedure is used on occasion, generally for relatively small blocks, and is referred to as a **specialist block purchase** or **specialist block sale,** depending on whether the institution is selling or buying shares.[10]

Larger blocks can be handled by the use of an **exchange distribution** (for sell orders) or **exchange acquisition** (for buy orders). Here a brokerage firm attempts to execute the order by finding enough offsetting orders from its customers. The block seller or buyer pays all brokerage costs, and the trade price is within the current bid and asked prices as quoted by the specialist. A similar procedure, known as a **special offering** (for sell orders) or **special bid** (for buy orders), involves letting all brokerage firms solicit offsetting orders from their customers.

Another way of selling blocks is to conduct a **secondary distribution,** where the shares are sold off the exchange after the close of trading in a manner similar to the sale of new issues of common stock. The exchange must give approval for such distributions and usually does so if it appears that the block could not be absorbed easily in normal trading on the exchange. Accordingly, secondary distributions generally involve the sale of exceptionally large blocks.

Whereas all of these ways of handling block orders are used at one time or another, most block orders are handled in what is known as the **upstairs dealer market.** By using **block houses,** which are set up to deal with large orders, institutions have been able to get better prices for their orders. This occurs because a block house, when informed that an institution wants to place a block order, will proceed to line up trading partners (including itself) to take the other side of the order. After this is done the block house will attempt to reach a mutually acceptable price with the original institution. Assuming that such a price is reached (if not, the institution can take the order to a different block house), the order will be "crossed" on the floor of the exchange, meaning that the specialist is given the opportunity to fill any limit orders that are in the specialist's book at the block's selling price.[11] However, there is a limit on the number of shares (1,000 shares or 5% of the size of the block, whichever is greater) that can be taken by the specialist to fill these limit orders.

For example, suppose that the PF Pension Fund informs a block house that it wishes to sell 20,000 shares of General Motors common stock. The block house then proceeds to find three institutional investors that want to buy, say, 5,000 shares apiece; the block house decides that it too will buy 5,000 shares of GM from PF. Noting that the buyers have said that they would be willing to pay $70 per share, the block house subsequently informs PF that it will buy the 20,000 shares for $69.75 each, less a commission of $8,000. Assuming that PF accepts the deal, the block house now becomes the owner of the shares but must first "cross" them on the NYSE, because the block house is a member of the exchange. In this example assume that when the block is crossed at $69.75, the specialist buys 500 shares at this price for a limit order that is in his or her book. After the cross, the block house gives 5,000 shares to each of the institutional buyers in exchange for $350,000 (= 5,000 shares × $70 per share) and hopes that the remaining 4,500 shares that it now owns can be sold in the near future at a favorable price. Needless to say, the possibility of not being able to sell them at a favorable price is one of the risks involved in operating a block house.

3.2.2 Other Exchanges

Table 3.2 shows the total trading volume of the securities listed on each of the active stock exchanges in the United States in 1992. Not surprisingly, the New York Stock Exchange dominates the list. Second in importance is the American Stock Exchange (AMEX), which lists shares of somewhat smaller companies of national interest (a few of which are also listed on the New York Stock Exchange). All the others are termed **regional exchanges,** because historically each served as the sole location for trading securities primarily of interest to investors in its region. However, the major regional exchanges now depend to a substantial extent on transactions in securities that are also listed on a national exchange. Interestingly, the regional exchanges are currently larger, in aggregate, than the AMEX. There are five major regional exchanges currently in existence, the Boston, Cincinnati, Chicago, Pacific, and Philadelphia exchanges.

Other stock exchanges use procedures similar to those of the New York Stock Exchange. The role of specialists and the extent of automation may differ slightly, but the approach is basically the same.

Options exchanges and futures exchanges utilize some procedures that differ significantly from those employed by stock exchanges. Futures exchanges

TABLE 3.2
TRADING VOLUME OF THE STOCK EXCHANGES

(a) 1992 Trading Volume

| | Shares[a] | | Dollars[a] | |
	Annual	Daily	Annual	Daily
NYSE	51,376	202	$1,745,466	$6,872
AMEX	3,600	14	42,238	166
Regionals	7,314	29	217,930	858
Nasdaq	48,455	191	890,785	3,507
Third market	4,554	18	154,719	609

(b) Five-Year Comparison

| | NYSE | | | Nasdaq | | |
Year	Companies	Issues	Daily Share Volume[a]	Companies	Issues	Daily Share Volume[a]
1992	2,089	2,658	202	4,113	4,764	191
1991	1,885	2,426	179	4,094	4,684	164
1990	1,774	2,284	157	4,132	4,706	132
1989	1,720	2,246	165	4,293	4,963	133
1988	1,681	2,234	161	4,451	5,144	123

[a]In millions.

Source: Adapted from *Fact Book: 1992 Data*, New York Stock Exchange, 1993, and *1993 Nasdaq Fact Book & Company Directory*, National Association of Security Dealers, 1993.

often have daily price limits instead of having specialists with directions to maintain "fair and orderly markets." The Chicago Board Options Exchange separates the two functions of the specialist: an order book official is charged with the maintenance of the book of limit orders and one or more registered market-makers are assigned the role of dealer. These exchanges will be discussed in more detail in Chapters 20 and 21.

3.2.3 Over-the-Counter Market

In the early days of the United States, banks acted as the primary dealers for stocks and bonds, and investors literally bought and sold securities "over the counter" at the banks. Transactions are more impersonal now, but the designation remains in use for transactions that are not executed on an organized exchange but, instead, involve the use of a dealer. Most bonds are sold over the counter, as are the securities of small (and some not so small) companies.

The over-the-counter (OTC) market for stocks is highly automated. In 1971 the **National Association of Securities Dealers** (NASD), which serves as a self-regulating agency for its members, put into operation the **National Association of Securities Dealers Automated Quotations** system (Nasdaq). This nationwide communications network allows brokers to know instantly the terms currently offered by all major dealers in securities covered by the system.

Dealers who subscribe to Level III of Nasdaq are given terminals with which to enter bid and asked prices for any stock in which they "make a market." Such dealers must be prepared to execute trades for at least one "normal unit of trading" (usually 100 shares) at the prices quoted. As soon as a bid or asked price is entered for a security, it is placed in a central computer file and may be seen by other subscribers (including other dealers) on their own terminals. When new quotations are entered, they replace the dealer's former prices.

When there is competition among dealers, those who are not well informed either price themselves out of the market by having too wide a bid-ask spread, or go out of business after incurring heavy losses. In the first situation, nobody does business with such a dealer, because there are better prices available with other dealers. The second situation occurs when the dealer accumulates a large inventory at too high a price or disposes of inventory at too low a price. Thus the dealer will be doing the opposite of the familiar Wall Street adage of "buy low, sell high."

It is argued that the interests of investors are best served by a market in which multiple dealers with unlimited access to all sources of information compete with one another, thereby leading to narrow bid-ask spreads around the "intrinsic" value of the security that provide investors with the "best" prices. However, organized exchanges counter with the argument that their system produces the "best" prices because all orders are sent to a central location for execution where they can be matched and bid on. Whereas trades in the over-the-counter market take place at the "best" quoted prices, the exchanges note that, although they have only one source of quoted prices (from the specialist), trades can (and often do) take place "inside" these prices.

Most brokerage firms subscribe to Level II of Nasdaq for their trading rooms, obtaining terminals that can display the current quotations on any security in the system. All bid and asked quotations are displayed, with the dealer offering each quotation being identified, so that orders can be routed to the dealer with the best price.[12] Imagine how difficult it would be to get the best price for a customer in the absence of such a terminal (as was the case before Nasdaq existed). A broker would have to contact dealers one by one to try to find the best price. After determining what appears to be the best price, the broker would then proceed to contact that dealer again. However, when this dealer is contacted, it may turn out that the price has gone up or down in the meantime and that the previously quoted price may no longer be the best one.

Level I of Nasdaq is used by individual account executives to get a feel for the market. It shows the **inside quotes,** meaning the highest bid and the lowest asked price for each security, along with last-sale reports and market summary data.

Nasdaq classifies stocks with larger trading volumes (which also meet certain other requirements) as belonging to the **National Market System** (Nasdaq/NMS). Every transaction made by a dealer for such a stock is reported directly, providing up-to-date detailed trading information to Nasdaq users. Furthermore, any stock included in Nasdaq/NMS is automatically eligible for margin purchases and short sales. Less active issues belong to the **Small Cap Issues** (Nasdaq Small Cap) section of Nasdaq; generally these issues are automatically "phased into" the National Market System when they meet the higher listing standards of NMS. For these issues, dealers report only the total transactions at the close of each day, and only certain ones are eligible for margin purchases and short sales. (The Federal Reserve Board determines which ones are eligible four times a year.)

As its name indicates, Nasdaq is primarily a quotation system. Actual transactions are often made via direct negotiation over the telephone between broker and dealer.[13] The price paid by a customer buying shares is likely to be higher than the amount paid by the broker to procure the shares, with the difference being known as a **markup.** When selling shares, the customer receives a price less than that received by the broker, with the difference being known as a **markdown.** (In both cases the customer may also be charged a commission.) The size of these markups and markdowns is usually less than 5% of the price paid or received. Brokers are examined periodically by the Securities and Exchange Commission to see that these markups and markdowns are "reasonable."

To be included in Nasdaq, a security must have at least two registered market-makers (that is, dealers) and a minimum number of publicly held shares. Moreover, the issuing firm must meet stated capital and asset requirements. As shown in Table 3.2, at the end of 1992, 4,764 issues were included in the system.[14] Although this total is more than double the total for the NYSE, trading volume is less than that of the NYSE, especially when measured in dollars.

The Nasdaq system covers only a portion of the outstanding OTC stocks and no bonds. Brokers with orders to buy or sell other OTC securities rely on quotations that are published daily on either Nasdaq's OTC Bulletin Board or what are known as **pink sheets** (there are also less formal communication networks) in order to obtain "best execution" for their clients.

3.2.4 Third and Fourth Markets

Until the 1970s the New York Stock Exchange required its member firms to trade all NYSE-listed stocks at the exchange and to charge fixed commissions. For large institutions this was expensive. In particular, the existence of a required minimum commission rate created a serious problem, since it exceeded the marginal cost of arranging large trades. Brokerage firms that were not members of the exchange faced no restrictions on the commissions they could charge and thus could compete effectively for large trades in NYSE-listed stocks. Such transactions were said to take place in the **third market.** More generally, the term *third market* now refers to the trading of any exchange-listed security in the over-the-counter market. The existence of such a market is enhanced today by the fact that its trading hours are not fixed (unlike exchanges), and that it can continue to trade securities even when trading is halted on an exchange. As can be seen in Table 3.2, on average 18 million shares were traded in the third market during each day of 1992.

Until 1976 NYSE member firms were prohibited by Rule 394 from either acting as dealers in the third market or executing orders involving NYSE-listed securities for their customers in the third market. In 1976 Rule 394 was replaced by Rule 390, which permits the execution of these orders in the third market but still prohibits member firms from acting as dealers in the third market. However, the Securities and Exchange Commission has issued a rule that permits member firms to act as dealers in securities that became listed on the NYSE after April 26, 1979. Controversy still exists over Rule 390, as some people argue that it should be abolished completely to spur competition between the NYSE and the over-the-counter market, whereas others argue that having all orders funneled to the NYSE will lead to the most competitive marketplace possible.

Many institutions have dispensed with brokers and exchanges altogether for transactions in exchange-listed stocks and other securities. Trades of this type, where the buyer and seller deal directly with each other, are sometimes said to take place in the **fourth market.** In the United States some of these transactions are facilitated by an automated computer/communications system called **Instinet,** which provides quotations and execution automatically.[15] A subscriber can enter a limit order in the computerized "book," where it can be seen by other subscribers who can, in turn, signal their desire to take it. Whenever two orders are matched, the system automatically records the transaction and sets up the paperwork for its completion. Subscribers can also use the system to find likely partners for a trade, then conduct negotiations by telephone. In recent years automated electronic facilities have been developed to permit institutional investors to trade *portfolios* of stocks directly with each other. The two largest such systems are POSIT and the Crossing Network. They are discussed further in this chapter's Institutional Issues section.

3.2.5 Foreign Markets

The two largest stock markets in the world outside New York are located in London and Tokyo. Both of these markets have recently undergone major changes in their rules and operating procedures. Furthermore, both of them have active markets in foreign securities. In particular, at the end of 1991 the London Stock Exchange listed 813 foreign stocks (in addition to 1,927 U.K. and Irish stocks) while the Tokyo Stock Exchange listed 125 foreign stocks (in addition to 1,650 Japanese stocks).

Crossing Systems: Evolution of the Fourth Market

Scientists define the evolution of a species as its gradual adoption of features that facilitate its long-term survival. In this context it is fitting to refer to the evolution of the fourth market. From its rudimentary beginnings the fourth market has evolved into a sophisticated trading mechanism where millions of shares change hands daily. Furthermore, the fourth market is posing a threat to existing species, in this case the organized security exchanges. How this competition plays out will influence the nature of trading well into the 21st century.

The fourth market, where large institutional investors deal directly with one another, began as a response to the high commission rates charged by brokerage firms. As discussed in the text, the original fourth market trading mechanism, run by Instinet, allows investors to trade with each other through an automated communications system at commissions that were originally only a small fraction of those charged by brokers.

However, this trading process (which is still very much alive and well) is rather cumbersome. Investors submit buy or sell limit orders (see Chapter 2) on individual securities at irregular times. If an interested investor on the "other side" of the trade happens to access the system at the right time, the trade may be completed. Although the commission costs of trading on the original fourth market are quite low (about a 3¢ to 4¢ per share), the odds of being able to complete large trades in numerous securities are small. Without improvement, the fourth market would surely have been pushed aside by other trading mechanisms, just as many promising, but ineffective, prehistoric creatures succumbed to competitors.

Nonetheless, the fourth market did evolve. Several electronic crossing systems now conduct regular market sessions in which investors may submit large packages of securities for trade. More specifically, current crossing systems work as follows:

1. Periodic trading sessions are established and widely announced.
2. Prior to these trading sessions, investors anonymously submit lists of stocks they wish to buy or sell and the associated quantities.
3. At the scheduled time (usually once or twice a day) the lists of desired trades are compared automatically by computer.
4. Trade prices are based on then current market prices as set on the organized security exchanges or the OTC market.
5. Offsetting buys and sells are matched. When buy orders do not equal sell orders for a security, matches are allocated based on the total dollar value of trades entered by each investor. Thus investors are encouraged to submit large trading volume requests.
6. Investors are notified of the completed trades, and the system handles the transfer of stocks.
7. Unmatched trades are returned to the investors for resubmission or execution elsewhere.

Crossing systems offer investors several key advantages over traditional trading methods. First, they provide anonymity. Investors' identities or intentions are not revealed, making it extremely difficult for other investors or market-makers to strategize against them. Second, as discussed, investors can trade entire portfolios at one time instead of individual securities on a piecemeal basis. Third, and most important, crossing networks are low-cost portfolio trading mechanisms.

The primary users of crossing networks are institutional investors with no urgent need to trade. Index funds (see Chapter 24), for example, trade only to adjust their portfolios so as to track the performance of a specific market index most effectively. Whether they trade this morning or this afternoon usually has little bearing on their results. Therefore, transaction costs are their primary concern. Crossing systems charge only 1¢ to 2¢ per share (as opposed to the 3¢ to 12¢ charged to institutional investors by brokerage firms). Furthermore, because trades are carried out at prevailing market prices, crossing systems permit investors to avoid the costs associated with bid-ask spread and price impact (discussed later in this chapter).

Crossing systems present some serious disadvantages as well. They do not offer liquidity in many stocks. Investors may not be able to complete trades in certain securities even after days of submitting those securities to the crossing networks. This problem is particularly acute for smaller-capitalization OTC stocks. In addition, the crossing systems require a certain amount of technological sophistication. Investors must submit trades computer to computer. Trading packages must be readied for entry at the appropriate times, and arrangements must be made for handling trades that cannot be completed through the crossing systems.

Currently, the two largest crossing systems are POSIT (run by Investment Technologies Group, a subsidiary of the brokerage firm Jefferies & Company, and BARRA, a consulting firm) and the Crossing Network (run by Instinet). Both systems work under the same basic procedures described earlier, although there are differences. For example, the Crossing Network conducts one session daily, in the early evening based on closing market prices. POSIT, on the other hand, conducts four daily crosses, two in the morning and two in the afternoon, based on prices prevailing in the market at the time of the crosses.

When both began operations in 1987, their trading volumes were insignificant. In subsequent years, however, volumes have increased. Currently, 5–6 million shares a day change hands through the crossing systems. Although this figure translates into only 1% to 2% of the New York Stock Exchange's daily volume, the potential for the crossing systems' long-term growth has created concern among members of the organized exchanges and OTC dealers.

The success of the large crossing systems has prompted several brokerage firms to initiate their own crossing operations, the most prominent being Fidelity (Investor's Liquidity Network) and Morgan Stanley (Match Plus). The NYSE has also entered the fray with an after-hours crossing system. However, each of these systems, unlike POSIT and the Crossing Network, requires revealing trading intentions to a brokerage firm. Despite assurances that their trading plans are confidential, institutional investors have generally been reluctant to work through these systems.

Many institutional investors have become sophisticated users of alternative trading mechanisms. For example, just after the NYSE's opening, an investor might send limit orders for a large set of stocks via the SuperDOT system (see this chapter) for immediate execution. The investor then withdraws uncompleted orders and submits them to POSIT for late morning and early afternoon crosses. Orders still unfilled are placed on the Crossing Network for that evening's session. Finally, the investor directs any orders still outstanding through traditional broker networks the next day.

The trading options available to institutional investors continue to grow as their per-unit trading costs continue to fall. Crossing systems have played an important role in these declining costs. Crossing systems are beginning to conduct global operations. Given that transaction costs on foreign markets are usually many times greater than they are in the United States, the room for crossing system growth appears enormous. The evolution of the fourth market continues.

Also of interest is the Toronto Stock Exchange, which by market value of securities listed is the fifth largest foreign stock market in the world (after Tokyo, London, Paris, and Frankfurt, according to the *Tokyo Stock Exchange 1993 Fact Book,* p. 83). Its electronic trading system has been adopted by many foreign markets, either directly (by Paris) or indirectly (by Tokyo). At the end of 1991 the Toronto Stock Exchange listed 74 foreign stocks (in addition to 1,464 Canadian stocks).

London

In October 1986 the "Big Bang" introduced several major reforms to the London Stock Exchange. Fixed brokerage commissions were eliminated, membership was opened up to corporations, and foreign firms were allowed to purchase existing member firms. Furthermore, an automated dealer quotation system similar to Nasdaq was introduced. This system, known as **SEAQ** (Stock Exchange Automated Quotations), involves competing market-makers whose quotes are displayed over a computer network. Small orders can be executed by using **SAEF** (SEAQ Automated Execution Facility), which functions like Nasdaq's SOES; large orders are handled over the telephone. Limit orders are not handled centrally but instead are handled by individual brokers or dealers who note when prices have moved sufficiently that they can be executed.

The London Stock Exchange's reforms have proved highly successful. The exchange has attracted trading in many non-U.K. stocks, thereby enhancing its status as the dominant European stock market. Even the U.S. stock markets have felt the competition. In an attempt to recapture some of the lost trading in U.S. securities from the London Stock Exchange, the NASD received approval from the SEC for a computer system like Nasdaq, which involves trading of many of the stocks listed on either the NYSE, AMEX, or Nasdaq/NMS. This system, known as **Nasdaq International,** opens for trading at 3:30 A.M., which corresponds to the opening time of the London Stock Exchange, and closes at 9 A.M., a half-hour before the NYSE opens.

Tokyo

Similar to the London Stock Exchange, the Tokyo Stock Exchange has recently experienced major reforms. **CORES** (Computer-assisted Order Routing and Execution System), a computer system for trading all but the 150 most active securities, was introduced in 1982. Then in 1986 the exchange began to admit foreign firms as members, and in 1990 **FORES** (Floor Order Routing and Execution System) was introduced as a computer system to facilitate trading in the most active stocks.

Interestingly, the system of trading both the most active and the relatively less active securities is quite different from any system found in either the United States or the United Kingdom. It is centered on members known as *saitori* who act, in a sense, as auctioneers in that they are neither dealers nor specialists. Instead they are intermediaries who accept orders from member firms and are not allowed to trade in any stocks for their own account.

At the opening of the exchange (because the exchange is open from 9 A.M. to 11 A.M. and 1 P.M. to 3 P.M., there are two openings per day) the *saitori* members follow a method called *itayose*, which operates like a call market in that the *saitori* seeks to set a single price so that the amount of trading is maximized (subject to certain constraints). This involves constructing supply and demand schedules for the market and limit orders that have been received, and noting where the two schedules intersect. (An example of how this is done is described in Chapter 4 and illustrated in Figures 4.1 through 4.4.)

After the opening of the exchange, the *saitori* follows a method known as *zaraba*, where orders are processed continually as they are received—that is, market orders are offset against previously unfilled limit orders. New limit orders are filled, if possible, against previously unfilled limit orders. If these new limit orders cannot be filled, then they are entered in the limit order book for possible future execution. Unlike the limit order book on the NYSE, the limit order book in Tokyo is available for inspection by member firms. Furthermore, unlike the NYSE, the Tokyo Stock Exchange prohibits trading at prices outside a given range based on the previous day's closing price. Hence there can be situations where trading in a stock ceases until the next day (when the price range is readjusted) unless two parties decide to trade within the current range.

Toronto

In 1977 the Toronto Stock Exchange began to use **CATS** (Computer-Assisted Trading System) on a trial basis with 30 stocks. Two years later CATS was expanded to cover about 700 stocks and was made permanent. All other listed stocks were traded in a specialist-driven system like the one in New York. However, the success of CATS has led to more and more stocks being traded on it. Indeed, plans are in place for trading in all stocks to be computerized so that the Toronto Stock Exchange will no longer have a central trading floor.

With CATS, orders are entered electronically in brokers' offices and then routed to a computer file. This computer file displays limit orders against which other investors may trade. Market orders are matched against the limit order with the best price that is in the file (that is, a market order to buy is matched against the lowest priced limit order to sell, and a market order to sell is matched against the highest priced limit order to buy). If insufficient volume is available in the file at the best price, the remainder of the market order is then put in the file as a limit order at that price. However, brokers, responding to the wishes of the investor, can change this price at any time.

At the daily opening CATS uses a different procedure. Like *itayose* in Tokyo, CATS sets an opening price so as to maximize the number of shares that are traded. While both market and limit orders are accepted, there are constraints on the size of each market order, and these orders must be from the public (meaning that member firms are not allowed to submit opening market orders).

3.3   INFORMATION-MOTIVATED AND LIQUIDITY-MOTIVATED TRADERS

There are two major reasons for most security transactions. An investor may believe that a security has become mispriced—meaning that its value is outside the current bid and asked prices. Anybody who feels this way believes (consciously or subconsciously) that he or she has information not known to (or understood by) the market in general and may be referred to as an *information-motivated trader.* On the other hand, an investor may simply want to sell some securities in order to buy something (such as a new car) or buy some securities with some newly acquired money (such as from an inheritance). Anybody acting in this manner may be referred to as a *liquidity-motivated trader.* In making security transactions, he or she does not presume that others in the market have incorrectly evaluated the prospects for a security.[16]

The Stock Exchange of Hong Kong: Another Asian Exchange Switches to Automated Matching

by Ann Guenther Sherman
Hong Kong University of Science and Technology

As the unrelenting march toward integration of the world's security markets continues, the competitive pressures on national stock exchanges to adopt efficient and low-cost trading mechanisms have grown stronger. The Stock Exchange of Hong Kong (SEHK) provides an interesting example of the conflict between entrenched business practices and external competition, and the ultimate resolution of that conflict.

Stock trading has a long history in Hong Kong, with informal trading dating back to 1866 and a formal exchange established in 1891 (the second in Asia, after Japan's). By 1973 four exchanges operated in the tiny city-state, far too many to justify from an economic perspective. Despite considerable controversy, the four exchanges were merged into the SEHK in 1986.

The newly created SEHK had many potential models for a trading system. It could have built on CATS (Computer-Assisted Trading System) of the Toronto Stock Exchange, which for some of its listed stocks is the world's first fully automated trading system. The SEHK could also have learned from CORES (Computer-Assisted Order Routing and Execution System), a modified version of CATS instituted by the Tokyo Stock Exchange. Other models include Nasdaq (National Association of Securities Dealers Automated Quotations), which was used as the basis for the Big Bang reorganization of the London Stock Market. Or, of course, Hong Kong could have followed one of the many auction/modified open-outcry systems in use around the world, including that of the New York Stock Exchange.

Instead, the SEHK chose an unusual way of arranging trades. Each member of the exchange has a booth or a desk on the exchange floor, at which it can have up to two representatives. Each booth has two telephones (an internal and an external line) and up to two computer terminals, only one of which operates in an interactive mode while the other is in display-only mode. Members enter buy and sell orders into the computer, and the orders are shown on the screen for that stock. The orders include price but not quantity. If another member of the exchange wishes to trade with the person who input the order, then he or she telephones that person. If the lines are full and the call cannot get through, then the trader may choose to get up and go to the other person's booth. The member who input the order is under no obligation to deal with the first person who calls or dashes over, and the quantity of any trade must be negotiated. After a trade has been made, the seller must enter the details into the system within 15 minutes. There is no order-matching facility, no designated market-maker, and no priority assigned to orders at the same price.

One of the system's weaknesses is that a person entering an order has less information than he or she would have in a simple open-outcry system. When a trader standing at a post on the NYSE shouts out an order, he or she can see how many other people at the post are ready to respond to the order and may even be able to judge how anxious they are to trade. When a trader enters an order into a terminal on the SEHK, he or she can only wait for the phone to ring. While talking to the first person who calls, the trader cannot tell how many others are also trying to get through—the only way to learn this is to hang up and wait for the phone to ring again, a method that may prove costly if in fact no one else is interested. This weakness is partially offset by the habit of traders' running over to each other's desks, a feature that was probably not in the original plan.

Another potential problem, especially during busy times, is that each order takes longer to arrange than in an automated order-matching system. Rather than simply entering a limit order into an automated system and receiving confirmation when the order is filled, traders must enter the order, wait for someone to contact them, negotiate a quantity, and then (if they are selling) enter the details into the computer. Most exchanges, such as those in Malaysia and Singapore, experienced sharp rises in turnover after they introduced automated trading systems. Taiwan, with fully automated trading, has handled daily volume levels close to Tokyo's (although Tokyo's market capitalization was then around 30 times larger). In spite of the possible reduction in trading capacity, however, the Hong Kong system may appeal to those who prefer private negotiation when arranging deals, rather than the impersonality of an order-matching system or the open competition of an open-outcry system.

A key disadvantage (or advantage, depending on your outlook) to the Hong Kong system is that it may facilitate manipulation of stock prices. Efficient and cheap price manipulation requires coordination on the part of the manipulators. They create a series of fake trades among themselves in the same stock at ever increasing (or decreasing) prices. In an automated matching system, price manipulators can still buy shares at above-market prices, but they cannot determine who gets those high prices, because orders are filled based on price and time priority. With the Hong Kong system, a price manipulator need only tell an accomplice when he or she plans to enter the order and make sure that the accomplice is ready to dial quickly. If the accomplice is not the first person to call, the manipulator can refuse to trade.

Although the SEHK fell behind many other Asian countries in updating trading methods, its members eventually recognized the necessity for reform. The Hong Kong securities industry was heavily influenced by the October 1987 crash, in which the Hong Kong stock and futures exchanges performed embarrassingly poorly. During the crash, the SEHK closed for 4 days, October 20–23 (the only stock exchange in the world to close for so long), and the chairman of the exchange was later arrested and convicted for accepting bribes in connection with a new listing on the exchange. In the aftermath of the crash, there have been major changes in Hong Kong, including the formation of the Securities and Futures Commission, which has tightened regulation of the market. Among other changes, some forms of insider trading are now illegal, and stock price manipulation is now prosecuted.

At the SEHK a new clearing system was adopted in 1992, and an automated order-matching system began operating on November 1, 1993, although it initially handled only a few stocks on an experimental basis. The order-matching system was originally expected to be introduced two years earlier, but complications in the replacement of the clearing system and the resistance of vested interests delayed its implementation. After automated order matching is fully implemented, members will have a choice between trading on the floor of the exchange and trading from terminals in their offices. Exchange officials expect the trading floor to soon be deserted, as happened in London after the Big Bang. The SEHK also has plans to introduce short selling and stock options, and it may extend trading hours beyond the current 3½ hours a day. Although these changes have taken many years, soon the SEHK will be as technologically advanced as other major exchanges around the world.

After control of Hong Kong switches from Great Britain to the People's Republic of China (PRC) in 1997, it is not clear what will happen to the SEHK. Most of the exchange's plans for expansion involve the listing of mainland companies, which it began in 1993. If the economic opening and development of the PRC continues, Hong Kong may be able to greatly enlarge its position as an international financial center. On the other hand, Hong Kong's stock market has a close rivalry with Singapore's, and Taiwan has announced its intention to supplant Hong Kong as an Asian financial center after 1997. There are already signs that the 1997 takeover may affect two of Hong Kong's key advantages, the rule of law and press freedom, in which case Singapore and Taiwan would gain a great competitive advantage. By the end of 1994, the SEHK should have completed the many reforms planned after the 1987 crash, but it will still face many challenges.

Dealers can make money by transacting with liquidity-motivated traders or with inept information-motivated traders, but on average, they can only lose money by transacting with clever information-motivated traders. The larger a dealer's bid-ask spread, the less business he or she will do; but whatever the spread, when a clever information-motivated trader makes a transaction, the dealer may expect to lose money. In the absence of unwise traders, the very existence of a dealer depends on investors' desires for liquidity. A dealer must select a bid-ask spread wide enough to limit the number of transactions with traders possessing superior information, but narrow enough to attract an adequate number of liquidity-motivated transactions.

A dealer can take either a passive or an active role. For example, tentative bid and asked prices can be established. Then as orders come in and are filled, the dealer's inventory (or "position") will vary and may even become negative when promises to deliver securities exceed promises to accept delivery. But any clear trend suggests that the bid and asked prices should be altered. In effect, a *passive dealer* lets the market indicate the appropriate bid and asked prices.

An *active dealer* tries to get as much information as possible and to alter bid and asked prices in advance so as to keep the flow of orders more in balance. The better a dealer's information, the smaller the bid-ask spread required to make a profit. Poorly informed dealers will either price themselves out of the market by having too low a bid price or too high an asked price, or go out of business after suffering losses by being "picked off" by more knowledgeable traders.

3.4   PRICES AS INFORMATION SOURCES

The usual description of a market assumes that every trader knows how much of a given item he or she will buy or sell at every price at which the item might trade. All the traders come together, and in one way or another a price is found that "clears" the market for that item—that is, it makes the quantity demanded as close as possible to the quantity supplied.

This may or may not be an adequate description of the market for consumer goods, but it is clearly inadequate when describing security markets. The value of any financial asset depends on future prospects that are almost always uncertain. Any information that bears on such prospects may lead to a revised estimate of the security's value. The fact that a knowledgeable trader is willing to buy or sell some quantity of a security at a particular price is likely to be information of just this sort. Offers to trade may thus affect other offers. Prices may both clear markets *and* convey information.

The dual role of prices has a number of implications. For example, it behooves the liquidity-motivated trader to publicize his or her motives in order to avoid an adverse effect that his or her trade may have on the price at which it is executed. Thus an institution purchasing securities for a pension fund that intends to hold a representative cross section of securities should make it clear that it does not consider the securities underpriced. On the other hand, any firm trying to buy or sell a large number of shares that it considers to be mispriced should try to conceal either its motives, its identity, or both (and many do try). Such attempts may be ineffective, however, as those asked to take the other side of these trades try to find out exactly what is going on (and many do find out).

<table>
<tr><td>**3.5**</td><td>CENTRAL MARKET</td></tr>
</table>

The Securities Acts Amendments of 1975 mandated that the U.S. Securities and Exchange Commission move as rapidly as possible toward the implementation of a truly nationwide competitive central security market:

> *The linking of all markets for qualified securities through communication and data processing facilities will foster efficiency, enhance competition, increase the information available to brokers, dealers, and investors, facilitate the offsetting of investors' orders, and contribute to best execution of such orders.* [17]

Implementation of these objectives has proceeded in steps. In 1975 a **consolidated tape** began to report trades in stocks listed on the New York and American stock exchanges that took place on the two exchanges, on major regional exchanges, in the over-the-counter market using the Nasdaq system, and in the fourth market using the Instinet system. Since 1976 this information has been used to produce the **composite stock price tables** published in the daily press.

The second step involved the setting of commissions charged to investors by brokerage firms that are members of the NYSE. Prior to 1975 investors were charged the same commission by all NYSE member firms for a given order because the NYSE required its members to levy a fixed commission. However, as a result of the Securities Acts Amendments of 1975, this system of fixed commissions was abolished and all brokerage firms were free to set their commissions at whatever level they desired.

The next step involved quotations. To obtain the best possible terms for a client, a broker must know the prices currently available on all major markets. To facilitate this, the Securities and Exchange Commission instructed stock exchanges to make their quotations available for use in the **Consolidated Quotations System** (CQS). With the implementation of this system in 1978, bid and asked prices (along with the corresponding volume limits) were made more accessible to those subscribing to quotation services. Increasingly a broker is able to rely on electronics to determine the best available terms for a trade, thus avoiding the need for extensive "shopping around."

In 1978 the **Intermarket Trading System** (ITS) was inaugurated. This electronic communications network links eight exchanges (NYSE, AMEX, the Boston, Cincinnati, Chicago, Pacific, and Philadelphia stock exchanges, and the Chicago Board Options Exchange) and certain over-the-counter security dealers, thereby enabling commission and floor brokers, specialists, and dealers at various locations to interact with one another. ITS display monitors provide the bid and asked prices quoted by market-makers (these quotes are obtained from

CQS), and the system allows the commission and floor brokers, specialists, and dealers to route orders electronically to where the best price exists at that moment. However, the market-maker providing the best price may withdraw it on receipt of an order. Another drawback is that the customer's broker is not required to route the order to the market-maker providing the best price. At the end of 1992, 2,532 exchange-listed stocks were included on the system, and daily trading volume averaged 10.8 million shares.

The final step in the process has not been implemented. It involves the establishment of a single centralized limit order book (CLOB), with associated procedures for linking markets electronically and the setting of rules concerning its use and disclosure. In implementing this step, many issues must be settled: Should there be specialists, and if so, how should they operate? What requirements (if any) should be imposed on market-makers? Who should operate the central market system?

There are many long-entrenched and powerful institutions in the securities industry. The eventual nature of the overall set of markets will undoubtedly depend in part on the relative political power of the various vested interests.

3.6   CLEARING PROCEDURES

Most stocks are sold the "regular way," which requires delivery of certificates within five business days. On rare occasions a sale may be made as a "cash" transaction, requiring delivery the same day, or as a "seller's option," giving the seller the choice of any delivery day within a specified period (typically, no more than 60 days). On other occasions extensions to the five-day time limit are granted.

It would be extremely inefficient if every security transaction had to end with a physical transfer of stock certificates from the seller to the buyer. A brokerage firm might sell 500 shares of AT&T stock for one client, Mr. A, and later that day buy 500 shares for Ms. B, another client. Mr. A's 500 shares could be delivered to the buyer, and Ms. B's shares could be obtained by accepting delivery from the seller. However, it would be much easier to transfer Mr. A's shares to Ms. B and instruct Ms. B's seller to deliver 500 shares directly to Mr. A's buyer. This would be especially helpful if the brokerage firm's clients, Mr. A and Ms. B, held their securities in street name. Then the 500 shares would not have to be moved and their ownership would not have to be changed on the books of AT&T.

3.6.1 Clearinghouses

The process can be facilitated even more by a **clearinghouse,** the members of which are brokerage firms, banks, and other financial institutions. Records of transactions made by members during the day are sent there shortly afterward. At the end of the day, both sides of the trades are verified for consistency, then all transactions are netted out. Each member receives a list of the net amounts of securities to be delivered or received along with the net amount of money to be paid or collected. Every day each member settles with the clearinghouse instead of with various other firms.

A centralized clearinghouse, operated by the National Securities Clearing Corporation, handles trades made on the New York and American stock exchanges and in the over-the-counter market. Some regional exchanges also maintain clearinghouses. Not all exchange members join such organizations; some choose to use the services of other members. Some banks belong in order to facilitate delivery of securities which, for example, serve as collateral for call loans.

By holding securities in street name and using clearinghouses, brokers can reduce the cost of transfer operations. But even more can be done: Certificates can be immobilized almost completely. The **Depository Trust Company** (DTC) accomplishes this by maintaining computerized records of the securities "owned" by its member firms (brokers, banks, and so on). Members' stock certificates are credited to their accounts at the DTC, while the certificates are transferred to the DTC on the books of the issuing corporation and remain registered in its name unless a member subsequently withdraws them. Whenever possible, one member will "deliver" securities to another by initiating a simple bookkeeping entry in which one account is credited and the other debited for the shares involved. Dividends paid on securities held by the DTC are simply credited to members' accounts based on their holdings and may be subsequently withdrawn in cash.

The Securities Acts Amendments of 1975 instructed the Securities and Exchange Commission to develop a central system of this sort to eliminate the movement of stock certificates and possibly eliminate stock certificates entirely. Eventually, when cash dividends are to be paid by a corporation, instead of writing checks, its computers may transfer money directly using other computers that are in touch with still other computers in banks, brokerage firms, and other financial institutions. Moreover, the central market system may be integrated with the central clearing system so that agreement of two parties to the terms of a transaction will automatically bring about the transfer of ownership required to complete the trade.

3.7   INSURANCE

In the late 1960s many brokerage firms were confronted with an unexpectedly large volume of transactions. Unfortunately, at that time computerized systems were unable to handle the work load. This gave rise to back-office problems and resulted in a rash of **fails to deliver**—instances in which a seller's broker did not deliver certificates to a buyer's broker on or before the required settlement date.

Worse yet, several brokerage firms subsequently collapsed, and some of their clients discovered for the first time that certificates "in their accounts" were not physically available. Such events led to serious concern about the desirability of any procedure that kept certificates out of the hands of the investor. To avoid erosion of investor confidence, member firms of the New York Stock Exchange spent substantial sums to cover the losses of failed firms or to merge them with successful firms. But such remedies were only temporary; insurance provided a more permanent solution.

3.7.1   Securities Investor Protection Corporation (SIPC)

The Securities Investor Protection Act of 1970 established the **Securities Investor Protection Corporation** (SIPC), a quasi-governmental agency that insures the accounts of clients of all brokers and members of exchanges registered with the Securities and Exchange Commission against loss due to a brokerage firm's failure. Each account is insured up to a stated amount ($500,000 per customer in 1994). The cost of the insurance is supposed to be borne by the covered brokers and members through premiums. Should this amount be insufficient, the SIPC can borrow up to $1 billion from the U.S. Treasury. A number of brokerage firms have gone further, arranging for additional coverage from private insurance companies.

3.8   COMMISSIONS

3.8.1   Fixed Commissions

In the 1770s people interested in buying and selling stocks and bonds met under a buttonwood tree at 68 Wall Street in New York City. In May 1792 a group of brokers pledged "not to buy or sell from this day for any person whatsoever, any kind of public stock at a less rate than one quarter percent commission on the specie value, and that we will give preference to each other in our negotiations."[18] A visitor to the New York Stock Exchange today can see a copy of this "buttonwood agreement" publicly displayed. This is not surprising, since the exchange is a lineal descendant of the group that met under the buttonwood tree. Also, until 1968 the exchange required its member brokers to charge fixed minimum commissions for stocks, with no "rebates, returns, discounts or allowances in 'any shape or manner,' direct or indirect."[19] The terms had changed, but the principle established 180 years earlier remained in effect.

In the United States most cartels designed to limit competition by fixing prices are illegal. But this one was exempted from prosecution under the antitrust laws. Before 1934 the exchange was, in essence, considered a private club for its members. This changed with passage of the Securities Exchange Act of 1934, which required most exchanges to be registered with the Securities and Exchange Commission (SEC). The commission, in turn, encouraged exchanges to "self-regulate" their activities, including the setting of minimum commissions.

3.8.2   Competitive Commissions

As mentioned earlier in this chapter, the system of fixed commissions was finally terminated by the Securities Acts Amendments of 1975 (but only after repeated challenges by the NYSE). Since May 1, 1975 (known in the trade as **May Day**), brokers have been free to set commissions at any desired rate or to negotiate with customers concerning the fees charged for particular trades. The former procedure is more commonly employed in "retail" trades executed for small investors, whereas the latter is used more often when handling large trades involving institutional investors.

In the era of fixed commissions, brokerage firms did not compete with one another over commissions. However, those brokerage firms that belonged to the New York Stock Exchange competed with one another in a different manner, namely, by offering a panoply of ancillary services to customers. Large institutions were provided with security analysis, performance measurement services, and the like in return for **soft dollars**—brokerage commissions ostensibly paid for having the brokerage firm execute their trades and indirectly designated as payment for services rendered. It appears that for every $3 in commissions received on large trades, brokerage firms were willing to spend up to roughly $2 to provide ancillary services to their customers. Thus it follows that it cost brokerage firms roughly $1 per $3 of commissions received just to execute a large trade for a customer. Apparently up to two-thirds of the fixed commission rate ($2 out of $3) on such large orders was pure (marginal) profit.

Experience after May Day provided confirmation. Rates for large trades fell substantially. So did those charged for small trades by firms offering only "bare-bones" brokerage services. On the other hand, broad-line firms that provided extensive services to small investors for no additional fee continued to charge commissions similar to those specified in the earlier fixed schedules. In succeeding years, as costs have risen, charges for smaller transactions have increased, whereas those for large trades have not.

During the 1960s and 1970s a number of procedures were used to subvert the fixed commission rates. In particular, the third and fourth markets expanded their operations while regional exchanges invented ways to serve as conduits to return a portion of the fixed commissions to institutional investors.

No legal restriction gave the New York Stock Exchange its monopoly power in the first instance. Instead, the situation has been attributed to the natural monopoly arising from economies of scale in bringing together many people (either physically or via modern communications technology) to trade with one another. The potential profits from such a monopoly are limited by the advantages it confers. The increasing institutionalization of security holdings and progress in communications and computer technology have diminished the advantages associated with a centralized physical exchange. Thus the removal of legal protection for this particular type of price fixing may have accelerated a trend already under way.

Increased competition among brokerage firms has resulted in a wide range of alternatives for investors. Following May Day, some firms "unbundled"—meaning that they priced their services separately from their pricing of order execution. Other firms "went discount," meaning that they dropped almost all ancillary services and cut commissions accordingly. Still others "bundled" new services into comprehensive packages. Some of these approaches have not stood the test of time, but just as mail-order firms, discount houses, department stores, and expensive boutiques coexist in the retail clothing trade, many different combinations are viable in the brokerage industry.

Soft Dollars

Suppose that you have decided to build a new home. As your first step you hire a general contractor to oversee the different construction phases. The general contractor, in turn, hires various subcontractors to lay the foundation, frame the house, install wiring, and so on.

You compensate the general contractor in large part based on the charges billed by the subcontractors. Now assume that the general contractor allowed the subcontractors to charge more than the true costs of their services. The difference between the billed costs and the true costs was then rebated to the general contractor in the form of payments for goods and services only indirectly related to the general contractor's work on your home, such as accounting services or transportation vehicles.

Presumably you would find such an arrangement objectionable. After all, fairness dictates that the general contractor's charges to you include only the actual cost of the subcontractors' labor and materials. The general contractor should pay for its accounting services directly out of its own pocket. The efficiency and equity of such an arrangement seems unquestionable, except perhaps in the investment management business, where each year institutional investors pay hundreds of millions of "soft" dollars to brokerage firms in a situation analogous to our hypothetical home-building example.

Soft dollars are brokerage commissions paid by institutional investors in excess of amounts required to compensate brokers for simply executing trades. As the text describes, soft dollars had their origin in the fixed commission rates imposed by the New York Stock Exchange prior to May 1, 1975. Large institutional investors paid the same commission rates as small retail investors, despite the obvious economies of scale present in carrying out large trades as opposed to small trades.

Brokerage firms competed with one another, not by lowering commission rates, but by rebating a portion of the commissions to large investors. These brokerage firms did so by offering a plethora of "free" services to the investors. These services typically involved various types of investment research, although on occasion they included such ethically questionable items as airline tickets and lodging for trips abroad.

After the deregulation of commission rates in 1975, it was widely assumed that soft dollars would disappear. Investors would pay brokers only for executing their trades in the most cost-effective manner. Other services, such as investment research, would be purchased directly from the supplying firms. This decoupling of payments for trade execution from other services is known as "unbundling."

Surprisingly, the soft dollar industry, despite some initial rough going following May Day, did not wither away. In fact, it flourished. Its prosperity was facilitated by two factors. First, Congress legislated in 1975 that commissions could continue to be used to pay for investment research, not just for trade execution. The conditions under which soft dollars could be used and the general types of investment research that can be purchased are specified (and occasionally modified) by the Securities and Exchange Commission. Although the legislation had the effect of curbing some of the most egregious soft dollar abuses, it left soft dollar users with wide latitude.

The second factor was the general trend of institutional investors toward hiring external investment managers to invest their assets. These managers, in a loose sense, act as the general contractor referred to earlier. The managers have discretion over the allocation of their clients' commissions. They are permitted (and, in fact, have a strong incentive) to use soft dollars to pay for various forms of investment research. That research includes primarily fundamental company analyses, data on expected earnings, and economic forecasts. It also includes computer software and hardware, performance measurement, and educational services. By using soft dollars to pay for such research, the costs are effectively shifted to the managers' clients, rather than paid for by the managers themselves.

Establishing the size of the soft dollar industry is difficult, but estimates of total soft dollar commissions in the range of $500 million to $1 billion annually appear reasonable. The soft dollar industry is large and lucrative enough to support a number of brokerage firms devoted solely to supplying third-party research services to investors in exchange for soft dollars. These brokerage firms make arrangements with providers of investment research to funnel payments for services rendered to investment managers in exchange for having the managers' execute trades through the brokerage firms.

In the investment industry, prices for research services are often quoted on two levels: hard (straight cash payment) or soft (price in commission dollars). The ratio of the two prices implies a conversion rate. Although this conversion rate is negotiable, a standard figure is 1.8 commission dollars paid to receive one dollar in services.

The stated rationale behind managers' use of soft dollars is that their clients benefit from the research services purchased. Presumably, in the absence of soft dollars managers would raise their fees to enable them to purchase the necessary research directly, yet maintain their current profit margins. However, managers are not required to provide their clients with a detailed accounting of their soft dollar use. (Some institutional investors do insist on such detailed reporting. Furthermore, Congress is considering requiring this disclosure.)

Thus it is difficult for clients to assess whether their commission dollars are being wisely allocated by their managers. One is hard-pressed to imagine how clients are better off under a system of unidentified, implicit fees than they would be if commission payments were completely unbundled.

Why don't institutional clients insist that soft dollar use be prohibited or at least be fully divulged? Inertia and ignorance appear to be two explanations. For another reason, many institutional investors have themselves become beneficiaries of soft dollars. They use soft dollars by directing their managers to purchase various services for their immediate benefit. (Soft dollars generated in this manner are sometimes called "directed commissions.") For example, a corporate pension fund staff may use their managers' soft dollars to purchase performance measurement services that the corporate budget would not normally allow.

Over the years, soft dollars have been criticized as being inefficient and ripe for abuse. Calls for prohibition of soft dollars have occasionally been heard. However, the soft dollar industry is powerful and to date has been able to ward off any substantive changes.

Figure 3.2 shows typical commission rates charged by retail brokerage firms for small- to medium-sized trades. These rates are representative of those charged by full-line retail brokers that provide offices with quotation devices, research reports, account executives available for advice and information, and the like. The rates also apply to trades made by customers whose volume of business is small. Discount firms with little but execution capability typically charge 30% to 70% less. As in any other competitive industry, it behooves the customer to decide what is worth paying for and then to shop around to obtain the best possible price.

3.9 TRANSACTION COSTS

3.9.1 Bid-Ask Spread

Commission costs are only a portion of the total cost associated with buying or selling a security. Consider a "round-trip" transaction, in which a stock is

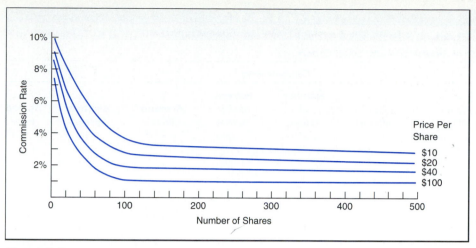

Figure 3.2
Typical Commission Rates for Selected Transactions; Dollar Commission as a Percentage of Order Value

purchased and then sold during a period in which no new information causes investors to collectively reassess the value of the stock (more concretely, the bid and asked prices quoted by dealers do not change). The stock will be purchased typically at the dealers' asked price and sold at the bid price, which is lower. The **bid-ask spread** thus constitutes a portion of the round-trip transaction costs.

How large is the spread between bid and asked prices for a typical stock? According to one study, the spread is approximately $.30 per share for the securities of large, actively traded companies. This amounts to less than 1% of the price per share for most stocks of this type—a reasonably small amount to pay for the ability to buy or sell in a hurry.

However, not all securities enjoy this type of liquidity. Shares of smaller firms tend to sell at lower prices but at similar bid-ask spreads. As a result, the percentage transaction cost is considerably larger. This is shown in panel (a) of Table 3.3. Stocks were assigned to sectors based on each firm's **market capitalization,** which is equal to the market value of the firm's outstanding equity (that is, its share price times the number of shares outstanding). For example, if the total market value of the common stock of a company was less than $10 million, it was considered to be in sector 1 (the smallest capitalization sector), and if the market value was greater than $1.5 billion, the company was included in sector 9 (the largest capitalization sector). As the table shows, the larger the capitalization, the greater was the average price per share. Note also that the average spread in dollars was actually greater for the smallest capitalization stocks than for the largest. Most importantly, however, the ratio of the average spread to the average price fell continuously from 6.55% for the smallest sector to .52% for the largest sector. This means that the larger the capitalization of the firm, the greater the liquidity will be for that investment.

Another study looked at NYSE stocks, based on their trading activity, and found similar-sized spreads. Specifically, the 20% most active stocks had a spread

TABLE 3.3
BID-ASK SPREADS AND ROUND-TRIP TRANSACTION COSTS

(a) Common Stock Bid-Ask Spreads: Small Orders

Capitalization

Sector	From (millions)	To (millions)	Number of Issues	Percent of U.S. Market	Average Price	Average Spread	Spread Price
1 (small)	$ 0	$ 10	1,009	.36%	$ 4.58	$.30	6.55%
2	10	25	754	.89	10.30	.42	4.07
3	25	50	613	1.59	15.16	.46	3.03
4	50	75	362	1.60	18.27	.34	1.86
5	75	100	202	1.27	21.85	.32	1.46
6	100	500	956	15.65	28.31	.32	1.13
7	500	1,000	238	12.29	35.43	.27	.76
8	1,000	1,500	102	8.87	44.34	.29	.65
9 (large)	1,500	99,999	180	57.48	52.40	.27	.52

(b) Percentage Round-Trip Transaction Costs, Common Stock

Capitalization

Dollar Value of Block ($ thousands)

Sector	5	25	250	500	1,000	2,500	5,000	10,000	20,000
1 (small)	17.3%	27.3%	43.8%						
2	8.9	12.0	23.8	33.4%					
3	5.0	7.6	18.8	25.9	30.0%				
4	4.3	5.8	9.6	16.9	25.4	31.5%			
5	2.8	3.9	5.9	8.1	11.5	15.7	25.7%		
6	1.8	2.1	3.2	4.4	5.6	7.9	11.0	16.2%	
7	1.9	2.0	3.1	4.0	5.6	7.7	10.4	14.3	20.0%
8	1.9	1.9	2.7	3.3	4.6	6.2	8.9	13.6	18.1
9 (large)	1.1	1.2	1.3	1.7	2.1	2.8	4.1	5.9	8.0

Source: Thomas F. Loeb, "Trading Cost: The Critical Link Between Investment Information and Results," *Financial Analysts Journal*, 39, no. 3 (May/June 1983): 41–42.

of .62%. The spreads increased uniformly thereafter, with the 20% least active stocks having the largest spread of 2.06%.[20]

The inverse relationship between the amount of trading activity (or market value) and spread size can be explained once it is recognized that the spread is the dealer's compensation for providing investors with liquidity. The smaller the amount of trading, the less frequently the dealer will capture the spread (by buying at the bid and selling at the asked). Hence the dealer will need a wider spread in order to generate a level of compensation commensurate with more frequently traded securities.

3.9.2 Price Impact

Brokerage commissions and bid-ask spreads represent transaction costs for small orders (typically 100 shares). For larger sized orders the possibility of **price impacts** must also be considered. Consider purchase orders. Due to the law of supply and demand, the larger the size of the order, the more likely the investor's purchase price will be higher. Furthermore, the more rapidly the order is to be completed and the more knowledgeable the individual or organization placing the order, the higher the purchase price charged by the dealer.

Panel (b) of Table 3.3 provides estimates of average costs for transactions in the upstairs dealer market. All three sources of costs are included: bid-ask spreads, brokerage commissions, and price impacts. The figures refer to the total cost for a "round-trip"—a purchase followed by a sale—and reveal that for any capitalization sector, larger block sizes are associated with larger percentage transaction costs. The figures also reveal that for any given dollar-size block, larger capitalization sectors are associated with smaller percentage transaction costs. [A similar observation can be made upon examination of panel (a).]

Panel (a) of Figure 3.3 on page 74 plots the percentage transaction costs for blocks of $25,000 each, which correspond to the values in the third column from the left in panel (b) of Table 3.3. Values range from 27.3% (for small-capitalization stocks) to 1.2% (for large-capitalization stocks).

Panel (b) of Figure 3.3 shows the relationship between order size and transaction cost for each of the three largest capitalization sectors, which correspond to the last three rows of panel (b) of Table 3.3. The figure shows that the impact of a very large order on price can be substantial, and the impact is greater for smaller capitalizations.

3.10   INVESTMENT BANKING

The discussion so far has focused on secondary markets for securities, where securities that were initially issued at some previous point in time are subsequently traded. The focus will now shift to the **primary market** for securities, which is the name given to the markets where the initial issuance itself takes place. Some issuers deal directly with purchasers in this market, but many rely on **investment bankers,** who serve as intermediaries between issuers and the ultimate purchasers of their securities.

3.10.1   Private Placements

Investment banking services are typically performed by brokerage firms and, to a limited extent, by commercial banks. In some instances only a few large institutional investors are solicited, and the entire issue is sold to one or a few of them. Indeed, such **private placements** are often announced only after the fact, via advertisements in the financial press. As long as relatively few potential buyers are contacted (say, fewer than 25), requirements for detailed disclosure, public notice, and so on, may be waived, considerably reducing the cost of floating an issue. However, such investments are illiquid because the investor is typically prohibited from selling the security within two years of the purchase date. This has resulted in few equities being sold in this manner. Instead, most private placements involve fixed-income securities that are purchased by investors who are attracted by their coupon payments, not the prospect of capital gains.

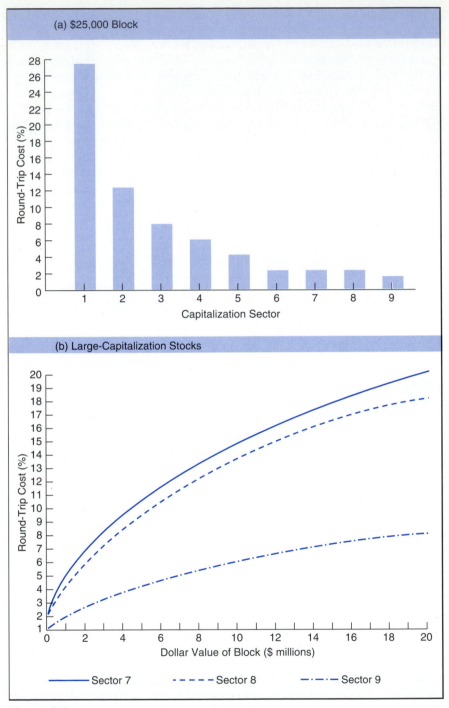

Figure 3.3
Round-Trip Transaction Costs

3.10.2 Public Sale

When public sale is contemplated, much more must be done than with private placements. Many firms may serve as intermediaries in the process. One, acting as the "lead" investment banker, will put together a syndicate (or purchase group) and a selling group. The **syndicate** includes firms that purchase the securities from the issuing corporation and are thus said to **underwrite** the offering. The **selling group** includes firms that contact potential buyers and do the actual selling, usually on a commission basis.

The process begins with discussions between the issuing corporation and one or more investment bankers. Some issuers utilize **competitive bidding,** then select the investment banker offering the best overall terms. This procedure is used for many government bond issues and is required by law for securities issued by firms in certain regulated industries. However, many corporations maintain a continuing relationship with a single investment banker and negotiate the terms of each new offering with that firm. The investment banker is likely to be heavily involved in the planning of an offering, the terms involved, the amount to be offered, and so on, serving, in effect, as a financial consultant to the corporation.

Once the basic characteristics of an offering have been established, a **registration statement** is filed with the Securities and Exchange Commission, and a preliminary **prospectus** disclosing material relevant to the prospective buyer is issued. (This prospectus is often referred to as a **red herring,** since it has a disclaimer printed in red ink across the first page, which informs the reader that it is not an offer to sell.) The actual price of the security is not included in the preliminary prospectus, and no final sales may be made until the registration becomes effective and a final prospectus is issued, indicating the "offer" price at which the stock will be sold. The final prospectus may be issued as soon as, in the opinion of the Securities and Exchange Commission, there has been adequate disclosure and a reasonable waiting period has passed (usually 20 days). The commission, however, does not take a position regarding the investment merits of an offering or the reasonableness of the price.

A security issue may be completely underwritten by an investment banker and the other members of the syndicate. If it is, the issuing corporation receives the public offering price less a stated percentage spread (although underwriters will occasionally be compensated with some combination of shares and warrants, perhaps in addition to a smaller spread). The underwriters, in turn, sell the securities at the public offering price (or less) and may buy some of the securities themselves. Underwriters who provide this sort of **firm commitment** bear all the risk, because the public may not be willing to buy the entire issue.

Not all agreements are of this type. In the case of a **rights offering** (where the current stockholders are given the opportunity to buy the new shares first), an underwriter may agree to purchase at a fixed price all securities not taken by current stockholders. This is termed a **standby agreement.** In the case of a nonrights offering (where the shares are offered to the general public first), members of an investment banking group may serve as agents instead of dealers, agreeing only to handle an offering on a **best-efforts basis.**

During the period when new securities remain unsold, the investment banker is allowed to attempt to "stabilize" the price of the security in the secondary market by standing ready to make purchases at a particular price. Such **pegging** may continue for up to ten days after the official offering date. There is a limit to the amount that can be purchased in this manner, usually stated in the agreement under which the underwriting syndicate is formed, because the members typically share the cost of such transactions. If there is to be any pegging, a statement to that effect must be included in the prospectus.

In any security transaction there may be explicit and implicit costs. In a primary distribution, the explicit cost is the underwriting spread, and the implicit cost is any difference between the public offering price and the price that might have been obtained otherwise. The spread provides the investment banking syndicate with compensation for selling the issue and bearing the risk that the issue may not be completely sold to the public, thereby leaving it with ownership of the unsold shares. The lower the public offering price, the smaller the risk that the issue will not be sold quickly at that price. If an issue is substantially underpriced, the syndicate can be assured that the securities will sell rapidly, requiring little or no support in the secondary market. Because many corporations deal with only one investment banking firm and because the larger investment banking firms rely on one another for inclusion in syndicates, it has been alleged that issuers pay too much in spreads, given the prices at which their securities are offered. In other words, the returns to underwriting are alleged to be overly large relative to the risks involved due to ignorance on the part of issuers or the existence of an informal cartel among investment banking firms.

3.10.3 Underpricing of Ipo's

Whether or not returns to underwriting are overly large, a number of **initial public offerings** (ipo's) do appear to have been underpriced. Ipo's are the company's first offerings of shares to the public and are sometimes referred to as **unseasoned offerings.** The abnormal rate of return for a sample of ipo's are shown in Figure 3.4. Each one of the first 60 months after the initial offering is shown on the horizontal axis, and the corresponding average abnormal return (meaning the average return over and above that of stocks of equal risk) is shown on the vertical axis. The leftmost point indicates the average abnormal return obtained by an investor who purchased such a stock at its offering price and sold it for the bid price at the end of the month during which it was offered. The average abnormal return was substantial: 11.4%. The remaining points show the average abnormal returns that could have been obtained by an investor who purchased the security in the secondary market at the beginning of the month after its offering, which is indicated on the horizontal axis, and sold it at the end of that month. Some of these postoffering abnormal returns were positive, but most were negative.

A subsequent study found that the initial abnormal return, measured over the time period beginning with the offering and ending when the first closing price was reported, was 14.1%.[21] Although there is evidence that the average abnormal returns remained positive over the next two months, the average abnormal return over the three-year period after the first close was −37.4%. Three

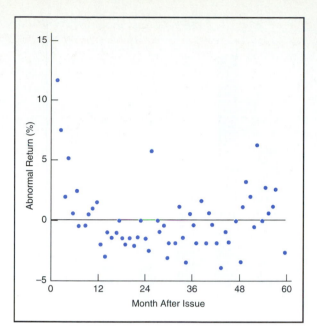

Figure 3.4
Average Abnormal Returns: 112 Common Stock Initial Public Offerings, 1960–1969
Source: Roger G. Ibbotson, "Price Performance of Common Stock New Issues," *Journal of Financial Economics* 2, no. 3 (September 1975): 252.

other interesting observations were that (1) offerings of smaller firms had lower three-year abnormal returns than those of larger firms, (2) firms that had the highest positive initial abnormal return had the worst performance over the subsequent three-year period, and (3) younger firms going public had both higher initial abnormal returns and lower subsequent three-year abnormal returns than older firms going public.

It would appear then that offerings of these unseasoned securities are typically underpriced (and then overpriced). Investors able to purchase a cross section of such shares at their offering prices might thus expect better performance over the first two months than those holding other securities of equal risk. It is not surprising that such offerings are often rationed to "favored" customers by the members of the selling group. It is "not uncommon for underwriters to receive, prior to the effective date, 'public indication of interest' for five times the number of shares available."[22] Unfavored customers are presumably allowed to buy only the new issues that are not substantially underpriced. And because costs may be incurred in becoming a "favored" customer, it is not clear that even such an investor obtains abnormally large returns overall.

Whereas the initial return obtained by the purchaser of a new issue may be substantial *on average,* the amount may be very good or very bad in any particular instance, as Figure 3.5 shows. Although the odds may be in the purchaser's favor, a single investment of this type is far from a sure bet.

3.10.4 Seasoned Offerings

Interestingly, the announcement of a seasoned stock offering seems to result in a decline of roughly 2% to 4% in the firm's stock price. This could be because managers tend to issue stock when they think it is overpriced in the marketplace.

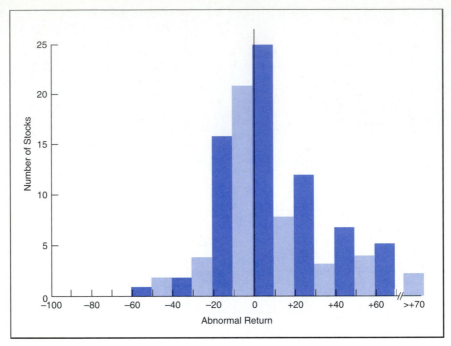

Figure 3.5
Average Abnormal Returns from Offering Date to End of Month: 112 Common Stock Initial Public Offerings, 1960–1969

Source: Roger G. Ibbotson, "Price Performance of Common Stock New Issues," *Journal of Financial Economics* 2, no. 3 (September 1975): 248.

Thus the announcement of the offering causes investors to revise downward their assessment of the value of the stock, leading to a price decline.[23] This decline is larger for stocks of industrial firms than for stocks of public utilities, probably due to the fact that the typical utility has seasoned offerings far more often than the typical industrial firm.[24]

3.10.5   Shelf Registration

A relatively recent change in regulations has made it possible for large corporations to foster greater competition among underwriters. Starting in 1982, the Securities and Exchange Commission allowed firms to register securities in advance of issuance under Rule 415. With such **shelf registration,** securities may be sold up to two years later. With securities "on the shelf," the corporation can require investment bankers to bid competitively, simply refusing to sell shares if desirable bids are not forthcoming. Thus one purpose of the SEC in allowing shelf registration was to reduce the costs of issuing securities. The evidence seems to suggest that indeed such costs have been reduced.[25]

3.10.6   Rule 144A Securities

As mentioned earlier, private placements are issued via direct negotiations between issuers and investors. These securities are not registered with the Securities and Exchange Commission, and issuers do not have to satisfy the stringent financial disclosure requirements. Prior to 1990 all investors had to wait two years before being permitted to trade private placements, making such securities highly illiquid.

In 1990 the Securities and Exchange Commission adopted Rule 144A, which permits privately placed securities issued under the provisions of the rule to be traded among large investors (those with assets in excess of $100 million—primarily institutional investors) at any time after their initial purchase. By removing the two-year requirement Rule 144A added liquidity to the private placement market, thereby increasing the attractiveness of these securities.

Historically, the private placement market has consisted predominantly of fixed-income securities. However, Rule 144A also applies to common stocks. Foreign corporations, who in many cases cannot or will not meet the SEC's disclosure rules, have been the primary issuers of common stock under Rule 144A. Whether the new rule will bring about an increase in private equity financing is still unclear.

3.10.7   Secondary Distributions

As mentioned earlier, an individual or institution wishing to sell a large block of stock can do so through a secondary distribution. An investment banking group buys the stock from the seller and then offers the shares to the public. Typically, the shares are first offered after normal trading hours at the day's closing price. The buyer often pays no commission, and the original seller receives the total proceeds less an underwriting spread.

The Securities and Exchange Commission requires that a secondary distribution be registered, with public announcement and disclosure and a 20–day waiting period, if the original seller has a "control relationship" with the issuer of the securities. Otherwise the distribution may be unregistered.

The impact of the sale of a large block on the market price of the stock provides information on the resiliency of the capital market. Figure 3.6 shows the av-

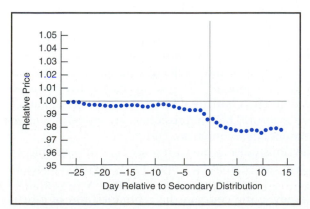

Figure 3.6

Prices for 345 Secondary Distributions, 1961–1965

Source: Myron S. Scholes, "The Market for Securities: Substitution versus Price Pressure and the Effects of Information on the Share Prices." *Journal of Business* 45, no. 2 (April 1972): 193.

TABLE 3.4		
AVERAGE PRICE DECLINE VERSUS TYPE OF SELLER: 345 SECONDARY DISTRIBUTIONS, 1961–1965		
Type of Seller	Percentage Change In Adjusted Price From Ten Days Before The Distribution To Ten Days After The Distribution
Corporations and officers	2.9%
Investment companies and mutual funds	2.5
Individuals	1.1
Estates	.7
Banks and insurance companies	.3

Source: Myron S. Scholes, "The Market for Securities: Substitution Versus Price Pressure and the Effects of Information on Share Prices," *Journal of Business*, 45, no. 2 (April 1972): 202.

erage prices (adjusted for market changes) for 345 secondary distributions, with the price 25 days prior to the distribution taken as 1.0. On average, a secondary distribution leads to a 2% to 3% decline in price. Because there is no evidence of a subsequent price rebound, this decline is most likely due to the information contained in the fact that someone has decided to sell. Additional analysis of these results, as shown in Table 3.4, supports the assertion. The size of the decline was related to the identity of the seller—being greater for sellers most likely to be information-motivated and smaller for sellers likely to be liquidity-motivated.[26]

3.11 REGULATION OF SECURITY MARKETS

Directly or indirectly, security markets in the United States are regulated under both federal and state laws. The Securities Act of 1933 was the first major legislation at the federal level. Sometimes called the "truth in securities" law, it requires registration of new issues and disclosure of relevant information by the issuer. Furthermore, the act prohibits misrepresentation and fraud in security sales. The Securities Exchange Act of 1934 extended the principles of the earlier act to cover secondary markets and required national exchanges, brokers, and dealers to be registered. It also made possible the establishment of self-regulatory organizations (SROs) to oversee the securities industry.

Since 1934 both acts (and subsequent amendments to them, such as the Securities Acts Amendments of 1975 that were discussed earlier in the chapter) have been administered by the **Securities and Exchange Commission** (SEC), a quasi-judicial agency of the U.S. government.[27] The SEC is run by five commissioners appointed by the President and confirmed by the Senate; each commissioner is appointed for a five-year term. The commissioners are aided by a large permanent staff of lawyers, accountants, economists, and others.

The SEC is the primary administrative agency for a number of other pieces of federal legislation. The Public Utility Holding Company Act of 1935 brought such corporations under the SEC's jurisdiction. The Bankruptcy Act of 1938 specified that the SEC should advise the court in the reorganization of a firm under bankruptcy proceedings whenever there is a substantial public interest in the firm's securities. The Maloney Act of 1938 extended the SEC's jurisdiction to include the over-the-counter market and recognized the National Association of Security Dealers as an SRO. The Trust Indenture Act of 1939 gave the SEC power to ensure that bond indenture trustees (individuals who represent bondholders in dealing with bond issuers) were free from any conflicts of interest. The Investment Company Act of 1940 extended disclosure and registration requirements to investment companies. (These are companies that use their funds primarily to purchase securities issued by the U.S. government, state governments, and corporations.) It was amended in 1970 in order to give certain rights to owners of investment companies who wanted to sell their shares before fulfilling the terms of a contractual purchase plan. The Investment Advisors Act of 1940 required the registration of those individuals who provide others with advice about security transactions. Advisors were also required to disclose any potential conflicts of interest. As mentioned earlier, the Securities Investor Protection Act of 1970 provided for the coverage of losses by investors in the event of the failure of a brokerage firm by establishing the Securities Investor Protection Corporation. The Insider Trading and Fraud Act of 1988 was passed to help define insider (a person who possesses material nonpublic information) trading and establish fines for insider trading violations.

As mentioned earlier, federal securities legislation relies heavily on the principle of **self-regulation.** The SEC has delegated its power to control trading practices for listed securities to the registered exchanges. However, the SEC has retained the power to alter or supplement any of the resulting rules or regulations. The SEC's power to control trading practices in over-the-counter securities has been similarly delegated to the National Association of Securities Dealers (NASD), a private association of brokers and dealers in OTC securities. In practice, the SEC staff usually discusses proposed changes with both the NASD and the registered exchanges in advance. Consequently, few rules are formally altered or rejected.

An important piece of legislation that makes security markets in the United States different from those in many other countries is the Banking Act of 1933, also known as the Glass-Steagall Act. This act prohibited commercial banks from engaging in investment banking activities because it was felt that there was an inherent conflict of interest in allowing banks to engage in both commercial and investment banking activities. Because of this act, banks have not played as prominent a role in security markets in the United States as elsewhere. Recently, however, their role has increased, as the federal government has taken action to spur competition among various types of financial institutions. Two key pieces of legislation were the Depository Institutions Deregulation and Monetary Control Act of 1980 and the Depository Institution Act of 1982. Many banks now offer security brokerage services, retirement funds, and the like via subsidiaries of their holding companies. Furthermore, long-standing limitations on rates paid on deposits and checking accounts were removed. As a result, the line between commercial banking and investment banking is becoming more blurred every day.

Initially, security regulation in the United States was the province of state governments. Beginning in 1911, state *blue sky laws* were passed to prevent "speculative schemes which have no more basis than so many feet of blue sky."[28]

Although such statutes vary substantially from state to state, most of them outlaw fraud in security sales and require the registration of certain securities as well as brokers and dealers (and, in some cases, investment advisors). Some order has been created by the passage in many states of all or part of the Uniform Securities Acts proposed by the National Conference of Commissions on Uniform State Laws in 1956.

Securities that are traded across state lines, as well as the brokers, dealers, and exchanges involved in such trading, typically fall under the purview of federal legislation. However, a considerable domain still comes under the exclusive jurisdiction of the states. Moreover, federal legislation only supplements state legislation; it does not supplant it. Some argue that the investor is overprotected as a result. Others suggest that the regulatory agencies (especially those that rely on "self-regulation" by powerful industry organizations) in fact protect the members of the regulated industry against competition, thereby damaging the interests of their customers instead of protecting them. Both positions undoubtedly contain some elements of truth.

3.12 SUMMARY

1. Security markets facilitate the trading of securities by providing a means of bringing buyers and sellers of financial assets together.
2. In the United States common stocks are traded primarily on organized security exchanges or on the over-the-counter market.
3. Organized security exchanges provide central physical locations where trading is done under a set of rules and regulations.
4. The primary organized security exchange is the New York Stock Exchange. Various regional exchanges also operate.
5. Trading on organized security exchanges is conducted only by members who transact in a specified group of securities.
6. Exchange members fall into one of four categories, depending on the type of trading activity in which they engage. Those categories are commission broker, floor broker, floor trader, and specialist.
7. Specialists are charged with maintaining an orderly market in their assigned stocks. In this capacity they perform two roles. They maintain a limit order book for unexecuted trades, and they act as a dealer, trading in their stocks for their own accounts.
8. In the OTC market, individuals act as dealers in a manner similar to specialists. However, unlike specialists, OTC dealers face competition from other dealers.
9. Most of the trading in the OTC market is done through a computerized system known as Nasdaq.
10. Trading in listed securities may take place outside the various exchanges on the third and fourth markets.
11. Foreign security markets each have their own particular operating procedures, rules, and customs.

12. Dealers typically make money trading with liquidity-motivated traders and lose money trading with adept information-motivated traders. A dealer must set a bid-ask spread that attracts sufficient revenue from the former group but avoids excessive losses to the latter.

13. Following legislation in 1975, the Securities and Exchange Commission has mandated procedures designed to create a truly nationwide central security market.

14. Clearinghouses facilitate the transfer of securities and cash between buyers and sellers. Most U.S. security transactions are now cleared electronically.

15. The SIPC is a quasi-governmental agency that insures the accounts of clients of all brokers and members of exchanges registered with the SEC against loss due to a brokerage firm's failure.

16. Following May Day (May 1, 1975), commissions have been negotiated between brokerage firms and their larger clients. In a competitive environment, commission rates typically vary inversely with the size of the order.

17. Transaction costs are a function of the stock's bid-ask spread, the price impact of the trade, and the commission.

18. The primary market for securities involves the initial issuance of securities.

19. Although some issuers deal directly with purchasers, most hire investment bankers to assist them in the sale of the securities.

20. The most prominent security market regulator is the SEC, a federal agency directed by five commissioners. Regulation of the U.S. security markets involves both federal and state laws.

21. The SEC has delegated to the various exchanges and the NASD the power to control trading practices through a system of self-regulation.

QUESTIONS AND PROBLEMS

1. What are ADRs? Why are they attractive to U.S. investors seeking to make investments in foreign corporations?

2. Discuss the advantages and disadvantages of the NYSE specialist system.

3. Differentiate between the role of a specialist on the NYSE and the role of a dealer on the OTC market.

4. Give several reasons why a corporation might desire to have its stock listed on the NYSE.

5. Describe the functions of commission brokers, floor brokers, and floor traders.

6. Pigeon Falls Fertilizer Company is listed on the NYSE. Gabby Hartnett, the specialist handling Pigeon Falls stock, is currently bidding 35¾ and asking 35⅞. What would be the likely outcomes of the following trading orders?
   a. Through a broker, Eppa Rixey places a market order to buy 100 shares of Pigeon Falls stock. No other broker from the crowd takes the order.
   b. Through a broker, Eppa places a limit order to sell 100 shares of Pigeon Falls stock at 36.
   c. Through a broker, Eppa places a limit order to buy 100 shares of Pigeon Falls stock at 35½. Another broker offers to sell 100 shares at 35½.

7. Bosco Snover is the NYSE specialist in Eola Enterprises' stock. Bosco's limit order book for Eola appears as follows:

Limit-Sell		Limit-Buy	
Price	Shares	Price	Shares
$30.250	200	$29.750	100
30.375	500	29.000	100
30.500	300	28.500	200
30.875	800	27.125	100
31.000	200	26.875	200

The last trade in the stock took place at $30.

    a. If a market order to sell 200 shares arrives, what will happen?

    b. If another market order to sell 100 shares arrives just moments later, what will happen?

    c. Do you think that Bosco would prefer to accumulate shares or reduce inventory, given the current orders in the limit order book?

8. Because specialists such as Chick Gandil are charged with maintaining a "fair and orderly" market, at times they will be required to sell when others are buying and buy when others are selling. How can Chick earn a profit when required to act in such a manner?

9. Why can't all security trades on the NYSE, no matter how large, be handled through the SuperDOT system?

10. Why is Nasdaq so important to the success of the OTC market?

11. What are some of the major steps that have been taken toward the ultimate emergence of a truly nationwide security market?

12. The NYSE has strongly opposed the creation of alternative market trading structures such as off-exchange crossing systems. The NYSE claims that these alternative structures undermine its ability to offer "best execution" to all investors. Discuss the merits of the NYSE's contention.

13. Distinguish between the third and fourth markets.

14. Why was May Day such an important event for the NYSE?

15. What is the purpose of SIPC insurance? Given the recent experience of the banking and savings and loan deposit insurance programs, under what conditions might SIPC insurance be expected to be effective? Under what conditions might it fail to accomplish its objectives?

16. After May Day, why did commission rates fall so sharply for large investors, but decline so little (or even increase) for small investors?

17. Transaction costs can be thought of as being derived from three sources. Identify and describe those sources.

18. What functions does a clearinghouse perform?

19. Fiddler Basinski is considering an investment in Poynette Lumber Company. Based on an analysis of Poynette's prospects, Fiddler expects the company's stock to rise from $40 to $45 over the next six months. Using data in Table 3.3(b), Poynette stock is in sector 1. Fiddler plans to invest $25,000 in the company and then liquidate the investment six months later. Given Fiddler's price appreciation expectations, is this investment likely to be profitable? Why?

20. Describe the primary conclusions of the results of the trading cost study presented in Table 3.3.

21. Why are liquid and continuous secondary security markets important to the effective functioning of primary security markets?

22. Describe the role of an underwriting syndicate in a public security offering.
23. Distinguish between a competitive bid underwriting and a negotiated underwriting.
24. Investment bankers frequently attempt to stabilize the price of a newly issued security in the secondary market.
    a. How is this stabilization accomplished?
    b. What is the purpose of the stabilization?
    c. What can go wrong with the stabilization attempts?
25. Why must companies that publicly issue securities file a prospectus with the SEC? What does the SEC's acceptance of the prospectus imply?
26. Discuss why ipo's appear to generate abnormal returns for investors. Are these returns a "sure thing"? What are the economic implications of these high returns for ipo issuers?

ENDNOTES

[1] Enough time is allowed to elapse between calls (for example, an hour or more) so that a substantial number of orders to buy and sell will accumulate.

[2] The applicant for membership must also pass a written examination, be sponsored by two current members of the exchange, and be approved by the board. Recently the NYSE began allowing members to lease their seats to individuals acceptable to the exchange. As of the end of 1992 there were 643 leased seats. In addition to the 1,366 full memberships, at the end of 1992 there were 54 individuals who held special memberships. In return for an annual fee, these members are granted access to the trading floor.

[3] During 1992 trading volume on the NYSE averaged, on a daily basis, 202.3 million shares, worth nearly $7 billion. The American Stock Exchange, the second largest organized exchange, had comparable daily values of less than one-tenth these amounts.

[4] *Fact Book: 1992 Data*, New York Stock Exchange, 1993: 29.

[5] ADRs are discussed in more detail in Chapters 17 and 26.

[6] The assignment is made by the board of directors and also includes any preferred stock or warrants that the company has listed on the exchange. At the end of 1992 there were 2,089 companies listed on the NYSE, with 2,658 stock issues being traded, meaning that there were over 500 different issues of preferred stock being traded on the NYSE. There were also 112 warrants on these companies' stock that were traded. Bonds are also listed on the NYSE but are traded in an entirely different manner, which does not involve the use of specialists. At the end of 1992 there were 636 companies that had 2,354 issues of bonds listed on the NYSE.

[7] The NYSE is currently open from 9:30 A.M. until 4 P.M. However, the NYSE is considering extending its hours of operation in order to overlap with the London and Tokyo stock markets. The NYSE does allow certain computerized trading to take place after close in Crossing Session I (4:15 P.M. to 5 P.M.) and Crossing Session II (4 P.M. to 5:15 P.M.) Trades in Crossing Session I are based on 4 P.M. closing prices, whereas each trade in Crossing Session II must involve a "basket" of at least 15 NYSE-listed stocks and an aggregate price of $15 million (prices are set for the baskets, not individual stocks).

[8] These GM orders may represent either orders for the specialist's own account or public orders. It should be noted that these orders may not be the "best" ones, as specialists are not required to display them on the screens of quotation machines. However, such

"hidden orders" would appear in the limit order book and would be revealed on the exchange floor. As a matter of NYSE policy, only the specialist is allowed to see the contents of the limit order book. However, in 1991 the NYSE began to allow the specialists to disclose to others on the floor some information about buying and selling interest at prices near the current bid and asked prices.

[9] Odd lot market orders are executed immediately by the specialist at the quoted bid or asked price. Odd lot limit orders are held by the specialist and executed immediately after there has been another trade at an acceptable price using that price. Typically, odd lot orders utilize the facilities of SuperDOT. There are special features of Super-Dot that are used to execute opening orders—that is, orders that are received up to the time the NYSE opens in the morning. It should be noted that small orders are often sent to third market dealers (this market is discussed later), in return for which the dealer pays a small fee to the broker. This practice is known as "payment for order flow." See James B. Cloonan, "'Payment for Order Flow' is No Deal For Investors," *AAII Journal,* 13, no. 3 (March 1991): 28–29.

[10] One alternative for the institution that is thinking of placing the block order is to place many small orders sequentially. However, institutions generally do not want to do this because it means that their block order will not be executed with due speed. Furthermore, other traders may anticipate these additional transactions and develop strategies to take advantage of them.

[11] The order must be crossed on an exchange where the stock is listed, provided that the block house is a member of that exchange.

[12] Generally the order will be a market order, since there is no central "limit order book" in the over-the-counter market except for small orders. Stop and stop limit orders are not allowed in the OTC market. See Endnote 13.

[13] Orders involving up to 1,000 shares of any Nasdaq/NMS security (for non-NMS securities, the limit is 500 shares) are handled by a computer system known as **SOES** (Small Order Execution System). Such orders can be either market or limit orders, because SOES maintains a composite limit order book.

[14] Of this total, 275 were foreign securities consisting of 88 ADRs and 187 non-ADRs. (Most of the non-ADRs were Canadian securities.)

[15] The use of an intermediary such as a computer system, makes it difficult to categorize such trades. Some people would refer to the market where trades involving a "matchmaker" take place as the "3.5 market." The term *fourth market* would then be used only when referring to the market where no matchmaker is involved.

[16] A similar classification of traders that has often been used by financial economists involves (1) informed speculative traders who possess both public and private information, (2) uninformed speculative traders who possess just public information, and (3) noise traders whose trades are not based on information. Hence the first two types can be viewed as information-motivated traders, the third as liquidity-motivated traders. See Sanford J. Grossman and Joseph E. Stiglitz, "On the Impossibility of Informationally Efficient Markets," *American Economic Review,* 70, no. 3 (June 1980): 393–408.

[17] From *Securities Acts Amendments of 1975,* section 11A.

[18] See Wilford J. Eiteman, Charles A. Dice, and David K. Eiteman, *The Stock Market* (New York: McGraw-Hill, 1969), p. 19.

[19] Eitemen, Dice, and Eiteman, *The Stock Market,* p. 138.

[20] Roger D. Huang and Hans R. Stoll, *Major World Equity Markets: Current Structure and Prospects for Change,* Monograph Series in Finance and Economics 1991–93, New York University Salomon Center, New York, 1991, p. 11.

[21] Investors who quickly sell their shares in order to capture this price spurt are known as "flippers." Jay R. Ritter, "The Long-Run Performance of Initial Public Offerings," *Journal of Finance,* 46, no. 1 (March 1991): 3–27. Also, see Roger G. Ibbotson, Jody L. Sindelar, and Jay R. Ritter, "Initial Public Offerings," *Journal of Applied Corporate Finance,* 1, no. 2 (Summer 1988): 37–45. An interesting explanation for the initial underpricing is provided by Kevin Rock, "Why New Issues Are Underpriced," *Journal of Financial Economics,* 15, no. 1/2 (January/February 1986): 187–212.

[22] Securities and Exchange Commission, *Report of Special Study on Security Markets,* 1973. Also see Roger G. Ibbotson, "Price Performance of Common Stock New Issues," *Journal of Financial Economics,* 2, no. 3 (September 1975): 235–272.

[23] See Stewart C. Myers and Nicholas S. Majluf, "Corporate Financing and Investment Decisions When Firms Have Information That Investors Do Not Have," *Journal of Financial Economics,* 13, no. 2 (June 1984): 187–221, and Wayne H. Mikkelson and M. Megan Partch, "Valuation Effects of Security Offerings and the Issuance Process," *Journal of Financial Economics,* 15, no. 1/2 (January/February 1986): 31–60.

[24] See Ronald W. Masulis and Ashok N. Korwar, "Seasoned Equity Offerings: An Empirical Investigation," *Journal of Financial Economics,* 15, no. 1/2 (January/February 1986): 91–118.

[25] See Sanjai Bhagat, M. Wayne Marr, and G. Rodney Thompson, "The Rule 415 Experiment: Equity Markets," *Journal of Finance,* 40, no. 5 (December 1985): 1385–1401.

[26] A more recent study has confirmed these findings. See Wayne H. Mikkelson and M. Megan Partch, "Stock Price Effects and Costs of Secondary Distributions," *Journal of Financial Economics,* 14, no. 2 (June 1985): 165–194.

[27] The Commodity Futures Trading Commission (CFTC) was established in 1974 by Congress to regulate futures markets, and the Municipal Securities Rulemaking Board (MSRB) was established in 1975 to regulate trading in municipal securities.

[28] See Hall v. Geiger-Jones Co., 242 U.S. 539 (1917).

KEY TERMS

security market	dealer
secondary markets	trading post
call markets	bid price
continuous markets	asked price
liquidity	double auction
organized exchanges	Super Designated Order Turnaround
seat	blocks
member firm	specialist block purchase
listed security	specialist block sale
delisted	exchange distribution
trading halt	exchange acquisition
American Depository Receipts	special offering
commission brokers	special bid
floor brokers	secondary distribution
floor traders	upstairs dealer market
specialists	block houses
limit order book	regional exchanges

National Association of Securities
  Dealers
National Association of Securities
  Dealers Automated Quotations
inside quotes
National Market System
Small Cap Issues
SOES
markup
markdown
pink sheets
third market
fourth market
Instinet
SEAQ
SAEF
Nasdaq International
CORES
FORES
CATS
consolidated tape
composite stock price tables
Consolidated Quotations System
Intermarket Trading System
clearinghouse
Depository Trust Company
fails to deliver

Securities Investor Protection
  Corporation
May Day
soft dollars
bid-ask spread
market capitalization
price impacts
primary market
investment bankers
private placements
syndicate
underwrite
selling group
competitive bidding
registration statement
prospectus
red herring
firm commitment
rights offering
standby agreement
best-efforts basis
pegging
initial public offerings
unseasoned offerings
shelf registration
Securities and Exchange Commission
self-regulation

REFERENCES

1. A good reference source for U.S. stock markets is:

    Robert A. Schwartz, *Equity Markets* (New York: Harper & Row, 1988).

2. Other valuable sources are the following fact books, which are updated annually:

    New York Stock Exchange, *Fact Book: 1992 Data,* 1993. (To order, write: New York Stock Exchange, Publications Department, 11 Wall St., New York, NY 10005.)

    American Stock Exchange, *American Stock Exchange 1992 Fact Book,* 1993. (To order, write: American Stock Exchange, Publications Department, 86 Trinity Place, New York, NY 10006.)

    National Association of Security Dealers, *1993 Nasdaq Fact Book & Company Directory,* 1993. (To order, write: National Association of Security Dealers, NASD MediaSource, P.O. Box 9403, Gaithersburg, MD 20898–9403.)

London Stock Exchange, *Stock Exchange Official Yearbook 1992–1993,* 1993. (To order, write: The Publicity and Promotions Department, The London Stock Exchange, London EC2N 1HP, U.K.)

Toronto Stock Exchange Press, *1992 Official Trading Statistics.* (To order, write: The Toronto Stock Exchange, Strategic Research & Planning, The Exchange Tower, 2 First Canadian Place, Toronto, Ontario M5X 1J2, Canada.)

Tokyo Stock Exchange, *Tokyo Stock Exchange 1993 Fact Book.* (To order, write: Tokyo Stock Exchange, New York Research Office, 45 Broadway, New York, NY 10006.)

3. For a description of foreign stock markets, see:

Guiseppe Tullio and Giorgio P. Szego, eds., "Equity Markets—An International Comparison: Part A," *Journal of Banking and Finance,* 13, nos. 4/5 (September 1989): 479–782.

Guiseppe Tullio and Giorgio P. Szego, eds., "Equity Markets—An International Comparison: Part B," *Journal of Banking and Finance,* 14, nos. 2/3 (August 1990): 231–672.

Roger D. Huang and Hans R. Stoll, *Major World Equity Markets: Current Structure and Prospects for Change,* Monograph Series in Finance and Economics 1991–1993, New York University Salomon Center, New York, 1991.

Roger D. Huang and Hans R. Stoll, "The Design of Trading Systems: Lessons from Abroad," *Financial Analysts Journal,* 48, no. 5 (September/October 1992): 49–54.

4. Other useful sources for information on market microstructure are:

James L. Hamilton, "Off-Board Trading of NYSE-Listed Stocks: The Effects of Deregulation and the National Market System," *Journal of Finance,* 42, no. 5 (December 1987): 1331–1345.

Ian Domowitz, "The Mechanics of Automated Execution Systems," *Journal of Financial Intermediation,* 1, no. 2 (June 1990): 167–194.

Lawrence E. Harris, *Liquidity, Trading Rules, and Electronic Trading Systems,* Monograph Series in Finance and Economics 1990–1994, New York University Salomon Center, New York, 1990.

Peter A. Abken, "Globalization of Stock, Futures, and Options Markets," *Federal Reserve Bank of Atlanta Economic Review,* 76, no. 4 (July/August 1991): 1–22.

Joel Hasbrouck, George Sofianos, and Deborah Sosebee, "New York Stock Exchange Systems and Procedures," NYSE Working Paper 93–01, 1993.

5. For a discussion of the effects of listing and delisting on a firm's stock, see:

Gary C. Sanger and John J. McConnell, "Stock Exchange Listings, Firm Value, and Security Market Efficiency: The Impact of NASDAQ," *Journal of Financial and Quantitative Analysis,* 21, no. 1 (March 1986): 1–25.

John J. McConnell and Gary C. Sanger, "The Puzzle in Post-Listing Common Stock Returns," *Journal of Finance,* 42, no. 1 (March 1987): 119–140.

Gary C. Sanger and James D. Peterson, "An Empirical Analysis of Common Stock Delistings," *Journal of Financial and Quantitative Analysis,* 25, no. 2 (June 1990): 261–272.

6. For more information on ADRs, see:

Narayanan Jayarman, Kuldeep Shatstri, and Kishore Tandon, "The Impact of International Cross Listings on Risk and Return," *Journal of Banking and Finance,* 17, no. 1 (February 1993): 91–103.

Albert Friedman and John Erickson, "Investing Abroad at Home: An Investor's Guide to ADRs," *AAII Journal,* 15, no. 10 (November 1993): 7–12.

Eric Fry, "A Guide to Investing Internationally Through the Use of ADRs," *AAII Journal,* 16, no. 2 (February 1994): 12–15.

7. Empirical studies that examine the costs of trading include:

Harold Demsetz, "The Cost of Transacting," *Quarterly Journal of Economics,* 82, no. 1 (February 1968): 33–53.

Walter Bagehot, "The Only Game in Town," *Financial Analysts Journal,* 27, no. 2 (March/April 1971): 12–14, 22.

Larry J. Cuneo and Wayne H. Wagner, "Reducing the Cost of Stock Trading," *Financial Analysts Journal,* 31, no. 6 (November/December 1975): 35–44.

Gilbert Beebower and William Priest, "The Tricks of the Trade," *Journal of Portfolio Management,* 6, no. 2 (Winter 1980): 36–42.

Jack L. Treynor, "What Does It Take to Win the Trading Game?" *Financial Analysts Journal,* 37, no. 1 (January/February 1981): 55–60.

Thomas F. Loeb, "Trading Cost: The Critical Link Between Investment Information and Results," *Financial Analysts Journal,* 39, no. 3 (May/June 1983): 39–44.

Wayne H. Mikkelson and M. Megan Partch, "Stock Price Effects and Costs of Secondary Distributions," *Journal of Financial Economics,* 14, no. 2 (June 1985): 165–194.

Robert W. Holthausen, Richard W. Leftwich, and David Mayers, "The Effect of Large Block Transactions on Security Prices," *Journal of Financial Economics,* 19, no. 2 (December 1987): 237–267.

Stephen A. Berkowitz, Dennis E. Logue, and Eugene E. Noser, Jr., "The Total Cost of Transactions on the NYSE," *Journal of Finance,* 43, no. 1 (March 1988): 97–112.

André F. Perold, "The Implementation Shortfall: Paper Versus Reality," *Journal of Portfolio Management,* 14, no. 3 (Spring 1988): 4–9.

Lawrence R. Glosten and Lawrence E. Harris, "Estimating the Components of the Bid/Ask Spread," *Journal of Financial Economics,* 21, no. 1 (May 1988): 123-142.

Joel Hasbrouck, "Trades, Quotes, Inventories, and Information," *Journal of Financial Economics,* 22, no. 2 (December 1988): 229–252.

Hans R. Stoll, "Inferring the Components of the Bid-Ask Spread: Theory and Empirical Tests," *Journal of Finance*, 44, no. 1 (March 1989): 115–134.

Robert W. Holthausen, Richard W. Leftwich, and David Mayers, "Large-Block Transactions, the Speed of Response, and Temporary and Permanent Stock-Price Effects," *Journal of Financial Economics*, 26, no. 1 (July 1990): 71–95.

F. Douglas Foster and S. Viswanathan, "Variations in Trading Volume, Return Volatility, and Trading Costs: Evidence on Recent Price Formation Models," *Journal of Finance*, 48, no. 1 (March 1993): 187–211.

Hans R. Stoll, "Equity Trading Costs In-The-Large," *Journal of Portfolio Management*, 19, no. 4 (Summer 1993): 41–50.

Joel Hasbrouck and George Sofianos, "The Trades of Market Makers: An Empirical Analysis of NYSE Specialists," *Journal of Finance*, 48, no. 5 (December 1993): 1565–1593.

Ananth Madhavan and Seymour Smidt, "An Analysis of Changes in Specialist Inventories and Quotations" *Journal of Finance*, 48, no. 5 (December 1993): 1595–1628.

8. For more on investment banking, see:

Richard A. Brealey and Stewart C. Myers, *Principles of Corporate Finance* (New York: McGraw-Hill, 1991), Chapter 15.

Stephen A. Ross, Randolph W. Westerfield, and Jeffrey F. Jaffee, *Corporate Finance* (Homewood, IL: Richard D. Irwin, 1993), Chapters 19–20.

9. For a historical essay on the development of American capital markets, which includes a significant discussion of regulation, see:

George David Smith and Richard Sylla, "The Transformation of Financial Capitalism: An Essay on the History of American Capital Markets," *Financial Markets, Institutions & Instruments*, 2, no. 2 (1993).

CHAPTER 4

Investment Value and Market Price

Payments provided by securities may differ in size, timing, and riskiness. Thus a security analyst must estimate the size of such payments along with when and under what conditions these payments will be received. This typically requires detailed analysis of the firm involved, the industry (or industries) in which the firm operates, and the economy as a whole.

Once such estimates have been made, the overall investment value of the security must be determined. This generally requires conversion of uncertain future values to certain present values. The current prices of other securities can often be utilized in this process. If it is possible to obtain a similar set of payments in some other way, the market price of doing so provides a benchmark for the investment value of the security being analyzed, because an investor would neither want to pay more than this for the security nor sell it for less. In some cases, however, equivalent alternatives may not exist, or the mere act of buying or selling the security in question in the quantities being considered might affect the price substantially. Under these conditions the preferences of the investor may have to be utilized explicitly in the process of estimating the security's investment value.

Later chapters discuss in detail the manner in which estimated future payments can be used to determine investment value. Methods for estimating the payments and finding equivalent alternatives will be discussed after the characteristics of the securities have been introduced. In this chapter some general principles of investment value are presented, leaving procedures designed for specific types of securities for later.

Although there are over 1 billion shares of AT&T common stock outstanding, on an average day fewer than 2 million shares will be traded. What determines the prices at which such trades take place? A simple (and correct) answer is: demand and supply. A more fundamental (and also correct) answer is: investors' estimates of AT&T's future earnings and dividends, for such estimates greatly influence demand and supply. Before dealing with such influences, it is useful to examine the role of demand and supply in the determination of security prices.

As shown in the previous chapter, securities are traded by many people in many different ways. Although the forces that determine prices are similar in all markets, they are slightly more obvious in markets using periodic "calls." One such market corresponds to the *itayose* method of price determination that is used by the *saitori* at the twice-a-day openings of the Tokyo Stock Exchange, as mentioned in Chapter 3.

4.1.1 Demand-to-Buy Schedule

At a designated time all brokers holding orders to buy or sell a given stock for customers gather at a specified location on the floor of the exchange. Some of the orders are market orders. For example, Mr. A may have instructed his broker to buy 100 shares of Minolta at the lowest possible price, whatever it may be. His personal **demand-to-buy schedule** at that time is shown in Figure 4.1(a): He wishes to buy 100 shares no matter what the price. Although this schedule captures the contractual nature of Mr. A's market order at a specific point in time, Mr. A undoubtedly has a good idea that his ultimate purchase price will be near the price for which orders were executed just before he placed his order. Thus his true demand schedule might be sloping downward from the upper left portion to the lower right portion of the graph. This is shown by the dashed line in the figure. It indicates his desire to buy more shares if the price is lower. However, to simplify his own tasks as well as his broker's tasks, he has estimated that the price for which his order will be ultimately executed will be in the range at which he would choose to hold 100 shares. In the example shown here, this price is 945 yen per share.

Other customers may place limit orders with their brokers. Thus Ms. B may have instructed her broker to buy 200 shares of Minolta at the lowest possible price if and only if that price is less than or equal to 940 yen per share. Her demand schedule is shown in Figure 4.1(b).

Some customers may give their broker two or more orders for the same security. Thus Mr. C may wish to buy 100 shares of Minolta at a price of 955 or less, plus an additional 100 shares if the price is at or below 945. To do this, Mr. C places a limit order for 100 shares at 955 and a second limit order for 100 shares at 945. Figure 4.1(c) portrays his demand schedule.

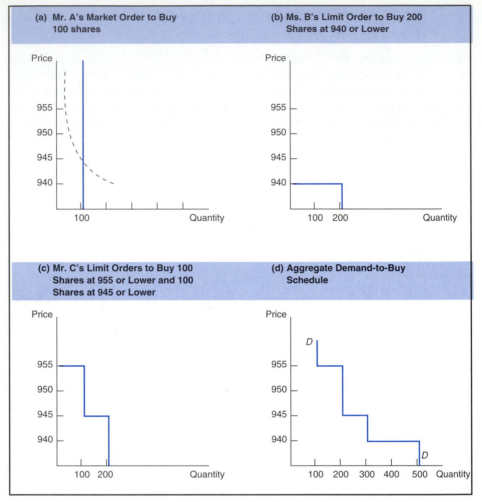

Figure 4.1
Individual Investors' Demand-to-Buy Schedules

If one could look at all the brokers' books and aggregate all the orders to buy Minolta (both market and limit orders), it would be possible to determine how many shares would be bought at every possible price. Assuming that only Mr. A, Ms. B, and Mr. C have placed buy orders, the resulting aggregate demand-to-buy schedule would look like line *DD* in Figure 4.1(d). Note that at lower prices more shares would be demanded.

4.1.2 Supply-to-Sell Schedule

Brokers will also hold market orders to sell shares of Minolta. For example, Ms. X may have placed a market order to sell 100 shares of Minolta at the highest possible price. Figure 4.2(a) displays her **supply-to-sell schedule.** As with market orders to

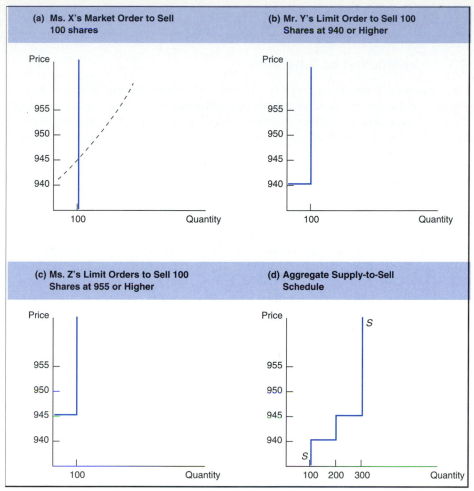

Figure 4.2
Individual Investors' Supply-to-Sell Schedules

buy, customers generally place such orders on the supposition that the actual price will be in the range in which their true desire would be to sell the stated number of shares. Thus Ms. X's actual supply schedule might appear more like the dashed line in Figure 4.2(a), indicating her willingness to sell more shares at higher prices.

Customers may also place limit orders to sell shares of Minolta. For example, Mr. Y may have placed a limit order to sell 100 shares at a price of 940 or higher, and Ms. Z may have placed a limit order to sell 100 shares at a price of 945 or higher. Panels (b) and (c) of Figure 4.2 illustrate these two supply-to-sell schedules.

Similar to the buy orders, if one could look at all the brokers' books and aggregate all the orders to sell Minolta (both market and limit orders), it would be possible to determine how many shares would be sold at every possible price. Assuming that only Ms. X, Mr. Y, and Ms. Z have placed sell orders, the resulting aggregate supply-to-sell schedule would look like line *SS* in Figure 4.2(d). Note that at higher prices more shares would be supplied.

4.1.3 Interaction of Schedules

The aggregate demand and supply schedules are shown on one graph in Figure 4.3. In general no one would have enough information to draw the actual schedules. However, this in no way diminishes their usefulness as representations of the underlying forces that are interacting to determine the market clearing price of Minolta.

What actually happens when all the brokers gather together with their order books in hand? A clerk of the exchange "calls out" a price—for example, 940 yen per share. The brokers then try to complete transactions with one another at that price. Those with orders to buy at that price signify the number of shares they wish to buy. Those with orders to sell do likewise. Some deals will be tentatively made, but as Figure 4.3 shows, more shares will be demanded at 940 than will be supplied. In particular, 300 shares will be demanded, but only 200 shares will be supplied. When trading is completed (meaning that all possible tentative deals have been made), there will be a number of brokers calling "buy," but nobody will stand ready to sell to them. The price of 940 was too low.

Seeing this, the clerk will cry out a different price—for example, 950. As the previous trades are all canceled at this point, the brokers will consult their order books once again and signify the extent to which they are willing to buy or sell shares at this new price. In this case, as Figure 4.3 shows, when trading is

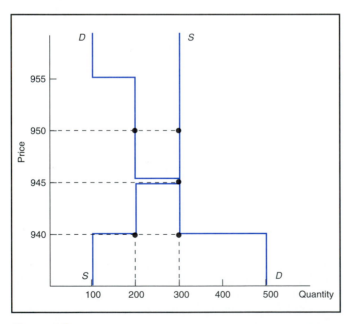

Figure 4.3
Determining a Security's Price by the Interaction of the Aggregate Demand-to-Buy and Supply-to-Sell Schedules

completed, there will be a number of brokers calling "sell," but nobody will stand ready to buy from them. In particular, 300 shares will be supplied, but there will be a demand for only 200 shares. The price of 950 was too high.

Undaunted, the clerk will try again. And again, if necessary. Only when there are relatively few unsatisfied brokers will the price (and the associated tentative deals) be declared final. As Figure 4.3 shows, 945 is such a price. At 945, customers collectively wish to sell 300 shares. Furthermore, there is a collective demand for 300 shares at this price. Thus quantity demanded equals quantity supplied. The price is "just right."

Another way to view this process is to focus on the quantity that would actually be traded at any given price. For any particular price, this would be the smaller of (1) the quantity people are willing to buy and (2) the quantity others are willing to sell, as shown in Figure 4.4. At the price where the quantity that would be traded is maximized, demand will equal supply. As can be seen in the figure, this occurs at a price of 945.

Trading procedures employed in security markets vary from auction markets to dealer markets and from call markets to continuous markets. However, the similarities are more important than the differences. In the United States, for example, specialists at the New York Stock Exchange and dealers in the over-the-counter market provide some of the functions of the *saitori* at the Tokyo Stock Exchange, and trades can take place at any time. Nevertheless, the basic principles of security price determination still operate. In general, market price equates quantity demanded with quantity supplied.

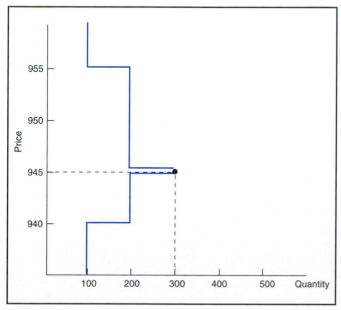

Figure 4.4
Aggregate Quantity Traded

For some purposes it is useful to ignore moment-to-moment changes in customers' orders and focus instead on the fundamental forces at work. Instead of asking how many shares an investor wishes to *buy or sell* at a given price, the number of shares the investor wishes to *hold* at that price can be determined. There is, of course, a close relationship between the two quantities. If an investor wishes to hold more shares than are currently held, the difference is the investor's demand-to-buy schedule. Conversely, if the investor wishes to hold fewer shares than are currently held, the difference is the investor's supply-to-sell schedule.

4.2.1   Demand-to-Hold Schedule

In Figure 4.5 one investor's **demand-to-hold schedule** for a security is shown by curve *dd*. This simply plots the number of shares that the investor wishes to hold at each possible price. In general, lower prices are associated with larger numbers of shares. Of course, the entire schedule is predicated on the investor's current feelings about the security's future prospects. If something makes the investor more optimistic about the security, then he or she will generally wish to hold more shares at any given price. In that case the entire schedule may shift to the right, as shown by curve *d'd'*. Alternatively, if something makes the investor more pessimistic about the security, then the entire curve may shift to the left, as shown by curve *d"d"*.

A factor that complicates analysis of this type is the tendency for some investors to regard sudden and substantial price changes in a security as indicators of changes in the future prospects of the issuer. In the absence of further information, an investor may interpret such a change as an indication that "someone knows something that I don't know." While exploring the situation, the investor may at least temporarily revise his or her own assessment of the issuer's prospects

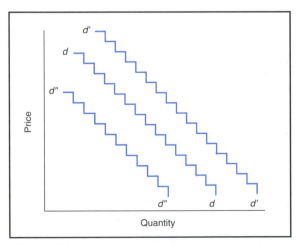

Figure 4.5
An Individual Investor's Demand-to-Hold Schedule

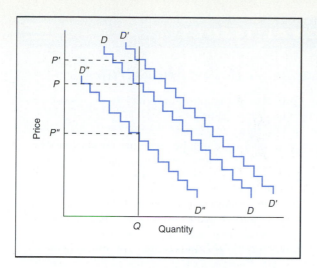

Figure 4.6

Aggregate Demand-to-Hold
and Available Quantity
Schedules

and, in doing so, may alter the demand-to-hold schedule. For this reason, few investors place limit orders at prices substantially different from the current price, for fear that such orders would be executed only if the security's prospects changed significantly. If such a large price change actually occurred, it would imply the need for a careful reevaluation of the security before buying or selling shares.

Despite this complication, it is possible to construct an aggregate schedule indicating the total number of shares of a given firm that investors will wish to hold at various prices, assuming no change in their views of the relative prospects of the firm. This overall demand-to-hold schedule, obtained by adding the individual investors' demand-to-hold schedules, would look like curve *DD* in Figure 4.6. In the short run, at least, the available number of shares is fixed—for example, at *Q* in the figure. Only one price will equate the aggregate demand to hold with the available number of shares. In Figure 4.6 it is *P.* At any higher price, current holders of the security will collectively wish to hold fewer shares than are outstanding. In their attempts to sell such shares, they will drive the price down until they or others are willing to hold all the shares. Conversely, if the price is below *P,* investors will collectively wish to hold more shares than are available. In their attempts to buy shares, they will drive the price up until they no longer want additional shares. Ultimately, the price will settle at *P,* where aggregate demand equals the available quantity.

4.2.2 Elasticity of Schedule

How elastic (that is, flat) will be the aggregate demand-to-hold schedule for a security? The answer depends in part on the extent to which the security is regarded as "unique." Securities are considered more unique when they have few close substitutes. Securities are considered less unique when they have more close substitutes. This means that the aggregate demand schedule will be more elastic (that is, more flat) for less unique securities. Equivalently, the less unique a security is, the greater will be the increase in the quantity demanded for a given fall in price. This is because these shares will produce a smaller increase in the typical portfolio's risk when substituted for other shares.

The Arizona Stock Exchange: A Better Mousetrap

So you think that supply and demand curves are merely esoteric figments of ivory-tower thinking. Perhaps a valid concept, you say, but they cannot possibly be of any practical use in establishing security prices. Well, do not tell that to AZX Inc. (AZX). Since early 1991 that organization (or its predecessor, Wunsch Auction Systems, Inc.) has been conducting regular security auctions among institutional investors for a broad list of common stocks. Market clearing prices in those auctions are determined by the explicit interaction of the investors' supply and demand preferences.

Step back for a moment and recall how prices are set on organized security exchanges or the OTC market (see Chapter 3). Dealers (whether specialists or OTC dealers) "make markets" in particular securities—that is, acting as intermediaries, they buy and sell from other investors for their own accounts. The dealers quote prices (bid-asked) to sellers and buyers on a continuous basis. They adjust prices as they sense supply and demand building and ebbing. It is the competitive efforts of these intermediaries that determine security prices.

AZX has developed a market mechanism quite different from that of the conventional dealer markets. AZX calls this mechanism the Arizona Stock Exchange, although it bears no resemblance to any existing stock exchange. (The name derives from financial support provided to AZX by the state of Arizona.) The concept behind the Arizona Stock Exchange is simple. Auctions are scheduled on a regular basis (currently daily at 5 P.M. EST, after the New York Stock Exchange closes). Prior to a scheduled auction, investors submit orders electronically to buy or sell specified quantities of a security at specified prices (essentially limit orders—see Chapter 2).

At the time of the auction, the orders of all participating investors are aggregated by computer—that is, the computer calculates supply and demand curves for each security being auctioned. The intersection of these curves determines the market clearing price for a security. At that price the maximum number of shares of stock will be exchanged. (All buy orders above and all sell orders below the equilibrium price are matched, whereas

orders at the equilibrium price are matched on a time priority basis.)

Investors are able to access the auction order information (in graphic or tabular form) up to the time of the auction through an open limit order book. As opposed to a specialist's proprietary closed limit order book, the Arizona Stock Exchange permits investors to examine the current supply and demand for a stock. This allows investors to raise their bid prices (or lower their asked prices) to adjust to the current market conditions. In order to prevent manipulative behavior, withdrawn orders incur a penalty charge.

The Arizona Stock Exchange possesses some intriguing advantages over traditional dealer markets:

1. It is simple and fair. All investors have access to the same auction information, and all investors trade at the same price.
2. Investors have direct access to the market. This feature removes the inherent conflicts of interest present in dealer markets.
3. Investors' orders are anonymous. Orders and trade executions are handled by computer.
4. It matches "natural" buyers and sellers (those with an explicit desire to transact), thereby perhaps establishing more robust and stable prices.
5. Transaction costs are low (about 1¢ per share versus 10¢ to 20¢ per share in dealer markets).

This last point warrants elaboration. Traditional dealer markets are continuous—trading can occur at any time during the trading day. Continuous trading mechanisms are expensive and require dealers because the "other side" of a trade is not always immediately available. Dealers provide liquidity to investors who wish to transact immediately.

With more frequent large trades having been made by institutional investors in the last decade, the ability of dealer markets to provide continuous liquidity has been severely tested. The market crash of October 1987 was an extreme, but not singular, example.

Many (and perhaps most) institutional investors do not require immediate liquidity. They can wait several hours to trade, particularly if by waiting their transaction costs are reduced significantly. In lieu of the continuous intervention of the dealer, the Arizona Stock Exchange substitutes a periodic call to market (akin to the crossing systems discussed in Chapter 3). Without the expensive overhead of the dealer, the Arizona Stock Exchange can afford to match buyers and sellers at a small fraction of the cost of the dealer market.

What are the disadvantages of the Arizona Stock Exchange? Conceptually, there are none to investors who do not require immediate liquidity. However, if you throw a party and no one comes, the party is a failure no matter how elaborate the preparations. Likewise, to be successful, AZX must attract enough institutional investors to generate sufficient liquidity and to contribute to the "discovery" of market prices. Consequently, AZX must

overcome investor inertia and ignorance. As with any fledgling trading mechanism, the Arizona Stock Exchange faces a catch-22: institutional investors want to see large trading volumes before they will participate, but those large volumes can occur only if institutional investors participate.

To date traders have not beaten a path to AZX's door. Currently 20 to 25 institutional investors use the system on any given day, and daily volume runs in the range of 300,000 to 700,000 shares traded. While these figures pale in comparison to the activity on the New York Stock Exchange, participating investors and trading volumes have been growing over the last few years. Regardless of whether or not the Arizona Stock Exchange succeeds in its present form, the concept of an electronic call to market is likely to gain increasing attention in the years ahead.

4.2.3 Shifts of Schedule

If one investor becomes more optimistic about the prospects for a security while another investor becomes more pessimistic about the same security, they may very likely trade with one another with no effect on the aggregate demand-to-hold schedule. In this situation there will be no change in the market price for the security. However, if more investors become optimistic rather than pessimistic, the schedule will shift to the right (for example, to $D'D'$ in Figure 4.6), causing an increase in price (to P'). Correspondingly, if more investors become pessimistic rather than optimistic, the schedule will shift to the left (for example, to $D''D''$ in Figure 4.6), causing a decrease in price (to P'').

| 4.3 | EFFECTS OF PROCEDURES FOR SHORT SALES |

Thus far the individual investor's demand-to-hold schedule has been drawn only in the region of positive quantities. But there is more to it: the higher the price, the smaller the quantity the investor will wish to hold. At some price the desired amount is zero, and at higher prices the investor may consider short selling the security.

If short sellers received the proceeds from such sales, an individual investor's demand-to-hold schedule for a given security would look like the curve in Figure 4.7(a). This curve can be thought of in either of two ways: as a demand

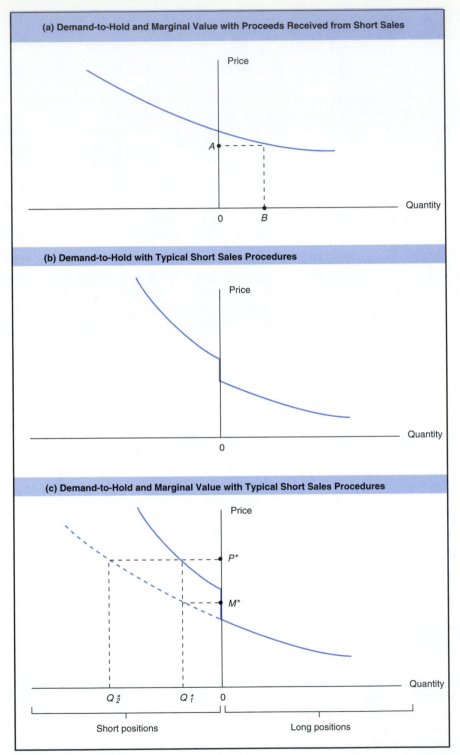

Figure 4.7
Demand-to-Hold Curves

curve (that is, at price A the investor wishes to hold quantity B) or as a marginal value curve (that is, if quantity B is held, the marginal value of one share more or less will be the amount A).

In fact, however, short sellers generally do not receive the proceeds of such sales. As mentioned in Chapter 2, these proceeds are held by the short seller's brokerage firm as collateral. In many instances the short seller does not even receive interest on this money and, furthermore, short sellers must meet initial margin requirements on the face amount of the short sale proceeds. This changes the situation from that shown in Figure 4.7(a). Selling a security one owns generates cash that can be used for other purposes, but selling a security that one does not own requires an investment of cash. Thus the decision to go short requires a higher price than it would if the short seller received full use of the proceeds. The effective demand-to-hold schedule would look like the curve in Figure 4.7(b). To the right of the vertical axis the curve is the same as in Figure 4.7(a), but to the left it is higher.

The effect of this is shown in Figure 4.7(c). The solid curve is the effective demand-to-hold schedule. The dashed curve is the portion of the original demand curve in Figure 4.7(a) that is to the left of the vertical axis. If the current price of the security is P^*, this investor will go short only Q_1^* shares, not Q_2^* shares. Thus his or her pessimism about the security will not have as much impact on the market as it would if short sellers received full use of the short sale proceeds. In a sense, the investor chooses a holding (Q_1^*) at which he or she considers the marginal value (M^*) to be less than the current market price (P^*).

4.4   PRICE AS A CONSENSUS

However one chooses to analyze the determination of a security's price, it is important to remember that a free market price for a security reflects a kind of consensus. This can be seen in Figure 4.8. Assume that the current market price for this particular security is P^*. Some individuals hold the security. For each of them, the situation is like that shown in Figure 4.8(a), where it can be seen that the investor has adjusted his or her portfolio so that the marginal value of a share (M^*) equals its market price.

A few investors may be short sellers. Their situation is like that shown in Figure 4.8(b). Because of the short sale rules, each short seller will have taken a position at which the marginal value of a share is less than the price. Many investors will choose to hold no shares, and thus their position is neither long nor short. Their situation is shown in Figure 4.8(c). For each of them the marginal value is equal to or, as in the case shown here, somewhat below the market price.

Were it not for short selling rules, every investor would adjust his or her portfolio holdings until the marginal value of a security equaled its current market price. Because the market price is the same for everyone, so would be the marginal value for all investors (assuming that all investors pay attention to the market). Price would clearly represent a consensus of investor opinion about value.

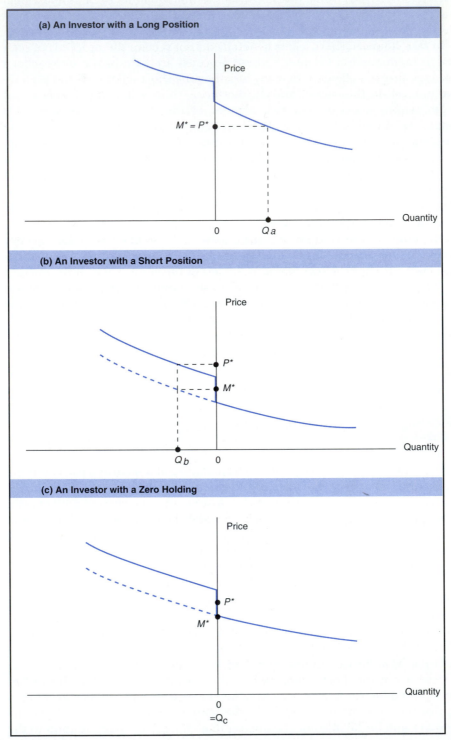

Figure 4.8
Price of a Security as a Consensus

CHAPTER 4

Current short selling rules in the United States change this situation, but only slightly. As some investors (primarily pessimists) might choose holdings at which the marginal value is below the market price, this market price could be slightly higher than an average of investors' marginal values. Accordingly, securities may be slightly "overpriced." (It should be noted that certain countries have more onerous short selling rules that could result in more notable instances of security overpricing.)

However, current short sale rules in the United States are likely to have a small impact on market prices. Even for the short seller, the disparity between market price and marginal value may be small. For those who hold no shares it would be smaller yet (or even zero). And for those who hold shares it will be zero. Moreover, short positions are typically a small fraction of long positions. For practical purposes, price can reasonably be considered equal to a consensus opinion of investors concerning marginal value. For it to be seriously in error as an estimate of that value, many investors must be poorly informed or poor analysts. Moreover, there must be either (1) a preponderance of such investors with overly optimistic forecasts or (2) a preponderance of such investors with overly pessimistic forecasts. Otherwise the actions of such investors will offset each other, making price a good estimate of the present value of the security's future prospects.

4.5	MARKET EFFICIENCY

Imagine a world in which (1) all investors have costless access to currently available information about the future, (2) all investors are good analysts, and (3) all investors pay close attention to market prices and adjust their holdings appropriately.[1] In such a market a security's price will be a good estimate of its **investment value,** where investment value is the present value of the security's future prospects, as estimated by well-informed and capable analysts, and can be thought of as the security's fair value.

An **efficient market** can now be defined:

> *A (perfectly) efficient market is one in which every security's price equals its investment value at all times.*

That is, each security sells for its fair value at all times. Hence any attempt to identify mispriced securities is futile.

In an efficient market a set of information is fully and immediately reflected in market prices. But what information? A popular definition is the following[2]:

Form of Efficiency	Set of Information Reflected in Security Prices
Weak	Previous prices of securities
Semistrong	All publicly available information
Strong	All information, both public and private

An equivalent definition of an efficient market is the following:

> *A market is efficient with respect to a particular set of information if it is impossible to make abnormal profits by using this set of information to formulate buying and selling decisions.*

That is, in an efficient market investors should expect to make only normal profits and earn a normal rate of return on their investments. For example, a market would be described as having **weak-form efficiency** if it is impossible to make abnormal profits by using past prices to make decisions about when to buy and sell securities. The evidence suggests that major security markets in the United States are weak-form efficient. However, U.S. markets do not conform so well to the definition of **semistrong-form efficiency** (although the lack of a precise meaning for "publicly available" makes this form of efficiency somewhat ambiguous). They conform even less well to the definition of **strong-form efficiency.**

In an efficient market any new information is immediately and fully reflected in prices. New information is just that: new, meaning a surprise. (Anything that is not a surprise is predictable and should have been anticipated before the fact.) Since happy surprises are about as likely as unhappy ones, price changes in an efficient market are about as likely to be positive as negative. While a security's price might be expected to move upward by an amount that provides a reasonable return on capital (when considered in conjunction with dividend payments), anything above or below this would, in such a market, be unpredictable. In a perfectly efficient market, price changes are close to random.[3]

Now consider an irrational market in which prices never bear any particular relationship to investment value. In such a world, price changes might also appear to be random. However, major security markets in the United States are not irrational. They may not attain perfect efficiency, but they are certainly much closer to it than to irrationality. To understand financial markets, it is important to understand perfectly efficient markets.

As mentioned earlier, in an efficient market a security's price will be a good estimate of its investment value, where investment value is the present value of the security's future prospects as estimated by well-informed and capable analysts. Any substantial disparity between price and value would reflect market inefficiency. In a well-developed and free market, major inefficiencies are rare. The reason is not hard to find. Major disparities between price and investment value will be noted by alert analysts who will seek to take advantage of their discoveries. Securities priced below value (known as underpriced or undervalued securities) will be purchased, creating pressure for price increases due to the increased demand to buy. Securities priced above value (known as overpriced or overvalued securities) will be sold, creating pressure for price decreases due to the increased supply to sell. As investors seek to take advantage of opportunities created by temporary inefficiencies, they will cause the inefficiencies to be reduced, denying the less alert and the less informed a chance to obtain large abnormal profits.

In the United States there are thousands of professional security analysts and even more amateurs. Not surprisingly, due to their actions the major U.S.

security markets appear to be much closer to efficiency than to irrationality. As a consequence it is extremely difficult to make abnormal profits by buying and selling securities in these markets.

4.6 SUMMARY

1. The forces of supply and demand interact to determine a security's market price.
2. An investor's demand-to-buy schedule indicates the quantity of a security that the investor wishes to purchase at various prices.
3. An investor's supply-to-sell schedule indicates the quantity of a security that the investor wishes to sell at various prices.
4. The demand and supply schedules for individual investors can be aggregated to create aggregate demand and supply schedules for a security.
5. The intersection of the aggregate demand and supply schedules determines the market clearing price of a security. At that price the quantity traded is maximized.
6. An investor's demand-to-hold schedule indicates the quantity of a security that the investor wishes to own at various prices, assuming no change in the investor's views concerning the relative prospects for the security.
7. The market price of a security can be thought of as representing a consensus opinion about the future prospects for the security.
8. In an efficient market a security's market price will fully reflect all available information relevant to the security's value at that time.
9. The concept of market efficiency can be expressed in three forms: weak, semistrong, and strong.
10. The three forms of market efficiency make different assumptions about the set of information reflected in security prices.

QUESTIONS AND PROBLEMS

1. What is the difference between call security markets and continuous security markets?
2. What is the relationship between the demand-to-hold schedule and the demand-to-buy and supply-to-sell schedules for a particular security?
3. At two separate points in time, Deerfoot Bay drew up the following personal demand-to-hold schedules for an investment in Lisle Bakery stock. Calculate Deerfoot's demand-to-buy schedule at the end of Year 2.

Year 1		Year 2	
Price	Quantity	Price	Quantity
$30	1,000	$30	1,100
40	900	40	990
50	800	50	880
60	700	60	770
70	600	70	660

4. Using an aggregate demand-to-hold schedule and associated demand-to-buy or supply-to-sell schedules, explain and illustrate the effect of the following events on the equilibrium price and quantity traded of Fairchild Corporation's stock.

   a. Fairchild officials announce that next year's earnings are expected to be significantly higher than analysts had previously forecast.

   b. A wealthy shareholder initiates a large secondary offering of Fairchild stock.

   c. Another company, quite similar to Fairchild in all respects except for being privately held, decides to offer its outstanding shares for sale to the public.

5. Is it true that in the short run the supply schedule for a security is perfectly inelastic, whereas the demand-to-hold schedule is typically elastic? Explain.

6. Short sellers do not receive the proceeds from their short sales, must put up initial margin, and often do not receive interest on these sums held by their brokers. How does this affect the aggregate demand-to-hold schedules for securities?

7. Imp Begley is pondering the statement, "The pattern of security price behavior might appear the same whether markets were efficient or if security prices bore no relationship whatsoever to investment value." Explain the meaning of this statement to Imp.

8. We all know that investors have widely diverse opinions about the future course of the economy and earnings forecasts for various industries and companies. How then is it possible for all these investors to arrive at an equilibrium price for any particular security?

9. Distinguish between the three forms of market efficiency.

10. Does the fact that a market exhibits weak-form efficiency necessarily imply that it is also strong-form efficient? How about the converse statement? Explain.

11. Consider the following types of information. If this information is immediately and fully reflected in security prices, what form of market efficiency is implied?

   a. A company's recent quarterly earnings announcement.

   b. Historical bond yields.

   c. Deliberations of a company's board of directors concerning a possible merger with another company.

   d. Limit orders in a specialist's book.

   e. A brokerage firm's published research report on a particular company.

   f. Movements in the Dow Jones Industrial Average as plotted in the *Wall Street Journal*.

12. Would you expect that fundamental security analysis makes security markets more efficient? Why?

13. Would you expect that NYSE specialists should be able to earn an abnormal profit in a semistrong efficient market? Why?

14. Is it true that in a perfectly efficient market no investor would consistently be able to earn a profit?

15. Although security markets may not be perfectly efficient, what is the rationale for expecting them to be highly efficient?

16. When a corporation announces its earnings for a period, the volume of transactions in its stock may increase, but frequently that increase is not associated with significant moves in the price of its stock. How can this be explained?

17. What are the implications of the three forms of market efficiency for technical and fundamental analysis (discussed in Chapter 1)?

18. The years 1986 and 1987 will probably be long remembered for the insider trading scandals that were exposed.
    a. Is successful insider trading consistent with the three forms of market efficiency? Explain.
    b. Play the role of devil's advocate and present a case outlining the benefits to financial markets of insider trading.

CFA EXAM QUESTION

19. Discuss the role of a portfolio manager in a perfectly efficient market.

ENDNOTES

[1] Actually, not all investors need to meet these three conditions in order for security prices to equal their investment values. Instead, what is needed is for marginal investors to meet these conditions, since their trades would correct the mispricing that would occur in their absence.

[2] Eugene F. Fama, "Efficient Capital Markets: A Review of Theory and Empirical Work," *Journal of Finance,* 25, no. 5 (May 1970): 383–417.

[3] Some people assert that daily security prices follow a **random walk,** meaning that security price changes (say, from one day to the next) are independently and identically distributed. That is, the price change from day t to day $t + 1$ is not influenced by the price change from day $t - 1$ to day t; and the size of the price change from one day to the next can be viewed as being determined by the spin of a roulette wheel (with the same roulette wheel being used every day).

KEY TERMS

demand-to-buy schedule	weak-form efficiency
supply-to-sell schedule	semistrong-form efficiency
demand-to-hold schedule	strong-form efficiency
investment value	random walk
efficient market	

REFERENCES

1. A discussion and examination of the demand curves for stocks is contained in:

   Andrei Shleifer, "Do Demand Curves Slope Down?" *Journal of Finance*, 41, no. 3 (July 1986): 579–590.

   Lawrence Harris and Eitan Gurel, "Price and Volume Effects Associated with Changes in the S&P 500: New Evidence for the Existence of Price Pressures," *Journal of Finance*, 41, no. 4 (September 1986): 815–829.

   Stephen W. Pruitt and K. C. John Wei, "Institutional Ownership and Changes in the S&P 500," *Journal of Finance*, 44, no. 2 (June 1989): 509–513.

2. For articles presenting arguments that securities are "overpriced" due to short sale restrictions, see:

   Edward M. Miller, "Risk, Uncertainty, and Divergence of Opinion," *Journal of Finance*, 32, no. 4 (September 1977): 1151–1168.

   Douglas W. Diamond and Robert E. Verrecchia, "Constraints on Short-Selling and Asset Price Adjustment to Private Information," *Journal of Financial Economics*, 18, no. 2 (June 1987): 277–311.

3. Many people believe that the following articles are the seminal pieces on efficient markets:

   Harry V. Roberts, "Stock Market 'Patterns' and Financial Analysis: Methodological Suggestions," *Journal of Finance*, 14, no. 1 (March 1959): 1–10.

   Eugene F. Fama, "Efficient Capital Markets: A Review of Theory and Empirical Work," *Journal of Finance*, 25, no. 5 (May 1970): 383–417.

   Eugene F. Fama, "Efficient Capital Markets: II," *Journal of Finance*, 46, no. 5 (December 1991): 1575–1617.

4. For an extensive discussion of efficient markets and related evidence, see:

   George Foster, *Financial Statement Analysis* (Englewood Cliffs, NJ: Prentice Hall, 1986), Chapters 9 and 11.

   Stephen F. LeRoy, "Capital Market Efficiency: An Update," *Federal Reserve Bank of San Francisco Economic Review*, no. 2 (Spring 1990): 29–40. A more detailed version of this paper can be found in: Stephen F. LeRoy, "Efficient Capital Markets and Martingales," *Journal of Economic Literature*, 27, no. 4 (December 1989): 1583–1621.

   Peter Fortune, "Stock Market Efficiency: An Autopsy?" *New England Economic Review* (March/April 1991): 17–40.

   Richard A. Brealey and Stewart C. Myers, *Principles of Corporate Finance* (New York: McGraw-Hill, 1991), Chapter 13.

   Stephen A. Ross, Randolph W. Westerfield, and Jeffrey F. Jaffe, *Corporate Finance* (Homewood, IL: Richard D. Irwin, 1993), Chapter 13.

5. Interesting overviews of efficient market concepts are presented in:

Robert Ferguson, "An Efficient Stock Market? Ridiculous!" *Journal of Portfolio Management,* 9, no. 4 (Summer 1983): 31–38.

Bob L. Boldt and Harold L. Arbit, "Efficient Markets and the Professional Investor," *Financial Analysts Journal,* 40, no. 4 (July/August 1984): 22–34.

Fischer Black, "Noise," *Journal of Finance,* 41, no. 3 (July 1986): 529–543.

The Valuation of Riskless Securities

A useful first step in understanding security valuation is to consider those fixed-income securities that are certain of making their promised payments in full and on time. The obvious candidates are the securities representing the debt of the U.S. government. Because the government can print money whenever it chooses, the promised payments on such securities are virtually certain to be made on schedule. However, there is a degree of uncertainty as to the purchasing power of the promised payments. Although U.S. government bonds may be riskless in terms of their nominal payments, they may be quite risky in terms of their real (or inflation-adjusted) payments. This chapter begins with a discussion of the relationship between nominal and real interest rates.

Despite the concern with inflation risk, it will be assumed that there are fixed-income securities whose nominal and real payments are certain. Specifically, it will be assumed that the magnitude of inflation can be accurately predicted. Such an assumption makes it possible to focus on the impact of *time* on bond valuation. The influence of other attributes on bond valuation can then be considered.

5.1 NOMINAL VERSUS REAL INTEREST RATES

Modern economies gain much of their efficiency through the use of money—a generally agreed-upon medium of exchange. Instead of trading present corn for a future Toyota, as in a barter economy, the citizen of a modern economy can trade his or her corn for money (that is, "sell it"), trade the money for future money (that is, "invest it"), and finally trade the future money for a Toyota (that is, "buy it"). The rate at which he or she can trade present money for future money is the nominal (or "monetary") interest rate—usually simply called the interest rate.

In periods of changing prices, the nominal interest rate may prove a poor guide to the real return obtained by the investor. Although there is no completely satisfactory way to summarize the many price changes that take place in such periods, most governments attempt to do so by measuring the cost of a specified bundle of major items. The "overall" price level computed for this representative combination of items is usually called a *cost-of-living index,* or *consumer price index.*

Whether or not the index is relevant for a given individual depends to a major extent on the similarity of his or her purchases to the bundle of goods and services used to construct the index. Moreover, such indices tend to overstate increases in the cost of living for people who do purchase the chosen bundle of items. There are two reasons for this. First, improvements in quality are seldom taken adequately into account. Perhaps more important, little or no adjustment is made in the composition of items in the bundle as relative prices change. The rational consumer can reduce the cost of attaining a given standard of living as prices change by substituting relatively less expensive items for those that have become relatively more expensive.

Despite these drawbacks, cost-of-living indices provide at least rough estimates of changes in prices. And such indices can be used to determine an overall real rate of interest. For example, assume that during a year in which the nominal rate of interest is 7%, the cost-of-living index increases from 121 to 124. This means that the bundle of goods and services that cost $100 in some base year and $121 at the beginning of the year now cost $124 at year end. The owner of such a bundle could have sold it for $121 at the start of the year, invested the proceeds at 7% to obtain $129.47 (= $121 × 1.07) at the end of the year, and then immediately purchased 1.0441 (= $129.47/$124) bundles. The real rate of interest was, thus, 4.41% (= 1.0441 − 1).

These calculations can be summarized in the following formula:

$$\frac{C_0 (1 + \text{NIR})}{C_1} = 1 + \text{RIR} \tag{5.1}$$

where:

C_0 = *level of the cost-of-living index at the beginning of the year,*
C_1 = *level of the cost-of-living index at the end of the year,*
NIR = *the nominal interest rate,*
RIR = *the real interest rate.*

Alternatively, Equation (5.1) can be written as:

$$\frac{1 + \text{NIR}}{1 + \text{CCL}} = 1 + \text{RIR} \tag{5.2}$$

---

where CCL = the rate of change in the cost of living index, or $(C_1 - C_0)/C_0$. In this case, CCL = .02479 = $(124 - 121)/121$, so prices increased by about 2.5%.

For quick calculation, the real rate of interest can be estimated by simply subtracting the rate of change in the cost of living index from the nominal interest rate:

$$RIR \cong NIR - CCL \qquad (5.3)$$

where $\cong$ means "is approximately equal to." In this case the quick calculation results in an estimate of 4.5% (= 7% − 2.5%), which is reasonably close to the true value of 4.41%.

Sad to say, inflation seems to be here to stay, but its precise magnitude is hard to forecast much in advance. For this reason, further discussion of real versus nominal interest rates is deferred until Chapter 13. Suffice it to say here that it may be best to view the expected real interest rate as determined by the underlying forces described in earlier sections, with the nominal interest rate approximately equal to this amount plus the expected rate of change in prices.

5.2   YIELD-TO-MATURITY

There are many interest rates, not just one. Furthermore, there are many ways that interest rates can be calculated. One such method results in an interest rate that is known as the yield-to-maturity. Another results in an interest rate known as the spot rate, which will be discussed in the next section.

In describing yields-to-maturity and spot rates, three hypothetical Treasury securities that are available to the public for investment will be considered. Such securities are widely believed to be free from default risk, meaning that investors have no doubts about being paid fully and on time. Thus, the impact of differing degrees of default risk on yields-to-maturity and spot rates is removed by considering these securities.

The three Treasury securities to be considered will be referred to as bonds *A, B,* and *C.* Bond *A* matures in a year, at which time the investor will receive $1,000. Similarly, bond *B* matures in two years, at which time the investor will receive $1,000. Bond *C* is a coupon bond that pays the investor $50 one year from now and matures two years from now, paying the investor $1,050 at that time. The prices at which these bonds are currently being sold in the market are:

Bond *A* (the one-year pure-discount bond): $934.58

Bond *B* (the two-year pure-discount bond): $857.34

Bond *C* (the two-year coupon bond): $946.93.

The **yield-to-maturity** on any fixed-income security is the single interest rate (with interest compounded at some specified interval) that, if paid by a bank on the amount invested, would enable the investor to obtain all the payments promised by the security in question. It is a simple matter to determine the yield-to-maturity on the one-year security, bond A. Since an investment of $934.58 will pay $1,000 one year later, the yield-to-maturity on this bond is the rate r_A that a bank would have to pay on a deposit of $934.58 in order for the account to have a balance of $1,000 after one year. Thus the yield-to-maturity on bond A is the rate r_A that solves the following equation:

$$(1 + r_A) \times \$934.58 = \$1,000 \qquad (5.4)$$

which is 7%.

In the case of bond B, assuming annual compounding at a rate r_B, an account with $857.34 invested initially (the cost of B) would grow to $(1 + r_B) \times$ $857.34 in one year. Leaving this total intact, the account would grow to $(1 + r_B)$ $\times [(1 + r_B) \times \$857.34]$ by the end of the second year. The yield-to-maturity is the rate r_B that makes this amount equal to $1,000. In other words, the yield-to-maturity on bond B is the rate r_B that solves the following equation:

$$(1 + r_B) \times [(1 + r_B) \times \$857.34] = \$1,000 \qquad (5.5)$$

which is 8%.

For bond C, consider investing $946.93 in an account. At the end of one year, the account would grow in value to $(1 + r_C) \times \$946.93$. Then the investor would remove $50, leaving a balance of $[(1 + r_C) \times \$946.93] - \$50$. At the end of the second year this balance would have grown to an amount equal to $(1 + r_C) \times \{[(1 + r_C) \times \$946.93] - \$50\}$. The yield-to-maturity on bond C is the rate r_C that makes this amount equal to $1,050:

$$(1 + r_C) \times \{[(1 + r_C) \times \$946.93] - \$50\} = \$1,050 \qquad (5.6)$$

which is 7.975%.

Equivalently, yield-to-maturity is the discount rate that makes the present value of the promised future cash flows equal in sum to the current market price of the bond.[1] When viewed in this manner, yield-to-maturity is analogous to internal rate of return, a concept used for making capital budgeting decisions and often described in introductory finance textbooks. This can be seen for bond A by dividing both sides of Equation (5.4) by $(1 + r_A)$, resulting in:

$$\$934.58 = \frac{\$1,000}{(1 + r_A)} . \qquad (5.7)$$

Similarly, for bond B both sides of Equation (5.5) can be divided by $(1 + r_B)^2$, resulting in:

$$\$857.34 = \frac{\$1,000}{(1 + r_B)^2} \qquad (5.8)$$

whereas for bond C both sides of Equation (5.6) can be divided by $(1 + r_C)^2$:

$$\$946.93 - \frac{\$50}{(1 + r_C)} = \frac{\$1,050}{(1 + r_C)^2}$$

or

$$\$946.93 = \frac{\$50}{(1 + r_C)} + \frac{\$1,050}{(1 + r_C)^2} . \qquad (5.9)$$

Because Equations (5.7), (5.8), and (5.9) are equivalent to Equations (5.4), (5.5), and (5.6), respectively, the solutions must be the same as before, with $r_A = 7\%$, $r_B = 8\%$, and $r_C = 7.975\%$.

For coupon-bearing bonds, the procedure for determining yield-to-maturity involves trial and error. In the case of bond C, a discount rate of 10% could be tried initially, resulting in a value for the right-hand side of Equation (5.9) of $913.22, a value that is too low. This indicates that the number in the denominator is too high, so a lower discount rate is used next—say 6%. In this case, the value on the right-hand side is $981.67, which is too high and indicates that 6% is too low. This means that the solution is between 6% and 10%, and the search could continue until the answer, 7.975%, is found.

Fortunately, computers are good at trial-and-error calculations. One can describe a very complex series of cash flows to a computer and get an answer concerning yield-to-maturity in short order. In fact, many hand-held calculators come with built-in programs to find yield-to-maturity, where you simply enter the number of days to maturity, the annual coupon payments, and the current market price, then press the key that indicates yield-to-maturity.

Yield-to-maturity is the most commonly used measure of a bond's "interest rate" or "return." It can be computed for any bond, and it facilitates comparisons among different investments. However, it has some serious drawbacks. In order to understand these drawbacks, the concept of spot rates must be introduced.

5.3   SPOT RATES

A **spot rate** is measured at a given point in time as the yield-to-maturity on a pure-discount security, and can be thought of as the interest rate associated with a spot contract. Such a contract, when signed, involves the immediate loaning of money from one party to another. The loan, along with interest, is to be repaid in its entirety at a specific time in the future. The interest rate that is specified in the contract is the spot rate.

Bonds A and B in the previous example were pure-discount securities, meaning that an investor who purchased either one would expect to receive only one cash payment from the issuer. Accordingly, in this example the one-year spot rate is 7% and the two-year spot rate is 8%. In general, the t-year spot rate s_t is the solution to the following equation:

$$P_t = \frac{M_t}{(1 + s_t)^t} \tag{5.10}$$

where P_t is the current market price of a pure-discount bond that matures in t years and has a maturity value of M_t. For example, the values of P_t and M_t for bond B would be $857.34 and $1,000, respectively, with $t = 2$.

Spot rates can also be determined in another manner if only coupon-bearing Treasury bonds are available for longer maturities. Generally the one-year spot rate (s_1) is known, as there typically is a one-year pure-discount

Treasury security available for making this calculation. However, it may be that no two-year pure-discount Treasury security exists. Instead, only a two-year coupon-bearing bond may be available for investment, having a current market price of P_2, a maturity value of M_2, and a coupon payment one year from now equal to C_1. In this situation, the two-year spot rate (s_2) is the solution to the following equation:

$$P_2 = \frac{C_1}{(1 + s_1)^1} + \frac{M_2}{(1 + s_2)^2}. \qquad (5.11)$$

For example, assume that only bonds A and C exist. In this situation it is known that the one-year spot rate, s_1, is 7%. Now, Equation (5.11) can be used to determine the two-year spot rate, s_2, where $P_2 = \$946.93$, $C_1 = \$50$, and $M_2 = \$1,050$:

$$\$946.93 = \frac{\$50}{(1 + .07)^1} + \frac{\$1,050}{(1 + s_2)^2}.$$

The solution to this equation is $s_2 = .08 = 8\%$. Thus, the two-year spot rate is determined to be the same in this example, regardless of whether it is calculated directly by analyzing pure-discount bond B or indirectly by analyzing coupon-bearing bond C in conjunction with bond A. Although this will not always be the case when actual bond prices are examined, typically the differences are insignificant.

5.4 DISCOUNT FACTORS

Having determined a set of spot rates, it is a straightforward matter to determine the corresponding set of **discount factors.** A discount factor d_t is equivalent to the present value of $1 to be received t years in the future from a Treasury security, and is equal to:

$$d_t = \frac{1}{(1 + s_t)^t}. \qquad (5.12)$$

The set of these factors is sometimes referred to as the **market discount function,** and it changes day to day as spot rates change. In the example, $d_1 = 1/(1 + .07)^1 = .9346$; and $d_2 = 1/(1 + .08)^2 = .8573$.

Once the market discount function has been determined, it is fairly straightforward to find the present value of any Treasury security (or, for that matter, any default-free security). Let C_t denote the cash payment to be made to the investor at year t on the security being evaluated. The multiplication of C_t by d_t is termed **discounting:** converting the given future value into an equivalent present value. The latter is equivalent in the sense that P present dollars can be converted into C_t dollars in year t via available investment instruments, given the currently prevailing spot rates. An investment paying C_t dollars in year t with certainty should sell for $P = d_t C_t$ dollars today. If it sells for more, it is overpriced; if it sells for less, it is underpriced. These statements rest solely on comparisons with equivalent opportunities in the marketplace. Valuation of default-free

Almost Riskless Securities

Unless we wish to remain on a purely abstract level, our discussion concerning the valuation of riskless securities requires an actual riskless security to value. Surprisingly, no such financial asset can be found in the U.S. financial markets.

A riskless security provides the investor with a certain return over the investor's time horizon. As an investor is ultimately interested in the purchasing power of his or her investments, the riskless security's return should be certain on a real (inflation-adjusted) basis.

As the text notes, although U.S. Treasury securities have zero risk of default, even they do not provide riskless real returns. Their principal and interest payments are not adjusted for inflation over the securities' lives. As a result, unexpected inflation may produce real returns different from those expected at the time the securities were purchased.

However, assume that U.S. inflation remains low and fairly predictable. Will Treasury securities provide investors with riskless returns? The answer is generally "no."

An investor's time horizon usually will not coincide with the life of a particular Treasury security. If that time horizon is shorter than the security's life, then the investor must purchase another Treasury security when the first security matures. If interest rates have changed in the interim, the investor will earn a different return than he or she originally anticipated. (This risk is known as reinvestment-rate risk—see Chapter 9.)

If the Treasury security's life exceeds the investor's time horizon, then the investor will have to sell the security before it matures. If interest rates change prior to the sale, the price of the security will change, thereby causing the investor to earn a different return from the one originally anticipated. (This risk is known as interest-rate risk—see Chapter 9.)

Even if the Treasury security's life matches the investor's time horizon, it generally will not provide a riskless return. With the exception of Treasury bills, all Treasury securities make periodic interest payments (see Chapter 14), which the investor must reinvest. If interest rates change over

the security's life, then the investor's reinvestment rate will change, causing the investor's return to differ from that originally anticipated at the time of the security's purchase.

Clearly, what investors need are Treasury securities that make only one payment (which includes principal and all interest) when those securities mature. Investors could then select a security whose life matched their investment time horizons. These securities would be truly riskless, at least on a nominal basis.

A fixed-income security that makes only one payment at maturity is called a zero coupon bond. Until the 1980s, however, Treasury zero coupon bonds did not exist, except for Treasury bills (which have a maximum maturity of one year). Today, over $200 billion of Treasury zero coupon bonds have been created. The growth of this market has been fueled by the unique advantages of riskless securities and the strong demand for those securities by institutional investors.

A coupon-bearing Treasury security can be viewed as a portfolio of zero coupon bonds. Each interest payment, as well as the principal, can be considered as a separate bond. In 1982, several brokerage firms came to a novel realization: a Treasury security's payments could be segregated and sold piecemeal through a process known as coupon stripping.

For example, brokerage firm XYZ could purchase a newly issued 20-year Treasury bond and deposit the bond with a custodian bank. Assuming semiannual interest payments, XYZ can create 41 separate zero coupon bonds (40 interest payments plus one principal repayment). Naturally, XYZ could create larger zero coupon bonds by buying and depositing more securities of the same Treasury issue. These zero coupon bonds, in turn, can be sold to investors (for a fee, of course). As the Treasury makes its required payments on the bond, the custodian bank remits the payments to the zero coupon bondholders of the appropriate maturity and effectively retires that particular bond. The process continues until all interest and principal payments have been made and all of the zero coupon bonds associated with this Treasury bond have been extinguished.

Brokerage firms have issued zero coupon bonds based on Treasury securities under a number of exotic names, such as LIONs (Lehman Investment Opportunity Notes), TIGRs (Merrill Lynch's Treasury Investment Growth Receipts), and CATs (Salomon Brothers' Certificates of Accrual on Treasury Securities). Not surprisingly, these securities have come to be known in the trade as "animals."

Brokerage firms and investors benefit from coupon stripping. The brokerage firms found that the sum of the parts was worth more than the whole, as the zero coupon bonds could be sold to investors at a higher combined price than could the source Treasury security. Investors benefited from the creation of a liquid market in riskless securities.

True to form, the U.S. Treasury only belatedly recognized the popularity of stripped Treasury securities. In 1985, the Treasury introduced a program called STRIPS (Separate Trading of Registered Interest and Principal Securities). This program allows purchasers of certain interest-bearing Treasury securities to keep whatever cash payments they want and to sell the rest. The stripped bonds are "held" in the Federal Reserve System's computer (called the *book entry system*), and payments on the bonds are made electronical-

ly. Any financial institution that is registered on the Federal Reserve System's computer may participate in the STRIPS program.

Brokerage firms soon found that it was much less expensive to create zero coupon bonds through the STRIPS program than to use bank custody accounts. As a result, virtually all stripped Treasuries are now created through the STRIPS program.

The values of zero coupon Treasury securities depend on many factors, including tax rates and regulations, the life of the securities, the relationship of long to short interest rates, and the market demand for certain bonds. Accounting for these valuation factors, the market maintains an equilibrium between the values of underlying Treasury securities and the stripped bonds. Just as financial organizations have found it profitable to produce stripped bonds, those same zero coupon bonds can be bundled to reconstitute the underlying securities if market prices warrant. The inexpensive operation of the STRIPS program has increased the efficiency of the zero coupon Treasury bond market.

Some day the Treasury may issue inflation-indexed bonds and permit them to be stripped. Such bonds would be truly riskless. Until then, stripped Treasury bonds offer investors the closest thing to a riskless security.

investments thus requires no assessment of individual preferences, only careful analysis of available opportunities in the marketplace.

The simplest and, in a sense, most fundamental characterization of the market structure for default-free bonds is given by the current set of discount factors, referred to earlier as the market discount function. With this set of factors, it is a simple matter to evaluate a default-free bond that provides more than one payment, for it is, in effect, a package of bonds, each of which provides only one payment. Each amount is simply multiplied by the appropriate discount factor and the resultant present values summed.

For example, assume that the Treasury is preparing to offer for sale a two-year coupon-bearing security that will pay $70 in one year and $1,070 in two years. What is a fair price for such a security? It is simply the present value of $70 and $1,070. How can this be determined? By multiplying the $70 and $1,070 by the one-year and two-year discount factors, respectively. Doing so results in ($70 × .9346) + ($1,070 × .8573), which equals $982.73.

No matter how complex the pattern of payments, this procedure can be used to determine the value of any default-free bond of this type. The general formula for a bond's present value (PV) is:

$$PV = \sum_{t=1}^{n} d_t C_t \qquad (5.13)$$

where the bond has promised cash payments C_t for each year from year 1 through year n.

At this point, it has been shown how spot rates and, in turn, discount factors can be calculated. However, no link between different spot rates (or different discount factors) has been established. For example, it has yet to be shown how the one-year spot rate of 7% is related to the two-year spot rate of 8%. The concept of forward rates makes the link.

5.5   FORWARD RATES

In the example, the one-year spot rate was determined to be 7%. This means that the market has determined that the present value of $1 to be paid by the Treasury department in one year is $1/1.07, or $.9346. That is, the relevant discount rate for converting a cash flow one year from now to its present value is 7%. Since it was also noted that the two-year spot rate was 8%, the present value of $1 to be paid by the Treasury department in two years is $1/1.08^2$, or $.8573.

An alternative view of $1 to be paid in two years is that it can be discounted in two steps. The first step determines its equivalent one-year value. That is, $1 to be received in two years is equivalent to $1/(1 + f_{1,2})$ to be received in one year. The second step determines the present value of this equivalent one-year amount by discounting it at the one-year spot rate of 7%. Thus its current value is:

$$\frac{\$1/(1 + f_{1,2})}{(1 + .07)} \; .$$

However, this value must be equal to $.8573, as it was mentioned earlier that, according to the two-year spot rate, $.8573 is the present value of $1 to be paid in two years. That is,

$$\frac{\$1/(1 + f_{1,2})}{(1 + .07)} = \$.8573 \qquad (5.14)$$

which has a solution for $f_{1,2}$ of 9.01%.

The discount rate $f_{1,2}$ is known as the **forward rate** from year one to year two. That is, it is the discount rate for determining the equivalent value of a dollar one year from now if it is to be received two years from now. In the example, $1 to be received two years from now is equivalent in value to $1/1.0901 = \$.9174$ to be received one year from now (in turn, note that the present value of $.9174 is $.9174/1.07 = \$.8573$).

Symbolically, the link between the one-year spot rate, two-year spot rate, and one-year forward rate is:

$$\frac{\$1/(1 + f_{1,2})}{(1 + s_1)} = \frac{\$1}{(1 + s_2)^2} \qquad (5.15)$$

which can be rewritten as:

$$(1 + f_{1,2}) = \frac{(1 + s_2)^2}{(1 + s_1)} \qquad (5.16)$$

or

$$(1 + s_1)(1 + f_{1,2}) = (1 + s_2)^2. \qquad (5.17)$$

Figure 5.1 illustrates this by referring to the example and then generalizing from it.

More generally, for year $t - 1$ and year t spot rates, the link to the forward rate between years $t - 1$ and t is:

$$(1 + f_{t-1,t}) = \frac{(1 + s_t)^t}{(1 + s_{t-1})^{t-1}} \qquad (5.18)$$

or

$$(1 + s_{t-1})^{t-1} \times (1 + f_{t-1,t}) = (1 + s_t)^t. \qquad (5.19)$$

Figure 5.1
Spot and Forward Rates

There is another interpretation that can be given to forward rates. Consider a contract made now where money will be loaned a year from now and paid back two years from now. Such a contract is known as a forward contract. The interest rate on the one-year loan that is specified in it (note that the interest will be paid when the loan matures in two years) is known as the forward rate.

It is important to distinguish this rate from the rate for one-year loans that will prevail for deals made a year from now (the spot rate at that time). A forward rate applies to contracts made now but relating to a period "forward" in time. By the nature of the contract, the terms are certain now, even though the actual transaction will occur later. If instead one were to wait until next year and sign a contract to borrow money in the spot market at that time, the terms might turn out to be better or worse than today's forward rate, since the future spot rate is not perfectly predictable.

In the example, the marketplace has priced Treasury securities such that a representative investor making a two-year loan to the government would demand an interest rate equal to the two-year spot rate, 8%. Equivalently, the investor would be willing to simultaneously (1) make a one-year loan to the government at an interest rate equal to the one-year spot rate, 7%; and (2) sign a forward contract with the government to loan the government money one year from now, being repaid two years from now when the interest rate to be paid is the forward rate, 9.01%.

When viewed in this manner, forward contracts are implicit. However, forward contracts are sometimes made explicitly. For example, a contractor might obtain a commitment from a bank for a one-year construction loan a year hence at a fixed rate of interest. Financial futures markets (discussed in Chapter 21) provide standardized forward contracts of this type. For example, in September one could contract to pay approximately $970 in December to purchase a 90-day Treasury bill that would pay $1,000 in the following March.

5.6   FORWARD RATES AND DISCOUNT FACTORS

In Equation (5.12) it was shown that a discount factor for t years could be calculated by adding one to the spot rate for t years, raising this sum to the power t, and then taking the reciprocal of the result. For example, it was shown that the two-year discount factor associated with the two-year spot rate of 8% was equal to $1/(1 + .08)^2 = .8573$.

Equation (5.17) suggests an equivalent method for calculating discount factors. In the case of the two-year factor, this method involves multiplying the one-year spot rate by the forward rate and taking the reciprocal of the result:

$$d_2 = \frac{1}{(1 + s_1) \times (1 + f_{1,2})} \tag{5.20}$$

which in the example is:

$$d_2 = \frac{1}{(1 + .07) \times (1 + .0901)}$$

$$= .8573.$$

More generally, the discount factor for year t that is shown in Equation (5.12) can be restated as follows:

$$d_t = \frac{1}{(1 + s_{t-1})^{t-1} \times (1 + f_{t-1, t})} . \qquad (5.21)$$

Thus, given a set of spot rates, it is possible to determine the market discount function in either of two ways, both of which will provide the same figures. First, the spot rates can be used in Equation (5.12) to arrive at a set of discount factors. Alternatively, the spot rates can be used to determine a set of forward rates, and then the spot rates and forward rates can be used in Equation (5.21) to arrive at a set of discount factors.

5.7   COMPOUNDING

Thus far, the discussion has concentrated on annual interest rates by assuming that cash flows are compounded (or discounted) annually. This is often appropriate, but for more precise calculations a shorter period may be more desirable. Moreover, some lenders explicitly compound funds more often than once each year.

Compounding is the payment of "interest on interest." At the end of each compounding interval, interest is computed and added to principal. This sum becomes the principal on which interest is computed at the end of the next interval. The process continues until the end of the final compounding interval is reached.

No problem is involved in adapting the previously stated formulas to compounding intervals other than a year. The simplest procedure is to count in units of the chosen interval. For example, yield-to-maturity can be calculated using any chosen compounding interval. If payment of P dollars now will result in the receipt of F dollars ten years from now, the yield-to-maturity can be calculated using annual compounding by finding a value r_a that satisfies the equation:

$$P(1 + r_a)^{10} = F \qquad (5.22)$$

since F will be received ten annual periods from now. The result, r_a, will be expressed as an annual rate with annual compounding.

Alternatively, yield-to-maturity can be calculated using semiannual compounding by finding a value r_s that satisfies the equation:

$$P(1 + r_s)^{20} = F \qquad (5.23)$$

since F will be received twenty semiannual periods from now. The result, r_s, will be expressed as a semiannual rate with semiannual compounding. It can be doubled to give an annual rate with semiannual compounding. Alternatively, the annual rate with annual compounding can be computed for a given value of r_s by using the following equation:

$$1 + r_a = (1 + r_s)^2. \tag{5.24}$$

For example, consider an investment costing $2,315.97 that will pay $5,000 ten years later. Applying Equations (5.22) and (5.23) to this security results in, respectively:

$$\$2,\!315.97(1 + r_a)^{10} = \$5,\!000$$

and

$$\$2,\!315.97(1 + r_s)^{20} = \$5,\!000$$

where the solutions are $r_a = 8\%$ and $r_s = 3.923\%$. Thus this security can be described as having an annual rate with annual compounding of 8%, a semiannual rate with semiannual compounding of 3.923%, and an annual rate with semiannual compounding of 7.846% ($= 2 \times 3.923\%$).[2]

To reduce the massive confusion caused by the many different methods that can be used to express interest rates, the Federal Truth-in-Lending Act requires every lender to compute and disclose the **annual percentage rate** (APR) implied by the terms of a loan. This is simply the annualized yield-to-maturity, computed by (1) determining the periodic yield-to-maturity based on a compounding interval that is equal to the most frequent time between payments on the loan, and (2) multiplying the resulting periodic yield by the number of compounding intervals in a year. Although some complications arise when payments are required at irregular intervals, the use of APRs has simplified the task of comparing lenders' terms.

Semiannual compounding is commonly used to determine the yield-to-maturity for bonds, since coupon payments are usually made twice each year. Most preprogrammed calculators and computers use this approach.[3]

5.8   THE BANK DISCOUNT METHOD

Despite the truth-in-lending law, other methods are still used to summarize interest rates. One time-honored procedure is the *bank discount method*. If someone "borrows" $100 from a bank, to be repaid a year later, the bank may subtract the interest payment of, for instance, $8, and give the borrower $92. According to the bank discount method, this is an interest rate of 8%. The borrower receives only $92, for which he or she must pay $8 in interest after one year. The true interest rate (APR) must be based on the money the borrower actually gets to use, which in this case is 8.70% ($= \$8/\$92$).

It is a simple matter to convert an interest rate quoted on the bank discount method to a true interest rate. (In this situation, the true interest rate is often called the bond equivalent yield.) If the bank discount rate is denoted BDR, the true rate is simply $BDR/(1 - BDR)$. Since $BDR > 0$, the bank discount rate understates the true cost of borrowing [that is, BDR $<$ BDR/(1 $-$ BDR)]. The previous example provides an illustration: 8.70% = .08/(1 $-$ .08). Note how the bank discount rate of 8% understates the true cost of borrowing by .70% in this example.

5.9   YIELD CURVES

At any point in time, Treasury securities will be priced approximately in accord with the existing set of spot rates and the associated discount factors. Although there have been times when all the spot rates are roughly equal in size, generally they have different values. Often the one-year spot rate is less than the two-year spot rate, which in turn is less than the three-year spot rate, and so on (that is, s_t increases as t increases). At other times, the one-year spot rate is greater than the two-year spot rate, which in turn is greater than the three-year spot rate, and so on (that is, s_t decreases as t increases). It is wise for the security analyst to know which case currently prevails, as this is a useful starting point in valuing fixed-income securities.

Unfortunately, this is easier said than done. Only the bonds of the U.S. government are clearly free from default risk. However, such bonds differ in tax treatment, as well as in callability and other features. Despite these problems, a summary of the approximate relationship between yields-to-maturity on Treasury securities of various terms-to-maturity is presented in each issue of the *Treasury Bulletin*. This summary is given in the form of a graph illustrating the current yield curve. Figure 5.2 provides an example.

A **yield curve** is a graph that shows the yields-to-maturity (on the vertical axis) for Treasury securities of various maturities (on the horizontal axis) as of a particular date. This provides an estimate of the current **term structure** of interest rates, and will change daily as yields-to-maturity change. Figure 5.3 illustrates some of the commonly observed shapes that the yield curve has taken in the past.[4]

While not shown in Figure 5.2, this relationship between yields and maturities is less than perfect. That is, not all Treasury securities lie exactly on the yield curve. Part of this is because of the previously mentioned differences in tax treatment, callability, and the like. Part is because of the fact that the yield-to-maturity on a coupon-bearing security is not clearly linked to the set of spot rates currently in existence. Since the set of spot rates is a fundamental determinant of the price of any Treasury security, there is no reason to expect yields to lie exactly on the curve. Indeed, a more meaningful graph would be one where spot rates are measured on the vertical axis instead of yields-to-maturity. With this in mind, two interesting questions to ponder are these: Why are the spot rates of different magnitudes? And why do the differences in these rates change over time, where sometimes long-term spot rates are greater than short-term spot rates and sometimes the opposite occurs? Attempts to answer such questions can be found in various term structure theories.

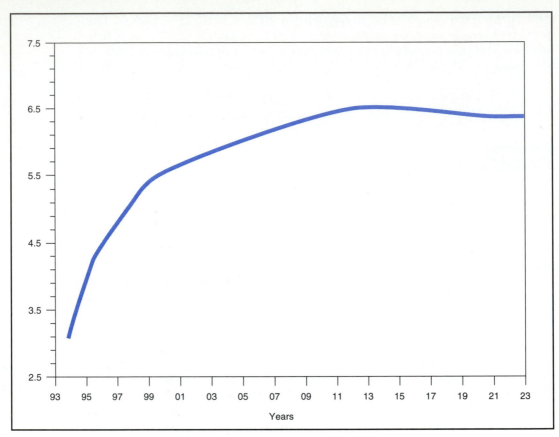

Figure 5.2
Yield Curve of Treasury Securities, June 30, 1993 (based on closing bid quotations)
Source: *Treasury Bulletin,* March 1994, p. 67.

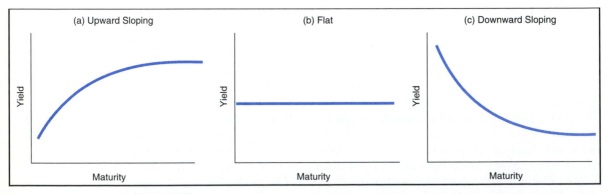

Figure 5.3
Typical Yield Curve Shapes

Three primary theories are used to explain the term structure of interest rates. In discussing them, the focus will be on the term structure of spot rates, because these rates (not yields-to-maturity) are critically important in determining the price of any Treasury security.

5.10.1   The Unbiased Expectations Theory

The **unbiased expectations theory** (or pure expectations theory, as it is sometimes called) holds that the forward rate represents the average opinion of the expected future spot rate for the period in question. Thus, a set of spot rates that is rising can be explained by arguing that the marketplace (that is, the general opinion of investors) believes that spot rates will be rising in the future. Conversely, a set of decreasing spot rates is explained by arguing that the marketplace expects spot rates to fall in the future.[5]

Upward-Sloping Yield Curves

In order to understand this theory more fully, consider the earlier example where the one-year spot rate was 7% and the two-year spot rate was 8%. The basic question is this: Why are these two spot rates different? Equivalently, why is the yield curve upward sloping?

Consider an investor with $1 to invest for two years (for ease of exposition, it will be assumed that any amount of money can be invested at the prevailing spot rates). This investor could follow a "maturity strategy," investing the money now for the full two years at the two-year spot rate of 8%. With this strategy, at the end of two years the dollar will have grown in value to $1.1664 (= $1 × 1.08 × 1.08). Alternatively, the investor could invest the dollar now for one year at the one-year spot rate of 7%, so that the investor knows that one year from now he or she will have $1.07 (= $1 × 1.07) to reinvest for one more year. Although the investor does not know what the one-year spot rate will be one year from now, the investor has an *expectation* about what it will be (this expected future spot rate will hereafter be denoted $es_{1,2}$). If the investor thinks that it will be 10%, then his or her $1 investment has an expected value two years from now of $1.177 (= $1 × 1.07 × 1.10). In this case, the investor would choose a "rollover strategy," meaning that the investor would choose to invest in a one-year security at 7% rather than in the two-year security, since he or she would expect to have more money at the end of two years by doing so (note that $1.177 > $1.1664).

However, an expected future spot rate of 10% cannot represent the general view in the marketplace. This is because if it did, people would not be willing to invest money at the two-year spot rate, as a higher return would be expected from investing money at the one-year rate and using the rollover strategy. Thus the two-year spot rate would quickly rise as the supply of funds for two-year loans at 8% would be less than the demand. Conversely, the supply of funds for one year at 7% would be more than the demand, causing the one-year rate to fall quickly. Thus, a one-year spot rate of 7%, a two-year spot rate of 8%, and an expected future spot rate of 10% cannot represent an equilibrium situation.

What if the expected future spot rate is 6% instead of 10%? In this case, according to the rollover strategy the investor would expect $1 to be worth $1.1342 (= $1 × 1.07 × 1.06) at the end of two years. Since this is less than the value the dollar will have if the maturity strategy is followed ($1.1342 < $1.664), the investor would choose the maturity strategy. Again, however, an expected future spot rate of 6% cannot represent the general view in the marketplace because if it did, people would not be willing to invest money at the one-year spot rate.

Earlier, it was shown that the forward rate in this example was 9.01%. What if the expected future spot rate was of this magnitude? At the end of two years the value of $1 with the rollover strategy would be $1.1664 (= $1 × 1.07 × 1.0901), the same as the value of $1 with the maturity strategy. In this case, equilibrium would exist in the marketplace because the general view would be that both strategies have the same expected return. Accordingly, investors with a two-year holding period would not have an incentive to choose one strategy over the other.

Note that an investor with a one-year holding period could follow a maturity strategy by investing $1 in the one-year security and receiving $1.07 after one year. Alternatively, a "naive strategy" could be followed, where a two-year security could be purchased now and sold after one year. If so, the expected selling price would be $1.07 (= $1.1664/1.0901), for a return of 7% (the security would have a maturity value of $1.1664 = $1 × 1.08 × 1.08, but since the spot rate is expected to be 9.01% in a year, its expected selling price is just the discounted value of its maturity value). Because the maturity and naive strategies have the same expected return, investors with a one-year holding period would not have an incentive to choose one strategy over the other.

Thus the unbiased expectations theory asserts that the expected future spot rate is equal in magnitude to the forward rate. In the example, the current one-year spot rate is 7%, and, according to this theory, the general opinion is that it will rise to a rate of 9.01% in one year. This expected rise in the one-year spot rate is the reason behind the upward-sloping term structure where the two-year spot rate (8%) is greater than the one-year spot rate (7%).

Equilibrium

In equation format, the unbiased expectations theory states that in equilibrium the expected future spot rate is equal to the forward rate:

$$es_{1,2} = f_{1,2}. \tag{5.25}$$

Thus Equation (5.17) can be restated with $es_{1,2}$ substituted for $f_{1,2}$ as follows:

$$(1 + s_1)(1 + es_{1,2}) = (1 + s_2)^2 \tag{5.26}$$

which can be conveniently interpreted to mean that the expected return from a maturity strategy must equal the expected return on a rollover strategy.[6]

The previous example dealt with an upward-sloping term structure, where the longer the term, the higher the spot rate. It is a straightforward matter to deal with a downward-sloping term structure, where the longer the term, the lower the spot rate. Whereas the explanation for an upward-sloping term structure was that investors expect spot rates to rise in the future, the reason for the downward-sloping curve is that investors expect spot rates to fall in the future.

Changing Spot Rates and Inflation

An interesting follow-up question is this: Why do investors expect spot rates to change, either rising or falling, in the future? A possible answer to this question can be found by noting that the spot rates that are observed in the marketplace are nominal rates. That is, they are a reflection of the underlying real rate and the expected inflation rate.[7] If either (or both) of these rates is expected to change in the future, then the spot rate will be expected to change.

For example, assume a constant real rate of 3%. Since the current one-year spot rate is 7%, this means that the general opinion in the marketplace is that the expected rate of inflation over the next year is approximately 4% (the nominal rate is approximately equal to the sum of the real rate and expected inflation rate; see Equation 5.3). Now, according to the unbiased expectations theory, the expected future spot rate is 9.01%, an increase of 2.01% from the current one-year spot rate of 7%. Why is the spot rate expected to rise by 2.01%? Because the inflation rate is expected to rise by 2.01%. That is, the expected inflation rate over the next 12 months is approximately 4%, and over the following 12 months it is expected to be higher, at approximately 6.01%.

To recapitulate, the two-year spot rate (8%) is greater than the one-year spot rate (7%) because investors expect the future one-year spot rate to be greater than the current one-year spot rate. They expect it to be greater because of an anticipated rise in the rate of inflation, from approximately 4% to approximately 6.01%.

In general, when current economic conditions make short-term spot rates abnormally high (owing, say, to a relatively high current rate of inflation), according to the unbiased expectations theory, the term structure should be downward sloping. This is because inflation would be expected to abate in the future. Conversely, when current conditions make short-term rates abnormally low (owing, say, to a relatively low current rate of inflation), the term structure should be upward sloping, as inflation would be expected to rise in the future. Examination of historical term structures suggests that this is what has actually happened, since the structure has been upward sloping in periods of lower interest rates and downward sloping in periods of higher interest rates.

However, examining historical term structures uncovers a problem. In particular, with this theory, it is logical to expect that over time there will be roughly as many occurrences of upward-sloping term structures as downward-sloping term structures. In reality, upward-sloping structures tend to be more frequent. The liquidity preference theory (also known as the liquidity premium theory) provides an explanation for this observation.

5.10.2   The Liquidity Preference Theory

The **liquidity preference theory** starts with the notion that investors are primarily interested in purchasing short-term securities. That is, even though some investors may have longer holding periods, there is a tendency for them to prefer short-term securities. This is because these investors realize that they may need their funds earlier than anticipated and recognize that they face less "price risk" (that is, "interest rate risk") if they invest in shorter-term securities.

Price Risk

For example, an investor with a two-year holding period would tend to prefer the rollover strategy because he or she would be certain of having a given amount of cash at the end of one year when it may be needed. If a maturity strategy had been followed, then the investor would have to sell the two-year security after one year if cash were needed. However, it is not known now what price the investor would get if he or she were to sell the two-year security in one year. Thus there is an extra element of risk associated with the maturity strategy that is absent from the rollover strategy.[8]

The upshot is that investors with a two-year holding period will not choose the maturity strategy if it has the same expected return as the rollover strategy, because it is riskier. The only way investors will follow the maturity strategy and buy the two-year securities is if the expected return is higher. That is, borrowers are going to have to pay the investors a risk premium in the form of a greater expected return in order to get them to purchase two-year securities.

Will borrowers be inclined to pay such a premium when issuing two-year securities? Yes, they will. First, frequent refinancing may be costly in terms of registration, advertising, and paperwork. These costs can be lessened by issuing relatively long-term securities. Second, some borrowers will realize that relatively long-term bonds are a less risky source of funds than relatively short-term bonds because they will not have to be as concerned about the possibility of refinancing in the future at higher interest rates. Thus borrowers may be willing to pay more (via higher expected interest costs) for relatively long-term funds.

In the example, the one-year spot rate was 7% and the two-year spot rate was 8%. As mentioned earlier, according to the liquidity preference theory, the only way investors will agree to follow a maturity strategy is if the expected return from doing so is higher than the expected return from following the rollover strategy. This means that the expected future spot rate must be something *less* than the forward rate of 9.01%—perhaps it is 8.6%. If so, then the value of a $1 investment in two years is expected to be $1.1620 ($= \$1 \times 1.07 \times 1.086$), if the rollover strategy is followed. Because the value of a $1 investment with the maturity strategy is $1.1664 ($= \$1 \times 1.08 \times 1.08$), it can be seen that this strategy has a higher expected return for the two-year period that can be attributed to its greater degree of price risk.

Liquidity Premium

The difference between the forward rate and the expected future spot rate is known as the **liquidity premium.**[9] It is the "extra" return given investors in order to entice them to purchase the more risky longer-maturity two-year security. In the example, it is equal to .41% ($= 9.01\% - 8.6\%$). More generally,

$$f_{1,2} = es_{1,2} + L_{1,2} \tag{5.27}$$

where $L_{1,2}$ is the liquidity premium for the period commencing one year from now and ending two years from now.[10]

How does the liquidity preference theory explain the slope of the term structure? In order to answer this question, note that with the rollover strategy the expected value of a dollar at the end of two years is $\$1 \times (1 + s_1) \times (1 + es_{1,2})$. Alternatively, with the maturity strategy, the expected value of a dollar at the end of two years is $\$1 \times (1 + s_2)^2$. As mentioned earlier, according to the liquidity preference theory, there is more risk with the maturity strategy, which in turn means that it must have a higher expected return. That is, the following inequality must hold:

$$\$1 \, (1 + s_1)(1 + es_{1,2}) < \$1(1 + s_2)^2 \tag{5.28}$$

or:

$$(1 + s_1)(1 + es_{1,2}) < (1 + s_2)^2. \tag{5.29}$$

This inequality is the key to understanding how the liquidity preference theory explains the term structure.[11]

Downward-Sloping Yield Curves

Consider the downward-sloping case first, where $s_1 > s_2$. The above inequality will hold in this situation only if the expected future spot rate ($es_{1,2}$) is substantially lower than the current one-year spot rate (s_1).[12] Thus a downward-sloping yield curve will be observed only when the marketplace believes that interest rates are going to decline substantially.

As an example, assume that the one-year spot rate (s_1) is 7% and the two-year spot rate (s_2) is 6%. Because 7% is greater than 6%, this is a situation where the term structure is downward sloping. Now, according to the liquidity preference theory, Equation (5.29) indicates that,

$$(1 + .07)(1 + es_{1,2}) < (1.06)^2$$

which can be true only if the expected future spot rate ($es_{1,2}$) is substantially less than 7%. Given the one-year and two-year spot rates, the forward rate ($f_{1,2}$) is equal to 5.01%. Assuming the liquidity premium ($L_{1,2}$) is .41%, then according to Equation (5.27), $es_{1,2}$ must be 4.6% (= 5.01% − .41%). Thus, the term structure is downward sloping because the current one-year spot rate of 7% is expected to decline to 4.6% in the future.

In comparison, the unbiased expectations theory also would explain the term structure by saying it was downward sloping because the one-year spot rate was expected to decline in the future. However, the unbiased expectations theory would expect the spot rate to decline to only 5.01%, not 4.6%.

Flat Yield Curves

Consider next the case of a flat yield curve, where $s_1 = s_2$. Equation (5.29) will be true in this situation only if $es_{1,2}$ is less than s_1. Thus a flat term structure will occur only when the marketplace expects interest rates to decline. Indeed, if $s_1 = s_2 = 7\%$ and $L_{1,2} = .41\%$, then $f_{1,2} = 7\%$, and according to Equation (5.27), the expected future spot rate is 6.59% (= 7% − .41%), a decline from the current one-year spot rate of 7%. This is in contrast to the unbiased expectations theory, where a flat term structure would be interpreted to mean that the marketplace expected interest rates to remain at the same level.

Upward-Sloping Yield Curves

The last case is an upward-sloping yield curve where $s_1 < s_2$. If it is slightly upward sloping, this can be consistent with an expectation that interest rates are going to decline in the future. For example, if $s_1 = 7\%$ and $s_2 = 7.1\%$, then the forward rate is 7.2%. In turn, if the liquidity premium is .41%, then the expected future spot rate is 6.79% (= 7.2% − .41%), a decline from the current one-year spot rate of 7%. Thus the reason for the slight upward slope to the term structure is that the marketplace expects a small decline in the spot rate. In contrast, the unbiased expectations theory would argue that the reason for the slight upward slope was the expectation of a small increase in the spot rate.

If the term structure is more steeply sloped, then it is more likely that the marketplace expects interest rates to rise in the future. For example, if $s_1 = 7\%$ and $s_2 = 7.3\%$, then the forward rate is 7.6%. Continuing to assume a liquidity premium of .41%, Equation (5.27) indicates that the marketplace expects the one-year spot rate to rise from 7% to 7.19% (= 7.6% − .41%). The unbiased expectations theory also would explain this steep slope by saying that the spot rate was expected to rise in the future, but by a larger amount. In particular, the unbiased expectations theory would state that the spot rate was expected to rise to 7.6%, not 7.19%.

In summary, with the liquidity preference theory, downward-sloping term structures are indicative of an expected decline in the spot rate, whereas upward-sloping term structures may indicate either an expected rise or decline, depending on how steep the slope is. Generally, the steeper the slope, the more likely it is that the marketplace expects spot rates to rise. If roughly half the time investors expect that spot rates will rise and half the time investors expect that spot rates will decline, then the liquidity preference theory suggests that there should be more occurrences of upward-sloping term structures than downward-sloping ones. As mentioned earlier, this is indeed what has happened.

5.10.3 The Market Segmentation Theory

A third explanation for the determination of the term structure rests on the assumption that there is **market segmentation.** Various investors and borrowers are thought to be restricted by law, preference, or custom to certain maturities. Perhaps there is a market for short-term securities, another for intermediate-term securities, and a third for long-term securities. According to the market segmentation theory, spot rates are determined by supply and demand conditions in each market. Furthermore, in the theory's most restrictive form, investors and borrowers will not leave their market and enter a different one even when the current rates suggest to them that there is a substantially higher expected return available by making such a move.[13]

With this theory, an upward-sloping term structure exists when the intersection of the supply and demand curves for shorter-term funds is at a lower interest rate than the intersection for longer-term funds. Conversely, a downward-sloping term structure would exist when the intersection for shorter-term funds was at a higher interest rate than the intersection for longer-term funds.

5.10.4 Empirical Evidence on the Theories

Empirical evidence provides some insight into the determinants of the term structure, but it is difficult to assess the relative importance of these three theories with a high degree of precision.

The market segmentation theory receives relatively slight empirical validation. This is understandable when it is realized that the theory will not hold if there are some investors and borrowers who are flexible enough to be willing to move into whatever segment has the highest expected return. By their actions, these investors and borrowers will give the term structure a continuity that is linked to expectations of future interest rates.

There does appear to be some evidence that the term structure conveys information about expected future spot rates, as hypothesized by both the unbiased expectations and liquidity preference theories. However, the evidence tends to favor the latter theory, because liquidity premiums also appear to exist.[14] In particular, there appear to be liquidity premiums of increasing size associated with Treasury securities of up to roughly one year in maturity (meaning that, for example, $L_{.5,.75} < L_{.75,1}$), but the premiums beyond one year are not larger than those for one-year periods. That is, investors seem to demand a premium in order to get them to purchase a one-year security instead of, say, a six-month security. However, the premium needed in order to get them to purchase an eighteen-month security (even though the eighteen-month security has more price risk than a one-year security) is no larger than the premium needed to get them to purchase the one-year security (meaning that $L_{.5,1} = L_{1,1.5}$).

A word of caution is in order here regarding estimating the size of liquidity premiums. Undoubtedly these premiums (if they exist) change in size over time. Hence trying to estimate their average size accurately is very difficult, and any observations must be made cautiously.

In summary, it appears that expectations about future spot rates are important determinants of the term structure. Liquidity premiums appear to exist, but they do not increase in size beyond roughly a year, meaning that investment strategies involving securities with maturities of one year or more will have roughly the same expected return.

Examining the term structure of interest rates is important for determining the current set of spot rates, which can be used as a basis for valuing any fixed-income security. Such an examination is also important because it provides some information about what the marketplace expects regarding the level of future interest rates.

1. The nominal (or monetary) interest rate is the rate at which an investor can trade present money for future money.
2. The real interest rate is a function of the difference between the nominal interest rate and the inflation rate.
3. In order to understand how bonds are valued in the marketplace, it is convenient to examine initially those fixed-income securities that are free from default risk—namely, Treasury securities.
4. The yield-to-maturity of a security is the discount rate that makes the present value of the security's promised future cash flows equal to the current market price of the security.
5. The spot rate is the yield-to-maturity on a pure discount security.
6. Once spot rates (each one associated with a different maturity) have been calculated, they can be used, for example, to value coupon-bearing Treasury securities.
7. A forward rate is the interest rate, established today, that will be paid on money to be borrowed at some specific time in the future, and to be repaid at an even more distant time in the future.
8. The payment of interest on interest is known as compounding.
9. Increasing the number of compounding intervals within a year will increase the effective annual interest rate.
10. A yield curve shows the relationship between yield-to-maturity and term-to-maturity for Treasury securities. This relationship is also known as the term structure of interest rates.
11. Three theories have generally been used to explain the term structure of interest rates: the unbiased expectations theory, the liquidity preference theory, and the market segmentation theory.
12. The unbiased expectations theory states that forward rates represent the consensus opinion about what spot rates will be in the future.
13. The liquidity preference theory states that forward rates overstate the consensus opinion about future spot rates by an amount necessary to compensate investors for holding longer-maturity securities.
14. The market segmentation theory states that different spot rates have different values because of the interaction of supply and demand for funds in markets that are separated from each other by maturity.
15. Evidence tends to favor the liquidity preference theory, at least over maturities up to roughly one year.

QUESTIONS AND PROBLEMS

1. If the real return on an investment in a given year was 6.0%, while its nominal return was 11.3%, what must have been the inflation rate during the year?
2. At the end of 1974, Emil Bildilli held a portfolio of long-term U.S. government bonds valued at $14,000. At the end of 1981, Emil's portfolio was

worth $16,932. Referring to Table 1.1, calculate the annualized real rate of return on Emil's bond portfolio over this seven-year period.

3. Consider two bonds, each with a $1,000 face value and each with three years remaining to maturity.

   a. The first bond is a pure-discount bond that currently sells for $816.30. What is its yield-to-maturity?

   b. The second bond currently sells for $949.37 and makes annual coupon payments at a rate of 7% (that is, it pays $70 in interest per year). The first interest payment is due one year from today. What is this bond's yield-to-maturity?

4. Camp Douglas Dirigibles has a bond outstanding with four years to maturity, a face value of $1,000, and an annual coupon payment of $100. What is the price of the Camp Douglas bond if its yield-to-maturity is 12%? If its yield-to-maturity is 8%?

5. The concept of yield-to-maturity is based on two crucial assumptions. What are those assumptions? What will happen to the bondholder's return if those assumptions are violated?

6. Patsy Dougherty bought a $1,000-face-value bond with a 9% annual coupon and three years to maturity that makes its first interest payment one year from today. Patsy bought the bond for $975.13.

   a. What is the bond's yield-to-maturity?

   b. If Patsy is able to invest the bond's cash flows at only 7%, what is Patsy's actual annual compounded return on the bond investment, assuming that it is held to maturity? (Hint: Think in terms of the cash flows paid to Patsy, the bond's purchase price, and the term of the investment.)

7. Consider three pure-discount bonds with maturities of one, two, and three years and prices of $930.23, $923.79, and $919.54, respectively. Each bond has a $1,000 face value. Based on this information, what are the one-year, two-year, and three-year spot rates?

8. What are the discount factors associated with three-year, four-year, and five-year $1,000-face-value pure-discount bonds that sell for $810.60, $730.96, and $649.93, respectively?

9. Distinguish between spot rates and forward rates.

10. Given the following spot rates for various periods of time from today, calculate forward rates from years one to two, two to three, and three to four.

Years From Today	Spot Rate
1	5.0%
2	5.5
3	6.5
4	7.0

11. Given the following forward rates, calculate the one-, two-, three-, and four-year spot rates.

Forward Time Period	Forward Rate
$f_{0,1}$	10.0%
$f_{1,2}$	9.5
$f_{2,3}$	9.0
$f_{3,4}$	8.5

12. Assume that the current one-year spot rate is 6% and the forward rates for one year hence and two years hence are, respectively:

$$f_{1,2} = 9\%$$
$$f_{2,3} = 10\%$$

What should be the market price of an 8% coupon bond, with a $1,000 face value, maturing three years from today? The first interest payment is due one year from today. Interest is payable annually.

13. Assume that the government has issued three bonds. The first, which pays $1,000 one year from today, is now selling for $909.09. The second, which pays $100 one year from today and $1,100 one year later, is now selling for $991.81. The third, which pays $100 one year from today, $100 one year later, and $1,100 one year after that, is now selling for $997.18.
    a. What are the current discount factors for dollars paid one, two, and three years from today?
    b. What are the forward rates?
    c. Honus Wagner, a friend, offers to pay you $500 one year from today, $600 two years from today, and $700 three years from today in return for a loan today. Assuming that Honus will not default on the loan, how much should you be willing to loan?
14. Mercury National Bank offers a passbook savings account that pays interest at a stated annual rate of 6%. Calculate the effective annual interest rate paid by Mercury National if it compounds interest:
    a. Semiannually
    b. Daily (365 days in a year).
15. Marty Marion is considering placing $30,000 in a three-year, default-free fixed-income investment that promises to provide interest at the rate of 8% during the first year, 10% in the second year, and 12% in the third year. Coupon payments can be reinvested at the rate in effect for the following year.
    a. Assuming annual compounding and repayment of principal at the end of the third year, to what value is Marty's investment expected to grow after three years?
    b. Recalculate your answer to part (a) assuming semiannual compounding.
16. Using the *Wall Street Journal* as a data source, turn to the table entitled "Treasury Bonds, Notes & Bills." Find the yield-to-maturity for Treasury securities maturing in one month, three months, one year, five years, ten years, and twenty years. With this information, construct the yield curve as of the paper's publication date.
17. Is it true that an observed downward-sloping yield curve is inconsistent with the liquidity preference theory of the term structure of interest rates? Explain.
18. Assume that the current structure of forward interest rates is upward sloping. Which will have a lower yield-to-maturity:
    a. A 15-year pure-discount bond or a 10-year pure-discount bond?
    b. A 10-year 5% coupon bond or a 10-year 6% coupon bond?
19. How would your answers to question 18 change if the forward interest rate structure were downward sloping?

20. Three theories explaining the term structure of interest rates are described in the chapter. Which theory do you believe best explains the relationship between spot rates and term-to-maturity? Provide supporting arguments for your answer.

21. Assume that the current spot rates are as follows:

Years From Today	Spot Rate
1 year	8%
2 years	9%
3 years	10%

If the unbiased expectations theory holds, what should be the yields-to-maturity on one- and two-year pure discount bonds one year from today?

22. (Appendix Question) Recalculate the answers to questions 14 and 15 assuming that interest compounds continuously.

23. (Appendix Question) What is the intrinsic value of a pure-discount bond with a $1,000 face value maturing one year from today, assuming an 8% discount rate with continuous compounding?

CFA EXAM QUESTIONS

24. The following are the average yields on U.S. Treasury bonds at two different points in time.

	Yield-to-Maturity	
Term to Maturity	January 15, 19XX	May 15, 19XX
1 year	7.25%	8.05%
2 years	7.50	7.90
3 years	7.90	7.70
10 years	8.30	7.45
15 years	8.45	7.30
20 years	8.55	7.20
25 years	8.60	7.10

a. Assuming a pure expectations hypothesis, define a forward rate. Describe how you would calculate the forward rate for a three-year U.S. Treasury bond two years from May 15, 19XX, using the actual term structure above.

b. Discuss how each of the three major term structure hypotheses could explain the January 15, 19XX term structure shown above.

c. Discuss what happened to the term structure over the time period and the effect of this change on the U.S. Treasury bonds of two and ten years.

d. Assume that you invest solely on the basis of yield spreads, and in January 19XX acted upon the expectation that the yield spread between one-year and twenty-five year U.S. Treasuries would return to a more typical spread of 170 basis points. Explain what you would have done on January 15, 19XX, and describe what happened between January 15, 19XX and May 15, 19XX.

25. a. Calculate the two-year spot rate implied by the U.S. Treasury yield curve data given below. Assume that interest is paid annually for purposes of this calculation. Show all calculations.

Years to Maturity	Current Coupon Yield-to-Maturity	Spot Rate
1	7.5%	7.5%
2	8.0	—

b. Explain why a spot rate curve can be derived entirely from the current coupon (yield-to-maturity) yield curve.

c. Given a U.S. Treasury one-year spot rate of 9.0% and a U.S. Treasury two-year spot rate of 9.5%, calculate the implied one-year forward rate for the two-year U.S. Treasury security with one year remaining to maturity. Explain why a one-year forward rate of 9.6% would not be expected to prevail in a market given these spot rates.

d. Describe one practical application of the spot rate concept and one practical application of the forward rate concept.

APPENDIX

CONTINUOUS COMPOUNDING

When computing an investment's return, the compounding interval can make a difference. For example, regulations may limit a savings institution to paying a fixed rate of interest, but make no specifications about the compounding interval. This was the situation in early 1975, when the legal limit on interest paid by savings and loan companies on deposits committed from six to ten years was 7.75% per year. Initially, most savings and loans paid "simple interest." Thus $1 deposited at the beginning of the year would grow to $1.0775 by the end of the year. Later, in an attempt to attract depositors, some enterprising savings and loans announced that they would pay 7.75% per year, compounded semiannually at a rate of 3.3875% (= 7.75%/2). This meant that $1 deposited at the beginning of the year would grow to $1.03875 at the end of six months, and this total would then grow to $1.079 (= $1.03875 × 1.03875) by the end of the year, for an effective annual interest rate of 7.9%. This procedure was considered within the letter, if not the spirit, of the law.

Before long, other competitors offered 7.75% per year compounded quarterly (that is, 7.75%/4 = 1.938% per quarter), giving an effective annual interest rate of 7.978%. Then others offered to compound the 7.75% rate on a monthly basis (at $7.75\%/12 = .646\%$ per month), for an effective annual interest rate of 8.031%. The end was reached when one company offered continuous compounding of the 7.75% annual rate. This rather abstract procedure represents the limit as interest is compounded more and more frequently. If r represents the annual rate of interest (in this case, 7.75%) and n the number of times compounding takes place per year, the effective annual rate, r_e, is given by:

$$\left(1 + \frac{r}{n}\right)^n = 1 + r_e. \tag{5.30}$$

Thus, with semiannual compounding of 7.75%,

$$\left(1 + \frac{.0775}{2}\right)^2 = (1 + .03875)^2 = 1.079$$

and with quarterly compounding,

$$\left(1 + \frac{.0775}{4}\right)^2 = (1 + .01938)^4 = 1.07978$$

and so on. As the compounding interval grows shorter, the number of times compounding takes place (n) grows larger, as does the effective interest rate, r_e.

Mathematicians can prove that as n grows larger, the quantity $[1 + (r/n)]^n$ becomes increasingly close to e^r where e stands for the number 2.71828 (rounded to five-place accuracy). In this case, $e^{.0775} = 1.0806$, indicating an effective annual rate of 8.06%.[15]

A more general formula for continuous compounding can also be derived. At an annual rate of r, with continuous compounding, P dollars will grow to F_t dollars t years from now, where the relationship between P, r, and F_t is:

$$Pe^{rt} = F_t. \tag{5.31}$$

Similarly, the present value of F_t dollars received t years later at an annual rate of r that is continuously compounded will be:

$$P = \frac{F_t}{e^{rt}}. \tag{5.32}$$

Thus if spot rates are expressed as annual rates with continuous compounding, then the discount factors d_t can be calculated as:

$$d_t = \frac{1}{e^{rt}}. \tag{5.33}$$

These last three formulas can be used for any value of t, including fractional amounts (for example, if F_t is to be received in 2½ years, then $t = 2.5$).

ENDNOTES

[1] This calculation assumes that the bond will not be called prior to maturity. If it is assumed that the bond will be called as soon as possible, then the discount rate that

makes the present value of the corresponding cash flows equal to the current market price of the bond is known as the bond's *yield-to-call*.

[2] Note how, using Equation (5.24), $r_a = (1.03923)^2 - 1 = 8\%$, a solution that is the same as the one provided by Equation (5.22).

[3] Consider what would happen if the number of compounding intervals in a year becomes arbitrarily large so that each interval is very small. In the limit there will be an infinite number of infinitely small intervals; such a situation involves *continuous compounding*, and is discussed in the appendix.

[4] Occasionally, the yield curve will be "humped," where it rises for a short while and then declines, perhaps leveling off for intermediate to long-term maturities.

[5] Recently, a "modern" expectations theory has been developed that is economically more logical than the "unbiased" expectations theory. However, it provides approximately the same empirical implications and explanations of the term structure as those given by the unbiased expectations theory. Thus, given the similarities of the two theories, only the unbiased expectations theory is presented.

[6] Equation (5.25) can be expressed more generally as $es_{t-1,t} = f_{t-1,t}$. Thus, using Equation (5.19), the unbiased expectations theory states that, in general, $(1 + s_{t-1})^{t-1} \times (1 + es_{t-1,t}) = (1 + s_t)^t$.

[7] See Equations (5.1) – (5.3) and Chapter 13 for a discussion of the nature of the relationship between nominal rates, real rates, and expected inflation rates.

[8] Unfortunately, this risk is often referred to as "liquidity risk" when it more appropriately should be called "price risk," because it is the price volatility associated with longer-term securities that is of concern to investors. Partially offsetting this price risk is a risk that is present in the rollover strategy and absent from the maturity strategy—namely, the risk associated with the uncertainty of the reinvestment rate at the end of the first year when the rollover strategy is chosen. The liquidity preference theory assumes that this risk is of relatively little concern to investors.

[9] Sometimes the difference is referred to as the *term premium*. See Bradford Cornell, "Measuring the Term Premium: An Empirical Note," *Journal of Economics and Business*, 42, no. 1 (February 1990): 89–92.

[10] It should be noted that although the forward rate can be determined, neither the expected future spot rate nor the liquidity premium can be observed. All that can be done is to estimate their respective values.

[11] Equation (5.27) can be expressed more generally as $f_{t-1,t} = es_{t-1,t} + L_{t-1,t}$. Thus, using Equation (5.19), the liquidity preference theory states that:

$$(1 + s_{t-1})^{t-1} \times (1 + es_{t-1,t} + L_{t-1,t}) = (1 + s_t)^t.$$

Since $L_{t-1,t} > 0$, it follows that, in general:

$$(1 + s_{t-1})^{t-1} \times (1 + es_{t-1,t}) < (1 + s_t)^t.$$

[12] If $es_{1,2}$ were equal to or greater than s_1, then the inequality would not hold in the correct direction because it was assumed that $s_1 > s_2$.

[13] A more moderate version is the *preferred habitat theory*, where borrowers and investors will leave their desired maturity segment if there are significant differences in the yields in the various segments.

[14] The empirical evidence is not without dispute. Fama has argued that the evidence is inconsistent with both the unbiased expectations and liquidity preference theories, while McCulloch refutes Fama's findings and argues in favor of the latter theory. See Eugene F. Fama, "Term Premiums in Bond Returns," *Journal of Financial Economics*, 13, no. 4 (De-

cember 1984): 529–546; and J. Huston McCulloch, "The Monotonicity of the Term Premium: A Closer Look," *Journal of Financial Economics,* 18, no. 1 (March 1987): 185–192, and "An Estimate of the Liquidity Premium," *Journal of Political Economy,* 83, no. 1 (February 1975): 95–119. McCulloch's findings are supported by Matthew Richardson, Paul Richardson, and Tom Smith in "The Monotonicity of the Term Premium: Another Look," *Journal of Financial Economics,* 31, no. 1 (February 1992): 97–105.

[15] Tables of natural logarithms may be used for such calculations. The natural logarithm of 1.0806 is .0775, and the antilogarithm of .0775 is 1.0806.

KEY TERMS

yield-to-maturity	annual percentage rate
spot rate	yield curve
discount factors	term structure
market discount function	unbiased expectations theory
discounting	liquidity preference theory
forward rate	liquidity premium
compounding	market segmentation

REFERENCES

1. Many of the fundamental concepts having to do with bonds are discussed in:

   Homer Sidney and Martin L. Leibowitz, *Inside the Yield Book: New Tools for Bond Market Strategy* (Englewood Cliffs, NJ: Prentice Hall, 1972).

   Marcia Stigum, *The Money Market* (Homewood, IL: Business One Irwin, 3rd ed., 1990).

   Frank J. Fabozzi, ed., *The Handbook of Fixed-Income Securities* (Homewood, IL: Business One Irwin, 3rd ed., 1991).

2. A discussion of the zero coupon Treasury bond market is presented in:

   Deborah W. Gregory and Miles Livingston, "Development of the Market for U.S. Treasury STRIPS," *Financial Analysts Journal,* 48, no. 2 (March/April 1992): 68–74.

3. For a thorough review of term structure theories and the associated empirical evidence, see:

   John H. Wood and Norma L. Wood, *Financial Markets* (San Diego, CA: Harcourt Brace Jovanovich, 1985), Chapter 19.

   Frederic S. Mishkin, *The Economics of Money, Banking, and Financial Markets* (Glenview, IL: Scott, Foresman, 1989), Chapter 7.

   Peter A. Abken, "Innovations in Modeling the Term Structure of Interest Rates," Federal Reserve Bank of Atlanta, *Economic Review,* 75, no. 4 (July/August 1990): 2–27.

Frank J. Fabozzi and Franco Modigliani, *Capital Markets: Institutions and Instruments* (Englewood Cliffs, NJ: Prentice Hall, 1992), Chapter 12.

Steven Russell, "Understanding the Term Structure of Interest Rates: The Expectations Theory," Federal Reserve Bank of St. Louis, *Review,* 74, no. 4 (July/August 1992): 36–50.

James C. Van Horne, *Financial Market Rates and Flows* (Englewood Cliffs, NJ: Prentice Hall, 1994), Chapter 5.

4. For a comparison of the traditional unbiased expectations theory and the modern expectations theory of the term structure of interest rates, see:

John H. Wood and Norma L. Wood, *Financial Markets* (San Diego, CA: Harcourt Brace Jovanovich, 1985), pp. 645–651.

5. For a discussion of the preferred habitat theory of the term structure of interest rates, see:

Frank J. Fabozzi and Franco Modigliani, *Capital Markets: Institutions and Instruments* (Englewood Cliffs, NJ: Prentice Hall, 1992), pp. 387–388.

James C. Van Horne, *Financial Market Rates and Flows* (Englewood Cliffs, NJ: Prentice Hall, 1994), pp. 101, 112–113.

6. For an intriguing tax-based explanation of why the yield curve has usually been upward sloping, see:

Richard Roll, "After-Tax Investment Results from Long-Term vs. Short-Term Discount Coupon Bonds," *Financial Analysts Journal,* 40, no. 1 (January/February 1984): 43–54.

Ricardo J. Rodriguez, "Investment Horizon, Taxes and Maturity Choice for Discount Coupon Bonds," *Financial Analysts Journal,* 44, no. 5 (September/October 1988): 67–69.

CHAPTER 6

The Valuation of Risky Securities

Payments received from riskless securities can be accurately predicted: Neither their amounts nor their timing is uncertain. But many securities do not meet such high standards. Some or all of their payments are *contingent* on events with respect to amount, timing, or both. A bankrupt corporation may not make its promised bond payments in full or on time. A worker who is laid off may pay his or her bills late (or not at all). A corporation may reduce or eliminate its dividend if its business becomes unprofitable.

The security analyst must try to evaluate the circumstances affecting a risky investment's payments and enumerate the key events upon which such payments are contingent. For example, an aircraft manufacturer's fortunes may depend on whether or not the firm is awarded a major contract by the government, whether or not its recently introduced commercial aircraft is accepted by the airlines, or whether or not there is an upturn in the economy with a concomitant increase in demand for airline travel. To value the stock of such a company properly, the analyst must consider each of these contingencies and estimate the corresponding effect on the firm and its stock.

The identification of important influences and the evaluation of their impact are exceedingly difficult. Among other things, the appropriate level of detail must be determined. The number of potentially relevant events is almost

143

always very large, and the analyst must attempt to focus on the relatively few that appear to be most important. In some cases it may be best to differentiate only a few alternatives (for example, whether the economy will turn up, turn down, or stay the same). In some cases, finer distinctions may be needed (for example, whether the gross domestic product will be up 1%, 2%, or 3%).

The process of identifying and evaluating key influences is central to security analysis. The use of such estimates is of concern in this chapter. After the contingencies have been identified and the corresponding payments estimated, how can the value of the security be determined?

6.1 MARKET VERSUS PERSONAL VALUATION

One approach to the valuation of risky securities focuses on the investor's personal attitudes and circumstances. Given his or her assessment of the likelihood of various contingencies, and feelings about the corresponding risks involved in an investment, an investor might determine the amount he or she would be willing to pay by some sort of introspection. This would be a "personal" valuation of the security.

Such an approach would be appropriate if there were only one investment in the world, but such is not the case. A security need not and should not be valued without considering available alternatives. Current market values of other securities provide important information, because a security is seldom so unique that nothing else is comparable. Security valuation should not be done in a vacuum; it should instead be performed in a market context.

Key to this approach is the comparison of one investment or combination of investments with others having comparable characteristics. For example, assume that A and B in Figure 6.1(a) are the same in this respect; then the two should be equal in value.

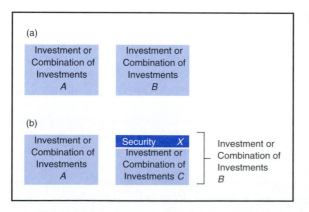

Figure 6.1
Comparing Investments

Now imagine that alternative B includes a security that an investor wishes to value—call it X. Moreover, assume that all other securities included in A and B are regularly traded and that their market values (prices) are widely reported and easily determined. Combination B can be thought to have two components: security X and the rest, which will be represented by C, as in Figure 6.1(b). Combination C might include many securities, only one, or, as a very special case, none at all.

If people are willing to purchase combination A for V_A, they should be willing to purchase combination B for the same amount, since the two provide comparable prospects. Thus

$$V_A = V_B.$$

The value of B, however, will simply be the sum of the values of its components:

$$V_B = V_X + V_C.$$

This implies that the value of security X can be determined solely by reference to market values placed on the securities comprising combinations A and C. Since $V_A = V_B$, it follows that

$$V_A = V_X + V_C$$

or, by rearranging,

$$V_X = V_A - V_C$$

meaning that the value of X can be determined by subtracting the value of C from the value of A.

6.2 APPROACHES TO SECURITY VALUATION

It is reasonable enough to say that market prices of "comparable investments" should be used to determine the value of a security. But when are two investments truly comparable?

An obvious case arises when investments provide identical payments in every possible contingency. If an investment's outcome is affected by relatively few events, it may be possible to purchase a set of other investments, each of which pays off in only one of the relevant contingencies. A properly selected mix of such investments may thus be completely comparable to the one to be valued. The next section illustrates this approach with an example drawn from the field of insurance.

A much more common approach to valuation is less detailed but more useful. Two alternatives are considered comparable if they offer similar expected returns and contribute equally to portfolio risk. Central to this view is the need to assess the probabilities of various contingencies. The remainder of this chapter and the next four chapters are devoted to this more widely used *risk-return approach*.

6.3.1 Insurance

Insurance policies are highly explicit examples of contingent payments. One can buy a $100,000 one-year "term" life insurance policy on a reasonably healthy 60–year-old for about $2,300. This, of course, can be viewed as an investment (albeit a morbid one): The sum of $100,000 will be paid by the insurance company if the insured dies within a year. Otherwise nothing at all will be paid. Involved is the sacrifice of a present certain value ($2,300) for a future uncertain value. The only relevant event is the possible death of the insured, and the relationship between that event and the amount to be paid is crystal clear.

Now imagine that a reasonably healthy 60-year-old executive asks you for a one-year loan. The executive would like as much as possible now; in return he or she promises to pay you $100,000 at the end of the year. Your problem is to determine the present value of that promise—that is, how much to advance now. Put somewhat differently, you must determine an appropriate interest rate for the loan.

To keep the example simple, assume that the only source of uncertainty is the borrower's ability to remain in this position and thus earn the requisite money, and that this depends only on his or her continued presence among the living. In other words, if the borrower lives, the $100,000 will be repaid in full and on time; otherwise, you will receive nothing.

The piece of paper representing the executive's promise to pay $100,000 is your security X. What is it worth? The answer clearly depends significantly on the available alternatives. And a crucial factor is the current rate of interest.

Assume that the going rate for riskless one-year loans is 8%. If there were no doubt whatsoever that the executive would repay the loan, it would be reasonable to advance $92,592.59 (since $100,000/$92,592.59 = 1.08$). However, the uncertainty connected with the loan makes this inadvisable. The appropriate amount is obviously less. But how much less?

In this case an answer can easily be determined. It would be entirely reasonable to advance at least $90,292.59, making the "promised" interest rate on the

Item	Event		
	Executive Dies	Executive Lives	Cost
Loan	0	$100,000	$90,292.59
Insurance policy	$100,000	0	2,300.00
Total	$100,000	$100,000	$92,592.59

TABLE 6.1
COSTS AND PAYMENTS FOR A LOAN AND AN INSURANCE POLICY

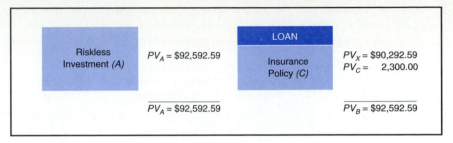

Figure 6.2
Comparing Two Riskless Investments

loan approximately 10.75% (since 100,000/90,292.59 = 1.1075). The basis for this calculation is quite simple. It relies on the fact that an investor can insure against the relevant risk, obtaining an overall position that is completely riskless.

Table 6.1 provides the details. The relevant event is whether or not the executive survives the year. The loan is thus a risky investment, paying $100,000 only if the executive lives. The life insurance policy is also a risky investment, paying $100,000 only if the executive dies. But a portfolio that includes both investments is totally riskless: Its owner will receive $100,000, no matter what happens! By paying $90,292.59 for the loan and $2,300 for the insurance policy, an investor could give up $92,592.59 now for a certain payment of $100,000 a year hence—obtaining a riskless return of 8%, which is the going rate on other riskless ventures.

This is, of course, an application of the general procedure described in the previous section. Figure 6.2 summarizes the details in the format used earlier, for purposes of comparison.

6.3.2 Valuation in a Complete Market

Assume, for the present, that market values can be used to estimate the present value of any contingent payment. A market in which such detailed quotations are available is termed a **complete market.** While no real market conforms to this specification, it is useful to see how valuation would be done in such circumstances.

First, a way to represent the present value of a guaranteed commitment to pay $1 at a specified time if (and only if) a specified event or "state of the world" occurs is needed. The following will suffice:

$$PV(\$1, t, e)$$

where:

$t =$ *the time at which the dollar is to be paid,*
$e =$ *the event that must occur if the dollar is to be paid.*

Armed with this notation, any risky investment can now be analyzed. Every possible contingency could, in theory, be considered separately, giving a (probably very lengthy) list of contingent payments of the following form:

Time Of Payment	Event On Which Payment Is Contingent	Amount Of Payment
t_1	e_1	D_1
t_2	e_2	D_2
.	.	.
.	.	.
.	.	.

Of course, some of the events might be the same, as might some of the times and amounts.

To find the present value of the investment, the present value of each of its contingent payments must be found and then added:

(1) Time Of Payment	(2) Event On Which Payment Is Contingent	(3) Amount Of Payment	(4) Discount Factor	(5) = (3) × (4) Present Value
t_1	e_1	D_1	$PV(\$1, t_1, e_1)$	$D_1 \times PV(\$1, t_1, e_1)$
t_2	e_2	D_2	$PV(\$1, t_2, e_2)$	$D_2 \times PV(\$1, t_2, e_2)$
.	.	.	.	.
.	.	.	.	.
.	.	.	.	.

Total value = _____

This **state-preference method** begins with the assumption that people's preferences are for *state-contingent claims* and concludes that securities will be valued on the basis of their payoffs in different "states of the world."

6.3.3 The Limitations of Insurance

Some believe that Lloyd's of London will insure almost anything. Perhaps so. This could ease the security analyst's task considerably. He or she would only (!) have to determine the payments $(D_1, D_2, \ldots)$ associated with an investment, the times at which they could be made $(t_1, t_2, \ldots)$, and the events on which they were contingent $(e_1, e_2, \ldots)$. The analyst could then use the premiums specified for the relevant insurance policies as estimates of appropriate discount factors $[PV(\$1,t_1,e_1), (PV(\$1,t_2,e_2), \ldots]$, and perform the required calculations.

But even if Lloyd's will insure anything, the premiums charged for many policies might not attract any takers. There are a number of interrelated reasons for this. As a case in point, imagine an aerospace company, the future profits of which depend heavily on whether or not the firm will be awarded a major government contract. Why not buy an appropriate insurance policy from Lloyd's, guaranteed to pay off if the firm loses the contract? Then only Lloyd's and the other firms in the industry would care about the outcome.

The idea is obviously whimsical. If Lloyd's were even willing to issue such a policy, the cost would be more than anyone would be likely to pay. Why? First, because of differences in information. Those familiar with the company or the government or both have better information about the likely outcome and can better assess the likelihood of various alternatives. Lloyd's operates at least partly in the dark. To protect itself, it will charge more than otherwise.

Second, there is the likelihood of **adverse selection.** If a policy of this sort is offered at a price low enough to attract anyone at all, the insurer can expect the firms that are least likely to win the contract to buy insurance, whereas those most likely to get the contract take their chances. This occurs frequently with life insurance. The less healthy an individual, the more likely he or she is to buy a policy. For this reason, the insured is usually required to pass a medical examination as a condition of sale. An examination of the health of a company's bid to win a government award might be much more difficult or expensive, so an insurance company must set its fees for such a policy on the assumption that it would end up insuring the riskiest client or clients.

Another factor is the thoroughly modern phenomenon described by the term **moral hazard.** The purchase of insurance may affect the likelihood of the event in question. If the manager of a firm is insured against the loss of the contract, he or she may well put less effort into the attempt to win it, increasing the likelihood of its loss and the insurance company's obligation to pay off. This explains the reluctance of an insurance company to insure a house or a car for more than its replacement value and the desire of many stockholders to have a corporation's officers own some of the firm's stock and none of its competitors' issues. Here again, the insurance company will account for this effect when setting prices.

Finally, there is the simple matter of overhead. Insurance people like to eat, as do investors who provide the capital that insurance companies need. The costs of doing business will, over the long pull, be reflected in the prices charged for that business. No financial service is free, and insurance is no exception.

For all these reasons securities markets do not conform to the specifications of the complete-market state-preference model. Although the approach is helpful for addressing certain theoretical issues, it is less useful for investment purposes than the risk-return (or "mean-variance") approach, to which the discussion now turns.

6.4   PROBABILISTIC FORECASTING

6.4.1 Assessing Probabilities

Lacking a plethora of widely available and low-cost insurance policies, it is not possible to value an investment without explicitly considering the likelihood of various outcomes. Instead, the analyst must attempt to assess directly the likelihood of each major event that can affect an investment. In short, he or she must engage in *probabilistic forecasting.*

The idea is simple enough, although its implementation is exceedingly difficult. The analyst expresses his or her assessment of the likelihood of every relevant event as a *probability*. If he or she feels that the chances of an event's taking place are 50–50, a probability of .50 is attached to the event. If the chances seem to be 3 out of 4, the probability is ¾, or .75 (another way of expressing this is to say that the *odds* are 3 to 1 that the event will take place). If the analyst considers an event to be absolutely certain, a probability of 1.0 should be assigned. If he or she feels that an event is completely impossible, its probability of occurrence is zero.

It is important, of course, to be consistent in one's estimates. For example, if the events on a list are *mutually exclusive and exhaustive* (that is, one of them, but only one, will take place), the probabilities should sum to 1.0.

Probability is, fundamentally, a subjective concept. Even simple cases fall under this heading. For example, a gambler may assess the probability of a coin's coming up heads at .5, based on knowledge of coins and past observations of the coin in question. But the estimate is still subjective, involving the implicit assumption that the coin really is "fair" and that the past is an appropriate guide to the future. Similar cases arise frequently in security analysis. Relative frequencies of various returns in the past are sometimes used as estimates of the probabilities of such returns in the future. Clearly this procedure relies on assumptions that require subjective judgment and may in some circumstances be totally inappropriate. Forecasts based on the extrapolation of past relationships are neither wholly objective nor necessarily preferable to predictions obtained in more subtle ways.

Probabilistic forecasting entails a decision to confront uncertainty head-on, acknowledge its existence, and try to measure its extent. Instead of attempting to answer a question such as "What will General Motors earn next year?", the analyst explicitly considers some of the more likely alternatives and the likelihood of each one. This brings the analysis out in the open, allowing both the estimator and the users of such estimates to assess the reasonableness of the values. Insistence on a single number for each estimate, with no measure of associated uncertainty, would suggest naivete or insecurity on the part of the producer or the consumer of such predictions.

In some organizations, analysts engage in explicit probabilistic forecasting, passing on all their detailed assessments to others charged with bringing together the estimates made within the group. In other organizations, the analysts make explicit probabilistic forecasts but summarize their evaluations in a relatively few key estimates, sending only the latter to others. In still other organizations, analysts do not engage in explicit probabilistic forecasting. Instead, they produce estimates that summarize their implicit beliefs about the probabilities of various events. As always, it is not the form but the substance that matters.

6.4.2 Probability Distributions

It is often convenient to portray probabilistic forecasts graphically. The possible outcomes are represented on the horizontal axis and the associated probabilities on the vertical axis. Figure 6.3 provides an example. In this case the outcomes are qualitatively different in nature and can be listed only on the horizontal axis; the ordering and spacing are arbitrary.

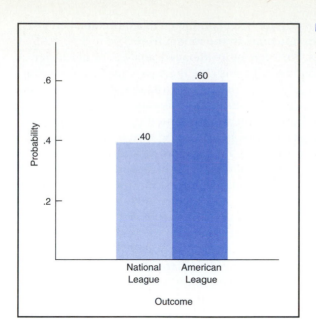

Figure 6.4 shows a somewhat different case. Here the alternative outcomes differ quantitatively and with regard to only one variable: earnings per share next year. In this instance the analyst has chosen to group together all possibilities from $.90 to $.99, assess the probability that the actual amount will fall within that range, and then repeat the process for the range from $1.00 to $1.09, the range from $1.10 to $1.19, and other $.10 ranges.

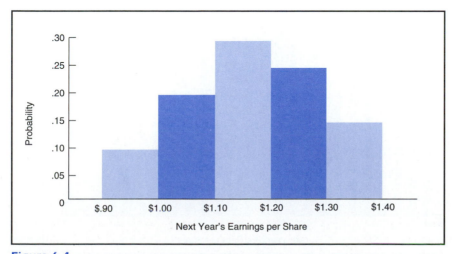

Figure 6.4
Probabilities of Next Year's Earnings per Share
(Using Wide Ranges)

The analysis could, of course, have been conducted at a more detailed level, with probabilities estimated for outcomes in the ranges from $.90 to $.94, $.95 to $.99, and similar $.05 ranges. An even more detailed analysis would assign a probability to every possible outcome. In this case the bars would be numerous, and each would be very thin, as shown in Figure 6.5. Note that the more numerous the number of bars, the smaller the sizes of associated probabilities.

The ultimate in a detailed prediction is represented by a *continuous probability distribution*. Such a curve represents, in effect, the tops of many thin bars. (Technically, the curve represents what happens when there is an infinite number of such bars.) Three examples of curves of this type are shown in Figure 6.6. Note that the vertical axis now measures probability density (instead of probability).

If continuous probability distributions are used, the analyst can forgo explicitly assessing particular individual outcomes. Instead, the analyst must draw a curve that seems to represent the situation as he or she sees it. The relative likelihood of any single outcome (such as earnings per share of $1.035) is zero. However, the relative likelihood of any range of earnings is found by simply finding the size of the area under the curve but above the horizontal axis. Thus the likelihood of earnings being between $1.03 and $1.04 could be found by measuring the area under the curve between $1.03 and $1.04, which in this case is approximately .07 (that is, there is a chance of 7 out of 100 that earnings will be between $1.03 and $1.04 next year). With a discrete probability distribution such as those shown in Figures 6.4 and 6.5, it was noted that the sum of the probabilities had to be 1.0. Now, with a continuous probability distribution, the total area under the curve must sum to 1.0.

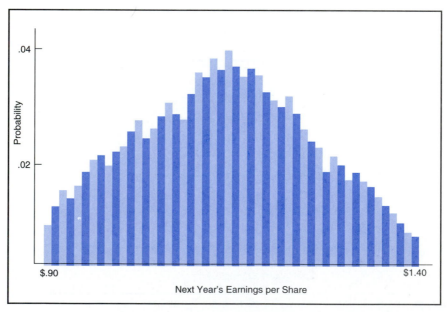

Figure 6.5
Probabilities of Next Year's Earnings per Share (Using Narrow Ranges)

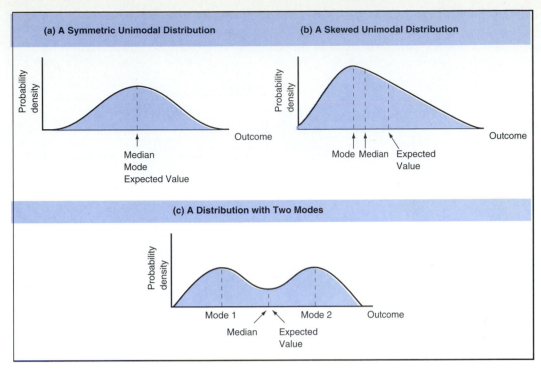

Figure 6.6
Continuous Probability Distributions

6.4.3 Event Trees

When events follow one another over time or are in any sense dependent on one another, it is often useful to describe the alternative sequences with a tree diagram. Figure 6.7 provides an example.

A borrower has promised to pay $15 one year hence and $8 two years hence, if possible. The analyst feels that the odds are only 40–60 that the first payment will in fact be made in full. Otherwise, the analyst feels that the borrower will be able to pay only $10 one year hence.

As far as the second year is concerned, the likely situation depends, in this analyst's judgment, on the outcome in the first year. If the borrower manages to pay the full $15 in the first year, the analyst feels that the odds are only 1–9 that the borrower will be able to meet the $8 commitment at the end of two years. Otherwise, the borrower will pay less: $6. On the other hand, if the borrower pays out $10 in the first year, although there appears to be no chance of recovering the $5 shortfall, the analyst feels that the odds are about even (50–50) that the promised $8 will be paid in the second year. If this does not happen, the analyst feels that $4 will be paid instead.

Figure 6.7 also shows the probability of each of the four possible sequences, or paths, through the tree. For example, the probability that both payments will be made in full is only .04, because there are only 40 chances out of 100 that the first payment will be made, and of those, only 1 out of 10 is expected to be followed by payment in full of the final obligation. This gives 4 out of 100 chances for the sequence: a probability of .04.

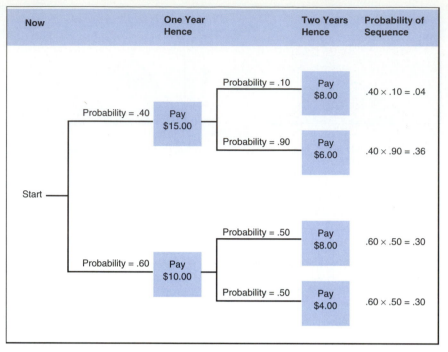

Now	One Year Hence	Two Years Hence	Probability of Sequence
		Probability = .10 Pay $8.00	.40 × .10 = .04
	Probability = .40 Pay $15.00		
		Probability = .90 Pay $6.00	.40 × .90 = .36
Start			
		Probability = .50 Pay $8.00	.60 × .50 = .30
	Probability = .60 Pay $10.00		
		Probability = .50 Pay $4.00	.60 × .50 = .30

Figure 6.7
An Event Tree

6.4.4 Expected Value

Often an analyst is uncertain about an outcome but wishes (or is required) to summarize the situation with one or two numbers—one indicating the *central tendency* of the distribution of outcomes and one measuring *relevant risk*. Both return and risk are discussed in subsequent chapters; the remainder of this chapter concentrates on the former.

How might a single number intended to summarize a set of possible outcomes be obtained? Obviously, no satisfactory way can be found if the alternative outcomes differ qualitatively (for example, the National League versus the American League in winning the World Series). But if the outcomes differ quantitatively, and especially if they differ in only one dimension, a number of possibilities present themselves.

Perhaps the most common procedure is to adopt the *most likely* value. This is known as the **mode** of the probability distribution (for a continuous probability distribution, the mode is the outcome with the highest probability density). Figure 6.6 shows the mode of each of the distributions. Note that in Figure 6.6(c) there are two modes: In this case, no single number can be used to answer the question in this manner.

Another alternative is to provide a "50–50" number—a value that is as likely to be too low as it is to be too high. This is called the **median** of the probability distribution. As shown in Figure 6.6, it may differ significantly from the mode(s).

A third alternative is to use an **expected value** (also known as the **mean**), a weighted average of all the possible outcomes, using the associated probabilities as weights. It takes into account all the information expressed in the distribution, both the magnitude and the probability of occurrence of each possible outcome. Almost any change in an investment's prospects or probabilities will affect the expected value of its outcomes (as it should).

In many instances there are no differences among these three measures. If the distribution is symmetric (each half is a mirror image of the other) and unimodal (there is one most likely value), then the median, mode, and expected value coincide, as in the case shown in Figure 6.6(a). Thus an analyst may choose to think in terms of, say, a 50–50 (median) value, even though the number wanted is the expected value. Only if the underlying probability distribution is highly skewed [as in Figure 6.6(b)] might this procedure lead to difficulties.

In those cases in which the values do differ, there are good reasons to prefer the expected value. As stated earlier, it takes all the estimates into account. But it has another advantage. Estimates about the prospects for securities serve as inputs for the process of portfolio construction or revision. The expected value of the return for a portfolio is related in a straightforward way to the expected values of the returns for its securities, but neither the median nor the mode for a portfolio can, in general, be determined from comparable values for its securities.

Table 6.2 provides an example of the computation of expected values. An analyst is trying to predict the impact on the prices of two securities of a surprise television address scheduled by the President. The analyst has delineated a number of possible announcements, ranging from changes in the situation in the Middle East through a decision concerning the federal deficit. The alternatives represented in the table have been defined to be mutually exclusive and exhaustive (that is, every possible combination is shown in a different row). After much thought and with some trepidation, the analyst has also estimated the probability of each announcement and the resultant effect on the prices of the two securities. Finally, the analyst has computed the associated values of a portfolio containing one share of each stock.

TABLE 6.2

ANALYSIS OF EFFECTS OF ANNOUNCEMENTS ON TWO SECURITIES AND A PORTFOLIO OF BOTH SECURITIES

Announcement	Probability	Predicted Price of Security A	Predicted Price of Security B	Predicted Value of A Portfolio of A and B
a	.10	$40.00	$62.00	$102.00
b	.20	42.00	65.00	107.00
c	.10	40.50	60.00	100.50
d	.25	41.00	61.00	102.00
e	.15	38.00	65.00	103.00
f	.10	40.50	59.00	99.50
g	.05	45.00	58.00	103.00
h	.05	40.50	58.00	98.50
	Expected Values:	$40.73	$61.90	$102.63

Cognitive Psychology

The bedrock on which theories of risky security valuation rest is the presumed existence of rational investors who respond in a predictable manner to the opportunities for gain and the risks of loss. As the text discusses, these investors are assumed to assess potential investments on the basis of expected outcomes derived from estimates of the investments' probability distributions of returns. Furthermore, the investors' estimates are assumed to exhibit no systematic biases relative to the "true" probability distributions. That is, investors do not consistently make mistakes in one direction or another when examining potential investments.

If such assumptions of rationality make sense for individual investors, then we might reasonably believe that they apply even more appropriately to institutional investors. After all, institutional investors bring to bear extensive analytical resources on the investment management problem. Moreover, the decision-making structures of institutional investors—such as hierarchies of personnel, committees, and performance reviews—are all designed to promote consistent and rational investment choices.

The view of investors as objective decision-makers has traditionally gone unchallenged in the academic world. While many professional investors have argued that investing is dominated by the emotions of fear and greed, their opinions have been dismissed by academics as anecdotal and self-serving. More recently, however, a school of thought has developed among certain academics which argues that investors may not deal with risky choices in a totally rational manner. This line of reasoning is based on a branch of psychology known as *cognitive psychology*, which studies the capacity of human beings for perception and judgment.

Applied to the study of economic decision-making, and investments in particular, cognitive psychology draws some intriguing conclusions. Most fundamentally, people do not appear to be consistent in how they treat economically equivalent choices if the choices are presented in significantly different contexts. These differences are referred to as *framing effects*. Two prominent cognitive psychology researchers, Daniel Kahneman and Amos Tversky, cite a simple example of framing effects (see "The Psychology of Preferences," *Scientific American,* January 1982).

Suppose that you are walking to a Broadway play carrying a ticket that cost $40. On reaching the theater you discover that you have lost your ticket. Would you pay another $40 for a ticket at the door? Now suppose that you were planning to buy the ticket at the door. On arriving you find that you have lost $40 on the way. Would you still buy a ticket?

The economic consequences of these two situations are identical. You have lost $40 and now must decide whether to spend another $40. Interestingly, however, most people buy a ticket in the second case, but not in the first. People therefore appear to "frame" the choices differently. They treat the loss of cash differently from the loss of a ticket.

In terms of investing, these framing effects have been suggested to cause deviations from rational decision-making. For example, it appears that people react differently to situations involving the prospects for large gains as opposed to large losses. That is, investors are assumed to choose a more risky investment over a less risky one only if the expected return of the more risky investment is greater than that of the less risky investment. (This trait is known as risk aversion—see Chapter 7.) Indeed, this assumption seems to hold well for situations involving large gains. For example, consider a situation where you have invested in a start-up company and have a 90% chance of receiving $1 million and a 10% chance of receiving nothing. Hence the expected payoff is $900,000 [= (.9 × $1 million) + (.1 × $0)]. If somebody offered to buy you out for $850,000, most likely you would accept the offer, since it has nearly the same expected payoff but much less risk. That is, you would be exhibiting risk-averse behavior.

Now, however, consider a situation involving large losses. Suppose that you had invested in another start-up company. Things are going poorly, and if nothing changes there is a 90% chance of losing $1 million, but a 10% chance that things might work out well enough to not lose (or gain) anything. Thus the expected loss is $900,000 [=

(.9 × \$1 million) + (.1 × \$0)]. Another investor offers to take over the company if you pay him or her \$850,000—a certain \$850,000 loss. Most people would reject the offer and choose to remain with the risky option even though it has a lower expected value (-\$900,000 versus -\$850,000). Thus in a situation involving large expected losses, people do not seem to exhibit risk-averse behavior—a framing effect.

People also seem to overestimate the probability of unlikely events occurring and underestimate the probability of moderately likely events occurring. These traits may explain the popularity of lotteries but may also have direct ramifications for the pricing of investments when the chances of success are low—such as bonds and stocks of bankrupt companies, start-up companies, and options whose strike prices are far above the underlying securities' prices.

Framing effects may also be involved in the observed tendency of investors to overreact to good and bad news. That is, some studies indicate that investors bid up the prices of companies reporting unexpectedly good earnings beyond the amount fairly warranted by the improved earnings. The converse seems to occur for companies reporting unexpectedly poor earnings.

Are the observations of cognitive psychologists relevant to the study of financial markets? Do these framing effects produce market anomalies that produce exploitable investment opportunities or even undermine commonly accepted theories of security valuation? Or are these framing effects merely interesting stories whose impacts are overwhelmed by the sophistication and profit motive of avaricious investors? Certainly, investors as a whole are far from irrational, for large and persistent disparities between "fair" values and market values are difficult to find. Nevertheless, the behavioral observations of cognitive psychologists are likely to provide a better understanding of how investors make decisions and help to explain certain apparent market inefficiencies.

The expected values are shown at the bottom of Table 6.2. Each is obtained by multiplying the probability of every announcement by the associated price, then summing. For example, the expected price of security A is determined by computing [(.10 × \$40.00) + (.20 × \$42.00) + . . .]; that of security B by computing [(.10 × \$62.00) + (.20 × \$65.00) + . . .]; and that of the portfolio by computing [(.10 × \$102.00) + (.20 × \$107.00) + . . .]. Not surprisingly, the expected value of the portfolio equals the sum of the expected values of its component securities. When the expected values for the securities are added together, one is, in effect, adding (.10 × \$40.00 + . . .) to (.10 × \$62.00 + . . .). Clearly this will give the expected value of the portfolio, which is .10 × (\$40.00 + \$62.00) + ...

6.4.5 Expected versus Promised Yield-to-Maturity

If payments from a bond are certain, there is no difference between the expected yield-to-maturity and the promised yield-to-maturity. However, many bonds fail to meet these standards. Two types of risk may be involved. First, the issuer may defer some payments. A dollar received further in the future is, of course, worth less in present value than a dollar received on schedule. Thus the present value of a bond will be smaller, the greater the likelihood of deferred payments. The second type of risk is potentially more serious. The borrower may default, in whole or in part, on some of the interest payments or on the principal at maturity. A firm becomes bankrupt when it is clearly unable to meet such obligations. The courts then divide the remaining assets among the various creditors in accordance with provisions agreed upon when the debts were issued.

To estimate the expected yield-to-maturity for a risky debt instrument, in principle all possible outcomes and the probability of each one should be considered. The simple example shown in Figure 6.7 can be used to illustrate the procedure. Assume that the security in question costs $15; that is, the borrower wants $15 now in return for a commitment to pay $15 one year hence and $8 two years hence. The promised yield-to-maturity is the interest rate that makes the present value of these payments equal $15. In this case it is 38.51% per year, a substantial figure indeed.

But the analyst feels that the probability of actually receiving this yield-to-maturity is only .04. Table 6.3 shows the possible sequences (paths in the event tree), as well as the probability and the yield-to-maturity for each one. The expected yield-to-maturity is simply the weighted average of these values, using the probabilities as weights [for example, (.04 × 38.51%) + (.36 × 30.62%) + (.30 × 13.61%) + (.30 × -5.20%) = 15.09%].

The expected yield-to-maturity is considerably less than the promised amount: 15.09% as opposed to 38.51%. And the former is the more relevant figure for investment analysis. This is an important point. The yield-to-maturity, as normally calculated, is based on promised payments, made at the promised times. If there is any risk that the borrower's commitments will not be paid fully and on time, the expected yield-to-maturity is less than this figure; and the greater the risk, the greater the disparity. This is illustrated in Table 6.4, which shows the (promised) yield-to-maturity values for six groups of industrial bonds classified by Standard & Poor's, a major rating service, as having different degrees of risk. Although the levels of all six yields reflect general interest rates at the time, the differences among them are primarily due to differences in risk. If the promised yields of all bonds were the same, the expected yields of high-risk bonds would be less than those of low-risk ones—an unlikely situation indeed. Instead, riskier bonds promise higher yields so that their expected yields can be at least as large as those of less risky ones.

The nature of most debt obligations would be more obvious if contracts were written somewhat differently. At present, a standard bond with no extra features "guarantees" that the borrower will pay the lender, say, $90 per year for 20 years, then $1,000 20 years hence. A more appropriate statement would indicate that the borrower guarantees to pay *no more than* $90 per year for 20 years, and $1,000 20 years hence.

TABLE 6.3
PROMISED VERSUS EXPECTED YIELD-TO-MATURITY

Payment One Year Hence	Payment Two Years Hence	Probability	Yield-to-Maturity
$15	$8	.04	38.51%
15	6	.36	30.62
10	8	.30	13.61
10	4	.30	−5.20
		Expected yield-to-maturity =	15.09%

TABLE 6.4
STANDARD & POOR'S INDUSTRIAL BOND YIELDS FOR AUGUST 1993

Rating	Yield-to-Maturity
AAA	6.68%
AA	7.32
A	7.80
BBB	8.45
BB	9.11
B	10.57

Source: Standard & Poor's *Bond Guide,* September 1993, p. 3.

6.5   EXPECTED HOLDING-PERIOD RETURN

6.5.1   Calculating Holding-Period Return

Yield-to-maturity calculations do not take into account any changes in the market value of a security prior to maturity. This might be interpreted as implying that the owner has no interest in selling the instrument prior to maturity, no matter what happens to its price or his or her situation. The calculation also fails to treat intermediate payments in a fully satisfactory way. If the owner does not wish to spend interest payments, he or she might choose to buy more of these securities. But the number that can be bought at any time depends on the price at that time, and yield-to-maturity calculations fail to take this into account.

While few dispute the value of yield-to-maturity as an indicator of a bond's overall return, it should be recognized as no more than this. For some purposes other measures may prove more useful. Moreover, for other types of securities there is no maturity: Common stocks provide the most important example.

A measure that can be used for any investment is its **holding-period return.** The idea is to specify a holding period of major interest, and then assume that any payments received during the period are reinvested. Although assumptions may differ from case to case, the usual procedure assumes that any payment received from a security (for example, a dividend from a stock, a coupon payment from a bond) is used to purchase more units of that security at the then current market price. Using this procedure, the performance of a security can be measured by comparing the value obtained in this manner at the end of the holding period with the value at the beginning. This **value-relative** can be converted to a holding-period return by subtracting 1 from it:[1]

$$r_{hp} = \frac{\text{value at the end of the holding period}}{\text{value at the beginning of the holding period}} - 1.$$

Holding-period return can be converted to an equivalent return per period. Allowing for the effect of compounding, the appropriate procedure is to find the value that satisfies the relationship

$$(1 + r_g)^N = 1 + r_{hp}$$

or

$$r_g = (1 + r_{hp})^{1/N} - 1$$

where:

N = the number of periods in the holding period,
r_{hp} = the holding-period return,
r_g = the equivalent return per period, compounded every period.

Suppose that a stock sold for $46 per share at the beginning of one year, paid dividends of $1.50 during that year, sold for $50 at the end of the year, paid dividends of $2 during the next year, and sold for $56 at the end of that year. What was the return over the two-year holding period?

To simplify the calculations, assume that all dividend payments are received at year-end. Then the $1.50 received during the first year could have bought .03 (= $1.50/$50) shares of the stock at the end of the first year. In practice, of course, this would be feasible only if the money were pooled with other similarly invested funds—for example, in a mutual fund (the dividends from 100 shares could have been used to buy three additional shares). In any event, for each share originally held, the investor would have obtained $2.06 (= 1.03 × $2) in dividends in the second year, and have had stock with value of $57.68 (= 1.03 × $56) at the end of the second year. The ending value would thus have been $59.74 (= $57.68 + $2.06), giving a value-relative of:

$$\frac{\$59.74}{\$46.00} = 1.2987.$$

The holding-period return was thus 29.87% per two years. This is equivalent to $(1.2987)^{1/2} - 1 = .1396$, or 13.96% per year.

An alternative method of computation treats the overall value-relative as the product of value-relatives for the individual periods. For example, if V_0 is the value at the beginning, V_1 the value at the end of the first year, and V_2 the value at the end of the second year:

$$\frac{V_2}{V_0} = \frac{V_2}{V_1} \times \frac{V_1}{V_0}.$$

Moreover, there is no need to carry the expansion in number of shares from period to period, as the factor (1.03 in the example) will simply cancel out in the subsequent periods' value-relatives. Each period can be analyzed in isolation, an appropriate value-relative calculated, and the set of such value-relatives multiplied together.

In our example, during the first year, ownership of a stock with an initial value of $46 led to stock and cash with a value of $50 + $1.50 at the end of the year. Thus,

$$\frac{V_1}{V_0} = \frac{\$51.50}{\$46.00} = 1.1196.$$

During the second year, ownership of stock with an initial value of $50 led to stock and cash with a value of $56 + $2 at year-end. Thus:

$$\frac{V_2}{V_1} = \frac{\$58}{\$50} = 1.16.$$

The two-year holding-period value-relative was therefore:

$$1.1196 \times 1.16 = 1.2987$$

which is exactly equal to the value obtained earlier.

The value-relative for each period can be viewed as 1 plus the return for that period. Thus the return on the stock being analyzed was 11.96% in the first year and 16% in the second. The holding-period value-relative is the product of 1 plus each return. If N periods are involved,

$$\frac{V_N}{V_0} = (1 + r_1)(1 + r_2) \ldots (1 + r_N).$$

To convert the result to a holding-period return stated as an amount per period, with compounding, one can find the *geometric mean return* of the periodic returns:

$$1 + r_g = [(1 + r_1)(1 + r_2) \ldots (1 + r_N)]^{1/N}.$$

More sophisticated calculations may be employed within this overall framework. Each dividend payment can be used to purchase shares immediately upon receipt, or, alternatively, it can be allowed to earn interest in a savings account until the end of the period. Brokerage and other costs associated with reinvestment of dividends can also be taken into account, although the magnitude of such costs will undoubtedly depend on the overall size of the holdings in question. The appropriate degree of complexity will, as always, be a function of the use for which the values are obtained.

Unfortunately, the most appropriate holding period is often at least as uncertain as the return over any given holding period. Neither an investor's situation nor his or her preferences can usually be predicted with certainty. Moreover, from a strategic viewpoint, an investment manager would like to hold a given security only as long as it outperforms available alternatives. Attempts to identify such periods in advance are seldom completely successful, but managers quite naturally continue to try to discover them. Holding-period return, like yield-to-maturity, provides a useful device for simplifying the complex reality of investment analysis. Although no panacea, it allows an analyst to focus on the most relevant horizon in a given situation and offers a good measure of performance over such a period.

6.5.2 Estimating Expected Holding-Period Return

It is a relatively straightforward matter to calculate a holding-period return after the fact. It is quite another thing to estimate it in advance. Any uncertainty surrounding payments by the issuer of a security during the period must be taken into account, but this is usually much simpler than the task of estimating the end-of-period market values, which often constitute a large portion of overall return. For example, it might seem a simple matter to estimate the return over

---

the next year for a share of Xerox stock. Dividends to be paid are often relatively easy to predict. But the price at year-end will depend on investors' attitudes toward the company and its stock at that time. To predict even a one-year holding-period return one must consider a much longer period and assess not only the company's future but also investors' future attitudes about that future—a formidable task indeed.

Quite clearly, estimation of holding-period return must account in some way for uncertainty. If a single estimate is required, it should conform to the principles stated earlier. Explicitly, an expected value should be provided by considering both the various possibilities along with their probabilities. More specifically, a security's expected holding-period return is calculated as a weighted average of possible holding-period returns, using probabilities as weights.[2]

6.6 EXPECTED RETURN AND SECURITY VALUATION

There is a very simple relationship between expected holding-period return, expected end-of-period value, and current value:

$$\text{Expected holding-period return} = \frac{\text{expected end-of-period value}}{\text{current value}} - 1.$$

Thus

$$\text{Current value} = \frac{\text{expected end-of-period value}}{1 + \text{expected holding-period return}}.$$

In words: To value a security, one needs to estimate the expected value at the end of a holding period and the expected return for the holding period that is appropriate for such a security.

The final phase is crucial. What is the "appropriate" expected return, and on what does it depend? Therein lies the remainder of the theory of valuation.

6.7 SUMMARY

1. The valuation of risky securities involves the explicit or implicit analysis of the events on which the securities' payments are contingent.
2. A contingent payment is a guaranteed cash flow that will be made if, and only if, a particular event (or state of the world) occurs.
3. A risky security's value could be calculated by aggregating the premiums corresponding to insurance policies written on each of its contingent payments, if such policies existed.
4. Due to the limitations of the insurance policy approach, for investment purposes the risk-return (mean-variance) approach to risky security valuation is most often employed.
5. Probabilistic forecasting involves identifying various alternative outcomes and the probabilities that those outcomes will occur. These forecasts may be

estimated using only past observations or by combining past observations with judgments about the future.

6. Probability distributions express (numerically or graphically) the likelihood of various possible outcomes occurring.

7. Event trees describe the likelihood of alternative sequences of outcomes occurring.

8. The expected value (mean), median, and mode are measures of central tendency of a probability distribution. In general, the expected value is the preferred measure because it takes into account all possible outcomes and their associated probabilities.

9. The expected yield-to-maturity of a bond will differ from the bond's promised yield-to-maturity if any of the bond's payments are uncertain. This difference will vary directly with the uncertainty of those payments.

10. A security's holding-period return compares the expected value of all of the security's cash flows over a given time period (with those cash flows reinvested at an assumed interest rate), relative to the current market price of the security.

QUESTIONS AND PROBLEMS

1. In March, a major bookmaker in Las Vegas accepted bets on the baseball teams that would eventually go to the World Series. For example, one could pay $10 at the time to bet that the Minnesota Twins would represent the American League in the World Series. The payoff on such a bet was set at $1,500 if the Twins did go to the World Series, and zero otherwise. Payoffs for bets on all teams in the American League Central Division were:

Team	Payoff per $1 Bet
Chicago White Sox	$180
Cleveland Indians	210
Kansas City Royals	60
Milwaukee Brewers	250
Minnesota Twins	150

a. What was the present value of $1 contingent on the event (state of the world) "The Twins go to the World Series"?

b. What was the present value of $1 contingent on the event "The Brewers go to the World Series"?

c. Why did the answers for (a) and (b) differ?

d. If someone had offered to pay you $1 if any team in the American League Central Division went to the World Series, how much would you have paid for this bet ("security")? If you had been virtually certain that one of these teams would go to the World Series, would your answer differ? Why?

2. Mondovi Optical is a small business. Its owner, Tully Sparks, has requested that the local bank loan the firm $25,000 for two years. The federal government's Small Business Administration will fully guarantee such a loan for a $1,000 fee. If the riskfree two-year interest rate is 5% per annum, what is the interest rate that the bank should charge Mondovi?

3. Why is the insurance policy approach to risky security valuation so difficult to implement in practice?
4. From the perspective of an insurance company, provide two examples of adverse selection and two examples of moral hazard.
5. Distinguish between continuous and discrete probability distributions.
6. What are the advantages and disadvantages of using past investment results to assess the probabilities of future investment outcomes?
7. The average annualized return on the S&P 500 index of common stocks from 1926 through 1993 was 12.34%. If, on January 1, 1994, you had been required to provide an estimate of the expected return on the S&P 500 over the coming year, would you have chosen 12.34%? Why or why not?
8. What is the value of event trees for investment decision-making?
9. Consider Fort McCoy Company, whose stock currently sells for $10 per share. Dode Paskert, a financial analyst, has estimated the stock's potential year-end prices and associated probabilities over the next two years:

Year 1   The stock has a 30% chance of rising to $20. It has a 60% chance of rising to $12. It has a 10% chance of falling to $8.

Year 2   If the stock rises to $20 in Year 1, it has a 50% chance of rising to $25 and a 50% chance of falling to $15. If the stock rises to $12 in Year 1, it has a 70% chance of rising to $15 and a 30% chance of falling to $10. If it falls to $8 in Year 1, it has a 40% chance of falling to $4 and a 60% chance of rising to $12.

   a. Draw an event tree for Fort McCoy Company stock.
   b. Based on this event tree, calculate the stock's expected price at the end of Year 2.
10. Calculate the expected return, mode, and median for a stock having the following probability distribution:

Return	Probability of Occurrence
−40%	.03
−10	.07
0	.30
15	.10
30	.05
40	.20
50	.25

11. Bear Tracks Schmitz has estimated the following probability distribution of next year's dividend payments for Mauston Inc.'s stock. According to Bear Tracks, what is the expected value of Mauston's dividend?

Dividend	Probability
$1.90	.05
1.95	.15
2.00	.30
2.05	.30
2.10	.15
2.15	.05

12. The probability distribution in Figure 6.6(b) is "skewed to the right." Explain why the distribution's expected value is greater than the median, which in turn is greater than the mode.

13. Dupee Shaw is a fixed-income security analyst who is reviewing a bond issued by Wyeville Corporation. The bond has one year to maturity, at which time the company promises to pay $100. It currently sells for $90. Dupee believes that Wyeville may not pay the full $100 at year-end. Dupee has estimated the following probability distribution of year-end payments. What is expected yield-to-maturity of the Wyeville bond according to Dupee?

Payment	Probability
$82	.05
90	.10
95	.30
98	.30
100	.25

14. If an investment returns 7% per year, how long does it take for the investment's value to double?

15. Pol Perritt purchased 100 shares of Waunakee Inc. and held the stock for four years. Pol's holding-period returns over these four years were:

Year	Return
1	+20%
2	+30
3	+50
4	−90

   a. What was the value-relative of Pol's investment over the four-year period?
   b. What was Pol's geometric mean return for the four-year period?

16. Stoughton Services' stock currently sells for $40. It is expected to pay a dividend of $2 each year for the next several years. It just made its latest dividend payment. Pinky O'Neill expects to sell Stoughton stock two years from today at $50. The reinvestment rate is 5%. If this outcome occurs, what will be the equivalent compound annual return from holding Stoughton stock over this two-year period?

17. Distinguish between expected holding-period return and yield-to-maturity.

ENDNOTES

[1] The term **price-relative** refers to the ratio of a security's price on a given day to its price on some previous day. Hence it is the same as the value-relative if there are no cash flows associated with the security between the two days.

[2] Expected return is also the mean of the probability distribution of holding-period returns—hence the "mean" in the *mean-variance approach,* which is the cornerstone of modern portfolio theory.

REFERENCES

1. The state-preference approach to asset pricing was developed by two previous winners of the Nobel prize in economics. See:

   Gerard Debreu, *Theory of Value: An Axiomatic Analysis of Economic Equilibrium* (New York: John Wiley, 1959).

   Kenneth J. Arrow, "The Role of Securities in the Optimal Allocation of Risk-Bearing," *Review of Economic Studies*, 31, no. 86 (April 1964): 91–96.

2. For a discussion of the application of the state-preference approach to finance, see:

   Thomas E. Copeland and J. Fred Weston, *Financial Theory and Corporate Policy* (Reading, MA: Addison-Wesley, 1988), Chapter 5.

3. The statistical concepts discussed in this chapter can be found in most introductory statistics textbooks, such as:

   James T. McClave and P. George Benson, *Statistics for Business and Economics* (San Francisco: Dellen, 1991).

The Portfolio Selection Problem

In 1952, Harry M. Markowitz published a landmark paper that is generally viewed as the origin of the *modern portfolio theory* approach to investing. Markowitz's approach begins by assuming that an investor has a given sum of money to invest at the present time. This money will be invested for a particular length of time known as the investor's **holding period.** At the end of the holding period, the investor will sell the securities that were purchased at the beginning of the period and then either spend the proceeds on consumption or reinvest the proceeds in various securities (or do some of both). Thus Markowitz's approach can be viewed as a single-period approach, where the beginning of the period is denoted $t = 0$ and the end of the period is denoted $t = 1$. At $t = 0$, the investor must make a decision on what particular securities to purchase and hold until $t = 1$.[1] Because a portfolio is a collection of securities, this decision is equivalent to selecting an optimal portfolio from a set of possible portfolios. Hence it is often referred to as the *portfolio selection problem.*

In making this decision at $t = 0$, the investor should recognize that security returns (and thus portfolio returns) over the forthcoming holding period are unknown. Nevertheless, the investor could estimate the **expected** (or mean) **returns** on the various securities under consideration, and then invest in the one with the highest expected return. (Methods for estimating expected returns will be discussed in Chapter 18.) Markowitz notes that this would generally be an unwise decision because the typical investor, although wanting "returns to be high," also wants "returns to be as certain as possible." This means that the investor, in seeking to both maximize expected return and minimize uncertainty (that is, **risk**), has two conflicting objectives that must be balanced against each other when making the purchase decision at $t = 0$. The Markowitz approach for how the investor should go about making this decision gives full consideration to both of these objectives.

One interesting consequence of having these two conflicting objectives is that the investor should diversify by purchasing not just one security but several. The ensuing discussion of Markowitz's approach to investing begins by defining more specifically what is meant by initial and terminal wealth.

7.1   INITIAL AND TERMINAL WEALTH

In Equation (1.1) of Chapter 1 it was noted that the one-period rate of return on a security could be calculated as:

$$\text{return} = \frac{\text{end-of-period wealth} - \text{beginning-of-period wealth}}{\text{beginning-of-period wealth}} \qquad (1.1)$$

where beginning-of-period wealth is the purchase price of one unit of the security at $t = 0$ (for example, one share of a firm's common stock), and end-of-period wealth is the market value of the unit at $t = 1$, along with the value of any cash (and cash equivalents) paid to the owner of the security between $t = 0$ and $t = 1$.

7.1.1   Determining the Rate of Return on a Portfolio

Because a portfolio is a collection of securities, its return r_p can be calculated in a similar manner:

$$r_p = \frac{W_1 - W_0}{W_0} . \qquad (7.1)$$

Here W_0 denotes the aggregate purchase price at $t = 0$ of the securities contained in the portfolio; W_1 denotes the aggregate market value of these securities at $t = 1$, as well as the aggregate cash (and cash equivalents) received between $t = 0$ and $t = 1$ from owning these securities. Equation (7.1) can be manipulated algebraically, resulting in:

$$W_0 (1 + r_p) = W_1. \qquad (7.2)$$

From Equation (7.2) it can be seen that beginning-of-period or **initial wealth** (as W_0 is sometimes called), when multiplied by one plus the rate of return on the portfolio, equals end-of-period or **terminal wealth** (as W_1 is sometimes called).

Earlier it was noted that the investor must make a decision regarding what portfolio to purchase at $t = 0$. In doing so, the investor does not know what the value of W_1 will be for most of the various alternative portfolios under consideration because the investor does not know what the rate of return will be for most of these portfolios.[2] Thus, according to Markowitz, the investor should view the rate of return associated with any one of these portfolios as what is called in statistics a **random variable;** such variables can be "described" by their moments, two of which are **expected value** (or mean) and **standard deviation.**[3]

Markowitz asserts that investors should base their portfolio decisions solely on expected returns and standard deviations. That is, the investor should estimate the expected return and standard deviation of each portfolio and then choose the "best" one based on the relative magnitudes of these two parameters. The intuition behind this is actually quite straightforward. Expected return can be viewed as a measure of the potential reward associated with any portfolio, and standard deviation can be viewed as a measure of the risk associated with any portfolio. Thus, once each portfolio has been examined in terms of its potential rewards and risks, the investor is in a position to identify the one portfolio that appears most desirable to him or her.

7.1.2 An Example

Consider the two alternative portfolios denoted *A* and *B,* shown in Table 7.1. Portfolio *A* has an expected annual return of 8% and portfolio *B* has an expected annual return of 12%. Assuming that the investor has initial wealth of $100,000 and a one-year holding period, this means that the expected levels of terminal wealth associated with *A* and *B* are $108,000 and $112,000, respectively. It would appear, then, that *B* is the more desirable portfolio. However, *A* and *B* have annual standard deviations of 10% and 20%, respectively. Table 7.1 shows that this means that there is a 2% chance that the investor will end up with terminal wealth of $70,000 or less if he or she purchases *B,* whereas there is virtually no chance that the investor's terminal wealth will be less than $70,000 if *A* is purchased. Similarly, *B* has a 5% chance of being worth less than $80,000, whereas *A* again has no chance. Continuing, *B* has a 14% chance of being worth less than $90,000, whereas *A* has only a 4% chance. Going on, *B* has a 27% chance of being worth less than $100,000, while *A* has only a 21% chance. Because the investor has initial wealth of $100,000, this last observation means that there is a greater probability of having a negative return if *B* (27%) is purchased instead of *A* (21%). Overall, it can be seen from Table 7.1 that *A* is less risky than *B,* meaning that on this dimension *A* would be more desirable. The ultimate decision about whether to purchase *A* or *B* will depend on this particular investor's attitude toward risk and return, as will be shown next.

| **7.2** | INDIFFERENCE CURVES |

The method that should be used in selecting the most desirable portfolio involves the use of **indifference curves.** These curves represent an investor's preferences for risk and return, and thus can be drawn on a two-dimensional figure where the horizontal axis indicates risk as measured by standard deviation (denoted σ_p) and the vertical axis indicates reward as measured by expected return (denoted $\bar{r}_p$).

TABLE 7.1

**A COMPARISON OF TERMINAL WEALTH LEVELS FOR
TWO HYPOTHETICAL PORTFOLIOS**

Level of Terminal Wealth	Percent Chance of Being Below This Level of Terminal Wealth	
	Portfolio A[a]	Portfolio B[b]
$ 70,000	0%	2%
$ 80,000	0%	5%
$ 90,000	4%	14%
$100,000	21%	27%
$110,000	57%	46%
$120,000	88%	66%
$130,000	99%	82%

[a] The expected return and standard deviation of A are 8% and 10%, respectively.

[b] The expected return and standard deviation of B are 12% and 20%, respectively. Initial wealth is assumed to be $100,000, and both portfolios are assumed to have normally distributed returns.

Figure 7.1 illustrates a "map" of indifference curves that a hypothetical investor might possess. Each curved line indicates one indifference curve for the investor and represents all combinations of portfolios that provide the investor with a given level of desirability. For example, the investor with the indifference curves in Figure 7.1 would find portfolios A and B (the same two portfolios that were shown in Table 7.1) equally desirable, even though they have different expected returns and standard deviations, because they both lie on the same indifference curve, I_2. Portfolio B has a higher standard deviation (20%) than portfolio A (10%) and is therefore less desirable on that dimension. However, exactly offsetting this loss in desirability is the gain in desirability provided by the

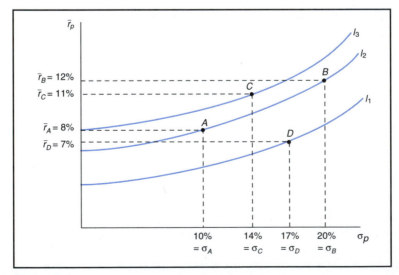

Figure 7.1
Map of Indifference Curves for a Risk-Averse Investor

higher expected return of B (12%) relative to A (8%). This example leads to the first important feature of indifference curves: *all portfolios that lie on a given indifference curve are equally desirable to the investor.*

An implication of this feature is that *indifference curves cannot intersect.* To see that this is so, consider two curves that do intersect, such as those that are shown in Figure 7.2. Here the point of intersection is represented by X. Remember that all the portfolios on I_1 are equally desirable. This means they are all as desirable as X, because X is on I_1. Similarly, all the portfolios on I_2 are equally desirable, and are as desirable as X, because X is also on I_2. Given that X is on both indifference curves, all the portfolios on I_1 must be as desirable as those on I_2. But this presents a contradiction, because I_1 and I_2 are two curves that are supposed to represent different levels of desirability. Thus, in order for there to be no contradiction, these curves cannot intersect.

Although the investor represented in Figure 7.1 would find portfolios A and B equally desirable, he or she would find portfolio C, with an expected return of 11% and a standard deviation of 14%, preferable to both of them. This is because portfolio C happens to be on an indifference curve, I_3, that is located to the "northwest" of I_2. Now C has a sufficiently larger expected return relative to A to more than offset its higher standard deviation and, on balance, make it more desirable than A. Equivalently, C has a sufficiently smaller standard deviation than B to more than offset its smaller expected return and, on balance, make it more desirable than B. This leads to the second important feature of indifference curves: *an investor will find any portfolio that is lying on an indifference curve that is "further northwest" to be more desirable than any portfolio lying on an indifference curve that is "not as far northwest."*

Lastly, it should be noted that *an investor has an infinite number of indifference curves.* This simply means that whenever there are two indifference curves that have been plotted on a graph, it is possible to plot a third indifference curve that lies between them. As can be seen in Figure 7.3, given indifference curves I_1 and I_2, it is possible to graph a third curve, I^*, lying between them. It also means that another indifference curve can be plotted above I_2 and yet another below I_1.

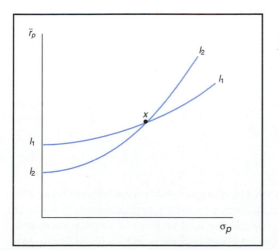

Figure 7.2
Intersecting Indifference Curves

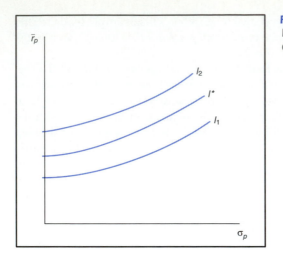

Figure 7.3
Plotting a Third Indifference Curve between Two Others

A good question to ask at this point is: How does an investor determine what his or her indifference curves look like? After all, each investor has a map of indifference curves that, while having the previously noted features, is nevertheless unique to that individual. One method, as will be shown in Chapter 24, involves presenting the investor with a set of hypothetical portfolios, along with their expected returns and standard deviations.[4] Then he or she would be asked to choose the most desirable one. Given the choice that is made, the shape and location of the investor's indifference curves can be estimated. This is because it is presumed that the investor would have acted as if he or she has indifference curves in making this choice, even though indifference curves would not have been explicitly used.

In summary, every investor has an indifference map representing his or her preferences for expected returns and standard deviations.[5] This means that the investor should determine the expected return and standard deviation for each potential portfolio, plot them on a graph such as Figure 7.1, and then select the one portfolio that lies on the indifference curve that is "furthest northwest." As shown in this example, from the set of the four potential portfolios—*A, B, C,* and *D*—the investor should select *C.*

7.3 NONSATIATION AND RISK AVERSION

7.3.1 Nonsatiation

Two assumptions are implicit in this discussion of indifference curves. First, it is assumed that investors, when given a choice between two otherwise identical portfolios, will always choose the one with the higher level of expected return. More fundamentally, an assumption of **nonsatiation** is made in utilizing the

Markowitz approach, meaning that investors are assumed to prefer higher levels of terminal wealth to lower levels of terminal wealth. This is because higher levels of terminal wealth allow the investor to spend more on consumption at $t = 1$ (or in the more distant future). Thus given two portfolios with the same standard deviation, such as A and E in Figure 7.4, the investor will choose the portfolio with the higher expected return. In this case, it is portfolio A.

However, it is not quite so obvious what the investor will do when having to choose between two portfolios having the same level of expected return but different levels of standard deviation, such as A and F. This is where the second assumption enters the discussion.

7.3.2 Risk Aversion

Generally it is assumed that investors are **risk-averse,** which means that the investor will choose the portfolio with the smaller standard deviation, A.[6] What does it mean to say that an investor is risk-averse? It means that the investor, when given the choice, will not want to take fair gambles, where a *fair gamble* is defined to be one that has an expected payoff of zero. For example, consider flipping a coin where "heads" means that you win $5 and "tails" means that you lose $5. Because the coin has a 50–50 chance of being "heads" or "tails," the expected payoff is $0 [$= (.5 \times \$5) + (.5 \times -\$5)$]. Accordingly, the risk-averse investor will choose to avoid this gamble. Intuitively, the reason is that the potential loss represents an amount of "displeasure" that is greater than the amount of "pleasure" associated with the potential gain.

The two assumptions of nonsatiation and risk aversion cause indifference curves to be positively sloped and convex.[7] Although it is assumed that all investors are risk-averse, it is not assumed that they have identical degrees of risk

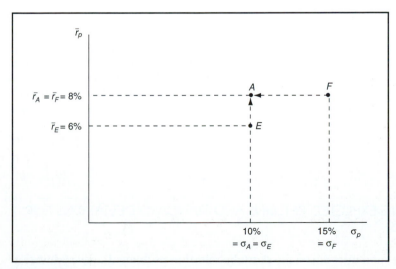

Figure 7.4
Nonsatiation, Risk Aversion, and Portfolio Choice

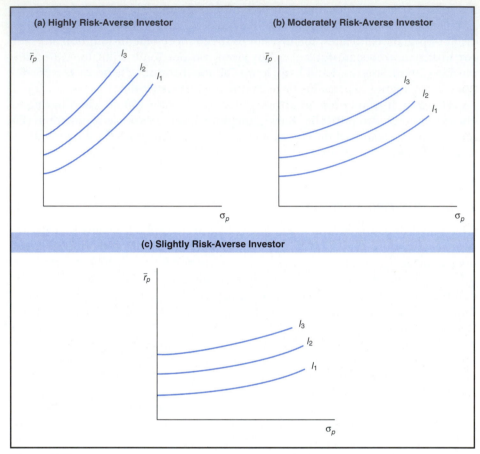

Figure 7.5
Indifference Curves for Different Types of Risk-Averse Investors

aversion. Some investors may be highly risk-averse, whereas others may be only slightly so. This means that different investors will have different maps of indifference curves. Panels (a), (b), and (c) of Figure 7.5 display maps for investors who are highly risk-averse, moderately risk-averse, and slightly risk-averse, respectively. As can be seen in these figures, a more risk-averse investor has more steeply sloped indifference curves.

7.4   CALCULATING EXPECTED RETURNS AND STANDARD DEVIATIONS FOR PORTFOLIOS

The previous section introduced the portfolio selection problem that every investor faces. It also introduced the investment approach of Harry Markowitz as a method of solving that problem. With this approach, an investor should evaluate alternative portfolios on the basis of their expected returns and standard deviations by using indifference curves. In the case of a risk-averse investor, the portfolio on the indifference curve that is "furthest northwest" would be the one selected for investment.

However, certain questions remain unanswered. In particular, how does the investor calculate the expected return and standard deviation for a portfolio?

7.4.1 Expected Returns

With the Markowitz approach to investing, the focus of the investor is on terminal (or end-of-period) wealth, W_1. That is, in deciding which portfolio to purchase with his or her initial (or beginning-of-period) wealth, W_0, the investor should focus on the effect that the various portfolios have on W_1. This effect can be measured by the expected return and standard deviation of each portfolio.

As mentioned previously, a portfolio is a collection of securities. Thus it seems logical that the expected return and standard deviation of a portfolio should depend on the expected return and standard deviation of each security contained in the portfolio. It also seems logical that the amount invested in each security should be important. Indeed, this is the case.

In order to show how the expected return on a portfolio depends on both the expected return on the individual securities and the amount invested in these securities, consider the three-security portfolio shown in Table 7.2(a). Assume that the investor has a one-year holding period, and that for this period he or she has estimated the expected returns on Able, Baker, and Charlie stock to be 16.2%, 24.6%, and 22.8%, respectively. This is equivalent to stating that the investor has estimated the end-of-period values of these three stocks to be, respectively, $46.48 [because ($46.48 − $40)/$40 = 16.2%], $43.61 [because ($43.61 − $35)/$35 = 24.6%], and $76.14 [because ($76.14 − $62)/$62 = 22.8%].[8] Furthermore, assume that this investor has initial wealth of $17,200.

Using End-of-Period Values

The expected return on this portfolio can be calculated in several ways, all of which give the same answer. Consider the method shown in Table 7.2(b). This method involves calculating the expected end-of-period value of the portfolio, and then using the formula for calculating the rate of return that was shown in Chapter 1. That is, first the initial portfolio value (W_0) is subtracted from the expected end-of-period value of the portfolio (W_1), and then this difference is divided by the initial portfolio value (W_0), the result of which is the portfolio's expected return. While the example shown in Table 7.2(b) involves three securities, the procedure can be generalized to any number of securities.

Using Security Expected Returns

An alternative method for calculating the expected return on this portfolio is shown in Table 7.2(c). This procedure involves calculating the expected return on a portfolio as the weighted average of the expected returns on its component securities. The relative market values of the securities in the portfolio are used as weights. In symbols, the general rule for calculating the expected return on a portfolio consisting of N securities is:

$$\bar{r}_P = \sum_{i=1}^{N} X_i \bar{r}_i \qquad (7.3a)$$

$$= X_1\bar{r}_1 + X_2\bar{r}_2 + \ldots + X_N\bar{r}_N \qquad (7.3b)$$

where:

$\bar{r}_p$ = the expected return of the portfolio,
X_i = the proportion of the portfolio's initial value invested in security i,
$\bar{r}_i$ = the expected return of security i, and
N = the number of securities in the portfolio.

TABLE 7.2

CALCULATING THE EXPECTED RETURN ON A PORTFOLIO

(a) Security and Portfolio Values

Security Name	Number of Shares in Portfolio	Initial Market Price Per Share	Total Investment	Proportion of Initial Market Value of Portfolio
Able Co.	100	$40	$4,000	$4,000/$17,200 = .2325
Baker Co.	200	35	7,000	7,000/ 17,200 = .4070
Charlie Co.	100	62	6,200	6,200/ 17,200 = .3605

Initial Market Value of Portfolio = W_0 = $17,200   Sum of Proportions = 1.0000

(b) Calculating the Expected Return for a Portfolio Using End-of-Period Values

Security Name	Number of Shares in Portfolio	Expected End-of-Period Value Per Share	Aggregate Expected End-of-Period Value
Able Co.	100	$46.48	$46.48 × 100 = $4,648
Baker Co.	200	43.61	$43.61 × 200 = 8,722
Charlie Co.	100	76.14	$76.14 × 100 = 7,614

Expected End-of-Period Value of Portfolio = $\overline{W}_1$ = $20,984
Portfolio Expected Return = $\bar{r}_p$ = ($20,984 − $17,200)/$17,200 = 22.00%

(c) Calculating the Expected Return for a Portfolio Using Security Expected Returns

Security Name	Proportion of Initial Market Value of Portfolio	Security Expected Returns	Contribution To Portfolio Expected Return
Able Co.	.2325	16.2%	.2325 × 16.2% = 3.77%
Baker Co.	.4070	24.6	.4070 × 24.6 = 10.01
Charlie Co.	.3605	22.8	.3605 × 22.8 = 8.22

Portfolio Expected Return = $\bar{r}_p$ = 22.00%

Thus, an **expected return vector** can be used to calculate the expected return for any portfolio formed from the N securities. This vector consists of one column of numbers, where the entry in row i contains the expected return of security i. In the previous example, the expected return vector was estimated by the investor to be:

$$
\begin{array}{ll}
\text{Row 1} \\
\text{Row 2} \\
\text{Row 3}
\end{array}
\begin{bmatrix}
16.2\% \\
24.6\% \\
22.8\%
\end{bmatrix}
$$

where the entries in rows 1, 2, and 3 denote the expected returns for securities 1, 2, and 3, respectively.

Because a portfolio's expected return is a weighted average of the expected returns of its securities, *the contribution of each security to the portfolio's expected return depends on its expected return and its proportionate share of the initial portfolio's market value.* Nothing else is relevant. It follows from Equation (7.3a) that an investor who simply wants the greatest possible expected return should hold one security: the one he or she considers to have the greatest expected return. Very few investors do this, and very few investment advisors would counsel such an extreme policy. Instead, investors should diversify, meaning that their portfolios should include more than one security. This is because diversification can reduce risk, as measured by standard deviation.

7.4.2 Standard Deviations

A useful measure of risk should somehow take into account both the probabilities of various possible "bad" outcomes and their associated magnitudes. Instead of measuring the probability of a number of different possible outcomes, the measure of risk should somehow estimate the extent to which the actual outcome is likely to diverge from the expected outcome. Standard deviation is a measure that does this, since it is an estimate of the likely divergence of an *actual* return from an *expected* return.

It may seem that any single measure of risk would provide at best a very crude summary of the "bad" possibilities. But in the more common situation where a portfolio's prospects are being assessed, standard deviation may prove to be a very good measure of the degree of uncertainty. The clearest example arises when the **probability distribution** for a portfolio's returns can be approximated by the familiar bell-shaped curve known as a **normal distribution.** This is often considered a plausible assumption for analyzing returns on diversified portfolios when the holding period being studied is relatively short (say, a quarter or less).

A question about standard deviation as a measure of risk is: Why count "happy" surprises (those above the expected return) at all in a measure of risk? Why not just consider the deviations *below* the expected return? Measures that do so have merit. However, the results will be the same if the probability distribution is symmetric, as is the normal distribution. Why? Because the left side of a symmetric distribution is a mirror image of the right side. Thus, a list of portfolios ordered on the basis of "downside risk" will not differ from one ordered on the basis of standard deviation if returns are normally distributed.[9]

Alternative Risk Measures

Virtually all investment textbooks (this one being no exception) define a portfolio's investment risk to be its volatility of returns, measured by the standard deviation (or, equivalently, the variance) of the portfolio's return distribution. This definition's pedagogical dominance reflects the practice of academics and to a lesser extent those investment professionals steeped in quantitative portfolio management techniques.

Yet ask the average person on the street to define investment risk, and he or she will invariably refer to the chances of something "bad" happening. To suggest to this person that risk also has some association with the possible occurrence of good outcomes will almost certainly draw a disbelieving look.

If, on the surface, the textbook definition of risk appears to have only an indirect relationship with an intuitive sense of risk, why has this "risk as standard deviation" definition so thoroughly dominated investment research? Further, why have alternative risk measures that directly address the likelihood of experiencing undesirable outcomes not been more widely considered and applied?

The straightforward answer to the first question is that standard deviation is computationally easier to work with than any alternative. Proofs and applications of various risk-return investment principles are typically simpler to derive using standard deviation as the measure of risk. For example, Harry Markowitz originally suggested a risk measure involving only negative outcomes when he developed his pioneering work on efficient sets (see Chapters 7–9). He rejected that approach in favor of standard deviation in order to simplify the calculations.

As our average person on the street intuitively understands, the biggest problem with standard deviation is that it "discriminates" against investments with volatility on the "upside." As the text describes, we assume that investors dislike risk. Therefore, if we define risk to incorporate both good and bad results, then our risk-reward evaluation of potential investments penalizes investments that might give us positive surprises just as we penalize those investments for the possibility of giving us negative surprises.

All of this concern is moot if investment returns are symmetrically distributed, particularly in the form of a normal distribution (or "bell-shaped" curve). In that case, the chances of a positive outcome a certain distance away from the center of the distribution are just as great as the chances of a negative outcome an equal distance in the opposite direction. The fact that results above the expected value are included with those below the expected value becomes irrelevant. The standard deviation accurately summarizes the "bad" part of an investment's return distribution.

However, what if investment returns are not normally distributed? For example, we have good reason to believe that common stock returns do not conform to this pattern. Consider that common stock investors face limited liability (see Chapter 17)—the most that they can lose is their original investment. Further, the potential upside gains on their investments are unlimited. Finally, most common stock returns are expected to fall near the market average. What we have just described is a "right-skewed" distribution rather than a normal distribution. Standard deviation insufficiently characterizes the risk of a right-skewed security, ignoring the fact that most of the security's volatility is on the "good" side of the security's expected return.

Interestingly, a simple mathematical transformation can often convert a right-skewed distribution to a normal distribution. If we add 1.0 to a security's return and then compute the natural logarithm of this value, the resulting transformed return distribution may appear to be normally distributed. Consequently, researchers are often concerned with whether security returns are "lognormally" distributed rather than normally distributed. Although the empirical evidence is open to debate, most observers consider lognormality to adequately characterize common stock returns.

Unfortunately, the returns on certain types of securities are neither normally nor lognormally distributed. The most obvious are options (see Chapter 20). For example, a call option allows the owner, for a price, to participate in positive returns on an underlying asset, but avoid the asset's negative returns.

Essentially, a call option truncates the underlying asset's return distribution at the point where losses begin. The investor then owns only the "good" or right side of the return distribution. The returns on a call option are definitely not normally distributed.

Moreover, some securities have options embedded in them. For example, callable bonds (see Chapter 14) allow issuers to redeem them at the issuers' discretion. They do so only if interest rates move in their favor. Home mortgages (which are often packaged and sold in pass-through securities—see Chapter 14) have similar prepayment features. Therefore, their returns are also not normally distributed.

If we wish to explicitly focus only on the likelihood of undesirable investment results in defining and measuring risk, what alternatives are available? The simplest answer is called *shortfall probability*. It measures the chances that a security's return will fall short of the expected return. Essentially, it is the proportion of the probability distribution lying to the left of the expected return.

More complex downside risk measures are provided by a family of statistics known as *lower partial moments,* or LPMs. For example, *mean shortfall* measures the average deviation of a security's returns below the expected return. Mean shortfall is more useful than shortfall probability because it takes into account the distance of each downside return from the expected return. That is, shortfall probability tells us only how likely it is that a security's return may fall below the expected return. Mean shortfall tells us how far below the expected return that shortfall is likely to be.

Semivariance is analogous to variance, but only those potential returns below the expected return are used in its calculation. As semivariance is the average squared deviation below the expected return, it penalizes securities with relatively large potential shortfalls.

Applied to securities with non-normal (and non-lognormal) return distributions, these downside risk measures are not only more intuitively appealing but are more flexible in their application than the traditional risk measures. Standard deviation is measured from the mean of the return distribution. However, an investor may want to evaluate investments using some other value as a target, such as the return on a market index or an absolute number such as 0%. Downside risk measures can accommodate these preferences.

However, downside risk measures have their own problems. In particular, they ignore the nature of an investment's possible outcomes above the target return. An alternative to using downside risk measures is to directly bring skewness into the evaluation of an investment. That is, we might assume that investors analyze potential investments not only on the basis of their expected returns and standard deviations, but also on their amount of right-skewness. In essence, risk becomes multidimensional; it includes both standard deviation and skewness. If two investments have the same expected return and standard deviation, the most right-skewed investment would be preferred.

No one risk measure can be expected to function well in all circumstances. Standard deviation has proved effective in the majority of the situations encountered by practitioners. In those cases where it is inadequate, alternatives must be considered not only in light of how well they describe the return distribution, but also in terms of the complexity that they add to the analysis.

Formula for Standard Deviation

Now just how is the standard deviation of a portfolio calculated? For the three-security portfolio consisting of Able, Baker, and Charlie, the formula is:

$$\sigma_P = \left[\sum_{i=1}^{3} \sum_{j=1}^{3} X_i X_j \sigma_{ij} \right]^{1/2} \tag{7.4}$$

where σ_{ij} denotes the **covariance** of the returns between security i and security j.

Covariance

What is covariance? It is a statistical measure of the relationship between two random variables. That is, it is a measure of how two random variables, such as the returns on securities i and j, "move together." A positive value for covariance indicates that the securities' returns tend to move in the same direction—for example, a better-than-expected return for one is likely to occur along with a better-than-expected return for the other. A negative covariance indicates a tendency for the returns to offset one another—for example, a better-than-expected return for one security is likely to occur along with a worse-than-expected return for the other. A relatively small or zero value for the covariance indicates that there is little or no relationship between the returns for the two securities.

Correlation

Closely related to covariance is the statistical measure known as correlation. In fact, the covariance between two random variables is equal to the correlation between the two random variables times the product of their standard deviations:

$$\sigma_{ij} = \rho_{ij}\sigma_i\sigma_j \qquad (7.5)$$

where ρ_{ij} (the Greek letter *rho*) denotes the **correlation coefficient** between the return on security i and the return on security j. The correlation coefficient rescales the covariance to facilitate comparison with corresponding values for other pairs of random variables.

Correlation coefficients always lie between -1 and $+1$. A value of -1 represents perfect negative correlation, and a value of $+1$ represents perfect positive correlation. Most cases lie between these two extreme values.

Figure 7.6(a) presents a scatter diagram for the returns on hypothetical securities A and B when the correlation between these two securities is perfectly positive. Note how all the points lie precisely on a straight upward-sloping line.

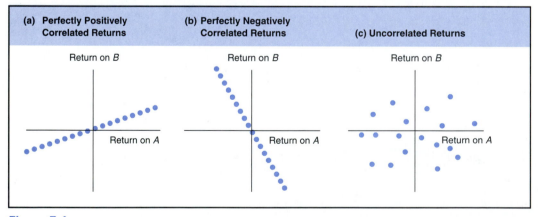

Figure 7.6
Returns on Two Securities

This means that when one of the two securities has a relatively high return, then so will the other. Similarly, when one of the two securities has a relatively low return, then so will the other.

Alternatively, the returns on the two securities will have a perfectly negative correlation when the scatter diagram indicates that the points lie precisely on a straight downward-sloping line, as shown in Figure 7.6(b). In such a case the returns on the two securities can be seen to move opposite each other. That is, when one security has a relatively high return, then the other will have a relatively low return.

A case of special importance arises when the scatter diagram of security returns shows a dispersion that cannot be represented even approximately by an upward-sloping or downward-sloping line. In such an instance, the returns are uncorrelated, meaning that the correlation coefficient is zero. Figure 7.6(c) provides an example. In this situation, when one security has a relatively high return, then the other can have either a relatively high, low, or average return.

Double Summation

Given an understanding of covariance and correlation, it is important to understand how the *double summation* indicated in Equation (7.4) is performed. Although there are many ways of performing double summation, all of which lead to the same answer, one way is perhaps more intuitive than the others. It starts with the first summation and sets i at its initial value of 1. Then the second summation is performed for j going from 1 to 3. At this point, i in the first summation is increased by 1, so that now $i = 2$. Again the second summation is performed by letting j go from 1 to 3, except that now $i = 2$. Continuing, i in the first summation is again increased by 1, so that $i = 3$. Then the second summation is once again performed by letting j go from 1 to 3. At this point, note that i and j are each at their upper limits of 3. This means that it is time to stop, as the double summation has been finished. This process can be shown algebraically as follows:

$$\sigma_P = \left[\sum_{j=1}^{3} X_1 X_j \sigma_{1j} + \sum_{j=1}^{3} X_2 X_j \sigma_{2j} + \sum_{j=1}^{3} X_3 X_j \sigma_{3j} \right]^{1/2} \tag{7.6a}$$

$$= [X_1 X_1 \sigma_{11} + X_1 X_2 \sigma_{12} + X_1 X_3 \sigma_{13}$$
$$+ X_2 X_1 \sigma_{21} + X_2 X_2 \sigma_{22} + X_2 X_3 \sigma_{23} \tag{7.6b}$$
$$+ X_3 X_1 \sigma_{31} + X_3 X_2 \sigma_{32} + X_3 X_3 \sigma_{33}]^{1/2}.$$

Each term in the double sum involves the product of the weights for two securities, X_i and X_j, and the covariance between these two securities. Note how there are nine terms to be added together in order to calculate the standard deviation of a portfolio consisting of three securities. It is no coincidence that the number of terms to be added together (9) equals the number of securities squared (3^2).

In general, calculating the standard deviation for a portfolio consisting of N securities involves performing the double sum indicated in Equation (7.4) over N securities, thereby involving the addition of N^2 terms:

$$\sigma_P = \left[\sum_{i=1}^{N} \sum_{j=1}^{N} X_i X_j \sigma_{ij} \right]^{1/2}. \tag{7.7}$$

An interesting feature of the double sum occurs when the subscripts i and j refer to the same security. In Equation (7.6), this occurs in the first $(X_1 X_1 \sigma_{11})$, fifth $(X_2 X_2 \sigma_{22})$, and ninth $(X_3 X_3 \sigma_{33})$ terms. What does it mean to have the subscripts for covariance refer to the same security? For example, consider security one (Able) so that $i = j = 1$. Since σ_{11} denotes the covariance of security one (Able) with security one (Able), Equation (7.5) indicates that:

$$\sigma_{11} = \rho_{11} \sigma_1 \sigma_1. \tag{7.8}$$

Now the correlation of any security with itself, in this case ρ_{11}, can be shown to be equal to $+1$.[10] This means that Equation (7.8) reduces to:

$$\begin{aligned} \sigma_{11} &= 1 \times \sigma_1 \times \sigma_1 \\ &= \sigma_1^2 \end{aligned}$$

which is just the standard deviation of security one squared, known as the variance of security one. Thus the double sum involves both variance and covariance terms.

Variance-Covariance Matrix

As an example, consider the following **variance-covariance matrix** for the stocks of Able, Baker, and Charlie:

	Column 1	Column 2	Column 3
Row 1	146	187	145
Row 2	187	854	104
Row 3	145	104	289

The entry in cell (i, j) denotes the covariance between security i and security j. For example, the entry in $(1,3)$ denotes the covariance between the first and third securities, which in this case is 145. Also, the entry in cell (i,i) denotes the variance of security i. For example, the variance of security 2 appears in cell $(2,2)$, and is equal to 854. Using this variance-covariance matrix along with the formula given in Equation (7.6b), the standard deviation of any portfolio that consists of investments in Able, Baker, and Charlie can now be calculated.

For example, consider the portfolio given in Table 7.2 that had proportions $X_1 = .2325$, $X_2 = .4070$, and $X_3 = .3605$:

$$\sigma_P = [X_1 X_1 \sigma_{11} + X_1 X_2 \sigma_{12} + X_1 X_3 \sigma_{13}$$
$$+ X_2 X_1 \sigma_{21} + X_2 X_2 \sigma_{22} + X_2 X_3 \sigma_{23}$$
$$+ X_3 X_1 \sigma_{31} + X_3 X_2 \sigma_{32} + X_3 X_3 \sigma_{33}]^{1/2}$$
$$= [(.2325 \times .2325 \times 146) + (.2325 \times .4070 \times 187)$$
$$+ (.2325 \times .3605 \times 145)$$
$$+ (.4070 \times .2325 \times 187) + (.4070 \times .4070 \times 854)$$
$$+ (.4070 \times .3605 \times 104)$$
$$+ (.3605 \times .2325 \times 145) + (.3605 \times .4070 \times 104)$$
$$+ (.3605 \times .3605 \times 289)]^{1/2}$$
$$= [277.13]^{1/2}$$
$$= 16.65\%.$$

Several interesting features about variance-covariance matrices deserve mention. First, such matrices are square, meaning that the number of columns equals the number of rows, and that the total number of cells for N securities equals N^2.

Second, the variances of the securities appear on the diagonal of the matrix, which are the cells that lie on a line going from the upper-left-hand corner to the lower-right-hand corner of the matrix. In the previous example, the variance of security 1 (146) appears in row one of column one. Similarly, the variances of securities 2 and 3 appear in row two of column two (854) and row three of column three (289), respectively.

Third, the matrix is symmetric, meaning that the number appearing in row i of column j also appears in row j of column i. That is, the elements in the cells above the diagonal also appear in the corresponding cells below the diagonal. In the previous example, note that the element in row one of column two, 187, also appears in row two of column one. Similarly, 145 appears in both row one of column three and row three of column one, and 104 appears in both row two of column three and row three of column two. The reason for this feature is quite simple—the covariance between two securities does not depend on the order in which the two securities are specified. This means that, for example, the covariance between the first and second securities is the same as the covariance between the second and first securities.[11]

7.5   SUMMARY

1. The Markowitz approach to portfolio selection assumes that investors seek both maximum expected return for a given level of risk and minimum uncertainty (risk) for a given level of expected return.
2. Expected return serves as the measure of potential reward associated with a portfolio. Standard deviation is viewed as the measure of a portfolio's risk.
3. An indifference curve represents the various combinations of risk and return that the investor finds equally desirable.
4. Investors are assumed to consider any portfolio lying on an indifference curve "further to the northwest" more desirable than any portfolio lying on an indifference curve that is "not as far northwest."

5. The assumptions of investor nonsatiation and risk aversion cause indifference curves to be positively sloped and convex.

6. The expected return on a portfolio is a weighted average of the expected returns of its component securities, with the relative portfolio proportions of the component securities serving as weights.

7. Covariance and correlation measure the extent to which two random variables "move together."

8. The standard deviation of a portfolio depends on the standard deviations and proportions of the component securities as well as their covariances with one another.

QUESTIONS AND PROBLEMS

1. Listed below are a number of portfolios and expected returns, standard deviations, and the amount of satisfaction (measured in utils) these portfolios provide Arky Vaughn. Given this information, graph Arky's identifiable indifference curves.

Portfolio	Expected Return	Standard Deviation	Utility
1	5%	0%	10 utils
2	6	10	10
3	9	20	10
4	14	30	10
5	10	0	20
6	11	10	20
7	14	20	20
8	19	30	20
9	15	0	30
10	16	10	30
11	19	20	30
12	24	30	30

2. Why are the indifference curves of typical investors assumed to slope upward to the right?

3. What does a set of convex indifference curves imply about an investor's trade-off between risk and return as the amount of risk varies?

4. Why are typical investors assumed to prefer portfolios on indifference curves lying to the "northwest"?

5. What is meant by the statement that "risk-averse investors exhibit diminishing marginal utility of income"? Why does diminishing marginal utility cause an investor to refuse to accept a "fair bet"?

6. Explain why an investor's indifference curves cannot intersect.

7. Why are the indifference curves of more risk-averse investors more steeply sloped than those of investors with less risk aversion?

8. Consider the following two sets of indifference curves for investors Hack Wilson and Kiki Cuyler. Determine whether Hack or Kiki:

a. Is more risk-averse,
b. Prefers investment A to investment B,
c. Prefers investment C to investment D.
Explain the reasons for your answers.

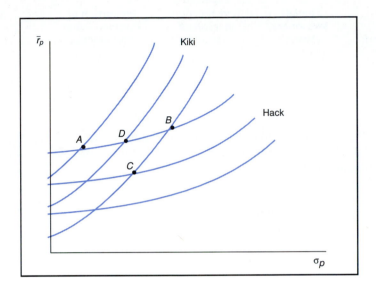

9. Consider four stocks with the following expected returns and standard deviations.

Stock	Expected Return	Standard Deviation
A	15%	12%
B	13	8
C	14	7
D	16	11

Are any of these stocks preferred over another by a risk-averse investor?
10. Do you agree with the assumptions of nonsatiation and risk aversion? Make a case for or against these assumptions.
11. At the beginning of the year, Corns Bradley owned four securities in the following amounts and with the following current and expected end-of-year prices:

Security	Share Amount	Current Price	Expected Year-End Price
A	100	$50	$60
B	200	35	40
C	50	25	50
D	100	100	110

What is the expected return on Corns's portfolio for the year?

12. Given the following information about four stocks comprising a portfolio, calculate each stock's expected return. Then, using these individual security's expected returns, calculate the portfolio's expected return.

Stock	Initial Investment Value	Expected End-of-Period Investment Value	Proportion of Portfolio Initial Market Value
A	$ 500	$ 700	19.2%
B	200	300	7.7
C	1,000	1,000	38.5
D	900	1,500	34.6

13. Squeaky Bluege has been considering an investment in Oakdale Merchandising. Squeaky has estimated the following probability distribution of returns for Oakdale stock:

Return	Probability
− 10%	.10
0	.25
10	.40
20	.20
30	.05

Based on Squeaky's estimates, calculate the expected return and standard deviation of Oakdale stock.

14. The expected returns and standard deviations of stocks A and B are:

Stock	Expected Return	Standard Deviation
A	13%	10%
B	5	18

Mox McQuery buys $20,000 of stock A and sells short $10,000 of stock B, using *all* of the proceeds to buy more of stock A. The correlation between the two securities is .25. What are the expected return and standard deviation of Mox's portfolio?

15. Both the covariance and the correlation coefficient measure the extent to which the returns on securities move together. What is the relationship between the two statistical measures? Why is the correlation coefficient a more convenient measure?

16. Give an example of two common stocks that you would expect to exhibit a relatively low correlation. Then give an example of two that would have a relatively high correlation.

17. Gibby Brock has estimated the following joint probability distribution of returns for investments in the stock of Lakeland Halfway Homes and Afton Brewery:

Lakeland	Afton	Probability
−10%	15%	.15
5	10	.20
10	5	.30
20	0	.35

Based on Gibby's estimates, calculate the covariance and correlation coefficient between two investments.

18. Calculate the correlation matrix that corresponds to the variance-covariance matrix given in the text for Able, Baker, and Charlie.

19. Given the following variance-covariance matrix for three securities, as well as the percentage of the portfolio that each security comprises, calculate the portfolio's standard deviation.

	Security A	Security B	Security C
Security A	459	−211	112
Security B	−211	312	215
Security C	112	215	179
	$X_A = .50$	$X_B = .30$	$X_C = .20$

20. Rube Bressler owns three stocks and has estimated the following joint probability distribution of returns:

Outcome	Stock A	Stock B	Stock C	Probability
1	−10	10	0	.30
2	0	10	10	.20
3	10	5	15	.30
4	20	−10	5	.20

Calculate the portfolio's expected return and standard deviation if Rube invests 20% in stock A, 50% in stock B, and 30% in stock C. Assume that each security's return is completely uncorrelated with the returns of the other securities.

21. If a portfolio's expected return is equal to the weighted average of the expected returns of the component securities, why is a portfolio's risk not generally equal to the weighted average of the component securities' standard deviations?

22. When is the standard deviation of a portfolio equal to the weighted average of the standard deviation of the component securities? Show this mathematically for a two-security portfolio. (Hint: Some algebra is necessary to solve this problem. Remember that $\sigma_{ij} = \rho_{ij}\sigma_i\sigma_j$. Try different values of ρ_{ij}.)

23. Consider two securities, A and B, with expected returns of 15% and 20%, respectively, and standard deviations of 30% and 40%, respectively. Calculate the standard deviation of a portfolio weighted equally between the two securities if their correlation is:
    a. 0.9
    b. 0.0
    c. −0.9

---

24. Listed here are estimates of the standard deviations and correlation coefficients for three stocks.

Stock	Standard Deviation	Correlation with Stock:		
		A	B	C
A	12%	1.00	−1.00	0.20
B	15	−1.00	1.00	−0.20
C	10	0.20	−0.20	1.00

a. If a portfolio is composed of 20% of stock A and 80% of stock C, what is the portfolio's standard deviation?

b. If a portfolio is composed of 40% of stock A, 20% of stock B, and 40% of stock C, what is the portfolio's standard deviation?

c. If you were asked to design a portfolio using stocks A and B, what percentage investment in each stock would produce a zero standard deviation? [Hint: Some algebra is necessary to solve this problem. Remember that $X_B = (1 - X_A)$.]

APPENDIX

RISK-NEUTRAL AND RISK-SEEKING INVESTORS

Earlier, it was mentioned that the Markowitz approach assumes that investors are risk-averse. Although this is a reasonable assumption to make, it is not necessary to do so. Alternatively, it can be assumed that investors are either risk-neutral or risk-seeking.

Consider the risk-seeking investor first. This investor, when faced with a fair gamble, will want to take the gamble. Furthermore, larger gambles are more desirable than smaller gambles. This is because the "pleasure" derived from winning is greater than the "displeasure" derived from losing. Because there is an equal chance of winning and losing, on balance the risk-seeking investor will want to take the gamble. What this means is that when faced with two portfolios that have the same expected return, this type of investor will choose the one with the higher standard deviation.

For example, in choosing between A and F in Figure 7.4, the risk-seeking investor will choose F. This suggests that the risk-seeking investor will have negatively sloped indifference curves.[12] In addition, risk-seeking investors will prefer to be on the indifference curve that is "furthest northeast". Figure 7.7 illustrates

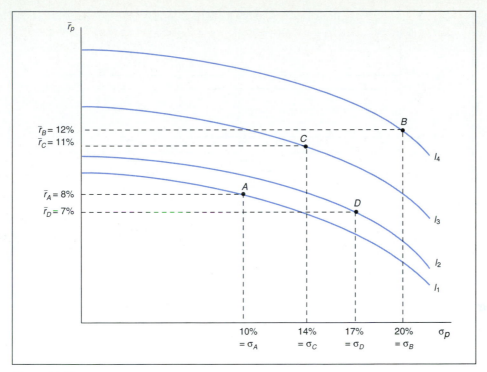

Figure 7.7
Map of Indifference Curves for a Risk-Seeking Investor

a map of the indifference curves for a hypothetical risk-seeking investor. As shown in the figure, when choosing between A, B, C, and D (the same four portfolios shown in Figure 7.1), this investor will choose B.

The risk-neutral case lies between the risk-seeking and risk-averse cases. While the risk-averse investor does not want to take fair gambles and the risk-seeking investor does want to take such gambles, the risk-neutral investor does not care whether or not the gamble is taken. This means that risk, or more specifically, standard deviation, is unimportant to the risk-neutral investor in evaluating portfolios. Accordingly, the indifference curves for such investors are horizontal lines as shown in Figure 7.8. These investors prefer to be on the indifference curve that is "furthest north." When faced with the choice of A, B, C, and D, such an investor will choose B, because it has the highest expected return.

Whereas investors can be either risk-seeking or risk-neutral, there is evidence to suggest that they are more accurately characterized as being, in general, risk-averse. One piece of evidence is the observation that equities have historically had higher average returns than bonds, suggesting that investors have had to be induced with higher rewards in order to get them to make riskier purchases.

The Portfolio Selection Problem

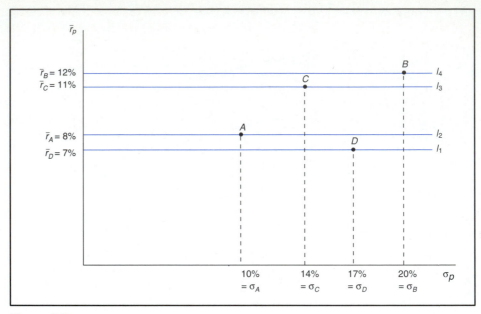

Figure 7.8
Map of Indifference Curves for a Risk-Neutral Investor

[1] Markowitz recognized that investing was generally a multiperiod activity, where at the end of each period, part of the investor's wealth was consumed and part was reinvested. Nevertheless, his one-period approach is optimal under a variety of reasonable circumstances. See Edwin J. Elton and Martin J. Gruber, *Finance as a Dynamic Process* (Englewood Cliffs, NJ: Prentice Hall, 1975), particularly Chapter 5.

[2] One portfolio that would not have an uncertain rate of return would involve the investor's putting all of his or her initial wealth in a pure discount government security that matures at $t = 1$. However, for almost all other portfolios the rate of return would be uncertain. See Chapter 4 for a discussion of this riskless security.

[3] A random variable's expected value is, in a sense, its "average" value. Thus the expected value for the return of a portfolio can be thought of as its expected or average return. The standard deviation of a random variable is a measure of the dispersion (or "spread") of possible values the random variable can take on. Accordingly, the standard deviation of a portfolio is a measure of the dispersion of possible returns that could be earned on the portfolio. Sometimes **variance** is used as a measure of the dispersion instead of standard deviation. However, because the variance of a random variable is simply the squared value of the standard deviation of the random variable, this distinction is not of importance here. These concepts will be discussed in more detail later on.

[4] For an alternative procedure, see Ralph O. Swalm, "Utility Theory: Insights into Risk Taking," *Harvard Business Review,* 44, no. 6 (November–December 1966): 123–136. Also see Endnote 5.

[5] At some point the reader may wonder why an investor's preferences are based only on expected returns and standard deviations. For example, it may seem logical that the investor's preferences should be based on expected returns, standard deviations, and the probability that a portfolio will lose money. The assertion that an investor's preferences are not based on anything other than expected returns and standard deviations follows from some specific assumptions coupled with *utility theory.* See Gordon J. Alexander and Jack Clark Francis, *Portfolio Analysis* (Englewood Cliffs, NJ: Prentice Hall, 1986), particularly Chapters 2 and 3, for more details. It should be noted that there is some dispute about the validity of using utility theory to describe people's behavior. Those holding the opposing viewpoints are typically economists and psychologists, and they are often referred to as rationalists and behaviorists, respectively. For a discussion of their views, see the entire second part of the October 1986 issue of the *Journal of Business* and the Institutional Issues section in Chapter 6 of this book.

[6] Investors who are **risk-seeking** would choose *F,* whereas investors who are **risk-neutral** would find *A* and *F* to be equally desirable. The appendix to this chapter discusses both risk-neutral and risk-seeking investors.

[7] Convexity of indifference curves means that their slopes increase when moving from left to right along any particular one. That is, they "bend upward." The underlying rationale for convexity lies in utility theory; see Endnote 5.

[8] The figures given for the expected end-of-period values include both the expected prices and the expected dividends for the period. For example, Able has an expected end-of-period value of $46.48, which could consist of a hypothetical expected cash dividend of $2 and share price of $44.48. These expected returns and values are estimated by use of security analysis, which will be discussed in Chapter 18.

[9] If returns are not normally distributed, the use of standard deviation can still be justified in an approximate sense, provided that there are small probabilities of extremely high and low returns. See H. Levy and H. M. Markowitz, "Approximating Expected Utility by a Function of Mean and Variance," *American Economic Review,* 69, no. 3 (June 1979): 308–317; and Yoram Kroll, Haim Levy, and Harry M. Markowitz, "Mean-Variance versus Direct Utility Maximization," *Journal of Finance,* 39, no. 1 (March 1984): 47–61. Some researchers have argued that the best model for a stock's returns is a mixture of normal distributions; for a discussion and references, see Richard Roll, "R^2," *Journal of Finance,* 43, no. 3 (July 1988): 541–566, particularly Footnote 11 on p. 561.

[10] Remember that correlation refers to how two random variables move together. If the two random variables are the same, then they must move exactly together with each other. This can be visualized by graphing the values of the same random variable on both the X-axis and the Y-axis. In such a graph, all points would lie on a straight 45-degree line passing through the origin, thereby implying a correlation of $+1$.

[11] For any variance-covariance matrix there is an implied correlation matrix that can be determined by using the data in the variance-covariance matrix and Equation (7.5). Specifically, this equation can be used to show that the correlation between any two securities i and j is equal to $\sigma_{ij}/\sigma_i\sigma_j$. The values for σ_{ij}, σ_i, and σ_j can be obtained from the variance-covariance matrix. For example, $\rho_{12} = 187/(\sqrt{146} \times \sqrt{854}) = .53$.

[12] It can also be shown that for a risk-seeking investor, these indifference curves will be concave, meaning that their slopes decrease when moving from left to right along any particular one. The underlying rationale for concavity lies in utility theory; see Endnotes 5 and 7.

holding period	nonsatiation
expected returns	risk-averse investor
risk	risk-seeking investor
initial wealth	risk-neutral investor
terminal wealth	expected return vector
random variable	probability distribution
expected value	normal distribution
standard deviation	covariance
variance	correlation coefficient
indifference curves	variance-covariance matrix

REFERENCES

1. The seminal work developing the mean-variance model is credited to Harry Markowitz, co-winner of the 1990 Nobel prize in economics, who developed his ideas in a paper and later in a book:

   Harry M. Markowitz, "Portfolio Selection," *Journal of Finance*, 7, no. 1 (March 1952): 77–91.

   Harry M. Markowitz, *Portfolio Selection: Efficient Diversification of Investments* (New York: John Wiley, 1959). (A reprint of this book that also contains some new material is available from Basil Blackwell, in Cambridge, MA; its copyright date is 1991.)

2. While utility theory can be traced back to the work of Daniel Bernoulli in the early part of the 18th century, the modern notion of utility theory was developed in:

   John von Neumann and Oskar Morgenstern, *Theory of Games and Economic Behavior* (New York: John Wiley, 1944).

   Kenneth J. Arrow, *Essays in the Theory of Risk-Bearing* (Chicago: Markham, 1971).

3. Significant other work in utility theory is reviewed in:

   Paul J. H. Schoemaker, "The Expected Utility Model: Its Variants, Purposes, Evidence and Limitations," *Journal of Economic Literature*, 20, no. 2 (June 1982): 529–563.

4. For an introduction to uncertainty and utility theory, see:

   Mark P. Kritzman, " . . . About Uncertainty," *Financial Analysts Journal*, 47, no. 2 (March/April 1991): 17–21.

   Mark Kritzman, " . . . About Utility," *Financial Analysts Journal*, 48, no. 3 (May/June 1992): 17–20.

Portfolio Analysis

The previous chapter introduced the portfolio selection problem that every investor faces. It also introduced the investment approach of Harry Markowitz as a method of solving that problem. With this approach, an investor should evaluate alternative portfolios on the basis of their expected returns and standard deviations by using indifference curves. In the case of a risk-averse investor, the portfolio with the indifference curve that is "furthest northwest" would be the one selected for investment.

However, the previous chapter left certain questions unanswered. In particular, how can Markowitz's approach be used once it is recognized that there are an infinite number of portfolios available for investment? What happens when the investor considers investing in a set of securities, one of which is riskless? What happens if the investor is allowed to buy securities on margin? This chapter and the next one will provide the answers to these questions, beginning with the first one.

As mentioned earlier, an infinite number of portfolios can be formed from a set of N securities. Consider the situation with Able, Baker, and Charlie companies where N is equal to 3. The investor could purchase just shares of Able, or just shares of Baker. Alternatively, the investor could purchase a combination of shares of Able and Baker. For example, the investor could put 50% of his or her money in each company, or 25% in one company and 75% in the other, or 33% in one and 67% in the other, or any percent (between 0% and 100%) in one company with the rest going into the other company. Without even considering investing in Charlie, there are already an infinite number of possible portfolios that could be purchased.[1]

Does the investor need to evaluate all these portfolios? Fortunately, the answer to this question is "no." The key to why the investor needs to look at only a subset of the available portfolios lies in the **efficient set theorem,** which states that:

> *An investor will choose his or her optimal portfolio from the set of portfolios that*
>
> 1. *Offer maximum expected return for varying levels of risk, and*
> 2. *Offer minimum risk for varying levels of expected return.*

The set of portfolios meeting these two conditions is known as the **efficient set** or efficient frontier.

8.1.1 The Feasible Set

Figure 8.1 provides an illustration of the location of the **feasible set,** also known as the opportunity set, from which the efficient set can be identified. The feasible set simply represents all portfolios that could be formed from a group of N securities. That is, all possible portfolios that could be formed from the N securities lie either on or within the boundary of the feasible set (the points denoted G, E, S, and H in the figure are examples of such portfolios). In general, this set will have an umbrella-type shape similar to the one shown in the figure. Depending on the particular securities involved, it may be more to the right or left, or higher or lower, or fatter or skinnier than indicated here. The point is that its shape will, except in perverse circumstances, look similar to what appears here.

8.1.2 The Efficient Set Theorem Applied to the Feasible Set

The efficient set can now be located by applying the efficient set theorem to this feasible set. First, the set of portfolios that meet the first condition of the efficient set theorem must be identified. Looking at Figure 8.1, there is no portfolio

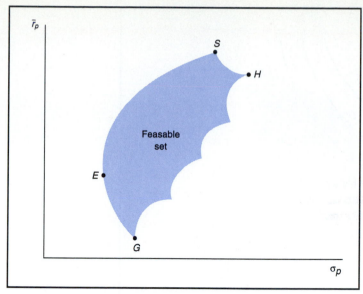

Figure 8.1
Feasible and Efficient Sets

offering less risk than that of portfolio *E*. This is because if a vertical line were drawn through *E*, there would be no point in the feasible set that was to the left of the line. Also, there is no portfolio offering more risk than that of portfolio *H*. This is because if a vertical line were drawn through *H*, there would be no point in the feasible set to the right of the line. Thus the set of portfolios offering maximum expected return for varying levels of risk is the set of portfolios lying on the "northern" boundary of the feasible set between points *E* and *H*.

Considering the second condition next, there is no portfolio offering an expected return greater than portfolio *S*, because no point in the feasible set lies above a horizontal line going through *S*. Similarly, there is no portfolio offering a lower expected return than portfolio *G*, because no point in the feasible set lies below a horizontal line going through *G*. Thus the set of portfolios offering minimum risk for varying levels of expected return is the set of portfolios lying on the "western" boundary of the feasible set between points *G* and *S*.

Remembering that both conditions have to be met in order to identify the efficient set, it can be seen that only those portfolios lying on the "northwest" boundary between points *E* and *S* do so. Accordingly, these portfolios form the efficient set, and it is from this set of **efficient portfolios** that the investor will find his or her optimal one.[2] All the other feasible portfolios are **inefficient portfolios** and can be safely ignored.

8.1.3 Selection of the Optimal Portfolio

How will the investor select an **optimal portfolio?** As shown in Figure 8.2, the investor should plot his or her indifference curves on the same figure as the efficient set and then proceed to choose the portfolio that is on the indifference

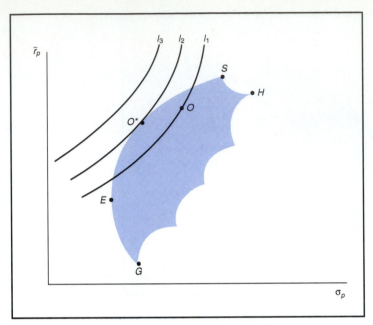

Figure 8.2
Selecting an Optimal Portfolio

curve that is "furthest northwest." This portfolio will correspond to the point where an indifference curve is just tangent to the efficient set. As can be seen in the figure, this is portfolio O^* on indifference curve I_2. Although the investor would prefer a portfolio on I_3, no such feasible portfolio exists; wanting to be on this indifference curve is just wishful thinking. In regard to I_1, there are several portfolios that the investor could choose (for example, O). However, the figure shows that portfolio O^* dominates such portfolios, because it is on an indifference curve that is "further northwest." Figure 8.3 shows how the highly risk-averse investor will choose a portfolio close to E. Figure 8.4 shows that the investor who is only slightly risk-averse will choose a portfolio close to S.[3]

Upon reflection, the efficient set theorem is quite rational. In Chapter 7, it was shown that the investor should select the portfolio that put him or her on the indifference curve "furthest northwest." The efficient set theorem, stating that the investor need not be concerned with portfolios that do not lie on the "northwest" boundary of the feasible set, is a logical consequence.

Indifference curves for the risk-averse investor were shown to be positively sloped and convex in Chapter 7. Now it will be shown that the efficient set is generally positively sloped and concave, meaning that if a straight line is drawn between any two points on the efficient set, the straight line will lie below the efficient set. This feature of the efficient set is important because it means that there will be only one tangency point between the investor's indifference curves and the efficient set.

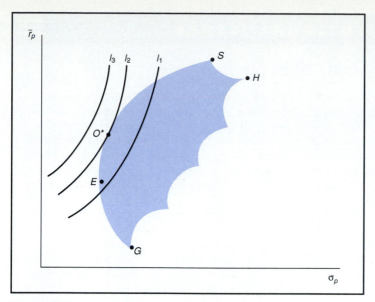

Figure 8.3
Portfolio Selection for a Highly Risk-Averse Investor

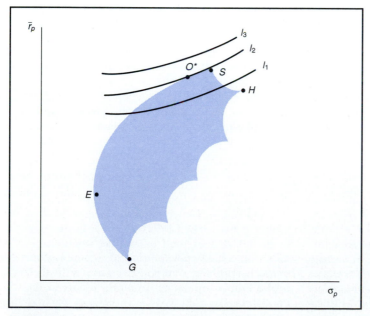

Figure 8.4
Portfolio Selection for a Slightly Risk-Averse Investor

The Trouble With Optimizers

Suppose that the captain of a modern luxury liner chose not to use the ship's state-of-the-art navigational system (a system that employs computers to triangulate off geostationary-orbiting satellites, thereby estimating the ship's position accurately to within a few feet). Instead, suppose that the captain chose to rely on the old-fashioned method of navigating by the stars, an antiquated method fraught with problems and imprecision. Most people would view the captain's choice as, at best, eccentric and, at worse, highly dangerous.

When it comes to constructing portfolios, many investment managers make a choice analogous to that of the ship's captain. They reject computer-based portfolio construction methods in favor of traditional approaches. Are their decisions as foolhardy as the captain's? Or is there a method to their apparent madness?

As this chapter discusses, the concepts of the efficient set and the investor's optimal portfolio are central to modern investment theory. But how can investors actually go about estimating the efficient set and selecting their optimal portfolios? Harry Markowitz first described the solution in the early 1950s. Using a mathematical technique called *quadratic programming*, investors can process expected returns, standard deviations, and covariances to calculate the efficient set. (See Appendix A to this chapter.) Given an estimate of their indifference curves (as reflected in their individual risk tolerances—see Chapter 24), they can then select a portfolio from the efficient set.

Simple, right? Certainly not in the 1950s. Given the data processing facilities available to investors at that time, calculating the efficient set for even a few hundred securities was essentially impossible. However, with the advent of low-cost, high-speed computers in the 1980s and the development of sophisticated risk models (see Chapter 11), an efficient set can be created for thousands of securities in a matter of minutes. The necessary computer hardware and software are available to virtually every institutional investor at a relatively low cost. In fact, the process has become so commonplace that it has acquired its own terminology. Using a computer to identify the efficient set and select an optimal portfolio is colloquially known as using an "optimizer." Portfolios are "optimized" and investors are said to apply "optimization techniques."

Despite the technology's widespread availability, relatively few investment managers actually use an optimizer to build portfolios. Instead, they rely for the most part on a series of qualitative rules and judgments.

Why do investment managers resist applying optimization techniques to portfolio building? Ignorance is not the answer. Most investment managers are well aware of Markowitz's portfolio selection concepts and the available technology, having graduated from business schools where these ideas are discussed in detail. Instead, the resistance derives from two sources: territorial concerns and implementation inadequacies.

From a territorial perspective, many investment managers are simply not comfortable with a quantitative approach to investing. Their decision-making emphasizes intuition and complex subjective judgments. The application of optimization techniques to portfolio construction imposes a very systematic and formal decision-making structure. Security analysts must become responsible for generating quantifiable expected return and risk forecasts. Portfolio managers must implement the decisions of a computer. As a result, the optimizer destroys the "artistry and grace" of investment management.

Further, with the introduction of an optimizer, a new breed of investment professional gains influence—the quantitative analyst (derisively called a "quant")—who coordinates the collection and application of risk and return estimates. Authority gained by quantitative analysts diminishes the influence of the traditional security analysts and portfolio managers, much to their consternation.

From the implementation perspective, serious problems have arisen with optimizers in practice. In particular, they tend to produce counterintuitive, uninvestable portfolios. This situation is not so much a problem with optimizers as it is the fault of the human operators supplying inputs to the optimizers. Here the GIGO (garbage in, garbage out) paradigm rules.

By their design, optimizers are attracted to securities with high expected returns, low standard deviations, and low covariances with other securities. Often this information is derived from historical databases covering thousands of securities. Unless the risk and return data are carefully checked, errors (for example, understating a security's standard deviation) can easily lead the optimizer to recommend purchases of securities for erroneous reasons. Even if the data are "clean," extreme historical values for some securities may lead the optimizer astray.

Unless programmed to take transaction costs into account, optimizers also display a nasty habit of generating high turnover and recommending investments in illiquid securities. *High turnover* refers to significant changes in portfolio composition from one period to the next. High turnover can result in unacceptably large transaction costs (see Chapter 3), thereby hindering portfolio performance. *Liquidity* refers to the ability to actually buy the securities selected by the optimizer. Selected securities may possess desirable risk-return characteristics but may not trade in sufficient volume to permit institutional investors to purchase them without incurring sizable transaction costs.

Solutions to these implementation problems do exist, ranging from careful data checking to placing constraints on maximum turnover or minimum liquidity. In the end, however, nothing can substitute for skillful judgmental forecasts of security returns and risks, balanced by properly applied notions of market equilibrium.

Territorial and implementation problems have given investment managers convenient reasons to avoid optimizers and stick to traditional portfolio construction methods. Nevertheless, the outlook for quantitative portfolio construction techniques is actually quite bright. The increasing efficiency of capital markets has forced institutional investment managers to process more information about more securities more rapidly than ever before. In response, they have generally increased their use of quantitative investment tools. While most do not directly integrate optimizers into their portfolio construction procedures, virtually all have become more sensitive to the objective of creating diversified portfolios that display the highest levels of expected return at acceptable levels of risk.

8.2 CONCAVITY OF THE EFFICIENT SET

In order to see why the efficient set is concave, consider the following two-security example. Security 1, the Ark Shipping Company, has an expected return of 5% and standard deviation of 20%. Security 2, the Gold Jewelry Company, has an expected return of 15% and standard deviation of 40%. Their respective locations are indicated by the letters A and G in Figure 8.5.

8.2.1 Bounds on the Location of Portfolios

Now consider all possible portfolios that an investor could purchase by combining these two securities. Let X_1 denote the proportion of the investor's funds invested in Ark Shipping and X_2 ($= 1 - X_1$) the proportion invested in Gold Jewelry. Thus, if the investor purchased just Ark Shipping, then $X_1 = 1$ and $X_2 = 0$. Alternatively, if the investor purchased just Gold Jewelry, then $X_1 = 0$ and $X_2 = 1$. A combination of .17 in Ark Shipping and .83 in Gold Jewelry is also possible, as are

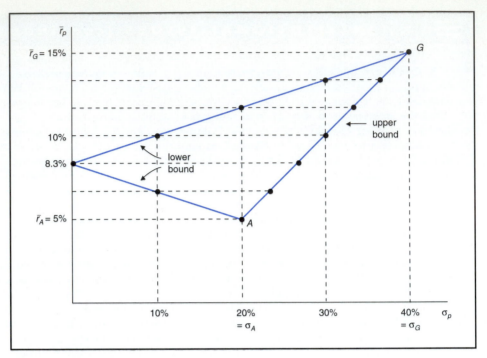

Figure 8.5
Upper and Lower Bounds to Combinations of Securities A and G

the respective combinations of .33 and .67, and .50 and .50. While there are many other possibilities, only the following seven portfolios will be considered:

	Portfolio A	Portfolio B	Portfolio C	Portfolio D	Portfolio E	Portfolio F	Portfolio G
X_1	1.00	.83	.67	.50	.33	.17	.00
X_2	.00	.17	.33	.50	.67	.83	1.00

In order to consider these seven portfolios for possible investment, their expected returns and standard deviations must be calculated. All the necessary information to calculate the expected returns for these portfolios is at hand, because all that is needed in order to utilize Equation (7.3a) has been provided:

$$\bar{r}_p = \sum_{i=1}^{N} X_i \bar{r}_i$$

$$= \sum_{i=1}^{2} X_i \bar{r}_i \tag{7.3a}$$

$$= X_i \bar{r}_1 + X_2 \bar{r}_2$$

$$= (X_1 \times 5\%) + (X_2 \times 15\%).$$

For portfolios A and G, this calculation is trivial, because the investor is purchasing shares of just one company. Thus their expected returns are 5% and 15%, respectively. For portfolios B, C, D, E, and F, the expected returns are, respectively:

$$\overline{r}_B = (.83 \times 5\%) + (.17 \times 15\%)$$
$$= 6.70\%$$
$$\overline{r}_C = (.67 \times 5\%) + (.33 \times 15\%)$$
$$= 8.30\%$$
$$\overline{r}_D = (.50 \times 5\%) + (.50 \times 15\%)$$
$$= 10\%$$
$$\overline{r}_E = (.33 \times 5\%) + (.67 \times 15\%)$$
$$= 11.70\%$$
$$\overline{r}_F = (.17 \times 5\%) + (.83 \times 15\%)$$
$$= 13.30\%.$$

In calculating the standard deviation of these seven portfolios, Equation (7.7) must be utilized:

$$\sigma_p = \left[\sum_{i=1}^{N} \sum_{j=1}^{N} X_i X_j \sigma_{ij} \right]^{1/2}$$
$$= \left[\sum_{i=1}^{2} \sum_{j=1}^{2} X_i X_j \sigma_{ij} \right]^{1/2} \tag{7.7}$$
$$= [X_1 X_1 \sigma_{11} + X_1 X_2 \sigma_{12} + X_2 X_1 \sigma_{21} + X_2 X_2 \sigma_{22}]^{1/2}$$
$$= [X_1^2 \sigma_1^2 + X_2^2 \sigma_2^2 + 2 X_1 X_2 \sigma_{12}]^{1/2}$$
$$= [(X_1^2 \times 20\%^2) + (X_2^2 \times 40\%^2) + 2 X_1 X_2 \sigma_{12}]^{1/2}.$$

Again, for portfolios A and G, this calculation is trivial, because the investor is purchasing shares of just one company. Thus their standard deviations are 20% and 40%, respectively.

For portfolios B, C, D, E, and F, application of Equation (7.7) indicates that the standard deviations depend on the magnitude of the covariance between the two securities. As shown in Equation (7.5), this covariance term is equal to the correlation between the two securities multiplied by the product of their standard deviations:

$$\sigma_{ij} = \rho_{ij} \times \sigma_i \times \sigma_j \tag{7.5}$$

so letting $i = 1$ and $j = 2$,

$$\sigma_{12} = \rho_{12} \times \sigma_1 \times \sigma_2$$
$$= \rho_{12} \times 20\% \times 40\%$$
$$= 800 \rho_{12}.$$

This means that the standard deviation of any portfolio consisting of Ark Shipping and Gold Jewelry can be expressed as:

$$\sigma_p = [(X_1^2 \times 20\%^2) + (X_2^2 \times 40\%^2) + (2 X_1 X_2 \times 800 \rho_{12})]^{1/2} \tag{8.1}$$
$$= [400 X_1^2 + 1{,}600 X_2^2 + 1{,}600 X_1 X_2 \rho_{12}]^{1/2}.$$

Consider portfolio D first. The standard deviation of this portfolio will be somewhere between 10% and 30%, the exact value depending upon the size of the correlation coefficient. How were these bounds of 10% and 30% determined? First, note that for portfolio D, Equation (8.1) reduces to:

$$\sigma_D = [(400 \times .25) + (1,600 \times .25) + (1,600 \times .5 \times .5\, \rho_{12})]^{1/2} \qquad (8.2)$$
$$= [500 + 400\rho_{12}]^{1/2}.$$

Inspection of Equation (8.2) indicates that σ_D will be at a minimum when the correlation coefficient, ρ_{12}, is at a minimum. Now remembering that the minimum value for any correlation coefficient is -1, it can be seen that the lower bound on σ_D is:

$$\sigma_D = [500 + (400 \times -1)]^{1/2}$$
$$= [500 - 400]^{1/2}$$
$$= [100]^{1/2}$$
$$= 10\%.$$

Similarly, inspection of Equation (8.2) indicates that σ_D will be at a maximum when the correlation coefficient is at a maximum, which is $+1$. Thus the upper bound on σ_D is:

$$\sigma_D = [500 + (400 \times 1)]^{1/2}$$
$$= [500 + 400]^{1/2}$$
$$= [900]^{1/2}$$
$$= 30\%.$$

In general, it can be seen from Equation (8.1) that for any given set of weights X_1 and X_2, the lower and upper bounds will occur when the correlation between the two securities is -1 and $+1$, respectively. Proceeding to apply the same analysis to the other portfolios reveals that their lower and upper bounds are:

	Standard Deviation of Portfolio	
Portfolio	Lower Bound	Upper Bound
A	20.00%	20.00%
B	10.00	23.33
C	0.00	26.67
D	10.00	30.00
E	20.00	33.33
F	30.00	36.67
G	40.00	40.00

These values are shown in Figure 8.5.

Interestingly, the upper bounds all lie on a straight line connecting points A and G. This means that any portfolio consisting of these two securities cannot have a standard deviation that plots to the right of a straight line connecting the two securities. Instead, the standard deviation must lie on or to the left of the straight line. This observation suggests a motivation for diversifying a portfolio. Namely, *diversification generally leads to risk reduction*, because the standard deviation of a portfolio will generally be less than a weighted average of the standard deviations of the securities in the portfolio.

Also interesting is the observation that the lower bounds all lie on one of two line segments that go from point *A* to a point on the vertical axis corresponding to 8.30% and then to point *G*. This means that any portfolio consisting of these two securities cannot have a standard deviation that plots to the left of either of these two line segments. For example, portfolio *B* must lie on the horizontal line going through the vertical axis at 6.70%, but bounded at the values of 10% and 23.33%.

In sum, any portfolio consisting of these two securities will lie within or on the boundary of the triangle shown in Figure 8.5, with its actual location depending on the magnitude of the correlation coefficient between the two securities.

8.2.2 Actual Locations of the Portfolios

What if the correlation were zero? In this case, Equation (8.1) reduces to:

$$\sigma p = [(400X_1^2) + (1,600X_2^2) + (1,600X_1X_2 \times 0)]^{1/2}$$
$$= [400X_1^2 + 1,600X_2^2]^{1/2}.$$

Applying the appropriate weights for X_1 and X_2, the standard deviation for portfolios *B, C, D, E,* and *F* can therefore be calculated as follows:

$$\sigma_B = [(400 \times .83^2) + (1,600 \times .17^2)]^{1/2}$$
$$= 17.94\%$$
$$\sigma_C = [(400 \times .67^2) + (1,600 \times .33^2)]^{1/2}$$
$$= 18.81\%$$
$$\sigma_D = [(400 \times .50^2) + (1,600 \times .50^2)]^{1/2}$$
$$= 22.36\%$$
$$\sigma_E = [(400 \times .33^2) + (1,600 \times .67^2)]^{1/2}$$
$$= 27.60\%$$
$$\sigma_F = [(400 \times .17^2) + (1,600 \times .83^2)]^{1/2}$$
$$= 33.37\%.$$

Figure 8.6 indicates the location of these portfolios, along with the upper and lower bounds that were shown in Figure 8.5. As can be seen, these portfolios, as well as all other possible portfolios consisting of Ark Shipping and Gold Jewelry, lie on a line that is curved or bowed to the left. While not shown here, if the correlation were less than zero, the line would curve more to the left. If the correlation were greater than zero, it would not curve quite as much to the left. The important point about this figure is that as long as the correlation is less than $+1$ and greater than -1, the line representing the set of portfolios consisting of various combinations of the two securities will have some degree of curvature to the left. Furthermore, the "northwest" portion will be concave.

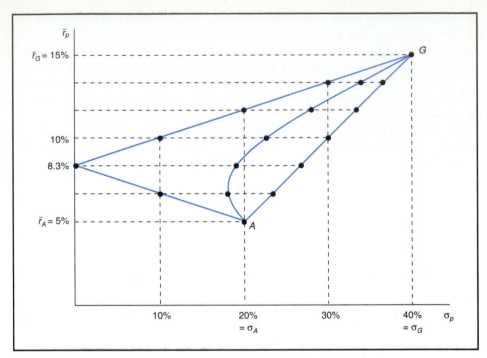

Figure 8.6
Portfolios Formed by Combining Securities A and G

Similar analysis can be applied to a situation where there are more than two securities under consideration. When this is done, as long as the correlations are less than $+1$ and greater than -1, the "northwest" portion must be concave, just as it is in the two-security example.[4] Thus in general the efficient set will be concave.

8.2.3 Impossibility of Having "Dents" in the Efficient Set

The previous example indicated what happens when two securities (such as Ark Shipping and Gold Jewelry) are combined to form a portfolio. It is important to recognize that the same principles hold if two portfolios are combined to form a third portfolio. That is, point A in Figure 8.6 could represent a portfolio of securities with an expected return of 5% and a standard deviation of 20%, and point G could represent another portfolio of securities with an expected return of 15% and a standard deviation of 40%. Combining these two portfolios will result in a third portfolio that has an expected return and standard deviation dependent on the proportions invested in A and G. Assuming that the correlation between A and G is zero, the location of the third portfolio will lie on the curved line connecting A and G.

Recognizing this, it can now be shown why the efficient set is concave. One way to do this is to show that it cannot have any other shape. Consider the efficient set shown in Figure 8.7. Note that there is a "dent" in it between points U and V. That is, between U and V there is a region on the efficient set where it is not concave. Can this truly be an efficient set? No, because an investor could put part of his or her funds in the portfolio located at U and the rest of his or her funds in the portfolio located at V. The resulting portfolio, a combination of U and V, would have to lie to the left of the alleged efficient set. Thus the new portfolio would be "more efficient" than a portfolio with the same expected return that was on the alleged efficient set between U and V.

For example, consider the portfolio on the alleged efficient set that lies halfway between U and V; it is indicated as point W in Figure 8.8. If it truly is an efficient portfolio, then it would be impossible to form a portfolio with the same expected return as W but with a lower standard deviation. However, by putting 50% of his or her funds in U and 50% in V, the investor would have a portfolio that dominates W, since it would have the same expected return but a lower standard deviation. Why will it have a lower standard deviation? Remember, if the correlation between U and V were $+1$, this portfolio would lie on the straight line connecting U and V and would thus have a lower standard deviation than W. Z denotes this point in Figure 8.8. Because the actual correlation is less than or equal to $+1$, it would have a standard deviation as low as or lower than Z's standard deviation. This means that the alleged efficient set was constructed in error, because it is easy to find "more efficient" portfolios in the region where it is not concave.

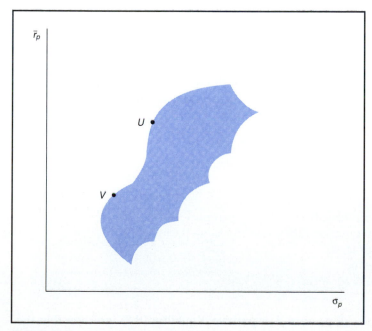

Figure 8.7
Concavity of the Efficient Set

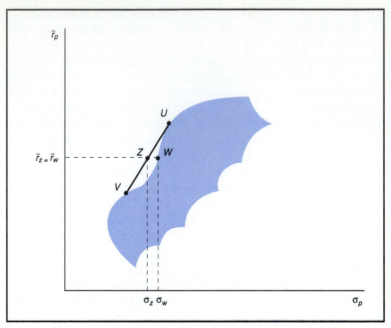

Figure 8.8
Removing a "Dent" from the Efficient Set

THE MARKET MODEL

Suppose that the return on a common stock over a given time period (say, a month) is related to the return over the same period that is earned on a market index such as the widely cited S&P 500.[5] That is, if the market has gone up then it is likely that the stock has gone up, and if the market has gone down then it is likely that the stock has gone down. One way to capture this relationship is with the **market model**:

$$r_i = \alpha_{iI} + \beta_{iI} r_I + \epsilon_{iI} \tag{8.3}$$

where:

r_i = return on security i for some given period,
r_I = return on market index I for the same period,
α_{iI} = intercept term,
β_{iI} = slope term,
ϵ_{iI} = random error term.

Assuming that the slope term β_{iI} is positive, Equation (8.3) indicates that the higher the return on the market index, the higher the return on the security is likely to be (note that the expected value of the random error term is zero).

The Active Manager Portfolio Selection Problem

The classic formulation of the portfolio selection problem depicts an investor who must choose a portfolio on the efficient set that exhibits the optimal combination of expected return and standard deviation, given the investor's risk-return preferences. In practice, however, this description inadequately characterizes the situation faced by most organizations that manage money for institutional investors. We want to consider how the portfolio selection problem can be modified to fit the concerns of institutional investors.

Certain types of institutional investors, such as pension and endowment funds (to whom we will refer as the "clients"), typically hire outside firms (to whom we will refer as the "managers") as agents to invest their assets. These managers usually specialize in a particular asset class, such as common stocks or fixed-income securities. The clients establish performance benchmarks for their managers. These benchmarks may be market indices (such as the S&P 500) or specialized benchmarks that reflect specific investment styles (such as small-capitalization growth stocks).

The clients hire some managers to simply match the performance of the benchmarks. These managers are called *passive managers* (see Chapter 24). The clients hire other managers to exceed the returns produced by the benchmarks. These managers are called *active managers*.

In the case of passive managers, the portfolio selection problem is trivial. They simply buy and hold those securities that constitute their assigned benchmarks. Their portfolios are called *index funds*. Passive managers need make no reference to the efficient set or risk-return preferences. Those issues must be dealt with by their clients. (Whether the benchmarks chosen by the clients are efficient is a separate, although important, subject that we will not address in this discussion.)

Active managers face a much more difficult task. They must create portfolios that produce returns exceeding the returns on their assigned benchmarks in sufficient magnitude and consistency to satisfy their clients.

The greatest obstacle confronting active managers is their lack of omniscience. Even the most capable of them make numerous errors in their security selections. Despite fables about managers who outperform the market's return every year by 10 percentage points, common stock managers who exceed their benchmarks' returns (after all fees and expenses) by 1–2 percentage points per annum are considered exceptional performers. Managers lacking skill (with skill defined in this case as the ability to accurately forecast security returns) will lose to their benchmarks as their fees and trading costs diminish their returns.

We refer to the returns that active managers earn above those of their benchmarks as *active returns*. For example, a manager whose portfolio and benchmark generate returns of 7% and 4%, respectively, has earned a 3% active return (= 7% − 4%). The expected active return for highly skillful managers exceeds that of less talented managers. Nevertheless, in any given period, through sheer chance, the less capable manager's active return may exceed that of the highly skillful manager.

Because the results of active managers' investment decisions are uncertain, their returns relative to their benchmarks exhibit variability over time. We refer to the standard deviation of active return as *active risk*.

Active managers (at least those with some investment forecasting ability) can increase their expected active returns by taking on more active risk. Suppose that Manager X forecasts that IBM stock will earn a return above that of the benchmark. IBM constitutes 2% of the benchmark. Manager X could "bet" on IBM by holding a portfolio with a 4% position in IBM stock. The difference between the actual portfolio's position in IBM and the benchmark's position (+2% = 4% − 2%) we call an *active position*. If IBM does perform well, Manager X's active return will be enhanced by the positive active position in IBM. However, if IBM performs poorly, then Manager X's active return will be diminished. The larger Manager X's active position is in IBM, the greater is his or her expected active return. However, the larger also is Manager X's active risk.

Active risk (and, hence, expected active return) can be eliminated by owning every benchmark security at weights matching those of the same securities in the benchmark. Passive managers follow this approach. Active managers assume active risk when they deviate in their portfolio holdings relative to their benchmarks. Rational and skillful active managers will take on active risk only with the expectation of earning positive active return.

The outline of the portfolio selection problem for an active manager now becomes clear. The manager is not concerned with the trade-off between portfolio expected return and standard deviation. Rather, the manager chooses between higher expected active return and lower active risk.

This process requires that we make an assumption about the manager's ability to forecast security returns. With that information, we can construct a manager's "efficient set" (based on expected active return and active risk) that exhibits the highest combination of expected active return per unit of active risk and the lowest active risk per unit of ex-

pected active return. Managers with greater skill will have efficient sets that lie further to the "northwest" than managers with less skill.

Indifference curves, analogous to those applied in the classical portfolio selection problem, indicate various combinations of active return and active risk that the manager finds equally desirable. The steepness of these indifference curves reflects the manager's degree of risk aversion, which is directly related to the manager's assessment of how his or her clients will respond to various investment outcomes.

The manager's optimal combination of active return and risk is that point on the efficient set which is tangent to one of the indifference curves. We can view this point as the manager's desired level of aggressiveness in implementing his or her security return forecasts. Managers (and their clients) with higher risk aversion will choose portfolios with lower levels of active risk. Conversely, managers (and their clients) with lower risk aversion will choose portfolios with higher levels of active risk.

Consider stock A, for example, which has $\alpha_{iI} = 2\%$ and $\beta_{iI} = 1.2$. This means that the market model for stock A is:

$$r_A = 2\% + 1.2r_I + \epsilon_{AI} \tag{8.4}$$

so that if the market index has a return of 10%, the return on the security is expected to be 14% [= 2% + (1.2 × 10%)]. Similarly, if the market index's return is −5%, then the return on security A is expected to be −4% = [2% + (1.2 × −5%)].

8.3.1 Random Error Terms

The term ϵ_{iI}, known as the **random error term** in Equation (8.3), simply shows that the market model does not explain security returns perfectly. That is, when the market index goes up by 10% or down by 5%, the return on security A is not going to be exactly 14% or −4%, respectively. The difference between what the return actually is and what it is expected to be, given the return on the market index, is attributed to the effect of the random error term. Hence, if the security's return were 9% instead of 14%, the 5% difference would be attributed to the random error term (that is, $\epsilon_{AI} = -5\%$; this will be illustrated shortly in Figure 8.11). Similarly, if the security return were −2% instead of −4%, the 2% difference would be attributed to the random error term (that is, $\epsilon_{AI} = +2\%$).

The random error term can be viewed as a random variable that has a probability distribution with a mean of zero and a standard deviation denoted $\sigma_{\epsilon i}$.[6] That is, it can be viewed as the outcome that results from the spin of a special kind of roulette wheel.

For example, security A might be thought of as having a random error term corresponding to a roulette wheel with integer values on it that range from -10% to $+10\%$, with the values evenly spaced.[7] This means that there are 21 possible outcomes, each of which has an equal probability of occurring. Given the range of numbers, it also means that the expected outcome of the random error term is zero:

$$[-10 \times \tfrac{1}{21}] + [-9 \times \tfrac{1}{21}] + \ldots + [9 \times \tfrac{1}{21}] + [10 \times \tfrac{1}{21}] = 0.$$

As can be seen, this calculation involves multiplying each outcome by its probability of occurring and then summing up the resulting products. The standard deviation of this random error term can now be shown to equal 6.06%:

$$\{[(-10 - 0)^2 \times \tfrac{1}{21}] + [(-9 - 0)^2 \times \tfrac{1}{21}] + \ldots + [(9 - 0)^2 \times \tfrac{1}{21}] + [(10 - 0)^2 \times \tfrac{1}{21}]\}^{1/2} = 6.06\%.$$

This calculation involves subtracting the expected outcome from each possible outcome, then squaring each one of these differences, multiplying each square by the probability of the corresponding outcome occurring, adding the products, and finally taking the square root of the resulting sum.

Figure 8.9 illustrates the roulette wheel corresponding to this random error term. In general, securities will have random error terms whose corresponding roulette wheels have different ranges and different forms of uneven spacing. While all of them will have an expected value of zero, they will typically have different standard deviations. For example, security B may have a random error term whose expected value and standard deviation are equal to zero and 4.76%, respectively.[8]

8.3.2 Graphical Representation of the Market Model

The solid line in panel (a) of Figure 8.10 provides a graph of the market model for security A. This line corresponds to Equation (8.4), but without the random error term. Accordingly, the line that is graphed for security A is:

$$r_A = 2\% + 1.2r_I. \tag{8.5}$$

Here the vertical axis measures the return on the particular security (r_A) whereas the horizontal axis measures the return on the market index (r_I). The line goes through the point on the vertical axis corresponding to the value of α_{AI}, which in this case is 2%. In addition, the line has a slope equal to β_{AI}, or 1.2.

Panel (b) of Figure 8.10 presents the graph of the market model for security B. The line can be expressed as the following equation:

$$r_B = -1\% + .8r_I. \tag{8.6}$$

This line goes through the point on the vertical axis corresponding to the value of α_{BI}, which in this case is -1%. Note that its slope is equal to β_{BI}, or .8.

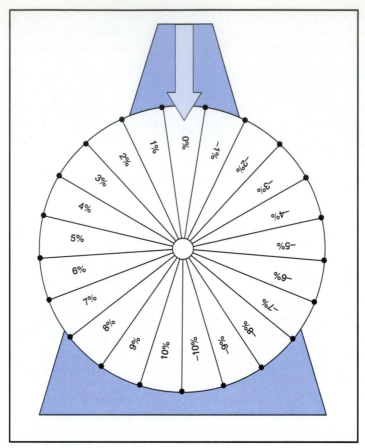

Figure 8.9
Security A's Random Error Term

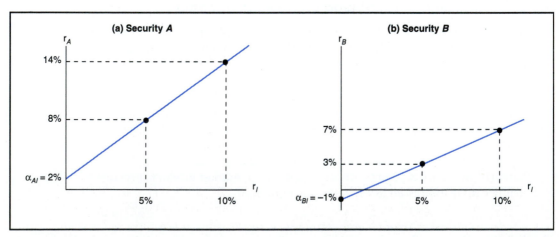

Figure 8.10
Market Model

8.3.3 Beta

At this point it can be seen that the slope in a security's market model measures the sensitivity of the security's returns to the market index's returns. Both lines in Figure 8.10 have positive slopes, indicating that the higher the returns of the market index, the higher the returns of the two securities. However, the two securities have different slopes, indicating that they have different sensitivities to the returns of the market index. Specifically, A has a higher slope than B, indicating that the returns of A are more sensitive than the returns of B to the returns of the market index.

For example, assume that the market index's expected return is 5%. If the market index subsequently has an actual return of 10%, it will have returned 5% more than expected. Panel (a) of Figure 8.10 shows that security A should have a return that is 6% ($= 14\% - 8\%$) greater than initially expected. Similarly, panel (b) shows that security B should have a return that is 4% ($= 7\% - 3\%$) greater than initially expected. The reason for the 2% ($= 6\% - 4\%$) difference is that security A has a higher slope than security B—that is, A is more sensitive than B to returns on the market index.

The slope term in the market model is often referred to as **beta**, and is equal to:

$$\beta_{iI} = \sigma_{iI}/\sigma_I^2 \tag{8.7}$$

where σ_{iI} denotes the covariance of the returns on stock i and the market index, and σ_I^2 denotes the variance of returns on the market index. A stock that has a return that mirrors the return on the market index will have a beta equal to one (and an intercept of zero, resulting in a market model that is $r_i = r_I + \epsilon_{iI}$). Hence stocks with betas greater than one (such as A) are more volatile than the market index and are known as **aggressive stocks.** In contrast, stocks with betas less than one (such as B) are less volatile than the market index and are known as **defensive stocks.**[9]

8.3.4 Actual Returns

The random error term suggests that for a given return on the market index, the actual return on a security will usually lie off its market model line.[10] If the actual returns on securities A and B turn out to be 9% and 11%, respectively, and the market index's actual return turns out to be 10%, then the actual return on A and B could be viewed as having the following three components:

	Security A	Security B
Intercept	2%	−1%
Actual return on the market index × beta	12% = 10% × 1.2	8% = 10% × .8
Random error outcome	−5% = 9% − (2% + 12%)	4% = 11% − (−1% + 8%)
Actual return	9%	11%

In this case, the roulette wheels for A and B can be thought of as having been "spun," resulting in values (that is, random error outcomes) of -5% for A and $+4\%$ for B. These values can be viewed as being equal to the vertical distance by which each security's actual return ended up being off its market model line, as shown in Figure 8.11.

Figure 8.11
Market Model and Actual Returns

DIVERSIFICATION

According to the market model, the total risk of any security i, measured by its variance and denoted σ_i^2, consists of two parts: (1) **market** (or systematic) **risk;** and (2) **unique** (or unsystematic) **risk.** That is, σ_i^2 equals the following:

$$\sigma_i^2 = \beta_{iI}^2 \sigma_I^2 + \sigma_{\epsilon i}^2 \tag{8.8}$$

where σ_I^2 denotes the variance of returns on the market index. Thus $\beta_{iI}^2 \sigma_I^2$ denotes the market risk of security i, and $\sigma_{\epsilon i}^2$ denotes the unique risk of security i as measured by the variance of the random error term, ϵ_{iI}, appearing in Equation (8.3).

8.4.1 Portfolio Total Risk

When the return on every risky *security* in a portfolio is related to the return on the market index as specified by the market model, what can be said about the total risk of the *portfolio*? If the proportion of funds invested in security i for a given portfolio p is denoted X_i, then the return on this portfolio will be:

$$r_p = \sum_{i=1}^{N} X_i r_i. \tag{8.9}$$

Substituting the right-hand side of Equation (8.3) for r_i in Equation (8.9) results in the following market model for the portfolio:

CHAPTER 8

$$r_p = \sum_{i=1}^{N} X_i(\alpha_{iI} + \beta_{iI}r_I + \epsilon_{iI})$$

$$= \sum_{i=1}^{N} X_i\alpha_{iI} + \left(\sum_{i=1}^{N} X_i\beta_{iI}\right) r_I + \sum_{i=1}^{N} X_i\epsilon_{iI})$$

$$= \alpha_{pI} + \beta_{pI}r_I + \epsilon_{pI} \qquad (8.10a)$$

where:

$$\alpha_{pI} = \sum_{i=1}^{N} X_i\alpha_{iI} \qquad (8.10b)$$

$$\beta_{pI} = \sum_{i=1}^{N} X_i\beta_{iI} \qquad (8.10c)$$

$$\epsilon_{pI} = \sum_{i=1}^{N} X_i\epsilon_{iI} \qquad (8.10d)$$

In Equations (8.10b) and (8.10c), the portfolio's vertical intercept (α_{pI}) and beta (β_{pI}) are shown to be weighted averages of the intercepts and betas of the securities, respectively, using their relative proportions in the portfolio as weights. Similarly, in Equation (8.10d), the portfolio's random error term (ϵ_{pI}) is a weighted average of the random error terms of the securities, again using the relative proportions in the portfolio as weights. Thus the portfolio's market model is a straightforward extension of the market model for individual securities given in Equation (8.3).[11]

From Equation (8.10a), it follows that the total risk of a portfolio, measured by the variance of the portfolio's returns and denoted σ_p^2, will be:

$$\sigma_p^2 = \beta_{pI}^2\sigma_I^2 + \sigma_{\epsilon p}^2 \qquad (8.11a)$$

where:

$$\beta_{pI}^2 = \left[\sum_{i=1}^{N} X_i\beta_{iI}\right]^2 \qquad (8.11b)$$

and, assuming the random error components of security returns are uncorrelated:

$$\sigma_{\epsilon p}^2 = \sum_{i=1}^{N} X_i^2\sigma_{\epsilon i}^2 \qquad (8.11c)$$

Equation (8.11a) shows that the total risk of any portfolio can be viewed as having two components, similar to the two components of the total risk of an individual security. These components are again referred to as market risk ($\beta_{pI}^2\sigma_I^2$) and unique risk ($\sigma_{\epsilon p}^2$).

Next, it will be shown that increased **diversification** can lead to the reduction of a portfolio's total risk. This occurs due to a reduction in the size of the portfolio's unique risk while the portfolio's market risk remains approximately the same size.

8.4.2 Portfolio Market Risk

Generally, the more diversified a portfolio (that is, the larger the number of securities in the portfolio), the smaller will be each proportion X_i. This will not cause β_{pI} to either decrease or increase significantly unless a deliberate attempt is made to do so by adding either relatively low or high beta securities, respectively, to the portfolio. That is, because a portfolio's beta is an average of the betas of its securities, there is no reason to suspect that increasing the amount of diversification will cause the portfolio beta, and thus the market risk of the portfolio, to change in a particular direction. Accordingly,

Diversification leads to averaging of market risk.

This makes sense because when prospects for the economy turn sour (or rosy), most securities will fall (or rise) in price. Regardless of the amount of diversification, portfolio returns will always be susceptible to such marketwide influences.

8.4.3 Portfolio Unique Risk

The situation is entirely different for unique risk. In a portfolio, some securities will go up as a result of unexpected good news specific to the company that issued the securities (such as an unexpected approval of a patent). Other securities will go down as a result of unexpected company-specific bad news (such as an industrial accident). Looking forward, approximately as many companies can be expected to have good news as bad news, leading to little anticipated net impact on the return of a "well-diversified" portfolio. This means that as a portfolio becomes more diversified, the smaller will be its unique risk and, in turn, its total risk.

This can be quantified precisely if the random error components of security returns are assumed to be uncorrelated, as was done when Equation (8.11c) was written. Consider the following situation. If the amount invested in each security is equal, then the proportion X_i will equal $1/N$, and the level of unique risk, as shown in Equation (8.11c), will be equal to:

$$\sigma_{\epsilon p}^2 = \sum_{i=1}^{N} \left[\frac{1}{N}\right]^2 \sigma_{\epsilon i}^2 \tag{8.12a}$$

$$= \frac{1}{N}\left[\frac{\sigma_{\epsilon 1}^2 + \sigma_{\epsilon 2}^2 + \ldots \sigma_{\epsilon N}^2}{N}\right]. \tag{8.12b}$$

The value inside the square brackets in Equation (8.12b) is simply the average unique risk of the component securities. But the portfolio's unique risk is only one-Nth as large as this, since the term $1/N$ appears outside the square brackets. Now as the portfolio becomes more diversified, the number of securities in it (that is, N) becomes larger. In turn, this means that $1/N$ becomes smaller, resulting in the portfolio having less unique risk.[12] That is,

Diversification can substantially reduce unique risk.

Roughly speaking, a portfolio that has 30 or more randomly selected securities in it will have a relatively small amount of unique risk. This means that its total risk will be only slightly greater than the amount of market risk that is present. Thus such portfolios are "well diversified." Figure 8.12 illustrates how diversification results in the reduction of unique risk but the averaging of market risk.

8.4.4 An Example

Consider the two securities, *A* and *B*, that were referred to earlier. These two securities had betas of 1.2 and .8, respectively; the standard deviations of their random error terms were, respectively, 6.06% and 4.76%. Thus, given that $\sigma_{\epsilon A}$ = 6.06% and $\sigma_{\epsilon B}$ = 4.76%, it follows that $\sigma_{\epsilon A}^2 = 6.06^2 = 37$ and $\sigma_{\epsilon B}^2 = 4.76^2 = 23$. Now assume that the standard deviation of the market index, σ_I, is 8%, which implies that the variance of the market index is $8^2 = 64$. Using Equation (8.8), this means that the variances of securities *A* and *B* are as follows:

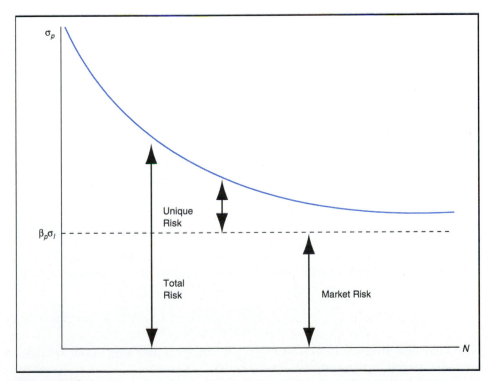

Figure 8.12
Risk and Diversification

$$\sigma_A^2 = (1.2^2 \times 64) + 37$$
$$= 129$$
$$\sigma_B^2 = (.8^2 \times 64) + 23$$
$$= 64.$$

A Two-Security Portfolio

Consider combining securities A and B into a portfolio, with an equal amount of the investor's money going into each security. That is, consider a portfolio that has $X_A = .5$ and $X_B = .5$. Since $\beta_{AI} = 1.2$ and $\beta_{BI} = .8$, the beta of this portfolio can be calculated using Equation (8.10c):

$$\beta_{pI} = (.5 \times 1.2) + (.5 \times .8)$$
$$= 1.0.$$

Using Equation (8.11c), the variance of the portfolio's random error term, $\sigma_{\epsilon p}^2$, equals:

$$\sigma_{\epsilon p}^2 = (.5^2 \times 37) + (.5^2 \times 23)$$
$$= 15.$$

From Equation (8.11a), it can be seen that this portfolio will have the following variance:

$$\sigma_p^2 = (1.0^2 \times 64) + 15$$
$$= 79.$$

This represents the total risk of the two-security portfolio.

A Three-Security Portfolio

Consider what would happen if a third security (C) was combined with the other two to form a three-security portfolio having $X_A = X_B = X_C = .33$. This third security has a beta of 1.0 and a random error term whose standard deviation $(\sigma_{\epsilon C})$ is 5.50%. Thus the variance of the random error term is $\sigma_{\epsilon C}^2 = 5.5^2 = 30$, and the security's variance is:

$$\sigma_C^2 = (1.0^2 \times 64) + 30$$
$$= 94.$$

First of all, note that the three-security portfolio has the same amount of market risk as the two-security portfolio, because both portfolios have a beta of 1.0:

$$\beta_{pI} = (.33 \times 1.2) + (.33 \times .8) + (.33 \times 1.0)$$
$$= 1.0.$$

Thus increased diversification has not led to a change in the level of market risk. Instead it has led to an averaging of market risk.

Using Equation (8.11c), the variance of the portfolio's random error term equals:

$$\sigma^2_{\epsilon p} = (.33^2 \times 37) + (.33^2 \times 23) + (.33^2 \times 30)$$
$$= 10.$$

Note that the variance of this three-security portfolio's random error term is less than the variance of the two-security portfolio's random error term (that is, $10 < 15$). Thus, in this example, increased diversification has indeed reduced unique risk.

From Equation (8.11a), it can be seen that this three-security portfolio will have the following variance:

$$\sigma^2_p = (1.0^2 \times 64) + 10$$
$$= 74.$$

This represents the total risk of the portfolio and is less than the total risk of the two-security portfolio ($74 < 79$). Thus increased diversification has led to a reduction in total risk.

8.5   SUMMARY

1. The efficient set contains those portfolios that offer both maximum expected return for varying levels of risk and minimum risk for varying levels of expected return.

2. Investors are assumed to select their optimal portfolios from among the portfolios lying on the efficient set.

3. An investor's optimal portfolio is identified as the tangency point between the investor's indifference curves and the efficient set.

4. The proposition that the efficient set is concave follows from the definition of portfolio standard deviation and the existence of assets whose returns are not perfectly positively or perfectly negatively correlated.

5. Diversification usually leads to risk reduction, because the standard deviation of a portfolio generally will be less than a weighted average of the standard deviations of the component securities.

6. The relationship between the return on a security and the return on a market index is known as the market model.

7. The market index's return does not completely explain the return on a security. The unexplained elements are captured by the random error term of the market model.

8. The slope in a security's market model measures the sensitivity of the security's return to the market index's return. The slope term is known as the security's beta.

9. According to the market model, the total risk of a security consists of market risk and unique risk.

10. A portfolio's vertical intercept, beta, and random error term are weighted averages of the component securities' intercepts, betas, and random error terms, respectively, with the securities' relative proportions in the portfolio serving as weights.

11. Diversification leads to an averaging of market risk.
12. Diversification can substantially reduce unique risk.

1. Why would you expect individual securities to generally lie in the "eastern" portion of the feasible set, whereas only portfolios would lie in the "northwestern" portion?
2. Explain why most investors prefer to hold a diversified portfolio of securities as opposed to placing all of their wealth in a single asset. Use an illustration of the feasible and efficient sets to explain your answer.
3. Why would you expect most U.S. common stocks to have positive covariances? Give an example of two stocks that you would expect to have a very high positive covariance. Give an example of two stocks that you would expect to have a very low positive (or even negative) covariance.
4. Discuss why the concepts of covariance and diversification are closely related.
5. Mule Haas is a portfolio manager. On average, the expected returns on all securities that Mule is researching are positive. Under what conditions might Mule be willing to purchase a security with a negative expected return?
6. In terms of the Markowitz model, explain, using words and graphs, how an investor goes about identifying his or her optimal portfolio. What specific information does an investor need to identify this portfolio?
7. Dode Brinker owns a portfolio of two securities with the following expected returns, standard deviations, and weights:

Security	Expected Return	Standard Deviation	Weight
A	10%	20%	.35
B	15	25	.65

For varying levels of correlation between the two securities, what is the maximum portfolio standard deviation? What is the minimum?
8. Briefly explain why the efficient set must be concave.
9. Leslie Nunamaker owns a portfolio whose market model is expressed as:

$$r_p = 1.5\% + 0.90r_I + \epsilon_{pI}.$$

If the expected return on the market index is 12%, what is the expected return on Leslie's portfolio?
10. How is beta derived from a security's market model? Why are high beta securities termed "aggressive"? Why are low beta securities termed "defensive"?
11. In the following table you are presented with ten years of return data for the stock of Glenwood City Properties and for a market index. Plot the returns of Glenwood City and the market index on a graph, with the market index's returns on the horizontal axis and Glenwood City's returns on the vertical axis. Draw your best guess of the market model through these points. From this graph only, compute an estimate of the beta of Glenwood City stock.

Year	Glenwood City	Market Index
1	8.1%	8.0%
2	3.0	0.0
3	5.3	14.9
4	1.0	5.0
5	−3.1	−4.1
6	−3.0	−8.9
7	5.0	10.1
8	3.2	5.0
9	1.2	1.5
10	1.3	2.4

12. Consider the stocks of two companies, Woodville Weasel Farms and New Richmond Furriers.
    a. If you are told that the slope of Woodville's market model is 1.20 and that the slope of New Richmond's market model is 1.00, which stock is likely to be more risky in a portfolio context? Why?
    b. If you are now also told that the standard deviation of the random error term for Woodville stock is 10.0%, whereas it is 21.5% for New Richmond stock, does your answer change? Explain.

13. The market model specifies a very simple relationship between a security's return and the return on the market index. Discuss some "real world" complexities that might diminish the predictive power of the market model.

14. For two portfolios, one invested in electric utilities and the other in gold mining companies, each has the same beta of 0.60. Why would a security analyst be interested to know that the gold portfolio has a much larger standard deviation of the random error term (unique risk) than the utility portfolio?

15. Lyndon Station stock has a beta of 1.20. Over five years, the following returns were produced by Lyndon stock and a market index. Assuming a market model intercept term of 0%, calculate the standard deviation of the market model random error term over this period.

Year	Lyndon Return	Market Index
1	17.2%	14.0%
2	−3.1	−3.0
3	13.3	10.0
4	28.5	25.0
5	9.8	8.0

16. Why does diversification lead to a reduction in unique risk, but not in market risk? Explain both intuitively and mathematically.

17. Siggy Boskie owns a portfolio composed of three securities with the following characteristics:

Security	Beta	Standard Deviation Random Error Term	Proportion
A	1.20	5%	.30
B	1.05	8	.50
C	0.90	2	.20

If the standard deviation of the market index is 18%, what is the total risk of Siggy's portfolio?

18. Consider two portfolios, one composed of four securities and the other of ten securities. All the securities have a beta of one and unique risk of 30%. Each portfolio distributes weight equally among its component securities. If the standard deviation of the market index is 20%, calculate the total risk of both portfolios.

19. (Appendix Question) What is a corner portfolio? Why are corner portfolios important for identifying the composition of the efficient set?

20. (Appendix Question) Why is the market model approach a simpler technique than the original Markowitz approach for constructing the efficient set?

21. (Appendix Question) If the variance of the market index is 490 and the co-variance between securities A and B is 470, what is the beta of security B, knowing that security A's beta is 1.20?

22. (Appendix Question) How many parameters must be estimated to analyze the risk-return profile of a 50-stock portfolio using (a) the original Markowitz approach and (b) the market model approach?

APPENDIX A

THE MARKOWITZ MODEL

A.1   DETERMINING THE COMPOSITION AND LOCATION OF THE EFFICIENT SET

Previously, it was noted that there are an infinite number of possible portfolios available to the investor, but that the investor needs to be concerned with only those portfolios that are on the efficient set. However, Markowitz's efficient set is a curved line, which means that there are an infinite number of points along it. This, in turn, means that there are an infinite number of efficient portfolios! How can Markowitz's approach be used if an investor needs to identify the com-position of each one of an infinite number of portfolios? Fortunately, there is no need to despair. Markowitz saw this potential problem and, in a major contribu-tion, presented a method for solving it.[13] It involves the use of a quadratic pro-gramming algorithm known as the *critical-line method*.

Although the algorithm is beyond the scope of this book, it is important to recognize what it does. To begin with, the investor must estimate the expected return vector and variance-covariance matrix. For example, consider the three-security example presented earlier in the chapter.[14] The expected return vector, denoted by ER, and the variance-covariance matrix, denoted by VC, were estimated to be:

$$ER = \begin{bmatrix} 16.2 \\ 24.6 \\ 22.8 \end{bmatrix} \qquad VC = \begin{bmatrix} 146 & 187 & 145 \\ 187 & 854 & 104 \\ 145 & 104 & 289 \end{bmatrix}.$$

The algorithm then identifies a number of *corner portfolios* that are associated with these securities and completely describe the efficient set. A corner portfolio is an efficient portfolio with the following property: Any combination of two adjacent corner portfolios will result in a portfolio that lies on the efficient set between the two corner portfolios. Just what this means is illustrated in the example.

The algorithm begins by identifying the portfolio with the highest expected return. This portfolio corresponds to point S in Figure 8.1 and is an efficient portfolio. It is composed of just one security—the security with the highest expected return. That is, if the investor wanted to purchase that portfolio, all he or she would have to do is to purchase shares of the company whose stock has the highest expected return. Any other portfolio would have a lower expected return, since at least part of the investor's funds would be placed in shares of other companies that have an expected return lower than S.

In the example, the company whose shares have the highest expected return is the second one, Baker Company. The corresponding efficient portfolio is the first of several corner portfolios that the algorithm will identify. Its composition is given by the following weight vector, denoted by $X(1)$:

$$X(1) = \begin{bmatrix} .00 \\ 1.00 \\ .00 \end{bmatrix}.$$

Its expected return and standard deviation correspond to the expected return and standard deviation of Baker, which are equal to 24.6% and $(854)^{1/2} = 29.22\%$ respectively. In Figure 8.13, this corner portfolio is denoted by $C(1)$.

The algorithm then identifies the second corner portfolio. This portfolio is on the efficient set below the first corner portfolio and has a composition given by the following weight vector, denoted by $X(2)$:

$$X(2) = \begin{bmatrix} .00 \\ .22 \\ .78 \end{bmatrix}.$$

That is, the second corner portfolio is a portfolio where the investor puts 22% of his or her funds into Baker common stock and the remainder, 78%, into Charlie common stock. Applying these weights to Equations (7.3a) and (7.7), the expected return and standard deviation of this corner portfolio can be calculated; they are equal to 23.20% and 15.90%, respectively. In Figure 8.13, this corner portfolio is denoted by $C(2)$.

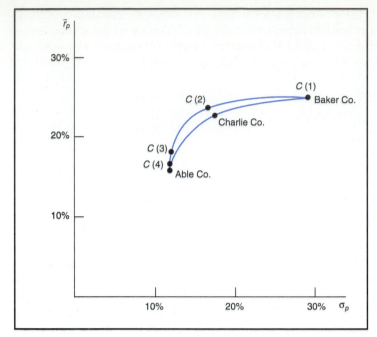

Figure 8.13
Corner Portfolios

What is important about the first and second corner portfolios is that they are *adjacent* efficient portfolios, and any efficient portfolio lying on the efficient set between them has a composition that is just a combination of their compositions. For example, the efficient portfolio lying halfway between them has the following composition:

$$[.5 \times X(1)] + [.5 \times X(2)] = .5 \times \begin{bmatrix} .00 \\ 1.00 \\ .00 \end{bmatrix} + .5 \times \begin{bmatrix} .00 \\ .22 \\ .78 \end{bmatrix} = \begin{bmatrix} .00 \\ .61 \\ .39 \end{bmatrix}.$$

That is, the portfolio has weights of .61 in Baker stock and .39 in Charlie stock. Using Equations (7.3a) and (7.7), the expected return and standard deviation of this portfolio turn out to be 23.9% and 20.28%, respectively.

Having identified the second corner portfolio, the algorithm then identifies the third one. Its composition is:

$$X(3) = \begin{bmatrix} .84 \\ .00 \\ .16 \end{bmatrix}.$$

These weights can now be used to calculate the expected return and standard deviation of this portfolio, which are 17.26% and 12.22%, respectively. As was noted for the previous two corner portfolios, this corner portfolio is an efficient portfolio and is denoted by $C(3)$ in Figure 8.13.

CHAPTER 8

Since they are adjacent, combinations of the second and third corner portfolios result in efficient portfolios that lie on the efficient set between them. For example, if the investor puts 33% of his or her money in the second corner portfolio and 67% in the third corner portfolio, then the resulting efficient portfolio has the following composition:

$$[.33 \times X(2)] + [.67 \times X(3)] = .33 \times \begin{bmatrix} .00 \\ .22 \\ .78 \end{bmatrix} + .67 \times \begin{bmatrix} .84 \\ .00 \\ .16 \end{bmatrix} = \begin{bmatrix} .56 \\ .07 \\ .36 \end{bmatrix}.$$

Using Equations (7.3a) and (7.7), this portfolio can be shown to have an expected return of 19.10% and a standard deviation of 12.88%.

Earlier it was mentioned that only combinations of *adjacent* corner portfolios will be efficient. This means that portfolios formed by combining *nonadjacent* corner portfolios will not lie on the efficient set. For example, the first and third corner portfolios are nonadjacent, which means that any portfolio formed by combining them will not be efficient. For example, if the investor put 50% of his or her funds in the first corner portfolio and 50% in the third corner portfolio, the resulting portfolio would have the following compositions:

$$[.5 \times X(1)] + [.5 \times X(3)] = .5 \times \begin{bmatrix} .00 \\ 1.00 \\ .00 \end{bmatrix} + .5 \times \begin{bmatrix} .84 \\ .00 \\ .16 \end{bmatrix} = \begin{bmatrix} .42 \\ .50 \\ .08 \end{bmatrix}.$$

With these weights, the expected return and standard deviation of this portfolio can be shown to be equal to 20.93% and 18.38%, respectively. However, this is an inefficient portfolio. Since its expected return (20.93%) lies between the expected return of the second (23.20%) and third (17.26%) corner portfolios, by combining these two adjacent corner portfolios the investor will be able to form an efficient portfolio that has the same expected return but lower standard deviation.[15]

Continuing, the algorithm now identifies the composition of the fourth corner portfolio:

$$X(4) = \begin{bmatrix} .99 \\ .00 \\ .01 \end{bmatrix}.$$

Its expected return and standard deviation can be calculated to be 16.27% and 12.08%, respectively. Having identified this portfolio as the one corresponding to point E in Figure 8.1 [and $C(4)$ in Figure 8.13], meaning that it is the portfolio that has the least standard deviation of all feasible portfolios, the algorithm stops. The four corner portfolios, summarized in Table 8.1 completely describe the efficient set associated with the stocks of Able, Baker, and Charlie.

It is a simple matter for the computer, using its capability for graphics, now to draw the graph of the efficient set. Perhaps it will find the composition, and in turn the expected return and standard deviation, for each of 20 efficient portfolios that are evenly spaced between the first and second corner portfolios. Then it will "connect the dots," tracing a straight line between each of the twenty successive portfolios. This will give the graph the appearance of a curved line, as shown in Figure 8.13, since these portfolios are located close to each other.

TABLE 8.1
CORNER PORTFOLIOS FOR A THREE-SECURITY EXAMPLE

Corner Portfolio	Weights			Corner Portfolio	
	Able Co.	Baker Co.	Charlie Co.	Expected Return	Standard Deviation
C(1)	.00	1.00	.00	24.60%	29.22%
C(2)	.00	.22	.78	23.20	15.90
C(3)	.84	.00	.16	17.26	12.22
C(4)	.99	.00	.01	16.27	12.08

Proceeding in a similar fashion, 20 efficient portfolios between the second and third corner portfolios will be located and the corresponding segment of the efficient set traced. Then the same procedure will be followed for the region between the third and fourth corner portfolios, at which point the graph has been completely drawn.

A.2   DETERMINING THE COMPOSITION OF THE OPTIMAL PORTFOLIO

Once the location and composition of Markowitz's efficient set have been determined, the composition of the investor's optimal portfolio can be determined. This portfolio, indicated by O^* in Figure 8.2, corresponds to the tangency point between the efficient set and one of the investor's indifference curves. The procedure for determining its composition starts by the investor noting graphically the level of its expected return. That is, from the graph the investor can note where O^* is located and then calibrate its expected return simply by using a ruler and extending a line from it to the vertical axis (with computers, more precise ways exist for doing this).

Having done so, the investor can now identify the two corner portfolios having expected returns "surrounding" this level. That is, the investor can identify the corner portfolio with the expected return nearest but greater than this level (the surrounding corner portfolio that is "above" O^*) and the corner portfolio with the expected return nearest but less than this level (the surrounding corner portfolio that is "below" O^*).

If the expected return of the optimal portfolio is denoted by $\bar{r}^*$ and the expected returns of these two surrounding portfolios are denoted by $\bar{r}^a$ and $\bar{r}^b$, respectively, then the composition of the optimal portfolio can be determined by solving the following equation for Y:

$$\bar{r}^* = (\bar{r}^a \times Y) + [\bar{r}^b \times (1 - Y)]. \tag{8.13}$$

The optimal portfolio will consist of a proportion Y of the "above" surrounding corner portfolio and a proportion $1 - Y$ of the "below" surrounding corner portfolio.

In the example, if the optimal portfolio had an expected return of 20%, then it can be noted that the second and third corner portfolios are the above and below surrounding corner portfolios, since they have expected returns of 23.20% and 17.26%, respectively. Equation (8.13) thus looks like:

$$20\% = (23.20\% \times Y) + [17.26\% \times (1 - Y)].$$

Solving this equation for Y results in $Y = .46$, meaning that the optimal portfolio consists of a proportion of .46 in the second corner portfolio and .54 in the third corner portfolio. In terms of the amount of investment in the securities of Able, Baker, and Charlie companies, this translates to:

$$[.46 \times X(2)] + [.54 \times X(3)] = .46 \times \begin{bmatrix} .00 \\ .22 \\ .78 \end{bmatrix} + .54 \times \begin{bmatrix} .84 \\ .00 \\ .16 \end{bmatrix} = \begin{bmatrix} .45 \\ .10 \\ .45 \end{bmatrix}.$$

Thus the investor should put 45%, 10%, and 45% of his or her funds in shares of Able, Baker, and Charlie, respectively.

More generally, if the weight vectors of the above and below surrounding corner portfolios are denoted by X^a and X^b, respectively, then the weights for the individual securities comprising the optimal portfolio will be equal to $(Y \times X^a) + [(1 - Y) \times X^b]$.

APPENDIX B

DETERMINING THE INPUTS NEEDED FOR LOCATING THE EFFICIENT SET

In order to construct the efficient set, the investor must estimate the expected returns for all the securities under consideration, as well as all of the variances and covariances. Subsequently, the optimal portfolio can be identified by noting where one of the investor's indifference curves is tangent to the efficient set, as shown in Figure 8.2.

Considerable effort is needed to construct this efficient set. First, the expected return for each security must be estimated. Given that there are N risky securities, this means that N parameters must be estimated. Second, the variance for each one of these securities must be estimated. Again, because there are N risky securities, this means that another N parameters must be estimated. Third, the covariance between each pair of risky securities must be estimated. There are $(N^2 - N)/2$ of these parameters to be estimated.[16] This means that the total number of parameters that need to be estimated is equal to $(N^2 + 3N)/2$, determined as follows:

Expected returns	N
Variances	N
Covariances	$(N^2 - N)/2$
Total	$(N^2 + 3N)/2$

For example, if there were 100 risky securities under consideration, then $[100^2 + (3 \times 100)]/2 = 5{,}150$ parameters would need to be estimated, consisting of 100 expected returns, 100 variances, and 4,950 covariances. These parameters can be estimated one by one, a task that will be quite time-consuming if not, practically speaking, impossible. Fortunately, alternatives exist, including one that is based on the market model.[17]

With the market model approach, the expected return on the market index must be estimated initially. Then, the vertical intercept and beta for each security must be estimated. At this point, $(1 + 2N)$ parameters have been estimated (1 for $\bar{r}_I$; $2N$ for the vertical intercept and beta for each of the N risky securities). In turn, these figures can be used to estimate the expected return for each security using Equation (8.3), restated as follows:

$$\bar{r}_i = \alpha_{iI} + \beta_{iI}\bar{r}_I. \tag{8.14}$$

Earlier, the expected return on the market index was estimated to be 5%. Given these figures, the expected return for security A was estimated to be 8%, because the vertical intercept and beta of this security were estimated to be 2% and 1.2, respectively:

$$\begin{aligned} \bar{r}_A &= 2\% + (5\% \times 1.2) \\ &= 8\%. \end{aligned}$$

Similarly, the expected return for security B was estimated to be 3%, because its vertical intercept and beta were estimated to be -1% and .8, respectively:

$$\begin{aligned} \bar{r}_B &= -1\% + (5\% \times .8) \\ &= 3\%. \end{aligned}$$

Using the market model approach, the variance of any security i can be estimated by multiplying the squared value of the security's beta by the variance of the market index and then adding the variance of the random error term to the product. The equation for doing this was given earlier:

$$\sigma_i^2 = \beta_{iI}^2 \sigma_I^2 + \sigma_{\epsilon i}^2 \tag{8.8}$$

where σ_I^2 denotes the variance of the market index and $\sigma_{\epsilon i}^2$ denotes the variance of the random error term for security i.

Assuming that the variance on the market index is 49, the respective variances of securities A and B can be estimated as follows:

$$\sigma_A^2 = (1.2^2 \times 49) + 6.06^2$$
$$= 107.28$$
$$\sigma_B^2 = (.8^2 \times 49) + 4.76^2$$
$$= 54.02.$$

This means that the standard deviations of these securities are estimated to be equal to $10.36\% = \sqrt{107.28}$ and $7.35\% = \sqrt{54.02}$, respectively.

Lastly, the covariance between any two securities i and j can be estimated by the product of the three numbers: the beta of security i, the beta of security j, and the variance of the market index. That is, the following formula can be used:

$$\sigma_{ij} = \beta_{iI}\beta_{jI}\sigma_I^2. \tag{8.15}$$

Thus for securities A and B, the estimated covariance would be:

$$\sigma_{A,B} = 1.2 \times .8 \times 49$$
$$= 47.04.$$

In summary, if the market model approach is used to estimate expected returns, variances, and covariances, then the following parameters must first be estimated:

For the market index:	
Expected return $(\bar{r}_I)$	1
Variance (σ_I^2)	1
For each security:	
Vertical intercept (α_{iI})	N
Beta (β_{iI})	N
Variance of random error term $(\sigma_{\epsilon i}^2)$	N
Total	3N + 2

Thus for 100 risky securities, $(3 \times 100) + 2 = 302$ parameters need to be estimated when the market model approach is used to determine the efficient set and tangency portfolio. With this approach, once these 302 parameters have been estimated, then it is a simple matter to use Equations (8.14), (8.8), and (8.15) to estimate the expected returns, variances, and covariances for the risky securities. Alternatively, the expected returns, variances, and covariances could be estimated one by one as noted earlier, in which case 5,150 parameters would need to be estimated. As can be seen with this example, the market model approach results in a notable reduction in the number of parameters that need to be estimated.

With the market model approach (or alternatively the one-by-one approach), after the expected returns, variances, and covariances have been estimated, a computer can be given these values. Then, using a "quadratic programming algorithm" the computer can proceed to identify the efficient set.[18] At this juncture, the investor's optimal portfolio can be determined by finding the point at which one of the indifference curves is tangent to the efficient set.

[1] This can be seen by noting that there are an infinite number of points on the real number line between 0 and 100. If these numbers are thought of as representing the percentage of the investor's funds going into shares of Able, with 100 minus this number going into Baker, it can be seen that there are an infinite number of portfolios that could be formed from just two different securities. In making this assertion, however, it has been assumed that an investor can buy a fraction of a share if he or she so desires. For example, the investor can buy not only one share of Able, but also 1.1 or 1.01 or 1.001 shares.

[2] In order to determine the compositions of the portfolios on the efficient set, the investor must solve a quadratic programming problem. See Markowitz's book entitled *Portfolio Selection* (cited at the end of the chapter), particularly pp. 176–185.

[3] The risk-neutral investor will choose portfolio *S*, while the risk-seeking investor will choose either *S* or *H*.

[4] This "curvature property" can also be used to explain why the right-hand side of the feasible set has the umbrella shape noted in Figure 8.2. A more rigorous demonstration of concavity is contained in Appendix A.

[5] This is an example of a single-factor model where the factor is the return on a market index (see Chapter 11 for more on factor models; see Chapters 10, 23, and 26 for more on market indices). The model is actually more general than indicated here in that the return need not be on a market index. It can be on any variable that is believed to have a major influence on individual stock returns, such as the predicted rate of increase in industrial production or gross domestic product.

[6] To be technically correct, the standard deviation of the random error term should be denoted $\sigma_{\epsilon iI}$, because it is measured relative to market index *I*. The subscript *I* is not shown here for ease of exposition.

[7] Because the range refers to the possible outcomes and the spacing refers to the probabilities of the various outcomes occurring, it can be seen that the roulette wheel is just a convenient way of referring to the random error term's probability distribution. Typically, it is assumed that a random error term has a normal distribution.

[8] This would be the case if security *B* had a random error term whose roulette wheel had integers from -9% to $+9\%$ on it, but the spacing for each integer between -5% and $+5\%$ was twice as large as the spacing for each integer from -9% to -6% and $+6\%$ to $+9\%$. This means that the probability of any specific integer between -5% and $+5\%$ occurring is equal to $\frac{2}{30}$, while the probability of any specific integer from -9% to -6% and $+6\%$ to $+9\%$ occurring is equal to $\frac{1}{30}$.

[9] Just how beta is estimated will be addressed in Chapter 17.

[10] If the random error term takes on a value of zero, then the security will lie *on* the line. However, the probability of this occurring is very small for most securities.

[11] Appendix B shows how the market model can be used to estimate expected returns, variances, and covariances for the securities in the feasible set; with these estimates in hand, the efficient set can subsequently be determined. See endnote 2.

[12] Actually, all that is necessary for this reduction in unique risk to occur is for the maximum amount invested in any one security to continually decrease as *N* increases.

[13] See Harry Markowitz, "The Optimization of a Quadratic Function Subject to Linear Constraints," *Naval Research Logistics Quarterly*, 3, nos. 1–2 (March–June 1956):111–133

[14] This example is based on one from Markowitz's book entitled *Portfolio Selection* (New Haven, CT: Yale University Press, 1959), 176–185.

[15] In this example, the efficient portfolio having an expected return of 20.93% can be determined by solving the following equation for Y: $(23.20\% \times Y) + [17.26\% \times (1 - Y)] = 20.93\%$. Because this is a linear equation with one unknown, it can easily be solved. The solution, $Y = .62$, indicates that by putting .62 of his or her funds in the second corner portfolio and .38 $(1.00 - .62)$ in the third corner portfolio, the investor will have an efficient portfolio with the same expected return but lower standard deviation (specifically, 14.09%) than the portfolio involving a 50-50 combination of the first and third corner portfolios.

[16] This number was arrived at in the following manner. The variance-covariance matrix has N rows and N columns, meaning that there are N^2 cells in it whose corresponding parameters need to be estimated. The cells on the diagonal contain the N variances mentioned earlier, leaving $(N^2 - N)$ covariances to be estimated. Because the variance-covariance matrix is symmetric, only those covariances below the diagonal need be estimated (this is because they also appear in corresponding locations above the diagonal), leaving a total of $(N^2 - N)/2$ parameters to be estimated.

[17] The market model approach is an approximate one (as are all the other alternatives) because it makes a number of simplifying assumptions. For example, this approach assumes that the random error terms for any two securities are uncorrelated [an assumption that was needed in deriving Equation (8.11c) and later in (8.15)]. This means that the outcome from a spin of the roulette wheel for one security (such as Mobil) has no bearing on the outcome from a spin of the roulette wheel for any other security (such as Exxon). It has been argued that this is not true for securities within certain industries. See Benjamin F. King, "Market and Industry Factors in Stock Price Behavior," *Journal of Business*, 39, no. 1 (January 1966): 139–170; and James L. Farrell, Jr., "Analyzing Covariation of Returns to Determine Homogeneous Stock Groupings," *Journal of Business*, 47, no. 2 (April 1974): 186–207.

[18] See Appendix B to Chapter 9 for a description of an algorithm that can be used in conjunction with the market model to determine the composition of the efficient set.

KEY TERMS

efficient set theorem

efficient set

feasible set

efficient portfolios

inefficient portfolios

optimal portfolio

market model

random error term

beta

aggressive stocks

defensive stocks

market risk

unique risk

diversification

REFERENCES

1. As mentioned at the end of Chapter 7, the seminal work developing the mean-variance model is credited to Harry Markowitz, who presented his ideas in a paper and later in a book:

Harry M. Markowitz, "Portfolio Selection," *Journal of Finance,* 7, no. 1 (March 1952): 77–91.

Harry M. Markowitz, *Portfolio Selection: Efficient Diversification of Investments* (New York: John Wiley, 1959). (A reprint of this book that also contains some new material is available from Basil Blackwell, in Cambridge, MA; its copyright date is 1991.)

2. The technique used for determining the location of the efficient set, along with the composition of the "corner portfolios" that lie on it, was developed in:

Harry M. Markowitz, "The Optimization of a Quadratic Function Subject to Linear Constraints," *Naval Research Logistics Quarterly,* 3, nos. 1–2 (March-June 1956): 111–133.

3. The market model, initially mentioned by Markowitz in a footnote on p. 100 of his book, was developed in:

William F. Sharpe, "A Simplified Model for Portfolio Analysis," *Management Science,* 9, no. 2 (January 1963): 277–293.

4. An extensive discussion of the market model can be found in Chapters 3 and 4 of:

Eugene F. Fama, *Foundations of Finance* (New York: Basic Books, 1976).

5. For discussions of how diversification reduces market risk, see:

John L. Evans and Stephen H. Archer, "Diversification and the Reduction of Dispersion: An Empirical Analysis," *Journal of Finance,* 23, no. 5 (December 1968): 761–767;

W. H. Wagner and S. C. Lau, "The Effect of Diversification on Risk," *Financial Analysts Journal,* 27, no. 6 (November-December 1971): 48–53.

Meir Statman, "How Many Stocks Make a Diversified Portfolio?" *Journal of Financial and Quantitative Analysis,* 22, no. 3 (September 1987): 353–363.

Gerald D. Newbould and Percy S. Poon, "The Minimum Number of Stocks Needed for Diversification," *Financial Practice and Education,* 3, no. 2 (Fall 1993): 85–87.

6. A discussion of some statistical problems that are encountered in partitioning total risk is contained in:

Bert Stine and Dwayne Key, "Reconciling Degrees of Freedom When Partitioning Risk: A Teaching Note," *Journal of Financial Education,* 19 (Fall 1990): 19–22.

7. Some of the statistical problems encountered in using optimization techniques to manage portfolios (specifically, the problem of how to cope with *estimation risk*) are discussed in:

J. D. Jobson and Bob Korkie, "Putting Markowitz Theory to Work," *Journal of Portfolio Management,* 7, no. 4 (Summer 1981): 70–74.

Gordon J. Alexander and Jack Clark Francis, *Portfolio Analysis* (Englewood Cliffs, NJ: Prentice Hall, 1986), Chapter 6.

Peter A. Frost and James E. Savarino, "Portfolio Size and Estimation Risk," *Journal of Portfolio Management,* 12, no. 4 (Summer 1986): 60–64.

Peter A. Frost and James E. Savarino, "For Better Performance: Constrain Portfolio Weights," *Journal of Portfolio Management,* 15, no. 1 (Fall 1988): 29–34.

Richard O. Michaud, "The Markowitz Optimization Enigma: Is 'Optimized' Optimal?" *Financial Analysts Journal,* 45, no. 1 (January/February 1989): 31–42.

Philippe Jorion, "Portfolio Optimization in Practice," *Financial Analysts Journal,* 48, no. 1 (January/February 1992): 68–74.

Vijay K. Chopra and William T. Ziemba, "The Effects of Errors in Means, Variances, and Covariances on Optimal Portfolio Choice," *Journal of Portfolio Management,* 19, no. 2 (Winter 1993): 6–11.

CHAPTER 9

Riskfree Lending and Borrowing

The previous two chapters focus on how an investor should go about determining what portfolio to select for investment. With Markowitz's approach, the investor is assumed to have a certain amount of initial wealth (W_0) to invest for a given holding period. Of all the portfolios that are available, the optimal one is shown to correspond to the point where one of the investor's indifference curves is tangent to the efficient set. At the end of the holding period, the investor's initial wealth will have either increased or decreased depending on the portfolio's rate of return. The resulting end-of-period wealth (W_1) can then be either completely reinvested, completely spent on consumption, or partially reinvested and partially consumed.

The Markowitz approach assumes that the assets considered for investment are individually risky—that is, each one of the N risky assets has an uncertain return over the investor's holding period. Because none of the assets has a perfectly negative correlation with any other asset, all the portfolios also have uncertain returns over the investor's holding period and thus are risky. Furthermore, the investor is not allowed to use borrowed money along with his or her initial wealth to purchase a portfolio of assets. This means that the investor is not allowed to use financial leverage, or margin.

In this chapter, the Markowitz approach to investing is expanded by first allowing the investor to consider investing in not only risky assets but also in a riskfree asset. This means there will now be N assets available for purchase, consisting of $N - 1$ risky assets and one riskfree asset. Second, the investor is allowed to borrow money but has to pay a given rate of interest on the loan. The next section considers the effect of adding a riskfree asset to the set of risky assets.

What exactly is a **riskfree asset** in the context of Markowitz's approach? Because this approach involves investing for a single holding period, it means that the return on the riskfree asset is certain. If the investor purchases a riskfree asset at the beginning of a holding period, then he or she knows exactly what the value of the asset will be at the end of the holding period. As there is no uncertainty about the terminal value of the riskfree asset, the standard deviation of the riskfree asset is, by definition, zero.

In turn, this means that the covariance between the rate of return on the riskfree asset and the rate of return on any risky asset is zero. This can be seen by remembering that the covariance between the returns on any two assets i and j is equal to the product of the correlation coefficient between the assets and the standard deviations of the two assets: $\sigma_{ij} = \rho_{ij}\sigma_i\sigma_j$. Given that $\sigma_i = 0$ if i is the riskfree asset, it follows that $\sigma_{ij} = 0$.

Because a riskfree asset has by definition a certain return, this type of asset must be some kind of fixed-income security with no possibility of default. As all corporate securities in principle have some chance of default, the riskfree asset cannot be issued by a corporation. Instead it must be a security issued by the federal government. However, not just any security issued by the U.S. Treasury qualifies as a riskfree security.

Consider an investor with a three-month holding period who purchases a Treasury security maturing in 20 years. Such a security is risky because the investor does not know what this security will be worth at the end of his or her holding period. As interest rates will very likely change in an unpredictable manner during the investor's holding period, the market price of the security will likewise change in an unpredictable manner. Because the presence of such **interest-rate risk** makes the value of the Treasury security uncertain, it cannot qualify as a riskfree asset. Indeed any Treasury security with a maturity date greater than the investor's holding period cannot qualify as a riskfree asset.

Next consider a Treasury security that matures before the end of the investor's holding period, such as a 30–day Treasury bill in the case of the investor with the three-month holding period. In this situation, the investor does not know at the beginning of the holding period what interest rates will be in 30 days. This means that the investor does not know the interest rate at which the proceeds from the maturing Treasury bill can be reinvested for the remainder of the holding period. The presence of such **reinvestment-rate risk** in all Treasury securities of shorter maturity than the investor's holding period means that these securities do not qualify as riskfree assets.

This leaves only one type of Treasury security to qualify as a riskfree asset: a Treasury security with a maturity that matches the length of the investor's holding period. For example, the investor with the three-month holding period would find that a Treasury bill with a three-month maturity date had a certain return. Because this security matures at the end of the investor's holding period, it provides the investor with an amount of money at the end of the holding period that is known for certain at the beginning of the holding period when an investment decision has to be made.[1]

Investing in the riskfree asset is often referred to as **riskfree lending,** because such an investment involves the purchase of Treasury bills and thus involves a loan by the investor to the federal government.

9.2	ALLOWING FOR RISKFREE LENDING

With the introduction of a riskfree asset, the investor is now able to put part of his or her money in this asset and the remainder in any of the risky portfolios contained in Markowitz's feasible set. Adding these new opportunities expands the feasible set significantly and, more importantly, changes the location of a substantial part of Markowitz's efficient set. The nature of these changes needs to be analyzed, since investors are concerned with selecting a portfolio from the efficient set. In so doing, consideration is given initially to determining the expected return and standard deviation for a portfolio that consists of combining an investment in the riskfree asset with an investment in a single risky security.

9.2.1   Investing in Both a Riskfree Asset and a Risky Asset

In Chapter 7, the companies of Able, Baker, and Charlie were assumed to have expected returns, variances, and covariances as indicated in the following expected return vector and variance-covariance matrix:

$$ER = \begin{bmatrix} 16.2 \\ 24.6 \\ 22.8 \end{bmatrix} \qquad VC = \begin{bmatrix} 146 & 187 & 145 \\ 187 & 854 & 104 \\ 145 & 104 & 289 \end{bmatrix}.$$

Defining the riskfree asset as security number 4, consider all portfolios that involve investing in just the common stock of Able and the riskfree asset. Let X_1 denote the proportion of the investor's funds invested in Able and $X_4 = 1 - X_1$ denote the proportion invested in the riskfree asset. If the investor put all his or her money in the riskfree asset, then $X_1 = 0$ and $X_4 = 1$. Alternatively, the investor could put all his or her money in just Able, in which case $X_1 = 1$ and $X_4 = 0$. A combination of .25 in Able and .75 in the riskfree asset is also possible, as are respective combinations of .50 and .50 or .75 and .25. While there are other possibilities, the focus here will be on these five portfolios:

	Portfolio A	Portfolio B	Portfolio C	Portfolio D	Portfolio E
X_1	.00	.25	.50	.75	1.00
X_4	1.00	.75	.50	.25	.00

Assuming that the riskfree asset has a rate of return (often denoted r_f) of 4%, all the necessary information for calculating the expected returns and standard deviations for these five portfolios is at hand. Equation (7.3a) from Chapter 7 can be used to calculate the expected returns for these portfolios:

$$\bar{r}_p = \sum_{i=1}^{N} X_i \bar{r}_i \qquad (7.3a)$$

$$= \sum_{i=1}^{4} X_i \bar{r}_i.$$

Portfolios A, B, C, D, and E do not involve investing in the second and third securities (that is, Baker and Charlie companies), meaning that $X_2 = 0$ and $X_3 = 0$ in these portfolios. Thus, the previous equation reduces to:

$$\bar{r}_p = X_1 \bar{r}_1 + X_4 \bar{r}_4$$
$$= (X_1 \times 16.2\%) + (X_4 \times 4\%)$$

where the riskfree rate is now denoted r_4.

For portfolios A and E this calculation is trivial because all the investor's funds are being placed in just one security. Thus their expected returns are just 4% and 16.2%, respectively. For portfolios B, C, and D, the expected returns are, respectively:

$$\bar{r}_B = (.25 \times 16.2\%) + (.75 \times 4\%)$$
$$= 7.05\%$$
$$\bar{r}_C = (.50 \times 16.2\%) + (.50 \times 4\%)$$
$$= 10.10\%$$
$$\bar{r}_D = (.75 \times 16.2\%) + (.25 \times 4\%)$$
$$= 13.15\%.$$

The standard deviations of portfolios A and E are simply the standard deviations of the riskfree asset and Able, respectively. Thus $\sigma_A = 0\%$ and $\sigma_E = 12.08\%$. In calculating the standard deviations of portfolios B, C, and D, Equation (7.7) from Chapter 7 must be utilized:

$$\sigma_p = \left[\sum_{i=1}^{N} \sum_{j=1}^{N} X_i X_j \sigma_{ij} \right]^{1/2} \qquad (7.7)$$

$$= \left[\sum_{i=1}^{4} \sum_{j=1}^{4} X_i X_j \sigma_{ij} \right]^{1/2}.$$

As $X_2 = 0$ and $X_3 = 0$ in these portfolios, this equation reduces to:

$$\sigma_p = [X_1 X_1 \sigma_{11} + X_1 X_4 \sigma_{14} + X_4 X_1 \sigma_{41} + X_4 X_4 \sigma_{44}]^{1/2}$$
$$= [X_1^2 \sigma_1^2 + X_4^2 \sigma_4^2 + 2X_1 X_4 \sigma_{14}]^{1/2}.$$

This equation can be reduced even further, because security number 4 is the riskfree security that, by definition, has $\sigma_4 = 0$ and $\sigma_{14} = 0$. Accordingly, it reduces to:

$$\sigma_p = [X_1^2 \sigma_1^2]^{1/2}$$
$$= [X_1^2 \times 146]^{1/2}$$
$$= X_1 \times 12.08\%.$$

Thus the standard deviations of portfolios B, C, and D are:

$$\sigma_B = .25 \times 12.08\%$$
$$= 3.02\%$$
$$\sigma_C = .50 \times 12.08\%$$
$$= 6.04\%$$
$$\sigma_D = .75 \times 12.08\%$$
$$= 9.06\%.$$

In summary, the five portfolios have the following expected returns and standard deviations:

Portfolio	X_1	X_4	Expected Return	Standard Deviation
A	.00	1.00	4.00%	0.00%
B	.25	.75	7.05	3.02
C	.50	.50	10.10	6.04
D	.75	.25	13.15	9.06
E	1.00	.00	16.20	12.08

These portfolios are plotted in Figure 9.1. It can be seen that they all lie on a straight line connecting the points representing the location of the riskfree asset and Able. Although only five particular combinations of the riskfree asset and Able have been examined here, it can be shown that any combination of the riskfree asset and Able will lie somewhere on the straight line connecting them; the exact location will depend on the relative proportions invested in these two assets. Furthermore, this observation can be generalized to combinations of the

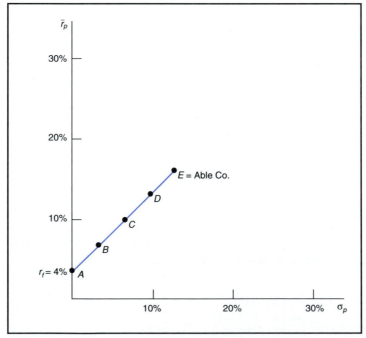

Figure 9.1
Combining Riskfree Lending with Investing in a Risky Asset

riskfree asset and any risky asset. This means that any portfolio consisting of a combination of the riskfree asset and a risky asset will have an expected return and standard deviation such that it plots somewhere on a straight line connecting them.

9.2.2 Investing in Both the Riskfree Asset and a Risky Portfolio

Next consider what happens when a portfolio consisting of more than just one risky security is combined with the riskfree asset. For example, consider the risky portfolio *PAC* that consists of Able and Charlie in proportions of .80 and .20, respectively. Its expected return (denoted $\bar{r}_{PAC}$) and standard deviation (denoted σ_{PAC}) are equal to:

$$\bar{r}_{PAC} = (.80 \times 16.2\%) + (.20 \times 22.8\%)$$
$$= 17.52\%$$
$$\sigma_{PAC} = [(.80 \times .80 \times 146) + (.20 \times .20 \times 289) +$$
$$(2 \times .80 \times .20 \times 145)]^{1/2}$$
$$= 12.30\%.$$

Any portfolio that consists of an investment in both *PAC* and the riskfree asset will have an expected return and standard deviation that can be calculated in a manner identical to that previously shown for combinations of an individual asset and the riskfree asset. A portfolio that has the proportion X_{PAC} invested in the portfolio *PAC* and the proportion $X_4 = 1 - X_{PAC}$ in the riskfree asset will have an expected return and standard deviation that are equal to, respectively:

$$\bar{r}_{PAC} = (X_{PAC} \times 17.52\%) + (X_4 \times 4\%)$$
$$\sigma_{PAC} = X_{PAC} \times 12.30\%.$$

For example, consider investing in a portfolio that consists of *PAC* and the riskfree asset in proportions of .25 and .75, respectively.[2] This portfolio will have an expected return of:

$$\bar{r}_p = (.25 \times 17.52\%) + (.75 \times 4\%)$$
$$= 7.38\%$$

and a standard deviation of:

$$\sigma_p = .25 \times 12.30\%$$
$$= 3.08\%.$$

Figure 9.2 shows that this portfolio lies on a straight line connecting the riskfree asset and *PAC*. In particular, it is indicated by the point *P* on this line. Other portfolios consisting of various combinations of *PAC* and the riskfree asset will also lie on this line, with their exact locations depending on the relative proportions invested in *PAC* and the riskfree asset. For example, a portfolio that involves investing a proportion of .50 in the riskfree asset and a proportion of .50 in *PAC* lies on this line exactly halfway between the two endpoints.

In summary, combining the riskfree asset with any risky portfolio can be viewed as being no different from combining the riskfree asset with an individual risky security. In both cases, the resulting portfolio has an expected return and standard deviation such that it lies somewhere on a straight line connecting the two endpoints.

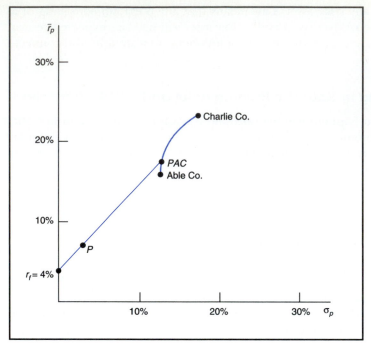

Figure 9.2
Combining Riskfree Lending with Investing in a Risky Portfolio

9.2.3 The Effect of Riskfree Lending on the Efficient Set

As mentioned earlier, the feasible set is changed significantly as a result of the introduction of riskfree lending. Figure 9.3 shows how it changes the feasible set for the example at hand. Here all risky assets and portfolios, not just Able and *PAC*, are considered in all possible combinations with the riskfree asset. In particular, note that there are two boundaries that are straight lines emanating from the riskfree asset. The bottom line connects the riskfree asset with Baker. Thus it represents portfolios formed by combining Baker and the riskfree asset.

The other straight line emanating from the riskfree asset represents combinations of the riskfree asset and a particular risky portfolio on the efficient set of the Markowitz model. It is a line that is just tangent to this efficient set, with the tangency point being denoted *T*. This tangency point represents a risky portfolio consisting of Able, Baker, and Charlie in proportions equal to, respectively, .12, .19, and .69. Substituting these proportions into Equations (7.3a) and (7.7) indicates that the expected return and standard deviation of *T* are 22.4% and 15.2%, respectively.

Although other risky efficient portfolios from the Markowitz model can also be combined with the riskfree asset, portfolio *T* deserves special attention. Why? Because there is no other portfolio consisting purely of risky assets that, when connected by a straight line to the riskfree asset, lies northwest of it. In other words, of all the lines that can be drawn emanating from the riskfree asset and

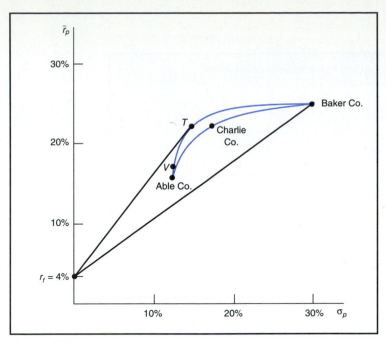

Figure 9.3
Feasible and Efficient Sets When Riskfree Lending Is Introduced

connecting with either a risky asset or risky portfolio, none has a greater slope than the line that goes to *T*.

This is important because part of the efficient set of the Markowitz model is dominated by this line. In particular, the portfolios on the Markowitz model efficient set going from the minimum risk portfolio, denoted *V*, to *T* are no longer efficient when a riskfree asset is made available for investment. Instead the efficient set now consists of a straight-line segment and a curved segment. The straight-line segment is the straight line going from the riskfree asset to *T* and thus consists of portfolios made up of various combinations of the riskfree asset and *T*. The curved segment consists of those portfolios to the northeast of *T* on the Markowitz model efficient set.

9.2.4   The Effect of Riskfree Lending on Portfolio Selection

Figure 9.4 shows how an investor would go about selecting an optimal efficient portfolio when there is a riskfree asset available for investment in addition to a number of risky assets. If the investor's indifference curves look like those shown in panel (a), the investor's optimal portfolio O* will involve investing part of his or her initial wealth in the riskfree asset and the rest in *T* because his or her indifference curves are tangent to the efficient set between the riskfree asset and *T*.[3] Alternatively, if the investor is less risk averse and has indifference curves that look like those shown in panel (b), then the investor's optimal portfolio O* will not involve any riskfree lending because his or her indifference curves are tangent to the curved segment of the efficient set that lies to the northeast of *T*.

Riskfree Lending and Borrowing   **239**

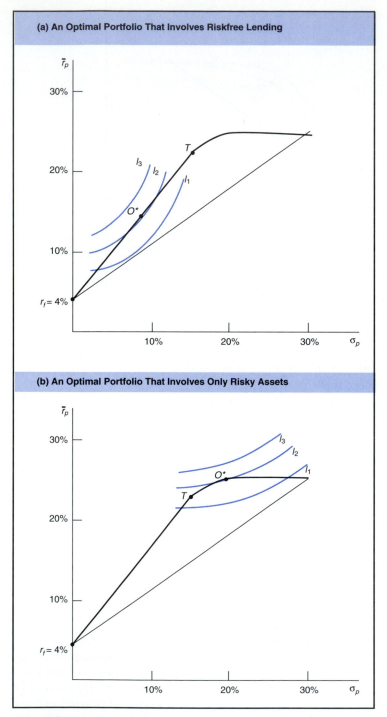

Figure 9.4
Portfolio Selection with Riskfree Lending

The analysis that was presented in the previous section can be expanded by allowing the investor to borrow money. This means that the investor is no longer restricted to his or her initial wealth when it comes time to decide how much money to invest in risky assets.[4] However, if the investor borrows money, then interest must be paid on the loan. Since the interest rate is known and there is no uncertainty about repaying the loan, it is often referred to as **riskfree borrowing.**

It will be assumed that the rate of interest charged on the loan is equal to the rate of interest that could be earned from investing in the riskfree asset.[5] In the earlier example, this means that the investor now has not only the opportunity to invest in a riskfree asset that earns a rate of return of 4% but alternatively may borrow money, for which the investor must pay a rate of interest equal to 4%.

Earlier the proportion invested in the riskfree asset was denoted X_4, and this proportion was constrained to be a nonnegative number between zero and one. Now with the opportunity to borrow at the same rate, X_4 will no longer be so constrained. In the earlier example, the investor had initial wealth of $17,200. If the investor borrows money, then he or she will have in excess of $17,200 to invest in the risky securities of Able, Baker, and Charlie.

For example, if the investor borrows $4,300, then he or she will have a total of $21,500 (= $17,200 + $4,300) to invest in these securities. In this situation, X_4 can be viewed as being equal to $-.25$ (= $-\$4,300/\$17,200$). However, the sum of the proportions must still equal one. This means that if the investor has borrowed money, the sum of the proportions invested in risky assets would be greater than one. For example, borrowing $4,300 and investing $21,500 in Able means that the proportion in Able, X_1, equals 1.25 (= $\$21,500/\$17,200$). Note how in this case $X_1 + X_4 = 1.25 + (-.25) = 1$.

9.3.1   Borrowing and Investing in a Risky Security

To evaluate the effect that the introduction of riskfree borrowing has on the efficient set, the example presented in the previous section will be expanded. In particular, consider portfolios *F, G, H,* and *I* where the investor will invest all the borrowed funds as well as his or her own funds in Able. Thus the proportions for these portfolios can be summarized as follows:

	Portfolio F	Portfolio G	Portfolio H	Portfolio I
X_1	1.25	1.50	1.75	2.00
X_4	−.25	−.50	−.75	−1.00

The expected returns of these portfolios are calculated in the same manner as was shown in the previous section. Equation (7.3a) is still used:

$$\bar{r}_p = \sum_{i=1}^{N} X_i \bar{r}_i \qquad\qquad (7.3a)$$

$$= \sum_{i=1}^{4} X_i \bar{r}_i.$$

$$= X_1 \bar{r}_1 + X_4 \bar{r}_4$$

$$= (X_1 \times 16.2\%) + (X_4 \times 4\%)$$

Thus portfolios *F, G, H,* and *I* have the following expected returns:

$$\bar{r}_F = (1.25 \times 16.2\%) + (-.25 \times 4\%)$$
$$= 19.25\%$$
$$\bar{r}_G = (1.50 \times 16.2\%) + (-.50 \times 4\%)$$
$$= 22.30\%$$
$$\bar{r}_H = (1.75 \times 16.2\%) + (-.75 \times 4\%)$$
$$= 25.35\%$$
$$\bar{r}_I = (2.00 \times 16.2\%) + (-1.00 \times 4\%)$$
$$= 28.40\%.$$

Similarly, the standard deviations of these portfolios are calculated by using Equation (7.7) as was done in the previous section:

$$\sigma_p = \left[\sum_{i=1}^{N} \sum_{j=1}^{N} X_i X_j \sigma_{ij} \right]^{1/2} \qquad\qquad (7.7)$$

$$= \left[\sum_{i=1}^{4} \sum_{j=1}^{4} X_i X_j \sigma_{ij} \right]^{1/2}$$

which was shown to reduce to:

$$\sigma_p = X_1 \times 12.08\%.$$

Thus the standard deviations of the four portfolios are:

$$\sigma_F = 1.25 \times 12.08\%$$
$$= 15.10\%$$
$$\sigma_G = 1.50 \times 12.08\%$$
$$= 18.12\%$$
$$\sigma_H = 1.75 \times 12.08\%$$
$$= 21.14\%$$
$$\sigma_I = 2.00 \times 12.08\%$$
$$= 24.16\%.$$

In summary, these four portfolios, as well as the five portfolios that involve risk-free lending, have the following expected returns and standard deviations:

Portfolio	X_1	X_4	Expected Return	Standard Deviation
A	.00	1.00	4.00%	0.00%
B	.25	.75	7.05	3.02
C	.50	.50	10.10	6.04
D	.75	.25	13.15	9.06
E	1.00	.00	16.20	12.08
F	1.25	−.25	19.25	15.10
G	1.50	−.50	22.30	18.12
H	1.75	−.75	25.35	21.14
I	2.00	−1.00	28.40	24.16

In Figure 9.5, it can be seen that the four portfolios that involve riskfree borrowing (F, G, H, and I) all lie on the same straight line that goes through the five portfolios that involve riskfree lending (A, B, C, D, and E). Furthermore, the larger the amount of borrowing, the further out on the line the portfolio lies; equivalently, the smaller the value of X_4, the further out on the line the portfolio lies.

Although only four particular combinations of borrowing and investing in Able have been examined here, it can be shown that any combination of borrowing and investing in Able will lie somewhere on this line with the exact location depending on the amount of borrowing. Furthermore, this observation can be generalized to combinations of riskfree borrowing and an investment in any particular risky asset. This means that borrowing at the riskfree rate and investing

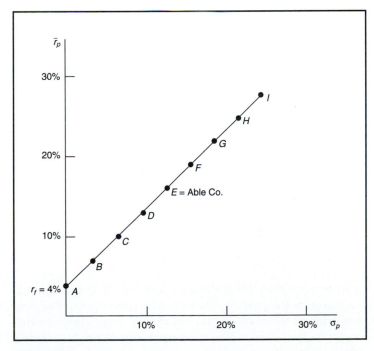

Figure 9.5
Combining Riskfree Borrowing and Lending with Investing in a Risky Asset

all the borrowed money and the investor's own money in a risky asset will result in a portfolio that has an expected return and standard deviation such that it lies on the extension of the straight line connecting the riskfree rate and the risky asset.

9.3.2 Borrowing and Investing in a Risky Portfolio

Next consider what happens when a portfolio of more than one risky asset is purchased with both the investor's own funds and borrowed funds. Earlier it was shown that the portfolio having proportions invested in Able and Charlie equal to .80 and .20, respectively, had an expected return of 17.52% and a standard deviation of 12.30%. This portfolio was referred to as *PAC*. Any portfolio that involves borrowing money at the riskfree rate and then investing these funds and the investor's own funds in *PAC* will have an expected return and standard deviation that can be calculated in a manner identical to that which was previously shown when borrowing was incurred and Able was purchased. A portfolio that involves borrowing the proportion X_4 and investing these funds and all the investor's own funds in *PAC* will have an expected return and standard deviation that are equal to, respectively:

$$\bar{r}_{PAC} = (X_{PAC} \times 17.52\%) + (X_4 \times 4\%)$$
$$\sigma_{PAC} = X_{PAC} \times 12.30\%.$$

For example, consider borrowing an amount of money equal to 25% of the investor's initial wealth and then investing all the investor's own funds and these borrowed funds in *PAC*. Thus, $X_{PAC} = 1 - X_4 = 1 - (-.25) = 1.25.$[6] This portfolio will have an expected return of:

$$\bar{r}_p = (1.25 \times 17.52\%) + (-.25 \times 4\%)$$
$$= 20.90\%$$

and a standard deviation of:

$$\sigma_p = 1.25 \times 12.30\%$$
$$= 15.38\%.$$

In Figure 9.6, it can be seen that this portfolio (denoted P) lies on the extension of the line that connects the riskfree rate with *PAC*. Other portfolios consisting of *PAC* and borrowing at the riskfree rate will also lie somewhere on this extension with their exact location depending on the amount of the borrowing. Thus borrowing to purchase a risky portfolio is no different from borrowing to purchase an individual risky asset. In both cases, the resulting portfolio lies on an extension of the line connecting the riskfree rate with the risky investment.

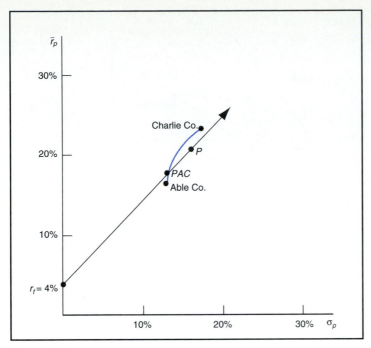

Figure 9.6
Combining Riskfree Borrowing and Lending with Investing in a Risky
Portfolio

ALLOWING FOR BOTH RISKFREE BORROWING AND LENDING

9.4.1 The Effect of Riskfree Borrowing and Lending on the Efficient Set

Figure 9.7 shows how the feasible set is changed when both borrowing and lending at the same riskfree rate are allowed. Here all risky assets and portfolios, not just Able and *PAC*, are considered. The feasible set is the entire area between the two lines emanating from the riskfree rate that go through the location of Baker and the portfolio denoted *T*. These two lines extend indefinitely to the right if it is assumed that there is no limit to the amount of borrowing that the investor can incur.

The straight line that goes through portfolio *T* is of special importance because it represents the efficient set. This means that it represents the set of portfolios that offer the best opportunities as it represents the set of feasible portfolios lying furthest northwest. Portfolio *T*, as was mentioned earlier, consists of investments in Able, Baker, and Charlie in proportions equal to, respectively, .12, .19, and .69.[7]

As before, the line going through *T* is just tangent to the Markowitz model efficient set. None of the portfolios, except for *T*, that were on the Markowitz model efficient set are efficient when riskfree borrowing and lending are intro-

---

Riskfree Lending and Borrowing   **245**

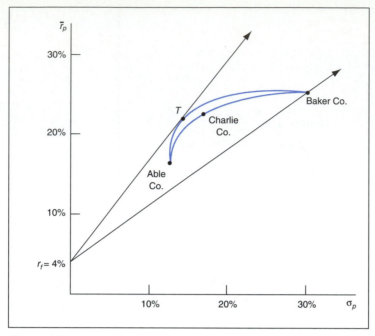

Figure 9.7
Feasible and Efficient Sets When Riskfree Borrowing and Lending Are
Introduced

duced. This can be seen by noting that every portfolio (except T) that lies on
the Markowitz model efficient set is dominated by a portfolio on this straight
line having the same standard deviation along with a higher expected return.

9.4.2 The Effect of Riskfree Borrowing and Lending on Portfolio Selection

Given the opportunity to either borrow or lend at the riskfree rate, an investor
would proceed to identify the optimal portfolio by plotting his or her indifference
curves on this graph and noting where one of them is tangent to the linear efficient set.[8] Figure 9.8 shows two alternative situations. If the investor's indifference
curves look like the ones in panel (a), then the investor's optimal portfolio O^* will
consist of an investment in the riskfree asset as well as in T. Alternatively, if the investor is less risk averse and has indifference curves that look like those shown in
panel (b), then the investor's optimal portfolio O^* will consist of borrowing at the
riskfree rate and investing these funds as well as his or her own funds in T.[9]

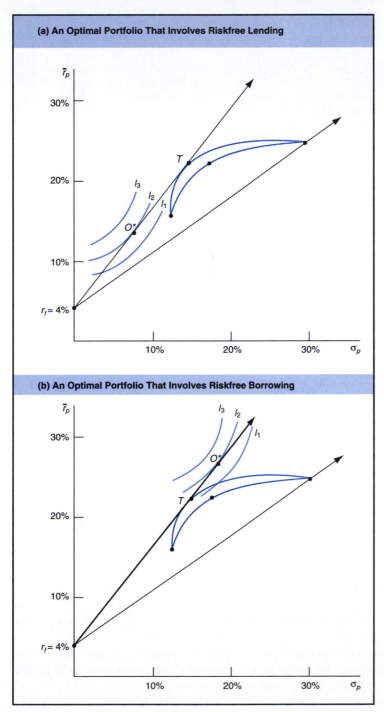

Figure 9.8
Portfolio Selection with Riskfree Borrowing and Lending

The Cost of Short-Term Borrowing

The extension of the Markowitz model to incorporate borrowing and lending assumes that investors can borrow or lend at the riskfree rate. Certainly, every investor has the opportunity to lend at the riskfree rate by simply purchasing U.S. Treasury securities with maturities corresponding to the length of his or her investment holding period.

Borrowing at the riskfree rate is another matter. In reality, only one entity has the option to borrow at the riskfree rate: the U.S. Treasury. Other investors, be they individuals or institutional investors, must borrow at interest rates exceeding those paid by the Treasury.

Just what level of interest rates do investors pay to borrow? To provide some perspective on this issue, we briefly survey some of the interest rates available in the market for short-term financial assets known as the *money market*.

The standard of comparison for all money market interest rates is the rate paid on short-term U.S. Treasury securities called U.S. Treasury bills (see Chapter 1). The return on Treasury bills is completely certain over the short term because the federal government will never default on its obligations. It always has the option to print money or raise taxes to pay off its debts.

Other borrowers, no matter how strong their current financial position, run at least some risk of defaulting on their short-term debts. Largely due to this fact, virtually all non-Treasury borrowers must pay interest rates exceeding those paid by the Treasury. The difference between what the Treasury pays to borrow money and what other borrowers pay is known as the *spread*. How large is the spread for non-Treasury borrowers?

If you as an individual investor wish to finance your investment in securities, you typically purchase them on margin from your broker. The same holds true for institutional investors. In such transactions the broker actually borrows money elsewhere in the money market (usually drawing down a line of credit at a bank and pledging securities as collateral). The interest rate paid by the broker is known as the *broker call money*, or broker call loan *rate* (see Chapter 3). Brokers add anywhere from 1% to 2% to the call money rate to determine the interest rate charged their margin

9.5 SUMMARY

1. The return on a riskfree asset is certain. The riskfree asset's standard deviation is zero as is its covariance with other assets.
2. In extending the Markowitz feasible set to include riskfree lending, investors are assumed to allocate their funds among a riskfree asset and a portfolio of risky assets.
3. With riskfree lending, the efficient set becomes a straight line from the riskfree rate to a point tangent to the curved Markowitz efficient set, in addition to the portion of the Markowitz efficient set that lies northeast of this tangency point.
4. Introducing riskfree borrowing permits an investor to engage in leverage. The investor may use all of his or her money, plus money borrowed at the riskfree rate, to purchase a portfolio of risky assets.
5. With riskfree lending and borrowing, the efficient set becomes a straight line from the riskfree rate through a point tangent to the curved Markowitz efficient set.

purchase customers. Larger investors can usually negotiate more favorable borrowing terms than smaller investors.

In 1992, the broker call money rate averaged roughly 5.62%. By comparison, the U.S. Treasury paid an average interest rate on 90–day Treasury bills of 3.43%. Thus the broker call money spread was 2.19 percentage points. Assuming a 1 percentage point markup over the broker call money rate, margin investors faced an average spread over 90–day Treasuries of 3.19 percentage points during 1992.

Large, financially strong corporations usually borrow in the money market through an instrument known as *commercial paper.* Commercial paper represents the negotiable, short-term, unsecured promissory notes of finance, industrial, utility, insurance, and bank holding companies. In 1992, three-month commercial paper interest rates averaged 3.75%, a spread of .32 percentage points over similar-maturity 90–day Treasury bills.

Corporations without the size and financial strength to borrow in the commercial paper market must obtain their short-term financing from banks. The interest rate officially quoted by banks on short-term unsecured loans to their best cus-

tomers is known as the *prime rate.* The prime rate is not always an accurate measure of short-term borrowing costs, as banks often discount from it on loans to their financially strong borrowers. Financially weaker clients, on the other hand, may be charged a premium above the prime rate. In 1992, the prime rate averaged 6.25%, a 2.82 percentage point spread over 90–day Treasuries.

Banks themselves borrow in the money market through large-denomination certificates of deposit (of usually $1 million or larger). Although these loans are unsecured and do not carry federal deposit insurance, the strong financial standing of most banks requires them to pay little more than the government for short-term borrowing. In 1992, rates for large, three-month certificates of deposit averaged 3.64%, only .21 percentage points above 90–day Treasuries.

From this brief money market survey, it is apparent that the Treasury bill rate is relevant to investor borrowing only as a base of comparison. Investors actually have to pay more, sometimes much more, to borrow in the money market, but then, of course, such borrowing is not considered riskfree, at least by the lenders.

6. With riskfree lending and borrowing, the efficient set consists of combinations of a single risky portfolio and various proportions of riskfree lending or borrowing.

7. The investor's optimal portfolio is determined by plotting his or her indifference curves against the efficient set.

8. The investor's optimal portfolio will include an investment in the risky portfolio and borrowing or lending at the riskfree rate.

9. Investors with higher levels of risk aversion will engage in less borrowing (or more lending) than investors with less risk aversion.

QUESTIONS AND PROBLEMS

1. Why is a pure discount government security (that is, one that does not make coupon payments, pays interest at maturity, and hence sells at a discount from par) with no risk of default still risky to an investor whose holding period does not coincide with the maturity date of the security?

2. Distinguish between reinvestment-rate risk and interest-rate risk.

Riskfree Lending and Borrowing

3. The covariance between a risk-free asset and a risky asset is zero. Explain why this is the case and demonstrate it mathematically.

4. Lindsay Brown owns a risky portfolio with a 15% expected return. The risk-free return is 5%. What is the expected return on Lindsay's total portfolio if Lindsay invests the following proportions in the risky portfolio and the remainder in the riskfree asset?
   a. 120%
   b. 90%
   c. 75%

5. Consider a risky portfolio with an expected return of 18%. With a riskfree return of 5%, how could you create a portfolio with a 24% expected return?

6. Happy Buker owns a risky portfolio with a 20% standard deviation. If Happy invests the following proportions in the riskfree asset and the remainder in the risky portfolio, what is the standard deviation of Happy's total portfolio?
   a. −30%
   b. 10%
   c. 30%

7. Oyster Burns's portfolio is composed of an investment in a risky portfolio (with a 12% expected return and a 25% standard deviation) and a riskfree asset (with a 7% return). If Oyster's total portfolio has a 20% standard deviation, what is its expected return?

8. Hick Cady argues that buying a risky portfolio with riskfree borrowing is equivalent to a purchase of the risky portfolio on margin. Patsy Cahill contends that such an investment can be viewed as selling the riskfree asset short and using proceeds to invest in the risky portfolio. Who is correct? Explain.

9. How does the efficient set change when riskfree borrowing and lending are introduced into the Markowitz model? Explain with words and graphs.

10. Why does the efficient set with the Markowitz model extended to include riskfree borrowing and lending have only one point in common with the efficient set of the Markowitz model without riskfree borrowing and lending? Why are the other points on the "old" efficient set no longer desirable? Explain with words and graphs.

11. Based on the assumptions developed in this chapter, is it true that all investors will hold the same risky portfolio? Explain.

12. How does the feasible set change when riskfree borrowing and lending are introduced into the Markowitz model? Explain with words and graphs.

13. With the Markowitz model extended to include riskfree borrowing and lending, draw the indifference curves, efficient set, and optimal portfolio for an investor with high risk aversion and an investor with low risk aversion.

14. Given the following expected return vector and variance-covariance matrix for three assets:

$$ER = \begin{bmatrix} 10.1 \\ 7.8 \\ 5.0 \end{bmatrix} \qquad VC = \begin{bmatrix} 210 & 60 & 0 \\ 60 & 90 & 0 \\ 0 & 0 & 0 \end{bmatrix}$$

and given the fact that Pie Traynor's risky portfolio is split 50–50 between the two risky assets:

a. Which security of the three must be the riskfree asset? Why?

b. Calculate the expected return and standard deviation of Pie's portfolio.

c. If the riskfree asset makes up 25% of Pie's total portfolio, what is the total portfolio's expected return and standard deviation?

15. What does the efficient set look like if riskfree borrowing is permitted but no lending is allowed? Explain with words and graphs.

16. What will be the effect on total portfolio expected return and risk if you borrow money at the riskfree rate and invest in the optimal risky portfolio?

17. Suppose that your level of risk aversion decreased as you grew richer. In a world of riskfree borrowing and lending, how would your optimal portfolio change? Would the types of risky securities you hold change? Explain with words and graphs.

18. (Appendix Question) How does the efficient set change when the condition of borrowing and lending at the same riskfree rate is changed to borrowing at a rate greater than the rate at which riskfree lending can be conducted? Explain with words and graphs.

19. (Appendix Question) Using the EGP algorithm, find the tangency portfolio associated with the following securities.

Security	Expected Return	Beta	Unsystematic Risk(σ_{ei}^2)
1	15.0%	1.50	500
2	11.0	1.10	625
3	10.0	1.00	600
4	9.0	0.90	800
5	7.0	0.70	600

The riskfree rate is 4.0%, and the variance of the market index is 400. (Use of a computer spreadsheet is recommended.)

APPENDIX A

ALLOWING FOR DIFFERENT BORROWING AND LENDING RATES

In this chapter it was assumed that the investor could borrow funds at the same rate that could be earned on an investment in the riskfree asset. As a result, the feasible set became the area bounded by two straight lines emanating from the riskfree rate. The upper line represented the efficient set and had one portfolio in common with the curved efficient set of the Markowitz model. This portfolio was located where the straight line from the riskfree rate was tangent to the curved efficient set. Now the concern will be with what happens if it is assumed that the investor can borrow but at a rate that is greater than the rate that can be earned by an investment in the riskfree asset. The rate on the riskfree asset will be denoted r_{fL}, where L indicates lending, because, as mentioned earlier, an investment in the riskfree asset is equivalent to lending money to the government. The rate at which the investor can borrow money will be denoted r_{fB} and is of a magnitude such that $r_{fB} > r_{fL}$.

One way to understand the effect on the efficient set of assuming that these two rates are different is as follows. First, consider what the efficient set would look like if riskfree borrowing and lending were possible at the same rate, r_{fL}. The resulting efficient set would be the straight line shown in Figure 9.9 that goes through the points r_{fL} and T_L.

Second, consider what the efficient set would look like if riskfree borrowing and lending were possible at the higher rate, r_{fB}. The resulting efficient set would be the straight line shown in Figure 9.9 that goes through the points r_{fB} and T_B. Note that the portfolio T_B lies on Markowitz's efficient set above the portfolio T_L, because it corresponds to a tangency point associated with a higher riskfree rate.

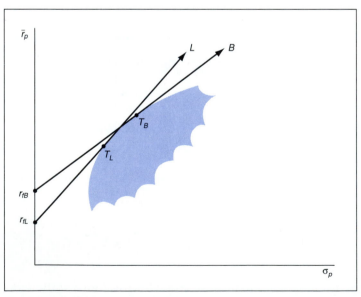

Figure 9.9
Evaluating Different Riskfree Rates

Third, as the investor cannot borrow at r_{fL}, that part of the line emanating from r_{fL} that extends to the right of T_L is not available to the investor and can thus be removed from consideration.

Fourth, as the investor cannot lend at the riskfree rate r_{fB}, that part of the line emanating from r_{fB} and going through T_B but lying to the left of T_B is not available to the investor and can thus be removed from consideration. The northwest boundary of what remains, shown in Figure 9.10, is the resulting efficient set.

This efficient set consists of three distinct but connected segments. The first segment is the straight line going from r_{fL} to T_L that represents various amounts of riskfree lending combined with investing in the portfolio of risky assets denoted T_L. The second segment is the curved line going from T_L to T_B that represents various risky portfolios that were also on Markowitz's curved efficient set. The third segment is the straight line extending outward from T_B that represents various amounts of borrowing combined with an investment in the risky portfolio denoted T_B.

The optimal portfolio for an investor will be, as before, the portfolio that corresponds to the point where an indifference curve is tangent to the efficient set. Depending on the investor's indifference curves, this tangency point could be on any one of the three segments that comprise the efficient set.

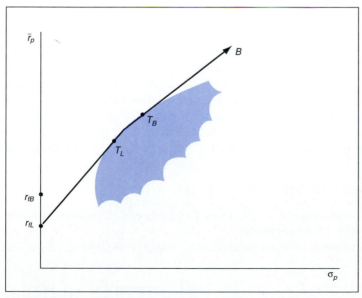

Figure 9.10
Efficient Set When the Riskfree Rates Are Different

APPENDIX B

DETERMINING THE COMPOSITION OF THE TANGENCY PORTFOLIO T

CORNER PORTFOLIOS AND T

When riskfree opportunities are added to the Markowitz model, the efficient set is a straight line going through portfolio T. This portfolio is known as the tangency portfolio as it lies at the point on the curved efficient set of Markowitz that is tangent to a straight line emanating from the riskfree rate.

Determining the composition of T (and hence its location) involves the same procedures that were presented in Appendix A to Chapter 8. In the example presented earlier in Figure 9.7, portfolio T was shown to lie on the curved efficient set of the Markowitz model. Specifically, it lies between the second and third corner portfolios that are shown in Figure 8.13, where they are denoted $C(2)$ and $C(3)$, respectively. Since T lies between these two corner portfolios, its composition is a weighted average of the compositions of $C(2)$ and $C(3)$ that are shown in Table 8.1. These weights [.86 in $C(2)$ and .14 in $C(3)$] can be determined graphically by drawing a horizontal line from T to the vertical axis where the expected return of T can then be measured.

In this example, the expected return of T is 22.4%. Since T lies between $C(2)$ and $C(3)$, its expected return must be a weighted average of the expected returns of $C(2)$, the above surrounding portfolio, and $C(3)$, the below surrounding portfolio. Thus its composition in terms of $C(2)$ and $C(3)$ can be determined by using Equation (8.13) with $\bar{r}^* = 22.4\%$, $\bar{r}^a = 23.20\%$, and $\bar{r}^b = 17.26\%$:

$$22.4\% = (23.20\% \times Y) + [17.26\% \times (1 - Y)].$$

The solution to this equation is $Y = .86$. Thus T consists of $C(2)$ and $C(3)$ in the proportions of .86 and .14, respectively.

In terms of the amount of investment in Able, Baker, and Charlie, this translates to:

$$[.86 \times X(2)] + [.14 \times X(3)] = .86 \times \begin{bmatrix} .00 \\ .22 \\ .78 \end{bmatrix} + .14 \times \begin{bmatrix} .84 \\ .00 \\ .16 \end{bmatrix} = \begin{bmatrix} .12 \\ .19 \\ .69 \end{bmatrix}.$$

That is, T consists of an investment of 12% in Able, 19% in Baker, and 69% in Charlie.

<table>
<tr><td>**B.2**</td><td>THE MARKET MODEL AND T</td></tr>
</table>

There is another method of determining the composition of T that does not involve the identification of corner portfolios and consequently is much simpler that the one just described. (Indeed all that is needed to use this method is some basic knowledge of how to use a spreadsheet.) It assumes that security returns can be described by the market model and that there is a riskfree borrowing and lending rate r_f available. The method, developed by Elton, Gruber, and Padberg (hereafter EGP), can be described by use of an example.[10]

Imagine that the investor wishes to locate the tangency portfolio T that is associated with the following ten securities.

Security Number i	Expected Return ($\bar{r}_i$)	Beta (β_{iI})	Unsystematic Risk (σ_{ei}^2)
1	15.0%	1.0	50
2	17.0	1.5	40
3	12.0	1.0	20
4	17.0	2.0	10
5	11.0	1.0	40
6	11.0	1.5	30
7	11.0	2.0	40
8	7.0	0.8	16
9	7.0	1.0	20
10	5.6	0.6	6

Furthermore, assume that the variance of the market index portfolio σ_I^2 is 10 and that the riskfree rate r_f is 5%.

The EGP algorithm begins by noting that the slope of a line emanating from r_f and going through any specific portfolio p will have a slope equal to the value of theta (Θ):

$$\Theta = \frac{\bar{r}_p - r_f}{\sigma_p}. \tag{9.1}$$

The algorithm recognizes that the portfolio p that has the maximum value of Θ is the tangency portfolio T and hence seeks to identify the portfolio that maximizes Θ. This is accomplished by using a five-step procedure.

1. Rank the securities in descending order based on the magnitude of the reward-to-volatility ratio:

$$RVOL_i = (\bar{r}_i - r_f)/\beta_{iI}. \tag{9.2}$$

(Note that the numerator represents the expected "reward" for buying the security and the denominator represents the security's beta. This ratio is sometimes known as the *Treynor Ratio*—see Chapter 25.)

In column (2) of the following table it can be seen that the ten securities are ranked in descending order of $RVOL_i$.

2. Starting at the top of the ranking, add securities one by one in calculating the following values of Φ_i:

$$\Phi_i = \sigma_I^2 \frac{\displaystyle\sum_{j=1}^{i} \frac{\bar{r}_j - r_f}{\sigma_{\epsilon j}^2} \beta_{jI}}{1 + \sigma_I^2 \displaystyle\sum_{j=1}^{i} \frac{\beta_{jI}}{\sigma_{\epsilon j}^2}}. \tag{9.3}$$

Column (3) of the following table displays these values.

3. Compare the values of Φ_i to the corresponding values of $RVOL_i$ one by one while moving down the ranked list of securities. Initially Φ_i will be the smaller of the two values but at some point it will become the larger one. Using k to denote the number of the last security before this happens, securities *1* through k will have nonzero weights in T whereas the others will have weights of zero. Hence Φ_k is the "cutoff rate" for $RVOL_i$.

In column (3), note how $RVOL_i$ is larger than Φ_i for the first five rows and then becomes smaller in the sixth row and remains smaller thereafter. This indicates that for this example, $k = 5$ and the cutoff rate [denoted by "*" in column (3)] is 5.45. This means that securities must have a reward-to-volatility ratio larger than 5.45 in order to have a nonzero weight in T.

4. Calculate the following values of Z_i in order to determine the size of the weights for the first k securities:

$$Z_i = \frac{\beta_{iI}}{\sigma_{\epsilon i}^2} \left[\frac{\bar{r}_i - r_f}{\beta_{iI}} - \Phi_K \right]. \tag{9.4}$$

The values of Z_i for $i = k + 1, k + 2, \ldots, N$ are set equal to zero.

The values of Z_i are shown in the fourth column. Because $k = 5$, note how the values of Z_6 through Z_{10} are equal to zero while those for the first five securities are positive numbers.

5. Divide each Z_i by the sum of the Z_i terms to transform them into the weights X_i for each security:

$$X_i = Z_i / \sum_{i=1}^{N} Z_i \tag{9.5}$$

This is necessary because the sum of the Z_i terms typically will not equal one.[11]

In the example, this sum equals .3879. Hence the weight of security one is simply $X_1 = .0910/.3879 = .2345$. This weight and the others are shown in the fifth column in the following table.

Security Number i (1)	RVOL$_i$ (2)	Φ_i (3)	Z$_i$ (4)	X$_i$ (5)
1	10	1.67	.0910	.2346
2	8	3.69	.0956	.2464
3	7	4.42	.0775	.1998
4	6	5.43	.1100	.2836
5	6	5.45*	.0138	.0356
6	4	5.30	.0000	.0000
7	3	5.02	.0000	.0000
8	2.5	4.91	.0000	.0000
9	2	4.75	.0000	.0000
10	1	4.52	.0000	.0000

APPENDIX C

DETERMINING THE COMPOSITION OF THE INVESTOR'S OPTIMAL PORTFOLIO O*

Once the investor has determined the location of the straight line efficient set by locating the tangency portfolio, he or she can move on to determine the composition of his or her optimal portfolio. This portfolio, denoted O^* in Figure 9.8, corresponds to the tangency point between the efficient set and one of the investor's indifference curves. The procedure for determining its composition is similar to that for the Markowitz model that was described in Appendix A of Chapter 8. It starts by the investor noting graphically the level of O^*'s expected return—that is, from the graph the investor can note where O^* is located and then calibrate its expected return by simply using a ruler and extending a horizontal line from O^* to the vertical axis.

If the expected return of the optimal portfolio is denoted by $\bar{r}^*$ and the riskfree rate and the expected return of the tangency portfolio are r_f and $\bar{r}_T$, respectively, then the composition of the optimal portfolio can be determined by first solving the following equation for Y:

$$\bar{r}^* = (\bar{r}_T \times Y) + [r_f \times (1 - Y)]. \tag{9.6}$$

The optimal portfolio will consist of a proportion Y of the tangency portfolio and a proportion $1 - Y$ of the riskfree rate. Thus the proportions to be invested in each risky security can be calculated by taking their proportions in T and multiplying them by Y.

In the example, if the optimal portfolio of the investor corresponds to the one shown in part (a) of Figure 9.8, then $\bar{r}^* = 14\%$. Thus Equation (9.6) would be:

$$14\% = (22.4\% \times Y) + [4\% \times (1 - Y)] \qquad (9.7)$$

because $\bar{r}_T = 22.4\%$ and $r_f = 4\%$. The solution to Equation (9.5) is $Y = .54$, meaning that the optimal portfolio consists of a proportion of .54 in the tangency portfolio and .46 in the riskfree asset.

In terms of the amount of investment in Able, Baker, and Charlie companies, this translates to:

$$[.54 \times X(T)] = .54 \times \begin{bmatrix} .12 \\ .19 \\ .69 \end{bmatrix} = \begin{bmatrix} .07 \\ .10 \\ .37 \end{bmatrix}.$$

Thus the investor should invest an amount of money that is equal to 7%, 10%, and 37% of his or her initial wealth in shares of Able, Baker, and Charlie, respectively. Furthermore, 46% of the investor's initial wealth should be used to buy Treasury bills, the riskfree asset.

Alternatively, if the optimal portfolio of the investor corresponds to the one shown in part (b) of Figure 9.8, then $\bar{r}^* = 27\%$. Thus Equation (9.6) would be:

$$27\% = (22.4\% \times Y) + [4\% \times (1 - Y)] \qquad (9.8)$$

and the solution would be $Y = 1.25$, meaning that the optimal portfolio consists of borrowing an amount of money equal to 25% of the investor's initial wealth and then investing the borrowed money and the initial wealth in T. In terms of the amount of investment in the securities of Able, Baker, and Charlie companies, this translates to:

$$[1.25 \times X(T)] = 1.25 \times \begin{bmatrix} .12 \\ .19 \\ .69 \end{bmatrix} = \begin{bmatrix} .15 \\ .24 \\ .86 \end{bmatrix}.$$

Thus the investor should invest an amount of money that is equal to 15%, 24%, and 86% of his or her initial wealth in shares of Able, Baker, and Charlie, respectively.

ENDNOTES

[1] To be truly riskfree, the security must not provide the investor with any coupon payments during the holding period. Instead it must provide the investor with only one cash inflow, and that inflow must occur at the end of the investor's holding period. Any intervening coupon payments would subject the investor to reinvestment-rate risk as he or she would not know the rate at which the coupon payments could be invested for the remainder of the holding period. It should also be noted that the discussion has focused on an asset that is riskfree in nominal terms because the presence of uncertain inflation means that virtually all U.S. Treasury securities are risky in real terms. These topics are considered further in the *Institutional Issues* section in Chapter 5.

^{2} Note that investing the proportion .25 in portfolio *PAC* is equivalent to investing the proportion .20 (= .25 × .80) in Able and the proportion .05 (= .25 × .20) in Charlie.

^{3} A more risk-averse investor (meaning an investor whose indifference curves have greater slopes) would choose an optimal portfolio that is closer to the riskfree asset on the line that connects the riskfree asset to *T*. Only if the investor is infinitely risk averse will the optimal portfolio consist of an investment in just the riskfree asset.

^{4} Allowing for borrowing can be viewed as giving the investor the opportunity to engage in margin purchases if he or she so desires. With borrowing the investor is allowed to use financial leverage.

^{5} Appendix A discusses what happens to the efficient set when the investor is able to borrow but at a rate that is greater than the rate that can be earned by investing in the riskfree asset.

^{6} Note that investing the proportion 1.25 in portfolio *PAC* is equivalent to investing the proportion 1.00 (= 1.25 × .80) in Able and the proportion .25 (= 1.25 × .20) in Charlie.

^{7} Appendix B illustrates how the composition of the tangency portfolio *T* is determined.

^{8} Appendix C illustrates how the composition of the investor's optimal portfolio O^* is determined.

^{9} The less risk averse the investor is, the smaller the proportion invested in the riskfree rate and the larger the proportion invested in *T*.

^{10} See Edwin J. Elton, Martin J. Gruber, and Manfred D. Padberg, "Simple Criteria for Optimal Portfolio Selection," *Journal of Finance*, 31, no. 5 (December 1976): 1341–1357. The example is taken from Edwin J. Elton and Martin J. Gruber, *Modern Portfolio Theory and Investment Analysis* (New York: John Wiley, 1991): 158–165.

^{11} By iteratively determining the composition of *T* for various riskfree rates, it is possible to determine the composition of many portfolios along the curved efficient set of the Markowitz model. Hence this algorithm can also be used to identify the efficient set when a riskfree rate is not present (as in Chapter 8) or when the riskfree borrowing rate is greater than the riskfree lending rate (as in Appendix A). It can also be used when short selling is permitted. See Gordon J. Alexander, "Short Selling and Efficient Sets," *Journal of Finance*, 48, no. 4 (September 1993): 1497–1506.

KEY TERMS

riskfree asset   riskfree lending
interest-rate risk   riskfree borrowing
reinvestment-rate risk

REFERENCES

1. Credit for extending Markowitz's model to include riskfree lending and borrowing belongs to:

James Tobin, "Liquidity Preference as Behavior Towards Risk," *Review of Economic Studies,* 26, no. 1 (February 1958): 65–86.

James Tobin, "The Theory of Portfolio Selection," in *The Theory of Interest Rates,* ed. F. H. Hahn and F. P. R. Brechling (London: Macmillan and Co., 1965).

2. For a discussion of various mean-variance models that involve different sets of assumptions regarding riskfree lending and borrowing, margin purchasing, and short selling, see:

Eugene F. Fama, *Foundations of Finance* (New York: Basic Books, 1976), Chapters 7 and 8.

Gordon J. Alexander and Jack Clark Francis, *Portfolio Analysis* (Englewood Cliffs, NJ: Prentice Hall, 1986), Chapter 4.

3. For a discussion of how to determine the composition of portfolios on the efficient set under a variety of different assumptions, see:

Edwin J. Elton, Martin J. Gruber, and Manfred D. Padberg, "Simple Criteria for Optimal Portfolio Selection," *Journal of Finance,* 31, no. 5 (December 1976): 1341–1357.

Edwin J. Elton and Martin J. Gruber, *Modern Portfolio Theory and Investment Analysis* (New York: John Wiley, 1991), Chapters 4 and 7.

Gordon J. Alexander, "Short Selling and Efficient Sets," *Journal of Finance,* 48, no. 4 (September 1993): 1497–1506.

The Capital Asset Pricing Model

Chapters 7, 8, and 9 presented a method for identifying an investor's optimal portfolio. With this method, the investor needs to estimate the expected returns and variances for all securities under consideration. Furthermore, all the covariances among these securities need to be estimated and the riskfree rate needs to be determined. Once this is done, the investor can identify the composition of the tangency portfolio as well as its expected return and standard deviation. At this juncture the investor can proceed to identify the optimal portfolio by noting where one of his or her indifference curves touches but does not intersect the efficient set. This portfolio involves an investment in the tangency portfolio along with a certain amount of either riskfree borrowing or lending because the efficient set is linear (that is, a straight line).

Such an approach to investing can be viewed as an exercise in **normative economics,** where investors are told what they should do. Thus, the approach is prescriptive in nature. In this chapter the realm of **positive economics** is entered, where a descriptive model of how assets are priced is presented. The model assumes among other things that all investors use the approach to investing given in Chapters 7, 8, and 9. The major implication of the model is that the expected return of an asset will be related to a measure of risk for that asset known as *beta*. The exact manner in which expected return and beta are related is specified by the **Capital Asset Pricing Model** (CAPM). This model provides the intellectual basis for a number of the current practices in the investment industry. Although many of these practices are based on various extensions and modifications of the CAPM, a sound understanding of the original version is necessary in order to understand them. Accordingly, this chapter presents the original version of the CAPM.[1]

10.1 ASSUMPTIONS

To see how assets are priced, a model (that is, a theory) must be constructed. This requires simplification in that the model-builder must abstract from the full complexity of the situation and focus only on the most important elements. The way this is achieved is by making certain assumptions about the environment. These assumptions need to be simplistic in order to provide the degree of abstraction that allows for some success in building the model. The *reasonableness* of the assumptions (or lack thereof) is of little concern. Instead the test of a model is its ability to help one understand and predict the process being modeled. As Milton Friedman, recipient of the 1976 Nobel Prize in Economics, has stated in a famous essay:

> [T]he relevant question to ask about the "assumptions" of a theory is not whether they are descriptively "realistic," for they never are, but whether they are sufficiently good approximations for the purpose in hand. And this question can be answered only by seeing whether the theory works, which means whether it yields sufficiently accurate predictions.[2]

Some of the assumptions behind the CAPM are also behind the normative approach to investing described in the previous three chapters. These assumptions are as follows:

1. Investors evaluate portfolios by looking at the expected returns and standard deviations of the portfolios over a one-period horizon.
2. Investors are never satiated, so when given a choice between two otherwise identical portfolios, they will choose the one with the higher expected return.
3. Investors are risk-averse, so when given a choice between two otherwise identical portfolios, they will choose the one with the lower standard deviation.
4. Individual assets are infinitely divisible, meaning that an investor can buy a fraction of a share if he or she so desires.
5. There is a riskfree rate at which an investor may either lend (that is, invest) money or borrow money.
6. Taxes and transaction costs are irrelevant.

To these assumptions the following ones are added:

7. All investors have the same one-period horizon.
8. The riskfree rate is the same for all investors.
9. Information is freely and instantly available to all investors.

10. Investors have **homogeneous expectations,** meaning that they have the same perceptions in regard to the expected returns, standard deviations, and covariances of securities.

As can be seen by examining these assumptions, the CAPM reduces the situation to an extreme case. Everyone has the same information and agrees about the future prospects for securities. Implicitly this means that investors analyze and process information in the same way. The markets for securities are **perfect markets,** meaning that there are no *frictions* to impede investing. Potential impediments such as finite divisibility, taxes, transaction costs, and different riskfree borrowing and lending rates have been assumed away. This allows the focus to change from how an individual should invest to what would happen to security prices if everyone invested in a similar manner. By examining the collective behavior of all investors in the marketplace, the nature of the resulting equilibrium relationship between each security's risk and return can be developed.

10.2　THE CAPITAL MARKET LINE

10.2.1　The Separation Theorem

Having made these ten assumptions, the resulting implications can now be examined. First, investors would analyze securities and determine the composition of the tangency portfolio. In so doing, *everyone would obtain in equilibrium the same tangency portfolio.* However, this is not surprising because there is complete agreement among investors on the estimates of the securities' expected returns, variances, and covariances, as well as on the size of the riskfree rate. This also means that the linear efficient set (described in Chapter 9) is the same for all investors because it simply involves combinations of the agreed-upon tangency portfolio and either riskfree borrowing or lending.

As all investors face the same efficient set, the only reason they will choose different portfolios is that they have different indifference curves. Thus different investors will choose different portfolios from the same efficient set because they have different preferences toward risk and return. For example, as was shown in Figure 9.8, the investor in panel (a) will choose a different portfolio than the investor in panel (b). Note, however, that although the chosen portfolios will be different, *each investor will choose the same combination of risky securities,* denoted T in Figure 9.8. This means that each investor will spread his or her funds among risky securities in the same relative proportions, adding riskfree borrowing or lending in order to achieve a personally preferred overall combination of risk and return. This feature of the CAPM is often referred to as the **separation theorem:**

> *The optimal combination of risky assets for an investor can be determined without any knowledge of the investor's preferences toward risk and return.*

In other words, the determination of the optimal combination of risky assets can be made without determining the shape of an investor's indifference curves.

The reasoning behind the separation theorem involves a property of the linear efficient set introduced in Chapter 9. There it was shown that all portfolios located on the linear efficient set involved an investment in a tangency portfolio combined with varying degrees of riskfree borrowing or lending. With the CAPM each person faces the same linear efficient set, meaning that each person will be investing in the same tangency portfolio (combined with a certain amount of either riskfree borrowing or lending that depends upon that person's indifference curves). It therefore follows that the risky portion of each person's portfolio will be the same.

In the example from Chapter 9, three securities were considered, corresponding to the stock of Able, Baker, and Charlie companies. With a riskfree rate of return of 4%, the tangency portfolio T was shown to consist of investments in Able, Baker, and Charlie in proportions equal to .12, .19, and .69, respectively. If the ten assumptions of the CAPM are made, then the investor shown in panel (a) of Figure 9.8 would invest approximately half of his or her money in the riskfree asset and the remainder in T. The investor shown in panel (b), on the other hand, would borrow an amount of money equal to approximately half the value of his or her initial wealth and proceed to invest these borrowed funds as well as his or her own funds in T.[3] Thus the proportions invested in the three stocks for panel (a) and (b) investors would equal:[4]

$$(.5) \times \begin{bmatrix} .12 \\ .19 \\ .69 \end{bmatrix} = \begin{bmatrix} .060 \\ .095 \\ .345 \end{bmatrix} \text{ for the investor in part (a),}$$

$$(1.5) \times \begin{bmatrix} .12 \\ .19 \\ .69 \end{bmatrix} = \begin{bmatrix} .180 \\ .285 \\ 1.035 \end{bmatrix} \text{ for the investor in part (b).}$$

Although the proportions to be invested in each of these three risky securities for the panel (a) investor (.060, .095, .345) can be seen to be different in size from their values for the panel (b) investor (.180, .285, 1.035), note how the relative proportions are the same, being equal to .12, .19, and .69, respectively.

10.2.2 The Market Portfolio

Another important feature of the CAPM is that in equilibrium each security must have a nonzero proportion in the composition of the tangency portfolio.[5] This mean that no security can in equilibrium have a proportion in T that is zero. The reasoning behind this feature lies in the previously mentioned separation theorem, where it was asserted that the risky portion of every investor's portfolio is independent of the investor's risk-return preferences. The justification for the theorem was that the risky portion of each investor's portfolio is simply an investment in T. If every investor is purchasing T and T does not involve an investment in each security, then nobody is investing in those securities with zero proportions in T. This means that the prices of these zero-proportion securities must fall, thereby causing the expected returns of these securities to rise until the resulting tangency portfolio has a nonzero proportion associated with them.

In the previous example, Charlie had a current price of $62 and an expected end-of-period price of $76.14. This meant that the expected return for Charlie was 22.8% [= ($76.14 − $62)/$62]. Now imagine that the current price of Charlie is $72, not $62, meaning that its expected return is 5.8% [= ($76.14 − $72)/$72]. If this were the case, the tangency portfolio associated with a riskfree rate of 4% would involve just Able and Baker in proportions of .90 and .10, respectively.[6] Because Charlie has a proportion of zero, nobody would want to hold shares of Charlie. Consequently, orders to sell would be received in substantial quantities with virtually no offsetting orders to buy being received. As a result, Charlie's price would fall as brokers would try to find someone to buy the shares. However, as Charlie's price falls, its expected return would rise because the same end-of-period price of $76.14 would be forecast for Charlie as before and it would now cost less to buy one share. Eventually, as the price falls, investors would change their minds and want to buy shares of Charlie. Ultimately, at a price of $62 investors will want to hold shares of Charlie so that in aggregate the number of shares demanded will equal the number of shares outstanding. Thus in equilibrium Charlie will have a nonzero proportion in the tangency portfolio.

Another interesting situation could also arise. What if each investor concludes that the tangency portfolio should involve a proportionate investment in the stock of Baker equal to .40, but at the current price of Baker there are not enough shares outstanding to meet the demand? In this situation orders to buy Baker will flood in, and brokers will raise the price in search of sellers. This will cause the expected return of Baker to fall, making it less attractive and thereby reducing its proportion in the tangency portfolio to a level where the number of shares demanded equals the number of shares outstanding.

Ultimately, everything will balance out. When all the price adjusting stops, the market will have been brought into equilibrium. First, each investor will want to hold a certain positive amount of each risky security. Second, the current market price of each security will be at a level where the number of shares demanded equals the number of shares outstanding.[7] Third, the riskfree rate will be at a level where the total amount of money borrowed equals the total amount of money lent. As a result, in equilibrium the proportions of the tangency portfolio will correspond to the proportions of what is known as the **market portfolio,** defined as follows:

> *The market portfolio is a portfolio consisting of all securities where the proportion invested in each security corresponds to its relative market value. The relative market value of a security is simply equal to the aggregate market value of the security divided by the sum of the aggregate market values of all securities.*[8]

The reason the market portfolio plays a central role in the CAPM is that the efficient set consists of an investment in the market portfolio, coupled with a desired amount of either riskfree borrowing or lending. Thus it is common practice to refer to the tangency portfolio as the market portfolio and to denote it as M instead of T. In theory, M consists not only of common stocks but also such other kinds of investments as bonds, preferred stocks, and real estate. However, in practice some people restrict M to just common stocks.

The Elusive Market Portfolio

The market portfolio holds a special place in modern investment theory and practice. It is central to the CAPM, which assumes that the market portfolio lies on the efficient set and that all investors hold the market portfolio in combination with a desired amount of riskfree borrowing and lending. Furthermore, the market portfolio represents the ultimate in diversification. Consequently, passive investors (or index fund managers—see Chapter 24), who do not *bet* on the performance of particular securities but rather desire broad diversification, seek to hold the market portfolio. The market portfolio also serves as a universal performance evaluation standard. Investment managers and their clients often compare the managers' results against the returns on the market portfolio.

Despite its widespread application, the market portfolio is surprisingly ill defined. In theory, the composition of the market portfolio is simple: All assets are weighted in proportion to their respective market values. In reality, actually identifying the *true* market portfolio (or even a close approximation) is beyond the capability of any individual or organization.

Consider how we might go about specifying the market portfolio. The process would involve two steps: enumerating the assets to be included and calculating the market values of those assets.

First, we must list the various types of assets that constitute the market portfolio. These days we should think globally by considering assets held by investors in both the United States and foreign countries. Of course we want to include all securities representing the assets of businesses. Therefore we should include common stocks, preferred stocks, and corporate bonds. In that vein we should also consider the value of proprietorships and partnerships. How about government debt? This should be considered if the debt is backed by real assets such as buildings. (Due to deficit spending, much of the government's debt is actually backed by future taxes and thus does not represent current wealth—a technical matter often overlooked.) We should also include real estate, cash holdings, monetary metals (primarily gold), and art. But we have not finished yet. We should also include consumer durable assets, such as autos, furniture, and major appliances. Last but certainly not least, we should include the largest asset of all, the training and education in which people have invested vast sums, called *human capital*.

Simply listing the composition of the market portfolio is a complex undertaking. Measuring its value is even more problematic. Given the sophistication of U.S. capital markets, the values of domestic publicly traded assets are relatively easy to

10.2.3 The Efficient Set

In the world of the Capital Asset Pricing Model it is a simple matter to determine the relationship between risk and return for efficient portfolios. Figure 10.1 portrays it graphically. Point M represents the market portfolio and r_f represents the riskfree rate of return. Efficient portfolios plot along the line starting at r_f and going through M and consist of alternative combinations of risk and return obtainable by combining the market portfolio with riskfree borrowing or lending. This linear efficient set of the CAPM is known as the **Capital Market Line** (CML). All portfolios other than those employing the market portfolio and riskfree borrowing or lending would lie below the CML, although some might plot very close to it.

The slope of the CML is equal to the difference between the expected return of the market portfolio and that of the riskfree security $(\bar{r}_M - r_f)$ divided by the difference in their risks $(\sigma_M - 0)$ or $(\bar{r}_M - r_f)/\sigma_M$.[9] Because the vertical in-

CHAPTER 10

collect. (We should be careful, however, to avoid double-counting—for example, when one corporation owns part of another corporation.) Data availability in foreign markets varies from country to country. In some markets, such as those in the United Kingdom and Japan, security data collection systems are just as sophisticated as those in the United States. In other markets, such as those in Third World countries, comprehensive security valuation data is difficult to acquire.

A similar situation exists with respect to non-publicly traded asset values. In some countries, such as the United States, the government attempts to make accurate estimates of a myriad of asset values from real estate to consumer durable goods. In other countries, little or no effort is made to compile this data.

Finally, with respect to estimating the value of human capital—well, good luck.

The difficulties involved in determining the composition and value of the *true* market portfolio have led to the use of market portfolio proxies. In dealing with common stocks, for example, most researchers and practitioners arbitrarily define the market portfolio to be a broad stock market index, such as the S&P 500 or the Wilshire 5000.

What are the ramifications of not knowing the market portfolio's true composition? From a theoretical perspective, the potential problems are significant. In two controversial articles (*Journal of Financial Economics*, March 1977, and *Journal of Finance*, September 1978), Richard Roll argued that the ambiguity of the market portfolio leaves the CAPM untestable. He contended that only if one knows the true market portfolio can one test whether it actually lies on the efficient set. Considering that the CAPM linear relationship between expected return and beta depends on the efficiency of the market portfolio, Roll's argument should not be taken lightly. Furthermore, Roll argues that the practice of using proxies for the market portfolio is loaded with problems. Different proxies, even if their returns are highly correlated, could lead to different beta estimates for the same security. Roll's arguments, it should be noted, were strongly contested by prominent CAPM defenders.

From a practical perspective, investors have generally been willing to overlook the market portfolio's ambiguity. Passive managers typically segment the market into various asset classes, such as stocks and bonds. They then define somewhat arbitrarily a market portfolio for each of those asset classes and construct portfolios to track the performance of the respective asset class market portfolios. Similarly, active managers frequently refer to a designated market portfolio when they devise their investment strategies. Performance evaluators employ market proxies in their CAPM-risk-adjusted return calculations (see Chapter 25).

tercept of the CML is r_f, the straight line characterizing the CML has the following equation:

$$\overline{r}_p = r_f + \left[\frac{\overline{r}_M - r_f}{\sigma_M}\right] \sigma_p \tag{10.1}$$

where $\overline{r}_p$ and σ_p refer to the expected return and standard deviation of an efficient portfolio.[10] In the previous example, the market portfolio associated with a riskfree rate of 4% consisted of Able, Baker, and Charlie (these stocks are assumed to be the only ones that exist) in the proportions of .12, .19, and .69, respectively. As it was shown in Chapter 9 that the expected return and standard deviation for a portfolio with these proportions was 22.4% and 15.2%, respectively, the equation for the resulting CML is:

$$\overline{r}_p = 4 + \left[\frac{22.4 - 4}{15.2}\right] \sigma_p = 4 + 1.21\sigma_p.$$

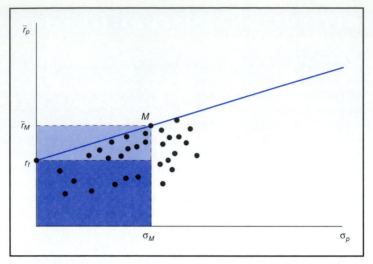

Figure 10.1
The Capital Market Line

Equilibrium in the security market can be characterized by two key numbers. The first is the vertical intercept of the CML (that is, the riskfree rate), which is often referred to as the *reward for waiting*. The second is the slope of the CML, which is often referred to as the *reward per unit of risk borne*. In essence, the security market provides a place where time and risk can be traded with their prices determined by the forces of supply and demand. Thus the intercept and slope of the CML can be thought of as the price of time and the price of risk, respectively. In the example, they are equal to 4% and 1.21, respectively.

10.3   THE SECURITY MARKET LINE

10.3.1   Implications for Individual Risky Assets

The Capital Market Line represents the equilibrium relationship between the expected return and standard deviation for efficient portfolios. Individual risky securities will always plot below the line because a single risky security when held by itself is an inefficient portfolio. The Capital Asset Pricing Model does not imply any particular relationship between the expected return and the standard deviation (that is, total risk) of an individual security. To say more about the expected return of an individual security, deeper analysis is necessary.

In Chapter 7 the following equation was given for calculating the standard deviation of any portfolio:

$$\sigma_p = \left[\sum_{i=1}^{N} \sum_{j=1}^{N} X_i X_j \sigma_{ij} \right]^{1/2} \tag{7.7}$$

where X_i and X_j denoted the proportions invested in securities i and j, respectively, and σ_{ij} denoted the covariance of returns between security i and j. Now consider using this equation to calculate the standard deviation of the market portfolio:

$$\sigma_M = \left[\sum_{i=1}^{N} \sum_{j=1}^{N} X_{iM} X_{jM} \sigma_{ij} \right]^{1/2} \tag{10.2}$$

where X_{iM} and X_{jM} denote the proportions invested in securities i and j in forming the market portfolio, respectively. It can be shown that another way to write equation (10.2) is as follows:

$$\sigma_M = \left[X_{1M} \sum_{j=1}^{N} X_{jM} \sigma_{1j} + X_{2M} \sum_{j=1}^{N} X_{jM} \sigma_{2j} + X_{3M} \sum_{j=1}^{N} X_{jM} \sigma_{3j} \right.$$
$$\left. + \ldots + X_{NM} \sum_{j=1}^{N} X_{jM} \sigma_{Nj} \right]^{1/2}. \tag{10.3}$$

At this point a property of covariance can be used: the covariance of security i with the market portfolio (σ_{iM}) can be expressed as the weighted average of every security's covariance with security i:

$$\sum_{j=1}^{N} X_{jM} \sigma_{ij} = \sigma_{iM}. \tag{10.4}$$

This property, when applied to each one of the N risky securities in the market portfolio, results in the following:

$$\sigma_M = [X_{1M} \sigma_{1M} + X_{2M} \sigma_{2M} + X_{3M} \sigma_{3M} + \ldots + X_{NM} \sigma_{NM}]^{1/2} \tag{10.5}$$

where σ_{1M} denotes the covariance of security 1 with the market portfolio, σ_{2M} denotes the covariance of security 2 with the market portfolio, and so on. Thus the standard deviation of the market portfolio is equal to the square root of a weighted average of the covariances of all the securities with it, where the weights are equal to the proportions of the respective securities in the market portfolio.

At this juncture an important point can be observed. Under the CAPM, each investor holds the market portfolio and is concerned with its standard deviation because this will influence the slope of the CML and hence the magnitude of his or her investment in the market portfolio. The contribution of each security to the standard deviation of the market portfolio can be seen in Equation (10.5) to depend on the size of its covariance with the market portfolio. Accordingly each investor will note that *the relevant measure of risk for a security is its covariance with the market portfolio, σ_{iM}.* This means that securities with larger values of σ_{iM} will be viewed by investors as contributing more to the risk of the market portfolio. It also means that securities with larger standard deviations should not be viewed as necessarily adding more risk to the market portfolio than those securities with smaller standard deviations.

From this analysis it follows that securities with larger values for σ_{iM} have to provide proportionately larger expected returns to interest investors in purchasing them. To see why, consider what would happen if such securities did not provide investors with proportionately larger levels of expected return. In this situation, these securities would contribute to the risk of the market portfolio while not contributing proportionately to the expected return of the market portfolio. This means that deleting such securities from the market portfolio would cause the expected return of the market portfolio relative to its standard deviation to rise. Because investors would view this as a favorable change, the market portfolio would no longer be the optimal risky portfolio to hold. Thus security prices would be out of equilibrium.

The exact form of the equilibrium relationship between risk and return can be written as follows:

$$\overline{r}_i = r_f + \left[\frac{\overline{r}_M - r_f}{\sigma_M^2}\right]\sigma_{iM}. \qquad (10.6)$$

As can be seen in panel (a) of Figure 10.2, Equation (10.6) represents a straight line having a vertical intercept of r_f and a slope of $[(\overline{r}_M - r_f)/\sigma_M^2]$. As the slope is positive, the equation indicates that securities with larger covariances with the market (σ_{iM}) will be priced so as to have larger expected returns (r_i). This relationship between covariance and expected return is known as the **Security Market Line** (SML).[11]

Interestingly, a risky security with $\sigma_{iM} = 0$ will have an expected return equal to the rate on the riskfree security, r_f. Why? Because this risky security, just like the riskfree security, does not contribute to the risk of the market portfolio. This is so even though the risky security has a positive standard deviation whereas the riskfree security has a standard deviation of zero.

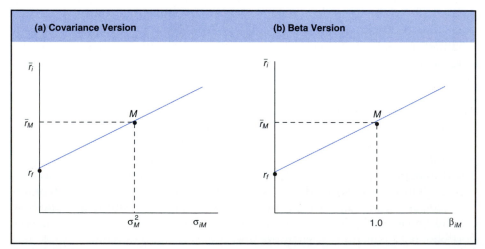

Figure 10.2
The Security Market Line

It is even possible for some risky securities (meaning securities with positive standard deviations) to have expected returns less than the riskfree rate. According to the CAPM, this will occur if $\sigma_{iM} < 0$, thereby indicating that they contribute a negative amount of risk to the market portfolio (meaning that they cause the risk of the market portfolio to be lower than it would be if less money were invested in them).

Also of interest is the observation that a risky security with $\sigma_{iM} = \sigma_M^2$ will have an expected return equal to the expected return on the market portfolio, $\bar{r}_M$. This is because such a security contributes an average amount of risk to the market portfolio.

Another way of expressing the SML is as follows:

$$\bar{r}_i = r_f + (\bar{r}_M - r_f)\, \beta_{iM} \tag{10.7}$$

where the term β_{iM} is defined as:

$$\beta_{iM} = \frac{\sigma_{iM}}{\sigma_M^2}. \tag{10.8}$$

The term β_{iM} is known as the **beta coefficient** (or simply the beta) for security i, and is an alternative way of representing the covariance of a security. Equation (10.7) is a different version of the SML as can be seen in panel (b) of Figure 10.2. Although having the same intercept as the earlier version shown in Equation (10.6), r_f, it has a different slope. The slope of this version is $(\bar{r}_M - r_f)$, whereas the slope of the earlier version was $[(\bar{r}_M - r_f)/\sigma_M^2]$.

One property of beta is that *the beta of a portfolio is simply a weighted average of the betas of its component securities, where the proportions invested in the securities are the respective weights.* That is, the beta of a portfolio can be calculated as:

$$\beta_{pM} = \sum_{i=1}^{N} X_i \beta_{iM}. \tag{10.9}$$

Earlier it was shown that the expected return of a portfolio is a weighted average of the expected returns of its component securities, where the proportions invested in the securities are the weights. This means that because every security plots on the SML, so will every portfolio. To put it more broadly, not only every security but also every portfolio must plot on an upward-sloping straight line in a diagram with expected return on the vertical axis and beta on the horizontal axis. This means that efficient portfolios plot on both the CML and the SML, although inefficient portfolios plot on the SML but below the CML.

Also of interest is that the SML must go through the point representing the market portfolio itself. Its beta is 1 and its expected return is $\bar{r}_M$, so its coordinates are $(1, \bar{r}_M)$. Because riskfree securities have beta values of 0, the SML will also go through a point with an expected return of r_f and coordinates of $(0, r_f)$. This means that the SML will have a vertical intercept equal to r_f and a slope equal to the vertical distance between these two points $(\bar{r}_M - r_f)$ divided by the horizontal distance between these two points $(1 - 0)$ or $(\bar{r}_M - r_f)/(1 - 0) = (\bar{r}_M - r_f)$. Thus these two points suffice to fix the location of the SML, indicating the *appropriate* expected returns for securities and portfolios with different beta values.

The equilibrium relationship shown by the SML comes to exist through the combined effects of investors' adjustments in holdings and the resulting pressures on security prices (as shown in Chapter 4). Given a set of security prices, investors calculate expected returns and covariances and then determine their optimal portfolios. If the number of shares of a security collectively desired differs from the number available, there will be upward or downward pressure on its price. Given a new set of prices, investors will reassess their desires for the various securities. The process will continue until the number of shares collectively desired for each security equals the number available.

For the individual investor, security prices and prospects are fixed while the quantities held can be altered. For the market as a whole, however, these quantities are fixed (at least in the short run), and prices are variable. As in any competitive market, equilibrium requires the adjustment of each security's price until there is consistency between the quantity desired and the quantity available.

It may seem logical to examine historical returns on securities to determine whether or not securities have been priced in equilibrium as suggested by the CAPM. However, the issue of whether or not such testing of the CAPM can be done in a meaningful manner is controversial. For at least some purposes, affirmative test results may not be necessary to make practical use of the CAPM.

10.3.2 An Example

In the example that was used earlier, Able, Baker, and Charlie were shown to form the market portfolio in proportions equal to .12, .19, and .69, respectively. Given these proportions, the market portfolio was shown to have an expected return of 22.4% and a standard deviation of 15.2%. The riskfree rate in the example was 4%. Thus for this example the SML as indicated in Equation (10.6) is:

$$\overline{r}_i = r_f + \left[\frac{\overline{r}_M - r_f}{\sigma_M^2} \right] \sigma_{iM} \tag{10.6}$$

$$= 4 + \left[\frac{22.4 - 4}{(15.2)^2} \right] \sigma_{iM}$$

$$= 4 + .08\sigma_{iM}. \tag{10.10}$$

The following expected return vector and variance-covariance matrix were used in the examples shown in Chapter 7, 8, and 9 are also used here:

$$ER = \begin{bmatrix} 16.2 \\ 24.6 \\ 22.8 \end{bmatrix} \qquad VC = \begin{bmatrix} 146 & 187 & 145 \\ 187 & 854 & 104 \\ 145 & 104 & 289 \end{bmatrix}.$$

At this point, the covariances of each security with the market portfolio can be calculated by using Equation (10.4). More specifically, the covariances with the market portfolio for Able, Baker, and Charlie are equal to:

$$\sigma_{1M} = \sum_{j=1}^{3} X_{jM}\sigma_{1j}$$

$$= (.12 \times 146) + (.19 \times 187) + (.69 \times 145)$$

$$= 153$$

$$\sigma_{2M} = \sum_{j=1}^{3} X_{jM}\sigma_{2j}$$

$$= (.12 \times 187) + (.19 \times 854) + (.69 \times 104)$$

$$= 257$$

$$\sigma_{3M} = \sum_{j=1}^{3} X_{jM}\sigma_{3j}$$

$$= (.12 \times 145) + (.19 \times 104) + (.69 \times 289)$$

$$= 236.$$

Note how the SML as given in Equation (10.10) states that the expected return for Able should be equal to $4 + (.08 \times 153) = 16.2\%$. Similarly, the expected return for Baker should be $4 + (.08 \times 257) = 24.6\%$, and the expected return for Charlie should be $4 + (.08 \times 236) = 22.8\%$. Each one of these expected returns corresponds to the respective value given in the expected return vector.

Alternatively, Equation (10.8) can be used to calculate the betas for the three companies. More specifically, the betas for Able, Baker, and Charlie are equal to:

$$\beta_{1M} = \frac{\sigma_{1M}}{\sigma_M^2}$$

$$= \frac{153}{(15.2)^2}$$

$$= .66$$

$$\beta_{2M} = \frac{\sigma_{2M}}{\sigma_M^2}$$

$$= \frac{257}{(15.2)^2}$$

$$= 1.11$$

$$\beta_{3M} = \frac{\sigma_{3M}}{\sigma_M^2}$$

$$= \frac{236}{(15.2)^2}$$

$$= 1.02.$$

Now Equation (10.7) indicated that the SML could be expressed in a form where the measure of risk for an asset was its beta. For the example under consideration, this reduces to:

$$\begin{aligned}
\bar{r}_i &= r_f + (\bar{r}_M - r_f)\,\beta_{iM} \\
&= 4 + (22.4 - 4)\beta_{iM} \\
&= 4 + 18.4\beta_{iM}
\end{aligned}$$

(10.11)

Note how the SML as given in this equation states that the expected return for Able should be equal to $4 + (18.4 \times .66) = 16.2\%$. Similarly, the expected return for Baker should be $4 + (18.4 \times 1.11) = 24.6\%$, and the expected return for Charlie should be $4 + (18.4 \times 1.02) = 22.8\%$. Each one of these expected returns correspond to the respective value given in the expected return vector.

It is important to realize that if any other portfolio is assumed to be the market portfolio, meaning that if any set of proportions other than .12, .19, and .69 is used, then such an equilibrium relationship between expected returns and betas (or covariances) will not hold. Consider a hypothetical market portfolio with equal proportions (that is, .333) invested in Able, Baker, and Charlie. Because this portfolio has an expected return of 21.2% and a standard deviation of 15.5%, the hypothetical SML would be as follows:

$$\begin{aligned}
\bar{r}_i &= r_f + \left[\frac{\bar{r}_M - r_f}{\sigma_M^2}\right]\sigma_{iM} \\
&= 4 + \left[\frac{21.2 - 4}{(15.5)^2}\right]\sigma_{iM} \\
&= 4 + .07\sigma_{iM}.
\end{aligned}$$

Able has a covariance with this portfolio of:

$$\begin{aligned}
\sigma_{1M} &= \sum_{j=1}^{3} X_{jM}\sigma_{1j} \\
&= (.333 \times 146) + (.333 \times 187) + (.333 \times 145) \\
&= 159,
\end{aligned}$$

which means that Able's expected return according to the hypothetical SML should be equal to $15.1\% = 4 + (.07 \times 159)$. However, because this does not correspond to the 16.2% figure that appears in the expected return vector, a portfolio with equal proportions invested in Able, Baker, and Charlie cannot be the market portfolio.[12]

10.4 THE MARKET MODEL

Chapter 8 introduced the market model, where the return on a common stock was assumed to be related to the return on a market index in the following manner:

$$r_i = \alpha_{iI} + \beta_{iI}r_I + \epsilon_{iI}$$

(8.3)

It is natural to think about the relationship between the market model and the Capital Asset Pricing Model. After all, both models have a slope term called "beta" in them, and both models somehow involve the market. However, there are two significant differences between the models.

First, the market model is a *factor model,* or to be more specific, a single-factor model where the factor is a market index. Unlike the CAPM, however, it is not an *equilibrium model* that describes how prices are set for securities.

Second, the market model utilizes a *market index* such as the S&P 500, whereas the CAPM involves the *market portfolio.* The market portfolio is a collection of all the securities in the marketplace, whereas a market index is in fact based on a sample of the market broadly construed (for example, 500 in the case of the S&P 500). Therefore, conceptually the beta of a stock based on the market model, β_{iI}, differs from the beta of the stock according to the CAPM, β_{iM}. This is because the market model beta is measured relative to a market index while the CAPM beta is measured relative to the market portfolio. In practice, however, the composition of the market portfolio is not precisely known, so a market index is used. Thus while conceptually different, betas determined with the use of a market index are treated as if they were determined with the use of the market portfolio. That is, β_{iI} is used as an estimate of β_{iM}.

In the example, only three securities were in existence—the common stocks of Able, Baker, and Charlie. Subsequent analysis indicated that the CAPM market portfolio consisted of these stocks in the proportions of .12, .19, and .69, respectively. It is against this portfolio that the betas of the securities should be measured. However, in practice they are likely to be measured against a market index (for example, one that is based on just the stocks of Able and Charlie in proportions of .20 and .80, respectively).

10.4.1   Market Indices

One of the most widely known indices is the Standard & Poor's Stock Price Index (referred to earlier as the S&P 500), a value-weighted average price of 500 large stocks. Complete coverage of the stocks listed on the New York Stock Exchange is provided by the NYSE Composite Index, which is broader than the S&P 500 in that it considers more stocks. The American Stock Exchange computes a similar index for the stocks it lists, and the National Association of Security Dealers provides an index of over-the-counter stocks traded on the Nasdaq system. The Russell 3000 and Wilshire 5000 stock indices are the most comprehensive indices of U.S. common stock prices published regularly in the United

States. Because they consist of both listed and over-the-counter stocks, they are closer than the others to representing the overall performance of American stocks.[13]

Without question the most widely quoted market index is the Dow Jones Industrial Average (DJIA). Although based on the performance of only 30 stocks and utilizing a less satisfactory averaging procedure, the DJIA provides at least a fair idea of what is happening to stock prices.[14] Table 10.1 provides a listing of the 30 stocks whose prices have been reflected in the DJIA.

10.4.2 Market and Non-Market Risk

In Chapter 8 it was shown that the total risk of a security σ_i^2 could be partitioned into two components as follows:

$$\sigma_i^2 = \beta_{iI}^2 \sigma_I^2 + \sigma_{\epsilon i}^2 \qquad (8.8)$$

where the components are:

$$\beta_{iI}^2 \sigma_I^2 = \text{market risk, and}$$
$$\sigma_{\epsilon i}^2 = \text{unique risk.}$$

Because beta, or covariance, is the relevant measure of risk for a security according to the CAPM, it is only appropriate to explore the relationship between it and the total risk of the security. It turns out that the relationship is identical to that given in Equation (8.8) *except that the market portfolio is involved instead of a market index:*

$$\sigma_i^2 = \beta_{iM}^2 \sigma_M^2 + \sigma_{\epsilon i}^2 \qquad (10.12)$$

TABLE 10.1	
STOCKS IN THE DOW JONES INDUSTRIAL AVERAGE AT YEAR-END, 1993	
Alcoa	Goodyear Tire
Allied Signal	IBM
American Express	International Paper
AT&T	McDonald's
Bethlehem Steel	Merck
Boeing	Minnesota Mining and Manufacturing (3M)
Caterpillar	J. P. Morgan
Chevron	Philip Morris
Coca-Cola	Procter & Gamble
Walt Disney	Sears, Roebuck
DuPont	Texaco
Eastman Kodak	Union Carbide
Exxon	United Technologies
General Electric	Westinghouse
General Motors	Woolworth

Source: Adapted from *The Wall Street Journal*, Dow Jones & Company, January 3, 1994, p.21.

As with the market model, the total risk of security i, measured by its variance and denoted σ_i^2, is shown to consist of two parts. The first component is the portion related to moves of the market portfolio. It is equal to the product of the square of the beta of the stock and the variance of the market portfolio, and also often referred to as the **market risk** of the security. The second component is the portion not related to moves of the market portfolio. It is denoted $\sigma_{\epsilon i}^2$ and can be considered **non-market risk.** Under the assumptions of the market model, it is also unique to the security in question and hence is termed *unique risk*. Note that if β_{il} is treated as an estimate of β_{iM}, then the decomposition of σ_i^2 is the same in Equations (8.8) and (10.12).

10.4.3 An Example

From the earlier example, the betas of Able, Baker, and Charlie were calculated to be .66, 1.11, and 1.02, respectively. As the standard deviation of the market portfolio was equal to 15.2%, this means that the market risk of the three firms is equal to $(.66^2 \times 15.2^2) = 100$, $(1.11^2 \times 15.2^2) = 285$, and $(1.02^2 \times 15.2^2) = 240$, respectively.

The non-market risk of any security can be calculated by solving Equation (10.12) for $\sigma_{\epsilon i}^2$:

$$\sigma_{\epsilon i}^2 = \sigma_i^2 - \beta_{iM}^2 \sigma_M^2 \tag{10.13}$$

Thus, Equation (10.13) can be used to calculate the non-market risk of Able, Baker, and Charlie, respectively:

$$\begin{aligned}
\sigma_{\epsilon 1}^2 &= 146 - 100 \\
&= 46 \\
\sigma_{\epsilon 2}^2 &= 854 - 285 \\
&= 569 \\
\sigma_{\epsilon 3}^2 &= 289 - 240 \\
&= 49.
\end{aligned}$$

Non-market risk is sometimes expressed as a standard deviation. This is calculated by taking the square root of $\sigma_{\epsilon i}^2$ and would be equal to $\sqrt{46} = 6.8\%$ for Able, $\sqrt{569} = 23.9\%$ for Baker, and $\sqrt{49} = 7\%$ for Charlie.

10.4.4 Motivation for the Partitioning of Risk

At this point one may wonder: why partition total risk into two parts? For the investor, it would seem that risk is risk—whatever its source. The answer lies in the domain of expected returns.

Market risk is related to the risk of the market portfolio and to the beta of the security in question. Securities with larger betas will have larger amounts of market risk. In the world of the CAPM, securities with larger betas will have larger expected returns. These two relationships together imply that securities with larger market risks should have larger expected returns.

Non-market risk is not related to beta. This means that there is no reason why securities with larger amounts of non-market risks should have larger expected returns. Thus according to the CAPM, investors are rewarded for bearing market risk but not for bearing non-market risk.

1. The Capital Assets Pricing Model (CAPM) is based on a specific set of assumptions about investor behavior and the existence of perfect security markets.
2. Based on these assumptions, all investors will hold the same efficient portfolio of risky assets.
3. Investors will differ only in the amounts of riskfree borrowing or lending they undertake.
4. The risky portfolio held by all investors is known as the market portfolio.
5. The market portfolio consists of all securities, each weighted in proportion to its market value relative to the market value of all securities.
6. The linear efficient set of the CAPM is known as the Capital Market Line (CML). The CML represents the equilibrium relationship between the expected return and standard deviation of efficient portfolios.
7. Under the CAPM the relevant measure of risk for a security is its covariance with the market portfolio.
8. The linear relationship between market covariance and expected return is known as the Security Market Line (SML).
9. The beta of a security is an alternative way of measuring the risk that a security adds to the market portfolio. Beta is a measure of covariance relative to the market portfolio's variance.
10. The beta from the CAPM is similar in concept to the beta from the market model. However, the market model is not an equilibrium model of security prices as is the CAPM. Furthermore, the market model uses a market index, which is a subset of the CAPM's market portfolio.
11. Under the CAPM, the total risk of a security can be separated into market risk and non-market risk. Under the market model, each security's non-market risk is unique to that security and hence is termed its unique risk.

QUESTIONS AND PROBLEMS

1. Describe the key assumptions underlying the CAPM.
2. Many of the underlying assumptions of the CAPM are violated to some degree in the "real world". Does that fact invalidate the model's conclusions? Explain.
3. What is the separation theorem? What implications does it have for the optimal portfolio of risky assets held by investors?
4. What constitutes the *market portfolio*? What problems does one confront in specifying the composition of the true market portfolio? How have researchers and practitioners circumvented these problems?
5. In the equilibrium world of the CAPM, is it possible for a security not to be part of the market portfolio? Explain.

6. Describe the price adjustment process that equilibrates the market's supply and demand for securities. What conditions will prevail under such an equilibrium?

7. Will an investor who owns the market portfolio have to buy and sell units of the component securities every time the relative prices of those securities change? Why?

8. Given an expected return of 12% for the market portfolio, a riskfree rate of 6%, and a market portfolio standard deviation of 20%, draw the Capital Market Line.

9. Explain the significance of the Capital Market Line.

10. Assume that two securities constitute the market portfolio. Those securities have the following expected returns, standard deviations, and proportions:

Security	Expected Return	Standard Deviation	Proportion
A	10%	20%	.40
B	15	28	.60

Based on this information, and given a correlation of .30 between the two securities and a riskfree rate of 5%, specify the equation for the Capital Market Line.

11. Distinguish between the Capital Market Line and the Security Market Line.

12. The market portfolio is assumed to be composed of four securities. Their covariances with the market and their proportions are shown below:

Security	Covariance with Market	Proportion
A	242	.20
B	360	.30
C	155	.20
D	210	.30

Given this data, calculate the market portfolio's standard deviation.

13. Explain the significance of the slope of the SML. How might the slope of the SML change over time?

14. Why should the expected return for a security be directly related to the security's covariance with the market portfolio?

15. The risk of a well-diversified portfolio to an investor is measured by the standard deviation of the portfolio's returns. Why shouldn't the risk of an individual security be calculated in the same manner?

16. A security with a high standard deviation of returns is not necessarily highly risky to an investor. Why might you suspect that securities with above-average standard deviations tend to have above-average betas?

17. Oil Smith, an investments student, argued, "A security with a positive standard deviation must have an expected return greater than the riskfree rate. Otherwise, why would anyone be willing to hold the security?" Based on the CAPM, is Oil's statement correct? Why?

18. Kitty Bransfield owns a portfolio composed of three securities. The betas of those securities and their proportions in Kitty's portfolio are shown on the next page. What is the beta of Kitty's portfolio?

Security	Beta	Proportion
A	.90	.30
B	1.30	.10
C	1.05	.60

19. Assume that the expected return on the market portfolio is 15% and its standard deviation is 21%. The riskfree rate is 7%. What is the standard deviation of a well-diversified (no non-market-risk) portfolio with an expected return of 16.6%?

20. Given that the expected return on the market portfolio is 10%, the riskfree rate of return is 6%, the beta of stock A is .85, and the beta of stock B is 1.20:
   a. Draw the SML.
   b. What is the equation for the SML?
   c. What are the equilibrium expected returns for stocks A and B?
   d. Plot the two risky securities on the SML.

21. You are given the following information on two securities, the market portfolio, and the riskfree rate:

	Expected Return	Correlation with Market Portfolio	Standard Deviation
Security 1	15.5%	0.90	20.0%
Security 2	9.2	0.80	9.0
Market Portfolio	12.0	1.00	12.0
Riskfree Rate	5.0	0.00	0.0

   a. Draw the SML.
   b. What are the betas of the two securities?
   c. Plot the two securities on the SML.

22. The SML describes an equilibrium relationship between risk and expected return. Would you consider a security that plotted above the SML to be an attractive investment? Why?

23. Assume that two securities, A and B, constitute the market portfolio. Their proportions and variances are .39, 160, and .61, 340, respectively. The covariance of the two securities is 190. Calculate the betas of the two securities.

24. The CAPM permits the standard deviation of a security to be segmented into market and non-market risk. Distinguish between the two types of risk.

25. Is an investor who owns any portfolio of risky assets other than the market portfolio exposed to some non-market risk? Explain.

26. Based on the risk and return relationships of the CAPM, supply values for the seven missing data in the following table.

Security	Expected Return	Beta	Standard Deviation	Non-market Risk ($\sigma_{\varepsilon i}^2$)
A	_____%	0.8	_____%	81
B	19.0	1.5	_____	36
C	15.0	_____	12	0
D	7.0	0	8	_____
E	16.6	_____	15	_____

27. (Appendix Question) Describe how the SML is altered when the riskfree borrowing rate exceeds the riskfree lending rate.

APPENDIX A

SOME EXTENDED VERSIONS OF THE CAPM

The original capital asset pricing model makes strong assumptions and gives strong implications. In the years since it was developed, more complex models have been proposed. These models generally involve relaxing some of the assumptions associated with the original CAPM and are often referred to as *extended versions of the CAPM,* or extended capital asset pricing models. Some of them are described in this appendix.

A.1 IMPOSING RESTRICTIONS ON RISKFREE BORROWING

A.1.1 The Capital Market Line

The original CAPM assumes that investors can lend or borrow at the same riskfree rate of interest. In reality, such borrowing is likely to be either unavailable or restricted in amount. What impact might the relaxation of this riskfree borrowing assumption have on the CAPM?

A useful way to answer the question makes the following alternative assumptions: (1) investors can lend money risklessly—that is, they can purchase assets that provide a riskfree return of r_{fL}; or (2) investors can borrow money without limit at a higher rate of interest, r_{fB}. These riskfree rates are shown on the vertical axis of Figure 10.3; the "umbrella area" represents risk-return combinations available from investment solely in risky assets.[15]

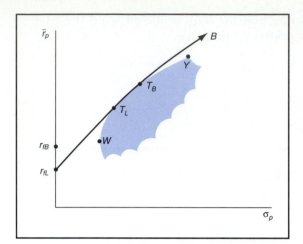

Figure 10.3
Efficient Set When the Riskfree Rates Are Different

If there are no opportunities to borrow or lend at the riskfree rate, the efficient set would be the curve WT_LT_BY, and many combinations of risky securities would be efficient. However, the availability of riskfree lending at the rate r_{fL} makes the risky portfolios between W and T_L inefficient, as combinations of riskfree lending and the portfolio plotting at T_L provide more return for the same risk.

Similarly, the ability to borrow money at rate r_{fB} makes another portfolio, denoted by T_B, of special interest. Risky portfolios between T_B and Y are now inefficient, because levered holdings of T_B dominate them by providing more return for the same risk.

Investors with attitudes toward risk that suggest neither borrowing nor lending should hold efficient combinations of risky securities plotting along curve T_LT_B. Accordingly, their holdings should be tailored to be consistent with differences in their degrees of aversion to risk.

In this situation the CML is now two lines and a curve, corresponding to the line going from r_{fL} to T_L, then the curve from T_L to T_B, and then the line from T_B on out to the northeast in Figure 10.3.

A.1.2 The Security Market Line

What becomes of the Security Market Line when the riskfree borrowing rate exceeds the riskfree lending rate? The answer depends on whether or not the market portfolio is in fact one of the efficient combinations of risky securities along the boundary between T_L and T_B in Figure 10.3.[16] If it is not, little more can be said. If it is, a great deal can be said.

Figure 10.4 shows a case in which the market portfolio (shown by point M) is efficient. In part (a) a line has been drawn that is tangent to the efficient set at point M. When this line is extended to the vertical axis, the resulting intercept is denoted $\bar{r}_z$. In part (b) only this tangency line is shown.

A striking characteristic of Figure 10.4(b) is this: It is precisely the same picture that would be produced in a market in which investors could borrow and lend without limit at a hypothetical riskfree rate equal in value to $\bar{r}_z$. Whereas only point M along the line emanating from $\bar{r}_z$ would be attainable, the expected

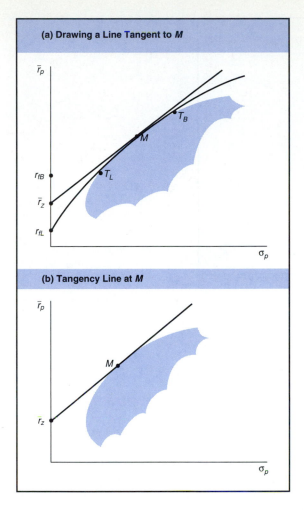

Figure 10.4
Risk and Return When the
Market Portfolio Is Efficient

returns of risky securities would be the same as they would be in a hypothetical market with borrowing and lending at $\bar{r}_z$. That is, all risky securities (and portfolios consisting of these securities) would plot along an SML going through point $\bar{r}_z$, as shown in Figure 10.5.

The vertical intercept of the SML indicates the expected return on a security or portfolio with a beta of zero. Accordingly, this extension of the CAPM is termed the *zero-beta capital asset pricing model*. This version of the CAPM implies that the SML will be flatter than implied by the original version, because $\bar{r}_z$ will be above r_{fL}. As a practical matter, it means that $\bar{r}_z$ must be inferred from the prices of risky securities, as it cannot simply be found in the quotations of current prices on, for example, Treasury bills. Many organizations that estimate the SML generally find that it conforms more to the zero-beta CAPM than to the original CAPM.

Cases in which borrowing is either impossible or costs more as one borrows larger amounts lead to only minor modifications in the conclusions. As long as the market portfolio is efficient, all securities will plot along an SML, but the "zero-beta return" will exceed the riskfree rate at which funds can be invested.

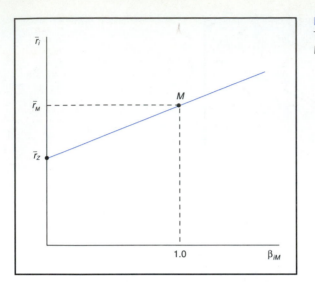

Figure 10.5
The Zero-Beta Security Market Line

A.2   INTRODUCING HETEROGENEOUS EXPECTATIONS

A number of researchers have examined the implications of assuming that different investors have different perceptions about expected returns, standard deviations, and covariances. More specifically, the assumption of homogeneous expectations has been replaced by these researchers with an assumption of *heterogeneous expectations.*

In one such study, it was noted that each investor would face an efficient set that was unique to him or her.[17] This means that the tangency portfolio (denoted by T in Chapter 9) is unique to each investor, because the optimal combination of risky assets for an investor depends on that investor's perceptions about expected returns, standard deviations, and covariances. Furthermore, an investor will likely determine that his or her tangency portfolio does not involve an investment in some securities (that is, certain securities may have zero proportions in the tangency portfolio). Nevertheless, the SML will still exist. This was shown by aggregating the holdings of all investors, and remembering that in equilibrium each security's price has to be at a level where the amount of the security demanded equals the supply of the security. Now, however, the equilibrium expected return for each security will be a complex weighted average of all investors' perceptions of its expected return. That is, from the viewpoint of a representative, or average, investor, each security will be priced fairly, so its expected return (as perceived by this investor) will be linearly and positively related to its beta.

The original CAPM assumes that investors are concerned only with risk and return. However, other characteristics may also be important to investors. For example, *liquidity* may be important. Here, liquidity refers to the cost of selling or buying a security "in a hurry." A house is regarded as a relatively illiquid investment, because usually a "fair" price for it cannot be obtained quickly. In terms of securities, liquidity may be measured by the size of the spread between the bid and asked prices, with smaller spreads suggesting greater liquidity. Furthermore, it is reasonable to assume that many investors would find more liquid securities to be more attractive, keeping everything else the same. However, investors undoubtedly differ in their attitudes toward liquidity. For some it is very important; for others, somewhat important; and for yet others, of little importance.

Under these conditions, security prices would adjust until, overall, investors would be content to hold the outstanding securities. The expected return of a security would be based on two characteristics of the security:

1. The marginal contribution of the security to the risk of an efficient portfolio. This would be measured by the familiar beta (β_{iM}) of the security.
2. The marginal contribution of the security to the liquidity of an efficient portfolio. This would be measured by the liquidity (L_i) of the security.

Now, other things being equal, investors dislike large values of β_{im} but like large values of L_i. This means that two securities with the same beta but different liquidities would not have the same level of expected return. To understand why they would have different levels of expected return, consider what would happen if they had the same level of expected return. In such a situation investors would buy the security with the greater liquidity and sell the one with the lesser liquidity. This would push the price of the first security up and the second one down. Ultimately, in equilibrium the quantity demanded would equal the quantity supplied, and the security with the greater liquidity would have a relatively lower expected return. Similarly, two securities with the same liquidity but different betas would not have the same level of expected return. Instead, the security with the higher beta would have a higher expected return.[18]

Figure 10.6 shows the equilibrium relationship one might expect among $\overline{r}_i$, β_{im}, and L_i. For a given level of β_{im}, more liquid securities have lower expected returns. And for a given level of L_i, more risky securities have higher expected returns as in the original CAPM. Lastly, there are securities with various levels of β_{im} and L_i that provide the same level of $\overline{r}_i$. The figure is three-dimensional, because now expected returns are related to two characteristics of securities. Accordingly, it is sometimes referred to as a *Security Market Plane*.[19]

If expected returns are based on beta, liquidity, and a third characteristic, then a four-dimensional CAPM would be necessary to describe the corresponding equilibrium.[20] Although a diagram cannot be drawn for this type of extended CAPM, an equation can be written for it. Such an equation, by analogy to the three-dimensional plane, is termed a *hyperplane*.

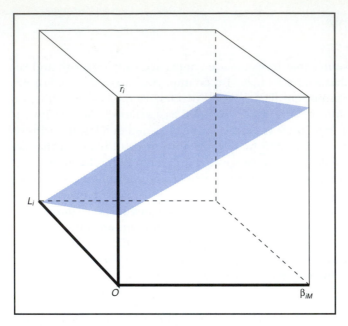

Figure 10.6
Security Market Plane

In equilibrium, all securities will plot on a Security Market Hyperplane, *where each axis measures the contribution of a security to a characteristic of efficient portfolios that matter (on average) to investors.*

The relationship between the expected return of a security and its contribution to a particular characteristic of efficient portfolios depends on the attitudes of investors to the characteristic:

If, on the average, a characteristic (such as liquidity) is liked by investors, then those securities that contribute more to that characteristic will, other things being equal, offer lower expected returns. Conversely, if a characteristic (such as beta) is disliked by investors, then those securities that contribute more to that characteristic will offer higher expected returns.

In a capital market with many relevant characteristics, the task of tailoring a portfolio for a specific investor is more complicated, because only an investor with average attitudes and circumstances should hold the market portfolio. In general:

If an investor likes a characteristic more (or dislikes it less) than the average investor, he or she should generally hold a portfolio with relatively more of that characteristic than is provided by holding the market portfolio. Conversely, if an investor likes a characteristic less (or dislikes it more) than the average investor, he or she should generally hold a portfolio with relatively less of that characteristic than is provided by holding the market portfolio.

For example, consider an investor who likes having a relatively liquid portfolio. Such an investor should hold a portfolio consisting of relatively liquid securities. Conversely, an investor who has relatively little need for liquidity should hold a portfolio of relatively illiquid securities.

The right combination of "tilt" away from market proportions will depend on the extent of the differences between the investor's attitudes and those of the average investor and on the added risk involved in such a strategy. A complex capital market requires all the tools of modern portfolio theory for managing the money of any investor who is significantly different from the "average investor." On the other hand, in such a world, investment management should be relatively passive: After the selection of an initial portfolio, there should be minor and infrequent changes.

APPENDIX B

A DERIVATION OF THE SECURITY MARKET LINE

Figure 10.7 shows the location of the feasible set of the Markowitz model along with the riskfree rate and the associated efficient set that represents the Capital Market Line. Within the feasible set of the Markowitz model lies every individual risky security. An arbitrarily chosen risky security, denoted i, has been selected for analysis and is shown on the figure.

Consider any portfolio, denoted p, that consists of the proportion X_i invested in security i and the proportion $(1 - X_i)$ invested in the market portfolio M. Such a portfolio will have an expected return equal to:

$$\bar{r}_p = X_i \bar{r}_i + (1 - X_i) \bar{r}_M \tag{10.14}$$

and a standard deviation equal to:

$$\sigma_p = [X_i^2 \sigma_i^2 + (1 - X_i)^2 \sigma_M^2 + 2 X_i (1 - X_i) \sigma_{iM}]^{1/2}. \tag{10.15}$$

All such portfolios will lie on a curved line connecting i and M such as the one shown in Figure 10.7.

Of concern is the slope of this curved line. Because it is a curved line, its slope is not a constant. However, its slope can be determined with the use of calculus. First, using Equation (10.14), the derivative of $\bar{r}_p$ with respect to X_i is taken:

$$\frac{d\bar{r}_p}{dX_i} = \bar{r}_i - \bar{r}_M. \tag{10.16}$$

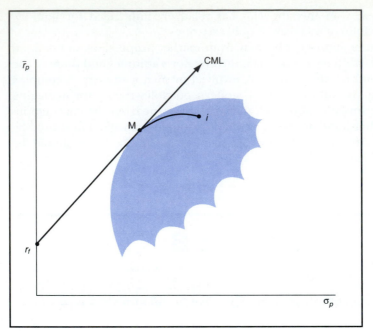

Figure 10.7
Deriving the Security Market Line

Second, using Equation (10.15), the derivative of σ_p with respect to X_i is taken:

$$\frac{d\sigma_p}{dX_i} = \frac{X_i\sigma_i^2 - \sigma_M^2 + X_i\sigma_M^2 + \sigma_{iM} - 2X_i\sigma_{iM}}{[X_i^2\sigma_i^2 + (1 - X_i)^2\sigma_M^2 + 2X_i(1 - X_i)\sigma_{iM}]^{1/2}}. \tag{10.17}$$

Third, it can be noted that the slope of the curved line iM, $d\bar{r}_p/d\sigma_p$, can be written as:

$$\frac{d\bar{r}_p}{d\sigma_p} = \frac{d\bar{r}_p/dX_i}{d\sigma_p/dX_i} \tag{10.18}$$

This means that the slope of iM can be calculated by substituting Equations (10.16) and (10.17) into the numerator and denominator of Equation (10.18), respectively:

$$\frac{d\bar{r}_p}{d\sigma_p} = \frac{[\bar{r}_i - \bar{r}_M][X_i^2\sigma_i^2 + (1 - X_i)^2\sigma_M^2 + 2X_i(1 - X_i)\sigma_{iM}]^{1/2}}{X_i\sigma_i^2 - \sigma_M^2 + X_i\sigma_M^2 + \sigma_{iM} - 2X_i\sigma_{iM}}. \tag{10.19}$$

Of interest is the slope of the curved line iM at the endpoint M. Because the proportion X_i is zero at this point, the slope of iM can be calculated by substituting zero for X_i in Equation (10.19). After doing so, many terms drop out, leaving:

$$\frac{d\bar{r}_p}{d\sigma_p} = \frac{[\bar{r}_i - \bar{r}_M][\sigma_M]}{\sigma_{iM} - \sigma_M^2}. \tag{10.20}$$

At M the slope of the CML, $(\bar{r}_M - r_f)/\sigma_M$, must equal the slope of the curved line iM. This is because the slope of the curved line iM increases when moving from the endpoint i, converging with the slope of the CML at the endpoint M. Accordingly, the slope of the curve iM at M, as shown on the right-hand side of Equation (10.20), is set equal to the slope of the CML:

$$\frac{[\bar{r}_i - \bar{r}_M][\sigma_M]}{\sigma_{iM} - \sigma_M^2} = \frac{\bar{r}_M - r_f}{\sigma_M}. \tag{10.21}$$

Solving Equation (10.21) for $\bar{r}_i$ results in the covariance version of the SML:

$$\bar{r}_i = r_f + \left[\frac{\bar{r}_M - r_f}{\sigma_M^2}\right]\sigma_{iM}. \tag{10.6}$$

The beta version of the SML is derived by substituting β_{iM} for σ_{iM}/σ_M^2 in Equation (10.6).

ENDNOTES

[1] Some extended versions of the CAPM are discussed in Appendix A.

[2] Milton Friedman, *Essays in the Theory of Positive Economics* (Chicago: University of Chicago Press, 1953): p.15.

[3] If the investor had initial wealth of $40,000, this means that he or she would borrow $20,000 and then invest $60,000 (= $40,000 + $20,000) in T.

[4] Note how the proportions in these three stocks sum to .5 for the panel (a) investor and 1.5 for the panel (b) investor. Because the respective proportions for the riskfree rate are .5 and −.5, the aggregate proportions for the stocks and riskfree rate sum to 1.0 for each investor.

[5] Securities that have zero net amounts outstanding will not appear in the tangency portfolio. Options and futures, discussed in Chapters 20 and 21, are examples of such securities.

[6] Although the expected return of Charlie has been changed, all the variances and covariances as well as the expected returns for Able and Baker are assumed to have the same values that were given in Chapters 7, 8 and 9. The singular change in the expected return of Charlie alters not only the composition of the tangency portfolio but, more generally, the location and shape of the efficient set.

[7] In this situation the market for each security is said to have *cleared*.

[8] The aggregate market value for the common stock of a company is equal to the current market price of the stock multiplied by the number of shares outstanding.

[9] The slope of a straight line can be determined if the location of two points on the line are known. It is determined by *rise over run,* meaning that it is determined by dividing the vertical distance between the two points by the horizontal distance between the two points. In the case of the CML, two points are known, corresponding to the riskfree rate and the market portfolio, so its slope can be determined in this manner.

[10] The equation of a straight line is of the form: $y = a + bx$, where a is the vertical intercept and b is the slope. Because the vertical intercept and slope of the CML are known, its equation can be written as shown here by making the appropriate substitutions for a and b.

[11] A more rigorous derivation of the SML is provided in Appendix B.

[12] Baker and Charlie have covariances of 382 and 179, respectively, which means that their expected returns should be equal to 30.74% = 4 + (.07 × 382) and 16.53% = 4 + (.07 × 179). However, these figures do not correspond to the respective ones (24.6% and 22.8%) appearing in the expected return vector, indicating that there are discrepancies for all three securities. Although this example has used the covariance version of the SML, the analysis is similar for the beta version of SML that is shown in Equation (10.7).

[13] Other indices of common stocks are commonly reported in the daily press. Many of these are components of the major indices mentioned here. For example, the *Wall Street Journal* reports on a daily basis not only the level of the S&P 500 but also the levels of the Standard & Poor's Industrials, Transportations, Utilities, and Financials. These last four indices reflect the performance of particular sectors of the stock market. Their components, 500 stocks in total, make up the S&P 500; Standard & Poor's also reports the level of a 400 MidCap index based on the stock prices of middle-sized companies. See Chapters 23 and 26 for a more thorough discussion of stock market indices.

[14] Charles Dow started this index in 1884 by simply adding the prices of 11 companies and then dividing the sum by 11. In 1928 securities were added to bring the total number up to 30. Since then the composition of these 30 has been changed periodically. Due to corporate actions such as stock dividends and splits as well as changes in the index's companies, the divisor is no longer simply equal to the number of stocks in the index.

[15] A more rigorous development of this figure is presented in Appendix A to Chapter 9.

[16] Assume that initial margin requirements for short sales do not exist, investors can obtain the proceeds from short sales, and neither riskfree borrowing nor lending is possible. In such a situation the feasible set would be bounded by a hyperbola that opens to the right. Furthermore, the efficient set would be the upper half of this boundary. Introducing riskfree borrowing and lending changes the shape and location of the efficient set to one that is similar to what appears in Figure 10.3. In such a situation the market portfolio would definitely plot on the efficient set between T_L and T_B. See Fischer Black, "Capital Market Equilibrium with Restricted Borrowing," *Journal of Business*, 45, no. 3 (July 1972): 444–455.

[17] See John Lintner, "The Aggregation of Investor's Diverse Judgements and Preferences in Purely Competitive Markets," *Journal of Financial and Quantitative Analysis*, 4, no. 4 (December 1969): 347–400.

[18] Investors possess completely illiquid assets in the form of human capital. This means that the ability that an investor has to produce a stream of income by working shows that the investor possesses an asset known as human capital and that different investors have different amounts of human capital. As slavery is outlawed, this asset cannot be sold and hence is nonmarketable. Nevertheless, because human capital is an asset, certain researchers have argued that it is relevant to each investor in identifying his or her optimal portfolio. Accordingly, the market portfolio should consist of all marketable and nonmarketable assets (like human capital), and each security's beta should be measured relative to it. See David Mayers, "Nonmarketable Assets and Capital Market Equilibrium under Uncertainty," in *Studies in the Theory of Capital Markets,* ed. Michael C. Jensen (New York: Praeger Publishers, 1972), and "Nonmarketable Assets and the Determination of Capital Asset Prices in the Absence of a Riskless Asset," *Journal of Business,* 46, no. 2 (April 1973): 258–267.

[19] The term *Security Market Plane* is a trademark of Wells Fargo Bank. For more on the relationship between liquidity and stock returns, see Yakov Amihud and Haim Mendelson, "Liquidity and Stock Returns," *Financial Analysts Journal*, 42, no. 3 (May/June 1986): 43–48; "Asset Pricing and the Bid-Ask Spread," *Journal of Financial Economics,* 17, no. 2 (December 1986): 223–249; and "Liquidity, Asset Prices and Financial Policy," *Financial Analysts Journal,* 47, no. 6 (November/December 1991): 56–66.

[20] Taxes might be such a third characteristic if the tax rate on income from capital gains is less than the tax rate on dividend income. In considering such taxes, one study found that the before-tax expected return of a security was a positive linear function of its beta and dividend yield. This means that securities with higher betas or dividend yields tended to have higher before-tax expected returns than securities with lower betas or dividend yields. The reason securities with higher dividend yields would have had higher before-tax expected returns was that they would be taxed more heavily. See M. J. Brennan, "Taxes, Market Valuation and Corporate Financial Policy," *National Tax Journal*, 23, no. 4 (December 1970): 417–427. The issue of whether or not dividends influence before-tax expected returns has been contentious. It is discussed in Chapters 15 and 16 of Thomas E. Copeland and J. Fred Weston, *Financial Theory and Corporate Policy*, (Reading, MA: Addison-Wesley, 1988).

KEY TERMS

normative economics

positive economics

Capital Asset Pricing Model

homogeneous expectations

perfect markets

separation theorem

market portfolio

Capital Market Line

Security Market Line

beta coefficient

market risk

non-market risk

REFERENCES

1. Credit for the initial development of the CAPM is usually given to:

William F. Sharpe, "Capital Asset Prices: A Theory of Market Equilibrium Under Conditions of Risk," *Journal of Finance*, 19, no. 3 (September 1964): 425–442.

John Lintner, "The Valuation of Risk Assets and the Selection of Risky Investments in Stock Portfolios and Capital Budgets," *Review of Economics and Statistics*, 47, no. 1 (February 1965): 13–37; and "Security Prices, Risk, and Maximal Gains from Diversification," *Journal of Finance*, 20, no. 4 (December 1965): 587–615.

Jan Mossin, "Equilibrium in a Capital Asset Market," *Econometrica*, 34, no. 4 (October 1966): 768–783.

2. The Sharpe and Lintner papers were compared in:

Eugene F. Fama, "Risk, Return, and Equilibrium: Some Clarifying Comments," *Journal of Finance*, 23, no. 1 (March 1968): 29–40.

3. Some extended versions of the CAPM are described in:

Gordon J. Alexander and Jack Clark Francis, *Portfolio Analysis* (Englewood Cliffs, NJ: Prentice Hall, 1986), Chapter 8.

Edwin J. Elton and Martin J. Gruber, *Modern Portfolio Theory and Investment Analysis* (New York: John Wiley, 1991), Chapter 12.

4. For a comparison of the market model and CAPM betas, see:

Harry M. Markowitz, "The 'Two Beta' Trap," *Journal of Portfolio Management*, 11, no. 1 (Fall 1984): 12–20.

5. It has been argued that the CAPM is virtually impossible to test because (a) the only testable hypothesis of the CAPM is that the "true" market portfolio lies on the efficient set (when this happens securities' expected returns and betas have a positive linear relationship) and (b) the "true" market portfolio cannot be meaningfully measured. See:

Richard Roll, "A Critique of the Asset Pricing Theory's Tests; Part I. On Past and Potential Testability of the Theory," *Journal of Financial Economics*, 4, no. 2 (March 1977): 129–176.

6. In spite of Roll's critique, several tests of the CAPM have been conducted. Some of them are summarized in:

Gordon J. Alexander and Jack Clark Francis, *Portfolio Analysis* (Englewood Cliffs, NJ: Prentice Hall, 1986), Chapter 10.

Edwin J. Elton and Martin J. Gruber, *Modern Portfolio Theory and Investment Analysis* (New York: John Wiley, 1991), Chapter 13.

7. Recently some people have concluded that the CAPM is no longer relevant based on the following test results that show that the relationship between beta and average stock returns is flat:

Eugene F. Fama and Kenneth R. French, "The Cross-Section of Expected Stock Returns," *Journal of Finance*, 47, no. 2 (June 1992): 427–465.

Eugene F. Fama and Kenneth R. French, "Common Risk Factors in the Returns on Stocks and Bonds," *Journal of Financial Economics*, 33, no. 1 (February 1993): 3–56.

8. However, these test results have been challenged by others, such as those listed below. For example, the third study shows that average returns and betas have a positive linear relationship when the market portfolio includes human capital (see Endnote 18) and betas are allowed to vary over the business cycle:

Louis K. C. Chan and Josef Lakonishok, "Are the Reports of Beta's Death Premature?", *Journal of Portfolio Management*, 19, no. 4 (Summer 1993): 51–62.

Fischer Black, "Beta and Return," *Journal of Portfolio Management*, 20, no. 1 (Fall 1993): 8–18.

Ravi Jagannathan and Zhenyu Wang, "The CAPM is Alive and Well," unpublished paper, Carlson School of Management, University of Minnesota, Minneapolis, MN, November 22, 1993.

9. For an assertion that the use of modern portfolio theory does not depend upon successful testing of the CAPM, see:

Harry M. Markowitz, "Nonnegative or Not Nonnegative: A Question about CAPMs," *Journal of Finance*, 38, no. 2 (May 1983): 283–295.

Factor Models

The objective of modern portfolio theory is to provide a means by which the investor can identify his or her optimal portfolio when there are an infinite number of possibilities. Using a framework involving expected returns and standard deviations shows that the investor needs to estimate the expected return and standard deviation for each security under consideration for inclusion in the portfolio along with all the covariances between securities. With these estimates the investor can derive the curved efficient set of Markowitz. Then for a given riskfree rate the investor can identify the tangency portfolio and determine the location of the linear efficient set. Finally, the investor can proceed to invest in this tangency portfolio and borrow or lend at the riskfree rate, with the amount of borrowing or lending depending on the investor's risk-return preferences.

11.1 FACTOR MODELS AND RETURN-GENERATING PROCESSES

The task of identifying the curved Markowitz efficient set can be greatly simplified by introducing a **return-generating process**. A return-generating process is a statistical model that describes how the return on a security is produced. Chapter 8 presented a type of return-generating process known as the market model. The market model states that a security's return is a function of the return on a market index. However, there are many other types of return-generating processes for securities.

11.1.1 Factor Models

Factor models or index models assume that the return on a security is sensitive to the movements of various factors or indices. The market model assumes that there is one factor—the return on a market index. However, in attempting to accurately estimate expected returns, variances, and covariances for securities, multiple-factor models are potentially more useful than the market model. They have this potential because it appears that actual security returns are sensitive to more than movements in a market index. This means that there probably is more than one pervasive factor in the economy that affects security returns.

As a return-generating process, a factor model attempts to capture the major economic forces that systematically move the prices of all securities. Implicit in the construction of a factor model is the assumption that the returns on two securities will be correlated—that is, will move together—only through common reactions to one or more of the factors specified in the model. Any aspect of a security's return unexplained by the factor model is assumed to be unique or specific to the security and therefore uncorrelated with the unique elements of returns on other securities. As a result, a factor model is a powerful tool for portfolio management. It can supply the information needed to calculate expected returns, variances, and covariances for every security—a necessary condition for determining the curved Markowitz efficient set. It can also be used to characterize a portfolio's sensitivity to movements in the factors.

11.1.2 Application

As a practical matter, all investors employ factor models whether they do so explicitly or implicitly. It is impossible to consider separately the interrelationship of every security with every other. Numerically, the problem of calculating covariances among securities rises exponentially as the number of securities analyzed increases.[1]

Conceptually, thinking about the tangled web of security variances and covariances becomes mind-boggling as the number of securities increases beyond just a few securities, let alone hundreds or thousands. Even the vast data processing capabilities of high-speed computers are strained when they are called upon to construct efficient sets from a large number of securities.

Abstraction is therefore an essential step in identifying the curved Markowitz efficient set. Factor models supply the necessary level of abstraction. They provide investment managers with a framework to identify important factors in the economy and the marketplace and to assess the extent to which different securities and portfolios will respond to changes in these factors.

Given the belief that one or more factors influence security returns, a primary goal of security analysis is to determine these factors and the sensitivities of security returns to movements in these factors. A formal statement of such a relationship is termed a *factor model of security returns*. The discussion begins with the simplest form of such a model, a one-factor model.

CHAPTER 11

Some investors argue that the return-generating process for securities involves a single factor. For example, they may contend that the returns on securities respond to the predicted growth rate in the gross domestic product (GDP).[2] Table 11.1 and Figure 11.1 illustrate one way of providing substance for such statements.

TABLE 11.1
FACTOR MODEL DATA

Year	Growth Rate in GDP	Rate of Inflation	Return on Widget Stock
1	5.7%	1.1%	14.3%
2	6.4	4.4	19.2
3	7.9	4.4	23.4
4	7.0	4.6	15.6
5	5.1	6.1	9.2
6	2.9	3.1	13.0

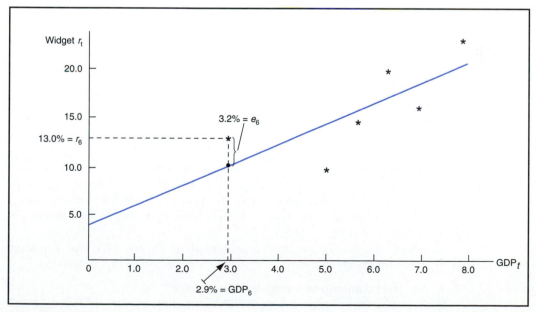

Figure 11.1
A One-Factor Model

11.2.1 An Example

On the horizontal axis of Figure 11.1 is the predicted growth rate in GDP, whereas the vertical axis measures the return on Widget's stock. Each point in the graph represents the combination of Widget's return and GDP growth rate for a particular year as reported in Table 11.1. A line has been statistically fitted to the data by using a technique known as *simple-regression analysis*. (*Simple* refers to the fact that there is one variable—GDP in this example—on the right-hand side of the equation).[3] This line has a positive slope of 2, indicating that there exists a positive relationship between GDP growth rates and Widget's returns. Higher rates of GDP growth are associated with higher returns.

In equation form, the relationship between predicted GDP growth and Widget's return can be expressed as follows:

$$r_t = a + b\text{GDP}_t + e_t \tag{11.1}$$

where:

> r_t = *the return on Widget in period* t,
> GDP_t = *the predicted rate of growth in GDP in period* t,
> e_t = *the unique or specific return on Widget in period* t,
> b = ***sensitivity*** *of Widget to predicted GDP growth,*[4]
> a = *the zero factor for GDP.*

In Figure 11.1 the zero factor is 4% per period. This is the return that would be expected for Widget if predicted GDP growth equaled zero. The sensitivity of Widget to predicted GDP growth b is 2, and is the same as the slope of the line in Figure 11.1. This value indicates that, in general, higher predicted growth in GDP is associated with higher returns for Widget. If predicted GDP growth equaled 5%, Widget should generate a return of 14% [= 4% + (2 × 5%)]. If predicted GDP growth were 1% higher—that is, 6%—Widget's return should be 2% higher, or 16%.

In this example, predicted GDP growth in year 6 was 2.9%, and Widget actually returned 13%. Therefore Widget's unique return (given by e_t) in this particular year was +3.2%. This was determined by subtracting an amount that represents Widget's expected return, given that GDP was predicted to grow by 2.9%, from Widget's actual return of 13%. In this case, Widget would have an expected return of 9.8% [= 4 + (2 × 2.9%)], thereby resulting in a unique return of +3.2% (= 13% − 9.8%).

In effect, the one-factor model presented in Figure 11.1 and Equation (11.1) attributes Widget's return in any particular period to three elements:

1. An effect common in any period (the term a)
2. An effect that differs across periods depending on the predicted growth rate of GDP (the term $b\text{GDP}_t$)
3. An effect specific to the particular period observed (the term e_t)

11.2.2 Generalizing the Example

This example of a one-factor model can be generalized in equation form for any security i in period t:

$$r_{it} = a_i + b_i F_t + e_{it} \tag{11.2}$$

where F is the predicted value of the factor in period t and b_i is the sensitivity of security i to this factor. If the predicted value of the factor were zero, the return on the security would equal $a_i + e_{it}$. Note that e_{it} is a random error term just like the random error term discussed in Chapter 8. This means that it is a random variable with an expected value of zero and a standard deviation σ_{ei}. It can be thought of as the outcome occurring from a spin of a roulette wheel.

Expected Return

According to the one-factor model, the expected return on security i can be written as:

$$\overline{r}_i = a_i + b_i \overline{F} \tag{11.3}$$

where $\overline{F}$ denotes the expected value of the factor.

This equation can be used to estimate the expected return on the security. For example, if the expected growth rate in GDP is 3%, then the expected return for Widget equals 10% [= 4% + (2 × 3%)].

Variance

With the one-factor model, it can also be shown that the variance of any security i is equal to:

$$\sigma_i^2 = b_i^2 \sigma_F^2 + \sigma_{ei}^2 \tag{11.4}$$

where σ_F^2 is the variance of the factor F and σ_{ei}^2 is the variance of the random error term e_i. Thus if the variance of the factor σ_F^2 equals 3 and the residual variance σ_{ei}^2 equals 15.2, then according to this equation Widget's variance equals:

$$\sigma_i^2 = (2^2 \times 3) + 15.2$$
$$= 27.2.$$

Covariance

With a one-factor model the covariance between any two securities i and j can be shown to equal:

$$\sigma_{ij} = b_i b_j \sigma_F^2. \tag{11.5}$$

In the example of Widget, Equation (11.5) can be used to estimate the covariance between Widget and another hypothetical security, such as the stock of Whatever Company. Assuming that the factor sensitivity of Whatever is 4.0, the covariance between Widget and Whatever equals:

$$\sigma_{ij} = 2 \times 4 \times 3$$
$$= 24$$

Assumptions

Equations (11.4) and (11.5) are based on two critical assumptions. The first assumption is that the random error term and the factor are uncorrelated. This means that the outcome of the factor has no bearing on the outcome of the random error term.

The second assumption is that the random error terms of any two securities are uncorrelated. This means that the outcome of the random error term of one security has no bearing on the outcome of the random error term of any other security. In other words, the returns of two securities will be correlated—that is, will move together only through common responses to the factor. If either of these two assumptions is invalid, then the model is an approximation, and a different factor model (perhaps one with more factors) will theoretically be a more accurate model of the return-generating process.

11.2.3 The Market Model

The market model can now be shown to be a specific example of a one-factor model where the factor is the return on a market index. In Chapter 8, the market model appeared as:

$$r_i = \alpha_{iI} + \beta_{iI} r_I + \epsilon_{iI} \qquad (8.3)$$

Comparing Equation (8.3) with the general form of the one-factor model in Equation (11.2), the similarity between the two equations is readily apparent. The intercept term α_{iI} from the market model equation corresponds to the zero factor term a_i from Equation (11.2). Furthermore, the slope term β_{iI} from the market model equates to the sensitivity term b_i from the generalized one-factor model. Each equation has a random error term: e_{it} in the factor model and ϵ_{iIt} in the market model.[5] Finally, the market index return plays the role of the single factor.

However, as mentioned earlier, the concept of a one-factor model does not restrict the investor to using a market index as the factor. Many other factors are plausible, such as predicted GDP or industrial production.

11.2.4 Two Important Features of One-Factor Models

Two features of one-factor models are of particular interest.

The Tangency Portfolio

First, the assumption that the returns on all securities respond to a single common factor greatly simplifies the task of identifying the tangency portfolio. To determine the composition of the tangency portfolio, the investor needs to estimate all the expected returns, variances, and covariances. This can be done with a one-factor model by estimating a_i, b_i, and σ_{ei} for each of the N risky securities.[6]

Also needed are the expected value of the factor $\overline{F}$ and its standard deviation, σ_F. With these estimates, Equations (11.3), (11.4), and (11.5) can subsequently be used to calculate expected returns, variances, and covariances for the securities. Using these values, the curved efficient set of Markowitz can be derived. Finally, the tangency portfolio can be determined for a given riskfree rate.

The common responsiveness of securities to the factor eliminates the need to estimate directly the covariances between the securities. Those covariances are captured by the securities' sensitivities to the factor and the factor's variance.

Diversification

The second interesting feature of one-factor models has to do with diversification. Earlier it was shown that diversification leads to an averaging of market risk and a reduction in unique risk. This feature is true of any one-factor model except that instead of market and unique risk, the words factor and nonfactor risk are used. In Equation (11.4) the first term on the right-hand side ($b_i^2 \sigma_F^2$) is known as the **factor risk** of the security, and the second term (σ_{ei}^2) is known as the **nonfactor** (or idiosyncratic) **risk** of the security.

With a one-factor model, the variance of a portfolio is given by:

$$\sigma_P^2 = b_P^2 \sigma_F^2 + \sigma_{ep}^2 \tag{11.6a}$$

where:

$$b_p = \sum_{i=1}^{N} X_i b_i \tag{11.6b}$$

$$\sigma_{ep}^2 = \sum_{i=1}^{N} X_i^2 \sigma_{ei}^2. \tag{11.6c}$$

Equation (11.6a) shows that the total risk of any portfolio can be viewed as having two components similar to the two components of the total risk of an individual security shown in Equation (11.4). In particular, the first and second terms on the right-hand side of Equation (11.6a) are the factor risk and nonfactor risk of the portfolio, respectively.

As a portfolio becomes more diversified (meaning that it contains more securities), each proportion X_i will become smaller. However, this will not cause b_p to either decrease or increase significantly unless a deliberate attempt is made to do so by adding securities with values of b_i that are either relatively low or high, respectively. As Equation (11.6b) shows, this is because b_p is simply a weighted average of the sensitivities of the securities b_i with the values of X_i serving as the weights. Thus *diversification leads to an averaging of factor risk*.

However, as a portfolio becomes more diversified, there is reason to expect σ_{ep}^2, the nonfactor risk, to decrease. This can be shown by examining Equation (11.6c). Assuming that the amount invested in each security is equal, then this equation can be rewritten by substituting $1/N$ for X_i:

$$\sigma_{ep}^2 = \sum_{i=1}^{N} \left(\frac{1}{N}\right)^2 \sigma_{ei}^2$$

$$= \left(\frac{1}{N}\right) \left[\frac{\sigma_{e1}^2 + \sigma_{e2}^2 + \ldots + \sigma_{eN}^2}{N}\right].$$

The value inside the square brackets is the average nonfactor risk for the individual securities. But the portfolio's nonfactor risk is only one-Nth as large as this because the term $1/N$ appears outside the brackets. As the portfolio becomes more diversified, the number of securities in it, N, becomes larger. This means that $1/N$ becomes smaller, which in turn reduces the nonfactor risk of the portfolio. Simply stated, *diversification reduces nonfactor risk*.[7]

11.3 MULTIPLE-FACTOR MODELS

The health of the economy affects most firms. Thus changes in expectations concerning the future of the economy can be expected to have profound effects on the returns of most securities. However, the economy is not a simple, monolithic entity. Several common influences with pervasive effects might be identified.

1. The growth rate of gross domestic product
2. The level of interest rates
3. The inflation rate
4. The level of oil prices

11.3.1 Two-Factor Models

Instead of a one-factor model, a multiple-factor model for security returns that considers these various influences may be more accurate. As an example of a multiple-factor model, consider a two-factor model. This means assuming that the return-generating process contains two factors.

In equation form, the two-factor model for period t is:

$$r_{it} = a_i + b_{i1}F_{1t} + b_{i2}F_{2t} + e_{it} \qquad (11.7)$$

where F_{1t} and F_{2t} are the two factors that are pervasive influences on security returns and b_{i1} and b_{i2} are the sensitivities of security i to these two factors. As with the one-factor model, e_{it} is a random error term and a_i is the expected return on security i if each factor has a value of zero.

Figure 11.2 provides an illustration of Widget Company's stock, whose returns are affected by expectations concerning both the growth rate in GDP and the rate of inflation. As was the case in the one-factor example, each point in the figure corresponds to a particular year. This time, however, each point is a combination of Widget's return, the rate of inflation, and the growth in GDP in that year as given in Table 11.1. To this scatter of points is fit a two-dimensional plane by using the statistical technique of *multiple-regression analysis*. (*Multiple* refers to the fact that there are two predicted variables, GDP and inflation, in this example on the right-hand side of the equation.) The plane for a given security is described by the following adaptation of Equation (11.7):

$$r_t = a + b_1 \text{GDP}_t + b_2 \text{INF}_t + e_t.$$

The slope of the plane in the GDP growth-rate direction (the term b_1) represents Widget's sensitivity to changes in GDP growth. The slope of the plane in the inflation rate direction (the term b_2) is Widget's sensitivity to changes in the inflation rate. Note that the sensitivities b_1 and b_2 in this example are positive

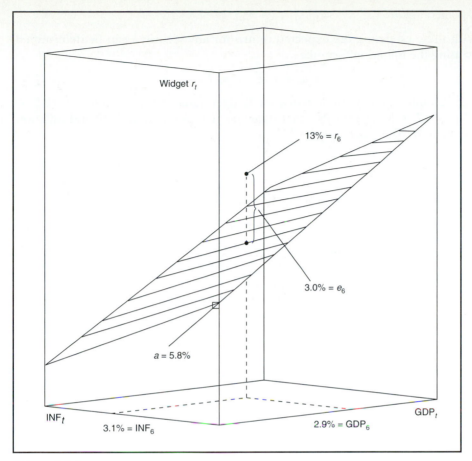

Figure 11.2
A Two-Factor Model

and negative, respectively, having corresponding values of 2.2 and $-.7$.[8] This indicates that as predicted GDP growth or inflation rises, Widget's return should increase or decrease, respectively.

The intercept term (the zero factor) in Figure 11.2 of 5.8% indicates Widget's expected return if both GDP growth and inflation are zero. Finally, in a given year the distance from Widget's actual point to the plane indicates its unique return (e_{it}), the portion of Widget's return not attributed to either GDP growth or inflation. For example, given that GDP grew by 2.9% and inflation was 3.1%, Widget's expected return in year 6 equals 10% [$= 5.8\% + (2.2 \times 2.9\%) - (.7 \times 3.1\%)$]. Hence its unique return for that year is equal to $+3\%$ ($= 13\% - 10\%$).

Four parameters need to be estimated for each security with the two-factor model: a_i, b_{i1}, b_{i2}, and the standard deviation of the random error term denoted σ_{ei}. For each of the factors, two parameters need to be estimated. These parameters are the expected value of each factor ($\overline{F}_1$ and $\overline{F}_2$) and the variance of each factor (σ_{F1}^2 and σ_{F2}^2). Finally, the covariance between the factors $COV(F_1, F_2)$ needs to be estimated.

Expected Return

With these estimates, the expected return for any security i can be determined by using the following formula:

$$\bar{r}_i = a_i + b_{i1}\bar{F}_1 + b_{i2}\bar{F}_2. \tag{11.8}$$

For example, the expected return for Widget equals 8.9% [= 5.8% + (2.2 × 3%) − (.7 × 5%)] provided that the expected increases in GDP and inflation are 3% and 5%, respectively.

Variance

According to the two-factor model, the variance for any security i is:

$$\sigma_i^2 = b_{i1}^2\sigma_{F1}^2 + b_{i2}^2\sigma_{F2}^2 + 2b_{i1}b_{i2}\,\mathrm{COV}(F_1, F_2) + \sigma_{ei}^2. \tag{11.9}$$

If, in the example, the variances of the first (σ_{F1}^2) and second (σ_{F2}^2) factors are equal to 3 and 2.9, respectively, and their covariance [$\mathrm{COV}(F_1, F_2)$] equals .65, then the variance of Widget equals 32.1 [= (2.2² × 3) + (−.7² × 2.9) + (2 × 2.2 × −.7 × .65) + 18.2], since its two sensitivities and random error term variance are 2.2, − .7, and 18.2, respectively.

Covariance

Similarly, according to the two-factor model the covariance between any two securities i and j can be determined by:

$$\sigma_{ij} = b_{i1}b_{j1}\sigma_{F1}^2 + b_{i2}b_{j2}\sigma_{F2}^2 + (b_{i1}b_{j2} + b_{i2}b_{j1})\,\mathrm{COV}\,(F_1, F_2). \tag{11.10}$$

Thus continuing with the example, the covariance between Widget and Whatever is estimated to equal 39.9 { = (2.2 × 6 × 3) + (−.7 × −5 × 2.9) + [(2.2 × −5) + (−.7 × 6)] × .65} because the sensitivities of Whatever to the two factors are 6 and −5, respectively.

The Tangency Portfolio

As with the one-factor model, once the expected returns, variances, and covariances have been determined using these equations, the investor can proceed to use an *optimizer* (a special kind of mathematical routine) to derive the curved efficient set of Markowitz. Then for a given riskfree rate, the tangency portfolio can be identified, after which the investor can determine his or her optimal portfolio.

Diversification

Everything said earlier regarding one-factor models and the effects of diversification applies here as well.

1. Diversification leads to an averaging of factor risk.
2. Diversification can substantially reduce nonfactor risk.
3. For a *well-diversified portfolio,* nonfactor risk will be insignificant.

As with a one-factor model, the sensitivity of a portfolio to a particular factor in a multiple-factor model is a weighted average of the sensitivities of the securities where the weights are equal to the proportions invested in the securities. This can be seen by remembering that the return on a portfolio is a weighted average of the returns of its component securities:

$$r_{pt} = \sum_{i=1}^{N} X_i r_{it}. \tag{11.11}$$

Substituting the right-hand side of Equation (11.7) for r_{it} on the right-hand side of Equation (11.11) results in:

$$r_{pt} = \sum_{i=1}^{N} X_i(a_i + b_{i1}F_{1t} + b_{i2}F_{2t} + e_{it})$$

$$= \left[\sum_{i=1}^{N} X_i a_i \right] + \left[\sum_{i=1}^{N} X_i b_{i1} F_{1t} \right] + \left[\sum_{i=1}^{N} X_i b_{i2} F_{2t} \right] + \left[\sum_{i=1}^{N} X_i e_{it} \right]$$

$$= a_p + b_{p1}F_{1t} + b_{p2}F_{2t} + e_{pt} \tag{11.12}$$

where:

$$a_p = \sum_{i=1}^{N} X_i a_i$$

$$b_{p1} = \sum_{i=1}^{N} X_i b_{i1}$$

$$b_{p2} = \sum_{i=1}^{N} X_i b_{i2}$$

$$e_{pt} = \sum_{i=1}^{N} X_i e_{it}.$$

Note that the portfolio sensitivities b_{p1} and b_{p2} are weighted averages of the respective individual sensitivities b_{i1} and b_{i2}.

11.3.2 Sector-Factor Models

The prices of securities in the same industry or economic sector often move together in response to changes in prospects for that sector. Some investors acknowledge this by using a special kind of multiple-factor model referred to as a **sector-factor model.** To create a sector-factor model, each security under consideration must be assigned to a sector. For a two-sector-factor model, there are two sectors and each security must be assigned to one of them.

For example, let sector-factor 1 consist of all industrial companies and sector-factor 2 consist of all nonindustrial companies (such as utility, transportation, and financial companies). Thus F_1 and F_2 can be thought of as representing the returns on an industrial stock index and a nonindustrial stock index, respectively. (They could, for example, be components of the S&P 500.) It should be kept in mind, however, that both the number of sectors and what each sector consists of is an open matter that is left to the investor to decide.[9]

With this two-sector-factor model, the return-generating process for securities is of the same general form as the two-factor model given in Equation (11.7). However, with the two-sector-factor model, F_1 and F_2 now denote sector-factors 1 and 2, respectively. Furthermore, any particular security belongs to either sector-factor 1 or sector-factor 2 but not both. By definition, a value of zero is given to the sensitivity term corresponding to the sector-factor to which the security is not assigned. This means that either b_{i1} or b_{i2} is set equal to zero, depending on the sector-factor to which security i is not assigned. The value of the other sensitivity term must be estimated. (To make matters simple, some people simply give it a value of one.)

As an illustration, consider General Motors (GM) and Delta Air Lines (DAL). The two-sector-factor model for GM (the time subscript t has been deleted for ease of exposition here) would be:

$$r_{GM} = a_{GM} + b_{GM1}F_1 + b_{GM2}F_2 + e_{GM}. \tag{11.13}$$

However, because GM belongs to sector-factor 1 as an industrial security, the coefficient b_{GM2} is assigned a value of zero. Once this assignment is made, Equation (11.13) reduces to:

$$r_{GM} = a_{GM} + b_{GM1}F_1 + e_{GM}. \tag{11.14}$$

Thus only the values of a_{GM}, b_{GM1}, and σ_{eGM} need to be estimated for GM with the two-sector-factor model. In comparison with the two-factor model, values of a_{GM}, b_{GM1}, b_{GM2}, and σ_{eGM} need to be estimated.

Similarly, as DAL belongs to the nonindustrial sector, it would have the following two-sector-factor model:

$$r_{DAL} = a_{DAL} + b_{DAL1}F_1 + b_{DAL2}F_2 + e_{DAL} \tag{11.15}$$

which would reduce to:

$$r_{DAL} = a_{DAL} + b_{DAL2}F_2 + e_{DAL} \tag{11.16}$$

as b_{DAL1} would be assigned a value of zero. Thus only the values of a_{DAL}, b_{DAL2}, and σ_{eDAL} need to be estimated with the two-sector-factor model.

In general, whereas four parameters need to be estimated for each security with a two-factor model (a_i, b_{i1}, b_{i2}, and σ_{ei}), only three parameters need to be estimated with a two-sector-factor model (a_i, σ_{ei}, and either b_{i1} or b_{i2}). With these estimates in hand, along with estimates of F_1, F_2, σ_{F1}, and σ_{F2}, the investor can use Equations (11.8) and (11.9) to estimate expected returns and variances for each security. Pairwise covariances can be estimated using Equation (11.10). This will then enable the investor to derive the curved efficient set of Markowitz from which the tangency portfolio can be determined for a given riskfree rate.

11.3.3 Extending the Model

To extend the discussion to more than two factors requires the abandonment of diagrams as the analysis moves beyond three dimensions. Nevertheless, the concepts are the same. If there are k factors, the multiple-factor model can be written as:

$$r_{it} = a_i + b_{i1}F_{1t} + b_{i2}F_{2t} + \ldots + b_{ik}F_{kt} + e_{it} \qquad (11.17)$$

where each security has k sensitivities, one for each of the k factors.

It is possible to have both factors and sector factors represented in Equation (11.17). For example, F_1 and F_2 could represent GDP and inflation as in Table 11.1, whereas F_3 and F_4 could represent the returns on industrial stocks and nonindustrial stocks, respectively. Hence each stock would have three sensitivities: b_{i1}, b_{i2}, and b_{i3} for industrials and b_{i1}, b_{i2}, and b_{i4} for nonindustrials.[10]

11.4   ESTIMATING FACTOR MODELS

Although many methods of estimating factor models are used, these methods can be grouped into three primary approaches:

1. Time-series approaches
2. Cross-sectional approaches
3. Factor-analytic approaches

11.4.1 Time-Series Approaches

Time-series approaches are perhaps the most intuitive to investors.[11] The model builder begins with the assumption that he or she knows in advance the factors that influence security returns. Identification of the relevant factors typically proceeds from an economic analysis of the firms involved. Aspects of macroeconomics, microeconomics, industrial organization, and fundamental security analysis will play a major role in the process.

For example, as discussed earlier, certain macroeconomic variables might be expected to have a pervasive impact on security returns, including such things as predicted growth in GDP, inflation, interest rates, and oil prices. With these factors specified, the model builder collects information concerning the values of the factors and security returns from period to period. Using this data, the model builder can calculate the sensitivities of the securities' returns to the factors, the securities' zero factors and unique returns, and the standard deviations of the factors and their correlations. In this approach, accurate measurement of factor values is crucial. In practice, this can be quite difficult.

The Barra U.S. Equity Multiple-Factor Model

For the quantitatively inclined investment professional, multiple-factor models are intuitively appealing tools. They capture the essence of the fundamental economic and financial forces that affect security returns in a concise and readily testable form. However, moving from abstract discussions to the development of factor models that are sufficiently comprehensive and robust to serve the varied needs of institutional investors is a difficult task. An overview of the BARRA U.S. equity multiple-factor model offers insights into the complex elements of factor model implementation.

The BARRA model is based on the pioneering work of Barr Rosenberg, an econometrician and former finance professor. In the early 1970s while at the University of California, Berkeley, he and Vinay Marathe formulated a sophisticated factor model. The model related common stock returns to a variety of factors derived primarily from the underlying companies' business operations.

Rosenberg is more than your typical ivory tower academic. Instead of being content to publish his results and receive the accolades of his colleagues, he recognized the commercial applications of his model. He formed a firm, now called BARRA, to enhance and sell the model to institutional investors.

Both the model and the firm proved successful beyond anyone's imagination. BARRA has grown into a worldwide consulting organization with annual revenues exceeding $40 million. Its stock is publicly traded and today has a market capitalization of over $50 million. Although Rosenberg left the firm in 1985 to pursue his own investment management ambitions, BARRA has continued to leverage off of its factor-model expertise by designing additional factor models for the global equity market and various foreign stock markets. The firm has also built factor models for the U.S. and several foreign bond markets.

Rosenberg's original U.S. equity multiple-factor model underwent a major revision in 1982 and is referred to by factor-model aficionados as the *E2 model*. Currently 630 institutional investors (over 50% of them outside of the United States) subscribe to the E2 model service. These investors range from large investment managers to pension

funds, and in total they manage over one trillion dollars of U.S. common stocks.

All factor models are based on the assumption that securities with similar exposures to specific factors will exhibit similar investment behavior. The factor model builder must translate this basic concept into practice. The process of constructing factor models is far from an exact science. While certain statistical tests can be applied to gauge the explanatory power of a particular factor model, the model builder retains wide latitude to include or exclude potential factors.

It is instructive, therefore, to review how BARRA developed the E2 model. The process by which the model was specified is summarized by five steps.

1. Data collection and checking
2. Factor selection
3. Creation of composite factors
4. Estimation of factor returns and the factor variance-covariance matrix
5. Model testing

The E2 model's construction began with the collection of relevant security data. BARRA gathered monthly components of security returns, such as prices, dividends, and shares outstanding, for the largest 1,400 common stocks (the "HICAP estimation universe") over an extended period of time. BARRA also acquired a wide array of income and balance sheet information on the underlying companies. This financial data came largely from the annual and quarterly financial statements issued by the companies.

As part of this collection process, BARRA checked the data for quality. Although this task may seem mundane, it was a critical step, as a small amount of bad data can produce a disproportionately large impact on a factor model's accuracy.

The second step involved factor selection. Literally hundreds of potential factors were available for inclusion in the model. BARRA sought to identify those factors that had a pervasive influence on the returns and risks of individual securities. Using historical security return data, BARRA isolated 70 market-related, income statement, and balance sheet factors that demonstrated statistically significant relationships with security prices.

The particular factors selected by BARRA ranged from the obvious to the novel. Examples included a company's historical equity beta, its consensus forecasted earnings growth, its historical variability in earnings, its debt to total assets, the number of security analysts covering a company's stock, and the proportion of a company's operating income derived from foreign sources.

The third step in the E2 model's construction entailed creating a set of composite factors from the 70 individual factors. BARRA employed 13 composite factors: Variability in Markets; Success; Size; Trading Activity; Growth; Earnings/Price; Book/Price; Earnings Variation; Financial Leverage; Foreign Income; Labor Intensity; Yield; and Low Capitalization. The individual factors were assigned to and weighted within the composite factors based on both judgment and statistical analyses.

The purpose of creating these composite factors was largely statistical convenience. As the text describes, a factor model builder must estimate the variance of each factor and the covariances among all the factors. The number of variances and covariances grows exponentially as the number of factors increases. Therefore, instead of having to calculate variances and covariances for dozens of factors, BARRA's task was considerably reduced by combining the individual factors into a handful of composite factors.

To these 13 composite factors, BARRA added 55 industry factors. (In the E2 model, a security can be assigned to as many as six industries, with total weights summing to 1, based on analysis of the company's sales, earnings, and assets.) Thus in its final form, the BARRA E2 factor model contains 68 fundamental and industry factors.

The fourth step involved estimating factor returns for each of the 68 factors and developing forecasts of nonfactor risk. Given return data on the model's estimation universe, for every month in its test period BARRA effectively estimated the returns on 68 portfolios that each had unit exposure to one particular factor and zero exposure to all other 67 factors. The returns to these unit-exposure portfolios represented the monthly returns to the respective factors. At this point, a forecasting model of nonfactor risk was developed, allowing BARRA to calculate the variance-covariance matrix for the 68 factors.

The last step involved testing the performance of the E2 model. BARRA was concerned with how effective its forecasts of security risk were outside of the test period. Cutting through the statistical jargon, BARRA found that the model performed well.

The BARRA E2 model is applied by institutional investors in a variety of situations. Investment managers use the model to forecast the variability of their portfolios' returns, both in an absolute sense and relative to a benchmark. The model allows the managers to dissect this forecasted risk into factor and nonfactor components. Managers can make informed judgments about the expected rewards offered by their particular portfolio strategies relative to the forecasted risks.

Managers and their clients also use the E2 model for performance attribution (see Chapter 25). Here an analyst uses the model to calculate a portfolio's historical exposure to the various factors. Then using BARRA's calculated factor returns, the contribution of each of those exposures to the portfolio's total return is computed. Finally, comparing the portfolio's exposures and the contributions of those exposures to the portfolio's performance against a relevant benchmark provides clues to the success or failure of the manager's strategies.

Institutional investors also use the E2 model to characterize the investment styles of their managers. Similar investment styles tend to exhibit similar E2 factor exposures. For example, large capitalization growth managers typically have large Size and Growth exposures and low Book/Price exposures. By analyzing a series of past returns for various portfolios with the E2 model, a client can more accurately identify the investment styles of its current and potential managers. This process aids in both performance evaluation and manager structuring (see Chapters 24 and 25).

The BARRA U.S. equity multiple-factor model has contributed to the rigor and sophistication with which institutional investors approach the task of managing large pools of U.S. common stocks. Perhaps the most impressive testament to the model's utility and robustness is that in the highly competitive and fickle world of investments, no alternative factor model has gained the widespread acceptance that the E2 model has achieved.

The Importance of Expectations

Security prices reflect investors' estimates of the present values of firms' future prospects. At any given time the price of Widget stock is likely to depend on the projected growth rate of GDP, the projected rate of inflation, and other factors. If investors' projections of such fundamental economic conditions change, so too will the price of Widget. Because the return on a stock is influenced heavily by changes in its price, stock returns are expected to be more highly correlated with changes in expected future values of fundamental economic variables than with the actual changes that occur contemporaneously.

For example, a large increase in inflation that was fully anticipated might have no effect on the stock price of a company whose earnings are highly sensitive to inflation. However, if the consensus expectation was for a low inflation rate, then the subsequent large increase would have a large effect on the company's stock price.

For this reason, whenever possible it is desirable to select factors that measure changes in expectations rather than realizations, as the latter typically include both changes that were anticipated and those that were not. One way to accomplish this goal is to rely on variables that involve changes in market prices. Thus the difference in the returns on two portfolios—one consisting of stocks thought to be unaffected by inflation and the other consisting of stocks thought to be affected by inflation—can be used as a factor that measures revisions in inflation expectations. Those who construct factor models using the time-series approach often rely on market-based surrogates for changes in forecasts of fundamental economic variables in this manner.

An Example

Table 11.1 and Figure 11.2 presented an example of how to use the time-series approach to estimate a factor model. In this example, returns on individual stocks such as Widget were related to two factors—gross domestic product and inflation—by comparing over time each stock's returns to the predicted values of the factors.

Recently, Fama and French conducted a study that used a time-series approach to identify the factors that explain stock and bond returns.[12] In their study, monthly stock returns were found to be related to three factors: a market factor, a size factor, and a book-to-market equity factor. In equation form, their factor model for stocks appears as:

$$r_{it} - r_{ft} = a_i + b_{i1}(r_{Mt} - r_{ft}) + b_{i2}\text{SMB}_t + b_{i3}\text{HML}_t + e_{it}. \qquad (11.18)$$

The first factor $(r_{Mt} - r_{ft})$ is simply the monthly return on a broad stock market over and above the return on one-month Treasury bills on a broad stock index. The size factor (SMB_t) can be thought of as the difference in the monthly return on two stock indices—a small stock index and a big-stock index. (Here a stock's size is measured by its stock price at the end of June each year times the number of shares it has outstanding at that time. The small-stock index consists of stocks that are below the median NYSE size and the big-stock index consists of stocks that are above the median.) The book-to-market equity factor (HML_t) is also the difference in the monthly return on two stock indices—an index of stocks with high book-to-market equity ratios and an index of stocks with low book-to-market equity ratios. (Here book equity is stockholders' equity taken from the firm's balance sheet and market equity is the same as the stock's size used in determining the previous factor. The high ratio index consists of stocks that are in the top third, and the low ratio index consists of stocks that are in the bottom third.)

Fama and French also identified two factors that seem to explain monthly bond returns. In equation form, their factor model for bonds appears as:

$$r_{it} - r_{ft} = a_i + b_{i1}\text{TERM}_t + b_{i2}\text{DEF}_t + e_{it}. \qquad (11.19)$$

These two factors are a term-structure factor and a default factor.[13] The term-structure factor $(TERM_t)$ is simply the difference in the monthly returns on long-term Treasury bonds and one-month Treasury bills. The default factor (DEF_t) is the difference in the monthly returns on a portfolio of long-term corporate bonds and long-term Treasury bonds.[14]

11.4.2 Cross-Sectional Approaches

Cross-sectional approaches are less intuitive than time-series approaches but can often be just as powerful a tool. The model builder begins with estimates of securities' sensitivities to certain factors. Then in a particular time period, the values of the factors are estimated based on securities' returns and their sensitivities to the factors. This process is repeated over multiple time periods, thereby providing an estimate of the factors' standard deviations and their correlations.

Note that the cross-sectional approach is entirely different from the time-series approach. With the latter approach, the values of the factors are known and the sensitivities are estimated. Furthermore, the analysis is conducted for one security over multiple time periods, then another security, then another, and so on. With the former approach the sensitivities are known and the values of the factors are estimated. Accordingly, the sensitivities in the cross-sectional approach are sometime referred to as **attribute**. Furthermore, the analysis is conducted over one time period for a group of securities, then another time period for the same group, then another, and so on. Examples of one-factor and two-factor models will be shown next to illustrate the cross-sectional approach.[15]

One-Factor Models

Figure 11.3 provides a hypothetical example of the relationship between the returns for a number of different stocks in a given time period and one security attribute—dividend yield—for each stock. Each point represents one particular stock, showing its return and dividend yield for the time period under evaluation. In this case, stocks with higher-dividend yields tended to do better—that is, have higher returns—than those with lower-dividend yields. Whereas Figure 11.3 (an example of the cross-sectional approach) is based on many stocks for one time period, Figure 11.1 (an example of the time-series approach) is based on one stock for many time periods.

To quantify the relationship shown in Figure 11.3, a straight line has been fitted to the diagram by using the statistical technique of simple-regression analysis. The equation of the line in Figure 11.3 is:

$$\bar{r}_{it} = 4 + .5b_{it} \tag{11.20}$$

or, more generally

$$\bar{r}_{it} = a_t + b_{it}F_t \tag{11.21}$$

where

$\bar{r}_{it}$ = *the expected return on stock* i *in period* t, *given that the factor had an actual value of* F_t,
a_t = *the zero factor in period* t,
b_{it} = *the dividend yield of stock* i *in period* t,
F_t = *the actual value of the factor in period* t.

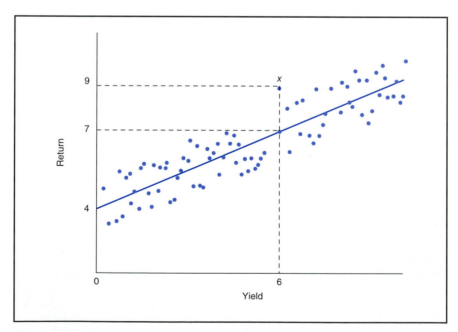

Figure 11.3
A Cross-Sectional One-Factor Model

The vertical intercept a_t indicates the expected return on a typical stock with a dividend yield of zero. Hence it is called the zero factor as in Equation (11.1). In Figure 11.3 it is equal to 4%. The slope of .5 indicates the increase in expected return for each percent of dividend yield. Hence it represents the actual value of the dividend yield factor (F_t) in this time period.

From this example it can be seen that the cross-sectional approach uses sensitivities to provide estimates of the values of the factors. Hence these factors are known as empirical factors. In comparison it was shown earlier that the time-series approach uses known values of factors to provide estimates of a security's sensitivities. Hence these factors are known as *fundamental factors*.

The actual return on any given security may lie above or below the line due to its nonfactor return. A complete description of the relationship for this one-factor model is:

$$r_{it} = 4 + .5b_{it} + e_{it} \qquad (11.22)$$

where e_{it} denotes the nonfactor return during period t on security i. In Figure 11.3, security x had a dividend yield of 6%. Hence from Equation (11.18) it had an expected return during this time period of 7% $[= 4 + (.5 \times 6)]$. Because it actually had a return of 9%, its nonfactor return was $+2\% = 9\% - 7\%$.

In periods such as the one shown in Figure 11.3, high-yield stocks tended to outperform low-yield stocks. This indicates that the yield factor F_t was positive at this time. However, in another time period it is possible that low-yield stocks will tend to outperform high-yield stocks. The regression line in the corresponding diagram will be downward-sloping, and the yield factor will be negative. In still other time periods, there will be no relationship between yield and return, resulting in a flat regression line and a yield factor of zero.

A Two-Factor Example

In some time periods small stocks tend to outperform large stocks. In other months the converse is true. Hence many cross-sectional models use a *size attribute* that is often computed by taking the logarithm of the total market value of the firm's outstanding equity measured in millions, which is, in turn, calculated by taking the firm's stock price and multiplying it by the number of shares outstanding and then dividing the resulting figure by one million.[16] Thus a $1-million stock would be assigned a size attribute value of zero; a $10-million stock a size attribute value of one; a $100-million stock a size attribute value of two, and so on. This convention is based on the empirical observation that the impact of the size factor on a security with a large total market value is likely to be twice as great as that on a security with one-tenth the value. More succinctly, the size effect appears to be *linear in the logarithms*.

To estimate the size factor in a given month, the procedure used in Figure 11.3 to estimate the yield factor can be employed. The size attributes of securities can be plotted on the horizontal axis and their returns for the given time period plotted (as in Figure 11.3) on the vertical axis. The slope of the resultant regression line provides an estimate of the size factor for the time period.

This procedure has drawbacks, however. Large stocks tend to have high yields. Thus differences in returns between large and small stocks may be due to some extent to differences in yield, not size. The estimated size factor may be in part a reflection of a true yield factor. The problem is symmetrical in that the estimated yield factor may also be in part a reflection of the true size factor.

To mitigate this problem, returns can be compared with both size and yield attributes simultaneously by using the statistical technique of multiple regression. Figure 11.4 provides an illustration. Each security is represented by a point in a three-dimensional graph with return during the time period shown on the vertical axis, dividend yield for the time period shown on one of the bottom axes, and size for the period shown on the other.

Multiple-regression analysis is typically used to fit a plane to the data. In the example shown in Figure 11.4, this results in the following regression equation:

$$r_{it} = 7 + .4b_{i1t} - .3b_{i2t} + e_{it} \tag{11.23}$$

where b_{i1t} and b_{i2t} denote, respectively, the dividend yield and size of stock i in time period t. In general, the regression equation for a two-factor model is:

$$r_{it} = a_t + b_{i1t}F_{1t} + b_{i2t}F_{2t} + e_{it} \tag{11.24}$$

where a_t denotes the zero factor in time period t and the two factors are denoted F_{1t} and F_{2t}.

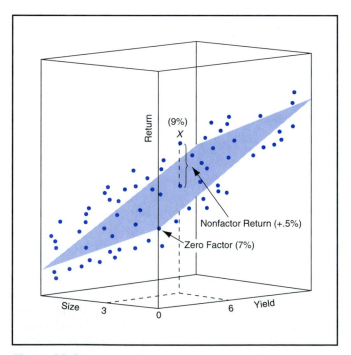

Figure 11.4
A Cross-Sectional Two-Factor Model

The equation of the plane shown in Figure 11.4 is:

$$\bar{r}_{it} = 7 + .4b_{i1t} - .3b_{i2t} \tag{11.25}$$

or, more generally,

$$\bar{r}_{it} = a_t + b_{i1t}F_{1t} + b_{i2t}F_{2t}. \tag{11.26}$$

This means that the zero factor a_t was 7%, indicating that a stock with zero-dividend yield and zero size (meaning a market value of $1 million) would have been expected to have a return of 7%. Note that the estimated values of the dividend yield-factor (F_{1t}) and size factor (F_{2t}) are .4 and $-.3$, respectively. Thus during this time period, higher-dividend yields and smaller sizes were both associated with larger returns.

Using Equations (11.23) and (11.25), a given security x with a dividend yield of 6% and a size of 3 would have been expected to have a return of 8.5% [= 7 + (.4 × 6) − (.3 × 3)]. With an actual return of 9% its nonfactor return e_{it} is thus +.5% (= 9% − 8.5%) during this time period, as shown in Figure 11.4.

The inclusion of size and dividend yield along with the use of multiple-regression analysis can help sort out the effects of differences in yield and size on differences in security returns. It cannot deal adequately with influences that are not represented at all, nor can it guarantee that the included attributes are not simply serving as *proxies* for other, more fundamental attributes. Statistical tests can indicate the ability of the variables included in the analysis to explain or predict past security returns. But judgment and luck are required to identify variables that can help predict future security returns, risks, and covariances. The extension to more than two variables follows in a straightforward manner from what has been indicated in Equations (11.23) through (11.26).

An Example

Sharpe conducted a study that used a cross-sectional approach to identify the factors that explain stock returns.[17] In his study, stock returns were related monthly to five security sensitivities (and eight sector-factors) that were measured for each stock. These sensitivities consisted of firm size (measured like Fama and French), the stock's historic beta when measured against a stock market index, the stock's dividend yield, the stock's historic beta when measured against a bond market index, and a measure of how much of the stock's historical return was due to mispricing.

Over the period 1931 to 1979, Sharpe collected monthly data for over 2,000 common stocks. Among other results, his analysis produced a value of .237 (annualized) for the dividend yield factor. By implication then, a stock with a 5% dividend yield outperformed a stock with a 4% dividend yield (but with similar exposures to all the other factors) by almost .24% per year.

11.4.3 Factor-Analytic Approaches

Finally, with factor-analytic approaches the model builder knows neither the factor values nor the securities' sensitivities to those factors. A statistical technique called *factor analysis* is used to extract the number of factors and securities' sensitivities based simply on a set of securities' past returns. Factor analysis takes the returns over many time periods on a sample of securities and attempts to identify one or more statistically significant factors that could have generated the covariances of returns observed within the sample. In essence, the return data tells the model builder about the structure of the factor model. Unfortunately, factor analysis does not specify what economic variables the factors represent.

11.4.4   Limitations

There is no reason to assume that a good factor model for one period will be a good one for the next period. Key factors change as in the effect of energy prices on security markets in the 1970s and more recently during the war in the Persian Gulf. The risks and returns associated with various factors and the sensitivities of securities to factors can change over time.[18]

It would be convenient if neither the relevant factors nor their magnitudes were to change from period to period. If this were so, mechanical procedures could be applied to security returns over an extended past period and the factor model inferred along with all the needed magnitudes. As it is, statistical estimation methods should be tempered with the judgment of the model builder to account for the dynamic nature of the investment environment.

11.5	FACTOR MODELS AND EQUILIBRIUM

It should be kept in mind that a factor model is not an equilibrium model of asset pricing. Compare, for example, the expected return on a stock using a one-factor model from Equation (11.3) with that of the Capital Asset Pricing Model (CAPM) from Equation (10.7):[19]

$$\overline{r}_i = a_i + b_i\overline{F} \tag{11.3}$$

$$\overline{r}_i = r_f + (\overline{r}_M - r_f)\,\beta_{iM}. \tag{10.7}$$

Both equations show that the expected return on the stock is related to a characteristic of the stock, b_i or β_i. Assuming that the expected return on the factor $\overline{F}$ and $\overline{r}_M - r_f$, is positive, the larger the size of the characteristic, the larger the security's expected return. Hence at this point there appears to be little to differentiate these two equations of expected return.

The key is in the other term on the right-hand side of each equation: a_i and r_f. The only characteristic of the stock that determines its expected return according to the CAPM is β_i, as r_f denotes the riskfree rate and is the same for all securities. However, with the factor model there is a second characteristic of the stock that needs to be estimated to determine the stock's expected return—namely, a_i. As the size of a_i differs from one stock to another, it prevents the factor model from being an equilibrium model.

Stated differently, two stocks with the same value of b_i can have dramatically different expected returns according to a factor model. For example, if GDP is expected to rise by 5%, then the expected return on Widget is 14% because a_i

and b_i for Widget are 4 and 2 [14% = 4% + (2 × 5%)]. In comparison, even though ABC has the same sensitivity to GDP as Widget ($b_i = 2$), it has an expected return of only 8% because its value of a_i is −2% [8% = −2% + (2 × 5%)].

In contrast, two stocks with the same value of β_i will have the same expected return according to the equilibrium-based CAPM. If Widget and XYZ both have a beta of 1.2, then they both will have an expected return of 14%, given that the riskfree rate is 8% and the expected return on the market is 13% [14% = 8% + (13% − 8%) × 1.2].

Having established that a factor model is not an equilibrium model, it seems appropriate to investigate the relationship between the parameters a_i and b_i of the one-factor model and the single parameter β_i of the CAPM.

For example, if actual returns can be viewed as being generated by a one-factor model where the factor F is the return on the market portfolio r_M, then according to Equation (11.3), expected returns will be equal to:

$$\bar{r}_i = a_i + b_i \bar{r}_M \qquad (11.27)$$

because $\bar{F} = \bar{r}_M$. But if equilibrium exists according to the CAPM, then Equation (10.7) can be rewritten to state that expected returns will also be equal to :

$$\bar{r}_i = (1 - \beta_{iM}) r_f + \bar{r}_M \beta_{iM}. \qquad (11.28)$$

This means that the parameters of the one-factor model and the CAPM must have the following relationships:

$$a_i = (1 - \beta_{iM}) r_f \qquad (11.29)$$

$$b_i = \beta_{iM}. \qquad (11.30)$$

This means that if expected returns are determined according to the CAPM and actual returns are generated by the one-factor market model, then a_i and b_i must be equal to $(1 - \beta_{iM}) r_f$ and β_{iM}, respectively.[20]

11.6   SUMMARY

1. A factor model is a return-generating process that relates returns on securities to the movement in one or more common factors.
2. Any aspect of a security's return unexplained by the factor model is assumed to be unique to the security and therefore uncorrelated with the unique element of returns on other securities.
3. The market model is a specific example of a factor model where the factor is the return on a market index.
4. The assumption that the returns on securities respond to common factors greatly simplifies the task of calculating the curved Markowitz efficient set.
5. The sensitivity of a portfolio to a factor is the weighted average of the sensitivities of the component securities with the securities' proportions in the portfolio serving as weights.
6. The total risk of a security is composed of factor risk and nonfactor risk.
7. Diversification leads to an averaging of factor risk.

8. Diversification reduces nonfactor risk.
9. Three basic methods are used to estimate factor models: the time-series approach, the cross-sectional approach, and the factor-analytic approach.
10. A factor model is not an equilibrium model of asset prices as is the CAPM. However, if equilibrium exists, certain relationships will hold between the factor model and the equilibrium asset-pricing model.

1. Included among the factors that might be expected to be pervasive are expectations regarding growth in real GNP, real interest rates, inflation, and oil prices. For each factor, provide an example of an industry that is expected to have a high (either positive or negative) sensitivity to the factor.
2. Why do factor models greatly simplify the process of deriving the curved Markowitz efficient set?
3. Many investment management firms assign each of their security analysts to research a particular group of stocks. (Usually these assignments are organized by industry.) How are these assignments an implicit recognition of the validity of factor-model relationships?
4. What are two critical assumptions underlying any factor model? Cite hypothetical examples of violations of those assumptions.
5. Cupid Childs, a wise investment statistician, once said with respect to factor models, "Similar stocks should display similar returns." What did Cupid mean by this statement?
6. Based on a one-factor model, consider a security with a zero-factor value of 4% and a sensitivity to the factor of .50. The factor takes on a value of 10%. The security generates a return of 11%. What portion is related to nonfactor elements?
7. Based on a one-factor model, consider a portfolio of two securities with the following characteristics:

Security	Factor Sensitivity	Nonfactor Risk (σ_{ei}^2)	Proportion
A	.20	49	.40
B	3.50	100	.60

   a. If the standard deviation of the factor is 15%, what is the factor risk of the portfolio?
   b. What is the nonfactor risk of the portfolio?
   c. What is the portfolio's standard deviation?
8. Recalculate the answers to Problem 7 assuming that the portfolio is also invested in the riskfree asset so that its investment proportions are:

Security	Proportion
Riskfree	.10
A	.36
B	.54

9. Based on a one-factor model, security A has a sensitivity of $-.50$, whereas security B has a sensitivity of 1.25. If the covariance between the two securities is -312.50, what is the standard deviation of the factor?

10. Based on a one-factor model, for two securities A and B:

$$r_A = 5\% + .8F + e_A$$
$$r_B = 7\% + 1.2F + e_B$$
$$\sigma_F = 18\%$$
$$\sigma_{eA} = 25\%$$
$$\sigma_{eB} = 15\%.$$

Calculate the standard deviation of each security.

11. Based on a one-factor model, if the average nonfactor risk (σ_{ei}^2) of all securities is 225, what is the nonfactor risk of a portfolio with equal weights assigned to its 10 securities? 100 securities? 1,000 securities?

12. Based on the discussion of factor and nonfactor risk and given a set of securities that can be combined into various portfolios, what might be a useful measure of the relative diversification of each of the alternative portfolios?

13. With a five-factor model (assuming uncorrelated factors) and a 30-stock portfolio, how many parameters must be estimated to calculate the expected return and standard deviation of the portfolio? How many additional parameter estimates are required if the factors are correlated?

14. Beyond the factors discussed in the text, speculate as to other factors that could reasonably be expected to pervasively affect security returns.

15. Based on a three-factor model, consider a portfolio composed of three securities with the following characteristics:

Security	Factor 1 Sensitivity	Factor 2 Sensitivity	Factor 3 Sensitivity	Proportion
A	$-.20$	3.60	.05	.60
B	.50	10.00	.75	.20
C	1.50	2.20	.30	.20

What are the sensitivities of the portfolio to factors 1, 2, and 3?

16. Smiler Murray, a quantitative security analyst, remarked, "The structure of any factor model concerns surprise, in particular the nature of correlations between surprises in different securities' returns." What does Smiler mean by this statement?

17. Dode Cicero owns a portfolio of two securities. Based on a two-factor model, the two securities have the following characteristics:

Security	Zero Factor	Factor 1 Sensitivity	Factor 2 Sensitivity	Non-Factor Risk (σ_{ei}^2)	Proportion
A	2%	.30	2.0	196	.70
B	3	.50	1.8	100	.30

The factors are uncorrelated. Factor 1 has an expected value of 15% and a standard deviation of 20%. Factor 2 has an expected value of 4% and a standard deviation of 5%. Calculate the expected return and standard deviation of Dode's portfolio. [Hint: Think about how Equation (11.6a) could be extended to a two-factor model by considering Equation (11.9).]

18. Compare and contrast the three approaches to estimating factor models.

19. Consider a factor model with earnings yield (or earnings/price ratio) and book-price (or book value/market price ratio) as the two factors. Stock A has an earnings yield of 10% and a book-price of 2. Stock B's earnings yield is 15% and it's book-price is .90. The zero factors of stocks A and B are 7% and 9%, respectively. If the expected returns of stocks A and B are 18% and 16.5%, respectively, what are the expected earnings-yield and book-price factor values?

20. Based on a two-factor model, consider two securities with the following characteristics:

Characteristic	Security A	Security B
Factor 1 sensitivity	1.5	.7
Factor 2 sensitivity	2.6	1.2
Nonfactor risk (σ_{ei}^2)	25.0	16.0

The standard deviations of factor 1 and factor 2 are 20% and 15%, respectively, and the factors have a covariance of 225. What are the standard deviations of securities A and B? What is their covariance?

21. Are factor models consistent with the CAPM? If returns are determined by a one-factor model (where that factor is the return on the market portfolio) and the CAPM holds, what relationships must exist between the two models?

ENDNOTES

[1] See Appendix B to Chapter 8.

[2] GDP is similar to gross national product (GNP) in that it is a measure of a country's total output of goods and services. However, GDP treats imports and exports slightly differently than GNP and, as a result, requires fewer revisions after it is initially reported. Furthermore, international comparisons are straightforward with GDP, as most countries report GDP instead of GNP. Consequently, only GDP is currently reported by the U.S. government.

[3] Only six data points are shown in the figure for ease of exposition. The standard statistical procedure of simple linear regression is discussed in Chapter 17 and in Mark Kritzman, ". . . About Regression," *Financial Analysts Journal*, 47, no. 3 (May/June 1991), 12–15. It can be found in most statistics books, such as James T. McClave and P. George Benson, *Statistics for Business and Economics* (San Francisco: Dellen, 1991), Chapter 11.

[4] Sometimes b is referred to as the **factor loading** or attribute of the security.

[5] The time subscript t was deleted from the market model simply for ease of exposition. Technically speaking, the random error term should be written as ϵ_{ilt}.

[6] This is shown in more detail in Appendix B to Chapter 8.

[7] Actually, all that is necessary for this reduction in nonfactor risk to occur is for the maximum amount invested in any one security to continually decrease as N increases. An example based on the market model is given in Chapter 8.

[8] These values were arrived at by applying multiple regression (see McClave and Benson, *Statistics*, Chapter 12) to the data given in Table 11.1.

[9] Attempts have been made to identify stock groups, or clusters, where stocks within any group have returns that are more highly correlated with one another than the returns of stocks from different groups. See, for example, Benjamin F. King, "Market and Industry factors in Stock Price Behavior," *Journal of Business*, 39, no. 1 (January 1966): 139–170; James L. Farrell, Jr., "Analyzing Covariation of Returns to Determine Stock Groupings," *Journal of Business*, 47, no. 2 (April 1974): 186–207; "Homogeneous Stock Groupings: Implications for Portfolio Management," *Financial Analysts Journal*, 31, no. 3 (May/June 1975): 50–62; and Robert D. Arnott, "Cluster Analysis and Stock Price Comovement," *Financial Analysts Journal*, 36, no. 6 (November/December 1980): 56–62.

[10] Another example of such a model expands the market model to include sector-factors where the sectors are selected to represent "industries." Hence each stock has two sensitivities that indicate how the stock responds to returns on the stock index and an industry index to which the stock belongs. See Gordon J. Alexander and Jack Clark Francis, *Portfolio Analysis* (Englewood Cliffs, NJ: Prentice Hall), 83–92.

[11] The examples given earlier in the chapter are examples of this approach.

[12] Eugene F. Fama and Kenneth R. French, "Common Risk Factors in the Returns on Stocks and Bonds," *Journal of Financial Economics*, 33, no. 1 (February 1993): 3–56. Other time series examples are presented in Chapter 12.

[13] Speculative-grade bonds were found to also be related to the three stock factors.

[14] Interestingly, Fama and French also found that the market factor ($r_{Mt} - r_{ft}$) was related to these two bond factors. In light of this, they constructed a revised market factor that basically consisted of the market factor less the influence of the two bond factors and the two other stock factors, and they found that stock returns were related to five factors: the revised market factor, SML_t, HML_t, $TERM_t$, and DEF_t. Bond returns continued to be related to just the two bond factors.

[15] Note that in the time-series approach, a security's sensitivity to a factor is its "attribute," and the factor is a given macroeconomic variable. Hence the attribute's value is unknown and must be estimated whereas the value of the factor is known. In the cross-sectional approach, a security's attribute is usually some microeconomic variable measuring the security's exposure to the factor (a stock's dividend yield and market capitalization can be thought of as examples of attributes). Hence the attribute's value is known whereas the factor is unknown and must be estimated.

[16] Size has also been used as a factor in the time-series approach but in a different manner. See the previous discussion of the Fama and French study that is mentioned in Endnote 12.

[17] William F. Sharpe, "Factors in New York Stock Exchange Security Returns, 1931–1979," *Journal of Portfolio Management*, 8, no. 4 (Summer 1982): 5–19. An application is presented in Blake R. Grossman and William F. Sharpe, "Financial Implications of South African Divestment," *Financial Analysts Journal*, 42, no. 4 (July-August 1986): 15–29.

[18] One study found that the factors that appear to explain security returns on even dates generally do not explain security returns on odd dates. See Dolores A. Conway and Marc R. Reinganum, "Stable Factors in Security Returns: Identification Using Cross Validation," *Journal of Business and Economic Statistics*, 6, no. 1 (January 1988): 1–15.

[19] Time subscripts have been removed for ease of exposition.

[20] If the factor in a one-factor world is the return on the market portfolio (as shown here), then technically the random error term for any security cannot be completely uncorrelated with the factor. This is because the market portfolio consists of all securities and hence is influenced by the nonfactor return of each security. See Eugene F. Fama, *Foundations of Finance* (New York: Basic Books, 1976), Chapter 3.

return-generating process	factor risk
factor models	nonfactor risk
sensitivity	sector-factor model
factor loading (attribute)	attribute

REFERENCES

1. General discussions of factor models can be found in:

   William F. Sharpe, "Factors in New York Stock Exchange Security Returns, 1931–1979," *Journal of Portfolio Management,* 8, no. 4 (Summer 1982): 5–19; and "Factor Models, CAPMs, and the ABT [*sic*]," *Journal of Portfolio Management,* 11, no. 1 (Fall 1984): 21–25.

   Mark Kritzman, " . . . About Factor Models," *Financial Analysts Journal,* 49, no. 1 (January/February 1993): 12–15.

2. Empirical papers that attempt to identify relevant factors and estimate the magnitudes of the associated values include:

   Benjamin F. King, "Market and Industry Factors in Stock Price Behavior," *Journal of Business,* 39, no. 1 (January 1966): 139–170.

   George J. Feeney and Donald D. Hester, "Stock Market Indices: A Principal Components Analysis," in Donald D. Hester and James Tobin, eds., *Risk Aversion and Portfolio Choice* (New York: John Wiley, 1967).

   Edwin J. Elton and Martin J. Gruber, "Estimating the Dependence Structure of Share Prices—Implications for Portfolio Selection," *Journal of Finance,* 28, no. 5 (December 1973): 1203–1232.

   James J. Farrell, Jr., "Analyzing Covariation of Returns to Determine Homogeneous Stock Groupings," *Journal of Business,* 47, no. 2 (April 1974): 186–207.

   Barr Rosenberg and Vinay Marathe, "The Prediction of Investment Risk: Systematic and Residual Risk," in *Proceedings of the Seminar on the Analysis of Security Prices* (Center for Research in Security Prices, Graduate School of Business, University of Chicago, November 1975).

   Robert D. Arnott, "Cluster Analysis and Stock Price Movement," *Financial Analysts Journal,* 36, no. 6 (November/December 1980): 56–62.

   Tony Estep, Nick Hanson, and Cal Johnson, "Sources of Value and Risk in Common Stocks," *Journal of Portfolio Management,* 9, no. 4 (Summer 1983): 5–13.

   Nai-Fu Chen, Richard Roll, and Stephen A. Ross, "Economic Forces and the Stock Market," *Journal of Business,* 59, no. 3 (July 1986): 383–403.

Robert D. Arnott, Charles M. Kelso, Jr., Stephen Kiscadden, and Rosemary Macedo, "Forecasting Factor Returns: An Intriguing Possibility," *Journal of Portfolio Management,* 16, no. 1 (Fall 1989): 28–35.

Eugene F. Fama and Kenneth R. French, "Common Risk Factors in the Returns on Stocks and Bonds," *Journal of Financial Economics,* 33, no. 1 (February 1993): 3–56.

3. Fixed-income factor models are discussed in:

Ronald N. Kahn and Deepak Gulrajani, "Risk and Return in the Canadian Bond Market," *Journal of Portfolio Management,* 19, no. 3 (Spring 1993): 86–92.

CHAPTER 12

Arbitrage Pricing Theory

The Capital Asset Pricing Model (CAPM) is an equilibrium model that describes why different securities have different expected returns. In particular, this positive economic model of asset pricing asserts that securities have different expected returns because they have different betas. However, there exists an alternative model of asset pricing that was developed by Stephen Ross. It is known as **Arbitrage Pricing Theory** (APT), and in some ways it is less complicated than the CAPM.

The CAPM requires a large number of assumptions, including those initially made by Harry Markowitz when he developed the basic mean-variance model. For example, each investor is assumed to choose his or her optimal portfolio by the use of indifference curves based on portfolio expected returns and standard deviations. In contrast, APT makes fewer assumptions. One primary APT assumption is that each investor, when given the opportunity to increase the return of his or her portfolio without increasing its risk, will proceed to do so. The mechanism for doing so involves the use of arbitrage portfolios.

12.1 FACTOR MODELS

APT starts out by making the assumption that security returns are related to an unknown number of unknown factors.[1] For ease of exposition, imagine that there is only one factor and that factor is the predicted rate of increase in industrial production. In this situation, security returns are related to the following one-factor model:

$$r_i = a_i + b_i F_1 + e_i \qquad (12.1)$$

where:

In this equation, b_i is known as the **sensitivity** of security i to the factor. (It is also known as the factor loading for security i or the attribute of security i.)[2]

Imagine that an investor owns three stocks and the current market value of his or her holdings in each one is $4,000,000. In this case, the investor's current investable wealth W_0 is equal to $12,000,000. Everyone believes that these three stocks have the following expected returns and sensitivities:

i	$\bar{r}_i$	b_i
Stock 1	15%	.9
Stock 2	21	3.0
Stock 3	12	1.8

Do these expected returns and factor sensitivities represent an equilibrium situation? If not, what will happen to stock prices and expected returns to restore equilibrium?

12.1.1 Principle of Arbitrage

In recent years, baseball card conventions have become commonplace events. Collectors gather to exchange baseball cards with one another at negotiated prices. Suppose that Ms. *A* attends such a gathering where in one corner she finds *S* offering to sell a 1951 Mickey Mantle rookie card for $400. Exploring the convention further, she finds *B* bidding $500 for the same card. Recognizing a financial opportunity, Ms. *A* agrees to sell the card to *B*, who gives her $500 in cash. She races back to give $400 to *S*, receives the card, and returns with it to *B*, who takes possession of the card. Ms. *A* pockets the $100 in profit from the two transactions and moves on in search of other opportunities. Ms. *A* has engaged in a form of arbitrage.

Arbitrage is the earning of riskless profit by taking advantage of differential pricing for the same physical asset or security. As a widely applied investment tactic, arbitrage typically entails the sale of a security at a relatively high price and the simultaneous purchase of the same security (or its functional equivalent) at a relatively low price.

Arbitrage activity is a critical element of modern, efficient security markets. Because arbitrage profits are by definition riskless, all investors have an incentive to take advantage of them whenever they are discovered. Granted, some investors have greater resources and inclination to engage in arbitrage than others. However, it takes relatively few of these active investors to exploit arbitrage situations and, by their buying and selling actions, eliminate these profit opportunities.

The nature of arbitrage is clear when discussing different prices for an individual security. However, "almost arbitrage" opportunities can involve "similar" securities or portfolios. That similarity can be defined in many ways. One interesting way is the exposure to pervasive factors that affect security prices.

A factor model implies that securities or portfolios with equal-factor sensitivities will behave in the same way except for nonfactor risk. Therefore, securities or portfolios with the same factor sensitivities should offer the same expected returns. If not, then "almost arbitrage" opportunities exist. Investors will take advantage of these opportunities, causing their elimination. That is the essential logic underlying APT.

12.1.2 Arbitrage Portfolios

According to APT, an investor will explore the possibility of forming an **arbitrage portfolio** substantially to increase the expected return of his or her current portfolio without increasing its risk. Just what is an arbitrage portfolio? First of all, it is a portfolio that does not require any additional funds from the investor. If X_i denotes the *change* in the investor's holdings of security i (and hence the weight of security i in the arbitrage portfolio), this requirement of an arbitrage portfolio can be written as:

$$X_1 + X_2 + X_3 = 0. \qquad (12.2)$$

Second, an arbitrage portfolio has no sensitivity to any factor. Because the sensitivity of a portfolio to a factor is just a weighted average of the sensitivities of the securities in the portfolio to that factor, this requirement of an arbitrage portfolio can be written as:

$$b_1 X_1 + b_2 X_2 + b_3 X_3 = 0 \qquad (12.3a)$$

or, in the current example:

$$.9X_1 + 3.0X_2 + 1.8X_3 = 0. \qquad (12.3b)$$

Thus, in this example, an arbitrage portfolio will have no sensitivity to industrial production.

Strictly speaking, an arbitrage portfolio should also have zero nonfactor risk. However, the APT assumes that such risk is small enough to be ignored. In its terminology, an arbitrage portfolio has "zero factor exposures."

At this point many potential arbitrage portfolios can be identified. These candidates are simply portfolios that meet the conditions given in Equations (12.2) and (12.3b). Note that there are three unknowns (X_1, X_2, and X_3) and two equations in this situation, which means that there is an infinite number of combinations of values for X_1, X_2, and X_3 that satisfy these two equations.[3] As a way of finding one combination, consider arbitrarily assigning a value of .1 to X_1. Doing so results in two equations and two unknowns:

$$.1 + X_2 + X_3 = 0 \qquad (12.4a)$$

$$.09 + 3.0X_2 + 1.8X_3 = 0. \qquad (12.4b)$$

The solution to Equations (12.4a) and (12.4b) is $X_2 = .075$ and $X_3 = -.175$. Hence a potential arbitrage portfolio is one with these weights.

In order to see if this candidate is indeed an arbitrage portfolio, its expected return must be determined. If it is positive, then an arbitrage portfolio will have been identified.[4] Mathematically, this third and last requirement for an arbitrage portfolio is:

$$X_1 \bar{r}_1 + X_2 \bar{r}_2 + X_3 \bar{r}_3 > 0 \qquad (12.5a)$$

or, for this example,

$$15 X_1 + 21 X_2 + 12 X_3 > 0. \qquad (12.5b)$$

Using the solution for this candidate, it can be seen that its expected return is $(15\% \times .1) + (21\% \times .075) + (12\% \times -.175) = .975\%$. Because this is a positive number, an arbitrage portfolio has indeed been identified.

The arbitrage portfolio just identified involves buying \$1,200,000 of stock 1 and \$900,000 of stock 2. How were these dollar figures arrived at? The solution comes from taking the current market value of the portfolio ($W_0 = \$12,000,000$) and multiplying it by the weights for the arbitrage portfolio of $X_1 = .1$ and $X_2 = .075$. Where does the money come from to make these purchases? It comes from selling \$2,100,000 of stock 3. (Note that $X_3 W_0 = -.175 \times \$12,000,000 = -\$2,100,000$.)

In summary, this arbitrage portfolio is attractive to any investor who desires a higher return and is not concerned with nonfactor risk. It requires no additional dollar investment, it has no factor risk, and it has a positive expected return.

12.1.3   The Investor's Position

At this juncture the investor can evaluate his or her position from either one of two equivalent viewpoints: (1) holding both the old portfolio and the arbitrage portfolio or (2) holding a new portfolio. Consider, for example, the weight in stock 1. The old portfolio weight was .33 and the arbitrage portfolio weight was .10, with the sum of these two weights being equal to .43. Note that the dollar value of the holdings of stock 1 in the new portfolio rises to \$5,200,000 ($= \$4,000,000 + \$1,200,000$), so its weight is .43 ($= \$5,200,000/\$12,000,000$), equivalent to the sum of the old and arbitrage portfolio weights.

Similarly, the portfolio's expected return is equal to the sum of the expected returns of the old and arbitrage portfolios, or 16.975% ($= 16\% + .975\%$). Equivalently, the new portfolio's expected return can be calculated using the new portfolio's weights and the expected returns of the stocks, or 16.975% [$= (.43 \times 15\%) + (.41 \times 21\%) + (.16 \times 12\%)$].

The sensitivity of the new portfolio is 1.9 [$= (.43 \times .9) + (.41 \times 3.0) + (.16 \times 1.8)$]. This is the same as the sum of the sensitivities of the old and arbitrage portfolios ($= 1.9 + 0.0$).

What about the risk of the new portfolio? Assume that the standard deviation of the old portfolio was 11%. The variance of the arbitrage portfolio will be small because its only source of risk is nonfactor risk. Similarly, the variance of the new portfolio will differ from that of the old only as a result of changes in its nonfactor risk. Thus it can be concluded that the risk of the new portfolio will be approximately 11%.[5] Table 12.1 summarizes these observations.

TABLE 12.1
HOW AN ARBITRAGE PORTFOLIO AFFECTS AN INVESTOR'S POSITION

	Old Portfolio	+	Arbitrage Portfolio	=	New Portfolio
Weights					
X_1	.333		.100		.433
X_2	.333		.075		.408
X_3	.333		−.175		.158
Properties:					
$\bar{r}_p$	16.000%		.975%		16.975%
b_p	1.900		.000		1.900
σ_p	11.000%		small		approx. 11.000%

12.2   PRICING EFFECTS

What are the consequences of buying stocks 1 and 2 and selling stock 3? As everyone will be doing so, their market prices will be affected and, accordingly, their expected returns will adjust. Specifically, the prices of stocks 1 and 2 will rise because of increased buying pressure. In turn, this will cause their expected returns to fall. Conversely, the selling pressure put on stock 3 will cause its stock price to fall and its expected return to rise.

This can be seen by examining the equation for estimating a stock's expected return:

$$\bar{r} = \frac{\overline{P}_1}{P_0} - 1 \qquad (12.6)$$

where P_0 is the stock's current price and $\overline{P}_1$ is the stock's expected end-of-period price. Buying a stock such as stock 1 or 2 will push up its current price P_0 and thus result in a decline in its expected return $\bar{r}$. Conversely, selling a stock such as stock 3 will push down its current price and result in a rise in its expected return.

This buying-and-selling activity will continue until *all* arbitrage possibilities are significantly reduced or eliminated. At this point there will exist an approximately linear relationship between expected returns and sensitivities of the following sort:

$$\bar{r}_i = \lambda_0 + \lambda_1 b_i \qquad (12.7)$$

where λ_0 and λ_1 are constants. This equation is the asset pricing equation of the APT when returns are generated by one factor.[6] Note that it is the equation of a straight line, meaning that in equilibrium there will be a linear relationship between expected returns and sensitivities.

In the example, one possible equilibrium setting could have $\lambda_0 = 8$ and $\lambda_1 = 4$.[7] Consequently, the pricing equation is:

$$\bar{r}_1 = 8 + 4b_i. \qquad (12.8)$$

This would result in the following equilibrium levels of expected returns for stocks 1, 2, and 3:

$$\bar{r}_1 = 8 + (4 \times .9) = 11.6\%$$
$$\bar{r}_2 = 8 + (4 \times 3.0) = 20.0\%$$
$$\bar{r}_3 = 8 + (4 \times 1.8) = 15.2\%.$$

As a result, the expected returns for stocks 1 and 2 will have fallen from 15% and 21%, respectively, to 11.6% and 20% because of increased buying pressure. Conversely, increased selling pressure will have caused the expected return on stock 3 to rise from 12% to 15.2%. The bottom line is that the expected return on any security is, in equilibrium, a linear function of the security's sensitivity to the factor b_i.

12.2.1 A Graphical Illustration

Figure 12.1 illustrates the asset pricing equation of Equation (12.7). Any security that has a factor sensitivity and expected return such that it lies off the line will be mispriced according to the APT and will present investors with the opportunity of forming arbitrage portfolios. Security B is an example. If an investor buys security B and sells security S in equal dollar amounts, then the investor will have formed an arbitrage portfolio.[8] How can this be?

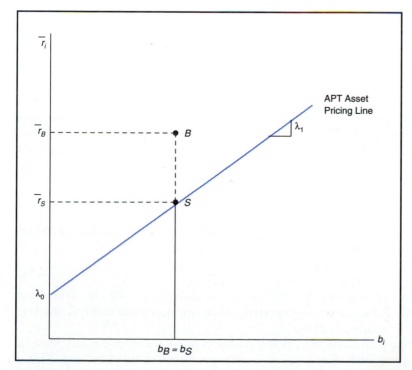

Figure 12.1
APT Asset Pricing Line

First of all, by selling an amount of security S to pay for the long position in security B the investor will not have committed any new funds. Second, because securities B and S have the same sensitivity to the factor, the selling of security S and buying of security B will constitute a portfolio with no sensitivity to the factor. Finally, the arbitrage portfolio will have a positive expected return because the expected return of security B is greater than the expected return of security S.[9] As a result of investors buying security B, its price will rise and, in turn, its expected return will fall until it is located on the APT asset pricing line.[10]

12.2.2 Interpreting the APT Pricing Equation

How can the constants λ_0 and λ_1 that appear in the APT pricing Equation (12.7) be interpreted? Assuming that there is a riskfree asset in existence, such an asset will have a rate of return that is a constant. Therefore this asset will have no sensitivity to the factor. From Equation (12.7) it can be seen that $\bar{r}_i = \lambda_0$ for any asset with $b_i = 0$. In the case of the riskfree asset, it is also known that $\bar{r}_i = r_f$, implying that $\lambda_0 = r_f$. Hence the value of λ_0 in Equation (12.7) must be r_f, allowing this equation to be rewritten as:

$$\bar{r}_i = r_f + \lambda_1 b_i. \tag{12.9}$$

In terms of λ_1, its value can be seen by considering a **pure factor portfolio** (or pure factor play) denoted p^* that has unit sensitivity to the factor, meaning $b_{p^*} = 1.0$. (If there were other factors, such a portfolio would be constructed so as to have no sensitivity to them.) According to Equation (12.9), such a portfolio will have the following expected return:

$$\bar{r}_{p^*} = r_f + \lambda_1. \tag{12.10a}$$

Note that this equation can be rewritten as:

$$\bar{r}_{p^*} - r_f = \lambda_1. \tag{12.10b}$$

Thus λ_1 is the expected excess return (meaning the expected return over and above the riskfree rate) on a portfolio that has unit sensitivity to the factor. Accordingly, it is known as a **factor risk premium** (or factor-expected return premium). Letting $\delta_1 = \bar{r}_{p^*}$ denote the expected return on a portfolio that has unit sensitivity to the factor, Equation (12.10b) can be rewritten as:

$$\delta_1 - r_f = \lambda_1. \tag{12.10c}$$

Inserting the left-hand side of Equation (12.10c) for λ_1 in Equation (12.9) results in a second version of the APT pricing equation:

$$\bar{r}_i = r_f + (\delta_1 - r_f) b_i. \tag{12.11}$$

In the example, because $r_f = 8\%$ and $\lambda_1 = \delta_1 - r_f = 4\%$, it follows that $\delta_1 = 12\%$. This means that the expected return on a portfolio that has unit sensitivity to the first factor is 12%.

In order to generalize the pricing equation of APT, the case where security returns are generated by more than one factor needs to be examined. This is done by considering a two-factor model next and then expanding the analysis to k factors where $k > 2$.

In the case of two factors, denoted F_1 and F_2 and representing predicted industrial production and inflation, each security will have two sensitivities, b_{i1} and b_{i2}. Thus security returns are generated by the following factor model:

$$r_i = a_i + b_{i1}F_1 + b_{i2}F_2 + e_i. \qquad (12.12)$$

Consider a situation where there are four securities that have the following expected returns and sensitivities.

i	$\bar{r}_i$	b_{i1}	b_{i2}
Stock 1	15%	.9	2.0
Stock 2	21	3.0	1.5
Stock 3	12	1.8	.7
Stock 4	8	2.0	3.2

In addition, consider an investor who has $5,000,000 invested in each of the securities. (Thus the investor has initial wealth W_0 of $20,000,000.) Are these securities priced in equilibrium?

12.3.1   Arbitrage Portfolios

To answer this question, the possibility of forming an arbitrage portfolio must be explored. First of all, an arbitrage portfolio must have weights that satisfy the following equations:

$$X_1 + X_2 + X_3 + X_4 = 0 \qquad (12.13)$$

$$.9X_1 + 3X_2 + 1.8X_3 + 2X_4 = 0 \qquad (12.14)$$

$$2X_1 + 1.5X_2 + .7X_3 + 3.2X_4 = 0. \qquad (12.15)$$

This means that the arbitrage portfolio must not involve an additional commitment of funds by the investor and must have zero sensitivity to each factor.

Note that there are three equations that need to be satisfied and that each equation involves four unknowns. Because there are more unknowns than equations, there are an infinite number of solutions. One solution can be found by setting X_1 equal to .1 (an arbitrarily chosen amount) and then solving for the remaining weights. Doing so results in the following weights: $X_2 = .088$, $X_3 = -.108$, and $X_4 = -.08$.

These weights represent a potential arbitrage portfolio. What remains to be done is to see if this portfolio has a positive expected return. Calculating the expected return of the portfolio reveals that it is equal to 1.41% [= (.1 × 15%) + (.088 × 21%) + (−.108 × 12%) + (−.08 × 8%)]. Hence an arbitrage portfolio has been identified.

This arbitrage portfolio involves the purchase of stocks 1 and 2, funded by selling stocks 3 and 4. Consequently, the buying-and-selling pressures will drive the prices of stocks 1 and 2 up and stocks 3 and 4 down. In turn, this means that the expected returns of stocks 1 and 2 will fall and stocks 3 and 4 will rise.

Investors will continue to create such arbitrage portfolios until equilibrium is reached. This means that equilibrium will be attained when any portfolio that satisfies the conditions given by Equations (12.13), (12.14), and (12.15) has an expected return of zero. This will occur when the following linear relationship between expected returns and sensitivities exists:

$$\bar{r}_i = \lambda_0 + \lambda_1 b_{i1} + \lambda_2 b_{i2}. \tag{12.16}$$

As in Equation (12.7), this is a linear equation except that it now has three dimensions, $\bar{r}_i$, b_{i1}, and b_{i2}. Hence it corresponds to the equation of a two-dimensional plane.

In the example, one possible equilibrium setting is where $\lambda_0 = 8$, $\lambda_1 = 4$, and $\lambda_2 = -2$. Thus the pricing equation is:

$$\bar{r}_i = 8 + 4b_{i1} - 2b_{i2}. \tag{12.17}$$

As a result, the four stocks have the following equilibrium levels of expected returns:

$$\bar{r}_1 = 8 + (4 \times .9) - (2 \times 2) = 7.6\%$$
$$\bar{r}_2 = 8 + (4 \times 3) - (2 \times 1.5) = 17.0\%$$
$$\bar{r}_3 = 8 + (4 \times 1.8) - (2 \times .7) = 13.8\%$$
$$\bar{r}_4 = 8 + (4 \times 2) - (2 \times 3.2) = 9.6\%.$$

The expected returns of stocks 1 and 2 have fallen from 15% and 21% while the expected returns of stocks 3 and 4 have risen from 12% and 8%, respectively. Given the buying-and-selling pressures generated by investing in arbitrage portfolios, these changes are in the predicted direction.

One consequence of Equation (12.17) is that a stock with higher sensitivity to the first factor than another stock will have a higher expected return if the two stocks also have the same sensitivity to the second factor because $\lambda_1 > 0$. Conversely, since $\lambda_2 < 0$, a stock with higher sensitivity to the second factor will have a lower expected return than another stock with a lower sensitivity to the second factor, provided that both stocks have the same sensitivity to the first factor. However, the effect of two stocks having different sensitivities to both factors can be confounding. For example, stock 4 has a lower expected return than stock 3 even though both of its sensitivities are larger. This is because the advantage of having a higher sensitivity to the first factor ($b_{41} = 2.0 > b_{31} = 1.8$) is not of sufficient magnitude to offset the disadvantage of having a higher sensitivity to the second factor ($b_{42} = 3.2 > b_{32} = .7$).

12.3.2 Pricing Effects

Extending the one-factor APT pricing Equation (12.7) to this two-factor situation is relatively uncomplicated. As before, λ_0 is equal to the riskfree rate. This is because the riskfree asset has no sensitivity to either factor, meaning that its values of b_{i1} and b_{i2} are both zero. Hence it follows that $\lambda_0 = r_f$. Thus Equation (12.16) can be rewritten more generally as:

$$\bar{r}_i = r_f + \lambda_1 b_{i1} + \lambda_2 b_{i2}. \tag{12.18}$$

In the example given in Equation (12.16), it can be seen that $r_f = 8\%$.

Next consider a well-diversified portfolio that has unit sensitivity to the first factor and zero sensitivity to the second factor. As mentioned earlier, such a portfolio is known as a pure factor portfolio or pure factor play because it has: (1) unit sensitivity to one factor, (2) no sensitivity to any other factor, and (3) zero nonfactor risk. Specifically, it has $b_1 = 1$ and $b_2 = 0$. It can be seen from Equation (12.18) that the expected return on this portfolio, denoted δ_1, will be equal to $r_f + \lambda_1$. As it follows that $\delta_1 - r_f = \lambda_1$, Equation (12.18) can be rewritten as:

$$\bar{r}_i = r_f + (\delta_1 - r_f)b_{i1} + \lambda_2 b_{i2}. \tag{12.19}$$

In the example given in Equation (12.16), it can be seen that $\delta_1 - r_f = 4$. This means that $\delta_1 = 12$ because $r_f = 8$. In other words, a portfolio that has unit sensitivity to predicted industrial production (the first factor) and zero sensitivity to predicted inflation (the second factor) would have an expected return of 12%, or 4% more than the riskfree rate of 8%.

Finally, consider a portfolio that has zero sensitivity to the first factor and unit sensitivity to the second factor, meaning that it has $b_1 = 0$ and $b_2 = 1$. It can be seen from Equation (12.18) that the expected return on this portfolio, denoted δ_2, will be equal to $r_f + \lambda_2$. Accordingly, $\delta_2 - r_f = \lambda_2$, thereby allowing Equation (12.19) to be rewritten as:

$$\bar{r}_i = r_f + (\delta_1 - r_f)b_{i1} + (\delta_2 - r_f)b_{i2}. \tag{12.20}$$

In the example given in Equation (12.16), it can be seen that $\delta_2 - r_f = -2$. This means that $\delta_2 = 6$ since $r_f = 8$. In other words, a portfolio that has zero sensitivity to predicted industrial production (the first factor) and unit sensitivity to predicted inflation (the second factor) would have an expected return of 6%, or 2% less than the riskfree rate of 8%.

12.4   MULTIPLE-FACTOR MODELS

When returns were generated by a two-factor model instead of a one-factor model, APT pricing Equations (12.7) and (12.11) were simply expanded to accommodate the additional factor in Equations (12.16) and (12.20). What happens to these APT pricing equations when returns are generated by a multiple-factor model where the number of factors k is greater than two? It turns out that the basic pricing equations are expanded once again in a relatively straightforward manner.

In the case of k factors $(F_1, F_2, \ldots, F_k)$ each security will have k sensitivities $(b_{i1}, b_{i2}, \ldots, b_{ik})$ in the following k-factor model:

$$r_i = a_i + b_{i1}F_1 + b_{i2}F_2 + \ldots + b_{ik}F_k + e_i. \tag{12.21}$$

In turn, this suggests that securities will be priced by the following equation, which is similar to Equations (12.7) and (12.16):

$$\bar{r}_i = \lambda_0 + \lambda_1 b_{i1} + \lambda_2 b_{i2} + \ldots + \lambda_k b_{ik}. \tag{12.22}$$

As before, this is a linear equation, except now it is in $k + 1$ dimensions with the dimensions being $\bar{r}_i, b_{i1}, b_{i2}, \ldots,$ and b_{ik}.

Extending the APT pricing Equations (12.11) and (12.20) to this situation is relatively uncomplicated. As before, λ_0 is equal to the riskfree rate as the riskfree asset has no sensitivity to any factor. Each value of δ_j represents the expected return on a portfolio of stocks that has unit sensitivity to factor j and zero sensitivity to all the other factors. As a result, Equations (12.11) and (12.20) can be expanded as follows:

$$\bar{r}_i = r_f + (\delta_1 - r_f)b_{i1} + (\delta_2 - r_f)b_{i2} + \ldots + (\delta_k - r_f)b_{ik}. \qquad (12.23)$$

Hence a stock's expected return is equal to the riskfree rate plus k risk premiums based on the stock's sensitivities to the k factors.

12.5   A SYNTHESIS OF THE APT AND THE CAPM

Unlike the APT, the CAPM does not assume that returns are generated by a factor model. However, this does not mean that the CAPM is inconsistent with a world in which returns are generated by a factor model. Indeed, it is possible to have a world where returns are generated by a factor model, where the remaining assumptions of the APT hold, and where all the assumptions of the CAPM hold. This situation will now be examined.

12.5.1   One-Factor Models

Consider what would happen if returns are generated by a one-factor model and that factor is the **market portfolio.** In such a situation, δ_1 will correspond to the expected return on the market portfolio and b_i will represent the beta of stock i measured relative to the market portfolio. Hence the CAPM will hold.

What if returns are generated by a one-factor model and that factor is *not* the market portfolio? Now δ_1 will correspond to the expected return on a portfolio with unit sensitivity to the factor, and b_i will represent the sensitivity of stock i measured relative to the factor.[11] However, if the CAPM also holds, then security i's expected return will be related to both its beta *and* sensitivity:

$$\bar{r}_i = r_f + (\bar{r}_M - r_f)\beta_{iM} \qquad (12.24)$$

$$\bar{r}_i = r_f + (\delta_1 - r_f)b_i. \qquad (12.25)$$

This suggests that betas and sensitivities must somehow be related to each other; just how they are related is shown next.

Applying APT

Since its inception in the mid-1970s, Arbitrage Pricing Theory (APT) has provided researchers and practitioners with an intuitive and flexible framework through which to address important investment management issues. As opposed to the Capital Asset Pricing Model (CAPM), with its specific assumptions concerning investor preferences as well as the critical role played by the market portfolio, APT operates under relatively weaker assumptions. Because of its emphasis on multiple sources of systematic risk, APT has attracted considerable interest as a tool for better explaining investment results and more effectively controlling portfolio risk.

Despite its attractive features, APT has not been widely applied by the investment community. The reason lies largely with APT's most significant drawback: the lack of specificity regarding the multiple factors that systematically affect security returns as well as the long-term return associated with each of these factors. Rightly or wrongly, the CAPM unambiguously states that a security's covariance with the market portfolio is the only systematic source of its investment risk within a well-diversified portfolio. APT, conversely, is conspicuously silent regarding the particular systematic factors affecting a security's risk and return. Investors must fend for themselves in determining those factors.

The number of institutional investors actually using APT to manage assets is small. The most prominent organization is Roll & Ross Asset Management Corporation (R&R). As Stephen Ross invented the APT, it is interesting to briefly review how R&R translates this theory into practice.

R&R begins with a statement of the systematic sources of risk (or factors) that it believes are *currently* relevant in the capital markets. Specifically, R&R has identified five factors that pervasively affect common stock returns:

- The business cycle
- Interest rates
- Investor confidence
- Short-term inflation
- Long-term inflationary expectations

R&R quantifies these factors by designating certain measurable macroeconomic variables as proxies. For example, the business-cycle factor is represented by real (inflation-adjusted) percentage changes in the index of industrial production, whereas short-term inflation is measured by monthly percentage changes in the consumer price index.

At the heart of the R&R approach are several assumptions. First, each source of systematic risk has a certain current volatility and reward. Factor volatilities and rewards, and even the factors themselves, may change over time. Second, individual securities and portfolios possess different sensitivities to each factor. These sensitivities may also vary through time. Third, a well-diversified portfolio's exposures to the factors will determine its expected return and total risk. Fourth, a portfolio should be constructed that offers the most attractive total reward-to-risk ratio, given the current rewards and volatilities exhibited by the factors.

R&R has developed a security database (updated monthly) that covers roughly 15,000 individual common stocks across 17 countries. For each country's stock market, R&R applies the database to create a pure factor portfolio (discussed in this chapter) for each of the five factors. R&R uses the historical returns on these pure factor portfolios not only to estimate the sensitivity of every security in its database to each of the factors, but also to estimate factor standard deviations, correlations, and risk premiums as well as calculate nonfactor returns and risk for every security.

Attention at this point turns to a client's benchmark. Typically, a U.S. institutional investor will select a market index such as the S&P 500 as its common stock benchmark. R&R's standard assignment is to devise a more efficient portfolio that exceeds the benchmark's expected return by a prespecified (reasonable) amount, yet maintains a similar standard deviation. R&R does this by employing portfolio optimization techniques (see Chapter 8) that combine securities in a way that attempts to set portfolio standard deviation near that of the benchmark; reduce nonfactor risk to minimal levels; emphasize stocks with high nonfactor reward-to-risk; increase exposure to risk factors with attractive reward-to-risk; and minimize buying and selling of securities (to control transaction costs). The process is repeated monthly to keep the portfolio properly aligned with the benchmark.

The R&R approach is highly quantitative and, intriguingly, involves no judgmental forecasts of factor returns or risks. Rather, historical data on the factors and securities' factor sensitivities is mechanically manipulated to determine the desired portfolio composition. This approach may prove effective if the future mimics the past, but it can produce disappointing results if past factor data display no stable relationship with future values.

R&R has captured considerable U.S. institutional investor interest since the firm was organized in 1986. Furthermore, the firm has expanded to take on foreign partners who now apply its techniques abroad. Thus R&R provides an interesting example of converting theoretical investment concepts into practical investment products.

Beta Coefficients and Factor Sensitivities

How can expected returns be linearly related to both betas and sensitivities? This will happen because betas and sensitivities will be related to each other in the following manner:

$$\beta_{iM} = \frac{\text{COV}(F_1, r_M)}{\sigma_M^2} b_i \qquad (12.26)$$

where $\text{COV}(F_1, r_M)$ denotes the covariance between the factor and the market portfolio and σ_M^2 denotes the variance of the return on the market portfolio.[12] Because the quantity $\text{COV}(F_1, r_M)/\sigma_M^2$ is a constant and does not change from one security to another, Equation (12.26) is equivalent to saying that β_{iM} will be equal to a constant times b_i when Equations (12.24) and (12.25) both hold. Hence if the factor is industrial production, then Equation (12.26) states that each security's beta is equal to a constant times the security's sensitivity to industrial production. The constant will be a positive number if industrial production and the returns on the market portfolio are positively correlated, as then $\text{COV}(F_1, r_M)$ will be positive.[13] Conversely, the constant will be negative if the correlation is negative because then $\text{COV}(F_1, r_M)$ will be negative.

Factor Risk Premiums

Continuing with this discussion, note what happens if the right-hand side of Equation (12.26) is substituted for β_{iM} on the right-hand side of Equation (12.24):

$$\bar{r}_i = r_f + \left[(\bar{r}_M - r_f)\frac{\text{COV}(F_1, r_M)}{\sigma_M^2}\right]b_i. \qquad (12.27)$$

Comparing this equation with Equation (12.9) reveals that if the assumptions of both APT (with one factor) and the CAPM hold, then the following relationship must hold:

$$\lambda_1 = (\overline{r}_M - r_f) \frac{\text{COV}(F_1, r_M)}{\sigma_M^2}. \qquad (12.28)$$

By itself, APT says nothing about the size of the factor risk premium λ_1. However, if the CAPM also holds, it can provide some guidance. This guidance is given in Equation (12.28), which has been shown to hold if the assumptions of both APT and the CAPM are taken as given.

Imagine that the factor moves with the market portfolio, meaning that it is positively correlated with the market portfolio so that $\text{COV}(F_1, r_M)$ is positive.[14] As σ_M^2 and $(\overline{r}_M - r_f)$ are both positive, it follows that the right-hand side of Equation (12.28) is positive and hence λ_1 is positive. Furthermore, because λ_1 is positive, it can be seen in Equation (12.9) that the higher the value of b_i, the higher will be the expected return of the security.[15] To generalize, if a factor is positively correlated with the market portfolio, then a security's expected return will be a positive function of the security's sensitivity to that factor.

Using the same kind of argument, if the factor moves against the market portfolio, meaning that F_1 is negatively correlated with $\overline{r}_M$, then λ_1 will be negative. This means that the higher the value of b_i, the lower will be the expected return on the security. Generalizing, if a factor is negatively correlated with the market portfolio, then a security's expected return will be a negative function of the security's sensitivity to that factor.

A Market Index as the Factor

What if returns are generated by a one-factor model and instead of industrial production, the factor is the return on a market index such as the S&P 500? Consider a situation where the following two conditions are met: (1) the returns on the index and market portfolio are perfectly correlated and (2) the variance of the returns on the market portfolio and the market index are identical.

First of all, a stock's beta will be equal to its sensitivity. This can be seen by examining Equation (12.26). Given the two conditions just described, $\text{COV}(F_1, r_M) = \sigma_{F1}\sigma_M = \sigma_M^2$ so that $\text{COV}(F_1, r_M)/\sigma_M^2 = 1$. Hence Equation (12.26) would reduce to $\beta_{iM} = b_i$.

Second, λ_1 will equal $\overline{r}_M - r_f$ under these two conditions. This can be seen by again noting that $\text{COV}(F_1, r_M)/\sigma_M^2 = 1$, which in turn means that Equation (12.28) reduces to $\lambda_1 = \overline{r}_M - r_f$. Because Equation (12.10c) states that $\delta_1 - r_f = \lambda_1$, this means that $\delta_1 = \overline{r}_M$. Hence the expected return on a portfolio that has unit sensitivity to the returns on the S&P 500 will be equal to the expected return on the market portfolio.

In summary, if a proxy for the market portfolio could be found such that the two conditions given previously were met, then the CAPM would hold where the role of the market portfolio could be replaced by the proxy. Unfortunately, because the market portfolio is unknown, it cannot be verified whether or not any proxy meets the two conditions.

12.5.2 Multiple-Factor Models

It is possible for the CAPM to hold even though returns are generated by a multiple-factor model such as a two-factor model. Again, Equations (12.24) and (12.25) can be extended to show that security i's expected return will be related to its beta and two sensitivities:

$$\bar{r}_i = r_f + (\bar{r}_M - r_f)\beta_{iM} \tag{12.29}$$

$$\bar{r}_i = r_f + (\delta_1 - r_f)b_{i1} + (\delta_2 - r_f)b_{i2}. \tag{12.30}$$

In this situation, Equation (12.26) can be extended to show that betas will be linearly related to sensitivities in the following manner:

$$\beta_{iM} = \frac{COV(F_1, r_M)}{\sigma_M^2} b_{i1} + \frac{COV(F_2, r_M)}{\sigma_M^2} b_{i2} \tag{12.31}$$

where $COV(F_1, r_M)$ and $COV(F_2, r_M)$ denote the covariance between the first factor and the returns on the market portfolio and covariance between the second factor and the returns on the market portfolio, respectively. As the quantities $COV(F_1, r_M)/\sigma_M^2$ and $COV(F_2, r_M)/\sigma_M^2$ are constants, it can be seen from Equation (12.31) that β_{iM} will be a function of b_{i1} and b_{i2} when Equations (12.29) and (12.30) hold. This means that a stock's beta will be a linear combination of its sensitivities to the two factors, which means that, in this example, the size of a stock's beta will be dependent of the size of its sensitivities to predicted industrial production and inflation.

Note what happens if the right-hand side of Equation (12.31) is substituted for β_{iM} on the right-hand side of Equation (12.29):

$$\bar{r}_i = r_f + (\bar{r}_M - r_f)\left[\frac{COV(F_1, r_M)}{\sigma_M^2} b_{i1} + \frac{COV(F_2, r_M)}{\sigma_M^2} b_{i2}\right] \tag{12.32a}$$

which can be rewritten as:

$$\bar{r}_i = r_f + \left[(\bar{r}_M - r_f)\frac{COV(F_1, r_M)}{\sigma_M^2}\right]b_{i1} + \left[(\bar{r}_M - r_f)\frac{COV(F_2, r_M)}{\sigma_M^2}\right]b_{i2}. \tag{12.32b}$$

Comparing this equation with Equation (12.18) reveals that if the assumptions of both APT (with two factors) and the CAPM hold, then the following relationships must hold:

$$\lambda_1 = (\bar{r}_M - r_f)\frac{COV(F_1, r_M)}{\sigma_M^2} \tag{12.33a}$$

$$\lambda_2 = (\bar{r}_M - r_f)\frac{COV(F_2, r_M)}{\sigma_M^2}. \tag{12.33b}$$

Hence the size of λ_1 and λ_2 will be dependent upon both the market premium $(\bar{r}_M - r_f)$, a positive number, and the covariance of the factor with the market portfolio, which may be positive or negative. This means that λ_1 and λ_2 will have positive values if the factors are positively correlated with the returns on the market portfolio.[16] However, if either factor is negatively correlated with the returns on the market portfolio, then the corresponding value of λ will be negative (as was the case with λ_2 in the example).

12.6 IDENTIFYING THE FACTORS

Left unanswered by APT are the number and identity of the factors that are "priced"—that is, have values of lambda (λ) that are sufficiently positive or negative in magnitude so that they need to be included when estimating expected returns. Several researchers have investigated stock returns and estimated that there are anywhere from three to five factors. Subsequently, various people attempted to identify these factors.[17] In one paper by Chen, Roll, and Ross, the following factors were identified:

1. Growth rate in industrial production,
2. Rate of inflation (both expected and unexpected),
3. Spread between long-term and short-term interest rates,
4. Spread between low-grade and high-grade bonds.[18]

Another paper by Berry, Burmeister, and McElroy identifies five factors. Of these five factors, three correspond closely to the last three identified by Chen, Roll, and Ross. The other two are the growth rate in aggregate sales in the economy and the rate of return on the S&P 500.[19]

Finally, consider the five factors used by Salomon Brothers in what they refer to as their Fundamental Factor Model. Only one factor, inflation, is in common with the factors identified by the others. The remaining factors are as follows:

1. Growth rate in gross national product,
2. Rate of interest,
3. Rate of change in oil prices,
4. Rate of growth in defense spending.[20]

In summary, it is interesting to note that the three sets of factors have some common characteristics. First, they contain some indication of aggregate economic activity (industrial production, aggregate sales, and GNP). Second, they contain inflation. Third, they contain some type of interest rate factor (either spreads or a rate itself). Considering the fact that stock prices can be thought of as being equal to the discounted value of future dividends, the factors make intuitive sense.[21] Future dividends will be related to aggregate economic activity, and the discount rate used to determine present value will be related to inflation and interest rates.

12.7 SUMMARY

1. Arbitrage Pricing Theory (APT) is an equilibrium model of security prices, as is the Capital Asset Pricing Model (CAPM).

2. APT makes fewer assumptions about investor preferences than does the CAPM.
3. APT assumes that security returns are generated by a factor model but does not identify the factors.
4. An arbitrage portfolio includes long and short positions in securities. It must have a net market value of zero, no sensitivity to any factor, and a positive expected return.
5. Investors will invest in arbitrage portfolios, driving up the prices of the securities held in long positions and driving down the prices of securities held in short positions, until all arbitrage possibilities are eliminated.
6. When all arbitrage possibilities are eliminated, the equilibrium-expected return on a security will be a linear function of its sensitivities to the factors.
7. A factor-risk premium is the equilibrium return over the riskfree rate expected to be generated by a portfolio with a unit sensitivity to the factor and no sensitivity to any other factor.
8. APT and the CAPM are not necessarily inconsistent with each other. If security returns are generated by a factor model and the CAPM holds, then a security's beta will depend on the security's sensitivity to the factors and the covariances between the factors and the market portfolio.
9. APT does not specify the number or identity of the factors that affect expected returns. Most research into factors focuses on indicators of aggregate economic activity, inflation, and interest rates.

QUESTIONS AND PROBLEMS

1. In what significant ways does the APT differ from the CAPM?
2. Why would an investor wish to form an arbitrage portfolio?
3. What three conditions define an arbitrage portfolio?
4. Assuming a one-factor model of the form:

$$r_i = 4\% + b_i F + e_i$$

consider three well-diversified portfolios (zero nonfactor risk). The expected value of the factor is 8%.

Portfolio	Factor Sensitivity	Expected Return
A	0.80	10.4%
B	1.00	10.0
C	1.20	13.6

Is one of the portfolio's expected return not in line with the factor model relationship? Which one? Can you construct a combination of the other two portfolios that has the same factor sensitivity as the "out-of-line" portfolio? What is the expected return of that combination? What action would you expect investors to take with respect to these three portfolios?

5. Socks Seybold owns a portfolio with the following characteristics. (Assume that returns are generated by a one-factor model.)

Security	Factor Sensitivity	Proportion	Expected Return
A	2.0	.20	20%
B	3.5	.40	10
C	0.5	.40	5

Socks decides to create an arbitrage portfolio by increasing the holdings of security A by .20 (Hint: Remember, X_B must equal $-X_C - X_A$.)

   a. What must be the weights of the other two securities in Socks's arbitrage portfolio?
   b. What is the expected return on the arbitrage portfolio?
   c. If everyone follows Socks's buy-and-sell decisions, what will be the effects on the prices of the three securities?

6. Assume that security returns are generated by a one-factor model. Hap Morse holds a portfolio whose component securities have the following characteristics:

Security	Factor Sensitivity	Proportion	Expected Return
A	.60	.40	12%
B	.30	.30	15
C	1.20	.30	8

Specify an arbitrage portfolio in which Hap might invest. (Remember that there are an infinite number of possibilities—choose one.) Demonstrate that this portfolio satisfies the conditions of an arbitrage portfolio.

7. Why must the variance of a well-diversified arbitrage portfolio be small?

8. Why is the concept of arbitrage central to the asset-pricing mechanism of the APT?

9. Based on a one-factor model, Wyeville Labs' stock has a factor sensitivity of 3. Given a riskfree rate of 5% and a factor risk premium of 7%, what is the equilibrium expected return on Wyeville stock?

10. According to the APT, why must the relationship between a security's equilibrium return and its factor sensitivities be linear?

11. Based on a one-factor model, two portfolios, A and B, have equilibrium expected returns of 9.8% and 11.0%, respectively. If the factor sensitivity of portfolios A and B is 0.80 and 1.00, respectively, what must be the riskfree rate?

12. What is a pure factor portfolio? How may such a portfolio be constructed?

13. Based on a one-factor model, assume that the riskfree rate is 6% and the expected return on a portfolio with unit sensitivity to the factor is 8.5%. Consider a portfolio of two securities with the following characteristics:

Security	Factor Sensitivity	Proportion
A	4.0	.30
B	2.6	.70

According to the APT, what is the portfolio's equilibrium expected return?

14. Assume that security returns are generated by a factor model in which two factors are pervasive. The sensitivities of two securities and of the riskfree asset to each of the two factors is shown below, along with the expected return on each security.

Security	b_{i1}	b_{i2}	Expected Return
A	0.50	0.80	16.2%
B	1.50	1.40	21.6
r_f	0.00	0.00	10.0

   a. If Dots Miller has $100 to invest and sells short $50 of security B and purchases $150 of security A, what is the sensitivity of Dots's portfolio to the two factors? (Ignore margin requirements.)
   b. If Dots now borrows $100 at the riskfree rate and invests the proceeds of the loan along with the original $100 in securities A and B in the same proportions as described in Part a, what is the sensitivity of this portfolio to the two factors?
   c. What is the expected return on the portfolio created in Part b?
   d. What is the expected return premium of factor 2?
15. Dandelion Pfeffer owns a portfolio with the following characteristics:

Security	Factor 1 Sensitivity	Factor 2 Sensitivity	Proportion	Expected Return
A	2.50	1.40	.30	13%
B	1.60	0.90	.30	18
C	0.80	1.00	.20	10
D	2.00	1.30	.20	12

   Assume that the returns are generated by a two-factor model. Dandelion decides to create an arbitrage portfolio by increasing the holding of security B by .05.
   a. What must be the weights of the other three securities in Dandelion's portfolio?
   b. What is the expected return on the arbitrage portfolio?
16. Is it true that if one believes that the APT is a correct theory of asset pricing, then the risk-return relationship derived from the CAPM is necessarily incorrect? Why?
17. If the CAPM and APT both hold, why must it be the case that the factor-risk premium is negative for a factor that is negatively correlated with the market portfolio? Explain both mathematically and intuitively.
18. Some people have argued that the market portfolio can never be measured and that the CAPM, therefore, is untestable. Others have argued that the APT specifies neither the number of factors nor their identity and, hence, is also untestable. If these views are correct, does this mean that the theories are of no value? Explain.
19. Although the APT does not specify the identity of the relevant factors, most empirical APT research has focused on certain types of factors. What are some of the common characteristics of those factors?

20. Assume that the CAPM holds and that returns on securities are generated by a single-factor model. You are given the following information:

$$\sigma_M^2 = 400 \qquad b_A = 0.70 \qquad b_B = 1.10 \qquad \text{COV}(F, r_M) = 370$$

   a. Calculate the beta coefficients of securities A and B.
   b. If the riskfree rate is 6% and the expected return on the market portfolio is 12%, what is the equilibrium expected return on securities A and B?

21. Assume that the CAPM holds and that returns are generated by a two-factor model. You are given the following information:

$$\sigma_M^2 = 324 \qquad b_{A1} = .80 \qquad b_{B1} = 1.00 \qquad \text{COV}(F_1, r_M) = 156$$
$$b_{A2} = 1.10 \qquad b_{B2} = .70 \qquad \text{COV}(F_2, r_M) = 500.$$

Calculate the beta coefficients of securities A and B.

CFA EXAM QUESTION

22. As the manager of a large, broadly diversified portfolio of stocks and bonds, you realize that changes in certain macroeconomic variables may directly affect the performance of your portfolio. You are considering using an arbitrage pricing theory (APT) approach to strategic portfolio planning and want to analyze the possible impacts of the following four factors:
   - industrial production;
   - inflation;
   - risk premia or quality spreads;
   - yield curve shifts.

   a. Indicate how each of these four factors influences the cash flows and the discount rates in the traditional discounted cash flow valuation model. Explain how unanticipated changes in each of these four factors could affect portfolio returns.
   b. You now use a constant-proportion allocation strategy of 60% stock and 40% bonds, which you rebalance monthly. Compare and contrast an active portfolio approach that incorporates macroeconomic factors, such as the four factors listed above, to the constant-proportion strategy currently in use.

ENDNOTES

[1] Factor models are discussed in detail in Chapter 11.

[2] There are other ways to write the equation for a factor model. Note that from Equation (12.1) it follows that $\overline{r}_i = a_i + b_i \overline{F}_1$, where $\overline{r}_i$ and $\overline{F}_1$ are the expected return for security i and the expected value of the factor, respectively. Substituting $\overline{r}_i - b_i \overline{F}_1$ for a_i in Equation (12.1) results in the following alternative formulation of a one-factor model: $r_i = \overline{r}_i + b_i(F_1 - \overline{F}_1) + e_i$. Letting $f_1 = F_1 - \overline{F}_1$, a third formulation of a one-factor model is: $r_i = \overline{r}_i + b_i f_1 + e_i$ where f_1 can be interpreted as the unexpected change in the value of the factor.

[3] There will always be an infinite number of solutions whenever there are more unknowns than equations. For example, consider a situation where there is one equation with two unknowns: $Y = 3X$. Note that there is an infinite number of paired values of X and Y that solve this equation, such as $(1, 3)$, $(2, 6)$, and $(3, 9)$.

[4] If its expected return is negative, then simply changing the signs of the weights will cause the expected return to become positive. Note that the new weights will also sum to zero and will still represent a portfolio that has zero sensitivity to the factor. Thus the new weights will represent an arbitrage portfolio.

[5] The APT ignores nonfactor risk. Because the total risk of a portfolio σ_p^2 is equal to $b_p^2 \sigma_F^2 + \sigma_{ep}^2$ according to the one-factor model [see Equation (11.6a) in Chapter 11], and given that the arbitrage portfolio has no factor risk by design, meaning that $b_p^2 \sigma_F^2 = 0$ because $b_p = 0$, this means that the arbitrage portfolio must be sufficiently diversified so as to have insignificant nonfactor risk and, consequently, insignificant total risk.

[6] Technically, this pricing equation is only approximately true and may be significantly wrong for a small number of assets.

[7] Why choose 8 and 4 for λ_0 and λ_1, respectively? The magnitudes that these two parameters assume in equilibrium will depend on many things, such as investors' relative degrees of risk aversion, wealth, and time preferences.

[8] If B were to plot below the APT asset pricing line, then investors would do just the opposite of what is described here. This means that they would buy S and sell B.

[9] A simpler way of viewing this transaction is as a stock swap where S is being swapped for B. Because it is a swap, no new funds are needed. Furthermore, because both B and S have the same factor sensitivity, the swap will not alter the sensitivity of the currently held portfolio. Finally, the replacement of S with B will increase the currently held portfolio's expected return because B has a higher level of expected return than S.

[10] Technically, the APT asset pricing line would shift upward a bit due to the selling of S.

[11] If the factor is a market index (instead of the market portfolio) such as the S&P 500, then δ_1 will correspond to the expected return on the index and b_i will represent the beta of stock i measured relative to the index, denoted previously in Chapter 8 as β_{iI}.

[12] This can be seen by noting that $\text{COV}(r_i, r_M) = \text{COV}(a_i + b_i F_1 + e_i, r_M)$, which simplifies to $\text{COV}(r_i, r_M) = b_i \text{COV}(F_1, r_M) + \text{COV}(e_i, r_M)$. As the last term is approximately zero, this equation reduces to $\text{COV}(r_i, r_M) = b_i \text{COV}(F_1, r_M)$. Dividing both sides by σ_M^2 and recognizing from Chapter 10 that $\text{COV}(r_i, r_M)/\sigma_M^2 = \beta_{iM}$ produces Equation (12.26).

[13] $\text{COV}(F_1, r_M)$ will be positive if the correlation is positive because it is equal to the product of the correlation and the standard deviations of F_1 and r_M.

[14] See Endnote 13.

[15] The greater the extent to which the factor moves with the market portfolio (meaning the higher the correlation between F_1 and r_M), the greater will be the associated expected return premium λ_1.

[16] For the reasoning behind this assertion, see Endnote 13.

[17] In Chapter 11 a three-factor model that was developed by Fama and French was described. In their model, the factors represented returns on (1) a general market index, (2) the difference between small and large stock indices, and (3) the difference between high and low book-to-market equity ratio stock indices.

[18] Note that the third factor can be interpreted as a measure of the term structure of interest rates, and the fourth factor can be interpreted as a measure of the default risk premium that investors demand for holding risky corporate bonds instead of Treasury bonds.

[19] Technically, they used the part of the rate of return of the S&P 500 that could not be attributed to the other four factors.

[20] Technically, they used inflation-adjusted figures for all the variables except the rate of interest.

[21] Dividend discount models are discussed in depth in Chapter 18.

Arbitrage Pricing Theory	pure factor portfolio
sensitivity	factor risk premium
arbitrage	market portfolio
arbitrage portfolio	

REFERENCES

1. Credit for the initial development of the APT belongs to:

   Stephen A. Ross, "The Arbitrage Theory of Capital Asset Pricing," *Journal of Economic Theory,* 13, no. 3 (December 1976): 341–360 and "Risk, Return, and Arbitrage," in *Risk and Return in Finance,* Vol. I, ed. Irwin Friend and James L. Bicksler (Cambridge, MA: Ballinger Publishing, 1977), Section 9.

2. Ross's initial presentation of the APT was clarified in:

   Gur Huberman, "A Simple Approach to Arbitrage Pricing Theory," *Journal of Economic Theory,* 28, no. 1 (October 1982): 183–191.

3. The fundamental asset pricing equation of Ross's APT is approximately correct for all but a small number of assets. By making additional assumptions all assets will be priced with, at most, negligible error. Some of the papers (also see the papers cited in References 7 and 8) that address this issue are:

   Nai-fu Chen and Jonathan E. Ingersoll, Jr., "Exact Pricing in Linear Factor Models with Finitely Many Assets: A Note," *Journal of Finance,* 38, no. 3 (June 1983): 985–988.

   Gary Chamberlain and Michael Rothschild, "Arbitrage, Factor Structure, and Mean-Variance Analysis on Large Asset Markets," *Econometrica,* 51, no. 5 (September 1983): 1281–1304.

   Gary Chamberlain, "Funds, Factors, and Diversification in Arbitrage Pricing Models," *Econometrica,* 51, no. 5 (September 1983): 1305–1323.

   Philip H. Dybvig, "An Explicit Bound on Individual Assets' Deviations from APT Pricing in a Finite Economy," *Journal of Financial Economics,* 12, no. 4 (December 1983): 483–496.

   Mark Grinblatt and Sheridan Titman, "Factor Pricing in a Finite Economy," *Journal of Financial Economics,* 12, no. 4 (December 1983): 497–507.

   Gregory Connor, "A Unified Beta Pricing Theory," *Journal of Economic Theory,* 34, no. 1 (October 1984): 13–31.

4. Nontechnical descriptions of the APT can be found in:

   Richard W. Roll and Stephen A. Ross, "Regulation, the Capital Asset Pricing Model, and the Arbitrage Pricing Theory," *Public Utilities Fortnightly,* 111, no. 11 (May 26, 1983): 22–28.

Richard Roll and Stephen A. Ross, "The Arbitrage Pricing Theory Approach to Strategic Portfolio Planning," *Financial Analysts Journal,* 40, no. 3 (May-June 1984): 14–26.

Dorothy H. Bower, Richard S. Bower, and Dennis E. Logue, "A Primer on Arbitrage Pricing Theory," *Midland Corporate Finance Journal,* 2, no. 3 (Fall 1984): 31–40.

5. Some of the attempts to identify the number of factors that are priced are:

Richard Roll and Stephen A. Ross, "An Empirical Investigation of the Arbitrage Pricing Theory," *Journal of Finance,* 35, no. 5 (December 1980): 1073–1103.

Stephen J. Brown and Mark I. Weinstein, "A New Approach to Testing Asset Pricing Models: The Bilinear Paradigm," *Journal of Finance,* 38, no. 3 (June 1983): 711–743.

Phoebus J. Dhrymes, Irwin Friend, and N. Bulent Gultekin, "A Critical Reexamination of the Empirical Evidence on the Arbitrage Pricing Theory," *Journal of Finance,* 39, no. 2 (June 1984): 323–346.

Richard Roll and Stephen A. Ross, "A Critical Reexamination of the Empirical Evidence on the Arbitrage Pricing Theory: A Reply," *Journal of Finance,* 39, no. 2 (June 1984): 347–350.

Charles Trzcinka, "On the Number of Factors in the Arbitrage Pricing Model," *Journal of Finance,* 41, no. 2 (June 1986): 347–368.

Dolores A. Conway and Marc R. Reinganum, "Stable Factors in Security Returns: Identification Using Cross Validation," *Journal of Business and Economic Statistics,* 6, no. 1 (January 1988): 1–15.

Bruce N. Lehmann and David M. Modest, "The Empirical Foundations of the Arbitrage Pricing Theory," *Journal of Financial Economics,* 21, no. 2 (September 1988): 213–254.

Gregory Connor and Robert A. Korajczyk, "Risk and Return in an Equilibrium APT: Application of a New Test Methodology," *Journal of Financial Economics,* 21, no. 2 (September 1988): 255–289.

Stephen J. Brown, "The Number of Factors in Security Returns," *Journal of Finance,* 44, no. 5 (December 1989): 1247–1262.

Eugene F. Fama and Kenneth R. French, "Common Risk Factors in the Returns on Stocks and Bonds," *Journal of Financial Economics,* 33, no. 1 (February 1993): 3–56.

Gregory Connor and Robert A. Korajczyk, "A Test for the Number of Factors in an Approximate Factor Model," *Journal of Finance,* 48, no. 4 (September 1993): 1263–1291.

6. A few of the previous papers also identified factors. Some other papers that also identified factors are:

Tony Estep, Nick Hansen, and Cal Johnson, "Sources of Value and Risk in Common Stocks," *Journal of Portfolio Management,* 9, no. 4 (Summer 1983): 5–13.

Nai-fu Chen, Richard Roll, and Stephen A. Ross, "Economic Forces and the Stock Market," *Journal of Business,* 59, no. 3 (July 1986): 383–403.

Marjorie B. McElroy and Edwin Burmeister, "Arbitrage Pricing Theory as a Restricted Nonlinear Multivariate Regression Model," *Journal of Business and Economic Statistics,* 6, no. 1 (January 1988): 29–42.

Michael A. Berry, Edwin Burmeister, and Marjorie B. McElroy, "Sorting Out Risks Using Known APT Factors," *Financial Analysts Journal,* 44, no. 2 (March-April 1988): 29–42.

7. It has been argued that the APT cannot be meaningfully tested and hence is of questionable practical use by:

Jay Shanken, "The Arbitrage Pricing Theory: Is It Testable?" *Journal of Finance,* 37, no. 5 (December 1982): 1129–1140.

Christian Gilles and Stephen F. LeRoy, "On the Arbitrage Pricing Theory," *Economic Theory,* 1, no. 3 (1991): 213–229.

Jay Shanken, "The Current State of Arbitrage Pricing Theory," *Journal of Finance,* 47, no. 4 (September 1992): 1569–1574.

8. For a discussion of the relationships between the APT and the CAPM, see:

William F. Sharpe, "Factor Models, CAPMs, and the ABT *(sic),*" *Journal of Portfolio Management,* 11, no. 1 (Fall 1984): 21–25.

Jay Shanken, "Multi-Beta CAPM or Equilibrium-APT?: A Reply," *Journal of Finance,* 40, no. 4 (September 1985): 1189–1196.

K. C. John Wei, "An Asset-Pricing Theory Unifying the CAPM and APT," *Journal of Finance,* 43, no. 4 (September 1988): 881–892.

Taxes and Inflation

Neither taxation nor inflation should be regarded as an unmitigated evil. Each provides benefits to some individuals that may outweigh the associated costs that others have to bear. Regardless of whether the benefits outweigh the costs, both taxes and inflation have a significant impact on investment decisions and investment results. This chapter provides an overview of some of the more important aspects of taxation and inflation from the viewpoint of the investor.

Federal and state tax laws play a major role in the way securities are priced in the marketplace because investors are understandably concerned with after-tax returns, not before-tax returns. Accordingly, the investor should determine the tax rate applicable to him or her before making any investment decision. This tax rate is not the same for all securities for a given individual investor: it can be as low as 0% in the case of certain tax-exempt securities issued by states and municipalities, and well over 40% for corporate bonds when both federal and state taxes are considered. After determining the applicable tax rate, the investor can estimate a security's expected after-tax return and risk. Upon doing so, an investment decision can be made wisely.

Many of the specific tax rates and provisions in the United States were enacted with the Tax Reform Act of 1986 and amended with the Omnibus Budget Reconciliation Acts of 1990 and 1993. Changes do occur from year to year, and current regulations should, of course, be consulted when preparing tax returns or considering major investment decisions. However, the material given here can be considered broadly representative of current taxation (primarily federal) in the United States.

Generally speaking, the most important taxes for investment decision-making are personal and corporate income taxes. The essential elements of each will be described, and the manner in which they influence the pricing of securities will be considered.

13.1.1   Corporate Income Taxes

There are three forms of business organizations in the United States and in most other countries—corporations, partnerships, and single proprietorships. The corporate form of organization is the largest in terms of the dollar value of assets owned, even though there are more firms organized as partnerships or single proprietorships. Legally, a corporation is regarded as a separate entity, whereas a proprietorship or partnership is considered an extension of its owner or owners. Income earned by proprietorships and partnerships is taxed primarily through the personal income tax levied on their owners. Income earned by a corporation may be taxed twice—once when it is earned, via the corporate income tax, and again when it is received as dividends by holders of the firm's securities, via the personal income tax.[1]

This double taxation of corporate income may at first seem inefficient, if not unfair. It also raises questions about the efficiency of the corporate form of organization. Suffice it to say that limited liability and the ability to subdivide ownership and to transfer shares of that ownership appear to be of sufficient value to more than offset the tax law disadvantages. Moreover, without the corporate income tax, personal tax rates would have to be increased if the level of government expenditures were to remain constant without increasing the national debt.

Corporate Tax Rates

Before 1993 the corporate income tax was relatively simple in one respect—there were only a few basic rates. However, in 1993 even this feature was made more complex, as there are now eight basic rates. The rates and applicable levels of taxable annual income are as follows:

1. A tax rate of 15% is applicable to the first $50,000;
2. A tax rate of 25% to the next $25,000;
3. A tax rate of 34% to the next $25,000;
4. A tax rate of 39% to the next $235,000;

---

5. A tax rate of 34% to the next $9,665,000;

6. A tax rate of 35% to the next $5,000,000;

7. A tax rate of 38% to the next $3,333,333;

8. A tax rate of 35% on all additional income.

Figure 13.1 illustrates what are known as the **marginal tax rate** and **average tax rate** schedules for corporations. A corporation's marginal tax rate is the tax rate it would pay on an additional dollar of income. For example, a corporation earning $85,000 would pay $17,150 in income taxes:

$$
\begin{aligned}
0.15 \times \$50,000 &= \$\ 7,500 \\
0.25 \times \quad 25,000 &= \quad 6,250 \\
0.34 \times \quad 10,000 &= \quad 3,400 \\
\hline
\text{Total income tax} &= \$17,150
\end{aligned}
$$

For this corporation, the marginal tax rate is 34% because an additional dollar of income would be taxed at this rate. In other words, if this firm had income of $85,001 instead of $85,000, its tax bill would have been $17,150.34 instead of $17,150. Thus $.34 (= $17,150.34 − $17,150.00) more in taxes would be paid as a result of earning $1 (= $85,001 − $85,000) more in income.

The average tax rate is equal to the total amount of taxes paid divided by the total income subject to tax. The average tax rate for the previous example would thus be 20.18% = $17,150/$85,000. That is, 20.18% of this firm's total income would be taken by the government in the form of corporate income taxes. As can be seen in Figure 13.1, the average rate is exactly equal to the marginal rate

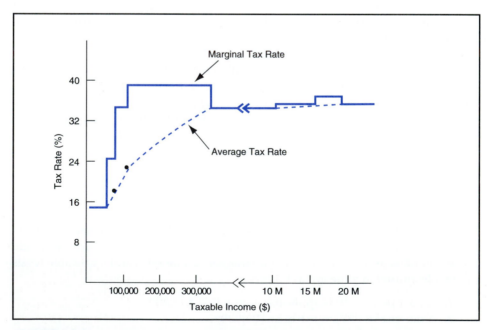

FIGURE 13.1

Marginal and Average Corporate Tax Rates, 1993

at three places: (1) the rates are equal to 15% for incomes below $50,000, (2) the rates are equal to 34% for incomes between $335,000 and $10,000,000, and (3) the rates are equal to 35% for incomes above $18,333,333.

The average rate measures the overall impact of taxes, but the marginal rate is more relevant for most decisions. For example, if a corporation were considering an investment that would increase its income from $85,000 to $90,000 each year, the increase in income after taxes would be $3,300 $[= (1 - .34) \times \$5,000]$, not $3,991 $[= (1 - .2018) \times \$5,000]$.

Corporate Income from Dividends, Interest, and Capital Gains

Congress has provided that 80% of the dividends received by a corporation can be excluded from income when calculating the corporation's income tax liability.[2] The effective tax rate on an additional dollar of dividends received by a corporation with an income in the 35% range is thus 7% $[= (1 - .80) \times .35]$. The reason for this special treatment of dividends is to avoid the triple taxation of income. Consider how dividends would be taxed if this 80% exclusion did not exist. Corporation A is taxed on its income and then pays dividends to one of its stockholders, corporation B. Corporation B then pays taxes on its income, which includes the dividends received from A. Finally, the stockholders of B pay income taxes on the dividends received from B. Thus a dollar of income earned by A would be taxed three times—a tax on A, then a tax on B, then a tax on the stockholders of B—if the dividend exclusion did not exist. With the dividend exclusion, a dollar of income earned by A is taxed, for all practical purposes, "only" a little more than twice.

Bonds versus Preferred Stocks

No deduction is allowed for interest received on bonds bought by a corporate investor. It is simply added to income and taxed at the regular rates. This means that the maximum effective tax rate on interest received from bonds is 35%, an amount substantially greater than the 7% effective tax rate on common and preferred stock dividends. This differential tax treatment has an effect on the relative prices that corporate and individual investors are willing to pay for these securities, because their concern is with relative after-tax yields.

Table 13.1 provides an example of preferred stock that illustrates the before-tax and after-tax yields for both a corporate investor with a marginal tax rate of 35% and an individual investor with a marginal personal tax rate of 28%. Note that the preferred stock has a lower before-tax yield in spite of being riskier than the bond. The table shows that the individual investor will be better off purchasing the bond, because its after-tax yield of 5.76% exceeds the after-tax yield of 5.04% on the preferred stock. (Careful scrutiny reveals that this is true for *any* marginal tax rate for the individual investor because dividend and interest income of any individual are taxed equally.) However, the corporate investor will be better off purchasing the preferred stock, because its after-tax yield of 6.51% exceeds the after-tax yield on bonds of 5.20%.

TABLE 13.1

COMPARISON OF YIELDS OF PREFERRED STOCKS AND CORPORATE BONDS

	Investment	
	Preferred Stock	Corporate Bond
A. Features		
Price	$10 per share	$1,000 per bond
Annual dollar yield	$.70 per share	$80 per bond
Aggregate investment	100 shares	1 bond
Cost of aggregate investment	$1,000	$1,000
Aggregate annual dollar yield	$70	$80
Before-tax percentage yield	7% = $70/$1,000	8% = $80/$1,000
B. Corporate Investor[a]		
After-tax dollar yield	$65.10 = $70[1 − (.20 x .35)]	$52 = $80 (1 − .35)
After-tax percentage yield	6.51% = $65.10/$1,000	5.20% = $52/$1,000
C. Individual Investor[b]		
After-tax dollar yield	$50.40 = $70 (1 − .28)	$57.60 = $80 (1 − .28)
After-tax percentage yield	5.04% = $50.40/$1,000	5.76% = $57.60/$1,000

[a] Assuming a marginal corporate income tax rate of 35%.

[b] Assuming a marginal individual income tax rate of 28%.

Tax-exempt Organizations

Many organizations are wholly or partly exempt from federal income taxes. Non-profit religious, charitable, or educational foundations generally qualify. A small tax (2% in 1993) is levied on the net investment income of such a foundation. In addition, the foundation should pay out either all income received by the end of the year following receipt, or a minimum percentage of its assets (5% in 1993), whichever is higher, as failure to do so can result in a confiscatory tax on the difference.

Investment companies, often called *mutual funds,* may elect to be treated as regulated investment companies for tax purposes. This privilege is granted if certain conditions are met. For example, the funds of the investment company must be invested primarily in securities, without undue concentration in any one. Thus its income takes the form of dividends and interest received on its investments, as well as capital gains from price appreciation realized when investments are sold at a price that is higher than their purchase price. A regulated investment company pays income tax only on income and capital gains not distributed to its shareholders. As a result of this tax treatment, such companies distribute substantially all income and gains, and in doing so end up not having to pay any taxes.

Employee pension, profit-sharing, and stock-bonus plans may also qualify for tax-exempt status. Such a plan may entrust its assets, which are usually securities, to a *fiduciary* (for example, a bank). The fiduciary receives new contributions, makes required payments, and manages the investments owned by the plan. A fiduciary under a qualified plan (that is, a plan that meets all the requirements of applicable legislation) pays no taxes on either income or capital gains.

Another example of a tax-exempt entity is the *personal trust.* Here, funds are provided for the benefit of one or more individuals by another individual or individuals with a fiduciary serving as a trustee. Some trusts are created by wills, others by contracts among living persons. Whatever the origin, trusts generally pay taxes only on income that is not distributed to the designated beneficiaries.

Income and capital gains earned by investment companies, pension funds, and personal trusts do not go untaxed forever. Payments made to investment company shareholders, pension fund beneficiaries, and the beneficiaries of personal trusts are subject to applicable personal income tax rules. The exemptions apply only to taxes that might otherwise be levied at the previous stage.

13.1.2 Personal Income Taxes

Although the corporate income tax is an important feature of the investment scene, its impact on most individuals is indirect. This is not so for the personal income tax. Few investors avoid dealing with it in detail, at both an economic and an emotional level. Its provisions have major and direct impacts on investment behavior.

Personal Tax Rates

Taxes must be paid on an individual's income, defined as "all wealth which flows to the taxpayer other than as a mere return of capital. It includes gains and profits from any source, including gains from the sale or other disposition of capital assets."[3] Certain items are excluded from the definition of income; others are deducted from it before computing the tax due. Moreover, capital gains and losses are subject to special procedures, which will be described in a later section. Deductions and exclusions of special importance for investment purposes are described in this section as well as in later sections.

Two figures are relevant for tax purposes. Adjusted gross income is obtained by subtracting certain allowed deductions (for example, business expenses and contributions to certain retirement funds) from gross income. This amount, less a number of personal expense deductions, equals taxable income, the figure on which tax liability is based. The amount of tax calculated on this basis must be paid unless the taxpayer is able to claim tax credits, which may be subtracted directly from the tax liability to obtain a final amount due the government.

Although the Tax Reform Act of 1986 (as amended in 1990 and 1993) brought sweeping changes aimed at simplification, many people are still of the opinion that almost nothing about personal income taxes in the United States is simple. Four different schedules of tax rates are currently in effect, the appropriate one depending on whether the particular taxpayer is single, married and filing a joint return with his or her spouse, married but filing a separate return, or a head of a household. Table 13.2 shows the tax rates in effect in 1993 for the first two types of taxpayers. (Note that the figures shown here—and elsewhere—are indexed to inflation, and hence will change over time.) The rates are plotted in Figures 13.2(a) and 13.2(b).[4] For comparison, the 1913 federal tax form applicable to individuals, the first one ever needed by U.S. taxpayers, is shown in Figure 13.3. Its relative simplicity is striking and emphasizes the complexity of modern personal income taxation.

Taxes and Inflation

TABLE 13.2
PERSONAL INCOME TAX RATES, 1993

Taxable Income

At Least	But Not More Than	Amount of Taxes
Single Taxpayers:		
$ 0	$ 22,100	$ 0 + 15% of income over $ 0
22,100	53,500	3,315 + 28 of income over 22,100
53,500	115,000	12,107 + 31 of income over 53,500
115,000	250,000	31,172 + 36 of income over 115,000
250,000	. . .	79,772 + 39.6 of income over 250,000
Married Taxpayers Filing Jointly:		
$ 0	$ 36,900	$ 0 + 15% of income over $ 0
36,900	89,150	5,535 + 28 of income over 36,900
89,150	140,000	20,165 + 31 of income over 89,150
140,000	250,000	35,929 + 36 of income over 140,000
250,000	. . .	75,529 + 39.6 of income over 250,000

The top line in each panel of Figure 13.2 shows the marginal tax rate, which was defined earlier when corporate income taxes were discussed. A similar definition applies here: the marginal tax rate is the tax rate an individual would pay on an additional dollar of taxable income. Although this rate is constant over certain ranges of income, it increases as the taxpayer moves to higher taxable income brackets, topping out at 39.6% for income over $250,000 for both individuals and married couples filing jointly. Interestingly, Figure 13.3 indicates that the highest marginal tax rate in 1913 was 6% and was applicable to any income over $500,000 that was earned by individuals.

The lower line in both Figures 13.2(a) and 13.2(b) shows the average tax rate, which was also defined earlier when corporate income taxes were being discussed. Again, a similar definition applies here: the average tax rate is the ratio of total tax paid to total taxable income and is generally smaller than the marginal tax rate. Although the average rate is less than the marginal rate for all levels of income above that specified for the lowest tax bracket of 15%, it becomes very close in size to the top marginal rate of 39.6% as income becomes very high.

Earlier, it was mentioned that for corporations, the marginal tax rate is generally more relevant than the average tax rate in making certain kinds of decisions. This observation is also true for individuals and married couples. For example, consider a married couple with taxable income of $80,000 who are evaluating an investment opportunity that is expected to increase their taxable income by $3,000. This increase in taxable income will result in an increase of $840 (= $3,000 × .28) in taxes, leaving a net increase in spendable income of $2,160 (= $3,000 − $840). The calculations for this particular example are simple because the change in taxable income left the taxpayer in the same bracket. Thus 28% of the additional income will be taxed away, leaving 72% to be spent. The average tax rate before and after the increase is irrelevant to this couple in deciding whether or not to make the investment.

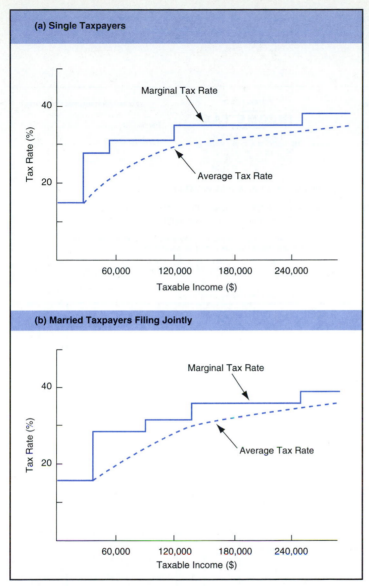

(a) Single Taxpayers

Marginal Tax Rate

Average Tax Rate

Tax Rate (%)

40

20

60,000   120,000   180,000   240,000

Taxable Income ($)

(b) Married Taxpayers Filing Jointly

Marginal Tax Rate

Average Tax Rate

Tax Rate (%)

40

20

60,000   120,000   180,000   240,000

Taxable Income ($)

FIGURE 13.2

Marginal and Average Personal Tax Rates, 1993

When an investment moves income into a higher bracket, the computations are more complex. For example, assume that the opportunity in question would increase the couple's income by $20,000. This increase in taxable income will result in an increase of $5,925.50 [= (.28 × $9,150) + (.31 × $10,850)] in taxes, leaving a net increase in spendable income of $14,074.50 ($20,000 − $5,925.50). Thus 29.63% (= $5,925.50/$20,000) of the additional income will be taxed away, an amount greater than the 28% figure that was applicable to the previous example. As before, average tax rates are irrelevant to the couple in making their decision.

TO BE FILED BY COLLECTOR

List No..........................

..................District of..

Date received...

FORM 1040

INCOME TAX

THE PENALTY
FOR FAILURE TO HAVE THIS RETURN IN
THE HANDS OF THE COLLECTOR OF
INTERNAL REVENUE ON OR BEFORE
MARCH 1 IS $20 TO $1,000
(SEE INSTRUCTIONS ON PAGE 4.)

UNITED STATES INTERNAL REVENUE.

TO BE FILLED IN BY MUNICIPAL COUNTY CLERK

File No..

Assessment List.......................................

Page.................... Line.......................

RETURN OF ANNUAL NET INCOME OF INDIVIDUALS.

(As provided by Act of Congress, approved October 3, 1913.)

RETURN OF NET INCOME RECEIVED OR ACCRUED DURING THE YEAR ENDED DECEMBER 31, 191....
(FOR THE YEAR 1913, FROM MARCH 1. TO DECEMBER 31.)

Filed by (or for) -- of --------------------------------------
(Full name of individual)   (Street and No.)

in the City, Town, or Post Office of -- State of -----------------------------
(Fill in page 2 and 3 before making entries below.)

1. GROSS INCOME (see page 2, line 12) -- $---------------------

2. GENERAL DEDUCTIONS (see page 3, line 7) -- $---------------------

3. NET INCOME -- $---------------------

Deductions and exemptions allowed in computing income subject to the normal tax of 1 percent.

4. Dividends and net earnings received or accrued, of corpora-
   tions, etc. subject to like tax. (See page 2, line 11) ---------- $---------------------

5. Amount of income on which the normal tax has been deducted
   and withheld at the source. (See page 2, line 9, column A) --

6. Specific exemptions of $3,000 or $4,000, as the case may be.
   (See Instructions 3 and 19) ----------------------------------

Total deductions and exemptions. (Items 4,5 and 6).----- $---------------------

7. TAXABLE INCOME on which the normal tax of 1 per cent is to be calculated (See Instruction 3). $---------------------

8. When the net income shown above on line 3 exceeds $20,000, the additional tax thereon must be calculated as per schedule below:

	INCOME	TAX
1 per cent on amount over $20,000 and not exceeding $50,000___	$---------------------	$---------------------
2 " " $50,000 " " $75,000___		
3 " " $75,000 " " $100,000___		
4 " " $100,000 " " $250,000___		
5 " " $250,000 " " $500,000___		
6 " " $500,000___		
Total additional or super tax_____		$---------------------
Total normal tax (1 per cent of amount entered on line 7)__		
Total tax liability_____		

Figure 13.3
1913 Federal Income Tax Form 1040

Tax-exempt Bonds

A major consideration for investors with large taxable incomes is the possibility of obtaining tax-exempt income. The simplest way to accomplish this is to purchase **tax-exempt bonds.** These securities exist because the notion of federalism has been interpreted to imply that the federal government should not tax states and municipalities, nor the income produced from their bonds.[5] Although the legal basis is complex, the facts are simple. Interest income from most bonds issued by states, municipalities, and their agencies need not be included in taxable income in determining the amount of federal taxes that are owed. The benefit for a high-bracket taxpayer is significant.

Consider again the couple in the previous example. Assume that for the same cost they can obtain an increase in taxable income of either $20,000 per year by investing in corporate bonds or $16,000 per year by purchasing tax-exempt bonds. As shown earlier, their effective tax rate on an increase of $20,000 in taxable income would be 29.62%, leaving 70.38% or $14,074.50 to be spent. But all $16,000 in tax-exempt income could be spent—clearly a preferable investment opportunity.

This relationship is no secret. Not surprisingly, tax-exempt bonds offer lower before-tax rates of interest than taxable bonds. Thus they are not attractive for investors with low marginal tax rates. For example, if the couple had a marginal tax rate of 15% instead of 29.62%, they would prefer the corporate bonds. This is because their after-tax return would be $17,000 [= $20,000 × (1 − .15)], an amount greater than the $16,000 provided by the tax-exempt bonds.

If couples with a marginal tax rate of 29.62% find the tax-exempt bonds more attractive, and couples with a marginal tax rate of 15% find the corporate bonds more attractive, then there should be a marginal tax rate in between these two rates that makes couples in that bracket indifferent between the two types of bonds. In this example, if the couple had a marginal tax rate of 20%, they would be indifferent between the corporate bonds and the tax-exempt bonds, because both would provide an after-tax return of $16,000. However, a 20% marginal tax rate does not currently exist. What this means is that couples with rates equal to or greater than the next highest tax rate (28%) would prefer the tax-exempt bonds; couples with rates equal to or less than the next lowest tax rate (15%) would prefer the corporate bonds (unless the additional income from the bond pushed them into the 28% bracket).

The 20% marginal tax rate figure was determined by solving the following equation for t:

$$\$20,000 \times (1 - t) = \$16,000.$$

More generally, the marginal tax rate that makes an investor indifferent between a taxable and a tax-exempt investment can be arrived at by solving the following equation for t:

$$\text{taxable bond yield} \times (1 - t) = \text{tax-exempt bond yield} \qquad (13.1a)$$

or:

$$1 - t = \text{tax-exempt bond yield/taxable bond yield} \qquad (13.1b)$$

---

or:

$$t = 1 - \text{ratio of tax-exempt to taxable bond yields.} \qquad (13.1c)$$

Figure 13.4 shows the ratio, over time, of the yield-to-maturity for a group of tax-exempt bonds issued by municipalities to that of a group of taxable bonds issued by public utilities.[6] On this basis, tax-exempt bonds appear to be competitive with taxable bonds for investors subject to marginal tax rates between 20% (when the ratio of bond yields is 80%) and 40% (when the ratio of bond yields is 60%). For those wealthy enough to be considering investments that provide income subject to the higher ranges, tax-exempt bonds are well worth investigation. Less wealthy investors are likely to find them unattractive.

Capital Gains and Losses

The provisions of the personal income tax laws that deal with the treatment of capital gains and losses have had a great impact on investor behavior. Only the basic elements of these provisions can be described here. Complete understanding of the details would require an effort sufficient to keep many lawyers, tax accountants, and investment advisors busy.

A change in the market value of a capital asset is not relevant for tax purposes until it is **realized** as a **capital gain** (or loss) by sale or exchange. If a security purchased for $50 appreciates to a value of $100 in a year, no tax is due on the **unrealized capital gain.** But if it is sold for $120 two years after purchase, the

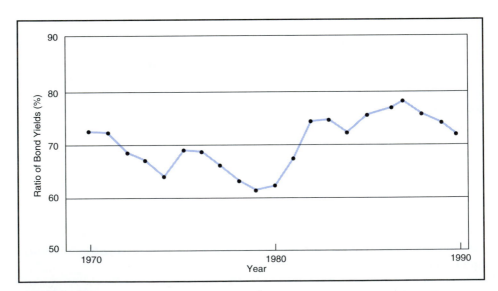

FIGURE 13.4

Ratio of Prime Long-Term Municipal Bond Yield to New Aa Long-Term Public Utility Bond Yield, 1970–1990

Source: Adapted from *Analytical Record of Yields and Yield Spreads,* Salomon Brothers Inc., various issues, Part III, Table 4.

difference of $70 must be declared as capital gains realized at the time of sale, and tax must be paid at the rate applicable to it.

This rule makes the end of the year an interesting time for stockbrokers. Depending on their situations, taxpayers may be either eager or reluctant to realize capital gains or losses before a new tax year begins. Consider, for example, a taxpayer who earlier in the year had sold 1,000 shares of stock A for $50 per share, having purchased it three years ago for $20 per share. This investor has a capital gain of $30,000 [= 1,000 × ($50 − $20)] and will have to pay taxes on this gain if nothing is done. However, it is now December, and the investor currently owns 1,000 shares of stock B, which is selling for $65 per share. Having purchased it four years ago for $95 per share, the investor has an unrealized loss of $30,000 [= 1,000 × ($65 − $95)] on the investment in B. Nevertheless, the investor believes that stock B will rebound in the near future and, hence, wants to continue owning it. It might seem at first glance that the investor should sell B on December 31 and then buy it back January 1, thereby establishing a capital loss of $30,000 on B to offset the capital gain on A. This would remove the tax liability associated with the investor's gain on A, while essentially maintaining his or her position in B. However, the same stock cannot be bought and sold simultaneously in such tax exchanges. This is because the tax laws preclude a deduction associated with a loss on a **wash sale** where a security is sold and a "substantially identical" one is bought within 30 days.

Brokerage firms publish lists pairing similar stocks for those investors who wish to sell a particular stock for tax purposes. By selling a stock and simultaneously purchasing the matching stock, the investor may be able to continually maintain a portfolio with similar investment characteristics. In the previous example, a brokerage firm may have stocks B and C matched together. These two stocks have different issuers but may be in the same industry and, in the opinion of the brokerage firm, be poised for a similar rebound next year. Accordingly, the investor might sell B and purchase C.

End-of-year sales and purchases motivated by tax considerations are fairly common. At this time, securities that experienced substantial price changes during the year tend to have large numbers of trades as investors sell to realize gains or losses. If buyers recognize that the sellers are motivated by knowledge of the tax laws, and not some previously unrecognized bad news affecting the company in question, such "selling pressure" should not seriously depress the company's stock price.

Capital gains and losses are, of course, those realized on capital assets, but the regulations define capital assets rather narrowly. Capital assets include all kinds of property, except that held in conjunction with the taxpayer's trade or business (for example, inventories). Gains or losses on property that is an integral part of a taxpayer's business are considered regular income. Gains on the sale of one's personal residence are capital gains, but, owing to special provisions in the tax law, some gains on property held only to rent to others may be considered income.[7] Pro rata appreciation of a fixed-income security issued at a significant discount (for example, a 90-day Treasury bill) may also be considered income, as it is more like interest than capital gains.

The capital gain or loss realized when an asset is sold or exchanged is the difference between the value received and the asset's *basis*. For an asset purchased outright, the (initial) basis is equal to the actual cost of the asset. For an asset received as a gift or inheritance, the recipient's basis may be the donor's adjusted basis or the value at the time of receipt, depending on the relationship between the two and the value at the time of the sale. Gains and losses are categorized as *short-term* if the asset is held for a year or less and *long-term* if the asset is held for more than a year.

While an asset is held, improvements may be made and their cost added to the basis. On the other hand, any return of capital must be deducted from the basis, as must depreciation. The basis is adjusted to account for such changes. The accounting required can become rather complicated. For example, if an investor buys 100 shares at $40 each, then buys another 100 at $50, and later sells 100 shares at $60, what is the realized capital gain? If the two round lots had been kept separate and only the shares that cost the higher amount were sold, the gain is $10 per share. This is the preferred alternative, because it minimizes current tax outlays. If, however, adequate identification of the lots is not possible, regulations require first-in, first-out (FIFO) accounting, which would place the basis at $40 per share and the gain at $20 per share.

The ability to control the realization of capital gains and losses has a number of obvious advantages. Most important, tax can be paid at the most opportune time. The clearest case involves the realization of capital gains around the time of retirement. Shortly before retirement is usually a time when the taxpayer's income is relatively high, which in turn means that the taxpayer's marginal tax rate is relatively high. After retirement the taxpayer's income and, in turn, marginal tax rate are usually substantially lower. Accordingly, it is generally advantageous for the taxpayer who is near retirement to wait until after retirement to realize any capital gains.

The tax treatment of capital gains begins by bringing all short-term capital gains and losses together to obtain either a net short-term capital gain or a loss. Similarly, all long-term gains and losses are brought together to obtain either a net long-term capital gain or a loss. Finally, all gains and losses are brought together to obtain a net aggregate capital gain or loss. Having made these calculations, the taxpayer will fall into one of the following categories and will be taxed as indicated:

1. Net aggregate capital gain attributable to net short-term capital gains being greater than net long-term capital losses.

   Taxation: The aggregate gain is taxed as ordinary income.

2. Net aggregate capital gain attributable to net short-term capital losses being less than net long-term capital gains.

   Taxation: The aggregate gain is taxed as ordinary income, subject to a maximum rate of 28%.

3. Net aggregate capital gain attributable to having both net short-term capital gains and net long-term capital gains.

Taxation: Both the net short-term capital gains and the net long-term capital gains are taxed as ordinary income, but the net long-term capital gains are subject to a maximum rate of 28%.

4. Net aggregate capital loss attributable to having either (a) both net short-term capital losses and long-term capital losses or (b) net short-term capital losses being greater than net long-term capital gains or (c) net short-term capital gains being less than net long-term capital losses.

Taxation: Under any of these circumstances, if the aggregate loss is less than or equal to $3,000, then the entire amount may be deducted from the taxpayer's ordinary income this year. Any excess over $3,000 can in future years be deducted from ordinary income or used to offset capital gains.

As an example, assume that Mr. and Mrs. Smith have taxable income of $300,000, which includes $40,000 of net aggregate capital gains. Their tax bill can be determined by first noting in Table 13.2 that their marginal tax rate appears to be 39.6%. Because this is greater than 28%, their tax bill can be calculated by taking advantage of the 28% maximum tax rate on capital gains, provided that they have at least $40,000 of net long-term capital gains. There are three cases to consider.

In case 1, the $40,000 was determined by aggregating a net short-term capital gain and a net long-term capital loss (such as $60,000 and $20,000, respectively), causing the full $300,000 to be treated as ordinary income. Hence the resulting tax bill is $95,329 [= $75,529 + .396 × ($300,000 − $250,000)], and the net capital gain is taxed at a rate of 39.6%. Hence the couple is unable to take advantage of the lower 28% capital gains tax rate.

In case 2, the $40,000 was determined by aggregating a net short-term capital loss and a net long-term capital gain (such as $10,000 and $50,000, respectively). Note from Table 13.2 that their taxable income before net aggregate capital gain is equal to $260,000 (= $300,000 − $40,000) and will be subject to taxes amounting to $79,489 [= $75,529 + .396 × ($260,000 − $250,000)]. The net aggregate capital gain will be subject to a rate of 28%, resulting in taxes amounting to $11,200 (= .28 × $40,000). Hence the Smiths' total tax bill comes to $90,689 (= $79,489 + $11,200).

In case 3, the $40,000 was determined by aggregating a net short-term capital gain and a net long-term capital gain (such as $20,000 each). The Smiths' taxable income before the net long-term capital gain is equal to $280,000 (= $300,000 − $20,000) and will be subject to taxes amounting to $87,409 [= $75,529 + .396 × ($280,000 − $250,000)]. The net long-term capital gain will be subject to a rate of 28%, resulting in taxes amounting to $5,600 (= .28 × $20,000). Hence the Smiths' total tax bill comes to $93,009 (= $87,409 + $5,600).

In summary, note that the tax bill of the Smiths is different for the three cases. It amounts to either $95,329 or $90,689 or $93,009, depending upon how the net aggregate capital gain of $40,000 was determined. The best situation from the Smiths' viewpoint is if it is due entirely to a net long-term capital gain (the tax bill would thus be minimized at $90,689), whereas the worst situation is if it is due entirely to a net short-term capital gain (the tax bill would thus be maximized at $95,329).

State Income Taxes

Most states levy personal income taxes, following a format similar to that of the federal government. Although lower, state taxes are also likely to be progressive. The impact of these taxes is not quite as large as it might first appear, because income taxes paid to state governments may be deducted from income before computing federal income tax. For example, consider an investor whose marginal rates for state and federal income taxes are 10% and 31%, respectively. Assume in this example that federal taxes are not deductible in computing state taxes. An additional $100 of income will result in $10 of state tax. This leaves $90 subject to federal income tax, thereby increasing the investor's federal income taxes by $27.90. Overall, $37.90 will be taxed away, giving an effective combined marginal rate of 37.9%. More generally:

$$\text{combined marginal tax rate} = s + (1 - s)f \qquad (13.2)$$

where s and f denote the marginal state and federal tax rates, respectively.

The situation becomes a bit more complicated if the state allows the taxpayer to deduct the amount of federal taxes paid in determining the amount of taxable income. In this situation there is **cross-deductibility,** because state taxes are deductible for federal tax purposes and federal taxes are deductible for state tax purposes. Now, using the previous $100 example, $7.12 $\{= \$100 \times [.1 - (.1 \times .31)]/[1 - (.1 \times .31)]\}$ will be paid in state income taxes, and $28.79 $\{= \$100 \times [.31 - (.1 \times .31)]/[1 - (.1 \times .31)]\}$ will be paid in federal income taxes, for a combined total of $35.91. Thus the effective combined marginal tax rate is 35.91%. More generally, the amount of state tax paid per additional dollar earned equals $[s - (s \times f)]/[1 - (s \times f)]$, and the corresponding amount of federal tax paid equals $[f - (s \times f)]/[1 - (s \times f)]$. Therefore:

$$\text{combined marginal tax rate} = \frac{s + f - (2 \times s \times f)}{1 - (s \times f)}. \qquad (13.3)$$

Another interesting feature of state taxation is that the interest income from bonds issued by municipalities within a state may be exempt from that state's income tax. Some states extend this exemption to include dividends from certain corporations domiciled within the state. Furthermore, cities that levy personal income taxes typically exempt from taxation the interest income on any municipal bonds they have issued. In this situation, the resident of the city who purchases such a bond escapes taxation on three levels—federal, state, and local.

13.1.3 Before-Tax Investing

There are features of the tax code that virtually all investors should consider. Specifically, investors should take advantage of the opportunities available to invest their money on a before-tax basis where, in addition, the income earned on the initial investment grows tax-free. If this is not possible, then they should consider doing just the latter—investing in such a manner that the income earned on the initial investment can grow tax-free.

Two examples can be used to illustrate the point. First, the tax code allows individuals who are self-employed to set aside as much as 25% of their income each year on a before-tax basis, subject to a maximum of $30,000, in what is known as a **Keogh plan** (also known as an H.R. 10 plan). This money can be invested according to the investor's desires and can be withdrawn after the investor reaches an age of 59½ (such withdrawals must begin by the age of 70½; penalties exist if withdrawals do not take place between the ages of 59½ and 70½). The key feature of Keogh plans is that neither the amount invested nor the income earned on this investment is subject to taxation until funds are withdrawn from the plan, at which point the funds are taxed as ordinary income.[8] Hence the investor benefits by deferring the payment of income taxes on both the amount invested and the income earned on the investment until a later date.

The second example is what is known as an **individual retirement account** or IRA, which can be set up by anyone. According to the tax code, an individual who is employed can contribute up to $2,000 per year to an IRA. Hence a married couple with both husband and wife working can set aside $4,000; if only one spouse works, a maximum of $2,250 can be set aside. Although the amount contributed to an IRA comes out of after-tax income (except in special circumstances), the earnings on the investment are allowed to grow without the payment of taxes until withdrawn.[9]

Consider an individual who is thinking about investing $2,000 of gross income in a 20-year bond. This investor is in the 31% marginal tax bracket and anticipates being in it for the rest of his or her life. Bonds currently earn 10% and are anticipated to continue earning this amount indefinitely. If the investor deposits the $2,000 in a Keogh plan, which in turn buys the bonds, it will grow to be worth $13,455 [$= \$2,000 \times (1.10)^{20}$] at the end of 20 years. Assuming that the money is withdrawn at that time, the investor will receive $9,284 [$= \$13,455 \times (1 - .31)$] after taxes.

Alternatively, the investor could consider investing in an IRA, which, in turn, buys the bonds. However, taxes on the $2,000 amounting to $620 ($= \$2,000 \times .31$) must be paid first. Depositing the remaining $1,380 ($= \$2,000 - \$620$) results in the IRA's having a balance of $9,284 [$= \$1,380 \times (1.10)^{20}$] at the end of 20 years. Assuming that the money is withdrawn at that time, the investor will receive $6,815 \{$= \$1,320 + [(\$9,284 - \$1,320) \times (1 - .31)]$\}$ after taxes.

As a basis for comparison, consider what would happen if the investor avoids using either a Keogh plan or an IRA and invests directly in bonds. Doing so means that only $1,380 is available for investment, and that each year the investor will get to keep earnings amounting to only 6.9% [$= 10\% \times (1 - .31)$] of the amount invested. Hence after 20 years the investor will have an amount available after taxes equal to $5,241 [$= \$1,380 \times (1.069)^{20}$].

In summary, the after-tax payoffs for the three alternatives discussed are:

Keogh plan:	$9,284
IRA:	6,815
Direct investment:	5,241

Note that the Keogh plan and the IRA provide the investor with 77% and 30% more money after taxes, respectively, than could be earned by investing directly. Another way to view these payoffs is to note that the direct investment would have to earn 14.5% before taxes in order to provide the same after-tax payoff provided by investing in a Keogh plan that earns 10%. Similarly, the direct investment would have to earn 12% before taxes in order to provide the same after-tax payoff provided by the IRA. It is no surprise that a popular book on investing advises readers that "one of the best ways to obtain extra investment funds is to avoid taxes legally."[10]

13.2 INFLATION IN THE UNITED STATES

The story is told of the modern-day Rip Van Winkle, who awoke in the year 2050 and immediately called his broker. (Fortunately, pay phones at the time permitted a call of up to three minutes without charge.) He first asked what had happened to the $10,000 he had instructed the broker to put in short-term Treasury bills, continually reinvesting the proceeds. The broker promptly informed him that due to high interest rates and the power of compounding, his initial $10,000 investment had grown to be worth over $1 million. Stunned, Mr. Van Winkle inquired about his stocks, which were also worth about $10,000 when he dozed off. The broker told him that he was in for an even more pleasant surprise: they were now worth $2.5 million. "In short, Mr. Van Winkle," said the broker, "you are a millionaire 3.5 times over." At this point an operator cut in: "Your three minutes are over, please deposit $100 for an additional three minutes." While this clearly overstates the case, there is no doubt that inflation is a major concern for investors. By and large, people have come to fear significant inflation, particularly when it is unpredictable.

This section begins by describing how **inflation** is typically measured. Then the benefits and costs of inflation are discussed, along with who gains and who loses when it is present.

13.2.1 Measuring Inflation

There is no completely satisfactory way to summarize the price changes that have occurred over a given time period for the large number of goods and services available in the United States. Nevertheless, the federal government has attempted to do so by measuring the cost of a specific mix of major items (a "basket of goods") at various points in time. The "overall" price level computed for this representative combination of items is termed a **cost-of-living index.** The percentage change in this index over a given time period can then be viewed as a measure of the inflation (or deflation) that took place from the beginning of the period to the end of the period.

Whether or not this measure of inflation is relevant for a given individual depends to a major extent on the similarity of his or her purchases to the mix of items used to construct the index. Even if an individual finds the mix to be appropriate at the beginning of a period, the rate of increase in the price of the mix over the time period is likely to overstate the increase in the cost of living for the individual. There are two reasons for this. First, improvements in the quality of the items in the mix are seldom taken adequately into account. This means the end-

Taxing Pension Funds

The battle over reducing the federal budget deficit continues unabated. Despite much political rhetoric and the large 1993 tax increases and spending cuts, many economists expect the government's budget deficit to remain above $200 billion and continue to grow for the foreseeable future.

Further expenditure reductions seem unlikely as politicians make few friends by chopping favored programs. Although additional tax increases may be more palatable, the choice of targets for those increases will be a volatile issue. The well-to-do were tapped for the 1993 increases, leaving politicians the unpleasant task of asking middle-class voters to pay more. What is a desperate politician to do?

One of the last unexploited sources of significant tax revenue is pension plans. Currently, private and public pension plans hold over $3 trillion in assets. Virtually all of those pension plans conform to specific government regulations and as a result are "qualified." These qualified pension plans offer their sponsors and participants several important tax advantages:

1. Employers may treat pension fund contributions as tax-deductible expenses.
2. Employees defer paying taxes on contributions that their employers make to the pension funds on their behalf.
3. Pension fund investment earnings are not taxed until they are withdrawn.

Under present laws, employers (and in some cases employees) make tax-deductible contributions to a pension plan to prefund pension benefits that are to be paid upon employees' subsequent retirements. These employer contributions clearly represent a form of income to employees. After all, employers could just as easily increase the employees' paychecks by the amount of the contributions and let the employees invest those dollars for themselves. Moreover, this income is invested and grows untaxed over the employees' working lives. Eventually the employees pay taxes on their invested pension contributions, but not until they receive their pension benefits during their retirement years.

This tax-advantaged status of pension funds is quite valuable. The U.S. Treasury estimates that the exclusion of pension contributions and plan earnings from taxation results in an annual loss to government coffers of over $50 billion. The exclusion of employer contributions from the payroll tax base adds several billion dollars more to this figure. These lost taxes constitute the largest single source of forgone revenues experienced by the federal government and considerably exceed the losses associated with such higher profile tax subsidies as mortgage interest deductions, accelerated depreciation, and exclusion of employer contributions for medical insurance.

Proponents of taxing pension plans contend that the costs of exempting pension plans from taxation far exceed the benefits (for example, Alicia Munnell, "Current Taxation of Qualified Pension Plans: Has the Time Come?" *New England Economic Review*, March/April 1992). Their primary argument is that pension funds do not increase national savings significantly. This contention may seem counterintuitive at first. After all, annual contributions to U.S. pension plans total roughly $150 billion. For a nation with a puny personal savings rate of under 5%, this $150 billion would seem to be an important source of funds for investment. But pension fund taxation proponents believe that employees save less outside of their pension funds because of their savings accumulated inside the pension funds. That is, pension savings offset other personal savings. Proponents estimate that this offset, while not dollar-for-dollar, effectively reduces net savings from pension plans to "only" about $50 billion per year (see the Munnell article)—roughly the same amount as the Treasury forgoes in lost tax revenues each year.

Taxation proponents also contend that exempting pension funds from taxation violates fundamental tax fairness principles. Not quite half of the U.S. working population is covered by pension plans. Moreover, those persons covered tend to be in the higher income categories. Further, as these higher income persons are subject to higher marginal tax rates, the benefit of tax-exempt pension funds is greatest for them.

Most proposals to tax pension funds involve levying a tax on each pension plan expressed as a percentage of the plan's annual contributions and investment earnings. Benefits would then not be subject to tax. As a transition to the tax scheme, a one-time tax on the plans' assets would be charged, thus taxing employees who have already accrued benefits tax-free.

Opponents of taxing pension funds contend that pension savings are a critical source of total U.S. savings. They take issue with the crowding-out theory of taxation proponents. That theory is difficult to substantiate empirically, and the crowding-out effect may be much less than proponents contend.

Moreover, even if some personal savings are crowded out by pension savings, adding $50 billion or more to U.S. savings represents roughly one-quarter of the country's annual personal savings. As savings ultimately have a multiplier effect on national income, accepting a $1 revenue loss for $1 of additional savings may be a sound long-term trade-off.

As for the equity issue, taxation opponents point out that higher income persons in all economies always provide the bulk of the economies' savings. It may be unrealistic and counterproductive to add to the existing disincentives to save in the name of wealth equity.

Opponents also point to the technical difficulties of taxing pension plans. Over one-third of pension assets are held by state and local pension plans. Constitutionally, it may be difficult to tax those plans. Even if it can be accomplished, cash-strapped state and local governments may respond to taxation by lowering their contributions to pension plans—surely an undesirable outcome.

Taxation of pension funds, if and when it ever occurs, may not take the form of radical legislation. Rather, it may begin with seemingly innocuous dips into pension fund coffers. In recent years, for example, taxes on pension fund holdings of foreign securities above a certain threshold have been proposed. Also discussed have been taxes on pension funds' security transactions as well as on their short-term capital gains.

of-period price for a good is not comparable to the beginning-of-period price, because the good is different. For example, a new Toyota may have a 5% higher sticker price than a similar model had the previous year, but the newer model may have better tires on it than the older model. Hence it would be inaccurate to conclude that the price of this particular model rose by 5% over the year.

Second, and perhaps more important, little or no adjustment is made in the mix as relative prices change. The rational customer can reduce the cost of attaining a given standard of living as prices change by substituting relatively less expensive goods for those that have become relatively more expensive. For example, if the price of beef rises 20% over a given year while the price of chicken rises only 10% over the same year, then the customer may start to eat more chicken and less beef. Failure to take into account this change in the mix will result in an overstatement in the rate of inflation. Despite these two drawbacks, cost-of-living indices provide at least rough estimates of changes in prices.

13.2.2 Price Indices

Most governments compute a number of alternative price indices in order to provide a wider choice for analysis. Nevertheless, many people tend to focus on one index as an indicator of the price level. In the United States the **Consumer**

Price Index (CPI) often fills this role, despite some attempts by government officials to discourage such widespread use.[11] Recognizing its importance, the composition of the market basket of goods used to make up the CPI has been changed from time to time in order to provide a more representative basket. Furthermore, the process by which the relevant data is gathered and verified has periodically been improved. Currently it is calculated monthly by the Bureau of Labor Statistics in the U.S. Department of Commerce.

In Chapter 1, Table 1.1 provided some historical perspective on the rate of inflation in the United States. It showed the annual rate of increase in the CPI from 1926 through 1993. As an aid to interpretation, these rates are plotted on a graph shown in panel (a) of Figure 13.5. As can be seen in the figure, the CPI did not grow at a constant rate over the period of 1926 to 1993. Following the substantial deflation from 1926 to 1933, prices increased in almost every year. Generally speaking, there were four subperiods with different rates of inflation: mild (but notably uneven) inflation from 1934 to 1952, negligible inflation from 1953 to 1965, and fairly rapid (but somewhat uneven) inflation from 1966 to 1981, followed again by mild inflation from 1982 to 1993.

Table 13.3 shows the average annual rate of growth of the CPI for each of these subperiods, measured by what is known as the **geometric mean** growth rate of the CPI. This growth rate, when compounded over the subperiod and applied to the beginning index value, results in the ending index value. For example, at the end of 1965 the CPI was 95.5, and at the end of 1981 it was at 281.5 (here the CPI is adjusted so that its value in 1967 was 100). Thus the geometric mean growth rate was 7.0%, because 95.5, when compounded at this rate over 16 years, equals 281.5:

$$281.5 = 95.5 \times (1 + .070)^{16}.$$

More generally, the geometric mean (g) can be calculated by solving the following equation for g:

$$C_e = C_b(1 + g)^y \tag{13.4}$$

which results in

$$g = (C_e/C_b)^{1/y} - 1 \tag{13.5}$$

where y denotes the number of years and C_e and C_b denote the ending and beginning CPI values, respectively.

TABLE 13.3		
GROWTH RATES OF THE U.S. CONSUMER PRICE INDEX		
From	To	Rate of Growth (% Per Year)
1926	1933	−3.8%
1934	1952	3.8
1953	1965	1.4
1966	1981	7.0
1982	1993	3.7

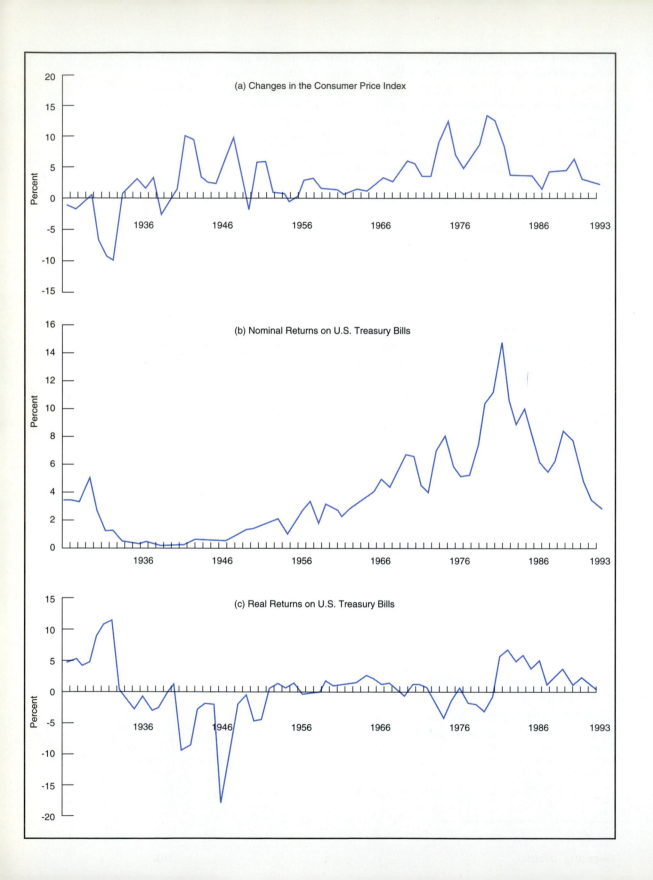

(a) Changes in the Consumer Price Index

(b) Nominal Returns on U.S. Treasury Bills

(c) Real Returns on U.S. Treasury Bills

13.3.1   Nominal Returns

Modern economies gain much of their efficiency through the use of money—a generally agreed-upon medium of exchange. Instead of trading corn for a stereo to be delivered in one year, as in a barter economy, the citizen of a modern economy can trade his or her corn for money, then trade this "current" money for "future" money by investing it. Later, the "future" money can be used to buy a stereo. The rate at which the citizen can trade "current" money for "future" money depends on the investment he or she makes and is known as the **nominal return** (also known as the nominal rate).

13.3.2   Fisher Model of Real Returns

In times of changing prices, the nominal return on an investment may be a poor indicator of the **real return** (also known as the real rate) obtained by the investor.[12] This is because part of the additional dollars received from the investment may be needed to recoup the investor's lost purchasing power due to inflation that has occurred over the investment period. As a result, adjustments to the nominal return are needed to remove the effect of inflation in order to determine the real return. Frequently, the CPI is used for this purpose.

For example, assume that at the start of a given year the CPI is at a level of 121, and that at the end of the year it is at a level of 124. This means that it costs $124 at the end of the year to buy the same amount of the CPI market basket of goods that at the start of the year could have been purchased for $121. Assuming that the nominal return is 8% for this year, the investor who started the year with $121 and invested it would have $121 × 1.08 = $130.68 at year-end. At this point, the investor could purchase ($130.68/$124) − 1 = .0539 = 5.39% more of the CPI market basket of goods than at the beginning of the year. Thus the real return for this investment was 5.39%.

These calculations can be summarized in the following formula:

$$[C_0 \times (1 + NR)/C_1] - 1 = RR \qquad (13.6)$$

where:

C_0 = *CPI at the beginning of the year,*
C_1 = *CPI at the end of the year,*
NR = *the nominal return for the year,*
RR = *the real return for the year.*

FIGURE 13.5

Nominal and Real Returns on Short-Term Default-Free Investments, 12-Month Periods Ending in December, From 1926 to 1993

Source: *Stocks, Bonds, Bills, and Inflation 1994 Yearbook* (Chicago Ibbotson Associates: 1994). All rights reserved.

Alternatively, the citizen could note that an increase in the CPI from 121 to 124 can be translated into an inflation rate of $(124/121) - 1 = .0248$ or 2.48%. Denoting this inflation rate as IR, the real return can be calculated using the following formula, known as the Fisher model:[13]

$$[(1 + NR)/(1 + IR)] - 1 = RR. \qquad (13.7)$$

Note that for the example, $RR = (1.08/1.0248) - 1 = .0539$ or 5.39%.

For quick calculation involving the Fisher model, the real return can be estimated by simply subtracting the inflation rate from the nominal return:

$$NR - IR \cong RR \qquad (13.8)$$

where $\cong$ means "is approximately equal to." In this example, the "quick method" results in an estimate of the real return of $.08 - .0248 = .0552$ or 5.52%. Thus the error resulting from use of this method is $.0552 - .0539 = .0013$ or .13%.[14]

13.3.3 The Effect of Investor Expectations

The simplest view of investors' attitudes toward inflation is that they are concerned with real returns, not nominal returns, and that a single price index is adequate to characterize the difference. Looking to the future, investors do not know what the rate of inflation will be, nor do they know what the nominal return on an investment will be. However, in both cases they have expectations about what these figures will be, which are denoted as EIR (expected inflation rate) and ENR (expected nominal return), respectively. Thus the Fisher model implies that ERR (the expected real return on an investment) can be approximated by:

$$ERR \cong ENR - EIR. \qquad (13.9)$$

If a security is to provide a given expected real return, the expected nominal return must be larger by the expected rate of inflation for the relevant holding period. This can be seen by rearranging Equation (13.9):

$$ENR \cong ERR + EIR. \qquad (13.10)$$

For example, if the expected rate of inflation is 4% and a given security is to provide investors with an expected real return of 6%, then the security must be priced in the marketplace so that its expected nominal return is approximately 10%. Furthermore, if the expected real rate remains constant, then a 1% increase in the expected rate of inflation from 4% to 5% will result in a 1% increase in the expected nominal rate of return from 10% to 11%. In summary, if investors are concerned with real returns, then securities will be priced in the marketplace so that expected nominal returns incorporate the expected rate of inflation.

At the start of a given investment holding period, nominal interest rates for securities having no risk of default should cover both a requisite expected real return and the expected rate of inflation for the period in question. At the end of the period, the real return actually received will be the difference between the nominal return and the rate of inflation actually experienced. Only when actual inflation equals expected inflation will the actual real return equal the expected real return on such securities.

As mentioned earlier, panel (a) of Figure 13.5 indicates the annual rate of inflation, as measured by changes in the Consumer Price Index, over the 68-year time period from 1926 to 1993. Panel (b) shows how short-term nominal interest rates varied over this time period; Treasury bill rates, taken from Table 1.1, are used for this purpose. Panel (c), derived by subtracting panel (a) from panel (b), represents real returns.

One cannot help being struck by the fact that those who invested in short-term securities over this period frequently ended up with less purchasing power than they started with because the real return was negative in 25 of the 68 years. Perhaps even more surprising, the average real return over the period was close to zero.

Although expected real returns may vary from year to year, this variation may be relatively small. If so, investors may have been willing to invest in short-term highly liquid securities even though they expected to earn very little in real terms. If they are currently willing to do so, such securities will be priced to give a very low expected real return.[15]

If this assumption is made, the "market's" predicted rate of inflation over the near future can be estimated by simply subtracting an estimate of the low expected real rate, say 1%, from the nominal interest rate (also known as the yield) on short-term government securities, namely, Treasury bills. In a sense, the resulting figure represents a consensus prediction of inflation—a prediction that an "average" investor in this market would make, and one that is likely to be more accurate over time than the predictions of any single forecaster.

Although deviations of actual inflation from expected inflation may have relatively little effect on the real return on investments in general, they may have a significant effect on specific investments. In fact, one would expect a direct impact on the real returns associated with investments whose payments are fixed in terms of dollars to be received.

A simple example will illustrate the relationship. Assume that everyone currently expects the rate of inflation to be 5% over the next year, and that a lender has agreed to make loans at a nominal rate of 5% (that is, the lender is content with having an expected real return of zero). Thus one can borrow $100 now and pay back one year later \$105 (= \$100 × 1.05) for a one-year loan. Note that if actual inflation equals expected inflation, a one-year loan would require a payment equivalent to \$100 in constant (current) dollars a year hence. In this case, the real rate of interest would turn out to be zero.

Now, imagine that an individual takes advantage of the lender's offer, borrowing \$100 for one year. How will the borrower and lender be affected if the actual rate of inflation differs from the expected rate of inflation?

Assume that in the first year prices rise by 9% instead of the expected 5%, meaning that unexpected inflation is 4% (= 9% − 5%). In this situation, the short-term borrower gains at the expense of the lender. Why? The borrower must still repay \$105, but in terms of constant dollars, this is only \$96.33 (= \$105/1.09), a figure that is less than the amount of the loan. As a result, the lender receives a real rate of interest of − 3.67% [= (\$96.33 − \$100)/\$100], instead of the anticipated rate of 0%.

What if first-year prices had risen by only 3%, meaning that unexpected inflation is − 2% (= 3% − 5%)? In this situation, the short-term lender gains at the expense of the borrower. While the borrower must repay \$105, in terms of constant dollars this amounts to \$101.94 (= \$105/1.03), a figure that is greater than the amount of the loan. As a result, the lender receives a real rate of interest of 1.94% [= (\$101.94 − \$100)/\$100], instead of the anticipated rate of 0%.

These results can be generalized: When the actual rate of inflation exceeds the expected rate of inflation, those with commitments to make payments that are fixed in nominal terms (debtors) gain in real terms at the expense of those to whom payments are to be made (creditors). Conversely, when actual inflation is less than expected inflation, creditors gain and debtors lose.[16] This uncertainty in the real return on fixed-income securities that is due to uncertain inflation is frequently referred to as **purchasing-power risk.**

13.6 INDEXATION

The previous section suggests that in a world of uncertain inflation, even default-free bonds are subject to purchasing-power risk. Contractual nominal interest rates can cover expected inflation, but the subsequent real return from any investment with fixed nominal payments will depend on the actual amount of inflation. As long as the two inflation rates differ, the expected real return will be uncertain. However, there is a way to design a bond so that its expected real return is certain. It involves the use of **indexation.**

If a specified price index can adequately measure purchasing power, there is no reason why a contract cannot be written with specified real payments instead of specified nominal payments. Thus, if the CPI currently stands at C_0, and will be C_1 one year later, C_2 two years later, and so on, in return for a loan of \$100, a borrower might promise to pay amounts that are currently unknown but will be equal to \$10 × C_1 one year later, \$10 × C_2 two years later, . . . , and \$110 × C_{10} ten years later. To convert these payments to constant real dollars, each one must be divided by the corresponding price level:

Adjusting Capital Gains Taxes for Inflation

A look back at recent U.S. taxation of capital gains reveals a picture of vacillating economic and social policies. Tax rates on long-term capital gains (hereafter, simply "capital gains") have fluctuated radically as various political groups and ideologies have come and gone in Washington, D.C. Over the last 20 years, capital gains tax rates on individuals in the highest personal income tax brackets have ranged from a high of 49% in 1977 to a low of 20% in 1982. Currently, capital gains are taxed at a 28% rate, but only the most naive investor would assume that that figure will remain constant for long.

Economists agree that taxing any commodity or activity reduces the output of that commodity or activity. Taxing gains on capital assets, therefore, reduces the amount of capital assets "produced." Other things remaining the same (always a tenuous assumption), lower capital gains tax rates will encourage savings, increase investment, and thus enhance economic productivity. However, as the vast proportion of taxable capital assets is directly or indirectly held by a minority of relatively affluent people, proponents of wealth redistribution view capital gains taxes as symbolic of their effort to create a more egalitarian society.

No particular capital gains tax rate will satisfy all interested groups. The politics of the issue are much too entangled with the economics. Despite this conflict, at least one inequitable aspect of the current capital gains tax structure calls for a remedy: the taxation of returns to capital that merely compensates investors for inflation experienced over the periods in which they hold their capital assets.

Suppose that you purchased a share of *XYZ* Corporation for $100. One year later you sell the stock for $110, giving you a 10% [= ($110 − $100)/$100] before-tax nominal return. With a 28% capital gains tax rate, your after-tax nominal return is 7.2% {=[($110 − $100) − (.28 × $10)]/$100}.

Now assume that the inflation rate was 5% during the year. Presuming that you are concerned with real returns, then you require a 5% return simply to make yourself "whole" in a purchasing power sense. The first 5% of your 10% before-tax nominal return is effectively a return of capital, not a source of profit. Therefore your before-tax real return should be calculated from a base value of $105, not $100, to take into account the 5% inflation rate. Consequently, your before-tax real return is 4.8% [= ($110 − $105)/$105].

However, the government levies capital gains taxes on both the inflation-compensation component of investment returns as well as the real profit component. Therefore your after-tax real return is 2.1% {= [($110 − $105) − (.28 × $10)]/$105}. From another perspective, because your before-tax real profits are $5 and the government has collected $2.80 in capital gains taxes from you, the effective tax rate on your capital gains is 56% (= $2.80/$5), not 28%.

The tax assessed on your capital, as distinguished from the tax imposed on the profits from your capital, is more akin to a property tax than an income tax. Moreover, the level of that tax changes with the inflation rate, producing an arbitrary and capricious tax structure. Over some holding periods, a capital asset's value may actually suffer a decline in real terms, yet inflation boosts its nominal value sufficiently to generate a gain for tax reporting purposes. An investor selling this asset could find himself or herself paying capital gains taxes on an inflation-adjusted capital loss.

The solution to this inequity involves indexing the base value (that is, the original cost) of the capital asset to the inflation rate. The base value is adjusted upward by the inflation rate experienced over the period the capital asset is held. Only gains above this adjusted base are subject to tax.

In our earlier example, the inflation-adjusted base value of *XYZ* common stock after one year is $105 (= $100 × 1.05), so your taxable gain is now $5 instead of $10. Thus your after-tax nominal return is 8.6% {= [($110 − $100) − (.28 × $5)]/$100}. Furthermore, your after-tax real return is 3.4% {= [($110 − $105) − (.28 × $5)]/$105}, for an effective tax rate of 28% (= $1.40/$5).

The fairness and simplicity of adjusting capital gains taxes for inflation seems indisputable. Why has such a proposal not received popular support? Several explanations are plausible. First, in periods of relatively low inflation, such as has been witnessed since the early 1980s, the inflation-compensation component of capital gains is relatively small, making the issue less pressing. Second, in periods of large budget deficits, any cut in taxes, even in the name of equity and increased long-term investment, causes short-term problems. Current government spending would have to be reduced or other taxes increased if the budget deficit were not to grow in the short term due to the effective capital gains tax cut. Finally, if one accepts the argument for adjusting capital gains for inflation, should not the same logic apply to interest income as well? After all, this investment income has its own inflation-compensation component. However, the tax revenue lost over the short term from such a change in the taxation of interest income would far exceed the revenue losses caused by altering the capital gains tax structure.

Time	Amount In Nominal Dollars	Price Level (CPI)	Amount In Real Dollars
1	$10 \times C_1$	C_1	10
2	$10 \times C_2$	C_2	10
.	.	.	.
.	.	.	.
.	.	.	.
10	$110 \times C_{10}$	C_{10}	110

The real value of each payment is the amount shown in the final column, regardless of what happens to prices (that is, regardless of the actual values of C_1, C_2, and so on). Thus the loan is said to be fully indexed, because all amounts are tied to a stated price index on a one-for-one basis. This means that when the price index goes up by 10%, for example, all of the subsequent payments go up by 10%.

In some countries, a great many contracts are tied to standard price indices (two notable examples are Israel and Brazil). Government bonds, returns on savings accounts, wage contracts, pension plans, insurance contracts—all have been indexed at various times and places. In the United States, social security payments are indexed, as are the wages and pension plans of many employees. Some of these are fully indexed, while others are only partially indexed, meaning that, for example, payments might be increased by 7% when the price index increases by 10%.

The key advantage of indexation is its role in reducing or eliminating purchasing-power risk. Typically, higher expected inflation is accompanied by increased uncertainty about the actual rate of inflation. This increased uncertainty means that the potential gains and losses to both nonindexed borrowers and nonindexed lenders are larger. Because both borrowers and lenders dislike the prospect of losses more than they like the prospect of gains, there will be increased pressure for indexation by both borrowers and lenders when a country moves into periods of high inflationary expectations.

Thus when uncertainty about inflation is substantial, one would expect indexation to become widespread. However, laws regulating interest rates may prevent the issuance of fully indexed debt if these laws place a ceiling on the nominal rate but not the real rate. This leads to predictable inefficiencies when expected inflation increases because rationing of credit that is subject to such ceilings is required. Rationing is necessary because a ceiling on the nominal rate means that the real rate declines as inflationary expectations increase, which in turn makes this type of credit attractive to borrowers.[17]

A notable example occurred in the 1970s in the United States. At that time, ceilings placed on nominal rates paid by savings and loan companies, coupled with increased inflationary expectations, caused a substantial outflow of funds from such companies and a corresponding reduction in the amount of money made available by them for home mortgages. On the other side were those issuers of securities that were not subject to rate ceilings and that offered an appropriate nominal rate and, thus, had little difficulty in attracting funds. The term **disintermediation** was invented to describe this pattern of funds flow.

Because inflation is generally harder to predict for longer time periods, uncertainty about inflation often leads to a reduction in the average term-to-maturity of newly issued fixed-income securities. For example, the average term-to-maturity of fixed-coupon debt issued in periods of great inflationary uncertainty is usually shorter than in more stable times.

Alternatively, debt with long maturities can be written with **variable rates** (also known as floating rates) of interest. Such instruments provide long-term debt at short-term rates. Interest payments are allowed to vary, with each one determined by adding a fixed number of percentage points (say, 2%) to a specified base rate that changes periodically. Two base rates frequently used are the prime rate and the yield on 90-day U.S. Treasury bills. If short-term interest rates anticipate inflation reasonably well, such a variable-rate security is an effective substitute for a fully indexed bond.

13.7 STOCK RETURNS AND INFLATION

13.7.1 Long-Term Historical Relationships

It is reasonable to assume that investors are more concerned with real returns than with nominal returns because real returns reflect how much better off they are after adjusting for inflation. Accordingly, real returns of securities need to be analyzed. This is done in Table 13.4 for common stocks and Treasury bills for the long-term period of 1802 to 1993 and five relatively long subperiods.

Column (2) of the table shows that, on average, the rate of return on common stocks has substantially exceeded the rate of inflation, providing a real return of nearly 8% for the entire period examined and in excess of 7% in all of the subperiods. In comparison, the rate of return on Treasury bills exceeded the rate of inflation by over 3% in the entire period. However, the subperiods show substantial variation, as the real return ranged from .49% over the period from 1926 to 1993 to 5.62% in the period from 1802 to 1888.

Also of interest is the **equity premium** shown in column (4), which is simply the difference between the real rate of return on stocks and bills. Although less than 2% from 1802 to 1888, it has since then been nearly 7%, an amount that some researchers believe is inexplicably large. In summary, Table 13.4 shows that

TABLE 13.4
RATES OF RETURN ON STOCKS, BILLS AND THE EQUITY PREMIUM

Period (1)	Real Return On Stocks (2)	Real Return On Bills (3)	Equity Premium (2) − (3) = (4)
1802-1990[1]	**7.81%**	**3.19%**	**4.62%**
1802–1888[1]	7.52	5.62	1.90
1889–1978[1]	7.87	.91	6.96
1979–1990[1]	9.44	2.73	6.71
1926–1993[2]	9.09	.49	8.60
1950–1993[2]	9.29	.92	8.37

[1] **Source:** Andrew B. Abel, "The Equity Premium Puzzle," *Federal Reserve Bank of Philadelphia Business Review* (September-October 1991), p. 8.
[2] **Source:** Table 1.1.

common stocks have historically returned substantially more than the rate of inflation and Treasury bills. That is, in the long run, common stocks have had a large positive real return.

13.7.2 Short-Term Historical Relationships

Another interesting question to investigate is the relationship between the short-term rate of return on stocks and the rate of inflation. Conventional wisdom suggests that stock returns should be relatively high when inflation is relatively high and relatively low when inflation is relatively low. Why? Because stocks represent claims on real assets that should increase in value with inflation.

Figure 13.6 displays the relationship between annual stock returns and rates of inflation for the period from 1926 to 1993. The figure shows that there is no discernible relationship between the rate of inflation and stock returns. Indeed, the correlation coefficient between these two variables is − .02, which for all practical purposes is equal to zero and indicates that there is no significant statistical relationship between the rate of inflation and stock returns.[18] That is, when inflation is relatively high, there is no tendency for stock returns to be either relatively high or low. Similarly, when inflation is relatively low, there is no tendency for stock returns to be either relatively high or low.[19] Accordingly, stocks are not good hedges against inflation in the short term.

13.7.3 Relationships Involving Expected Inflation

The previous results used historical (or *ex post*) rates of inflation and stock returns. Also of interest are tests of the relationship between expected (or *ex ante*) rates of inflation and stock returns. For example, if expected inflation for the forthcoming year is relatively high, what effect does that have on stock returns over the forthcoming year?

One recent study explored this relationship by using time horizons of one and five years.[20] The major difficulty in performing such a test is that expected inflation rates are not observable—only subsequent actual inflation rates are observed. This was overcome by constructing and testing four models for arriving

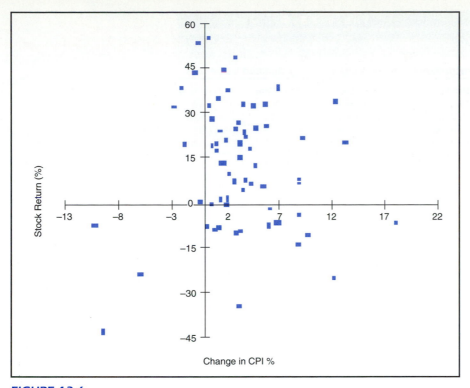

FIGURE 13.6

Annual Stock Returns and Rates of Inflation (1926–1993)

Source: *Stocks, Bonds, Bills, and Inflation 1994 Yearbook* (Chicago Ibbotson Associates: 1994). All rights reserved.

at estimates of expected inflation. These models used past inflation rates and interest rates as "instrumental variables" to estimate expected inflation.

To simplify, the tests involved the following model:

$$r_t = \alpha + \beta\pi_t + e_t \tag{13.11}$$

where r_t and π_t denote, respectively, the rate of return on stocks and the expected inflation rate over time period t. In this equation the variable of interest is the
coefficient β. If there is a one-for-one relationship between expected inflation
and stock returns, then the estimated value of β will be approximately equal to
1.0. In such a situation, an increase of 1% in the expected inflation rate would
result in a 1% increase in stock returns, indicating that the Fisher model is appropriate when stated in terms of expectations.

Equation (13.11) was first tested using one-year stock returns and inflation
rates from 1802 to 1990 and then tested again using overlapping five-year returns and rates.[21] Table 13.5 presents the results. In two of the four cases involving one-year expectations, the value of β appears to be significantly less than 1.0.
This suggests that, in the short term, stock returns do not respond to changes in
expected rates of inflation. However, in all four cases involving five-year expectations, the value of β is not significantly different from 1.0, suggesting that stock
returns do respond to changes in expected rates of inflation over long horizons.

TABLE 13.5

TESTING THE RELATIONSHIP BETWEEN EXPECTED INFLATION RATES AND STOCK RETURNS, 1802–1990

Instrumental Variables Used		Estimated Value of β	
One-Year	**Five-Year**	**One-Year**	**Five-Year**
ST int rates	LT int rates	−2.781	1.394
ST inf rates	LT inf rates	−.048*	1.820
ST int rates	ST, LT int rates	−2.531	2.072
ST inf rates	ST, LT int rates	.061*	.380

Notes: ST = past year; LT = past five years; int = interest; inf = inflation.
*Denotes number is significantly different from 1.0 at .10 level of significance.
Source: Jacob Boudoukh and Matthew Richardson, "Stock Returns and Inflation: A Long-Horizon Perspective," *American Economic Review*, 83, no. 5 (December 1993): 1352.

Hence the Fisher model appears to be validated when applied over long horizons but not when applied over short horizons.[22] That is, there appears to be a positive relation between expected rates of inflation and stock returns over long periods of time but not over short periods. These findings are consistent with those observed when actual rates of inflation were compared with stock returns.

13.8 SUMMARY

1. Because investors concern themselves with after-tax returns, federal and state tax laws play a major role in the way securities are priced.
2. Income earned by a corporation may be taxed twice—once when it is earned, via the corporate income tax, and again when it is received as dividends by the stockholders, via the personal income tax.
3. In the case of both individuals and corporations, the marginal tax rate is more relevant than the average tax rate for making investment decisions.
4. Tax-exempt bonds generally pay lower interest rates than equivalent-risk taxable bonds. Comparable tax-exempt and taxable bonds should be evaluated on an after-tax basis.
5. The calculation of capital gains taxes involves netting all short-term gains and losses; netting all long-term gains and losses; and netting short-term net gains (losses) against long-term net gains (losses). The outcome of these computations determines how an investor's capital gains are taxed.
6. Because state taxes are deductible on a federal level and vice versa for some states, the combined marginal tax rate is not the sum of the state and federal marginal tax rates.
7. Some tax shelters, such as Keogh plans and IRAs, permit the deferment of taxes on the investor's wage income and investment earnings.
8. Inflation measures the percentage change in a specific cost-of-living index at various points in time.

9. Whether a measure of inflation is relevant for a given individual depends to a large extent on the similarity of his or her purchases to the composition of the price index.

10. An investor's real return is a function of the difference between the investor's nominal return and the inflation rate.

11. Real returns are important to an investor because they represent how much the investor's purchasing power has increased (or decreased) and thus how much better (or worse) off the investor is.

12. If investors are concerned with real returns, securities will be priced so that expected nominal returns incorporate the expected inflation rate.

13. When the actual inflation rate exceeds the expected inflation rate, debtors gain in real terms at the expense of creditors. The opposite is the case when actual inflation is less than expected inflation.

14. Investment returns can be indexed by tying security payments to changes in the price level. Indexation reduces or removes an investment's purchasing-power risk.

15. Over long periods of time, common stocks have generated large, positive real returns. Treasury bills have produced much lower, but still positive, real returns.

16. Over short periods of time, stock returns are not positively related to either actual or expected rates of inflation. However, over long periods of time, stock returns are positively related to both actual and expected rates of inflation.

QUESTIONS AND PROBLEMS

1. Why is the marginal tax rate more relevant to investment decision-making than the average tax rate?

2. Given the following income tax schedule, draw a graph illustrating the marginal and average tax rates as a function of income level.

Income	Tax Rate
$0 – $10,000	10%
$10,001 – $20,000	13
$20,001 – $30,000	15
$30,001 – $50,000	20
$50,001 and above	25

3. Minneapolis Pipelines pays an annual dividend of $0.80 per share on its preferred stock. The stock currently sells for $12 per share. Maplewood Chemicals is considering investing idle cash in either Minneapolis's preferred stock or a bond yielding 9.8%. If Maplewood's marginal tax rate is 34%, which investment is more attractive?

4. U.S. federal personal income tax rates are progressive in that the marginal tax rate increases with income (see Figure 13.2). What is the justification for this tax structure? Make a case for or against progressive tax rates.

5. Footsie Belardi earned $60,000 last year. Using the single filer tax schedule in Table 13.2, calculate Footsie's income tax.

6. Heine Groh expects consumer prices to rise at a 7% rate next year, and has negotiated a 9.5% pay increase. Given a 35% marginal income tax bracket, will this pay increase cause Heine's real income (that is, purchasing power) to grow? Explain.

7. A corporate bond is selling for $950. It matures in a year, at which time the holder will receive $1,000. In addition, the bond will pay $50 in interest during the year. What would be the after-tax return on the bond to an investor in the 50% marginal income tax bracket? (Assume that capital gains do not receive preferential tax treatment.) What would be the after-tax return if the bond had been a tax-free municipal bond?

8. Consider a tax-exempt municipal bond yielding 6%. To an investor in the following marginal tax brackets, what is the equivalent before-tax interest rate that a taxable bond would have to offer to be considered equivalent to the municipal bond?
   a. 10%
   b. 28%
   c. 33%

9. Spot Bethea must choose between investing in a tax-free municipal bond yielding 5% and a taxable bond yielding 7.5%. Spot's marginal tax rate is 30%. Which bond should Spot choose?

10. Pinky Higgins and spouse had taxable income of $100,000 last year, which includes a net capital gain of $80,000. What is their tax bill if the gain is entirely long-term? What is their tax bill if the gain is entirely short-term? What is their tax bill if the gain is half short-term and half long-term?

11. Pinky Higgins and spouse had taxable income of $100,000 last year, which includes net aggregate capital gains of $20,000. The $20,000 consists of a net short-term capital loss of $5,000 and a net long-term capital gain of $25,000. What is their tax bill?

12. Jean Dubuc lives in a state where the tax schedule lists an 8% marginal tax rate. The federal tax schedule lists a 25% marginal tax rate. Accounting for cross-deductibility:
   a. What is Jean's effective state marginal tax rate?
   b. What is Jean's effective federal marginal tax rate?
   c. What is Jean's effective combined marginal tax rate?

13. Would you expect tax shelters to be as attractive to lower income persons as to higher income persons? Should lower income persons invest in tax shelters at all? Why?

14. Given the following beginning and ending values for a particular price index, and the respective number of years between the measurement of the two values, calculate the annual compounded (geometric mean) inflation rates during the three periods.

Price Index Beginning Value	Price Index Ending Value	Years Covered
100	120	1
120	175	3
175	150	2

15. Calculate the arithmetic (that is, the simple) mean rate of inflation using the data in Table 1.1 for the same time periods given in Table 13.3. What is the relationship between the arithmetic and geometric means?

16. Given the following average compound annual inflation rates, how much would $1 be worth in terms of purchasing power five years from today expressed in today's dollars?
    a. 5%
    b. 10%
    c. 15%

17. Bingo Binks's portfolio earned an 8% average compound annual return over an eight-year period. The average compound annual inflation rate over this time period was 4%. Bingo's portfolio was worth $15,000 at the beginning of the period. At the end of the period, what was the portfolio worth expressed in beginning-of-period dollars?

18. Kirby Higbe started the year with investments valued at $11,500. At the end of two years those same investments were worth $16,000. During the same time period the price index rose from 210 to 250. What was Kirby's annual real rate of return over the two-year period?

19. How are economywide inflation rates calculated? Are all consumers affected equally by the increase in overall prices measured by the price index? Explain.

20. Assume that your portfolio grows 9% in value per year and annual inflation is 5%. How many years will it take for the nominal value of your portfolio to triple? How many years will it take for the real value of your portfolio to triple?

21. Why is it reasonable to assume that rational investors will build an expected inflation premium into the returns they require from their investments?

22. In the late 1970s and early 1980s, a period of unexpectedly high inflation, Happy Felsch referred to long-term bonds issued by U.S. corporations and the Treasury as "certificates of confiscation." Why would Happy make such a comment?

23. Also in the late 1970s and early 1980s, there was considerable discussion concerning the "quality" of corporate earnings. Straight-line depreciation and the FIFO inventory valuation methods were often cited as the causes of "poor quality" earnings. Further, it was argued that these accounting methods effectively resulted in tax overpayments. Discuss the reasons for both contentions.

24. From the perspective of after-tax returns, what is the problem with fully inflation-indexed securities?

25. Explain why the returns on bonds are found to be negatively correlated with unexpected inflation. Why does this relationship become progressively more negative as one considers longer-lived bonds?

26. Common stocks, in general, do not appear to be effective hedges against either expected or unexpected short-run inflation. Explain why the stocks of some companies might be better hedges against inflation than others.

---

¹ Certain corporations with 35 or fewer shareholders may elect to be treated as partnerships for tax purposes. Such firms, often called "Subchapter S corporations" (after the enabling provision of the Internal Revenue Code), constitute an exception to the general rule.

² This assumes that the corporate investor owns between 20% and 80% of the stock of the firm issuing the dividends. If less than 20% is owned, than only 70% of the dividends are excluded from income. If 80% or more is owned, then 100% of the dividend is excluded.

³ *1988 Federal Tax Course* (Englewood Cliffs, NJ: Prentice Hall, 1987): 89.

⁴ Some subtle yet complicated changes made in 1990 and 1993 cause the tax rate schedules to be slightly different from what is shown here.

⁵ Chapter 14 describes various types of bonds that are available for investment and gives a more detailed discussion of how they are taxed.

⁶ These yields are also compared in Chapter 14 (see, in particular, Figure 14.7).

⁷ When a residence is sold, the homeowner will not have to recognize a capital gain if either another more expensive home is bought within two years or if the homeowner is at least 55 years old and certain other conditions are met.

⁸ Other plans that are treated similarly with respect to taxation are known as 401(k) plans, run by corporations, 403(b) plans, run by certain nonprofit organizations and school districts, and 457 plans, run by state and local governments.

⁹ Variable annuities, available from many insurance companies, are treated similarly for tax purposes. See Endnote 15 in Chapter 22.

¹⁰ Burton G. Malkiel, *A Random Walk Down Wall Street* (New York: W.W. Norton, 1990): 279.

¹¹ A number of authorities prefer "deflators" derived from gross domestic product figures, but such indices have not received the publicity accorded the Consumer Price Index.

¹² Here real return refers to the increase (or decrease) in purchasing power that the investor has received as a result of making a particular investment.

¹³ The Fisher model is named after its creator, Irving Fisher, who derived the model in *The Theory of Interest* (New York: Macmillan, 1930).

¹⁴ This error will be larger for higher rates of inflation. Thus, in those countries with "hyperinflation," the quick method will have a substantial amount of error associated with it. For example, if the nominal return is 110% and the inflation rate is 100%, then the true real return is 5% but the quick method will indicate that it is twice as large, 10%.

¹⁵ However, there apparently are periods of time when such securities have an expected real return that is relatively large. For example, in the 1981-1986 period, Treasury bill returns actually exceeded the rate of change in the CPI by over 5%. This suggests that investors probably expected a positive real return over the latter part of the period.

¹⁶ More specifically, it can be shown that long-term borrowers are likely to gain somewhat more than short-term borrowers when actual inflation exceeds expected inflation and lose somewhat more when actual inflation falls below expectations. Similarly, long-term lenders are likely to lose somewhat more than short-term lenders when actual inflation exceeds expectations and gain somewhat more when actual inflation falls below expectations.

¹⁷ Actually, rationing might not occur as lenders may simply refuse to make those kinds of loans that are subject to ceilings when inflationary expectations are high.

¹⁸ The correlation coefficient for the period from 1950 to 1993 is equal to $-.3$. Similar results occur when monthly data is used. Hence some people argue that there is an inverse relationship between historical rates of inflation and stock returns.

[19] Interestingly, there appears to be a significantly negative relationship between the real return on stocks and the rate of inflation. That is, higher rates of inflation seem to be accompanied by lower real stock returns. A number of explanations (some of them conflicting) have been offered to account for this observation. For a survey, see David P. Ely and Kenneth J. Robinson, "The Stock Market and Inflation: A Synthesis of the Theory and Evidence," *Federal Reserve Bank of Dallas Economic Review* (March 1989): 17–29.

[20] Jacob Boudoukh and Matthew Richardson, "Stock Returns and Inflation: A Long-Horizon Perspective," *American Economic Review,* 83, no. 5 (December 1993): 1346–1355.

[21] Equation (13.11) was also tested using actual inflation rates and stock returns from 1802 through 1990. The estimated value of β when one-year rates were used was .07, which was significantly less than 1.0 and not significantly different from zero. When five-year rates were used, its estimated value was .52, which was not significantly different from 1.0. These results are consistent with the earlier results about the observed short-term and long-term relationship between inflation rates and stock returns.

[22] Similar results were obtained when both subperiods and U.K. data were analyzed.

KEY TERMS

marginal tax rate	cost-of-living index
average tax rate	Consumer Price Index
tax-exempt bonds	geometric mean
realized capital gain	nominal return
unrealized capital gain	real return
wash sale	purchasing-power risk
capital gains and losses	indexation
cross-deductibility	disintermediation
Keogh plan	variable rates
individual retirement account	equity premium
inflation	

REFERENCES

1. A good reference source for reading about the federal tax code is:

John L. Kramer and Lawrence C. Phillips, eds., *Prentice Hall's Federal Taxation, 1992* (Englewood Cliffs, NJ: Prentice Hall, 1991).

2. For a valuable book that provides a framework for analyzing how tax rules affect decision-making, see:

Myron S. Scholes and Mark A. Wolfson, *Taxes and Business Strategy* (Englewood Cliffs, NJ: Prentice Hall, 1992).

3. Portfolio management and taxation are discussed in:

Robert H. Jeffrey and Robert D. Arnott, "Is Your Alpha Big Enough to Cover Its Taxes?" *Journal of Portfolio Management,* 19, no. 3 (Spring 1993): 15–25.

4. The seminal work linking interest rates and inflationary expectations is:

Irving Fisher, *The Theory of Interest* (New York: Macmillan, 1930).

5. For a review article and test of this linkage, see, respectively:

Herbert Taylor, "Interest Rates: How Much Does Expected Inflation Matter?" *Federal Reserve Bank of Philadelphia Business Review* (July/August 1982): 3–12.

Jacob Boudoukh and Matthew Richardson, "Stock Returns and Inflation: A Long-Horizon Perspective," *American Economic Review,* 83, no. 5 (December 1993): 1346–1355.

6. The relationship between real interest rates and inflation is discussed in:

George G. Pennachi, "Identifying the Dynamics of Real Interest Rates and Inflation: Evidence Using Survey Data," *Review of Financial Studies,* 4, no. 1 (1991): 53–86.

7. The following papers present an analysis of the effect of inflation on the accounting treatment of corporate earnings:

Franco Modigliani and Richard A. Cohn, "Inflation and the Stock Market," *Financial Analysts Journal,* 35, no. 2 (March/April 1979): 24–44.

Kenneth R. French, Richard S. Ruback, and G. William Schwert, "Effects of Nominal Contracting on Stock Returns," *Journal of Political Economy,* 91, no. 1 (February 1983): 70–96.

William H. Beaver, Paul A. Griffin, and Wayne R. Landsman, "How Well Does Replacement Cost Income Explain Stock Return [sic]?" *Financial Analysts Journal,* 39, no. 2 (March/April 1983): 26–30, 39.

William C. Nordby, "Applications of Inflation-Adjusted Accounting Data," *Financial Analysts Journal,* 39, no. 2 (March/April 1983): 33-39.

Charles G. Callard and David C. Kleinman, "Inflation-Adjusted Accounting: Does It Matter?" *Financial Analysts Journal,* 41, no. 3 (May/June 1985): 51–59.

8. For a discussion of the relationship of the inflation rate to the returns on stocks, bonds, and real estate, see:

Eugene F. Fama and G. William Schwert, "Asset Returns and Inflation," *Journal of Financial Economics,* 5, no. 2 (November 1977): 115–146.

9. Other papers dealing with the relationship between inflation and stock returns can be found at the end of the following survey articles:

David P. Ely and Kenneth J. Robinson, "The Stock Market and Inflation: A Synthesis of the Theory and Evidence," *Federal Reserve Bank of Dallas Economic Review* (March 1989): 17–29.

Andrew B. Abel, "The Equity Premium Puzzle," *Federal Reserve Bank of Philadelphia Business Review* (September/October 1991): 3–14.

10. The equity premium has also been reviewed and analyzed in:

> Jeremy J. Siegel, "The Equity Premium: Stock and Bond Returns Since 1802," *Financial Analysts Journal*, 48, no. 1 (January/February 1992): 28–38, 46.

11. The tendency of certain types of common stocks to offer better inflation hedges is discussed in:

> Douglas K. Pearce and V. Vance Roley, "Firm Characteristics, Unanticipated Inflation, and Stock Returns," *Journal of Finance*, 43, no. 4 (September 1988): 965–981.

> Christopher K. Ma and M. E. Ellis, "Selecting Industries as Inflation Hedges," *Journal of Portfolio Management*, 15, no. 4 (Summer 1989): 45–48.

> Yaman Asikoglu and Metin R. Ercan, "Inflation Flow-Through and Stock Prices," *Journal of Portfolio Management*, 18, no. 3 (Spring 1992): 63-68.

12. International evidence on the relationship between stock returns and inflation is provided by:

> Bruno Solnik, "The Relation Between Stock Prices and Inflationary Expectations: The International Evidence," *Journal of Finance*, 38, no. 1 (March 1983): 35–48.

> N. Bulent Gultekin, "Stock Market Returns and Inflation: Evidence From Other Countries," *Journal of Finance*, 38, no. 1 (March 1983): 49–65.

CHAPTER 14

Fixed-Income Securities

This chapter surveys the major types of fixed-income securities, with an emphasis on those currently popular in the United States. Such a survey cannot be exhaustive. A security is, after all, a contract giving the investor certain rights to the future prospects of the issuer. Because the rights given to the investor can differ from one security to another, and because the future prospects of issuers can differ substantially, the number of different types of fixed-income securities is quite large (and growing), making a complete survey virtually impossible.

The term *fixed-income* is commonly used to cover the types of securities discussed in this chapter, but is a bit misleading. Typically, these securities promise the investor that he or she will receive certain specified cash flows at certain specified times in the future. It may be one cash flow, in which case the security is known as a **pure-discount security.** Alternatively, it may involve multiple cash flows. If all of these cash flows (except for the last one) are of the same size, they are generally referred to as **coupon payments.** The specified date beyond which the investor will no longer receive cash flows is known as the **maturity date.** On this date, the investor receives the **principal** (also known as the par value or face value) associated with the security, along with the last coupon payment. However, all the cash flows are *promised,* and thus may not be received. That is, in many cases there is at least some risk that a promised payment will not be made in full and on time.

Perhaps the most familiar type of fixed-income investment is the personal savings account at a bank, savings and loan company, or credit union. Such an account provides substantial (if not complete) safety of principal and interest, high liquidity, and a relatively low return.

14.1.1 Commercial Banks

Many people maintain a checking account at a commercial bank. Formally, these accounts are termed **demand deposits,** because money can be withdrawn on demand by the depositors. Although the bookkeeping required to keep track of withdrawals and deposits is costly to the bank, the balance in such an account is available to support interest-earning loans made by the bank. Within bounds set by regulations, banks offer terms for checking accounts that reflect these aspects. Customers with small balances who write many checks pay the bank, whereas those with large balances who write few checks are paid by the bank. Often, the two elements are identified separately, with service charges assessed for check writing and interest paid on average balances. In some cases the amount of interest paid increases substantially if a larger minimum balance is maintained.

An alternative to a checking account is a standard savings account. Although a written request for a withdrawal may be required up to 30 days in advance, in practice, requests for withdrawals are almost always honored immediately. Almost any amount may be invested in a savings account. No security is issued; instead, the current balance plus interest earned is posted to the bank's records and (if desired) to the depositor's "passbook."

Almost all banks also offer money market accounts and negotiable order of withdrawal (NOW) accounts, which pay interest and on which checks may be written. Credit unions offer services similar to these accounts, via share draft accounts, and many investment companies (described in Chapter 22) provide at least limited check-writing services.

The standard ("passbook") savings account is only one of many types of **time deposits.** A single-maturity deposit may be withdrawn at a stated maturity date (for example, one year after the initial deposit). A multiple-maturity deposit may be withdrawn at a stated date or left for one or more periods of equal length (thus, a 90-day multiple-maturity deposit can be withdrawn roughly every three months after the date of the initial deposit). In practice, most single-maturity and multiple-maturity deposits can be withdrawn at any time. However, a penalty must be paid when this is done prior to maturity. Often, the penalty takes the form of recomputing the interest earned using a lower rate. Sometimes, an additional penalty may be deducted from the recomputed account balance.

Some types of time deposits may be made in almost any amount, whereas others may be made only in units of, say, $1,000 each. The latter may be represented by **certificates of deposit** (CDs), which clearly qualify to be called securities. Large-denomination CDs (generally $100,000 or more and known as "jumbos") may be negotiable—that is, the original depositor may sell the certificate to someone else before maturity. In most cases all interest is paid, along with the principal, at maturity.[1] The top part of Figure 14.1 shows average yields of CDs with various maturities, issued by major banks in certain big states, as published each Wednesday in the *Wall Street Journal*.

Most bank accounts in the United States are insured by the Federal Deposit Insurance Corporation (FDIC), a government agency that guarantees the payment of principal on any account up to a stated limit ($100,000 in 1994) if the bank is closed and liquidated. The FDIC, created in 1933, levies insurance premiums on its member banks and is authorized to borrow funds from the U.S. Treasury, if needed, although it has never done so. By opening certain kinds of multiple accounts, each under the limit, an investor can have a considerable amount covered by deposit insurance.

14.1.2 Savings and Loan Companies and Mutual Savings Banks

Savings and loan companies and mutual savings banks accept relatively short-term deposits, then use the money primarily to make relatively long-term loans, often for home mortgages. All mutual savings banks and mutual savings and loan companies are nominally owned by their members, whereas stock savings and loan companies are owned by stockholders (like commercial banks) who may or may not deposit funds or obtain loans there.

In the United States, most accounts in savings companies are insured by the same government agency that insures most bank accounts, the FDIC. The principal of each account is insured up to the same limit used for bank accounts, but here, too, judicious use of multiple accounts makes it possible to have even more covered by deposit insurance.

The terms for deposits offered by institutions of this type are generally similar to those offered by commercial banks. The bottom part of Figure 14.1 presents the highest yields on CDs of various maturities that are issued by federally insured "thrift institutions," as reported weekly in the *Wall Street Journal*.

14.1.3 Credit Unions

A credit union accepts deposits from members of the credit union (membership is limited to individuals sharing some kind of "common bond," often a common employer) and then loans these funds to other members. Typically, loans are relatively small and relatively short-term (for example, to finance the purchase of an automobile). Excess funds are invested in highly liquid short-term assets.

Each credit union is owned by its members, who elect a board of directors. Deposits are generally similar to passbook accounts in a bank or a savings and loan company, and also earn "dividends" instead of interest. Many credit unions also offer CDs and checking accounts to their members.

Deposits in all federally chartered credit unions are insured by the National Credit Union Administration (NCUA), a U.S. government agency that serves the same function as the FDIC. The amount and type of insurance coverage provided by both of these agencies is essentially identical.

BANXQUOTE® MONEY MARKETS

Survey ended Tuesday, December 14, 1993
AVERAGE YIELDS OF MAJOR BANKS

	MMi*	One Month	Two Months	Three Months	Six Months	One Year	Two Years	Five Years
NEW YORK								
Savings	1.95%	z	z	2.45%	2.56%	2.81%	3.43%	4.53%
Jumbos	2.70%	2.61%	2.66%	2.59%	2.68%	2.95%	3.55%	4.49%
CALIFORNIA								
Savings	2.25%	z	z	2.40%	2.53%	2.77%	3.12%	4.27%
Jumbos	2.31%	2.37%	2.39%	2.47%	2.62%	2.87%	3.35%	4.50%
PENNSYLVANIA								
Savings	2.49%	z	z	2.55%	2.89%	3.05%	3.18%	4.47%
Jumbos	2.66%	2.44%	2.43%	2.54%	2.65%	2.80%	3.19%	z
ILLINOIS								
Savings	2.41%	z	z	2.81%	2.96%	3.18%	3.69%	4.84%
Jumbos	2.65%	2.84%	2.91%	3.05%	3.15%	3.33%	3.85%	4.96%
TEXAS								
Savings	2.69%	z	z	2.52%	2.73%	2.83%	3.13%	4.09%
Jumbos	2.69%	2.76%	2.76%	2.83%	2.98%	3.38%	3.73%	4.49%
FLORIDA								
Savings	2.30%	z	z	2.32%	2.78%	3.05%	3.60%	4.54%
Jumbos	2.42%	2.31%	2.33%	2.48%	2.84%	3.03%	3.74%	4.69%
BANK AVERAGE								
Savings	2.35%	z	z	2.51%	2.74%	2.95%	3.36%	4.46%
Jumbos	2.57%	2.55%	2.58%	2.66%	2.82%	3.06%	3.60%	4.65%
WEEKLY CHANGE (in percentage point)								
Savings	+0.01	z	z	−0.01	−0.01	....	+0.02	....
Jumbos	....	−0.01	−0.01	−0.01	....	....	+0.02	+0.02

SAVINGS CD YIELDS OFFERED THROUGH LEADING BROKERS

	Three Months	Six Months	One Year	Two Years	Five Years
BROKER AVERAGE	3.17%	3.28%	3.55%	3.95%	4.62%
WEEKLY CHANGE	....	+0.05	+0.10	−0.02	+0.06

*Money Market Investments include MMDA, NOW, savings deposits, passbook and other liquid accounts.
Each depositor is insured by the Federal Deposit Insurance Corp. (FDIC) up to $100,000 per issuing institution.
COMPOUND METHODS: c-Continuously. d-Daily. w-Weekly. m-Monthly. q-Quarterly. s-Semi-annually. a-Annually. si-Simple interest.
F-Floating rate. P-Prime CD. T-T-Bill CD.BD-Broker-Dealer.

YIELD BASIS: A-365/365. B-360/360. C-365/360.
The information included in this table has been obtained directly from broker-dealers, banks and savings institutions, but the accuracy and validity cannot be guaranteed. Rates are subject to change. Yields, terms and capital adequacy should be verified before investing. Only well capitalized or adequately capitalized depository institutions are quoted. APY-Annual percentage yield.
z-Unavailable.

HIGH YIELD SAVINGS

Small minimum balance/opening deposit, generally $500 to $25,000

Money Market Investments*	Rate		APY
Loyola Federal, Baltimore Md	3.36%	dA	3.42%
Columbia First, Arlington Va	3.30%	dC	3.40%
Washington Mutual, Seattle Wa	3.25%	mA	3.30%
Washington Savings, Waldorf Md	3.25%	dA	3.30%
New South FSB, Birmingham Al	3.25%	qA	3.29%

One Month CDs	Rate		APY
Washington Mutual, Seattle Wa	3.15%	mA	3.20%
Firstrust Bank, Philadelphia Pa	2.96%	w	3.00%
Bay Savings, Newport News Va	2.96%	dA	3.00%
New South FSB, Birmingham Al	2.90%	siA	2.94%
Providence Savings, Vienna Va	2.86%	dA	2.90%

Two Months CDs	Rate		APY
Washington Mutual, Seattle Wa	3.15%	mA	3.20%
New South FSB, Birmingham Al	2.90%	siA	2.94%
Providence Savings, Vienna Va	2.86%	dA	2.90%
Safra National, New York NY	2.80%	dA	2.84%
Lasalle Bk Lake View, Chicago Il	2.75%	siA	2.78%

Three Months CDs	Rate		APY
Acacia Federal, Annandale Va	3.35%	dA	3.41%
Lasalle Bk Lake View, Chicago Il	3.32%	FT	3.36%
Washington Mutual, Seattle Wa	3.15%	mA	3.20%
Paine Webber -BD-, New York NY	3.15%	siA	3.19%
Bay Savings, Newport News Va	3.10%	dA	3.15%

Six Months CDs	Rate		APY
First Deposit, Tilton NH	3.63%	dA	3.70%
Acacia Federal, Annandale Va	3.55%	dA	3.61%
Colonial National, Wilmington De	3.44%	dA	3.50%
Continental Svgs, San Fran Ca	3.44%	dA	3.50%
Guaranty Bank, Milwaukee WI	3.46%	siA	3.49%

One Year CDs	Rate		APY
Continental Svgs, San Fran Ca	4.02%	dA	4.10%
First Deposit, Tilton NH	3.92%	dA	4.00%
Acacia Federal, Annandale Va	3.85%	dA	3.92%
Guaranty Bank, Milwaukee WI	3.83%	qA	3.89%
MBNA America, Newark De	3.80%	dA	3.87%

Two Years CDs	Rate		APY
Home Federal, Washington DC	4.40%	dA	4.50%
Acacia Federal, Annandale Va	4.35%	dA	4.45%
Continental Svgs, San Fran Ca	4.31%	dA	4.40%
Premium Federal, Gibbsboro NJ	4.26%	dA	4.35%
New South FSB, Birmingham Al	4.26%	dA	4.33%

Five Years CDs	Rate		APY
American Federal, Rockville Md	5.45%	aA	5.45%
Metropolitan Bank, Arlington Va	5.27%	dA	5.41%
Eastern Savings, Baltimore Md	5.27%	mA	5.40%
Continental Svgs, San Fran Ca	5.26%	dA	5.40%
MBNA America, Newark De	5.25%	dA	5.39%

HIGH YIELD JUMBOS

Large minimum balance/opening deposit, generally $95,000 to $100,000

Money Market Investments*	Rate		APY
Loyola Federal, Baltimore Md	3.36%	dA	3.42%
Columbia First, Arlington Va	3.30%	dC	3.40%
First Signature, Portsmouth NH	3.28%	dA	3.33%
Eastern Savings, Baltimore Md	3.25%	dA	3.30%
Washington Mutual, Seattle Wa	3.25%	mA	3.30%

One Month Jumbo CDs	Rate		APY
Greenwood Trust, Wilmington De	3.30%	siA	3.35%
Colonial National, Wilmington De	3.25%	siA	3.30%
Pacific Heritage, Torrance Ca	3.25%	siA	3.30%
Washington Mutual, Seattle Wa	3.25%	mA	3.30%
Frst Comonwelth, Alexandria Va	3.25%	siA	3.30%

Two Months Jumbo CDs	Rate		APY
Colonial National, Wilmington De	3.35%	siA	3.40%
Pacific Heritage, Torrance Ca	3.35%	siA	3.40%
Frst Comonwelth, Alexandria Va	3.35%	siA	3.40%
Greenwood Trust, Wilmington De	3.30%	siA	3.35%
Washington Mutual, Seattle Wa	3.25%	mA	3.30%

Three Months Jumbo CDs	Rate		APY
Colonial National, Wilmington De	3.45%	siA	3.49%
First Federal, Rochester NY	3.35%	siC	3.44%
Continental Svgs, San Fran Ca	3.40%	siA	3.44%
Topa Savings, Los Angeles Ca	3.40%	siA	3.44%
Acacia Federal, Annandale Va	3.35%	dA	3.41%

Six Months Jumbo CDs	Rate		APY
First Deposit NCCB, Concord NH	3.92%	dA	4.00%
Topa Savings, Los Angeles Ca	3.75%	siA	3.79%
First Deposit, Tilton NH	3.68%	dA	3.75%
Continental Svgs, San Fran Ca	3.60%	siA	3.63%
Acacia Federal, Annandale Va	3.55%	dA	3.61%

One Year Jumbo CDs	Rate		APY
First Deposit NCCB, Concord NH	4.02%	dA	4.10%
First Deposit, Tilton NH	3.95%	dA	4.03%
First USA, Wilmington De	3.95%	siC	4.00%
Topa Savings, Los Angeles Ca	4.00%	siA	4.00%
MBNA America, Newark De	3.90%	dA	3.98%

Two Years Jumbo CDs	Rate		APY
First USA, Wilmington De	4.85%	siC	4.80%
Acacia Federal, Annandale Va	4.35%	dA	4.45%
New South FSB, Birmingham Al	4.26%	qA	4.33%
Topa Savings, Los Angeles Ca	4.40%	siA	4.31%
Key Bank USA, Albany NY	4.20%	mA	4.28%

Five Years Jumbo CDs	Rate		APY
MBNA America, Newark De	5.35%	dA	5.50%
Eastern Savings, Baltimore Md	5.27%	mA	5.40%
Washington Savings, Waldorf Md	5.25%	qA	5.35%
Apple Bank, New York NY	5.13%	qA	5.23%
Acacia Federal, Annandale Va	5.10%	dA	5.23%

For more information call MASTERFUND at (800) 666-2000. MASTERFUND is registered with the FDIC as a deposit broker.

Source: BANXQUOTE, Wilmington, De. BANXQUOTE is a registered trademark and service mark of MASTERFUND INC.

FIGURE 14.1

Yields on Certificates of Deposit

Source: Reprinted by permission of *The Wall Street Journal*, Dow Jones & Company, Inc., December 15, 1993, p. C18. All rights reserved worldwide.

14.1.4 Other Types of Personal Savings Accounts

A number of institutions similar to those just described can be found. For example, there are companies chartered to accept deposits and use the proceeds to make consumer loans. In some countries, the government-run post office accepts savings deposits. Certain kinds of life insurance policies include a savings component, as payments often exceed the amount strictly required to pay for just the insurance involved. The "cash value" of such a policy may be obtained by cancellation; alternatively, some or all of it may be "borrowed" without canceling the policy. The implicit rate of return on the cash value of an insurance policy is typically quite low, reflecting the extremely low risk to the policyholder and the length of the insurance company's commitment.[2]

14.2   MONEY MARKET INSTRUMENTS

Certain types of short-term (meaning, arbitrarily, one year or less), highly marketable loans play a major role in the investment and borrowing activities of both financial and nonfinancial corporations. Individual investors with substantial funds may invest in such money market instruments directly, but most do so indirectly via money market accounts at various financial institutions.[3]

Some money market instruments are negotiable and are traded in active secondary dealer markets; others are not. Some may be purchased by anyone with adequate funds; others only by particular types of institutions. Many are sold on a discount basis—for example, a 90-day note with a face value of $100,000 might be sold for $98,000, where the face value of $100,000 is to be paid to the investor at maturity and the difference of $2,000 represents interest income.

Interest rates on such money market instruments are often reported on what is known as a **bank discount basis.** In the example, this means that the note will be described in the media as having a discount of 2% per quarter, or 8% per year. However, the discount does not represent the true interest rate on the note. In such a situation, the true interest rate is higher—in this case it equals $2,000/$98,000 = 2.04\%$ per quarter, or the equivalent of 8.16% per year (with quarterly compounding, it would equal $8.41\% = 1.0204^4 - 1$).

The *Wall Street Journal* publishes on a daily basis a list of the current interest rates on a number of money market instruments. Figure 14.2 presents such a list. Some of the types of money market instruments mentioned on this list are described next.

14.2.1   Commercial Paper

Commercial paper is an unsecured short-term promissory note issued by both financial and nonfinancial companies. The dollar amount of commercial paper outstanding exceeds the amount of any other type of money market instrument except for Treasury bills, with the majority being issued by financial companies such as bank holding companies as well as companies involved in sales and personal finance, insurance, and leasing. Such notes are often issued by large firms that have unused lines of credit at banks, making it highly likely that the loan will

FIGURE 14.2
Interest Rates on Money Market Instruments

Source: Reprinted by permission of *The Wall Street Journal*, Dow Jones & Company, Inc., December 14, 1993, p. C19. All rights reserved worldwide.

MONEY RATES

Monday, December 13, 1993

The key U.S. and foreign annual interest rates below are a guide to general levels but don't always represent actual transactions.

PRIME RATE: 6%. The base rate on corporate loans posted by at least 75% of the nation's 30 largest banks.

FEDERAL FUNDS: 3% high, 2⅞% low, 2⅞% near closing bid, 2 15/16% offered. Reserves traded among commercial banks for overnight use in amounts of $1 million or more. Source: Prebon Yamane (U.S.A.) Inc.

DISCOUNT RATE: 3%. The charge on loans to depository institutions by the Federal Reserve Banks.

CALL MONEY: 5%. The charge on loans to brokers on stock exchange collateral. Source: Telerate Systems Inc.

COMMERCIAL PAPER placed directly by General Electric Capital Corp.: 3.22% 30 to 59 days; 3.20% 60 to 119 days; 3.25% 120 to 149 days; 3.27% 150 to 179 days; 3.28% 180 to 239 days; 3.38% 240 to 270 days.

COMMERCIAL PAPER: High-grade unsecured notes sold through dealers by major corporations: 3.35% 30 days; 3.35% 60 days; 3.35% 90 days.

CERTIFICATES OF DEPOSIT: 2.61% one month; 2.66% two months; 2.69% three months; 2.78% six months; 3.02% one year. Average of top rates paid by major New York banks on primary new issues of negotiable C.D.s, usually on amounts of $1 million and more. The minimum unit is $100,000. Typical rates in the secondary market: 3.30% one month; 3.32% three months; 3.35% six months.

BANKERS ACCEPTANCES: 3.19% 30 days; 3.19% 60 days; 3.20% 90 days; 3.22% 120 days; 3.25% 150 days; 3.28% 180 days. Offered rates of negotiable, bank-backed business credit instruments typically financing an import order.

LONDON LATE EURODOLLARS: 3 1/16% - 2 15/16% one month; 3 5/16% - 3 3/16% two months; 3⅜% - 3¼% three months; 3⅜% - 3¼% four months; 3 7/16% - 3 5/16% five months; 3½% - 3⅜% six months.

LONDON INTERBANK OFFERED RATES (LIBOR): 3 5/16% one month; 3⅜% three months; 3½% six months; 3 13/16% one year. The average of interbank offered rates for dollar deposits in the London market based on quotations at five major banks. Effective rate for contracts entered into two days from date appearing at top of this column.

FOREIGN PRIME RATES: Canada 5.50%; Germany 6.05%; Japan 3%; Switzerland 7.50%; Britain 6%. These rate indications aren't directly comparable; lending practices vary widely by location.

TREASURY BILLS: Results of the Monday, December 13, 1993, auction of short-term U.S. government bills, sold at a discount from face value in units of $10,000 to $1 million: 3.06%, 13 weeks; 3.26%, 26 weeks.

FEDERAL HOME LOAN MORTGAGE CORP. (Freddie Mac): Posted yields on 30-year mortgage commitments. Delivery within 30 days 7.07%, 60 days 7.14%, standard conventional fixed-rate mortgages; 3.875%, 2% rate capped one-year adjustable rate mortgages. Source: Telerate Systems Inc.

FEDERAL NATIONAL MORTGAGE ASSOCIATION (Fannie Mae): Posted yields on 30 year mortgage commitments (priced at par) for delivery within 30 days 7.02%, 60 days 7.12%, standard conventional fixed rate-mortgages; 5.10%, 6/2 rate capped one-year adjustable rate mortgages. Source: Telerate Systems Inc.

MERRILL LYNCH READY ASSETS TRUST: 2.70%. Annualized average rate of return after expenses for the past 30 days; not a forecast of future returns.

be paid off when it becomes due. As a result, the interest rates on commercial paper reflect this, being relatively low in comparison with other corporate fixed-income securities.

Commercial paper is usually sold in denominations of $100,000 or more with maturities of up to 270 days (the maximum allowed by the Securities and Exchange Commission without registration) to large institutional investors such as money market mutual funds. Typically these investors hold onto the paper until maturity, resulting in a very small secondary market. Generally the terms of commercial paper are not negotiable, but the issuer may be willing to prepay the note (perhaps by issuing another) if necessary.

14.2.2 Certificates of Deposit

These are the certificates representing time deposits at commercial banks or savings and loan associations that were mentioned earlier. Large-denomination (or jumbo) CDs are issued in amounts of $100,000 or more, have a specified maturity, and generally are negotiable, meaning that they can be sold by one investor to another. Such certificates are insured by the FDIC or NCUA, but only for $100,000 (in 1994).

Interestingly, foreign banks that have branches in the United States also offer dollar-denominated CDs to investors. Such CDs have been dubbed Yankee CDs by the media.

14.2.3 Bankers' Acceptances

Historically, these instruments were created to finance goods in transit; currently they are generally used to finance foreign trade. For example, the buyer of the goods may issue a written promise to the seller to pay a given sum within a short period of time (for example, 180 days or less). A bank then "accepts" this promise, obligating itself to pay the amount when requested, and obtains in return a claim on the goods as collateral. The written promise becomes a liability of both the bank and the buyer of the goods and is known as a **bankers' acceptance.**

The seller of the goods, having received the written promise from the buyer that the bank has "accepted," need not wait until the promise is due in order to receive payment. Instead, the acceptance can be sold to someone else at a price that is less than the amount of the promised payment to be made in the future. Thus such instruments are pure discount securities.

14.2.4 Eurodollars

In the world of international finance, large short-term CDs denominated in dollars and issued by banks outside the United States (most often in London) are known as **Eurodollar CDs** (or simply Euro CDs). Also available for investment are dollar-denominated time deposits in banks outside the United States, known as **Eurodollar deposits.** A key distinction between Euro CDs and Eurodollar deposits is that Euro CDs are negotiable, meaning that they can be traded, whereas Eurodollar deposits are nonnegotiable, meaning that they cannot be traded.

The demand and supply conditions for such instruments may differ from the conditions for other U.S. money market instruments, owing to restrictions imposed (or likely to be imposed) by the United States and other governments. However, enough commonality exists to keep interest rates from diverging too much from rates available on domestic alternatives. One difference from CDs issued by U.S. banks is that the Euro CDs do not have federal deposit insurance.

14.2.5 Repurchase Agreements

Often one investor (usually a financial institution) will sell another investor (usually another financial institution) a money market instrument, and agree to repurchase it for an agreed-upon price at a later date. For example, investor A might sell investor B a number of Treasury bills that mature in 180 days for a price of $10 million. As part of the sale, investor A has signed a **repurchase agreement** (or "repo") with investor B (from the perspective of the purchaser, investor B, the agreement is referred to as a "reverse repo"). This agreement specifies that after 30 days, investor A will repurchase these Treasury bills for $10.1 million. Thus investor A will have paid investor B $100,000 in interest for 30 days' use of $10 million, meaning that investor B has, in essence, purchased a money market instrument that matures in 30 days. The annualized interest rate is known as the **repo rate,** which in this case is equal to 12% [= ($100,000/$10,000,000) $\times$ (360/30)].

Note how this repurchase agreement is like a collateralized loan from B to A, with the Treasury bills serving as the collateral. Such loans involve very little risk to the lender (B), because the money market instruments typically used in repurchase agreements are of high quality.

14.3   U.S. GOVERNMENT SECURITIES

It should come as no surprise that the U.S. government relies heavily on debt financing. Since the 1960s, revenues have seldom covered expenses, and the differences have been financed primarily by issuing debt instruments. Moreover, new debt must be issued in order to get the necessary funds to pay off old debt that comes due. Such **debt refunding** sometimes allows the holders of the maturing debt to exchange it directly for new debt, and in the process receive beneficial treatment for tax purposes.

Some idea of the magnitude and ownership structure of U.S. Treasury debt can be gained by examining Table 14.1. Through the U.S. Treasury, federal agencies, and various trust funds, the federal government itself is a large holder, as is the Federal Reserve System. However, a large amount is held by state and local governments as well as private investors of one sort or another. For example, these securities are a major factor in the portfolios of commercial banks and other financial institutions. To a lesser extent, business corporations also invest in them, primarily as outlets for relatively short-term excess working capital. The amount held by individual households is also substantial, with over half of their investment in U.S. government securities being in savings bonds and notes. Lastly, foreign holdings have become quite large in recent years.

About two-thirds of the public debt is marketable, meaning that it is represented by securities that can be sold at any time by the original purchaser through government security dealers.[4] The major nonmarketable issues are held by U.S. government agencies, foreign governments, state and local governments, and individuals (the latter in the form of U.S. Savings Bonds). Marketable issues include Treasury bills, notes, and bonds. Table 14.2 shows the amounts of interest-bearing U.S. public debt in each category at the end of 1992 (there was an additional $3.1 billion of non-interest-bearing U.S. public debt outstanding at that time, so total U.S. public debt amounted to $4,177.0 billion).

TABLE 14.1
OWNERSHIP OF OUTSTANDING PUBLIC DEBT OF U.S. TREASURY, END OF 1992

Held By		Dollar Amount (in Billions)	Percent of Total Amount
U.S. Treasury, federal agencies, and trust funds		$1,047.8	25.1%
Federal Reserve Banks		302.5	7.2
Private investors:			
Commercial banks	$293.4		7.0
Money market funds	80.6		1.9
Insurance companies	190.3		4.6
Other companies	192.5		4.6
State and local treasuries	534.8		12.8
Individuals	289.2		6.9
Foreign and international	512.5		12.3
Other miscellaneous	746.6		17.9
Total private investors		2,839.9	68.0
Total gross public debt[1]		$4,177.0	100.0%

[1]According to the Federal Reserve Bulletin, the components do not sum to the total shown because of rounding.

Source: *Federal Reserve Bulletin*, November 1993, p. A30.

The relative maturity dates for U.S. government debt are influenced by a number of factors. As time passes, of course, the **term-to-maturity** (that is, the remaining time until maturity) of an outstanding issue will decrease. Moreover, the Treasury has considerable latitude in selecting maturities for new issues and can also engage in refunding operations. From time to time, congressional limits on amounts issued or interest paid on certain types of instruments may force reliance on other types of instruments. Debt operations may also be employed as a

TABLE 14.2
INTEREST-BEARING U.S. PUBLIC DEBT, END OF 1992

	Category	Amount (In Billions)
Nonmarketable:		
Government account series	$1,043.5	
U.S. Savings Bonds	155.0	
Foreign series	37.4	
State and local government series	153.5	
Total Nonmarketable Debt		$1,419.8
Marketable:		
Bills	$ 657.7	
Notes	1,608.9	
Bonds	472.5	
Total Marketable Debt		2,754.1
Total Debt[1]		$4,173.9

[1] According to the Federal Reserve Bulletin, the components do not sum to the total shown because of rounding.

Source: *Federal Reserve Bulletin*, November 1993, p. A30.

conscious instrument of governmental economic policy in an attempt to influence the current interest rates for securities of various maturities.

Table 14.3 shows that the maturity structure of marketable, interest-bearing U.S. public debt in June 1993 is not long. For example, slightly over 30% was short-term debt, maturing in less than one year. Furthermore, about 70% had a maturity date within five years.

Many types of debt have been issued by the U.S. government as well as by U.S. government agencies and organizations sponsored by the federal government. Figure 14.3 shows a typical list of price quotations for certain types of debt securities that have been issued by the U.S. government. These securities will be discussed next.

14.3.1   U.S. Treasury Bills

Treasury bills are issued on a discount basis, with maturities of up to 52 weeks and in denominations of $10,000 or more (although at times denominations as small as $1,000 have been offered). All are issued in book-entry form, where the buyer receives a receipt at time of purchase and the bill's face value at maturity. Although Treasury bills are sold at discount, their dollar yield (that is, the difference between the purchase price and the face value if the bill is held to maturity) is treated as interest income for tax purposes.

Offerings of 13-week and 26-week bills are usually made once each week; 52-week bills are usually offered every fourth week. All are sold by auction. Bids may be entered on either a competitive or a noncompetitive basis. With a competitive bid, the investor states a price that he or she is willing to pay (which can be converted to the interest rate that would be earned if the bid is accepted). For example, an investor might enter a bid for a stated number of 13-week bills at a price of 98.512. If the bid is accepted, the investor will pay $9,851.20 for each $10,000 of face value, meaning that an investment of $9,851.20 will generate a receipt of $10,000 if held to maturity 13 weeks later. With a noncompetitive bid, the investor agrees to pay the average price of all bids that will be accepted by the Treasury.

TABLE 14.3

MATURITY STRUCTURE OF MARKETABLE, INTEREST-BEARING U.S. PUBLIC DEBT HELD BY PRIVATE INVESTORS, JUNE 1993

Maturity	Amount (in Billions)	Percent of Total Amount
Within 1 year	$ 849.7	33.8%
1–5 years	949.1	37.7
5–10 years	309.3	12.3
10–20 years	84.2	3.3
20 years and over	323.2	12.9
Total	$2,515.5	100.0%

Source: *Treasury Bulletin*, September 1993, p. 34.

TREASURY BONDS, NOTES & BILLS

Monday, December 13, 1993

Representative Over-the-Counter quotations based on transactions of $1 million or more.

Treasury bond, note and bill quotes are as of mid-afternoon. Colons in bid-and-asked quotes represent 32nds; 101:01 means 101 1/32. Net changes in 32nds. n-Treasury note. Treasury bill quotes in hundredths, quoted on terms of a rate of discount. Days to maturity calculated from settlement date. All yields are to maturity and based on the asked quote. Latest 13-week and 26-week bills are boldfaced. For bonds callable prior to maturity, yields are computed to the earliest call date for issues quoted above par and to the maturity date for issues below par. *-When issued.
Source: Federal Reserve Bank of New York.

U.S. Treasury strips as of 3 p.m. Eastern time, also based on transactions of $1 million or more. Colons in bid-and-asked quotes represent 32nds; 101:01 means 101 1/32. Net changes in 32nds. Yields calculated on the asked quotation. ci-stripped coupon interest. bp-Treasury bond, stripped principal. np-Treasury note, stripped principal. For bonds callable prior to maturity, yields are computed to the earliest call date for issues quoted above par and to the maturity date for issues below par.
Source: Bear, Stearns & Co. via Street Software Technology Inc.

GOVT. BONDS & NOTES

Rate	Maturity Mo/Yr	Bid	Asked	Chg.	Ask Yld.
5	Dec 93n	100:02	100:04	− 1	2.08
7⅝	Dec 93n	100:06	100:08	− 1	1.81
7	Jan 94n	100:09	100:11	− 1	2.83
4⅞	Jan 94n	100:07	100:09	....	2.62
6⅞	Feb 94n	100:19	100:21	− 1	2.89
8⅞	Feb 94n	100:30	101:00	− 1	2.83
9	Feb 94	100:31	101:01	− 1	2.77
5¾	Feb 94n	100:14	100:16	− 1	2.90
5¾	Mar 94n	100:23	100:25	....	3.01
8½	Mar 94n	101:17	101:19	− 1	2.93
7	Apr 94n	101:07	101:09	− 1	3.07
5⅞	Apr 94n	100:24	100:26	− 1	3.17
7	May 94n	101:16	101:18	− 1	3.19
9⅛	May 94n	102:17	102:19	− 1	3.17
13⅛	May 94n	104:01	104:03	− 3	3.15
5⅛	May 94n	100:26	100:28	....	3.18
5	Jun 94n	100:28	100:30	+ 1	3.25
8½	Jul 94n	102:24	102:26	....	3.24
8	Jul 94n	102:20	102:22	....	3.32
4¼	Jul 94n	100:16	100:18	− 1	3.34
6⅞	Aug 94n	102:07	102:09	....	3.40
8⅝	Aug 94n	103:12	103:14	− 1	3.39

Rate	Maturity Mo/Yr	Bid	Asked	Chg.	Ask Yld.
7⅞	Nov 99n	112:27	112:29	− 8	5.31
6⅜	Jan 00n	105:08	105:10	− 6	5.34
7⅞	Feb 95-00	104:13	104:17	− 2	3.87
8½	Feb 00n	116:10	116:12	− 8	5.35
5½	Apr 00n	101:00	101:02	− 7	5.30
8⅞	May 00n	118:22	118:24	− 10	5.38
8⅜	Aug 95-00	106:18	106:22	− 1	4.19
8¾	Aug 00n	118:09	118:11	− 9	5.43
8½	Nov 00n	117:05	117:07	− 10	5.48
7¾	Feb 01n	113:01	113:03	− 10	5.51
11¾	Feb 01	136:23	136:27	− 10	5.47
8	May 01n	114:23	114:25	− 10	5.54
13⅛	May 01	145:27	145:31	− 9	5.50
7⅞	Aug 01n	114:03	114:05	− 12	5.58
8	Aug 96-01	108:08	108:12	− 3	4.63
13⅜	Aug 01	148:13	148:17	− 15	5.53
7½	Nov 01n	111:28	111:30	− 12	5.61
15¾	Nov 01	164:26	164:30	− 16	5.52
14⅛	Feb 02	156:05	156:09	− 21	5.58
7½	May 02n	112:07	112:09	− 11	5.65
6⅜	Aug 02n	104:19	104:21	− 11	5.69
11⅝	Nov 02	140:31	141:03	− 14	5.69
6¼	Feb 03n	103:20	103:22	− 11	5.73

Rate	Maturity Mo/Yr	Bid	Asked	Chg.	Ask Yld.
	Nov 01 np	63:21	63:26	− 8	5.76
	Feb 02 ci	62:13	62:18	− 8	5.82
	May 02 ci	61:17	61:22	− 7	5.82
	Aug 02 ci	61:23	61:28	− 8	5.79
	Aug 02 ci	60:10	60:15	− 9	5.89
	Aug 02 np	60:24	60:29	− 7	5.80
	Nov 02 ci	59:10	59:15	− 7	5.91
	Feb 03 ci	58:06	58:11	− 9	5.97
	Feb 03 bp	58:26	58:31	− 8	5.84
	May 03 ci	57:06	57:11	− 9	5.99
	Aug 03 ci	56:04	56:09	− 8	6.03
	Nov 03 ci	55:09	55:14	− 8	6.03
	Feb 04 ci	54:03	54:08	− 9	6.11
	May 04 ci	53:03	53:08	− 9	6.14
	Aug 04 ci	52:03	52:09	− 10	6.18
	Nov 04 bp	51:07	51:12	− 10	6.20
	Nov 04 ci	51:14	51:20	− 9	6.15
	Feb 05 ci	50:07	50:12	− 8	6.24
	May 05 ci	49:10	49:15	− 8	6.26
	May 05 bp	49:18	49:23	− 13	6.22
	Aug 05 ci	48:13	48:18	− 8	6.28
	Aug 05 np	48:31	49:04	− 10	6.19
	Nov 05 ci	47:18	47:23	− 8	6.30
	Feb 06 ci	46:24	46:29	− 8	6.32
	Feb 06 np	47:22	47:27	− 8	6.15
	May 06 ci	45:24	45:30	− 10	6.36
	Aug 06 ci	44:28	45:02	− 10	6.39
	Nov 06 ci	44:03	44:08	− 10	6.41
	Feb 07 ci	43:08	43:14	− 12	6.43
	May 07 ci	42:13	42:19	− 12	6.47
	Aug 07 ci	41:22	41:27	− 12	6.47
	Nov 07 ci	40:29	41:03	− 12	6.49
	Feb 08 ci	40:02	40:07	− 12	6.53
	May 08 ci	39:10	39:15	− 13	6.55
	Aug 08 ci	38:18	38:24	− 12	6.57
	Aug 08 ci	37:28	38:01	− 13	6.61
	May 09 ci	37:04	37:09	− 13	6.61
	Aug 09 ci	36:15	36:20	− 13	6.62
	Nov 09 ci	35:24	35:30	− 14	6.64
	Nov 09 ci	35:04	35:10	− 13	6.65
	Nov 09 np	35:10	35:16	− 17	6.61
	Feb 10 ci	34:14	34:19	− 10	6.68
	May 10 ci	33:24	33:29	− 12	6.70
	Aug 10 ci	33:05	33:10	− 11	6.70
	Nov 10 ci	32:18	32:23	− 12	6.72

Rate	Maturity Mo/Yr	Bid	Asked	Chg.	Ask Yld.
7⅜	May 96n	106:25	106:27	− 2	4.36
7⅝	May 96n	107:16	107:18	− 1	4.35
7⅞	Jun 96n	108:27	108:29	− 3	4.15
7⅞	Jul 96n	108:10	108:12	− 1	4.41
7⅛	Jul 96n	108:13	108:15	− 1	4.43
4⅜	Aug 96n	99:26	99:28	− 2	4.43
7¼	Aug 96n	106:30	107:00	− 3	4.48
7	Sep 96n	106:21	106:23	− 2	4.42
8	Oct 96n	109:03	109:05	− 2	4.52
6⅞	Oct 96n	106:07	106:09	− 3	4.52
4⅜	Nov 96n	99:18	99:20	− 2	4.51
7¼	Nov 96n	107:09	107:11	− 3	4.53
6½	Nov 96n	105:11	105:13	− 1	4.53
6⅛	Dec 96n	104:17	104:19	− 1	4.49
8	Jan 97n	109:19	109:21	− 2	4.61
6¼	Jan 97n	104:22	104:24	− 2	4.60
6¾	Feb 97n	106:06	106:08	− 3	4.63
6⅜	Mar 97n	106:21	106:23	− 2	4.65
8½	Apr 97n	111:19	111:21	− 1	4.68
6⅞	Apr 97n	106:23	106:25	− 1	4.68
8½	May 97n	111:25	111:27	− 2	4.71
6¾	May 97n	106:10	106:12	− 3	4.73
6⅜	Jun 97n	105:08	105:10	− 4	4.73
8½	Jul 97n	112:02	112:04	− 3	4.78
5½	Jul 97n	102:13	102:15	− 3	4.75
8⅝	Aug 97n	112:21	112:23	− 3	4.80
5⅞	Aug 97n	102:21	102:23	− 4	4.82
5½	Sep 97n	102:09	102:11	− 2	4.82
8¾	Oct 97n	113:13	113:15	− 4	4.86
5¾	Oct 97n	103:01	103:03	− 4	4.86
8⅞	Nov 97n	114:00	114:02	− 4	4.89
6	Nov 97n	103:29	103:31	− 4	4.89
6	Dec 97n	103:28	103:30	− 6	4.91
7⅞	Jan 98n	110:19	110:21	− 9	4.96
5⅝	Jan 98n	102:12	102:14	− 5	4.96
8⅛	Feb 98n	111:22	111:24	− 4	4.97
5⅛	Feb 98n	100:16	100:18	− 4	4.98
5⅛	Mar 98n	100:14	100:16	− 3	4.99
7⅞	Apr 98n	110:29	110:31	− 5	5.03
5⅛	Apr 98n	100:11	100:13	− 3	5.01
9	May 98n	115:18	115:20	− 6	5.01
5⅜	May 98n	101:07	101:09	− 3	5.05
5⅛	Jun 98n	100:06	100:08	− 4	5.06
8⅛	Jul 98n	112:24	112:26	− 5	5.08
5¼	Jul 98n	100:19	100:21	− 4	5.08
9¼	Aug 98n	117:02	117:04	− 6	5.08
4¾	Aug 98n	98:17	98:19	− 4	5.08
4¾	Sep 98n	98:17	98:19	− 4	5.08
7⅛	Oct 98n	108:13	108:15	− 4	5.13
4¾	Oct 98n	98:10	98:12	− 5	5.13
3½	Nov 98	99:02	100:02	− 4	3.49
8⅞	Nov 98n	116:02	116:04	− 5	5.14
5⅜	Nov 98n	99:28	99:30	− 4	5.14
6⅜	Jan 99n	105:06	105:08	− 4	5.19
8⅞	Feb 99n	116:14	116:16	− 7	5.19
7	Apr 99n	108:02	108:04	− 7	5.23
8½	May 94-99	102:08	102:12	....	2.72
9⅛	May 99n	118:05	118:07	− 7	5.22
6⅜	Jul 99n	105:08	105:10	− 4	5.26
8	Aug 99n	113:07	113:09	− 6	5.26
6	Oct 99n	103:11	103:13	− 7	5.31

U.S. TREASURY STRIPS

Mat.	Type	Bid	Asked	Chg.	Ask Yld.
Feb 94	ci	99:15	99:16	....	3.07
May 94	ci	98:21	98:21	....	3.26
Aug 94	ci	97:23	97:24	....	3.45
Nov 94	ci	96:24	96:25	....	3.60
Nov 94	np	96:26	96:27	+ 2	3.55
Feb 95	ci	95:22	95:23	....	3.77
Feb 95	np	95:23	95:24	+ 2	3.74
May 95	ci	94:20	94:21	+ 1	3.90
May 95	np	94:20	94:22	+ 1	3.90
Aug 95	ci	93:18	93:19	....	4.01
Aug 95	np	93:17	93:19	....	4.02
Nov 95	ci	92:16	92:17	....	4.08
Nov 95	np	92:14	92:16	....	4.11
Feb 96	ci	91:05	91:07	− 1	4.28
Feb 96	np	91:03	91:05	....	4.32
May 96	np	90:00	90:02	− 1	4.38
May 96	ci	89:31	90:01	− 1	4.39
Aug 96	ci	88:26	88:28	− 1	4.47
Nov 96	np	87:19	87:22	....	4.56
Nov 96	ci	87:20	87:22	− 1	4.55
Feb 97	ci	86:08	86:11	− 2	4.69
May 97	ci	85:00	85:03	− 2	4.78
May 97	np	85:00	85:03	....	4.78
Aug 97	ci	83:24	83:27	− 2	4.86
Aug 97	np	82:16	82:19	− 2	4.95
Aug 97	np	83:23	83:26	− 1	4.88
Nov 97	np	82:15	82:18	− 1	4.95
Feb 98	ci	81:06	81:09	− 1	5.03
Feb 98	np	81:04	81:08	− 3	5.05
May 98	ci	79:30	80:01	− 3	5.10
May 98	np	80:00	80:03	− 3	5.09
May 98	ci	78:25	78:29	− 3	5.14
Aug 98	np	78:24	78:27	− 3	5.15
Nov 98	ci	77:18	77:22	− 5	5.20
Nov 98	np	77:17	77:21	− 3	5.21
Feb 99	ci	76:10	76:13	− 3	5.27
May 99	np	76:10	76:13	− 3	5.27
May 99	ci	75:06	75:09	− 3	5.31
Aug 99	np	75:03	75:07	− 3	5.33
Aug 99	ci	74:04	74:08	− 3	5.32
Aug 99	np	74:00	74:04	− 3	5.35
Nov 99	ci	72:27	72:31	− 4	5.40
Nov 99	np	72:25	72:29	− 5	5.41
Feb 00	ci	71:20	71:24	− 5	5.45
Feb 00	ci	71:17	71:21	− 8	5.47
May 00	np	70:14	70:18	− 5	5.49
May 00	ci	70:14	70:18	− 6	5.51
Aug 00	ci	69:06	69:14	− 5	5.54
Aug 00	np	69:06	69:10	− 8	5.57
Nov 00	ci	68:06	68:11	− 5	5.58
Nov 00	np	67:31	68:03	− 7	5.63
Feb 01	ci	67:00	67:05	− 7	5.64
May 01	ci	66:28	67:02	− 8	5.65
May 01	ci	65:31	66:04	− 7	5.66
May 01	np	65:16	65:20	− 8	5.69
Aug 01	ci	64:28	65:00	− 7	5.70
Nov 01	np	64:24	64:28	− 9	5.72
Nov 01	ci	63:26	63:31	− 7	5.72

Mat.	Type	Bid	Asked	Chg.	Ask Yld.
Feb 21	bp	16:11	16:15	− 3	6.75
May 21	ci	16:00	16:04	− 4	6.77
May 21	bp	16:04	16:08	− 4	6.74
Aug 21	ci	15:25	15:29	− 5	6.76
Aug 21	bp	15:28	16:00	− 5	6.73
Nov 21	ci	15:18	15:22	− 6	6.72
Nov 21	bp	15:22	15:26	− 6	6.72
May 22	ci	15:22	15:26	− 5	6.66
Aug 22	ci	15:19	15:23	− 5	6.61
Aug 22	ci	15:11	15:15	− 5	6.61
Aug 22	bp	15:12	15:16	− 5	6.61
Nov 22	bp	15:12	15:06	− 5	6.61
Nov 22	bp	15:03	15:07	− 5	6.61
Feb 23	ci	15:12	15:16	− 5	6.49
Feb 23	bp	15:12	15:16	− 5	6.49

TREASURY BILLS

Maturity	Days to Mat.	Bid	Asked	Chg.	Ask Yld.
Dec 16 '93	1	2.99	2.89	+ 0.08	2.93
Dec 23 '93	8	2.72	2.62	− 0.03	2.66
Dec 30 '93	15	2.80	2.70	− 0.01	2.74
Jan 06 '94	22	2.82	2.72	− 0.04	2.76
Jan 13 '94	29	2.93	2.83	− 0.01	2.88
Jan 20 '94	36	2.94	2.90	− 0.03	2.95
Jan 27 '94	43	2.95	2.91	− 0.04	2.96
Feb 03 '94	50	2.98	2.94	− 0.03	2.99
Feb 10 '94	57	2.99	2.95	− 0.02	3.01
Feb 17 '94	64	3.01	2.99	− 0.01	3.05
Feb 24 '94	71	3.01	2.99	− 0.01	3.05
Mar 03 '94	78	3.02	3.00	− 0.01	3.06
Mar 10 '94	85	3.05	3.03	....	3.09
Mar 17 '94	92	3.05	3.03	− 0.01	3.10
Mar 24 '94	99	3.04	3.02	....	3.09
Mar 31 '94	106	3.04	3.02	....	3.09
Apr 07 '94	113	3.10	3.08	− 0.02	3.15
Apr 14 '94	120	3.12	3.10	− 0.01	3.18
Apr 21 '94	127	3.14	3.12	....	3.20
Apr 28 '94	134	3.16	3.14	+ 0.01	3.22
May 05 '94	141	3.17	3.15	− 0.01	3.23
May 12 '94	148	3.19	3.17	....	3.26
May 19 '94	155	3.21	3.19	....	3.28
May 26 '94	162	3.22	3.20	+ 0.01	3.28
Jun 02 '94	169	3.21	3.19	....	3.28
Jun 09 '94	176	3.25	3.23	+ 0.01	3.33
Jun 30 '94	197	3.23	3.21	....	3.31
Jul 28 '94	225	3.29	3.27	+ 0.01	3.37
Aug 25 '94	253	3.33	3.31	....	3.42
Sep 22 '94	281	3.35	3.33	....	3.45
Oct 20 '94	309	3.40	3.38	....	3.50
Nov 17 '94	337	3.45	3.43	+ 0.01	3.56
Dec 15 '94	365	3.48	3.46	....	3.60

◄──

Before each auction, the Treasury announces the total face value and the maturities of all bills that it plans to issue. At the auction itself, having received the bids, the Treasury proceeds to accept all noncompetitive bids. For example, if $6 billion of 13-week bills are to be issued, perhaps $2 billion of noncompetitive bids will have been received by the time of the auction. Because all of these bids will be accepted, the Treasury will accept only $4 billion of competitive bids, taking the highest prices offered by competitive-bidding investors. The average price on the accepted competitive bids will be the price charged to the noncompetitive bidders.

Each Tuesday the *Wall Street Journal* publishes the results of the auction that took place on the previous day. Figure 14.4 presents the results of the auction that took place on December 13, 1993. Individuals may purchase new issues of Treasury bills directly from one of the 12 Federal Reserve Banks, or indirectly via a bank or broker. Government security dealers maintain an active secondary market in bills, and it is a simple matter to buy or sell one prior to maturity (especially if the original purchase was through a bank or a broker). Terms offered by government security dealers are reported daily in the financial press, stated on a "bank discount" basis. To determine the actual dollar prices, an investor needs to "undo" the bank discount computation.

For example, a bill with 120 days left to maturity might be listed as "7.48% bid, 7.19% ask." Both of these discounts were obtained by multiplying the actual discount by 360/120 (the inverse of the portion of a 360-day year involved). Thus, to find the actual discount associated with the 7.48% bid, multiply 7.48% by 120/360, resulting in a figure of 2.493%. This means that the dealer is bidding 97.507% ($= 100\% - 2.493\%$) of face value, or equivalently that the dealer is willing to pay $9,750.70 for this $10,000 Treasury bill.

Similarly, the dealer is offering to sell such a bill at a discount of 2.397% $\{= 100\% - [7.19\% \times (120/360)]\}$, meaning that the dealer is willing to sell such a bill for $9,760.30 $[= \$10,000 \times (100\% - 2.397\%)]$. The difference between

Here are the details of yesterday's auction by the Treasury of 13-week and 26-week bills:

Rates are determined by the difference between the purchase price and face value. Thus, higher bidding narrows the investor's return while lower bidding widens it. The percentage rates are calculated on a 360-day year, while the coupon equivalent yield is based on a 365-day year.

	13-Week	26-Week
Applications	$55,775,696,000	$48,878,949,000
Accepted bids	$13,073,996,000	$13,080,408,000
Accepted at low price	22%	76%
Accepted noncompet'ly ...	$1,118,192,000	$861,519,000
Average price (Rate)	99.227 (3.06%)	98.352 (3.26%)
High price (Rate)	99.229 (3.05%)	98.362 (3.24%)
Low price (Rate)	99.227 (3.06%)	98.352 (3.26%)
Coupon equivalent	3.12%	3.36%
CUSIP number	912794J54	912794L28

Both issues are dated Dec. 16. The 13-week bills mature March 17, 1994, and the 26-week bills mature June 16, 1994.

FIGURE 14.4

Treasury Bill Auction Results for December 13, 1993

the prices—$9.60 (= $9,760.30 − $9,750.70)—is known as the **dealer's spread,** and it serves as compensation for carrying inventories of bills, taking associated risks, and bearing the clerical and other costs associated with being a market-maker.

In addition to the bid and asked discounts, the *Wall Street Journal* and other media provide an **equivalent yield** that is based on the asked price. In the example, the equivalent yield would be calculated by determining the dollar discount on the security ($10,000 − $9,760.30 = $239.70) and then dividing this figure by the purchase price ($239.70/$9,760.30 = 2.455%) in order to arrive at the rate of return associated with purchasing the security. Then this rate of return would be annualized by multiplying it by 365, and dividing the product by the number of days until maturity. The resulting figure would be the equivalent yield. In the example, the equivalent yield would be 7.47% [= 2.455% × (365/120)].[5]

14.3.2 U.S. Treasury Notes

Treasury notes are issued with maturities from one to ten years and generally make coupon payments semiannually. Some, issued prior to 1983, were in *bearer* form, with coupons attached; the owner simply submitted each coupon on its specified date to receive payment for the stated amount. Beginning in 1983, the Treasury ceased the issuance of bearer notes (and bonds). All issues since then are in *registered* form; the current owner is registered with the Treasury, which sends him or her each coupon payment when due and the principal value at maturity. When a registered note is sold, the new owner's name and address are substituted for those of the old owner on the Treasury's books.

Treasury notes are issued in denominations of $1,000 or more. Coupon payments are set at an amount so that the notes will initially sell close to par value. In most cases an auction is held, with both competitive and noncompetitive bids being submitted.

Treasury notes are traded in an active secondary market made by dealers in U.S. government securities. For example, as shown in Figure 14.3, the December 14, 1993, issue of the *Wall Street Journal* carried the following quotation from the day before, December 13, 1993:

Rate	Mat. Date	Bid	Asked	Chg.	Ask Yield
7⅞	Nov 99n	112:27	112:29	−8	5.31

The quotation indicated that a note (n), maturing in November 1999, carried a coupon rate of 7⅞%. It could be sold to a dealer for $112\frac{27}{32}$% of par value, which is equivalent to $1,128.4375 per $1,000 of par value. Alternatively, it could be purchased from a dealer for $112\frac{29}{32}$% of par value, which is equivalent to $1,129.0625 per $1,000 of par value (thus the dealer's spread was equal to $.6250 = $1,129.0625 − $1,128.4375). On December 13, 1993, the bid price was $\frac{8}{32}$ less than it had been on the previous trading day, resulting in a reported "Chg." of −8 (note how numbers are expressed in 32nds, reflecting an old tradition). The effective yield-to-maturity at the time, based on the asked price, was approximately 5.31% per year.[6]

In practice, the situation facing a potential buyer (or seller) is a little more complicated. The buyer is generally expected to pay the dealer not only the stated price ($1,129.0625) but also any **accrued interest.** For example, if 122 days have elapsed since the last coupon payment and 61 days remain, then an amount equal to $\frac{2}{3}$ [= 122/(122 + 61)] of the semiannual coupon ($\frac{2}{3} \times \frac{1}{2} \times$ $78.75 = $26.25) is added to the stated purchase price to determine the total amount required (in this case, $26.25 + $1,129.0625 = $1,155.3125). Similarly, if an investor were to sell a note to the dealer, the dealer would pay the investor the stated bid price plus accrued interest (in this case, $1,128.4375 + $26.25 = $1,154.6875). This procedure is commonly followed with both government and corporate bonds.[7]

14.3.3 U.S. Treasury Bonds

Treasury bonds have maturities greater than ten years at the time of issuance. Those issued prior to 1983 may be in either bearer or registered form; more recent issues will be in registered form. Denominations range from $1,000 upward. Unlike Treasury notes, some Treasury bond issues have **call provisions** that allow them to be "called" during a specified period (usually the period begins five to ten years prior to maturity and ends at the maturity date). This means that at any scheduled coupon payment date during this period, the Treasury has the right to force the investor to sell the bonds back to the government at par value.

Callable issues can be identified in Figure 14.3 by noting which issues have a range of years given as the maturity date (this "range of years" indicates the call period). For example, the 7⅛ of February 95–00 mature in 2000 but may be called beginning in 1995 (the "7⅛" indicates that the bonds have a coupon rate of 7⅛%, paid semiannually, just like the Treasury notes from earlier).

For callable issues, the yield-to-maturity is calculated using the asked price. If this price is greater than par, then the yield-to-maturity is based on an assumption that the bond will be called at the earliest allowable date. Otherwise, Treasury bonds are comparable to Treasury notes, with dealers' bid and asked quotations being stated in the same form.

14.3.4 U.S. Savings Bonds

These nonmarketable bonds are offered only to individuals and selected organizations. No more than a specified amount (currently $15,000 of issue price) may be purchased by any person in a single year. Two types are available. Series EE bonds are essentially pure discount bonds, meaning that no interest is paid on them prior to maturity. The term-to-maturity at the date of issuance has varied from time to time. For bonds issued in 1994, it was 18 years. (However, they may be held as long as an additional 12 years before they must be redeemed or exchanged for an HH bond.) Series HH bonds mature in 20 years and pay interest semiannually but can be redeemed for par value at any time. Both types are registered.

Series EE bonds are available in small denominations (the smallest one has a maturity value of $50) and may be purchased from commercial banks and many other financial institutions. Some employers even allow employees to obtain them through payroll savings plans. Series HH bonds are available only in exchange for eligible Series EE bonds (that is, a Series EE bond must be purchased first and then held for the minimum time period of six months before it can be exchanged) and can be obtained only from the Treasury department or one of the 12 Federal Reserve Banks.

Series EE bonds utilize a floating market-based rate with a minimum pre-specified floor known as a *guaranteed rate*. The floating market-based rate is determined every six months (on May 1 and November 1) and is applicable for the next six months. This rate is set equal to 85% of the average market yield over the previous six months on Treasury bonds and notes with about five years remaining to maturity. If the bond is held for five or more years, the redemption value of the bond will be determined by using the floating rates that were in place since the bond's issuance or the guaranteed rate, whichever is higher. Should the bond be held for less than five years, the guaranteed rate is used to determine the redemption value of the bond; in 1994 this rate was 4%. Series HH bonds issued in 1994 also provided a fixed annual rate of 4%.

Unlike most other discount bonds, no taxes are paid on the interest as it accumulates semiannually on the Series EE bonds. Only when these bonds are redeemed is the interest subject to federal income tax; no state or local income taxes are involved.[8] Thus a $15,000 investment that grows to $30,000 in 12 years will create a tax obligation only at the end of the 12th year. Furthermore, should a Series EE bond be exchanged for a Series HH bond, this tax obligation on the interest earned on the Series EE bond can be deferred until the Series HH bond is redeemed. However, the HH bond interest is subject to federal income tax annually. Hence, the tax obligation on the $30,000 would be deferred if the EE bond is exchanged for an HH bond, but the $1,800 (= .06 × $30,000) annual HH interest would be immediately taxable.

The terms on which Savings Bonds are offered have been revised from time to time. In some cases, improved terms have been offered to holders of outstanding bonds. Terms have sometimes been inferior to those available on less well-known or less accessible instruments with similar characteristics. At such times, the Treasury department sells Savings Bonds by appealing more to patriotism than to the desire for high return.

14.3.5 Zero Coupon Treasury Security Receipts

A noncallable Treasury note or bond is, in effect, a portfolio of pure-discount bonds (or, equivalently, a portfolio of zero coupon bonds). That is, each coupon payment, as well as the principal, can be viewed as a bond unto itself; the investor who owns the bond can therefore be viewed as holding a number of individual pure-discount bonds. In 1982, a number of brokerage firms began separating these components, using a process known as **coupon stripping.** (Chapter 5's Institutional Issues also discusses zero coupon Treasury securities.)

With this process, Treasury bonds of a given issue are purchased and placed in trust with a custodian (for example, a bank). Sets of *receipts* are then issued, one set for each coupon date. For example, an August 15, 2001, receipt might entitle its holder to receive $1,000 on that date (and nothing on any other date). The amount required to meet the payments on all the August 15, 2001, receipts would exactly equal the total amount received on that date from coupon payments on the Treasury securities held in the trust account.

In addition to issuing a set of receipts corresponding to coupon dates, another set of receipts would be issued that mature on the date the principal of the securities held in trust is due. Thus holders of these receipts share in the principal payment.[9]

Noting the favorable market reaction to the offering of these stripped securities, in 1985 the Treasury department introduced a program for investors called Separate Trading of Registered Interest and Principal Securities (STRIPS). This program allows purchasers of certain coupon-bearing Treasury securities to keep whatever cash payments they want and to sell the rest. The prices at which such pure-discount securities sold on December 13, 1993, are shown in Figure 14.3.

Figure 14.5 shows typical market prices for a set of stripped Treasury securities, where price is expressed as a percent of maturity value. As the figure shows, the longer the investor has to wait until maturity, the lower the price of the security.

The Internal Revenue Service requires that taxes be paid annually on the accrued interest earned on such securities. That is, such securities are treated for tax purposes as **original issue discount securities,** also known as OID debt instruments. They are securities that were issued at a discount from par due to their relatively small (or nonexistent) coupon payments.[10]

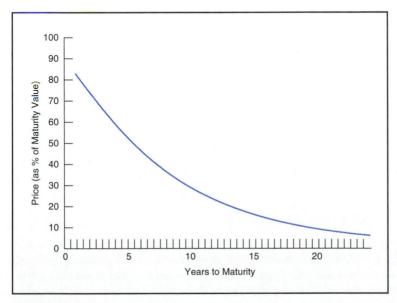

FIGURE 14.5
Typical Market Prices for a Set of Stripped Treasury Securities

For example, a STRIP that matures in two years for $1,000 might be purchased currently for $900. Thus the investor would earn $100 in interest over two years, realizing it when the STRIP matures. However, the IRS would make the investor pay taxes on a portion of the $100 each year. The amount to be recognized must be calculated using the *constant interest method* that reflects the actual economic accrual of interest. This means that the investor cannot report $50 (=$100/2) per year as interest income. Instead, first the yield needs to be calculated, which in this case is 5.4% [= ($1,000/$900)$^{1/2}$ − 1]. This means that the implied value of the STRIP at the end of the first year would be $948.60 (= $900 × 1.054. Thus the amount of interest income to be recognized then is $48.60 (= $948.60 − $900). The amount of interest income to be recognized in the second year, assuming that the STRIP is held to maturity, will be $51.40 (= $1,000 − $948.60). (Note that $1,000 = $948.60 × 1.054). Consequently, the taxable investor has a cash outflow not only when purchasing the STRIP, but also every year until it matures. Only at that time does the investor experience a cash inflow. As a result, such securities are attractive primarily for tax-exempt investors and for investors in low tax brackets. (For example, some people purchase them as investments that are held in the names of their children.)

14.4 FEDERAL AGENCY SECURITIES

Although much of the federal government's activity is financed directly, via taxes and debt issued by the Treasury department, a substantial amount is financed in other ways. In some situations, various government departments provide explicit or implicit backing for the securities of quasi-governmental agencies. In other situations, the federal government has guaranteed both the principal and coupon payments on bonds issued by certain private organizations. In both cases, some of the arrangements are so convoluted that cynics suggest that the original legislative intent was to obscure the nature and extent of government backing. In any event, a wide range of bonds with different degrees of government backing has been created in this manner. Many of the bonds are considered second in safety only to the debt obligations of the U.S. government itself.

Table 14.4 lists the issuers of these securities and the amounts outstanding at the end of 1992. A partial list of typical price quotations is shown in Figure 14.6; these quotations can be interpreted in a manner similar to Treasury security quotations.

14.4.1 Bonds of Federal Agencies

Bonds issued by federal agencies provide funds to support such activities as housing (through either direct loans or the purchase of existing mortgages); export and import activities (via loans, credit guarantees, and insurance); the postal service; and the activities of the Tennessee Valley Authority. Many issues are guaranteed by the full faith and credit of the U.S. government, but some (for example, those of the Tennessee Valley Authority) are not.

TABLE 14.4

DEBT OUTSTANDING OF FEDERAL AND FEDERALLY SPONSORED AGENCIES, END OF 1992

Debt of Federal Agencies	Amount (In Millions)
Defense Department: Family Housing and Homeowner's Assistance	$ 7
Export-Import Bank	7,208
Federal Housing Administration	374
Postal Service	10,660
Tennessee Valley Authority	23,580
Total	$41,829

Debt of Federally Sponsored Agencies	Amount (In Millions)
Federal Home Loan Banks	$114,733
Federal National Mortgage Association	166,300
Federal Home Loan Mortgage Corporation	29,631
Student Loan Marketing Association	39,650
Farm Credit Banks	51,910
Financing Corporation	8,170
Farm Credit Financial Assistance Corporation	1,261
Resolution Funding Corporation	29,996
Other	490
Total	$442,141

Source: *Federal Reserve Bulletin*, November 1993, p. A33.

14.4.2 Bonds of Federally Sponsored Agencies

Federally sponsored agencies are privately owned agencies that issue securities and use the proceeds to support the granting of certain types of loans to farmers, homeowners, and others. A common procedure involves the creation of a series of governmental "banks" to buy securities issued by private organizations that grant the loans in the first instance. Some or all of the initial capital for these "banks" may be provided by the government, but subsequent amounts typically come from bonds issued by the "banks."

Although the debts of agencies of this type are usually not guaranteed by the federal government, governmental control is designed to ensure that each debt issue is backed by extremely safe assets (for example, mortgages insured by another quasi-governmental agency). Moreover, it is generally presumed that governmental assistance of one sort or another would be provided if there were any danger of default on such debt.

As shown in Table 14.4, there are eight federally sponsored agencies. Federal Home Loan Banks make loans to thrift institutions, primarily savings and loan associations. The Federal National Mortgage Association (FNMA, also known as "Fannie Mae") purchases and sells real estate mortgages—not only those insured by the Federal Housing Administration or guaranteed by the Veterans Administration, but also conventional mortgages. The Federal Home Loan Mortgage Corporation (known as "Freddie Mac") deals only in conventional mortgages. The Student Loan Marketing Association (known as "Sallie Mae") purchases federally guaranteed loans made to students by other lenders, such as

GOVERNMENT AGENCY & SIMILAR ISSUES

Monday, December 13, 1993

Over-the-Counter mid-afternoon quotations based on large transactions, usually $1 million or more. Colons in bid-and-asked quotes represent 32nds; 101:01 means 101 1/32.

All yields are calculated to maturity, and based on the asked quote. * -- Callable issue, maturity date shown. For issues callable prior to maturity, yields are computed to the earliest call date for issues quoted above par, or 100, and to the maturity date for issues quoted below par.

Source: Bear, Stearns & Co. via Street Software Technology Inc.

FNMA Issues

Rate	Mat.	Bid	Asked	Yld.
7.55	1-94	100:09	100:13	1.64
9.45	1-94	100:13	100:17	1.72
7.65	4-94	101:10	101:14	3.10
9.60	4-94	102:00	102:04	2.89
9.30	5-94	102:08	102:12	3.30
8.60	6-94	102:13	102:17	3.31
7.45	7-94	102:05	102:09	3.37
8.90	8-94	103:10	103:14	3.50
10.10	10-94	105:00	105:08	3.54
9.25	11-94	104:13	104:21	3.93
5.50	12-94	101:06	101:10	4.16
9.00	1-95	105:04	105:12	3.81
11.95	1-95	108:06	108:18	3.70
11.50	2-95	108:07	108:19	3.80
8.85	3-95	105:27	106:03	3.75
11.70	5-95	110:03	110:15	3.94
11.15	6-95	109:29	110:09	3.98
4.75	8-95	100:26	100:30	4.16
10.50	9-95	110:09	110:21	4.08
8.80	11-95	108:05	108:13	4.15
10.60	11-95	111:13	111:21	4.16
9.20	1-96	109:13	109:21	4.27
7.00	2-96	104:28	105:04	4.47
7.70	2-96*	100:17	100:21	3.44
9.35	2-96	109:21	109:29	4.48
8.00	4-96*	101:05	101:09	3.88
8.05	6-96*	101:21	101:25	4.30
8.50	6-96	108:27	109:03	4.59
8.75	6-96	109:14	109:22	4.58
8.00	7-96	107:29	108:05	4.60
7.90	8-96	107:30	108:06	4.59
8.15	8-96	108:18	108:26	4.59
8.20	8-96*	102:14	102:18	4.19
7.70	9-96	107:18	107:22	4.67
8.63	9-96	109:29	110:05	4.63
7.05	10-96	106:04	106:08	4.66
8.45	10-96	109:27	110:03	4.63
6.90	11-96*	102:08	102:12	4.20
7.70	12-96	107:26	108:02	4.77
8.20	12-96	109:28	110:04	4.57
6.20	1-97*	101:31	102:07	4.05
7.60	1-97	108:04	108:12	4.64
7.05	3-97*	103:05	103:09	4.29
7.00	4-97*	103:01	103:05	4.50
9.25	4-97*	101:13	101:17	4.32
6.75	4-97	105:18	105:22	4.89
9.20	6-97	113:17	113:25	4.85
8.95	7-97	113:01	113:09	4.85
8.80	7-97	112:21	112:29	4.86
9.15	9-97*	103:09	103:17	4.20
9.55	9-97	114:04	114:12	5.26
5.70	9-97*	100:22	100:26	5.20
5.35	10-97*	100:19	100:23	4.93
6.05	10-97	102:00	102:06	4.81
6.05	11-97	102:17	102:21	5.29
9.55	11-97	114:17	114:25	5.30
7.10	12-97*	104:14	106:22	5.22
8.60	12-97*	104:05	104:13	3.99
9.55	12-97	115:17	115:25	5.12
6.30	12-97*	103:12	103:16	4.44
6.05	1-98	103:10	103:14	5.10
8.65	2-98	112:21	112:29	5.16
8.20	3-98	110:31	111:03	5.24
5.30	3-98*	100:08	100:12	5.12
5.25	3-98	100:04	100:08	5.18
9.15	4-98	114:16	114:24	5.28
8.38	4-98*	104:20	104:24	4.71
8.15	5-98	111:08	111:12	5.22
5.25	5-98*	99:12	99:20	5.34
5.40	5-98*	99:30	100:02	5.38
5.38	6-98	100:18	100:22	5.20
5.10	7-98*	98:29	99:01	5.34
8.20	8-98	105:17	105:21	4.60
5.35	8-98*	99:26	99:30	5.36
4.70	9-98*	97:14	97:18	5.29
7.85	9-98	110:09	110:13	5.33
4.95	9-98*	98:11	98:13	5.33
4.88	10-98*	98:01	98:03	5.33
5.05	11-98	99:04	99:06	5.24
5.30	12-98*	99:20	99:22	5.37
7.05	12-98*	107:11	107:15	5.32
7.05	12-98*	104:23	104:27	4.50
7.50	3-99*	105:01	105:05	5.03
9.55	3-99	118:15	118:31	5.34
8.70	6-99	114:23	114:31	5.50
8.45	7-99	113:03	113:11	5.63
8.65	7-99*	102:06	102:14	4.29
6.35	8-99	103:21	103:25	5.56
8.55	8-99	114:16	114:24	5.50
9.00	10-99*	102:22	102:30	5.28
8.35	11-99	114:07	114:15	5.45
8.65	12-99*	103:24	104:04	4.33
6.10	2-00	103:19	103:23	5.38
9.30	2-00*	104:04	104:12	5.32
9.05	4-00	118:15	118:23	5.50
9.80	5-00*	106:25	107:01	4.56
8.90	6-00	118:07	118:15	5.48
9.20	9-00	119:21	119:29	5.61
8.25	12-00	115:14	115:22	5.52
8.88	1-01*	104:17	104:25	3.62
8.50	2-01*	105:00	105:08	2.02
8.70	3-01*	100:28	101:08	3.58
8.63	4-01*	108:02	108:06	4.84
8.70	6-01*	108:05	108:09	5.11
8.88	7-01*	111:01	111:05	4.24
7.80	12-01*	102:19	102:27	4.76
7.20	1-02*	105:00	105:08	5.32
7.50	2-02	110:09	110:17	5.86
7.90	4-02*	106:03	106:11	5.77
7.55	4-02	110:14	110:22	5.91
7.80	6-02*	106:09	106:17	5.71
7.30	7-02*	105:24	106:00	5.43
7.00	8-02*	104:06	104:14	5.64
6.95	9-02*	103:21	103:29	5.77
7.30	10-02*	106:06	106:14	5.43
6.80	10-02*	102:28	103:09	4.92
7.05	11-02	107:02	107:10	5.98
6.80	1-03	105:25	105:29	5.65
6.40	3-03*	100:25	100:29	6.15
6.63	4-03*	102:11	102:15	5.97
6.45	6-03*	101:04	101:08	6.13
6.20	7-03*	99:20	99:24	6.23
6.25	8-03*	99:27	99:31	6.25
5.45	10-03	96:20	96:22	5.90
6.20	11-03*	99:03	99:05	6.32
5.80	12-03	99:00	99:04	5.92
12.65	3-14*	101:24	102:08	2.95
0.00	7-14	24:02	24:10	7.00
10.35	12-15	144:21	145:05	6.47
8.20	3-16	116:02	116:10	6.77
8.95	2-18	129:00	129:08	6.53
8.10	8-19	118:16	118:24	6.58
0.00	10-19	16:25	17:01	6.97
9.65	8-20*	116:13	116:21	3.26
9.50	11-20*	115:30	116:06	3.98

Federal Home Loan Bank

Rate	Mat.	Bid	Asked	Yld.
7.38	12-93	100:04	100:08	0.00
7.50	12-93	100:04	100:08	0.00
12.15	12-93	100:10	100:14	0.00
5.00	1-94	100:05	100:09	2.41
7.30	1-94	100:13	100:17	2.44
7.55	1-94	100:14	100:18	2.40
9.30	2-94	100:30	101:02	2.81
7.45	2-94	100:23	100:27	3.02
9.60	2-94	101:05	101:09	2.89
12.00	2-94	101:19	101:23	3.00
7.58	3-94	101:03	101:07	3.10
5.48	4-94	100:21	100:25	3.27
7.28	4-94	101:09	101:13	3.31
8.50	4-94	101:23	101:27	3.30
9.55	4-94	102:03	102:07	3.29
7.20	5-94	101:19	101:23	3.26
7.50	6-94	102:00	102:04	3.42
8.60	6-94	102:18	102:22	3.44
8.63	6-94	102:19	102:23	3.40
8.30	7-94	102:23	102:27	3.53
6.70	8-94	101:30	102:02	3.65
8.60	8-94	103:08	103:12	3.61
6.58	9-94	102:01	102:05	3.73
8.30	10-94	103:13	103:19	3.99
4.75	11-94	100:18	100:22	4.00
5.89	11-94	101:21	101:25	3.94
8.20	11-94	103:19	103:25	4.07
8.05	12-94	103:31	104:05	3.89
5.45	1-95	101:16	101:20	3.93
8.40	1-95	104:24	104:27	3.89
5.94	2-95	102:08	102:12	3.89
8.60	2-95	105:09	105:17	3.83
6.45	3-95	102:31	103:03	3.95
7.88	3-95	104:25	104:27	3.96
9.00	3-95	106:05	106:13	3.82
6.04	4-95	102:17	102:25	3.92
8.88	6-95	106:26	107:02	4.06
10.00	6-95	108:15	108:23	4.06
10.30	7-95	109:11	109:19	4.08
4.60	8-95	100:16	100:20	4.21
4.50	9-95	100:10	100:14	4.24
5.00	10-95	101:08	101:12	4.22
5.38	11-95	102:00	102:04	4.23
5.47	12-95*	100:00	100:04	0.00
7.95	12-95*	100:00	100:04	3.72
9.50	12-95	110:01	110:09	4.16
8.10	3-96	107:19	107:27	4.44
9.80	3-96	111:16	111:24	4.32
6.68	4-96	104:14	104:18	4.61
4.36	4-96*	99:17	99:21	4.51
7.75	4-96	106:31	107:07	4.49
8.25	5-96	108:10	108:18	4.52
8.25	6-96	108:20	108:28	4.59
4.41	7-96*	99:08	99:12	4.67
8.00	7-96	108:00	108:08	4.61
7.70	8-96	107:18	107:26	4.58
8.25	9-96	109:07	109:15	4.58
7.10	10-96	106:10	106:14	4.67
8.25	11-96	109:20	109:28	4.62
6.85	2-97	105:29	106:05	4.75
9.15	3-97	112:20	112:28	4.85
6.99	4-97	106:10	106:14	4.89
9.20	8-97	113:29	114:05	4.95
5.26	4-98*	99:23	99:27	5.30
9.25	11-98	116:24	117:00	5.30
9.30	1-99	117:06	117:14	5.35
8.60	6-99	114:11	114:19	5.50
8.45	7-99	113:25	114:01	5.51
8.60	8-99	114:26	115:02	5.48
8.38	10-99	113:17	113:25	5.58
8.60	1-00	116:01	116:09	5.43
9.50	2-04	122:29	123:13	6.34

Federal Farm Credit Bank

Rate	Mat.	Bid	Asked	Yld.
7.38	12-93	100:04	100:08	0.00
3.00	1-94	100:00	100:04	0.50
3.30	1-94	100:00	100:04	0.79

Rate	Mat.	Bid	Asked	Yld.
3.63	1-94	100:00	100:04	1.11
3.21	2-94	100:00	100:04	2.22
3.36	2-94	100:00	100:04	2.35
3.43	2-94	99:31	100:03	2.66
7.19	2-94	100:16	100:20	2.85
3.19	3-94	100:00	100:04	2.57
3.21	3-94	100:01	100:05	2.46
12.35	3-94	101:27	101:31	2.87
3.33	4-94	99:30	100:02	3.10
3.15	4-94	100:00	100:04	2.72
5.80	4-94	100:22	100:26	3.06
14.25	4-94	103:22	103:26	3.09
3.31	5-94	100:00	100:04	2.97
3.32	5-94	99:29	100:01	3.22
3.37	6-94	100:00	100:04	3.09
3.56	6-94	100:00	100:04	3.28
3.60	7-94	99:30	100:02	3.48
3.64	8-94	100:00	100:04	3.43
3.40	9-94	99:27	99:31	3.44
4.31	9-94	100:10	100:14	3.67
8.63	9-94	103:11	103:15	3.61
13.00	9-94	106:12	106:16	3.61
3.43	10-94	99:25	99:27	3.63
3.48	11-94	99:27	99:29	3.59
3.62	12-94	99:31	100:01	3.59
11.45	12-94	106:30	107:06	3.75
8.30	1-95	104:15	104:23	3.86
6.38	4-95	102:29	103:01	3.95
5.50	12-95	102:09	102:13	4.22
5.08	1-96	101:11	101:15	4.33
4.49	3-96*	99:31	100:02	4.46
6.65	5-96	104:19	104:23	4.53
11.90	10-97	122:12	122:24	5.28
5.88	2-98*	100:02	100:06	4.34
8.65	10-99	114:27	115:03	5.56
8.70	6-01*	101:24	101:28	8.36
7.95	4-02*	109:25	109:29	4.67

Student Loan Marketing

Rate	Mat.	Bid	Asked	Yld.
7.38	1-94	100:09	100:13	1.69
16.00	2-94	102:00	102:04	2.82
7.43	4-94	101:08	101:12	3.08
7.35	5-94	101:19	101:23	3.29
7.30	5-94	101:19	101:23	3.31
8.50	7-94	102:21	102:25	3.40
7.50	7-94	102:05	102:09	3.42
8.10	7-94	102:16	102:20	3.58
8.30	9-94	103:10	103:14	3.69
7.54	10-94	102:30	103:06	3.56
0.00	11-94	96:03	96:09	4.37
8.55	2-95	104:27	104:31	3.99
5.28	2-95	101:10	101:14	3.96
7.63	3-95	104:11	104:17	3.80
7.74	3-96*	100:28	101:04	3.42
9.50	9-97*	103:18	103:26	4.16
9.34	7-98*	100:13	100:25	9.12
9.78	1-99*	100:18	100:26	1.12
8.75	8-00*	103:09	103:17	3.47
9.80	9-00*	108:21	109:05	4.34
7.00	12-02	106:20	106:28	6.00
0.00	5-14	21:01	21:09	7.72
0.00	10-22	14:00	14:08	6.88

World Bank Bonds

Rate	Mat.	Bid	Asked	Yld.
11.63	12-94	107:09	107:13	4.00
8.63	10-95	107:04	107:08	4.37
7.25	10-96	106:09	106:17	4.72
8.75	3-97	111:02	111:10	4.89
5.88	7-97	103:03	103:11	4.85
9.88	10-97	116:06	116:14	5.05
8.38	10-99	113:20	113:28	5.54
8.13	3-01	113:26	113:28	5.74
6.75	1-02	106:23	106:27	5.68
12.38	10-02	141:23	141:31	6.14
8.25	9-16	118:04	118:12	6.67
8.63	10-16	122:17	122:25	6.67
9.25	7-17	129:20	129:28	6.71

FIGURE 14.6

Price Quotations for Government Agency Issues (Excerpts)

Source: Reprinted by permission of *The Wall Street Journal*, Dow Jones & Company, Inc., December 14, 1993, p. C17. All rights reserved worldwide.

commercial banks, and may make direct student loans under special circumstances. The Farm Credit Banks lend to farmers as well as farm associations and cooperatives, and the Farm Credit Financial Assistance Corporation was created in 1987 to help the Farm Credit Bank System. The Financing Corporation was established in August 1987 to recapitalize the Federal Savings and Loan Insurance Corporation (FSLIC). Lastly, the Resolution Funding Corporation was created in 1989 to assist in the recovery of the thrift industry, mainly by assisting bankrupt or near-bankrupt savings and loans.

14.4.3 Participation Certificates

To support credit for home purchases, the government has authorized the issuance of **participation certificates.** A group of assets (for example, mortgages) is placed in a pool, and certificates representing ownership of those assets are issued to pay for them. The holders of the certificates receive the interest and principal payments as they are made, minus a small service charge. The most important certificates of this type are those issued by the Government National Mortgage Association (GNMA, or "Ginnie Mae") and are known as GNMA Modified Pass-Through Securities. These securities are guaranteed by GNMA and backed by the full faith and credit of the U.S. government.

GNMA pass-through securities are created by certain private organizations such as savings and loans and mortgage bankers that bundle a package of similar (in terms of maturity date and interest rate) mortgages together. These mortgages must be individually guaranteed by either the Federal Housing Administration or the Veterans Administration (thus making them free from default risk) and have, in aggregate, a principal amount of at least $1 million. After these mortgages have been bundled together, an application is made to GNMA for a guarantee on the pass-through securities. Typically each security represents $25,000 worth of principal. Once the guarantee is received, the securities are sold to the public through brokers. The interest rate paid on the securities is .5% less than the interest rate paid on the mortgages, with GNMA keeping .1% and the creator .4%.

Unlike most bonds, GNMA pass-through securities pay investors on a monthly basis an amount of money that represents both a pro rata return of principal and interest on the underlying mortgages. For example, the holder of a $25,000 certificate from a $1 million pool would indirectly "own" 2½% of each mortgage in the pool. Each month the homeowners make mortgage payments that consist of part principal and part interest. In turn, each month the investor receives 2½% of the aggregate amount paid by the homeowners. Because the mortgages are free from default risk, there is no default risk on the pass-through securities. (If homeowner payments are late, GNMA will either use excess cash or borrow money from the Treasury to make sure that the investors are paid in a timely fashion.)

Prepayment Risk

There is one particular risk to investors, however, that arises because homeowners are allowed to prepay their mortgages. This prepayment allowance means that typical pass-through securities, although initially having a stated life of 30 years, may actually have much shorter lives. This can cause losses if the investor buys an existing pass-through that is selling at a premium, a situation that can happen if interest rates have fallen since the time the pass-through security was created. In such a situation, homeowners may start to prepay their mortgages. This means that the investor will receive par value on the security shortly after paying a premium for it, thereby causing the investor to incur a loss.

Consider a pass-through security of $25,000, initially issued with a stated interest rate of 12%. Suppose that interest rates subsequently fall so that new pass-throughs carry a stated rate of 10%. At this time the older pass-through security has $20,000 of principal outstanding, but as a consequence of the fall in interest rates it is selling at a premium, perhaps for $22,000. Now suppose that interest rates fall further to 8%. At this point many homeowners prepay their mortgages in order to refinance them at the current rate of 8%. As a result an investor who purchased the older pass-through security for $22,000 ends up shortly thereafter receiving $20,000, thereby quickly losing $2,000.[11]

Innovations

The interest the investing public has shown in GNMA pass-through securities has caused a number of similar securities to be created. One, typically issued in denominations of $100,000 or more, is the "guaranteed mortgage certificate" sold by the Federal Home Loan Mortgage Corporation ("Freddie Mac"), a federally sponsored agency that was mentioned earlier. A number of banks have offered similar pass-through mortgage certificates backed by private insurance companies. Some of them have repackaged the cash flows that are paid by the homeowners so that investors can receive something other than a pro rata share of them. Examples of such innovations include collateralized mortgage obligations (CMOs), real estate mortgage investment conduits (REMICs), floaters, inverse floaters, interest-only securities (IOs), and principal-only securities (POs).

14.5　STATE AND LOCAL GOVERNMENT SECURITIES

The 1992 Census of Governments showed that there were 86,742 governmental units in the United States in addition to the federal government itself:[12]

State Government		50
Local Government:		
County	3,043	
Municipal	19,296	
Township or Town	16,666	
School District	14,556	
Special District	33,131	
Total Local Governmental Units		86,692
Total Governmental Units		86,742

Collateralized Mortgage Obligations

Twenty years ago the market for securities backed by residential mortgages was a fledgling. Today it stands as a behemoth, dwarfing the corporate bond market in terms of outstanding market value and daily trading volume. Moreover, the market has considerable growth capacity left. Only about one-third of the roughly $2 trillion in single-family mortgages has been converted into tradable securities. Further, the trillion-dollar market for commercial and multifamily residential mortgages remains largely untapped.

The key to the mortgage-backed security market's success has been the creation of financial instruments that appeal to investors who would not or could not invest directly in mortgages. (The process of packaging the cash flows from individual mortgages into various financial securities is referred to as the "securitization" of mortgages.) The mainstay of the mortgage-backed security market has always been the traditional pass-through security. However, mortgage-backed securities also take other forms, and the pace of innovation is increasing.

Originally designed to help liquify the home mortgage market and thereby increase the availability and lower the cost of home financing, pass-through securities have succeeded beyond anyone's wildest imagination. Investors have been attracted by the higher yields available relative to Treasury securities, combined with the pass-through securities' safety and liquidity.

However, one aspect of traditional pass-through securities has always proven particularly troublesome to investors: the cash flows produced by these securities are uncertain. As the text describes, homeowners have the option to prepay their mortgages. These prepayments may occur because the homeowner decides to sell his or her house. More disconcerting to the pass-through securityholder, however, is that homeowners are more likely to refinance their mortgages as interest rates decline. The pass-through securityholder thus may receive sizable principal repayments at the most inopportune time—when interest rates decline significantly. (This phenomenon was witnessed on a large scale from late 1991 to mid 1993, when long-term interest rates tumbled.)

In an effort to overcome this undesirable feature of traditional pass-through securities, many organizations have repackaged these securities into a different form of mortgage-backed security: collateralized mortgage obligations (CMOs).

There are many different variations of CMOs, but the underlying concept behind all of them is relatively simple. Mortgages generate two types of payments: interest and principal. If a pension fund, for example, owns a traditional pass-through security, it receives a pro rata share of the interest and principal payments made on the various mortgages that have been pooled together. On a monthly basis, the pension fund's investment declines in size as it receives regularly scheduled principal payments. Moreover, if a mortgage in the pool prepays in full, the pension fund receives a pro rata portion of the prepaid principal and no more interest from that mortgage. The pool is now smaller by the amount of the paid-off mortgage. The pension fund's interest payments from the pool decline, and it must find an alternative investment for its prepaid principal.

CMOs are simply a means to allocate principal and interest payments among investors in a mortgage pool. A CMO originator (or sponsor) transforms a traditional mortgage pool into a set of securities, called CMO *tranches* (French for "slice"), that have different priority claims on the interest and principal paid by the mortgages underlying the CMO.

Although there is no "typical" form of CMO, consider a common CMO structure that involves four tranches—*A, B, C,* and *Z.* Each tranche is initially allocated a specific proportion of the underlying mortgage pool's outstanding principal value. Interest payments, as with any bond, are paid as a percentage of the outstanding principal corresponding to each tranche.

The tranches differ in terms of how they are retired (that is, how principal payments are allocated among them). The *A* tranche receives all principal payments made by the pool until the tranche is retired. The *B* and *C* tranches receive only interest payments as long as the *A* tranche has not been fully paid off. Once it has, the *B* tranche receives all principal payments until it is retired; afterwards, principal payments go to the *C* tranche.

The last tranche, the Z (or accrual) tranche, receives neither principal nor interest payments until the other three tranches have been extinguished. Its earned interest goes to retire the principal of the other tranches. Thus the Z tranche's principal actually grows over time at a compound rate in a manner similar to the way interest accrues on pure-discount bonds. When the other three tranches have finally been retired, it receives all remaining interest and principal payments.

The primary purpose of dividing a mortgage pass-through pool's principal and income flows into various tranches is to create a set of securities with varying levels of interest rate and prepayment risk. Investors can match their risk preferences and predictions with the appropriate securities. The CMO originator expects that investors will pay a premium for this flexibility, with the sum of the parts being worth more than the whole. Investors desiring short-maturity bonds with very predictable cash flows invest in the A tranche, whereas investors seeking intermediate-maturity bonds with less predictable cash flows look to the B and C tranches. Finally, investors willing to bear the substantial interest-rate risk of long-maturity deep-discount bonds purchase the Z tranche. Of course, the mar-

ket sets prices of the various tranches accordingly, with the A tranche exhibiting the lowest yields, while the Z tranche sells at the highest yields. (The higher-yielding tranches of certain CMOs have been popular among investors in recent years as interest rates have fallen. Some observers contend that this popularity results from a misunderstanding of the true risks of these securities.)

The risk of principal prepayments can be allocated across various tranches, but in the final analysis it cannot be reduced. Thus, although holders of the slower-pay tranches may be less exposed to prepayment risk, if interest rates drop sharply they may still receive unexpectedly early prepayments, which can adversely affect the values of their investment. Evaluating this risk can prove extremely difficult, especially for some of the more complex CMO structures, which may include various combinations of such esoteric securities as planned amortization classes (PACs), companion tranches, floaters, inverse floaters, and jump-Z tranches. Despite this caveat, CMOs represent an excellent example of how the financial markets respond to the needs of suppliers and users of funds by creating flexible new securities.

A great many of these units borrow money, with their securities called **municipal bonds** or simply "municipals" or "muni's." (Only the securities of the U.S. government are referred to as "governments.") Table 14.5 provides estimates of

TABLE 14.5	
ESTIMATED AMOUNTS OF VARIOUS FIXED-INCOME SECURITIES OUTSTANDING, END OF 1992	
Type of Security	**Amount (In Billions)**
U.S. government securities	$ 4,795.5
Corporate and foreign obligations	1,966.4
State and local obligations	1,197.3
Mortgages	4,005.6
Consumer credit	809.2
Other	2,210.7
Total	$14,984.7

Source: *Federal Reserve Bulletin*, November 1993, p. A43.

TABLE 14.6
NEW SECURITY ISSUES OF STATE AND LOCAL GOVERNMENTS IN 1992, CLASSIFIED BY ISSUER

Issuer	Amount (In Billions)
States	$ 25.3
Special districts and statutory authorities	129.7
Municipalities, counties, and townships	60.2
Total	$215.2

Source: *Federal Reserve Bulletin*, November 1993, p. A34.

the amounts of various types of fixed-income securities outstanding at the end of 1992. With over one trillion dollars in outstanding value, municipals clearly warrant attention.

14.5.1 Issuing Agencies

Table 14.6 shows the dollar values of municipal bonds issued in 1992 by various agencies, whereas Table 14.7 shows the purposes for the issuance of such debt. States generally issue debt to finance capital expenditures, primarily for highways, housing, and education.[13] The concept behind the issuance of such debt is that the revenue generated by the resulting facilities will be used to make the required debt payments. In some cases, the link is direct (for example, tolls may be used to pay for a bridge). In other cases it is somewhat indirect (for example, gasoline taxes may be used to pay for highway construction) or very indirect (for example, state sales taxes or income taxes may be used to pay for the construction of new government buildings).

States cannot be sued without their consent. Thus bondholders may have no legal recourse in the event of default. This means that state-issued bonds that are dependent on particular revenues from some capital project may involve considerable risk. However, bonds backed by the "full faith and credit" of a state government are generally considered quite safe in spite of the inability of the bondholders to sue. This is because it is anticipated that state legislatures will do whatever is necessary to see that such bonds are paid off in a timely manner.

TABLE 14.7
NEW SECURITY ISSUES OF STATE AND LOCAL GOVERNMENTS IN 1992, CLASSIFIED BY PURPOSE

Purpose	Amount (In Billions)
Education	$22.1
Transportation	17.3
Utilities and conservation	20.1
Social welfare	21.8
Industrial aid	5.4
Other	33.6
Total	$120.3

Source: *Federal Reserve Bulletin*, November 1993, p. A34.

Unlike state governments, local governments can be sued against their will, making it possible for bondholders to force officials to collect whatever amount is needed in order to meet required debt payments. In many cases, only revenues from specific projects may be used (for example, the tolls collected on a particular highway). In other cases, collections from a particular tax may be used, although possibly only up to some statutory limit.

Some local governments (for example, Cleveland in 1978–1979) have defaulted on their debts, and others (for example, New York City in 1975) have "restructured" their debt, giving holders new certificates offering lower or deferred interest and longer maturities in exchange for currently outstanding certificates.

Counties and municipalities are familiar to most people, but other forms of local government also exist. Examples include school districts as well as other districts and authorities that have been created to finance and operate seaports or airports. All are created by state charter and may be granted monopoly powers as well as rights to collect certain types of taxes. However, limits are often placed on the amount of taxes collected, the tax rate charged, and the amount (or type) of debt issued.

The primary source of funding for such agencies is the property tax. Because a given property may be liable for taxes levied by several agencies (such as a city, a county, a school district, a port authority, and a sewer district), the risk of an agency's bonds may depend on both the value of property subject to its taxes and the amount of other debt dependent on the same property.

14.5.2 Types of Municipal Bonds

In 1992, new municipal bonds with a par value of $215.2 billion were issued. Of this total, $78.6 billion were general obligation bonds (GOs) and $136.6 billion were revenue bonds.[14]

General obligation bonds are backed by the full faith and credit (and thus the full taxing power) of the issuing agency. Most are issued by agencies with unlimited taxing power, although in a minority of cases the issuer is subject to limits on the amount of taxes or the tax rate (or both).

Revenue bonds are backed by revenues from a designated project, authority, or agency or by the proceeds from a specific tax. In many cases, such bonds are issued by agencies that hope to sell their services, pay the required expenses, and have enough left over to meet required payments on outstanding debt. Except for the possible granting of monopoly powers, the authorizing state and local government may provide no further assistance to the issuer. Such bonds are only as creditworthy as the enterprise associated with the issuer.

Many revenue bonds are issued to finance capital expenditures for publicly owned utilities (for example, water, electricity, or gas). Others are issued to finance quasi-utility operations (for example, public transportation). Some are financed by special assessments levied on properties benefiting from the original expenditure (for example, those connected to a new sewer system). **Industrial development bonds** (IDBs) are used to finance the purchase or construction of industrial facilities that are to be leased to firms on a favorable basis. In effect, such bonds provide cheap financing to businesses choosing to locate in the geographical area of the issuer.

Although most municipal financing involves the issuance of long-term securities, a number of different types of short-term securities have been issued in order to meet short-term demands for cash. Traditionally used types include tax anticipation notes (TANs), revenue anticipation notes (RANs), grant anticipation notes (GANs), and tax and revenue anticipation notes (TRANs). In each case, the name of the security refers to the source of repayment. Thus some can be classified as general obligation securities and others as revenue securities.

More recently, municipalities have started to issue two other kinds of short-term securities. Tax-exempt commercial paper is similar to corporate commercial paper, having a fixed interest rate and a maturity typically within 270 days. Variable-rate demand obligations have an interest rate that changes periodically (perhaps weekly) as some prespecified market interest rate changes. Furthermore, they can be redeemed at the desire of the investor within a prespecified number of days after giving notice to the issuer (for example, seven days after notification of intent).

14.5.3 Tax Treatment

Through a reciprocal arrangement with the federal government, coupon payments on state and local government securities are exempt from federal taxation, and coupon payments on Treasury and agency (except FNMA) securities are exempt from state and local taxation. Similar tax treatment is accorded to the price appreciation on short-term and long-term issues that are original issue discount securities (as mentioned earlier, OID securities are securities that were issued for a below-par price).

However, a different tax treatment is generally given to coupon-bearing securities that were issued at par value but were subsequently bought at a discount in the marketplace. Such securities, known as **market discount bonds,** provide the investor with income not only from the coupons but also from the difference between the purchase price and the par value. Unlike the coupons, which are tax-exempt, this difference is treated as taxable interest income (if the bond was purchased before May 1, 1993, it is treated as a taxable capital gain).

Another interesting tax feature of municipals is that if the investor resides in the state of the issuer, then he or she is generally exempt not only from paying federal taxes on the coupon payments, but also from paying state taxes. Furthermore, if the investor resides in a city with an income tax and purchases municipals issued by the city, then usually he or she is exempt from paying city taxes on the coupon payments. Thus a resident of New York City who purchases a municipal security issued by the city (or one of its political subdivisions) will not have to pay federal, state, or city income taxes on the coupon payments. However, if the New York City resident were to purchase a California municipal, then both New York State and New York City income taxes would have to be paid on the coupon payments. Although state and city income tax rates are much lower than those of the federal government, this feature nevertheless tends to make local issues more advantageous from an after-tax return viewpoint (an advantage that is offset to a certain degree by the resulting lack of diversification).

The avoidance of federal income tax on interest earned on a municipal bond makes such a security attractive to wealthy individual investors as well as corporate investors. As shown in Figure 14.7, this has resulted in municipal

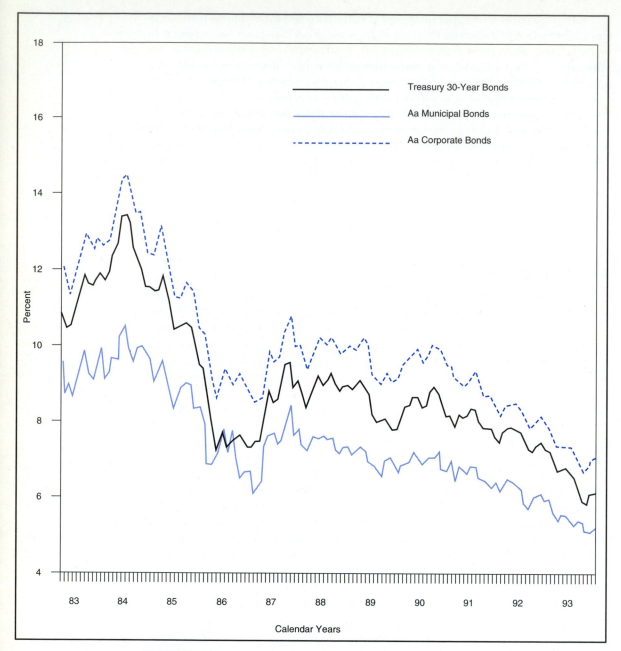

FIGURE 14.7

Average Yields of Long-Term Fixed-Income Securities (Monthly Averages)

Source: *Treasury Bulletin,* September 1993, p. 68.

securities having yields that are considerably lower than those on taxable securities.[15] Consequently, the cost of financing to municipal issuers is lower, suggesting that a federal subsidy has been provided to the issuers.

Over the years, this subsidy has been used to support activities deemed worthy of encouragement (even though the encouragement is somewhat hidden). For example, private universities may issue tax-exempt bonds to finance certain types of improvements, and private firms may do so to finance certain pollution-reducing activities. Such bonds are generally backed only by the resources of the issuer, with government involvement limited to the granting of favorable tax treatment. The Tax Reform Act of 1986 greatly restricted the granting of such tax treatment, leading to the emergence of **taxable municipals,** which are typically issued to finance projects that are not viewed as essential under the tax law.

14.5.4 The Market for Municipal Bonds

Municipals are usually issued as **serial bonds,** where one prespecified group matures a year after issue, another two years after issue, another three years after, and so on. Alternatively, **term bonds** (that is, bonds that all mature on the same date) or a mixture of serial and term bonds may be issued. The overall package is generally offered by the issuer on a competitive basis to various underwriters. The winning bidder then reoffers the individual bonds to investors at a higher price.

Unlike corporate bonds, municipal bonds do not need to be registered with the SEC before public issuance.[16] Indeed, the federal government leaves most regulation in this market to state and local authorities.

Municipal bonds may be callable at specified dates and prices. Occasionally, the issuing authority is obligated to make designated payments into a **sinking fund,** which is used to buy similar bonds (or perhaps even its own bonds). As the issuing authority's bonds mature, the money for paying them off will come from having the sinking fund sell some of its holdings.

A secondary market in municipal bonds is made by various dealers. Standard & Poor's Corporation publishes on a daily basis a listing of municipal bond quotations by various dealers in the *Blue List.* In addition, the *Bond Buyer* has a teletype system that provides dealer quotations. However, the relatively small amounts of particular issues and maturities outstanding limit the size of the market. Many individuals who invest in municipals simply buy new issues and hold them to maturity.

14.5.5 Municipal Bond Insurance

An investor concerned about possible default of a municipal bond can purchase an insurance policy to cover any losses that would be incurred if coupons or principal are not paid in full and on time. That is, an investor can contract with a company to have a specific portfolio of bonds insured. Alternatively, the issuer of the bonds can purchase such insurance from one of the firms that specialize in issuing this type of insurance. Generally the cost of this insurance is more than offset by the lower interest rate that the issuer has to pay as a result of insuring its bonds. In either case, the cost of the insurance will depend on the bonds included and their ratings.

Corporate bonds are similar to other kinds of fixed-income securities in that they promise to make specified payments at specified times and provide legal remedies in the event of default. Restrictions are often placed on the activities of the issuing corporation in order to provide additional protection for bondholders (for example, there may be restrictions on the amount of additional bonds that can be issued in the future).

14.6.1 Tax Treatment

Corporate bonds that are original issue discount securities generally have the discount taxed as ordinary income by the federal government. The constant interest method is to be used to determine the portion of the discount that must be reported as taxable interest each year. (This method was described earlier when stripped Treasury bonds were discussed.) With this method a portion of the discount must be recognized as income each year that the security is held, thereby causing the investor to have to pay taxes on that amount.

Corporate bonds carrying coupon payments have the coupon taxed as income each year. Furthermore, if the bond was originally sold at par but later bought at a discount in the marketplace (as mentioned earlier, such bonds are known as market discount bonds), then the investor generally will have to pay ordinary income taxes on both the coupon payments and the discount. Using either the constant interest method or straight-line method where the discount is spread out evenly over the remaining life of the bond, the investor can recognize a portion of the discount as interest income each year that the bond is held, and pay taxes on it. Alternatively, the investor can wait until the bond is disposed of and at that time recognize the market discount as taxable interest income.[17]

From the viewpoint of the issuing corporation, debt differs from equity in two crucial respects. First, principal and interest payments are obligatory. Failure to make any payment in full and on time can expose the issuer to expensive, time-consuming, and potentially disruptive legal actions. Second, unlike dividend payments, interest payments are considered expenses to the corporation, and hence can be deducted from earnings before calculating the corporation's income tax liability. As a result, each dollar paid in interest reduces earnings before taxes by a dollar, thereby reducing corporate taxes by 35 cents for a firm in the 35% marginal tax bracket. This leads to less than a dollar decline in earnings after taxes (in the 35% tax bracket example, the decline in earnings is 65 cents).

14.6.2 The Indenture

An issue of bonds is generally covered by an **indenture,** in which the issuing corporation promises a specified **trustee** that it will comply with a number of stated provisions. Chief among these is the timely payment of required coupons and principal on the issue. Other terms are often included to control the sale of pledged property, the issuance of other bonds, and the like.

The trustee for a bond issue, usually a bank or a trust company, acts on behalf of the bondholders. Some actions may be required by the indenture, while others may be done at the trustee's discretion, such as acting in response to a request from specific bondholders.

If the corporation defaults on an interest payment, then after a relatively short period of time (perhaps one to six months) the entire principal typically becomes due and payable—a procedure designed to enhance the bondholders' status in any forthcoming bankruptcy or related legal proceedings.

14.6.3 Types of Bonds

An exhaustive list of the names used to describe bonds would be intolerably long. Different names are often used for the same type of bond, and occasionally the same name will be used for two quite different bonds. A few major types do predominate, however, with relatively standard nomenclature.

Mortgage Bonds

Mortgage bonds represent debt that is secured by the pledge of specific property. In the event of default, the bondholders are entitled to obtain the property in question and sell it to satisfy their claims on the firm. In addition to the property itself, the holders of mortgage bonds have an unsecured claim on the corporation.

Mortgage bondholders are usually protected by a number of terms included in the bond indenture. The corporation may be constrained from pledging the property for other bonds (or such bonds, if issued, must be "junior" or "second" mortgages, with a claim on the property only after the first mortgage is satisfied). Certain property acquired by the corporation after the bonds were issued may also be pledged to support the bonds.

Collateral Trust Bonds

Collateral trust bonds are backed by other securities that are usually held by the trustee. A common situation of this sort arises when the securities of a subsidiary firm are pledged as collateral by the parent firm.

Equipment Obligations

Known also as equipment trust certificates, **equipment obligations** are backed by specific pieces of equipment (for example, railroad cars and commercial aircraft). If necessary, the equipment can be readily sold and delivered to a new owner. The legal arrangements used to facilitate the issuance of such bonds can be very complex. The most popular procedure uses the "Philadelphia Plan," in which the trustee initially holds the equipment and issues obligations and then leases the equipment to a corporation. Money received from the lessee is subsequently used to make interest and principal payments to the holders of the obligations. Ultimately, if all payments are made on schedule, the leasing corporation takes title to the equipment.

Debentures

Debentures are general obligations of the issuing corporation and thus represent unsecured credit. To protect the holders of such bonds, the indenture will usually limit the future issuance of secured debt as well as any additional unsecured debt.

Subordinated Debentures

When more than one issue of debenture is outstanding, a hierarchy may be specified. For example, **subordinated debentures** are junior to unsubordinated debentures, meaning that in the event of bankruptcy, junior claims are to be considered only after senior claims have been fully satisfied.

Other Types of Bonds

Income bonds are more like preferred stock (described in a later section) than bonds. Payment of interest in full and on schedule is not absolutely required, and failure to do so need not send the corporation into bankruptcy. Interest on income bonds may or may not qualify as a tax-deductible expense for the issuing corporation. This type of bond has rarely been used, except in reorganizations of bankrupt railroads.

Guaranteed bonds are issued by one corporation but backed in some way by another (for example, by a parent firm). **Participating bonds** require stated interest payments and provide additional amounts if earnings exceed some stated level. **Voting bonds,** unlike regular bonds, give the holders some voice in management. Serial bonds, with different portions of the issue maturing at different dates, are sometimes used by corporations for equipment financing (as mentioned earlier, they are also used by municipalities).

Convertible bonds may, at the holder's option, be exchanged for other securities, often common stock. Such bonds, which have become very popular in recent years, are discussed in more detail in the appendix to Chapter 20.

14.6.4   Call Provisions

Management would like to have the right to pay off the corporation's bonds at par at any time prior to maturity. This would provide management with flexibility, as debt could be reduced or its maturity altered via refunding. Most important, expensive high-coupon debt that was issued during a time of high interest rates could be replaced with cheaper low-coupon debt if rates decline.

Not surprisingly, investors hold quite a different opinion on the matter. The issuer's ability to redeem an issue at par at any time virtually precludes a rise in price over par and robs the holder of potential gains from price appreciation associated with declining interest rates. Moreover, it introduces a new form of uncertainty. A bond with such a feature will almost certainly sell for less than one without it.

Despite the cost of obtaining this sort of flexibility, many corporations include call provisions in their bond indentures that give the corporation the option to call some or all of the bonds from their holders at stated prices during specified periods prior to maturity. In a sense, the firm sells a bond and simultaneously buys an option from the holders. The net price of the bond is thus the difference between the value of the bond and the option. (Interestingly, some recent corporate issues have given the investor the option of forcing the issuer to call the security.)

The indenture usually gives investors two kinds of call protection. First of all, during the first few years after being issued, a bond may not be callable. Secondly, a **call premium** may be specified in the call provision. Such a premium indicates that if the issue is called, the issuer must pay the bondholders a **call price** that is a stated amount above par. Often, the amount above par becomes smaller as time passes and the maturity date approaches.

An entire issue may be called, or only specific bonds that are chosen randomly by the trustee. In either case, a notice of redemption will appear in advance in the financial press.

14.6.5 Sinking Funds

A bond indenture will often require the issuing corporation to make annual payments into a sinking fund. The idea is to pay part of the principal of the debt (as well as the interest) each year, thereby reducing the amount outstanding at maturity.

Sinking funds operate by having the corporation transmit cash to the trustee, who can then purchase bonds in the open market. Alternatively, the corporation may obtain the bonds itself, by either purchase or call, and deposit them with the trustee. Call prices for sinking fund purchases may differ from those specified when the entire issue is to be repaid prior to maturity.

Required contributions to a sinking fund may or may not be the same each year. In some cases, the required amount may depend on earnings, output, and so on; in others, the goal is to make the total paid for interest and principal the same each year.

14.6.6 Private Placements

Bonds intended for eventual public sale are usually issued in denominations of $1,000 each. Both bearer and registered forms may be utilized. Often, however, a single investor (or a small group of investors) will buy an entire issue. Such **private placements** are typically purchased by large financial institutions.

14.6.7 Bankruptcy

When a corporation fails to make a scheduled coupon or principal payment on a bond, the corporation is said to be in default on that obligation. If the payment is not made within a relatively short period, some sort of litigation almost inevitably follows.

A corporation unable to meet its obligatory debt payments is said to be technically insolvent (or insolvent in the equity sense). If the value of the firm's assets falls below its liabilities, it is said to be insolvent (or insolvent in the bankruptcy sense).

Behind these definitions lie much legislation, many court cases, and varied legal opinions. While the details differ, the usual situation begins with a default on one or more required coupon payments. If voluntary agreements with creditors cannot be obtained, this usually leads to a filing of bankruptcy—usually "voluntary"—by the corporation itself. Subsequent developments involve courts, court-appointed officials, representatives of the firm's creditors, and the management of the firm, among others.

Liquidation

A question that arises in most bankruptcy cases is whether or not the firm's assets should be liquidated (that is, sold) and the proceeds divided among the creditors. Such an action is taken only if the court feels that the resulting value would exceed that likely to be obtained if the firm continued in operation (perhaps after substantial reorganization).

If the firm's assets are liquidated in a "straight bankruptcy," secured creditors receive either the property pledged for their loans or the proceeds from the sale of the secured property. If this amount falls short of their claims, the difference is considered an unsecured debt of the firm; on the other hand, any excess is made available for other creditors. Next, assets are used to pay the claims of priority creditors to the extent possible. These include claims for such items as administrative expenses, wages (up to a stated limit per person), uninsured pension claims, taxes, and rents. Anything left over is used to pay unsecured creditors in proportion to their claims on the firm.

Reorganization

If the value of a firm's assets when employed as part of a "going concern" appears to exceed the value of the assets in liquidation, a reorganization of the firm and its liabilities may be undertaken. Such proceedings, conducted under the provisions of the Federal Bankruptcy Act, may be voluntary (initiated by the firm) or involuntary (initiated by three or more creditors). A number of parties must concur in the proposed reorganization, including the holders of two-thirds of the value in each general class of creditor that is affected by the reorganization.

Among the goals of reorganization are "fair and equitable" treatment of various classes of securities, and the elimination of "burdensome" debt obligations. Typically, creditors are given new claims on the reorganized firm, with the amounts of the new claims intended to be at least equal in value to the amounts that the creditors would have received in liquidation. For example, holders of debentures might receive bonds of longer maturity, holders of subordinated debentures might become stockholders, and stockholders might be left without any claims on the firm.

Arrangements

A third procedure is available to financially distressed corporations. The Federal Bankruptcy Act authorizes *arrangements,* in which debts may be extended (to longer maturities) or reduced.

Although the subject is far too complex for detailed treatment here, two aspects of bankruptcy deserve some discussion. First, the choice between continuation of a firm and liquidation of its assets should be unrelated to considerations of bankruptcy. If an asset can be sold for more than the present value of its future earnings, it should be. Management may have to be taken to court to be forced to do this, but the issue is not really one of solvency or lack thereof.

Second, the definition of insolvency is rather vague. Assume, for the sake of argument, that assets can be adequately valued at the larger of liquidating or going-concern value. A firm is said to be insolvent if this value is less than that of the firm's liabilities. But how should the liabilities be valued? Their current market value will inevitably be less than the value of the assets, while their book value can be greater than the value of the assets.

14.6.8   Trading in Corporate Bonds

Although most of the trading in corporate bonds takes place utilizing dealers in the over-the-counter market, many corporate bonds are listed on the New York Stock Exchange (a notably smaller number are listed on the American Stock Exchange). However, trading in corporate bonds on the NYSE takes place at a location that is different from the location where common stocks are traded. Furthermore, no specialists are involved in the trading of corporate bonds on the NYSE. Instead, orders for "active" issues are traded in a "ring" in the Bond Room. Here, the member announces a bid or asked price, depending on whether the member is buying or selling. This invites other members to make counteroffers or to accept the announced price.

"Inactive" issues of bonds that are listed on the NYSE are traded through a computer system known as the **Automated Bond System** (ABS). With this system, members enter their bid or asked prices, along with the quantities, into computer terminals located on the floor of the Bond Room. Other members can see these orders by looking at display terminals and can respond by entering an order at a terminal.

Because some corporate bonds are traded on the NYSE, the prices at which such trades are made can be found in the financial press. Figure 14.8 provides an example. Consider the following entry in this figure:

Bonds	Current Yield	Volume	Close	Net Change
ATT 4⅜99	4.6	17	94½	−¾

This entry indicates that AT&T bonds carrying a 4⅜% coupon (paid semiannually) and maturing in 1999 last traded on December 13, 1993, at 94½. As these bonds have a par value of $1,000, this means that the last trade was at $945.00. The **current yield,** meaning the annual coupon rate divided by the current closing price, was approximately 4.6% (= $40/$945.00). In all, 17 bonds traded hands on the exchange during the day, and the closing price was down ¾ (= $7.50) from that of the previous trading day.

FIGURE 14.8

Price Quotations for Corporate Bonds (Excerpts)

Source: Reprinted by permission of *The Wall Street Journal*, Dow Jones & Company, Inc., December 14, 1993, p. C16. All rights reserved worldwide.

In a sense, the NYSE is the "odd lot" market for bonds, even though at the end of 1992 it had nearly 2,400 bonds available for trading (1,462 of them being U.S. corporate debt issues with an aggregate par value of $262.5 billion).[18] That is, major trades of bonds are generally negotiated elsewhere by dealers and institutional investors, either directly or through brokers. Thus reported prices on the NYSE may be poor guides to values associated with large transactions.

14.7 FOREIGN BONDS

The foreign bond market refers to bonds issued and denominated in the currency of a country other than the one in which the issuer is primarily located. For example, the Mexican government has issued bonds that are denominated in U.S. dollars, mature in 1997, and carry an 8⅛% coupon rate. Although a brief listing of some of these bonds sometimes appears daily at the end of the "New York Exchange Bonds" quotations section in the *Wall Street Journal,* the amount of trading is often so small that all that is reported is the total volume, as shown in Figure 14.8. Foreign bonds that are issued in the United States and are denominated in U.S. dollars are referred to as Yankee bonds, and foreign (that is, non-Japanese) bonds that are issued in Japan are referred to as Samurai bonds.

In issuing foreign bonds, the issuer must abide by the rules and regulations imposed by the government of the country in which the bonds are issued. This may be relatively easy or difficult, depending on the country involved.

One of the main advantages of purchasing foreign bonds is the opportunity to obtain international diversification of the default risk of a bond portfolio while not having to be concerned about foreign exchange fluctuations. For example, an American investor might be able to buy a Toyota bond in Japan that is denominated in yen, but in doing so would have to worry about the yen-dollar exchange rate. This is because the coupon payments and ultimately the principal would be paid to the investor in yen, which would then have to be converted into dollars at a currently unknown exchange rate. However, the investor could avoid such worries by purchasing a Toyota bond that is denominated in U.S. dollars.

14.8 EUROBONDS

Owing in part to government restrictions on investment in foreign securities, a number of borrowers have found it advantageous to sell securities in other countries. The term **Eurobond** is loosely applied to bonds that are offered outside the country of the borrower and outside the country in whose currency the securities are denominated.[19] Thus a bond issued by a U.S. corporation that is denominated in Japanese yen (or U.S. dollars) and sold in Germany would be referred to as a Eurobond.

As the Eurobond market is neither regulated nor taxed, it offers substantial advantages for many issuers and buyers of bonds. For example, a foreign subsidiary of a U.S. corporation may issue a Eurobond in "bearer" form. No tax will be withheld by the corporation, and the tax (if any) paid by the purchaser will depend on his or her country of residence. For tax reasons, interest rates on Eurobonds tend to be somewhat lower than those on domestic bonds denominated in the same currency.

14.9   PREFERRED STOCK

In some respects, **preferred stock** is like a perpetual bond. A given dollar amount is to be paid each year by the issuer to the investor. This amount may be stated as a percent of the stock's par value (for example, 8% of $100, meaning $8 per year) or directly as a dollar figure (for example, $2.75 per year). Because the security is a "stock," such payments are called dividends instead of interest and hence do not qualify as a tax-deductible expense for the issuing corporation. Furthermore, failure to make such payments does not constitute grounds for bankruptcy proceedings.

A recent innovation is adjustable rate preferred stock (ARPS), where the dividend is reset periodically in terms of an applicable rate. For example, the annualized "percent of par" for the dividend might be reset every three months to be equal to the largest of the rates on (1) three-month Treasury bills, (2) ten-year Treasury bonds, and (3) twenty-year Treasury bonds. Related to ARPS are Dutch auction rate preferred stocks (DARPS), where the dividend is reset periodically (more often than for ARPS) at a level determined by bidding from current and potential owners.[20]

Preferred stock generally receives preferential treatment when it comes to dividends. Specified payments must be made on the preferred stock before any dividends may be paid to holders of the firm's common stock. Failure to pay a preferred dividend in full does not constitute default, but unpaid dividends are usually **cumulative.** This means that all previously unpaid preferred stock dividends must be paid (but seldom with interest) before any dividends may be paid on the common stock.

No indenture is provided with a preferred stock issue. However, various provisions protecting the preferred stockholders against potentially harmful actions may be written into the corporation's charter. For example, one provision may limit the dollar amount of senior securities that can be issued in the future. Although preferred stockholders typically do not have voting rights, there may be another provision that gives them voting rights when the corporation is in arrears on its preferred dividends.

Many issues of preferred stock are callable at a stated redemption price. *Participating preferred stock* entitles the holder to receive extra dividends when earnings permit. *Convertible preferred stock* may, at the option of the holder, be converted into another security (usually the firm's common stock) on stated terms. Some firms issue more than one class of preferred stock, with preference accorded the various classes in a specified order.

In the event of a dissolution of the firm, preferred stock often receives preferential treatment as to assets. Generally this means that preferred stockholders are entitled to receive the stock's par value before any payment is made to common stockholders.

As preferred stock has many features of a bond without the substantial tax advantage that bonds give to the issuer, it is used less often than debt. In 1992, $21.3 billion of preferred stock was issued, compared with $377.7 billion of publicly offered domestic corporate debt.[21]

As indicated in Chapter 13, interest income from bonds held by a corporate investor is subject to the corporate income tax, but 80% of any dividend income received is exempt from taxation.[22] For a corporate investor this makes the effective tax rate on dividends from preferred stock approximately 7% (= .35 × .20), compared with 35% for interest received on bonds. For this reason, preferred stocks tend to sell at prices that give lower before-tax returns than long-term bonds, even though bonds may be considerably lower in risk. As a result, preferred stocks are generally unattractive holdings for noncorporate investors, such as individuals and tax-exempt investors.

Many preferred stocks are traded on major exchanges in a manner similar to common stocks. Typically, they are assigned to the same specialist that is responsible for the firm's common stock. Trading prices are reported in the financial press in the same format used for common stocks.

14.10   SUMMARY

1. The most familiar types of fixed-income securities are personal savings deposits. These include demand deposits, time deposits, and certificates of deposit issued by commercial banks, savings and loan companies, mutual savings banks, and credit unions.
2. Highly marketable, short-term securities are referred to as money market instruments. These securities include commercial paper, large-denomination certificates of deposit, bankers' acceptances, repurchase agreements, and Eurodollar CDs.
3. The U.S. Treasury issues debt securities to finance the government's borrowing needs. These securities are issued in various maturities—short-term (Treasury bills), intermediate-term (Treasury notes), and long-term (Treasury bonds). The Treasury also issues Savings Bonds to individual investors.
4. Treasury notes or bonds can be converted into a set of pure-discount bonds by issuing marketable receipts entitling the holder to a specific coupon payment or the bond's principal payment. Separating a bond into its component payments is known as coupon stripping.
5. Federal agencies also issue securities to finance their operations. In some cases this debt is explicitly backed by the U.S. Treasury. In other cases the government guarantee is implicit.

6. Participation certificates represent ownership of a pool of securities. The holders receive cash flows from the pool's securities in proportion to their ownership in the pool.

7. State and local governments issue a wide variety of fixed-income securities. These securities may be backed solely by the full faith and credit of the issuer or by a specific revenue source.

8. Because municipal securities are generally exempt from federal taxation, those securities usually offer lower yields than taxable securities.

9. Corporate bonds, such as mortgage bonds or equipment obligations, may be backed by specific assets. Alternatively, corporate bonds, such as debentures, may represent general obligations of the issuing corporations.

10. Corporate bonds (and some federal government and municipal bonds) may contain call provisions, giving the issuer the right to redeem the security prior to maturity under specified terms.

11. Corporations entering bankruptcy may undergo liquidation or reorganization, or enter into arrangements.

12. Preferred stock dividends are generally fixed but do not represent legal obligations of the issuers. Most preferred stock dividends are cumulative, requiring payment of all unpaid preferred dividends before common stock dividends can be paid.

QUESTIONS AND PROBLEMS

1. What is the annual equivalent yield on a 13-week Treasury bill selling at a price of 96?

2. Consider a 13-week Treasury bill, issued today, which is selling for $9,675. (Its face value is $10,000.)
   a. What is the annual discount based on the selling price of the security?
   b. What is the annual equivalent yield of the security?

3. If a three-month Treasury bill sells for a price of 98, whereas a six-month Treasury bill sells for 96, is the equivalent yield (unannualized) for the six-month bill twice that of the three-month bill? Why?

4. Rank the various money market instruments discussed in the text in terms of default risk. Explain the reasoning behind your rankings. Find the latest interest rates for these securities. Do they correspond with your default-risk rankings?

5. The U.S. Treasury once issued notes and bonds only in bearer form. Now its notes and bonds are issued only in registered form. Given the characteristics of bearer and registered bonds, speculate as to what reasons might have prompted the Treasury to change the form of issuance.

6. Using the *Wall Street Journal* as a data source, identify a particular Treasury note or bond. What is its coupon rate? What is its maturity date? What is the latest bid-ask spread for the security? What is the security's yield-to-maturity?

7. Describe the standard practice by which sellers of government and corporate bonds are compensated for accrued interest.

8. What is the rationale for including a call provision in the indenture of a bond issue? How do bond investors typically respond to the inclusion of a call provision?

9. How do zero-coupon fixed-income securities provide returns to investors?

10. Consider a ten-year zero-coupon Treasury security selling for a price of $300, with a face value of $1,000. What is the before-tax annual rate of return to an investor who buys and holds this security to maturity?

11. Why does the IRS treat the difference between the price of a bond purchased at a discount and its face value as ordinary income to the investor, as opposed to treating it as a capital gain?

12. Bonds issued by federal agencies carry an explicit or implicit promise that the federal government will ensure payment of interest and principal. Why then are these securities usually priced by the market to offer yields above Treasury securities?

13. What is a mortgage participation certificate? What is the primary risk that such securities present to investors?

14. Cozy Dolan, an amateur investor, said, "I prefer investing in GNMA pass-through securities. Their government guarantee gives me a riskfree return." Comment on Cozy's remark.

15. Distinguish between a general obligation municipal bond and a revenue bond.

16. Pigeon Falls Airlines was in difficult financial shape owing to ongoing recession and labor problems. To this point the firm had issued no debt but management believed that borrowing in the bond market was the only way to get through the tough times. Because of its poor financial condition, Pigeon Falls's investment bankers advised management that a debenture issue would not be well received. What other bond issuance options might Pigeon Falls pursue?

17. Is any mortgage bond necessarily a more secure investment than any debenture? Explain.

18. A callable bond is sometimes described as a combination of a noncallable bond and an option. Explain why this description is appropriate. Further, explain how these two features impact the price of a callable bond.

19. Muddy Ruel is considering purchasing one of two bonds: a corporate bond with a 9% coupon interest rate, selling at par, or a tax-free municipal bond with a 6% coupon interest rate, likewise selling at par. Given that Muddy is in the 30% tax bracket, and assuming that all other relevant factors are the same between the two bonds, which bond should Muddy select?

20. Is it true that most corporations that default on their debt eventually enter bankruptcy and see their assets liquidated to repay creditors? Explain.

21. Eurobonds have become very popular forms of financing in recent years. What features of the Eurobond market make Eurobonds attractive to issuers and bondholders?

22. In trying to explain the concept of preferred stock to a novice investor, Patsy Donovan referred to it as a "hybrid" security. What did Patsy mean by this term?

23. What is the purpose of the cumulative restriction of most preferred stock?

24. The preferred stock of Clinton Foods carries a dividend of $8 per share. The stock currently sells for $50. If one year from today the Clinton preferred stock's price remains unchanged, what is the return from holding the stock for:

a. A corporation in the 35% tax bracket?

b. An individual in the 35% tax bracket?

CFA Exam Question

25. A portfolio manager at Superior Trust Company is structuring a fixed-income portfolio to meet the objectives of a client. The client plans on retiring in 15 years and wants a substantial lump sum at that time. The client has specified the use of AAA-rated securities.

The portfolio manager compares U.S. Treasuries with zero-coupon stripped U.S. Treasuries and observes a significant yield advantage for the stripped bonds.

Maturity	Coupon U.S. Treasuries	Zero Coupon Stripped U.S. Treasuries
3 year	5.50%	5.80%
5 year	6.00	6.60
7 year	6.75	7.25
10 year	7.25	7.60
15 year	7.40	8.80
30 year	7.75	7.75

Briefly discuss two reasons why zero coupon stripped U.S. Treasuries could yield more than coupon U.S. Treasuries with the same final maturity.

ENDNOTES

[1] One recent innovation is the issuance of "equity-linked CDs" that provide the investor with a return based on the performance of a given market index, coupled with a guarantee that the investor will not experience a loss (some even guarantee the investor some minimal interest rate if the market index performs poorly). See Michael D. Joehnk, "Short-Term Investing: Socking It Away in CDs," *AAII Journal,* 12, no. 8 (September 1990): 7–9. See also Jeffrey Cohn and Michael E. Edieson, "Banking on the Market: Equity-Linked CDs," *AAII Journal,* 15, no. 3 (March 1993): 11–15.

[2] Many insurance companies sell *guaranteed investment contracts* (GICs) that are similar to CDs in that they typically pay a stated interest rate for a given number of years. Other types of financial institutions offer contracts similar to GICs. See Robert T. Kleiman and Anandi P. Sahu, "The ABCs of GICs for Retirement Plan Investing," *AAII Journal,* 14, no. 3 (March 1992): 7–10.

[3] Short-term obligations of the U.S. government and its agencies are also considered money market instruments; they will be described in the next section.

[4] For more on trading Treasuries, see Jay Goldinger, "Trading Treasuries: Know the Risks Before You Invest," *AAII Journal,* 11, no. 10 (November 1989): 12–15.

[5] This approach to calculating equivalent yields for Treasury bills is applicable only if the maturity is six months or less; a more complicated approach is necessary for T-bills with longer lives. See Richard J. Kish, "Discrepancy in Treasury Bill Yield Calculations," *Financial Practice and Education,* 2, no. 1 (Spring/Summer 1992): 41–45.

[6] The yield-to-maturity on a bond is the discount rate that makes the present value of the future coupon payments and par value equal to its current market price (which in this case is the asked price). Chapter 15 will discuss yields more fully.

[7] The procedure for calculating accrued interest on corporate bonds is different in that it is based on an assumption that there are 30 days in each month and 180 days in each semiannual period. Specifically, (1) the number of complete months left until the next coupon payment is determined and multiplied by 30; (2) the number of days left in the current month is determined and added to the previous figure; (3) the resulting figure is subtracted from 180, thereby giving the number of days that have elapsed since the last coupon payment; (4) this figure is divided by 180, giving the fraction of the period that has elapsed; and (5) this fraction is multiplied by the semiannual coupon, resulting in the amount of accrued interest. See "Dividends and Interest: Who Gets Payments After a Trade?" *AAII Journal,* 12, no. 4 (April 1990): 8–11.

[8] If the bonds are used to pay for certain educational expenses the interest may be completely taxfree. For more on savings bonds, see Paul F. Jessup, "The Purloined Investment: EE Savings Bonds Make Sense," *AAII Journal,* 12, no. 8 (September 1990): 10–13; and Phillip R. Daves and Robert A. Kunkel, "After the Fall: Savings Bonds Are Still Attractive Short Term," *AAII Journal,* 15, no. 4 (April 1993): 11–12.

[9] If the underlying Treasury security is callable, this set of receipts would provide the holders with all coupon payments received after the date of first call as well as the principal.

[10] OID securities can have either no coupons (in which case they are pure discount securities) or small coupons. The key distinguishing feature of an OID security is that at issuance it was sold for a significant discount from par value. *De minimus rules* indicate that, for tax purposes, small discounts can be ignored until the security is sold or matures.

[11] Determining an appropriate price for a pass-through security is quite complicated. For an analysis, see Richard J. Kish and James Greenleaf, "Teaching How Mortgage Pass-Through Securities Are Priced," *Financial Practice and Education,* 3, no. 1 (Spring/Summer 1993): 85–94.

[12] *1993 Statistical Abstract of the United States,* Table 466, p. 291.

[13] In some cases no capital expenditure is involved. (For example, the proceeds from the debt issue may be used to refund an outstanding debt issue.)

[14] *Federal Reserve Bulletin,* November 1993, p. A34.

[15] As noted in Chapter 13 (see Figure 13.4 and the related discussion), the yields on municipal bonds have historically been 20% to 40% below the yields on similar taxable bonds.

[16] However, municipal bonds that are unregistered with respect to ownership cannot be issued (this prohibition began July 1, 1983). See Hildy Richelson, "Municipal Bonds: A Guide to the Various Forms of Ownership," *AAII Journal,* 13, no. 4 (April 1991): 13–16.

[17] This assumes that the bond was purchased on or after May 1, 1993. For more on the taxation of bonds, see Chapter 13 or Clark Blackman II and Donald Laubacher, "The Basics of Bond Discounts and Premiums," *AAII Journal,* 15, no. 3 (March 1993): 24–27, or IRS Publications 550 and 1212. The taxation of securities in general and bonds in

particular is a complex matter, with many exceptions and alternative procedures. Any investor would be well advised to check carefully beforehand to be certain of the method of taxation involved for any security being considered for purchase.

[18] New York Stock Exchange *Fact Book 1992 Data,* pp. 44, 48.

[19] There are also fixed-income securities of this nature that have shorter lives; they are sometimes referred to as Euronotes or Euro-commercial paper. The market where they (and Eurobonds) are issued and traded is known as the Eurocredit market.

[20] For a discussion of ARPS and DARPS, see Michael J. Alderson, Keith C. Brown, and Scott L. Lummer, "Dutch Auction Rate Preferred Stock," *Financial Management,* 16, no. 2 (Summer 1987), 68–73. See also Michael J. Alderson and Donald R. Fraser, "Financial Innovations and Excesses Revisited: The Case of Auction Rate Preferred Stock," *Financial Management,* 22, no. 2 (Summer 1993): 61–75.

[21] *Federal Reserve Bulletin,* November 1993, p. A34.

[22] This assumes that the corporate investor owns between 20% and 80% of the firm's common stock. If less than 20% is owned, only 70% of the dividend is exempt from taxation whereas if more than 80% is owned, then all of the dividend is exempt.

KEY TERMS

pure-discount security
coupon payments
maturity date
principal
demand deposits
time deposits
certificates of deposit
bank discount basis
commercial paper
bankers' acceptance
Eurodollar CDs
Eurodollar deposits
repurchase agreement
repo rate
debt refunding
term-to-maturity
dealer's spread
equivalent yield
accrued interest
call provisions
coupon stripping
original issue discount
    securities
federally sponsored agencies
participation certificates
municipal bonds
general obligation bonds

revenue bonds
industrial development bonds
market discount bonds
taxable municipals
serial bonds
term bonds
sinking fund
indenture
trustee
mortgage bonds
collateral trust bonds
equipment obligations
debentures
subordinated debentures
income bonds
guaranteed bonds
participating bonds
voting bonds
convertible bonds
call premium
call price
private placements
Automated Bond System
current yield
Eurobond
preferred stock
cumulative dividends

1. A concise summary description of the various types of money market instruments is contained in:

   Timothy Q. Cook and Timothy D. Rowe, *Instruments of the Money Market* (Federal Reserve Bank of Richmond, 1986).

2. The following contain thorough descriptions of the various types of fixed-income securities discussed in this chapter:

   Frank J. Fabozzi and Franco Modigliani, *Capital Markets: Institutions and Instruments* (Englewood Cliffs, NJ: Prentice Hall, 1992), Chapters 13–18;

   Frank J. Fabozzi, Franco Modigliani, and Michael G. Ferri, *Foundations of Financial Markets and Institutions* (Englewood Cliffs, NJ: Prentice Hall, 1994), Chapters 16, 17, 20–24.

3. For a discussion of coupon stripping, see:

   Miles Livingston and Deborah Wright Gregory, *The Stripping of U.S. Treasury Securities,* Monograph Series in Finance and Economics #1989–1, New York University Salomon Center, Leonard N. Stern School of Business.

   Deborah W. Gregory and Miles Livingston, "Development of the Market for U.S. Treasury STRIPS," *Financial Analysts Journal,* 48, no. 2 (March/April 1992): 68–74.

   Phillip R. Daves, Michael C. Ehrhardt, and John M. Wachowicz, Jr., "A Guide to Investing in U.S. Treasury STRIPS," *AAII Journal,* 15, no. 1 (January 1993): 6–10.

   Phillip R. Daves and Michael C. Ehrhardt, "Liquidity, Reconstitution, and the Value of U.S. Treasury STRIPS," *Journal of Finance,* 47, no. 1 (March 1993): 315–329.

4. For a discussion of the market for securities issued by the U.S. Treasury, see:

   Peter Wann, *Inside the US Treasury Market* (New York: Quorum Books, 1989).

5. For a discussion of mortgage-backed securities, see:

   Earl Baldwin and Saundra Stotts, *Mortgage-Backed Securities: A Reference Guide for Lenders & Issuers* (Chicago: Probus Publishing, 1990).

   Sean Becketti and Charles S. Morris, *The Prepayment Experience of FNMA Mortgage-Backed Securities,* Monograph Series in Finance and Economics #1990–3, New York University Salomon Center, Leonard N. Stern School of Business.

   Eduardo S. Schwartz and Walter N. Torous, "Prepayment, Default, and the Valuation of Mortgage Pass-through Securities," *Journal of Business,* 65, no. 2 (April 1992): 221–239.

   Andrew Carron, "Understanding CMOs, REMICs, and Other Mortgage Derivatives," *Journal of Fixed Income,* 2, no. 1 (June 1992): 25–43.

Albert J. Golly, Jr., "An Individual Investor's Guide to the Complex World of CMOs," *AAII Journal*, 14, no. 6 (July 1992): 7–10.

Frank J. Fabozzi and Franco Modigliani, *Mortgage & Mortgage-Backed Securities Markets* (Boston: Harvard Business School Press, 1992).

Michael D. Joehnk and Matthew J. Hassett, "Getting a Grip on the Risks of CMO Prepayments," *AAII Journal*, 15, no. 5 (June 1993): 8–12.

Frank J. Fabozzi, Charles Ramsey, and Frank R. Ramirez, *Collateralized Mortgage Obligations: Structure and Analysis* (Summit, NJ: Frank J. Fabozzi Associates, 1993).

6. For a discussion of municipal bonds, see:

Peter Fortune, "The Municipal Bond Market, Part I: Politics, Taxes, and Yields," Federal Reserve Bank of Boston, *New England Economic Review*, (September/October 1991): 13–36.

Peter Fortune, "The Municipal Bond Market, Part II: Problems and Policies," Federal Reserve Bank of Boston, *New England Economic Review*, (May/June 1992): 47–64.

7. For a discussion of the foreign bond and Eurobond markets, see:

J. Orlin Grabbe, *International Financial Markets* (New York: Elsevier Science Publishing, 1991), Chapters 16–18.

Bruno Solnik, *International Investments* (Reading, MA: Addison-Wesley, 1991), Chapters 6–7.

8. For a discussion of the Eurocredit market, see:

Arie L. Melnik and Steven E. Plaut, *The Short-Term Eurocredit Market*, Monograph Series in Finance and Economics #1991–1, New York University Salomon Center, Leonard N. Stern School of Business.

9. For a discussion of how government bond markets function in the United Kingdom, Japan, and Germany, see:

Thomas J. Urich, *U.K., German and Japanese Government Bond Markets*, Monograph Series in Finance and Economics #1991–2, New York University Salomon Center, Leonard N. Stern School of Business.

10. The accuracy of reported prices for corporate bonds is analyzed in:

Kenneth P. Nunn, Jr., Joanne Hill, and Thomas Schneeweis, "Corporate Bond Price Data Sources and Risk/Return Measurement," *Journal of Financial and Quantitative Analysis*, 21, no. 2 (June 1986): 197–208.

Oded Sarig and Arthur Warga, "Bond Price Data and Bond Market Liquidity," *Journal of Financial and Quantitative Analysis*, 24, no. 3 (September 1989): 367–378.

Arthur D. Warga, "Corporate Bond Price Discrepancies in the Dealer and Exchange Markets," *Journal of Fixed Income*, 1, no. 3 (December 1991): 7–16.

11. The market for preferred stock is discussed in:

   Arthur L. Houston, Jr., and Carol Olson Houston, "Financing with Preferred Stock," *Financial Management,* 19, no. 3 (Autumn 1990): 42–54.

12. An extensive discussion of the private placement market for corporate debt is contained in:

   Mark Carey, Stephen Prowse, John Rea, and Gregory Udell, "The Economics of Private Placements: A New Look," *Financial Markets, Institutions & Instruments,* 2, no. 3 (1993).

Bond Analysis

Consider an investor who believes that there are situations where public information can be used to identify mispriced bonds. To translate that belief into action about which bonds to buy and sell, an analytical procedure is needed. One procedure involves comparing a bond's yield-to-maturity with a yield-to-maturity that the investor feels is appropriate, based on the characteristics of the bond as well as on current market conditions. If the yield-to-maturity is higher than the appropriate yield-to-maturity, then the bond is said to be underpriced (or undervalued), and it is a candidate for buying. Conversely, if the yield-to-maturity is lower than the appropriate one, then the bond is said to be overpriced (or overvalued), and it is a candidate for selling (or even short selling).

Alternatively, the investor could estimate the bond's "true" or "intrinsic" value and compare it with the bond's current market price. Specifically, if the current market price is less than the bond's intrinsic value, then the bond is underpriced, and if it is greater, then the bond is overpriced.

Both procedures for analyzing bonds are based on the capitalization of income method of valuation. The first procedure involving yields is analogous to the internal rate of return method that is discussed in most introductory finance textbooks, whereas the second procedure involving intrinsic value is analogous to the net present value method, which also appears in such books. While the focus in those books is on making an investment decision involving some type of real asset (such as whether or not a new piece of machinery should be purchased), the focus here is on making an investment decision involving a particular type of financial asset—bonds.

An investor who believes that the bond market is efficient would question the ability of other investors to identify mispriced situations. However, if an investor believes that such situations exist, then an economically sensible and logical approach to valuation is needed to identify them. One such approach is the **capitalization of income method of valuation.**

This method of valuation states that the intrinsic value of any asset is based on the discounted value of the cash flows that the investor expects to receive in the future from owning the asset. As mentioned earlier, one way that this method has been applied to bond valuation is to compare the bond's yield-to-maturity y with the appropriate yield-to-maturity y^*. Specifically, if $y > y^*$, then the bond is underpriced, and if $y < y^*$, then the bond is overpriced. However, if $y = y^*$, then the bond is said to be fairly priced.

15.1.1 Promised Yield-to-Maturity

Letting P denote the current market price of a bond with a remaining life of n years, and promising cash flows to the investor of C_1 in year $1, C_2$ in year 2, and so on, the yield-to-maturity (more specifically, the **promised yield-to-maturity**) of the bond is the value of y that solves the following equation:

$$P = \frac{C_1}{(1 + y)^1} + \frac{C_2}{(1 + y)^2} + \frac{C_3}{(1 + y)^3} + \cdots + \frac{C_n}{(1 + y)^n}.$$

Using summation notation, this equation can be rewritten as:

$$P = \sum_{t=1}^{n} \frac{C_t}{(1 + y)^t}. \tag{15.1}$$

For example, consider a bond that is currently selling for $900 and has a remaining life of three years. For ease of exposition, assume that it makes annual coupon payments amounting to $60 per year and has a par value of $1,000—that is, $C_1 = \$60$, $C_2 = \$60$, and $C_3 = \$1,060 \ (= \$1,000 + \$60)$. Using Equation (15.1), the yield-to-maturity on this bond is the value of y that solves the following equation:

$$\$900 = \frac{\$60}{(1 + y)^1} + \frac{\$60}{(1 + y)^2} + \frac{\$1,060}{(1 + y)^3}$$

which is $y = 10.02\%$. If subsequent analysis indicates that the yield-to-maturity should be 9.00%, then this bond is underpriced because $y = 10.02\% > y^* = 9.00\%$.

15.1.2 Intrinsic Value

Alternatively, the intrinsic value of a bond can be calculated using the following formula:

$$V = \frac{C_1}{(1 + y^*)^1} + \frac{C_2}{(1 + y^*)^2} + \frac{C_3}{(1 + y^*)^3} + \cdots + \frac{C_n}{(1 + y^*)^n}$$

or, using summation notation,

$$V = \sum_{t=1}^{n} \frac{C_t}{(1 + y^*)^t}. \tag{15.2}$$

Because the purchase price of the bond is its market price P, the **net present value** (NPV) to the investor is equal to the difference between the value of the bond and the purchase price:

$$NPV = V - P = \left[\sum_{t=1}^{n} \frac{C_t}{(1 + y^*)^t} \right] - P. \tag{15.3}$$

The NPV of the bond in the previous example is the solution to the following equation:

$$NPV = \left[\frac{\$60}{(1 + .09)^1} + \frac{\$60}{(1 + .09)^2} + \frac{\$1,060}{(1 + .09)^3} \right] - \$900$$

$$= \$24.06.$$

Because this bond has a positive NPV, it is underpriced. This will always be the case when a bond has a yield-to-maturity that is higher than the appropriate one. (Earlier it was shown that this bond's yield-to-maturity was 10.02%, which is more than 9.00%, the appropriate yield-to-maturity.) That is, in general, any bond with $y > y^*$ will always have a positive NPV and vice versa, so that under either method it would be underpriced.[1]

Alternatively, if the investor had determined that y^* was equal to 11.00%, then the bond's NPV would have been $-\$22.19$. This would suggest that the bond was overpriced, just as would have been noted when the yield-to-maturity of 10.02% was compared with 11.00%. This will always be the case—a bond with $y < y^*$ will always have a negative NPV and vice versa, so that under either method it would be found to be overpriced.

It should also be pointed out that if the investor had determined that y^* had a value of approximately the same magnitude as the bond's yield-to-maturity of 10%, then the NPV of the bond would be approximately zero. In such a situation the bond would be viewed as being fairly priced.

Note that in order to use the capitalization of income method of valuation, the values of C_t, P, and y^* must be determined. It is generally quite easy to determine the values for C_t and P because they are the bond's promised cash flows and current market price, respectively. However, determining the value of y^* is difficult because it will depend on the investor's subjective evaluation of certain characteristics of the bond as well as on current market conditions. Given that the key ingredient in bond analysis is determining the appropriate value of y^*, the next section will discuss what attributes should be considered in making such a determination.

15.2   BOND ATTRIBUTES

Six primary attributes of a bond are of significant importance in bond valuation: (1) length of time until maturity, (2) coupon rate, (3) call provisions, (4) tax status, (5) marketability, and (6) likelihood of default. At any time the structure of market prices for bonds differing in these dimensions can be examined and described in terms of yields-to-maturity. This overall structure is sometimes referred to as the **yield structure.** Often attention is confined to differences along a single dimension, holding the other attributes constant. For example, the set of yields of bonds of different maturities constitutes the **term structure** (discussed in Chapter 5), and the set of yields of bonds of different default risk is referred to as the **risk structure.**

Most bond analysts consider the yields-to-maturity for default-free bonds to form the term structure. "Risk differentials" are then added to obtain the relevant yields-to-maturity for bonds of lower quality. Although subject to some criticism, this procedure makes it possible to think about a complicated set of relationships sequentially.

The differential between the yields of two bonds is usually called a **yield spread.** Most often it involves the bond that is under analysis and a comparable default-free bond (that is, a Treasury security of similar maturity and coupon rate). Yield spreads are sometimes measured in **basis points,** where one basis point equals .01%. If the yield-to-maturity for one bond is 11.50% and that of another is 11.90%, the yield spread is 40 basis points.

15.2.1   Coupon Rate and Length of Time until Maturity

These attributes of a bond are important because they determine the size and timing of the cash flows that are promised to the bondholder by the issuer. Given a bond's current market price, these attributes can be used to determine the bond's yield-to-maturity, which will subsequently be compared with what the investor thinks that it should be. More specifically, if the market for Treasury securities is viewed as being efficient, then the yield-to-maturity on a Treasury security that is similar to the bond under evaluation can form a starting point in the analysis of the bond.

Consider the previously mentioned bond that is selling for $900 and has promised cash flows over the next three years of $60, $60, and $1,060, respectively. In this case, perhaps a Treasury security with a cash flow over the next three years of $50, $50, and $1,050 that is currently selling for $910.61 would form the starting point of the analysis. Because the yield-to-maturity on this security is 8.5%, the yield spread between the bond and the Treasury security is 10.02% − 8.50% = 1.52%, or 152 basis points. Figure 15.1 illustrates the yield spread between an index of long-term Aaa-rated corporate bonds and U.S. Treasury bonds from March 1993 until April 1994. Note that the spread declined from roughly 100 basis points to 50 basis points over this time period.

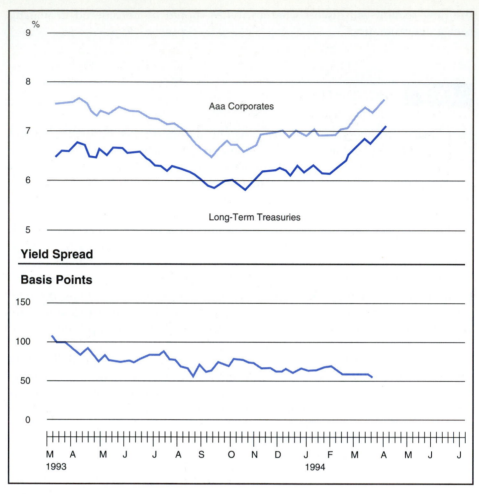

FIGURE 15.1
U.S. Treasury Bond Yields and Aaa Corporate Bond Yields
Source: *Moody's Bond Records,* April 1994, p. 704.

15.2.2 Call Provisions

There are times when, by historical standards, yields-to-maturity are relatively high. Bonds issued during such times may, at first glance, appear to be unusually attractive investments. However, deeper analysis indicates that this is not necessarily the case. Why? Because most corporate bonds have a **call provision** that enables the issuer to redeem the bonds prior to maturity, usually for a price somewhat above par.[2] This price is known as the **call price,** and the difference between it and the par value of the bond is known as the **call premium.** An issuer will often find it financially advantageous to call the existing bonds if yields drop substantially after the bonds were initially sold because the issuer will be able to replace them with lower-yielding securities that are less costly.[3]

For example, consider a ten-year bond issued at par ($1,000) that has a coupon rate of 12% and is callable at $1,050 any time after it has been outstanding for five years.[4] If, after five years, yields on similar five-year bonds were 8%, the bond would probably be called. This means that an investor who had planned on receiving annual coupon payments of $120 for ten years would instead actually receive $120 annual coupon payments for five years and the call price of $1,050 after five years. At this time the investor could take the $1,050 and reinvest it in the 8% bonds, thereby receiving $84 per year in coupon payments over the remaining five years (it is assumed here that the investor can purchase a fraction of a bond, so that the full $1,050 can be invested in the 8% bonds) and $1,050 at the end of the tenth year as a return of principal. Given this pattern of cash flows, the actual yield-to-maturity (otherwise known as the *realized return*) over the ten years would be 10.96%.

This example suggests that the higher the coupon rate of a callable bond, the greater is the likely divergence between actual and promised yields. This is borne out by experience. Figure 15.2 plots the coupon rate, set at the time of issue, on the horizontal axis. As most bonds are initially sold at (or very close to) par, the coupon rate is also a measure of the yield-to-maturity that an investor may have thought was obtainable by purchasing one of the newly issued bonds.

The vertical axis in this figure plots the subsequent actual yields-to-maturity obtained up to the original maturity date by an investor, assuming that the payments received in the event of a call were reinvested in noncallable bonds with appropriate maturities. The curve is based on experience for a group of callable bonds issued by utility companies during a period of fluctuating interest rates. As can be seen, the coupon rate and actual yield are quite similar in magnitude until the coupon rate gets near 5%. At this point, higher coupon rates are no

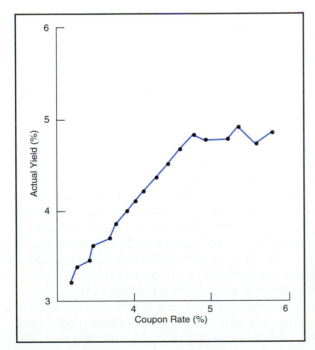

FIGURE 15.2

Promised and Actual Yields of Callable Aa Utility Bonds, 1956–1964

Source: Frank C. Jen and James E. Wert, "The Effect of Call Risk on Corporate Bond Yields," *Journal of Finance*, 22, no. 4 (December 1967): p. 646.

longer associated with higher actual yields because these coupon rates were relatively high during the time period examined. As a consequence, most of the bonds with coupon rates above 5% were ultimately called.

The upshot is that a bond with a greater likelihood of being called should have a higher yield-to-maturity—that is, the higher the coupon rate or the lower the call premium, the higher the yield-to-maturity should be. Equivalently, bonds with higher coupon rates or lower call premiums will have lower intrinsic values, keeping everything else equal.

15.2.3 Tax Status

In Chapter 13 it was noted that tax-exempt municipal bonds have had yields-to-maturity that were approximately 20% to 40% lower than the yields-to-maturity on similar taxable bonds because the coupon payments on muni's are exempt from federal income taxation. However, taxation can also affect bond prices and yields in other ways. For example, any low-coupon taxable bond selling at a discount provides return in two forms: coupon payments and gains from price appreciation. In the United States both are taxable as ordinary income, but taxes on the latter may be deferred until the bond either is sold or matures if the bond was initially sold at par.[5] This suggests that such **market discount bonds** have a tax advantage because of this deferral. As a result, they should have slightly lower before-tax yields than high-coupon taxable bonds, other things being equal—that is, such low-coupon bonds will have a slightly higher intrinsic value than high-coupon bonds.

15.2.4 Marketability

Marketability (sometimes also referred to as liquidity) refers to the ability of an investor to sell an asset quickly without having to make a substantial price concession. An example of an illiquid asset would be a *collectible*, such as a piece of artwork. An investor who owns a van Gogh painting may have to settle for a relatively low price if he or she has to sell it within an hour. If the sale can be postponed for a length of time in order to set up a public auction, undoubtedly a much higher price could be obtained. Alternatively, an investor with $1,000,000 worth of IBM common stock who has to sell these shares within an hour will probably be able to receive a price close to the price that other sellers of IBM stock recently received. Furthermore, it is quite unlikely that waiting would increase the expected selling price of such a security.

Because most bonds are bought and sold in dealer markets, one measure of a bond's marketability is the bid-ask spread that the dealers are quoting on the bond. Bonds that are being actively traded will tend to have lower bid-ask spreads than bonds that are inactive. This is because the dealer is more exposed to risk when making a market in an inactive security than when making a market in an active security. The source of this risk is the inventory that the dealer holds, and the fact that interest rates in general may move in a way that causes the dealer to lose money on his or her inventory. Accordingly, bonds that are actively traded should have a lower yield-to-maturity and a higher intrinsic value than bonds that are inactive, keeping everything else equal.

15.2.5 Likelihood of Default

Currently a number of corporations—the two largest being Standard & Poor's Corporation and Moody's Investors Service, Inc.—provide ratings of the credit-worthiness of thousands of corporate and municipal bonds. Such **bond ratings** are often interpreted as an indication of the likelihood of default by the issuer. Figure 15.3 provides details on the ratings assigned by Standard & Poor's, and Figure 15.4 provides similar details for Moody's.[6]

A broader set of categories is often employed, with bonds classified as being of either **investment grade** or **speculative grade.** Typically, investment-grade bonds are bonds that have been assigned to one of the top four ratings (AAA through BBB by Standard & Poor's; Aaa through Baa by Moody's). In contrast, speculative-grade bonds are bonds that have been assigned to one of the lower ratings (BB and below by Standard & Poor's; Ba and below by Moody's). Sometimes these low-rated securities are called, derisively, **junk bonds.**[7] Furthermore, if the junk bonds were of investment grade when originally issued, they are often called **fallen angels.**

At times certain regulated financial institutions, such as banks, savings and loans, and insurance companies, have been prohibited from purchasing bonds that were not of investment grade. As a consequence, investment-grade bonds are sometimes thought to command "superpremium" prices, and hence disproportionately low yields. However, a major disparity in yields could attract a great many new issuers, who would increase the supply of such bonds, thereby causing bond prices to fall and yields to rise. For a significant superpremium to persist, rather substantial market segmentation on both the buying and the selling sides would be required. As there is no clear evidence that such segmentation exists, it seems more likely that the differences in yields between investment-grade bonds and speculative-grade bonds are roughly proportional to differences in default risk.

According to Moody's, ratings are designed to provide "investors with a simple system of gradation by which the relative investment qualities of bonds may be noted."[8] Moreover:

> Since ratings involve judgments about the future, on the one hand, and since they are used by investors as a means of protection, on the other, the effort is made when assigning ratings to look at "worst" potentialities in the "visible" future, rather than solely at the past record and the status of the present. Therefore, investors using the ratings should not expect to find in them a reflection of statistical factors alone, since they are an appraisal of long-term risks, including the recognition of many non-statistical factors.[9]

Despite this disclaimer, the influence of "statistical factors" on the ratings is apparently significant. Several studies have investigated the relationship between historical measures of a firm's performance and the ratings assigned its bonds. Many of the differences in the ratings accorded various bonds can in fact be attributed to differences in the issuers' situations, measured in traditional ways. For corporate bonds, better ratings are generally associated with lower financial leverage (that is, debt to total assets); smaller past variation in earnings over time; larger asset base (firm size); more profitable operations; and lack of subordination to other debt issues. One use of these findings is in the development of models for predicting the initial ratings that will be given to forthcoming bond issues as well as for predicting changes in the ratings of outstanding bonds.

A Standard & Poor's corporate or municipal debt rating is a current assessment of the creditworthiness of an obligor with respect to a specific obligation. This assessment may take into consideration obligors such as guarantors, insurers, or lessees.

The debt rating is not a recommendation to purchase, sell, or hold a security, inasmuch as it does not comment as to market price or suitability for a particular investor.

The ratings are based on current information furnished by the issuer or obtained by Standard & Poor's from other sources it considers reliable. Standard & Poor's does not perform any audit in connection with any rating and may, on occasion, rely on unaudited financial information. The ratings may be changed, suspended or withdrawn as a result of changes in, or unavailability of, such information, or based on other circumstances.

The ratings are based, in varying degrees, on the following considerations:

I. Likelihood of default-capacity and willingness of the obligor as to the timely payment of interest and repayment of principal in accordance with the terms of the obligation;

II. Nature of and provisions of the obligation;

III. Protection afforded by, and relative position of, the obligation in the event of bankruptcy, reorganization or other arrangement under the laws of bankruptcy and other laws affecting creditors' rights.

AAA Debt rated 'AAA' has the highest rating assigned by Standard & Poor's. Capacity to pay interest and repay principal is extremely strong.

AA Debt rated 'AA' has a very strong capacity to pay interest and repay principal and differs from the higher-rated issues only in small degree.

A Debt rated 'A' has a strong capacity to pay interest and repay principal although it is somewhat more susceptible to the adverse effects of changes in curcumstances and economic conditions than debt in higher-rated categories.

BBB Debt rated 'BBB' is regarded as having an adequate capacity to pay interest and repay principal. Whereas it normally exhibits adequate protection parameters, adverse economic conditions or changing circumstances are more likely to lead to a weakened capacity to pay interest and repay principal for debt in this category than in higher rated categories.

BB, B, CCC, CC, C Debt rated 'BB', 'B', 'CCC', 'CC', and 'C' is regarded, on balance, as predominantly speculative with respect to capacity to pay interest and repay principal in accordance with the terms of the obligation. 'BB' indicates the lowest degree of speculation and 'C' the highest degree of speculation. While such debt will likely have some quality and protective characteristics, these are outweighed by large uncertainties or major risk exposures to adverse conditions.

CI The rating CI is reserved for income bonds on which no interest is being paid.

D Debt rated D is in payment default.

FIGURE 15.3
Standard & Poor's Debt Rating Definitions
Source: *Standard & Poor's Bond Guide,* November 1993, p. 10.

Default Premiums

Because common stocks do not "promise" any cash flows to the investor, they are not subject to default. To assess the investment prospects for a common stock, all possible holding-period returns might be considered. By multiplying each return by its perceived probability of occurrence and then adding up the products, an estimate of the expected holding-period return can be determined.

Aaa

Bonds which are rated **Aaa** are judged to be of the best quality. They carry the smallest degree of investment risk and are generally referred to as "gilt edge." Interest payments are protected by a large or by an exceptionally stable margin and principal is secure. While the various protective elements are likely to change, such changes as can be visualized are most unlikely to impair the fundamentally strong position of such issues.

Aa

Bonds which are rated **Aa** are judged to be of high quality by all standards. Together with the **Aaa** group they comprise what are generally known as high grade bonds. They are rated lower than the best bonds because margins of protection may not be as large as in **Aaa** securities or fluctuation of protective elements may be of greater amplitude or there may be other elements present which make the long term risks appear somewhat larger than in **Aaa** securities.

A

Bonds which are rated **A** possess many favorable investment attributes and are to be considered as upper medium grade obligations. Factors giving security to principal and interest are considered adequate but elements may be present which suggest a susceptibility to impairment sometime in the future.

Baa

Bonds which are rated **Baa** are considered as medium grade obligations, i.e., they are neither highly protected nor poorly secured. Interest payments and principal security appear adequate for the present but certain protective elements may be lacking or may be characteristically unreliable over any great length of time. Such bonds lack outstanding investment characteristics and in fact have speculative characteristics as well.

Ba

Bonds which are rated **Ba** are judged to have speculative elements; their future cannot be considered as well assured. Often the protection of interest and principal payments may be very moderate and thereby not well safeguarded during other good and bad times over the future. Uncertainty of position characterizes bonds in this class.

B

Bonds which are rated **B** generally lack characteristics of the desired investment. Assurance of interest and principal payments or of maintenance of other terms of the contract over any long period of time may be small.

Caa

Bonds which are rated **Caa** are of poor standing. Such issues may be in default or there may be present elements of danger with respect to principal or interest.

Ca

Bonds which are rated **Ca** represent obligations which are speculative in a high degree. Such issues are often in default or have other marked shortcomings.

C

Bonds which are rated **C** are the lowest rated class of bonds and issues so rated can be regarded as having extremely poor prospects of ever attaining any real investment standing.

FIGURE 15.4

Moody's Corporate Bond Ratings

Source: *Moody's Bond Record,* November 1993, p. 3.

Taking Advantage of the Bond Rating Process

"**Y**our bond rating: don't try to issue debt without it," might read the motto of U.S. bond rating agencies. Receiving an investment-grade bond rating has long been a prerequisite for any U.S. debt issuer desiring easy access to the domestic bond market. Without such a rating, debt issuers are forced to seek financing from more expensive sources: banks, the market for privately placed debt, or the high-yield (junk) bond market.

Once they have acquired an investment-grade bond rating, debt issuers strive to maintain that rating or even improve it. The benefits of an improved rating (and the costs of a lower rating) can be substantial. The difference in yields between the highest and lowest rated investment-grade bonds fluctuates over time but is often well over a full percentage point (as is illustrated in Figure 15.5). Yield differences between investment-grade and non-investment-grade bonds are even greater. As U.S. corporations have increased the amount of debt on their balance sheets in recent decades, the financial ramifications of bond rating changes have increased commensurately.

Most institutional bond investors focus their efforts on forecasting changes in interest rates and structuring their portfolios to benefit from those expected movements. However, the emphasis placed by the bond market on both a debt issue's initial rating and subsequent changes in that rating present insightful investors with another approach to bond management: searching for bonds whose "true" credit quality is different from their assigned ratings. In discussing those opportunities, we first consider some additional information on the bond rating process.

Two companies dominate the bond rating business: Standard & Poor's and Moody's. At least one of these organizations rates virtually every corporate debt security that comes to the public market. Over 2,000 debt issuers submit financial data to

FIGURE 15.5
Corporate Bond Yields by Ratings
Source: *Moody's Bond Record*, November 1993, p. 3.

these organizations. For all practical purposes, no bond can be considered an investment-grade security without the acquiescence of S&P's or Moody's.

In addition, a relatively small market exists for "third opinions." Three other firms—Fitch Investors; Duff & Phelps; and McCarthy, Crisanti & Maffei—produce ratings on a portion of the bonds that are rated by the two big firms. Although their ratings rarely differ significantly from S&P's and Moody's, in some situations investors and issuers are comforted by a confirmation of the two big firms' ratings or believe that the smaller rating agencies may uncover aspects of the debt issuers' financial conditions overlooked by S&P's and Moody's.

The text describes many of the financial factors that rating agencies use in assigning bond ratings, including the issuers' leverage, earnings variability, and profitability. Research has shown that such factors systematically "explain" a large portion of bond rating differences among debt issues, implying that there is a significant "mechanical" aspect to the rating process.

Despite this dominant formulistic element of bond ratings, qualitative judgments by the rating agencies still appear to play an important role in rating assignments. Interestingly, as corporations have increased the leverage on their balance sheets, a firm's ability to generate future cash flow to meet its interest expenses has come to play a major role in setting bond ratings. However, evaluating the prospective, rather than contemporaneous, cash flow strength of an issuer is an uncertain process and requires more subjective interpretations of the financial data on the part of the rating agencies.

Some institutional bond investors attempt to take advantage of the uncertainty surrounding a bond's rating. They recognize that, all other factors being equal, a bond with a lower rating will sell for a lower price (equivalently, a higher yield) than a bond with a higher rating. If bonds can be discovered whose credit quality supports a higher rating, then these bonds will offer premium yields relative to bonds with the same "actual" credit quality. Conversely, bonds that deserve a lower rating will provide yields below those with the same

"actual" credit quality. Thus an investor who purchases underrated bonds and avoids overrated bonds can construct a portfolio that will outperform a passively managed portfolio of similar risk.

Owners of underrated bonds may benefit even further if their bonds are subsequently upgraded by the rating agencies. Such upgrades are usually associated with substantial price increases, although those increases usually occur in advance of rating changes, rather than subsequently.

Why do such institutional bond investors expect to beat the ratings game? They believe that with intensive security analysis they can understand a debt issuer's financial condition more accurately and on a more timely basis than can the rating agencies. Essentially, these investors make their moves and wait for the market and the rating agencies to catch up to them.

Security analysis of this type is similar to fundamental stock analysis (see Chapters 18 and 23), although less emphasis is placed on an issuer's long-term growth prospects and more attention is paid to the issuer's ability to cover near- and medium-term obligations. Nevertheless, an interpretation of a debt issuer's "true" financial condition is based on a wide range of disparate variables, from the quality of the debt issuer's management to the market for its products.

To a certain extent, these bond investors also play a numbers game with the rating agencies. Both S&P and Moody's employ fewer than 100 analysts (the smaller rating agencies employ far fewer). Thus the rating agencies cannot cover all debt issuers at all times. Significant positive or negative news about an issuer may cause the rating agencies to immediately reevaluate their bond ratings. However, at other times a debt issuer's financial condition may change slowly, without full recognition by the market and the rating agencies.

Of course, as with successful common stock analysis, identifying misrated bonds consistently and accurately requires skills possessed by few investors in an efficient market. But also as with common stock analysis, the potential profits to bond investors who correctly diverge from the current consensus can be large.

A similar procedure can be employed with bonds, with the analysis usually focusing on yield-to-maturity. Formally all possible yields are considered, along with their respective probabilities, and a weighted average computed to determine the **expected yield-to-maturity.** As long as there is any possibility of default or late payment, the expected yield will fall below the promised yield. In general, the greater the risk of default and the greater the amount of loss in the event of default, the greater will be this disparity in yields.

This is illustrated in Figure 15.6 for a hypothetical risky bond. Its promised yield-to-maturity is 12% but, owing to a high default risk, the expected yield is only 9%. The 3% difference between promised and expected yields is the **default premium.** Any bond that has some probability of default should offer such a premium, and it should be greater, the greater the probability of default.

Just how large should a bond's default premium be? According to one model, the answer depends on both the probability of default and the likely financial loss to the bondholder in the event of default.[10] Consider a bond that is perceived to be equally likely to default in each year (given that it did not default in the previous year), with the probability that it will default in any given year denoted by p_d. Assume that if the bond does default, a payment equal to $(1 - \lambda)$ times its market price a year earlier will be made to the owner of each bond. According to this model, a bond will be fairly priced if its promised yield-to-maturity y is

$$y = \frac{\bar{y} + \lambda p_d}{1 - p_d} \tag{15.4}$$

where $\bar{y}$ denotes the bond's expected yield-to-maturity. The difference d between a bond's promised yield-to-maturity y and its expected yield-to-maturity $\bar{y}$ was referred to earlier as the bond's default premium. Using Equation (15.4), this difference for a fairly priced bond will be equal to

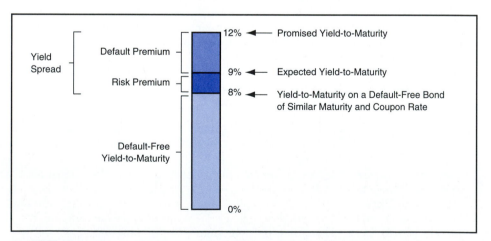

FIGURE 15.6
Yield-to-Maturity for a Risky Bond

$$d = y - \bar{y}$$

$$= \left(\frac{\bar{y} + \lambda p_d}{1 - p_d}\right) - \bar{y}. \tag{15.5}$$

As an example, consider the bond illustrated in Figure 15.4. Assume that this bond has a 6% annual default probability, and that it is estimated that if the bond does default, each bondholder will receive an amount equal to 60% of the bond's market price a year earlier (meaning that $1 - \lambda = .60$, which in turn means that $\lambda = .40$). Using Equation (15.5), this bond would be fairly priced if its default premium were equal to

$$d = \left[\frac{.09 + (.40 \times .06)}{1 - .06}\right] - .09$$

$$= .0313$$

or 3.13%. Because the actual default premium earlier was estimated to be 3%, it can be seen that the two figures are similar. This suggests that the actual default premium is appropriate, according to this model.

What sort of default experience might the long-run bond investor anticipate, and how is this experience likely to be related to the ratings of the bonds held? In a massive study of all large bond issues and a sample of small bond issues, Hickman attempted to answer these questions.[11] He analyzed investor experience for each bond from 1900 through 1943 to determine the actual yield-to-maturity, measured from the date of issuance to the date on which the bond matured, defaulted, or was called, whichever came first. He then compared this actual yield with the promised yield-to-maturity based on the price at the time of issue. Every bond was also classified according to the ratings assigned at the time of issue. Panel (a) of Table 15.1 shows the major results.

As might be expected, Hickman found that, in general, the riskier the bond, the higher the promised yield at the time of issue and the higher the percentage of bonds that subsequently defaulted. However, a surprise was uncovered when the actual yields-to-maturity were compared with promised yields-to-maturity. As the last column on the right of the table shows, in four out of five rating classifications, the actual yield was found to *exceed* the promised yield. Fortunately, a convenient explanation exists for this finding—the period studied by Hickman was one in which a substantial drop in interest rates occurred. This is important because the drop made it attractive for issuers to call their outstanding bonds, paying the bondholders a call premium in the process, which resulted in an actual yield above the promised yield.

To see what might have happened had this not been the case, Fraine and Mills reanalyzed the data for large investment-grade issues.[12] Their results are shown in panel (b) of Table 15.1. The initial columns differ from those in panel (a) because smaller issues were excluded. The major difference between the panels appears in the right-hand column, where Fraine and Mills substituted a bond's promised yield for its actual yield whenever the latter was larger, thereby removing the effects of most calls. Unlike Hickman's, their results suggest that there was little difference in actual yields within the highest rating classifications.

More recently, Edward Altman examined the default experience of corporate bonds over the period from 1971 through 1990.[13] His methodology was

TABLE 15.1
ACTUAL AND REALIZED BOND YIELDS-TO-MATURITY, 1900–1943

(a) All Large and a Sample of Small Issues

Composite Rating	Comparable Moody's Rating	Promised Yield-to-Maturity at Issue	Percent Defaulting Prior to Maturity	Actual Yield-to-Maturity
I	Aaa	4.5%	5.9%	5.1%
II	Aa	4.6	6.0	5.0
III	A	4.9	13.4	5.0
IV	Baa	5.4	19.1	5.7
V–IX	below Baa	9.5	42.4	8.6

(b) All Large Issues

Composite Rating	Comparable Moody's Rating	Promised Yield-to-Maturity	Actual Yield-to-Maturity	Modified Actual Yield-to-Maturity
I	Aaa	4.5%	5.1%	4.3%
II	Aa	4.5	5.1	4.3
III	A	4.9	5.0	4.3
IV	Baa	5.4*	5.8	4.5

Source: (a) W. Braddock Hickman, *Corporate Bond Quality and Investor Experience* (Princeton, NJ: Princeton University Press, 1958), p. 10. (b) Harold G. Fraine and Robert H. Mills, "The Effect of Defaults and Credit Deterioration on Yields of Corporate Bonds," *Journal of Finance*, 16, no. 3 (September 1961): p. 433.

somewhat different from Hickman's in that for each bond he noted its rating when it was originally issued and then how many years later it went into default (if at all). From this he compiled "mortality tables," such as Table 15.2, which shows the percentage of bond issues that went into default within various numbers of years after issuance.

There are several interesting observations that can be made upon inspection of this table. First, in looking down any particular column, it can be seen that the cumulative rate of default increases as one moves further from the date

TABLE 15.2
DEFAULT RATES OF U.S. BONDS, 1971–1990

Years After Issuance	Original Rating						
	AAA	AA	A	BBB	BB	B	CCC
1	.00%	.00%	.00%	.03%	.00%	.87%	1.31%
2	.00	.00	.30	.57	.93	3.22	4.00
3	.00	1.11	.60	.85	1.36	9.41	19.72
4	.00	1.42	.65	1.34	3.98	16.37	36.67
5	.00	1.70	.65	1.54	5.93	20.87	38.08
6	.14	1.70	.73	1.81	7.38	26.48	40.58
7	.19	1.91	.87	2.70	10.91	29.62	NA
8	.19	1.93	.94	2.83	10.91	31.74	NA
9	.19	2.01	1.28	2.99	10.91	39.38	NA
10	.19	2.11	1.28	3.85	13.86	40.86	NA

Source: Edward I. Altman, "Defaults and Returns on High-Yield Bonds Through the First Half of 1991," *Financial Analysts Journal*, 47, no. 6 (November/December 1991): Table X, pp. 74–75.

of issuance. Second, with the exception of those bonds originally rated AA, by looking across any row it can be seen that lower rated bonds had higher default rates. Third, the default rates for the speculative grades of bonds are strikingly high. Indeed, it raises a question of whether or not such bonds make good investments, as their higher yields might not make up for their higher default rates. This question will be addressed shortly.

Risk Premiums

It is useful to compare the expected return of a risky security with the certain return of a default-free security. In an efficient market, the difference in these returns will be related to the relevant systematic (or nondiversifiable) risk of the security. Consider common stocks, where the investor has a holding period of one year or less. In this situation the expected return on a share is typically compared with the yield of a Treasury bill having a maturity date corresponding with the end of the holding period. (Note that the yield on such a Treasury bill is equal to its holding period return.)

Traditionally, a risky bond's expected yield-to-maturity is compared with that of a default-free bond of similar maturity and coupon rate. The difference between these yields is known as the bond's **risk premium.** In the example shown in Figure 15.6, default-free bonds of similar maturity and coupon rate offer a certain 8% yield-to-maturity. Because the risky bond's expected yield-to-maturity is 9%, its risk premium is 1% (that is, 100 basis points).

Every bond that might default will offer a default premium. But the risk premium is another matter. Any security's expected return should be related only to its systematic risk, for it is this risk that measures its contribution to the risk of a well-diversified portfolio; its total risk is not directly relevant.

For example, if a group of companies all faced the possibility of bankruptcy, but from totally unrelated causes, a portfolio that included all of their bonds would subsequently provide an actual return very close to its expected return. This is because the default premiums earned on the bonds that did not default would offset the losses incurred from those bonds that did default. Consequently, there should be little reason for this expected return to differ significantly from that of a default-free bond, because there is little doubt concerning what its actual return will be. Accordingly, each bond should be priced to offer little or no risk premium (but each bond should have a substantive default premium).

However, the risks associated with bonds are not unrelated. Figure 15.7 shows the ratio of the par value of corporate bonds defaulting during the year to the par value outstanding at the beginning of the year for each year from 1900 to 1965. Not surprisingly, the peaks coincide with periods of economic distress.[14] When business is bad, most firms are affected. The market value of a firm's common stock will decline when an economic downturn is anticipated. If the likelihood of default on its debt also increases, the market value of its outstanding bonds will follow suit. Thus the holding-period return on a bond may be correlated with the returns of other bonds and with those of stocks. Most important, a risky bond's holding-period return is likely to be correlated, at least to some extent, with the return on a widely diversified "market portfolio" that includes both corporate bonds and stocks. It is this part of the risk of a bond that is known as systematic risk and causes a bond to have a risk premium in the form of an expected return that is greater than the default-free rate because it is not diversifiable.

FIGURE 15.7
Default Rates, 1900–1965
Source: Adapted from Thomas R. Atkinson and Elizabeth T. Simpson, *Trends in Corporate Bond Quality*
(New York: Columbia University Press, 1967), p. 5.

Bonds with greater likelihood of default will have greater potential sensitivity to market declines, which, in turn, represent lowered assessments of prospects for the economy as a whole. This is illustrated in Table 15.3, which summarizes the investment performance of three portfolios of bonds, known as bond funds, in the Keystone group.[15] All values shown in the table are based on annual returns earned over a 24-year period by each portfolio. As might be anticipated, the bond portfolio with the lowest rated bonds (fund B4) had the highest average return and highest standard deviation, while the bond portfolio with the highest rated bonds (fund B1) had the lowest average return and lowest standard deviation.

To estimate each portfolio's sensitivity to changes in stock prices, each portfolio's returns were compared with those of Standard & Poor's 500. Specifically, a beta was calculated for each portfolio in order to measure the sensitivity of each portfolio to swings in the stock market. As can be seen in the table, the lower the bond rating of the portfolio, the higher the estimated beta, indicating that lower rated bonds moved more with stocks and thus should have had higher average returns.

	Table 15.3		
	Risk and Return, Keystone Bond Funds, 1968–1991		
	Fund B1	**Fund B2**	**Fund B4**
	Conservative Bonds	**Investment Grade Bonds**	**Discount Bonds**
Average return (% per year)	7.84	8.53	8.64
Standard deviation of return (% per year)	8.27	9.35	13.68
Beta value, relative to S&P 500	.26	.38	.54
Proportion of variance explained by S&P 500	.28	.45	.42

CHAPTER 15

The final row in the table shows the proportion of the year-to-year variation in bond portfolio returns that was associated with stock market swings. As indicated, relatively more of the B2 and B4 portfolios' variation was associated with the stock market than was the case with the B1 portfolio. Thus for higher rated bonds, interest-rate risk appears to have been more important than stock market risk.[16]

15.3 THE RISK STRUCTURE OF INTEREST RATES

The greater a bond's risk of default, the greater its default premium. This alone will cause a bond with a higher default risk to offer a higher promised yield-to-maturity. If it is also true that the greater a bond's risk of default, the greater its risk premium, then the promised yield-to-maturity will have to be even higher. As a result, bonds given lower agency ratings should have higher promised yields-to-maturity if such ratings really do reflect the risk of default.

Figure 15.5 shows that this is indeed the case. Each of the curves plots the promised yield-to-maturity for a group of corporate bonds assigned the same ratings by Moody's. Note that the scale is "upside down," so that higher promised yields plot at lower positions on the diagram. (Such a procedure is often employed for bonds.)

Figure 15.5 shows not only that bonds are priced so that higher promised yields go with lower ratings, it also shows that the differences between the yields in the rating categories vary considerably over time. This suggests that agency ratings indicate *relative* levels of risk instead of *absolute* levels of risk.

If an absolute level of risk were indicated by a rating classification, then each classification would be associated with a particular probability of default (or, more accurately, a range of probabilities of default). Consequently, as the economy became more uncertain in terms of such factors as the near-term level of gross domestic product, bonds would be reclassified, with most moving to lower ratings. In this situation, yield spreads between classifications would change only slightly, as each classification would still reflect bonds having the same probability of default. However, Figure 15.5 shows that these spreads change over time, an observation that can be interpreted as evidence that the ratings do not reflect absolute levels of risk. Further evidence is provided in Table 15.4, which shows the historical difference in the returns on junk bonds and U.S. Treasuries for various holding periods. As shown in the table, at times these differences are positive and at other times they are negative. (For example, the average annual differences for 1978–1983 and 1984–1991 are +5.82% and −2.31%, respectively.)

It is known that rating agencies prefer to avoid making a large number of rating changes as the economy becomes more uncertain. Instead, they prefer to use the classifications to indicate relative levels of risk. This means that an overall increase in economic uncertainty would not result in a significant number of reclassifications. Thus the probability of default associated with bonds in a given rating classification would be greater at such a time. In turn, the yield spreads between classifications of corporate bonds and the yield spreads between corporate and government bonds would increase. Indeed, there is evidence that the spread between the promised yields of bonds of different rating classifications increases when the degree of uncertainty about the economy increases.

Bond Analysis

TABLE 15.4

HISTORICAL RETURN DIFFERENCES BETWEEN JUNK BONDS AND U.S. TREASURIES

Terminal Period (December 31)

Base Period (Jan.1)	1978	1979	1980	1981	1982	1983	1984	1985	1986	1987	1988	1989	1990	1991
1978	8.68%	6.60%	5.01%	5.51%	3.17%	5.82%	4.13%	2.70%	1.59%	2.22%	2.41%	0.98%	(0.04%)	1.37%
1979		4.55	3.23	4.48	1.71	5.22	3.32	1.77	0.62	1.44	1.73	0.23	(0.82)	0.74
1980			1.96	4.45	0.67	5.39	3.05	1.24	(0.02)	1.01	1.38	(0.25)	(1.35)	0.37
1981				7.08	(0.13)	6.74	3.36	1.07	(0.42)	0.85	1.29	(0.54)	(1.73)	0.19
1982					(9.63)	6.49	1.93	(0.69)	(2.16)	(0.33)	0.36	(1.60)	(2.80)	(0.60)
1983						19.57	6.62	1.84	(0.56)	1.22	1.74	(0.65)	(2.11)	0.26
1984							(6.32)	7.60	(7.73)	(3.48)	(1.89)	(4.06)	(5.19)	(2.31)
1985								(9.03)	(8.50)	(2.50)	(0.76)	(3.60)	(5.00)	(1.70)
1986									(7.99)	0.34	1.64	(2.41)	(4.30)	(0.54)
1987										7.34	5.89	(0.76)	(3.49)	0.93
1988											4.27	(5.16)	(7.31)	(1.04)
1989												(14.37)	(12.76)	(3.11)
1990													(11.24)	4.34
1991*														19.01

*First six months of 1991.

Source: Edward I. Altman, "Defaults and Returns on High-Yield Bonds Through the First Half of 1991," *Financial Analysts Journal*, 47, no. 6 (November/December 1991): Table XIV, p. 77.

Matrix Bond Pricing

Many institutional investors must periodically determine the market values of their bond portfolios. For example, a pension fund may wish to keep beneficiaries abreast of the value of their fixed-income investments. Further, the pension fund needs accurate market valuations to evaluate fixed-income managers' investment results and to compute their compensation. (Managers' fees are typically based on the market values of their portfolios.)

In some cases, valuing a bond portfolio is a straightforward matter. Prices of most Treasury bonds, many government agency bonds, and certain actively traded corporate bonds are available through real-time electronic quotation systems and the print media. Unlike common stocks, however, where an active market usually exists for all but the smallest issues, many bond issues (even some with large face values outstanding) do not trade frequently. It is not uncommon to find entire bond issues held to maturity by investors. The limited trading of these securities inhibits efforts to accurately determine their current market prices.

How can an institutional investor establish market prices for thinly traded fixed-income securities in its possession? It could ask its fixed-income managers to supply their best estimates of the bonds' market prices. After all, these managers constantly compare their perceptions of the bonds' intrinsic values to the bonds' estimated market prices as part of their portfolio management processes. However, a manager has an inherent conflict of interest in providing such valuations because his or her financial well-being is directly related to those values.

Alternatively, the pension fund might canvass bond dealers who trade the bonds under question (or similar securities) and solicit representative bid prices. Unfortunately, this procedure is too time-consuming to conduct on a regular basis for hundreds of bonds. Furthermore, the dealers have no incentive to participate.

In response to this dearth of pricing data, institutional investors have turned to various commercial bond valuation services. For a fee, these organizations provide third-party security valuations for tens of thousands of fixed-income securities on a daily, weekly, or monthly basis.

Some bond pricing services "lever off" of their own trading operations. (Merrill Lynch, for example, runs one of the largest pricing services.) They use their bond traders to submit bid-side valuations daily for any securities that its traders regularly see traded in the market. This "hand pricing" by traders offers perhaps the best estimate that institutional investors can readily obtain as to the "true" market price, or liquidation value, of their bonds. Note, however, that the pricing services do not offer to transact at their price quotations. An actual bid for an institutional investor's fixed-income portfolio would involve an assessment by the trader of many factors, including the trader's current inventory, the price risk of the portfolio, and available hedges on the portfolio.

Oftentimes, however, a bond pricing service does not have immediate access to current prices for certain securities, either because it does not maintain a trading desk or because its traders do not deal in the securities. In those cases, various mechanical procedures, generally known as *matrix pricing*, are used to estimate market prices. The particular matrix pricing formulas vary among the pricing services and among the types of bonds valued by the services. Nevertheless, the pricing of corporate bonds provides a good example of the essential aspects of matrix bond pricing.

The price matrix for investment grade corporate bonds is typically three-dimensional with sector, quality, and term-to-maturity as the three primary variables. Each cell in the matrix represents a unique three-way combination of these variables. For example, one cell might contain industrial bonds with A ratings and three years to maturity.

Each cell in the matrix is assigned an incremental yield (or "spread") over comparable maturity Treasury securities, based on an analysis of current market conditions. (For example, three-year, A-rated industrial bonds might be assigned a 100 basis point spread over Treasuries.) These spreads may change over time at the discretion of the pricing service.

Once the matrix spreads are established, a corporate bond is priced by finding the cell in which it resides and using the associated yield to discount the bond's promised cash flows and thereby compute an estimated price. Adjustments may be made for special factors, such as coupon rates, call features, and sinking fund provisions.

Mortgage pass-through securities create particular problems for matrix pricing systems, especially complex mortgage-backed bonds, such as various forms of collateral mortgage obligations (CMOs). There exist literally hundreds of variations of mortgage pass-through securities that differ in terms of coupon rate, payment terms, years since issuance (called "seasoning"), underlying collateral, and expected prepayment speed. The existing matrix pricing procedures are relatively primitive compared to the state-of-the-art option-adjusted pricing models used by many fixed-income managers.

For standard mortgage pass-through securities, the bond pricing services may supply valuations for various generic securities based on issuer type, coupon rate, and seasoning (for example, GNMA single-family, moderately seasoned, 8% coupon mortgage pools). Any mortgage pass-through security that matches the characteristics of one of the generic securities is assigned the same price.

For CMOs, the matrix-pricing systems use simple prepayment assumptions to generate a stream of expected cash flows for the particular CMO tranche under consideration (see Chapter 14 for a further discussion of CMOs). With these expected cash flows, the expected life of the security is calculated, and a yield spread from a comparable term-to-maturity Treasury security is established. The pass-through security's expected cash flows are then discounted at the assigned yield to produce an estimated market price.

Current matrix-pricing procedures for pass-through securities have been criticized for not explicitly accounting for the imbedded option contained in those securities (that is, the ability of homeowners to prepay their mortgages at their discretion). This option has an implicit value, and failing to adequately incorporate it into a pass-through securities price will produce systematic errors.

As one might expect, the accuracy of matrix bond pricing depends on the uniqueness of the security under analysis. Those securities that do not deviate significantly in terms of investment characteristics from their actively traded counterparts are relatively easy to price accurately. Securities with relatively unique or complicated features are more difficult to price accurately, and their matrix prices are often considered suspect by fixed-income managers.

Some models have attempted to take advantage of this observation in order to predict the amount of economic uncertainty. In particular, these models use the size of the yield spread between, say, bonds rated AAA and those rated BBB by Standard & Poor's as an indication of the degree of economic uncertainty. For example, if this spread is widening, then that might be taken as an indication that the near-term future of the economy was becoming more uncertain. It should be noted that there are other models that look not at yield spreads but at differences in the holding-period returns of AAA and BBB bonds.

15.4   DETERMINANTS OF YIELD SPREADS

As mentioned previously, when bond analysts refer to a corporate bond's yield spread, they are typically referring to the difference between the corporate bond's promised yield-to-maturity and that of another bond (often a Treasury security) having a similar maturity and coupon rate. The greater the risk of default, the greater this spread should be. Moreover, bonds that have more marketability might command an additional "premium" in price, and hence offer a lower yield-to-maturity with a corresponding lower spread. Given a large enough sample of bonds, it should be possible to see whether these relationships really do exist.

One study of corporate bond prices did just this.[17] Four measures were used to assess the probability of default:

1. The extent to which the firm's net income had varied over the preceding nine years (measured by the coefficient of variation of earnings—that is, the ratio of standard deviation of earnings to average earnings)
2. The length of time that the firm had operated without forcing any of its creditors to take a loss
3. The ratio of the market value of the firm's equity to the par value of its debt
4. The market value of the firm's outstanding debt (an indication of marketability)

First, these measures were calculated, along with the yield spread, for each of 366 bonds. Second, the logarithm of every yield spread and measure was calculated. Third, statistical methods were used to analyze the relationship between a bond's yield spread and these measures. The one that was found to describe this relationship most accurately was:

$$\begin{aligned} \text{yield spread} = \quad &.987 + .307 \text{ (earnings variability)} \\ &-.253 \text{ (time without default)} - .537 \text{ (equity/debt ratio)} \\ &-.275 \text{ (market value of debt)}. \qquad (15.6) \end{aligned}$$

This form of the relationship accounted for roughly 75% of the variation in the bonds' yield spreads.

The advantage of an equation such as this is that the coefficients can be easily interpreted. Because all yield spreads and values had been converted to logarithms, the effect is similar to that of using ratio scales on all axes of a diagram. This means that a 1% increase in a bond's earnings variability can be expected to bring about an increase of .307% in the bond's yield spread, other things being equal. Similarly, a 1% increase in a bond's time without default can be expected to cause a decrease of approximately .253% in the bond's yield spread, and so on. Each coefficient is an elasticity, indicating the percentage change in a bond's yield spread likely to accompany a 1% change in the associated measure. As every measure was found to be related in the expected direction to the yield spread, the study provides substantial support for the notion that bonds with higher default risk and less marketability have higher yield spreads.

15.5 FINANCIAL RATIOS AS PREDICTORS OF DEFAULT

For years, security analysts have used accounting ratios to indicate the probability that a firm will fail to meet its financial obligations. Specific procedures have been developed to predict default with such ratios. Univariate analysis attempts to find the best single predictor for the purpose, whereas multivariate analysis searches for the best combination of two or more predictors.

15.5.1 Univariate Methods

Cash inflows can be viewed as contributions to the firm's cash balance, while cash outflows can be viewed as drains on this balance. When the balance falls below zero, default is likely to occur. This means that the probability of default will be greater for the firm when (1) the existing cash balance is smaller, (2) the expected net cash flow (measured before payments to creditors and stockholders) is smaller, and (3) the net cash flow is more variable.

In an examination of various measures used to assess these factors, it was found that the ratio of net cash flow (income before depreciation, depletion, and amortization charges) to total debt was particularly useful.[18] Panel (a) of Figure 15.8 shows the mean value of this ratio for a group of firms that defaulted on a promised payment and for a companion group that did not. As early as five years before default the two groups' ratios diverged, and the spread widened as the year of default approached.

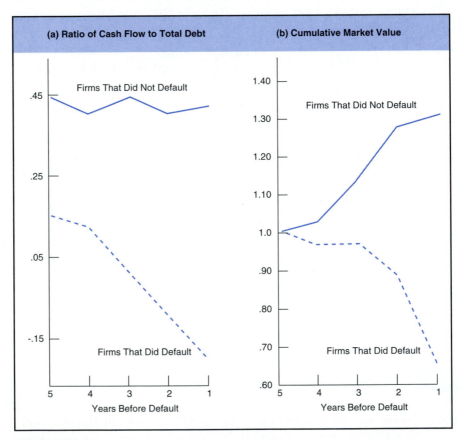

FIGURE 15.8

Financial Ratios and Market Prices for Firms That Defaulted and Those That Did Not

Source: William H. Beaver, "Market Prices, Financial Ratios and the Prediction of Failure," *Journal of Accounting Research*, 6, no. 2 (Autumn 1968): pp. 182, 185.

This changing spread suggests that the probability of default may not be constant through time. Instead, warning signals may indicate an increase in the probability, which should, in turn, cause a fall in the market price of the firm's bonds along with a fall in the market price of its common stock. Panel (b) of Figure 15.8 shows that such signals are indeed recognized in the marketplace. The median market value of common stock in the firms that did not default went up, while that of the firms that subsequently defaulted went down as the date of default approached.

15.5.2 Multivariate Methods

Combinations of certain financial ratios and cash flow variables have been considered as possible predictors of default. In one of the first studies, statistical analysis indicated that the most accurate method of predicting default involved calculating a firm's default-risk rating, known as its *Z-score*, from some of its financial ratios as follows:

$$Z = 1.2X_1 + 1.4X_2 + 3.3X_3 + .6X_4 + .99X_5 \tag{15.7}$$

where the following five ratios were calculated from information contained in the firm's most recent income statement and balance sheet:

X_1 = *(current assets − current liabilities)/total assets,*
X_2 = *retained earnings/total assets,*
X_3 = *earnings before interest and taxes/total assets,*
X_4 = *market value of equity/book value of total debt,*
X_5 = *sales/total assets.*

Any firm with a *Z*-score below 1.8 was considered a likely candidate for default, and the lower the score, the greater the likelihood.[19]

15.5.3 Investment Implications

Does this mean that securities of firms whose cash-flow-to-total-debt ratio or *Z*-score had declined should have been avoided? Hardly. It should be remembered that the firms represented by the dashed lines in Figure 15.7 were chosen because they eventually defaulted. Had all firms with declining ratios been selected, corresponding decreases in their market prices would undoubtedly have been observed, reflecting the increased probability of future default. However, only some of these firms would have ultimately defaulted, while the others would have recovered. Consequently, the gains on the firms that recovered might well have offset the losses on the firms that defaulted. In summary, the net result from purchasing a portfolio of stocks that had declining ratios or *Z*-scores could easily have been the achievement of an average return.

What about purchasing bonds of companies that have just had their ratings increased, and selling (or avoiding) bonds of companies that have just had their ratings decreased? After all, such changes in ratings should be related to a change in the default risk of the issuer. In a study that looked at the behavior of bond prices around the time of ratings changes, some evidence was found that the bond price adjustment to a rating change occurred in the period from eighteen to seven months *before* the rating change. Little or no evidence of a substantive price change was found either during the month of the rating change or in the period from six months before to six months after the rating change.[20] These findings are consistent with the notion that the bond market is semistrong-form efficient, because bond ratings are at least partly predictable from publicly available information.

15.6 SUMMARY

1. The capitalization of income method of valuation is a commonly used approach to identify mispriced bonds. It is based on the discounted value of the cash flows that the investor expects to receive from owning a bond.
2. Given the bond's current market price and promised cash flows, the investor can calculate the bond's promised yield-to-maturity and compare it to an appropriate discount rate.
3. Alternatively, the investor can use an appropriate discount rate to discount the bond's promised cash flows. The sum of the present value of these cash flows is compared to the bond's market price.
4. Six primary attributes are of significance in bond valuation: length of time to maturity, coupon rate, call provisions, tax status, marketability, and likelihood of default.
5. Time to maturity, call provisions, tax status, and likelihood of default tend to be directly related to promised yield-to-maturity. Coupon rate and marketability tend to be inversely related to promised yield-to-maturity.
6. Several organizations provide ratings of the creditworthiness of thousands of corporate and municipal bonds. These ratings are often interpreted as an indication of the issuer's likelihood of default.
7. Bond ratings indicate relative levels of risk instead of absolute levels of risk.
8. A bond's promised yield-to-maturity can be decomposed into a default-free yield-to-maturity and a yield spread. Furthermore, the yield spread can be decomposed into a risk premium and a default premium.
9. Various statistical models have been developed to predict the probability that a bond issuer will default. These models typically use financial ratios derived from the issuer's balance sheet and income statement.

QUESTIONS AND PROBLEMS

1. Bones Ely owns a $1,000 face-value bond with three years to maturity. The bond makes annual interest payments of $75, the first to be made one year from today. The bond is currently priced at $975.48. Given an appropriate discount rate of 10%, should Bones hold or sell the bond?
2. A broker has advised Jewel Ens to purchase a ten-year $10,000 face-value bond that makes 8% annual coupon payments. The appropriate discount

rate is 9%. The first interest payment is due one year from today. If the bond currently sells for $8,560, should Jewel follow the broker's advice?

3. Patsy Tebeau is considering investing in a bond currently selling for $8,785.07. The bond has four years to maturity, a $10,000 face value, and an 8% coupon rate. The next annual interest payment is due one year from today. The appropriate discount rate for investments of similar risk is 10%.
   a. Calculate the intrinsic value of the bond. Based on this calculation, should Patsy purchase the bond?
   b. Calculate the yield-to-maturity of the bond. Based on this calculation, should Patsy purchase the bond?

4. Consider two bonds with $1,000 face values that carry coupon rates of 8%, make annual coupon payments, and exhibit similar risk characteristics. However, the first bond has five years to maturity whereas the second has ten years to maturity. The appropriate discount rate for investments of similar risk is 8%. If this discount rate rises by two percentage points, what will be the respective percentage price changes of the two bonds?

5. Why is it convenient to use Treasury securities as a starting point for analyzing bond yields?

6. Bond A's yield-to-maturity is 9.80%; bond B's yield-to-maturity is 8.73%. What is the difference in yields stated in basis points?

7. Bibb Falk recently purchased a bond with a $1,000 face value, a 10% coupon rate, and four years to maturity. The bond makes annual interest payments, the first to be received one year from today. Bibb paid $1,032.40 for the bond.
   a. What is the bond's yield-to-maturity?
   b. If the bond can be called two years from now at a price of $1,100, what is its yield-to-call?

8. Burleigh Grimes purchased at par a bond with a face value of $1,000. The bond had five years to maturity and a 10% coupon rate. The bond was called two years later for a price of $1,200, after making its second annual interest payment. Burleigh then reinvested the proceeds in a bond selling at its face value of $1,000, with three years to maturity and a 7% coupon rate. What was Burleigh's actual yield-to-maturity over the five-year period?

9. Nellie Fox acquired at par a bond for $1,000 that offered a 9% coupon rate. At the time of purchase, the bond had four years to maturity. Assuming annual interest payments, calculate Nellie's actual yield-to-maturity if all the interest payments were reinvested in an investment earning 15% per year. What would Nellie's actual yield-to-maturity be if all interest payments were spent immediately upon receipt?

10. Distinguish between yield-to-first-call and yield-to-maturity.

11. What is the effect of a call provision on a bond's potential for price appreciation?

12. What is the purpose of bond ratings? Given the importance attached to bond ratings by bond investors, why don't common stock investors focus on quality ratings of entire companies in making their investment decisions?

13. According to Lave Cross, "Agency ratings indicate *relative* levels of risk instead of *absolute* levels of risk." Explain the meaning of Lave's statement.

14. Based on the default premium model presented in the text, what is the fair value default premium for a bond with an expected yield-to-maturity of

8.5%, a 10% annual default probability, and an expected loss as a percent of market value of 60%?

15. Corporate default appears to be an event specific to an individual company. Yet despite the apparent diversifiable nature of corporate default (meaning that relatively few bonds would default in a well-diversified portfolio), the bond market systematically adds default premiums when valuing corporate bonds. Explain why.

16. Junk bonds are often viewed by investors as having financial characteristics much more akin to common stocks than to high-grade corporate bonds. Why?

17. Examining Equation (15.6), explain the rationale underlying the observed relationship (positive or negative) between each of the variables and the yield spread.

18. How would you expect yield spreads to respond to the following macroeconomic events: recession, high inflation, tax cuts, stock market decline, improved trade balance? Explain the reasoning behind each of your answers.

19. Urban Shocker has noted that the spread between the yield-to-maturity on BBB-rated bonds and that on AAA-rated bonds has recently widened considerably. Explain to Urban what this change might indicate.

CFA Exam Question

20. [In 1990,] Barney Gray, CFA, is Director of Fixed-Income Securities at Piedmont Security Advisors. In a recent meeting, one of his major endowment clients suggested investing in corporate bonds yielding 9%, rather than U.S. government bonds yielding 8%. Two bond issues—one U.S. Treasury and one corporate—were compared to illustrate the point.

U.S. Treasury bond	8% due 6/15/2010	Priced at 100
AJAX Manufacturing	9.5% due 6/15/2015	Priced at 105
Rated AAA		
Callable @ 107.5 on 6/15/1995		

Gray wants to prepare a response based upon his expectation that long-term U.S. Treasury interest rates will fall sharply (at least 100 basis points) over the next three months.

Evaluate the return expectations for each bond under this scenario, and support an evaluation of which bond would be the superior performer. Discuss the price-yield measures that affect your conclusion.

ENDNOTES

[1] A more accurate method of determining a bond's intrinsic value involves the use of spot rates. That is, in determining the NPV of this bond, the investor might have determined that the relevant spot rates for the one-year, two-year, and three-year cash flows are 8.24%, 8.69%, and 9.03%, respectively. Using these values, the bond's intrinsic value equals $924.06 \{= [\$60/(1.0824)] + [\$60/(1.0869)^2] + [\$1,060/(1.0903)^3]\}$. Although V is the same in this example when either spot rates or y^* are used in the calculations, this need not always be the case.

[2] Many corporate bonds have, in addition to a call provision, a provision for a sinking fund where each year the issuer retires a prespecified portion of the original bond issue.

[3] The investor generally can escape having his or her bonds called if either Treasury securities or discounted corporate bonds are purchased. However, because these securities have less "call risk," they are likely to have lower yields-to-maturity than similar bonds with higher levels of "call risk."

[4] In this example, the **yield-to-call** (or, to be more specific, the yield-to-first-call) is 12.78%. That is, 12.78% is the discount rate that makes the present value of $120 received after each of the first four years and $1,170 (= $1,050 + $120) at the end of five years equal to the issue price of the bond, $1,000. Note how the yield-to-call is greater than the bond's promised yield-to-maturity at the time of issue of 12%.

[5] Any gains from price appreciation realized by an investor in municipal bonds is also taxable as ordinary income. For more on the taxation of fixed-income securities, see Chapter 13 or Clark Blackman II and Donald Laubacher, "The Basics of Amortizing Bond Premiums and Discounts," *AAII Journal,* 15, no. 3 (March 1993): 24–27.

[6] Both rating agencies actually use finer gradations than those shown in the figures. Standard & Poor's sometimes places a + or − next to its letter rating if a bond is in a category ranging from AA to CCC. Similarly, Moody's may place a 1, 2, or 3 next to its letter rating if a bond is in a category ranging from Aa down to B. Both agencies also rate certain types of short-term debt instruments.

[7] For a primer on junk bonds and their analysis, see Stanley Block, "High-Yielding Securities: How Appropriate Are They?" *AAII Journal,* 11, no. 10 (November 1989): 7–11; Glenn E. Atkins and Ben Branch, "A Qualitative Look at High-Yield Bond Analysis," *AAII Journal,* 13, no. 12 (October 1991): 12–15. Also see the articles cited in notes 13 and 14.

[8] *Moody's Bond Record* (New York: Moody's Investors Service, April 1994): p. 3.

[9] *Moody's Bond Record,* p. 3.

[10] The model was developed by Gordon Pye in "Gauging the Default Premium," *Financial Analysts Journal,* 30, no. 1 (January/February 1974): 49–52.

[11] W. Braddock Hickman, *Corporate Bond Quality and Investor Experience* (Princeton, NJ: Princeton University Press, 1958).

[12] Harold G. Fraine and Robert H. Mills, "The Effect of Defaults and Credit Deterioration on Yields of Corporate Bonds," *Journal of Finance,* 16, no. 3 (September 1961): 423–434.

[13] Edward I. Altman, "Defaults and Returns on High-Yield Bonds Through the First Half of 1991," *Financial Analysts Journal,* 47, no. 6 (November/December 1991): 67–77.

[14] See Marshall E. Blume and Donald B. Keim, "Realized Returns and Defaults on Low-Grade Bonds: The Cohort of 1977 and 1978," *Financial Analysts Journal,* 47, no. 2 (March/April 1991): 63–72; Marshall E. Blume, Donald B. Keim, and Sandeep A. Patel, "Returns and Volatility of Low-Grade Bonds, 1977–1989," *Journal of Finance,* 46, no. 1 (March 1991): 49–74; and Marshall E. Blume and Donald B. Keim, "The Risk and Return of Low-Grade Bonds: An Update," *Financial Analysts Journal,* 47, no. 5 (September/October 1991). A similar observation has been made for municipal bonds. See George H. Hempel, *The Postwar Quality of State and Local Debt* (New York: Columbia University Press, 1971).

[15] For an in-depth analysis of such bond portfolios, see Bradford Cornell and Kevin Greene, "The Investment Performance of Low-Grade Bond Funds," *Journal of Finance,* 46, no. 1 (March 1991): 29–48; and Bradford Cornell, "Liquidity and the Pricing of Low-Grade Bonds," *Financial Analysts Journal,* 48, no. 1 (January/February 1992): 63–67, 74.

[16] In a study of preferred stocks, it was found that the price movements of low-rated preferred stocks were related more to the price movements of common stocks than to the price movements of bonds; for high-rated preferred stocks, the findings were just the

opposite. See John S. Bildersee, "Some Aspects of the Performance of Non-Convertible Preferred Stocks," *Journal of Finance,* 28, no. 5 (December 1973): 1187–1201.

[17] Lawrence Fisher, "Determinants of Risk Premiums on Corporate Bonds," *Journal of Political Economy,* 67, no. 3 (June 1959): 217–237.

[18] William H. Beaver, "Market Prices, Financial Ratios and the Prediction of Failure," *Journal of Accounting Research,* 6, no. 2 (Autumn 1968): 179–192.

[19] Edward I. Altman, "Financial Ratios, Discriminant Analysis and the Prediction of Corporate Bankruptcy," *Journal of Finance,* 23, no. 4 (September 1968): 589–609.

[20] Mark I. Weinstein, "The Effect of a Rating Change Announcement on Bond Price," *Journal of Financial Economics,* 5, no. 3 (December 1977): 329–350. Another study that examined rating change announcements that were "noncontaminated by other news releases found a small but statistically significant upward movement in daily bond prices around upgrades; downgrades produced no significant movements." See John R. M. Hand, Robert W. Holthausen, and Richard W. Leftwich, "The Effect of Bond Rating Agency Announcements on Bond and Stock Prices," *Journal of Finance,* 47, no. 2 (June 1992): 733–752.

KEY TERMS

capitalization of income method of valuation	basis points	investment-grade bonds
promised yield-to-maturity	call provision	speculative-grade bonds
net present value	call price	junk bonds
yield structure	call premium	fallen angels
term structure	yield-to-call	expected yield-to-maturity
risk structure	market discount bonds	default premium
yield spread	marketability	risk premium
	bond ratings	

REFERENCES

1. For a detailed discussion of bond valuation and the attributes of bonds that are important in their pricing, see:

   Karlyn Mitchell, "The Call, Sinking Fund, and Term-To-Maturity Features of Corporate Bonds: An Empirical Investigation," *Journal of Financial and Quantitative Analysis,* 26, no. 2 (June 1991): 201–222.

   James C. Van Horne, *Financial Market Rates and Flows* (Englewood Cliffs, NJ: Prentice Hall, 1994).

   Frank J. Fabozzi, *Valuation of Fixed Income Securities* (Summit, NJ: Frank J. Fabozzi Associates, 1994).

2. Some of the many studies that have investigated the relationship between historical measures of a firm's performance and its bond ratings are:

   Thomas F. Pogue and Robert M. Soldofsky, "What's in a Bond Rating?" *Journal of Financial and Quantitative Analysis,* 4, no. 2 (June 1969): 201–228.

R. R. West, "An Alternate Approach to Predicting Corporate Bond Ratings," *Journal of Accounting Research,* 8, no. 1 (Spring 1970): 118–125.

George E. Pinches and Kent A. Mingo, "A Multivariate Analysis of Industrial Bond Ratings," *Journal of Finance,* 30, no. 1 (March 1975): 201–206.

Robert S. Kaplan and Gabriel Urwitz, "Statistical Models of Bond Ratings: A Methodological Inquiry," *Journal of Business,* 52, no. 2 (April 1979): 231–261.

Ahmed Belkaoui, *Industrial Bonds and the Rating Process* (Westport, CT: Quorum Books, 1983).

3. Changes in bond ratings have been studied in:

Steven Katz, "The Price Adjustment Process of Bonds to Rating Reclassifications: A Test of Bond Market Efficiency," *Journal of Finance,* 29, no. 2 (May 1974): 551–559.

Paul Grier and Steven Katz, "The Differential Effects of Bond Rating Changes Among Industrial and Public Utility Bonds by Maturity," *Journal of Business,* 49, no. 2 (April 1976): 226–239.

Mark I. Weinstein, "The Effect of a Rating Change Announcement on Bond Price," *Journal of Financial Economics,* 5, no. 3 (December 1977): 329–350.

Douglas J. Lucas and John G. Lonski, "Changes in Corporate Credit Quality 1970–1990," *Journal of Fixed Income,* 1, no. 4 (March 1992): 7–14.

Edward I. Altman and Duen Li Kao, "Rating Drift in High-Yield Bonds," *Journal of Fixed Income,* 1, no. 4 (March 1992): 15–20.

Edward I. Altman, "The Implications of Bond Ratings Drift," *Financial Analysts Journal,* 48, no. 3 (May/June 1992): 64–75.

John R. M. Hand, Robert W. Holthausen, and Richard W. Leftwich, "The Effect of Bond Rating Agency Announcements on Bond and Stock Prices," *Journal of Finance,* 47, no. 2 (June 1992): 733–752.

4. Municipal bond ratings are discussed in:

John E. Petersen, *The Rating Game* (New York: The Twentieth Century Fund, 1974).

Robert W. Ingram, Leroy D. Brooks, and Ronald M. Copeland, "The Information Content of Municipal Bond Rating Changes: A Note," *Journal of Finance,* 38, no. 3 (June 1983): 997–1003.

George Foster, *Financial Statement Analysis* (Englewood Cliffs, NJ: Prentice Hall, 1986), Chapter 14.

5. Default premiums and risks are discussed in:

W. Braddock Hickman, *Corporate Bond Quality and Investor Experience* (Princeton, NJ: Princeton University Press, 1958).

Harold G. Fraine and Robert H. Mills, "The Effect of Defaults and Credit Deterioration on Yields of Corporate Bonds," *Journal of Finance,* 16, no. 3 (September 1961): 423–434.

Thomas R. Atkinson and Elizabeth T. Simpson, *Trends in Corporate Bond Quality* (New York: Columbia University Press, 1967).

Gordon Pye, "Gauging the Default Premium," *Financial Analysts Journal,* 30, no. 1 (January/February 1974): 49–52.

Ricardo J. Rodriguez, "Default Risk, Yield Spreads, and Time to Maturity," *Journal of Financial and Quantitative Analysis,* 23, no. 1 (March 1988): 111–117.

Edward I. Altman, "Measuring Corporate Bond Mortality and Performance," *Journal of Finance,* 44, no. 4 (September 1989): 909–922.

Paul Asquith, David W. Mullins, Jr., and Eric D. Wolff, "Original Issue High Yield Bonds; Aging Analysis of Defaults, Exchanges, and Calls," *Journal of Finance,* 44, no. 4 (September 1989): 923–952.

Marshall E. Blume and Donald B. Keim, "Realized Returns and Defaults on Low-Grade Bonds: The Cohort of 1977 and 1978," *Financial Analysts Journal,* 47, no. 2 (March/April 1991): 63–72.

Marshall E. Blume, Donald B. Keim, and Sandeep A. Patel, "Returns and Volatility of Low-Grade Bonds, 1977–1989," *Journal of Finance,* 46, no. 1 (March 1991): 49–74.

Bradford Cornell and Kevin Greene, "The Investment Performance of Low-Grade Bond Funds," *Journal of Finance,* 46, no. 1 (March 1991): 29–48.

Jerome S. Fons and Andrew E. Kimball, "Corporate Bond Defaults and Default Rates 1970–1990," *Journal of Fixed Income,* 1, no. 1 (June 1991): 36–47.

Marshall E. Blume and Donald B. Keim, "The Risk and Return of Low-Grade Bonds: An Update," *Financial Analysts Journal,* 47, no. 5 (September/October 1991): 85–89.

Edward I. Altman, "Defaults and Returns on High-Yield Bonds Through the First Half of 1991," *Financial Analysts Journal,* 47, no. 6 (November/December 1991): 67–77.

Bradford Cornell, "Liquidity and the Pricing of Low-Grade Bonds," *Financial Analysts Journal,* 48, no. 1 (January/February 1992): 63–67, 74.

Edward I. Altman, "Revisiting the High-Yield Bond Market," *Financial Management,* 21, no. 2 (Summer 1992): 79–92.

6. The classic study on yield spreads is:

Lawrence Fisher, "Determinants of Risk Premiums on Corporate Bonds," *Journal of Political Economy,* 67, no. 3 (June 1959): 217–237.

7. Yield spreads for municipal bonds are discussed in:

George Foster, *Financial Statement Analysis* (Englewood Cliffs, NJ: Prentice Hall, 1986), pp. 510–511.

8. Predicting bankruptcy has been a subject of much research; see the following papers and their citations:

William H. Beaver, "Financial Ratios as Predictors of Failure," *Empirical Research in Accounting: Selected Studies, 1966,* supplement to *Journal of Accounting Research:* 71–111.

William H. Beaver, "Market Prices, Financial Ratios and the Prediction of Failure," *Journal of Accounting Research,* 6, no. 2 (Autumn 1968): 179–192.

Edward I. Altman, "Financial Ratios, Discriminant Analysis and the Prediction of Corporate Bankruptcy," *Journal of Finance,* 23, no. 4 (September 1968): 589–609.

Edward B. Deakin, "A Discriminant Analysis of Predictors of Business Failure," *Journal of Accounting Research,* 10, no. 1 (Spring 1972): 167–179.

R. Charles Moyer, "Forecasting Financial Failure: A Re-examination," *Financial Management,* 6, no. 1 (Spring 1977): 11–17.

Edward I. Altman, Robert G. Haldeman, and P. Narayanan, "Zeta Analysis: A New Model to Identify Bankruptcy Risk of Corporations," *Journal of Banking and Finance,* 1, no. 1 (June 1977): 29–54.

James A. Ohlson, "Financial Ratios and the Probabilistic Prediction of Bankruptcy," *Journal of Accounting Research,* 18, no. 1 (Spring 1980): 109–131.

Joseph Aharony, Charles P. Jones, and Itzhak Swary, "An Analysis of Risk and Return Characteristics of Corporate Bankruptcy Using Capital Market Data," *Journal of Finance,* 35, no. 4 (September 1980): 1001–1016.

Ismael G. Dambolena and Sarkis J. Khoury, "Ratio Stability and Corporate Failure," *Journal of Finance,* 35, no. 4 (September 1980): 1017–1026.

Edward I. Altman, "The Success of Business Failure Prediction Models: An International Survey," *Journal of Banking and Finance,* 8, no. 2 (June 1984): 171–198.

Cornelius J. Casey and Norman J. Bartczak, "Cash Flow—It's Not the Bottom Line," *Harvard Business Review,* 62, no. 4 (July-August 1984): 61–66.

Cornelius Casey and Norman Bartczak, "Using Operating Cash Flow Data to Predict Financial Distress: Some Extensions," *Journal of Accounting Research,* 23, no. 1 (Spring 1985): 384–401.

James A. Gentry, Paul Newbold, and David T. Whitford, "Classifying Bankrupt Firms with Funds Flow Components," *Journal of Accounting Research,* 23, no. 1 (Spring 1985): 146–160.

James A. Gentry, Paul Newbold, and David T. Whitford, "Predicting Bankruptcy: If Cash Flow's Not the Bottom Line, What Is?" *Financial Analysts Journal,* 41, no. 5 (September/October 1985): 47–56.

Maggie Queen and Richard Roll, "Firm Mortality: Using Market Indicators to Predict Survival," *Financial Analysts Journal,* 43, no. 3 (May/June 1987): 9–26.

Ismael G. Dambolena and Joel M. Shulman, "A Primary Rule for Detecting Bankruptcy: Watch the Cash," *Financial Analysts Journal,* 44, no. 5 (September/October 1988): 74–78.

James M. Gahlon and Robert L. Vigeland, "Early Warning Signs of Bankruptcy Using Cash Flow Analysis," *Journal of Commercial Bank Lending,* 71, no. 4 (December 1988): 4–15.

Abdul Aziz and Gerald H. Lawson, "Cash Flow Reporting and Financial Distress Models: Testing of Hypothesis," *Financial Management,* 18, no. 1 (Spring 1989): 55–63.

CHAPTER 16

Bond Portfolio Management

The methods currently in use for managing bond portfolios can be divided into two general categories—passive and active. Methods in the passive category rest on the basic assumption that bond markets are semistrong-form efficient—that is, current bond prices are viewed as accurately reflecting all publicly available information. Thus bonds are felt to be priced fairly in the marketplace, providing a return that is commensurate with the risk involved. In addition to believing that individual bonds are not mispriced, passive investors also believe that attempting to predict interest rates is, in general, futile. In summary, passive management rests on the belief that attempts at both security selection (that is, identifying mispriced bonds) and market timing (for example, buying long-term bonds when interest rates are predicted to fall and replacing them with short-term bonds when interest rates are predicted to rise) will be unsuccessful in providing the investor with above-average returns.

Active methods of bond portfolio management are based on the assumption that the bond market is not so efficient, thereby giving some investors the opportunity to earn above-average returns. That is, active management is based on the ability of the portfolio manager either to identify mispriced bonds or to "time" the bond market by accurately predicting interest rates.

This chapter will discuss these two general approaches to bond portfolio management. It begins by reviewing some of the findings regarding the efficiency of the bond market.

In assessing the efficiency of the bond market, only a few of the major studies will be mentioned. The impression obtained from reading them is that bond markets appear to be highly, but not perfectly, semistrong-form efficient—that is, bond prices tend to reflect almost all publicly available information. Not surprisingly, this impression is similar to the one that is obtained from studies of the efficiency of stock markets.

16.1.1   Price Behavior of Treasury Bills

An early study of bond market efficiency focused on the price behavior of Treasury bills. In particular, the prices of Treasury bills were analyzed on a weekly basis from October 1946 through December 1964, a total of 796 weeks. The study found that knowledge of how Treasury bill prices changed in the past was of little use in trying to predict how they would change in the future. Consequently, the results from this study are consistent with the notion that the market for Treasury bills is weak-form efficient.[1]

16.1.2   Expert Predictions of Interest Rates

Bond market efficiency has also been studied by examining the accuracy of interest-rate predictions that have been made by experts. These people use a wide range of techniques and a number of different sources of information. As it is reasonable to assume that their information is publicly available, such studies can be viewed as tests of semistrong-form efficiency.

One way these tests have been conducted involves the building of statistical models that are based on what the experts have said in regard to how interest rates should be predicted. Once these models have been constructed, their predictive accuracy can be evaluated. In one study six different models were constructed, and their one-month-ahead predictions were tested over the two-year period of 1973 and 1974. Consistent with the notion of efficient markets, it was found that a simple model of "no change" was more accurate in predicting interest rates than any of the six statistical models.[2]

Another way these tests have been conducted involves comparing a set of explicit predictions with what subsequently occurred. One source of such predictions is the quarterly survey of interest-rate expectations that appears in the *Goldsmith-Nagan Bond and Money Market Newsletter*, published by Goldsmith-Nagan, Inc. Specifically, this survey reports the predictions made by a number (roughly 50) of "money market professionals" regarding three-month-ahead and six-month-ahead levels of ten different interest rates. In one study the predictions made from September 1969 through December 1972 (that is, 14 sets of quarterly predictions) were compared with those of a no-change model—that is, a model that forecasts no change from the current level of interest rates.[3] Interestingly, the professionals seemed to forecast better than the no-change model for short-term interest rates (such as forecasting what the three-month Treasury bill rate will be three months in the future), but did worse than the no-change model for longer-term interest rates (such as forecasting what the intermediate-term Treasury note rate will be three months in the future).

A subsequent study examined the Goldsmith-Nagan predictions of three-month Treasury bill rates six months in the future during the time period from March 1970 through September 1979 (39 predictions).[4] These predictions were compared with those of three "simple" models, the first one being the no-change model. The second model was based on the liquidity preference theory of the term structure of interest rates (discussed in Chapter 5). According to this theory, the forward rate implicit in current market rates should be equal to the expected future interest rate plus a liquidity premium. Thus a forecast of the expected future rate can be obtained by subtracting an estimate of the liquidity premium from the forward rate. The third model was what statisticians refer to as an autoregressive model. Basically, a forecast of the future Treasury bill rate was formed from the current Treasury bill rate as well as what the Treasury bill rate was one, two, three, and six quarters ago. The study found that the professionals were more accurate than both the no-change model and the liquidity premium model, but less accurate than the autoregressive model.

Another study evaluated the six-month-ahead predictions of three-month Treasury bill rates that were made by nine economists and reported semi-annually in *The Wall Street Journal*. Evaluating the forecasts published from December 1981 through June 1986, it was found that the no-change model was more accurate.[5]

In summary, it appears from this evidence that the no-change model sometimes provides the most accurate forecasts of future interest rates, whereas at other times the experts are more accurate. On balance, a reasonable interpretation of these results is that the bond market is nearly semistrong-form efficient. Although the bond market may not be perfectly efficient, the evidence clearly suggests that it is hard to forecast interest rates consistently with greater accuracy than a no-change model.[6]

16.1.3 Price Reaction to Bond Rating Changes

A different test of market efficiency concerned the reaction of bond prices to rating changes. If ratings are based on public information, then any rating change would follow the release of such information. This suggests that in a semistrong-form efficient market, a bond's price would react to the release of the public information rather than the subsequent announcement of the rating change. Thus an announcement of a rating change should not trigger a subsequent adjustment in the associated bond's price.

In a study that examined 100 rating changes that took place during the period of 1962 through 1974, no significant changes in bond prices were detected in the period from six months before through six months after the announcement of the change. However, a significant change was observed in the period from 18 months through 7 months before the announcement. Specifically, rating increases were preceded by price increases, and rating decreases were preceded by price decreases.[7]

16.1.4 Money Supply Announcements

Every week, generally on Thursday, the Federal Reserve Board announces the current size of the money supply in the economy. It is known that interest rates are related to, among other things, the availability of credit and that the money supply affects this availability. This means that if the money supply figures are surprisingly high or low, then the announcement should trigger adjustments in the levels of various interest rates.[8] Furthermore, such adjustments should take place rapidly in a semistrong-form efficient market. Past studies indicate that such adjustments are indeed rapid, generally taking place within a day after the announcement.[9]

16.1.5 Summary

In summary, the evidence on the efficiency of the bond market is consistent with the notion that it is highly, but not perfectly, semistrong-form efficient.[10] Statistical tests of past prices of Treasury bills suggest that it is efficient. It appears that corporate bonds reflect the information leading to a rating change in a timely fashion and that interest rates change rapidly when there is a surprise in the announced size of the money supply, observations that are also consistent with the notion of efficiency.

However, there is some evidence that suggests that certain professionals are occasionally able to forecast interest rates in an accurate manner. With this in mind, it is not surprising that while some bond managers have opted to follow a passive approach to investing, others have decided to be more active in their approach. These two approaches will be presented next, beginning with a discussion of some bond pricing theorems. In turn, these theorems will be related to a concept known as duration, which is the basis for one method of passively managing a bond portfolio.

16.2	BOND PRICING THEOREMS

Bond pricing theorems deal with how bond prices move in response to changes in the bonds' yields-to-maturity. Before presenting the theorems, a brief review of some terms associated with bonds will be given.

The typical bond is characterized by a promise to pay the investor two types of cash flows. The first involves the payment of a fixed dollar amount periodically (usually every six months), with the last payment being on a stated date. The second type of cash flow involves the payment of a lump sum on this stated date. The periodic payments are known as **coupon payments,** and the lump-sum payment is known as the bond's principal (or par value or face value). A bond's **coupon rate** is calculated by taking the dollar amount of the coupon payments a bondholder would receive over the course of a year, and dividing this total by the par value of the bond. Finally, the amount of time left until the last promised payment is made is known as the bond's **term-to-maturity,** while the discount rate that makes the present value of all the cash flows equal to the market price of the bond is known as the bond's **yield-to-maturity** (or, simply, yield).

Note that if a bond has a market price that is equal to its par value, then its yield-to-maturity will be equal to its coupon rate. However, if the market price is less than par value (a situation where the bond is said to be selling at a discount), then the bond will have a yield-to-maturity that is greater than the coupon rate. Conversely, if the market price is greater than par value (a situation where the bond is said to be selling at a premium), then the bond will have a yield-to-maturity that is less than the coupon rate.

With this in mind, five theorems that deal with bond pricing have been derived.[11] For ease of exposition, it is assumed that there is one coupon payment per year (that is, coupon payments are made every 12 months). The theorems are as follows:

1. If a bond's market price increases, then its yield must decrease; conversely, if a bond's market price decreases, then its yield must increase.

    As an example, consider bond *A*, which has a life of five years, a par value of $1,000, and pays coupons annually of $80. Its yield is 8% because it is currently selling for $1,000. However, if its price increases to $1,100, then its yield will fall to 5.76%. Conversely, if its price falls to $900, then its yield will rise to 10.68%.

2. If a bond's yield does not change over its life, then the size of its discount or premium will decrease as its life gets shorter.

    This can be seen by examining Figure 16.1. Note how the price of a bond that is selling at either a premium or a discount today will converge over time to its par value. Ultimately the premium or discount will completely disappear at the maturity date.

    As an example, consider bond *B*, which has a life of five years, has a par value of $1,000, and pays coupons annually of $60. Its current market price is $883.31, indicating that it has a yield of 9%. After one year, if it still has a yield of 9%, it will be selling for $902.81. Thus its discount has decreased from $116.69 (= $1,000 − $883.31) to $97.19 (= $1,000 − $902.81), for a change of $19.50 (= $116.69 − $97.19).

    An equivalent interpretation of this theorem is that if two bonds have the same coupon rate, par value, and yield, then the one with the shorter life will sell for a smaller discount or premium. Consider two bonds, one with a life of five years and the other with a life of four years. Both bonds have a par value of $1,000, pay annual coupons of $60, and yield 9%. In this situation, the one with a five-year life has a discount of $116.69, whereas the one with a four-year life has a smaller discount of $97.19.

3. If a bond's yield does not change over its life, then the size of its discount or premium will decrease at an increasing rate as its life gets shorter.

    Figure 16.1 can also be used to illustrate this theorem. Note how the size of the premium or discount does not change much at first when time passes from today to tomorrow. In contrast, note how the size changes much more notably when time passes just before the maturity date.

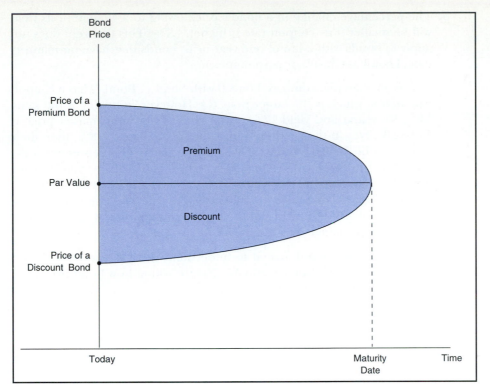

FIGURE 16.1
Changes in a Bond's Price over Its Life*
*Assuming that the bond's yield-to-maturity remains constant through time.

As an example, consider bond *B* again. After two years, if it still has a yield of 9%, it will be selling for $924.06. Thus its discount has decreased to $75.94 (= $1,000 − $924.06). Now the amount of the change in the discount from five years to four years was $19.50 ($116.90 − $97.19) for a percentage change from par of 1.950%. However, the amount of the change from four years to three years is larger, going from $97.19 to $75.94 for a dollar change of $21.25 and a percentage change from par of 2.125%.

4. A decrease in a bond's yield will raise the bond's price by an amount that is greater in size than the corresponding fall in the bond's price that would occur if there were an equal-sized increase in the bond's yield.

As an example, consider bond *C*, which has a life of five years and a coupon rate of 7%. Because it is currently selling at its par value of $1,000, its yield is 7%. If its yield rises by 1% to 8%, then it will be selling for $960.07, a change of $39.93. Alternatively, if its yield falls by 1% to 6%, then it will be selling for $1,042.12, a change of $42.12, which is of greater magnitude than the $39.93 associated with the 1% rise in the bond's yield.

5. The percentage change in a bond's price owing to a change in its yield will be smaller if its coupon rate is higher. (*Note:* This theorem does not apply to bonds with a life of one year or to bonds that have no maturity date, known as consols or perpetuities.)

As an example, compare bond *D* with bond *C*. Bond *D* has a coupon rate of 9%, which is 2% larger than *C*'s. However, bond *D* has the same life (five years) and yield (7%) as *C*. Thus *D*'s current market price is $1,082.00. Now if the yield on both *C* and *D* increases to 8%, then their prices will be $960.07 and $1,039.93, respectively. This represents a decrease in the price of *C* equal to $39.93 (= $1,000 − $960.07), or 3.993%. (*Note:* 3.993% = $39.93/$1,000.) For *D*, the decrease in price is equal to $42.07 (= $1,082 − $1,039.93), or 3.889%. (*Note:* 3.889% = $42.07/$1,082.) Because *D* had the higher coupon rate, it has the smaller percentage change in price.

It is important for a bond analyst to understand these properties of bond prices thoroughly because they are valuable in forecasting how bond prices will respond to changes in interest rates.

16.3   CONVEXITY

The first and fourth bond pricing theorems have led to the concept in bond valuation known as **convexity.** Consider what happens to the price of a bond if its yield increases or decreases. According to Theorem 1, bond prices and yields are inversely related. However, this relationship is not linear, according to Theorem 4. The size of the rise in a bond's price associated with a given decrease in its yield is greater than the drop in the bond's price for a similar-sized increase in the bond's yield.

This can be seen by examining Figure 16.2. The current yield-to-maturity and the price for the bond are denoted by P and y, respectively. Consider what would happen to the bond's price if the yield increased or decreased by a fixed amount (for example, 1%), denoted y^+ and y^-. The associated bond prices are denoted by P^- and P^+, respectively.

Two observations can be made by examining this figure. First, an increase in the yield to y^+ is associated with a drop in the bond's price to P^-, and a decrease in the yield to y^- is associated with a rise in the bond's price to P^+. This is in accord with the first bond theorem. (Hence the symbols $+$ and $-$ are paired inversely so that, for example, y^+ is associated with P^-.) Second, note that the size of the rise in the bond's price $(P^+ - P)$ is greater than the size of the drop in the bond's price $(P - P^-)$. This is in accord with the fourth bond theorem.

The curved line in the figure that shows the relationship between bond prices and yields is convex because it opens upward. Accordingly, the relationship is frequently referred to as convexity. Although this relationship is true for standard types of bonds, it should be mentioned that the degree of curvature (or convexity) is not the same for all bonds. Instead, it depends on, among other things, the size of the coupon payments, the life of the bond, and its current market price.

FIGURE 16.2
Bond Convexity

<hr>

16.4   DURATION

Duration is a measure of the "average maturity" of the stream of payments associated with a bond. More specifically, it is a weighted average of the lengths of time until the remaining payments are made. Consider, for example, a bond with annual coupon payments of $80, a remaining life of three years, and a par value of $1,000. Because it has a current market price of $950.25, it has a yield-to-maturity of 10.00%. As shown in Table 16.1, its duration is 2.78 years. Note that this is calculated by taking the present value of each cash flow, multiplying each one by the respective amount of time until it is received, summing the resulting figures, and then dividing this sum ($2,639.17) by the market price of the bond ($950.25).

16.4.1 The Formula

Specifically, the formula for a bond's duration D is

$$D = \frac{\sum_{t=1}^{T} PV(C_t) \times t}{P_0} \tag{16.1}$$

<hr>

TABLE 16.1

CALCULATION OF DURATION

Time Until Receipt of Cash Flow	Amount of Cash Flow	Present Value Factor	Present Value of Cash Flow	Present Value of Cash Flow × Time
1	$ 80	.9091	$ 72.73	$ 72.73
2	80	.8264	66.12	132.23
3	1,080	.7513	811.40	2,434.21
			$950.25	$2,639.17

$$\text{Duration} = \frac{\$2,639.17}{\$950.25} = 2.78 \text{ years}$$

where $PV(C_t)$ denotes the present value of the cash flow to be received at time t, calculated using a discount rate equal to the bond's yield-to-maturity; P_0 denotes the current market price of the bond; and T denotes the bond's remaining life.[12]

Why is duration thought of as the "average maturity of the stream of payments associated with a bond"? This can be seen by realizing that the current market price of the bond, P_0, is equal to the sum of the present values of the cash flows, $PV(C_t)$, where the discount rate is the bond's yield-to-maturity,

$$P_0 = \sum_{t=1}^{T} PV(C_t). \tag{16.2}$$

Thus there is an equivalent method for calculating a bond's duration that can be seen by rewriting Equation (16.1) in a slightly different manner,

$$D = \sum_{t=1}^{T} \left[\frac{PV(C_t)}{P_0} \times t \right]. \tag{16.3}$$

First, the present value of each cash flow, $PV(C_t)$, is expressed as a proportion of the market price P_0. Second, these proportions are multiplied by the respective amount of time until the cash flows are received. Third, these figures are summed, with the sum being equal to the bond's duration.

In the example shown in Table 16.1, note that .07653 ($= \$72.73/\$950.25$) of the bond's market price is to be received in one year. Similarly, .06958 ($= \$66.12/\$950.25$) is to be received in two years, and .85388 ($= \$811.40/\$950.25$) is to be received in three years. Note how these proportions sum to 1, which means that they can be interpreted as weights in calculating a weighted average. Thus to calculate the average maturity of the payments associated with a bond, each weight needs to be multiplied by the respective amount of time until the corresponding cash flow is to be received, and then the products need to be summed: $(1 \times .07653) + (2 \times .06958) + (3 \times .85388) = 2.78$ years.

Note how a zero coupon bond will have a duration equal to its remaining life T because there is only one cash flow associated with such a bond—that is, because $P_0 = PV(C_T)$ for such bonds, Equation (16.3) reduces to

$$D = \frac{\text{PV}(C_T)}{P_0} \times T$$
$$= 1 \times T$$
$$= T.$$

For any coupon-bearing bond its duration will always be less than the amount of time to its maturity date T. Again, examination of Equation (16.3) indicates why this is so. Because the largest value that t can have is T, and each value of t is multiplied by a weight equal to $\text{PV}(C_t)/P_0$, it follows that D must be less than T.

16.4.2 Relationship to Bond Price Changes

One implication of Theorem 5 is that bonds having the same maturity date but different coupon sizes may react differently to a given change in interest rates. That is, the prices of these bonds may adjust by notably different amounts when there is a given change in interest rates. However, bonds with the same duration will react quite similarly. Specifically, the percentage change in a bond's price is related to its duration in the following fashion:

$$\text{Percentage change in price} \cong -D \times \text{percentage change in (1+ the bond's yield)} \qquad (16.4a)$$

where the symbol $\cong$ means "is approximately equal to." This formula implies that when the yields of two bonds having the same duration change by the same percentage, then the prices of the two bonds will change by approximately equal percentages. Equivalently, Equation (16.4a) is written as

$$\frac{\Delta P}{P} \cong -D\left(\frac{\Delta y}{1 + y}\right) \qquad (16.4b)$$

where ΔP denotes the change in the bond's price, P is the bond's initial price, Δy is the change in the bond's yield-to-maturity, and y is the bond's initial yield-to-maturity.

As an example, consider a bond that is currently selling for \$1,000 with a yield-to-maturity of 8%. Given that the bond has a duration of ten years, by how much will the bond's price change if its yield increases to 9%? Using Equation (16.4b), it can be seen that $\Delta y = 9\% - 8\% = 1\% = .01$, so that $\Delta y/(1 + y) = .01/1.08 = .00926 = .926\%$ and $-D[\Delta y/(1 + y)] = -10[.926\%] = -9.26\%$. Hence the one-percentage-point rise in the yield will cause approximately a 9.26% drop in the bond's price to \$926 [= \$1,000 - (.0926 \times \$1,000)].

16.4.3 Relationship between Convexity and Duration

At this point it is useful to consider just what kind of relationship the concepts of convexity and duration have to each other. After all, both have something to do with measuring the association of the change in a bond's price with a change in the bond's yield-to-maturity. Figure 16.3 shows the nature of the relationship.

Like Figure 16.2, this figure represents a bond that is currently selling for P and has a yield-to-maturity of y. Note the straight line that is tangent to the curve at the point associated with the current price and yield.

If the bond's yield increases to y^+, then the associated price of the bond will fall to P^-. Conversely, if the bond's yield decreases to y^-, then the associated price of the bond will rise to P^+. However, by using Equation (16.4b), the estimated prices will be P_D^- and P_D^+, respectively. This is because the equation, as mentioned earlier, is not exact. Instead, it is an approximation that states that the percentage change in the bond's price is a linear function of its duration. Hence the equation approximates the new price in a linear fashion represented by the straight line and leading to an error that is a consequence of convexity. [In the example, the sizes of the respective errors are $(P^- - P_D^-)$ and $(P^+ - P_D^+)$.] That is, because the relationship between yield changes and bond price changes is convex, not linear, the use of Equation (16.4b) will underestimate the new price associated with either an increase or a decrease in the bond's yield.[13] However, for small changes in yields the error is relatively small, and thus, as an approximation, Equation (16.4b) works reasonably well. This can be seen by observing in Figure 16.3 that the size of the pricing error becomes smaller as the size of the yield change gets smaller. (Note that the distance between the linear approximating line and the convex curve will be smaller for smaller changes in yields from y.)

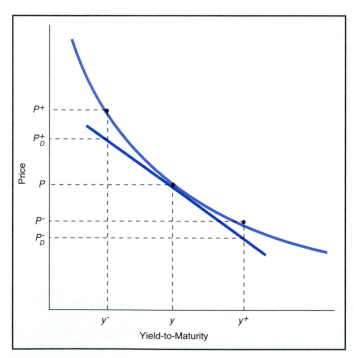

FIGURE 16.3
Bond Convexity and Duration

16.4.4 Changes in the Term Structure

As mentioned earlier, when yields change, most bond prices also change, but some react more than others. Even bonds with the same maturity date can react quite differently to a given change in yields. However, it was shown in Equations (16.4a) and (16.4b) that the percentage change in a bond's price is related to its duration. Hence the prices of two bonds that have the same duration will react similarly to a given change in yields.

For example, the bond shown in Table 16.1 has a duration of 2.78 and a yield of 10%. If its yield changes to 11%, then the percentage change in (1 + the bond's yield) is .91% [= (1.11 − 1.10)/1.10]. Thus its price should change by approximately −2.53% (= −2.78 × .91%). Using a discount rate of 11%, its price can be calculated to equal $926.69, for an actual price change of −$23.56 (= $926.69 − $950.25) and a percentage change of −2.48% (= −$23.56/$950.25). Any other bond having a duration of 2.78 years will experience a similar price change if it has a similar percentage change in its yield.

Consider a bond with a maturity of four years that also has a duration of 2.78 years. When there is a shift in interest rates, and the yields on the three-year and four-year bonds change by the same amount, then their prices will change similarly. For example, if the yield on the four-year bond goes from 10.8% to 11.81% at the same time the yield on the three-year bond is going from 10% to 11%, then the percentage change in the present value of the four-year bond will be approximately −2.53% {= −2.78 × [(1.1181 − 1.108)/1.108] = 2.78 × .91%}, which is the same percentage as the three-year bond.

What if the "percentage change in (1 + the bond's yield)" is different? That is, what happens if the term structure shifts in a manner so that "the percentage change in (1 + the bond's yield)" is not the same for all bonds? Perhaps when the three-year bond goes from a yield of 10% to a yield of 11% [a percentage change of .91% = (1.11 − 1.10)/1.10], the four-year bond will go from a yield of 10.8% to a yield of 11.5% [a percentage change of .63% = (1.115 − 1.108)/1.108]. In this case the percentage change in price for the four-year bond will be approximately −1.75% {= −2.78 × [(1.115 − 1.108)/1.108]}, which is a smaller change than the −2.53% associated with the three-year bond. Accordingly, even though the two bonds have the same duration, it does not automatically follow that their prices will react identically to *any* change in yields, as these yield changes can be different for two bonds having the same duration.

16.5 IMMUNIZATION

The introduction of the concept of duration led to the development of the technique of bond portfolio management known as **immunization.** Specifically, this technique allegedly allows a bond portfolio manager to be relatively certain of being able to meet a given promised stream of cash outflows. Thus once the portfolio has been formed, it is "immunized" from any adverse effects associated with future changes in interest rates.

16.5.1 How Immunization Is Accomplished

Immunization is accomplished simply by calculating the duration of the promised outflows and then investing in a portfolio of bonds that has an identical duration. In doing so, this technique takes advantage of the observation that *the duration of a portfolio of bonds is equal to the weighted average of the durations of the individual bonds in the portfolio.* For example, if a portfolio has one-third of its funds invested in bonds having a duration of six years and two-thirds in bonds having a duration of three years, then the portfolio itself has a duration of four years $[= (\frac{1}{3} \times 6) + (\frac{2}{3} \times 3)]$.

Consider a simple situation where a portfolio manager has one and only one cash outflow to make from his or her portfolio—an amount equal to $1,000,000, which is to be paid in two years. Because there is only one cash outflow, its duration is simply two years. Now the bond portfolio manager is considering investing in two different bond issues. The first bond issue is the one shown in Table 16.1, where the bonds have a maturity of three years. The second bond issue involves a set of bonds that mature in one year, providing the holder of each bond with a single payment of $1,070 (consisting of a single coupon payment of $70 and a par value of $1,000). As these bonds are currently selling for $972.73, their yield-to-maturity is 10%.

Consider the choices open to the portfolio manager. All of the portfolio's funds could be invested in the one-year bonds, with the notion of reinvesting the proceeds from the maturing bonds one year from now in another one-year issue. However, doing so would entail risks. In particular, if interest rates were to decline over the next year, then the funds from the maturing one-year bonds would have to be reinvested at a lower rate than the currently available 10%. Thus the portfolio manager faces reinvestment-rate risk owing to the possibility that the funds one year from now could be reinvested only at a lower rate.[14]

A second alternative would be for the portfolio manager to invest all of the funds in the three-year issue. However, this also entails risks. In particular, the three-year bonds will have to be sold after two years in order to come up with the $1,000,000. The risk is that interest rates will have risen before then, meaning that bond prices, in general, will have fallen and the bonds will not have a selling price that is at least $1,000,000. Thus the portfolio manager faces interest-rate risk with this strategy.

One proposed solution is to invest part of the portfolio's funds in the one-year bonds and the rest in the three-year bonds. How much should be placed in each issue? If immunization is to be used, the solution can be found by solving simultaneously a set of two equations involving two unknowns,

$$W_1 + W_3 = 1 \qquad (16.5)$$

$$(W_1 \times 1) + (W_3 \times 2.78) = 2. \qquad (16.6)$$

Here W_1 and W_3 denote the weights (or proportions) of the portfolio's funds that are to be invested in the bonds with maturities of one and three years, respectively. Note how Equation (16.5) states that the sum of the weights must equal 1, whereas Equation (16.6) states that the weighted average of the durations of the bonds in the portfolio must equal the duration of the cash outflow, which is two years.

The solution to these two equations is easily found. First, Equation (16.5) is rewritten as:

$$W_1 = 1 - W_3. \tag{16.7}$$

Then $1 - W_3$ is substituted for W_1 in Equation (16.6), resulting in

$$[(1 - W_3) \times 1] + (W_3 \times 2.78) = 2. \tag{16.8}$$

As this is one equation with one unknown, W_3, it can be solved easily. Doing so results in $W_3 = .5618$. Inserting this value into Equation (16.7) indicates that $W_1 = .4382$. Thus the portfolio manager should put 43.82% of the portfolio's funds in the one-year bonds and 56.18% in the three-year bonds.

In this case, the portfolio manager would need $826,446 [= $1,000,000/ $(1.10)^2$] in order to purchase bonds that would create a fully immunized portfolio. With this money, $362,149 (= .4382 × $826,446) would be used to buy one-year bonds and $464,297 (= .5618 × $826,446) would be used to buy three-year bonds. Because the current market prices of the one-year and three-year bonds are $972.73 and $950.25, respectively, this means that 372 one-year bonds (= $362,149/$972.73) and 489 three-year bonds (= $464,297/$950.25) would be purchased.

What does immunization accomplish? According to theory, if yields rise, then the portfolio's losses owing to the selling of the three-year bonds at a discount after two years will be exactly offset by the gains from reinvesting the maturing one-year bonds (and first-year coupons on the three-year bonds) at the higher rate. Alternatively, if yields fall, then the loss from being able to reinvest the maturing one-year bonds (and first-year coupons on the three-year bonds) at a lower rate will be exactly offset by being able to sell the three-year bonds after two years at a premium. Thus the portfolio is *immunized* from the effect of any movements in interest rates in the future.

Table 16.2 shows more explicitly what would happen to the portfolio. The second column shows what the portfolio would be worth at the end of two years if yields remained at 10% over the next two years. As can be seen, the value of the portfolio of one-year and three-year bonds would be approximately equal to the promised cash outflow of $1,000,000. Alternatively, if yields fell to 9% or rose to 11% before one year had passed and remained at the new level, then the value of the portfolio would be slightly more than the needed $1,000,000.[15]

16.5.2 Problems with Immunization

The previous paragraph described what immunization accomplishes in theory. This leaves open the possibility that it might not work quite as well in practice. What can cause it to work less than perfectly? Underlying this issue is this question: Why might duration fail to measure the interest-rate risk of a bond accurately? In terms of the example, what can cause the value of the portfolio to be less than $1,000,000 at the end of two years?

TABLE 16.2

EXAMPLE OF AN IMMUNIZED PORTFOLIO

	Yield-to-Maturity At the End of One Year		
	9%	10%	11%
Value at t = 2 from reinvesting one-year bond proceeds:			
[$1,070 × 372.3 × (1 + y)] =	$ 434,213	$438,197	$ 442,181
Value at t = 2 of three-year bonds:			
Value from reinvesting coupons received at t = 1:			
[$80 × 488.6 × (1 + y)] =	42,606	42,997	43,388
Coupons received at t = 2:			
[$80 × 488.6] =	39,088	39,088	39,088
Selling price at t = 2:			
[$1,080 × 488.6/(1 + y)] =	484,117	479.716	475,395
Aggregate portfolio value at t = 2:	$1,000,024	$999,998	$1,000,052

Default and Call Risk

To begin with, immunization (and duration) are based on the belief that all of the bonds' promised cash flows will subsequently be paid in full and on time. This means that immunization is based on the assumption that the bonds will not default and will not be called before maturity—that is, the bonds are assumed to be free from both call risk and default risk. Consequently, if a bond in the portfolio either enters into default or is called, the portfolio will not be immunized.

Multiple Nonparallel Shifts in a Nonhorizontal Yield Curve

Immunization (and duration) are also based on the assumption that the yield curve is horizontal and that any shifts in it will be parallel and will occur before any payments are received from the bonds that were purchased. In the example, both the one-year and the three-year bonds had the same 10% yield-to-maturity at the start, and the shift of 1% in yields was assumed to be the same for both bond issues. Furthermore, this shift was assumed to occur sometime before one year had passed.

In reality, the yield curve will not be horizontal at the start, and shifts in it are not likely to be either parallel or restricted in when they occur. Perhaps the one-year and the three-year bonds will have initial yields of 10% and 10.5%, respectively, with the yields on the one-year and three-year bonds falling by 1% and .8%, respectively, after one year. Indeed, there is evidence of greater volatility in yields of shorter term securities. If these kinds of shifts occur, then it is possible that the portfolio will not be immunized.[16]

If the bond portfolio manager followed a special kind of immunization known as **cash matching,** then frequent nonparallel shifts in a nonhorizontal yield curve would have no adverse effect on the portfolio. This is because cash matching involves the purchase of bonds so that the cash received each period from the bonds is identical in size to the promised cash outflow for that period.

Surplus Management

Corporate pension funds are established to secure the funding of retirement benefits promised to corporate employees. Therefore the primary investment objective of these funds is to accumulate sufficient assets, through contributions and investment income, to satisfy all pension obligations on a timely basis.

The management of corporate pension funds has traditionally focused solely on the asset side of the asset-liability equation. Those organizations charged with the oversight of pension funds (often referred to as "plan sponsors") have typically defined their investment policies in terms of seeking maximum returns subject to their tolerance for volatility of returns (see Chapter 24). This philosophy has led many plan sponsors to invest heavily in equity assets, particularly common stocks, based on their perceived superior long-run risk-return characteristics (see Chapter 1).

The foundation of this investment philosophy received a jolt in 1986 when the Financial Accounting Standards Board issued FAS 87, a directive requiring corporations to more fully disclose pension obligations on their financial statements beginning in 1989. Prior to FAS 87, corporate reporting on pension obligations was consigned to annual report footnotes. This level of disclosure seemed inadequate, given that pension assets and liabilities would represent the largest items on many corporations' balance sheets if they were reported there, and that annual pension expenses often represent a large portion of a corporation's earnings. FAS 87 was designed to address this deficiency.

FAS 87 requires that companies report any negative difference between their pension assets and their pension liabilities on their balance sheets as liabilities. (There is no corresponding balance sheet asset if pension assets exceed pension liabilities.) Moreover, the way in which companies state pension expenses on their income statements was redefined. The expense includes costs associated with pension benefits earned in the current year, plus interest on past obligations, plus the amortization of any unfunded liabilities (that is, liabilities not offset by pension assets), less the expected earnings on the pension fund's assets.

As a result of FAS 87, a corporation's earnings have become sensitive to changes in its pension fund's surplus, which is the difference in value between the fund's assets and liabilities. A significant decrease in pension surplus will result in an earnings reduction, whereas a significant increase can boost earnings. Thus FAS 87 created for the first time a source of reported earnings variability directly attributable to changes in a pension fund's assets and liabilities.

This new source of earnings variability has caused some companies to emphasize control of pension surplus volatility through a process known as *surplus management*. How does a plan sponsor manage pension surplus? By developing an investment strategy that causes the value of the pension fund's assets to move more closely with the pension fund's liabilities. That is, the plan sponsor wishes to "immunize" the pension fund's liabilities by creating an appropriately structured portfolio of assets. In this way the variability of changes in pension surplus will be reduced, thereby lowering the pension fund's impact on the variability of the corporation's earnings.

In order to specify the appropriate composition of the pension fund's portfolio that will immunize the fund's pension liabilities, the plan sponsor must determine what factors can cause the value of these liabilities to change. In the short run, when promised pension benefits can be viewed as fixed, only movements in interest rates will alter the value of pension liabilities. FAS 87 mandates that the value of pension liabilities be calculated as the discounted value of pension benefits earned to date by the company's employees (plus, in some cases, projected salary increases for current employees). The discount rate applied to these earned pension benefits is related to current market interest rates. Therefore as those interest rates fluctuate so too does the value of a company's pension liabilities. Interest-rate increases reduce the value of pension liabilities, whereas interest-rate declines increase pension liabilities.

As described in the text, a simple means of at least partially immunizing a set of interest-sensitive liabilities is to create a portfolio of bonds whose duration equals that of the liabilities. As interest rates change, the value of the assets will rise and fall more or less in line with the value of the liabilities, maintaining a relatively constant pension surplus.

FAS 87 has given rise to numerous sophisticated strategies designed to reduce pension surplus volatility. To implement these strategies, some plan sponsors have significantly reduced their pension funds' allocations to equity assets and purchased fixed-income securities.

Such shifts in asset allocation have led critics of surplus management to argue that by maintaining large fixed-income investments, pension plans are sacrificing the superior returns available from equity assets. These critics contend that surplus management is shortsighted. If one views pension liabilities on a longer term basis, they are not fixed. Rather, they grow with inflation and worker productivity (which translate into pay raises and higher benefits). Thus, in the long run, equity assets may be more effective in hedging against these changes in pension liabilities than fixed-income investments.

Such a cash-matched portfolio of bonds is often referred to as a **dedicated portfolio.** Note that there is no need to reinvest any cash inflows with a dedicated portfolio, so there is no reinvestment-rate risk. Furthermore, because bonds do not have to be sold prior to maturity, there is no interest-rate risk either.

In the simplest situation where there is one promised cash outflow, the dedicated portfolio would consist of zero coupon bonds where each bond has a life corresponding to the date of the promised cash outflow. In the previous example, where there was a promised cash outflow of $1,000,000 after two years, this would be accomplished by purchasing the requisite number of zero coupon bonds having a maturity of two years.

However, cash matching is often not so easily accomplished. This is because the promised cash outflows may involve an uneven stream of payments for which no zero coupon bonds exist. Indeed, it can be difficult (if not impossible) and expensive to exactly match cash inflows with promised outflows.

Another potential way around the problem of nonhorizontal yield curves that experience nonparallel shifts is to use one of a variety of more complicated immunization models. These models involve various other assumptions about the current shape of the yield curve and how it will shift in the future. Consequently, the bond portfolio manager must choose the one that he or she personally views as being most accurate. Interestingly, various studies have found that the best performer was the version of immunization that has been described in this chapter, and not the more complicated models. Thus some researchers argue that the portfolio manager interested in immunization would be well advised to use this version.[17]

An implication is that regardless of the model being used, the bond portfolio manager must recognize that there is a risk being incurred—the risk that the yield curve will shift in a way that does not correspond with the way assumed by the model. For example, if the model presented here is used, then the bond portfolio is facing risk in that the yield curve will not shift in a parallel manner. Consequently, some people have argued that none of the immunization models are useful.[18] Others have argued that there are ways to use immunization in the presence of such risk, which has been called **stochastic process risk.**[19]

Rebalancing

Another problem with the use of immunization is the effect of the passage of time on the duration of the bonds held and on the duration of the promised cash outflows. As time passes and yields change, these durations can change at different rates so that the portfolio is no longer immunized. This means that the portfolio may need to be rebalanced fairly often.

Here rebalancing refers to selling some bonds currently held and replacing them with others so that afterward the duration of the portfolio matches the duration of the promised cash outflows. However, because rebalancing causes the portfolio manager to incur transaction costs, the manager might not want to rebalance whenever the durations do not match, as the costs might outweigh the perceived gains from rebalancing. Ultimately, the bond portfolio manager will have to decide how frequently to rebalance the portfolio, taking into consideration the risk of being unbalanced along with the transaction costs associated with rebalancing.

Many Candidates

Finally, there are usually many portfolios that have a duration of the requisite length. Which one is the bond portfolio manager to choose? In the example, imagine that in addition to the one-year and three-year bonds, there is a zero coupon bond having a life of four years (thus its duration is also four years) that the manager is considering. Now the manager faces a choice of which portfolio to hold, as there are many that have the requisite duration of two years. In addition to the one previously described that consisted of just one-year and three-year bonds, there is also one where two-thirds and one-third of the portfolio's funds are invested in one-year bonds and four-year bonds, respectively. [Note how the duration of this portfolio is also two years: $(\frac{2}{3} \times 1) + (\frac{1}{3} \times 4) = 2$.] Furthermore, there are many other candidate portfolios.

One possible solution is to choose the portfolio having the highest average yield-to-maturity (or, alternatively, the lowest cost). Here the yield of each issue is multiplied by the percentage of the portfolio's funds invested in that issue. Another possible solution is to choose the portfolio that most closely resembles a "bullet" or "focused" portfolio, because it has been argued that such a portfolio has less stochastic process risk than any other. Such a portfolio is one where the bonds in it have durations (or, alternatively, terms-to-maturity) most closely matching the duration of the promised outflows. In the example the portfolio consisting of just one-year and three-year bonds would be more "focused" than the one consisting of the one-year and four-year bonds.

16.6 ACTIVE MANAGEMENT

As mentioned earlier, active management of a bond portfolio is based on the belief that the bond market is not perfectly efficient. Such management can involve security selection, where attempts are made at identifying mispriced bonds. Alternatively, it can involve market timing, where attempts are made at forecasting general movements in interest rates. It is also possible for an active portfolio manager to be involved in both security selection and market timing. Although there are a large number of methods of actively managing a bond portfolio, some general types of active management can be described.

16.6.1 Horizon Analysis

The return on a bond over any given holding period, sometimes referred to as the bond's realized return, depends on its price at the beginning of the period and its price at the end of the period, as well as on its coupon rate. Thus the return on a bond over a one-year holding period will depend on the yield structure at the beginning of the year and the yield structure at the end of the year, as the price of the bond at these two points in time will depend on these structures. It follows that possible subsequent changes to the beginning-of-period yield structure must be analyzed in order to estimate possible bond returns over a given holding period. Bond portfolio managers who believe that they are able to identify such changes will want to translate their beliefs into action.

One way of doing this is known as **horizon analysis,** where a single holding period is selected for analysis and possible yield structures at the end of the period (that is, at the "horizon") are considered. The possible returns for two bonds—one currently held and one candidate to replace it—are then analyzed. In doing so, neither bond is assumed to default up to the horizon date. In the process of the analysis, the sensitivities of the returns to changes in key assumptions regarding yields are estimated, allowing at least a rough assessment of some of the relevant risks.

Horizon analysis can be viewed as another way of implementing the capitalization of income method of valuation that was discussed in Chapter 15. By focusing on the estimated end-of-period price of a bond, it seeks to determine whether the current market price is relatively high or low. That is, for a given estimated end-of-period price, a bond will have a relatively high expected return if its current price is relatively low. Conversely, a bond will have a relatively low expected return if its current price is relatively high.

Figure 16.4 represents a page from a standard yield book for bonds with a 4% coupon. As indicated, a 4% bond with ten years remaining to maturity that is currently priced at $67.48 (for ease of exposition, a par of $100 is used here) will have a 9% promised annual yield-to-maturity (or 4.5% semiannually). Five years into the future, such a bond's term-to-maturity will have decreased, and the relevant promised yield-to-maturity will probably have changed. Thus as time passes, the bond might follow a path "through the table" such as that shown by the dashed line. If so, it would end up at a price of $83.78 at the *horizon* (five years hence) with an 8% promised annual yield-to-maturity (or 4% semiannually).

Over any holding period, a bond's return will typically be affected by both the passage of time and a change in yield. Horizon analysis breaks this into two parts: one owing solely to the passage of time, whereby the bond's price moves toward the par value to be paid at maturity (assuming no change in yield), and the other owing solely to a change in yield (assuming no passage of time). This is illustrated in Figure 16.4. The total price change from $67.48 to $83.78 (or $16.30) is broken into a change from $67.48 to $80.22 (or $12.74) followed by

FIGURE 16.4

The Effect of Time and Yield Change on a 4% Coupon Bond

Note: y_0 and P_0 denote the bond's annual yield-to-maturity and price at the beginning of the period; y_H and P_H denote the bond's annual yield-to-maturity and price at the horizon (that is, the end of the period); P_A denotes the bond's price at the horizon if its annual yield had remained at $y_0 = 9\%$; yields are compounded semiannually.

Source: Martin L. Leibowitz, "Horizon Analysis for Managed Bond Portfolio," *Journal of Portfolio Management*, 1, no. 3 (Spring 1975): p. 26.

an instantaneous change from $80.22 to $83.78 (or $3.56). The intermediate value is the price the bond would command at the horizon if its promised yield-to-maturity had remained unchanged at its initial level of 9%. The actual price is that which it commands at its actual yield-to-maturity of 8%. In summary, the total price change can be broken into two parts, representing the two effects:

$$\text{Price change} = \text{time effect} + \text{yield change effect}. \qquad (16.9)$$

Thus far no account has been taken of the coupon payments to be received before the horizon date. In principle, one should consider all possible uses of such cash flows or at least analyze possible alternative yield structures during the period to determine likely reinvestment opportunities. In practice, this is rarely done. Instead, a single reinvestment rate is assumed, and the future value of all coupon payments at the horizon date is determined by compounding each one using this rate.[20]

For example, if $2 is received every six months (as in Figure 16.4), with the first payment occurring six months from now and the last payment occurring five years from now, and if each payment is reinvested at 4.25% per six months, then the value at the end of five years will be approximately $24.29. Of this amount, $20 can be considered interest (coupon payments of $2 for ten six-month periods), with the remaining $4.29 being "interest on interest."

In summary, a bond's overall dollar return has four components—the time effect, the yield change effect, the coupons, and the interest from reinvesting the coupons. In the example, the overall dollar return is

$$\begin{array}{c}\text{Overall}\\ \text{dollar}\\ \text{return}\end{array} = \begin{array}{c}\text{time}\\ \text{effect}\end{array} + \begin{array}{c}\text{yield}\\ \text{change}\\ \text{effect}\end{array} + \text{coupons} + \begin{array}{c}\text{interest on}\\ \text{coupons}\end{array}$$

$$= (\$80.22 - \$67.48) + (\$83.78 - \$80.22) + \$20.00 + \$4.29$$
$$= \$12.74 + \$3.56 + \$20.00 + \$4.29$$
$$= \$40.59.$$

This overall dollar return can be converted into an overall rate of return by dividing it by the market price of the bond at the beginning of the period, $67.48. Thus it can be seen that a bond's overall rate of return consists of four components:

$$\begin{array}{c}\text{Overall}\\ \text{rate of}\\ \text{return}\end{array} = \frac{\$12.74}{\$67.48} + \frac{\$3.56}{\$67.48} + \frac{\$20.00}{\$67.48} + \frac{\$4.29}{\$67.48}$$

$$= .1888 + .0528 + .2964 + .0635$$
$$= .6015$$

or 60.15%. The first term is the return owing to the passage of time, the second term is the return owing to yield change, the third term is coupon return, and the fourth term is the return owing to the reinvestment of the coupon payments.

Because the second term is uncertain, it is important to analyze it further. In the example, a change in yield from 9.0% to 8.0% will result in a change in the market price from $80.22 to $83.78. Given that 8.0% was the expected yield at the horizon, an expected overall rate of return of 60.15% was computed. By using different end-of-period yields, different overall rates of return can be calculated. Then, with estimates of the probabilities of these yields occurring, a sense of the bond's risk can be obtained. Indeed, it can now be seen why bond portfolio managers devote a great deal of attention to making predictions of future yields.

16.6.2   Bond Swaps

Given a set of predictions about future bond yields, holding-period returns over one or more horizons for one or more bonds can be estimated. The goal of **bond swapping** is to actively manage a portfolio by exchanging bonds to take advantage of any superior ability to predict such yields.[21] In making a swap, the portfolio manager believes that an overpriced bond is being exchanged for an underpriced bond. Some swaps are based on the belief that the market will correct for its mispricing in a short period of time, whereas other types of swaps are based on a belief that corrections either will never take place or will take place, but over a long period of time.

There are several categories for classifying swaps, and the distinctions between the categories are often blurry. Nevertheless, many bond swaps can be placed in one of four general categories:

1. **Substitution swap:** Ideally, this swap is an exchange of a bond for a perfect substitute or "twin" bond. The motivation here is temporary price advantage, presumably resulting from an imbalance in the relative supply and demand conditions in the marketplace.

2. **Intermarket spread swap:** This type of swap involves a more general movement out of one market component and into another with the intention of exploiting a currently advantageous yield relationship. The idea here is to benefit from a forecasted changing relationship between the two market components. Although such swaps will almost always have some sensitivity to the direction of the overall market, the idealized focus of this type of swap is the spread relationship itself.

3. **Rate anticipation swap:** Such swaps, on the other hand, are geared toward profiting from an anticipated movement in overall market rates.

4. **Pure yield pickup swap:** These swaps are oriented toward yield improvements over the long term, with little heed being paid to interim price movements in either the respective market components or the market as a whole.[22]

Consider a hypothetical portfolio manager who holds some of a 30-year AA utility bond issue that has a 7% coupon rate. As these bonds are currently selling at par, their yield-to-maturity is 7%. Now imagine that there is another 30-year AA utility bond issue with a 7% coupon rate that is being made available to the manager at a price that provides a yield-to-maturity of 7.10%. An example of a substitution swap is where the manager exchanges a given dollar amount of the currently held bonds for an equivalent dollar amount of the second bond issue, thereby picking up 10 basis points in yield.

Alternatively, the manager might note that there is a 10-year AA utility bond issue outstanding that carries a 6% coupon and is priced at par; thus its yield is 6%. In this case there is a 100-basis-point yield spread between the currently held 30-year bonds and the 10-year bonds. If the manager feels that this spread is too low, then an intermarket spread swap might be used, where some of the 30-year bonds are exchanged for an equivalent dollar amount of the 10-year bonds. Because the manager expects the spread to increase in the future, the yield on the 10-year bonds is expected to fall. This means that the price on these bonds is expected to rise by an abnormal amount, resulting in an abnormally high holding-period return.

Another possibility is that the manager feels that yields in general are going to rise. In such a situation, the manager will recognize that the currently held portfolio is in a very risky position. This is because longer term bonds generally move downward further in price for a given rise in yields than do shorter term bonds, because they generally have a longer duration. Accordingly, the manager might use a rate anticipation swap to exchange a given dollar amount of the 30-year bonds for an equivalent amount of some short-term bonds.

Finally, the manager might not want to make any predictions about future yields or yield spreads. Instead, it might simply be noted that some 30-year AA industrial bonds are currently priced to yield 8%. In this case the manager might want to enter a pure yield pickup swap where some of the 7% utility bonds are exchanged for an equivalent dollar amount of the 8% industrial bonds, the motivation being to earn the extra 100 basis points in yield from the industrials.

16.6.3 Contingent Immunization

One method of bond portfolio management that has both passive and active elements is **contingent immunization.** In the simplest form of contingent immunization, the portfolio will be actively managed as long as favorable results are obtained. However, if unfavorable results occur, then the portfolio will be immunized immediately.

As an illustration, consider the earlier example where the portfolio manager had to come up with $1,000,000 at the end of two years, and the current yield curve was horizontal at 10%. In this situation it was mentioned that the portfolio manager could immunize the portfolio by investing $826,446 in one-year and three-year bonds. However, the portfolio manager might convince the client that the portfolio should be *contingently* immunized with $841,680. This means that the portfolio manager must be certain that the portfolio will be worth at least $1,000,000 at the end of the two years, with any excess going to the client and the manager being compensated accordingly. Equivalently, the portfolio manager must earn a minimum average return of 9% (note that $841,680 \times 1.09^2 = \$1,000,000$) over the two years. Here, the client is willing to settle for a return as low as 9% but hopes that the portfolio manager will be able to exceed the 10% return that could have been locked in with an immunized portfolio.

In this situation the manager would proceed to actively manage the portfolio by engaging in either selectivity or timing, or both. Perhaps the arrangement with the client is that the status of the portfolio will be reviewed weekly, and yields that are currently available will be determined.

Consider how the review would be conducted after one year has elapsed and the yield curve is still horizontal but at 11%. First, it is noted that $900,901 ($= \$1,000,000/1.11$) would be needed to immunize the portfolio at that point in time. Second, the market value of the current portfolio is determined to be $930,000. Now in this example, the arrangement between the client and the portfolio manager is that the manager can continue to actively manage the portfolio as long as it is worth at least $10,000 more than the amount needed for immunization. Because it is worth $930,000, an amount greater than $910,901 ($= \$900,901 + \$10,000$), the portfolio manager can continue being active. However, if the portfolio had been worth less than $910,901, then, according to the agreement, the manager would immediately immunize the portfolio.

16.6.4 Riding the Yield Curve

This method of bond portfolio management is sometimes used by people who, having liquidity as a primary objective, invest in short-term fixed-income securities. One way of investing is to simply purchase these securities and hold them until they mature, and then reinvest the proceeds. An alternative way is to ride the yield curve, provided that certain conditions exist.

One condition is that the yield curve be upward sloping, indicating that longer term securities have higher yields. Another condition is that the investor believe that the yield curve will remain upward sloping. Given these two conditions, the investor who is riding the yield curve will purchase securities that have a somewhat longer term-to-maturity than desired, and then sell them before they mature, thereby capturing some capital gains.

For example, consider an investor who prefers investing in 90-day Treasury bills. Currently such bills are selling for $98.25 per $100 of face value, indicating that they have a yield of 7.00% [note that $98.25 = $100 − (7.00 × 90/360)]. However, 180-day Treasury bills are currently selling for $96.00, indicating that they have a higher yield of 8.00% [note that $96 = $100 − (8.00 × 180/360)]. Given that this investor believes that the yield curve will remain upward sloping over the next three months, it can be shown that riding the yield curve will result in a higher return than simply buying and holding the 90-day Treasury bills.

If the investor buys and holds the 90-day Treasury bills, then the resulting annualized rate of return will be:

$$\frac{\$100 - \$98.25}{\$98.25} \times \frac{365}{90}$$

which is 7.22%. Alternatively, if the investor buys the 180-day Treasury bills and subsequently sells them after 90 days, then the expected selling price will be $98.25. (Note that this is the same as the current price of 90-day bills, because it is assumed that the yield curve will not have changed after 90 days have elapsed.) This means that the expected return is:

$$\frac{\$98.25 - \$96.00}{\$96.00} \times \frac{365}{90}$$

which is 9.50%. In comparison, the expected return from riding the yield curve is higher. This is because the investor expects to benefit from a decline in yield, a decline that does not result from a shift in the yield curve but is attributable to the shortening of the maturity of the 180-day Treasury bills that were initially purchased.

It should be kept in mind that if the yield curve does change, then "riding it" might be detrimental to the investor's return.[23] That is, riding the yield curve has more risk than simply buying securities that mature at the appropriate time. Similarly, there are two transactions necessary (buying and then selling the security) when riding the yield curve, whereas a maturity strategy has only one transaction (buying the security). Thus there are going to be larger transaction costs associated with riding the yield curve.

BONDS VERSUS STOCKS

Bonds and stocks are different kinds of securities, with quite different characteristics. Making an investment decision between them should not be based on some simple one-dimensional comparison. In many cases this decision, known as **asset allocation,** will involve investing in both bonds and stocks.[24]

Although historical relationships may not be useful for predicting future relationships accurately, it is instructive to examine the average values, standard deviations, and correlations of past stock and bond returns. These statistics are presented in Table 16.3, based on quarterly excess returns during one time period, 1926–1985, and two subperiods, 1926–1945 and 1946–1985. (The returns were published by Ibbotson Associates; see Figure 1.1 and Table 1.1 in Chapter 1.)

Based on average returns, stocks appear to have a substantial advantage for the investor with a reasonably long horizon.[25] However, there is good reason to believe that the average returns on long-term bonds are not representative of investors' expectations for future returns. The returns show the results obtained by purchasing a long-term bond, holding it for a period of time, then replacing it with another long-term bond. The total returns include both income and capital gains or losses. During this period, bond price changes were negative more often than positive, averaging roughly −1% per year.[26] A better estimate of investors' expectations might be obtained by assuming that the expected price would be as likely to increase as to decrease. Expected future returns on bonds might then have been roughly 1% per year (.25% per quarter) greater than shown in the table.

For an investor concerned with month-to-month variation (such as an investor with a possible need for liquidity or with a known short horizon), bonds look relatively more attractive than stocks. This can be seen by examining the standard deviation of returns. In this sense stocks were riskier than bonds during

TABLE 16.3			
HISTORICAL RELATIONSHIPS BETWEEN BONDS AND STOCKS			
	Stocks	**Bonds**	**Correlation**
A. 1926–1985:			
Average Quarterly Excess Return	2.20%	.41%	
Standard Deviation	12.39	3.98	
Correlation			.30
B. 1926–1945:			
Average Quarterly Excess Return	2.94%	1.11%	
Standard Deviation	18.68	1.99	
Correlation			.45
C. 1946–1985:			
Average Quarterly Excess Return	1.83%	0.06%	
Standard Deviation	7.54	4.65	
Correlation			.40

Source: Adapted from Meir Statman and Neal L. Ushman, "Bonds Versus Stocks: Another Look," *Journal of Portfolio Management,* 13, no. 2 (Winter 1987): pp. 33–38.

the period and both subperiods. Note that the increased uncertainty concerning the rate of inflation during the postwar subperiod has increased the variability of bond returns.

The correlation between stock and bond returns has been low, and during various 26-year periods it has even had negative values. This indicates that portfolios combining both stocks and bonds benefited considerably from the resulting diversification. More recently, however, correlations have been positive (and substantially so), owing in part to common reactions to changes in inflationary expectations. Consequently, the gains from diversification have recently been reduced substantially. Nevertheless, from the historical record it would be reasonable to expect that, in the future, bonds will still offer diversification benefits.

16.8   SUMMARY

1. Similar to the U.S. common stock market, the U.S. bond market appears to be highly, but not perfectly, semistrong-form efficient.
2. For a typical bond making periodic interest payments and a final principal repayment on a stated date, five bond pricing theorems apply:
   a. If a bond's market price increases, then its yield must decrease; conversely, if a bond's market price decreases, then its yield must increase.
   b. If a bond's yield does not change over its life, then the size of its discount or premium will decrease as its life gets shorter.
   c. If a bond's yield does not change over its life, then the size of its discount or premium will decrease at an increasing rate as its life gets shorter.
   d. A decrease in a bond's yield will raise the bond's price by an amount that is greater in size than the corresponding fall in the bond's price that would occur if there were an equal-sized increase in the bond's yield. (That is, the price–yield relationship is convex.)
   e. The percentage change in a bond's price owing to a change in its yield will be smaller if its coupon rate is higher.
3. Duration is a measure of the "average maturity" of the stream of payments associated with a bond. It is a weighted average of the length of time until the bond's remaining payments are made, with the weights equal to the present value of each cash flow relative to the price of the bond.
4. The duration of a portfolio of bonds is equal to the weighted average of the durations of the individual bonds in the portfolio.
5. A bond portfolio manager can be fairly confident of being able to meet a given promised stream of cash outflows by creating a bond portfolio with a duration equal to the liabilities. This procedure is known as immunization.
6. Problems with immunization include default and call risk, multiple nonparallel shifts in a nonhorizontal yield curve, costly rebalancings, and a wide range of candidate bond portfolios.
7. Active bond management may involve security selection, market timing (where attempts are made to forecast general movements in interest rates), or combinations of the two.

8. Active management strategies include horizon analysis, bond swaps, contingent immunization, and riding the yield curve.

1. A $10,000 face-value pure-discount bond with a ten-year term-to-maturity currently sells so as to produce an 8% yield-to-maturity. What is the bond's price? Calculate the bond's price if its yield rises to 10%; if its yield falls to 5%.

2. Both bonds A and B have $10,000 face values, have 10% coupon rates, and sell with yields-to-maturity of 9%. However, bond A has a 20-year term-to-maturity while bond B has a five-year term-to-maturity. Calculate the prices of the two bonds. Despite having the same yields, why is one bond's price different from the other's?

3. Consider three pure-discount bonds, each with a $1,000 face value; 7% yield-to-maturity; and terms-to-maturity of 5, 10, and 20 years, respectively. Calculate each bond's price. Graph the bond's discounts versus their terms-to-maturity. Is the relationship linear? Why?

4. Consider two bonds with 10% coupon rates and $1,000 face values. One of the bonds has a term-to-maturity of 4 years, whereas the other has a term-to-maturity of 15 years. Both make annual interest payments. Assuming that yields on the two bonds rise from 10% to 14%, calculate the intrinsic values of the two bonds before and after the change in interest rates. Explain the difference in percentage price changes.

5. Consider a five-year term-to-maturity bond with a $1,000 face value and $100 annual coupon interest payments. The bond sells at par. What is the bond's percentage price change if the yield-to-maturity rises to 12%; if it falls to 8%?

6. Consider two bonds, one with 5 years to maturity and the other with 20 years to maturity. Both have $1,000 face values and 8% coupon rates (with annual interest payments), and both sell at par. Assume that the yields of both bonds fall to 6%. Calculate the dollar increases in the bonds' prices. What percentage of this increase in each case comes from a change in the present value of the bonds' principals, and what percentage comes from a change in the present value of the bonds' interest payments?

7. Both bonds A and B have $10,000 face values, 8% yields-to-maturity, and ten-year terms-to-maturity. However, bond A has a 10% coupon rate whereas bond B sells at par. (Both make annual interest payments.) If the yields on both bonds decline to 6%, calculate the percentage price changes of the two bonds.

8. Consider a bond selling at its par value of $1,000, with six years to maturity and a 7% coupon rate (with annual interest payments). Calculate the bond's duration.

9. If the yield-to-maturity on the bond in Problem 8 increases to 8%, what happens to the bond's duration? Why does this change occur?

10. Why must the duration of a coupon-bearing bond always be less than the time to its maturity date?

---

11. Liz Funk owns a portfolio of four bonds with the following durations and proportions:

Bond	Duration	Proportion
A	4.5 years	.20
B	3.0	.25
C	3.5	.25
D	2.8	.30

What is the duration of Liz's bond portfolio?

12. Rank order the following bonds in terms of duration. Explain the rationale behind your rankings. (You do not have to actually calculate the bonds' durations. Logical reasoning will suffice.)

Bond	Term-to-Maturity	Coupon Rate	Yield-to-Maturity
1	30 years	10.0%	10.0%
2	30	0.0	10.0
3	30	10.0	7.0
4	5	10.0	10.0

13. What impact would you expect the option features of callable bonds and mortgage participation certificates to have on the expected durations of such bonds as opposed to the durations calculated based on the bonds' stated maturity dates?

14. Consider a bond with a 3.5-year duration. If its yield-to-maturity increases from 8.0% to 8.3%, what is the expected percentage change in the price of the bond?

15. The price-yield relationship for a typical bond is convex, opening upward as shown in Figure 16.2. Investment professionals often describe the price-yield relationship of mortgage pass-through securities as being "negatively convex"—that is, a graph of the relationship opens downward. What features of these securities could produce such a relationship?

16. Explain why immunization permits a bond investor to be confident of meeting a given liability on a predetermined future date.

17. What are the advantages and disadvantages of meeting promised cash outflows through cash matching as opposed to duration matching?

18. Why can nonparallel shifts in the yield curve cause problems for an investor seeking to construct an immunized bond portfolio?

19. Old True Blue Richardson is planning to offset a single-payment liability with an immunized bond portfolio. Old True Blue is considering buying either bonds with durations close to that of the liability (a "bullet" strategy) or bonds with durations considerably above and below that of the liability (a "barbell" strategy). Why is the "bullet" strategy a lower risk strategy for Old True Blue? What are its disadvantages relative to the "barbell" strategy?

20. Describe the four components of return on a bond investment over a given holding period.

21. Consider a bond with a $1,000 face value, ten years to maturity, and $80 annual coupon interest payments. The bond sells so as to produce a 10%

yield-to-maturity. That yield is expected to decline to 9% at the end of four years. Interest income is assumed to be invested at 9.5%. Calculate the bond's four-year holding period return and the four components of that return.

22. Distinguish between a substitution swap and an intermarket swap.

23. Compare contingent immunization to the strategy of using stop orders (discussed in Chapter 2) to protect a portfolio's value.

CFA Exam Questions

24. Bill Peters is the investment officer of a $60 million pension fund. He has become concerned about the big price swings that have occurred lately in the fund's fixed-income securities. Peters has been told that such price behavior is only natural given the recent behavior of market yields. To deal with the problem, the pension fund's fixed-income money manager keeps track of exposure to price volatility by closely monitoring bond duration. The money manager believes that price volatility can be kept to a reasonable level as long as portfolio duration is maintained at approximately seven to eight years.

Discuss the concepts of duration and convexity and explain how each fits into the price/yield relationship. In the situation described above, explain why the money manager should have used both duration and convexity to monitor the bond portfolio's exposure to price volatility.

25. As a continuation of your analysis of Monticello's debt you are asked to evaluate two specific bond issues held in Cavalier managed accounts, as shown in the table below.

    a. Using the duration and yield information in the table, compare the price and yield behavior of the two bonds under each of the following two scenarios:

       • Scenario 1—strong economic recovery with rising inflation expectations; and
       • Scenario 2—economic recession with reduced inflation expectations.

    b. Using the information in the table, calculate the projected price change for Bond B if the yield-to-maturity for this bond falls by 75 basis points.

    c. Describe the shortcoming of analyzing Bond A strictly to call or to maturity. Explain an approach to remedy this shortcoming.

	Bond A (Callable)	Bond B (Non-callable)
Maturity	2002	2002
Coupon	11.50%	7.25%
Current price	125.75	100.00
Yield-to-maturity	7.70%	7.25%
Modified duration to maturity	6.20	6.80
Convexity to maturity	0.50	0.60
Call date	1996	—
Call price	105	—
Yield-to-call	5.10%	—
Maturity duration to call	3.10	—
Convexity to call	0.10	—

APPENDIX

EMPIRICAL REGULARITIES IN THE BOND MARKET

Certain empirical regularities in the stock market are well known among investment professionals.[27] Because these regularities cannot be explained by any of the currently known asset pricing models, they are referred to as "anomalies." An interesting question to ponder is this: do such regularities also exist in the bond market? One study looked at this question by examining the daily performance from January 1963 through December 1986 of the Dow Jones Composite Bond Average. (This bond index consists of 20 investment-grade U.S. corporate bonds, divided evenly between industrials and utilities.)[28]

A.1   THE JANUARY EFFECT

Table 16.4 presents evidence that, as with common stocks, there is a January effect in bonds—that is, on average, corporate bonds have a notably higher return during the month of January than during the other 11 months of the

TABLE 16.4
SEASONALITY IN BOND RETURNS

	Average Return in January	Average Monthly Return in Other Months
(a) 1963–1986[1]	4.34%	−.56%
(b) 1963–1979[2]		
Aaa	1.15%	.22%
Aa	1.21	.29
A	1.18	.30
Baa	1.55	.30
Ba	3.32	.27
B	5.09	.36

[1] **Source:** Susan D. Jordan and Bradford D. Jordan, "Seasonality in Daily Bond Returns," *Journal of Financial and Quantitative Analysis,* 26, no. 2 (June 1991): Table 5, p. 281.

[2] **Source:** Eric C. Chang and Roger D. Huang. "Time-Varying Return and Risk in the Corporate Bond Market," *Journal of Financial and Quantitative Analysis,* 25, no. 3 (September 1990): Table 1, p. 331.

year. Furthermore, this table also shows that this observation was true across all investment-grade (Aaa to Baa) and two speculative-grade (Ba and B) risk classes. Interestingly, the effect is extremely pronounced for the speculative classes.

A.2 THE DAY-OF-THE-WEEK EFFECT

Table 16.5 presents the average daily returns for each business day of the week over the period from 1963 to 1986. As with common stocks, the average return on Monday is negative. However, it is also negative for every day except Thursday, and the average returns for all five days are not statistically significantly different from one another.[29] Hence in contrast to common stocks, the day-of-the-week effect does not appear to exist for corporate bonds.

TABLE 16.5
ANALYSIS OF DAILY RETURN

Day of Week	Average Daily Return
Monday	− .20%
Tuesday	− .93
Wednesday	− .00
Thursday	.44
Friday	− .00

Source: Susan D. Jordan and Bradford D. Jordan, "Seasonality in Daily Bond Returns," *Journal of Financial and Quantitative Analysis,* 26, no. 2 (June 1991): Table 5, p. 281.

ENDNOTES

[1] For details, see Richard Roll, *The Behavior of Interest Rates* (New York: Basic Books, 1970). Interestingly, this study also produced evidence rejecting the unbiased expectations theory of the term structure of interest rates (see Chapter 5 for a discussion of this theory). Also of interest is that U.S. Treasury bonds appear to have been mispriced in May and June of 1986. See Bradford Cornell and Alan C. Shapiro, "The Mispricing of U.S. Treasury Bonds: A Case Study," *Review of Financial Studies,* 2, no. 3 (1989): 297–310.

[2] J. Walter Elliott and Jerome R. Baier, "Econometric Models and Current Interest Rates: How Well Do They Predict Future Rates?" *Journal of Finance,* 34, no. 4 (September 1979): 975–986. It should be noted that the models used by major economic forecasting firms tend to have similar amounts of accuracy. See Stephen K. McNees, "Forecasting Accuracy of Alternative Techniques: A Comparison of U.S. Macroeconomic Forecasts," *Journal of Business & Economic Statistics,* 4, no. 1 (January 1986): 5–15, particularly Table 6, where 90-day Treasury bill rate forecasts are evaluated, and Dean Croushore, "Introducing: The Survey of Professional Forecasters," Federal Reserve Bank of Philadelphia *Business Review,* November-December 1993: 3–15.

[3] Michael J. Prell, "How Well Do the Experts Forecast Interest Rates?" *Federal Reserve Bank of Kansas City Monthly Review,* September-October 1973: 3–13.

[4] Adrian W. Throop, "Interest Rate Forecast and Market Efficiency," *Federal Reserve Bank of San Francisco Economic Review,* Spring 1981: 29–43. This article contains a useful reference list of other studies concerning the prediction of interest rates.

[5] Forecasts implicit in the futures market (to be discussed in Chapter 21) for Treasury bills were also found to be more accurate than those of the economists, but less accurate than those of the no-change model over this time period. For a longer time period, the futures market and no-change model forecasts were of comparable accuracy; see Michael T. Belognia, "Predicting Interest Rates: A Comparison of Professional and Market-Based Forecasts," *Federal Reserve Bank of St. Louis Review,* 69, no. 3 (March 1987): 9–15.

[6] The reported accuracy of macroeconomic forecasters in regard to Treasury bill rates (see the Early Quarter results for a two-quarter horizon in Table 6 of McNees, "Forecast Accuracy") can be compared to the reported accuracy of the no-change model (see Table 1 of Belognia, "Predicting Interest Rates"). Although such a comparison should be done with caution, it does suggest that the no-change model is of similar, and in some cases superior, accuracy. There is also indirect evidence about the superiority of the no-change model in that bond portfolio managers apparently have not been able to generate returns exceeding those of bond market indices. See Christopher R. Blake, Edwin J. Elton, and Martin J. Gruber, "The Performance of Bond Mutual Funds," *Journal of Business,* 66, no. 3 (July 1993): 371–403. It also appears that the record of the experts in predicting the level of the stock market is of little value. See Werner F. De Bondt, "What Do Economists Know About the Stock Market?" *Journal of Portfolio Management,* 17, no. 2 (Winter 1991): 84–91.

[7] See Mark I. Weinstein, "The Effect of a Rating Change Announcement on Bond Price," *Journal of Financial Economics,* 5, no. 3 (December 1977): 329–350. A study of the prices of the common stocks associated with bonds that had rating changes reported similar results—stock prices tended to change several months prior to the announcement dates of the rating changes. See George E. Pinches and J. Clay Singleton, "The Adjustment of Stock Prices to Bond Rating Changes," *Journal of Finance,* 33, no. 1 (March 1978): 29–44. Another study that examined rating change announcements that were "noncontaminated" by other news releases found a small but statistically significant upward movement in daily bond prices around upgrades; downgrades produced no significant movements. Oddly, these findings were reversed when stock prices were examined in that no significant movements were found around upgrades but marginally significant downward movements were observed around downgrades. See John R. M. Hand, Robert W. Holthausen, and Richard W. Leftwich, "The Effect of Bond Rating Agency Announcements on Bond and Stock Prices," *Journal of Finance,* 47, no. 2 (June 1992): 733–752. Further analysis revealed that one type of downgrade—namely, "downgrades associated with deteriorating financial prospects"—resulted in a significant downward movement in the price of the associated firm's stock. See Jeremy C. Goh and Louis H. Ederington, "Is a Bond Downgrade Bad News, Good News, or No News for Stockholders?" *Journal of Finance,* 48, no. 5 (December 1993): 2001–2008.

[8] For an explanation and empirical investigation of this adjustment process, see Richard G. Sheehan, "Weekly Money Announcements: New Information and Its Effects," *Federal Reserve Bank of St. Louis Review,* 67, no. 7 (August/September 1985): 25–34; and Anthony M. Santomero, "Money Supply Announcements: A Retrospective," *Journal of Economics and Business,* 43, no. 1 (February 1991): 1–23.

[9] See, for example, Thomas Urich and Paul Wachtel, "Market Response to Weekly Money Supply Announcements in the 1970s," *Journal of Finance,* 36, no. 5 (December 1981): 1063–1072, and "The Effects of Inflation and Money Supply Announcements on Interest Rates," *Journal of Finance,* 39, no. 4 (September 1984): 1177–1188; and Bradford Cornell, "Money Supply Announcements and Interest Rates: Another View," *Journal of Business,* 56, no. 1 (January 1983): 1–23.

[10] Like the stock market, the bond market has some anomalies. However, they are fewer in number and less pronounced. These anomalies are briefly discussed in the Appendix.

[11] Burton G. Malkiel, "Expectations, Bond Prices, and the Term Structure of Interest Rates," *Quarterly Journal of Economics,* 76, no. 2 (May 1962): 197–218.

[12] There are other methods of calculating a bond's duration. For example, instead of using the bond's yield to calculate $PV(C_t)$, the appropriate current spot rates could be used.

[13] It follows that if there are two bonds that are identical in all aspects except that one has "more convexity," then the one with more convexity would be more desirable. This is because if yields rise, its price will drop by a smaller amount than the other bonds. Conversely, if yields drop, its price will rise by a larger amount than the other bonds. In either case, the investor is better off with the bond having more convexity.

[14] If there were two-year coupon-bearing bonds available for investment, then there would be no reinvestment-rate risk associated with the principal. However, the investor would still face reinvestment-rate risk in terms of the coupon payments received after one year. While such risk appears to be relatively minor in this example, such risk becomes much more substantial in situations involving promised cash outflows that are more than two years into the future.

[15] The reason that the value is more than $1,000,000 is due to the convexity property of bonds, discussed earlier.

[16] See the articles by Jeffrey Nelson and Stephen Schaefer, "The Dynamics of the Term Structure and Alternative Portfolio Immunization Strategies," pp. 61–101; and Jonathan E. Ingersoll, Jr., "Is Immunization Feasible? Evidence from the CRSP Data," pp. 163–182 in George G. Kaufman, G. O. Bierwag, and Alden Toevs, eds., *Innovations in Bond Portfolio Management: Duration Analysis and Immunization* (Greenwich, CT: JAI Press 1983); and Robert R. Reitano, "Non-Parallel Yield Curve Shifts and Spread Leverage," *Journal of Portfolio Management,* 17, no. 3 (Spring 1991): 82–87.

[17] For a summary and set of references, see G. O. Bierwag, George G. Kaufman, Robert Schweitzer, and Alden Toevs, "The Art of Risk Management in Bond Portfolios," *Journal of Portfolio Management,* 7, no. 3 (Spring 1981): 27–36; G. O. Bierwag, George G. Kaufman, and Alden Toevs, "Duration: Its Development and Use in Bond Portfolio Management," *Financial Analysts Journal,* 39, no. 4 (July–August 1983): 15–35; and Stephen M. Schaefer, "Immunization and Duration: A Review of Theory, Performance and Applications," *Midland Corporate Finance Journal,* 2, no. 3 (Fall 1984): 41–58.

[18] See N. Bulent Gultekin and Richard J. Rogalski, "Alternative Duration Specifications and the Measurement of Basis Risk," *Journal of Business,* 57, no. 2 (April 1984): 241–264. For rebuttals and responses, see G. O. Bierwag, George G. Kaufman, Cynthia M. Latta, and Gordon S. Roberts, "Duration: Response to Critics," *Journal of Portfolio Management,* 13, no. 2 (Winter 1987): 48–52; N. Bulent Gultekin and Richard J. Rogalski, "Duration: Response to Critics: Comment," *Journal of Portfolio Management,* 15, no. 3 (Spring 1989): 83–87; G. O. Bierwag, George G. Kaufman, Cynthia M. Latta, and Gordon S. Roberts, "Duration as a Measure of Basis Risk: The Wrong Answer at Low Cost—Rejoinder," Journal of Portfolio Management, 15, no. 4 (Summer 1989): 82–85; and N. Bulent Gultekin and Richard J. Rogalski, "Duration as a Measure of Basis Risk: The Wrong Answer at Low Cost—Answer to Rejoinder," *Journal of Portfolio Management,* 15, no. 4 (Summer 1989): 86–87.

[19] G. O. Bierwag, George G. Kaufman, and Alden Toevs, "Bond Portfolio Immunization and Stochastic Process Risk," *Journal of Bank Research,* 13 (Winter 1983), 282–291; and G. O. Bierwag, George G. Kaufman, and Cynthia M. Latta, "Duration Models: A Taxonomy," *Journal of Portfolio Management,* 15, no. 1 (Fall 1988): 50–54.

[20] The longer the horizon, the greater the importance of the size of the reinvestment rate in determining a bond's return. This means that if the investor's horizon is greater than, say, ten years, then alternative reinvestment rates should be considered.

[21] Bond swaps should not be confused with interest-rate swaps, where two issuers of debt keep the respective amounts raised but make each other's coupon payments. That is, issuer *A* makes the coupon payments on issuer *B*'s debt, and issuer *B* makes the coupon payments on issuer *A*'s debt, perhaps because *A* has fixed-rate debt and *B* has floating-rate debt. See, for example, Stuart M. Turnbull, "Swaps: A Zero Sum Game?," *Financial Management,* 16, no. 1 (Spring 1987): 15–21; and Clifford W. Smith, Jr., Charles W. Smithson, and D. Sykes Wilford, *Managing Financial Risk* (New York: Harper & Row, 1990), Chapters 9–12.

[22] Martin L. Leibowitz, "Horizon Analysis for Managed Bond Portfolios," *Journal of Portfolio Management,* 1, no. 3 (Spring 1975): 32–33.

[23] According to the unbiased expectations theory (discussed in Chapter 5), the yield curve would be expected to shift in such a manner that the expected return of both strategies (in the example, buy and hold the 90-day T-bills versus buy and sell 90 days later the 180-day T-bills) would be the same.

[24] Chapter 24 presents a discussion of some methods for making the asset allocation decision. For a model on how to measure the interest-rate sensitivity of a portfolio consisting of both stocks and bonds, see Martin L. Leibowitz, "Total Portfolio Duration: A New Perspective on Asset Allocation," *Financial Analysts Journal,* 42, no. 5 (September/October 1986): 18–29.

[25] Another study involving simulation found that, based on historical returns, an investor with a 20-year horizon had about a 5% probability of earning less when investing in a common stock index as opposed to investing in a long-term Treasury bond index. For a ten-year horizon the probability was 11%. See Kirt C. Butler and Dale L. Domian, "Risk, Diversification, and the Investment Horizon," *Journal of Portfolio Management,* 17, no. 3 (Spring 1991): 41–47.

[26] The observation is based on data through 1985, as reflected in Table 16.3. More recent data indicates that bond price changes have more often been positive than negative.

[27] Some of these regularities are discussed in the Appendix to Chapter 17.

[28] Susan D. Jordan and Bradford D. Jordan, "Seasonality in Daily Bond Returns," *Journal of Financial and Quantitative Analysis,* 26, no. 2 (June 1991): 269–285. Note that this study did not examine the bond market in order to see whether the "size effect" (observed for common stocks) was present. Hence only two of the anomalies discussed in the Appendix to Chapter 17 are discussed here.

[29] The returns on Wednesday and Friday are shown to be zero, but this is only because of rounding, as they are slightly negative.

KEY TERMS

coupon payments	immunization	substitution swap
coupon rate	cash matching	intermarket spread swap
term-to-maturity	dedicated portfolio	rate anticipation swap
yield-to-maturity	stochastic process risk	pure yield pickup swap
convexity	horizon analysis	contingent immunization
duration	bond swapping	asset allocation

REFERENCES

1. There have been many tests of efficiency in the bond market. Endnotes 1 through 9 contain citations of several of them, whereas some of the others are cited in:

   Frank J. Fabozzi and T. Dessa Fabozzi, *Bond Markets, Analysis and Strategies* (Englewood Cliffs, NJ: Prentice Hall, 1989): 300–303. Chapter 4 of this book also contains an extensive discussion of the concepts of convexity and duration.

2. A book that discusses convexity, duration, and many related investment strategies is:

   Gerald O. Bierwag, *Duration Analysis* (Cambridge, MA: Ballinger Publishing, 1987).

3. A method for measuring convexity is given by:

   Robert Brooks and Miles Livingston, "A Closed-Form Equation for Bond Convexity," *Financial Analysts Journal,* 45, no. 6 (November/December 1989): 78–79.

4. The concept of duration and its use to measure interest-rate risk was initially developed by:

   Frederick R. Macauley, *Some Theoretical Problems Suggested by the Movement of Interest Rates, Bond Yields, and Stock Prices in the United States Since 1856* (New York: National Bureau of Economic Research, 1938).

   J. R. Hicks, *Value and Capital,* 2d ed. (Oxford, England: Clarendon Press, 1946; the first edition was published in 1939).

   Michael H. Hopewell and George G. Kaufman, "Bond Price Volatility and Term to Maturity: A Generalized Respecification," *American Economic Review,* 63, no. 4 (September 1973): 4749–4753.

5. For interesting articles describing the development of the concept of duration (as well as immunization), see:

   Roman L. Weil, "Macauley's Duration: An Appreciation," *Journal of Business,* 46, no. 4 (October 1973): 589–592.

   Frank K. Reilly and Rupinder S. Sidhu, "The Many Uses of Bond Duration," *Financial Analysts Journal,* 36, no. 4 (July/August 1980): 58–72.

   G. O. Bierwag, George G. Kaufman, and Alden Toevs, "Duration: Its Development and Use in Bond Portfolio Management," *Financial Analysts Journal,* 39, no. 4 (July/August 1983): 15–35.

6. For alternative methods of calculating duration, see:

   Jess H. Chua, "A Generalized Formula for Calculating Bond Duration," *Financial Analysts Journal,* 44, no. 5 (September/October 1988): 65–67.

   Sanjay K. Nawalkha and Nelson J. Lacey, "Closed-Form Solutions of Higher-Order Duration Measures," *Financial Analysts Journal,* 44, no. 6 (November/December 1988): 82–84.

7. For the initial development and subsequent supportive tests of immunization, see:

F. M. Redington, "Review of the Principles of Life-Office Valuations," *Journal of the Institute of Actuaries*, 78, no. 3 (1952): 286–315.

Lawrence Fisher and Roman L. Weil, "Coping with the Risk of Interest-Rate Fluctuations: Returns to Bondholders from Naive and Optimal Strategies," *Journal of Business*, 44, no. 4 (October 1971): 408–431.

G. O. Bierwag and George G. Kaufman, "Coping with the Risk of Interest-Rate Fluctuations: A Note," *Journal of Business*, 50, no. 3 (July 1977): 364–370.

Charles H. Gushee, "How to Immunize a Bond Investment," *Financial Analysts Journal*, 37, no. 2 (March/April 1981): 44–51.

G. O. Bierwag, George G. Kaufman, Robert Schweitzer, and Alden Toevs, "The Art of Risk Management in Bond Portfolios," *Journal of Portfolio Management*, 7, no. 2 (Spring 1981): 27–36.

Gerald O. Bierwag, *Duration Analysis* (Cambridge, MA: Ballinger Publishing, 1987), Chapter 12.

Donald R. Chambers, Willard T. Carleton, and Richard W. McEnally, "Immunizing Default-Free Bond Portfolios with a Duration Vector," *Journal of Financial and Quantitative Analysis*, 23, no. 1 (March 1988): 89–104.

Iraj Fooladi and Gordon S. Roberts, "Bond Portfolio Immunization," *Journal of Economics and Business*, 44, no. 1 (February 1992): 3–17.

8. For some interesting articles on the relationship of duration and convexity, see:

Mark L. Dunetz and James M. Mahoney, "Using Duration and Convexity in the Analysis of Callable Bonds," *Financial Analysts Journal*, 44, no. 3 (May/June 1988): 53–72.

Bruce J. Grantier, "Convexity and Bond Portfolio Performance: The Benter the Better," *Financial Analysts Journal*, 44, no. 6 (November/December 1988): 79–81.

Jacques A. Schnabel, "Is Benter Better: A Cautionary Note on Maximizing Convexity," *Financial Analysts Journal*, 46, no. 1 (January/February 1990): 78–79.

Robert Brooks and Miles Livingston, "Relative Impact of Duration and Convexity on Bond Price Changes," *Financial Practice and Education*, 2, no. 1 (Spring/Summer 1992): 93–99.

Mark Kritzman, " . . . About Duration and Convexity," *Financial Analysts Journal*, 48, no. 6 (November/December 1992): 17–20.

Gerald O. Bierwag, Iraj Fooladi, and Gordon S. Roberts, "Designing an Immunized Portfolio: Is M-Squared the Key?" *Journal of Banking and Finance*, 17, no. 6 (December 1993): 1147–1170.

9. Some of the research that is critical of the use of duration, convexity, and immunization is mentioned in Endnote 18. Other critical research includes:

Jonathan E. Ingersoll, Jr., Jeffrey Skelton, and Roman L. Weil, "Duration Forty Years Later," *Journal of Financial and Quantitative Analysis,* 13, no. 4 (November 1977): 627–650.

Ronald N. Kahn and Roland Lochoff, "Convexity and Exceptional Return," *Journal of Portfolio Management,* 16, no. 2 (Winter 1990): 43–47.

Antti Ilmanen, "How Well Does Duration Measure Interest Rate Risk?" *Journal of Fixed Income,* 1, no. 4 (March 1992): 43–51.

10. For a discussion of how to use nondefault-free bonds in an immunized portfolio, see:

Gordon J. Alexander and Bruce G. Resnick, "Using Linear and Goal Programming to Immunize Bond Portfolios," *Journal of Banking and Finance,* 9, no. 1 (March 1985): 35–54.

G. O. Bierwag and George G. Kaufman, "Durations of Nondefault-Free Securities," *Financial Analysts Journal,* 44, no. 4 (July/August 1988): 39–46, 62.

Gerald O. Bierwag, Charles J. Corrado, and George G. Kaufman, "Computing Durations for Bond Portfolios," *Journal of Portfolio Management,* 17, no. 1 (Fall 1990): 51–55.

Gerald O. Bierwag, Charles J. Corrado, and George G. Kaufman, "Durations for Portfolios of Bonds Priced on Different Term Structures," *Journal of Banking and Finance,* 16, no. 4 (August 1992): 705–714.

11. For a discussion of the effect of call risk on duration (and immunization), see:

Kurt Winkelmann, "Uses and Abuses of Duration and Convexity," *Financial Analysts Journal,* 45, no. 5 (September/October 1989): 72–75.

12. For a discussion of how to use duration to measure the risk of foreign bonds, see:

Steven I. Dym, "Measuring the Risk of Foreign Bonds," *Journal of Portfolio Management,* 17, no. 2 (Winter 1991): 56–61.

Steven Dym, "Global and Local Components of Foreign Bond Risk," *Financial Analysts Journal,* 48, no. 2 (March/April 1992): 83–91.

13. Dedicated bond portfolios and contingent immunization are discussed in:

Martin L. Leibowitz and Alfred Weinberger, "Contingent Immunization—Part I: Risk Control Procedures," *Financial Analysts Journal,* 38, no. 6 (November/December 1982): 17–31.

Martin L. Leibowitz and Alfred Weinberger, "Contingent Immunization—Part II: Problem Areas," *Financial Analysts Journal,* 39, no. 1 (January/February 1983): 39–50.

Martin L. Leibowitz, "The Dedicated Bond Portfolio in Pension Funds—Part I: Motivations and Basics," *Financial Analysts Journal,* 42, no. 1 (January/February 1986): 69–75.

Martin L. Leibowitz, "The Dedicated Bond Portfolio in Pension Funds—Part II: Immunization, Horizon Matching, and Contingent Procedures," *Financial Analysts Journal,* 42, no. 2 (March/April 1986): 47–57.

14. For a discussion of horizon analysis and bond swaps, see:

Sidney Homer and Martin L. Leibowitz, *Inside the Yield Book* (Englewood Cliffs, NJ: Prentice Hall, 1972), Chapters 6–7.

Martin L. Leibowitz, "Horizon Analysis for Managed Bond Portfolios," *Journal of Portfolio Management,* 1, no. 3 (Spring 1975): 23–34.

Martin L. Leibowitz, "An Analytic Approach to the Bond Market," in *Financial Analyst's Handbook,* ed. Sumner N. Levine (Homewood, IL: Dow Jones-Irwin, 1975), pp. 226–277.

Marcia Stigum and Frank J. Fabozzi, *The Dow Jones-Irwin Guide to Bond and Money Market Investments* (Homewood, IL: Dow Jones-Irwin, 1987), Chapter 16.

15. For a discussion of various yield curve strategies, see:

Jerome S. Osteryoung, Gordon S. Roberts, and Daniel E. McCarty, "Ride the Yield Curve When Investing Idle Funds in Treasury Bills?" *Financial Executive,* 47, no. 4 (April 1979): 10–15.

Edward A. Dyl and Michael D. Joehnk, "Riding the Yield Curve: Does It Work?" *Journal of Portfolio Management,* 7, no. 3 (Spring 1981): 13–17.

Marcia Stigum and Frank J. Fabozzi, *The Dow Jones-Irwin Guide to Bond and Money Market Investments* (Homewood, IL: Dow Jones-Irwin, 1987), 270–272.

Frank J. Jones, "Yield Curve Strategies," *Journal of Fixed Income,* 1, no. 2 (September 1991): 43–51.

Robin Grieves and Alan J. Marcus, "Riding the Yield Curve: Reprise," *Journal of Portfolio Management,* 18, no. 4 (Summer 1992): 67–76.

16. More on bond investment strategies is contained in:

Ehud I. Ronn, "A New Linear Programming Approach to Bond Portfolio Management," *Journal of Financial and Quantitative Analysis,* 22, no. 4 (December 1987): 439–466.

Michael C. Ehrhardt, "A New Linear Programming Approach to Bond Portfolio Management: A Comment," *Journal of Financial and Quantitative Analysis,* 24, no. 4 (December 1989): 533–537.

Randall S. Hiller and Christian Schaack, "A Classification of Structured Bond Portfolio Modeling Techniques," *Journal of Portfolio Management,* 17, no. 1 (Fall 1990): 37–48.

Frank J. Fabozzi, *Bond Markets, Analysis and Strategies* (Englewood Cliffs, NJ: Prentice Hall, 1993), in particular Chapters 20–22.

17. For an interesting discussion of what mix of bonds and stocks is appropriate for investors, see:

Martin L. Leibowitz and William S. Krasker, "The Persistence of Risk: Stocks Versus Bonds Over the Long Term," *Financial Analysts Journal,* 44, no. 6 (November/December 1988): 40–47.

Paul A. Samuelson, "The Judgment of Economic Science on Rational Portfolio Management: Indexing, Timing and Long-Horizon Effects," *Journal of Portfolio Management,* 16, no. 1 (Fall 1989): 4–12.

Martin L. Leibowitz and Terence C. Langetieg, "Shortfall Risk and the Asset Allocation Decision: A Simulation Analysis of Stock and Bond Profiles," *Journal of Portfolio Management,* 16, no. 1 (Fall 1989): 61–68.

Keith P. Ambachtscheer, "The Persistence of Investment Risk," *Journal of Portfolio Management,* 16, no. 1 (Fall 1989): 69–71.

Kirt C. Butler and Dale L. Domian, "Risk, Diversification, and the Investment Horizon," *Journal of Portfolio Management,* 17, no. 3 (Spring 1991): 41–47.

18. Pension fund management is discussed in:

Martin L. Leibowitz, "Total Portfolio Duration: A New Perspective on Asset Allocation," *Financial Analysts Journal,* 42, no. 5 (September/October 1986): 18–29, 77.

Martin L. Leibowitz and Roy D. Henriksson, "Portfolio Optimization Within a Surplus Framework," *Financial Analysts Journal,* 44, no. 2 (March/April 1988): 43–51.

William F. Sharpe, "Liabilities—A New Approach," *Journal of Portfolio Management,* 16, no. 2 (Winter 1990): 4–10.

19. Empirical regularities in the bond market have been investigated by:

Eric C. Chang and J. Michael Pinegar, "Return Seasonality and Tax-Loss Selling in the Market for Long-Term Government and Corporate Bonds," *Journal of Financial Economics,* 17, no. 2 (December 1986): 391–415.

Eric C. Chang and Roger D. Huang, "Time-Varying Return and Risk in the Corporate Bond Market," *Journal of Financial and Quantitative Analysis,* 25, no. 3 (September 1990): 323–340.

Susan D. Jordan and Bradford D. Jordan, "Seasonality in Daily Bond Returns," *Journal of Financial and Quantitative Analysis,* 26, no. 2 (June 1991): 269–285.

Common Stocks

Common stocks are easier to describe than fixed-income securities such as bonds, but they are harder to analyze. Fixed-income securities almost always have a limited life and an upper dollar limit on cash payments to investors. Common stocks have neither. Although the basic principles of valuation apply to both, the role of uncertainty is larger for common stocks, so much so that it often dominates all other elements in their valuation.

Common stock represents equity, or an ownership position in a corporation. It is a residual claim, in the sense that creditors and preferred stockholders must be paid as scheduled before common stockholders can receive any payments. In bankruptcy, common stockholders are in principle entitled to any value remaining after all other claimants have been satisfied. (However, in practice, courts sometimes violate this principle.)

The great advantage of the corporate form of organization is the **limited liability** of its owners. Common stocks are generally "fully paid and nonassessable," meaning that common stockholders may lose their initial investment, but not more. That is, if the corporation fails to meet its obligations, the stockholders cannot be forced to give the corporation the funds that are needed to pay off the obligations. However, as a result of such a failure, it is possible that the value of a corporation's shares will be negligible. This will result in the stockholders' having lost an amount equal to the price previously paid to buy the shares.

A corporation exists only when it has been granted a **charter,** or certificate of incorporation, by a state. This document specifies the rights and obligations of stockholders. It may be amended with the approval of the stockholders, perhaps by a majority or a two-thirds vote, where each share of stock generally entitles its owner to one vote. Both the initial terms of the charter and the terms of any amendment must also be approved by the state in which the corporation is chartered. The State of Delaware has captured a disproportionate number of corporate charters because it is particularly hospitable in this respect as well as in levying corporate taxes.

17.1.1 Stock Certificates

The ownership of a firm's stock has typically been represented by a single certificate, with the number of shares held by the particular investor noted on it. Such a stock certificate is usually registered, with the name, address, and holdings of the investor included on the corporation's books. Dividend payments, voting material, annual and quarterly reports, and other mailings are then sent directly to the investor, taking into account the size of his or her holdings.

Shares of stock held by an investor may be transferred to a new owner with the assistance of either the issuing corporation or, more commonly, its designated **transfer agent.** This agent will cancel the old stock certificate and issue a new one in its place, made out to the new owner. Frequently, a **registrar** will make sure that this canceling and issuing of certificates has been done properly. Usually, banks and trust companies act as transfer agents and registrars. Many stockholders have chosen to avoid these rather cumbersome procedures. Instead, depository arrangements (discussed in Chapter 3) are used, which substitute computerized records for embossed certificates.

17.1.2 Voting

Because an owner of a share of common stock is one of the owners of a corporation, he or she is entitled to vote on matters brought up at the corporation's annual meeting, and to vote for the corporation's directors. Any owner may attend and vote in person, but most choose instead to vote by **proxy.** That is, the incumbent directors and senior management will typically solicit all the stockholders, asking each one to sign a proxy statement. Such a statement is a power of attorney authorizing the designated party listed on the statement to cast all of the investor's votes on any matter brought up at the meeting. Occasionally, desired positions on specific issues are solicited on the proxy statement. However, most of the time the positions held by the incumbents are made known with the proxy solicitation. As the majority of votes are generally controlled by the incumbents via proxy statements, the actual voting turns out to be perfunctory, leaving little if any controversy or excitement.[1]

17.1.3 Proxy Fight

Once in a while, however, a **proxy fight** develops. Insurgents from outside the corporation solicit proxies to vote against the incumbents, often in order to effect a takeover of some sort. Stockholders are deluged with literature and appeals for their proxies. The incumbents usually win, but the possibility of a loss in such a skirmish tends to curb activities clearly not in the stockholders' best interests.

When proposals are to be voted on, the number of votes given an investor equals the number of shares held. Thus when a yes or no vote is called for, anyone controlling a majority of the shares will be able to make sure that the outcome he or she favors will receive a majority of the votes. When directors are to be elected, however, there are two types of voting systems that can be used, one of which does not give a majority owner complete control of the outcome. This type of voting system is known as a **cumulative voting system,** whereas the other type of voting system that does allow a majority owner to control the outcome completely is known as a **majority voting system** (or straight voting system).

Under both systems, the winners of the election are those candidates who have received the highest vote totals. Thus if six candidates were running for the three directorships, the three receiving the largest number of votes would be elected.

Majority Voting System

With both voting systems, a stockholder receives a total number of votes that equals the number of directors to be elected times the number of shares owned. However, with the majority voting system, the stockholder may give any one candidate, as a maximum, only a number of votes equal to the number of shares owned. This means that in a situation where three directors are to be elected, a stockholder with 400 shares would have 1,200 votes but could give no more than 400 of these votes to any one candidate. Note that if there are a total of 1,000 shares outstanding and one stockholder owns, or has proxies for, 501 shares, then he or she can give 501 votes to each of the three candidates he or she favors. In doing so, this stockholder will be certain that they are elected, regardless of how the remaining 499 shares are voted. The majority shareholder's candidates would each have 501 votes, whereas the most any other candidate could receive is 499 votes. Thus with a majority voting system, a stockholder owning (or controlling with proxies) one share more than 50% is certain of electing all the candidates that he or she favors.

Cumulative Voting System

The cumulative voting system differs from the majority voting system in that a stockholder can cast his or her votes in any manner. As a result, a minority stockholder is certain of having some representation on the board of directors, provided that the number of shares owned is sufficiently large. In the previous example, the minority owner of the 400 shares could now cast all of his or her 1,200 votes for one candidate. Imagine that this owner wanted to elect director *A*, but the majority owner of 501 shares wanted to elect candidates *B, C,* and *D.*

In this situation, the minority stockholder could give all 1,200 votes to A and be certain that A would be one of the three directors elected, regardless of what the majority stockholder did. Why? If the majority owner held the remaining 600 shares, he or she would have 1,800 votes. There is no way that candidate A, favored by the minority stockholder, can come in lower than second place in the vote totals. This is because A will receive 1,200 votes, and there is no way that the 1,800 votes of the majority stockholder can be cast to give more than one of his or her favored candidates a vote total in excess of 1,200. Thus the minority stockholder is assured that A will be elected, whereas the majority stockholder is assured that only two of his or her favorites will be elected.

How many shares, as a minimum, must a stockholder own in order to be able to elect a specific number of candidates under a cumulative voting system? In general, the formula for making such a determination is

$$n = \left(\frac{ds}{D + 1} \right) + 1 \tag{17.1}$$

> where: n = minimum number of shares that must be owned,
> d = number of directors the stockholder wants to be certain of electing,
> s = number of shares outstanding,
> D = number of directors to be elected.

Thus the minimum number of shares a stockholder needs in order to ensure the election of one director when three are to be elected and there are 1,000 shares outstanding is 251 {= [(1 × 1,000)/(3 + 1)] + 1}. Because in the example the minority stockholder owned 400 shares, it can be seen from the formula that he or she is certain of being able to elect one director. Note that the minimum number of shares that must be owned in order to be certain of electing two directors is 501 {= [(2 × 1,000)/(3 + 1)] + 1}. The minimum number owned to be certain of electing all three directors is 751 {= [(3 × 1,000)/(3 + 1)] + 1}.

In summary, the cumulative voting system gives minority stockholders the right to have some representation on the board of directors, provided that the number of shares owned is sufficiently large. In contrast, the majority voting system does not give minority stockholders the right to such representation, even if 49.9% of the shares are owned by the minority stockholder.

The voting system that a corporation decides to use depends not only on the desires of the corporate founders but also on the state in which the firm is incorporated. Some states require cumulative voting systems. In Delaware, however, there is no cumulative voting unless it is specifically stated in the corporate charter.

17.1.4 Takeovers

Periodically, a firm or a wealthy individual who is convinced that the management of a corporation is not fully exploiting its opportunities will attempt a **takeover.** This is frequently done with a **tender offer** being made by a **bidder** to a

target firm.[2] Before this offer is announced, some of the target firm's shares are usually acquired by the bidder in the open market through the use of brokers. (Once 5% of the stock is so acquired, the bidder has ten days to report the acquisition to the SEC on a 13d form.) Then in its quest to acquire a substantial number of the target's shares, the bid is announced to the public. Advertisements to purchase shares are placed in the financial press, and material describing the bid is mailed to the target's stockholders. The bidder generally offers to buy at a stated price some or all shares offered ("tendered") by the current stockholders of the target. This buying offer is usually contingent on the tender of a minimum number of shares by the target's stockholders by a fixed date. When the buying offer is first made, the offered price ("tender price") is generally set considerably above the current market price, although the offer itself usually leads to a subsequent price increase.

Management of the target firm frequently responds to tender offers with advertisements, mailings, and the like, urging its stockholders to reject the bidder's offer. Sometimes a **white knight** will be sought, meaning that another firm that is favorably inclined toward current management will be invited to make a better offer to the target's stockholders. Another type of response by management is to pay **greenmail** to the bidder, meaning that any shares held by the bidder will be bought by the target firm at an above-market price. Still another type of response is for management of the target firm to issue a tender offer of its own, known as a **repurchase offer,** where the firm offers to buy back some of its own stock. (Repurchase offers are also made by firms that have not received tender offers from outside bidders.) Other types of corporate defenses include the **Pac-Man defense,** where the initial target turns around and makes a tender offer for the initial acquirer; the **crown jewel defense,** where the target sells its most attractive assets to make the firm less attractive; and the use of **poison pills,** where the target gives its shareholders certain rights that can be exercised only in the event of a subsequent takeover and that, once exercised, will be extremely onerous to the acquirer.

17.1.5 Ownership versus Control

Much has been written about the effect of the separation of ownership and control of the modern corporation.[3] This separation gives rise to what is known as a principal-agent problem. In particular, stockholders can be viewed as principals who hire management to act as their agent. The agent is to make decisions that maximize shareholder wealth as reflected in the firm's stock price. No problem would exist if stockholders could monitor the managers costlessly, because the stockholders would then be capable of determining for certain whether or not management had acted in their best interests. However, monitoring is not costless, and complete monitoring of every decision is, practically speaking, impossible.[4] As a result, some, but not complete, monitoring is done. This gives management considerable latitude in making decisions and leaves open the possibility that some decisions will not be in the stockholders' best interests.[5] However, the possibility of a proxy fight or tender offer provides at least some check on such decisions.

To align the interests of management with their own, stockholders frequently offer certain incentives to management. An example is the use of stock options. These options are given to certain high-level managers and allow them to purchase a specified number of shares at a stated price (often above the market price when the options are initially issued) by a stated date. Thus they motivate these managers to make decisions that will increase the stock price of the firm as much as possible. Furthermore, given their relatively long initial lifespan (in comparison with listed options, discussed in Chapter 20), stock options implicitly exert pressure on management to take a long-term view in making decisions.

17.1.6 Stockholders' Equity

Par Value

When a corporation is first chartered, it is authorized to issue up to a stated number of shares of common stock, each of which will often carry a specified **par value.** Legally a corporation may be precluded from making payments to common stockholders if doing so would reduce the balance-sheet value of stockholders' equity below the amount represented by the par value of outstanding stock. For this reason the par value is typically low relative to the price for which the stock is initially sold. Some corporations issue no-par stock. (If so, a stated value must be recorded in place of the par value.)

When stock is initially sold for more than its par value, the difference may be carried separately on the corporation's books under stockholders' equity. Frequently the entry is for "capital contributed in excess of par value" or "paid-in capital." The par value of the stock is carried in a separate account, generally entitled simply "common stock," with an amount that is equal to the number of shares outstanding times the par value per share (for no-par stock, the stated value).

Book Value

With the passage of time, a corporation will generate income, much of which is paid out to creditors (as interest) and to stockholders (as dividends). Any remainder is added to the amount shown as cumulative retained earnings on the corporation's books. The sum of the cumulative retained earnings and other entries (such as "common stock" and "capital contributed in excess of par value") under stockholders' equity is the **book value of the equity.** The **book value per share** is obtained by dividing the book value of the equity by the number of shares outstanding.

Reserved and Treasury Stock

Typically, a corporation will issue only part of its authorized stock. Some of the remainder may be specifically reserved for outstanding options, convertible securities, and so on. However, if a corporation wishes to issue new stock in excess of the amount originally authorized, the charter must be amended. This requires approval by both the state and the stockholders.

Corporate Governance

Conflicts between corporate managements and shareholders surfaced as a major public policy issue in the 1980s. The potentially adversarial principal-agent relationship between corporation owners and managers has long been recognized. In the last decade, however, two major developments brought this issue to greater prominence.

First, corporate managements, responding to a wave of hostile corporate takeovers, instituted various defensive strategies such as poison pill provisions, the sale of key corporate assets, and staggered board of directors terms. These defenses were designed to prevent the target companies from being acquired easily, thereby protecting the jobs of existing management. Indeed, they appear to have had the intended result of making those companies worth less to prospective acquirers. However, they also reduced the value of the companies to their existing shareholders.

Second, large shareholders came to realize that they wielded considerable corporate voting power. The growth of institutional investors has concentrated corporate ownership in the hands of a relatively few organizations. (See the Institutional Issues discussion in Chapter 1.) The resources of these large organizations enabled them to actively oppose management decisions that diminished the value of their investments. *Corporate governance,* a particularly bureaucratic sounding term, has become the catchall description for institutional investor efforts to influence the fundamental business policies of corporate managements.

Until recently, the attitude of most company managements toward shareholders was simply, "If you don't like the way we run the company, then sell our stock and quit complaining." Institutional investors, however, came to realize that they had nowhere else to go. For example, they place hundreds of billions of dollars in portfolios designed to track the U.S. stock market (see Chapter 24). As a result, they effectively hold permanent positions in all large U.S. corporations. Corporate governance (or "shareholder rights") activities expressed institutional investors' desires to stand and fight for their financial interests.

State and local pension funds (that is, "public"

pension funds) are the leading shareholder rights proponents. Their activism can be traced to the early and mid 1980s, when many of them sponsored shareholder resolutions that urged corporations to end their involvement in South Africa. Although none of those resolutions passed, their mere introduction embarrassed the confronted corporate managements. Many prominent U.S. companies voluntarily sold their South African business investments or considerably lowered their profile in the country.

The organizational lessons acquired in this South African "divestment" debate proved valuable when the battle against corporate takeover defenses began soon after. In 1984 several public pension funds, along with various union pension funds, formed the Council of Institutional Investors (CII). The goal of the CII is to provide a forum for institutional investors to discuss and organize efforts to encourage enlightened shareholder rights policies by corporate managements. Although the CII is still dominated by public and union pension funds, several large corporate pension funds have joined in recent years. Today the CII has over 80 members who, in total, control more than $600 billion in assets.

The CII and other shareholder rights organizations have become forces to be reckoned with on corporate governance issues. Shareholder victories have begun to mount. Under pressure from institutional investors, chief executives from such large organizations as General Motors, American Express, and Westinghouse have been ousted. IBM restructured its board of directors to give more power to outsiders. Sears revamped its business strategy, eliminating unprofitable operations.

Many large corporations have seen the handwriting on the wall and have moved to negotiate directly with their large institutional shareholders. Thus although direct victories by institutional investors in proxy battles remain extremely rare, shareholder rights proponents are increasingly accomplishing their objectives away from the publicity of annual meetings. In fact, some institutional investors have espoused a controversial concept known as "relationship investing," whereby they take large minority positions in poorly performing companies with the intention of assisting the corporate managements in improving financial results.

Interestingly, the motives of institutional shareholders in the corporate governance debate are not always clear-cut. For example, public pension funds may be sensitive to political pressures to support companies domiciled in their states or localities, regardless of the companies' shareholder rights record. Managers of corporate pension funds may wish to avoid opposing other corporations' shareholder rights practices for fear that their own companies may face similar pressures some day. Insurance companies and mutual funds, newcomers to the corporate governance debate, may be directly employed by the companies whose shareholder policies they oppose.

Given these potentially conflicting motivations, it is perhaps surprising that the shareholder rights movement has achieved its current prominence. Recent actions on the part of the federal government seem likely to ensure that the debate continues. In 1988 the Department of Labor ruled that a pension fund's proxy votes are a plan asset and must be managed accordingly. In 1992 the Securities and Exchange Commission issued regulations making it easier for institutional investors to communicate with one another to enlist support for various shareholder proposals. Congress is considering legislation formalizing certain shareholder rights.

While shareholder rights activists still oppose blatantly anti-shareholder takeover defenses, they have begun to focus their attention on more subtle issues, such as executive compensation, independent boards of directors, and secret balloting in proxy fights. The future may see debates moving to such non-shareholder issues as product liability, health care, and the environment. To what extent institutional investors should involve themselves with corporate business decision-making remains a hotly contested subject. One thing is certain, however: Corporate managements will never again be able to run their businesses oblivious to the wishes of their largest shareholders.

Sometimes a corporation will repurchase some of its outstanding stock, either in the open market through the services of a broker or with a tender offer. Afterward, this stock may be "held in the treasury." Such **treasury stock** is not entitled to voting rights or dividends and is equivalent economically (though not legally) to unissued stock.

A major study of over 1,300 stock repurchases found that nearly 90% of the repurchases analyzed were executed in the open market, with the remainder being "self-tender offers."[6] There were two types of self-tender offers that occurred with approximately equal frequency. The first type is a "fixed-price" self-tender offer, where the corporation makes an offer to repurchase a stated number of shares at a set, predetermined price. The second type is a "Dutch-auction" self-tender offer, where the corporation again makes an offer to repurchase a stated number of shares, but at a price that is determined by inviting existing shareholders to submit offers to sell. The ultimate repurchase price is the lowest offered price at which the previously stated number of shares can be repurchased from those shareholders that have submitted offers.[7]

Figure 17.1 shows the average stock price behavior surrounding the announcement date for the three types of stock repurchases just mentioned. For each repurchase the stock's "abnormal" return was determined by relating daily returns on the stock to the corresponding returns on the stock market index.

This was done for the 50-day period immediately prior to the repurchase announcement and the 50-day period immediately following it. These abnormal returns were averaged across firms for each day relative to the announcement and then cumulated across time. The figure shows that open-market repurchases are typically made after the stock price has had an abnormal decline. However, fixed-price and Dutch-auction repurchases are made after a period of fairly normal returns. Also of interest is the observation that the stock price jumped upward on the announcement of the repurchase offer for all three types. (The average size of the abnormal return on the announcement date was 11% for fixed-price, 8% for Dutch-auction, and 2% for open-market repurchases.) Finally, after the repurchase offer expired, the stock price did not tend to fall back to its preannouncement level.

Interestingly, another study found that investors could form profitable investment strategies to take advantage of the observed abnormal return associated with the announcement of a stock repurchase.[8] Specifically, the strategy involves fixed-price self-tender offers where the stock is purchased by the investor in the open market shortly before the offer's expiration date if it is selling at least 3% below the repurchase price. Then the investor tenders the stock to the firm on the expiration date. If the repurchase is oversubscribed (meaning that more shares are submitted for repurchase than the corporation has indicated it

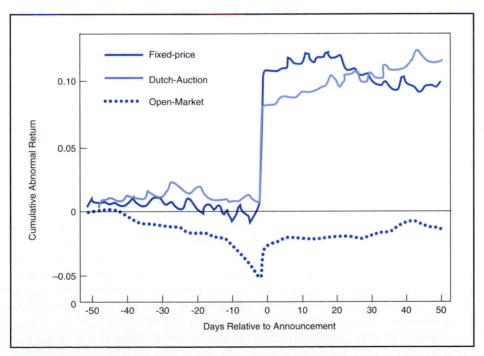

Figure 17.1

Abnormal Stock Price Behavior around Repurchase Announcements

Source: Robert Comment and Gregg A. Jarrell, "The Relative Signalling Power of Dutch-Auction and Fixed-Price Self-Tender Offers and Open-Market Share Repurchases," *Journal of Finance*, 46, no. 4 (September 1991): p. 1254.

will buy), then the number of shares that the corporation does not buy are sold in the marketplace shortly after the expiration date. The result is that for an investment of less than a week, this strategy will generate an abnormal return of more than 9%.

Why do firms repurchase their stock? Previously it was mentioned that one motive was to repel a takeover attempt. Two other explanations have been offered. First, management may be attempting to send a signal to the shareholders (and the public) that the corporation's stock is undervalued in the marketplace. Second, it may be beneficial taxwise to the current shareholders for the firm to use excess cash to repurchase stock instead of using it to pay a cash dividend.

For example, consider a shareholder who bought 10 shares of stock at $40 per share that are now worth $50 per share, resulting in an unrealized capital gain of $10 per share, or $100 in total. Furthermore, the shareholder could receive a $10 per share cash dividend from the firm as part of a general disbursement of excess cash. As a result, the stock price will drop $10 per share, removing the capital gain, but all of this dividend will be treated as taxable income to the shareholder. Alternatively, the corporation could spend the same amount to repurchase its stock. If the shareholder tenders his or her pro rata share, then the investor will receive $100 for two shares of stock (= $100 cash dividend/$50 share price, assuming perfect markets) and have to pay capital gains on only the amount of $100 that exceeds the $80 (= 2 shares × $40) cost of the two shares that were repurchased. Hence the shareholder would have to pay capital gains taxes on only $20 of the $100 at that time but would have unrealized capital gains of $10 per share on the eight shares still owned (as the stock price would remain at $50 per share), upon which capital gains taxes will have to be paid at some later date when they are sold. Thus the shareholder benefits taxwise from a repurchase in two ways in that a *smaller* amount is taxed at that time at a capital gains tax rate which is potentially a *lower* rate than the ordinary income tax rate.

Classified Stock

Some corporations issue two or more classes of common stock. For example, class *A* stock might have a preferred position in regard to dividends but might not have any voting rights. In contrast, class *B* stock might have full voting rights but a lower position in regard to dividends. Often this is equivalent to an issue of preferred stock, along with a normal issue of common stock.

An interesting example involves the three classes of General Motors common stock. These classes are referred to as $1⅔ par value, class *E*, and class *H* stock. One share in each class has 1, ¼, and ½ vote, respectively. In terms of dividends, the class *E* and class *H* stocks are allowed to receive an amount that does not exceed the "adjusted earnings" of GM's Electronic Data Systems and Hughes Electronics subsidiaries, respectively. The $1⅔ par value stock is allowed to receive dividends that do not exceed the remainder of GM's earnings.

Another example involves Canadian corporations. Because of the Canada Income Tax Act of 1971, Canadian firms are allowed to have class *A* and class *B* shares. The only difference between the two classes is that class *A* shares receive cash dividends whereas class *B* shares receive stock dividends. Furthermore, owners of either class can swap their shares one-for-one for shares of the other class at any time.

Americus Trust Securities

An unusual type of security, somewhat like classified stock, involves Americus Trust securities. These securities have been issued by the Americus Shareowner Service Corporation (it should be noted that they are no longer allowed to be issued), and are listed on the American Stock Exchange. They can be described most easily with an example.

Americus buys some of the outstanding shares of Exxon and then issues two kinds of trust securities, *Exxon primes* and *Exxon scores.* An investor can subsequently buy either of these securities through a broker and can find them listed on the American Stock Exchange as "A-xonpr" and "A-xonsc," respectively. Note that Exxon itself has nothing to do with either the creation or subsequent trading of the primes and scores.

The owner of an Exxon prime is entitled to all cash dividends that Exxon pays to Americus, and any price appreciation in Exxon up to a set limit (the "termination claim") at the expiration of the trust security. The owner of an Exxon score is entitled to all of the remaining (if any) price appreciation on Exxon. Given a price limit of $60 and a five-year expiration date, this means that if Exxon is selling for $50 on the expiration date, the prime owner will receive $50 and the score owner will receive nothing. However, if Exxon is selling for $100, then the prime owner will receive $60 and the score owner will receive $40. Currently, there are in excess of 20 companies that have some of their shares divided into primes and scores by Americus.

Letter or Restricted Stock

In the United States, security regulations require that most stock be registered with the SEC before it may be sold in a public offering. Under some conditions, unregistered stock may be sold directly to a purchaser, but its subsequent sale is **restricted.** Such **letter stock** must be held for at least two years and cannot be sold even at that time unless ample information on the company is available and the amount sold is a relatively small percentage of the total amount outstanding. (Indeed, it is called letter stock because the purchaser must provide the SEC with a letter indicating that the shares will be held as an investment and will not be for resale.) However, as mentioned in Chapter 3, under certain circumstances (defined by SEC Rule 144A) large institutional investors are allowed to trade non-public securities issued under this rule among themselves at any time after their issuance.

17.2 CASH DIVIDENDS

Payments made in cash to stockholders are termed **dividends.** These are typically declared quarterly by the board of directors and paid to the stockholders of record at a date specified by the board, known as the **date of record.** The dividends may be of almost any size, subject to certain restrictions such as those contained in the charter or in documents given to creditors. Thus even though this is unusual, dividends may even be larger than the current earnings of the corporation. (If so, they are usually paid out of past earnings.)

Compiling a list of stockholders to receive the dividend is not as simple as it may initially seem, because for many firms the list changes almost constantly as shares are bought and sold. The way of identifying those stockholders who are to receive the dividend is by use of an **ex-dividend date.** Because of the time required to record the transfer of ownership of common stock, major stock exchanges specify an ex-dividend date that is four business days prior to the date of record. Investors purchasing shares before an ex-dividend date are entitled to receive the dividend in question; those purchasing on or after the ex-dividend date are not entitled to the dividend.

For example, a dividend may be declared on May 15 with a date of record of Friday, June 15. In this situation Monday, June 11, would become the ex-dividend date. If an investor bought shares on Friday, June 8, he or she would subsequently receive the cash dividend (unless the shares were sold later in the day on the 8th, in which case the new owner would receive the dividend). However, if the shares were bought on Monday, June 11, the investor would not receive the cash dividend. Besides a declaration date (May 15), an ex-dividend date (June 11), and a date of record (June 15), there is also a fourth date, the "payment date." On this date (perhaps June 25) the checks for the cash dividends are put in the mail or deposited electronically in the accounts of custodian banks.

17.3   STOCK DIVIDENDS AND STOCK SPLITS

Occasionally, the board of directors decides to forgo a cash dividend and "pays" a **stock dividend** instead. For example, if a 5% stock dividend is declared, the owner of 100 shares receives five additional shares that are issued for this occasion. The accounting treatment of a stock dividend is to increase the "common stock" and "capital contributed in excess of par" accounts by an amount equal to the market value of the stock at the time of the dividend times the number of new shares issued. (The "common stock" account would increase by an amount equal to the par value times the number of new shares. The remainder of the increase would go into the "capital contributed in excess of par" account.) In order to keep the total book value of stockholders' equity the same, the "retained earnings" account is reduced by an equivalent amount.

A **stock split** is similar to a stock dividend in that the stockholder owns more shares afterward. However, it is different in both magnitude and accounting treatment. With a stock split, all the old shares are destroyed and new ones are issued with a new par value. Afterwards the number of new shares outstanding is usually larger than the previous number of old shares by 25% or more, with the exact amount depending on the size of the split. In contrast, a stock dividend usually results in an increase of less than 25%. Whereas a stock dividend results in adjustments to the dollar figures in certain stockholders' equity accounts, no adjustments are made for a split. For example, if a $1 par value stock is split 2-for-1, the holder of 200 old shares will receive 400 new $.50 par value shares, and none of the dollar figures in stockholders' equity would change.

A **reverse stock split** reduces the number of shares and increases the par value per share. For example, in a reverse 2-for-1 split, the holder of 200 $1 par value shares would exchange them for 100 $2 par value shares. Again there would not be any change in the dollar figures in stockholders' equity.

Stock dividends and splits must be taken into account when following the price of a company's shares. For example, a fall in price per share may be due solely to a large stock split. To reduce confusion, most financial services provide data adjusted for at least some of these changes. Thus if a stock split 2-for-1 on January 30, 1994, prices prior to that date might be divided by 2 to facilitate comparison.

17.3.1 Ex-Distribution Dates

Similar to the payment of cash dividends, the corporation specifies three dates associated with either stock dividends or stock splits: a declaration date, a date of record, and a payment date. However, there is now an **ex-distribution date** instead of an ex-dividend date. For stock dividends of less than 20%, the procedure is identical to the one described previously for cash dividends—the ex-distribution date is four business days before the date of record, meaning that if you buy the stock after that date, you do not get the additional shares.

For larger stock dividends and all stock splits, the procedure is a bit different in that the ex-distribution date is usually the business day after the payment date (which, in turn, is after the date of record). Hence if a 25% stock dividend is declared on May 15 with a date of record of June 15 and a payment date of June 25, then anyone buying the stock before June 26 will receive the stock dividend. However, those who wait until June 26 to buy the stock will not receive the stock dividend.[9]

17.3.2 Reasons for Stock Dividends and Splits

Why do corporations issue stock dividends and split their stocks? Nothing of importance would appear to be changed, as such actions do not increase revenues or reduce expenses. All that happens is that there is a change in the size of the units in which ownership may be bought and sold. Moreover, because the process involves administrative effort, and costs something to execute, one wonders why it is done.

It is sometimes argued that stockholders respond positively to "tangible" evidence of the growth of their corporation. Another view holds that splits and stock dividends, by decreasing the price per share, may bring the stock's price into a more desirable trading range and hence increase the total value of the amount outstanding.[10]

Figure 17.2 presents the average behavior of stock returns for 219 stock splits that occurred between 1945 and 1965. For each split, the stock's "abnormal" return was determined by relating monthly returns on the stock to the corresponding returns in the stock market. This was done month by month for the

54-month period immediately prior to the split and the 54-month period immediately following it. These abnormal returns were averaged across firms for each month relative to the firm's split and then cumulated across time.

As the figure shows, the stocks tended to have a positive abnormal return of about 30% during the 54 months prior to splitting. Was this due to anticipation of the coming split? Not likely, as these splits are not announced until roughly two months before the effective date (denoted by 0 in the figure). The causal relationship could well be just the reverse: stocks split after unusual price increases. That is, unexpected positive developments (such as unexpected large increases in earnings) caused abnormal increases in the stock prices of these firms, after which the firms decided to split their stock. The behavior of the post-split prices indicates that afterward investors did not continue to receive positive abnormal returns. In the study shown in Figure 17.2, investors actually lost some ground. Other studies, using different stocks and time periods, found either no abnormal returns or slightly positive abnormal returns after the split.[11]

The evidence also suggests that rather than *decreasing* transaction costs, stock splits actually *increased* them. A study of presplit and postsplit behavior showed that after splits, trading volume rose less than proportionately, and both commission costs and bid-ask spreads, expressed as a percentage of value, increased—hardly reactions that are favorable to stockholders.[12] For example, after a 2-for-1 stock split there will be twice as many shares outstanding, so it is reasonable to expect the daily number of shares that are traded to double. It is also reasonable to expect the commission for buying 200 shares after the split to be the same as the commission for buying 100 shares before the split. Instead, it was found that after the split the number of shares traded daily was less than twice as large and the commission was larger.

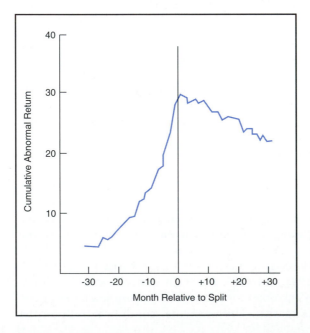

Figure 17.2
Abnormal Stock Returns before and after Stock Splits
Source: Sasson Bar-Yosef and Lawrence D. Brown, "A Re-examination of Stock Splits Using Moving Betas," *Journal of Finance*, 32, no. 4 (September 1977): p. 1074.

CHAPTER 17

Another study of stock splits and stock dividends uncovered an apparent market inefficiency.[13] This study examined the performance of stocks around the "ex" dates associated with their stock splits and dividends. If an investor bought shares of a firm the day before its ex date and sold them the day after the ex date, then on average the investor would make an abnormal return of roughly 2% for stock dividends and 1% for stock splits. Such an observance appears to violate the notion of efficient markets because it suggests that an investor can make abnormal returns by trading stocks using a simple strategy based on publicly available information.

17.4   PREEMPTIVE RIGHTS

Under common law (and most state laws), a stockholder has an inherent right to maintain his or her proportionate ownership of the corporation. The existence of these **preemptive rights** means that when new shares are to be sold, the current stockholders must be given the right of first refusal in regard to the purchase of the new shares.[14] This is accomplished by issuing a certificate to each stockholder that indicates the number of new shares he or she is authorized to purchase. This number will be proportional to the number of existing shares currently owned by the stockholder. Usually, the new shares will be priced below the current market price of the stock, making such **rights** valuable. The stockholder can exercise the rights by purchasing his or her allotted amount of new shares, thereby maintaining his or her proportional ownership in the firm, but at the cost of providing additional capital. Alternatively, the rights can be sold to someone else.[15]

For example, if a firm needs $10,000,000 for new equipment, it may decide to sell new shares in order to raise the capital. Given that the current market price of the stock is $60 per share, a **rights offering** may be used to raise the capital, where the **subscription price** is set at $50 per share.[16] Accordingly, 200,000 (= $10,000,000/$50) new shares are to be sold. Assuming that the firm has 4,000,000 shares outstanding, this means that the owner of one share will receive the right to buy 1/20 (= 200,000/4,000,000) of a new share. Because the number of rights received is equal to the number of shares owned, it can be seen that 20 shares must be owned in order to be able to buy one new share. Thus if a stockholder owns 100 shares, he or she will receive 100 rights allowing him or her to buy 5 [= (1/20) × 100] new shares. These rights are valuable because their owner can buy stock at $50 a share when the market price is significantly higher. The current owner of 100 shares can either use the 100 rights by coming up with cash equal to $250 (= 5 × $50) or sell the 100 rights to someone else. But this raises a question: What is a fair price for the rights?

Rights are distributed in a manner similar to cash dividends. That is, there is a date of record and, four business days earlier, an **ex-rights date.** Before the ex-rights date, the value of a right can be calculated by using the following equation:

$$C_o - (RN + S) = R \qquad (17.2)$$

> where: C_o = *"rights-on" market price of stock,*
> R = *value of a right,*
> N = *number of rights needed to buy one share,*
> S = *subscription price.*

Equation (17.2) can be interpreted in the following manner. If an investor purchases one share before the ex-rights date, by definition he or she pays the market price of C_o, shown on the left-hand side of the equation. Alternatively, the investor could purchase the number of rights necessary to buy one share of the new stock at a cost of RN and set aside an amount of money equal to the subscription price S. The total cost of doing this is $(RN + S)$. The only difference between the two alternatives is that the first one gives the investor not only one share of stock but also one right. Thus, the difference in the cost of the two alternatives, $C_o - (RN + S)$, must equal the value of a right R, as shown in Equation (17.2).

Equation (17.2) can be rewritten as:

$$R = \frac{C_o - S}{N + 1}. \qquad (17.3)$$

Thus in the previous example, the value of a right when the stock is selling for $60 would be equal to approximately $.48 [= ($60 − $50)/(20 + 1)].

On or after the ex-rights date, the value of a right can be calculated by using the following equation:

$$C_e - (RN + S) = 0 \qquad (17.4)$$

where C_e is the ex-rights market price of the stock. The reasoning behind this equation is similar to the reasoning behind Equation (17.2). That is, an investor can purchase one share by either buying it in the open market at a cost of C_e or purchasing the requisite number of rights and setting aside the subscription price, for a total cost of $RN + S$. Because the purchase of one share ex-rights means that the investor does not receive a right, the two alternatives provide the investor with the same item. Thus the cost of these two alternatives should be equivalent, so the difference in their cost should be zero.

Equation (17.4) can be rewritten as:

$$R = \frac{C_e - S}{N}. \qquad (17.5)$$

In the previous example, if the stock is selling for $56 after the ex-rights date, then the value of a right at that time would be approximately $.30 [= ($56 − $50)/20].

Figures 17.3 through 17.6 provide examples of quotations summarizing a day's transactions in stocks traded over-the-counter and on various stock exchanges.

17.5.1 Nasdaq

Active stocks traded with the aid of the National Association of Securities Dealers' Automated Quotation system (Nasdaq) are summarized in the forms shown in Figure 17.3(a) and (b). Transactions in securities designated National Market Issues are summarized in detail, as shown in Figure 17.3(a). High and low prices for trades over the preceding 52 weeks are given, along with the annual per-share amount of dividends, in dollars, based on the latest declared amount. (Letters refer to footnotes providing details concerning extra or special dividends and yields. The footnotes also explain the sporadic entries in the extreme left column and why certain rows are either emboldened or underlined.) This dollar amount is divided by the **closing price** (the price at which the last trade of the day was made) to obtain the figure shown for **dividend yield.** The price–earnings ratio (the closing price divided by the last 12 months' earnings per share) is given next. The remaining entries summarize the day's transactions in the major markets in which the stock is traded. Sales, in hundreds of shares, are indicated, followed by the highest and lowest prices at which trades were completed during the day. The next entry is the closing price, and the final entry shows the difference between the day's closing price and that of the preceding day.

Over-the-counter Nasdaq stocks with somewhat less activity are referred to as Small-Cap Issues; transactions in these stocks are summarized in Figure 17.3(b). Annual per-share dividends are reported first, followed by trading volume (in hundreds of shares) and the price at which the last trade of the day took place. The net change in the last price from the previous day is shown in the right-hand column. It should be noted that investors in these securities transact with dealers, paying the asked price when purchasing shares and receiving the bid price when selling shares. Hence the last price and net change figures may reflect bid or asked prices. It should also be noted that the investor may also have to bear markdowns or markups and commissions, which may be added by the retail broker.[17]

17.5.2 U.S. Stock Exchanges

Activity in stocks traded on U.S. stock exchanges is shown in Figure 17.4. Stocks listed on the New York Stock Exchange are shown in the upper left of the figure. Those listed on the American Stock Exchange are shown in the upper right. The information provided for both of these exchanges is identical in format to the information provided for Nasdaq National Market Issues shown in Figure 17.3(a).

(a) NASDAQ NATIONAL MARKET ISSUES

Quotations as of 4 p.m. Eastern Time
Monday, December 13, 1993

-A-A-A-

(Stock quotation table — NASDAQ National Market Issues listings, columns: 52 Weeks Hi Lo, Stock, Sym, Yld Div % PE, Vol 100s, Hi Lo Close, Net Chg)

(b) NASDAQ SMALL-CAP ISSUES

Quotes at 4 p.m. Eastern Time
Monday, December 13, 1993

(Stock quotation table — NASDAQ Small-Cap Issues listings, columns: Issue, Div, Vol 100s, Last, Chg)

Figure 17.3

Summary of Stocks Traded with the Aid of the Nasdaq System

Source: Reprinted by permission of *The Wall Street Journal*, Dow Jones & Company, Inc., December 14, 1993, pp. C6, C8. All rights reserved worldwide.

Figure 17.4

Summary of Activities in Stocks Traded on U.S. Exchanges

Source: Reprinted by permission of *The Wall Street Journal*, Dow Jones & Company, Inc., December 14, 1993, pp. C3, C10. All rights reserved worldwide.

The bottom panel of Figure 17.4 describes the activity in various regional stock exchanges in the United States. However, any trading that involves securities that are also listed on either the NYSE or AMEX ("dually listed securities") is excluded, because these trades are reflected in either panel (a) or (b). Less information is provided for trading on the regional exchanges than on organized exchanges, as all that is reported are the daily sales and the high, low, and closing prices, along with the change in the close from the previous day.

Figure 17.5 displays trading activity in the "Emerging Company Marketplace" on the American Stock Exchange. Such trading began on March 18, 1992, and involves smaller start-up companies that do not meet the AMEX's regular listing requirements. Previously these stocks were traded on Nasdaq but were not National Market Issues. The information provided in the figure is identical in format to the information presented for the regularly listed AMEX stocks shown in Figure 17.4(b).

17.5.3 Foreign Stock Exchanges

Figure 17.6 displays the trading activities in various foreign stock markets. The top part of the figure shows the trading activities in the two major Canadian markets—Toronto and Montreal. The bottom part shows some of the trading activities in a few other foreign markets. In both parts of the figure the prices given are stated in the local currency of the country in which the exchange is located. The U.S. financial press provides more information for the Canadian markets, presumably because of the greater interest among Americans in the securities traded in these markets.

Figure 17.5

Emerging Company Marketplace on the AMEX

Source: Reprinted by permission of *The Wall Street Journal*, Dow Jones & Company, Inc., December 14, 1993, p. C10. All rights reserved worldwide.

(a) CANADIAN MARKETS

TORONTO

Quotations in Canadian Funds
Quotations in cents unless marked $
Monday, December 13, 1993

Sales	Stock	High	Low	Close	Chg.
358846	Abti Prce	$15	14⅞	15	
35100	Agnico E	$19½	19¼	19¼ + ⅛
46800	Air Canada	$5¼	5⅛	5¼ + ⅛
79414	Alt Energy	$19¼	18½	18¾ − ½
7923	Alta Nat	$16¾	16	16¼ − ⅜
58750	Anderson	$28¼	26	26 − 2
695562	A Barick	$37¼	37¼	37⅞ + ⅞
5700	Atco I f	$16½	16	16½ + ⅛
28051	Aur Res o	$5¾	5½	5¾
263194	BCE Inc	$46	45¾	45¾ − ⅛
19331	BC Gas	$16¾	16½	16¾
655131	Bank N S	$30	29⅝	30
300	Baton	$7⅜	7¾	7⅜
17694	BCE Mobl	$40⅞	40⅜	40⅞ + ¼
852500	Bramalea	39	38	38 − 1
57147	BC Telcom	$23¾	23½	23⅞ + ¼
69250	CAE	$7	6⅞	7 − ⅛
200	CCL A	$10	10	10 − ⅜
10830	CCL B f	$10¼	10⅛	10½ − ⅛
6407	Cabre	$14½	13⅝	13⅞ − ¼
86110	Cambridg	$18¼	18	18¼ + ¼
210350	Cameco	$28	27¼	27¼ − ⅞
320221	CI Bk Com	$32⅜	31¾	32¼ + ⅛
122400	Cdn Nat Res	$16¼	15¾	15¾ − ¼
21500	CP Forest	$19¾	19½	19¾
248114	CP Ltd	$22¾	22	22½
375111	CTire A f	$18	17⅞	17¾ + ⅛
3850	C Util B	$25½	25½	25½
20261	Canfor	$41¾	41½	41½
1200	Cara	490	485	485 − 5
50	Celanese	$59	59	59 − ¾
34600	Cineplex	385	380	380 − 5
1447	Camdev	475	475	475 − 25
27300	Co Steel f	$26½	26¼	26¼ − ⅜
12400	CocaCBev	$5⅝	5½	5½ − ⅛
2473	Conwest	$20⅜	20⅜	20⅝ + ⅛
2434	Crownx	$13¼	13¼	13¼ − ¾
570447	Crownx f	$6⅞	6⅝	6¾ − ⅛
45214	Corel	$26	25⅜	25⅜ − ⅛

Sales	Stock	High	Low	Close	Chg.
88165	DY 4 syst	$27½	27	27¾ − ⅛
64700	Delrina C o	$26¼	26⅛	26¼ + ½
16600	Derlan	$5½	5	5⅛ + ⅛
2800	Dicknsn A f	$6⅞	6⅝	6⅞ + ¼
356686	Dofasco	$22¾	23⅝	22½ + ⅛
61619	Dundee A f	$9⅞	8⅞	9⅛ + ⅜
4540	Dupont A f	$48	47½	48 + ¼
100300	Dylex A f	150	145	147 + 3
60400	ELAN Eng	$9⅞	9⅝	9¾
114726	Euro Nev	$48¾	47½	47¾ + ½
14673	FCA Intl	350	340	350 + 20
1600	FPI Ltd	325	325	325
27600	Fahnstk A f	$11⅞	11½	11¾ + ¼
233983	Fed Ind A	$8½	8¼	8⅜
1700	Finning L	$19¾	18⅞	19¾
44270	Flet CCan A	$21½	21⅜	21½ + ⅛
139120	FSesn HI f	$14¼	13⅜	13⅜ − ⅞
69711	Franco	$94¼	92½	93¼ + ¾
64350	Geac Comp	$17¼	16½	17¾ + ⅝
6000	Gendis A	$20¼	20	20 − ½
150984	Gentra Inc	43½	42	42½ − ½
103750	Goldcorp f	$9¼	9	9¼
8218	Hayes D	$17⅜	16⅜	17¾ + ⅛
90801	Hees Intl	$14¼	13⅝	14⅛ + ⅜
237138	Hemlo Gld	$14⅜	14½	14⅜ − ¼
1200	Hollinger I	$13¾	13¾	13¾
9775	Horsham f	$19¾	19½	19½
93307	H Bay Co	$40⅞	40¼	40⅝ + ½
2200	ISM Info	$13	13	13
129253	Imasco L	$38½	38¼	38⅜
197074	IForest A f	$20¼	19¼	19⅝ + ⅛
103801	Intrprov P	$32¼	32	32½ − ½
21750	I SemiT Af	$17¾	17½	17½ − ½
112945	Ipsco	$26	25½	25½ − ½
2399	ISG Tech	$16½	16	16½
472	Ivaco A f	$6½	6½	6½
593950	Jannock	$18½	18	18½ + ⅜
5548	Labatt	$23⅝	22⅝	23⅜ + ½
81446	Loblaw Co	$23	22¾	23 − ¼
138410	Mackenzie	$11½	11¼	11½ + ⅛
17396	Magna A f	$60½	59½	59¾ − ⅝
81525	M L Foods	$12⅞	12⅝	12¾ − ⅛
1750	MDS H A	$13¼	13⅛	13¼ + ⅛

Sales	Stock	High	Low	Close	Chg.
46182	Maclean H	$12½	12¼	12%
7162	Maritime f	$25⅜	25¼	25¼ − ⅛
237600	Mark Res	$8⅞	8¾	8⅞ + ⅛
166462	Molson A f	$26¼	26⅜	26⅝ + ¼
200	Molson B	$26¼	26¼	26¼
30400	Morisn P	$8¾	8⅜	8⅝
159798	Mlnd Wlyn	$13½	13¼	13⅜ − ⅛
11250	Noma A f	$7	6⅞	7
126600	Noranda F	$12	11⅞	11⅞
158674	Noranda f	$26½	25½	26 + ⅝
53304	Norcen	$16⅝	16½	16¼ − ⅜
6800	NA palldm o	$7½	7¼	7½ + ½
567720	Nova Cor f	$9¼	9	9¼
79443	NS Power	$13	12⅞	12⅞ − ¼
52275	Nowsco W	$20½	20¼	20½ − ¾
60949	Onex C f	$17¼	17¼	17¼
18840	Oshawa A f	$21¾	21½	21¾ + ⅛
201087	PWA Corp	145	134	136 + 5
28200	Pgurin A f	315	305	310 − 5
29390	PanCan P	$40	39½	39½ − ½
88873	Petro Cdn	$12	11½	11½ − ⅛
476082	Placer Dm	$34	33¼	33⅞ + 1
65782	Poco Pete	$8⅞	8⅜	8¾ − ⅛
75687	Ptash Cor	$30	29⅞	30 + ⅛
1144	QSR o	205	202	205
21000	Rayrock f	16½	15⅞	15⅞
85674	Renisanc	$26⅞	25¼	25¼ − ⅞
25300	Rogers Cn bf	$34⅝	34½	34⅝ + ½
5020	Rogers A	$22½	22¼	22⅝ − ⅝
209659	Rogers B f	$22¼	21⅞	22¼ − ⅛
422626	Royal Bnk	$28¼	27¾	28
120004	Sceptre R	$12½	12	12 − ⅜
3300	Scotts f	$9⅝	9½	9½ − ⅜
78116	Sears Can	$10	9¾	9¾ + ½
35700	SHL Systm	$9	8⅞	9 + ½
60125	Shell Can	$36¼	36¼	36½ + ½
183304	Sherritt	10⅛	10¾	10⅞ + ½
7545	Southam	$17¼	17½	17⅝ − ¼
10200	Spar Aero	$17⅞	17¾	17¾ + ¼
279301	Stelco A	$8½	7½	8 + ½
139059	Talisman	$27¾	26¼	27 − ⅝
166700	Teck B f	$23¼	23⅜	23⅜ − ¼
259844	Telus Cor	$16½	15⅞	16

Sales	Stock	High	Low	Close	Chg.
184700	ThomCor	$16½	15⅞	16⅛ + ⅛
846041	Tor Dm Bk	$21¾	21¼	21⅝ + ⅛
336675	TIPS	2195	2180	2185 + 10
16540	Torstar B f	$24¾	24	24¾ + ⅜
334113	TrAlt corp	$15½	15	15½
192905	TrCan PL	$20½	19⅝	20 + ⅛
57770	Trilon A	345	330	330 − 10
22130	Trimac	$15½	15	15½
241450	Trizec A f	92	88	90 − 1
4266	Unicorp A f	50	50	50
96796	Wascana	$8¾	8½	8½ − ¼
100	Westmin	$5¾	5⅝	5⅝ − ⅛
7676	Weston	$38⅞	38½	38½

Total sales 84,526,552 shares.

f-No voting rights or restricted voting rights.

MONTREAL

Sales	Stock	High	Low	Close	Chg.
77588	Bank Mont	$27½	27½	27⅝
36000	Bio Pha	$13½	13½	13¼ + ¼
2924	BombrdrA	$19⅞	19¼	19⅝ − ¼
85387	BombrdrB	$19¾	19¼	19⅝ − ¼
20551	Cambior	$20½	20	20
20803	Cascades	$06⅝	06½	06½ − ⅛
4603	DomTxtA	$09¼	09⅛	09⅛
130228	NatBk Cda	$11	10¾	10¾ − ¼
218807	Power Corp	$21½	21	21¼ + ¼
29350	Quebecr A	$18½	17⅞	17⅞ − ¼
93134	Quebecr B	$18¾	18	18 − ⅛
1075	Quebecr Pr	$25½	24⅞	24⅞ − ⅛
21217	Teleglobe	20	19¼	20 + ¼
27384	U V A	$07⅞	07¾	07¾ − ⅛
114474	Videotron	$25¾	25½	25⅝

Total Sales 11,122,742 shares; as of 4:00 pm.

(b) OTHER FOREIGN MARKETS

Monday, December 13, 1993

TOKYO
(in yen)

	Close	Prev. Close
ANA	1090	1090
Aiwa	1840	1820
Ajinomoto	1170	1180
Alps Elec	941	891
Amada Co	885	876
Anritsu	1020	1010
Asahi Chem	612	605
Asahi Glass	1090	1070
Bank of Tokyo	1570	1570
Bk of Yokohama	971	995
Banyu Pharm	898	906
Bridgestone	1300	1230
Brother Ind	420	416
CSK	2420	2430
Canon Inc	1440	1420
Canon Sales	2970	2890
Casio Computer	985	965
Chubu Pwr	2910	2990
Chugai Pharm	1260	1250
Citizen Watch	792	786
Dai Nippon Prnt	1620	1610
Dai-ichi Kangyo	1900	1930
Daiei	1430	1450
Daiichi Seiyaku	1480	1410
Dainippon Ink	446	460
Dainippon Pharm	1000	1010
Daiwa House	1500	1510
Daiwa Securities	1280	1280
Eisai	1810	1810
Ezaki Glico	1100	1130
Fanuc	3760	3660
Fuji Bank	1930	1920
Fuji Hi	280	281
Fuji Photo Film	2480	2430
Fujisawa Pharm	1030	1070
Fujitsu	835	815
Furukawa Elec	513	510
Green Cross	972	975
Haseko	665	681
Hirose Elec	6010	5860
Hitachi Cable	700	685
Hitachi Credit	1820	1860
Hitachi Ltd	840	810
Hitachi Maxell	1720	1700
Hitachi Metals	875	874
Hitachi Sales	512	518
Honda Motor	1480	1430
Hosiden Elec	1780	1790
Hoya	1790	1800
IHI	405	421

	Close	Prev. Close
Mitsubishi Kasei	450	445
Mitsubishi Matl	383	387
Mitsubishi Trust	1210	1210
Mitsubishi Whse	1440	1420
Mitsui Fudosan	1160	1170
Mitsui Mar&Fire	775	775
Mitsui Trust	915	916
Mitsui & Co	716	691
Mitsukoshi	805	790
Mochida Pharm	2150	2160
NCR Japan	905	879
NEC	904	880
NGK Spark	951	950
NIFCO	1280	1280
NKK	240	237
NSK	560	535
NTN	498	520
NTT	735000	730000
New Oji Paper	928	925
Nihon Unisys Ltd	1270	1200
Nikko Securities	1110	1130
Nikon Corp	829	812
Nintendo	6870	6860
Nippon Chemi-con	535	521
Nippon Columbia	475	460
Nippon El Glass	1140	1140
Nippon Express	985	988
Nippon Hodo	1950	2000
Nippon Meat	1540	1580
Nippon Oil	657	669
Nippon Paper	506	518
Nippon Sanso	470	455
Nippon Shinpan	925	910
Nippon Steel	311	313
Nissan Motor	717	723
Nissin Food	2930	2910
Nitsuko	790	780
Nomura Securities	1840	1850
OKK	400	363
Obayashi Corp	607	615
Odakyu Railway	701	695
Oki Elec Ind	456	443
Okuma Corp	569	570
Olympus Optical	978	949
Omron	1430	1380
Ono Pharm	5100	5200
Onoda Cement	513	506
Onward	1060	1060
Orient Corp	705	726
Pioneer Electron	2710	2670
Renown	465	456
Ricoh Co	656	665

LONDON
(in pence)

	Close	Prev. Close
Toyoda Mach	536	550
Toyota Motor	1790	1700
Tsugami	335	342
Uny	1340	1320
Ushio	759	740
Wacoal	1320	1320
Yamaha	892	930
Yamaichi Sec	650	654
Yamanouchi Phm	2120	2080
Yamatake-Hnywl	1310	1360
Yamato Transport	1130	1130
Yamazaki Baking	2220	2260
Yasuda Fire	734	734
Yokogawa Elec	770	760

	Close	Prev. Close
Abbey National	461	467
Albert Fisher	64	64
Allied-Lyons	617	624
Argyll Group	258	261
Arlo Wiggins	240	240
Assoc Brit Fds	539	539
BAA PLC	996	994
Barclays	609	612
Bass	527	543
BAT Indus	515	523
Blue Circle	338	345
BOC Group	632	635
Body Shop	214	212.5
Boots	550	550
Borland	1200	1200
Bowater Indus	474	457
BPB Indus	316	313
British Aero	417	421
British Airws	438	435
British Gas	352.5	346
British Pete	324	315
British Steel	134	134
British Telcom	464	469.5
BTR	338	348.5
Burmah Castrol	801	799
Cable&Wireless	488	498
Cadbury Schwp	489	489
Caradon	367	370
Charter Cons	710	722
Coats Viyella	267	269
Commercial Un	647	653
Courtaulds	462	459

	Close	Prev. Close
Sedgwick Grp	186	186
Shell Trnspt	697	693
Siebe PLC	571	570
SmithKln Bchm	375	375
Smith&Nephew	145.5	146.5
Std Chartrd	1195	1212
Storehouse	232	231
Sun Alliance	373	380
TI Group	390	386
Tarmac	165	166
Tate & Lyle	399	398
Tesco	205	199
Thorn EMI	992	997
Tomkins	231	229
Trafalgar Hse	87.5	85.5
TSB Group	248	243
Utd Biscuits	349	347
Unilever	1174	1180
Vodafone	567	568
Warburg	894	900
Wellcome	627	627
Williams Hldgs	348	352
WPP Group	94	94

South African Mines
(in U.S. dollars)

	Close	Prev. Close
Bracken	0.55	0.55
Deelkraal	2.05	2.15
Doornfontein	1.10	1.05
Durban Deep	11.25	11.00
E. Rand Gold	2.38	2.08
E. Rand Prop	1.31	1.12
Elandsrand	6.50	6.25
Grootvlei	2.45	2.25
Harmony	5.05	4.95
Hartebstftn	6.25	6.00
Impala Pltm	12.88	12.50
Kinross	17.75	16.88
Leslie	1.88	1.73
Loraine	5.35	4.80
Randfontein	10.00	9.44
Rustenburg	16.88	16.62
Southvaal	30.62	29.38
Stilfontein	1.28	1.23
Unisel	2.33	2.23
West Areas	9.35	9.15
Winkelhaak	16.50	16.00

MILAN
(in lire)

	Close	Prev. Close
Banca Com	5075	5100
Benetton	25015	24710
CIR	1620	1595
FIAT Com	4276	4165
FIAT Pref	2240	2170
Generali	38350	38250
Mediobanca	14300	13995
Montedison	812	771
Olivetti Com	1999	1978
Olivetti NC	1450	1394
Pirelli Co	3649	3661
Pirelli SpA	2090	2079
Rinascente	8220	8350
RAS	27995	27850
Saipem	3300	3249
SIP	3410	3345
Snia	1425	1365

PARIS
(in French francs)

	Close	Prev. Close
Accor	585	583
Air Liquide	831	832
Alcatel Alstm	803	808
AXA Group	1549	1569
BSN-Gervais	880	871
Carrefour	4110	4090
Club Med	343.4	337
Dassault Avitn	480	484.2
Elf Aquitaine	417.8	420.4
Elf Sanofi	1012	1013
Euro Disneyld	35.25	35.35
Generale Eaux	2746	2760
Havas	461	458.5
Imetal	555	565
Lafarge Coppe	435.3	437
LVMH	3776	3810
Machines Bull	27.1	24.9
Matra-Hachette	142.3	144.2
Michelin	192	190.2
L'Oreal	1248	1250
Paribas	474	476
Pernod Ricard	393.8	390
Peugeot	732	730
Saint Gobain	588	591
Schneider	418.2	410
Soc Generale	744	744
Suez	345.7	344

	Close	Prev. Close
Elsevier	161.60	164.30
Fokker	20.10	20.20
Gist-Brocades	51.90	51.90
Heineken	208.40	209.50
Hoogovens	44.70	45.30
Hunter Douglas	74.40	74.60
Intl Ndrindn Gr	89.50	89.30
KLM	40.10	40.20
KNP BT	42.50	42.40
Nedlloyd	53.10	53.50
Oce-van Grntn	60.50	60.20
Pakhoed Hldg	49.10	47.60
Philips	38.90	39.30
Robeco	119.50	119.30
Rodamco	60	60
Rolinco	121.20	121
Rorento	97	97.10
Royal Dutch	196.70	195.80
Unilever	219.20	221.80
VOC	42.60	41.50
VNU	152.70	151.60
Wolters Kluwer	113.90	113.60

HONG KONG
(in Hong Kong dollars)

	Close	Prev. Close
Bank E Asia	48	47.50
Cathay Pacific	12.70	12.40
Cheung Kong	41.25	40.75
China L & P	51.50	52
Dairy Farm	13.60	13.80
Hang Seng Bk	64.50	64.50
HK Electric	27.10	26.70
HK Land	21.80	21.70
HK Telecom	15.90	16
HSBC Hldgs	96.50	95.50
Hutchsn Whmp	37.50	37
Hysan Develop	25.40	25.50
Jardine Mathsn	72	72.50
Sun Hung Kai	55.50	55.50
Swire Pacific	61	61.50
Wharf Holdings	30.25	30.25

SYDNEY
(in Australian dollars)

	Close	Prev. Close
Amcor	9.34	9.38
ANZ Group	5	5.06
Ashton	2.42	2.42
Boral	4.19	4.12
Bougainville	0.64	0.63

Figure 17.6

Summary of Trading Activities on Selected Foreign Exchanges

Source: Reprinted by permission of *The Wall Street Journal*, Dow Jones & Company, Inc., December 14, 1993, p. C12. All rights reserved worldwide.

The Securities and Exchange Commission requires the officers and directors of a corporation whose securities are traded on an organized exchange to report any transactions they have made in the firm's shares. Such a report, known as form 4, must be filed within ten days following the month in which the transaction takes place. This reporting requirement is also applicable to any stockholder who owns 10% or more of a firm's shares.[18] Such stockholders, officers, and directors are often referred to as **insiders.** The information they provide about their trading is subsequently reported in the Securities and Exchange Commission's monthly *Official Summary of Insider Transactions*.[19] For example, the summary of trades made in January (and reported by early February) is published early in March. Thus up to two months may elapse before knowledge of such trades becomes widespread.

The Securities Exchange Act of 1934 prohibits corporate insiders from short selling (discussed in Chapter 2). Furthermore, it requires them to return all short-term profits from security transactions in their own stocks to the corporation. For this purpose, "short term" is defined as less than six months, meaning that the shares were both bought and sold within a six-month time period.[20] As a result of this requirement, few insiders buy and sell within a six-month time period. Instead, most prefer to spread their buy-and-sell orders over longer time periods so that they do not have to return their profits.

In the United States it is illegal for anyone to enter into a security transaction if he or she has taken advantage of material "inside" information (that is, substantive nonpublic information) about the corporation that is unavailable to other people involved in the transaction. This proscription includes not only insiders but also those to whom they give such secret information. (The recipient of such a "tip" is termed the "tippee".)

Legally there are two types of nonpublic information: that which is "private" (that is, legal) and that which is "inside" (that is, possibly illegal). Unfortunately, the distinction between the two types is highly ambiguous, causing continuous problems for security analysts.

Legal issues aside, two questions of relevance to outside investors may be posed: (1) Do insiders make unusual profits on transactions in their own stocks? and (2) If they do, can others profit by following their example as soon as it becomes public knowledge?

Insiders trade their stock for many reasons. For example, some purchases result from the exercise of options, and some sales result from the need for cash. Moreover, it is not unusual to find some insiders purchasing a stock during a month in which other insiders are selling it. However, when a major piece of inside information suggests that a stock's value differs significantly from its current market price, it is reasonable to expect a preponderance of insider trades on one side of the market (that is, either purchases or sales).

One way to search for such situations is to examine the *Official Summary* and count the number of days during a month that each insider traded his or her firm's stock (excluding the exercise of options).[21] If the number of days on which purchases were made exceeds those on which sales were made, the individual can be counted as a net purchaser during that month; and if the converse holds, the individual would be a net seller. Next the number of net purchasers and sellers for the firm's stock can be considered. If there were at least, say, three more net purchasers than net sellers, it might be inferred that, on balance, favorable insider information motivated the insider trades during the month. Conversely, if there are at least three more net sellers than net purchasers, it might be inferred that, on balance, unfavorable insider information motivated the insider trades.

Different cutoff levels could be used in this process to reflect the intensity of insider trading. A cutoff of 1 would require a simple majority of trades of one type, whereas a cutoff of 5 would require a "supermajority" of trades of one type.

Such a procedure was used in a detailed study of insider transactions during the 1950s and 1960s.[22] Table 17.1 summarizes the key results. The two columns on the right-hand side of the table indicate the "abnormal" returns over an eight-month period on securities that exceeded the cutoff level for insider trading. For example, during the 1960s, if an investor purchased every stock in the sample for which there were three or more net purchasers, and sold every stock for which there were three or more net sellers during a month, more or less coincident with the transactions of the insiders themselves, then the investor would have earned, on average, an abnormal return of 5.07% over the subsequent eight months. If the transactions had been made instead at roughly the time the information was published in the *Official Summary*, an average abnormal return of 4.94% would have been earned over the next eight months.

As the first row in the table shows, a bare majority of insider trades does not appear to isolate possible effects of insider information. But a majority of 3, 4, or 5 does seem to do so. The figures shown are gross of any transaction costs; but even so, it appears that insiders can and do make money from their special knowledge of their companies. This is not surprising, because if anyone can know the true value of a firm, it should be the insiders. As the information these insiders presumably are using is nonpublic in nature, these findings suggest that markets are not strong-form efficient. (The notion of market efficiency was introduced in Chapter 4.)

TABLE 17.1
ABNORMAL RETURNS ASSOCIATED WITH INSIDER TRADING

Sample			Average Abnormal Return (%) Over Eight Months Following	
Cutoff (No. of Net Purchasers or Sellers)	No. of Cases	Period	Month of Transaction	Month Information Became Publicly Available
1	362	1960s	1.36	.70
3	861	1960s	5.07	4.94
4	293	1950s	5.14	4.12
5	157	1950s	4.48	4.08

Source: Jeffrey F. Jaffe, "Special Information and Insider Trading," *Journal of Business*, 47, no. 3 (July 1974): pp. 421, 426. © 1974, The University of Chicago.

On the other hand, the abnormal returns associated with transactions that could have been made by outsiders, using only publicly available information on insider trading, are quite surprising. Moreover, those associated with cutoffs of 3, 4, or 5 pass statistical tests designed to see if they might result simply from chance. After transaction costs, trades designed to capitalize on such information appear to still produce abnormal returns (although not highly so), suggesting that markets are not even semistrong-form efficient. However, more recent studies have found that outsiders cannot use the publicly available information about insider trading to make abnormal profits, and thus support the notion that markets are semistrong-form efficient.[23] With such conflicting evidence it appears that whether or not insider trading information can be profitably used by outsiders remains an open question.

17.7   EX ANTE AND EX POST VALUES

Equilibrium theories such as the Capital Asset Pricing Model and the Arbitrage Pricing Theory imply that in the opinion of well-informed investors, securities with different attributes will have different expected returns. Thus the focus of these theories is on future or *ex ante* (Latin for "before the fact") expected returns. However, only historical or *ex post* (Latin for "after the fact") actual returns are subsequently observed. These historical returns are undoubtedly different from the expected returns, making it extremely difficult to tell whether security attributes and expected returns do in fact go together in the manner implied by either the CAPM or the APT. Moreover, such theories are relatively silent concerning simple ways in which a security's future expected return and attributes might be estimated by examining historical returns.

To bridge this gap, investigators have used the average historical return of a security as an estimate of its expected return. This requires an assumption that the expected return did not change over some arbitrary time period and that this time period contains a sufficient number of historical returns to make a reasonably accurate estimate of the expected return. However, an objection may be made in that expectations almost certainly would have changed over the time period needed to obtain a useful estimate of the expected return for any given security.[24] Despite this objection, it is worthwhile to examine historical returns to see how they might be used to come up with meaningful predictions about the future.[25] The next section explores the prediction of a firm's beta. It begins by discussing the estimation of the firm's historical beta by use of the market model.

17.8   COMMON STOCKS BETAS

For purposes of portfolio management, the relevant risk of a security concerns its impact on the risk of a well-diversified portfolio. In the world of the CAPM, such portfolios would be subject primarily to market risk. This suggests the importance of a security's beta, which measures its sensitivity to future market movements. To estimate beta, in principle the possible sources of such movements should be considered. Then the reaction of the security's price to each of these sources should be estimated, along with the probability of each reaction. In the process, the economics of the relevant industry and firm, the impact of both operating and financial leverage on the firm, and other fundamental factors should be taken into account.

But what about investigating the extent to which the security's price moved with the market in the past? Such an approach ignores myriad possible differences between the past and the future. However, it is easily done and provides a useful starting point.

As shown in Chapter 8, a security's beta can be regarded as the slope of the market model. If this line were constant over time, meaning that it was not changing from period to period, then the **historical beta** for a security could be estimated by examining the historical relationship between the returns on the security and on a market index. The statistical procedure used for making such estimates of *ex post* betas is **simple linear regression,** also known as ordinary least squares (OLS).[26]

As an example, consider estimating the *ex post* beta for Widget Manufacturing (WM) using a hypothetical market index. Table 17.2 presents the most recent 16 quarterly returns on both WM and the index, and the calculations necessary to determine WM's *ex post* beta and alpha, as well as certain other statistical parameters. As can be seen, WM's beta and alpha were equal to .63 and .79%, respectively, over this period.[27]

Given these values for alpha and beta, the market model for WM is:

$$r_{WM} = .79\% + .63 r_I + \epsilon_{WM}. \tag{17.6}$$

Figure 17.7 presents a scatter diagram of the returns on WM (r_{WM}) and the index r_I. Also shown in the figure is a graph of the market model except that the random error term is deleted—that is, the figure has a graph of the following line:

$$r_{WM} = .79\% + .63 r_I. \tag{17.7}$$

The vertical distance of each point in the scatter diagram from this line represents an estimate of the size of the random error term for the corresponding quarter. The exact distance can be found by rewriting Equation (17.6) as:

$$r_{WM} - (.79\% + .63 r_I) = \epsilon_{WM}. \tag{17.8}$$

For example, looking at part (B) of Table 17.2, three quarters ago (quarter 14) the return on WM and the index were 7.55% and 2.66%, respectively. The value of ϵ_{WM} for that quarter can be calculated by using Equation (17.8) as follows:

$$7.55\% - [.79\% + (.63 \times 2.66\%)] = 5.08\%.$$

The values of ϵ_{WM} can be similarly calculated for the other 15 quarters of the estimation period. The standard deviation of the resulting set of 16 numbers is an estimate of the **standard deviation of the random error term** (or residual standard deviation), and is shown in Table 17.2 to be equal to 6.67%. This number can be viewed as an estimate of the historical unique risk of WM.

TABLE 17.2
MARKET MODEL FOR WIDGET MANUFACTURING

(A) Data

Quarter		WM Returns = Y (1)	Index Returns = X (2)	Y^2 (3)	X^2 (4)	$Y \times X$ (5)
1	1	−13.38%	2.52%	178.92	6.35	−33.71
	2	16.79	5.45	282.00	29.71	91.54
	3	−1.67	0.76	2.77	0.57	−1.26
	4	−3.46	2.36	11.99	5.58	−8.18
2	5	10.22	8.56	104.53	73.36	87.57
	6	7.13	8.67	50.79	75.19	61.80
	7	6.71	10.80	45.07	116.59	72.49
	8	7.84	3.33	61.47	11.08	26.10
3	9	2.15	−5.07	4.62	25.66	−10.89
	10	7.95	7.10	63.22	50.42	56.46
	11	−8.05	−11.57	64.74	133.87	93.09
	12	7.68	4.65	58.97	21.58	35.67
4	13	4.75	14.59	22.55	212.97	69.29
	14	7.55	2.66	57.03	7.05	20.05
	15	−2.36	3.81	5.58	14.54	−9.01
	16	4.98	7.99	24.78	63.85	39.78
Sum (Σ) =		54.84	66.62	1039.03	848.38	590.80
		= ΣY	= ΣX	= ΣY^2	= ΣX^2	= ΣXY

(B) Calculations

1. Beta:

$$\frac{(T \times \Sigma XY) - (\Sigma Y \times \Sigma X)}{(T \times \Sigma X^2) - (\Sigma X)^2} = \frac{(16 \times 590.80) - (54.84 \times 66.62)}{(16 \times 848.38) - (66.62)^2} = .63$$

2. Alpha:

$$[\Sigma Y/T] - [Beta \times (\Sigma X/T)] = [54.84/16] - [.63 \times (66.62/16)] = .79\%$$

3. Standard Deviation of Random Error Term:

$$\{[\Sigma Y^2 - (Alpha \times \Sigma Y) - (Beta \times \Sigma XY)]/[T - 2]\}^{1/2}$$
$$= \{[1039.03 - (.79 \times 54.84) - (.63 \times 590.80)]/[16 - 2]\}^{1/2} = 6.67\%$$

4. Standard Error of Beta:

Standard Deviation of Random Error Term/$\{\Sigma X^2 - [(\Sigma X)^2/T]\}^{1/2}$
$$= 6.67/\{848.38 - [(66.62)^2/16]\}^{1/2} = .28$$

5. Standard Error of Alpha:

Standard Deviation of Random Error Term/$\{T - [(\Sigma X)^2/\Sigma X^2]\}^{1/2}$
$$= 6.67/\{16 - [(66.62)^2/848.38]\}^{1/2} = 2.03$$

6. Correlation Coefficient:

$$\frac{(T \times \Sigma XY) - (\Sigma Y \times \Sigma X)}{\{[(T \times \Sigma Y^2) - (\Sigma Y)^2] \times [(T \times \Sigma X^2) - (\Sigma X)^2]\}^{1/2}}$$

$$= \frac{(16 \times 590.80) - (54.84 \times 66.62)}{\{[(16 \times 1039.03) - (54.84)^2] \times [(16 \times 848.38) - (66.62)^2]\}^{1/2}} = .52$$

7. Coefficient of Determination:

$$(Correlation\ Coefficient)^2 = (.52)^2 = .27$$

8. Coefficient of Nondetermination:

$$1 - Coefficient\ of\ Determination = 1 - .27 = .73$$

*All summations are to be carried out over t, where t goes from 1 to T (in this example, t = 1, 2, . . ., 16).

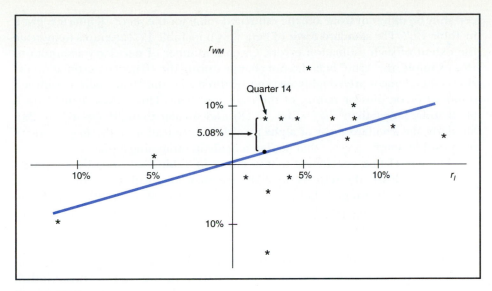

Figure 17.7
Market Model for WM

The market model for WM that is shown in Figure 17.7 corresponds to the regression line for the scatter diagram. Recalling that a straight line is defined by its intercept and slope, it can be shown that there are no other values for alpha and beta that will define a straight line that fits the scatter diagram any better than the regression line. This means that there is no line that could be drawn that would result in a smaller standard deviation of the random error term. Thus the regression line is often referred to as the line of "best fit."

Equivalently, the line of best fit is the line that has the smallest sum of squared values of the random error terms. That is, the 16 random error terms associated with the regression line can each be squared and then summed. This sum (the sum of squared errors) is smaller for the line of best fit than the sum associated with any other line.

For example, in Equation (17.8) if alpha equalled 1.5% and beta equalled .8, then the random error term ϵ_{WM} could be calculated for each of the 16 quarters. With these 16 values, the standard deviation of the random error term could be calculated by squaring each value, summing up the squared values, and dividing the sum by 14 $[= (16 - 2)]$. The standard deviation of the random error term would then be the square root of this number. However, it would be larger than 6.67%, which is the standard deviation of the random error term associated with the line of best fit—that is, the line with an alpha of .79% and a beta of .63.

It should be remembered that a security's "true" historical beta cannot be observed. All that can be done is to estimate its value. Thus even if a security's "true" beta remained the same forever, its estimated value, obtained in the manner shown in Table 17.2, would still change from time to time because of mistakes (known as sampling errors) in estimating it. For example, if a different set of 16 quarters were examined, the resulting estimated beta for WM would almost certainly be different from .63, the estimated value for the set of 16 quarters given in Table 17.2. The **standard error of beta** shown in Table 17.2 attempts to indicate the extent of such estimation errors. Given a number of necessary assumptions (for example, the "true" beta did not change during the 16-quarter estimation period), the chances are roughly two out of three that the "true" beta is within a standard error, plus or minus, of the estimated beta. Thus WM's "true" beta is likely to be larger than .35 (= .63 − .28) and smaller than .91 (= .63 + .28). Similarly, the **standard error of alpha** provides an indication of the magnitude of the possible sampling error that has been made in estimating alpha.

The **correlation coefficient** that is shown in Table 17.2 provides an indication of how closely the returns on WM were associated with the returns on the index. Because its range is between −1 and +1, the value for WM of .52 indicates a mildly strong positive relationship between WM and the index. This means that larger returns for WM seem to be associated with larger returns on the index.

The **coefficient of determination** represents the proportion of variation in the return on WM that is related to the variation in the return on the index. That is, it shows how much of the movements in WM's returns can be explained by movements in the returns on the index. With a value of .27 it can be seen that 27% of the movements in the return on WM during the 16-quarter estimation period can be attributed to movements in the return on the index.

Because the **coefficient of nondetermination** is 1 minus the coefficient of determination, it represents the proportion of movements in the return on WM that is not due to movements in the return on the index. Thus 73% of the movements in WM cannot be attributed to movements in the index.

Figure 17.8 shows a page from the Security Risk Evaluation report prepared by Merrill Lynch, Pierce, Fenner & Smith Inc. Percentage price changes for many stocks, calculated for each of 60 months (when available), were compared by means of the corresponding percentage changes in the Standard & Poor's 500 using the market model in Table 17.2. Seven of the resulting values from this analysis are of interest for each stock.

The values shown under *Beta* and *Alpha* indicate the slope and intercept, respectively, of the straight line that is the best fit for the scatter diagram of the percentage price changes for the stock and index. For example, during the 60-month period covered, the stock of Ask Computer had a beta and alpha of 1.65 and −.06%, respectively.

The value of *R-Sqr*, short for **R-squared,** is equivalent to the coefficient of determination shown in Table 17.2.[28] Having a value of .37 means that 37% of the variation in Ask Computer's price changes could be attributed to changes in the market index over the 60-month period.

The value for *Resid Std Dev-n* (**residual standard deviation**) corresponds to the standard deviation of the random error term in Table 17.2. Ask Computer can be seen to have a residual standard deviation of 10.82%.

Std. Err. of Beta (standard error of beta) indicates that there is roughly a two out of three chance that the "true" beta for Ask Computer is between 1.37 (= 1.65 − .28) and 1.93 (= 1.65 + .28). Similarly, the value under *Std. Err. of Alpha* indicates that there is roughly a two out of three chance that the "true" alpha for Ask Computer lies between −1.47 (= −.06 − 1.41) and 1.35 (= −.06 + 1.41).

Ticker Symbol	Security Name	92/04 Close Price	Beta	Alpha	R-Sqr	Resid Std Dev-n	Std. Err. of Beta	Std. Err. of Alpha	Adjusted Beta	Number of Observ
AOI	AOI COAL CO	0.500	1.11	−1.79	0.07	19.23	0.49	2.51	1.07	60
APAT	APA OPTICS INC	4.875	0.60	0.80	0.08	9.66	0.25	1.26	0.73	60
APIE	API ENTERPRISES INC	0.688	1.00	2.51	0.02	26.90	0.69	3.51	1.00	60
ASKI	ASK COMPUTER SYS INC	14.875	1.65	−0.06	0.37	10.82	0.28	1.41	1.43	60
ATV	ARC INTL CORP	0.813	1.22	−1.38	0.07	20.71	0.53	2.70	1.15	60
ASTA	AST RESEARCH INC	16.750	1.47	1.66	0.16	16.75	0.43	2.19	1.31	60
ARX	ARX INC	1.875	1.02	−1.90	0.07	17.02	0.43	2.22	1.01	60
ASAA	ASA INTL LTD	1.875	0.79	−1.03	0.01	23.55	0.60	3.07	0.86	60
RCH	ARCO CHEM CO	45.375	1.33	0.03	0.47	7.35	0.19	1.00	1.22	55
ANBC	ANB CORP	36.375	−0.02	1.80	0.10	1.90	0.13	0.56	0.32	12
ATCE	ATC ENVIRONMENTAL INC	2.813	−0.02	0.68	0.02	21.22	0.75	3.22	0.32	46
ATI	ATI MED INC	3.750	0.26	0.07	0.01	19.11	0.49	2.49	0.51	60
ATCIC	ATC INC	1.750	0.61	0.38	0.00	26.63	0.68	3.47	0.74	60
ATNN	ATNN INC	0.219	1.38	1.51	0.00	50.89	1.30	6.64	1.25	60
ATTNF	ATTN AVECA ENTERTAIN-MENT COR	1.750	2.81	0.39	0.05	42.49	1.59	6.97	2.20	39
AVSY	AVTR SYS INC	0.203	−0.54	6.23	0.06	55.49	3.33	14.41	−0.02	18
AWCSA	AW COMPUTER SYS INC CLASS A	5.875	1.23	7.08	0.01	71.41	1.85	9.29	1.15	60
ARON	AARON RENTS INC	13.125	0.92	−0.23	0.16	10.30	0.26	1.34	0.95	60
ABIX	ABATIX ENVIRONMENTAL CORP	1.750	0.00	0.36	0.03	17.54	0.67	2.96	0.34	37
ABT	ABBOTT LABS	66.000	0.87	0.87	0.51	4.31	0.11	0.56	0.92	60
ABERF	ABER RES LTD	0.969	1.53	3.52	0.02	29.18	1.11	4.93	1.35	37
AANB	ABIGAIL ADAMS NATL BANCORP I	11.000	−1.50	1.81	0.14	12.61	0.70	2.80	−0.66	24
ABBK	ABINGTON BANCORP INC	5.875	1.37	−0.15	0.09	20.09	0.51	2.62	1.24	60
ABD	ABIOMED INC	13.000	1.08	1.04	0.07	18.21	0.47	2.43	1.05	57
ABY	ABITIBI PRICE INC	12.625	0.65	−1.42	0.23	6.00	0.15	0.80	0.77	57
ABRI	ABRAMS INDS INC	4.313	1.28	1.90	0.07	20.91	0.53	2.73	1.18	60
ACAP	ACAP CORP	0.500	0.05	0.88	0.02	13.80	0.35	1.80	0.37	60
ACLE	ACCEL INTL CORP	6.750	1.12	−0.66	0.20	11.10	0.28	1.45	1.08	60
AKLM	ACCLAIM ENTHT INC	6.375	1.29	0.02	0.03	23.62	0.84	3.58	1.19	46
ACCU	ACCUHEALTH INC	5.438	0.53	0.60	0.00	13.47	0.49	2.17	0.69	41

Based on S&P 500 Index, Using Straight Regression   Page 3

Figure 17.8
Sample Page from Security Risk Evaluation by Merrill Lynch, Pierce, Fenner & Smith Inc.

The seventh value in Figure 17.8 that is of particular interest is the **adjusted beta** value, which is discussed next.

17.8.1 Adjusting Beta

Without any information at all it would be reasonable to estimate the beta of a stock to be equal to 1.0, the average size of beta. Given a chance to see how the stock moved relative to a market index over some time period, a modification of this prior estimate would seem appropriate. Such a modification would sensibly produce a final estimate of beta that would lie between the value of 1.0 and its initially estimated value based purely on historical price changes.

Formal procedures for making such modifications have been adopted by most investment firms that estimate betas. The specific adjustments made typically differ from time to time and, in some cases, from stock to stock. In Figure 17.8 the **adjusted beta** values were obtained by giving approximately 34% weight to the average marketwide beta of 1.0 and approximately 66% weight to the historical estimate of beta for each stock. Thus the adjusted beta for Ask Computer is 1.43 [= (.34 × 1.0) + (.66 × 1.65)]. More generally,

$$\beta_a = (.34 \times 1.0) + (.66 \times \beta_h) \tag{17.9}$$

where β_a and β_h are the adjusted and historical betas, respectively.[29] Examination of Equation (17.9) indicates that this procedure takes the historical beta for a security and adjusts it by giving it a value closer to 1.0. Thus historical betas less than 1.0 are made larger, but will still be less than 1.0, and historical betas greater than 1.0 are made smaller, but will still be greater than 1.0. The adjustments are in these directions because the weights (.66 and .34) are positive and add up to 1.0, indicating that the adjustment procedure is an averaging technique.

Table 17.3 shows the extent to which such a procedure anticipates differences between historical and future betas. The second column lists the unadjusted historical betas for eight portfolios of 100 securities each, based on monthly price changes from July 1947 through June 1954 (the portfolios were designed to have significantly different betas during this period). The third column of the table shows the values obtained when an adjustment of the type used by Merrill Lynch was applied. The betas in the fourth column are based on price changes over the subsequent seven years. For a majority of the portfolios, the adjusted betas are closer in magnitude to the subsequent historical betas than are the unadjusted betas. This suggests that the adjusted historical beta is a more accurate estimate of the future beta than the unadjusted historical beta.

The fifth column of Table 17.3 shows the historical betas estimated using data from a third seven-year period. Comparing the unadjusted betas in columns 2, 4, and 5, it can be seen that there is a continuing tendency for betas to shrink toward the mean value of 1.0 over time. Thus adjustment procedures seem to have some usefulness when it comes to estimating betas for a future time period.

TABLE 17.3
Ex Ante and Ex Post Beta Values for Portfolios of 100 Securities

Portfolio	July 1947–June 1954		July 1954–June 1961	July 1961 June 1968
	Unadjusted	Adjusted		
(1)	(2)	(3)	(4)	(5)
1	.36	.48	.57	.72
2	.61	.68	.71	.79
3	.78	.82	.88	.88
4	.91	.93	.96	.92
5	1.01	1.01	1.03	1.04
6	1.13	1.10	1.13	1.02
7	1.26	1.21	1.24	1.08
8	1.47	1.39	1.32	1.15

Source: Marshall E. Blume, "Betas and Their Regression Tendencies," *Journal of Finance*, 30, no. 3 (June 1975): p. 792.

CHAPTER 17

It seems plausible that "true" betas not only vary over time but have a tendency to move back toward average levels, as extreme values are likely to be moderated over time. A firm whose operations or financing make the risk of its equity considerably different from that of other firms is more likely to move back toward the average than away from it over time. Such changes in betas are due to real economic phenomena, not simply an artifact of overly simple statistical procedures. There is, however, no reason to expect every stock's "true" beta to move to the same average in the same manner at the same speed. In this regard, some fundamental analysis of the firm may prove more useful than the adoption of more sophisticated statistical methods for processing past price changes in estimating beta.

Although historical betas for portfolios can provide useful information about future betas, historical betas for individual securities are subject to great error and should be treated accordingly. This can be seen by noting the magnitude of the standard errors of the betas shown earlier in Figure 17.8.

Table 17.4 provides another view. Every stock listed on the New York Stock Exchange was assigned to one of ten classes in each year from 1931 through 1967, based on the magnitude of its historical beta calculated using data from the preceding five years. The stocks in the top 10% of each January's ranking were assigned to class 10, the next 10% to class 9, and so on. The table shows the percent of the stocks that were in the same class (column 1) and within one risk class (column 3) five years later. Also shown are the entries that would be expected if there were no relationship between such past and future beta classes. Examination of the table reveals that individual security betas have some but not a great deal of predictive value.

TABLE 17.4
MOVEMENT OF STOCKS AMONG BETA CLASSES

Risk Class	Percent Of Stocks In The Same Beta Class Five Years Later		Percent Of Stocks In The Same Beta Class Or Within One Risk Class Five Years Later	
	Actual (1)	Expected If There Were No Relationship (2)	Actual (3)	Expected If There Were No Relationship (4)
10 (highest beta values)	35.2%	10%	69.3%	20%
9	18.4	10	53.7	30
8	16.4	10	45.3	30
7	13.3	10	40.9	30
6	13.9	10	39.3	30
5	13.6	10	41.7	30
4	13.2	10	40.2	30
3	15.9	10	44.6	30
2	21.5	10	60.9	30
1 (lowest beta values)	40.5	10	62.3	20

Source: William F. Sharpe and Guy M. Cooper, "Risk-Return Classes of New York Stock Exchange Common Stocks, 1931–1967," *Financial Analysts Journal*, 28, no. 2 (March/April 1972): p. 53.

Figure 17.9
Percent of Differences in Beta Values Attributable to Differences in Prior Year's Betas
Source: Robert A. Levy, "On the Short-Term Stationarity of Beta Coefficients," *Financial Analysts Journal,*
27, no. 6 (November/December 1971): p. 57.

Figure 17.9 shows that the predictive ability of historical portfolio betas improves with the amount of diversification in a portfolio. The vertical axis plots the percentage of the differences in (measured) portfolio betas (based on weekly price changes) in one year that can be attributed to differences in their (measured) betas in the prior year. The horizontal axis indicates the number of securities in each portfolio. It can be seen in the figure that the historical betas for portfolios containing roughly 10 to 20 securities or more have a high degree of predictive ability. Thus individual security betas are worth estimating, even though they are rather inaccurate when viewed by themselves. This is because their individual inaccuracies seem to cancel out one another when the beta of a diversified portfolio is calculated, producing an accurate estimate of the portfolio's beta.

17.8.2   Leverage and Beta

The beta of a *firm* represents the sensitivity of the aggregate value of the firm to changes in the value of the market portfolio. It depends on both the demand for the firm's products and the firm's operating costs. However, most firms have both debt and equity outstanding. This means that the beta of a firm's *equity* (that is, stock) depends on the beta of the firm and the firm's financial leverage. For example, imagine that there are two firms that are identical in every way except that firm *A* has debt while firm *B* is free of debt. This means that even though they have the same earnings before interest and taxes (EBIT), they will have different earnings after taxes (EAT) because *A,* unlike *B,* has to make interest payments. In this situation, the firm betas for *A* and *B* are the same, but the stock beta for *A* will be greater than the stock beta for *B.* The difference in their debt levels is the reason for the difference in their stock betas. This is because the debt makes the earnings available to common stockholders more variable for *A* than for *B*. Thus the stock beta for *A* could be viewed as being equal to the stock beta it would have if it had no debt (that is, the beta of *B*) plus an adjustment for the amount of debt it actually has outstanding.

One method that has been suggested for determining the influence of debt on the beta of the stock of a firm involves a four-step procedure.[30] First, the current market values of the firm's outstanding debt *D* and equity *E* must be determined. Once this is done, the current market value of the levered firm V_L can be determined:

$$V_L = D + E. \tag{17.10}$$

Second, the market value of the firm *if it were unlevered* must be determined. This can be done by using the following formula:

$$V_u = V_L - \tau D \tag{17.11}$$

where: V_u = *market value of firm if it was unlevered,*
τ = *average corporate tax rate for the firm,*
D = *market value of firm's debt.*

Third, the beta of the firm can be calculated after estimating the betas of the firm's debt β_{debt} and equity β_{equity} by using the following formula:

$$\beta_{\text{firm}} = \beta_{\text{debt}} \frac{(1 - \tau)D}{V_u} + \beta_{\text{equity}} \frac{E}{V_u}. \tag{17.12}$$

Fourth, having used Equation (17.12) to estimate the beta of the firm, the effect of any degree of leverage on the equity beta of the firm can be determined by restating this equation. Specifically, solving Equation (17.12) for β_{equity} results in[31]

$$\beta_{\text{equity}} = \beta_{\text{firm}} + (\beta_{\text{firm}} - \beta_{\text{debt}}) \left(\frac{D}{E}\right)(1 - \tau). \tag{17.13}$$

In Evaluating Equation (17.13) it should be noted that the value of β_{firm} does not change as the firm's debt-equity ratio D/E is changed. Assuming that the value of β_{debt} also does not change, it can be seen that increasing the firm's debt-equity ratio will increase the beta of the firm's equity. Intuitively this makes sense, because a higher debt-equity ratio will make a firm's EAT more volatile. Conversely, lowering a firm's debt-equity ratio should lower the firm's equity beta because it makes EAT less volatile.

This property of beta can be useful in estimating the beta of a firm's equity if the firm has recently altered its debt-equity ratio (or is contemplating increasing the ratio). For example, imagine that ABC Inc. had until last month $60 million of equity and $40 million of debt outstanding for a total firm value of $100 million; its tax rate is 30%. Using the market model shown in Table 17.2, but applied to data before the recent equity issuance, it is determined that the equity beta and debt beta of ABC are 1.40 and .20, respectively. However, ABC has just issued $20 million of equity and used the proceeds to retire some of the debt so that the current values of ABC's debt and equity are $74 million and $20 million, respectively. (The $74 million value of equity represents the sum of $20 million in new equity and $54 million in old equity, which has decreased in value by $6 million due to the loss of tax shields resulting from the $20 million reduction in ABC's debt.) What is the equity beta of ABC likely to be in the immediate future?

The previously described four-step procedure can be used to answer this question. First, it is noted from Equation (17.10) that the value of ABC before the new equity issuance was $100 million. Second, it is noted from Equation (17.11) that the value of ABC if the firm were unlevered would be equal to $88 million [= $100 million − (.3 × $40 million)]. Third, the beta of the firm can be estimated using Equation (17.12):

$$\beta_{\text{firm}} = .20 \left[\frac{(1 - .3)\$40 \text{ million}}{\$88 \text{ million}} \right] + 1.40 \left(\frac{\$60 \text{ million}}{\$88 \text{ million}} \right)$$

$$= 1.02$$

Lastly, the current equity beta (that is, the equity beta after the recent issuance of $20 million of equity) can be estimated by using Equation (17.13),

$$\beta_{\text{equity}} = 1.02 + (1.02 - .20) \left(\frac{\$20 \text{ million}}{\$74 \text{ million}} \right) (1 - .3)$$

$$= 1.17.$$

Hence the reduction in the amount of debt that ABC has outstanding has reduced the beta of the equity from 1.40 to 1.17.[32]

17.8.3 Industry Beta Values

Firms in industries having highly cyclical demand or large fixed costs might be expected to have higher firm betas than those in industries with more stable demand or greater variable costs, because they will have greater variability in EBIT. Differences in financial leverage could wholly offset such factors, leaving few, if any, differences among the equity betas of firms in different industries. However, this does not seem to be the case. Firms in certain industries do tend to have higher equity betas than those in other industries, and, by and large, the classifications agree with prior expectations.

Table 17.5 shows the average equity betas for stocks in various industry classifications. Stock prices of firms whose products are termed "necessities" tend to respond less than the stock prices of most other firms when expectations about the future health of the economy are revised. That is, firms in necessities (such as utilities or food) tend to have low betas because they tend to have more stable earnings. Stock prices of firms that manufacture "luxuries" tend to respond more than most others when expectations about the future health of the economy are revised. That is, firms in luxuries (such as travel or electronics) tend to have high betas because they tend to have more cyclical earnings.

TABLE 17.5
AVERAGE VALUES OF BETA FOR STOCKS IN SELECTED INDUSTRIES, 1966–1974

Industry	Beta Value	Industry	Beta Value
Air transport	1.80	Energy, raw materials	1.22
Real property	1.70	Tires, rubber goods	1.21
Travel, outdoor recreation	1.66	Railroads, shipping	1.19
Electronics	1.60	Forest products, paper	1.16
Miscellaneous finance	1.60	Miscellaneous, conglomerate	1.14
Nondurables, entertainment	1.47	Drugs, medicine	1.14
Consumer durables	1.44	Domestic oil	1.12
Business machines	1.43	Soaps, cosmetics	1.09
Retail, general	1.43	Steel	1.02
Media	1.39	Containers	1.01
Insurance	1.34	Nonferrous metals	.99
Trucking, freight	1.31	Agriculture, food	.99
Producer goods	1.30	Liquor	.89
Aerospace	1.30	International oil	.85
Business services	1.28	Banks	.81
Apparel	1.27	Tobacco	.80
Construction	1.27	Telephone	.75
Motor vehicles	1.27	Energy, utilities	.60
Photographic, optical	1.24	Gold	.36
Chemicals	1.22		

Source: Barr Rosenberg and James Guy. "Prediction of Beta from Investment Fundamentals, *Financial Analysts Journal*, 32, no. 4 (July/August 1976): p. 66.

Forecasting Beta

Information of the type shown in Table 17.5 can be used to adjust historical equity betas. For example, the knowledge that a corporation is in the air transport industry suggests that a reasonable prior estimate of its equity beta is 1.8. Thus it makes more sense to adjust its historical equity beta toward a value of 1.8 than 1.0, the average for all stocks, as was suggested in Equation (17.9).

The procedure used to adjust historical betas involves an implicit prediction equation for future betas. Equation (17.9) can be written more generally as:

$$\beta_a = a + b\beta_h \qquad (17.14)$$

where a and b are constants. One way to consider the differences in industry betas is to alter Equation (17.14) as follows:

$$\beta_a = a\beta_{\text{ind}} + b\beta_h \qquad (17.15)$$

where β_{ind} denotes the average equity beta of the industry to which the stock belongs.

For example, consider the values of .33 and .67 for a and b, respectively. Air Express is an air transport firm whose historical beta is 2.0. What is its adjusted beta? Noting that the average equity beta for stocks in the air transport industry is 1.8, its adjusted beta can be calculated by using Equation (17.15) as follows:

$$\beta_a = (.33 \times 1.8) + (.67 \times 2.0)$$
$$= 1.93.$$

Thus Air Express has an adjusted beta of 1.93, which lies between its historical beta of 2.0 and the average equity beta in its industry of 1.8. Indeed, this is what Equation (17.15) accomplishes: It alters a historical beta to give an adjusted beta lying between β_h and β_{ind}.

Multiple-Industry Firms

What should be done if the firm has divisions that are in different industries? In a situation where there are two industries involved, Equation (17.15) could be modified as follows:

$$\beta_a = a(E_{ind1}\beta_{ind1} + E_{ind2}\beta_{ind2}) + b\beta_h \qquad (17.16)$$

where E_{ind1} and E_{ind2} denote the percentages of the firm's earnings that are from industries 1 and 2, respectively, and β_{ind1} and β_{ind2} are the betas for industries 1 and 2, respectively.[33]

As an example, consider Electrospace, a firm that has half of its earnings coming from a division that is in the electronics industry and half coming from a division that is in the aerospace industry. Assuming that a and b are equal to .33 and .67, respectively, and that the historical beta for Electrospace is 1.2, its adjusted beta can be calculated in two steps.

First, the value of $E_{ind1}\beta_{ind1} + E_{ind2}\beta_{ind2}$ needs to be calculated. Doing so produces a value of 1.45 [= (.5 × 1.6) + (.5 × 1.3)]. This can be interpreted as the average equity beta for any stock whose firm has equal business interests in the electronics and aerospace industries.

Second, the adjusted beta of Electrospace can be calculated using Equation (17.16) as 1.28 [= (.33 × 1.45) + (.67 × 1.20)]. Note that this value lies between the firm's historical beta of 1.20 and its "industry" beta of 1.45.

Adjustments Based on Financial Characteristics

Various financial characteristics can also be used to estimate an adjusted beta. For example, stocks with high dividend yields might have lower betas because more of their value is associated with near-term than far-term dividends. Equation (17.16) could thus be augmented to

$$\beta_a = a(E_{ind1}\beta_{ind1} + E_{ind2}\beta_{ind2}) + b\beta_h + cY \qquad (17.17)$$

where c is a constant and Y is the dividend yield of the firm's stock.

Table 17.6 shows a beta prediction equation of this form, using historic data from 1928 through 1982.[34] To estimate the beta of a security using this prediction equation, start with a constant based on the industry (referred to as the "sector") in which the security is classified. Then add to this constant an amount equal to the security's historical beta times 0.576. [Note that this is similar to the adjustment to historical beta shown in Equation (17.9).] Finally, add (1) the

TABLE 17.6

A BETA PREDICTION EQUATION DERIVED
FROM A FACTOR MODEL

Constant Term

Sector	Value
Basic industry	.455
Capital goods	.425
Consumer staple	.307
Consumer cyclical	.443
Credit cyclical	.429
Energy	.394
Finance	.398
Transportation	.255
Utilities	.340

Variable Terms

Attribute	Coefficient
Beta	.576
Yield	−.019
Size	−.105

Source: Blake Grossman and William F. Sharpe, "Factors in Security Returns," paper presented at the Center for the Study of Banking and Financial Markets, University of Washington, March 1984.

security's dividend yield times $-.019$, and (2) the security's "size attribute" times $-.105$.[35] Algebraically, the model is:

$$\beta_a = a_s + (.576 \times \beta_h) + (-.019 \times Y) + (-.105 \times S) \qquad (17.18)$$

where a_s denotes the constant associated with the sector to which the stock belongs, β_h is the historical beta, Y is the dividend yield, and S is the size of the firm. With this formula, securities having higher yields are predicted to have lower betas, as are those with larger market values of equity outstanding.

Example

As an example, consider a stock that is classified as belonging to the "basic industry." It has a historical beta of 1.2, a dividend yield over the previous 12 months of 4%, and an aggregate market value of $7 billion (that is, the firm has 100 million shares outstanding and the stock is selling for $70 per share). Using Equation (17.18), its adjusted beta is:

$$\begin{aligned}
\beta_a &= .455 + (.576 \times 1.2) + (-.019 \times 4) + [-.105 \times (\log 7)] \\
&= .455 + .69 - .08 - .09 \\
&= .98.
\end{aligned}$$

Such prediction equations, based on multifactor models, fit historical data considerably better than those that use only historical betas. One study reported an improvement of 86% over the more simple adjusted beta approach.[36] However, such figures describe only the extent to which the equations fit a given set

---

of data. As the true test of a prediction equation is its ability to *predict,* only extensive experience with such approaches can, in the final analysis, determine how well various models can predict beta values.

17.8.4 Beta Services

Services providing betas on a regular basis in published form are available in several countries. Many use only past price changes to form estimates. Some derive their estimates from more general factor models. One service uses weekly data for two years; another, monthly data for five years. One estimates betas for U.S. securities relative to Standard & Poor's 500; another, relative to the New York Stock Exchange composite index; and so on. In each case, estimates for individual securities are subject to error. Thus it is hardly surprising that estimated values for a given security obtained by different services using different procedures are not the same. This does not indicate that the various estimates are useless, only that they should be used appropriately and with caution.

17.9 GROWTH VERSUS VALUE

Common stocks are often divided into two categories—**growth stocks** and **value stocks.** Although there are no hard-and-fast rules on how they are divided and disagreement exists among investment professionals on what category certain stocks belong to, there are two financial measures that are often used to distinguish growth stocks from value stocks. These are the book-value-to-market-value ratio (BV/MV) and the earnings-to-price ratio (E/P).[37]

17.9.1 Book-Value-to-Market-Value Ratio

This ratio is typically calculated as follows. First, the book value of the firm's common stock is determined by using the most recent balance sheet data and calculating the total value of stockholders' equity. Second, the market capitalization of the firm's common stock is determined by taking the most recent market price for the firm's common stock and multiplying it by the number of shares outstanding. Lastly, the book value of stockholders' equity is divided by the market capitalization to arrive at the BV/MV ratio. Relatively low values of this ratio characterize growth stocks, and relatively high values characterize value stocks.[38]

An interesting question is whether there is a relationship between stock returns and their BV/MV ratios. Fama and French examined this issue and found that there was such a relationship.[39] Specifically, they found that on average the larger the size of the BV/MV ratio, the larger the rate of return. Table 17.7 presents their findings.

Panel (a) of Table 17.7 was constructed as follows. First, at the end of June 1963, the book value was determined for each stock on the NYSE, AMEX, and Nasdaq using the annual financial statements that involved the fiscal year ending

TABLE 17.7
GROWTH VERSUS VALUE STOCKS

	Portfolio Number*											
	1	2	3	4	5	6	7	8	9	10	11	12
(a) Portfolios Based on BV/MV Ratio:												
Return	.30	.67	.87	.97	1.04	1.17	1.30	1.44	1.50	1.59	1.92	1.83
BV/MV	.11	.22	.34	.47	.60	.73	.87	1.03	1.23	1.52	1.93	2.77
(b) Portfolios Based on E/P Ratio†												
Return	1.04	.93	.94	1.03	1.18	1.22	1.33	1.42	1.46	1.57	1.74	1.72
E/P	.01	.03	.05	.06	.08	.09	.11	.12	.14	.16	.20	.28
(c) Portfolios Based on Size:												
Return	1.64	1.16	1.29	1.24	1.25	1.29	1.17	1.07	1.10	.95	.88	.90
ln(MV)	1.98	3.18	3.63	4.10	4.50	4.89	5.30	5.73	6.24	6.82	7.39	8.44

* Portfolios formed based on rankings of indicated financial measure for stocks from smallest (1) to largest (12); return indicates the average monthly return, in percent, from July 1963 through December 1990.

† The portfolio of stocks that had negative earnings had an average monthly return of 1.46.

Source: Eugene F. Fama and Kenneth R. French, "The Cross-Section of Expected Stock Returns," *Journal of Finance*, 47, no. 2 (June 1992): Table II, pp. 436–437; Table IV, pp. 442–443.

in 1962. This value was then divided by the market capitalization for each firm, where the market capitalization was determined by using the market price for each firm as of the end of December 1962. Second, using these BV/MV ratios, the firms were ranked from smallest to largest and formed into 12 portfolios. Third, the return on each portfolio was tracked monthly from July 1963 through June 1964. Fourth, the entire process was updated by a year so that returns were calculated from July 1964 to June 1965 on 12 BV/MV-ranked portfolios that were formed based on data as of the end of 1963. The process was repeated until a set of monthly returns was available from July 1963 through December 1990 for each of the 12 portfolios.

Table 17.7(a) shows a clear relationship between average monthly return and the BV/MV ratio—higher values of the ratio are associated with higher average returns. Remembering that growth stocks tend to have low BV/MV ratios and value stocks tend to have high BV/MV ratios, this suggests that over the period analyzed, value stocks tended to outperform growth stocks.

17.9.2   Earnings-to-Price Ratio

This ratio is typically calculated as follows. First, the accounting value of the firm's earnings per share is determined by using the most recent income statement and dividing the firm's earnings after taxes by the number of shares outstanding. Second, the market price of the firm's common stock is determined by taking the most recent price at which the firm's common stock was traded. Lastly, the earnings per share figure is divided by the market price of the stock to arrive at the E/P ratio. Relatively low values of this ratio characterize growth stocks, and relatively high values characterize value stocks.

An interesting question is whether there is a relationship between stock returns and their E/P ratios. Fama and French also examined this issue and discovered such a relationship.[40] Specifically, they found that on average the larger the size of the E/P ratio, the larger the rate of return. Their results are shown in Table 17.7(b), which was constructed in the same manner as part (a) except that now at the end of each June, firms are ranked and assigned to portfolios on the basis of their E/P ratios.

Except for portfolio 1, part (b) shows a clear relationship between average monthly return and the E/P ratio—higher values of the ratio are associated with higher average returns. Remembering that growth stocks tend to have low E/P ratios and value stocks tend to have high E/P ratios, this data reinforces the conclusions drawn from the BV/MV data—namely, that value stocks tended to outperform growth stocks over the period analyzed.

There is one other interesting feature of this panel. When Fama and French assigned stocks to portfolios based on their E/P ratios, they assigned those stocks that had negative earnings and hence a negative E/P ratio to a separate portfolio. This portfolio had an average monthly return of 1.46%. Thus if one considers a portfolio with a negative E/P ratio to be the lowest E/P portfolio, then it can be seen from the table that as E/P gets larger, average returns at first decline and then rise. This has led Fama and French to refer to the relationship between average returns and the E/P ratio as being "U-shaped."

17.9.3 Size

Although firm size is not generally used as a criterion for distinguishing growth from value stocks, it is often used to sort stocks. For example, many investment professionals think of stocks in terms of two dimensions as follows:

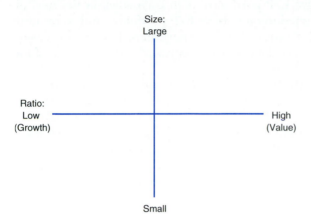

Hence stocks could be classified as growth or value using the BV/MV ratio and as large or small using their size. The result is that each stock could be located in a scatter diagram like the one shown.

Typically a stock's market capitalization is used as the measure of its size. This is what Fama and French did when they assigned stocks to one of 12 portfolios after ranking them at the end of each June based on size. Proceeding in a manner analogous to that discussed previously, they tracked the monthly returns for these 12 size-based portfolios from July 1963 to December 1990. Table 17.7(c) displays the average returns and sizes of these portfolios.

In contrast to parts (a) and (b), it can be seen that there is a clear inverse relationship between size and average return. That is, stocks of smaller firms tend to have higher returns than stocks of larger firms. Even more notable is the average return for the smallest portfolio (1). This return is significantly higher than for the next smallest portfolio (2) or for any other. Hence when some people refer to a **size effect** in stock returns, they are really referring to a "small firm effect."[41]

17.9.4 Interrelationships

The existence of a relationship between any one of three financial variables (BV/MV ratio, E/P ratio, and firm size) and stock returns suggests that there is at least one missing factor that is needed to explain the differences in returns.[42] Hence it is of interest to examine the interrelationships between the BV/MV ratio, the E/P ratio, firm size, and average returns. The joint effect of E/P ratio and firm size on stock returns is examined next.

Common Stocks

E/P, Size, and Average Returns

In order to examine the joint effect of these two financial variables on stock returns, one study noted at each year-end the breakpoints formed by sorting NYSE and AMEX stocks in quintiles based on just size and then on just the E/P ratio.[43] Then, using both of these sets of breakpoints, stocks were assigned to one of 25 size-E/P portfolios for the next year. That is, each stock in the smallest size quintile was assigned to one of five E/P portfolios, then each stock in the next-to-smallest size quintile was assigned to one of five E/P portfolios, and so on until there were 25 (= 5 sizes × E/P ratios) size—E/P portfolios. The process was repeated year after year until a set of daily returns was available for each one of the 25 portfolios from 1963 through 1977.

When average returns for the 25 portfolios were compared, it was found that there was a clear inverse relationship between size and average returns for any E/P quintile. For example, consider the five size-ranked portfolios that were formed from the lowest E/P quintile. It was found that when comparing these five portfolios, the larger the size, the smaller the average return.

However, there was no clear relationship between E/P ratios and average returns for any size quintile. For example, consider the five E/P-ranked portfolios that were formed from the smallest size quintile. In this case the largest and third largest average returns were associated with the lowest and next to lowest E/P portfolios. This was contrary to previous observations of the relationship between E/P ratios and average returns. As a consequence, it appears that there is a missing factor that is needed to explain differences in stock returns, and that this factor is more closely related to size than to the E/P ratio.[44]

BV/MV, Size, and Average Returns

Fama and French were interested in the joint effect of the BV/MV ratio and firm size on stock returns.[45] Accordingly, they formed 100 portfolios annually based on the rankings of stocks using size and BV/MV ratio. Monthly returns on these portfolios were then recorded for the period from July 1963 through the end of 1990.

When average returns for the 100 portfolios were compared, it was found that there was an inverse relationship between size and average return for almost every BV/MV decile. For example, consider the ten size-ranked portfolios that were formed from the largest BV/MV decile. It was found that when comparing these ten portfolios, in general the larger the size, the smaller the average return. The only exception was for the two smallest BV/MV deciles, where in each case there was no apparent relationship between size and return.

Furthermore, there was a clear direct relationship between BV/MV ratios and average returns for any size quintile. For example, consider the ten BV/MV-ranked portfolios that were formed from the smallest size decile. It was found that when comparing these ten portfolios, the larger the BV/MV ratio, the larger the average return. Consequently, Fama and French concluded that there are at least two missing factors that are needed to explain differences in stock returns, and that those factors are closely related to size and the BV/MV ratio.

1. Common stock represents an ownership position in a corporation. Common stockholders possess a residual claim on the corporation's earnings and assets. Furthermore, their liability for the corporation's obligations is limited.

2. Common stockholders elect the corporation's directors through either a majority or a cumulative voting system.

3. Corporations may at times repurchase some of their outstanding stock either in the open market or through a tender offer. Such actions may involve an attempt to repel a takeover, a signal to shareholders that the stock is undervalued, or a taxwise distribution of cash to shareholders.

4. Stock dividends and splits involve the issuance of additional shares of common stock to current stockholders, proportional to their ownership positions. No change in the total value of the corporation is caused by a stock dividend or split.

5. Preemptive rights give existing stockholders the right of first refusal to purchase new shares. Such shares are purchased in a rights offering.

6. Daily information regarding transactions in publicly traded stocks can be found in business newspapers and the business sections of most local newspapers.

7. In the United States, trading on inside information is illegal in public security markets. However, defining inside information is difficult.

8. A security's beta can be estimated using historical return data for the security and a market index. The beta is the slope of the security's market model, calculated by using simple linear regression.

9. Beta estimates based on historical return data are sometimes adjusted to account for a tendency of betas to drift toward an average value of 1.0 over time.

10. Estimates of betas are generally more accurate for diversified portfolios than for individual securities.

11. Forecasts of a security's beta can be improved by accounting for certain characteristics of the corporation, such as the industry (or industries) in which it operates, its financial leverage, and its market capitalization.

12. Firms that have either low book-value-to-market-value or earnings-to-price ratios, or both, are generally referred to as growth stocks, whereas firms that have either high book-value-to-market-value or earnings-to-price ratios, or both, are generally referred to as value stocks.

13. Firms that have either high book-value-to-market-value ratios, high earnings-to-price ratios, or are of smaller firm size historically have had higher stock returns.

14. When viewed jointly, there seems to be a relationship between stock returns and both firm size and the book-value-to-market-value ratio.

1. What is the significant advantage of the corporate form of business organization? Why would you expect that this advantage would be important to the success of a capitalist economy?

2. Fall Creek is conducting the annual election for its five-member board of directors. The firm has 1,500,000 shares of voting common stock outstanding.

   a. Under a majority voting system, how many shares must a stockholder own to ensure being able to elect his or her choices to each of the five director seats?

   b. Under a cumulative voting system, how many shares must a stockholder own to ensure being able to elect his or her choices to two of the director seats?

   c. Arlie Latham holds 20% of Fall Creek's outstanding stock. How many directors can Arlie elect under a cumulative voting system?

3. The issue of corporate ownership versus control has become quite controversial. Discuss the principal-agent problem as it relates to shareholder-management relations. Specifically, why is there a potential conflict between the two groups? What steps can be taken to mitigate this problem?

4. When a bidder makes a tender offer for a target firm, what types of defenses are often applied to fend off the bidder? Do these defenses generally seem to be in the best interests of the target firm's shareholders? Why?

5. Why might a corporation wish to issue more than one class of common stock?

6. With respect to the payment of corporate dividends, distinguish between declaration date, ex-dividend date, and date of record.

7. Theoretical arguments and empirical research support the case that stock dividends and splits do not enhance shareholder wealth. However, corporations continue to declare stock dividends and splits. Summarize the arguments for and against stock dividends and splits from the perspective of the shareholder.

8. Menomonie Publishing stock currently sells for $40 per share. The company has 1,200,000 shares outstanding. What would be the effect on the number of shares outstanding and on the stock price of the following:

   a. 15% Stock dividend

   b. 4-for-3 stock split

   c. Reverse 3-for-1 stock split

9. St. Paul Corporation is planning to raise $35,000,000 through the sale of new common stock under a rights offering. The subscription price is $70 per share while the stock currently sells for $80 per share, rights on. Total outstanding shares equal 10,000,000. Of this amount, Addie Joss owns 100,000 shares.

   a. How many shares of stock will each right permit its owner to purchase?

   b. What will be the total value of Addie's rights a day before the ex-rights date, assuming that the market price of St. Paul stock remains at $80 per share?

c. After the ex-rights date, if the market value of each St. Paul right equals $.20, what must be the ex-rights market price of St. Paul's stock?

10. Pep Clark owns stock in DeKalb Dairy. DeKalb is planning a rights offering in which seven shares must be owned to buy one additional share at a price of $15. DeKalb stock currently sells for $63 per share.

    a. What is the value of a DeKalb right?

    b. At the time of the offering announcement, Pep's assets consisted of $1,500 in cash and 490 shares of DeKalb. List and show the value of Pep's assets prior to the ex-rights date.

    c. List and show the value of Pep's assets on the ex-rights date if DeKalb stock sells for $60 per share on that date.

    d. List and show the value of Pep's assets if Pep sells the DeKalb rights on the ex-rights date.

11. Using a recent *Wall Street Journal* as a data source, select a NYSE-listed stock whose name begins with the same letter as the first letter of your last name. For this stock, calculate its rate of return for that day of the week. What was the stock's trading volume that day?

12. From the perspective of an efficient market proponent, why is it surprising that trades based on insider trading data found in the SEC's *Official Summary of Insider Transactions* appear to produce significant abnormal profits?

13. Tomah Electronics' stock price at the end of several quarters, along with the market index value for the same periods, is shown below. Tomah pays no dividends. Calculate the beta of Tomah's stock over the eight quarters.

Quarter	Quarter-End Tomah Stock Price	Quarter-End Market Index Value
0	60.000	210.00
1	62.500	220.50
2	64.375	229.87
3	59.875	206.88
4	56.875	190.33
5	61.500	209.36
6	66.500	238.67
7	69.750	257.76
8	68.375	262.92

14. Using the data from Problem 9 in Chapter 1, calculate the beta of the small stock portfolio over the 20-year period. Use the common stock returns from Table 1.1 as the returns on the market index.

15. Shown here are ten quarters of return data for Baraboo Associates stock, as well as return data over the same period for a broad stock market index. Using this information, calculate the following statistics for Baraboo Associates stock.

    a. beta

    b. alpha

    c. standard deviation of random error term

    d. coefficient of determination

Quarter	Baraboo Return	Market Return
1	3.8%	2.7%
2	5.3	3.1
3	−7.2	−4.9
4	10.1	9.9
5	1.0	2.7
6	2.5	1.2
7	6.4	3.8
8	4.8	4.0
9	6.0	5.5
10	2.2	2.0

16. What is the rationale for calculating "adjusted" betas as described in the text?

17. Sugar Grove Technologies has debt and equity with total market values of $120 million and $230 million, respectively. With a 35% corporate tax, what is the firm's unlevered value?

18. The market value of Oswego Computers' total debt outstanding is $10 million. Further, the unlevered market value of Oswego is $40 million. The firm's average corporate tax rate is 35%.

   a. If the beta of the firm's debt is .40 and the beta of its equity is 1.20, what is the firm's beta?

   b. If the firm borrows another $10 million and uses the proceeds to purchase an equivalent amount of its own equity, what will be the effect on the beta of its equity?

19. Why would one expect that the betas of companies within industries should be more similar than the betas of companies across industries?

20. Necedah Power is an electric utility company. Its historical beta is .70. Its stock offers a dividend yield of 7.6%. The market value of its outstanding equity is currently $140 million. Based on the data from Table 17.6, calculate Necedah's beta.

21. Explain the primary differences between multiple-factor models of beta and historical models of beta. In particular, why might you expect that the multiple-factor models would do a better job of forecasting betas than do the historical models?

22. Generally, stocks with relatively low price per share (roughly $5 per share or less) have higher betas than stocks with a higher price per share. What attributes of low-price stocks might you expect to be correlated with higher beta values?

23. (Appendix Question) The empirical regularities cited in this chapter have potentially troubling implications for the Capital Asset Pricing Model and the concept of highly efficient markets. Discuss some of these implications.

24. (Appendix Question) Boileryard Clarke, an astute investment observer, wrote, "Testing for empirical regularities is conceptually difficult because it is really a two-hypothesis test. One test relates to the validity of the underlying asset pricing model, and the other test relates to the existence of the empirical regularity." What does Boileryard mean by this statement?

25. You ask John Statdud, your research assistant, to analyze the relationship between the return on Coca-Cola Enterprises (CCE) common stock and the return on the market using the Standard & Poor's 500 Stock Index as a proxy for the market. The data include monthly returns for both CCE and S&P 500 over a recent five-year period. The results of the regression are indicated below:

$$R_{CCE,t} = .59 + .94(R_{S\&P,t}) + e_{CCE,t}$$
$$(.81) \quad (3.10)$$

> where: $R_{CCE,t}$ = return on CCE common stock in month t,
> $R_{S\&P,t}$ = return on S&P 500 stock index in month t,
> $e_{CCE,t}$ = residual error in month t.

The numbers in parentheses are the t-statistics (the .01 critical value is 2.66). The coefficient of determination R^2 for the regression is .215. Statdud wrote the following summary of the regression results:

1. The regression statistics indicate that during the five-year period under study, when the annual return on the S&P 500 was zero, CCE had an average annual return of 0.59%.
2. The alpha value of .59 is a measure of the variability of the return on the market.
3. The coefficient of .94 indicates CCE's sensitivity to the return on the S&P 500 and suggests that the return on CCE's common stock is less sensitive to market movements than the average stock.
4. The t-statistic of 3.10 for the slope coefficient indicates that the coefficient is not statistically significant at the .01 level.
5. The R^2 for the regression of .215 indicates that the average estimate deviates from the actual observation by an average of 21.5%.
6. There is no concern that the slope coefficient lacks statistical significance since beta values tend to be less stable (and therefore less useful) than alpha values.
7. The regression should be rerun using ten years of data. This would improve the reliability of the estimated coefficients while not sacrificing anything.

Identify which of the seven statements made by Statdud are incorrect and justify your answer(s).

26. You are a portfolio manager meeting a client. During the conversation that followed your formal review of her account, your client asked the following question: "My granddaughter, who is studying investments, tells me that one of the best ways to make money in the stock market is to buy the stocks of small-capitalization firms on a Monday morning late in December and to sell the stocks one month later." What is she talking about?
 a. Identify the apparent market anomalies (empirical regularities) that would justify the proposed strategy.
 b. Explain why you believe such a strategy might or might not work in the future.

APPENDIX

EMPIRICAL REGULARITIES IN THE STOCK MARKET

Researchers have uncovered certain **empirical regularities** in common stocks. That is, certain cross-sectional differences among stock returns have been found to occur with regularity. Some regularities should occur according to certain asset pricing models. For example, the CAPM asserts that different stocks should have different returns because different stocks have different betas. What makes the regularities that are about to be discussed of special interest is that they are not predicted by any of the traditional asset pricing models. Accordingly, they are sometimes also referred to as **anomalies.**

Earlier it was mentioned that returns were related to a firm's size as well as its book-value-to-market-value and earnings-to-price ratios. Hence these relationships are often used as examples of anomalies.[46] This appendix will examine some calendar anomalies and present some international evidence that indicates that such anomalies also exist in other countries.

A.1 SEASONALITY IN STOCK RETURNS

The desire of individuals for liquidity may be thought to change from day to day and from month to month. If so, there may be seasonal patterns in stock returns. One might presume that such patterns would be relatively unimportant. Indeed, according to the notion of efficient markets, such patterns should be quite minor (if they exist at all), because they are not suggested by traditional asset pricing models. However, the evidence indicates that at least two are significant: the **January effect** and the **day-of-the-week effect.**[47]

A.1.1 January Effect

There is no obvious reason to expect stock returns to be higher in certain months than in others. However, in a study that looked at average monthly returns on NYSE-listed common stocks, significant seasonalities were found.[48] In particular, the average return in January was higher than the average return in any other month. Table 17.8 indicates the average stock return in January and

---

TABLE 17.8
SEASONALITY IN STOCK RETURNS

Time Period	Average Stock Return In January	Average Stock Return In Other Months	Difference In Returns
1904–1928	1.30%	.44%	.86%
1929–1940	6.63	−.60	7.23
1941–1974	3.91	.70	3.21
1904–1974	3.48	.42	3.06

Source: Michael S. Rozeff and William R. Kinney, Jr., "Capital Market Seasonality: The Case of Stock Returns," *Journal of Financial Economics*, 3, no. 4 (October 1976): p. 388.

the other 11 months for various time periods. Although the difference in returns was minor in the early part of the century, more recently it appears that the average return in January has been approximately 3% higher than the average monthly returns in February through December.[49]

A.1.2 Day-of-the-Week Effect

It is often assumed that the expected daily returns on stocks are the same for all days of the week. That is, the expected return on a given stock is the same for Monday as it is for Tuesday as it is for Wednesday as it is for Thursday as it is for Friday. However, a number of studies have uncovered evidence that refutes this belief. Two early studies looked at the average daily return on NYSE-listed securities and found that the return on Monday was quite different.[50] In particular, the average return on Monday was found to be much lower than the average return on any other day of the week. Furthermore, the average return on Monday was negative, whereas the other days of the week had positive average returns. Table 17.9 displays these findings.

The rate of return on a stock for a given day of the week is typically calculated by subtracting the closing price on the previous trading day from the closing price on that day, adding any dividends for that day to the difference, and then dividing the resulting number by the closing price as of the previous trading day:

$$r_t = \frac{(P_t - P_{t-1}) + D_t}{P_{t-1}} \tag{17.19}$$

where P_t and P_{t-1} are the closing prices on days t and $t-1$, and D_t is the value of any dividends paid on day t. This means that the return for Monday uses the closing price on Monday as P_t and the closing price on Friday as P_{t-1}. Thus the change in the price of a stock for Monday ($P_t - P_{t-1}$) actually represents the change in price *over the weekend,* as well as during Monday. This observation has caused some people to refer to the day-of-the-week effect as the *weekend effect.* Other people use the *weekend effect* to refer to price behavior from Friday close to Monday open, and the *Monday effect* to refer to price behavior from Monday open to Monday close.

A refinement of the day-of-the-week effect involved an examination of NYSE stock returns over 15-minute intervals during trading hours over the period of December 1, 1981, through January 31, 1983.[51] Figure 17.10 displays the results

---

| TABLE 17.9 |||||
| ANALYSIS OF DAILY RETURNS |||||
	Monday	**Tuesday**	**Wednesday**	**Thursday**	**Friday**
A. French Study					
January 1953–December 1977	−.17%	.02%	.10%	.04%	.09%
B. Gibbons & Hess Study					
July 1962–December 1978	−.13%	.00%	.10%	.03%	.08%

Source: Kenneth R. French, "Stock Returns and the Weekend Effect," *Journal of Financial Economics,* 8, no. 1 (March 1980): p. 58; and Michael R. Gibbons and Patrick Hess, "Day of the Week Effects and Asset Returns," *Journal of Business,* 54, no. 4 (October 1981): pp. 582–583.

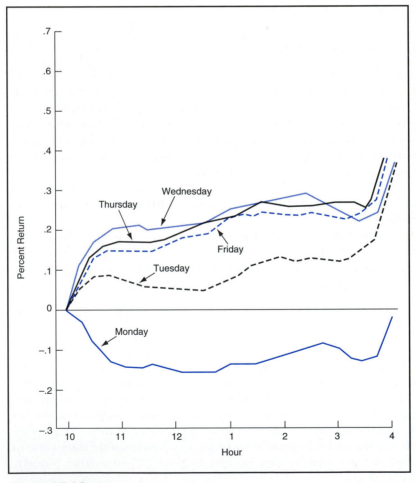

Figure 17.10

Cumulated 15-Minute Intraday Returns

Source: Lawrence Harris, "How to Profit From Intraday Stock Returns," *Journal of Portfolio Management,* 12, no. 2 (Winter 1986): p. 63.

when these returns were cumulated and examined on a day-of-the-week basis. Several observations can be made. First, the negative returns during trading hours on Monday occurred within an hour of the opening. Afterward, the behavior of stock prices on Monday was similar to the other days of the week. Second, on Tuesdays through Fridays there was a notable upward movement in prices in the first hour of trading. Third, on all days of the week there was a notable upward movement in prices during the last hour of trading.[52] Hence most of the daily price movement in a stock typically comes near the open and close.

Somewhat related to the day-of-the-week effect is the **holiday effect.** A study of this effect found that average stock returns on trading days immediately before federal holidays (the market is closed on these holidays; there are eight per year) are 9 to 14 times higher than the average daily returns during the rest of the year.[53] Furthermore, this abnormally high return is spread out from the closing price two days before the holiday to the opening price on the day after the holiday. Tests indicate that it is unrelated to the size, January, or day-of-the-week effects.

A.2   INTERRELATIONSHIPS

Given the presence of these regularities as well as those mentioned earlier in the chapter, researchers have attempted to see whether there are any interrelationships among them. For example, is the January effect more pronounced for small firms? A brief discussion of this interrelationship follows.[54]

A.2.1   Size and January Effects

Having observed that small firms have higher returns than large firms, and that returns are higher in January than in any other month of the year, it is interesting to ponder whether or not these two effects are somehow interrelated. One study that examined this issue found that the two effects were strongly interrelated.[55] All NYSE-listed and AMEX-listed stocks over the 17-year period of 1963 to 1979 were examined in this study. At the end of each year, each firm was ranked by the size of the aggregate market value of its equity (that is, the year-end market price per share times the number of shares outstanding). Ten portfolios were then formed based on size, with portfolio 1 containing the smallest 10% of the firms, portfolio 2 the next smallest 10%, and so on.

Abnormal returns were calculated subsequently for each portfolio on a monthly basis over the 17-year period and averaged for each month. Figure 17.11 displays the results.

It can be seen from this figure that the size effect was most pronounced in January, because the line for this month slopes down sharply from left to right. The other 11 months of the year appear to be quite similar to each other. Generally, each one of these months displays a slight downward slope, indicating that the size effect also existed for these months, but only to a minor degree. Also of interest is the observation that large firms had a negative abnormal return in

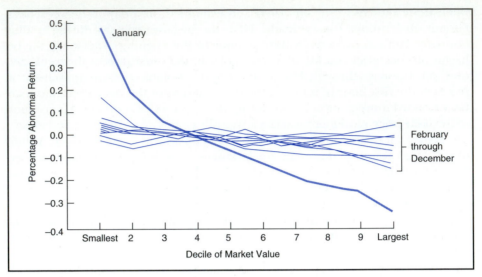

Figure 17.11

Interrelationship Between the Size Effect and the January Effect

Source: Donald B. Keim, "Size-related Anomalies and Stock Return Seasonality: Further Empirical Evidence," *Journal of Financial Economics,* 12, no. 1 (June 1983): p. 21.

January. Thus the January effect has been due primarily to the behavior of small firms, and the size effect has been concentrated mainly in the month of January.

Further examination of this interrelationship between the size effect and the January effect has revealed that it is concentrated in the first five trading days of January.[56] In particular, the difference in returns between the smallest firm portfolio and the largest firm portfolio over these five days was 8.0%, whereas over the entire year it was 30.4%. Thus 26.3% (= 8.0%/30.4%) of the annual size effect occurred during these five days. (If the size effect had been spread evenly over the year, then .4% of it would have been attributed to these five days.)

Attempts have been made to explain this interrelationship between the January effect and the size effect. One explanation that appears to have some merit has to do with "tax selling." This explanation begins by arguing that stocks that have declined during the year have downward pressure on their prices near year-end as investors sell them to realize capital losses in order to minimize tax payments. After the end of the year, this pressure is removed and the prices jump back to their "fair" values. A related argument asserts that some professional money managers wish to sell those stocks that have performed poorly during the past year in order to avoid their appearance on year-end reports. Such activity is often referred to as "window dressing." Note that these arguments fly in the face of the notion of efficient markets. (The notion of efficient markets would suggest that this cannot be true, because if investors sensed that stocks were becoming undervalued at year-end, they would flood the market with buy orders, thereby preventing any substantive undervaluation from occurring.) Nevertheless, it does appear to have some merit in that those stocks that declined during the previous year had the largest appreciation in January.[57] However, this association between January returns and previous year stock-price declines does not appear to be attributable solely to such downward tax-selling price pressure. This is because the biggest "losers" during a year appear to have abnormally high returns for as long as five Januaries thereafter. This contradicts such arguments, because according to them the abnormal price rebound should occur only in the first subsequent January.[58]

Contradictory evidence is also provided by noting that the January effect exists in Japan (as will be shown later), yet Japan has no capital gains tax and disallows any deduction for capital losses.[59] Rebutting this evidence is the observation that the January effect apparently did not exist prior to the imposition of income taxes in the United States.[60]

A second possible explanation is that small stocks may be relatively riskier in January than during the rest of the year. If this is true, then they should have a relatively higher average return in January. A study finding that the betas of small stocks tend to increase at the beginning of the year lends support to this explanation.[61]

A.3   INTERNATIONAL EVIDENCE

Several people have investigated foreign stock markets in order to see whether similar anomalies exist outside the United States.[62] Because the Tokyo Stock Exchange is the largest non-U.S. exchange, evidence concerning anomalies there will be discussed next. Overall, the anomalies that have been observed in the United States also appear, for the most part, in Japan.

A.3.1   Size Effect

Table 17.10 presents evidence that suggests that the size effect also exists in Japan.[63] The data used in panel (A) were based on all stocks in the first section of the Tokyo Stock Exchange. (The Tokyo Stock Exchange has two "sections"; the second is less than 10% of the size of the first, measured by the market value of the securities traded on it.) Two indices were prepared and examined over the period from 1952 to 1980; they include the same stocks but are compiled differently. The EW index weights all the stocks equally, and the VW index weights the stocks by market value. Hence the EW index is influenced much more by the performance of small stocks. As the table indicates, the EW index returned 5.1% more, suggesting the presence of a size effect.

Panel (B) of Table 17.10 also indicates the presence of a size effect between 3.4% and 8.4% for the period from 1973 to 1987. Here the performance of small firms is measured with two indices. [Large stocks are measured by the TOPIX index, which is computed in a manner similar to the VW index in panel (A).] First, the smallest quintile of stocks in the first section is formed into a value-weighted index denoted TSEsmall. Second, the stocks in the second section are formed into a value-weighted index denoted TSE2. Interestingly, over the same

| **TABLE 17.10** | | | |
| SIZE EFFECT ON THE TOKYO STOCK EXCHANGE | | | |
	Small Stocks	Large Stocks	Difference
A. 1952–1980: EW vs. VW[a]	22.7%	17.6%	5.1%
B. 1973–1987: TSEsmall vs. TOPIX[b]	21.7	13.3	8.4
TSE2 vs. TOPIX[b]	16.7	13.3	3.4

[a]Adapted from Kiyoshi Kato and James S. Schallheim, "Seasonal and Size Anomalies in the Japanese Stock Market," Journal of Financial and Quantitative Analysis, 20, no. 2 (June 1985): p. 248.

[b]Adapted from Yasushi Hamao, "Fifteen-Year Performance of Japanese Capital Markets," in Japanese Capital Markets, Edwin J. Elton and Martin J. Gruber, eds. (New York: Ballinger, 1990): p. 10.

time period the difference in the returns on the S&P 500 (a large stock-value-weighted index) and the returns on the smallest quintile of NYSE-listed stocks was 7.8%, comparable to the differences in Tokyo.

A.3.2   January Effect

Table 17.11 shows the presence of a January effect in the Tokyo Stock Exchange.[64] The first two rows involve the same indices used in panel (A) of Table 17.10; panel (C) uses a value-weighted index prepared by *Morgan Stanley Capital International Perspective*. In all three panels the average return in January is clearly higher than the average monthly return in the remaining 11 months. Interestingly, June also has an unusually high average return, but not nearly as dramatic as January's.

A.3.3   Day-of-the-Week Effect

Evidence regarding the day-of-the-week effect is provided in Table 17.12.[65] It should be noted that the Tokyo Stock Exchange was open on Saturday mornings during the periods examined; hence there is an average return reported for Saturday as well as for Monday through Friday. Two indices are involved. The first is the TOPIX index, which is a value-weighted index based on all stocks listed in the first section. The second is the Nikkei Dow, which is based on 225 large, well-established companies on the Tokyo Stock Exchange and is a price-weighted index like the Dow Jones Industrial Average.

The table indicates that Monday returns are, in general, negative, just as in the United States (see Table 17.9 for comparisons).[66] Furthermore, Wednesday returns are the largest, again similar to the United States. Second largest is Saturday, the last trading day of the week in Japan. This is similar to the United States in that the last trading day of the week is the second largest. What is surprising is that Tuesday is negative, and even more so than Monday. Otherwise the day-of-the-week effect in Japan is similar to that observed in the United States.[67]

TABLE 17.11						
JANUARY EFFECT ON THE TOKYO STOCK EXCHANGE						
	Jan.	**Feb.–Dec.**	**Difference**	**June**	**Feb.–May and July–Dec.**	**Difference**
A. 1952–1980: EW[a]	7.1%	1.4%	6.7%	2.8%	1.3%	1.5%
B. 1952–1980: VW[a]	4.5	1.2	3.3	2.5	1.1	1.4
C. 1959–1979: VW[b]	3.5	.7	2.8	2.1	.5	1.6

[a]Adapted from Kiyoshi Kato and James S. Schallheim, "Seasonal and Size Anomalies in the Japanese Stock Market." Journal of Financial and Quantitative Analysis, 20, no. 2 (June 1985): p. 248.

[b]Adapted from Mustafa N. Gultekin and N. Bulent Gultekin, "Stock Market Seasonality: International Evidence," Journal of Financial Economics, 12, no. 4 (December 1983): p. 475.

TABLE 17.12						
DAY-OF-THE-WEEK EFFECT ON THE TOKYO STOCK EXCHANGE						
	Monday	**Tuesday**	**Wednesday**	**Thursday**	**Friday**	**Saturday**
A. 1970–1983: Nikkei Dow[a]	−.02%	−.09%	.15%	.03%	.06%	.12%
B. 1970–1983: Topix[a]	−.01	−.06	.12	.03	.06	.10
C. 1978–1987: Topix[b]	.00	−.09	.14	.06	.10	.14

[a]Adapted from Jeffrey Jaffe and Randolph Westerfield, "Patterns in Japanese Common Stock Returns: Day of the Week and Turn of the Year Effects," Journal of Financial and Quantitative Analysis, 20, no. 2 (June 1985): p. 263.

[b]Kiyoshi Kato, Sandra L. Schwartz, and William T. Ziemba, "Day of the Week Effects in Japanese Stocks," in Japanese Capital Markets, Edwin J. Elton and Martin J. Gruber, eds. (New York: Ballinger, 1990): p. 253.

A.3.4 Size and January Effects

Examination of Table 17.11 reveals that the size effect occurs for the most part in January. Hence these two effects are interconnected in a manner similar to that in the United States, as can be seen by examining the average returns indicated in panels (A) and (B).

These panels show that there is a pronounced difference in the average returns between the equal-weighted and value-weighted indices of 2.6% (= 7.1% − 4.5%) in January, but a relatively small difference of .2% (= 1.4% − 1.2%) during the other 11 months of the year. This is notable because the EW index gives much larger weights to small stocks than the VW index, suggesting that the difference between the two indices can be attributed to the performance of the small stocks. In summary, it would appear that in Japan the size effect is primarily a January effect.

A.4 SUMMARY OF EMPIRICAL REGULARITIES

On balance, what do these regularities suggest that the investor should do? First, investors who want to buy stocks should avoid doing so late on Friday or early on Monday. Conversely, investors who want to sell stocks should try to sell late on

Friday or early on Monday. Second, if the stocks of small firms are to be purchased, they should be purchased in late December or somewhat earlier. If the stocks of small firms are to be sold, they should be sold in mid-January or somewhat later. Third, if the stocks of large firms are to be purchased, they should be purchased in early February or somewhat later. If the stocks of large firms are to be sold, they should be sold in late December or somewhat earlier.[68]

Two words of caution are in order here. First, none of these empirical regularities is of a sufficient magnitude to suggest that riches are to be made by exploiting them. Indeed, transaction costs would devour most if not all of any profits that might be made.[69] All that they suggest is that if, for whatever reason, a buy or sell order is to be placed, there are some times when it may be more advantageous to do so. Second, although these regularities have been found to exist in the past, and in some instances for long periods of time and in several foreign markets, there is no guarantee that they will continue to exist in the future.[70] It may be the case that as more investors become aware of them and time their trades accordingly, such regularities will cease to exist.

ENDNOTES

[1] For more information on proxies, see Paul Jessup and Mary Bochnak, "Exercising Your Rights: How to Use Proxy Material," *AAII Journal,* 14, no. 9 (October 1992): 8–11.

[2] Another form of a takeover is a **merger.** A merger occurs when two firms combine their operations, the result being that only one firm exists. Mergers usually are negotiated by the management of the two firms. Tender offers differ in that the management of the bidder makes a direct appeal to the stockholders of the target firm for their shares. Tender offers also differ in that afterward both firms will still exist, because most tender offers are not for all the shares of the target. **Management buyouts** are a special kind of tender offer, where the current management of the firm uses borrowed funds to buy the company. (Hence they are a type of **leveraged buyout**. LBOs can be executed by anyone, including incumbent management.)

[3] See, for example, Michael C. Jensen and William H. Meckling, "Theory of the Firm: Managerial Behavior, Agency Costs and Ownership Structure," *Journal of Financial Economics,* 3, no. 4 (October 1976): 305–360; Eugene F. Fama, "Agency Problems and the Theory of the Firm," *Journal of Political Economy,* 88, no. 2 (April 1980): 288–307; Eugene F. Fama and Michael C. Jensen, "Separation of Ownership and Control," *Journal of Law and Economics,* 26 (June 1983): 301–325; Eugene F. Fama and Michael C. Jensen, "Agency Problems and Residual Claims," *Journal of Law and Economics,* 26 (June 1983): 327–349; the entire issues of vol. 11 (April 1983) and vol. 20 (January/March 1988) of the *Journal of Financial Economics;* and Michael C. Jensen, "Eclipse of the Public Corporation," *Harvard Business Review,* 89, no. 5 (September-October 1989): 61–74.

[4] An example of monitoring is having the firm's financial statements audited independently.

[5] For example, management may decide to procure lavishly furnished offices and an executive jet when the conduct of business suggests that these actions are not merited. Furthermore, management may invest in negative net present value investment projects when the firm has "free cash flow" instead of paying it to the shareholders. See Michael C. Jensen, "Agency Costs of Free Cash Flow, Corporate Finance and Takeovers," *American Economic Review,* 76, no. 2 (May 1986): 323–329.

[6] Robert Comment and Gregg A. Jarrell, "The Relative Signalling Power of Dutch-

Auction and Fixed-Price Self-Tender Offers and Open-Market Share Repurchases," *Journal of Finance,* 46, no. 4 (September 1991): 1243–1271.

[7] It should be noted that whereas there were similar numbers of fixed-price and Dutch-auction tender offers, the Dutch-auction method is becoming increasingly popular, particularly among larger corporations.

[8] Such findings are inconsistent with the notion of efficient markets, and hence can be considered an "anomaly." See Josef Lakonishok and Theo Vermaelen, "Anomalous Price Behavior Around Repurchase Tender Offers," *Journal of Finance,* 45, no. 2 (June 1990): 455–477. The Appendix discusses several other anomalies uncovered by researchers.

[9] For more on "ex dates," see "Dividends and Interest: Who Gets Payments After a Trade?" *AAII Journal,* 12, no. 4 (April 1990): 8–11.

[10] Some evidence in support of this view is provided by Josef Lakonishok and Baruch Lev, "Stock Splits and Stock Dividends: Why, Who, and When," *Journal of Finance,* 42, no. 4 (September 1987): 913–932.

[11] See Eugene F. Fama, Lawrence Fisher, Michael C. Jensen, and Richard Roll, "The Adjustment of Stock Prices to New Information," *International Economic Review,* 10, no. 1 (February 1969): 1–21; and Guy Charest, "Split Information, Stock Returns and Market Efficiency—I," *Journal of Financial Economics,* 6, no. 2/3 (June/September 1978): 265–296.

[12] See Thomas E. Copeland, "Liquidity Changes Following Stock Splits," *Journal of Finance,* 34, no. 1 (March 1979): 115–141; and Robert M. Conroy, Robert S. Harris, and Bruce A. Benet, "The Effects of Stock Splits on Bid-Ask Spreads," *Journal of Finance,* 45, no. 4 (September 1990): 1285–1295.

[13] Mark S. Grinblatt, Ronald W. Masulis, and Sheridan Titman, "The Valuation Effects of Stock Splits and Stock Dividends," *Journal of Financial Economics,* 13, no. 4 (December 1984): 461–490.

[14] Current stockholders may not be given this right if there is a provision in the charter denying it, or if it is denied by the stockholders at the annual meeting.

[15] The investor could simply let the rights expire, causing that investor's proportion in the corporation to decline as others are given ownership in the expanded firm in return for the provision of new capital. Sometimes there is an **oversubscription privilege** given to the subscribing stockholders. This means that those stockholders who have exercised their rights will be given an opportunity to buy the shares that were not purchased; this opportunity can become important if the rights are not transferable.

[16] The subscription price is usually set at roughly 80% of the current market price of the stock.

[17] American Depository Receipts (ADRs) for foreign stocks that are traded on Nasdaq are shown after the Small-Cap Issues under a heading of "ADRs." Exchange-listed ADRs are not shown separately. Instead, they are integrated into the tables with listed U.S. securities. ADRs are discussed in more detail in Chapters 3 and 26.

[18] This reporting requirement should not be confused with SEC Rule 13d, which requires investors to disclose their holdings in a company once they are equal to 5% or more of the company's stock. Unlike form 4 investors, Rule 13d investors are not viewed as insiders by the SEC, and they do not have to report every transaction they subsequently make.

[19] The *Value Line Investment Survey* (published by Value Line, Inc., New York, NY) reports an "index of insider decisions" for each stock covered in its weekly service. In essence, this is a cumulative index of the net number of purchasers (including those who exercise options) and sellers. The *Weekly Insider Report* (published by Vickers Stock Research

Corp., Brookside, NJ) reports a ratio of total insider buying to total insider selling. For an article about what constitutes insider trading, see Gary L. Tidwell, "Here's a Tip—Know the Rules of Insider Trading," *Sloan Management Review,* 28, no. 4 (Summer 1987): 93–98.

[20] If the insider bought the stock by exercising an option that was given to him or her as part of his or her compensation, then the six-month period is measured from the day the option was granted.

[21] An alternative method is to examine stock returns on days of illegal insider trading. Looking at 183 SEC cases from 1980 to 1989, one study found that stock prices had an average abnormal return of 3.0% on each day that illegal insider buying took place and −3.5% on each day that illegal insider selling took place. See Lisa K. Meulbroek, "An Empirical Analysis of Illegal Insider Trading," *Journal of Finance,* 47, no. 5 (December 1992): 1661–1699.

[22] Jeffrey F. Jaffe, "Special Information and Insider Trading," *Journal of Business,* 47, no. 3 (July 1974): 410–428. Also see Joseph E. Finnerty, "Insiders and Market Efficiency," *Journal of Finance,* 31, no. 4 (September 1976): 1141–1148; and Aaron B. Feigen, "Information Opportunities from Insider Trading Laws," *AAII Journal,* 11, no. 8 (September 1989): 12–15.

[23] See Herbert S. Kerr, "The Battle of Insider Trading and Market Efficiency," *Journal of Portfolio Management,* 6, no. 4 (Summer 1980): 47–58; Wayne Y. Lee and Michael E. Solt, "Insider Trading: A Poor Guide to Market Timing," *Journal of Portfolio Management,* 12, no. 4 (Summer 1986): 65–71; H. Nejat Seyhun, "Insiders' Profits, Costs of Trading, and Market Efficiency," *Journal of Financial Economics,* 16, no. 2 (June 1986): 189–212; Michael S. Rozeff and Mir A. Zaman, "Market Efficiency and Insider Trading: New Evidence," *Journal of Business,* 61, no. 1 (January 1988): 25–44; and Ji-Chai Lin and John S. Howe, "Insider Trading in the OTC Market," *Journal of Finance,* 45, no. 4 (September 1990): 1273–1284.

[24] It has been argued that roughly 300 months (25 years) of historical returns are needed in order for a simple averaging technique to produce useful estimates of expected returns, provided that the "true" but unobserved expected return is constant during this entire period. See J. D. Jobson and Bob Korkie, "Estimation for Markowitz Efficient Portfolios," *Journal of the American Statistical Association,* 75, no. 371 (September 1980): 544–554; and "Putting Markowitz Theory to Work," *Journal of Portfolio Management,* 7, no. 4 (Summer 1981): 70–74.

[25] In doing so, a number of researchers have uncovered certain "empirical regularities" in common stocks; the Appendix discusses a number of them. For a more detailed summary, see Donald B. Keim, "The CAPM and Equity Return Regularities," *Financial Analysts Journal,* 42, no. 3 (May/June 1986): 19–34; Douglas K. Pearce, "Challenges to the Concept of Market Efficiency," *Federal Reserve Bank of Kansas City Economic Review,* 72, no. 8 (September/October 1987): 16–33; and Robert A. Haugen and Josef Lakonishok, *The Incredible January Effect* (Homewood, IL: Dow Jones-Irwin, 1988).

[26] For an introduction to regression, see Chapter 11 of James T. McClave and P. George Benson, *Statistics for Business and Economics* (San Francisco: Dellen Publishing, 1991); and Mark P. Kritzman, " . . . About Regressions," *Financial Analysts Journal,* 47, no. 3 (May/June 1991): 12–15.

[27] WM's beta and alpha would have been equal to .63 and .17%, respectively, if excess returns (that is, returns less the riskfree rate) had been used in the calculations instead of returns. Using returns or excess returns (as well as including or ignoring dividends in calculating returns) appears to make little difference in the estimated size of beta. However, there is a substantive difference in the estimated size of alpha. See William F. Sharpe and Guy M. Cooper, "Risk-Return Classes of New York Stock Exchange Common Stocks, 1931-1967," *Financial Analysts Journal,* 28, no. 2 (March/April 1972): 46–54.

[28] R is used here to denote the correlation coefficient; sometimes (as in Chapter 8) the Greek letter rho (ρ) is used instead. Thus R-squared is equivalent to ρ-squared, or the square of the correlation coefficient.

[29] Adjusted betas are also published in the *Value Line Investment Survey;* their adjusted beta is equal to $(.35 \times 1.0) + (.67 \times \beta_h)$. Thus the adjustment procedures of Value Line and Merrill Lynch are quite similar. See Meir Statman, "Betas Compared: Merrill Lynch vs. Value Line," *Journal of Portfolio Management,* 7, no. 2 (Winter 1981): 41–44; and Frank K. Reilly and David J. Wright, "A Comparison of Published Betas," *Journal of Portfolio Management,* 14, no. 3 (Spring 1988): 64–69.

[30] The method is developed more fully in Richard A. Brealey and Stewart C. Myers, *Principles of Corporate Finance* (New York: McGraw-Hill, 1991): 191–192, 468–469; and Thomas E. Copeland and J. Fred Weston, *Financial Theory and Corporate Policy* (Reading, MA: Addison-Wesley, 1988), Chapter 13.

[31] To derive Equation (17.13), note that Equation (17.11) can be written as $V_u = D + E - \tau D$ since $V_L = D + E$. Hence the quantity $D + E - \tau D$ can be substituted for V_u in Equation (17.12), and then the altered equation can be solved for β_{equity} and simplified, resulting in Equation (17.13).

[32] It is assumed here that ABC's bond beta and average tax rate were unaffected by the new issuance of equity. More complex analyses are sometimes utilized to take into account the possible impact of capital structure changes upon them.

[33] The term $(E_{ind1}\beta_{ind1} + E_{ind2}\beta_{ind2})$ would simply be expanded if more than two industries were involved.

[34] In this method, both historical and adjusted betas are calculated relative to a value-weighted index of the returns on all stocks listed on the New York Stock Exchange. All attributes were calculated using data available a full month prior to the beginning of the month in which stock returns are measured. This avoids statistical problems and provides results that can be used for actual portfolio management.

[35] The dividend yield is measured in percent per year. The "size attribute" is calculated by taking the logarithm (to the base 10) of the total market value of equity outstanding (that is, price per share times shares outstanding), expressed in billions of dollars.

[36] Barr Rosenberg and Vinay Marathe, "The Prediction of Investment Risk: Systematic and Residual Risk," *Proceedings of the Seminar on the Analysis of Security Prices,* University of Chicago, November 1975. Also see Barr Rosenberg, "Prediction of Common Stock Investment Risk," *Journal of Portfolio Management,* 11, no. 1 (Fall 1984): 44–53; and "Prediction of Common Stock Betas," *Journal of Portfolio Management,* 11, no. 2 (Winter 1985): 5–14.

[37] In general, growth stocks are stocks having rapid increases in earnings whereas value stocks are stocks whose market price seems to be low relative to measures of their worth. Hence other ratios (such as dividend yield and P/E ratios) are sometimes used in sorting out these two types of stocks.

[38] The S&P/BARRA Value Stock Index and the S&P/BARRA Growth Stock Index involve dividing the S&P 500 stocks into two groups based on the size of their BV/MV ratios every six months. The stocks in each group are then used to form these two market-capitalization-weighted indices. The construction of market indices is discussed in more detail in Chapter 23.

[39] Eugene F. Fama and Kenneth R. French, "The Cross-Section of Expected Stock Returns," *Journal of Finance,* 47, no. 2 (June 1992): 427–465. Also see Barr Rosenberg, Kenneth Reid, and Ronald Lanstein, "Persuasive Evidence of Market Inefficiency," *Journal of Portfolio Management,* 11, no. 3 (Spring 1985): 9–16.

[40] Also see S. Basu, "Investment Performance of Common Stocks in Relation to Their Price-Earnings Ratios: A Test of the Efficient Market Hypothesis," *Journal of Finance,* 32, no. 3 (June 1977): 663–682; and "The Relationship Between Earnings' Yield, Market Value and Return for NYSE Common Stocks: Further Evidence," *Journal of Financial Economics,* 12, no. 1 (June 1983): 129–156.

[41] Other studies of the size effect include Rolf Banz, "The Relationship Between Return and Market Value of Common Stocks," *Journal of Financial Economics,* 9, no. 1 (March 1981): 3–18; and Marc R. Reinganum, "Misspecification of Capital Asset Pricing: Empirical Anomalies Based on Earnings Yields and Market Values," *Journal of Financial Economics,* 9, no. 1 (March 1981): 19–46.

[42] The missing variable apparently is not beta, as the relationship between these variables and stock returns has been found to exist independent of differences in beta. See Fama and French, "The Cross-Section of Expected Stock Returns."

[43] Marc R. Reinganum, "Misspecification of Capital Asset Pricing." Also see Rolf W. Banz and William J. Breen, "Sample Dependent Results Using Accounting and Market Data: Some Evidence," *Journal of Finance,* 41, no. 4 (September 1986): 779–793.

[44] It should be noted that this view is not universally held. See Jeffrey Jaffe, Donald B. Keim, and Randolph Westerfield, "Earnings Yields, Market Values, and Stock Returns," *Journal of Finance,* 44, no. 1 (March 1989): 135–138.

[45] Fama and French, "The Cross-Section of Expected Stock Returns."

[46] Another anomaly involves financial leverage. More specifically, the stocks of firms with larger debt-to-equity ratios have, on average, larger stock returns. See Laxmi Chand Bhandari, "Debt/Equity Ratio and Expected Common Stock Returns: Empirical Evidence," *Journal of Finance,* 43, no. 2 (June 1988): 507–528.

[47] There is also evidence of a "weather effect" in that NYSE stock returns appear to be related to the amount of cloud cover in New York City. More specifically, the average daily return was .13% when the cloud cover was 0-20% and .02% when the the cloud cover was 100%. This has been interpreted to mean that investor psychology influences asset prices. See Edward M. Saunders, Jr., "Stock Prices and Wall Street Weather," *American Economic Review,* 83, no. 5 (December 1993): 1337–1345.

[48] Michael S. Rozeff and William R. Kinney, Jr., "Capital Market Seasonality: The Case of Stock Returns," *Journal of Financial Economics,* 3, no. 4 (October 1976): 379–402. For an argument that the market does not have a January effect, see Jay R. Ritter and Navin Chopra, "Portfolio Rebalancing and the Turn-of-the-Year Effect," *Journal of Finance,* 44, no. 1 (March 1989): 149–166.

[49] Interestingly, it appears that the returns over the first half of any month (defined to include the last day of the previous month) are significantly higher than the returns over the second half of the month. See Robert A. Ariel, "A Monthly Effect in Stock Returns," *Journal of Financial Economics,* 18, no. 1 (March 1987): 161–174. Another study found this effect to be concentrated in the first three trading days (plus the last trading day of the previous month) and labeled it the **turn-of-the-month effect.** See Josef Lakonishok and Seymour Smidt, "Are Seasonal Anomalies Real? A Ninety-Year Perspective," *Review of Financial Studies,* 1, no. 4 (Winter 1988): 403–425.

[50] Kenneth R. French, "Stock Returns and the Weekend Effect," *Journal of Financial Economics,* 8, no. 1 (March 1980): 55–69; and Michael R. Gibbons and Patrick Hess, "Day of the Week Effects and Asset Returns," *Journal of Business,* 54, no. 4 (October 1981): 579–596. For an argument that this effect disappeared in the mid 1970s, see Robert A. Connolly, "An Examination of the Robustness of the Weekend Effect," *Journal of Financial and Quantitative Analysis,* 24, no. 2 (June 1989): 133–169.

[51] Lawrence Harris, "How to Profit from Intradaily Stock Returns," *Journal of Portfolio Management,* 12, no. 2 (Winter 1986): 61–64; and "A Transaction Data Study of Weekly and Intradaily Patterns in Stock Returns," *Journal of Financial Economics,* 16, no. 1 (May 1986): 99–117.

[52] This rise in stock prices at the end of the day appears to be primarily due to a large price rise between the next to last and last trades; this observation appears to be widespread over firms and days of the week. See Lawrence Harris, "A Day-End Transaction Price Anomaly," *Journal of Financial and Quantitative Analysis,* 24, no. 1 (March 1989): 29–45.

[53] Robert A. Ariel, "High Stock Returns Before Holidays: Existence and Evidence on Possible Causes," *Journal of Finance,* 45, no. 5 (December 1990): 1611–1626. The holiday effect also exists in Japan and the U.K. See Chan-Wang Kim and Jinwoo Park, "Holiday Effects and Stock Returns: Further Evidence," *Journal of Financial and Quantitative Analysis,* 29, no. 1 (March 1994): 145–157.

[54] Other interrelationships are discussed in the previous edition (1990) of this book; see pp. 451–457.

[55] Donald B. Keim, "Size-related Anomalies and Stock Return Seasonality: Further Empirical Evidence," *Journal of Financial Economics,* 12, no. 1 (June 1983): 13–32.

[56] Rogalski also finds that the anomalous price behavior of stocks in January mostly occurs in the first five trading days. Roll has observed that the largest daily differences in the returns between small firms and large firms occur over the last trading day of the year and the first four trading days of the year. Furthermore, eight of the subsequent ten trading days also have notably large differences in returns. See Richard Rogalski, "New Findings Regarding Day-of-the-Week Returns Over Trading and Non-Trading Periods: A Note," *Journal of Finance,* 39, no. 5 (December 1984): 1603–1614; and Richard Roll, "Vas ist das?" *Journal of Portfolio Management,* 9, no. 2 (Winter 1983): 18–28.

[57] See Roll, "Vas ist das?"; Edward A. Dyl, "Capital Gains Taxation and Year-End Stock Market Behavior," *Journal of Finance,* 32, no. 1 (March 1977): 165–175; Ben Branch, "A Tax Loss Trading Rule," *Journal of Business,* 50, no. 2 (April 1977): 198–207; Dan Givoly and Arie Ovadia, "Year-End Tax-Induced Sales and Stock Market Seasonality," *Journal of Finance,* 38, no. 1 (March 1983): 171–185; Marc R. Reinganum, "The Anomalous Stock Market Behavior of Small Firms in January: Empirical Tests for Tax-Loss Selling Effects," *Journal of Financial Economics,* 12, no. 1 (June 1983): 89–104; Josef Lakonishok and Seymour Smidt, "Capital Gain Taxation and Volume of Trading," *Journal of Finance,* 41, no. 4 (September 1986): 951–974; Jay R. Ritter, "The Buying and Selling Behavior of Individual Investors at the Turn of the Year," *Journal of Finance,* 43, no. 3 (July 1988): 701–717; Joseph P. Ogden, "Turn-of-Month Evaluations of Liquid Profits and Stock Returns: A Common Explanation for the Monthly and January Effects," *Journal of Finance,* 45, no. 4 (September 1990): 1259–1272; and Greggory A. Brauer and Eric C. Chang, "Return Seasonality in Stocks and Their Underlying Assets: Tax-Loss Selling versus Information Explanations," *Review of Financial Studies,* 3, no. 2 (1990): 255–280.

[58] See K. C. Chan, "Can Tax-Loss Selling Explain the January Seasonal in Stock Returns?" *Journal of Finance,* 41, no. 5 (December 1986): 1115–1128; Werner F. M. DeBondt and Richard Thaler, "Does the Stock Market Overreact?" *Journal of Finance,* 40, no. 3 (July 1985), 793–805; and "Further Evidence on Investor Over-reaction and Stock Market Seasonality," *Journal of Finance,* 42, no. 3 (July 1987): 557–581.

[59] A similar observation has been made regarding Canada. See Angel Berges, John J. McConnell, and Gary G. Schlarbaum, "The Turn-of-the-Year in Canada," *Journal of Finance,* 39, no. 1 (March 1984): 185–192.

[60] See Steven L. Jones, Winson Lee, and Rudolf Apenbrink, "New Evidence on the January Effect Before Personal Income Taxes," *Journal of Finance,* 46, no. 5 (December 1991): 1909–1924.

[61] Richard J. Rogalski and Seha M. Tinic, "The January Size Effect: Anomaly or Risk Mismeasurement?" *Financial Analysts Journal*, 42, no. 6 (November-December 1986): 63–70. See also Avner Arbel, "Generic Stocks: An Old Product in a New Package," *Journal of Portfolio Management*, 11, no. 4 (Summer 1985): 4–13; and K. C. Chan and Nai-fu Chen, "Structural and Return Characteristics of Small and Large Firms," *Journal of Finance*, 46, no. 4 (September 1991): 1467–1484.

[62] The BV/MV ratio anomaly was found to exist in other countries, particularly France, Switzerland, and Japan, suggesting that value stocks have outperformed growth stocks outside the United States. See Carlo Capaul, Ian Rowley, and William F. Sharpe, "International Value and Growth Stock Returns," *Financial Analysts Journal*, 49, no. 1 (January/February 1993): 27–36.

[63] See Kiyoshi Kato and James S. Schallheim, "Seasonal and Size Anomalies in the Japanese Stock Market," *Journal of Financial and Quantitative Analysis*, 20, no. 2 (June 1985): 243–260; and Yasushi Hamao, "Fifteen-Year Performance of Japanese Capital Markets," in *Japanese Capital Markets*, Edwin J. Elton and Martin J. Gruber, eds. (New York: Ballinger, 1990): 3–26.

[64] See Kato and Schallheim, "Seasonal and Size Anomalies"; and Mustafa N. Gultekin and N. Bulent Gultekin, "Stock Market Seasonality: International Evidence," *Journal of Financial Economics*, 12, no. 4 (December 1983): 469–481.

[65] See Jeffrey Jaffe and Randolph Westerfield, "Patterns in Japanese Common Stock Returns: Day of the Week and Turn of the Year Effects," *Journal of Financial and Quantitative Analysis*, 20, no. 2 (June 1985): 261–272; "The Weekend Effect in Common Stock Returns: The International Evidence," *Journal of Finance*, 40, no. 2 (June 1985): 433–454; and Kiyoshi Kato, Sandra L. Schwartz, and William T. Ziemba, "Day of the Week Effects in Japanese Stocks," in *Japanese Capital Markets*: 249–281.

[66] More recently there has been some evidence that the day-of-the-week effect has become much less noticeable in both the United States and Japan. See Robert Connolly, "An Examination of the Robustness of the Weekend Effect"; and Eric C. Chang, J. Michael Pinegar, and R. Ravichandron, "International Evidence on the Robustness of the Day-of-the-Week Effect," *Journal of Financial and Quantitative Analysis*, 28, no. 4 (December 1993): 497–513.

[67] Additional patterns have been discovered. Imagine splitting the set of Mondays in two where one set corresponds to Mondays that follow a week where the market declined and the second set corresponds to Mondays that follow a week where the market rose. Interestingly, in both the United States and Japan, the average return for the first set of Mondays is significantly negative ($-.39\%$ in the United States and $-.18\%$ in Japan) whereas the average return for the second set of Mondays is slightly positive ($.06\%$ in the United States and $.11\%$ in Japan). See Jeffrey F. Jaffe, Randolph Westerfield, and Christopher Ma, "A Twist on the Monday Effect in Stock Prices: Evidence from the U.S. and Foreign Stock Markets," *Journal of Banking and Finance*, 13, no. 4/5 (September 1989): 641–650.

[68] These recommendations are based on studies that typically involved exchange-listed stocks. For over-the-counter stocks, Richard D. Fortin and O. Maurice Joy ["Buying and Selling OTC Stock: Fine-Tuning Your Trade Date," *AAII Journal*, 15, no. 3 (March 1993): 8–10] recommend (1) buying just before and selling just after the end of the month, (2) buying on Tuesday and selling on Friday, and (3) buying within two days on either side of a holiday and avoiding selling during this period.

[69] See Donald B. Keim, "Trading Patterns, Bid-Ask Spreads, and Estimated Security Returns: The Case of Common Stocks at Calendar Turning Points," *Journal of Financial Economics*, 25, no. 1 (November 1989): 75–97.

[70] The Appendix to Chapter 16 discusses regularities in the bond market.

common stock
limited liability
charter
transfer agent
registrar
proxy
proxy fight
cumulative voting system
majority voting system
takeover
tender offer
bidder
target firm
merger
management buyout
leveraged buyout
white knight
greenmail
repurchase offer
Pac-Man defense
crown jewel defense
poison pill defense
par value

book value of the equity
book value per share
treasury stock
restricted
letter stock
dividends
date of record
ex-dividend date
stock dividend
stock split
reverse stock split
ex-distribution date
preemptive rights
rights
oversubscription privilege
rights offering
subscription price
ex-rights date
closing price
dividend yield
insiders
ex ante
ex post

historical beta
simple linear regression
standard deviation of the
    random error term
standard error of beta
standard error of alpha
correlation coefficient
coefficient of determination
coefficient of
    nondetermination
R-squared
residual standard deviation
adjusted beta
growth stocks
value stocks
size effect
empirical regularities
anomalies
January effect
day-of-the-week effect
turn-of-the-month effect
holiday effect

REFERENCES

1. For a discussion of the motivations for takeovers and the associated consequences, see:

Michael C. Jensen and Richard S. Ruback, "The Market for Corporate Control: The Scientific Evidence," *Journal of Financial Economics,* 11, nos. 1–4 (April 1983): 5–50.

Richard Roll, "The Hubris Hypothesis of Corporate Takeovers," *Journal of Business,* 59, no. 1, pt. 2 (April 1986): 197–216.

J. Fred Weston, Kwang S. Chung, and Susan E. Hoag, *Mergers, Restructuring, and Corporate Control* (Englewood Cliffs, NJ: Prentice Hall, 1990).

Michael C. Jensen, "Corporate Control and the Politics of Finance," *Journal of Applied Corporate Finance,* 4, no. 2 (Summer 1991): 13–33.

Andrei Shleifer and Robert W. Vishny, "The Takeover Wave of the 1980s," *Journal of Applied Corporate Finance,* 4, no. 3 (Fall 1991): 49–56.

Jack Treynor, "The Value of Control," *Financial Analysts Journal,* 49, no. 5 (July/August 1993): 6–9.

2. For a study of how risk arbitrageurs (investors who buy and sell stocks of firms involved in takeovers and divestitures) are able to earn substantial returns, see:

David F. Larcker and Thomas Lys, "An Empirical Analysis of the Incentives to Engage in Costly Information Acquisition: The Case of Risk Arbitrage," *Journal of Financial Economics*, 18, no. 1 (March 1987): 111–126.

3. Three interesting studies of stock repurchases are:

Josef Lakonishok and Theo Vermaelen, "Anomalous Price Behavior Around Repurchase Tender Offers," *Journal of Finance*, 45, no. 2 (June 1990): 455–477.

Robert Comment and Gregg A. Jarrell, "The Relative Signalling Power of Dutch-Auction and Fixed-Price Self-Tender Offers and Open-Market Share Repurchases," *Journal of Finance*, 46, no. 4 (September 1991): 1243–1271.

Laurie Simon Bagwell, "Dutch Auction Repurchases: An Analysis of Shareholder Heterogeneity," *Journal of Finance*, 47, no. 1 (March 1992): 71–105.

4. Americus Trust Securities are discussed in:

Robert A. Jarrow and Maureen O'Hara, "Primes and Scores: An Essay on Market Imperfections," *Journal of Finance*, 44, no. 5 (December 1989): 1263–1287.

P. C. Venkatesh, "Trading Costs and Ex-Day Behavior: An Examination of Primes and Scores," *Financial Management*, 20, no. 3 (Autumn 1991): 84–95.

5. Stock splits and stock dividends are examined in:

Eugene F. Fama, Lawrence Fisher, Michael C. Jensen, and Richard Roll, "The Adjustment of Stock Prices to New Information," *International Economic Review*, 10, no. 1 (February 1969): 1–21.

Sasson Bar-Yosef and Lawrence D. Brown, "A Re-examination of Stock Splits Using Moving Betas," *Journal of Finance*, 32, no. 4 (September 1977): 1069–1080.

Guy Charest, "Split Information, Stock Returns, and Market Efficiency–I," *Journal of Financial Economics*, 6, no. 2/3 (June/September 1978): 265–296.

Thomas E. Copeland, "Liquidity Changes Following Stock Splits," *Journal of Finance*, 34, no. 1 (March 1979): 115–141.

J. Randall Woolridge, "Ex-Date Stock Price Adjustment to Stock Dividends: A Note," *Journal of Finance*, 38, no. 1 (March 1983): 247–255.

Mark S. Grinblatt, Ronald W. Masulis, and Sheridan Titman, "The Valuation Effects of Stock Splits and Stock Dividends," *Journal of Financial Economics*, 13, no. 4 (December 1984): 461–490.

Josef Lakonishok and Baruch Lev, "Stock Splits and Stock Dividends: Why, Who, and When," *Journal of Finance*, 42, no. 4 (September 1987): 913–932.

Robert S. Conroy, Robert S. Harris, and Bruce A. Benet, "The Effects of Stock Splits on Bid-Ask Spreads," *Journal of Finance*, 45, no. 4 (September 1990): 1285–1295.

David A. Dubofsky, "Volatility Increases Subsequent to NYSE and AMEX Stock Splits," *Journal of Finance,* 46, no. 1 (March 1991): 421–431.

6. Insider trading has been examined in a number of studies. Some of the major ones are:

Jeffrey F. Jaffe, "Special Information and Insider Trading," *Journal of Business,* 47, no. 3 (July 1974): 410–428.

Joseph E. Finnerty, "Insiders and Market Efficiency," *Journal of Finance,* 31, no. 4 (September 1976): 1141–1148.

Herbert S. Kerr, "The Battle of Insider Trading and Market Efficiency," *Journal of Portfolio Management,* 6, no. 4 (Summer 1980): 47–58.

Wayne Y. Lee and Michael Solt, "Insider Trading: A Poor Guide to Market Timing," *Journal of Portfolio Management,* 12, no. 4 (Summer 1986): 65–71.

H. Nejat Seyhun, "Insiders' Profits, Costs of Trading, and Market Efficiency," *Journal of Financial Economics,* 16, no. 2 (June 1986): 189–212.

H. Nejat Seyhun, "The Information Content of Aggregate Insider Trading," *Journal of Business,* 61, no. 1 (January 1988): 1–24.

Michael S. Rozeff and Mir A. Zaman, "Market Efficiency and Insider Trading: New Evidence," *Journal of Business,* 61, no. 1 (January 1988): 25–44.

Ji-Chai Lin and John S. Howe, "Insider Trading in the OTC Market," *Journal of Finance,* 45, no. 4 (September 1990): 1273–1284.

Lisa K. Meulbroek, "An Empirical Analysis of Illegal Insider Trading," *Journal of Finance,* 47, no. 5 (December 1992): 1661–1699.

Mustafa Chowdhury, John S. Howe, and Ji-Chai Lin, "The Relation between Aggregate Insider Transactions and Stock Market Returns," *Journal of Financial and Quantitative Analysis,* 28, no. 3 (September 1993): 431–437.

7. The behavior of beta coefficients has been extensively studied. See, for example:

Marshall Blume, "On the Assessment of Risk," *Journal of Finance,* 26, no. 1 (March 1971): 1–10.

Robert A. Levy, "On the Short-Term Stationarity of Beta Coefficients," *Financial Analysts Journal,* 27, no. 6 (November/December 1971): 55–62.

William F. Sharpe and Guy M. Cooper, "Risk-Return Classes of New York Stock Exchange Common Stocks, 1931–1967," *Financial Analysts Journal,* 28, no. 2 (March-April 1972): 46–54.

Robert S. Hamada, "The Effect of the Firm's Capital Structure on the Systematic Risk of Common Stocks," *Journal of Finance,* 27, no. 2 (May 1972): 435–452.

Marshall Blume, "Betas and Their Regression Tendencies," *Journal of Finance,* 30, no. 3 (June 1975): 785–795.

Barr Rosenberg and Vinay Marathe, "The Prediction of Investment Risk: Systematic and Residual Risk," *Proceedings of the Seminar on the Analysis of Security Prices,* Center for Research in Security Prices, Graduate School of Business, University of Chicago, November 1975.

Barr Rosenberg and James Guy, "Prediction of Beta from Investment Fundamentals," *Financial Analysts Journal,* 32, no. 3 (May–June 1976): 60–72, and no. 4 (July–August 1976): 62–70.

Meir Statman, "Betas Compared: Merrill Lynch vs. Value Line," *Journal of Portfolio Management,* 7, no. 2 (Winter 1981): 41–44.

Diana R. Harrington, "Whose Beta is Best?" *Financial Analysts Journal,* 39, no. 5 (July/August 1983): 67–73.

Barr Rosenberg, "Prediction of Common Stock Investment Risk," *Journal of Portfolio Management,* 11, no. 1 (Fall 1984): 44–53.

Barr Rosenberg, "Prediction of Common Stock Betas," *Journal of Portfolio Management,* 11, no. 2 (Winter 1985): 5–14.

Gordon J. Alexander and Jack Clark Francis, *Portfolio Analysis* (Englewood Cliffs, NJ: Prentice Hall, 1986): 185–192.

George Foster, *Financial Statement Analysis* (Englewood Cliffs, NJ: Prentice Hall, 1986), Chapter 10.

Frank K. Reilly and David J. Wright, "A Comparison of Published Betas," *Journal of Portfolio Management,* 14, no. 3 (Spring 1988): 64–69.

Thomas E. Copeland and J. Fred Weston, *Financial Theory and Corporate Policy* (Reading, MA: Addison-Wesley, 1988), Chapter 13.

Richard A. Brealey and Stewart C. Myers, *Principles of Corporate Finance* (New York: McGraw-Hill, 1991): 191–192, 468–469.

8. The characteristics of value and growth stocks are described in:

Ken Gregory, "Fund Investment Strategies: Growth vs. Value Investing," *AAII Journal,* 11, no. 9 (October 1989): 22–25.

David E. Tierney and Kenneth J. Winston, "Using Generic Benchmarks to Present Manager Styles," *Journal of Portfolio Management,* 17, no. 4 (Summer 1991): 33–36.

John Bajkowski, "A Question of Style: Growth and Value Investing," *AAII Journal,* 14, no. 5 (June 1992): 33–37.

John Bajkowski, "Creating Stock Screens That Make Practical Sense," *AAII Journal,* 15, no. 6 (July 1993): 34–37.

9. Many of the studies conducted concerning various empirical regularities are cited in the endnotes. Also see:

Donald B. Keim, "The CAPM and Equity Return Regularities," *Financial Analysts Journal,* 42, no. 3 (May/June 1986): 19–34.

Michael Smirlock and Laura Starks, "Day-of-the-Week and Intraday Effects in Stock Returns," *Journal of Financial Economics,* 17, no. 1 (September 1986): 197–210.

Richard H. Thaler, "Anomalies: The January Effect," *Journal of Economic Perspectives,* 1, no. 1 (Summer 1987): 197–201; and "Anomalies: Seasonal Movements in Security Prices II—Weekend, Holiday, Turn of the Month, and Intraday Effects," *Journal of Economic Perspectives,* 1, no. 2 (Fall 1987): 169–177.

Douglas K. Pearce, "Challenges to the Concept of Market Efficiency," *Federal Reserve Bank of Kansas City Economic Review*, 72, no. 8 (September/October 1987): 16–33.

Elroy Dimson, ed., *Stock Market Anomalies* (Cambridge, England: Cambridge University Press, 1988).

Robert A. Haugen and Josef Lakonishok, *The Incredible January Effect* (Homewood, IL: Dow Jones-Irwin, 1988).

Burton G. Malkiel, *A Random Walk Down Wall Street* (New York: W. W. Norton, 1990), Chapter 8.

Eugene F. Fama, "Efficient Capital Markets: II," *Journal of Finance*, 46, no. 5 (December 1991): 1575–1617.

Narasimhan Jegadeesh, "Does Market Risk Really Explain the Size Effect?" *Journal of Financial and Quantitative Analysis*, 27, no. 3 (September 1992): 337–351.

Mark D. Griffiths and Robert W. White, "Tax-Induced Trading and the Turn-of-the-Year Anomaly: An Intraday Study," *Journal of Finance*, 48, no. 2 (June 1993): 575–598.

10. For a tongue-in-cheek article on anomalies that shows that market returns are influenced by superstition because returns on Friday the 13th are, on average, abnormally low, see:

Robert W. Kolb and Ricardo J. Rodriguez, "Friday the Thirteenth: 'Part VII'—A Note," *Journal of Finance*, 42, no. 5 (December 1987): 1385–1387.

CHAPTER 18

The Valuation of Common Stocks

In Chapter 17 it was noted that one purpose of financial analysis is to identify mispriced securities. Fundamental analysis was mentioned as one approach for conducting a search for such securities. With this approach the security analyst makes estimates of such things as the firm's future earnings and dividends. If these estimates are substantially different from the average estimates of other analysts but are felt to be more accurate, then from the viewpoint of the security analyst, a mispriced security will have been identified. If it is also felt that the market price of the security will adjust to reflect these more accurate estimates, then the security will be expected to have an abnormal rate of return. Accordingly, the analyst will issue either a buy or sell recommendation, depending on the direction of the anticipated price adjustment. Based on the capitalization of income method of valuation, dividend discount models have been frequently used by fundamental analysts as a means of identifying mispriced stocks. This chapter will discuss dividend discount models and how they can be related to models based on price-earnings ratios.

18.1 CAPITALIZATION OF INCOME METHOD OF VALUATION

There are many ways to implement the fundamental analysis approach to identifying mispriced securities. A number of them are either directly or indirectly related to what is sometimes referred to as the **capitalization of income method of valuation.**[1] This method states that the "true" or "intrinsic" value of any asset is based on the cash flows that the investor expects to receive in the future from owning the asset. Because these cash flows are expected in the future, they are adjusted by a **discount rate** to reflect not only the time value of money but also the riskiness of the cash flows.

Algebraically, the intrinsic value of the asset V is equal to the sum of the present values of the expected cash flows:

$$V = \frac{C_1}{(1+k)^1} + \frac{C_2}{(1+k)^2} + \frac{C_3}{(1+k)^3} + \cdots$$

$$= \sum_{t=1}^{\infty} \frac{C_t}{(1+k)^t} \tag{18.1}$$

where C_t denotes the expected cash flow associated with the asset at time t and k is the appropriate discount rate for cash flows of this degree of risk. In this equation the discount rate is assumed to be the same for all periods. Because the symbol ∞ above the summation sign in the equation denotes infinity, all expected cash flows, from immediately after making the investment until infinity, will be discounted at the same rate in determining V.[2]

18.1.1 Net Present Value

For the sake of convenience, let the current moment in time be denoted as zero, or $t = 0$. If the cost of purchasing an asset at $t = 0$ is P, then its **net present value** (NPV) is equal to the difference between its intrinsic value and cost, or:

$$\text{NPV} = V - P$$

$$= \left[\sum_{t=1}^{\infty} \frac{C_t}{(1+k)^t} \right] - P. \tag{18.2}$$

The NPV calculation shown here is conceptually the same as the NPV calculation made for capital budgeting decisions that has long been advocated in introductory finance textbooks. Capital budgeting decisions involve deciding whether or not a given investment project should be undertaken. (For example, should a new machine be purchased?) In making this decision, the focal point is the NPV of the project. Specifically, an investment project is viewed favorably if its NPV is positive, and unfavorably if its NPV is negative. For a simple project involving a cash outflow now (at $t = 0$) and expected cash inflows in the future, a positive NPV means that the present value of all the expected cash inflows is greater than the cost of making the investment. Conversely, a negative NPV means that the present value of all the expected cash inflows is less than the cost of making the investment.

The same views about NPV apply when financial assets (such as a share of common stock), instead of real assets (such as a new machine), are being considered for purchase. That is, a financial asset is viewed favorably and said to be underpriced (or undervalued) if NPV > 0. Conversely, a financial asset is viewed unfavorably and said to be overpriced or (overvalued) if NPV < 0. From Equation (18.2), this is equivalent to stating that a financial asset is underpriced if $V > P$:

$$\sum_{t=1}^{\infty} \frac{C_t}{(1+k)^t} > P. \tag{18.3}$$

Conversely, the asset is overvalued if $V < P$:

$$\sum_{t=1}^{\infty} \frac{C_t}{(1 + k)^t} < P. \qquad (18.4)$$

18.1.2   Internal Rate of Return

Another way of making capital budgeting decisions in a manner that is similar to the NPV method involves calculating the **internal rate of return** (IRR) associated with the investment project. With IRR, NPV in Equation (18.2) is set equal to zero and the discount rate becomes the unknown that must be calculated. That is, the IRR for a given investment is the discount rate that makes the NPV of the investment equal to zero. Algebraically, the procedure involves solving the following equation for the internal rate of return k^*:

$$0 = \sum_{t=1}^{\infty} \frac{C_t}{(1 + k^*)^t} - P. \qquad (18.5)$$

Equivalently, Equation (18.5) can be rewritten as:

$$P = \sum_{t=1}^{\infty} \frac{C_t}{(1 + k^*)^t}. \qquad (18.6)$$

The decision rule for IRR involves comparing the project's IRR (denoted by k^*) with the required rate of return for an investment of similar risk (denoted by k). Specifically, the investment is viewed favorably if $k^* > k$, and unfavorably if $k^* < k$. As with NPV, the same decision rule applies if either a real asset or a financial asset is being considered for possible investment.[3]

18.1.3   Application to Common Stocks

This chapter is concerned with using the capitalization of income method to determine the intrinsic value of common stocks. Because the cash flows associated with an investment in any particular common stock are the dividends that are expected to be paid throughout the future on the shares purchased, the models suggested by this method of valuation are often known as **dividend discount models** (DDMs).[4] Accordingly, D_t will be used instead of C_t to denote the expected cash flow in period t associated with a particular common stock, resulting in the following restatement of Equation (18.1):

$$V = \frac{D_1}{(1 + k)^1} + \frac{D_2}{(1 + k)^2} + \frac{D_3}{(1 + k)^3} + \cdots$$

$$= \sum_{t=1}^{\infty} \frac{D_t}{(1 + k)^t} \qquad (18.7)$$

Usually the focus of DDMs is on determining the "true" or "intrinsic" value of one share of a particular company's common stock, even if larger size purchases are being contemplated. This is because it is usually assumed that larger size purchases can be made at a cost that is a simple multiple of the cost of one share. (For example, the cost of 1,000 shares is usually assumed to be 1,000 times the cost of one share.) Thus the numerator in DDMs is the cash dividends per share that are expected in the future.

However, there is a complication in using Equation (18.7) to determine the intrinsic value of a share of common stock. In particular, in order to use this equation the investor must forecast *all* future dividends. Because a common stock does not have a fixed lifetime, this suggests that an infinitely long stream of dividends must be forecast. Although this may seem to be an impossible task, with the addition of certain assumptions, the equation can be made tractable (that is, usable).

These assumptions center on dividend growth rates. That is, the dividend per share at any time t can be viewed as being equal to the dividend per share at time $t - 1$ times a dividend growth rate of g_t,

$$D_t = D_{t-1}(1 + g_t) \tag{18.8}$$

or, equivalently:

$$\frac{D_t - D_{t-1}}{D_{t-1}} = g_t. \tag{18.9}$$

For example, if the dividend per share expected at $t = 2$ is \$4 and the dividend per share expected at $t = 3$ is \$4.20, then $g_3 = (\$4.20 - \$4)/\$4 = 5\%$.

The different types of tractable DDMs reflect different sets of assumptions about dividend growth rates, and are presented next. The discussion begins with the simplest case, the zero-growth model.

18.2   THE ZERO-GROWTH MODEL

One assumption that could be made about future dividends is that they will remain at a fixed dollar amount. That is, the dollar amount of dividends per share that were paid over the past year D_0 will also be paid over the next year D_1, and the year after that D_2, and the year after that D_3, and so on—that is,

$$D_0 = D_1 = D_2 = D_3 = \cdots = D_\infty.$$

This is equivalent to assuming that all the dividend growth rates are zero, because if $g_t = 0$, then $D_t = D_{t-1}$ in Equation (18.8). Accordingly, this model is often referred to as the **zero-growth** (or no-growth) **model.**

18.2.1   Net Present Value

The impact of this assumption on Equation (18.7) can be analyzed by noting what happens when D_t is replaced by D_0 in the numerator:

$$V = \sum_{t=1}^{\infty} \frac{D_0}{(1 + k)^t}. \tag{18.10}$$

The Valuation of Common Stocks

Fortunately, Equation (18.10) can be simplified by noting that D_0 is a fixed dollar amount, which means that it can be written outside the summation sign,

$$V = D_0 \left[\sum_{t=1}^{\infty} \frac{1}{(1 + k)^t} \right]. \qquad (18.11)$$

The next step involves using a property of infinite series from mathematics. If $k > 0$, then it can be shown that:

$$\sum_{t=1}^{\infty} \frac{1}{(1 + k)^t} = \frac{1}{k}. \qquad (18.12)$$

Applying this property to Equation (18.11) results in the following formula for the zero-growth model:

$$V = \frac{D_0}{k_0}. \qquad (18.13)$$

Because $D_0 = D_1$, Equation (18.13) is written sometimes as:

$$V = \frac{D_1}{k}. \qquad (18.14)$$

Example

As an example of how this DDM can be used, assume that the Zinc Company is expected to pay cash dividends amounting to \$8 per share into the indefinite future and has a required rate of return of 10%. Using either Equation (18.13) or Equation (18.14), it can be seen that the value of a share of Zinc stock is equal to \$80 (= \$8/.10). With a current stock price of \$65 per share, Equation (18.2) would suggest that the NPV per share is \$15 (= \$80 − \$65). Equivalently, as $V = \$80 > P = \$65$, the stock is underpriced by \$15 per share and would be a candidate for purchase.

18.2.2 Internal Rate of Return

Equation (18.13) can be reformulated to solve for the IRR on an investment in a zero-growth security. First, the security's current price P is substituted for V, and second, k^* is substituted for k. These changes result in:

$$P = \frac{D_0}{k^*}$$

which can be rewritten as:

$$k^* = \frac{D_0}{P} \qquad (18.15a)$$

$$= \frac{D_1}{P}. \qquad (18.15b)$$

Applying this formula to the stock of Zinc indicates that $k^* = 12.3\%$ ($=$ $\$8/\$65$). Because the IRR from an investment in Zinc exceeds the required rate of return on Zinc ($12.3\% > 10\%$), this method also indicates that Zinc is underpriced.[5]

18.2.3 Application

The zero-growth model may seem quite restrictive. After all, it seems unreasonable to assume that a given stock will pay a fixed dollar-size dividend forever. Although such a criticism has validity for common stock valuation, there is one particular situation where this model is quite useful.

Specifically, whenever the intrinsic value of a share of high-grade preferred stock is to be determined, the zero-growth DDM will often be appropriate. This is because most preferred stock is nonparticipating, meaning that it pays a fixed dollar-size dividend that will not change as earnings per share change. Furthermore, for high-grade preferred stock these dividends are expected to be paid regularly into the foreseeable future. Why? Because preferred stock does not have a fixed lifetime, and, by restricting the application of the zero growth model to high-grade preferred stocks, the chance of a suspension of dividends is remote.[6]

18.3   THE CONSTANT-GROWTH MODEL

The next type of DDM to be considered is one that assumes that dividends will grow from period to period at the same rate forever, and is therefore known as the **constant growth model.**[7] Specifically, the dividends per share that were paid over the previous year D_0 are expected to grow at a given rate g, so that the dividends expected over the next year D_1 are expected to be equal to $D_0(1 + g)$. Dividends the year after that are again expected to grow by the same rate g, meaning that $D_2 = D_1(1 + g)$. Because $D_1 = D_0(1 + g)$, this is equivalent to assuming that $D_2 = D_0(1 + g)^2$ and, in general:

$$D_t = D_{t-1}(1 + g) \tag{18.16a}$$

$$= D_0(1 + g)^t. \tag{18.16b}$$

18.3.1 Net Present Value

The impact of this assumption on Equation (18.7) can be analyzed by noting what happens when D_t is replaced by $D_0(1 + g)^t$ in the numerator:

$$V = \sum_{t=1}^{\infty} \frac{D_0(1 + g)^t}{(1 + k)^t}. \tag{18.17}$$

The Valuation of Common Stocks

Fortunately, Equation (18.17) can be simplified by noting that D_0 is a fixed dollar amount, which means that it can be written outside the summation sign:

$$V = D_0 \left[\sum_{t=1}^{\infty} \frac{(1 + g)^t}{(1 + k)^t} \right]. \tag{18.18}$$

The next step involves using a property of infinite series from mathematics. If $k > g$, then it can be shown that:

$$\sum_{t=1}^{\infty} \frac{(1 + g)^t}{(1 + k)^t} = \frac{1 + g}{k - g}. \tag{18.19}$$

Substituting Equation (18.19) into Equation (18.18) results in the valuation formula for the constant-growth model:

$$V = D_0 \left(\frac{1 + g}{k - g} \right). \tag{18.20}$$

Sometimes Equation (18.20) is rewritten as:

$$V = \frac{D_1}{k - g} \tag{18.21}$$

because $D_1 = D_0(1 + g)$.

Example

As an example of how this DDM can be used, assume that during the past year the Copper Company paid dividends amounting to $1.80 per share. The forecast is that dividends on Copper stock will increase by 5% per year into the indefinite future. Thus dividends over the next year are expected to equal $1.89 [= $1.80 × (1 + .05)]. Using Equation (18.20) and assuming a required rate of return k of 11%, it can be seen that the value of a share of Copper stock is equal to $31.50 [= $1.80 × (1 + .05)/(.11 − .05) = $1.89/(.11 − .05)]. With a current stock price of $40 per share, Equation (18.2) would suggest that the NPV per share is −$8.50 (= $31.50 − $40). Equivalently, as V = $31.50 < P = $40, the stock is overpriced by $8.50 per share and would be a candidate for sale if currently owned.

18.3.2 Internal Rate of Return

Equation (18.20) can be reformulated to solve for the IRR on an investment in a constant-growth security. First, the current price of the security P is substituted for V and then k^* is substituted for k. These changes result in:

$$P = D_0 \left(\frac{1 + g}{k^* - g} \right). \tag{18.22}$$

which can be rewritten as:

$$k^* = \frac{D_0(1 + g)}{P} + g \qquad\qquad (18.23\text{a})$$

$$= \frac{D_1}{P} + g. \qquad\qquad (18.23\text{b})$$

Example

Applying this formula to the stock of Copper indicates that $k^* = 9.72\%$ $\{=$ [$\$1.80 \times (1 + .05)/\$40] + .05 = (\$1.89/\$40) + .05\}$. Because the required rate of return on Copper exceeds the IRR from an investment in Copper (11% > 9.72%), this method also indicates that Copper is overpriced.

18.3.3 Relationship to the Zero-Growth Model

The zero-growth model of the previous section can be shown to be a special case of the constant-growth model. In particular, if the growth rate g is assumed to be equal to zero, then dividends will be a fixed dollar amount forever, which is the same as saying that there will be zero growth. Letting $g = 0$ in Equations (18.20) and (18.23a) results in two equations that are identical to Equations (18.13) and (18.15a), respectively.

Even though the assumption of constant dividend growth may seem less restrictive than the assumption of zero dividend growth, it may still be viewed as unrealistic in many cases. However, as will be shown next, the constant-growth model is important because it is embedded in the multiple-growth model.

18.4   THE MULTIPLE-GROWTH MODEL

A more general DDM for valuing common stocks is the **multiple-growth model.** With this model, the focus is on a time in the future (denoted by T) after which dividends are expected to grow at a constant rate g. Although the investor is still concerned with forecasting dividends, these dividends do not need to have any specific pattern until this time, after which they will be assumed to have the specific pattern of constant growth. The dividends up until T $(D_1, D_2, D_3, \ldots, D_T)$ will be forecast individually by the investor. (The investor also forecasts when this time T will occur.) Thereafter dividends are assumed to grow by a constant rate g that the investor must also forecast, meaning that:

$$D_{T+1} = D_T(1 + g)$$
$$D_{T+2} = D_{T+1}(1 + g) = D_T(1 + g)^2$$
$$D_{T+3} = D_{T+2}(1 + g) = D_T(1 + g)^3$$

and so on. Figure 18.1 presents a time line of dividends and growth rates associated with the multiple-growth model.

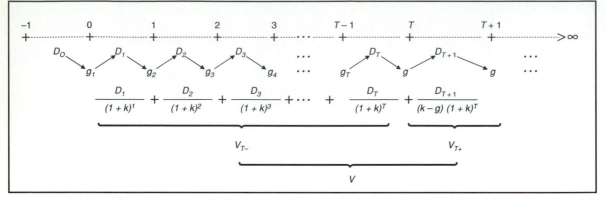

Figure 18.1
Time Line for Multiple-Growth Model

18.4.1 Net Present Value

In determining the value of a share of common stock with the multiple-growth model, the present value of the forecast stream of dividends must be determined. This can be done by dividing the stream into two parts, finding the present value of each part, and then adding these two present values together.

The first part consists of finding the present value of all the forecast dividends that will be paid up to and including time T. Denoting this present value by V_{T-}, it is equal to:

$$V_{T-} = \sum_{t=1}^{T} \frac{D_t}{(1 + k)^t}.$$

(18.24)

The second part consists of finding the present value of all the forecast dividends that will be paid after time T, and involves the application of the constant-growth model. The application begins by imagining that the investor is not at time zero but is at time T, and has not changed his or her forecast of dividends for the stock. This means that the next period's dividend D_{T+1} and all those thereafter are expected to grow at the rate g. Thus the investor would be viewing the stock as having a constant growth rate, and its value at time T, V_T, could be determined with the constant-growth model of Equation (18.21):

$$V_T = D_{T+1}\left(\frac{1}{k - g}\right).$$

(18.25)

One way to view V_T is that it represents a lump sum that is just as desirable as the stream of dividends after T. That is, an investor would find a lump sum of cash equal to V_T, to be received at time T, to be equally desirable as the stream of dividends D_{T+1}, D_{T+2}, D_{T+3}, and so on. Now given that the investor is at time zero, not at time T, the present value at $t = 0$ of the lump sum V_T must be determined. This is done simply by discounting it for T periods at the rate k, resulting in the following formula for finding the present value at time zero for all dividends after T, denoted V_{T+}:

$$V_{T+} = V_T \left[\frac{1}{(1 + k)^T} \right] \tag{18.26}$$

$$= \frac{D_{T+1}}{(k - g)(1 + k)^T}.$$

Having found the present value of all dividends up to and including time T with Equation (18.24), and the present value of all dividends after time T with Equation (18.26), the value of the stock can be determined by summing up these two amounts:

$$V = V_{T-} + V_{T+}$$

$$= \sum_{t=1}^{T} \frac{D_t}{(1 + k)^t} + \frac{D_{T+1}}{(k - g)(1 + k)^T}. \tag{18.27}$$

Figure 18.1 illustrates the valuation procedure for the multiple-growth DDM that is given in Equation (18.27).

Example

As an example of how this DDM can be used, assume that during the past year the Magnesium Company paid dividends amounting to $.75 per share. Over the next year, Magnesium is expected to pay dividends of $2 per share. Thus $g_1 = (D_1 - D_0)/D_0 = (\$2 - \$.75)/\$.75 = 167\%$. The year after that, dividends are expected to amount to $3 per share, indicating that $g_2 = (D_2 - D_1)/D_1 = (\$3 - \$2)/\$2 = 50\%$. At this time, the forecast is that dividends will grow by 10% per year indefinitely, indicating that $T = 2$ and $g = 10\%$. Consequently, $D_{T+1} = D_3 = \$3(1 + .10) = \$3.30$. Given a required rate of return on Magnesium shares of 15%, the values of V_{T-} and V_{T+} can be calculated as follows:

$$V_{T-} = \frac{\$2}{(1 + .15)^1} + \frac{\$3}{(1 + .15)^2}$$

$$= \$4.01$$

$$V_{T+} = \frac{\$3.30}{(.15 - .10)(1 + .15)^2}$$

$$= \$49.91.$$

Summing V_{T-} and V_{T+} results in a value for V of $4.01 + $49.91 = $53.92. With a current stock price of $55 per share, Magnesium appears to be fairly priced. That is, Magnesium is not significantly mispriced because V and P are nearly of equal size.

18.4.2 Internal Rate of Return

The zero-growth and constant-growth models have equations for V that can be reformulated in order to solve for the IRR on an investment in a stock. Unfortunately, a convenient expression similar to Equations (18.15a), (18.15b), (18.23a), and (18.23b) is not available for the multiple-growth model. This can be seen by noting that the expression for IRR is derived by substituting P for V, and k^* for k in Equation (18.27):

$$ P = \sum_{t=1}^{T} \frac{D_t}{(1 + k^*)^t} + \frac{D_{T+1}}{(k^* - g)(1 + k^*)^T}. \qquad (18.28) $$

This equation cannot be rewritten with k^* isolated on the left-hand side, meaning that a closed-form expression for IRR does not exist for the multiple-growth model.

However, all is not lost. It is still possible to calculate the IRR for an investment in a stock conforming to the multiple-growth model by using an "educated" trial-and-error method. The basis for this method is in the observation that the right-hand side of Equation (18.28) is simply equal to the present value of the dividend stream, where k^* is used as the discount rate. Hence the larger the value of k^*, the smaller the value of the right-hand side of Equation (18.28). The trial-and-error method proceeds by initially using an estimate for k^*. If the resulting value on the right-hand side of Equation (18.28) is larger than P, then a larger estimate of k^* is tried. Conversely, if the resulting value is smaller than P, then a smaller estimate of k^* is tried. Continuing this search process, the investor can hone in on the value of k^* that makes the right-hand side equal P on the left-hand side. Fortunately, it is a relatively simple matter to program a computer to conduct the search for k^* in Equation (18.28). Most spreadsheets include a function that does so automatically.

Example

Applying Equation (18.28) to the Magnesium Company results in:

$$ \$55 = \frac{\$2}{(1 + k^*)^1} + \frac{\$3}{(1 + k^*)^2} + \frac{\$3.30}{(k^* - .10)(1 + k^*)^2}. \qquad (18.29) $$

Initially a rate of 14% is used in attempting to solve this equation for k^*. Inserting 14% for k^* in the right-hand side of Equation (18.29) results in a value of $67.54. Earlier 15% was used in determining V and resulted in a value of $53.92. This means that k^* must have a value between 14% and 15%, since $55 is between $67.54 and $53.92. If 14.5% is tried next, the resulting value is $59.97, suggesting that a higher rate should be tried. If 14.8% and 14.9% are subsequently tried, the respective resulting values are $56.18 and $55.03. As $55.03 is the closest to P, the IRR associated with an investment in Magnesium is 14.9%. Given a required return of 15% and an IRR of approximately that amount, the stock of Magnesium appears to be fairly priced.

18.4.3 Relationship to the Constant-Growth Model

The constant-growth model can be shown to be a special case of the multiple-growth model. In particular, if the time when constant growth is assumed to begin is set equal to zero, then:

$$V_{T-} = \sum_{t=1}^{T} \frac{D_t}{(1 + k)^t} = 0$$

and

$$V_{T+} = \frac{D_{T+1}}{(k - g)(1 + k)^T} = \frac{D_1}{k - g}$$

because $T = 0$ and $(1 + k)^0 = 1$. Given that the multiple-growth model states that $V = V_{T-} + V_{T+}$, it can be seen that setting $T = 0$ results in $V = D_1/(k - g)$, a formula that is equivalent to the formula for the constant-growth model.

18.4.4 Two-Stage and Three-Stage Models

Two dividend discount models that investors sometimes use are the two-stage model and the three-stage model.[8] The two-stage model assumes that a constant growth rate g_1 exists only until some time T, when a different growth rate g_2 is assumed to begin and continue thereafter. The three-stage model assumes that a constant growth rate g_1 exists only until some time T_1, when a second growth rate is assumed to begin and last until a later time T_2, when a third growth rate is assumed to begin and last thereafter. By letting V_{T+} denote the present value of all dividends after the last growth rate has begun and V_{T-} the present value of all the preceding dividends, it can be seen that these models are just special cases of the multiple-growth model.

In applying the capitalization of income method of valuation to common stocks, it might seem appropriate to assume that the stock will be sold at some point in the future. In this case the expected cash flows would consist of the dividends up to that point as well as the expected selling price. Because dividends after the selling date would be ignored, the use of a dividend discount model may seem to be improper. However, as will be shown next, this is not so.

18.5   VALUATION BASED ON A FINITE HOLDING PERIOD

The capitalization of income method of valuation involves discounting all dividends that are expected throughout the future. Because the simplified models of zero growth, constant growth, and multiple growth are based on this method, they too involve a future stream of dividends. Upon reflection it may seem that such models are relevant only for an investor who plans to hold a stock forever, as only such an investor would expect to receive this stream of future dividends.

But what about an investor who plans to sell the stock in a year?[9] In such a situation, the cash flows that the investor expects to receive from purchasing a share of the stock are equal to the dividend expected to be paid one year from now (for ease of exposition, it is assumed that common stocks pay dividends annually) and the expected selling price of the stock. Thus it would seem appropriate to determine the intrinsic value of the stock to the investor by discounting these two cash flows at the required rate of return as follows:

$$V = \frac{D_1 + P_1}{1 + k}$$

$$= \frac{D_1}{1 + k} + \frac{P_1}{1 + k} \tag{18.30}$$

where D_1 and P_1 are the expected dividend and selling price at $t = 1$, respectively.

In order to use Equation (18.30), the expected price of the stock at $t = 1$ must be estimated. The simplest approach assumes that the selling price will be based on the dividends that are expected to be paid after the selling date. Thus the expected selling price at $t = 1$ is:

$$P_1 = \frac{D_2}{(1 + k)^1} + \frac{D_3}{(1 + k)^2} + \frac{D_4}{(1 + k)^3} + \cdots$$

$$= \sum_{t=2}^{\infty} \frac{D_t}{(1 + k)^{t-1}}. \tag{18.31}$$

Substituting Equation (18.31) for P_1 in the right-hand side of Equation (18.30) results in:

$$V = \frac{D_1}{1 + k} + \left[\frac{D_2}{(1 + k)^1} + \frac{D_3}{(1 + k)^2} + \frac{D_4}{(1 + k)^3} + \cdots \right] \left(\frac{1}{1 + k} \right)$$

$$= \frac{D_1}{(1 + k)^1} + \frac{D_2}{(1 + k)^2} + \frac{D_3}{(1 + k)^3} + \frac{D_4}{(1 + k)^4} + \cdots$$

$$= \sum_{t=1}^{\infty} \frac{D_t}{(1 + k)^t}$$

which is exactly the same as Equation (18.7). Thus valuing a share of common stock by discounting its dividends up to some point in the future and its expected selling price at that time is equivalent to valuing stock by discounting all future dividends. Simply stated, the two are equivalent because the expected selling price is itself based on dividends to be paid after the selling date. Thus Equation (18.7), as well as the zero-growth, constant-growth, and multiple-growth models that are based on it, is appropriate for determining the intrinsic value of a share of common stock regardless of the length of the investor's planned holding period.

Example

As an example, reconsider the common stock of the Copper Company. Over the past year it was noted that Copper paid dividends of $1.80 per share, with the forecast that the dividends would grow by 5% per year forever. This means that dividends over the next two years (D_1 and D_2) are forecast to be $1.89 [= $1.80 × (1 + .05)] and $1.985 [= $1.89 × (1 + .05)], respectively. If the investor plans to sell the stock after one year, the selling price could be estimated by noting that at $t = 1$, the forecast of dividends for the forthcoming year would be D_2, or $1.985. Thus the anticipated selling price at $t = 1$, denoted P_1, would be equal to $33.08 [= $1.985/(.11 − .05)]. Accordingly, the intrinsic value of Copper to such an investor would equal the present value of the expected cash flows, which are $D_1 = 1.89 and $P_1 = 33.08. Using Equation (18.30) and assuming a required rate of 11%, this value is equal to $31.50 [= ($1.89 + $33.08)/(1 + .11)]. Note that this is the same amount that was calculated earlier when all the dividends from now to infinity were discounted using the constant-growth model: $V = D_1/(k − g) = $1.89/(.11 − .05) = 31.50.

18.6 MODELS BASED ON PRICE-EARNINGS RATIOS

Despite the inherent sensibility of DDMs, many security analysts use a much simpler procedure to value common stocks. First, a stock's earnings per share over the forthcoming year E_1 are estimated, and then the analyst (or someone else) specifies a "normal" **price-earnings ratio** for the stock. The product of these two numbers gives the estimated future price P_1. Together with estimated dividends D_1 to be paid during the period and the current price P, the estimated return on the stock over the period can be determined:

$$\text{Expected return} = \frac{(P_1 − P) + D_1}{P} \qquad (18.32)$$

where $P_1 = (P_1/E_1) × E_1$.

Some security analysts expand this procedure, estimating earnings per share and price-earnings ratios for optimistic, most likely, and pessimistic scenarios to produce a rudimentary probability distribution of a security's return. Other analysts determine whether a stock is underpriced or overpriced by comparing the stock's actual price-earnings ratio with its "normal" price-earnings ratio, as will be shown next.[10]

In order to make this comparison, Equation (18.7) must be rearranged and some new variables introduced. To begin, it should be noted that earnings per share E_t are related to dividends per share D_t by the firm's **payout ratio** p_t,

$$D_t = p_t E_t. \qquad (18.33)$$

Furthermore, if an analyst has forecast earnings-per-share and payout ratios, then he or she has implicitly forecast dividends.

Equation (18.33) can be used to restate the various DDMs where the focus is on estimating what the stock's price-earnings ratio should be instead of on estimating the intrinsic value of the stock. In order to do so, $p_t E_t$ is substituted for D_t

in the right-hand side of Equation (18.7), resulting in a general formula for determining a stock's intrinsic value that involves discounting earnings:

$$V = \frac{D_1}{(1 + k)^1} + \frac{D_2}{(1 + k)^2} + \frac{D_3}{(1 + k)^3} + \cdots$$

$$= \frac{p_1 E_1}{(1 + k)^1} + \frac{p_2 E_2}{(1 + k)^2} + \frac{p_3 E_3}{(1 + k)^3} + \cdots$$

$$= \sum_{t=1}^{\infty} \frac{p_t E_t}{(1 + k)^t}. \tag{18.34}$$

Earlier it was noted that dividends in adjacent time periods could be viewed as being "linked" to each other by a dividend growth rate g_t. Similarly, earnings per share in any year t can be "linked" to earnings per share in the previous year $t - 1$ by a growth rate in earnings per share, g_{et},

$$E_t = E_{t-1}(1 + g_{et}). \tag{18.35}$$

This implies that

$$E_1 = E_0(1 + g_{e1})$$
$$E_2 = E_1(1 + g_{e2}) = E_0(1 + g_{e1})(1 + g_{e2})$$
$$E_3 = E_2(1 + g_{e3}) = E_0(1 + g_{e1})(1 + g_{e2})(1 + g_{e3})$$

and so on, where E_0 is the actual level of earnings per share over the past year, E_1 is the expected level of earnings per share over the forthcoming year, E_2 is the expected level of earnings per share for the year after E_1, and E_3 is the expected level of earnings per share for the year after E_2.

These equations relating expected future earnings per share to E_0 can be substituted into Equation (18.34), resulting in:

$$V = \frac{p_1[E_0(1 + g_{e1})]}{(1 + k)^1} + \frac{p_2[E_0(1 + g_{e1})(1 + g_{e2})]}{(1 + k)^2}$$

$$+ \frac{p_3[E_0(1 + g_{e1})(1 + g_{e2})(1 + g_{e3})]}{(1 + k)^3} + \cdots. \tag{18.36}$$

As V is the intrinsic value of a share of stock, it represents what the stock would be selling for if it were fairly priced. It follows that V/E_0 represents what the price-earnings ratio would be if the stock were fairly priced, and is sometimes referred to as the stock's "normal" price-earnings ratio. Dividing both sides of Equation (18.36) by E_0 and simplifying results in the formula for determining the "normal" price-earnings ratio:

$$\frac{V}{E_0} = \frac{p_1(1 + g_{e1})}{(1 + k)^1} + \frac{p_2(1 + g_{e1})(1 + g_{e2})}{(1 + k)^2}$$

$$+ \frac{p_3(1 + g_{e1})(1 + g_{e2})(1 + g_{e3})}{(1 + k)^3} + \cdots. \tag{18.37}$$

This shows that, other things being equal, a stock's "normal" price-earnings ratio will be higher:

The *greater* the expected payout ratios ($p_1, p_2, p_3, \ldots$),
The *greater* the expected growth rates in earnings per share ($g_{e1}, g_{e2}, g_{e3}, \ldots$),
The *smaller* the required rate of return (k).

The qualifying phrase "other things being equal" should not be overlooked. For example, a firm cannot increase the value of its shares by simply making greater payouts. This will increase $p_1, p_2, p_3, \ldots$, but will decrease the expected growth rates in earnings per share $g_{e1}, g_{e2}, g_{e3}, \ldots$. Assuming that the firm's investment policy is not altered, the effects of the reduced growth in its earnings per share will just offset the effects of the increased payouts, leaving its share value unchanged.

Earlier it was noted that a stock was viewed as underpriced if $V > P$ and overpriced if $V < P$. Because dividing both sides of an inequality by a positive constant will not change the direction of the inequality, such a division can be done here to the two inequalities involving V and P, where the positive constant is E_0. The result is that a stock can be viewed as being underpriced if $V/E_0 > P/E_0$ and overpriced if $V/E_0 < P/E_0$. Thus a stock will be underpriced if its "normal" price-earnings ratio is greater than its actual price-earnings ratio, and overpriced if its "normal" price-earnings ratio is less than its actual price-earnings ratio.

Unfortunately, Equation (18.37) is intractable, meaning that it cannot be used to estimate the "normal" price-earnings ratio for any stock. However, simplifying assumptions can be made that result in tractable formulas for estimating "normal" price-earnings ratios. These assumptions, along with the formulas, parallel those made previously regarding dividends and are discussed next.

18.6.1 The Zero-Growth Model

The zero-growth model assumed that dividends per share remained at a fixed dollar amount forever. This is most likely if earnings per share remain at a fixed dollar amount forever, with the firm maintaining a 100% payout ratio. Why 100%? Because if a lesser amount were assumed to be paid out, it would mean that the firm was retaining part of its earnings. These retained earnings would be put to some use, and would thus be expected to increase future earnings and hence dividends per share.

Accordingly, the zero-growth model can be interpreted as assuming $p_t = 1$ for all time periods and $E_0 = E_1 = E_2 = E_3$ and so on. This means that $D_0 = E_0 = D_1 = E_1 = D_2 = E_2$ and so on, allowing valuation Equation (18.13) to be restated as:

$$V = \frac{E_0}{k}. \tag{18.38}$$

Dividing Equation (18.38) by E_0 results in the formula for the "normal" price-earnings ratio for a stock having zero growth:

$$\frac{V}{E_0} = \frac{1}{k}. \tag{18.39}$$

Earlier it was assumed that the Zinc Company was a zero-growth firm paying dividends of $8 per share, selling for $65 a share, and having a required rate of return of 10%. Because Zinc is a zero-growth company, it will be assumed that it has a 100% payout ratio which, in turn, means that $E_0 = \$8$. At this point Equation (18.38) can be used to note that a "normal" price-earnings ratio for Zinc is $1/.10 = 10$. As Zinc has an actual price-earnings ratio of $\$65/\$8 = 8.1$, and because $V/E_0 = 10 > P/E_0 = 8.1$, it can be seen that Zinc stock is underpriced.

18.6.2 The Constant-Growth Model

Earlier it was noted that dividends in adjacent time periods could be viewed as being connected to each other by a dividend growth rate g_t. Similarly, it was noted that earnings per share can be connected by an earnings growth rate g_{et}. The constant-growth model assumes that the growth rate in dividends per share will be the same throughout the future. An equivalent assumption is that earnings per share will grow at a constant rate g_e throughout the future, with the payout ratio remaining at a constant level p. This means that:

$$E_1 = E_0(1 + g_e) = E_0(1 + g_e)^1$$
$$E_2 = E_1(1 + g_e) = E_0(1 + g_e)(1 + g_e) = E_0(1 + g_e)^2$$
$$E_3 = E_2(1 + g_e) = E_0(1 + g_e)(1 + g_e)(1 + g_e) = E_0(1 + g_e)^3$$

and so on. In general, earnings in year t can be connected to E_0 as follows:

$$E_t = E_0(1 + g_e)^t. \tag{18.40}$$

Substituting Equation (18.40) into the numerator of Equation (18.34) and recognizing that $p_t = p$ results in:

$$V = \sum_{t=1}^{\infty} \frac{pE_0(1 + g_e)^t}{(1 + k)^t}$$

$$= pE_0 \left[\sum_{t=1}^{\infty} \frac{(1 + g_e)^t}{(1 + k)^t} \right]. \tag{18.41}$$

The same mathematical property of infinite series given in Equation (18.19) can be applied to Equation (18.41), resulting in:

$$V = pE_0 \left(\frac{1 + g_e}{k - g_e} \right). \tag{18.42}$$

It can be noted that the earnings-based constant-growth model has a numerator that is identical to the numerator of the dividend-based constant-growth model, because $pE_0 = D_0$. Furthermore, the denominators of the two models are identical. Both assertions require that the growth rates in earnings and dividends be the same (that is, $g_e = g$). Examination of the assumptions of the models reveals that these growth rates must be equal. This can be seen by recalling that constant earnings growth means:

$$E_t = E_{t-1}(1 + g_e).$$

Now when both sides of this equation are multiplied by the constant payout ratio, the result is:

$$pE_t = pE_{t-1}(1 + g_e).$$

Because $pE_t = D_t$ and $pE_{t-1} = D_{t-1}$, this equation reduces to:

$$D_t = D_{t-1}(1 + g_e)$$

which indicates that dividends in any period $t - 1$ will grow by the earnings growth rate, g_e. Because the dividend-based constant-growth model assumed that dividends in any period $t - 1$ would grow by the dividend growth rate g, it can be seen that the two growth rates must be equal for the two models to be equivalent.

Equation (18.42) can be restated by dividing each side by E_0, resulting in the following formula for determining the "normal" price-earnings ratio for a stock with constant growth:

$$\frac{V}{E_0} = p\left(\frac{1 + g_e}{k + g_e}\right). \tag{18.43}$$

Example

Earlier it was assumed that the Copper Company had paid dividends of $1.80 per share over the past year, with a forecast that dividends would grow by 5% per year forever. Furthermore, it was assumed that the required rate of return on Copper was 11%, and the current stock price was $40 per share. Now assuming that E_0 was $2.70, it can be seen that the payout ratio was equal to 66⅔% (= $1.80/$2.70). This means that the "normal" price-earnings ratio for Copper, according to Equation (18.43), is equal to 11.7 [= .6667 × (1 + .05) /(.11 −.05)]. Because this is less than Copper's actual price-earnings ratio of 14.8 (= $40/$2.70), it follows that the stock of Copper Company is overpriced.

18.6.3 The Multiple-Growth Model

Earlier it was noted that the most general DDM is the multiple-growth model, where dividends are allowed to grow at varying rates until some point in time T, after which they are assumed to grow at a constant rate. In this situation the present value of all the dividends is found by adding the present value of all dividends up to and including T, denoted by V_{T-}, and the present value of all dividends after T, denoted by V_{T+}:

$$V = V_{T-} + V_{T+}$$

$$= \sum_{t=1}^{T} \frac{D_t}{(1 + k)^t} + \frac{D_{T+1}}{(k - g)(1 + k)^T}. \tag{18.27}$$

In general, earnings per share in any period t can be expressed as being equal to E_0 times the product of all the earnings growth rates from time zero to time t:

$$E_t = E_0(1 + g_{e1})(1 + g_{e2}) \cdots (1 + g_{et}). \qquad (18.44)$$

Because dividends per share in any period t are equal to the payout ratio for that period times the earnings per share, it follows from Equation (18.44) that:

$$\begin{aligned} D_t &= p_t E_t \\ &= p_t E_0(1 + g_{e1})(1 + g_{e2}) \cdots (1 + g_{et}). \end{aligned} \qquad (18.45)$$

Replacing the numerator in Equation (18.37) with the right-hand side of Equation (18.45) and then dividing both sides by E_0 gives the following formula for determining a stock's "normal" price-earnings ratio with the multiple-growth model:

$$\begin{aligned} \frac{V}{E_0} &= \frac{p_1(1 + g_{e1})}{(1 + k)^1} + \frac{p_2(1 + g_{e1})(1 + g_{e2})}{(1 + k)^2} + \cdots \\ &+ \frac{p_T(1 + g_{e1})(1 + g_{e2}) \cdots (1 + g_{eT})}{(1 + k)^T} \\ &+ \frac{p(1 + g_{e1})(1 + g_{e2}) \cdots (1 + g_{eT})(1 + g)}{(k - g)(1 + k)^T}. \end{aligned} \qquad (18.46)$$

Example

Consider the Magnesium Company again. Its share price is currently $55, and per share earnings and dividends over the past year were $3 and $.75, respectively. For the next two years, forecast earnings and dividends, along with the earnings growth rates and payout ratios, are:

$$\begin{array}{llll} D_1 = \$2.00 & E_1 = \$5.00 & g_{e1} = 67\% & p_1 = 40\% \\ D_2 = \$3.00 & E_2 = \$6.00 & g_{e2} = 20\% & p_2 = 50\%. \end{array}$$

Constant growth in dividends and earnings of 10% per year is forecast to begin at $T = 2$, which means that $D_3 = \$3.30$, $E_3 = \$6.60$, $g = 10\%$, and $p = 50\%$.

Given a required return of 15%, Equation (18.46) can be used as follows to estimate a "normal" price-earnings ratio for Magnesium:

$$\begin{aligned} \frac{V}{E_0} &= \frac{.40(1 + .67)}{(1 + .15)^1} + \frac{.50(1 + .67)(1 + .20)}{(1 + .15)^2} + \frac{.50(1 + .67)(1 + .20)(1 + .10)}{(.15 - .10)(1 + .15)^2} \\ &= .58 + .76 + 16.67 \\ &= 18.01. \end{aligned}$$

Because the actual price-earnings ratio of 18.33 (= $55/$3) is close to the "normal" ratio of 18.01, the stock of the Magnesium Company can be viewed as fairly priced.

So far no explanation has been given as to why earnings or dividends will be expected to grow in the future. One way of providing such an explanation uses the constant-growth model. Assuming that no new capital is obtained externally and no shares are repurchased (meaning that the number of shares outstanding does not increase or decrease), the portion of earnings not paid to stockholders as dividends will be used to pay for the firm's new investments. Given that p_t denotes the payout ratio in year t, then $(1 - p_t)$ will be equal to the portion of earnings not paid out, known as the **retention ratio.** Furthermore, the firm's new investments, stated on a per-share basis and denoted by I_t, will be:

$$I_t = (1 - p_t)E_t. \tag{18.47}$$

If these new investments have an average return on equity of r_t in period t and every year thereafter, they will add $r_t I_t$ to earnings per share in year $t + 1$ and every year thereafter. If all previous investments also produce perpetual earnings at a constant rate of return, next year's earnings will equal this year's earnings plus the new earnings resulting from this year's new investments:

$$
\begin{aligned}
E_{t+1} &= E_t + r_t I_t \\
&= E_t + r_t(1 - p_t)E_t \\
&= E_t[1 + r_t(1 - p_t)].
\end{aligned}
\tag{18.48}
$$

Because it was shown earlier that the growth rate in earnings per share is:

$$E_t = E_{t-1}(1 + g_{et}) \tag{18.35}$$

it follows that:

$$E_{t+1} = E_t(1 + g_{et+1}). \tag{18.49}$$

A comparison of Equations (18.48) and (18.49) indicates that:

$$g_{et+1} = r_t(1 - p_t). \tag{18.50}$$

If the growth rate in earnings per share g_{et+1} is to be constant over time, then the average return on equity for new investments r_t and the payout ratio p_t must also be constant over time. In this situation Equation (18.50) can be simplified by removing the time subscripts:

$$g_e = r(1 - p). \tag{18.51a}$$

Because the growth rate in dividends per share g is equal to the growth rate in earnings per share g_e, this equation can be rewritten as:

$$g = r(1 - p). \tag{18.51b}$$

From this equation it can be seen that the growth rate g depends on (1) the proportion of earnings that is retained $1 - p$, and (2) the average return on equity for the earnings that are retained r.

The constant-growth valuation formula given in Equation (18.20) can be modified by replacing g with the expression on the right-hand side of Equation (18.51b), resulting in:

$$V = D_0\left(\frac{1 + g}{k - g}\right) \qquad\qquad (18.52)$$

$$= D_0\left[\frac{1 + r(1 - p)}{k - r(1 - p)}\right].$$

$$= D_1\left[\frac{1}{k - r(1 - p)}\right].$$

Under these assumptions, a stock's value (and hence its price) should be greater, the greater its average return on equity for new investments, other things being equal.

Example

Continuing with the Copper Company, recall that $E_0 = \$2.70$ and $p = 66\frac{2}{3}\%$. This means that $33\frac{1}{3}\%$ of earnings per share over the past year were retained and reinvested, an amount equal to $\$.90$ ($= .3333 \times \$2.70$). The earnings per share in the forthcoming year E_1 are expected to be $\$2.835$ [$= \$2.70 \times (1 + .05)$] because the growth rate g for Copper is 5%.

The source of the increase in earnings per share of $\$.135$ ($= \$2.835 - \$2.70$) is the $\$.90$ per share that was reinvested at $t = 0$. The average return on equity for new investments r is 15%, because $\$.135/\$.90 = 15\%$. That is, the reinvested earnings of $\$.90$ per share can be viewed as having generated an annual increase in earnings per share of $\$.135$. This increase will occur not only at $t = 1$, but also at $t = 2$, $t = 3$, and so on. Equivalently, a $\$.90$ investment at $t = 0$ will generate a perpetual annual cash inflow of $\$.135$ beginning at $t = 1$.

Expected dividends at $t = 1$ can be calculated by multiplying the expected payout ratio p of $66\frac{2}{3}\%$ times the expected earnings per share E_1 of $\$2.835$, or $.6667 \times \$2.835 = \$1.89$. It can also be calculated by multiplying 1 plus the growth rate g of 5% times the past amount of dividends per share D_0 of $\$1.80$, or $1.05 \times \$1.80 = \$1.89$.

It can be seen that the growth rate in dividends per share of 5% is equal to the product of the retention rate ($33\frac{1}{3}\%$) and the average return on equity for new investments (15%), an amount equal to 5% ($= .3333 \times .15$).

Two years from now ($t = 2$), earnings per share are anticipated to be $\$2.977$ [$= \$2.835 \times (1 + .05)$], a further increase of $\$.142$ ($= \$2.977 - \$2.835$) that is due to the retention and reinvestment of $\$.945$ ($= .3333 \times \$2.835$) per share at $t = 1$. This expected increase in earnings per share of $\$.142$ is the result of earning (15%) on the reinvestment ($\$.945$), because $.15 \times \$.945 = \$.142$.

The expected earnings per share at $t = 2$ can be viewed as having three components. The first is the earnings attributable to the assets held at $t = 0$, an amount equal to $\$2.70$. The second is the earnings attributable to the reinvestment of $\$.90$ at $t = 0$, earning $\$.135$. The third is the earnings attributable to the reinvestment of $\$.945$ at $t = 1$, earning $\$.142$. These three components, when summed, can be seen to equal $E_2 = \$2.977$ ($= \$2.70 + \$.135 + \$.142$).

Dividends at $t = 2$ are expected to be 5% larger than at $t = 1$, or $\$1.985$ ($= 1.05 \times \$1.89$) per share. This amount corresponds to the amount calculated by multiplying the payout ratio times the expected earnings per share at $t = 2$, or $\$1.985$ ($= .6667 \times \$2.977$). Figure 18.2 summarizes the example.

Figure 18.2
Growth in Earnings for Copper Company

18.8   A THREE-STAGE DDM

As this chapter's Institutional Issues discusses, the three-stage DDM is the most widely applied form of the general multiple-growth DDM. Consider analyzing the *ABC* Company.

18.8.1   Making Forecasts

Over the past year, *ABC* has had earnings per share of $1.67 and dividends per share of $.40. After carefully studying ABC, the security analyst has made the following forecasts of earnings per share and dividends per share for the next five years:

$$E_1 = \$2.67 \quad E_2 = \$4.00 \quad E_3 = \$6.00 \quad E_4 = \$8.00 \quad E_5 = \$10.00$$
$$D_2 = \$\,.60 \quad D_2 = \$1.60 \quad D_3 = \$2.40 \quad D_4 = \$3.20 \quad D_5 = \$\,5.00.$$

These forecasts imply the following payout ratios and earnings-per-share growth rates:

$$p_1 = 22\% \quad p_2 = 40\% \quad p_3 = 40\% \quad p_4 = 40\% \quad p_5 = 50\%$$
$$g_{e1} = 60\% \quad g_{e2} = 50\% \quad g_{e3} = 50\% \quad g_{e4} = 33\% \quad g_{e5} = 25\%.$$

Furthermore, the analyst believes that *ABC* will enter a transition stage at the end of the fifth year (that is, the sixth year will be the first year of the transition stage), and that the transition stage will last three years. Earnings per share and the payout ratio for year 6 are forecast to be $E_6 = \$11.90$ and $p_6 = 55\%$. {Thus $g_{e6} = 19\% \,[= (\$11.90 - \$10.00)/\$10.00]$ and $D_6 = \$6.55 \,(= .55 \times \$11.90)$}.

The last stage, known as the maturity stage, is forecast to have an earnings-per-share growth rate of 4% and a payout ratio of 70%. Now it was shown in Equation (18.51b) that with the constant-growth model, $g = r(1 - p)$, where r is the average return on equity for new investment and p is the payout ratio. Given

---

Applying Dividend Discount Models

Over the last 30 years, dividend discount models (DDMs) have achieved broad acceptance among professional common stock investors. Although few investment managers rely solely on DDMs to select stocks, many have integrated DDMs into their security valuation procedures.

The reasons for the popularity of DDMs are twofold. First, DDMs are based on a simple, widely understood concept: The fair value of any security should equal the discounted value of the cash flows expected to be produced by that security. Second, the basic inputs for DDMs are standard outputs for many large investment management firms—that is, these firms employ security analysts who are responsible for projecting corporate earnings.

Valuing common stocks with a DDM technically requires an estimate of future dividends over an infinite time horizon. Given that accurately forecasting dividends three years from today, let alone 20 years in the future, is a difficult proposition, how do investment firms actually go about implementing DDMs?

One approach is to use constant or two-stage dividend growth models, as described in the text. However, although such models are relatively easy to apply, institutional investors typically view the assumed dividend growth assumptions as overly simplistic. Instead, these investors generally prefer three-stage models, believing that they provide the best combination of realism and ease of application.

Whereas many variations of the three-stage DDM exist, in general, the model is based on the assumption that companies evolve through three stages during their lifetimes. (Figure 18.3 portrays these stages.)

1. **Growth stage:** Characterized by rapidly expanding sales, high profit margins, and abnormally high growth in earnings per share. Because of highly profitable expected investment opportunities, the payout ratio is low. Competitors are attracted by the unusually high earnings, leading to a decline in the growth rate.
2. **Transition stage:** In later years, increased competition reduces profit margins and earnings growth slows. With fewer new investment opportunities, the company begins to pay out a larger percentage of earnings.

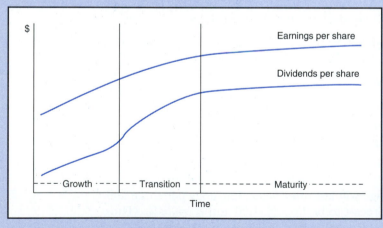

Figure 18.3
The Three Stages of the Multiple-Growth Model
Source: Adapted from Carmine J. Grigoli, "Demystifying Dividend Discount Models," *Merrill Lynch Quantitative Research*, April 1982.

3. **Maturity (steady-state) stage:** Eventually the company reaches a position where its new investment opportunities offer, on average, only slightly attractive returns on equity. At that time its earnings growth rate, payout ratio, and return on equity stabilize for the remainder of its life.

The forecasting process of the three-stage DDM involves specifying earnings and dividend growth rates in each of the three stages. Although one cannot expect a security analyst to be omniscient in his or her growth forecast for a particular company, one can hope that the forecast pattern of growth—in terms of magnitude and duration—resembles that actually realized by the company, particularly in the short run.

Investment firms attempt to structure their DDMs to make maximum use of their analysts' forecasting capabilities. Thus the models emphasize specific forecasts in the near term, when it is realistic to expect security analysts to project earnings and dividends more accurately. Conversely, the models emphasize more general forecasts over the longer term, when distinctions between companies' growth rates become less discernible. Typically, analysts are required to supply the following for their assigned companies:

1. expected annual earnings and dividends for the next several years;
2. after these specific annual forecasts end, earnings growth and the payout ratio forecasts until the end of the growth stage;
3. the number of years until the transition stage is reached;
4. the duration (in years) of the transition stage—that is, once abnormally high growth

ends, the number of years until the maturity stage is reached.

Most three-stage DDMs assume that during the transition stage, earnings growth declines and payout ratios rise linearly to the maturity-stage steady-state levels. (For example, if the transition stage is ten years long, earnings growth at the maturity stage is 5% per year, and earnings growth at the end of the growth stage is 25%, then earnings growth will decline 2% in each year of the transition stage.) Finally, most three-stage DDMs make standard assumptions that all companies in the maturity stage have the same growth rates, payout ratios, and return on equity.

With analysts' inputs, plus an appropriate required rate of return for each security, all the necessary information for the three-stage DDM is available. The last step involves merely calculating the discounted value of the estimated dividends to determine the stock's "fair" value.

The seeming simplicity of the three-stage DDM should not lead one to believe that it is without its implementation problems. Investment firms must strive to achieve consistency across their analysts' forecasts. The long-term nature of the estimates involved, the substantial training required to make even short-term earnings forecasts accurately, and the coordination of a number of analysts covering many companies severely complicate the problem. Considerable discipline is required if the DDM valuations generated by a firm's analysts are to be sufficiently comparable and reliable to guide investment decisions. Despite these complexities, if successfully implemented, DDMs can combine the creative insights of security analysts with the rigor and discipline of quantitative investment techniques.

---

that the maturity stage has constant growth, this equation can be reformulated and used to determine r:

$$r = g /(1 - p).$$

Thus r for *ABC* has an implied value of 13.33% [= 4%/(100% − 70%)], which is assumed to be consistent with the long-run growth forecasts for similar companies.

At this point there are only two missing pieces of information that are needed to determine the value of *ABC*—the earnings-per-share growth rates and the payout ratios for the transition stage. Taking earnings per share first, it has been forecast that $g_{e6} = 19\%$ and $g_{e9} = 4\%$. One method of determining how 19% will "decay" to 4% is to note that there are three years between the sixth and ninth years, and 15% between 19% and 4%. A "linear decay" rate would be determined by noting that 15%/3 years = 5% per year. This rate of 5% would be deducted from 19% to get g_{e7}, resulting in 14% (= 19% − 5%). Then it would be deducted from 14% to get g_{e8}, resulting in 9% (= 14% − 5%). Finally, as a check it can be noted that 4% (= 9% − 5%) is the value that was forecast for g_{e9}.

A similar procedure can be used to determine how the payout ratio of 55% in year 6 will grow to 70% in year 9. The "linear growth" rate will be (70% − 55%)/3 years = 15%/3 years = 5% per year, indicating that $p_7 = 60\%$ (= 55% + 5%) and $p_8 = 65\%$ (= 60% + 5%). Again a check indicates that 70% (= 65% + 5%) is the value that was forecast for p_9.

With these forecasts of earnings-per-share growth rates and payout ratios in hand, forecasts of dividends per share can now be made:

$$
\begin{aligned}
D_7 &= p_7 E_7 \\
&= p_7 E_6 (1 + g_{e7}) \\
&= .60 \times \$11.90 \times (1 + .14) \\
&= .60 \times \$13.57 \\
&= \$8.14 \\
D_8 &= p_8 E_8 \\
&= p_8 E_6 (1 + g_{e7})(1 + g_{e8}) \\
&= .65 \times \$11.90 \times (1 + .14) \times (1 + .09) \\
&= .65 \times \$14.79 \\
&= \$9.61 \\
D_9 &= p_9 E_9 \\
&= p_9 E_6 (1 + g_{e7})(1 + g_{e8})(1 + g_{e9}) \\
&= .70 \times \$11.90 \times (1 + .14) \times (1 + .09) \times (1 + .04) \\
&= .70 \times \$15.38 \\
&= \$10.76.
\end{aligned}
$$

18.8.2 Estimating the Intrinsic Value

Given a required rate of return on *ABC* of 12.4%, all the necessary inputs for the multiple-growth model have been determined. Hence it is now possible to estimate *ABC*'s intrinsic (or fair) value. To begin, it can be seen that $T = 8$, indicating that V_{T-} involves determining the present value of D_1 through D_8,

$$
\begin{aligned}
V_{T-} &= \left[\frac{\$.60}{(1 + .124)^1} \right] + \left[\frac{\$1.60}{(1 + .124)^2} \right] + \left[\frac{\$2.40}{(1 + .124)^3} \right] \\
&\quad + \left[\frac{\$3.20}{(1 + .124)^4} \right] + \left[\frac{\$5.00}{(1 + .124)^5} \right] + \left[\frac{\$6.55}{(1 + .124)^6} \right] \\
&\quad + \left[\frac{\$8.14}{(1 + .124)^7} \right] + \left[\frac{\$9.61}{(1 + .124)^8} \right] \\
&= \$18.89.
\end{aligned}
$$

Then V_{T+} can be determined using D_9:

$$V_{T+} = \frac{\$10.76}{(.124 - .04)(1 + .124)^8}$$

$$= \$50.28.$$

Combining V_{T-} and V_{T+} results in the intrinsic value of ABC:

$$V = V_{T-} + V_{T+}$$
$$= \$18.89 + \$50.28$$
$$= \$69.17.$$

Given a current market price for ABC of \$50, it can be seen that its stock is underpriced by \$19.17 ($= \$69.17 - \$50$) per share. Equivalently, it can be noted that the actual price-earnings ratio for ABC is 29.9 ($= \$50/\$1.67$) but that a "normal" price-earnings ratio would be higher, equal to 41.4 ($= \$69.17/\$1.67$), again indicating that ABC is underpriced.

18.8.3 Implied Returns

As shown with the previous example, once the analyst has made certain forecasts, it is relatively straightforward to determine a company's expected dividends for each year up through the first year of the maturity stage. Then the present value of these predicted dividends can be calculated for a given required rate of return. However, many investment firms use a computerized trial-and-error procedure to determine the discount rate that equates the present value of the stock's expected dividends with its current price. Sometimes this long-run internal rate of return is referred to as the security's **implied return.** In the case of ABC, its implied return is 14.8%.

18.8.4 The Security Market Line

After implied returns have been estimated for a number of stocks, the associated beta for each stock can be estimated. Then for all the stocks analyzed, this information can be plotted on a graph that has implied returns on the vertical axis and estimated betas on the horizontal axis.

At this point there are alternative methods for estimating the security market line (SML).[11] One method involves determining a line of best fit for this graph by using a statistical procedure known as simple regression (as discussed in Chapter 17). That is, the values of an intercept term and a slope term are determined from the data, thereby indicating the location of the straight line that best describes the relationship between implied returns and betas.[12]

Figure 18.4 provides an example of the estimated SML. In this case the SML has been determined to have an intercept of 8% and a slope of 4%, indicating that, in general, securities with higher betas are expected to have higher implied returns in the forthcoming period. Depending on the sizes of the implied returns, such lines can have steeper or flatter slopes, or even negative slopes.

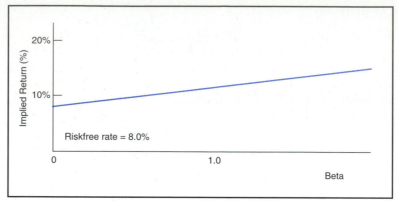

Figure 18.4
A Security Market Line Estimated from Implied Returns

The second method of estimating the SML involves calculating the implied return for a portfolio of common stocks. This is done by taking a value-weighted average of the implied returns of the stocks in the portfolio, with the resulting return being an estimate of the implied return on the market portfolio. Given this return and a beta of 1, the "market" portfolio can be plotted on a graph having implied returns on the vertical axis and betas on the horizontal axis. Next the riskfree rate, having a beta of 0, can be plotted on the same graph. Finally, the SML is determined by simply connecting these two points with a straight line.

Either of these SMLs can be used to determine the required return on a stock. However, they will most likely result in different numbers, as the two lines will most likely have different intercepts and slopes. For example, note that in the first method the SML may not go through the riskfree rate, whereas the second method forces the SML to go through this rate.

18.8.5 Required Returns and Alphas

Once a security's beta has been estimated, its required return can be determined from the estimated SML. For example, the equation for the SML shown in Figure 18.4 is:

$$k_i = 8 + 4\beta_i.$$

Thus if *ABC* has an estimated beta of 1.1, then it would have a required return equal to 12.4% [= 8 + (4 × 1.1)].

Once the required return on a stock has been determined, the difference between the stock's implied return (from the DDM) and this required return can be calculated. This difference is then viewed as an estimate of the stock's *alpha* and represents " . . . the degree to which a stock is mispriced. Positive alphas indicate undervalued securities and negative alphas indicate overvalued securities."[13] In the case of *ABC*, its implied and required returns were 14.8% and 12.4%, respectively. Thus its estimated alpha would be 2.4% (= 14.8% − 12.4%). Because this is a positive number, *ABC* can be viewed as being underpriced.

18.8.6 The Implied Return on the Stock Market

Another product of this analysis is that the implied return for a portfolio of stocks can be compared with the expected return on bonds. (The latter is typically represented by the current yield-to-maturity on long-term Treasury bonds.) Specifically, the difference between stock and bond returns can be used as an input for recommendations concerning asset allocation between stocks and bonds. That is, it can be used to form recommendations regarding what percent of an investor's money should go into stocks and what percent should go into bonds. For example, the greater the implied return on stocks relative to bonds, the larger the percentage of the investor's money that should be placed in common stocks.

18.9 DIVIDEND DISCOUNT MODELS AND EXPECTED RETURNS

The procedures described here are similar to those employed by a number of brokerage firms and portfolio managers.[14] A security's implied return, obtained from a DDM, is often treated as an expected return, which in turn can be divided into two components—the security's required return and alpha.

However, the expected return on a stock over a given holding period may differ from its DDM-based implied rate k^*. A simple set of examples will indicate why this difference can exist.

Assume that a security analyst predicts that a stock will pay a dividend of $1.10 per year forever. On the other hand, the consensus opinion of "the market" (most other investors) is that the dividend will equal $1.00 per year forever. This suggests that the analyst's prediction is a deviant or nonconsensus one.

Assume that both the analyst and other investors agree that the required rate of return for a stock of this type is 10%. Using the formula for the zero-growth model, the value of the stock is $D_1/.10 = 10D_1$, meaning that the stock should sell for ten times its expected dividend. Because other investors expect to receive $1.00 per year, the stock has a current price P of $10 per share. The analyst feels that the stock has a value of $1.10/.10 = $11 and thus feels that it is underpriced by $11 - $10 = $1 per share.

18.9.1 Rate of Convergence of Investors' Predictions

In this situation the implied return according to the analyst is $1.10/$10 = 11%. If the analyst buys a share now with a plan to sell it a year later, what rate of return might the analyst expect to earn? The answer depends on what assumption is made regarding the *rate of convergence of investors' predictions*—that is, the answer depends on the expected market reaction to the mispricing that the analyst believes currently exists.

The cases shown in Table 18.1 are based on an assumption that the analyst is confident that his or her forecast of future dividends is correct. That is, in all of the cases, the analyst expects that at the end of the year, the stock will pay the predicted dividend of $1.10.

TABLE 18.1
ALPHA AND THE CONVERGENCE OF PREDICTIONS

	Expected Amount of Convergence		
	0% (A)	100% (B)	50% (C)
Dividend predictions D_2			
Consensus of other investors	1.00	1.10	1.05
Analyst	1.10	1.10	1.10
Expected stock price P_1	10.00	11.00	10.50
Expected return:			
Dividence yield D_1/P	11%	11%	11%
Capital gain $(P_1 - P)/P$	0	10	5
Total expected return	11%	21%	16%
Less required return	10	10	10
Alpha	1%	11%	6%

Note: P_1 is equal to the consensus dividend prediction at t = 1 divided by the required return of 10%. The example assumes that the current stock price P is $10, and dividends are forecast by the consensus at t = 0 to remain constant at $1.00 per share, whereas the analyst forecasts the dividends at t = 0 to remain constant at $1.10 per share.

No Convergence

In column (A), it is assumed that other investors will regard the higher dividend as a fluke and steadfastly refuse to alter their projections of subsequent dividends from their initial estimate of $1.00. As a result, the security's price at $t = 1$ can be expected to remain at $10 (= $1.00/.10). In this case the analyst's total return is expected to be 11% (= $1.10/$10), which will be attributed entirely to dividends as no capital gains are expected.

The 11% expected return can also be viewed as consisting of the required return of 10% plus an alpha of 1% that is equal to the portion of the dividend unanticipated by other investors, $.10/$10. Accordingly, if it is assumed that there will be no convergence of predictions, the expected return would be set at the implied rate of 11% and the alpha would be set at 1%.

Complete Convergence

Column (B) shows a very different situation. Here it is assumed that the other investors will recognize their error and completely revise their predictions. At the end of the year, it is expected that they too will predict future dividends of $1.10 per year thereafter; thus the stock is expected to be selling for $11 (= $1.10/.10) at $t = 1$. Under these conditions, the analyst can expect to achieve a total return of 21% by selling the stock at the end of the year for $11, obtaining 11% (= $1.10/$10) in dividend yield and 10% (= $1/$10) in capital gains.

The 10% expected capital gains result directly from the expected repricing of the security because of the complete convergence of predictions. In this case the fruits of the analyst's superior prediction are expected to be obtained all in one year. Instead of 1% "extra" per year forever, as in column (A), the analyst expects to obtain 1% (= \$.10/\$10) in extra dividend yield plus 10% (= \$1/\$10) in capital gains this year. By continuing to hold the stock in subsequent years, the analyst would expect to earn only the required return of 10% over those years. Accordingly, the expected return is 21% and the alpha is 11% when it is assumed that there is complete convergence of predictions.

Partial Convergence

Column (C) shows an intermediate case. Here the predictions of the other investors are expected to converge only halfway toward those of the analyst (that is, from \$1.00 to \$1.05 instead of to \$1.10). Total return in the first year is expected to be 16%, consisting of 11% (= \$1.10/\$10) in dividend yield plus 5% (= \$.50/\$10) in capital gains.

Since the stock is expected to be selling for \$10.50 (= \$1.05/.10) at $t = 1$, the analyst will still feel that it is underpriced at $t = 1$ because it will have an intrinsic value of \$11 (= \$1.10/.10) at that time. To obtain the remainder of the "extra return" owing to this underpricing, the stock would have to be held past $t = 1$. Accordingly, the expected return would be set at 16% and the alpha would be set at 6% when it is assumed that there is halfway convergence of predictions.

In general, a security's expected return and alpha will be larger, the faster the assumed rate of convergence of predictions.[15] Many investors use the implied rate (that is, the internal rate of return k^*) as a surrogate for a relatively short-term (for example, one year) expected return, as in column (A). In doing so, they are assuming that the dividend forecast is completely accurate, but that there is no convergence. Alternatively, investors could assume that there is some degree of convergence, thereby raising their estimate of the security's expected return. Indeed, investors could further alter their estimate of the security's expected return by assuming that the security analyst's deviant prediction is less than perfectly accurate, as will be seen next.[16]

18.9.2 Predicted versus Actual Returns

An alternative approach does not simply use outputs from a model "as is," but *adjusts* them, based on relationships between previous predictions and actual outcomes. Panels (a) and (b) of Figure 18.5 provide examples.

Each point in Figure 18.5(a) plots a *predicted return* on the stock market as a whole (on the horizontal axis) and the subsequent *actual return* for that period (on the vertical axis). The line of best fit (determined by simple regression) through the points indicates the general relationship between prediction and outcome. If the current prediction is 14%, history suggests that an estimate of 15% would be superior.

Each point in Figure 18.5(b) plots a predicted alpha value for a security (on the horizontal axis) and the subsequent "abnormal return" for that period (on the vertical axis). Such a diagram can be made for a given security, or for all the securities that a particular analyst makes predictions about, or for all the securities that the investment firm makes predictions about. Again a line of best fit can be drawn through the points. In this case, if the current prediction of a security's

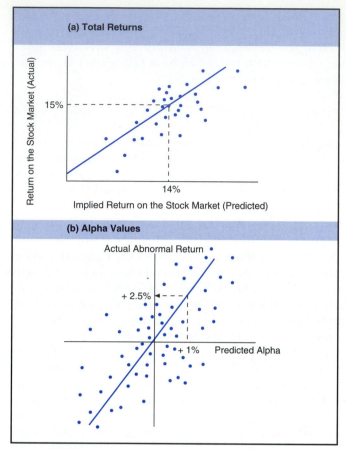

Figure 18.5
Adjusting Predictions

alpha is $+1\%$, this relationship suggests that an "adjusted" estimate of $+2.5\%$ would be superior.

An important by-product of this type of analysis is the measure of correlation between predicted and actual outcomes, indicating the nearness of the points to the line. This **information coefficient** (IC) can serve as a measure of predictive accuracy. If it is too small to be significantly different from zero in a statistical sense, the value of the predictions is subject to considerable question.[17]

18.10 SUMMARY

1. The capitalization of income method of valuation states that the intrinsic value of any asset is equal to the sum of the discounted cash flows investors expect to receive from that asset.

2. Dividend discount models (DDMs) are a specific application of the capitalization of income method of valuation to common stocks.
3. To use a DDM, the investor must implicitly or explicitly supply a forecast of all future dividends expected to be generated by a security.
4. Investors typically make certain simplifying assumptions about the growth of common stock dividends. For example, a common stock's dividends may be assumed to exhibit zero growth or growth at a constant rate. More complex assumptions may allow for multiple growth rates over time.
5. Instead of applying DDMs, many security analysts use a simpler method of security valuation that involves estimating a stock's "normal" price-earnings ratio and comparing it with the stock's actual price-earnings ratio.
6. The growth rate in a firm's earnings and dividends depends on its earnings retention rate and its average return on equity for new investments.
7. Determining whether a security is mispriced using a DDM can be done in one of two ways. First, the discounted value of expected dividends can be compared with the stock's current price. Second, the discount rate that equates the stock's current price to the present value of forecast dividends can be compared with the required return for stocks of similar risk.
8. The rate of return that an analyst with accurate non-consensus dividend forecasts can expect to earn depends on the rate of convergence of other investors' predictions to the predictions of the analyst.

QUESTIONS AND PROBLEMS

1. Consider five annual cash flows (the first occurring one year from today):

Year	Cash Flow
1	$5
2	$6
3	$7
4	$8
5	$9

   Given a discount rate of 10%, what is the present value of this stream of cash flows?
2. Alta Cohen is considering buying a machine to produce baseballs. The machine costs $10,000. With the machine, Alta expects to produce and sell 1,000 baseballs per year for $3 per baseball, net of all costs. The machine's life is five years (with no salvage value). Based on these assumptions and an 8% discount rate, what is the net present value of Alta's investment?
3. Hub Collins has invested in a project that promised to pay $100, $200, and $300, respectively, at the end of the next three years. If Hub paid $513.04 for this investment, what is the project's internal rate of return?
4. Afton Products currently pays a dividend of $4 per share on its common stock.

a. If Afton Products plans to increase its dividend at a rate of 5% per year indefinitely, what will be the dividend per share in 10 years?

b. If Afton Products' dividend per share is expected to be $5.87 per share at the end of five years, at what annual rate is the dividend expected to grow?

5. Hammond Pipes has issued a preferred stock that pays $12 per share. The dividend is fixed and the stock has no expiration date. What is the intrinsic value of Hammond preferred stock, assuming a discount rate of 15%?

6. Milton Information Services currently pays a dividend of $4 per share on its common stock. The dividend is expected to grow at 4% per year forever. Stocks with similar risk currently are priced to provide a 12% expected return. What is the intrinsic value of Milton stock?

7. Spring Valley Bedding stock currently sells for $53 per share. The stock's dividend is expected to grow at 6% per year indefinitely. Spring Valley just paid a dividend of $3 per share. Given this information, calculate the stock's internal rate of return.

8. Select a stock whose name begins with the first letter of your last name. From the *Value Line Investment Survey* find the average annual compounded growth rate in the stock's dividend over the last five years. Assume that this growth rate will continue indefinitely. Also from the *Value Line Investment Survey* find the beta of the stock. Using the current riskfree rate (90-day Treasury bills as found in the *Wall Street Journal*) and a 6% expected market risk premium, calculate the SML and the required return on the stock. Finally, using the dividend growth rate and the required return, calculate the intrinsic value of the stock. (*Note:* If the data for your stock is incompatible with the constant-growth DDM, select another stock.) Compare this intrinsic value to the latest closing price for the stock. Is the stock underpriced or overpriced? What potential problems are involved with this approach to making investment decisions?

9. The constant-growth model is an overly simplistic means of valuing most corporations' stocks. However, a number of market analysts believe that it is a useful means of estimating a fair value for the stock market as a whole. Why might the constant-growth DDM be a more reasonable valuation tool for the market in aggregate as opposed to individual stocks?

10. This year Monona Air Cleaners Inc. will pay a dividend on its stock of $6 per share. The following year the dividend is expected to be the same, increasing to $7 the year after. From that point on, the dividend is expected to grow at 4% per year indefinitely. Stocks with similar risk are currently priced to provide a 10% expected return. What is the intrinsic value of Monona stock?

11. Knapp Carpet recently paid an annual dividend on its stock of $2 per share. The dividend is expected to grow at $1 per share for the next four years. Thereafter the dividend is expected to grow at 5% per year indefinitely. The required return on stocks with similar risk is 12%. What is the intrinsic value of Knapp stock?

12. Chief Medical Inc. is a little-known producer of heart pacemakers. The earnings and dividend growth prospects of the company are disputed by analysts. Albert Bender is forecasting 5% growth in dividends indefinitely.

However, his brother John is predicting a 20% growth in dividends, but only for the next three years, after which the growth rate is expected to decline to 4% for the indefinite future. Chief dividends per share are currently $3. Stocks with similar risk are currently priced to provide a 14% expected return.

    a. What is the intrinsic value of Chief stock according to Albert?

    b. What is the intrinsic value of Chief stock according to John?

    c. Assume that Chief stock now sells for $39¾ per share. If the stock is fairly priced at the present time, what is the implied perpetual dividend growth rate? What is the implied P/E (price-earnings ratio) on next year's earnings, based on this perpetual dividend growth assumption and assuming a 25% payout ratio?

13. Elk Mound Candy Company currently pays a dividend of $3 per share. That dividend is expected to grow at a 6% rate indefinitely. Stocks with similar risk provide a 10% expected return. Calculate the intrinsic value of Elk Mound stock today using an interim computation based on the sale of the stock at its expected intrinsic value three years from now.

14. How would an increase in the perceived riskiness of a common stock's future cash flows affect its price-earnings ratio? Explain intuitively and mathematically.

15. Roberts Roofing currently earns $4 per share. Its return on equity is 20% and it retains 50% of its earnings (both figures are expected to be maintained indefinitely). Stocks of similar risk are priced to return 15%. What is the intrinsic value of Roberts' stock?

16. Osseo Operations recently paid an annual dividend of $4 per share. Earnings for the same year were $8 per share. The required return on stocks with similar risk is 11%. Dividends are expected to grow 6% per year indefinitely. Calculate Osseo's "normal" price-earnings ratio.

17. Reedsburg Associates is currently paying a dividend of $2 per share on earnings of $4 per share. Its stock is selling for $200 per share. Stocks of similar risk are priced to return 15%. What kind of return on equity could explain investors' willingness to pay a price equal to 50 times earnings on this stock?

18. Rochelle Corp. is expected to pay out 40% of its earnings and to earn an average of 15% per year on its incremental reinvested earnings forever. Stocks with similar risk are currently priced to provide a 12% expected return. By what percentage can Rochelle's earnings be expected to grow each year? What is an appropriate price-earnings multiple for the stock? What portion of the return on Rochelle stock is expected to come from capital gains?

19. A three-stage DDM has become a very popular common stock valuation model. It is used by a number of institutional investors and brokerage firms. What advantages does it offer relative to a simple constant-growth DDM? Despite its increased sophistication compared to the constant-growth DDM, what disadvantages does it still retain?

20. What explanations can you offer for the fact that the SML shown in Figure 18.4 is so flat?

---

21. Fay Thomas, a financial analyst, once remarked: "Even if your dividend estimates and discount rate assumption are correct, dividend discount models identify stocks that will produce positive risk-adjusted returns only if other investors eventually come to agree with the DDM's valuation conclusions." Is this statement correct? Why?

22. Some people assert that a "true" growth company is one whose dividends grow at a rate greater than its required rate of return. Why is the constant-growth DDM incapable of valuing such a "true" growth stock?

CFA EXAM QUESTIONS

23. The constant-growth dividend discount model can be used for both the valuation of companies and the estimation of the long-term total return of a stock.

> Assume: $20   =   *the price of a stock today,*
>   8%   =   *the expected growth rate of dividends,*
> $0.60 =   *the annual dividend one year forward.*

   a. Using only the above data, compute the expected long-term total return on the stock using the constant-growth dividend discount model. Show calculations.
   b. Briefly discuss three disadvantages of the constant-growth dividend discount model in its application to investment analysis.

24. As a firm operating in a mature industry, Arbot Industries is expected to maintain a constant dividend payout ratio and constant growth rate of earnings for the foreseeable future. Earnings were $4.50 per share in the recently completed fiscal year. The dividend payout ratio has been a constant 55% in recent years and is expected to remain so. Arbot's return on equity (ROE) is expected to remain at 10% in the future, and you require an 11% return on the stock.
   a. Using the constant-growth dividend discount model, calculate the current value of Arbot common stock. Show your calculations.
   After an aggressive acquisition and marketing program, it now appears that Arbot's earnings per share and ROE will grow rapidly over the next two years. You are aware that the dividend discount model can be useful in estimating the value of common stock even when the assumption of constant growth does not apply.
   b. Calculate the current value of Arbot's common stock, using the dividend discount model, assuming that Arbot's dividend will grow at a 15% rate for the next two years, returning in the third year to the historical growth rate and continuing to grow at the historical rate for the foreseeable future. Show your calculations.

APPENDIX

THE GRAHAM-REA MODEL

In 1934 a book that was to become the cornerstone of fundamental analysis was published by Benjamin Graham and David L. Dodd. This book, entitled *Security Analysis,* argued that the future earnings power of the firm was the most important determinant of a stock's value.[18] However, in 1974 Graham himself repudiated the book and the principles contained in it.[19] Instead of following his old approach, Graham, along with James Rea, developed a new approach to identifying underpriced common stocks.[20] The reason for his change in attitude was his belief that the stock market was becoming increasingly efficient, and that only smaller and smaller pockets of inefficiencies remained. Because Graham and Rea believed that these inefficiencies tended to be present in the stocks of certain identifiable firms, they developed a set of criteria to spot such stocks.

The Graham-Rea approach can be applied mechanically, as it involves examining the current financial statements of the firm under consideration and relating certain items from these statements to the firm's current stock price and the current yield on triple-A bonds. Ten questions that can be answered with a simple "yes" or "no" are involved. Table 18.2 lists them, indicating that the first five questions deal with "rewards" and the second five questions deal with "risks." The idea behind these questions is to identify stocks that have the highest reward-to-risk ratio. In order for a stock to be recommended for purchase by Graham and Rea, it need not provide a "yes" answer to all of the questions.

The simplest way to use the questions is to first remove all stocks that do not provide a "yes" answer to question 6. Then, of the remaining stocks, remove those that do not provide a "yes" answer to either question 1 or question 3 or question 5. The stocks that are left are candidates for purchase.

In determining when to sell, the Graham-Rea approach says that the investor should sell as soon as the stock has risen 50% or two years have passed since the stock was purchased, whichever occurs first. However, if neither of these two sell signals has occurred and the stock either stops paying dividends or no longer generates the appropriate "yes" answers to the questions, then it should be sold immediately.

How well has the Graham-Rea approach to investing worked? In a study of this approach which focused on New York Stock Exchange and American Stock Exchange securities, three observations were particularly interesting.[21] First, since the approach was publicized it was found that the number of stocks that

TABLE 18.2
GRAHAM-REA STOCK SELECTION QUESTIONS

A. Rewards

1. Is the price-earnings ratio less than one-half the reciprocal of the triple-A bond yield? (For example, if the current triple-A rate is 12%, then the reciprocal is $1/.12 = 8\frac{1}{3}$, and half of that is $4\frac{1}{6}$. Thus, for a stock to provide a "yes" answer to this question, its price-earnings ratio must be less than $4\frac{1}{6}$.)

2. Is the price-earnings ratio less than 40% of the highest "average" price-earnings ratio of the last five years? (Here, the "average" price-earnings ratio for a stock for a given year is the average stock price for the year divided by the earnings per share for that year.)

3. Is the dividend yield at least $\frac{2}{3}$ the triple-A bond yield?

4. Is the stock price below $\frac{2}{3}$ of the tangible book value per share? (Here tangible book value per share is simply total assets less total debt, with the difference divided by the number of shares outstanding.)

5. Is the stock price below $\frac{2}{3}$ of the net current asset value per share? (Here net current asset value per share is current assets less total debt, with the difference divided by the number of shares outstanding.)

B. Risks

6. Is the debt-to-equity ratio less than one? (Here the debt-to-equity ratio is simply total debt divided by total equity as shown on the balance sheet.)

7. Is the current ratio greater than two? (Here the current ratio is current assets divided by current liabilities.)

8. Is total debt less than twice the net current asset value? (Here net current asset value is current assets less total debt.)

9. Has the earnings-per-share growth rate of the last ten years averaged at least 7% per year? (If the earnings per share over the last year is denoted E_0 and the earnings per share over the year ending ten years ago is denoted E_{-10}, then the growth rate is the value of g that solves the equation $E_0 = E_{-10}(1 + g)^{10}$. To provide a "yes" answer to this question, g must be at least 7%.)

10. Over the time period examined in question 9, have eight or more of the annual growth rates in earnings per share been equal to -5% or more? (Here the ten annual growth rates in earnings per share would be calculated and then examined to see that no more than two of them were less than -5%.)

Source: Adapted from Paul Blustein, "Ben Graham's Last Will and Testament," *Forbes*, August 1, 1977: 43–45; and James B. Rea, "Remembering Benjamin Graham—Teacher and Friend," *Journal of Portfolio Management*, 3, no. 4 (Summer 1977): 66–72.

provided the appropriate "yes" answers declined dramatically. (For example, in 1980 only five securities had "yes" answers to questions 1 and 6.) Second, the historical record suggests that positive abnormal returns would have been earned had this approach been used subsequent to its publication. Third, because many of the firms recommended for purchase were small firms, it is possible that all that this approach does is capture the size effect (that is, the small-firm effect that was discussed in the appendix to Chapter 17). However, the study found that even after adjusting for the size effect, the approach would still have earned positive abnormal returns since its publication.[22]

In closing, it should be noted that a number of professional portfolio managers currently follow the Graham-Rea approach to investing. Examples include the Rea-Graham Fund, LMH Fund, Sequoia Fund, and Pacific Partners Fund.

[1] The appendix describes a model used by some fundamental analysts for identifying winners (that is, underpriced common stocks) that is not directly related to the capitalization of income method of valuation. For a description of the typical financial characteristics of stock market winners, see Marc R. Reinganum, "The Anatomy of Stock Market Winners," *Financial Analysts Journal*, 44, no. 2 (March/April 1988): 16–28.

[2] Sometimes the expected cash flows after some time period will be equal to zero, meaning that the summation only needs to be carried out to that point. Even if they are never equal to zero, in many cases the denominator in Equation (18.1) will become so large as t gets large (for example, if $t = 40$ or more for a discount rate of 15%) that the present value of all expected cash flows past an arbitrary time in the future will be roughly zero, and can be safely ignored. Furthermore, the discount rate may vary from period to period. It was assumed to be constant here for ease of exposition.

[3] With complex cash flows (such as a mix of positive and negative cash flows), the IRR method can be misleading. However, this is not a problem when it is applied to securities such as stocks and bonds. For a discussion of potential problems in other contexts, see Richard A. Brealey and Stewart C. Myers, *Principles of Corporate Finance* (New York: McGraw-Hill, 1991), Chapter 5.

[4] Because the focus of DDMs is on predicting dividends, there is a particular situation where using DDMs to value common stocks is exceptionally difficult. This is the case where the firm has not paid dividends on its stock in the recent past, which results in a lack of historical record on which to base a prediction of dividends. Examples include valuing the stock of a firm being sold to the public for the first time (known as an *initial public offering*, or *ipo*), valuing the stock of a firm that has not paid dividends recently (perhaps the firm has never paid dividends, or perhaps it has suspended paying them), and valuing the stock of a closely held firm. A more extensive discussion of DDMs is contained in the entire November-December 1985 issue of the *Financial Analysts Journal*. For articles that describe some of the current applications of DDMs, see Barbara Donnelly, "The Dividend Discount Model Comes into Its Own," *Institutional Investor*, 19, no. 3 (March 1985): 77–82; and Kent Hickman and Glen H. Petry, "A Comparison of Stock Price Predictions Using Court Accepted Formulas, Dividend Discount, and P/E Models," *Financial Management*, 19, no. 2 (Summer 1990): 76–87.

[5] A share of common stock has a positive NPV if and only if it has an IRR greater than its required rate of return. Thus there can never be inconsistent signals given by the two approaches. That is, there will never be a situation where one approach indicates that a stock is underpriced and the other approach indicates that it is overpriced. This is true not only for the zero-growth model, but for all DDMs.

[6] The formula for valuing *consols* (these are bonds that make regular coupon payments but have no maturity date) is identical to Equation (18.13), where the numerator now represents the annual coupon payment. Because it has been found that the price behavior of high-grade preferred stock is very similar to that of bonds, it is not surprising that the zero–growth model can be used to value high-grade preferred stocks. See John S. Bildersee, "Some Aspects of the Performance of Non-Convertible Preferred Stocks," *Journal of Finance*, 28, no. 5 (December 1973): 1187–1201; and Enrico J. Ferreira, Michael F. Spivey, and Charles E. Edwards, "Pricing New-Issue and Seasoned Preferred Stock: A Comparison of Valuation Models," *Financial Management*, 21, no. 2 (Summer 1992): 52–62.

⁷ For an extension of this model which introduces capital gains taxes, see Raymond Chiang and Ricardo J. Rodriguez, "Personal Taxes, Holding Period, and the Valuation of Growth Stocks," *Journal of Economics and Business,* 42, no. 4 (November 1990): 303–309.

⁸ For a discussion of these models, see Russell J. Fuller and Chi-Cheng Hsia, "A Simplified Common Stock Valuation Model," *Financial Analysts Journal,* 40, no. 5 (September/October 1984): 49–56; Eric H. Sorensen and David A. Williamson, "Some Evidence on the Value of Dividend Discount Models," *Financial Analysts Journal,* 41, no. 6 (November/December 1985): 60–69; Richard W. Taylor, "A Three-Phase Quarterly Dividend Discount Model," *Financial Analysts Journal,* 44, no. 5 (September/October 1988): 79–80, and "A Three-Phase Quarterly Earnings Model, *Financial Analysts Journal,* 45, no. 5 (September/October 1989): 79; and Michael S. Rozeff, "The Three-Phase Dividend Discount Model and the ROPE Model," *Journal of Portfolio Management,* 16, no. 2 (Winter 1990): 36–42.

⁹ The analysis is similar if it is assumed that the investor plans to sell the stock after some other length of time, such as six months or two years.

¹⁰ Alternatively, some analysts focus on the **earnings-price ratio,** which is the reciprocal of the price-earnings ratio. Accordingly, the formulas for a stock's "normal" earnings-price ratio can be found by simply taking the reciprocal of the forthcoming formulas for determining a stock's "normal" price-earnings ratio. In cases where earnings are close to zero, the earnings-price ratio is computationally preferred by analysts to the price-earnings ratio. This is because it approaches zero in such a situation, whereas the price-earnings ratio approaches infinity.

¹¹ There are numerous methods besides those described here. Some of them are based on more complicated versions of the CAPM, whereas others are based on the APT (discussed in Chapter 12).

¹² There are ways of forcing the intercept of the line to go through the riskfree rate in order to agree with the implications of the traditional CAPM.

¹³ Carmine J. Grigoli, "Common Stock Valuation," *Merrill Lynch Quantitative Analysis,* May/June 1984. A subsequent procedure divides the estimated alpha by an estimate of the security's unique risk (that is, nonmarket or unsystematic risk) to obtain a standardized alpha. Then, based on the magnitude of the standardized alpha, the security is classified into one of ten "standardized alpha deciles." See also Marshall E. Blume, "The Use of 'Alphas' to Improve Performance," *Journal of Portfolio Management,* 11, no. 1 (Fall 1984): 86–92.

¹⁴ An example of a similar procedure formerly used by Wells Fargo Investment Advisors is described by George Foster in *Financial Statement Analysis* (Englewood Cliffs, NJ: Prentice Hall, 1986), pp. 428–430.

¹⁵ In a perfectly efficient market (in the semistrong-form sense), these analysts would sometimes be right and sometimes be wrong, so that on balance their predictions would be of no value. In such a situation, the expected return for any security would be its required return and the alpha would be zero.

¹⁶ As an example of how to estimate alpha if it is assumed that the analyst has less than perfect forecasting ability and there is less than 100% convergence, reconsider the example given in Table 18.1. First, assume that the forecast accuracy of the security analyst is 60%. Remembering that the analyst's forecast of D_1 is $1.10, but the consensus forecast is $1.00, then 60% accuracy means that the forecast that should be used is $1.06 $[= \$1.00 + .60 \times (\$1.10 - \$1.00)]$. Second, assume that there will be 50% convergence. This means that the security's price at $t = 1$ is expected to be $10.30 = \{[\$1.00 + .50 \times (\$1.06 - \$1.00)]/.10\}$. Hence the expected return under 60% forecast accuracy and 50% convergence is 13.6% $\{= [(\$10.30 - \$10) + \$1.06]/\$10\}$, which translates into an alpha of 3.6% $(= 13.6\% - 10\%)$.

---

606 CHAPTER 18

[17] It has been argued that a value of .15 for an IC is indicative of good performance with regard to stock forecasting, and that several different forecasters have recorded ICs of this magnitude (a value of zero would be expected in a perfectly efficient market). See Keith P. Ambachtsheer, "Profit Potential in an 'Almost Efficient' Market," *Journal of Portfolio Management,* 1, no. 1 (Fall 1974): 84–87, and "Where Are the Customers' Alphas?" *Journal of Portfolio Management,* 4, no. 1 (Fall 1977): 52–56; Keith P. Ambachtsheer and James L. Farrell, Jr., "Can Active Management Add Value?" *Financial Analysts Journal,* 35, no. 6 (November–December 1979): 39–47; and S. D. Hodges and R. A. Brealey, "Portfolio Selection in a Dynamic and Uncertain World," *Financial Analysts Journal,* 29, no. 2 (March–April 1973): 50–65.

[18] Graham and Dodd also argued that each dollar of dividends is worth four times as much as each dollar of retained earnings. Subsequent examination of market data indicates that their argument has no support. See J. Ronald Hoffmeister and Edward A. Dyl, "Dividends and Share Value: Graham and Dodd Revisited," *Financial Analysts Journal,* 41, no. 3 (May/June 1985): 77–78; and Lewis D. Johnson, "Dividends and Share Value: Graham and Dodd Revisited, Again," *Financial Analysts Journal,* 41, no. 5 (September/October 1985): 79–80. For the most recent edition of the book, see Sidney Cottle, Roger F. Murray, and Frank E. Block, *Graham and Dodd's Security Analysis,* 5th ed. (New York: McGraw-Hill, 1988). For a brief discussion of their approach to investing, see Roger F. Murray, "Graham and Dodd: A Durable Discipline," *Financial Analysts Journal,* 40, no. 5 (September/October 1984): 18–23.

[19] See "A Conversation with Benjamin Graham," *Financial Analysts Journal,* 32, no. 5 (September/October 1976): 20–23.

[20] For a description of this approach, see Paul Blustein, "Ben Graham's Last Will and Testament," *Forbes,* August 1, 1977: 43–45; and James B. Rea, "Remembering Benjamin Graham—Teacher and Friend", *Journal of Portfolio Management,* 3, no. 4 (Summer 1977): 66–72.

[21] Henry R. Oppenheimer, "A Test of Ben Graham's Stock Selection Criteria," *Financial Analysts Journal,* 40, no. 5 (September/October 1984): 68–74.

[22] A subsequent study focused on only one of the ten Graham-Rea questions, number 5 in Table 18.2. It found that portfolios consisting of securities that had "yes" answers to this question would have earned above-market returns. See Henry R. Oppenheimer, "Ben Graham's Net Current Asset Values: A Performance Update," *Financial Analysts Journal,* 42, no. 6 (November/December 1986): 40–47.

KEY TERMS

capitalization of income method of valuation	multiple-growth model
discount rate	price-earnings ratio
net present value	earnings-price ratio
internal rate of return	payout ratio
dividend discount model	retention ratio
zero-growth model	implied return
constant-growth model	information coefficient

1. The foundation for dividend discount models was laid out in:

   John Burr Williams, *The Theory of Investment Value* (Amsterdam: North-Holland Publishing, 1964). The original edition was published in 1938.

2. The constant-growth and multiple-growth models were subsequently developed by, respectively:

   M. J. Gordon, "Dividends, Earnings, and Stock Prices," *Review of Economics and Statistics,* 41, no. 2 (May 1959): 99–105.

   Nicholas Molodovsky, Catherine May, and Sherman Chottiner, "Common Stock Valuation: Principles, Tables and Application," *Financial Analysts Journal,* 21, no. 2 (March/April 1965): 104–123.

3. For more on DDMs, see the entire November–December 1985 issue of the *Financial Analysts Journal.* Some of the problems involved in using dividend discount models are discussed in:

   Richard O. Michaud and Paul L. Davis, "Valuation Model Bias and the Scale Structure of Dividend Discount Returns," *Journal of Finance,* 38, no. 2 (May 1982): 563–573.

   Adam K. Gehr, Jr., "A Bias in Dividend Discount Models," *Financial Analysts Journal,* 48, no. 1 (January/February 1992): 75–80.

4. For more on how to measure and use P/E ratios, see:

   John Markese, "Will the Real P/E Please Stand Up?" *AAII Journal,* 11, no. 9 (October 1989): 32–34.

   Robert J. Angell and Alonzo Redman, "How to Judge a P/E? Examine the Expected Growth Rate," *AAII Journal,* 12, no. 3 (March 1990): 16–17.

   John Baijkowski, "Price-Earnings Ratios and Fundamental Stock Valuation," *AAII Journal,* 13, no. 6 (July 1991): 33–36.

5. For an interesting note on why Japanese P/E ratios appear to be overstated, see:

   Harold Bierman, Jr., "Price/Earnings Ratios Restructured for Japan," *Financial Analysts Journal,* 47, No. 2 (March/April 1991): 91–92.

6. For an article that ties DDMs, P/E ratios, and Graham and Dodd together, see:

   John Baijkowski, "From Theory to Reality: Applying the Valuation Models," *AAII Journal,* 15, no. 1 (January 1993): 34–37.

7. The issue of market volatility has been studied by utilizing dividend discount models. In essence, these studies compare the actual levels of various stock market indices with their intrinsic values, calculated by determining the present value of rational forecasts of subsequent dividends paid on the stocks in the indices. The main observation is that the actual levels fluctuate far more over time than the intrinsic values. A conclusion that some people draw from

these studies is that there is excess volatility in stock prices and hence markets are not efficient. This hotly debated topic was introduced in:

Stephen F. LeRoy and Richard D. Porter, "The Present-Value Relation: Tests Based on Implied Variance Bounds," *Econometrica,* 49, no. 3 (May 1981): 555–574.

Robert J. Shiller, "Do Stock Prices Move Too Much to Be Justified by Subsequent Changes in Dividends?" *American Economic Review,* 71, no. 3 (June 1981): 421–436.

8. For more on market volatility, see:

Robert J. Shiller, "Theories of Aggregate Stock Price Movements," *Journal of Portfolio Management,* 10, no. 2 (Winter 1984): 23–37.

Robert J. Shiller, *Market Volatility* (Cambridge, MA: MIT Press, 1989).

Stephen F. LeRoy, "Efficient Capital Markets and Martingales," *Journal of Economic Literature,* 27, no. 4 (December 1989): 1583–1621.

Stephen F. LeRoy, "Capital Market Efficiency: An Update," *Federal Reserve Bank of San Francisco Economic Review* (Spring 1990): 29–40.

Lucy F. Ackert and Brian F. Smith, "Stock Price Volatility, Ordinary Dividends, and Other Cash Flows to Shareholders," *Journal of Finance,* 48, no. 4 (September 1993): 1147–1160.

Earnings

Chapter 18 discussed how the intrinsic value of a share of common stock can be determined by discounting expected dividends per share at a rate of return that is appropriate for a security of similar risk. Alternatively, the implied return on a share of common stock can be determined by finding the discount rate that makes the present value of all the expected dividends equal to the current market price of the stock. In either case, a forecast of dividends per share is necessary. Because dividends per share are equal to earnings per share times a payout ratio, dividends can be forecast by forecasting earnings per share and payout ratios. Currently there are numerous methods that are used by security analysts for forecasting either earnings or dividends. This chapter presents a discussion of some of the important features of dividends and earnings that the analyst should be aware of in making such forecasts. It begins with a discussion of the relationship among earnings, dividends, and investment.

19.1 STOCK VALUATION BASED ON EARNINGS

A continual controversy in the investment community concerns the relevance of dividends versus earnings as the underlying source of value of a share of common stock. Clearly, earnings are important to stockholders because earnings provide the cash flow necessary for paying dividends. However, dividends are also important because dividends are what stockholders actually receive from the firm, and they are the focus of the dividend discount models discussed in Chapter 18. Indeed, it would seem that if management increased the proportion of earnings per share paid out as dividends, they could make their stockholders wealthier, suggesting that the **dividend decision** (deciding on the amount of dividends to pay) is a very important one.

Considerable light was shed on this controversy in 1961 when Merton Miller and Franco Modigliani published a seminal paper arguing that the underlying source of value of a share of common stock was earnings, not dividends. An implication of this conclusion is that the dividend decision is relatively unimportant to the stockholders, as it will not affect the value of their investment in the firm.

In the course of a year, a firm generates revenues and incurs costs. With cash accounting, the difference between revenues and costs would be termed *cash flow*. With accrual accounting, used by almost all firms, both revenues and costs are likely to include estimates made by accountants of the values of noncash items. Items such as depreciation charges are deducted from cash flow to obtain earnings. Moreover, each year some amount is invested in the business. Of the total (gross) investment, a portion will be equal in value to the estimated depreciation of various real assets (such as machines and buildings); the rest is new (net) investment.

The dollar amount of new investment each year should be based on the investment opportunities that are available to the firm, and they should be unaffected by the dollar amount of dividends that are to be paid out. In particular, any investment opportunity whose net present value (NPV) is positive should be undertaken. This means that the future prospects of the firm can be described by a stream of expected earnings ($E_1, E_2, E_3, \ldots$) and the expected net investment required to produce such earnings ($I_1, I_2, I_3, \ldots$). Taking these two streams as given, it can be shown that management can set the total dollar amount of current dividends (D_0) at any level without making the current stockholders either better or worse off.[1] This will be done next, with the focus on earnings and how they can be used to pay for new investments and dividends.

19.1.1 Earnings, Dividends, and Investment

Figure 19.1(a) shows one way that the firm can use total earnings for the current year (E_0). In this situation, new investment (I_0) is financed out of earnings, and the firm uses the remainder of the earnings to pay dividends (D_0) to its stockholders. For example, if the Plum Company has just earned $5,000 and has new investments it would like to make that cost $3,000, then Plum could pay for these investments out of earnings and declare a dividend of $2,000.

Issuing Stock

Whereas earnings are exactly equal to dividends and investment ($E_0 = D_0 + I_0$) in Figure 19.1(a), this need not be the case. In the situation shown in Figure 19.1(b), earnings are less than dividends and investment ($E_0 < D_0 + I_0$). Because the amount of investment has been determined by the number of positive NPV projects available to the firm, the reason for this inequality is that the firm has decided to pay its current stockholders a higher dividend than was paid in Figure 19.1(a). However, in order for higher dividends to be paid, additional funds must be obtained from outside the firm. This is accomplished by a new sale of common stock (it is assumed that the flotation costs associated with a new sale of common stock are negligible).

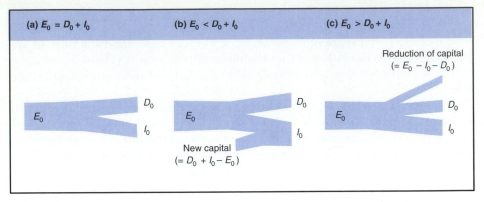

Figure 19.1
Earnings, Dividends, and Investment

The reason the funds are obtained through a new sale of common stock instead of through a new sale of debt is a desire to avoid the confounding effects of a change in the firm's debt-equity ratio. That is, if debt financing is to be allowed, then two things would be changing at the same time—the amount of the dividend and the debt-equity ratio for the firm. As a result, if stockholders appear to be made better off by a change in the amount of the dividend, their betterment may actually be due to a change in the debt-equity ratio. By prohibiting debt financing, the debt-equity ratio will remain constant, and only the amount of the dividend will be allowed to change. That is, each additional dollar in equity funds raised by issuing new stock is offset by a dollar in dividend payments. Thus if stockholders appear to be better off, it has to be due to the change in the amount of the dividend, because everything else (specifically, the amount of investment and the debt-equity ratio) has remained fixed.

Note that if investment is financed out of earnings, as in Figure 19.1(a), then it has been financed with equity obtained internally. In Figure 19.1(b), investment has also been financed with equity, but here some of the equity has been obtained externally. As a result, the debt-equity ratio for the firm is the same in both situations.

In the case of Plum, instead of paying dividends amounting to $2,000, the firm could decide to pay dividends amounting to $3,000. Because investment is equal to $3,000, Plum will have a cash outflow of $6,000 ($= $3,000 + $3,000$), with earnings amounting to only $5,000. This means that Plum will have to sell $1,000 ($= $6,000 - $5,000$) of new common stock.

Repurchasing Stock

In Figure 19.1(c), the situation is reversed from 19.1(b) as earnings are now greater than dividends and investment ($E_0 > D_0 + I_0$). Given that the amount of investment has been determined by the number of positive NPV projects available to the firm, the reason for this inequality is that the firm has decided to pay its stockholders a lower dividend than was paid in Figure 19.1(a). In paying this smaller dividend, the firm will be left with excess cash. It is assumed that the firm will use this cash to repurchase some of its outstanding shares in the market-place (and that the transaction costs associated with such repurchases are negligible).

The reason for this assumption is the desire to keep the situation comparable to the two earlier ones. Allowing the firm to keep the excess cash would be tantamount to letting the firm invest the cash, an investment decision that was not made in the two earlier cases and therefore does not have a positive NPV (remember that I_0 consists of all positive NPV projects). Allowing the firm to keep the excess cash would also mean that the firm has made a decision to lower its debt-equity ratio. This is because retention of the excess cash would increase the amount of equity for the firm, thereby decreasing the amount of debt outstanding relative to the amount of equity.

Continuing with the Plum Company, dividends could be set at $1,000 instead of $2,000 or $3,000. In this case, the firm would have a cash outflow for dividends and investment amounting to $4,000 (= $1,000 + $3,000). With earnings of $5,000, this means that there would be $1,000 (= $5,000 − $4,000) of cash left for the firm to use to repurchase its own stock.

The Dividend Decision

The firm has a decision to make regarding the size of its current dividends. The amount of current earnings E_0 and the amount of new investment I_0 have been determined. What is left to be decided is the amount of dividends, D_0. They can be set equal to earnings less investment [as in Figure 19.1(a)], or greater than this amount [as in Figure 19.1(b)], or less than this amount [as in Figure 19.1(c)]. The question that remains to be answered is this: Will one of these three levels of dividends make the current stockholders better off than the other two? That is, which level of dividends—$1,000, $2,000, or $3,000—will make the current stockholders better off?

The simplest way to answer this question is to consider a stockholder who presently holds 1% of the common stock of the firm and is determined to maintain this percentage ownership in the future.[2] If the firm follows a dividend policy as shown in Figure 19.1(a), the stockholder's current dividends will equal $.01D_0$ or, equivalently, $.01(E_0 − I_0)$. Similarly, the stockholder's future dividends will be equal to $.01D_t$ or, equivalently, $.01(E_t − I_t)$.

If the firm follows a dividend policy as shown in Figure 19.1(b), however, the stockholder must invest additional funds in the firm's common stock in order to avoid a diminished proportional ownership position in the firm. Why? Because in this situation the firm must raise funds by selling additional shares in order to pay for the larger cash dividends. As $E_0 < D_0 + I_0$, the total amount of funds that the firm needs to raise is the amount F_0 such that:

$$E_0 + F_0 = D_0 + I_0 \qquad (19.1)$$

or

$$F_0 = D_0 + I_0 − E_0. \qquad (19.2)$$

The amount of the additional investment that the stockholder needs to make in order to maintain a 1% position in the firm is $.01F_0$, which from Equation (19.2) is equal to $.01(D_0 + I_0 - E_0)$. Because the stockholder receives 1% of the dividends, the net amount the stockholder receives at time zero is equal to $.01D_0 - .01F_0$, or:

$$.01D_0 - .01(D_0 + I_0 - E_0) = .01E_0 - .01I_0. \qquad (19.3)$$

Interestingly, the net amount the stockholder receives, $.01E_0 - .01I_0$, is the same as in the first situation. This is because the amount of the extra cash dividend received is exactly offset by the amount the stockholder needs to spend to maintain his or her ownership position in the firm.

If the firm follows a dividend policy as shown in Figure 19.1(c), then the firm will repurchase shares. Accordingly, the stockholder must sell some shares back to the firm in order to avoid having an increased ownership position in the firm. As $E_0 > D_0 + I_0$, the total amount of funds that the firm will spend on repurchasing its own shares is the amount R_0 such that:

$$E_0 = D_0 + I_0 + R_0 \qquad (19.4)$$

or

$$R_0 = E_0 - D_0 - I_0. \qquad (19.5)$$

The amount of stock that the stockholder needs to sell back to the firm to maintain a 1% position in the firm is $.01R_0$, which from Equation (19.5) is equal to $.01(E_0 - D_0 - I_0)$. Because the stockholder receives 1% of the dividends, the net amount the stockholder receives at time zero is equal to $.01D_0 + .01R_0$, or:

$$.01D_0 + .01(E_0 - D_0 - I_0) = .01E_0 - .01I_0. \qquad (19.6)$$

Again this net amount, $.01E_0 - .01I_0$, is the same as in the first situation. That is, in the third situation, the smaller amount of the cash dividend received by the stockholder is exactly made up for by the amount of cash received from the repurchase of shares by the firm.

Thus no matter what the firm's dividend policy, a stockholder choosing to maintain a constant proportional ownership will be able to spend the same amount of money on consumption at time zero. This amount will be equal to the proportion times the quantity $E_0 - I_0$. Furthermore, this will also be true in the future. That is, in any year t the stockholder will be able to spend on consumption an amount that is equal to the proportion times the quantity $E_t - I_t$.

19.1.2 Earnings Determine Market Value

In determining the value of 1% of the current shares outstanding, remember that the firm is about to declare and pay current dividends. Regardless of the magnitude of these dividends, the stockholder will only be able to spend on consumption an amount equal to $.01(E_0 - I_0)$. Furthermore, the stockholder will be able to spend on consumption an amount equal to $.01(E_t - I_t)$ in any future year t. Discounting these expected amounts by a (constant) rate k reveals that the value (V) of 1% of the current shares outstanding will be:

$$.01V = \frac{.01(E_0 - I_0)}{(1 + k)^0} + \frac{.01(E_1 - I_1)}{(1 + k)^1} + \frac{.01(E_2 - I_2)}{(1 + k)^2} + \cdots$$

Multiplying both sides of this equation by 100 results in the following expression for the total market value of all shares outstanding:

$$V = \frac{(E_0 - I_0)}{(1 + k)^0} + \frac{(E_1 - I_1)}{(1 + k)^1} + \frac{(E_2 - I_2)}{(1 + k)^2} + \cdots \qquad (19.7)$$

Equation (19.7) shows that the aggregate market value of equity is equal to the present value of expected earnings net of investment. Note how the size of the dividends does not enter into the formula. This indicates that the market value of the stock is *independent* of the dividend decision made by the firm, meaning that the dividend decision is irrelevant to stock valuation. Instead, the market value of the firm is related to the earnings prospects of the firm, along with the required amounts of new investment needed to produce those earnings.[3]

Dividend Discount Models

In Chapter 18 it was shown that the value of a share of common stock was equal to the present value of all dividends expected in the future. Hence it is tempting to believe that, contrary to the assertion above, the market value of a firm's stock is *dependent* on the dividend decision. However, it turns out that there is nothing inconsistent between valuation being based on dividend discount models and the irrelevancy of the dividend decision.

The dividend irrelevancy argument suggests that if the firm decides to increase its current dividend, then new shares will need to be sold. This, in turn, suggests that future dividends will be smaller because the aggregate amount of dividends will have to be divided among an increased number of shares outstanding. Ultimately, the current stockholders will be neither better off nor worse off, as the increased current dividend will be exactly offset by the decreased future dividends. Conversely, if the firm decides to decrease its current dividend, then shares will be repurchased and future dividends will be increased due to the fewer shares outstanding. Ultimately, the decreased current dividend will be exactly offset by the increased future dividends, again leaving current stockholders neither better off nor worse off.

Example

All this can be illustrated with the earlier example of the Plum Company. Because Plum currently has reported earnings of $5,000 and investments totaling $3,000, if dividends amounting to $2,000 were paid, then the stockholder owning 1% of the firm would receive cash amounting to $20 (= .01 × $2,000).

Alternatively, if dividends amounting to $3,000 were paid, then Plum would have to raise $1,000 from the sale of new common stock. The stockholder would receive $30 (= .01 × $3,000) in dividends, but would have to pay $10 (= .01 × $1,000) to purchase 1% of the new stock, thereby maintaining his or her 1% ownership position. Consequently, the net cash flow to the stockholder would be $20 (= $30 − $10), the same amount as in the previous situation.

Lastly, if dividends amounting to $1,000 were paid, then Plum would have cash amounting to $1,000 to use to repurchase common stock. The stockholder, desirous of maintaining a 1% position, would thus sell shares amounting to $10 (= .01 × $1,000). As a result, the stockholder would have a cash inflow totaling $20 (= $10 + $10), again the same amount as in the two previous situations.

Under all three situations, the 1% stockholder would receive the same cash flow at the present time ($20) and have the same claim on the future earnings of Plum. That is, in all three cases, the stockholder would still own 1% of Plum and would therefore receive the same amount of dividends in the future. Accordingly, the 1% stockholder (and all the others) would be neither better off nor worse off if Plum pays a dividend amounting to $1,000, $2,000, or $3,000. In summary, the dividend decision is a nonevent—whatever the level of dividends, current stockholders will be neither better off nor worse off. This result is sometimes referred to as the "dividend irrelevancy theorem."

19.2 DETERMINANTS OF DIVIDENDS

Few firms attempt to maintain a constant ratio of dividends to current earnings because doing so would result in a fluctuating dollar amount of dividends. The reason the dividends would fluctuate is that earnings on a year-to-year basis are likely to be quite variable. Instead, firms attempt to maintain a desired ratio of dividends to earnings over some relatively long period, meaning that there is a target payout ratio of dividends to long-run or sustainable earnings. As a result, dividends are usually kept at a constant dollar amount and are increased only when management is confident that it will be relatively easy to keep paying this increased amount in the future.[4] Nonetheless, larger earnings are likely to be accompanied by some sort of increase in dividends, as Table 19.1 shows.

TABLE 19.1
EARNINGS AND DIVIDEND CHANGES*

Earnings Changes			Percent of Cases in Which Firms		
Current Year	Previous Year	Percent of Cases	Increased Dividends	Did Not Change Dividends	Decreased Dividends
+		59.3%	65.8%	13.9%	20.3%
−		40.7	42.8	17.9	39.5
+	+	33.4	74.8	11.4	13.8
+	−	25.9	54.1	17.2	28.7
−	+	24.7	49.7	16.9	33.4
−	−	16.0	31.8	19.4	48.8

*Based on 392 firms during the period 1946–1964.

Source: Eugene F. Fama and Harvey Babiak, "Dividend Policy: An Empirical Analysis," *Journal of the American Statistical Association,* 63, no. 324 (December 1968): p. 1134.

19.2.1 Changes in Earnings and Dividends

The first two lines of Table 19.1 indicate that 59.3% of the time the earnings of the firms examined rose, and the remaining 40.7% of the time earnings fell. The majority of the times when current earnings rose, firms increased their current dividends. However, whenever current earnings fell, firms would increase their current dividends as frequently as they would decrease their current dividends (note that, roughly speaking, 42.8% ≅ 39.5%).

The next two lines of the table suggest that firms are more likely to increase current dividends if they have had two consecutive years of rising earnings than if they have had falling and then rising earnings (74.8% > 54.1%). The last two lines of the table suggest that firms are more likely to decrease current dividends if they have had two consecutive years of falling earnings than if they have had rising and then falling earnings (48.8% > 33.4%). Overall, the table shows that firms in general are more likely to increase dividends than to decrease them.

19.2.2 The Lintner Model

A formal representation of the kind of behavior implied by a constant long-run target payout ratio begins by assuming that the goal of the firm is to pay out p^* (for example, $p^* = 60\%$) of long-run earnings. If this target ratio were maintained every year, total dividends paid in year t would be:

$$D_t^* = p^* E_t \qquad (19.8)$$

where D_t^* denotes the target amount for dividends to be paid in year t and E_t is the amount of earnings in year t. The difference between target dividends in year t and the previous year's actual dividends is determined by subtracting D_{t-1} from both sides of Equation (19.8), resulting in:

$$D_t^* - D_{t-1} = p^* E_t - D_{t-1}. \qquad (19.9)$$

Although firms would like to change their dividends from D_{t-1} to D_t^*, few (if any) firms would actually change their dividends by this amount. Instead, the actual change in dividends will be a proportion of the desired change:

$$D_t - D_{t-1} = a(D_t^* - D_{t-1}) \qquad (19.10)$$

where a is a "speed of adjustment" coefficient, a number between zero and one.

For example, if a firm has just earned $5 million ($E_t =$ $5 million) and has a target payout ratio of 60%, then it would like to pay dividends amounting to $3 million (= .6 × $5 million). Assuming that it paid dividends of $2 million last year, this represents an increase of $1 million (= $3 million − $2 million). However, if $a = 50\%$, then the firm will actually increase the dividends by $500,000 (= .5 × $1 million). Thus actual dividends will be equal to $2.5 million (= $2 million + $500,000), an amount equal to last year's dividends plus the change in dividends from last year to this year.

This model can be summarized by substituting $p^* E_t$ for D_t^* in Equation (19.10) and then solving the resulting expression for D_t:

$$D_t = ap^* E_t + (1 - a)D_{t-1}. \qquad (19.11)$$

Equation (19.11) indicates that the amount of current dividends is based on the amount of current earnings and the amount of the last year's dividends.[5] In the previous example, $a = 50\%$, $p^* = 60\%$, $E_t = \$5$ million, and $D_{t-1} = \$2$ million. Thus actual dividends D_t would be equal to $2.5 million ($= [.5 \times .6 \times \$5$ million$] + [1 - .5] \times \$2$ million).

By subtracting D_{t-1} from both sides of Equation (19.11), it can be seen that the change in dividends is equal to:

$$D_t - D_{t-1} = ap^*E_t - aD_{t-1}. \qquad (19.12)$$

When written in this form, the model suggests that the size of the *change* in dividends will be positively related to the current amount of earnings (because ap^* is a positive number) and negatively related to the amount of the previous period's dividends (since $-aD_{t-1}$ is a negative number). Thus the larger current earnings are, the larger the change in dividends, but the larger the previous period's dividends, the smaller the change in dividends.

19.2.3 Test Results

Statistical analysis has been used to test how well this model describes the way a sample of firms set the amount of their dividends. Table 19.2 summarizes some of the values obtained in one such study. The average firm had a target payout ratio of 59.1% and adjusted dividends 26.9% of the way toward its target each year. However, most firms' dividends varied substantially from the pattern implied by their targets and adjustment factors. Somewhat less than half (42%) of the annual variance in the typical firm's dividends could be explained in this manner. This means that the model, although explaining a portion of the changes in dividends that occurred, leaves a substantial portion unexplained.

TABLE 19.2					
TARGET PAYOUT RATIOS AND SPEED OF DIVIDEND ADJUSTMENT FACTORS[*]					
Speed of Adjustment Coefficient		**Target Payout Ratio**		**Percent of Variance Explained**	
Value	Percent of Firms with Smaller Value	Value	Percent of Firms with Smaller Value	Value	Percent of Firms with Smaller Value
.104	10%	.401	10%	11%	10%
.182	30	.525	30	32	30
.251	50	.584	50	42	50
.339	70	.660	70	54	70
.470	90	.779	90	72	90
average .269		average .591		average 42	

[*]Based on 298 firms during the period 1946–1968.

Source: Eugene F. Fama, "The Empirical Relationship Between the Dividend and Investment Decisions of Firms," *American Economic Review,* 64, no. 3 (June 1974): p. 310.

It is reasonable to believe that management has more information about the future earnings of the firm than does the public (which includes its own stockholders). This situation of **asymmetric information** suggests that managers will seek to convey the information to the public if they have an incentive to do so. Assuming that they have such an incentive, one way of doing so is by announcing a change in the amount of the firm's dividends. When used in this manner, dividend announcements are said to be a signaling device.[6]

19.3.1 Signaling

A relatively simple view of dividend changes is that an announced increase in dividends is a signal that management has increased its assessment of the firm's future earnings. The announced increase in dividends is therefore "good news" and will, in turn, cause investors to raise their expectations regarding the firm's future earnings. Conversely, an announced decrease in dividends is a signal that management has decreased its assessment of the firm's future earnings. The announced decrease in dividends is therefore "bad news" and will, in turn, cause investors to lower their expectations regarding the firm's future earnings. An implication is that an announced increase in dividends will cause the firm's stock price to rise, and an announced decrease will cause it to fall.

This simple model of dividend changes can be thought of as a special case of the model given in Equation (19.12), where the speed of adjustment, a, is zero. With this model, the expected change in dividends, $D_t - D_{t-1}$, is zero, suggesting that a simple increase in dividends will be viewed as good news. Conversely, a simple decrease in dividends will be viewed as bad news.

One way of testing to see if dividend changes do indeed convey information to the public is to see how stock prices react to announcements of changes in dividends. However, care must be exercised in conducting such a study because the firm's announcement of dividends is often made at the same time as the firm announces its earnings. Thus when such announcements are made at the same time, any price change in the firm's common stock may be attributable to either (or both) announcements.

One study attempted to avoid this problem of contamination by looking only at cases where the announcement of earnings was at least 11 trading days apart from the announcement of dividends. Figure 19.2 provides an illustration of the average abnormal return associated with a firm's dividend announcement for those firms that announced their dividends 11 or more days after they announced their earnings (similar results were obtained when the authors examined those cases where dividend announcements preceded earnings announcements).

In those cases where firms announced an increase in their dividends, there is a significant positive reaction in their stock prices. Conversely, in those cases where firms announced a decrease in their dividends, there is a significant negative reaction in their stock prices. These findings strongly support the **information**

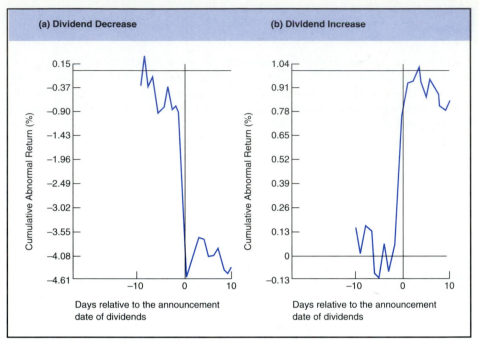

Figure 19.2

Cumulative Abnormal Returns Starting Ten Days before a Dividend Announcement

Source: Joseph Aharony and Itzhak Swary, "Quarterly Dividend and Earnings Announcements and Stockholders' Returns: An Empirical Analysis," *Journal of Finance*, 35, no. 1 (March 1980): p. 8.

content of dividends hypothesis, where dividend announcements are asserted to contain inside information about the firm's future prospects.

It should be noted that there is nothing inconsistent with dividends being used as a signal and with the dividend irrelevancy argument of Miller and Modigliani that was made earlier. In particular, stockholders will be neither better nor worse off if the *level* of dividends, relative to earnings, is high or low. *Changes* in dividends may, however, be important because they convey information to the public about the future earnings prospects for the firm.

19.3.2   Dividend Initiations and Omissions

One study looked at the relationship between dividend changes and past, current, and future changes in earnings.[7] Specifically, it focused on the most dramatic dividend announcements possible—dividend initiations and omissions—because the information being conveyed in these announcements is clearly unambiguous.

That is, if the information content of dividends hypothesis is correct, then firms that start to pay dividends for the first time in at least ten years must be signaling that they believe that earnings have recently increased to a permanently higher level, and that earnings may increase even more in the near future. The question to be addressed is this: Have firms actually experienced notably higher earnings around the time of such initiations and afterward?

Conversely, firms that have paid dividends for at least ten years and that suddenly stop paying any dividends must believe that their earnings have recently decreased to a permanently lower level, and that earnings may decrease even more in the future. For them the question is this: Have firms actually experienced notably lower earnings around the time of such omissions and afterward?

The answer supported the information content of dividends hypothesis. Specifically, the study found that earnings tended to increase for at least one year leading up to dividend initiations and to decrease for up to two years leading up to dividend omissions. Furthermore, earnings continued to increase for at least one year after initiations and to decrease for one year after omissions, and such changes appear to be permanent. Interestingly, the larger the change in the firm's stock price when the dividend initiation or omission is announced, the larger the change in the firm's earnings in both the year of the announcement and the year thereafter. Thus it seems that dividends do indeed convey information about earnings.

19.3.3 Dividends and Losses

In a similar vein to dividend initiations and omissions, it is interesting to examine situations where firms that have had a string of at least ten years of positive earnings and dividend payments suddenly experience negative earnings. In particular, do dividends in such a situation convey information about future earnings?

One study examined this situation by looking at firms that had at least one year of negative earnings during the 1980–1985 period but previously had at least ten consecutive years of positive earnings and dividend payments; 167 firms ("loss" firms) were uncovered meeting these criteria.[8] A comparison sample of 440 firms ("non-loss" firms) that had positive earnings during the 1980–1985 period as well as during a previous ten-year period was also formed.

Approximately half the "loss" firms reduced or omitted their dividends in the four subsequent quarters after the fiscal year-end of the loss. In comparison, fewer than 1% of the "non-loss" firms either reduced or omitted their dividends during the six-year period of 1980–1985. Further examination revealed that:

1. The "loss" firms that did not reduce their dividends were more likely to have unusual income items, indicating that their earnings problems were more likely to be temporary.
2. The "loss" firms that reduced their dividends had deeper losses than the "loss" firms that did not reduce their dividends.
3. The "loss" firms that reduced their dividends were much more likely to have negative earnings in the next two years than the nonreducing "loss" firms.

Hence knowing what happened to dividends for a "loss" firm tends to make it easier to predict its future earnings, thereby indicating that dividends have information content when a firm suddenly has negative earnings.

ACCOUNTING EARNINGS VERSUS ECONOMIC EARNINGS

Because the prediction of earnings is of critical importance in security analysis and investment research, a review of what is known about earnings and the relationship between earnings and security prices is essential. At a fundamental level, consideration of the concept of "earnings" itself is needed. Specifically, just what is meant by "earnings" to those who produce the figures, and how does this affect the valuation process?

19.4.1 Accounting Earnings

A firm's accountants operate under constraints and guidelines imposed by regulatory authorities and professional organizations such as the Securities and Exchange Commission (SEC) and the Financial Accounting Standards Board (FASB). In cooperation with management, the accountants produce, on a quarterly basis, a set of financial statements for the firm that ends with a figure for the firm's **accounting earnings** (also known as the firm's reported earnings). In a broad sense, such earnings represent the difference between revenues and expenses, including the expenses associated with nonequity sources of funds (such as debt). This difference, the "total earnings available for common stock," is divided by the number of shares outstanding to calculate **earnings per share** (EPS). It may also be divided by the book value per share to calculate the **return on equity** (ROE).

A basic principle of accounting makes the book value of a firm's equity at the end of a period (such as a quarter or a year) equal to (1) its value at the end of the previous period, plus (2) the portion of accounting earnings for the period that is retained by the firm (here it is assumed that there has been no change in the number of shares outstanding during the period). Letting B_t denote the book value of the equity of the firm at the end of period t, E_t^a denotes the accounting earnings for period t, and D_t denotes the dividends paid during period t, this relationship can be expressed algebraically as:

$$B_t = B_{t-1} + E_t^a - D_t \qquad (19.13)$$

From Equation (19.13), it can be seen that accounting earnings equal the change in book value of equity plus dividends paid:

$$E_t^a = B_t - B_{t-1} + D_t. \qquad (19.14)$$

19.4.2 Economic Earnings

Economic earnings (E_t^e) may be defined as the amount that would be obtained in Equation (19.14) if the change in the book value of the firm equaled the change in the **economic value of the firm:**

$$E_t^e = V_t - V_{t-1} + D_t. \tag{19.15}$$

Here the change in the economic value of the firm during period t, $V_t - V_{t-1}$, is defined as the change in the market value of the firm's common stock (assuming that there is no change in the market value of the firm's other securities).[9]

It is easy to show that reported book values and market values (that is, economic values) of stocks are often considerably different. Figure 19.3 shows the ratio of (1) the year-end market price per share for Standard & Poor's Industrial Stock Index, to (2) the corresponding year-end book value per share. It can be seen that the ratio is typically greater than 1.0 and has fluctuated considerably from year to year.

Figure 19.4 plots book values (horizontal axis) and market values (vertical axis) for the stocks in the Dow Jones Industrial Average. If investors viewed market and book values as essentially equivalent, the points would plot along a 45-degree line (that is, a line with a slope of 1) that emanates from the origin. However, as the extensive scatter of the points indicates, market values diverge from book values by different amounts for different stocks.

Both Figure 19.3 and Figure 19.4 indicate that there can be sizable differences between market and book values. Because Equations (19.14) and (19.15) show that accounting and economic earnings will be equal only if market and book values are equal, the evidence thus suggests that accounting and economic earnings differ by varying amounts for different firms.

It is sometimes contended that investors estimate the value of a firm's common stock by directly applying a formula to the firm's current and past accounting earnings.[10] Such a belief may tempt a firm's managers to try to "manage" such earnings in order to make a firm appear more valuable than it is, thereby fooling investors, at least temporarily. This is permissible since the **generally accepted accounting principles** (GAAP) set by the regulatory authorities (such as FASB) allow a large amount of discretion in how certain items are accounted for (examples include methods for depreciation and inventory valuation). As a result, management may pressure accountants to use those principles that maximize the level of reported earnings, or that result in a high growth rate of reported earnings, or that "smooth" earnings by reducing the year-to-year variability of earnings around a growth rate.[11] Some of these activities can be continued only for a limited number of years; others can go on indefinitely.

To obtain a truly independent estimate of value, analysts must dissect reported earnings. In doing so, they should not be fooled by any accounting illusions, meaning that they should ignore any manipulations that may have been made by the accountants at management's request.[12] Anyone who estimates value by applying a formula (no matter how complex) to reported earnings is not producing an estimate that is completely free from all possible manipulations by management. This is not to say that reported earnings are irrelevant for security valuation. Instead, they should be viewed as one source of information about the future prospects of a firm.

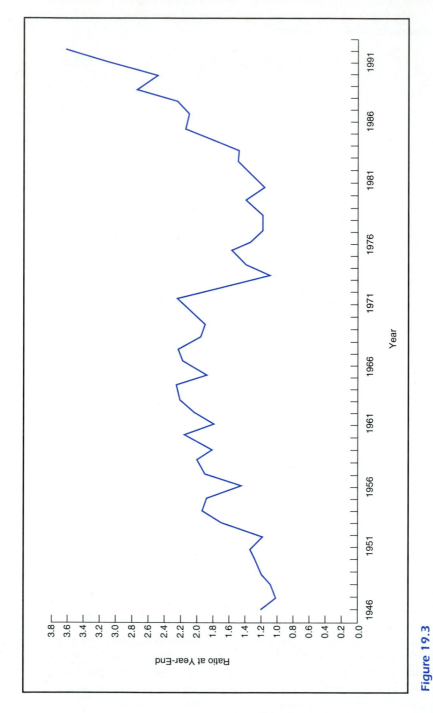

Figure 19.3
Ratio of Price to Book Value: Standard & Poor's Industrial Stock Index, 1946–1992
Source: Standard & Poor's *Statistical Service*, various issues.

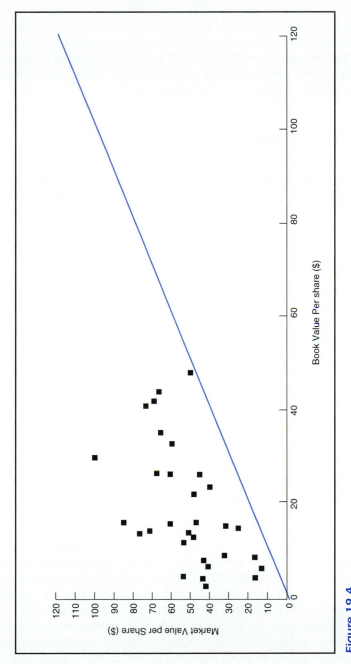

Figure 19.4
Market and Book Values, Stocks in Dow Jones Industrial Average, Year-end 1992

Chapter 18 discussed how dividend discount models could be used to determine if stocks were either underpriced or overpriced. One means of making this determination was to compare the actual price-earnings ratio for a firm with what the security analyst had determined it should be. In view of this use of price-earnings ratios, some evidence on the behavior of overall earnings, prices, and price-earnings ratios will now be presented.

19.5.1 The Historical Record

Panel (a) of Figure 19.5 presents a plot of the year-end price-earnings ratios for the Standard & Poor's 500. It can be seen from this plot that the variation in the ratio on a year-to-year basis is considerable, suggesting that investors do not simply apply a standard multiple to earnings in order to determine an appropriate value.

Panel (b) of Figure 19.5 presents a plot of earnings per share (the lower jagged line) and price (the upper jagged line) for the Standard & Poor's 500.[13] Both lines generally move upward to the right, showing a general trend for both earnings per share and prices to increase over time. However, the two lines are not parallel. This means that earnings per share and prices do not move together in a lockstep manner, an observation that is also apparent in panel (a).

19.5.2 Permanent and Transitory Components of Earnings

When individual common stocks are analyzed, they too show considerable variation in their price-earnings ratios over time. Furthermore, their ratios are quite different from each other at any point in time. One possible explanation notes that reported earnings can be viewed as having two components. The *permanent component* is the component that is likely to be repeated in the future, whereas the *transitory component* is not likely to be repeated.

Earlier, it was argued that the intrinsic value of a stock depends on the firm's future earnings prospects. This suggests that changes in a stock's intrinsic value, and in turn its price, will be correlated with changes in the permanent component of its earnings but not with changes in the transitory component. If the transitory component is positive, then the price-earnings ratio would be relatively low due to a relatively large number in the denominator. Conversely, if the transitory component is negative, then the price-earnings ratio would be relatively high due to a relatively small number in the denominator.

As an example, consider a firm whose current stock price is $30 per share. Its permanent component of earnings per share over the past year is $4, and its transitory component is $1, resulting in reported earnings of $5 (= $4 + $1) and a price-earnings ratio of 6 (= $30/$5). Remember that this stock's current price is based on its future prospects, which are in turn based on the permanent component of earnings per share over the past year. Thus if the firm had the same permanent component of $4 but had a transitory component of −$1

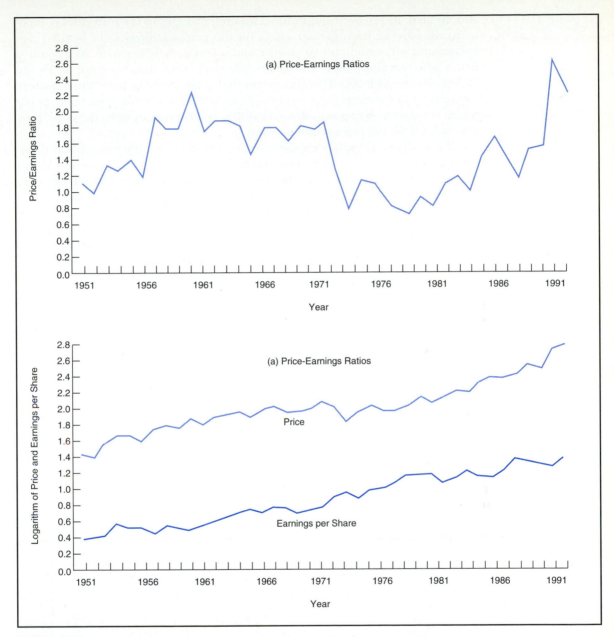

Figure 19.5

Price, Earnings, and Price-Earnings Ratios, Standard & Poor's 500, Year-end, 1951–1992

Source: Standard & Poor's *Statistical Service*, various issues.

instead of +\$1, the stock would still have a current price of \$30 per share. However, its reported earnings would have been \$3 (= \$4 − \$1) and its price-earnings ratio would have been 10 (= \$30/\$3).

The permanent component of earnings will change over time, causing investors to revise their forecasts. This will lead to a change in a firm's stock price and, in turn, its price-earnings ratio. However, changes in the transitory component will have an even greater effect on the price-earnings ratio because this component will sometimes be positive and sometimes be negative. As a result, a firm's price-earnings ratio will be variable over time, as was shown in Figure 19.5(a) for the S&P 500. This also means that at any point in time, the transitory component of earnings for a group of firms will have varying sizes, some being positive and some being negative. As a result, at any point in time, firms will have a range of different price-earnings ratios.

If this were a complete explanation for the considerable variation in price-earnings ratios over time and across firms, then most of the variation in a firm's price-earnings ratio would itself be transitory. That is, the ratio would vary over time around some average value. However, the evidence suggests that this is not the case. Figure 19.6 shows the behavior over time of price-earnings ratios for two groups of stocks. The first group includes stocks with high price-earnings ratios at the beginning of the period (that is, during a portfolio formation period). The other group includes stocks with low price-earnings ratios at the beginning of the period.

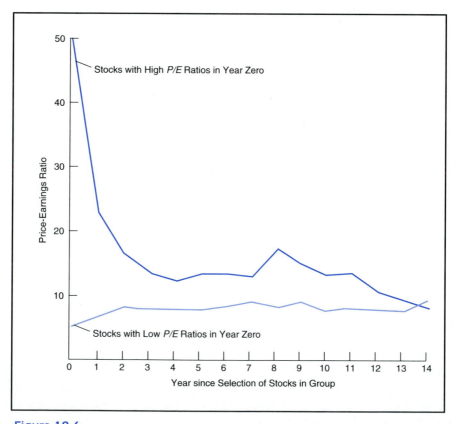

Figure 19.6

Price-Earnings Ratios over Time for Two Groups of Stocks

Source: William Beaver and Dale Morse, "What Determines Price-Earnings Ratios? *Financial Analysts Journal,* 34, no. 4 (July/August 1978): p. 68.

Over time, the price-earnings ratios tend to revert to an average ratio for the market as a whole. The changes are substantial in the first two years, owing undoubtedly to the influence of transitory components of earnings. That is, those stocks in the high price-earnings ratio group apparently had, on average, a negative transitory component in their earnings in the portfolio formation period. (Remember that such a component would tend to give a stock a high ratio.) Conversely, those stocks in the low price-earnings ratio group apparently had, on average, a positive transitory component. (Remember that such a component would tend to give a stock a low ratio.) Over future periods, each group of stocks would tend to have an equal number of stocks with positive and negative transitory components, resulting in an average transitory component for each group of roughly zero.

However, Figure 19.6 shows that the two groups of stocks have different price-earnings ratios for many years after the portfolio formation period. Three explanations can be offered for this persistent difference.

1. Appropriate discount rates (that is, required returns) differ because of differences in security attributes. For two firms with the same current and expected future earnings, the firm with the lower discount rate will have a higher stock price and hence a higher price-earnings ratio.

2. There may be permanent differences between economic and reported earnings due to the use of different accounting methods. As mentioned earlier, there is evidence that the market sees through such differences in reported earnings.

3. There may be persistent differences in the forecasts of long-term permanent earnings growth rates by security analysts. That is, firms with high price-earnings ratios may have high forecast long-term permanent earnings growth rates and hence relatively high prices. Conversely, firms with low price-earnings ratios may have low forecast long-term permanent earnings growth rates and hence relatively low prices.[14] If such forecasts persist over time, then firms with high price-earnings ratios would tend to continue having high ratios over time, while firms with low ratios would tend to continue having low ratios over time. Evidence suggests that indeed this is the case.

19.6 RELATIVE GROWTH RATES OF FIRMS' EARNINGS

Because security analysis typically involves forecasting earnings per share, it is useful to examine the historical record to see how earnings per share have changed over time. An interesting question about growth rates in firm earnings over time focuses on "growth stocks." The very idea of a growth stock suggests that growth in some firms' earnings will exceed the average growth of all firms' earnings in most years, while other firms' earnings will grow less than the average.

19.6.1 Earnings Growth Rates

The results of a study of the earnings growth rates for 610 industrial companies from 1950 to 1964 are shown in Table 19.3. In every year, each firm's earnings were compared with its earnings in the previous year and the percentage change calculated. The year was counted as "good" for the firm if its percentage change was in the top half of the changes for all firms that year, and "bad" if it was in the bottom half. If some firms tend to experience above-average earnings growth rates, then fairly long runs of good years should occur for these firms. Conversely, if some firms tend to experience below-average earnings growth rates, then they should have fairly long runs of bad years.

The middle two columns of Table 19.3 indicate the actual number of runs of various lengths. The right-hand column shows the number that would be expected if there were a 50–50 chance of either a good year or a bad year. The three columns are remarkably similar. Above-average earnings growth in the past does not appear to indicate above-average growth in the future; and below-average growth in the past does not appear to indicate below-average growth in the future. Flipping a coin seems to be as reliable a predictor of future growth as looking at past growth rates.

A study using longer time periods for measuring growth reached generally similar conclusions.[15] For each of 323 companies with positive earnings in each year from 1946 through 1965, average growth rates were computed for (1) the period from 1946 through 1955 and (2) the period from 1956 through 1965. Differences among firms' earnings growth rates in the first period accounted for less than 1% of the variation in the differences among their earnings growth rates in the second period.

TABLE 19.3
EARNINGS GROWTH RATES*

Length of Run	Actual Number of Good Runs	Actual Number of Bad Runs	Number of Good or Bad Runs Expected if the Odds Each Year Were 50–50 Regardless of Past Performance
1	1,152	1,102	1,068
2	562	590	534
3	266	300	267
4	114	120	133
5	55	63	67
6	24	20	33
7	23	12	17
8	5	6	8
9	3	3	4
10	6	0	2
11	2	0	1
12	1	0	1
13	0	0	0
14	0	1	0

*Based on 610 firms during the period 1950–1964.

Source: Richard A. Brealey, *An Introduction to Risk and Return from Common Stocks* (Cambridge, MA: MIT Press, 1983): p. 89.

19.6.2 Annual Earnings

The results of these and other studies suggest that *annual reported earnings* follow what is known in statistics as a **random walk model.** That is, annual earnings for the forthcoming year (E_t) can be thought of as being equal to annual earnings over the past year (E_{t-1}) plus a random error term. (Remember that a random error term can be thought of as a roulette wheel where the numbers on the wheel are distributed around zero.) Accordingly, next year's earnings can be described by the following statistical model:

$$E_t = E_{t-1} + \epsilon_t \qquad (19.16)$$

where ϵ_t is the random error term. With this model, the estimate of next year's earnings is simply the past year's earnings, E_{t-1}. Another way of viewing a random walk model for earnings is that the change in earnings is independent and identically distributed:

$$E_t - E_{t-1} = \epsilon_t. \qquad (19.17)$$

This means that the change in earnings, $E_t - E_{t-1}$, is unrelated to past changes in earnings and can be thought of as a spin from a roulette wheel that is perhaps unique to the firm but, more importantly, is used year after year. Because the expected outcome from a spin of the roulette wheel is zero, the expected change in earnings is zero. This implies that the expected level of earnings is equal to the past year's earnings, as was suggested earlier.[16]

19.6.3 Quarterly Earnings

In terms of *quarterly reported earnings*, consideration must be given to the fact that there is typically a seasonal component to a firm's earnings (for example, many firms have high earnings during the quarter that includes Christmas). As a result, a slightly different model appears to be best for forecasting purposes. This model forecasts the growth in earnings for the forthcoming quarter relative to the same quarter one year ago, a quantity denoted $QE_t - QE_{t-4}$. It does so by relating this growth to the growth during the most recent quarter relative to the comparable quarter one year before it, $QE_{t-1} - QE_{t-5}$. Formally, the model for the "seasonally differenced series" of quarterly earnings is known as an *autoregressive model of order one*, and is as follows:

$$QE_t - QE_{t-4} = a(QE_{t-1} - QE_{t-5}) + b + e_t \qquad (19.18)$$

where a and b are constants and e_t is a random error term.

Alternatively, the model can be rewritten by moving the term QE_{t-4} to the right-hand side:

$$QE_t = QE_{t-4} + a(QE_{t-1} - QE_{t-5}) + b + e_t. \qquad (19.19)$$

By estimating the constants a and b, this model can be used to forecast quarterly earnings.[17]

For example, assuming estimates for a and b of .4 and .05, respectively, the forecast of a firm's earnings for the next quarter would be equal to QE_{t-4} + $.4(QE_{t-1} - QE_{t-5})$ + \$.05. Thus if a firm had earnings per share for the last quarter $(t - 1)$ of $3, for four quarters before now $(t - 4)$ of $2, and for five quarters before now $(t - 5)$ of $2.60, then its forecasted earnings for the forthcoming quarter would be equal to $2.21 [$= $2 + .4(\$3 - \$2.60) + \$.05$]. Note how the forecast consists of three components—a component equal to last quarter's earnings ($2); a component that considers the year-to-year quarterly growth in earnings ($.16 $= .4[\$3 - \$2.60]$); and a component that is a constant ($.05).[18]

| 19.7 | COMOVEMENT OF EARNINGS |

Past changes in security prices are of limited value for the prediction of future changes. And past changes in the overall level of the market are of limited help in the prediction of future market moves. However, security price changes are related to concurrent changes in the prices of the market portfolio and, to a lesser extent, an "industry" portfolio.[19] Although the strength of these relationships differs among securities, historical data can generally be utilized to help estimate the relative future strengths of the relationships for different securities. For example, the relationship between a security's returns and market returns has been referred to as the security's *beta* and can be estimated by examining historical returns. Similarly, the industry that a security belongs to can be determined and a portfolio of stocks in that industry constructed. Then the historical returns on the security can be compared to this portfolio, and an industry beta can be estimated.

It has been argued that security prices are determined by economic earnings, and that security price movements are related to movements in market and industry prices. Thus an interesting issue is whether or not movements in the economic earnings of a firm are related to movements in the economic earnings of the market and industry portfolios. Such an issue has been explored by looking at accounting earnings and assuming that they are correlated with economic earnings.

Table 19.4 shows that such relationships do exist. Earnings reported by 217 corporations from 1948 through 1966 were compared first with the earnings for Standard & Poor's 425–stock index (which served as a surrogate for marketwide earnings) and then with the average earnings of all firms in the same industry. The proportion of each firm's earnings variations that could be attributed to each of these factors was determined. The results shown in the table are the average proportions for all the firms in each industry.

The results differ notably from one industry to another, with the marketwide factor ranging between 5% and 48% and the industry factor ranging from 5% to 49%. The bottom row of the table shows the values obtained by averaging over all 217 corporations. Changes in marketwide earnings accounted for 21% of the variation in the earnings of the typical firm, and changes in the earnings of firms in its industry accounted for another 21%.

Earlier, it was mentioned that a security's beta (sometimes known as its **market beta**) is a measure of how the price of the security will covary with the price

TABLE 19.4

THE PROPORTION OF THE VARIATION OF A FIRM'S EARNINGS ATTRIBUTABLE TO MARKET-WIDE AND INDUSTRY-WIDE EARNINGS CHANGES

Proportion Attributable to:

Industry	Market-wide Earnings Changes	Additional Influence of Changes in Industry-wide Earnings
Aircraft	11%	5%
Autos	48	11
Beer	11	7
Cement	6	32
Chemicals	41	8
Cosmetics	5	6
Department stores	30	37
Drugs	14	7
Electricals	24	8
Food	10	10
Machinery	19	16
Nonferrous metals	26	25
Office machinery	14	6
Oil	13	49
Paper	27	28
Rubber	26	48
Steel	32	21
Supermarkets	6	33
Textiles and clothing	25	29
Tobacco	8	19
All firms	21	21

Source: Richard Brealey, "Some Implications of the Comovement of American Company Earnings," *Applied Economics*, 3, no. 3 (September 1971): p. 187.

of the market portfolio. Similarly, a security's **accounting beta** is a measure of how the accounting earnings of the security will covary with the accounting earnings of the market portfolio. If security prices are related to earnings, then it seems reasonable to expect market betas to be related to accounting betas. Studies that have examined this issue have found that market and accounting betas are significantly correlated, with accounting betas explaining between 20% and 40% of the variation that is observed in market betas.

19.8   EARNINGS ANNOUNCEMENTS AND PRICE CHANGES

A number of studies have shown large price changes for stocks of companies that report earnings that differ substantially from consensus expectations. One study looked at three groups of 50 stocks.[20] The first group consisted of the 50 stocks listed on the New York Stock Exchange (NYSE) that experienced the greatest price rise during 1970. The second group consisted of 50 stocks chosen randomly from all those listed on the NYSE during 1970. The third group consisted of the 50 stocks listed on the NYSE that experienced the greatest price decline during 1970. As shown in Figure 19.7, the median changes in the prices of the stocks in the top, random, and bottom groups were 48.4%, −3.2%, and −56.7%, respectively.

Next, the study looked at the actual change in earnings per share from 1969 to 1970 for each stock in each group. As shown in Figure 19.7, the median changes in earnings per share for the top, random, and bottom groups were 21.4%, −10.5%, and −83.0%, respectively.

Lastly, the study determined the forecasted change in earnings per share at the beginning of 1970 for each stock in each group. This was done by using the predictions contained in Standard & Poor's *Earnings Forecaster*, where estimates made by a number of investment research organizations are reported. The median forecasted changes in earnings per share for the top, random, and bottom groups are shown in Figure 19.7 to be 7.7%, 5.8%, and 15.3%, respectively.

Interestingly, the forecasts of earnings per share hardly correspond to the price movements of the stocks. In fact, the earnings of the stocks in the bottom group were expected to increase more than the earnings of the stocks in the top group (15.3%, compared with 7.7%). However, the prediction for the bottom group was disastrously wrong, with a median earnings per share decline of 83.0%. And, as Figure 19.7 shows, prices definitely followed suit. Overall, it appears that unexpected changes in earnings do indeed affect security prices.[21]

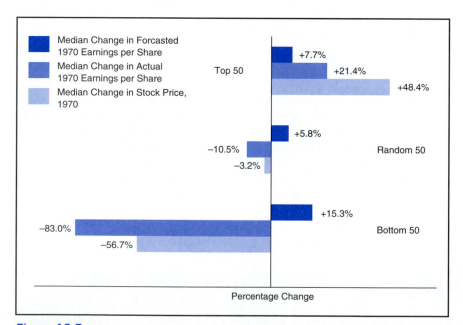

Figure 19.7

Earnings and Price Changes: Selected Stocks Listed on the New York Stock Exchange during 1970

Source: Victor Niederhoffer and Patrick J. Regan, "Earnings Changes, Analysts' Forecasts, and Stock Prices," *Financial Analysts Journal*, 28, no. 3 (May/June 1972): p. 67.

CHAPTER 19

But do earnings surprises affect prices before or after their announcement? In a completely efficient market, such information would be reflected in prices as soon as it had been disseminated to a few major market participants. The reaction of security prices around the time of earnings announcements has been examined by a number of authors and will be discussed next.

19.8.1 Deviations from Time-Series Models of Earnings

A comprehensive study involving 2,053 firms from 1974 through 1981 provided evidence concerning the speed of response of security prices to earnings announcements.[22] For each company, an expected earnings figure was computed for each quarter by using the model of the time-series behavior of earnings shown in Equation (19.19). With this model, the expected earnings for a firm during period t was equal to $QE_{t-4} + a(QE_{t-1} - QE_{t-5}) + b$. For example, the earnings expected for the firm in the second quarter of 1995 would equal (1) the firm's earnings in the second quarter of 1994, plus (2) the change in earnings from the first quarter of 1994 to the first quarter of 1995 times the parameter a, plus (3) the parameter b. The values of a and b would be determined by analysis of the behavior of earnings prior to the second quarter of 1995.

Given actual earnings and an estimate of expected earnings, a forecast error (FE_t) can be computed for the firm:

$$FE_t = QE_t - \overline{QE}_t \qquad (19.20)$$

where QE_t are the actual earnings for quarter t and $\overline{QE}_t$ are the expected earnings for quarter t, forecast at time $t - 1$. Simply stated, Equation (19.20) indicates that the forecast error for a quarter is the difference between actual earnings for that quarter and expected earnings.

The forecast error provides a measure of the "surprise" in the quarterly earnings announcement, but it fails to differentiate between stocks for which large forecast errors are routine and those for which they are rare. The important surprises are those associated with forecast errors that are large by historical standards. To account for this, a forecast error can be related to previous errors to obtain a measure of **standardized unexpected earnings** (SUE):

$$\text{SUE}_t = \frac{FE_t}{\sigma_{FEt}} \qquad (19.21)$$

where σ_{FEt} is the standard deviation of forecast errors over the twenty quarterly earnings of the firm prior to t. (That is, forecast errors were determined for each one of the 20 quarters before t, then the standard deviation for this set of 20 errors was estimated.)

For example, a firm with a forecast of earnings per share of $3 that subsequently reports actual earnings of $5 will have a forecast error of $2 (= $5 − $3). That is, the earnings announcement will "surprise" people by $2. Now if the standard deviation of past errors is $.80, this surprise will be notable, as the standardized unexpected earnings (SUE) equal 2.50 (= $2/$.80).[23] However, if the standard deviation is $4, then this surprise will be minor, because SUE will equal .50 (= $2/$4). Thus, a large positive value for SUE would indicate that the earnings announcement contained significant "good news," whereas a large negative SUE would indicate that the earnings announcement contained significant "bad news."

In the study, the SUEs associated with all the earnings announcements for all the sampled firms were ranked from smallest to largest. Then they were divided into ten equal-sized groups based on the ranking. Group 1 consisted of those announcements resulting in the most negative SUEs, and group 10 consisted of those with the most positive SUEs.

After forming these ten groups, the stock returns for each firm in each group were measured for the period from 60 days before its earnings announcement through 60 days after its announcement. Figure 19.8 shows the **abnormal return** for the average firm in each of the ten groups for three different time periods.

Panel (a) shows the average abnormal return for the period from 60 days before the earnings announcement through the day the announcement appeared in the *Wall Street Journal*. This period is denoted $(-60, 0)$.

Panel (b) shows the average abnormal return for the two-day period consisting of the day before the announcement appeared in the *Wall Street Journal* and the day the announcement appeared, a period that is denoted $(-1, 0)$. Because day 0 is the day the announcement appeared in the *Wall Street Journal*, day -1 is the day the announcement was made to the public. If this announcement was made after trading hours on day -1, investors would not have been able to buy or sell the stock until the next day, day 0. If the announcement was made during trading hours on day -1, then investors could have acted on that day. Due to the inability to pinpoint the hour of the announcement, the return over the two-day period was examined to see the immediate impact of the announcement on the price of the security.

Panel (c) shows the average abnormal return for the period from the day after the announcement through 60 days after the announcement, a period that is denoted $(1, 60)$.

Panel (a) shows that prices of firms that announced unexpectedly high earnings (such as SUE group 10) tended to increase *prior* to the announcement (day 0), suggesting that information relevant to the earnings announcement was becoming available to the market prior to the actual announcement. Conversely, prices of firms that announced unexpectedly low earnings (such as SUE group 1) tended to decrease *prior* to the announcement, undoubtedly for the same reason. In general, there seems to be a strong direct correspondence between the size of the unexpected earnings and the size of the abnormal return. Note that if an investor knew what the earnings were going to be 60 days before the announcement, then this information could be exploited by either buying the stock if the firm was going to announce unexpected large earnings, or short selling the stock if the firm was going to announce unexpected low earnings. However, because investors typically do not have prior access to earnings, such exploitation is generally impossible. Thus the existence of abnormal returns prior to the announcement date does not necessarily indicate some sort of market inefficiency.

Panel (b) shows that the larger the size of the unexpected earnings, the larger the price movement during the two-day period surrounding the announcement. For example, firms in SUE group 1 had an abnormal return of -1.34%, while those in SUE group 10 had an abnormal return of 1.26%. As in panel (a),

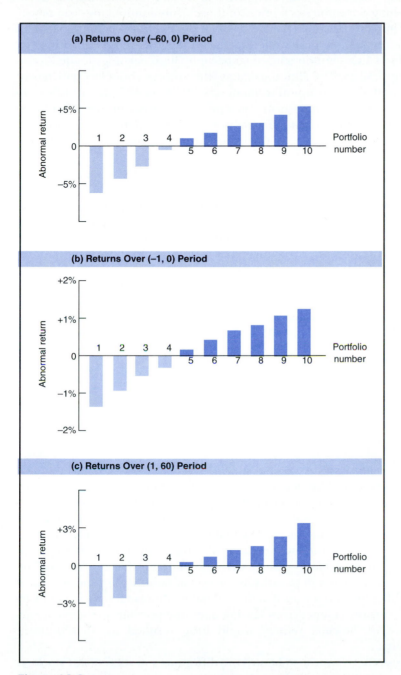

Figure 19.8

Security Returns in Period surrounding Earnings Announcements

Source: George Foster, Chris Olsen, and Terry Shevlin, "Earnings Releases, Anomalies, and the Behavior of Security Returns," *Accounting Review,* 59, no. 4 (October 1984): p. 587.

there is a direct relationship between the size of the unexpected earnings and the abnormal stock return.[24] Thus it appears that the market reacted in a predictable fashion, pushing up the stock prices of those firms announcing "good news" and pushing down the stock prices of those firms announcing "bad news."

As shown in panel (c), the changes in stock prices after the announcement dates are quite remarkable in that they appear to suggest a market inefficiency. Prices of stocks of firms announcing unexpectedly high earnings tended to increase for many days *after* the announcement (the average abnormal return over the 60–day period after the announcement was 3.23% for SUE group 10). Conversely, the prices of firms announcing unexpectedly low earnings tended to decrease for many days *after* the announcement (the average abnormal return over the 60–day period subsequent to the announcement was -3.08% for SUE group 1).

As was noted in the two previous panels, there seems to be a strong direct correspondence between the size of the unexpected earnings and the size of the abnormal return. This observation suggests that an investor could make abnormal returns by simply looking at quarterly earnings announcements and, based on the magnitude and sign of the unexpected component, acting appropriately. That is, if the firm announced earnings that were notably above expectations, the investor should subsequently purchase some of the firm's stock. In contrast, if the announced earnings were notably below expectations, the investor should subsequently sell any holdings and perhaps even short sell the firm's stock. Announcements of earnings that were reasonably close to expectations would not motivate either a buy or sell order. Accordingly, the "post-earnings-announcement drift" can be viewed as an empirical anomaly that is inconsistent with the notion of semistrong efficient markets.[25]

19.8.2 Unexpected Earnings and Abnormal Returns

One plausible explanation for the abnormal returns associated with large SUEs concerns the cost of information transfer. "New news" must reach a large number of investors before the appropriate new equilibrium price can be completely established. Although large institutional investors can obtain news quickly, it may take some time before it reaches smaller institutional investors and individuals. Thus after an earnings announcement there can be a period of abnormal price movement that is related in sign and magnitude to the nature of the announcement.

Alternatively, perhaps the measurement of "abnormal" returns has been in error. In making such a measurement, a determination of what is a "normal" return must be made. Such a determination is not straightforward but instead is fraught with difficulty. This means that the estimated abnormal returns could actually be due to measurement errors, leaving open the possibility that a more accurate measure of "normal return" would have resulted in no significant abnormal returns.

Nevertheless, there appear to be striking differences in subsequent stock returns for firms with different SUEs. Although the magnitudes of the return differences may be too small to warrant extensive trading, they do suggest the consideration of such things as SUE values and forecast revisions when money must be invested or a portion of an existing portfolio must be liquidated.

Consensus Earnings Expectations

Reference is frequently made in the financial press to "market" or "consensus" expectations. We may read that the "market" expects inflation to remain stable or that the "market" expects the Fed to raise interest rates. Given that the market is the amalgam of a large, diverse group of investors, how does anyone determine what the market really expects?

Of course, the most important market expectations are established and published daily—that is, the expected values of corporate assets as reflected in security prices. But what about market expectations regarding economic and financial variables that underlie security prices? In general, these expectations are reported anecdotally, perhaps through interviews with prominent investors or through a variety of surveys.

Investing based on such ambiguous information is problematic. Abnormal returns can be earned only by staking out positions based on expectations contrary to those of the market. Superior investors will consistently identify securities for which market expectations are somehow in error. But unless these investors can correctly interpret the market's expectations, they will not know whether their expectations are significantly different from those of the market.

As the text discusses, earnings expectations are the most important determinant of common stock prices. If an investor can identify companies for which the market is under- or overestimating future earnings, the investor can appropriately buy and sell these stocks to produce portfolio returns superior to those of the market on a risk-adjusted basis.

Many organizations publish earnings estimates, including Standard & Poor's, Value Line, and brokerage houses. However, individually these estimates do not represent market expectations; they are merely the opinions of specific analysts. What is needed is a means to collect the earnings estimates of many analysts following a particular company. That need has been satisfied for over 20 years by a firm called Institutional Brokers Estimate System, or I/B/E/S.

While I/B/E/S is not the only company collecting earnings expectations data (Zacks Investment Research is a prominent competitor), it was the first and it remains the leader in the field. I/B/E/S was formed in 1971. Its initial objectives were modest—to collect timely earnings estimates from brokerage firms on several hundred large, well-followed companies. These estimates were then compiled and the distributions of earnings estimates (high, low, median, measure of dispersion) were periodically reported to subscribers.

For example, suppose that an institutional investment firm was estimating earnings next year of $2.50 per share for *XYZ* company and $3.30 per share for *ABC* company. Through I/B/E/S, the institutional investor might find that the consensus earnings estimates for *XYZ* and *ABC* were currently $1.50 and $3.50, respectively. Further, the coefficient of variation (standard deviation divided by mean—a measure of the estimates' relative dispersion) was 0.20 for *XYZ* and 0.80 for *ABC*. If the institutional investor has confidence in its own estimates, then it should expect *XYZ* stock to perform relatively well. The market's earnings expectations are tight around the $1.50 level, which is $1.00 less than the investor's estimate. If the market comes to realize that $2.50 is the actual level of *XYZ* earnings, it will likely bid the company's stock price up.

ABC stock is much less attractive. The institutional investor's estimate is less than the consensus by $0.20, so it might wish to sell *ABC* out of its portfolio if it owned the stock or perhaps even short sell the stock. However, the relatively high dispersion of estimates around the median indicates that the market's expectations are not firm. If *ABC*'s earnings actually come in at $3.30, the result may not be a particularly unpleasant surprise to the market, and therefore may have little impact on *ABC*'s stock price.

The advantages of using consensus earnings expectations in common stock analysis quickly caught on among institutional investors. Today, I/B/E/S receives, compiles, and distributes earnings estimates from over 6,000 equity analysts in nearly 600 research departments in over 33 countries. Although by far the most intense analyst earnings coverage is for U.S. companies, the contributing I/B/E/S analysts now cover over 13,000 companies in 39 equity markets around the world. Even companies in emerging equity markets such as the People's Republic of China, Sri Lanka, and Chile have attracted institutional analysts' coverage and have been included in the I/B/E/S service.

I/B/E/S collects earnings estimates in a number of ways, including faxes, diskettes, telephone calls, and printed reports. Many research firms now provide I/B/E/S with data directly by computer. Upon receipt of analysts' earnings estimates, I/B/E/S staffers perform several quality checks to ensure the integrity of the data. At that point, the estimates are entered into the firm's database. Summary consensus numbers are updated daily and made available to I/B/E/S subscribers.

The original I/B/E/S reports were simply printed books containing summary data on individual company earnings estimates. Although the original printed format is still available, I/B/E/S now pro-vides data through a variety of electronic vendors. For example, I/B/E/S data can be accessed through an optical disk data delivery system that can easily bring earnings expectation data into an electronic spreadsheet for detailed analysis.

Customers can now receive I/B/E/S data diced and sliced in a number of ways. The firm makes available to subscribers analyst-by-analyst data, daily alerts of analyst changes, and custom-designed reports. The firm also provides commentaries and analyses of market trends that it discerns from the earnings estimate data.

The systematic collection of earnings estimates is an excellent example of the forces that have been increasing the efficiency of security markets. Before I/B/E/S collected such data, consensus earnings estimates were difficult to obtain and highly ambiguous. Now those estimates are rigorously quantified and widely distributed, decreasing the likelihood of investors' acting on incomplete or erroneous information.

19.8.3 Security Analysts' Forecasts of Future Earnings

In using only the historical record of past earnings to forecast future earnings, it was mentioned earlier that an autoregressive model of order one, as shown in Equation (19.19), seemed to work about as well as any other model. However, security analysts do not restrict themselves to just past earnings when developing their forecasts. Instead, they look at many different pieces of information. This raises several interesting questions. How well can analysts forecast earnings? And do their forecasts incorporate information other than that contained in past earnings? The results of two studies that provide some answers to these questions are shown in Tables 19.5 and 19.6.

Forecasts of Analysts

In one study, illustrated in Table 19.5, two sets of forecasts were examined for the quarterly earnings of 50 firms over the period from 1971 through 1975.[26] The first set was obtained by applying sophisticated mechanical models to each firm's previous earnings history [such as the autoregressive model of Equation (19.19)]. The second set was obtained from the earnings forecasts of security analysts as reported in the *Value Line Investment Survey*.[27] The results suggest that the analysts outperformed the mechanical model. For example, 63.5% of the analysts' forecasts were within 25% of the actual earnings values, while only 54.4% of the forecasts made via mechanical models came as close. Analysts appear to base

TABLE 19.5

ACCURACY OF MECHANICAL AND JUDGMENTAL EARNINGS FORECASTS

Earnings Forecast Error as a Percent of Actual Earnings	Percent of Forecasts with a Smaller Error	
	Mechanical Model	Analysts' Forecasts
5%	15.0%	18.0%
10	26.5	32.0
25	54.5	63.5
50	81.0	86.5
75	87.5	90.5
100	89.5	92.0

Source: Lawrence D. Brown and Michael S. Rozeff, "The Superiority of Analyst Forecasts as Measures of Expectations: Evidence from Earnings," *Journal of Finance,* 33, no. 1 (March 1978): pp. 7–8.

their forecasts on both past earnings and other information, and the latter appears to help.

In another study, forecasts of annual earnings made by security analysts approximately 240, 180, 120, and 60 days before the announcement date of actual earnings were examined.[28] Typically these days correspond to dates in each of the year's fiscal quarters before the announcement date. Hence, 240 days falls roughly between last year's earnings announcement and this year's first quarter earnings announcement, 180 days falls roughly between the first quarter and second quarter earnings announcement, and so on. These forecasts, made over the period from 1975 to 1982 by analysts at between 50 and 130 brokerage firms, were obtained from the Institutional Brokers Estimate System (I/B/E/S) database developed by the brokerage firm of Lynch, Jones, & Ryan.

Table 19.6 presents a comparison of the accuracy of four forecasts. The first forecast, denoted *RW*, is the annual forecast generated by using a model like the random walk model of Equation (19.16). The second, denoted *AR*, is the annual forecast produced by using an autoregressive model like the one shown in Equation (19.19). The third is the average forecast published by I/B/E/S, and the fourth is the single most current individual forecast published by I/B/E/S.

TABLE 19.6

FORECAST ACCURACY OF TIME-SERIES MODELS AND SECURITY MODELS

Model	Days before Annual Announcement Date			
	240	180	120	60
Random walk	$.963	$.781	$.620	$.363
Autoregressive	.975	.780	.592	.350
Average analyst	.747	.645	.516	.395
Current analyst	.742	.610	.468	.342

Source: Adapted from Patricia C. O'Brien, "Analysts' Forecasts as Earnings Expectations," *Journal of Accounting and Economics,* 10, no. 1 (January 1988): Table 4.

Forecast accuracy for a particular model and firm is measured by absolute forecast error, or:

$$FE = |A - F|. \tag{19.22}$$

where F denotes the forecast and A denotes the subsequent actual earnings of the firm.

There are several interesting observations to be made from Table 19.6. First, as the announcement date gets closer, all of the forecasting models become more accurate. This is hardly surprising, because more information is available as the announcement date gets closer. Second, for long horizons both the average and most current forecasts are more accurate than either of the time-series models. Third, the current forecast is more accurate than any of the other models. However, subsequent examination of the forecasts indicates that the average forecast was more accurate than the most current forecast, provided that none of the individual forecasts used to determine the average was "stale" (that is, more than roughly a week old). This is because such averaging reduces the forecast error by having individual forecast errors offset each other (that is, positive errors will offset negative errors, resulting in a smaller error for the average forecast).

Another interesting observation that has been uncovered about security analysts' forecasts is that they tend to be too optimistic, meaning that they tend to have an upward bias (more on this shortly). Hence most of the typical analysts' revisions are downward. One interpretation of this observation is that many of the analysts work for brokerage firms and thus find it in their employers' best interest (and thus their own) to avoid antagonizing any corporation that is or might become an investment banking client.[29]

All-American Analysts

The monthly publication *Institutional Investor* announces each October its All-American Research Team by querying 2,000 money managers.[30] These managers are asked to evaluate security analysts on the basis of (1) stock recommendations, (2) earnings forecasts, (3) written reports, and (4) overall performance. From these evaluations, analysts are selected for the Team (there is a First Team, a Second Team, a Third Team, and Runners-up) in over 60 industries as well as in such areas as portfolio strategy, quantitative analysis, economics, and market timing.

One study looked at the relative forecasting ability of All-American and NonAll-American industry analysts for the fiscal years 1981–1985. In doing so, each EPS forecast of an All-American was matched with a forecast by a NonAll-American for the same firm, where each forecast was made an identical number of days before the fiscal year-end. Forecast accuracy was measured by using Equation (19.22). Table 19.7(a) indicates that the average forecast error for All-Americans was $.95, while NonAll-Americans had an error of $.98. Hence, All-American EPS forecasts were more accurate by approximately $.03 per share.

TABLE 19.7
EPS FORECAST ACCURACY OF ALL-AMERICAN AND NONALL-AMERICAN ANALYSTS

	Average Absolute Forecast Error*		
	NonAll-Americans	**All-Americans**	**Difference**
(a) While on Team:	$.98	$.95	$.03
	(3.7%)	(3.6%)	(.1%)
	NonAll-Americans	**Future All-Americans**	**Difference**
(b) Before Gaining Membership:			
One Year Before	$.97	$.97	$.00
	(3.1%)	(3.1%)	(.0%)
Two Years Before	.95	.94	.01
	(3.2%)	(3.2%)	(.0%)
Three Years Before	.96	.94	.02
	(3.5%)	(3.5%)	(.0%)
	Former All-Americans	**Remaining All-Americans**	**Difference**
(c) Before Losing Membership:			
One Year Before	$1.03	$1.01	$.02
	(3.8%)	(3.7%)	(.1%)
Two Years Before	.91	.88	.03
	(3.3%)	(3.3%)	(.0%)
Three Years Before	.91	.87	.04
	(2.8%)	(2.7%)	(.1%)

*The numbers shown in parentheses below the average absolute forecast error represent the average of the percentage absolute forecast errors where the percentage is calculated as $|A - F|/A$ where A = actual and F = forecast.

Source: Scott E. Stickel, "Reputation and Performance Among Security Analysts," *Journal of Finance*, 47, no. 5 (December 1992): pp. 1818, 1819, 1821.

Also examined in the study were the records of analysts in the three-year period before they became All-Americans ("future" All-Americans) and the records of All-Americans in the three-year period before they lost their exalted status and became NonAll-Americans ("former" All-Americans).[31] This was done as follows.

1. The track records of future All-Americans were matched with analysts who were and remained NonAll-Americans. Table 19.7(b) indicates that future All-Americans were only slightly more accurate {by $.01[= ($.00+$.01+$.02)/3] per share, on average} than NonAll-Americans in the three-year period before they became All-Americans.
2. The track records of former All-Americans were matched with All-Americans who maintained their Team membership ("remaining" All-Americans). Table 19.7(c) indicates that former All-Americans were less accurate than the remaining All-Americans by between $.04 and $.02 per share in the three-year period before removal.

Given the nearly indistinguishable differences in earnings forecasting performance between All-Americans and NonAll-Americans, the reasons for Team membership appear to be explained by other factors, such as high-quality company research or good personal relationships with money managers.

The study also documented the existence of forecast bias. This bias was measured by the average forecast error where the forecast error for a given analyst is:

$$FE = A - F. \tag{19.23}$$

As before, F denotes the forecast, and A denotes the subsequent actual earnings of the firm. Note how Equation (19.23) is identical to Equation (19.22), except that absolute values are no longer used. The average forecast error for All-Americans was $\$-.73$ per share (or 2.9% of the actual EPS). For NonAll-Americans the comparable figure was $\$-.74$ (or 3.0%). Given that the average FE was negative, this means that both types of analysts tended to overestimate the level of EPS. As mentioned earlier, this is clear evidence of both All-Americans' and NonAll-Americans' being too optimistic in forecasting EPS.

19.8.4 Management Forecasts of Future Earnings

Often management itself will make a forecast of next year's earnings for the firm. Generally, the forecasts of security analysts are not as accurate as the forecasts of management when both sets of forecasts are made about the same time, as shown in Table 19.8.[32] Here average security analysts' forecasts, as reported weekly by Zacks Investment Research's Icarus Service, were compared with corresponding management forecasts.[33] The objective was to see who was the more accurate forecaster. To do this, forecast errors (FE) were calculated for both sets of forecasts as:

$$FE = |(F - A)/A| \tag{19.24}$$

where F is the earnings forecast and A is the actual earnings subsequently reported by the firm. Hence an earnings forecast of $3 per share that subsequently turned out to be $4 would have $FE = |(\$3 - \$4)/\$4| = .25$ or 25%.

Letting $t = 0$ denote the date that the management forecast is released, analysts' forecasts were collected weekly from 12 weeks before to 12 weeks after $t = 0$. As Table 19.8 shows at the bottom, the average forecast error for management was .150. Analyst forecast errors ranged from .224 at week -12 (meaning 12 weeks prior to the date of the management forecast) to .124 at week $+12$. Hence, as was shown in Table 19.6, analysts' forecasts became more accurate the closer they were to the date the actual earnings were announced, because the size of the average forecast error decreases fairly steadily from $t = -12$ to $t = +12$.

Most important, however, is the observation that management forecasts were more accurate than analyst forecasts from $t = -12$ to $t = +8$ (the difference was found to be statistically significant through $t = +4$). That is, forecasts issued by analysts before, coincident to, or up to four months after management's forecast were less accurate. This observation is not surprising up to $t = 0$, as management has private information about the firm that is not available to the analysts. However, it is surprising that management forecasts were superior from $t = +1$ through $t = +4$ because it suggests that analysts could improve their accuracy simply by using management's previously released forecast. After $t = +4$, the analysts' forecasts were more accurate (the difference was statistically

TABLE 19.8
SECURITY ANALYST AND MANAGEMENT FORECAST ERRORS

Week	Average Analyst Forecast Error	Average Analyst Forecast Error – Average Management Forecast Error[*]
−12	.224	.074
−11	.222	.072
−10	.221	.071
−9	.221	.071
−8	.214	.064
−7	.221	.071
−6	.222	.072
−5	.216	.066
−4	.210	.060
−3	.208	.058
−2	.211	.061
−1	.209	.059
0	.195	.045
+1	.186	.036
+2	.177	.027
+3	.174	.024
+4	.171	.021
+5	.166	.016
+6	.160	.010
+7	.153	.003
+8	.150	.000
+9	.141	−.009
+10	.133	−.017
+11	.129	−.021
+12	.124	−.026

*The size of the average management forecast error was .150.

Source: Adapted from John M. Hassell and Robert H. Jennings, "Relative Forecast Accuracy and the Timing of Earnings Forecast Announcements," *Accounting Review,* 61, no. 1 (January 1986): Tables 2 and 3.

significant beginning nine weeks after the release date of the management forecast—a finding that is not surprising, because the analysts probably had access to more timely information upon which to base their forecasts).

19.8.5 Sources of Errors in Forecasting

As security analysts' forecasts are not perfect, it is interesting to consider the major source of their errors. One study examined the I/B/E/S database and attempted to break down the forecast errors into three components: (1) errors that could be traced to misjudgments about the economy; (2) errors that could be traced to misjudgments about the firm's particular industry; and (3) errors that were purely due to misjudgments about the firm.[34]

The results indicated the following: less than 3% of the typical error was due to a misjudgment about the economy; roughly 30% of the typical error was due to a misjudgment about the industry; and over 65% of the typical error was due to a misjudgment about the firm.

1. Assuming that a firm undertakes positive NPV projects and maintains a constant debt-equity ratio, shareholders will be indifferent to the level of dividends.

2. If dividends and new investment are greater than earnings, the firm may issue new equity. If dividends and new investment are less than earnings, the firm may repurchase equity. In either case, a stockholder maintaining constant proportional ownership will be able to spend the same amount on consumption, regardless of the level of dividends.

3. Earnings, not dividends, are the source of a firm's value.

4. Few firms attempt to maintain a constant ratio of dividends to current earnings. It is often assumed that firms establish a long-run payout ratio and adjust current actual dividends based on the difference between current target dividends and the last period's actual dividends.

5. Corporate management often uses dividend changes as a signaling device, raising or lowering dividends based on its assessment of the firm's future earnings.

6. A firm has considerable discretion in calculating its accounting earnings. These accounting earnings may differ substantially from the firm's economic earnings. Similarly, a firm's book value may differ considerably from its market value.

7. Earnings can be divided into permanent and transitory components. A firm's intrinsic value will be based on the permanent component of earnings. The transitory component is a significant factor in short-run changes in a firm's price-earnings ratio.

8. There is a positive relationship between accounting betas and market betas. Firms whose earnings covary more with marketwide earnings are likely to have higher market betas.

9. Stocks with the highest returns typically have earnings that are substantially greater than expected, whereas those with the lowest returns have earnings substantially below expectations.

10. Stock prices tend to correctly anticipate earnings announcements by moving in the appropriate direction beforehand.

11. Stock prices tend to react correctly but not fully to earnings announcements immediately afterward.

12. Stock prices continue to move in a direction similar to their initial reaction for several months afterward. This phenomenon is known as post-earnings-announcement drift.

13. Analysts appear to forecast earnings better than sophisticated mechanical models.

14. Analysts tend to overestimate when forecasting earnings per share.

15. Management earnings forecasts are generally more accurate than analysts' forecasts.

1. For a given level of earnings (E), net new investment (I), and dividends (D), explain why a firm must issue new stock if $E < D + I$ and it desires to maintain a constant debt-equity ratio. Similarly, why must it repurchase shares if $E > D + I$ and it desires to maintain a constant debt-equity ratio?

2. Merrillan Motors had earnings of $8 million last year. It made $5 million of investments in projects with positive net present values. Pat Collins owns 20% of the firm's common stock. Assume that Pat desires no change in proportional ownership of Merrillan and the firm wishes to maintain a constant debt-equity ratio. What will be Pat's action in response to:
   a. Merrillan's paying out dividends of $5 million?
   b. Merrillan's paying out dividends of $1 million?
   c. Merrillan's paying out dividends of $3 million?

3. Why is an individual stockholder indifferent between the firm retaining $1 of earnings or paying out the $1 of earnings as a dividend, assuming that the firm and the stockholder maintain a constant debt-equity ratio and a constant proportional ownership position, respectively?

4. If the dividend decision is irrelevant to the valuation of a firm, then are not dividend discount models irrelevant to valuing a share of common stock? Why?

5. Scoops Cooney, a confused investment student, commented, "I understand the irrelevance of the dividend decision to the value of the firm. As a result, I calculate the value of a firm's stock based on the present value of the firm's expected earnings per share." Is Scoops correct? Why?

6. Why do most corporations not maintain a constant payout ratio? What payout strategy do most firms pursue?

7. Hixton Farms has a target payout ratio of 50%. Dividends paid last year amounted to $10 million. Its earnings were $20 million. Hixton's "speed of adjustment" factor for dividends is 60%. What will be its dividend payments over the next five years if its earnings display the following path:

Year	Earnings
1	$30 million
2	35 million
3	30 million
4	25 million
5	30 million

Draw a graph of Hixton's actual dividends paid versus the desired dividend payments over this five-year period.

8. Rockton Plastics has made changes to its dividends over the last 14 years. Based on a target payout ratio of 30%, according to the Lintner Model the firm would have preferred to make a different set of dividend changes. Both the actual and preferred dividend changes are shown on page 648. What "speed of adjustment" factor is implied by these two dividend change series? (Use of a computer regression program, such as one provided with an electronic spreadsheet, is recommended.)

Year	Actual Change in Dividends	Preferred Change in Dividends
1	$-0.28	$-0.47
2	-0.09	-0.16
3	-0.05	-0.08
4	-0.01	-0.02
5	0.01	0.02
6	0.04	0.07
7	0.01	0.01
8	0.03	0.05
9	0.03	0.05
10	0.01	0.02
11	0.04	0.07
12	0.03	0.06
13	0.03	0.05

9. How are dividends used as a signaling device by corporate management? To the extent that dividends are a signaling device, how are dividend changes related to stock prices?

10. Discuss why there generally does not exist a one-to-one relationship between corporations' book values and their market values.

11. The price per share of the Dells Deli Corporation is less than its book value. Does this indicate that those who now hold the firm's shares have lost money in the past? Does it indicate that they are likely to lose money in the future? Does it indicate that the Dells Deli should not undertake any further capital investment? Explain your answers.

12. Why might a steady trend in a firm's reported earnings from year to year suggest that the figures do not represent the firm's economic earnings?

13. Reported earnings typically differ, sometimes considerably, from economic earnings. Nevertheless, it is often argued that reported earnings are intended simply to provide a "source of information" to investors about the value of the firm. If so, might there not be many alternative accounting procedures of equal use to investors? How might one go about evaluating the usefulness of such procedures?

14. Distinguish between permanent and transitory earnings. Would you expect companies across industries to differ in terms of the relative importance of transitory earnings to total earnings? Explain.

15. Price-earnings ratios for individual companies vary over time and across firms. Discuss some of the possible reasons for this variability.

16. Why would you expect a security's market beta to be highly correlated with its accounting beta?

17. Harlond Clift once wrote in a market newsletter that, "I focus my research on consensus earnings forecasts. Those companies that the consensus believes will produce the largest earnings increases next year are most likely to produce the best returns." Is Harlond's opinion consistent with empirical evidence? Explain why or why not.

18. Calculate the relationship between the following series of quarterly earnings using an autoregressive model of order one (use of a computer regression program is recommended). What is your forecast for earnings in Quarter 21?

Quarter	Earnings	Quarter	Earnings
1	$4.00	11	$4.25
2	4.10	12	4.49
3	3.95	13	4.59
4	4.20	14	4.58
5	4.30	15	4.39
6	4.29	16	4.63
7	4.11	17	4.73
8	4.35	18	4.72
9	4.44	19	4.54
10	4.43	20	4.78

19. Oakdale Orchards has produced the following earnings over the last nine quarters:

Quarter	Earnings per Share
1	$2.00
2	1.95
3	2.05
4	2.10
5	2.40
6	2.24
7	2.67
8	2.84
9	2.64

The expected earnings for the current quarter are based on the equation $QE_t = QE_{t-4} + .75(QE_{t-1} - QE_{t-5})$. Calculate the standardized unexpected earnings in each of the last four quarters, given a standard deviation of $0.35.

20. Why might the price of a stock react only partially to an "earnings surprise" on the first day or two after the earnings announcement?

21. (Appendix Question) The Value Line ranking system has long shown a consistent ability to produce positive risk-adjusted returns. These results have been particularly disconcerting for efficient markets proponents. Why?

APPENDIX

VALUE LINE RANKINGS

It has been observed that investors can use the information contained in either a quarterly earnings announcement or a revision of an earnings forecast by security analysts to make abnormal returns. Another source of information that may be useful to investors is the *Value Line Investment Survey* (published weekly by Value

Line, Inc., New York, for $525 per year), which is reputed to be the largest stock investment advisory service in the United States.[35]

Each week, every one of approximately 1,700 stocks is assigned one of five possible ranks by Value Line. By design, the categories include the same number of stocks each week, as follows:

Rank		Number of Stocks
1	(highest)	100
2	(above average)	300
3	(average)	900
4	(below average)	300
5	(lowest)	100

Many factors go into the ranking procedure. Not surprisingly, the exact details have not been revealed. However, the key elements are all based on publicly available information:[36]

1. the most recent year's earnings and average stock price, relative to the comparable values for the previous ten years, and the stock's average price over the preceding ten weeks relative to that of the preceding 52 weeks;
2. a price momentum element that is based on the stock's current price-earnings ratio relative to that of the market, compared with the average of the corresponding figures over the last five years;
3. an earnings momentum element that is based on the most recent quarter's earnings relative to the amount reported four quarters earlier;
4. an earnings "surprise" element where the most recent quarter's earnings are compared with the amount forecast by Value Line's security analysts.

A test of the resulting rankings showed them to be of some value.[37] Beginning in November 26, 1965, five portfolios were formed (on paper). The first included all stocks ranked "1" at that time, in equal dollar values; the second included all stocks ranked "2" and so on. After six months each portfolio was altered as necessary to again include equal dollar values of all stocks with the appropriate ranks at that time. The procedure was continued until February 3, 1978, when the last set of portfolios was formed. Then, each portfolio's actual rate of return was measured and adjustments for risk were made to determine "abnormal" returns.

The results, shown in Table 19.9, indicate that both the actual and abnormal returns are perfectly ordered with the rankings of the securities in the portfolios. More in-depth analysis indicated that most of the abnormal returns occurred in the 13-week period subsequent to the formation date. Interestingly, this study shows that the only notable abnormal return is for the securities with a ranking of 5. This suggests that an investor should sell (or even short sell) any securities that have such a ranking.

This study also looked at those securities whose rank had been changed by Value Line. Roughly 70 to 80 securities change ranks each week, evenly split between those being upgraded and those being downgraded. Almost all the

TABLE 19.9
PERFORMANCE OF PORTFOLIOS FORMED ON THE BASIS OF VALUE LINE RANKINGS

	Ranking				
	1	**2**	**3**	**4**	**5**
Actual return over subsequent 26 weeks	7.38%	6.51%	4.10%	2.70%	.37%
Abnormal return over subsequent 26 weeks	.33%	.35%	− .57%	− 1.12%	− 3.05%

Source: Thomas E. Copeland and David Mayers, "The Value Line Enigma (1965–1978): A Case Study of Performance Evaluation Issues," *Journal of Financial Economics*, 10, no. 3 (November 1982): pp. 298, 301.

changes are of one rank (seldom does a security jump two ranks—for example, from 1 to 3, or vice versa).

Focusing the analysis on the time of the change in rank, it was determined that, on average, securities whose rank had been upgraded earned an abnormal return of .77% in the subsequent 13 weeks. Conversely, those securities whose rank had been downgraded earned an abnormal return of − 1.42% in the subsequent 13 weeks. Overall, most of the adjustment in the stock prices of these securities was found to be concentrated in the two-week period subsequent to the publication of the change in rank.[38]

These results do not suggest that Value Line provides a guaranteed formula for outstanding portfolio performance. No transaction costs were charged in the calculations, and turnover was high.[39] Thus it might not be possible to earn abnormal returns by continually using Value Line rankings when these costs are taken into consideration. But the results do suggest that, when initially investing in stocks, Value Line rankings may prove useful.[40] It can be conjectured that Value Line rankings "work" primarily because they use quarterly earnings in both the earnings momentum and surprise elements that go into the Value Line ranking procedure.[41] After all, it has been noted that there are abnormal price movements subsequent to the announcement of quarterly earnings.

To summarize, the results suggest that there is a two-part puzzle associated with Value Line ranks. First, Value Line appears to have superior forecasting ability that is based on public information. Second, the market takes time to adjust to the Value Line rankings. Both of these observations are puzzling because they are inconsistent with the notion of efficient markets.[42] To further complicate matters, one study found that most rank changes occur shortly after earnings announcements are made. Subsequent investigation revealed that Value Line's superior performance was attributable to the "post-earnings-announcement drift." Hence the two anomalies appear to be related.[43]

ENDNOTES

[1] In Chapter 18, D_0 denoted the per-share dividends that had been paid over the past year. Now D_0 is used to denote the aggregate amount of dividends that is about to be paid. Similarly, the quantities of earnings (E_t) and new investment (I_t) are measured

for the firm on an aggregate basis, not a per-share basis. Note that dividends cannot be set at an arbitrarily high value relative to earnings (for example, earnings of $10 million and dividends of $100 million), because the firm would then find it practically impossible to obtain the necessary funds to pay the dividends.

[2] The use of such a stockholder is for ease of exposition. The same answer would be obtained if other types of stockholders (such as those who are not interested in maintaining a constant proportional ownership position in the firm in the future) are considered.

[3] It has been argued that if the tax rate on dividends is greater than the tax rate on capital gains, then stockholders will earn more on an after-tax basis if the firm has a relatively low payout ratio. An additional benefit to stockholders if the firm has a low payout ratio is that capital gains taxes are paid only when the stock is sold, and can therefore be deferred. Thus it appears that stockholders will be better off if the firm has a relatively low payout ratio. For a more detailed discussion of the issue, along with the relevant citations, see pp. 128–135 of Gordon J. Alexander and Jack Clark Francis, *Portfolio Analysis* (Englewood Cliffs, NJ: Prentice Hall, 1986). Also see James S. Ang, David W. Blackwell, and William L. Megginson, "The Effect of Taxes on the Relative Valuation of Dividends and Capital Gains: Evidence from Dual-Class British Investment Trusts," *Journal of Finance*, 46, no. 1 (March 1991): 383–399.

[4] In addition to a regular dividend, sometimes a firm will declare a "special" or "extra" dividend, usually at year-end. By calling it a special dividend, the firm is conveying a message to its stockholders that such a dividend is a one-time event.

[5] Looking backward in time, it can be shown that current dividends D_t are a linear function of past earnings $E_{t-1}, E_{t-2}, E_{t-3}$, and so on. More specifically, it can be shown that:

$$D_t = ap^*[(1 - a)^0 E_{t-0} + (1 - a)^1 E_{t-1} + (1 - a)^2 E_{t-2} + (1 - a)^3 E_{t-3} + \dots].$$

Because the quantity $(1 - a)$ is a positive fraction (for example, $1/3$), when it is raised to a power it becomes smaller in value, with larger powers resulting in values closer to zero. Thus current dividends depend more on recent past earnings than on distant past earnings, and the equation can be approximated by using an arbitrary number of past earnings (the accuracy of the approximation depends on the number used).

[6] Other signaling devices include changes in the firm's capital structure (for example, announcing an issuance of debt with the proceeds being used to repurchase stock). It has been argued that in order for the signal to be useful to the public, (1) management must have an incentive to send a truthful signal; (2) the signal cannot be imitated by competitors in different financial positions; and (3) there cannot be a cheaper means of conveying the same information. See Stephen A. Ross, "The Determination of Financial Structure: The Incentive Signalling Approach," *Bell Journal of Economics*, 8, no. 1 (Spring 1977): 23–40.

[7] Paul M. Healy and Krishna G. Palepu, "Earnings Information Conveyed by Dividend Initiations and Omissions," *Journal of Financial Economics*, 21, no. 2 (September 1988): 149–175.

[8] Harry DeAngelo, Linda DeAngelo, and Douglas J. Skinner, "Dividends and Losses," *Journal of Finance*, 47, no. 5 (December 1992): 1837–1863. Also see Harry DeAngelo and Linda DeAngelo, "Dividend Policy and Financial Distress: An Empirical Investigation of Troubled NYSE Firms," *Journal of Finance*, 45, no. 5 (December 1990): 1415–1431.

[9] Sir John R. Hicks, winner in 1972 of the Nobel Prize in Economics, defined the weekly economic income of an individual as "the maximum value which he can consume

during a week and still be as well off at the end of the week as he was at the beginning" (*Value and Capital,* London: Oxford University Press, 1946, p. 172). The definition of the economic earnings of a firm that is given in Equation (19.15) can be viewed as an extension of Hicks's definition for an individual.

[10] Two assertions that have been made in regard to what investors look at when valuing stocks are known as the *mechanistic hypothesis* and the *myopic hypothesis.* The former asserts that investors look only at reported earnings, and the latter asserts that investors look only at the short-term future. Both these assertions seem to be invalid when data are analyzed. For an in-depth discussion, see George Foster, *Financial Statement Analysis* (Englewood Cliffs, NJ: Prentice Hall, 1986), 443–445.

[11] For a discussion of a number of related issues, see Ross Watts, "Does It Pay to Manipulate EPS?" in *Issues in Corporate Finance* (New York: Stern Stewart Putnam & Macklis, 1983).

[12] There is evidence that investors in publicly held firms are not fooled by such manipulations. See, for example, John R. M. Hand and Patricia Hughes, "The Motives and Consequences of Debt-Equity Swaps and Defeasances: More Evidence That It Does Not Pay to Manipulate Earnings," *Journal of Applied Corporate Finance,* 3, no. 3 (Fall 1990): 77–81.

[13] The vertical axis of this figure actually measures the logarithm of earnings per share and of the price index. In this type of diagram, a given vertical distance represents the same percentage change, no matter where it appears. If prices, for example, changed by the same percentage every year (like $10 to $20 to $40 to $80), then the plot of log prices would be a straight line sloping upward to the right whereas the plot of prices would curve upward.

[14] This suggests that firms will have high price-earnings ratios if they have either negative transitory current earnings or high forecasted long-term permanent earnings, or both. The converse holds for firms with low price-earnings ratios.

[15] John Lintner and Robert Glauber, "Higgledy Piggledy Growth in America," in James Lorie and Richard Brealey, eds., *Modern Developments in Investment Management* (Hinsdale, IL, Dryden Press, 1978). However, a more recent study came to a different conclusion concerning the predictability of earnings changes. This study divided a large number of companies into five groups based on their earnings-to-price (E/P) ratios, and found that lower E/P stock groups exhibited consistently higher long-term earnings growth rates. See Russell J. Fuller, Lex C. Huberts, and Michael Levinson, "It's Not Higgledy-Piggledy Growth!", *Journal of Portfolio Management,* 18, no. 2 (Winter 1992): 38–45. Also see H. Bradlee Perry, "Analyzing Growth Stocks: What's a Good Growth Rate?", *AAII Journal,* 13, no. 9 (October 1991): 7–10.

[16] Some people [for example, Jane Ou and Stephen H. Penman, "Financial Statement Analysis and the Prediction of Stock Returns," *Journal of Accounting and Economics,* 11, no. 4 (November 1989): 295–329] think that a "random walk with drift" model as follows is more accurate:

$$E_t - E_{t-1} = \delta + \epsilon_t$$

where δ is a positive constant that represents the "drift" term. With this model, the expected change in earnings is equal to δ. Note how the random walk model given in Equation (19.17) is a special case where $\delta = 0$.

[17] This model can also be used to forecast annual earnings by working forward one quarter at a time and then adding up the forecasts for the forthcoming four quarters. Doing so would result in a forecast of annual earnings (E_t) equal to $E_{t-1} + c(QE_{t-1} - QE_{t-5})$ + d, where $c = a^1 + a^2 + a^3 + a^4$ and $d = 4b + 3ab + 2a^2b + a^3b$. Note that the random walk model is a special case where a and b are equal to zero, thereby making c and d equal to zero.

[18] It has been argued that an improvement can be made in this model by either (1) adding to the right-hand side the term $c(QE_{t-4} - QE_{t-8})$ where c is a constant or (2) by multiplying the constant b term by the random error term that occurred four quarters ago now (e_{t-4}). See P. A. Griffin, "The Time-Series Behavior of Quarterly Earnings: Preliminary Evidence," *Journal of Accounting Research,* 15, no. 1 (Spring 1977): 71–83; Lawrence D. Brown and Michael S. Rozeff, "Univariate Time-Series Models of Quarterly Accounting Earnings per Share: A Proposed Model," *Journal of Accounting Research,* 17, no. 1 (Spring 1979): 179–189; and Allen W. Bathke, Jr. and Kenneth S. Lorek, "The Relationship Between Time Series Models and the Security Market's Expectations of Quarterly Earnings," *Accounting Review,* 59, no. 2 (April 1984): 163–176.

[19] Although the definition of what constitutes an "industry" differs from one study to another, various authors have found that security price movements can be attributed not only to market price movements but also to industry price movements. See Alexander and Francis, *Portfolio Analysis,* pp. 195–196, for a description of these studies and the relevant citations.

[20] Victor Niederhoffer and Patrick J. Regan, "Earnings Changes, Analysts' Forecasts, and Stock Prices," *Financial Analysts Journal,* 28, no. 3 (May–June 1972): 65–71. It should be noted that the entire June/September 1992 issue of the *Journal of Accounting and Economics* is devoted to an examination of how stock prices are related to earnings and other financial statement information.

[21] Another study using data from 1980 and 1981 reached similar conclusions. That is, the top 50 stocks had forecasted and actual earnings growth rates of 14.3% and 31.3%, respectively. For the bottom 50 stocks the respective rates were 17.4% and -10.3%. See Gary A. Benesh and Pamela P. Peterson, "On the Relation Between Earnings Changes, Analysts' Forecasts and Stock Price Fluctuations," *Financial Analysts Journal,* 42, no. 6 (November/December 1986): 29–39, 55.

[22] George Foster, Chris Olsen, and Terry Shevlin, "Earnings Releases, Anomalies, and the Behavior of Security Returns," *Accounting Review,* 59, no. 4 (October 1984): 574–603. For a related paper, see Roger Kormendi and Robert Lipe, "Earnings Innovations, Earnings Persistence, and Stock Returns," *Journal of Business,* 60, no. 3 (July 1987): 323–345.

[23] Assume that a firm's earnings are normally distributed and that this distribution remains unchanged over time. Accordingly, 67% of the actual earnings should fall within one standard deviation of the firm's expected earnings. Equivalently, 67% of the SUEs should be less than 1.0. Similarly, 95% of the SUEs should be less than 2.0.

[24] Studies have shown that earnings announcements containing "good news" are often made earlier than expected, while those containing "bad news" are often made later than expected. These studies also show that the "timeliness" (defined as the difference between the actual announcement date and the expected announcement date) affects the size of the abnormal return. Interestingly, around the time of earnings announcements there appears to be both increased trading volume and increased variability in security returns. See George Foster, *Financial Statement Analysis* (Englewood Cliffs, NJ: Prentice Hall, 1986): 377–386; and V. V. Chari, Ravi Jagannathan, and Aharon Ofer, "Seasonalities in Security Returns: The Case of Earnings Announcements," *Journal of Financial Economics,* 21, no. 1 (May 1988): 101–121.

[25] One article argues that the post-earnings-announcement drift should be listed with the set of empirical regularities described in the appendix to Chapter 17. See Charles P. Jones and Bruce Bublitz, "The CAPM and Equity Return Regularities: An Extension," *Financial Analysts Journal,* 43, no. 3 (May/June 1987): 77–79.

[26] Lawrence D. Brown and Michael S. Rozeff, "The Superiority of Analyst Forecasts as Measures of Expectations: Evidence from Earnings," *Journal of Finance,* 33, no. 1 (March 1978): 1–16.

[27] Value Line also ranks stocks in terms of their relative attractiveness as investments. For a discussion of the usefulness of the Value Line rankings, see the appendix.

[28] Patricia C. O'Brien, "Analysts' Forecasts as Earnings Expectations," *Journal of Accounting and Economics*, 10, no. 1 (January 1988): 53–83.

[29] The observation that analysts (1) tend to be too optimistic in their EPS forecasts, (2) tend to revise these forecasts downward, and (3) issue far more buy than sell recommendations has been documented in several places. See, for example, John C. Groth, Wilbur G. Lewellen, Gary Schlarbaum, and Ronald C. Lease, "An Analysis of Brokerage House Recommendations," *Financial Analysts Journal*, 35, no. 1 (January/February 1979): 32–40; and Werner F. De Bondt and Richard H. Thaler, "Do Security Analysts Overreact?" *American Economic Review*, 80, no. 2 (May 1990): 52–57. For a counterview, see Michael P. Keane and David E. Runkle, "Are Analysts' Forecasts Rational?", unpublished paper, November 1992, Federal Reserve Bank of Minneapolis.

[30] The discussion that follows draws from Scott E. Stickel, "Reputation and Performance Among Security Analysts," *Journal of Finance*, 47, no. 5 (December 1992): 1811–1836.

[31] The study also found that the median number of firms analyzed by All-Americans and NonAll-Americans was 14 and 8, respectively, and that All-Americans revised their forecasts within a given fiscal year on average every 86 days whereas NonAll-Americans revised them every 93 days.

[32] John M. Hassell and Robert H. Jennings, "Relative Forecast Accuracy and the Timing of Earnings Forecast Announcements," *Accounting Review*, 61, no. 1 (January 1986): 58–75.

[33] Similar to I/B/E/S, Zacks Investment Research provides weekly summaries of earnings forecasts for over 2,000 firms that are provided by analysts at roughly 50 brokerage firms. While Zacks dates forecasts by the date of issuance by the analysts' employers, I/B/E/S dates forecasts by when they receive them.

[34] Edwin J. Elton, Martin J. Gruber, and Mustafa N. Gultekin, "Professional Expectations: Accuracy and Diagnosis of Errors," *Journal of Financial and Quantitative Analysis*, 19, no. 4 (December 1984): 351–363.

[35] Value Line also has a service called *VALUE/SCREEN III* (formerly called *VALUE/SCREEN Plus*) that involves software and periodic updates of their rankings as well as other data. An annual subscription costs $325 for quarterly updates (available only by mail), $465 for monthly updates by mail, $495 for monthly electronic updates, and $1,995 for weekly updates (available only electronically).

[36] For details, see Arnold Bernhard, "Investing in Common Stocks with the Aid of the Value Line Rankings and other Criteria of Stock Value," Arnold Bernhard, New York, 1975.

[37] Thomas E. Copeland and David Mayers, "The Value Line Enigma (1965–1978): A Case Study of Performance Evaluation Issues," *Journal of Financial Economics*, 10, no. 3 (November 1982): 289–321.

[38] A later study found that most of the adjustment actually was in the three-day period after the change. The most notable price movement was associated with those stocks being upgraded from 2 to 1. Other notable but less sizable price movements were associated with upgrades from 3 to 2, and downgrades from 1 to 2 and 2 to 3. See Scott E. Stickel, "The Effect of Value Line Investment Survey Rank Changes on Common Stock Prices," *Journal of Financial Economics*, 14, no. 1 (March 1985): 121–143.

[39] A discussion of transaction costs is contained in Copeland and Mayers, "The Value Line Enigma," pp. 319–320; and Clark Holloway, "A Note on Testing an Aggressive Investment Strategy Using Value Line Ranks," *Journal of Finance*, 36, no. 3 (June 1981): 711–719.

[40] Value Line also provides a measure of the risk of individual securities that is known as Safety Rank. This risk measure was found to be more highly correlated with subsequent returns than either beta or standard deviation, suggesting that it is a more useful measure of risk. See Russell J. Fuller and G. Wenchi Wong, "Traditional versus Theoretical Risk Measures," *Financial Analysts Journal,* 44, no. 2 (March/April 1988): 52–57, 67.

[41] One speculation is that the rankings are simply capturing the size effect by giving higher ranks to smaller firms (the size effect is discussed in the appendix to Chapter 17). However, tests suggest that this is not true. See Gur Huberman and Shmuel Kandel, "Value Line Rank and Firm Size," *Journal of Business,* 60, no. 4 (October 1987): 577–589.

[42] For an argument on why these observations do not violate market efficiency, see Gur Huberman and Shmuel Kandel, "Market Efficiency and Value Line's Record," *Journal of Business,* 63, no. 2 (April 1990): 187–216.

[43] See John Affleck-Graves and Richard R. Mendenhall, "The Relation Between the Value Line Enigma and Post-Earnings-Announcement Drift," *Journal of Financial Economics,* 31, no. 1 (February 1992): 75–96.

KEY TERMS

dividend decision
asymmetric information
information content of dividends
   hypothesis
accounting earnings
earnings per share
return on equity
economic earnings

economic value of the firm
generally accepted accounting
   principles
random walk model
market beta
accounting beta
standardized unexpected earnings
abnormal return

REFERENCES

1. The seminal paper on dividend policy that established both the "dividend irrelevancy theorem" and the notion that earnings are the basis for the market value of the firm was written by two Nobel laureates in economics:

   Merton H. Miller and Franco Modigliani, "Dividend Policy, Growth, and the Valuation of Shares," *Journal of Business,* 34, no. 4 (October 1961): 411–433.

2. The Lintner Model of dividend behavior and some studies that empirically tested it are:

   John Lintner, "Distribution of Incomes of Corporations Among Dividends, Retained Earnings, and Taxes," *American Economic Review,* 46, no. 2 (May 1956): 97–113.

   John A. Brittain, *Corporate Dividend Policy* (Washington, DC: The Brookings Institution, 1966).

Eugene F. Fama and Harvey Babiak, "Dividend Policy: An Empirical Analysis," *Journal of the American Statistical Association,* 63, no. 324 (December 1968): 1132–1161.

Eugene F. Fama, "The Empirical Relationship Between the Dividend and Investment Decisions of Firms," *American Economic Review,* 64, no. 3 (June 1974): 304–318.

Terry A. Marsh and Robert C. Merton, "Dividend Behavior for the Aggregate Stock Market," *Journal of Business,* 60, no. 1 (January 1987): 1–40.

3. The determinants of recent dividend behavior appear to be similar to those in the Lintner Model from the 1950s, according to:

H. Kent Baker, Gail E. Farrelly, and Richard B. Edelman, "A Survey of Management Views on Dividend Policy," *Financial Management,* 14, no. 3 (Autumn 1985): 78–84.

4. A summary of the literature on signaling can be found in:

Thomas E. Copeland and J. Fred Weston, *Financial Theory and Corporate Policy* (Reading, MA: Addison-Wesley, 1988), 501–507, 584–588.

5. The information content of dividends hypothesis, closely linked to the signaling literature, has been the subject of much research. Some of the more important papers are:

R. Richardson Pettit, "Dividend Announcements, Security Performance, and Capital Market Efficiency," *Journal of Finance,* 27, no. 5 (December 1972): 993–1007.

Ross Watts, "The Information Content of Dividends," *Journal of Business,* 46, no. 2 (April 1973): 191–211.

Joseph Aharony and Itzak Swary, "Quarterly Dividend and Earnings Announcements and Stockholders' Returns: An Empirical Analysis," *Journal of Finance,* 35, no. 1 (March 1980): 1–12.

Clarence C. Y. Kwan, "Efficient Market Tests of the Informational Content of Dividend Announcements: Critique and Extension," *Journal of Financial and Quantitative Analysis,* 16, no. 2 (June 1981): 193–206.

Paul Asquith and David W. Mullins, Jr., "The Impact of Initiating Dividend Payments on Shareholders' Wealth," *Journal of Business,* 56, no. 1 (January 1983): 77–96.

James A. Brickley, "Shareholder Wealth, Information Signaling and the Specially Designated Dividend: An Empirical Study," *Journal of Financial Economics,* 12, no. 2 (August 1983): 187–209.

J. Randall Woolridge, "Dividend Changes and Stock Prices," *Journal of Finance,* 38, no. 5 (December 1983): 1607–1615.

Terry E. Dielman and Henry R. Oppenheimer, "An Examination of Investor Behavior During Periods of Large Dividend Changes," *Journal of Financial and Quantitative Analysis,* 19, no. 2 (June 1984): 197–216.

Paul M. Healy and Krishna G. Palepu, "Earnings Information Conveyed by Dividend Initiations and Omissions," *Journal of Financial Economics,* 21, no. 2 (September 1988): 149–175.

P. C. Venkatesh, "The Impact of Dividend Initiation on the Information Content of Earnings Announcements and Returns Volatility," *Journal of Business,* 62, no. 2 (April 1989): 175–197.

Larry H. P. Lang and Robert H. Litzenberger, "Dividend Announcements: Cash Flow Signalling vs. Free Cash Flow Hypothesis," *Journal of Financial Economics,* 24, no. 1 (September 1989): 181–191.

Harry DeAngelo, Linda DeAngelo, and Douglas J. Skinner, "Dividends and Losses," *Journal of Finance,* 47, no. 5 (December 1992): 1837–1863.

Keith M. Howe, Jia He, and G. Wenchi Kao, "One-Time Cash Flow Announcements and Free Cash-Flow Theory: Share Repurchases and Special Dividends," *Journal of Finance,* 47, no. 5 (December 1992): 1963–1975.

6. The relationship between economic and accounting earnings is discussed in:

Fischer Black, "The Magic in Earnings: Economic Earnings versus Accounting Earnings," *Financial Analysts Journal,* 36, no. 6 (November/December 1980): 19–24.

7. For a study on the timing of dividend announcements as well as a listing of other studies concerning dividend announcements, see:

Avner Kalay and Uri Loewenstein, "The Informational Content of the Timing of Dividend Announcements," *Journal of Financial Economics,* 16, no. 3 (July 1986): 373–388.

Aharon R. Ofer and Daniel R. Siegel, "Corporate Financial Policy, Information, and Market Expectations: An Empirical Investigation of Dividends," *Journal of Finance,* 42, no. 4 (September 1987): 889–911.

8. For a review of the literature dealing with dividends, see:

James S. Ang, *Do Dividends Matter? A Review of Corporate Dividend Theories and Evidence,* Monograph Series in Finance and Economics #1987–2, New York University Salomon Center, Leonard N. Stern School of Business.

9. For a discussion of price-earnings ratios, see:

William Beaver and Dale Morse, "What Determines Price-Earnings Ratios?" *Financial Analysts Journal,* 34, no. 4 (July/August 1978): 65–76.

William H. Beaver, *Financial Reporting: An Accounting Revolution* (Englewood Cliffs, NJ: Prentice Hall, 1981), Chapters 4 and 5.

George Foster, *Financial Statement Analysis* (Englewood Cliffs, NJ: Prentice Hall, 1986), 437–442.

Paul Zarowin, "What Determines Earnings-Price Ratios: Revisited," *Journal of Accounting, Auditing, and Finance,* 5, no. 3 (Summer 1990): 439–454.

Peter D. Easton and Trevor S. Harris, "Earnings as an Explanatory Variable for Returns," *Journal of Accounting Research,* 29, no. 1 (Spring 1991): 19–36.

10. Time-series models of annual and quarterly earnings per share are discussed in:

George Foster, "Quarterly Accounting Data: Time-Series Properties and Predictive-Ability Results," *Accounting Review,* 52, no. 1 (January 1977): 1–21.

George Foster, *Financial Statement Analysis* (Englewood Cliffs, NJ: Prentice Hall, 1986), Chapter 7.

Ross L. Watts and Jerold L. Zimmerman, *Positive Accounting Theory* (Englewood Cliffs, NJ: Prentice Hall, 1986), Chapter 6.

11. The relationship between market betas and accounting betas has been explored by:

Ray Ball and Philip Brown, "Portfolio Theory and Accounting," *Journal of Accounting Research,* 7, no. 2 (Autumn 1969): 300–323.

William Beaver and James Manegold, "The Association Between Market-Determined and Accounting-Determined Measures of Systematic Risk: Some Further Evidence," *Journal of Financial and Quantitative Analysis,* 10, no. 2 (June 1975): 231–284.

12. The relationship between earnings announcements and stock prices has been documented in many studies. See the following as well as their citations:

Ray Ball and Philip Brown, "An Empirical Evaluation of Accounting Income Numbers," *Journal of Accounting Research,* 6, no. 2 (Autumn 1968): 159–178.

William H. Beaver, "The Information Content of Annual Earnings Announcements," *Empirical Research in Accounting: Selected Studies,* Supplement to *Journal of Accounting Research,* 6 (1968): 67–92.

Leonard Zacks, "EPS Forecasts—Accuracy Is Not Enough," *Financial Analysts Journal,* 35, no. 2 (March/April 1979): 53–55.

Dale Morse, "Price and Trading Volume Reaction Surrounding Earnings Announcements: A Closer Examination," *Journal of Accounting Research,* 19, no. 2 (Autumn 1981): 374–383.

James M. Patell and Mark A. Wolfson, "The Ex Ante and Ex Post Effects of Quarterly Earnings Announcements Reflected in Stock and Option Prices," *Journal of Accounting Research,* 19, no. 2 (Autumn 1981): 434–458.

Richard J. Rendleman, Jr., Charles P. Jones, and Henry A. Latane, "Empirical Anomalies Based on Unexpected Earnings and the Importance of Risk Adjustments," *Journal of Financial Economics,* 10, no. 3 (November 1982): 269–287.

James M. Patell and Mark A. Wolfson, "The Intraday Speed of Adjustment of Stock Prices to Earnings and Dividend Announcements," *Journal of Financial Economics,* 13, no. 2 (June 1984): 223–252.

George Foster, Chris Olsen, and Terry Shevlin, "Earnings Releases, Anomalies, and the Behavior of Security Returns," *Accounting Review,* 59, no. 4 (October 1984): 574–603.

Catherine S. Woodruff and A. J. Senchack, Jr., "Intradaily Price-Volume Adjustments of NYSE Stocks to Unexpected Earnings," *Journal of Finance,* 43, no. 2 (June 1988): 467–491.

The entire issue of the *Journal of Accounting and Economics,* 15, no. 2/3 (June/September 1992).

13. Some of the studies that have examined possible explanations for the "post-earnings-announcement drift" in stock prices are:

Richard J. Rendleman, Jr., Charles P. Jones, and Henry A. Latane, "Further Insight into the Standardized Unexpected Earnings Anomaly: Size and Serial Correlation Effects," *Financial Review,* 22, no. 1 (February 1987): 131–144.

Victor L. Bernard and Jacob K. Thomas, "Post-Earnings-Announcement Drift: Delayed Price Response or Risk Premium?" *Journal of Accounting Research,* 27 (Supplement 1989): 1–36.

Robert N. Freeman and Senyo Tse, "The Multiperiod Information Content of Accounting Earnings: Confirmations and Contradictions of Previous Earnings Reports," *Journal of Accounting Research,* 27 (Supplement 1989): 49–79.

Victor L. Bernard and Jacob K. Thomas, "Evidence That Stock Prices Do Not Fully Reflect the Implications of Current Earnings for Future Earnings," *Journal of Accounting and Economics,* 13, no. 4 (December 1990): 305–340.

Richard R. Mendenhall, "Evidence on the Possible Underweighting of Earnings-Related Information," *Journal of Accounting Research,* 29, no. 1 (Spring 1991): 170–179.

Ray Ball, "The Earnings-Price Anomaly," *Journal of Accounting and Economics,* 15, no. 2/3 (June/September 1992): 319–345.

Jeffery S. Abarbanell and Victor L. Bernard, "Tests of Analysts' Overreaction/Underreaction to Earnings Information as an Explanation for Anomalous Stock Price Behavior," *Journal of Finance,* 47, no. 3 (July 1992): 1181–1207.

14. There have been numerous studies concerning the earnings forecasts made by security analysts and management. Some of the studies are:

Lawrence D. Brown and Michael S. Rozeff, "The Superiority of Analyst Forecasts as Measures of Expectations: Evidence from Earnings," *Journal of Finance,* 33, no. 1 (March 1978): 1–16.

Lawrence D. Brown and Michael S. Rozeff, "Analysts Can Forecast Accurately!", *Journal of Portfolio Management,* 6, no. 3 (Spring 1980): 31–34.

John G. Cragg and Burton G. Malkiel, *Expectations and the Structure of Share Prices* (Chicago: University of Chicago Press, 1982), particularly pp. 85–86 and 165.

Dan Givoly and Josef Lakonishok, "Properties of Analysts' Forecasts of Earnings: A Review and Analysis of the Research," *Journal of Accounting Literature,* 3 (Spring 1984): 117–152.

Dan Givoly and Josef Lakonishok, "The Quality of Analysts' Forecasts of Earnings," *Financial Analysts Journal,* 40, no. 5 (September/October 1984): 40–47.

Philip Brown, George Foster, and Eric Noreen, *Security Analyst Multi-Year Earnings Forecasts and the Capital Markets* (Sarasota, FL: American Accounting Association, 1985).

John M. Hassell and Robert H. Jennings, "Relative Forecast Accuracy and the Timing of Earnings Forecast Announcements," *Accounting Review*, 61, no. 1 (January 1986): 58–75.

Gary A. Benesh and Pamela P. Peterson, "On the Relation Between Earnings Changes, Analysts' Forecasts and Stock Price Fluctuations," *Financial Analysts Journal*, 42, no. 6 (November/December 1986): 29–39, 55.

Lawrence D. Brown, Robert L. Hagerman, Paul A. Griffin, and Mark Zmijewski, "Security Analyst Superiority Relative to Univariate Time-Series Models in Forecasting Quarterly Earnings," *Journal of Accounting and Economics*, 9, no. 1 (April 1987): 61–87.

Robert Conroy and Robert Harris, "Consensus Forecasts of Corporate Earnings: Analysts' Forecasts and Time-Series Methods," *Management Science*, 33, no. 6 (June 1987): 725–738.

Lawrence D. Brown, Robert L. Hagerman, Paul A. Griffin, and Mark Zmijewski, "An Evaluation of Alternative Proxies for the Market's Assessment of Unexpected Earnings," *Journal of Accounting and Economics*, 9, no. 2 (July 1987): 159–193.

Patricia C. O'Brien, "Analysts' Forecasts as Earnings Expectations," *Journal of Accounting and Economics*, 10, no. 1 (January 1988): 53–83.

Werner F. De Bondt and Richard H. Thaler, "Do Security Analysts Overreact?", *American Economic Review*, 80, no. 2 (May 1990): 52–57.

Lawrence D. Brown and Kwon-Jung Kim, "Timely Aggregate Analyst Forecasts as Better Proxies for Market Earnings Expectations," *Journal of Accounting Research*, 29, no. 2 (Autumn 1991): 382–385.

Ashiq Ali, April Klein, and James Rosenfeld, "Analysts' Use of Information about Permanent and Transitory Earnings Components in Forecasting Annual EPS," *Accounting Review*, 67, no. 1 (January 1992): 183–198.

Scott E. Stickel, "Reputation and Performance Among Security Analysts," *Journal of Finance*, 47, no. 5 (December 1992): 1811–1836.

15. For a description of the analyst forecasts published by Value Line, I/B/E/S, and others, see:

Donna R. Philbrick and William E. Ricks, "Using Value Line and IBES Analyst Forecasts in Accounting Research," *Journal of Accounting Research*, 29, no. 2 (Autumn 1991): 397–417.

John Markese, "The Role of Earnings Forecasts in Stock Price Behavior," *AAII Journal*, 14, no. 4 (April 1992): 30–32.

16. As the endnotes to the appendix show, the Value Line Investment Survey has been intensively scrutinized. Those who would like to learn more about Value Line can purchase the following software manual (directly from Value Line or in a shrink-wrap package with this textbook through Prentice Hall) and user's guide:

Value Line, Inc., *VALUE/SCREEN Plus* (Englewood Cliffs, NJ: Prentice Hall, 1990).

Gerald P. Madden, *Investment Analysis with VALUE/SCREEN Plus* (Englewood Cliffs, NJ: Prentice Hall, 1991).

Options

In the world of investments, an **option** is a type of contract between two people where one person grants the other person the right to buy a specific asset at a specific price within a specific time period. Alternatively, the contract may grant the other person the right to sell a specific asset at a specific price within a specific time period. The person who has received the right, and thus has a decision to make, is known as the option buyer because he or she must pay for this right. The person who has sold the right, and thus must respond to the buyer's decision, is known as the option writer.

The variety of contracts containing an option feature is enormous. Even within the domain of publicly traded securities, many types can be found. Traditionally only certain instruments are referred to as options; the others, though similar in nature, are designated differently. This chapter presents an introduction to the institutional features of option contracts, along with some basics regarding how they are valued in the marketplace.

20.1   TYPES OF OPTION CONTRACTS

The two most basic types of option contracts are known as calls and puts. Currently such contracts are traded on many exchanges around the world. Furthermore, many of these contracts are created privately (that is, "off exchange" or "over the counter"), typically involving financial institutions or investment banking firms and their clients. A brief introduction to calls and puts follows.

20.1.1 Call Options

The most prominent type of option contract is the **call option** for stocks. It gives the buyer the right to buy ("call away") a specific number of shares of a specific company from the option writer at a specific purchase price at any time up to and including a specific date. Note how the contract specifies four items:

1. the company whose shares can be bought;
2. the number of shares that can be bought;
3. the purchase price for those shares, known as the **exercise price** (or striking price);
4. the date when the right to buy expires, known as the **expiration date.**

Example

Consider a simple hypothetical example where investors B and W are thinking about signing a call option contract. This contract will allow B to buy 100 shares of Widget from W for $50 per share at any time during the next six months. Currently Widget is selling for $45 per share on an organized exchange. Investor B, the potential option buyer, believes that the price of Widget's common stock will rise substantially over the next six months. Investor W, the potential option writer, has a different opinion about Widget, believing that its stock price will not rise above $50 over this time period.

Will investor W be willing to sign this contract without receiving something in return from investor B? No. W is running a risk by signing the contract and would demand compensation for doing so. The risk is that Widget's stock price will subsequently rise above $50 per share, in which case W will have to buy the shares at that price and then turn them over to B for only $50 per share. Perhaps the stock will rise to $60, costing W $6,000 (= $60 × 100 shares) to buy the stock. Then W will give the 100 shares to B and receive in return $5,000 (= $50 × 100 shares). Consequently W will have lost $1,000 (= $6,000 − $5,000).

The point is that the buyer of a call option will have to pay the writer something in order to get the writer to sign the contract. The amount paid is known as the **premium,** although *option price* is a more appropriate term. In the example, perhaps the premium is $3 per share, meaning that investor B will pay $300 (= $3 × 100 shares) to investor W in order to induce W to sign the contract. Because investor B expects Widget's stock price to rise in the future, he or she would expect to make money by purchasing shares of Widget at $45 per share. The attraction of purchasing call options instead of shares is that investor B can apply a high degree of leverage, since only $3 per share needs to be spent in order to purchase the option.

At some point in time after investors B and W have signed the call option contract, investor W might like to get out of the contract. Because breaching the contract is illegal, how can this be done? Investor W could buy the contract back from investor B for a negotiated amount of money and then destroy the document. If Widget rises in one month to $55 per share, perhaps the amount will be $7 per share [or, in total, $700 (= $7 × 100 shares)]. In this case, W will have lost $400 (= $300 − $700) and B will have made $400. Alternatively, if Widget falls to $40 per share, perhaps the amount will be $.50 per share [or, in total, $50 (= $.50 × 100 shares)], in which case W will have made $250 (= $300 − $50) and B will have lost $250.

Another way that W can get out of the contract is to find someone else to take his or her position in the contract (assuming that the contract has a provision that allows this to be done). For example, if Widget has risen to $55 per share after one month, perhaps investor W will find an investor, denoted WW, who is willing to become the option writer if W will pay him or her $7 per share (or $700 in total). Assuming that they both agree, the contract will be amended so that WW is now the option writer, with W no longer being a party in the contract.

What if investor B subsequently wants to get out of the contract? In this case, B could look and see if someone is willing to pay an agreeable sum of money in order to possess the right to buy Widget stock under the terms of the contract—that is, B could attempt to sell the contract to someone else. In this situation, perhaps investor B will find another investor, denoted BB, who is willing to pay B $7 per share (or $700 in total) in return for the right to buy Widget under the terms of the call option contract. Provided that B is agreeable, the call option contract will be sold to BB and amended, making BB the option buyer.

In this example, both of the original parties, W and B, have "closed out" (or "offset" or "unwound") their positions and are no longer involved in the call option contract. However, the example suggests that the original writer and buyer must meet face to face in order to draw up the terms of the contract. It also suggests that if either the original writer or buyer wants to get out of the contract, then he or she must reach an agreeable price with the other original party or, alternatively, find a third investor to whom he or she can transfer the position in the contract. Thus it would appear that there is a great amount of effort involved if an investor wants to deal in options.

Role of Exchanges

Fortunately this is not the case in the United States because of the introduction of *standardized contracts* and the maintenance of a relatively liquid marketplace by organized exchanges for listed options.[1] The Options Clearing Corporation (OCC), a company that is jointly owned by several exchanges, greatly facilitates trading in these options. It does so by maintaining a computer system that keeps track of all of these options by recording the position of each investor in each one. Although the mechanics are rather complex, the principles are simple enough. As soon as a buyer and a writer decide to trade a particular option contract and the buyer pays the agreed-upon premium, the OCC steps in, becoming the effective writer as far as the buyer is concerned and the effective buyer as far as the writer is concerned. Thus at this time all direct links between original buyer and writer are severed. If a buyer chooses to exercise an option, the OCC will randomly choose a writer who has not closed his or her position and assign the exercise notice accordingly. The OCC also guarantees delivery of stock if the writer is unable to come up with the shares.

The OCC makes it possible for buyers and writers to "close out" their positions at any time. If a buyer subsequently becomes a writer of the same contract, meaning that the buyer later "sells" the contract to someone else, the OCC computer will note the offsetting positions in this investor's account and will simply cancel both entries. Consider an investor who buys a contract on Monday and then sells it on Tuesday. The computer will note that the investor's net position is zero and will remove both entries. The second trade is a **closing sale** because it serves to close out the investor's position from the earlier trade. Closing sales thus allow buyers to sell options rather than exercise them.

A similar procedure allows a writer to pay to be relieved of the potential obligation to deliver stock. Consider an investor who writes a contract on Wednesday and buys an identical one on Thursday. The latter is a **closing purchase** and, analogous to a closing sale, serves to close out the investor's position from the earlier trade.

Stock Split and Dividend Protection

Call options are protected against stock splits and stock dividends on the underlying stock. In the example where the option was on 100 shares of Widget stock with an exercise price of $50, a two-for-one stock split would cause the contract to be altered so that it was for 200 shares at $25 per share. The reason for this protection has to do with the effect that stock splits and stock dividends have on the share price of the firm. Since either of these events will cause the share price to fall below what it otherwise would have been, without adjustment they would work to the disadvantage of the call option buyer and to the advantage of the call option writer.

In terms of cash dividends, there is no protection for listed call options.[2] That is, the exercise price and the number of shares are unaffected by the payment of cash dividends. For example, the terms of the Widget call option would remain the same if Widget declared and paid a $4 per share cash dividend.

20.1.2 Put Options

A second type of option contract for stocks is the **put option.** It gives the buyer the right to sell ("put away") a specific number of shares of a specific company to the option writer at a specific selling price at any time up to and including a specific date. Note how the contract specifies four items that are analogous to those for call options:

1. the company whose shares can be sold;
2. the number of shares that can be sold;
3. the selling price for those shares, known as the exercise price (or striking price);
4. the date when the right to sell expires, known as the expiration date.

An Example

Consider an example where investors B and W are thinking about signing a put option contract. This contract will allow B to sell 100 shares of XYZ Company to W for $30 per share at any time during the next six months. Currently XYZ is

---

selling for $35 per share on an organized exchange. Investor B, the potential option buyer, believes that the price of XYZ's common stock will fall substantially over the next six months. Investor W, the potential option writer, has a different opinion about XYZ, believing that its stock price will not fall below $30 over this time period.

As with the call option on Widget, investor W would be running a risk by signing the contract and would demand compensation for doing so. The risk is that XYZ's stock price will subsequently fall below $30 per share, in which case W will have to buy the shares at $30 per share from B when they are not worth that much in the marketplace. Perhaps XYZ will fall to $20, costing W $3,000 (= $30 × 100 shares) to buy stock that is worth only $2,000 (= $20 × 100 shares). Consequently W would have lost $1,000 (= $3,000 − $2,000). In this case B would make $1,000, purchasing XYZ in the marketplace for $2,000 and then selling the shares to W for $3,000.

As with a call option, the buyer of a put option will have to pay the writer an amount of money known as a premium in order to get the writer to sign the contract and assume this risk. Also as with call options, the buyer and writer may "close out" (or "offset" or "unwind") their positions at any time by simply entering an offsetting transaction. As with calls, this is easily done for listed put options in the United States because these contracts are standardized.

Again, the OCC facilitates trading in listed puts, as these options exist only in the memory of its computer system. As with calls, as soon as a buyer and a writer decide to trade a particular put option contract and the buyer pays the agreed-upon premium, the OCC steps in, becoming the effective writer as far as the buyer is concerned and the effective buyer as far as the writer is concerned. If a buyer chooses to exercise an option, the OCC will randomly choose a writer who has not closed his or her position and assign the exercise notice accordingly. The OCC also guarantees delivery of the exercise price if the writer is unable to come up with the necessary cash.

Like calls, puts are protected against stock splits and stock dividends on the underlying stock. In the example where the option was on 100 shares of XYZ stock with an exercise price of $30, a two-for-one stock split would cause the contract to be altered so that it was for 200 shares at $15 per share. In terms of cash dividends, there is no protection for listed puts.

20.2 OPTION TRADING

Exchanges begin trading a new set of options on a given stock every three months. The newly created options have roughly nine months before they expire.[3] For example, options on Widget might be introduced in January, April, July, and October, with expiration dates in, respectively, September, December, March, and June. Furthermore, the exchange might decide to introduce long-term options on Widget (dubbed LEAPS by the exchanges for long-term equity anticipation securities) that expire as far into the future as two to three years.

Generally, two call options on a stock are introduced at the same time, the two being identical in all respects except for the exercise price. In terms of the exercise price, if the stock is selling for $200 or less at the time the options are to be introduced, then the two exercise prices will be set at $5 intervals bracketing the stock price.[4] Furthermore, a pair of put option contracts may also be introduced at the same time. For example, if Widget is selling for $43 in January, then two September call options may be introduced that have exercise prices of $40 and $45. Similarly, two September put options with exercise prices of $40 and $45 may also be introduced.

After an option has been introduced, new options having the same terms as the existing ones but with different exercise prices may be introduced when the stock price of the company moves up or down so much that it is substantially outside of the initial bracket. In terms of Widget, if its stock price rises in the next month to $49, perhaps September put and call options having a $50 exercise price will be introduced.

Once listed, an option remains listed until its expiration date. Specifically, listed options on common stocks generally expire at 10:59 P.M. Central Time on the Saturday after the third Friday of the specified month.

20.2.1   Trading Activity

In recent years common stock options have been traded on the Chicago Board Options Exchange (CBOE) and on the American, Pacific, Philadelphia, and New York stock exchanges. Figure 20.1 shows a portion of the daily listing of the trading activity on the CBOE. The first column lists the name of the company and, indented below it, the closing price on its common stock. The next column lists the exercise price for the option contracts on the company, followed by a column giving the expiration date. The next two columns give the trading volume and last trade premium for call options having the exercise price and expiration date shown on the left. The last two columns give the trading volume and last trade premium for the matching put option.

For example, Best Buy common stock closed at $40.125 on December 13, 1993. By the end of that day, 180 Best Buy call option contracts having an exercise price of $45 per share that expire on the third Friday of March of 1994 had been traded. The closing trade that day took place at $3.375 per share (or $337.50 per contract). Similarly, 120 Best Buy put option contracts with the same exercise price ($45) and expiration date (March 1994) had been traded. The closing trade was at $7.00 per share (or $700 per contract).

Some options are not traded during a day and are indicated by three periods " . . .". Others, while included because of the format of the report, have not been introduced and are therefore unavailable for trading. These contracts are also indicated by the three periods. Hence when nothing is reported (see, for example, Best Buy March 35 calls in Figure 20.1), it cannot be determined whether this is because there was no trading or the contracts simply do not exist.

At the bottom of the listings, the total volume (that is, the number of contracts traded) and the open interest (the number of contracts outstanding) for calls and puts are displayed for each exchange and overall.

Composite volume and close for actively traded equity and LEAPS, or long-term options, with results for the corresponding put or call contract. Volume figures are unofficial. Open interest is total outstanding for all exchanges and reflects previous trading day. Close when possible is shown for the underlying stock on primary market. CB-Chicago Board Options Exchange. AM-American Stock Exchange. PB-Philadelphia Stock Exchange. PC-Pacific Stock Exchange. NY-New York Stock Exchange. XC-Composite. p-Put.

Option/Strike	Exp.	Call Vol.	Call Last	Put Vol.	Put Last
A Hess 45	Jan	30	15/16	...	...
A M D 15	Apr	2	4¼	91	15/16
18⅛ 17½	Dec	...	...	35	3/16
18⅛ 17½	Jan	29	11/16	26	1
18⅛ 17½	Apr	37	2¾	45	2
18⅛ 17½	Jul	...	...	30	2¼
18⅛ 20	Dec	170	1/16	471	13/16
18⅛ 20	Jan	232	¾	20	2¾
18⅛ 20	Apr	36	1¾	4	3¾
18⅛ 30	Jan	...	...	42	12½
18⅛ 30	Apr	...	...	42	12⅝
A M R 65	Dec	13	3½	63	⅛
68⅜ 70	Dec	41	⅜	10	1⅞
68⅜ 70	Jan	24	1¾	...	...
68⅜ 70	Feb	23	2¾	...	...
68⅜ 70	May	157	4⅝	...	...
A S A 45	Dec	77	5	...	...
49⅞ 45	Jan	100	5⅝	52	⅜
49⅞ 45	Feb	97	5¾	14	15/16
49⅞ 45	May	5	7⅜	33	2
49⅞ 50	Dec	342	⅝	33	¾
49⅞ 50	Jan	309	2⅛	148	2¼
49⅞ 50	Feb	54	3	29	2¾
49⅞ 55	Dec	50	1/16	...	...
49⅞ 55	Jan	32	¾	15	5¼
49⅞ 55	Feb	67	1⅛	...	...
ABrrck 22½	Jan	5	6⅛	50	⅛
28⅜ 25	Dec	93	3½	...	...
28⅜ 25	Jan	91	3⅞	45	7/16
28⅜ 25	Apr	46	5	1017	1 1/16
28⅜ 30	Dec	57	⅛	101	13/16
28⅜ 30	Jan	341	15/16	107	2⅜
28⅜ 30	Apr	1204	2 1/16	112	3⅝
28⅜ 30	Jul	37	3¼	...	...
28⅜ 35	Apr	80	⅞	...	...
BestBuy 35	Dec	26	5⅝	11	¼
40⅛ 35	Mar	...	...	122	2⅛
40⅛ 40	Dec	286	1½	501	1 7/16
40⅛ 40	Jan	86	4	181	3¼
40⅛ 40	Mar	64	6	9	4⅜
40⅛ 45	Dec	994	¼	329	4¾
40⅛ 45	Jan	313	2	19	6
40⅛ 45	Mar	180	3⅜	120	7
40⅛ 50	Dec	605	1/16	189	9½
40⅛ 50	Jan	344	13/16	10	9½
40⅛ 50	Mar	92	2⅛	72	10⅝
40⅛ 55	Dec	...	...	38	14
40⅛ 55	Jan	90	⅜	...	...
40⅛ 55	Mar	31	½	...	...
Beth S 17½	Jan	71	1¼	...	...
18⅜ 20	Jan	50	5/16	...	...
BetzLb 45	Jan	50	⅞	...	...
Bevrly 12½	Dec	36	9/16	...	...
12⅞ 12½	Jan	33	1 1/16	10	7/16
12⅞ 15	Jun	35	¾	...	...
BioTcG 5	Feb	115	½	...	...
5 7½	May	90	⅜	...	...
Biogen 25	Apr	30	15¼	...	...
40⅛ 30	Jul	30	11¾	...	...
Biomet 10	Dec	100	1⅛	...	...
11⅛ 12½	Jan	54	⅜	5	1⅝
11⅛ 12½	Apr	153	15/16	...	...
11⅛ 12½	Jul	73	15/16	5	2 3/16
BkBost 22½	Dec	70	⅜	520	¼
22½ 22½	Jan	28	1	440	¾
BkrsLH 22½	Jan	...	...	200	1
22¾ 25	Jan	200	½	...	...
BkrsTr 80	Dec	...	...	24	3
Blk Dk 20	Jan	...	...	35	½
20⅛ 20	Feb	...	...	75	⅞
22⅞ 30	Feb	106	½	...	...
CmprsL 12½	Jan	...	...	25	9/16
Cnseco 50	Dec	40	6⅞	...	...
55¾ 50	Jan	10	7¾	157	1¼
55¾ 50	Feb	47	8½	80	2⅜
55¾ 55	Dec	70	1½	35	⅞
55¾ 55	Jan	60	3⅞	1	2⅝
55¾ 55	Feb	50	6¼	11	4
55¾ 60	Dec	35	5/16	10	4¼
55¾ 60	Jan	80	2	...	...
55¾ 65	Feb	127	1⅞	...	...
CntCrd 25	Dec	45	1⅞	...	...
Cntocr 7½	Apr	200	5½	...	...
12¼ 10	Jan	144	2¾	10	5/16
12¼ 12½	Dec	584	⅜	10	⅝
12¼ 12½	Jan	450	1¼	5	1 1/16
12¼ 12½	Apr	20	2⅝	55	2
12¼ 15	Dec	27	1/16	10	2 3/16
12¼ 15	Jan	37	½	10	2 7/16
12¼ 15	Apr	145	1¼	...	...
12¼ 15	Jul	25	1⅞	...	...
CocaCE 15	Feb	30	5/16	...	...
Coke 32½	Jan	57	11⅛	...	...
43¾ 40	Jan	50	3⅞	310	3/16
43¾ 40	Feb	1	4⅜	35	7/16
43¾ 45	Jan	163	⅝	15	1⅞
43¾ 45	Feb	51	15/16	...	...
43¾ 45	May	126	1¾	100	2¾
43¾ 50	Feb	100	⅛	...	...
ColHsp 30	Jan	5	2½	110	¼
33¼ 30	Feb	392	13/16	...	...
33¼ 35	Feb	71	¾	...	...
ColuGs 20	Jan	100	3¾	...	...
Comcst 30	Dec	50	3⅝	...	...
34½ 35	Jan	120	1 7/16	27	2⅛

Figure 20.1

Listed Options Quotations (Excerpt)

Source: Reprinted by permission of *The Wall Street Journal,* ©Dow Jones & Company, Inc., December 14, 1993, p. C13. All rights reserved worldwide.

20.2.2 Most Active Options

Additional information besides the trading activity for options that is shown in Figure 20.1 is provided every day for the "most active" options. Figure 20.2 provides an example of the most active options on December 13, 1993. After the name of the company and the contract specifications come the trading volume on the contract on that day, the exchange on which the option is traded, the closing price on the contract, the change this represents from the previous day's closing price, the closing price on the underlying stock, and the open interest in that contract.

For example, IBM December 55 calls that are traded on the CBOE were the most active issue on December 13, 1993. On that day, 9,869 of these contracts were traded. The premium on the last trade was $2.4375 per share (or $243.75 per contract). This represents an increase of $1.4375 from the last trade premium on the previous trading day. On December 13, 1993, the closing price on the common stock of IBM was $57.375 per share.

Investors may place the same kinds of orders for options as for stocks—market, limit, stop, and stop limit orders. (These were discussed in Chapter 2.) However, the way that the orders for options are executed on the exchanges is, in some cases, different from the way that orders for stocks are executed.

MOST ACTIVE CONTRACTS

Option/Strike		Vol	Exch	Last		Net Chg	a-Close	Open Int	Option/Strike		Vol	Exch	Last		Net Chg	a-Close	Open Int
I B M	Dec 55	9,869	CB	$2^{7}/_{16}$ +	$1^{7}/_{16}$	57⅜	18,971	Intel	Dec 55	p 2,248	AM	$^{5}/_{16}$ −	$^{5}/_{16}$	57½	13,576
TelMex	Dec 65	8,300	XC	$^{1}/_{16}$	...	61½	3,743	ParaCm	Jan 60	2,030	CB	20⅞ −	⅞	80⅜	3,689
I B M	Jan 60	7,597	CB	$1^{5}/_{16}$ +	$^{9}/_{16}$	57⅜	11,106	Merck	Jan 30	1,925	CB	3 −	¼	32⅞	18,264
I B M	Jan 55	6,281	CB	3⅝ +	1¼	57⅜	24,217	Seagte	Dec 20	1,858	AM	$1^{5}/_{16}$ +	$1^{1}/_{16}$	21	2,740
TelMex	Dec 60	5,511	XC	1⅝ +	$^{5}/_{16}$	61½	28,533	ParaCm	Jan 85	1,765	CB	1⅛ −	$^{3}/_{16}$	80⅜	15,808
ParaCm	Dec 80	5,057	CB	$1^{13}/_{16}$ −	⅞	80⅜	28,674	I B M	Jan 50	1,739	CB	7¾ +	2	57⅜	22,102
I B M	Jan 45	4,671	CB	12⅝ +	2⅛	57⅜	20,567	ParaCm	Dec 65	1,713	CB	15½ −	⅞	80⅜	11,789
ParaCm	Dec 85	4,460	CB	$^{3}/_{16}$ −	⅛	80⅜	24,715	F N M	Dec 75	1,704	PB	4⅛ +	⅜	79¼	7,574
I B M	Dec 45	4,103	CB	12½ +	2⅝	57⅜	7,164	F N M	Jan 75	1,687	PB	5⅛ +	¼	79¼	905
Intel	Jan 60	3,891	AM	$1^{15}/_{16}$ +	¼	57½	15,174	I B M	Dec 60	1,658	CB	¼ +	$^{3}/_{16}$	57⅜	5,067
Intel	Jan 50	p 3,584	AM	½ −	$^{5}/_{16}$	57½	9,803	TelMex	Jan 60	1,623	XC	3 +	$^{3}/_{16}$	61½	25,286
ParaCm	Jan 80	3,037	CB	3⅛ −	⅝	80⅜	13,602	ParaCm	Dec 75	p 1,613	CB	$^{3}/_{16}$ −	⅛	80⅜	14,403
LAC	Apr 7½	3,016	CB	2½ +	⅜	9⅛	1,470	Merck	Apr 30	p 1,596	CB	⅞	...	32⅞	5,084
Merck	Jan 35	2,756	CB	½	...	32⅞	37,167	I B M	Jan 55	p 1,547	CB	$1^{1}/_{16}$ −	⅞	57⅜	6,945
I B M	Dec 55	p 2,723	CB	⅛ −	⅝	57⅜	6,971	AppleC	Jan 30	1,540	AM	1⅞ +	⅜	29½	6,595
NMedE	Feb 15	2,722	AM	½ +	⅛	13⅝	305	Intel	Dec 60	1,499	AM	$^{3}/_{16}$ −	$^{1}/_{16}$	57½	12,741
NMedE	Dec 12½	2,698	AM	$1^{5}/_{16}$ +	$^{13}/_{16}$	13⅝	2,273	Chryslr	Dec 55	1,440	CB	1⅞ +	¼	56¾	7,117
ParaCm	Dec 75	2,692	CB	5½ −	1	80⅜	19,392	I B M	Apr 55	1,431	CB	5⅛ +	1⅛	57⅜	9,358
TimeW	Dec 45	2,415	PB	$^{3}/_{16}$ −	$^{1}/_{16}$	44½	13,935	BattlM	Jan 10	1,414	XC	$1^{5}/_{16}$ +	$^{3}/_{16}$	10⅝	11,937
Tex In	Dec 55	p 2,250	CB	⅛ −	¼	60	2,696	Willms	Jan 30	1,361	CB	1½ +	¾	26⅝	1,390

Figure 20.2
Most Active Options Quotations
Source: Reprinted by permission of *The Wall Street Journal*, ©Dow Jones & Company, Inc., December 14, 1993, p. C13. All rights reserved worldwide.

20.2.3 Trading on Exchanges

There are two types of exchange-based mechanisms in the United States for trading option contracts. The focal point for trading involves either specialists or market-makers, as will be discussed next.

Use of Specialists

As was mentioned in Chapter 3, trading on stock exchanges centers on specialists. These people serve two functions, acting as both dealers and brokers. As dealers they keep an inventory of the stocks that are assigned to them and buy and sell from that inventory at bid and asked prices, respectively. As brokers they keep the limit order book and execute the orders in it as market prices move up and down. Some option markets, such as the American Stock Exchange, function in a similar manner. These markets have specialists who are assigned specific option contracts, and these specialists act as dealers and brokers in their assigned options. As with the stock exchanges, there may also be **floor traders,** who trade solely for themselves, hoping to buy low and sell high, and **floor brokers,** who handle orders from the public.

Use of Market-Makers

Other option markets, such as the Chicago Board Options Exchange, do not involve specialists. Instead they involve **market-makers,** who act solely as dealers, and **order book officials** (previously known as board brokers), who keep the limit order book. The market-makers must trade with floor brokers, who are members of the exchange that handle orders from the public. In doing so, the market-makers have an inventory of options and quote bid and asked prices. Whereas there is one and only one specialist typically assigned to a stock, there usually is more than one market-maker assigned to the options on a given stock. Furthermore, a market-maker is prohibited from handling public orders in his or her assigned options but may handle public orders in other options. That is, market-makers can also act as floor brokers, but only in unassigned options.

The order book official, in keeping the limit order book, is not allowed to engage in any trading. Unlike the specialist, the order book official's limit order book can be shown to other members of the exchange. The order book official stands at the trading post for those options that are his or her responsibility. All orders must be executed by means of an auction at the trading post with "open outcry," meaning that the auction is conducted orally.

Like the organized stock exchanges in the United States, all option exchanges are continuous markets, meaning that orders can be executed any time the exchanges are open. However, actual trading in options is, on occasion, far from continuous. In the financial press it is not unusual to find prices for various options that appear to be "out of line" with one another or with the price of the underlying stock. It should be remembered that each listed price is that of the last trade of the day, and that these trades may have taken place at different times. Apparent price disparities may simply reflect trades that occurred before and after major news, rather than concurrent values at which obviously profitable trades could have been made.

20.2.4 Commissions

Whereas a commission must be paid to a stockbroker whenever an option is either written, bought, or sold, the size of the commission has been reduced substantially since options began to be traded on organized exchanges in 1973. Furthermore, this commission is typically smaller than the commission that would be paid if the underlying stock had been purchased instead of the option. This is probably due to the fact that clearing and settling are easier with options than with stocks (with options there are no share certificates that have to change hands with every trade) and that the order size is smaller (the total dollar amount paid for the option is much less than the total dollar amount of the underlying stock).[5]

However, the investor should be aware that exercising an option will typically result in the buyer's having to pay a commission equivalent to the commission that would be incurred if the stock itself were being bought or sold.

20.3   MARGIN

Any buyer of an option would like some assurance that the writer can deliver as required if the option is exercised. Specifically, the buyer of a call option would like some assurance that the writer is capable of delivering the requisite shares, and the buyer of a put option would like some assurance that the writer is capable of delivering the necessary cash. Because all option contracts are with the OCC, it is actually the institution concerned with the ability of the writer to fulfill the terms of the contract.

Open Outcry

Is it a scene from a Fellini movie? Or perhaps the crowd at a 90%-off sale at Bloomingdale's? No, it is simply the members of the Chicago Board Options Exchange (CBOE) participating in the time-honored tradition of open outcry.

As the text describes, at the CBOE and other option exchanges (as well as futures exchanges—see Chapter 21), members come together in various trading pits to conduct transactions in specific option contracts. Like the trading posts of the New York Stock Exchange (see Chapter 3), the CBOE trading pits serve as central locations where market-clearing prices for option contracts are continuously determined through an auction process. Unlike the NYSE trading posts, however, the CBOE and most other option exchanges do not use a specialist system. No one individual acts as a monopolistic dealer and auctioneer, ensuring the setting of market-clearing prices. Instead, those prices are established through *open outcry,* a public auction method involving verbal bids and offers initiated by the exchange members in the pit.

Open outcry is a raucous and colorful trading mechanism that combines the mental gymnastics of rapid-fire decision-making with a set of physical skills ranging from strategic positioning in the trading pit to shouting instructions to frenetic hand signaling.

To describe the open outcry system as "the pits" is no exaggeration. The process begins in the trading pits, large depressions in the exchange floor surrounded by several levels of stairs on which the members stand. Although no formal rules are involved, traders generally behave very territorially in the pit. Floor traders usually have certain market-makers with whom they prefer to trade, and these individuals position themselves to make convenient contact with one another. Further, the most senior and important traders take positions in the pit where they have most efficient access to their counterparts. Junior members must stand in less desirable positions, where they are less likely to catch the attention of other traders.

The trading pits are often crowded, noisy, and uncomfortable. Members may jostle each other for position. Hence such attributes as voice strength and physical endurance are important. The pits are dominated by men, and the disadvantages endured by women in this physical environment are not lost on critics of the open outcry system.

Members deliver their trading intentions through a system of verbal orders and hand signals. For example, a floor broker may enter the IBM trading pit and verbally announce his or her intention to purchase June IBM call option contracts at a specified price. At the same time, he or she will typically repeat the buy order and desired price through hand signals. If a market-maker wishes to sell at that price, he or she will signal the desired quantity by hand.

To the uninitiated, the hand gestures used by members appear wild and unintelligible. In actuality, the signals are simple and highly efficient. Buy and sell orders are indicated by the position of the trader's palm(s). If the trader's palms are facing him or her, a buy is signaled. The trader signals a sell by keeping his or her palms pointed outward.

The trader indicates the bid or asked price by holding his or her hand in a vertical position and using fingers to indicate the fraction of a dollar involved. For example, one finger indicates an eighth of a dollar, whereas a closed fist indicates a full dollar.

Traders likewise display their quantity intentions with their hands. In this case, however, fingers pointed vertically indicate one through five contracts, while fingers pointed horizontally indicate six through nine contracts. One finger to the forehead indicates ten contracts.

At any given time, members in the pit may be trading in different option contracts, shouting in an attempt to make their voices heard above the din, and flailing their arms about to signal their trading intentions. Add to this scene runners milling about the edge of the pit, time and sale clerks, price reporters, order book officials keeping track of transactions, and persons situated away from the pit signaling in orders to the floor brokers, and pandemonium hardly seems an adequate description of the trading process.

Open outcry is a controversial trading mechanism. It has been criticized as an archaic method designed primarily to perpetuate control over lucrative option trading by the exchanges' members. In an age of advanced electronics, there are readily available computer systems that could facilitate electronic auctions and permit wider access to the auction process. (For example, in mid-1992 the Chicago Board of Trade and the Chicago Mercantile Exchange initiated a trading system known as Globex. This system involves electronic trading in certain futures contracts that are listed on various exchanges during times when those exchanges are closed. When the exchanges are open, they use an open outcry system that is essentially the same as that used on the CBOE.) The benefits of such electronic auction systems would appear to be lower trading costs and greater liquidity.

Defenders of the open outcry system claim that it is the most efficient method of price discovery. They believe that the system's face-to-face contact permits traders to better ascertain the "true" intentions of buyers and sellers. Moreover, the defenders contend that price manipulation is less likely in an open environment. Whether or not this is true remains an open question.

To relieve the OCC of this concern, margin requirements have been set by the exchanges where the options are traded. However, brokerage firms are allowed to impose even stricter requirements if they so desire, since they are ultimately liable to the OCC for the actions of their investors.

In the case of a call, shares are to be delivered by the writer in return for the exercise price. In the case of a put, cash is to be delivered in return for shares. In either case the net cost to the option writer will be the absolute difference between the exercise price and the stock's market value at the time of exercise. As the OCC is at risk if the writer is unable to bear this cost, it is not surprising that the OCC would have a system in place protecting itself from the actions of the writers. This system is known as margin, and it is in some ways similar to the notion of margin associated with stock purchases and short sales that was discussed in Chapter 2.[6]

20.3.1 Calls

In a situation known as **covered call writing,** where the writer of a call owns the underlying stock, the writer does not need to come up with any cash. Instead, the premium paid by the buyer is given to the writer, but the writer's stock is kept in escrow by the brokerage firm. Thus if the buyer chooses to exercise the option, the requisite shares are at hand for delivery. If the option expires, or if the writer enters a closing purchase, then the writer will have access to the shares.

In a situation known as **naked call writing,** where the writer of a call does not own the underlying stock, the margin requirements are more complicated. Specifically, this involves determining the higher of two figures. The first figure is equal to the option premium plus 20% of the market value of the underlying stock, less an amount equal to the call's exercise price less the stock's market price (provided that the exercise price is larger than the stock's market price). The second figure is equal to the sum of the option premium and 10% of the market price of the underlying stock.

As an example of the margin required for naked call writing, consider an investor who writes a December 60 call and receives a premium of $3 per share. If the underlying stock is selling for $58, then the margin is the higher of two figures calculated as follows:

Method 1:	Option premium	
	= $3 × 100 shares	$300
	20% of market value of stock	
	= .20 × $58 × 100 shares	1,160
	Less amount by which call's exercise price exceeds stock's market price	
	= ($60 − $58) × 100 shares	−200
	Total	$1,260
Method 2:	Option premium	
	= $3 × 100 shares	$300
	10% of market value of stock	
	= .10 × $58 × 100 shares	580
	Total	$880

Because the first method results in a higher figure, it is applicable. Thus in this example the amount of margin required is equal to $1,260, meaning that the writer must deposit $1,260 in cash with his or her broker. Since the premium can be used for this purpose, the writer needs to come up with only $960 (= $1,260 − $300).

20.3.2 Puts

For puts the margin requirements are similar. If the brokerage account of the writer of a put contains cash (or other securities) amounting to the exercise price of the put, then no margin is required. Furthermore, the writer can remove from the account an amount of cash that is equal to the premium received from the buyer. The reason for this is that the account will still have collateral that is equal in value to the exercise price.

If the brokerage account of a put writer does not contain cash (or securities), then the situation is known as **naked put writing.** The amount of margin required for such a writer is calculated in a manner similar to that for the writer of a naked call option—that is, the put writer must come up with margin equal to the larger of two figures. The first figure is equal to the option premium plus 20% of the market value of the underlying stock, less an amount equal to the stock's market price less the put's exercise price. (Note that this last component is the reverse of the amount for a call, and it is subtracted only if the stock's market price is larger than the exercise price.) The second figure is calculated exactly as previously described for calls, being equal to the sum of the option premium and 10% of the market price of the underlying security.

As an example of the margin required for naked put writing, consider an investor who writes a March 40 put and receives a premium of $4 per share. If the underlying stock is selling for $41, then the margin is the higher of two figures calculated as follows:

Method 1: Option premium
         = $4 × 100 shares $400
       20% of market value of stock
         = .20 × $41 × 100 shares   820
       Less amount by which stock's market price
         exceeds put's exercise price
         = ($41 − $40) × 100 shares   − 100
       Total $1,120

Method 2: Option premium
         = $4 × 100 shares $400
       10% of market value of stock
         = .10 × $41 × 100 shares   410
       Total $810

Because the first method results in a higher figure, it is applicable. Thus in this example the amount of margin required is equal to $1,120, meaning that the writer must deposit $1,120 in cash with his or her broker. Since the premium can be used for this purpose, the writer needs to come up with only $720 (= $1,120 − $400).

It should be noted that maintenance margin requirements for options are the same as initial margin requirements. Furthermore, the calculation of margin requirements becomes much more complex when the individual is engaged in various investment activities (such as simultaneously buying and writing different put and call options as well as buying some common stocks on margin while short selling others). Finally, when index options are involved, the margin requirements are reduced (specifically, the 20% figure is reduced to 15%) owing to the fact that index options tend to be less volatile than individual stock options. (Index options are discussed later in the chapter.)

20.4   TAXATION OF OPTION PROFITS AND LOSSES

Although income tax regulations can be quite complex, the general approach to the taxation of profits and losses from option trading is reasonably easy to understand. Usually short-term capital gains and losses are involved because the buying and selling transactions are mostly within one year of each other. Hence the net amount is usually treated as ordinary income if it is a gain and is fully deductible (subject to a $3,000 cap) from ordinary income if it is a loss. Commissions paid are added to purchase prices and subtracted from selling prices in determining the amount of the capital gains and losses.

Consider a call option buyer first. If the call is exercised, the buyer is considered to have bought the stock for a total cost equal to the exercise price plus the premium paid for the option itself. When the stock is subsequently sold, the difference between this cost and the selling price will be the buyer's capital gain or loss.

If the call buyer later sells the option instead of exercising it, the difference between the buying and selling prices is the amount of the capital gain or loss. However, if the call expires unexercised, the buyer will have a capital loss equal to the premium paid on the option.

Consider the writer of a call option next. If the call is exercised, the writer is considered to have sold the stock for a total value equal to the exercise price plus the premium received for the option. The difference between this value and the price paid when the stock was purchased is the amount of the capital gain or loss incurred by the writer.

If the call writer later buys the option, thereby closing out his or her position, the difference between the premium that was received when the option was written and the premium that was paid to close out the position is the amount of the capital gain or loss. However, if the option expires unexercised, then the writer will have a capital gain equal to the amount of the premium received.

The treatment of puts is quite similar. If the put expires unexercised, then the buyer has a capital loss and the writer has a capital gain that are both equal to the premium on the put. If a closing transaction is entered, then the difference between the buying and selling prices is the amount of the capital gain or loss. If the put is exercised, then the buyer has a capital gain equal to the exercise price less the amount paid for both the stock and the put. The writer who receives the stock in this situation is treated as having made a stock purchase for an amount equal to the exercise price less the premium received on the put.

These and other rules give rise to a number of strategies that take tax consequences into account. For example, consider an investor who previously bought a stock and has seen its market price rise dramatically. If the investor sells it now, a capital gain will be incurred. However, the investor could buy a January put and hold off selling the stock until the turn of the year. By doing so, the capital gain will not be realized this year, so no taxes will need to be paid on the stock this year. However, the gain on the stock will have been protected by the use of the put. Once January arrives, the investor can decide to either exercise the put or sell the stock, realizing the gain at that time and thus having deferred tax payments for a year.

20.5.1 Valuation at Expiration

The value of an option is related to the value of the underlying security in a manner that is most easily seen just prior to expiration (which for simplicity will be referred to as "at expiration"). Figure 20.3(a) relates the value of a call option with an exercise price of $100 to the price of the underlying stock at expiration. If the stock price is below $100, the option will be worthless when it expires. If the price is above $100, the option can be exercised for $100 to obtain a security with a greater value, resulting in a net gain to the option buyer that will equal the difference between the security's market price and the $100 exercise price. However, there is no need for the option buyer to actually exercise the option. Instead, the option writer can simply pay the buyer the difference between the security price and the $100 exercise price, thereby allowing both parties to avoid

Figure 20.3
Values of Options at Expiration

the inconvenience of exercise. This is commonly done for listed options (by using the services of the OCC), although a minority of investors choose to exercise their options, possibly for tax purposes.

Figure 20.3(b) shows the value at expiration of a put option with an exercise price of $100. If the stock price is above $100, the option will be worthless when it expires. If the price is below $100, the option can be exercised to obtain $100 for stock having a lower value, resulting in a net gain to the option buyer that will equal the difference between the $100 exercise price and the stock's market price. As with a call option, neither the put option buyer nor the writer need actually deal in the stock. Instead, the writer of any put option that is worth exercising at expiration can simply pay the buyer of the option the difference between the stock price and the $100 exercise price.

In both panels of Figure 20.3, the lines indicating the value of a call and a put at expiration can also be interpreted to be the value of a call or a put *at the moment the option is exercised,* no matter when that occurs during the life of the option. In particular, for calls the kinked line connecting points 0, *E*, and *Z* is known as the **intrinsic value** of the call. Similarly, for puts the kinked line connecting points *Z*, *E*, and $200 is known as the intrinsic value of the put.

The kinked lines representing the intrinsic values of calls and puts such as those shown in Figure 20.3 can be expressed as IV_c and IV_p, respectively, as follows:

$$IV_c = \max \{0, P_s - E\} \tag{20.1a}$$

$$IV_p = \max \{0, E - P_s\} \tag{20.1b}$$

where P_s denotes the market price of the underlying stock and E denotes the exercise price of the option. (Here max means to use the larger of the two values in braces.)

Consider the call option in Figure 20.3(a). Its intrinsic value, according to Equation (20.1a), is max $\{0, P_s - \$100\}$ because its exercise price is $100. Note that for any market price of the stock that is below $100, such as $50, its intrinsic value is max $\{0, \$50 - \$100\} = 0$. Hence $IV_c = 0$ in such situations. Next imagine that the market price of the stock is above $100, for example, $150. In this situation its intrinsic value is max $\{0, \$150 - \$100\} = \$50$. Hence $IV_c = P_s - E$. Thus the kinked intrinsic value line has its kink at E, as it has two components that meet there: a horizontal line going through the origin out to the value E, and then a 45–degree line (and therefore having a slope of 1) going northeast from E. Similar analysis reveals that the kinked intrinsic value line for the put also has its kink at E, as shown in Figure 20.3(b).

Calls and puts will not sell for less than their intrinsic values, owing to the actions of shrewd investors. If an option sold for less than its intrinsic value, then such investors could instantaneously make riskless profits. For example, if the stock price was $150 and the call was selling for $40, which is $10 less than its intrinsic value of $50, then these investors would simultaneously buy these calls, exercise them, and sell the shares received from the writers. In doing so they would spend $140 on each call and exercise price and get $150 in return for each share sold, resulting in a net riskless profit of $10 per call. As a consequence, the call will not sell for less than $50 if the stock price is $150.

20.5.2 Profits and Losses on Calls and Puts

Figure 20.3 shows the values of call and put options at expiration. However, in order to determine profits and losses from buying or writing these options, the premiums involved must be taken into consideration.[7] Figure 20.4 does this for investors who engage in some of the more complicated option strategies. Each strategy assumes that the underlying stock is selling for $100 at the time an option is initially bought or written. It is also assumed that closing transactions are made just prior to the expiration date for the option being considered. Outcomes are shown for each of ten strategies. Because the profit obtained by a buyer is the writer's loss and vice versa, each diagram in the figure has a corresponding mirror image.

Panels (a) and (b) in Figure 20.4 show the profits and losses associated with buying and writing a call, respectively. Similarly, panels (c) and (d) show the profits and losses associated with buying and writing a put, respectively.

Consider panels (a) and (c) first. The kinked lines representing profits and losses in these two panels are simply graphs of the intrinsic value equations, Equations (20.1a) and (20.1b), shown in Figure 20.3, less the premiums on the options. Thus they are graphs of the following equations:

$$\begin{aligned}
\pi_c &= IV_c - P_c \\
&= \max\{0, P_s - E\} - P_c \\
&= \max\{-P_c, P_s - E - P_c\}
\end{aligned} \tag{20.2a}$$

$$\begin{aligned}
\pi_p &= IV_p - P_p \\
&= \max\{0, E - P_s\} - P_p \\
&= \max\{-P_p, E - P_s - P_p\}
\end{aligned} \tag{20.2b}$$

where π_c and π_p denote the profits associated with buying a call and a put, and P_c and P_p denote the premiums on the call and the put, respectively. This means

---

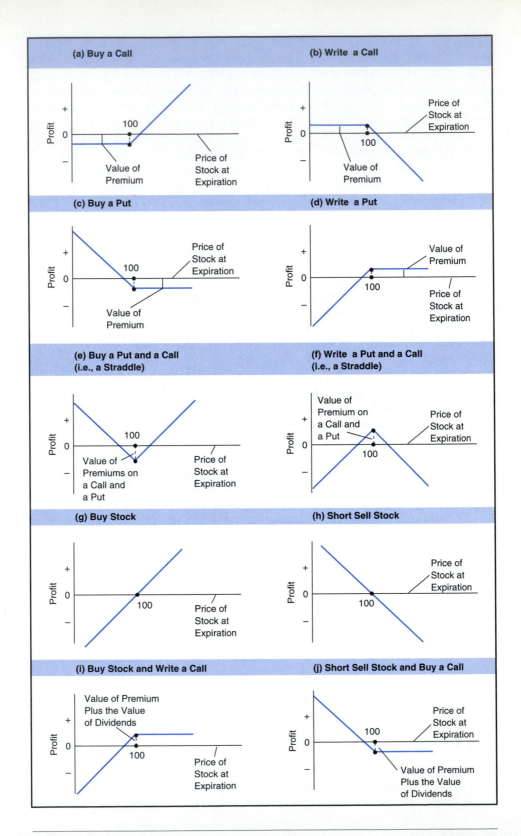

(a) Buy a Call

(b) Write a Call

(c) Buy a Put

(d) Write a Put

(e) Buy a Put and a Call (i.e., a Straddle)

(f) Write a Put and a Call (i.e., a Straddle)

(g) Buy Stock

(h) Short Sell Stock

(i) Buy Stock and Write a Call

(j) Short Sell Stock and Buy a Call

Figure 20.4

Profits and Losses from Various Strategies

that the kinked profit line for the call is simply the same kinked line for the intrinsic value but lowered by an amount equal to the call premium P_c. Similarly, the kinked profit line for the put is simply the kinked intrinsic value line for the put, lowered by an amount equal to the put premium P_p.

If the premium on the call and put options shown in Figure 20.3 were $5, then their profit lines would be graphs of the following two equations:

$$\pi_c = \max\{-\$5, P_s - \$100 - \$5\}$$
$$= \max\{-\$5, P_s - \$105\}$$
$$\pi_p = \max\{-\$5, \$100 - P_s - \$5\}$$
$$= \max\{-\$5, \$95 - P_s\}.$$

Therefore the kinked line for the call would be a horizontal line intersecting the vertical axis at $-\$5$, and it would have a kink at a stock price of $100, where it would turn upward to intersect the horizontal axis at $105. This indicates that the call buyer would not make a profit unless the stock price was above the breakeven point of $105 at expiration. Each dollar that the stock price is above $105 represents an additional dollar of profit. (Hence a price of $108 would represent a profit of $3, since the call buyer pays a premium of $5 and an exercise price of $100 to procure a share of stock that is worth $108.)

Similarly, the kinked line for the put would be a downward-sloping line that would have a kink at a stock price of $100 after intersecting the horizontal axis at $95. At the kink the line would become horizontal so that if this part of the line were extended leftward to the vertical axis, it would intersect it at $-\$5$. This indicates that the put buyer would not make a profit unless the stock price was below the breakeven point of $95 at expiration. Each dollar that the stock price is below $95 represents an additional dollar of profit. (Hence a price of $92 would represent a profit of $3, since the put buyer pays a premium of $5 and gives up a share of stock worth $92 in order to receive $100 in return.)

Panels (b) and (d) of Figure 20.4 are mirror images of panels (a) and (c), respectively. This is because options are zero-sum games, where the profits to one party occur at the expense of the other party. Hence if the stock price is at $108 so that the call buyer has a $3 profit, then the call writer has a $3 loss (because the writer receives the $5 premium and $100 exercise price but must give up a share of stock worth $108). Similarly, if the put buyer has a $3 profit, then the put writer has a loss of $3.

20.5.3 Profits and Losses from Some Option Strategies

Panels (e) and (f) of Figure 20.4 illustrate a more complicated options strategy known as a **straddle.** This strategy involves buying (or writing) both a call and a put on the same stock, with the options having the same exercise price and expiration date.[8] Note how panel (e) can be derived by adding the profits and losses shown in panels (a) and (c), whereas panel (f) can be derived by adding the profits and losses shown in panels (b) and (d). It can also be seen that panels (e) and (f) are mirror images of each other, again reflecting the fact that the profits to buyers equal the losses to writers and vice versa.

Panel (g) of Figure 20.4 shows the profit or loss made by an investor who avoids options entirely but buys a share of the underlying stock (at $100) at the same time that others buy or write options and sells the stock when the options expire. Assuming that no dividends are paid in the interim, the relationship is that shown by the solid line.[9] Similarly, panel (h) shows the profit or loss obtained by an investor who short sells the stock at the initial date and then buys it back at the expiration date.

Panel (i) of Figure 20.4 shows the results obtained by an investor who buys one share of stock and simultaneously writes a call on it. These results can be derived by adding the profits and losses shown in panels (b) and (g). As mentioned earlier, such an investor is said to have written a fully covered option. In contrast, the writer who does not hold the underlying stock, depicted in panel (b), is said to have written a naked option.

Panel (j) of Figure 20.4 shows the results obtained by an investor who short sells one share of stock and simultaneously buys a call option, and it can be derived by adding the profits and losses in panels (a) and (h). Note that this panel is the mirror image of panel (i).

Comparison of the diagrams in Figure 20.4 suggests that similar results can be obtained via alternative strategies. Panels (c) and (j) are similar, as are (d) and (i). Neither the premiums involved nor the initial investments required need be equal in every case. Nonetheless, the similarity of the results obtained with different "packages" of securities suggests that the total market values of the packages will be similar.

Having discussed the value of options (and option-based strategies) when they expire, it is appropriate to discuss next the value of options before they expire. Specifically, what is the fair (or true) value of an option today if it expires at some future date? A method utilizing the binomial option pricing model can be used to answer such a question. It is presented next.

20.6   THE BINOMIAL OPTION PRICING MODEL

The binomial option pricing model (BOPM) can be used to estimate the fair value of a call or put option. It is best presented through an example in which it is assumed that the options are **European options,** meaning that they can be exercised only on their expiration dates. In addition, it is assumed that the underlying stock does not pay any dividends during the life of the option. It should be noted that the model can be modified to value **American options,** which are options that can be exercised any time during their life and can also be used to value options on stocks that pay dividends during the life of the option.

20.6.1 Call Options

Assume that the price of Widget stock today ($t = 0$) is $100, and that after one year ($t = T$) its stock will be selling for either $125 or $80, meaning that the stock will either rise by 25% or fall by 20% over the year. In addition, the annual riskfree rate is 8% compounded continuously. Investors are assumed to be able to either lend (by purchasing these 8% bonds) or borrow (by shortselling the bonds) at this rate.

Now consider a call option on Widget that has an exercise price of $100 and an expiration date of one year from now. This means that on the expiration date the call will have a value of either $25 (if Widget is at $125) or $0 (if Widget is at $80). Panel (a) of Figure 20.5 illustrates the situation by use of a "price tree." It can be seen from this tree why this is called a binomial model, as there are only two branches that represent prices at the expiration date.

Valuation

The question that arises is this: What is a fair value for the call at time 0? The binomial option pricing model is designed to answer this question.

There are three investments that are of interest here: the stock, the option, and a riskfree bond. The prices and payoffs for the stock are known. It is also known that $100 invested in a riskfree bond will grow to approximately $108.33

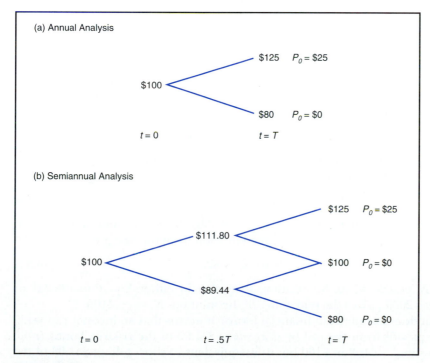

Figure 20.5
Binomial Model of Prices for Widget

given interest is continuously compounded at an annual rate of 8%.[10] Finally, the end-of-period payoffs associated with the option are known. What is to be determined is a fair price that the option should sell for now.

The key to understanding the situation is the observation that there are two possible future *states of nature*. The stock's price may go up or down. For simplicity, these two states are called the "up state" and the "down state," respectively. This essential information is summarized as follows:

Security	Payoff In Up State	Payoff In Down State	Current Price
Stock	$125.00	$80.00	$100.00
Bond	$108.33	$108.33	$100.00
Call	$25.00	$0.00	???

Note that at this juncture the current price of the call is unknown.

Replicating Portfolios

Although the Widget call option may seem exotic, its characteristics can in fact be replicated with an appropriate combination of the Widget stock and the risk-free bond. Moreover, the cost of this *replicating portfolio* constitutes the fair value of the option. Why? Because otherwise there would be an *arbitrage opportunity*— an investor could buy the cheaper of the two alternatives and sell the more expensive one, thereby achieving a guaranteed profit. (Just how this is done will be shown shortly.)

The composition of a portfolio that will precisely replicate the payoffs of the Widget call option needs to be determined. Consider a portfolio with N_s shares of Widget stock and N_b riskfree bonds. In the up state such a portfolio will have a payoff of $125N_s + $108.33N_b$, whereas in the down state it will have a payoff of $80N_s + $108.33N_b$. The call option is worth $25 in the up state. Thus N_s and N_b need to have values so that:

$$\$125N_s + \$108.33\,N_b = \$25. \tag{20.3a}$$

On the other hand, the call option is worthless in the down state. Thus N_s and N_b need to have values so that:

$$\$80N_s + \$108.33\,N_b = \$0. \tag{20.3b}$$

These two linear equations, (20.3a) and (20.3b), have two unknowns and can easily be solved. Subtracting the second equation from the first gives:

$$(\$125 - \$80)\,N_s = \$25 \tag{20.3c}$$

so that N_s equals .5556. Substituting this value in either Equation (20.3a) or Equation (20.3b) gives the remainder of the solution, $N_b = -.4103$.

What does this mean in financial terms? It means that an investor can replicate the payoffs from the call by *short selling* $41.03 of the riskfree bonds (note that investing $-.4103$ in $100 bonds is equivalent to short selling $41.03 of the bonds or borrowing $41.03 at the riskfree rate) and *purchasing* .5556 shares of Widget stock. This is indeed the case, as can be seen here:

CHAPTER 20

Portfolio Component	Payoff In Up State	Payoff In Down State
Stock investment	.5556 × $125 = $69.45	.5556 × $80 = $44.45
Loan repayment	− $41.03 × 1.0833 = − $44.45	− $41.03 × 1.0833 = − $44.45
Net payoff	$25.00	$0.00

Because the replicating portfolio provides the same payoffs as the call, only its cost needs to be calculated in order to find the fair value of the option. To obtain the portfolio, $55.56 must be spent to purchase .5556 shares of Widget stock (at $100 per share). However, $41.03 of this amount is provided by the proceeds from the short sale of the bond. Thus only $14.53 (= $55.56 − $41.03) of the investor's own funds must be spent. Accordingly, this is the fair value of the call option.

More generally, the value of the call option will be:

$$V_o = N_s P_s + N_b P_b \qquad (20.4)$$

where V_o represents the value of the option, P_s is the price of the stock, P_b is the price of a riskfree bond, and N_s and N_b are the number of shares and riskfree bonds required to replicate the option's payoffs.

Overpricing

To show that equilibrium will be attained if the call is selling for $14.53, consider what a shrewd investor would do if the call were selling for either more or less than this amount. Imagine that the call is selling for $20, so it is overpriced. In this case the investor would consider writing one call, buying .5556 shares, and borrowing $41.03. The net cash flow when this is done (that is, at $t = 0$) would be $5.47 [= $20 − (.5556 × $100) + $41.03], indicating that the investor has a net cash inflow. At the end of the year (that is, at $t = T$) the investor's net cash flow will be as follows:

Portfolio Component	Payoff In Up State	Payoff In Down State
Written call	− $25.00	$0.00
Stock investment	.5556 × $125 = $69.45	.5556 × $80 = $44.45
Loan repayment	− $41.03 × 1.0833 = − $44.45	− $41.03 × 1.0833 = − $44.45
Net payoff	$0.00	$0.00

Because the net aggregate value is zero regardless of the ending stock price, the investor has no risk of loss from this strategy. Thus the investor currently has a means for generating free cash as long as the call is priced at $20, since the investment strategy does not require any cash from the investor later on. This cannot represent equilibrium, as anyone can get free cash by investing similarly.

Underpricing

Next imagine that the call is selling for $10 instead of $20, so it is underpriced. In this case the investor would consider buying one call, short selling .5556 shares, and investing $41.03 at the riskfree rate. The net cash flow when this is done (that is, at $t = 0$) would be $4.53 $[= -$10 + (.5556 \times $100) - $41.03]$, indicating that the investor has a net cash inflow. At the end of the year (that is, at $t = T$) the investor's net cash flow will be as follows:

Portfolio Component	Payoff In Up State	Payoff In Down State
Call investment	$25.00	$0.00
Repay shorted stock	$-.5556 \times 125	$-.5556 \times 80
	$= -$69.45$	$= -$44.45$
Riskfree investment	41.03×1.0833	41.03×1.0833
	$= 44.45	$= 44.45
Net payoff	$0.00	$0.00

Once again, the net aggregate value is zero regardless of the ending stock price, indicating that the investor has no risk of loss from this strategy. Hence the investor currently has a means for generating free cash as long as the call is priced at $10. This cannot represent equilibrium, however, as anyone can get free cash by investing similarly.

The Hedge Ratio

To replicate the Widget call option, imagine borrowing $41.03 and purchasing .5556 shares of Widget stock. Now consider the effect of a change in the price of the stock tomorrow (not a year from now) on the value of the replicating portfolio. Because .5556 shares of stock are included in the portfolio, the value of the portfolio will change by $.5556 for every $1 change in the price of Widget stock. But because the call option and the portfolio should sell for the same price, it follows that the price of the call should also change by $.5556 for every $1 change in the price of the stock. This relationship is defined as the option's **hedge ratio.** It is equal to the value of N_s that was determined in Equation (20.3c).

In the case of the Widget call option, the hedge ratio was equal to .5556, which equals the value of $($25 - $0)/($125 - $80)$. Note that the numerator equals the difference between the option's payoffs in the up and down states, and the denominator equals the difference between the stock's payoffs in the two states. More generally, in the binomial model:

$$h = \frac{P_{ou} - P_{od}}{P_{su} - P_{sd}} \qquad (20.5)$$

where P represents the end-of-period price and the subscripts indicate the instrument (o for option, s for stock) and the state of nature (u for up, d for down).

To replicate a call option in a binomial world, h shares of stock [where h represents the hedge ratio determined by using Equation (20.5)] must be purchased. Simultaneously an amount must be risklessly borrowed by short selling bonds; this amount is equal to:

$$B = \text{PV}(hP_{sd} - P_{od}) \qquad (20.6)$$

where PV refers to taking the present value of the figure calculated in the following parentheses. (Note that the figure in parentheses is the value of the bond at the end of the period.)[11]

To summarize, the value of a call option is given to be:

$$V_o = hP_s - B \qquad (20.7)$$

where h and B are the hedge ratio and the current value of a short bond position in a portfolio that replicates the payoffs of the call, and they are calculated by using Equations (20.5) and (20.6).

More Than Two Prices

At this juncture it is reasonable to wonder about the accuracy of the BOPM if it is based on an assumption that the price of Widget stock can assume only one of two values at the end of a year. Realistically, Widget stock can assume any one of a great number of prices at year-end. It turns out that this is not a problem, as the model can be extended in a straightforward manner.

In the case of Widget, divide the year into two six-month periods. In the first period, assume that Widget can go up to $111.80 (an 11.80% increase) or down to $89.44 (a 10.56% decrease). For the second six-month period, the price of Widget can again go either up by 11.80% or down by 10.56%. Hence the price of Widget will follow one of the paths of the price tree shown in panel (b) of Figure 20.5 over the forthcoming year. Note how Widget can now assume one of three prices at year-end: $125, $100, or $80. The associated value of the call option is also given in the figure for each of these stock prices.

How can the value of the Widget call option at time 0 be calculated from the information given in the figure? The answer is remarkably simple. All that is done is that the problem is broken down into three parts, each of which is solved in a manner similar to that shown earlier when panel (a) was discussed. The three parts must be approached sequentially by working backward in time.

First, imagine that six months have passed and the price of Widget stock is $111.80. What is the value of the call option at this node in the price tree? The hedge ratio h is calculated to be 1.0 [= ($25 − $0)/($125 − $100)], and the amount of the borrowing B is calculated to be $96.08 [= (1 × $100 − $0)/1.0408]. (The 8% riskfree rate compounded continuously corresponds to a discrete discount rate of 4.08% for the six-month period.) Using Equation (20.7), the value of the call is determined to be $15.72 (= 1 × $111.80 − $96.08).

Second, again imagine that six months have passed but the price of Widget is $89.44. While Equations (20.5), (20.6), and (20.7) could be used to determine the value of the call at this node in the price tree, intuition gives the answer more quickly: the call has to be selling for $0. This is because in six months the price of Widget will be either $100 or $80, and regardless of which it is, the call will still be worthless. That is, investors will realize that the call will be worthless at the end of the year if the stock price is at $89.44 after six months, and hence they will be unwilling to pay anything for the call option.

Third, imagine that no time has elapsed, so that it is time 0. In this case the price tree can be simplified to:

$$\$100 \overset{\displaystyle \$111.80 \qquad P_o = \$15.72}{\underset{\displaystyle \$89.44 \qquad P_o = \$0}{}}$$

Applying Equations (20.5) and (20.6) indicates that the hedge ratio h is equal to .7030 [= ($15.72 − $0)/($111.80 − $89.44)] and the amount of borrowing B is equal to $60.41 [= (.7030 × $89.44 − $0)/1.0408]. Applying Equation (20.7) results in a value for the call at $t = 0$ of $9.89 (= .7030 × $100 − $60.41).

There is no need to stop here. Instead of analyzing two six-month periods, four quarterly periods can be analyzed, or 12 monthly periods. Note that the number of year-end stock prices for Widget is equal to one more than the number of periods in a year. Hence when annual periods were used in panel (a) of Figure 20.5, there were two year-end prices, and when semiannual prices were used, there were three year-end prices. It follows that if quarterly or monthly periods had been used, there would have been 5 or 13 year-end prices, respectively.

20.6.2 Put Options

Can the BOPM be used to value puts? Because the formulas cover any set of payoffs, they can be applied directly. Consider Widget once again from an annual perspective, where the put option has an exercise price of $100 and an expiration date of one year. Its price tree will be:

$$\$100 \overset{\displaystyle \$125 \qquad P_o = \$0}{\underset{\displaystyle \$80 \qquad P_o = \$20}{}}$$

Applying Equation (20.5) gives the hedge ratio for the put option as − .4444 [= ($0 − $20)/($125 − $80)]. Note that this is a negative number, indicating that a rise in the price of the stock will lower the price of the put.

Applying Equation (20.6) shows that B equals − $51.28, which is the present value of the year-end value of − $55.55. Because these are negative numbers, they denote the amount of bonds to be purchased (that is, the negative value of a short position should be interpreted as the value of a long position).

To replicate the put option, then, one *sells short* .4444 shares of Widget and *lends* (that is, invests in the riskfree bond) $51.28. As the short sale will generate $44.44 while the bond purchase will cost $51.28, the net cost of the replicating portfolio will be $6.84 (= $51.28 − $44.44). Accordingly, this is the fair value of the put.

This is the same value that is obtained when Equation (20.7) is used: $6.84 [= .4444 × $100 − (− $51.28)], where $h = .4444$, $B = − 51.28, and $P_s = 100. Hence Equations (20.5), (20.6), and (20.7) can be used to value not only calls but also puts. Furthermore, the procedure for extending the valuation of puts to the situation where there is more than one period between now and the expiration date is analogous to the one that was given for calls.

20.6.3 Put-Call Parity

Earlier it was shown that the call on Widget had a hedge ratio of .5556. Note that $.5556 - 1 = -.4444$, the hedge ratio for the put. This is not a coincidence. The hedge ratios of a European put and call having the same exercise price and expiration date are related in the following manner:

$$h_c - 1 = h_p \tag{20.8}$$

where h_c and h_p denote the hedge ratios for the call and the put, respectively.

Of even greater interest is the relationship between the market prices of a call and a put on a given stock that have the same exercise price and expiration date. Again consider the example involving Widget options that have an exercise price of \$100 and an expiration date of one year. Two investment strategies need to be compared. Strategy A involves buying a put and a share of stock. (This strategy is sometimes known as a "protective put" or a "married put.") Strategy B involves buying a call and investing an amount of money in the riskfree asset that is equal to the present value of the exercise price.

At the expiration date the values of these two investment strategies can be calculated under two scenarios: the price of Widget being below its exercise price of \$100, and the price of Widget being above its exercise price. (The case where it is exactly equal to its exercise price can be added to either scenario without affecting the results.) Table 20.1 does this. Note that if the stock of Widget is selling for less than the \$100 exercise price on the expiration date, both strategies have a payoff of \$100 in cash. Alternatively, if the price of Widget stock is above \$100, both strategies result in the investor's having possession of a share of stock that is worth more than \$100. Hence, because both strategies have the same payoffs, they must cost the same amount in equilibrium:

$$P_p + P_s = P_c + E/e^{RT} \tag{20.9}$$

where P_p and P_c denote the current market prices of the put and the call, respectively.

This equation represents what is known as **put-call parity.** In Table 20.1 it can be seen that the cost of each strategy is \$106.84, just as was suggested previously by the calculations using Equations (20.5), (20.6), and (20.7).

TABLE 20.1
PUT-CALL PARITY INVOLVING WIDGET

Strategy	Initial Cost	Value at Expiration Date $P_s < E = \$100$	Value at Expiration Date $E = \$100 > P_s$
A: Buy put	$P_p + P_s$	Exercise put, get \$100	Throw away put, have stock worth P_s
Buy share of stock	$= \$6.84 + \$100$		
	$= \$106.84$		
B: Buy call	$P_c + E/e^{RT}$	Throw away call, get \$100	Exercise call, get stock worth P_s
Invest present value	$= \$14.53 + \$92.31$	from riskfree asset	
of E in riskfree asset	$= \$106.84$		

Consider what would happen with the binomial option pricing model if the number of periods before the expiration date were allowed to increase. For example, with Widget's option for which the expiration date was a year in the future, there could be a price tree with periods for each one of the approximately 250 trading days in a year. Hence there would be 251 possible year-end prices for Widget stock. Needless to say, the fair value of any call associated with such a tree is found by using a computer to quickly perform calculations such as those shown earlier for Widget. If the number of periods were even larger, with each one representing a specific hour of each trading day, then there would be about 1,750 ($= 7 \times 250$) hourly periods (and 1,751 possible year-end prices). Note that the number of periods in a year gets larger as the length of each period gets shorter. In the limit there will be an infinite number of infinitely small periods (and, consequently, an infinite number of possible year-end prices). In this situation the BOPM given in Equation (20.7) reduces to the Black-Scholes model, so named in honor of its originators.[12]

20.7.1 Limitations on Its Use

At first this model might seem to have limited use, because almost all options in the United States are American options that can be exercised at any time up to their expiration date whereas the Black-Scholes model applies only to European options. Furthermore, strictly speaking, the model is applicable only to options on stocks that will not pay any dividends over the life of the option. However, most of the common stocks on which options are written do in fact pay dividends.

The first drawback of the Black-Scholes model—that it is only applicable to European options—can be dispensed with rather easily when the option is a call and the underlying stock does not pay dividends. This is because it can be shown that it is unwise for an investor holding an American call option on a non-dividend-paying stock to exercise it prior to maturity.[13] As there is no reason for exercising such an option prior to maturity, the opportunity to do so is worthless. Consequently there will be no difference in the values of an American and a European call option. In turn, this means that the Black-Scholes model can be used to estimate the fair value of American call options on non-dividend-paying stocks.

The reason for this can be seen in Figure 20.6, but first some terminology must be introduced. A call option is said to be **at the money** if the underlying stock has a market price roughly equal to the call's exercise price. If the stock's market price is below the exercise price, the call is said to be **out of the money,** and if the market price is above the exercise price, the call is said to be **in the money.** Occasionally, finer gradations are invoked, and one hears of "near the money," "deep in the money," or "far out of the money."

As mentioned earlier, the value of an option if it were exercised immediately is known as its intrinsic value. This value is equal to zero if the option is out of the money. However, it is equal to the difference between the stock price and the exercise price if the option is in the money. The excess of the option's price over its intrinsic value is the option's **time value** (or time premium). As shown in Figure 20.3(a), for call options at expiration the time value is zero. However, before then the time value is positive. Note that a call option's premium is simply the sum of its intrinsic and time values.

An investor considering exercising a call option on a non-dividend-paying stock prior to its expiration date will always find it cheaper to sell the call option and purchase the stock in the marketplace. This is because exercising the call will result in the investor's losing the time value of the option (hence the expression that call options are "worth more alive than dead").

For example, consider a stock that has a current price of $110. If this stock has a call option with an exercise price of $100 that is selling for $14, then the intrinsic and time values of this option are $10 (= $110 − $100) and $4 (= $14 − $10), respectively. An investor who owns one of these calls could exercise it by spending an additional $100. However, it would be cheaper for the investor to get the share of stock by selling the call option and buying the share of stock in the marketplace, because the additional cost would be only $96 (= $110 − $14).

The second drawback of the Black-Scholes model—that it is only applicable to non-dividend-paying stocks—cannot be easily dismissed, as many call options are written on stocks that will pay dividends over the life of the option. Some procedures have been suggested for amending this formula to value call options on such stocks.[14]

20.7.2 The Formula

In a world not bothered by taxes and transaction costs, the fair value of a call option can be estimated by using the valuation formula developed by Black and Scholes. It has been widely used by those who deal with options to search for situations where the market price of an option differs substantially from its fair value. A call option that is found to be selling for substantially less than its Black-Scholes value is a candidate for purchase, whereas one that is found to be selling for substantially more is a candidate for writing. The Black-Scholes formula for estimating the fair value of a call option V_c is:

$$V_c = N(d_1)P_s - \frac{E}{e^{RT}}N(d_2) \tag{20.10}$$

where:

$$d_1 = \frac{\ln(P_s/E) + (R + .5\sigma^2)T}{\sigma\sqrt{T}} \tag{20.11}$$

$$d_2 = \frac{\ln(P_s/E) + (R - .5\sigma^2)T}{\sigma\sqrt{T}} \tag{20.12a}$$

$$= d_1 - \sigma\sqrt{T} \tag{20.12b}$$

Note that E/e^{RT} is the present value of the exercise price where a continuous discount rate is used. The quantity $\ln(P_s/E)$ is the natural logarithm of P_s/E. Finally, $N(d_1)$ and $N(d_2)$ denote the probabilities that outcomes of less than d_1 and d_2, respectively, will occur in a normal distribution that has a mean of 0 and a standard deviation of 1.

Table 20.2 provides values of $N(d_1)$ for various levels of d_1.[15] Only this table and a pocket calculator are needed in order to use the Black-Scholes formula for valuing a call option. It should be noted that with this formula the interest rate R and the stock volatility σ are assumed to be constant over the life of the option. (More recently people have developed formulas where these assumptions have been relaxed.)

For example, consider a call option that expires in three months and has an exercise price of $40 (thus T = .25 and E = 40). Furthermore, the current price and the risk of the underlying common stock are $36 and 50%, respectively, whereas the riskfree rate is 5% (thus P_s = 36, R = .05, and σ = .50). Solving Equations (20.11) and (20.12b) provides the following values for d_1 and d_2:

$$d_1 = \frac{\ln(36/40) + [.05 + .5(.50)^2].25}{.50\sqrt{.25}} = -.25$$

$$d_2 = -.25 - .50\sqrt{.25} = -.50.$$

Now Table 20.2 can be used to find the corresponding values of $N(d_1)$ and $N(d_2)$:

$$N(d_1) = N(-.25) = .4013$$
$$N(d_2) = N(-.50) = .3085.$$

Finally, Equation (20.10) can be used to estimate the fair value of this call option:

$$V_c = (.4013 \times \$36) - \left(\frac{\$40}{e^{.05 \times .25}} \times .3085\right)$$

$$= \$14.45 - \$12.19 = \$2.26.$$

TABLE 20.2

TABLE 20.2								
VALUES OF N(d) FOR SELECTED VALUES OF d								
d	**N(d)**		**d**	**N(d)**		**d**	**N(d)**
			−1.00	.1587		1.00	.8413
−2.95	.0016		−.95	.1711		1.05	.8531
−2.90	.0019		−.90	.1841		1.10	.8643
−2.85	.0022		−.85	.1977		1.15	.8749
−2.80	.0026		−.80	.2119		1.20	.8849
−2.75	.0030		−.75	.2266		1.25	.8944
−2.70	.0035		−.70	.2420		1.30	.9032
−2.65	.0040		−.65	.2578		1.35	.9115
−2.60	.0047		−.60	.2743		1.40	.9192
−2.55	.0054		−.55	.2912		1.45	.9265
−2.50	.0062		−.50	.3085		1.50	.9332
−2.45	.0071		−.45	.3264		1.55	.9394
−2.40	.0082		−.40	.3446		1.60	.9452
−2.35	.0094		−.35	.3632		1.65	.9505
−2.30	.0107		−.30	.3821		1.70	.9554
−2.25	.0122		−.25	.4013		1.75	.9599
−2.20	.0139		−.20	.4207		1.80	.9641
−2.15	.0158		−.15	.4404		1.85	.9678
−2.10	.0179		−.10	.4602		1.90	.9713
−2.05	.0202		−.05	.4801		1.95	.9744
−2.00	.0228		.00	.5000		2.00	.9773
−1.95	.0256		.05	.5199		2.05	.9798
−1.90	.0287		.10	.5398		2.10	.9821
−1.85	.0322		.15	.5596		2.15	.9842
−1.80	.0359		.20	.5793		2.20	.9861
−1.75	.0401		.25	.5987		2.25	.9878
−1.70	.0446		.30	.6179		2.30	.9893
−1.65	.0495		.35	.6368		2.35	.9906
−1.60	.0548		.40	.6554		2.40	.9918
−1.55	.0606		.45	.6736		2.45	.9929
−1.50	.0668		.50	.6915		2.50	.9938
−1.45	.0735		.55	.7088		2.55	.9946
−1.40	.0808		.60	.7257		2.60	.9953
−1.35	.0885		.65	.7422		2.65	.9960
−1.30	.0968		.70	.7580		2.70	.9965
−1.25	.1057		.75	.7734		2.75	.9970
−1.20	.1151		.80	.7881		2.80	.9974
−1.15	.1251		.85	.8023		2.85	.9978
−1.10	.1357		.90	.8159		2.90	.9981
−1.05	.1469		.95	.8289		2.95	.9984

If this call option is currently selling for $5, the investor should consider writing some of them. This is because they are overpriced (according to the Black-Scholes model), suggesting that their price will fall in the near future. Thus the writer would receive a premium of $5 and would expect to be able to enter a closing buy order later for a lower price, making a profit on the difference. Conversely, if the call option were selling for $1, the investor should consider buying some of them. This is because they are underpriced and can be expected to rise in value in the future.

20.7.3 Comparison to BOPM

At this juncture the BOPM formula [given in Equation (20.7) where V_0 is now denoted V_c] can be compared with the Black-Scholes option pricing formula [given in Equation (20.10)]:

$$V_c = hP_s - B \tag{20.7}$$

$$V_c = \text{N}(d_1)P_s - \frac{E}{e^{RT}}\text{N}(d_2). \tag{20.10}$$

In comparing the two equations, the quantity $\text{N}(d_1)$ in Equation (20.10) can be seen to correspond to h in Equation (20.7). Remembering that h is the hedge ratio, the quantity $\text{N}(d_1)$ in the Black-Scholes formula can be interpreted in a similar manner. That is, it corresponds to the number of shares that an investor would need to purchase in executing an investment strategy that was designed to have the same payoffs as a call option. Similarly, the quantity $EN(d_2)/e^{RT}$ corresponds to B, the amount of money that the investor borrows as the other part of the strategy. This means that the quantity $EN(d_2)$ corresponds to the face amount of the loan, because it is the amount that must be paid back to the lender at time T, the expiration date. Hence e^{RT} is the present value (or discount) factor, indicating that the interest rate on the loan is R per period and that the loan is for T periods. Thus the seemingly complex Black-Scholes formula can be seen to have an intuitive interpretation. It simply involves calculating the cost of a buy-stock-and-borrow-money investment strategy that has the same payoffs at T as a call option.

In the example, $\text{N}(d_1)$ was equal to .4013 and $EN(d_2)/e^{RT}$ was equal to $12.19. Hence an investment strategy that involves buying .4013 shares and borrowing $12.19 at time 0 will have payoffs exactly equal to those associated with buying the call.[16] Because this strategy costs $2.26, it follows that in equilibrium the market price of the call must also be $2.26.

20.7.4 Static Analysis

Close scrutiny of the Black-Scholes formula reveals some interesting features of European call option pricing. In particular, the fair value of a call option is dependent on five inputs—the market price of the common stock P_s, the exercise price of the option E, the length of time until the expiration date T, the riskfree rate R, and the risk of the common stock σ. What happens to the fair value of a call option when one of these inputs is changed while the other four remain the same?

1. The higher the price of the underlying stock P_s, the higher the value of the call option.
2. The higher the exercise price E, the lower the value of the call option.
3. The longer the time to the expiration date T, the higher the value of the call option.
4. The higher the riskfree rate R, the higher the value of the call option.
5. The greater the risk σ of the common stock, the higher the value of the call option.

Of these five factors, the first three (P_s, E, and T) are readily determined. The fourth factor, the riskfree rate R, is often estimated by using the yield-to-maturity on a Treasury bill having a maturity date close to the expiration date of the option. The fifth factor, the risk of the underlying stock σ, is not readily observed; consequently various methods for estimating it have been proposed. Two of these methods will be presented next.

20.7.5 Estimating a Stock's Risk from Historical Prices

One method for estimating the risk of the underlying common stock associated with a call option involves analyzing historical prices of the stock. Initially a set of $n + 1$ market prices on the underlying stock must be obtained from either financial publications such as the *Wall Street Journal* or a computer database. These prices are then used to calculate a set of n continuously compounded returns as follows:

$$r_t = \ln\left(\frac{P_{st}}{P_{st-1}}\right) \tag{20.13}$$

where P_{st} and P_{st-1} denote the market price of the underlying stock at times t and $t - 1$, respectively. Here, ln denotes taking the natural logarithm of the quantity P_{st}/P_{st-1}, which thus results in a continuously compounded return.

For example, the set of market prices for the stock might consist of the closing price at the end of each of 53 weeks. If the price at the end of one week was $105 and the price at the end of the next week was $107, then the return for that week r_t will be equal to 1.886% [$= \ln(107/105)$]. Similar calculations will result in a set of 52 weekly returns.

Having calculated a set of n returns on the stock, the next step involves using them to estimate the stock's average return:

$$r_{av} = \frac{1}{n} \sum_{t=1}^{n} r_t. \tag{20.14}$$

The average return is then used in estimating the per-period variance—that is, the square of the per-period standard deviation:

$$s^2 = \frac{1}{n-1} \sum_{t=1}^{n} (r_t - r_{av})^2. \tag{20.15}$$

This is called the per-period variance because its size is dependent on the length of time over which each return is measured. In the example, weekly returns were calculated and would lead to the estimation of a weekly variance. Alternatively, daily returns could have been used, leading to a daily variance that would be of smaller magnitude than the weekly variance. However, what is needed is not a weekly or daily variance, but an annual variance. This is obtained by multiplying the per-period variance by the number of periods in a year. Thus an estimated weekly variance would be multiplied by 52 in order to estimate the annual variance σ^2 (that is, $\sigma^2 = 52s^2$).[17]

Alternative methods of estimating a stock's total risk exist. One such method involves subjectively estimating the probabilities of possible future stock prices. Another method involves combining the historical and subjective risk estimates.

For any estimate of future uncertainty, historical data are likely to prove more helpful than definitive. And because recent data may prove more helpful than older data, some analysts study daily price changes over the most recent 6 to 12 months, sometimes giving more weight to more recent data than to earlier ones. Others take into account the price histories of related stocks and the possibility that a stock whose price has recently decreased may be more risky in the future than it was in the past. Still others make explicit subjective estimates of the future, taking into account changes in uncertainty concerning the economy in general as well as uncertainty in specific industries and in stocks.

In some cases an analyst's estimate of a stock's risk over the next three months may differ from that for the following three months, leading to the use of different values of σ for call options on the same stock that have different expiration dates.

20.7.6 The Market Consensus of a Stock's Risk

Another way to estimate a stock's risk is based on the assumption that a currently outstanding call option is fairly priced in the marketplace. Because this means that $P_c = V_c$, the current market price of the call P_c can be entered on the left-hand side of Equation (20.10) in place of the fair value of the call V_c. Next all the other factors except for σ are entered on the right-hand side, and a value for σ, the only unknown variable, is found that satisfies the equation. The solution for σ can be interpreted as representing a consensus opinion in the marketplace on the size of the stock's risk, and it is sometimes known as the stock's **implicit** (or implied) **volatility.**[18]

For example, assume that the riskfree rate is 6%, and that a six-month call option with an exercise price of $40 sells for $4 when the price of the underlying stock is $36. Different estimates of σ can be "plugged into" the right-hand side of Equation (20.10) until a value of $4 for this side of the equation is obtained. In this example an estimated value of .40 (that is, 40%) for σ will result in a number for the right-hand side of Equation (20.10) that is equal to $4, the current market price of the call option that is on the left-hand side.

The procedure can be modified by applying it to several call options on the same stock. For example, σ can be estimated for each of several call options on the same stock that have different exercise prices but the same expiration date. Then the resulting estimates for σ can be averaged and, in turn, used to determine the fair value of another call option on the same stock having yet another exercise price but a similar expiration date.

In the example, σ can be estimated not only for a six-month option having an exercise price of $40, but also for six-month options having exercise prices of $35 and $45. Then the three estimates of σ can be averaged to produce a "best estimate" of σ that is used to value a six-month $50 option on the same stock.

Alternatively, the procedure can be modified by averaging the estimates for σ associated with each of several expiration dates. In the example, σ can be estimated not only for a six-month option having an exercise price of $40 but also for a three-month and a nine-month option that each have an exercise price of $40. The three estimates of σ can be averaged to produce a best estimate of σ that will subsequently be used to determine the fair value of a one-month $40 option on the same stock.

There are other ways of using a set of estimates of σ that correspond to different call options on the same stock. Perhaps σ will be estimated for a set of calls having different expiration prices and different exercise prices, and then averaged. Perhaps σ will be estimated from historical returns using Equation (20.15), with the resulting figure averaged with one or more estimates of the stock's implicit volatility. Although the evidence is still unclear, it appears that methods based on calculating implicit volatility are better than methods based on historical returns.[19] It should be remembered, however, that all of these methods assume that volatility remains constant over the life of the option—an assumption that can be challenged.

20.7.7 More on Hedge Ratios

The slope of the Black-Scholes value curve at any point represents the expected change in the value of the option per dollar change in the price of the underlying common stock. This amount corresponds to the hedge ratio of the call option and is equal to $N(d_1)$ in Equation (20.10). As can be seen in Figure 20.6 (assuming that the market price of the call is equal to its Black-Scholes value), the slope (that is, the hedge ratio) of the curve is always positive. Note that if the stock has a relatively low market price, the slope will be near zero. For higher stock prices the slope increases and ultimately approaches a value of 1 for relatively high prices.

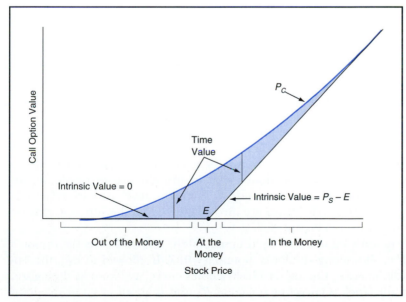

Figure 20.6
Option Terminology for Calls

Because the hedge ratio is typically less than 1, a $1 increase in the stock price will typically result in an increase in a call option's value of less than $1. However, the percentage change in the value of the call option will generally be much greater than the percentage change in the price of the stock. It is this relationship that leads people to say that options offer high leverage.

The reason for referring to the slope of the Black-Scholes value curve as the hedge ratio is that a "hedge" portfolio, meaning a nearly riskfree portfolio, can be formed by simultaneously writing one call option and purchasing a number of shares equal to the hedge ratio, $N(d_1)$. For example, assume that the hedge ratio is .5, indicating that the hedge portfolio consists of writing one call and buying .5 shares of stock. Now if the stock price rises by $1, the value of the call option will rise by approximately $.50. This means that the hedge portfolio would lose approximately $.50 on the written call option but gain $.50 from the rise in the stock's price. Conversely, a $1 decrease in the stock's price would result in a $.50 gain on the written call option but a loss of $.50 on the half-share of stock. Overall, it can be seen that the hedge portfolio will neither gain nor lose value when the price of the underlying common stock changes by a relatively small amount.[20]

Even if the Black-Scholes model is valid and all the inputs have been correctly specified, it should be noted that risk is not permanently eliminated in the hedge portfolio when the portfolio is first formed (or, for that matter, at any time). This is because the hedge ratio will change as the stock price changes and as the life of the option decreases with the passage of time. In order to eliminate risk from the hedge portfolio, the investor will have to alter its composition continuously. Altering it less often will reduce but not completely eliminate risk.

20.7.8 Adjustments for Dividends

Thus far the issue of dividend payments on the underlying stock during the life of an option has been avoided. Other things being equal, the greater the amount of the dividends to be paid during the life of a call option, the lower the value of the call option. This is because the greater the dividend that a firm declares, the lower its stock price will be. Since options are not "dividend protected," this lower stock price will result in a lower value for the call option.

Moreover it may pay to exercise an American call option just prior to an ex-dividend date. Earlier it was mentioned that in the absence of dividends, an American call option would be worth at least as much "alive" (not exercised) as "dead" (exercised). When dividends are involved, however, the situation may be different. This is shown in Figure 20.7.

The call option's value if exercised immediately, referred to as the option's "intrinsic value," lies along the lower boundary 0EZ. If allowed to live, the option's value will lie along the higher Black-Scholes curve, as shown in the figure. Imagine that the stock is currently priced at P_{s1} and is about to go ex-dividend for the last time prior to the option's expiration. Afterward it can be expected to sell for a lower price P_{s2}. The Black-Scholes formula can be used to estimate the

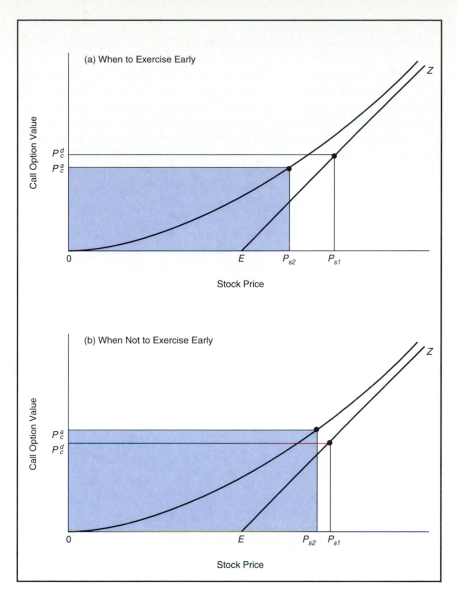

Figure 20.7
Option Values before and after an Ex-Dividend Date

option's value if it remains "alive" just after the ex-dividend date. In Figure 20.7, this alive value is P_c^a. If instead the option is exercised just before the ex-dividend date while the stock price is still P_{s1}, the investor will obtain the "dead" value (that is, the intrinsic value) of P_c^d. If P_c^d is greater than P_c^a [as is the case in panel (a)], the option should be exercised now, just before the ex-dividend date; if P_c^d is less than P_c^a [as is the case in panel (b)], the option should not be exercised. Hence for a call option on a dividend-paying stock, the possibility of early exercise must be taken into consideration.[21]

Similar to a call option, a put option is said to be at the money if the underlying stock has a market price roughly equal to the put's exercise price. However, the terms "out of the money" and "in the money" have, in one sense, *opposite meanings* for puts and calls. In particular, a put option is out of the money if the underlying stock has a market price above the exercise price and is in the money if the market price is below the exercise price. Figure 20.8 provides an illustration of how these terms apply to a put option.

As mentioned earlier, the value of either a call or a put, if it were exercised immediately, is known as its intrinsic value. This value is equal to zero if the option is out of the money, and is equal to the difference between the stock price and the exercise price if the stock is in the money. Thus in another sense, the terms "out of the money" and "in the money" have *similar meanings* for puts and calls.

The excess of the price of a call or a put over this intrinsic value is the option's time value (or time premium). As shown for calls and puts in panels (a) and (b) of Figure 20.3, respectively, the time value is 0 at expiration. However, Figures 20.6 and 20.8 show that the time value is generally positive before expiration. Note that an option's premium is simply the sum of its intrinsic value and its time value.

20.8.1 Put-Call Parity

Consider a put and a call on the same underlying stock that have the same exercise price and expiration date. Earlier it was shown in Equation (20.9) that their market prices should be related, with the nature of the relationship known as put-call parity. However, it should be noted that this relationship is valid only for European options on non-dividend-paying stocks.

Equation (20.9) can be rearranged in the following manner so that it can be used to estimate the value of European put options:

$$P_p = P_c + \frac{E}{e^{RT}} - P_s. \tag{20.16}$$

Thus the value of a put can be estimated by using either the BOPM or the Black-Scholes formula to estimate the value of a matching call option, then adding an amount equal to the present value of the exercise price to this estimate, and finally subtracting from this sum an amount that is equal to the current market price of the underlying common stock.

For example, consider a put option that expires in three months and has an exercise price of $40, while the current market price and the risk of the underlying common stock are $36 and 50%, respectively. Assuming that the riskfree rate is 5%, it was shown earlier that the Black-Scholes estimate of the value for a matching call option was $2.26. Because the 5% riskfree rate is a continuously compounded rate, the present value of the exercise price is equal to $39.50 [$= \$40/(e^{.05 \times .25})$]. At this point, since it has been determined that $P_c = \$2.26$, $E/e^{RT} = \$39.50$, and $P_s = \$36$, Equation (20.16) can be used to estimate the value of the put option as being equal to $5.76 ($= \$2.26 + \$39.50 - \$36$).

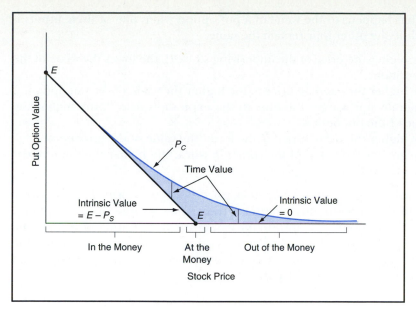

Figure 20.8
Option Terminology for Puts

Alternatively, the Black-Scholes formula for estimating the value of a call given in Equation (20.10) can be substituted for P_c in Equation (20.16). After doing so and simplifying, an equation that can be used directly for estimating the value of a put is obtained:

$$P_p = \frac{E}{e^{RT}} N(-d_2) - P_s N(-d_1) \tag{20.17}$$

where d_1 and d_2 are given in Equations (20.11) and (20.12a), respectively.

In the previous example, $d_1 = -.25$ and $d_2 = -.50$; thus $N(-d_1) = N(.25) = .5987$ and $N(-d_2) = N(.50) = .6915$. Applying Equation (20.17), the value of this put can be estimated directly:

$$P_p = \left(\frac{\$40}{e^{.05 \times .25}} \times .6915 \right) - (\$36 \times .5987)$$

$$= \$27.31 - \$21.55 = \$5.76$$

which is the same estimated value as indicated earlier when Equation (20.16) was used.

20.8.2   Static Analysis

Close scrutiny of the put-call parity equation reveals some interesting features of European put option pricing. In particular, the value of a put option is dependent on the values of the same five inputs used for call valuation—the market price of the common stock P_s, the exercise price of the option E, the length of time until the expiration date T, the riskfree rate R, and the risk of the common stock σ. What happens to the value of a put option when one of these inputs is changed while the other four remain the same?

1. The higher the price of the underlying stock P_s, the lower the value of the put option.
2. The higher the exercise price E, the higher the value of the put option.
3. Generally, the longer the time to the expiration date T, the higher the value of the put option.
4. The higher the riskfree rate R, the lower the value of the put option.
5. The greater the risk σ of the common stock, the higher the value of the put option.

The relationships for the underlying stock price P_s, exercise price E, and riskfree rate R are in the opposite direction from those shown earlier for call options, while the relationships for the time to the expiration date T and risk σ are in the same direction. It should be noted that exceptions can occur with T when the put is deep in the money. In such a situation a longer time to expiration could actually decrease the value of the put.

20.8.3 Early Exercise and Dividends

Equations (20.16) and (20.17) apply to a European put on a stock that will not pay dividends prior to the option's expiration. As with call options, complications arise when it is recognized that most put options are American, meaning that they can be exercised before expiration, and that often dividends on the underlying common stock will be paid before the expiration date.

Consider first the ability to exercise a put option at any time up to its expiration date. Earlier it was shown that if there were no dividends on the underlying stock, then a call option was worth more "alive" than "dead," meaning that call options should not be exercised prior to expiration. Such an argument does *not* hold for put options.

Specifically, if a put option is in the money, meaning that the market price of the stock is less than the exercise price, then the investor may want to exercise the put option. In doing so, the investor will receive an additional amount of cash equal to $E - P_s$. In turn, this cash can be invested at the riskfree rate to earn money over the remaining life of the option. Because these earnings may be greater than any additional profits received by the investor if the put option were held, it may be advantageous to exercise the put early and thereby receive the earnings.

An example can be used to illustrate the point. Consider a put option on Widget that has a year left until its expiration date. The exercise price on the put is $100, and the annual riskfree rate is 10%. Imagine that the stock price of Widget is now at $5 per share, having recently plunged in value. If an investor owned such a deep-in-the-money option, it would be in his or her best interest to exercise it immediately. The logic is as follows.

The intrinsic value of the put is currently $95 (= $100 − $5), indicating that if the put is exercised immediately, the buyer will receive $95. That is, the buyer will spend $5 to buy a share of Widget and then turn the share and the put over to the writer in return for the exercise price of $100. The net cash inflow to the put buyer of $95 could be invested in the riskfree asset so that in one year it would be worth $104.50 (= $95 × 1.10). Alternatively, if the put is held, what is the best that the buyer can hope to earn at year-end? If the stock price of Widget drops to $0, the buyer will receive $100 at expiration from the put writer. Clearly the buyer would be better off exercising the put now instead of holding onto it. Hence early exercise is merited in such a situation.

What will happen to the market price of the put in such a situation? In equilibrium it will be equal to the put's intrinsic value $E - P_s$ (in this instance, $95). Hence the put's time premium would be zero. This is because nobody would pay more than the intrinsic value for the put, knowing that they could get a better return by investing in the riskfree asset. In addition, nobody would be willing to sell a put for less than its intrinsic value because this would open up the opportunity for immediately earning riskfree profits by purchasing the put and exercising it right away. Hence the only price that the put could sell for would be its intrinsic value.

Consider next the impact of dividends on put valuation. Previously it was shown that the owner of a call may find it optimal to exercise just *before* an ex-dividend date, as doing so allowed the investor to receive the forthcoming dividends on the stock. With respect to a put, the owner may find it optimal to exercise just *after* the ex-dividend date, as the corresponding drop in the stock price will cause the value of the put to rise.[22]

20.9 INDEX OPTIONS

Not all options are written on individual issues of common stock. In recent years many new options have been created that have as an underlying asset something other than the stock of a particular company. One of them—index options—is discussed here. The appendix discusses others, while the next chapter discusses what are known as futures options.

20.9.1 Cash Settlement

A call option on General Motors stock is a relatively simple instrument. Upon exercise, the call buyer literally calls away 100 shares of GM stock. The call writer is expected to physically deliver the shares. In practice, both the buyer and the writer may find it advantageous to close their positions in order to avoid the costs associated with the physical transfer of shares. In this event the buyer may expect a gain (and the seller a loss) approximately equal to the difference between the current market price of the security and the option's exercise price.

It would be entirely feasible to use only a "cash settlement" procedure upon expiration for any option contract. Here the writer would be required to pay the buyer an amount equal to the difference between the current price of the security and the call option's exercise price (provided that the current price is larger than the exercise price). Similarly for puts, the writer could be expected to pay the buyer an amount equal to the difference between the option's exercise price and the current market price (provided that the exercise price is larger than the current price).

Although listed options on individual securities retain the obligation to "deliver," the realization that cash settlement can serve as a substitute has allowed the creation of index options.

20.9.2 The Contract

An index option is based on the level of an index of stock prices and thus allows investors to take positions in the market that the index represents. Some indices are designed to reflect movements in the stock market, broadly construed. Other "specialized" indices are intended to capture changes in the fortunes of particular industries or sectors. Figure 20.9 shows some of the major indices on which options were offered in 1993, along with their quotations. Some of the indices are highly specialized, consisting of only a few stocks. Others are broadly representative of major portions of the stock market. Roughly one-half are European and the other half are American. Generally, the options expire within a few months, but a few (the LEAPs, shown in the lower right part of Figure 20.9) expire in over a year.[23]

Contracts for index options are not stated in terms of numbers of shares. Instead, the size of a contract is determined by multiplying the level of the index by a multiplier specified by the exchange on which the option is traded. The premium (price) of an index option times the applicable multiplier indicates the total amount paid.

Consider, for example, the S&P 100 index call option that is traded on the Chicago Board Options Exchange with an exercise price of 400 and expiring in March 1994. Note that it has an indicated premium of $31\frac{1}{8}$ on December 13, 1993. Because the multiplier for S&P 100 option contracts is 100, this means that an investor would have to pay $3,112.50 $(= 31.125 \times 100)$ for this contract (plus a commission).

After purchasing this contract, the investor could later sell it or exercise it for its cash settlement value. Perhaps in February 1994 the S&P 100 will be at 450. In this case the investor could exercise the call, receiving its intrinsic value of $5,000 $[= (450 - 400) \times 100]$ for doing so. Alternatively, the investor could simply sell the call on the exchange. In doing so, the amount received would almost certainly be greater than $5,000 because it would sell for an amount equal to the sum of its intrinsic and time values (see Figure 20.6).

20.9.3 Flex Options

In an effort to counteract the growing off-exchange market for customized call and put options, the CBOE has recently started to list "flexible option contracts," called "flex options" for short. These contracts are on indices, and they allow an investor (typically an institution) to specify the exercise price and expiration date. Once the investor places the order, it is executed on the CBOE, where someone else takes the other side of the contract. Because the OCC is in the middle between the buyer and the writer, there is little risk of default on the

CHICAGO

Strike	Vol.	Last	Net Chg.	Open Int.
FINTIMES-SE100(FSX)				
Dec 325c	22	2⅜	– ⅜	160
Dec 325p	25	15/16	– 1/16	113
Dec 330c	5	7/16	– ⅝	5
Dec 330p	10	4¼	+ ⅝	96
Call vol. ...27	Open Int. ...778			
Put vol. ...35	Open Int. ...1,299			
RUSSELL 2000(RUT)				
Dec 240c	75	11½	– 3½	1,440
Dec 245c	25	6⅝	– ⅞	253
Jan 250c	16	5¼	– 1	310
Jan 250p	91	2⅜	– ⅜	3,119
Mar 250c	310	8⅜	– ¾	955
Mar 250p	300	5¼	+ ¼	950
Dec 250c	85	3⅛	+ 3/16	1,415
Dec 250p	25	⅞	+ 3/16	3,151
Jan 255c	25	2	– 13/16	803
Jan 255p	585	4½	– ⅛	755
Dec 255c	3	3/16	– 5/16	636
Dec 255p	572	2⅞	– ⅛	2,115
Jan 260p	346	8⅜	+ 1	1,264
Mar 260p	1	10⅛	– 1½	2
Dec 260p	61	8⅜	+ 1¼	3,461
Call vol. ...614	Open Int. ...15,548			
Put vol. ...1,981	Open Int. ...28,113			
S & P 100 INDEX(OEX)				
Jan 380p	385	⅜	– 1/16	7,301
Feb 380p	75	15/16	– ⅛	4,272
Mar 380c	4	51¾	+ 3	19
Mar 380p	17	1 9/16	– 3/16	2,069
Jan 385p	105	7/16	– ⅛	4,198
Feb 385p	5	1¼	...	1,587
Jan 390p	767	½	– 3/16	3,919
Feb 390p	210	1 7/16	– 1/16	1,574
Mar 390p	24	1 15/16	– 7/16	1,515
Dec 390p	156	1/16	...	18,922
Jan 395p	572	11/16	– ⅛	4,519
Dec 395p	1,218	1/16	...	23,617
Jan 400p	3,604	13/16	– ¼	11,108
Feb 400p	1,053	2	– ⅜	3,076
Mar 400c	5	31⅛	– ¼	5
Mar 400p	21	2⅞	– ⅜	824
Dec 400p	3,490	1/16	– 1/16	36,983
Jan 405c	3	25½	+ 1⅞	35
Jan 405p	4,347	1	– ⅜	12,174
Feb 405p	30	2¾	– ⅛	1,008
Dec 405c	3	25¼	+ 1	409
Dec 405p	2,071	1/16	– 1/16	31,747
Jan 410c	12	20⅝	...	388
Jan 410p	5,181	1 5/16	– 7/16	14,753
Feb 410c	3	21½	+ 1	140
Feb 410p	620	3	– ½	5,323
Mar 410p	105	4¾	– ⅜	3,375
Dec 410c	11	20¼	+ 2½	2,093
Dec 410p	1,616	⅛	...	39,274
Jan 415c	928	17½	+ 3	388
Jan 415p	2,870	1 11/16	– 11/16	13,144
Feb 415c	2	17	– ¼	93
Feb 415p	150	3¾	– ⅞	1,369
Dec 415c	926	16	+ 3½	6,379
Dec 415p	8,489	3/16	– ⅛	48,675
Jan 420c	2,120	13½	+ 2	11,626
Jan 420p	9,610	2 7/16	– 13/16	23,341
Feb 420p	1,592	4⅜	– ⅞	6,594
Mar 420c	18	15½	– ¼	53
Mar 420p	16	7	– ¼	2,443
Dec 420c	4,527	11	+ 2⅛	18,468
Dec 420p	12,285	¼	– 7/16	55,716
Jan 425c	4,601	9½	+ 1⅝	19,386

PACIFIC

WILSHIRE INDEX(WSX)					
Jan	300c	3,200	28	...	...
Jan	300p	3,200	5/16	– ⅛	25
Jan	320p	45	2⅝	+ 3/16	31
Dec	320c	5	6⅝	– 2	35
Jan	325c	5	6¼	+ ⅛	82
Jan	325p	23	3½	– ¾	70
Dec	325c	51	4	+ 1⅜	88
Dec	325p	30	1 1/16	– 9/16	75
Jan	330c	15	4⅛	– ¼	44
Jan	330p	20	6½	+ ⅞	17
Dec	330c	7	⅞	+ ¼	123
Dec	330p	59	4	– ⅜	141
Jan	350c	3,200	⅛	– ⅛	50
Jan	350p	3,400	22¼	...	...
Call vol. ...6,483	Open Int. ...909				
Put vol. ...6,777	Open Int. ...1,132				

NEW YORK

NYSE INDEX new(NYA)					
Jan	250p	9	1 9/16	– 1/16	28
Jan	255p	2	2½		314
Jan	260p	200	4¼	– ¼	303
Call vol. ...0	Open Int. ...760				
Put vol. ...211	Open Int. ...1,579				

LEAPS—LONG TERM OPTIONS

MAJOR MARKET — AM					
Dec 94	25p	20	1/16	– 1/16	5150
Dec 95	25p	15	3/16	– 1/16	2882
Dec 95	32½p	165	1	– ⅛	846
Dec 94	35p	10	⅞	...	11333
Dec 95	35p	40	1½	...	1722
Dec 94	37½p	17	1¾	– 3/16	5431
Dec 95	37½p	200	2 3/16	– 3/16	2793
Dec 95	40p	8	3⅛	...	490
Call vol. ...0	Open Int. ...49,823				
Put vol. ...475	Open Int. ...105,354				
S & P 100 INDEX — CB					
Dec 94	32½p	40	¼	...	9536
Dec 94	35p	10	7/16	...	20670
Dec 94	37½p	32	13/16	– 1/16	11918
Dec 94	40p	565	15/16	...	50567
Dec 93	42½p	135	⅛	– 1/16	8916
Dec 94	42½p	103	2⅛	...	9694
Dec 93	45p	1010	2	– ⅛	1536
Call vol. ...0	Open Int. ...7,965				
Put vol. ...1,897	Open Int. ...220,199				
S & P 500 INDEX — CB					
Dec 94	40p	74	⅝	...	20551
Dec 94	42½p	40	1	...	12113
Dec 93	45c	1	1¼	– ⅛	120
Dec 94	45p	57	1⅝	...	14190
Dec 94	50p	40	4⅛	...	1448
Call vol. ...1	Open Int. ...20,740				
Put vol. ...211	Open Int. ...257,443				

Figure 20.9

Index Options Quotations

Source: Reprinted by permission of *The Wall Street Journal*, ©Dow Jones & Company, Inc., December 14, 1993, p. C18. All rights reserved worldwide.

contract. This is an advantage to these customized options, since options created off-exchange (say between investors *A* and *B*) are only as good as the credit-worthiness of the parties themselves. (The possibility that the writer of one of these off-exchange options may default on his or her obligations is referred to as **counterparty risk.**)

In the mid 1980s one of the more popular uses of options, procuring **portfolio insurance,** was developed. Consider an investor who holds a highly diversified portfolio. This investor would like to be able to benefit from any upward movements that may subsequently occur in the stock market but would also like to be protected from any downward movements.[24] There are, in principle, at least three ways this might be accomplished.[25]

20.10.1 Purchase an Insurance Policy

One alternative is to sign a contract with an insurance company. For example, assume that the portfolio is currently worth $100,000. The insurance company might agree to cover any loss in value over some specified period, such as over the forthcoming year. At the end of the year, if the portfolio value was $95,000, the insurance company would pay the investor $5,000. On the other hand, if the value was $105,000, the insurance company would pay nothing.

Figure 20.10(a) illustrates this situation. The horizontal axis measures the value of the portfolio at year-end. The 45–degree line $0BC$ shows the value of the uninsured portfolio, while the kinked line ABC shows the value of the insured portfolio. As the figure shows, if the portfolio value at the end of the year is more than $100,000, then the insured portfolio will be worth the same amount as the uninsured portfolio. However, if the portfolio value is less than $100,000, then the insured portfolio is worth more, with the vertical difference between $0B$ and AB representing the size of the payment made to the investor by the insurance company.

Unfortunately insurance companies rarely sign contracts of this sort. However, this is not the only alternative. Instead of dealing with an insurance company, the investor could consider purchasing a put option.

20.10.2 Purchase a Protective Put

Assume that a put option is available on a stock market index that closely resembles the investor's portfolio. The kinked line ADE in Figure 20.10(b) shows the value to a buyer of such a put at the expiration date, where the put has an exercise price of $100,000 [note how it corresponds to Figure 20.3(b)]. Line $0BC$ is the value of the portfolio on the expiration date, assuming that the put was not purchased.

What would happen to an investor who (1) held the portfolio and (2) purchased this put? Figure 20.10(c) shows the answer. The value of the portfolio *(ABC)* is simply the sum of the values $0BC$ and ADE shown in Figure 20.10(b). Not surprisingly, it is precisely the same as the kinked line ABC in Figure 20.10(a).

In this case the purchase of a put provides protection against declines in portfolio value. In this role it is termed a protective put (or "married put"). In practice, stock indices may not closely correspond with an investor's portfolio. Thus the purchase of a put on a stock index may provide only imperfect insurance. In a graph such as that shown in Figure 20.10(c), the resulting curve

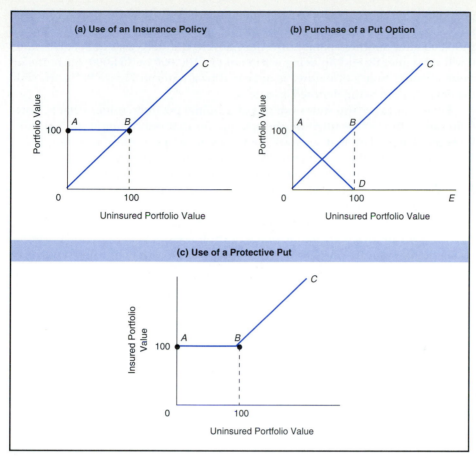

(a) Use of an Insurance Policy

(b) Purchase of a Put Option

(c) Use of a Protective Put

Figure 20.10
Portfolio Insurance

would be somewhat fuzzy owing to the possible divergence of values of the portfolio and the index. For example, the portfolio may decline in value by $25,000 whereas the index declines only by $10,000. In this case the portfolio would be insured for only 40% (= $10,000/$25,000) of its decline in value.

What if neither explicit insurance nor an appropriate put were available? Can something still be done to insure the portfolio's value against market declines? Yes, if the allocation of funds between the portfolio and a riskless security can be altered frequently enough (and at reasonable cost). This type of portfolio insurance involves the creation of a **synthetic put,** and its application involves the use of a dynamic strategy for asset allocation, which will be discussed next.

20.10.3 Create a Synthetic Put

Insuring a portfolio by creating a synthetic put can most easily be described with an example.[26] Assume that the investor has $100,000 and is considering the purchase of a portfolio of common stocks. It is believed that the market value of this portfolio will either increase to $125,000 or decrease to $80,000 in six months. If it does increase to $125,000, then it will end up being worth either $156,250 or $100,000 after another six months. Alternatively, if it decreases to $80,000, then it will subsequently end up being worth either $100,000 or $64,000. Each one of these possible "states of nature" is indicated by a letter in Figure 20.11(a), with the current state being denoted as state A.

Figure 20.11(a) also shows two sets of terminal portfolio values (that is, portfolio values after 12 months) on the assumption that the common stock portfolio is purchased. The first set gives the values of the portfolio if it is uninsured. The second shows the desired portfolio values—that is, the values of an insured portfolio. In this example the investor wants to be certain that the ending portfolio is worth at least $100,000, while also being able to earn the returns associated with state D, should that state occur.[27]

What should the investor do initially in order to be certain of this? Clearly, the investor cannot simply purchase the portfolio of stocks because the portfolio could be worth only $64,000 if state G occurs. However, the investor could

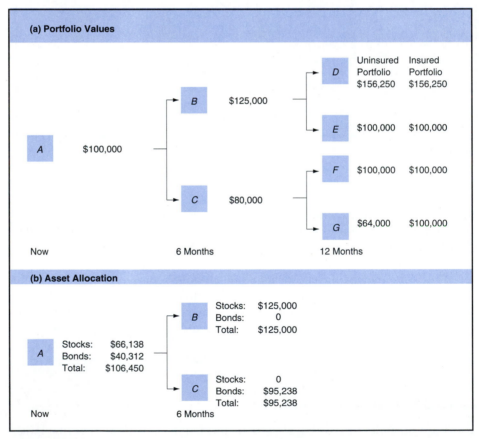

Figure 20.11
Creation of a Synthetic Put

consider purchasing portfolio insurance—that is, creating a synthetic put—by investing in both the stock portfolio and riskfree bonds.

The way this is done is to imagine that six months have passed and that state B has occurred. In this situation, how might one be certain to have $156,250 if the final state is D and $100,000 if the state is E? The answer is simple—if state B occurs, make sure that the portfolio at that point is worth $125,000. Thus an initial investment strategy is required that will provide $125,000 if the six-month state turns out to be state B.

It is also possible that after the first six months state C will occur. In this situation, how might one be certain to have $100,000 regardless of the final state? Assuming that riskfree bonds return 5% (compounded discretely) per six months, the investor should purchase $95,238 ($= \$100,000/1.05$) of these bonds if state C occurs. This means that an initial investment strategy is required that will provide $95,238 if the six-month state turns out to be state C.

Figure 20.11(b) shows the investments and the amounts required in situations B and C. It remains only to determine an appropriate initial set of investments (at point A).

An amount of $1 invested in the common stock portfolio at A will grow to $1.25 after six months if the state at that time is B. More generally, s invested in the common stock portfolio at A will grow to $1.25s$ if the six-month state is B. Similarly, b invested in bonds at A will grow to $1.05b$ after six months. Thus, a set of initial investments that will provide $125,000 if state B occurs can be found by solving the following equation for s and b:

$$1.25s + 1.05b = \$125,000. \tag{20.18}$$

If the six-month state is C, then s invested in the common stock portfolio will be worth $.8s$, while b invested in bonds will be worth $1.05b$. Thus a set of initial investments that will provide $95,238 if state C occurs can be found by solving the following equation for s and b:

$$.8s + 1.05b = \$95,238. \tag{20.19}$$

Solutions for s and b can now be found because there are two equations and two unknowns. The solution, shown in Figure 20.11(b), is that the investor should initially put $66,138 in common stocks and $40,312 in bonds (that is, $s = \$66,138$ and $b = \$40,312$), for a total initial investment of $106,450 ($= \$66,138 + \$40,312$).

Making this initial investment is equivalent to investing $100,000 in the common stock portfolio and buying a protective put option (or an insurance policy) for $6,450. Indeed, this analysis could be used to determine the appropriate price for such an option or insurance policy. Equivalently, the actions of the investor have resulted in the creation of a synthetic put where the stocks being held are the underlying asset.

By design, this initial investment will provide precisely the desired ending values, but only if the "mix" is altered as values change. The goal is achieved by using a *dynamic strategy* in which investments are bought and sold at intermediate points, depending on the returns of the underlying assets.

In the example, if state B occurs, the stocks will be worth $82,672 (= $66,138 × 1.25), and the bonds will be worth $42,328 (= $40,312 × 1.05), for an aggregate value of $125,000. In this situation the $42,328 of bonds would be sold and the proceeds used to make an additional investment in the common stock portfolio so that the investor is entirely invested in common stocks for the last six months.

However, if state C occurs, the stocks will be worth $52,910 (= $66,138 × .8), and the bonds will be worth $42,328 (= $40,312 × 1.05), for an aggregate value of $95,238. In this situation the $52,910 of stocks would be sold and the proceeds used to make an additional investment in the riskfree bonds for the last six months.

Thus more money is invested in common stocks if the initial portfolio rises in value, with the money obtained by selling bonds. However, if the initial portfolio falls in value, more money is invested in bonds, with the money obtained by selling stocks. In this example the percentage invested in stocks is initially 62.13% (= $66,138/$106,450) and subsequently goes to either 100% (if stocks go up) or 0% (if stocks go down).

More realistic applications involve many time intervals within the one-year period, with smaller stock price movements in each interval. Consequently there would be more changes in the mix of stocks and bonds after each interval, but the changes would be of smaller magnitude. Nevertheless, the essential nature of the strategy would be the same:

When stock prices rise, sell some bonds and buy more stocks.
When stock prices fall, sell some stocks and buy more bonds.

Often computers are used to monitor stock price movements of investors who have obtained portfolio insurance in this manner. When these movements are of sufficient magnitude, the computer is used to place the requisite buy and sell orders electronically. Because much of this monitoring and ordering is programmed into a computer, portfolio insurance is often referred to as a form of **program trading.**[28]

If there are only two states of nature in each interval, and reallocation is possible after every interval, and there are no transaction costs, then the values associated with any desired "insured portfolio" can be replicated exactly with a dynamic strategy. In practice, however, the results are likely to be only approximately equal. First there are transaction costs associated with buying and selling securities for the dynamic strategy.[29] Second, if an interval is defined as a length of time over which only two alternative states may occur, then the amount of time to an interval may be so short that reallocation is impossible after each interval.

In practice, arbitrary rules are applied to avoid frequent revisions and the associated high level of transaction costs while being reasonably certain of providing the portfolio with the desired level of insurance.[30] Unfortunately these arbitrary rules did not work very well on Black Monday and Terrible Tuesday (October 19–20, 1987). During these two days stock prices moved downward so fast that reallocation could not be performed in a timely fashion, resulting in a situation where portfolio insurance did not provide the protection that had been anticipated. As a result, some people believe that dynamic strategies will be used less frequently in the future, and that puts will be used more often.[31]

1. An option is a contract between two investors that grants one investor the right (but not the obligation) to sell to or buy from the other investor a specific asset at a specific price within a specific time period.

2. A call option for a stock gives the buyer the right to buy a specific number of shares of a specific company from the option writer at a specific purchase price at any time up to and including a specific date.

3. A put option for a stock gives the buyer the right to sell a specific number of shares of a specific company to the option writer at a specific selling price at any time up to and including a specific date.

4. Option trading is facilitated by standardized contracts traded on organized exchanges. These exchanges employ the services of a clearing corporation, which maintains records of all trades and acts as a buyer from all option writers and a writer to all option buyers.

5. Option writers are required to deposit margin to ensure performance of their obligations. The amount and form of the margin will depend on the particular option strategy involved.

6. The intrinsic value of a call option equals the difference between the stock's price and the option's exercise price, if this difference is positive. Otherwise the option's intrinsic value is zero.

7. The intrinsic value of a put option equals the difference between its exercise price and the stock's price, if this difference is positive. Otherwise, the option's intrinsic value is zero.

8. Calls and puts will not sell for less than their intrinsic values. However, they may sell for more than their intrinsic values owing to their time values.

9. The binomial option pricing model can be used to determine the fair value of an option based on the assumption that the underlying asset will attain one of two possible known prices at the end of each of a finite number of periods, given its price at the start of each period.

10. An option's hedge ratio indicates the change in the option's value resulting from a one-dollar change in the value of the underlying asset.

11. The Black-Scholes option valuation model shows that the fair value of an option is determined by five factors: the market price of the stock, the exercise price, the life of the option, the riskfree rate, and the risk of the common stock. It assumes that the riskfree rate and common stock risk are constant over the option's life.

12. Put-call parity states that buying both a put option on a stock and a share of the stock will produce the same payoff as buying both a call option on the stock and a riskfree bond (assuming that both options have the same exercise price and expiration date).

13. In addition to put and call options on individual common stocks, options on other assets are traded, such as options on stock indices, debt instruments, and foreign currency.

14. Synthetic options can be created by holding the underlying asset and a riskfree asset in relative amounts that vary with the market price of the underlying asset.

1. Why have organized options exchanges been so important to the growth in options trading?

2. How do organized options exchanges permit option buyers and writers to open and close positions without having to contact one another directly?

3. Consider the following stocks selling for the prices listed below:

Stock	Current Price
A	$26
B	$73
C	$215

Specify the likely exercise prices that will be set for newly created options on these stocks.

4. From the latest two consecutive issues of the *Wall Street Journal,* find the price of the General Motors call option with the nearest expiration date and the exercise price closest to the current price of GM stock. What is the premium on the call option? What has been the percentage change in the option's price from the previous day? From another part of the *Journal,* calculate the percentage change in the price of GM stock from the previous day. Compare this number to the option's percentage price change.

5. Polly Wolfe has written a September 45 naked call option on Albion software stock. When the option was written, the stock sold for $42 per share. The option premium was $2.75. Calculate how much margin Polly had to deposit upon writing the call.

6. Dasher Troy wrote a March 75 naked put option on Lodi Mines stock. When the option was written, the stock sold for $80 per share. The option premium was $.30. How much margin did Dasher have to deposit?

7. Draw a profit-loss graph for the following option strategies:
   a. Buy a put, $2 premium, $70 exercise price.
   b. Write a call, $3 premium, $40 exercise price.
   c. Buy a stock for $80 and buy a put on the same stock, $1 premium, $70 exercise price.

8. Elizabeth Stroud had only a few hours left to decide whether to exercise a call option on Carson Company stock. The call option has an exercise price of $54. Elizabeth originally purchased the call six months ago for $400 (or $4 per share).
   a. For what range of stock prices should Elizabeth exercise the call on the last day of the call's life?
   b. For what range of stock prices would Elizabeth realize a net loss (including the premium paid for the call)?
   c. If Elizabeth had purchased a put instead of a call, how would your answers to parts (a) and (b) change?

9. On November 18, three call options on Eden Prairie Associates stock, all expiring in December, sold for the following prices:

Exercise Price	Option Price
$50	$7½
$60	$3
$70	$1½

Firpo Marberry is considering a "butterfly spread" that involves the following positions:

Buy 1 call at $50 exercise price.

Sell (write) 2 calls at $60 exercise price.

Buy 1 call at $70 exercise price.

   a. What would be the values at expiration of Firpo's spread if Eden Prairie Associates' stock price is below $50? Between $50 and $60? Between $60 and $70? Above $70?

   b. What dollar investment would be required of Firpo to establish the spread?

10. What is the time value of an option? Why does an option's time value decline as the option approaches expiration?

11. Shorewood Systems stock currently sells for $50 per share. One year from today the stock will be worth either $58.09 or $43.04. The continuously compounded riskfree rate is 5.13% for one year. Based on the binomial option pricing model, what is the fair value for a call option on Shorewood stock with one year to expiration and a $50 exercise price?

12. Hopkins Pharmaceuticals stock is currently priced at $40 per share. Six months from now its price will be either $44.21 or $36.19. If the price rises to $44.21, then six months later the price will be either $48.86 or $40. If, however, the price initially falls to $36.19, then six months later the price will be either $40 or $32.75. The riskfree rate (continuously compounded) is 3.05% over each six-month period. Using the binomial option pricing model, what is the fair value of a one-year call option on Hopkins stock?

13. Given the information below, calculate the three-month call option price that is consistent with the Black-Scholes model:

$$P_s = \$47, \quad E = \$45, \quad R = .05, \quad \sigma = .40.$$

14. If the premium on a call option has recently declined, does this indicate that the option is a better buy than it was previously? Why?

15. List the variables needed to estimate the value of a call option. Describe how a change in the value of these variables affects the value of a call option.

16. Calculate the hedge ratio of a call option for a stock with a current price of $40, an exercise price of $45, a standard deviation of 34%, and a time to expiration of six months, given a riskfree return of 7% per annum.

17. Using the Black-Scholes model, calculate the implicit volatility of a stock with a three-month call option currently selling for $8.54 and:

$$P_s = \$83, \quad E = \$80, \quad R = .05.$$

18. Blondy Ryan owns 20,000 shares of Merrimac Monitoring Equipment stock. This stock makes up the bulk of Blondy's wealth. Concerned about the stock's near-term prospects, Blondy wishes to fully hedge the risk of the stock. Given a hedge ratio of .37 and a premium of $2.50 for the near Merrimac put option, how many put options should Blondy buy?

---

19. A six-month call option with an exercise price of $40 is selling for $5. The current price of the stock is $41.25. The hedge ratio of the option is .65.

    a. What percentage change in the option's price is likely to accompany a 1% change in the stock's price?

    b. If the beta of the stock is 1.10, what is the beta of the option? (*Hint:* Recall what the beta of a stock implies about the relationship between the stock's price and that of the market.)

20. The fair value of a three-month call option on Portage Industries stock is $1.50. The exercise price of the call option is $30. The riskfree rate is 5%, and the stock price of Portage is currently $28 per share. What is the fair value of a three-month put option on Portage stock with the same exercise price as the call option?

21. Given the following information, calculate the three-month put option price that is consistent with the Black-Scholes model:

$$P_s = \$32, \qquad E = \$45, \qquad R = .06, \qquad \sigma = .35.$$

22. Explain why call options on non-dividend-paying stocks are "worth more alive than dead."

23. In February Gid Gardner sold a September 55 call on Dane Corporation stock for $4.375 per share and simultaneously bought a September 55 put on the same stock for $6 per share. At the time, Treasury bills coming due in September were priced to yield 12.6%, and Dane stock sold for $53 per share.

    a. What value would put-call parity suggest was appropriate for the Dane put?

    b. Dane was expected to make three dividend payments between February and September. Could that account for the discrepancy between your answer to part (a) and the actual price of the put? Why or why not?

    c. If Dane stock were to fall to a very low value before September, might it pay for Gid to exercise the put? Why?

24. Why does a stock index option sell at a lower price than the cost of a portfolio of options on the constituent stocks (assuming that the index call option and the portfolio of call options control the same dollar value of stocks)?

25. Distinguish between portfolio insurance implemented through a protective put and through dynamic asset allocation.

26. (Appendix Question) What is the primary advantage to an investor of a warrant compared to a call option?

27. (Appendix Question) Wheeling Corp. has a 10% subordinated convertible debenture outstanding, maturing in 8 years. The bond's face value is $1,000. It currently sells for 99 of par. The bond is convertible into 15 shares of common stock. The company's common stock currently sells for $50 per share. Nonconvertible bonds of similar risk have a yield of 12%.

    a. What is the bond's conversion value?

    b. What is the bond's conversion premium?

    c. What is the bond's investment value?

APPENDIX

SECURITIES WITH OPTIONLIKE FEATURES

Many securities have features that are similar to stock options, particularly call options. In some cases the optionlike features are explicit. Examples include options on stock market indices (discussed earlier in the chapter), debt instruments, and foreign currencies.[32] These options let investors take positions based on their forecasts of movements of the stock market, interest rates, and foreign exchange rates. In other cases more subtle optionlike features are involved. This appendix discusses some of these securities.

A.1 WARRANTS

A stock purchase warrant (or, more simply, a warrant) is a call option issued by the firm whose stock serves as the underlying security.[33] At the time of issue, a warrant usually has a longer time to expiration (for example, five or more years) than a typical call option. Some perpetual warrants, with no expiration date, have also been issued. Generally, warrants may be exercised before expiration—that is, they are like American call options—but some require an initial waiting period.

The exercise price may be fixed, or it may change during the life of the warrant, usually increasing in steps. The initial exercise price is typically set to exceed the market price of the underlying security at the time the warrant is issued, often by a substantial amount.

At the time of issue, one warrant typically entitles the holder to purchase one share of stock for the appropriate exercise price. However, most warrants are protected against stock splits and stock dividends. This means that any warrant with such protection will enable the investor to buy more or less than one share at an altered exercise price if a stock dividend or stock split is declared. For example, a two-for-one stock split would allow the warrant holder to purchase two shares at one-half the original exercise price, whereas a one-for-two reverse stock split would allow the warrant holder to purchase one-half share at twice the original exercise price.

Warrants may be distributed to stockholders in lieu of a stock or cash dividend or sold directly as a new security issue. Alternatively, warrants may be issued in order to "sweeten" an offering of some other kind of security. For example, a bond may be sold by the firm with warrants attached to it. In some cases, the warrants are nondetachable, except upon exercise. This means that if an investor wants to sell one of the bonds, the warrants must be either exercised or sold with the bond. In other cases the warrants are detachable, meaning that after the initial sale of the bonds an investor may sell either the bonds or the warrants (or both).

Terms associated with a warrant are contained in a warrant agreement, which serves the same function as an indenture for a bond issue. In this agreement the scope of the warrant holder's protection is defined (for example, the treatment of warrants in the event of a merger). It may also specify certain restrictions on corporate behavior.

Some warrants that are issued with bonds have an additional attribute. Although they may be detached and exercised by paying cash to the corporation, an alternative method of payment is provided. This alternative allows bonds from the initial issue to be used in lieu of cash to pay the exercise price, with the bonds being valued at par for this purpose.

One difference between warrants and call options is the limitation on the amount of warrants that are outstanding. A specific number of warrants of a particular type will be issued. The total generally cannot be increased, and typically will be reduced as the warrants are exercised. In contrast, a call option can be created whenever two people wish to create one. Thus the number outstanding is not fixed. Exercise of a call option on its stock has no more effect on a corporation than a transaction in its stock on the secondary market. However, the exercise of a warrant does have an effect. In particular, it leaves the corporation with more cash, fewer warrants outstanding, and more stock outstanding.

Warrants are traded on major stock exchanges and on the over-the-counter market. Quotations for those with active markets are provided in the financial press in the sections devoted primarily to stocks.

A.2   RIGHTS

A right is similar to a warrant in that it also is like a call option issued by the firm whose stock serves as the underlying security. Rights, also known as subscription warrants, are issued to give existing stockholders their preemptive right to subscribe to a new issue of common stock before the general public is given an opportunity. Each share of stock receives one right. A stated number of rights plus cash equal to a specified subscription price are required in order to obtain one new share. To ensure the sale of the new stock, the subscription price is usually set below the stock's market price at the time the rights are issued. This does not mean that new subscribers get a bargain, as they must pay old stockholders for the required number of rights, which become valuable as a result.

Rights generally have short lives (from two to ten weeks when issued) and may be freely traded prior to exercise. Up to a specified date, old shares of the stock trade *cum rights*, meaning that the buyer of the stock is entitled to receive the rights when issued. Afterward the stock trades *ex rights* at a correspondingly lower price. Rights for popular issues of stock are sometimes traded on exchanges; others are available in the over-the-counter market. Often trading begins prior to actual availability, with the rights sold for delivery on a *when-issued* basis.

A right is, in effect, a warrant, although one with a rather short time before expiration. It also differs with regard to exercise price, which is typically set above the stock's market price at issuance for a warrant and below it for a right. Because of their short lives, rights need not be protected against stock splits and stock dividends. Otherwise they have all the attributes of a warrant and can be valued in a similar manner.[34]

A.3   BOND CALL PROVISIONS

Many firms issue bonds with call provisions that allow the firm to repurchase the bonds before maturity, usually at a price above par value. This amounts to the simultaneous sale of a straight bond and purchase of a call option that is paid by the corporation in the form of a relatively lower selling price for the bond. The writer of the option is the bond purchaser.

Bond call provisions usually can be exercised only after some specified date (for example, five years after issue). Moreover, the exercise price, known as the call premium, may be different for different exercise dates (typically shrinking in size the longer the bond is outstanding). The implicit call option associated with such a bond is thus both longer lived and more complex than those traded on the listed option markets.[35]

A.4   CONVERTIBLE SECURITIES

A particularly popular financial instrument is a security that can be converted into a different security of the same firm under certain conditions. The typical case involves a bond or a preferred stock convertible into shares of the firm's common stock, with a stated number of shares received for each bond or share of preferred stock. Usually no cash is involved: the old security is simply traded in, and the appropriate number of new securities is issued in return. Convertible preferred stocks are issued from time to time, but tax effects make them, like other preferred stock, attractive primarily to corporate investors. For other investors many issues of convertible bonds are more attractive.

If a $1,000 par-value bond can be converted into 20 shares of common stock, the *conversion ratio* is 20. Alternatively, the *conversion price* may be said to be $50 (= $1,000/20), because $50 of the bond's par value must be given up to obtain one common share. Neither the conversion ratio nor the conversion price is affected by changes in a bond's market value.

Conversion ratios are typically set so that conversion will not prove attractive unless the stock price increases substantially from its value at the time the convertible security was first issued. This is similar to the general practice used in setting exercise prices for warrants.

A convertible bond's *conversion value,* obtained by multiplying the conversion ratio by the stock's current market price, is the value that would be obtained by conversion; it is the bond's current "value as stock." The *conversion premium* is the amount by which the bond's current market price exceeds its conversion value, expressed as a percent of the latter. A related amount is the convertible's *investment value.* This value is an estimate—based on the convertible's maturity date, coupon rate, and credit rating—of the amount for which the bond might sell if it were not convertible. Equivalently, it is the convertible's "value as a straight bond."

Consider a $1,000 par-value bond convertible into 20 shares of stock. If the market price of the stock is $60 per share, then the conversion value of the bond is $1,200 (= $60 × 20). If the current market price of the convertible bond is $1,300, then its conversion premium is $100 (= $1,300 − $1,200). Its investment value might be estimated to be, say, $950, meaning that the bond would sell for this much if it did not provide the investor with the option of convertibility.

Convertible securities of great complexity can be found in the marketplace. Some may be converted only after an initial waiting period. Some may be converted up to the bond's maturity date; others, only for a stated, shorter period. Some have different conversion ratios for different years. A few can be converted into packages of two or more different securities; others require the additional payment of cash upon conversion.

Convertible bonds are usually protected against stock splits and stock dividends via adjustment in the conversion ratio. For example, a bond with an initial conversion ratio of 20 could be adjusted to have a ratio of 22 following a 10% stock dividend. Protection against cash dividends is not generally provided, but some indentures require that the holders of convertible bonds be notified prior to payment of cash dividends so that they may convert before the resultant fall in the stock's market price.

Convertible securities often contain a call provision, which may be used by the corporation to force conversion when the stock's market price is sufficiently high to make the value of the stock obtained on conversion exceed the call price of the bond. For example, if the conversion value of the bond is $1,200 (the bond is convertible into 20 shares of stock that are currently selling for $60 per share) and the call price is $1,100, the firm can force conversion by calling the bond. This is because a bondholder faces two choices when the call is received—either convert and receive 20 shares collectively worth $1,200 or receive cash of $1,100—and should choose the shares because they have a higher value.

A convertible bond is, for practical purposes, a bond with nondetachable warrants plus the restriction that *only* the bond is usable (at par) to pay the exercise price. If the bond were not callable, the value of this package would equal the value of a straight noncallable bond (that is, the estimated investment value) plus that of the warrants. However, most convertible bonds are callable and thus involve a double option: the holder has an option to convert the bond to stock, and the issuing corporation has an option to buy the bond back from the investors.

Endnotes

[1] Prior to 1973, options were traded over the counter through the efforts of dealers and brokers in a relatively illiquid market. These dealers and brokers brought buyers and writers together, arranged terms, helped with the paperwork, and charged fees for their efforts.

[2] However, there is protection for any cash dividend that is formally designated a "return of capital." Furthermore, options that are traded over the counter typically are protected from any type of cash dividend. In both cases the protection is in the form of a reduction in the exercise price.

[3] For some active stocks, options may be introduced that have only one or two months to expiration.

[4] If the stock sells for less than $25, then the interval may be $2.50 (for example, at $15 and $17.50 for a stock selling at $16). If the stock sells for more than $200, the interval will be for $10 (or perhaps even $20). It should be noted that exchange officials have latitude in setting the terms of the options.

[5] For more on commissions, see pp. 109–115 of John C. Cox and Mark Rubinstein, *Options Markets* (Englewood Cliffs, NJ: Prentice Hall, 1985).

[6] It should be noted that a call or put buyer is not allowed to use margin. Instead, the option buyer is required to pay 100% of the option's purchase price. In contrast, the stock buyer can use margin, where part of the cost of purchasing the stock is borrowed.

[7] Because the premium is paid by the buyer to the writer at the time the option is created, its value should be compounded to the expiration date using an appropriate rate of interest when calculating profits and losses.

[8] Strips and straps are option strategies similar to a straddle. The former involves combining two puts with one call, and the latter involves combining two calls with one put. Another kind of strategy is known as a spread, where one call is bought while another is written on the same underlying security. Specifically, a price spread involves two calls having the same expiration date but different exercise prices. A time spread involves two calls having the same exercise price but different expiration dates.

[9] If there are dividends, they should be expressed as a compounded value at the expiration date associated with the options (as they would have been previously received) and added to the line, thereby shifting it upward.

[10] In general, $1 will grow to $1e^{RT}$ at the end of T periods if it is continuously compounded at a rate of R. Here e represents the base of the natural logarithm, which is equal to approximately 2.71828. For a more detailed discussion, see the Appendix to Chapter 5.

[11] Equations (20.5) and (20.6) can be derived by solving the set of Equations (20.3a) and (20.3b) using symbols instead of numbers.

[12] Fischer Black and Myron Scholes, "The Pricing of Options and Corporate Liabilities," *Journal of Political Economy*, 81, no. 3 (May/June 1973): 637–654. Also see Fischer Black,

"How We Came Up with the Option Formula," *Journal of Portfolio Management,* 15, no. 2 (Winter 1989): 4–8, and "How to Use the Holes in Black-Scholes," *Journal of Applied Corporate Finance,* 1, no. 4 (Winter 1989): 67–73.

[13] See Robert C. Merton, "Theory of Rational Option Pricing," *Bell Journal of Economics and Management Science,* 4, no. 1 (Spring 1973): 141–183.

[14] These procedures are reviewed in the options textbooks cited at the end of the chapter.

[15] Table 20.2 is an abbreviated version of a standard cumulative normal distribution table. More detailed versions can be found in most statistics textbooks.

[16] It should be pointed out that the investment strategy is more complicated than it might appear because the number of shares that are to be held will change over time as the stock price changes and the expiration date gets closer. Similarly, the amount of the loan will change over time. Hence it is a *dynamic strategy.*

[17] If daily data are used, it is best to multiply the daily variance by 250 instead of 365 because there are about 250 trading days in a year. See Mark Kritzman, "About Estimating Volatility: Part I," *Financial Analysts Journal,* 47, no. 4 (July/August 1991): 22–25; and "About Estimating Volatility: Part II," *Financial Analysts Journal,* 47, no. 5 (September/October 1991): 10–11. For a method of estimating σ that uses high, low, opening, and closing prices as well as trading volume, see Mark B. Garman and Michael J. Klass, "On the Estimation of Security Price Volatilities from Historical Data," *Journal of Business,* 53, no. 1 (January 1980): 67–78.

[18] Alternatively, Equation (20.10) could be solved for the interest rate R; doing so gives an estimate of the *implied interest rate.* See Menachem Brenner and Dan Galai, "Implied Interest Rates," *Journal of Business,* 59, no. 3 (July 1986): 493–507.

[19] For a further discussion of these methods, see any of the options textbooks cited at the end of the chapter, or see Menachem Brenner and Marti Subrahmanyam, "A Simple Formula to Compute the Implied Standard Deviation," *Financial Analysts Journal,* 44, no. 5 (September/October 1988): 80–83.

[20] This explanation of a hedge ratio follows from the BOPM-based interpretation of the Black-Scholes formula that was given earlier. That is, if a call's payoffs can be duplicated by buying stock and borrowing at the riskfree rate, it follows that buying stock and writing a call will duplicate investing in the riskfree asset.

[21] See endnote 14.

[22] See Robert Geske and Kuldeep Shastri, "The Early Exercise of American Puts," *Journal of Banking and Finance,* 9, no. 2 (June 1985): 207–219, and endnote 14.

[23] A rather unusual kind of index option, referred to as a "warrant," has appeared recently on the American Stock Exchange. Usually the underlying asset is a foreign stock market index. Daily trading activity in these warrants is reported in the AMEX's stock tables, listed in the appropriate alphabetical place under the name of the issuer (such as under *S* for Salomon Brothers). Put warrants give the owner the right to "sell the index" at a stated exercise price, while call warrants give the owner the right to "buy the index" at a stated exercise price. Note that the warrants are only as good as the credit quality of the issuer, since the warrant owner might be left with an option that cannot be exercised if the issuer goes bankrupt. For a discussion of how the possibility of default by the writer affects the prices of such options, see Herb Johnson and Rene Stulz, "The Pricing of Options with Default Risk," *Journal of Finance,* 42, no. 2 (June 1987): 267–280.

[24] In an efficient market, investors with "average" attitudes toward risk should not purchase portfolio insurance. Those who are especially averse to "downside risk" (relative to "upside potential") may find it useful to buy insurance. The key is the nature of the investor's attitudes toward risk and return. See Hayne E. Leland, "Who Should Buy Portfolio Insurance?" *Journal of Finance,* 35, no. 2 (May 1980): 581–594.

[25] Some people would argue that the use of stop orders represents a fourth way.

[26] For an exposition, see Mark Rubinstein and Hayne E. Leland, "Replicating Options with Positions in Stock and Cash," *Financial Analysts Journal*, 37, no. 4 (July/August 1981): 63–72; Mark Rubinstein, "Alternative Paths to Portfolio Insurance," *Financial Analysts Journal*, 41, no. 4 (July/August 1985): 42–52; Robert Ferguson, "How to Beat the S&P 500 (Without Losing Sleep)," *Financial Analysts Journal*, 42, no. 2 (March/April 1986): 37–46; and Thomas J. O'Brien, "The Mechanics of Portfolio Insurance," *Journal of Portfolio Management*, 14, no. 3 (Spring 1988): 40–47.

[27] In this example, portfolio insurance is sought for a one-year horizon with a floor of 0% (meaning that the investor does not want to lose any of the initial investment over the next 12 months). Other horizons and floors, such as a two-year horizon with a floor of −5% (meaning that the investor does not want to lose more than 5% of the initial investment over the next 24 months), are possible. Note the parallel to the discussion of the BOPM, which provides a theoretical basis for the development of portfolio insurance.

[28] The next chapter discusses another form of program trading that is known as index arbitrage.

[29] There is another dynamic strategy for insuring the portfolio that is often preferred because it has smaller transaction costs. It involves index futures, which are a type of financial contract that is discussed in the next chapter. For a survey of dynamic trading strategies, see Robert R. Trippi and Richard B. Harriff, "Dynamic Asset Allocation Rules: Survey and Synthesis," *Journal of Portfolio Management*, 17, no. 4 (Summer 1991): 19–26.

[30] For a discussion of transaction costs, see John E. Gilster, Jr., and William Lee, "The Effects of Transactions Costs and Different Borrowing and Lending Rates on the Option Pricing Model: A Note," *Journal of Finance*, 39, no. 4 (September 1984): 1215–1222; Hayne E. Leland, "Option Pricing and Replication with Transactions Costs," *Journal of Finance*, 40, no. 5 (December 1985): 1283–1301; Fischer Black and Robert Jones, "Simplifying Portfolio Insurance," *Journal of Portfolio Management*, 14, no. 1 (Fall 1987): 48–51; and Phelim P. Boyle and Ton Yorst, "Option Replication in Discrete Time with Transactions Costs," *Journal of Finance*, 47, no. 1 (March 1992): 271–293.

[31] See Mark Rubinstein, "Portfolio Insurance and the Market Crash," *Financial Analysts Journal*, 44, no. 1 (January/February 1988): 38–47. For a discussion of various types of dynamic strategies, see André F. Perold and William F. Sharpe, "Dynamic Strategies for Asset Allocation," *Financial Analysts Journal*, 44, no. 1 (January/February 1988): 16–27; and Philip H. Dybvig, "Inefficient Dynamic Portfolio Strategies or How to Throw Away a Million Dollars in the Stock Market," *Review of Financial Studies*, 1, no. 1 (Spring 1988): 67–88.

[32] See the textbooks cited at the end of the chapter for more on these types of options. For more on foreign exchange options, see Ian Giddy, "The Foreign Exchange Option as a Hedging Tool," *Midland Corporate Finance Journal*, 1, no. 3 (Fall 1983): 32–42; Niso Abauf, "Foreign Exchange Options: The Leading Hedge," *Midland Corporate Finance Journal*, 5, no. 2 (Summer 1987): 51–58; and Mark Kritzman, "About Option Replication," *Financial Analysts Journal*, 48, no. 1 (January/February 1992): 21–23.

[33] These warrants should not be confused with the put warrants and call warrants on foreign stock market indices that were discussed in endnote 23. Those warrants are issued by some entity such as a brokerage firm. These warrants are issued by the firm whose shares can be purchased by the owner of the warrant.

[34] Rights are also discussed in Chapter 17. Valuation of rights is relatively simple if it is assumed that there is no chance that they will end up being out of the money on the expiration date and the time value of money is ignored (meaning that the riskfree rate is assumed to be zero).

[35] Bond call provisions are also discussed in Chapters 14 and 15.

option	intrinsic value
call option	straddle
exercise price	European options
expiration date	American options
premium	hedge ratio
closing sale	put-call parity
closing purchase	at the money
put option	out of the money
floor traders	in the money
floor brokers	time value
market-makers	implicit volatility
order book officials	counterparty risk
covered call writing	portfolio insurance
naked call writing	synthetic put
naked put writing	program trading

REFERENCES

1. Investment strategies involving options are discussed in many papers. Here are three of the most notable ones:

   Robert C. Merton, Myron S. Scholes, and Mathew L. Gladstein, "The Returns and Risk of Alternative Call Option Portfolio Investment Strategies," *Journal of Business,* 51, no. 1 (April 1978): 183–242.

   Robert C. Merton, Myron S. Scholes, and Mathew L. Gladstein, "The Returns and Risk of Alternative Put-Option Portfolio Investment Strategies," *Journal of Business,* 55, no. 1 (January 1982): 1–55.

   Aimee Gerberg Ronn and Ehud I. Ronn, "The Box Spread Arbitrage Conditions: Theory, Tests, and Investment Strategies," *Review of Financial Studies,* 2, no. 1 (1989): 91–107.

2. A description and comparison of the specialist and market-maker systems for trading options are presented by:

   Robert Neal, "A Comparison of Transaction Costs Between Competitive Market-Maker and Specialist Structures," *Journal of Business,* 65, no. 2 (July 1992): 317–334.

3. The binomial option pricing model was initially developed in:

   William F. Sharpe, *Investments* (Englewood Cliffs, NJ: Prentice Hall, 1978), Chapter 14.

4. A short while later the following two papers expanded upon Sharpe's model:

John C. Cox, Stephen A. Ross, and Mark Rubinstein, "Option Pricing: A Simplified Approach," *Journal of Financial Economics,* 7, no. 3 (September 1979): 229–263.

Richard J. Rendleman, Jr., and Brit J. Bartter, "Two-State Option Pricing," *Journal of Finance,* 34, no. 5 (December 1979): 1093–1110.

5. For more on the theory of binomial models, see:

Daniel B. Nelson and Krishna Ramaswamy, "Simple Binomial Processes as Diffusion Approximations in Financial Models," *Review of Financial Studies,* 3, no. 3 (1990): 393–430.

6. Two seminal papers on option pricing are:

Robert C. Merton, "Theory of Rational Option Pricing," *Bell Journal of Economics and Management Science,* 4, no. 1 (Spring 1973): 141–183.

Fischer Black and Myron Scholes, "The Pricing of Options and Corporate Liabilities," *Journal of Political Economy,* 81, no. 3 (May/June 1973): 637–654.

7. The Black-Scholes option pricing model assumes that the riskfree rate is constant over the life of the option. For three interesting papers that relax this assumption, see:

Ramon Rabinovitch, "Pricing Stock and Bond Options When the Default-Free Rate Is Stochastic," *Journal of Financial and Quantitative Analysis,* 24, no. 4 (December 1989): 447–457.

Stuart M. Turnbull and Frank Milne, "A Simple Approach to Interest-Rate Option Pricing," *Review of Financial Studies,* 4, no. 1 (1991): 87–121.

Jason Z. Wei, "Valuing American Equity Options with a Stochastic Interest Rate: A Note," *Journal of Financial Engineering,* 2, no. 2 (June 1993): 195–206.

8. The Black-Scholes model also assumes that the volatility of the underlying asset is constant over the life of the option. For papers that relax this assumption, see:

John Hull and Alan White, "The Pricing of Options on Assets with Stochastic Volatilities," *Journal of Finance,* 42, no. 2 (June 1987): 281–300.

Herb Johnson and David Shanno, "Option Pricing When the Variance Is Changing," *Journal of Financial and Quantitative Analysis,* 22, no. 2 (June 1987): 143–151.

Louis O. Scott, "Option Pricing When the Variance Changes Randomly: Theory, Estimation, and an Application," *Journal of Financial and Quantitative Analysis,* 22, no. 4 (December 1987): 419–438.

James B. Wiggins, "Option Values Under Stochastic Volatility: Theory and Empirical Estimates," *Journal of Financial Economics,* 19, no. 2 (December 1987): 351–372.

Marc Chesney and Louis Scott, "Pricing European Currency Options: A Comparison of the Modified Black-Scholes Model and a Random Variance Model," *Journal of Financial and Quantitative Analysis,* 24, no. 3 (September 1989): 267–284.

Thomas J. Finucane, "Black-Scholes Approximations of Call Option Prices with Stochastic Volatilities: A Note," *Journal of Financial and Quantitative Analysis,* 24, no. 4 (December 1989): 527–532.

Steven L. Heston, "A Closed-Form Solution for Options in Stochastic Volatility with Applications to Bond and Currency Options," *Review of Financial Studies,* 6, no. 2 (1993): 327–343.

9. Portfolio insurance has received much attention. In addition to the citations given in the chapter, see:

M. J. Brennan and R. Solanki, "Optimal Portfolio Insurance," *Journal of Financial and Quantitative Analysis,* 16, no. 3 (September 1981): 279–300.

Ethan S. Etzioni, "Rebalance Disciplines for Portfolio Insurance," *Journal of Portfolio Management,* 13, no. 1 (Fall 1986): 59–62.

Richard J. Rendelman, Jr., and Richard McEnally, "Assessing the Costs of Portfolio Insurance," *Financial Analysts Journal,* 43, no. 3 (May/June 1987): 27–37.

C. B. Garcia and F. J. Gould, "An Empirical Study of Portfolio Insurance," *Financial Analysts Journal,* 43, no. 4 (July/August 1987): 44–54.

Robert Ferguson, "A Comparison of the Mean-Variance and Long-Term Return Characteristics of Three Investment Strategies," *Financial Analysts Journal,* 43, no. 4 (July/August 1987): 55–66.

Fischer Black and Robert Jones, "Simplifying Portfolio Insurance," *Journal of Portfolio Management,* 14, no. 1 (Fall 1987): 48–51.

Yu Zhu and Robert C. Kavee, "Performance of Portfolio Insurance Strategies," *Journal of Portfolio Management,* 14, no. 3 (Spring 1988): 48–54.

Fischer Black and Robert Jones, "Simplifying Portfolio Insurance for Corporate Pension Plans," *Journal of Portfolio Management,* 14, no. 4 (Summer 1988): 33–37.

Thomas J. O'Brien, *How Option Replicating Portfolio Insurance Works: Expanded Details,* Monograph Series in Finance and Economics #1988–4, New York University Salomon Center, Leonard N. Stern School of Business.

Erol Hakanoglu, Robert Koppraseh, and Emmanuel Roman, "Constant Proportion Portfolio Insurance for Fixed-Income Investment," *Journal of Portfolio Management,* 15, no. 4 (Summer 1989): 58–66.

Michael J. Brennan and Eduardo Schwartz, "Portfolio Insurance and Financial Market Equilibrium," *Journal of Business,* 62, no. 4 (October 1989): 455–472.

Sanford J. Grossman and Jean-Luc Vila, "Portfolio Insurance in Complete Markets: A Note," *Journal of Business,* 62, no. 4 (October 1989): 473–476.

Robert R. Trippi and Richard B. Harriff, "Dynamic Asset Allocation Rules: Survey and Synthesis," *Journal of Portfolio Management,* 17, no. 4 (Summer 1991): 19–26.

Charles J. Jacklin, Allan W. Kleidon, and Paul Pfleiderer, "Underestimation of Portfolio Insurance and the Crash of October 1987," *Review of Financial Studies,* 5, no. 1 (1992): 35–63.

10. A great deal has been written on warrants and convertibles. For an introduction to this literature, see:

Richard A. Brealey and Stewart C. Myers, *Principles of Corporate Finance* (New York: McGraw-Hill, 1991), Chapter 22.

11. Many textbooks are devoted exclusively to options or have options as one of their primary subjects. Most cover everything discussed in this chapter, but in more detail and with a more complete list of citations. Here are a few:

Robert A. Jarrow and Andrew Rudd, *Option Pricing* (Homewood, IL: Richard D. Irwin, 1983).

John C. Cox and Mark Rubinstein, *Options Markets* (Englewood Cliffs, NJ: Prentice Hall, 1985).

Richard M. Bookstaber, *Option Pricing and Investment Strategies* (Chicago: Probus Publishing, 1987).

Peter Ritchken, *Options: Theory, Strategy, and Applications* (Glenview, IL: Scott, Foresman, 1987).

Don M. Chance, *An Introduction to Options and Futures* (Fort Worth, TX: The Dryden Press, 1991).

Robert W. Kolb, *Options: An Introduction* (Miami, FL: Kolb Publishing, 1991).

Alan L. Tucker, *Financial Futures, Options, and Swaps* (St. Paul, MN: West Publishing, 1991).

David A. Dubofsky, *Options and Financial Futures* (New York: McGraw-Hill, 1992).

John C. Hull, *Options, Futures, and Other Derivative Securities* (Englewood Cliffs, NJ: Prentice Hall, 1993).

Hans R. Stoll and Robert E. Whaley, *Futures and Options* (Cincinnati, OH: South-Western Publishing, 1993).

12. A useful software package and manual for valuing options is:

Stuart M. Turnbull, *Option Valuation* (Toronto: Holt, Rinehart and Winston of Canada, 1987).

Futures

Consider a contract that involves the delivery of some specific asset by a seller to a buyer at an agreed-upon future date. While such a contract also specifies the purchase price, the asset is not to be paid for until the delivery date. However, the buyer and the seller will both be requested to make a security deposit at the time the contract is signed. The reason for this deposit is to protect each person from experiencing any losses, should the other person renege on the contract. Hence the size of the deposit is checked daily to see that it provides sufficient protection. If it is insufficient, it will have to be increased. If it is more than sufficient, the excess can be withdrawn.

These contracts are often referred to as **futures** (short for futures contract), and in the United States they involve assets such as agricultural goods (for example, wheat), natural resources (for example, copper), foreign currencies (for example, Swiss francs), fixed-income securities (for example, Treasury bonds), and market indices (for example, the Standard & Poor's 500).[1] As with options, standardization of the terms in these contracts makes it relatively easy for anyone to create and subsequently trade the contracts.

21.1 HEDGERS AND SPECULATORS

There are two types of people who deal in futures (and options)—speculators and hedgers. **Speculators** buy and sell futures for the sole purpose of making a profit by closing out their positions at a price that is better than the the initial price (or so they hope). Such people neither produce nor use the asset in the ordinary course of business. In contrast, **hedgers** buy and sell futures to offset an otherwise risky position in the spot market. In the ordinary course of business, they either produce or use the asset.

21.1.1 Example of Hedging

For example, consider wheat futures. A farmer might note today that the market price for a wheat futures contract with delivery around harvest time is $4 per bushel, a price that is high enough to ensure a profitable year. Although the farmer could sell wheat futures today, alternatively the farmer could wait until harvest and sell the wheat on the spot market at that time.[2] However, waiting until harvest entails risk because the spot price of wheat could fall by then, perhaps to $3 per bushel, which would bring financial ruin to the farmer. In contrast, selling wheat futures today will allow the farmer to "lock in" a $4 per bushel selling price. Doing so would remove an element of risk from the farmer's primary business of growing wheat. Thus a farmer who sells futures is known as a hedger or, more specifically, a **short hedger.**

Perhaps the buyer of the farmer's futures contract is a baker who uses wheat in making bread. Currently the baker has enough wheat in inventory to last until harvest season. In anticipation of the need to replenish the inventory at that time, the baker could buy a wheat futures contract today at $4 per bushel. Alternatively, the baker could simply wait until the inventory runs low and then buy wheat in the spot market. However, there is a chance that the spot price will be $5 per bushel at that time. Should this happen, the baker would have to raise the selling price of bread and perhaps lose sales in doing so. Alternatively, by purchasing wheat futures, the baker can "lock in" a $4 per bushel purchase price, thereby removing an element of risk from the bread business. Thus a baker who buys futures is also known as a hedger or, more specifically, a **long hedger.**

21.1.2 Example of Speculating

The farmer and the baker can be compared with a speculator—a person who buys and sells wheat futures, based on the forecast price of wheat, in the pursuit of relatively short-term profits. As mentioned earlier, such a person neither produces nor uses the asset in the ordinary course of business.

A speculator who thinks that the price of wheat is going to rise substantially will buy wheat futures. Later this person will enter a **reversing trade** by selling wheat futures. If the forecast was accurate, a profit will have been made on an increase in the wheat futures price.

For example, consider a speculator expecting at least a $1 per bushel rise in the spot price of wheat. Whereas this person could buy wheat, store it, and hope to sell it later at the anticipated higher price, it would be easier and more profitable to buy a wheat futures contract today at $4 per bushel. Later, assuming that the spot price of wheat rises by $1, the speculator would enter a reversing trade by selling the wheat futures contract for perhaps $5 per bushel. (A $1 rise in the spot price of wheat will cause the futures price to rise by about $1.) Thus the speculator will make a profit of $1 per bushel, or $5,000 in total, because these contracts are for 5,000 bushels. As will be shown later, the speculator might need to make a security deposit of $1,000 at the time the wheat futures contract is bought. As this is returned when the reversing trade is made, the speculator's rate of return is quite high (500%) relative to the percentage rise in the price of wheat (25%).

Alternatively, if a speculator forecasts a substantial price decline, then initially wheat futures would be sold. Later the person would enter a reversing trade by purchasing wheat futures. Assuming that the forecast was accurate, a profit will have been made on the decrease in the wheat futures price.

21.2 THE FUTURES CONTRACT

Futures contracts are standardized in terms of delivery as well as the type of asset that is permissible for delivery. For example, the Chicago Board of Trade specifies the following requirements for its July wheat contract:

1. The seller agrees to deliver 5,000 bushels of either no. 2 soft red wheat, no. 2 hard red winter wheat, no. 2 dark northern spring wheat, or no. 1 northern spring wheat at the agreed-upon price. Alternatively, a number of other grades can be delivered at specified premiums or discounts from the agreed-upon price. In any case, the seller is allowed to decide which grade shall be delivered.
2. The grain will be delivered by registered warehouse receipts issued by approved warehouses in Chicago or Toledo, Ohio. (Toledo deliveries are discounted $.02 per bushel.)
3. Delivery will take place during the month of July, with the seller allowed to decide the actual date.
4. Upon delivery of the warehouse receipt from the seller to the buyer, the latter will pay the former the agreed-upon price in cash.

After an organized exchange has set all the terms of a futures contract except for its price, the exchange will authorize trading in the contract.[3] Buyers and sellers (or their representatives) meet at a specific place on the floor of the exchange and try to agree on a price at which to trade. If they succeed, one or more contracts will be created, with all the standard terms plus an additional one—the price involved. Prices are normally stated on a per-unit basis. Thus if a buyer and a seller agree to a price of $4 per bushel for a contract of 5,000 bushels of wheat, the amount of money involved is $20,000.

Figure 21.1 shows a set of daily quotations giving the prices at which some popular futures contracts were traded and the total volume of sales for each type of contract. Such listings of active futures markets are published regularly in the financial press, with each item for delivery (such as corn) having a heading that indicates the number of units per contract (5,000 bushels) and the terms on which prices are stated (cents per bushel).

Below the heading for the asset are certain details for each type of contract. Moving from left to right in Figure 21.1, the first column shows the delivery

Figure 21.1
Quotations for Futures Prices (Excerpts)
Source: Reprinted by permission of *The Wall Street Journal,* ©Dow Jones & Company, Inc., December 14, 1993, p. C14. All rights reserved worldwide.

Monday, December 13, 1993.

Open Interest Reflects Previous Trading Day.

GRAINS AND OILSEEDS

CORN (CBT) 5,000 bu.; cents per bu.

	Open	High	Low	Settle	Change	Lifetime High	Lifetime Low	Open Interest
Dec	285½	285¾	283¾	284¾	— 1½	290¾	225¼	7,276
Mr94	292½	292½	290½	291¼	— 2¼	297	232¾	161,247
May	295½	296	293½	293¾	— 2¼	299¾	250½	66,510
July	295¼	295½	293¾	293¾	— 3	299¼	241	54,336
Sept	279½	279¾	277¾	277¾	— 2¼	274¾	240¾	8,416
Dec	264¾	265	262¾	263	— 2¼	267½	236½	29,989
Mr95	270¼	270½	268½	268¾	— 2	274¼	253½	943

Est vol 55,000; vol Fri 245,860; open int 328,717, +1,694.

OATS (CBT) 5,000 bu.; cents per bu.

	Open	High	Low	Settle	Change	Lifetime High	Lifetime Low	Open Interest
Dec	132	132½	129	129	...	161	127	638
Mr94	138¼	138¾	134	134¼	+ 4¼	163½	134	14,455
May	142½	142½	138¼	138½	+ ...	164	138	3,831
July	144½	145	141¾	142	+ 3½	161¼	140	1,298
Sept	145	145	143	143	— 3¾	152½	141	90

Est vol 2,500; vol Fri 1,593; open int 20,368, +30.

SOYBEANS (CBT) 5,000 bu.; cents per bu.

	Open	High	Low	Settle	Change	Lifetime High	Lifetime Low	Open Interest
Jan	683½	683½	675½	675½	— 10¼	756	576½	57,534
Mar	689½	689½	681½	682	— 10	754	589¾	41,897
May	691½	691½	684½	684½	— 9¼	751	592½	26,818
July	691¾	693	688½	688½	— 10¼	750	594½	25,261
Aug	686	688	680½	680½	— 10¼	735	628	4,191
Sept	660	660	654½	654½	— 8¼	676	617	2,712
Nov	636	637	631½	632	— 5¾	650	581½	6,946
Ja95	641½	641½	638	638	— 5½	656	618½	100
July	647	647	645½	644	— 4½	654½	645½	100
Nov	620	620	617	616	— 5½	628	614	119

Est vol 50,000; vol Fri 40,407; open int 170,060, +126.

METALS AND PETROLEUM

GOLD (CMX)-100 troy oz.; $ per troy oz.

	Open	High	Low	Settle	Change	Lifetime High	Lifetime Low	Open Interest
Dec	387.40	388.50	386.10	387.00	+ 3.80	414.00	331.70	897
Fb94	389.20	390.40	387.70	388.60	+ 3.70	415.70	333.80	87,699
Apr	391.20	391.80	389.60	390.50	+ 3.80	418.50	335.20	12,494
June	393.00	393.90	392.90	392.40	+ 3.80	417.20	339.40	21,114
Aug	395.20	395.20	393.40	393.40	+ 3.80	415.00	341.50	5,515
Oct	...	...	...	396.30	+ 3.80	417.00	344.00	3,653
Dec	400.00	400.00	397.50	398.30	+ 3.70	426.50	343.00	11,459
Fb95	401.50	401.50	400.60	400.60	+ 3.70	411.00	363.50	1,115
Apr	...	...	...	402.90	+ 3.70	425.00	363.50	1,942
June	...	...	...	405.30	+ 3.70	430.00	351.00	3,716
Aug	...	...	...	407.70	+ 3.70	404.00	380.50	177
Dec	413.50	413.50	413.50	412.80	+ 3.70	439.50	358.00	2,010
Ju96	...	...	...	420.70	+ 3.70	447.00	370.60	830
Dec	431.00	431.00	431.00	430.20	+ 3.70	443.00	379.60	650
Dc97	...	...	...	450.80	+ 3.70	477.00	402.00	458

Est vol 32,000; vol Fri 20,771; open int 153,745, −325.

CRUDE OIL, Light Sweet (NYM) 1,000 bbls.; $ per bbl.

	Open	High	Low	Settle	Change	Lifetime High	Lifetime Low	Open Interest
Jan	15.06	15.20	14.50	14.52	— .55	21.15	14.40	78,420
Feb	na	15.46	14.84	14.84	— .45	21.10	14.69	87,126
Mar	15.70	15.75	15.23	15.23	— .45	21.10	15.04	52,235
Apr	15.70	15.75	15.47	15.51	— .44	20.88	15.33	23,209
May	16.00	16.01	15.74	15.77	— .41	20.78	15.60	21,423
June	16.27	16.50	16.20	16.02	— .40	21.35	15.88	38,454
July	16.47	16.35	16.35	16.23	— .39	20.78	16.00	14,604
Aug	16.61	16.88	16.45	16.43	— .39	20.78	16.16	10,354
Sept	17.05	17.05	16.66	16.62	— .38	20.78	16.16	11,180
Oct	16.85	16.90	16.85	16.81	— .39	20.73	16.63	7,034
Nov	17.05	17.30	17.00	16.99	— .39	20.69	16.85	10,601
Dec	17.50	17.58	17.20	17.15	— .39	21.25	16.90	18,753
Ja95	17.75	17.75	17.50	17.29	— .39	20.78	17.10	4,343
Feb	17.50	17.55	17.43	17.43	— .39	19.21	17.35	1,659
Mar	17.95	17.96	17.57	17.57	— .39	19.21	17.50	5,684
Apr	17.68	17.85	17.72	17.72	— .39	19.68	17.50	183
May	18.00	18.00	18.00	17.87	— .39	19.23	18.00	494
June	18.31	18.31	18.02	18.02	— .39	21.21	18.08	17,981
Sept	18.50	18.50	18.40	18.29	— .41	19.84	18.45	2,812
Dec	...	...	...	18.54	— .42	20.80	18.37	12,513
Ju96	...	...	...	19.03	— .43	20.26	19.03	13,852
Dec	19.96	19.96	19.75	19.52	— .44	20.40	19.31	3,054

Est vol 136,645; vol Fri 113,988; open int 435,968, −519.

CURRENCY

JAPAN YEN (CME)-12.5 million yen; $ per yen (.00)

	Open	High	Low	Settle	Change	Lifetime High	Lifetime Low	Open Interest
Dec	.9170	.9186	.9165	.9178	+ .0012	.9950	.7970	31,549
Mr94	.9204	.9215	.9191	.9200	+ .0005	.9930	.8700	67,441
June	.9230	.9245	.9230	.9240	+ .0005	.9945	.8540	744
Sept	...	...	...	.9290	+ .0006	.9610	.9240	182

Est vol 18,171; vol Fri 31,613; open int 99,916, +4,630.

DEUTSCHEMARK (CME)-125,000 marks; $ per mark

	Open	High	Low	Settle	Change	Lifetime High	Lifetime Low	Open Interest
Dec	.5892	.5905	.5875	.5881	— .0013	.6650	.5657	62,691
Mr94	.5853	.5871	.5814	.5816	— .0037	.6205	.5646	120,086
June	.5820	.5820	.5787	.5788	— .0037	.6162	.5607	662
Sept	...	...	...	.5770	— .0037	.6130	.5735	129

Est vol 43,571; vol Fri 72,934; open int 183,468, −6,559.

INTEREST RATE

TREASURY BONDS (CBT)-$100,000; pts. 32nds of 100%

	Open	High	Low	Settle	Chg	Yield Settle	Yield Chg	Open Interest
Dec	116-14	116-17	116-00	116-11	— 13	6.525	+ .033	52,945
Mr94	115-07	115-11	114-24	115-05	— 12	6.622	+ .031	247,989
June	113-30	114-09	113-24	114-04	— 11	6.707	+ .028	10,317
Sept	113-00	113-10	112-27	113-05	— 11	6.788	+ .008	14,239
Dec	112-24	112-30	112-18	112-28	— 11	6.812	+ .029	12,394
Mr95	...	...	...	112-05	— 11	6.873	+ .030	51

Est vol 280,000; vol Fri 404,489; op int 338,001, +4,277.

EURODOLLAR (CME)-$1 million; pts of 100%

	Open	High	Low	Settle	Chg	Yield Settle	Yield Chg	Open Interest
Dec	96.62	96.63	96.62	96.62	— .01	3.38	+ .01	250,486
Mr94	96.43	96.45	96.43	96.45	— .01	3.55	...	393,918
June	96.11	96.12	96.09	96.11	— .01	3.89	+ .01	244,362
Sept	95.77	95.79	95.76	95.78	— .01	4.22	+ .01	155,284
Dec	95.36	95.37	95.33	95.37	— .01	4.63	+ .01	179,929
Mr95	95.24	95.27	95.23	95.27	— .01	4.73	+ .01	118,926
June	95.05	95.07	95.02	95.06	— .02	4.94	+ .02	103,768
Sept	94.88	94.89	94.86	94.88	— .02	5.12	+ .03	82,141
Dec	94.55	94.57	94.53	94.58	— .03	5.42	+ .03	77,127
Mr96	94.54	94.55	94.53	94.54	— .04	5.46	+ .04	58,117
June	94.38	94.39	94.37	94.38	— .04	5.62	+ .04	53,171
Sept	94.25	94.26	94.24	94.25	— .04	5.75	+ .04	43,456
Dec	93.98	94.00	93.98	93.99	— .04	6.01	+ .04	42,054
Mr97	93.97	93.99	93.97	93.98	— .04	6.02	+ .04	34,056
June	93.85	93.86	93.84	93.85	— .04	6.15	+ .04	31,259
Sept	93.76	93.76	93.75	93.76	— .04	6.24	+ .04	24,518
Dec	93.53	93.55	93.53	93.54	— .04	6.46	+ .04	21,155
Mr98	93.56	93.57	93.55	93.56	— .04	6.44	+ .04	14,847
June	93.46	93.47	93.45	93.46	— .04	6.54	+ .04	8,076
Sept	93.39	93.40	93.38	93.39	— .04	6.61	+ .04	2,554
Dec	93.22	93.23	93.21	93.20	— .04	6.80	+ .04	2,187
Mr99	93.19	93.26	93.18	93.24	— .04	6.76	+ .04	2,492
June	93.19	93.19	93.14	93.17	— .04	6.83	+ .04	2,639
Sept	93.15	93.15	93.13	93.13	— .04	6.87	+ .04	2,019
Dec	92.97	92.98	92.97	92.96	— .04	7.04	+ .04	1,644
Mr00	93.01	93.02	93.01	93.00	— .04	7.00	+ .04	2,019
June	92.95	92.96	92.95	92.94	— .04	7.06	+ .04	1,644
Sept	92.91	92.92	92.90	92.90	— .04	7.10	+ .04	2,072
Dec	92.76	...	...	92.76	— .04	7.24	+ .04	1,549

Est vol 199,085; vol Fri 310,398; open int 2,270,051, +11,777.

INDEX

S&P 500 INDEX (CME) $500 times index

	Open	High	Low	Settle	Chg	High	Low	Open Interest
Dec	463.10	466.55	463.10	466.50	+ 2.60	471.55	429.70	94,306
Mr94	464.30	467.60	464.10	467.50	+ 2.60	472.50	434.00	110,574
June	464.90	468.90	464.85	468.50	+ 2.70	473.30	444.50	2,403
Sept	466.45	469.90	466.00	469.75	+ 2.85	474.00	452.20	642

Est vol 66,732; vol Fri 63,823; open int 207,925, −100.
Index prelim High 465.71; Low 462.71; Close 465.71 +1.78

TREASURY BILLS (CME)-$1 mil.; pts. of 100%

	Open	High	Low	Settle	Chg	Discount Settle	Discount Chg	Open Interest
Mar	96.74	96.76	96.73	96.76	...	3.24	...	22,771
June	96.48	96.49	96.47	96.48	— .01	3.52	+ .01	4,756
Sept	...	...	...	96.20	— .02	3.80	+ .02	196

EXCHANGE ABBREVIATIONS
(for commodity futures and futures options)

CBT-Chicago Board of Trade; CME-Chicago Mercantile Exchange; CSCE-Coffee, Sugar & Cocoa Exchange, New York; CMX-Commodity Exchange, New York; IPE-International Petroleum Exchange; KC-Kansas City Board of Trade; LIFFE-London International Financial Futures Exchange; ME-Montreal Exchange; MCE-MidAmerica Commodity Exchange; MPLS-Minneapolis Grain Exchange; CTN-New York Cotton Exchange; NYM-New York Mercantile Exchange; PBOT-Philadelphia Board of Trade; WPG-Winnipeg Commodity Exchange.

dates for the contracts. For example, there are seven different futures contracts for corn, each one involving the same item but having different delivery dates. Next comes *open,* denoting the price at which the first transaction was made; *high* and *low,* representing the highest and lowest prices during the day; and *settle* (short for settlement price), a price that is a representative price (for example, the average of the high and low prices) during the "closing period" designated by the exchange in question (for example, the last two minutes of trading). After *change* from the previous day's settlement price come the highest and lowest prices recorded during the lifetime of the contract. The last column on the right shows the **open interest** (the number of outstanding contracts) on the previous day.

For each futures contract, summary figures are given below the figures for the last delivery date. (In the case of corn, these summary figures are below the March 1995 delivery date figures.) They indicate the total volume (that is, the number of contracts) traded on that day and on the previous trading day as well as the total open interest in such contracts on that day and the change in total open interest from the previous day.

21.3 FUTURES MARKETS

The futures contracts shown in Figure 21.1 are traded on various organized exchanges. The Chicago Board of Trade (CBT) was the earliest one, founded in 1848, and currently is the largest futures exchange in the world. Other futures exchanges are listed in the lower right-hand corner of Figure 21.1.

The method of trading futures on organized exchanges is similar in some ways to and different in other ways from the way stocks and options are traded. As with stocks and options, customers can place market, limit, and stop orders. Furthermore, once an order is transmitted to an exchange floor, it must be taken to a designated spot for execution by a member of the exchange, just as is done for stocks and options. This spot is known as a *pit* because of its shape, which is circular with a set of interior descending steps on which members stand. What transpires in the pit is what distinguishes trading in futures from trading in stocks and options.

First, there are no specialists or market-makers on futures exchanges. Instead, members can be floor brokers, meaning that they execute customers' orders. In doing so, they (or their phone clerks) each keep a file of any stop or limit orders that cannot be immediately executed. Alternatively, members can be floor traders (those with very short holding periods, of less than a day, are known as **locals** or scalpers), meaning that they execute orders for their own personal accounts in an attempt to make profits by "buying low and selling high." Floor traders are in some ways similar to market-makers, because a floor trader may have an inventory of futures contracts and may act as a dealer. However, unlike a market-maker, a floor trader is not required to do so.

Second, all futures orders must be announced by "open outcry," meaning that any member wishing to buy or sell any futures contract must verbally announce the order and a price at which the member is willing to trade. This way, the order is exposed to everyone in the pit, thereby enabling an auction to take place that will lead to the order being filled at the best possible price.

21.3.1 The Clearinghouse

Each futures exchange has an associated clearinghouse that becomes the "seller's buyer" and the "buyer's seller" as soon as a trade is concluded. The procedure is similar to that used for options. This is not surprising, because the first market in listed options was organized by people associated with a futures exchange. (Specifically, the Chicago Board Options Exchange was set up by the Chicago Board of Trade.)

In order to understand how a clearinghouse operates, consider the futures market for wheat. Assume that on the first day of trading in July wheat, buyer B agrees to purchase 5,000 bushels (one contract) from seller S for $4 per bushel, or $20,000 in total. (Actually, what happens is that a floor broker working for B's brokerage firm and a floor broker working for S's brokerage firm meet in the wheat pit and agree on a price.) In this situation, B might believe that the price of wheat is going to rise whereas S might believe that it is going to fall.

After B and S reach their agreement, the clearinghouse will immediately step in and break the transaction apart—that is, B and S no longer deal directly with each other. Now it is the obligation of the clearinghouse to deliver the wheat to B and to accept delivery from S. At this point there is an open interest of one contract (5,000 bushels) in July wheat, because only one contract exists at this time. (Technically there are two, since the clearinghouse has separate contracts with B and S.) Figure 21.2 summarizes the creation of this contract.

It is important to realize that if nothing else is done at this point, the clearinghouse is in a potentially risky position. For example, if the price of wheat rises to $5 per bushel by July, what happens if S does not deliver the wheat? The clearinghouse will have to buy the wheat on the spot market for $25,000 ($= 5,000 \times$ $5) and then deliver it to B. Because the clearinghouse will receive the selling price of $20,000 ($= 5,000 \times$ $4) from B in return, it will have lost $5,000. Even though the clearinghouse has a claim on S for the $5,000, it faces protracted

Figure 21.2
Creating a Futures Contract

legal battles in trying to recover this amount and may end up with little or nothing from S.

Alternatively, if the price of wheat falls to $3 per bushel by July, then B will be paying $20,000 for delivery of wheat that is only worth $15,000 (= 5,000 × $3) on the spot market. What happens if B refuses to make payment? In this case the clearinghouse will not deliver the wheat that it received from S. Instead, it will have to sell the wheat for $15,000 on the spot market. Because the clearinghouse paid S $20,000 for the wheat, it will have lost $5,000. Again, although the clearinghouse has a claim on B for the $5,000, it may end up with little or nothing from B.

The procedures that protect the clearinghouse from such potential losses involve having brokers (1) impose initial margin requirements on both buyers and sellers; (2) mark to market the accounts of buyers and sellers every day; and (3) impose daily maintenance margin requirements on both buyers and sellers.

21.3.2 Initial Margin

In order to buy and sell futures, an investor must open a futures account with a brokerage firm. This type of account must be kept separate from other accounts (such as a cash account or a margin account) that the investor might have. Whenever a futures contract is signed, both buyer and seller are required to post initial margin. That is, both buyer and seller are required to make security deposits that are intended to guarantee that they will in fact be able to fulfill their obligations; accordingly, initial margin is often referred to as **performance margin.** The amount of this margin is roughly 5% to 15% of the total purchase price of the futures contract. However, it is often stated as a given dollar amount regardless of the purchase price.[4]

For example, a July wheat futures contract for 5,000 bushels at $4 per bushel would have a total purchase price of $20,000 (= 5,000 × $4). With a 5% initial margin requirement, buyer B and seller S would each have to make a deposit of $1,000 (= .05 × $20,000). This deposit can be made in the form of either cash, cash equivalents (such as Treasury bills), or a bank line of credit, and it forms the equity in the account on the first day.

Whereas initial margin provides some protection to the clearinghouse, it does not provide complete protection. As indicated earlier, if the futures price of wheat rises to $5 per bushel by July, the clearinghouse faces a potential loss of $5,000, only $1,000 of which can be quickly recovered owing to the margin deposit. This is where the use of marking to market, coupled with a maintenance margin requirement, provides the requisite amount of additional protection.

21.3.3 Marking to Market

In order to understand marking to market, the previous example, where B and S were, respectively, a buyer and a seller of a 5,000–bushel wheat futures contract at $4 per bushel, will be continued. Assume now that on the second day of trading the settlement price of July wheat is $4.10 per bushel. In this situation, S has "lost" $500 owing to the rise in the price of wheat from $4 to $4.10 per bushel, while B has "made" $500 (= $.10 × 5,000). Thus the equity in the account of S is reduced by $500, and the equity in the account of B is increased by $500. Because the initial equity was equal to the initial margin requirement of $1,000, this means that S has equity of $500 whereas B has equity of $1,500. This process of adjusting the equity in an investor's account in order to reflect the change in the settlement price of the futures contract is known as **marking to market.** It should also be noted that as part of the marking-to-market process, the clearinghouse every day replaces each existing futures contract with a new one that has as the purchase price the settlement price as reported in the financial press.

In general, the equity in either a buyer's or a seller's account is (1) the initial margin deposit and (2) the sum of all daily gains, less losses, on open positions in futures. As the amount of the gains (less losses) changes every day, the amount of equity changes every day.

In the example, if the settlement price of the July wheat futures contract had fallen to $3.95 per bushel the third day (that is, the day after rising to $4.10), then B would have "lost" $750 $[= 5,000 \times (\$4.10 - \$3.95)]$ whereas S would have "made" $750 on that day. When their accounts are marked to market at the end of the day, the equity in B's account has dropped from $1,500 to $750, whereas S's equity has risen from $500 to $1,250.

21.3.4 Maintenance Margin

Another key concept is maintenance margin. According to the maintenance margin requirement, the investor must keep the account's equity equal to or greater than a certain percentage of the amount deposited as initial margin. Because this percentage is roughly 65%, the investor must have equity equal to or greater than 65% of the initial margin. If this requirement is not met, the investor will receive a margin call from his or her broker. This call is a request for an additional deposit of cash (nothing else can be deposited for this purpose) known as **variation margin** to bring the equity up to the initial margin level. If the investor does not (or cannot) respond, then the broker will close out the investor's position by entering a reversing trade in the investor's account.

For example, reconsider investors B and S, who had, respectively, bought and sold a July wheat futures contract at $4 per bushel. Each investor had made a deposit of $1,000 in order to meet the initial margin requirement. The next day the price of the wheat futures contract rose to $4.10 per bushel, or $20,500. Thus the equity of B increased to $1,500 while the equity of S decreased to $500. If the maintenance margin requirement is 65% of initial margin, both B and S are required to have equity of at least $650 $(= .65 \times \$1,000)$ in their accounts every day. Because the actual level of equity for B clearly exceeds this amount, B does not need to do anything. Indeed, B may withdraw an amount of cash equal to the amount by which the equity exceeds the initial margin; in this example, B can withdraw cash of $500.

However, S is undermargined and will be asked to make a cash deposit of at least $500, because this will increase the equity from $500 to $1,000, the level of the initial margin. In the event that S refuses to make this deposit, the broker will enter a reversing trade for S by purchasing a July wheat futures contract. The result is that S will simply receive an amount of money approximately equal to the account's equity, $500, and the account will be closed. As S initially deposited $1,000, this represents a personal loss of $500.

On the third day the price of the July wheat futures contract is assumed to settle at \$3.95 per bushel, representing a \$750 loss for B and a \$750 gain for S (see Table 21.1). As a consequence, B is now undermargined and will be asked to deposit \$750 so that the equity in B's account is \$1,000. Conversely, S can withdraw \$750, as the equity in S's account is over the \$1,000 initial margin requirement by this amount.

21.3.5 Reversing Trades

Suppose that on the next day B finds that people are paying \$4.15 per bushel for July wheat. This represents daily profit to B of \$.20 per bushel, because the price was \$3.95 the previous day. If B believes that the price of July wheat will not go any higher, then B might sell a July wheat futures contract for \$4.15 to someone else. (Conversely, S might buy a July wheat futures contract since S's equity has been reduced to zero.) In this situation B has made a reversing trade, because B now has offsetting positions with respect to July wheat. (Equivalently, B is said to have unwound or closed out or offset his or her position in July wheat.)

At this point the benefit to B of having a clearinghouse involved can be seen. Nominally, B is obligated to deliver 5,000 bushels of wheat to the clearinghouse in July, which in turn is obligated to deliver it back to B. Why? Because B is involved in two July wheat contracts, one as a seller and one as a buyer. However, the clearinghouse will note that B has offsetting positions in July wheat, and it will immediately cancel both of them. Furthermore, once the reversing trade has been made, B will be able to withdraw \$2,000, consisting of (1) the initial margin of \$1,000; (2) a variation margin deposit owing to the daily marking to market of \$250; and (3) the \$750 [= 5,000 × (\$4.15 − \$4)] net profit that has been made. Table 21.1 illustrates the effect these events have had on the equity in the account of B (and that of S).

TABLE 21.1

MARGIN REQUIREMENTS FOR A FUTURES CONTRACT

Day	Price of Wheat	Event	Buyer B Amount	Buyer B Equity In Account	Seller S Amount	Seller S Equity In Account
(a) If Maintenance Margin Were Not Required:						
1	\$4	Deposit initial margin	\$ 1,000	\$1,000	\$ 1,000	\$1,000
2	\$4.10	Mark to market	+500	1,500	−500	500
3	\$3.95	Mark to market	−750	750	+750	1,250
4	\$4.15	Mark to market	+1,000	1,750	−1,000	250
(b) With Required Maintenance Margin:						
1	\$4	Deposit initial margin	\$ 1,000	\$1,000	\$1,000	\$1,000
2	\$4.10	Mark to market:	+500	1,500	−500	500
		Buyer withdraws cash	−500	1,000	—	—
		Seller deposits cash	—	—	+500	1,000
3	\$3.95	Mark to market:	−750	250	+750	1,750
		Buyer deposits cash	+750	1,000	—	—
		Seller withdraws cash	—	—	−750	1,000
4	\$4.15	Mark to market:	+1,000	2,000	−1,000	0
		Reversing trade and withdrawal of cash	−2,000	0	—	—

In effect, a futures contract is replaced every day by (1) adjusting the equity in the investor's account and (2) drawing up a new contract that has a purchase price equal to the current settlement price. This daily marking-to-market procedure, coupled with margin requirements, results in the clearinghouse's always having a security deposit of sufficient size to protect it from losses owing to the actions of the individual investors.[5]

These rather complex arrangements make it possible for futures traders to think in very simple terms. In the example, B bought a contract of July wheat at $4 and sold it on day 4 for $4.15, making a profit of $.15 per bushel. If S, having initially sold a contract of July wheat at $4, later made a reversing trade for $4.25, then S's position can also be thought of in simple terms—specifically, S sold July wheat for $4 and later bought it back for $4.25—suffering a loss of $.25 per bushel in the process.

21.3.6 Futures Positions

In the previous example, B was the person who initially bought a July wheat futures contract. Accordingly, B now has a long position and is said to be **long** one contract of July wheat. In contrast S, having initially sold a July wheat futures contract, has a short position and is said to be **short** one contract of July wheat.

The process of marking to market every day means that changes in the settlement price are realized as soon as they occur. When the settlement price rises, those with long positions realize profits equal to the change and those who are short realize losses. Conversely, when the settlement price falls, those with long positions realize losses, while those with short positions realize profits. In either event, total profits always equal total losses. Thus either the buyer gains and the seller loses, or the seller gains and the buyer loses because both parties are involved in a "zero-sum game" (as was also the case with buyers and writers of options, discussed in Chapter 20).

21.3.7 Taxation

Earlier it was mentioned that there are two types of people who deal in futures—speculators and hedgers. These two types of investors are treated differently by the Internal Revenue Service.

A speculator in futures is considered to have a capital asset for tax purposes, whether he or she is long or short. When the position is closed out, the resultant profit or loss is treated as a capital gain or loss and is taxed accordingly. In comparison, because a hedger has dealt in futures as part of normal business activities, the resulting profit or loss is generally viewed as ordinary income or loss for the business and is taxed accordingly.

21.3.8 Open Interest

When trading is first allowed in a contract, there is no open interest because no contracts are outstanding. Subsequently, as people begin to make transactions, the open interest grows. At any time open interest equals the amount that those with short positions (the sellers) are currently obligated to deliver. It also equals the amount that those with long positions (the buyers) are obligated to receive.

Open-interest figures are typically shown with futures prices in the financial press. For example, Figure 21.1 indicates that on December 13, 1993, a total of 161,247 contracts in March 1994 corn was outstanding on the Chicago Board of Trade (CBT). Note the substantial differences in the open-interest figures for the other corn contracts on the Chicago Board of Trade on that day. This is quite typical. Figure 21.3 shows why. Open interest in a wheat contract is shown for every month from the preceding January until the contract expired at the end of the delivery month, December. From January until the end of September, more trades were generally made to open new positions than to reverse old ones, and open interest continued to increase. As the delivery month came closer, reversing trades began to outnumber trades intended to open new positions, and the open interest began to decline. The amount remaining at the beginning of December was the maximum number of bushels of wheat that could have been delivered against futures contracts at that time, but most of these contracts were also settled by reversing trades instead of delivery.

Relatively few futures positions—less than 3% of the total—end in actual delivery of the asset involved.[6] However, the fact that delivery is a possibility makes a contract's value in the delivery month differ only slightly, if at all, from the spot price (that is, the current market price) of the asset.

If not reversed, most futures contracts require delivery of the corresponding asset. Notable exceptions are market index futures—they do not require delivery of the set of securities comprising the corresponding index. Instead, an amount equal to the difference between the level of the index and the purchase price must be paid *in cash* on the delivery date. Nevertheless, similar to other

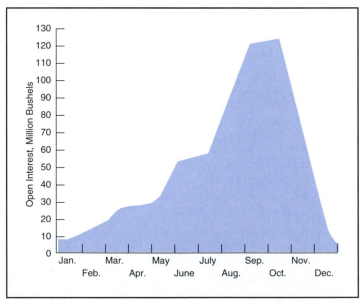

Figure 21.3
Open Interest, December 1978, Chicago Board of Trade Wheat
Contract: January 3, 1978, through December 28, 1978

types of futures, most positions in market index futures are closed out with reversing trades prior to the date at which delivery (in cash) is required.

21.3.9 Price Limits

The futures exchanges, subject to approval by the **Commodity Futures Trading Commission** (CFTC), place dollar limits on the extent to which futures prices are allowed to vary from day to day. For example, if July wheat closed at $4 on the previous day and the daily price limit is $.20, then on the following day contracts at prices outside the range from $3.80 to $4.20 would not be allowed to be traded on the exchange. If a major piece of news during the day led traders to consider $4.25 a reasonable price for the contract, they would have to either (1) trade privately, forgoing the advantages offered by the exchange; (2) trade on the exchange at the limit price of $4.20; or (3) let the contract settle at $4.20 and then wait until the next day, when the range of acceptable prices would be from $4 to $4.40.

One result of the "limit move" to $4.20 is that it is entirely possible that no contracts will be traded at all on that day. This is because nobody will want to sell these wheat contracts for a below-market price of $4.20, preferring to wait until the next day when the range of acceptable prices is raised. Indeed, if the news is important enough (such as a massive freeze in Florida, destroying many orange trees and dramatically affecting orange juice futures), there can be limit moves for a number of successive days, with no trading taking place for several days.

The futures exchanges impose price limits on futures because of a belief that traders may overreact to major news and should be "protected" from voluntarily entering into agreements under such conditions. Interestingly, initial margins are usually set at an amount that is roughly equal to the price limit times the size of the contract. In the case of wheat having a $.20 price limit and a contract for 5,000 bushels, the initial margin is usually about $1,000 (= $.20 × 5,000). Thus if the price of wheat moves the limit against the investor, no more than the initial margin of $1,000 will be lost on the day of the adverse limit move. In a sense, the price limit has "protected" the investor (and the clearinghouse) from losing more than $1,000 on that day. However, it is possible that the investor cannot enter a reversing trade as soon as prices have moved the limit, meaning that much larger losses can be incurred later (as in the case of the "Florida freeze" and orange juice futures).

21.4   BASIS

The difference between the current spot price on an asset (that is, the price of the asset for immediate delivery) and the corresponding futures price (that is, the purchase price stated in the futures contract) is known as the **basis** for the futures:

$$\text{Basis} = \text{current spot price} - \text{futures price.} \qquad (21.1)$$

A person with a short position in a futures contract and a long position in the deliverable asset (meaning that he or she owns the asset) will profit if the basis is positive and widens (or is negative and narrows). This is because the futures price will be falling or the spot price will be rising (or both). A falling futures price benefits those who are short futures, and a rising spot price benefits those who own the asset. Using the same type of reasoning, it can be shown that this person will lose if the basis is positive and narrows (or is negative and widens).

21.4.1 Speculating on the Basis

As an example, consider the situation previously discussed where the July futures price of wheat was $4 per bushel and the contract was for 5,000 bushels. Assuming that the current spot price of wheat is $4.30 per bushel, the basis is +$.30 (= $4.30 − $4.00). Now imagine that the basis widens by $.10 to +$.40 owing to the futures price falling to $3.95 and the spot price rising to $4.35. (Note that other combinations of price movements could cause the $.10 widening of the basis.) A person who has a short position in one futures contract and a long position of 5,000 bushels of wheat will make a profit of $500 (= $.10 × 5,000 bushels). This is because he or she gains on both the short position in the futures contract (owing to the $.05 fall in the futures price) and the long position in the asset (owing to the $.05 rise in its spot price).

However, if the basis narrows by $.10 to +$.20, then the person will have a loss of $500 (= $.10 × 5,000 bushels). Perhaps the narrowing resulted from both (1) a $.05 rise in the futures price to $4.05, causing a $250 loss on the person's short position, and (2) a $.05 fall in the spot price to $4.25, causing a $250 loss on his or her long position.

Note that if the $.30 basis was negative because the spot price was $3.70 and it subsequently widened by $.10 to −$.40, then the person would have a loss of $500 (= $.10 × 5,000 bushels). However, if it narrowed by $.10 to −$.20, then he or she would have a gain of $500. Hence the person gains if the basis is positive and widens or is negative and narrows, but he or she loses if the basis is positive and narrows or is negative and widens:

Long in Spot Market, Short in Futures Market

	Positive Basis	Negative Basis
Basis widens	Gain	Loss
Basis narrows	Loss	Gain

Conversely, a person with a long position in a futures contract and a short position in the deliverable asset (meaning that he or she has borrowed the asset and sold it, and now has an obligation to buy the asset in order to repay the loan or has contracted to purchase it at a fixed price) will profit if the basis is positive and narrows (or is negative and widens). However, a loss would be incurred if a positive basis widened (or a negative basis narrowed).

Short in Spot Market, Long in Futures Market

	Positive Basis	Negative Basis
Basis widens	Loss	Gain
Basis narrows	Gain	Loss

The risk that the basis will narrow or widen, causing gains or losses to these people, is known as **basis risk.** The only type of uncertainty they face concerns the difference between the spot price of the deliverable asset and the price of the futures contract. Such a person is said to be **speculating on the basis.**[7]

21.4.2 Spreads

It is quite possible to take a long position in a futures contract and a short position in another futures contract in the same asset, but with a different delivery date. The person who does this is speculating on changes in the difference between the prices of the two contracts, a difference that constitutes the "basis" for these particular positions.

Others attempt to profit from temporary imbalances among the prices of futures contracts on different but related assets. For example, one might take a long position in soybeans along with a short position in an item produced from soybeans, such as soybean meal. Another possibility involves a position in wheat with an offsetting position in corn, which serves as a substitute for wheat in many applications.

Such people are known as *spreaders*, and, like those who speculate on the basis, they reduce or eliminate the risk associated with general price moves. Instead, they take on the risk associated with changes in price *differences* in the hope that their alleged superior knowledge will enable them to consistently make profits from such changes.

21.5	RETURNS ON FUTURES

During the period from 1950 through 1976, a portfolio made up of positions in 23 different commodity futures contracts was compared with a diversified portfolio of common stocks.[8] The average rates of return and risk level of the two portfolios were found to be of similar magnitude:

Portfolio	Average Annual Return	Standard Deviation
Futures	13.83%	22.43%
Common stocks	13.05	18.95

Given these results, an investor might view the two alternatives as equally desirable. Better yet, during the period from 1950 to 1976, a combination of the two portfolios was found to be more desirable than either portfolio by itself. This resulted from the fact that the returns of the commodity futures and stock portfolios were negatively correlated, suggesting that the return on a combined portfolio would have had considerably less variation than on either portfolio separately. Specifically, the correlation coefficient was −.24, resulting in the following standard deviations for portfolios with different combinations:

Percent in Stocks	Percent in Futures	Standard Deviation	Average Annual Return
0%	100%	22.43%	13.83%
20	80	17.43	13.67
40	60	13.77	13.52
60	40	12.68	13.36
80	20	14.74	13.21
100%	0	18.95	13.05

Whereas there was little difference in the average returns of the various portfolios, there was a noticeable difference in their risks. In particular, the portfolio with 60% in stocks and 40% in futures seems to have had much less risk than the others.

Also of interest was the observation that commodity futures have been at least a partial hedge against inflation. During the period from 1950 to 1976, the returns on the portfolio of 23 futures were positively correlated with changes in the Consumer Price Index, having a correlation coefficient of .58. In contrast, the returns on the portfolio of common stocks were negatively correlated with changes in the Consumer Price Index, having a correlation coefficient of $-.43$. (See the accompanying *Institutional Issues* section for a further discussion of commodity futures returns.)

At this point it is appropriate to discuss the pricing of futures contracts. Specifically, what is the relationship between the futures price and investors' expectations of what the spot price will be on the delivery date? And what is the relationship between the futures price and the current spot price of the deliverable asset? The next two sections explore these relationships and provide some answers to the questions.

21.6   FUTURES PRICES AND EXPECTED SPOT PRICES

21.6.1   Certainty

If future spot prices could be predicted with certainty, there would be no reason for anyone to be either a buyer or a seller of a futures contract. To understand why, imagine what a futures contract would look like in a world of certainty. First, the purchase price of the futures contract would simply equal the (perfectly predictable) expected spot price on the delivery date. This means that neither buyers nor sellers would be able to make profits from the existence of futures. Second, the purchase price would not change as the delivery date got closer.[9] Finally, no margin would be necessary because there would not be any unexpected "adverse" price movements.

21.6.2   Uncertainty

While it is useful to know something about the way in which futures prices and expected spot prices are related to each other in a world of certainty where forecasting is done with complete accuracy, the real world is uncertain. Given this, how are futures prices related to expected spot prices? While there are several possible explanations, no definitive answer has been provided.

Expectations Hypothesis

One possible explanation is given by the **expectations hypothesis:** The current purchase price of a futures contract equals the consensus expectation of the spot price on the delivery date. In symbols:

$$P_f = \bar{P}_s$$

where P_f is the current purchase price of the futures contract and $\bar{P}_s$ is the expected spot price of the asset on the delivery date. Thus if a July wheat futures contract is currently selling for $4 per bushel, then it can be inferred that the consensus opinion is that in July the spot price of wheat will be $4.

If the expectations hypothesis is correct, a speculator should not expect to either win or lose from a position in the futures market, be it long or short. Neglecting margin requirements, a speculator who takes a long position in futures agrees to pay P_f at the delivery date for an asset that is expected to be worth $\bar{P}_s$ at that time. Thus the long speculator's expected profit is $\bar{P}_s - P_f$, which equals zero. Conversely, a speculator with a short position will have sold an asset at a price of P_f and will expect to enter a reversing trade at $\bar{P}_s$ on the delivery date. Thus the short speculator's expected profit is $P_f - \bar{P}_s$, which also equals zero.

The expectations hypothesis is often defended on the grounds that speculators are indifferent to risk and are thus happy to accommodate hedgers without any compensation in the form of the risk premium. The reason for their indifference has to do with the belief that the impact of a specific futures position on the risk of a diversified portfolio that includes many types of assets will be very small. Thus speculators holding diversified portfolios may be willing to take over some risk from hedgers with little (if any) compensation in the form of a risk premium.

Figure 21.4 shows the pattern of futures prices implied by the expectations hypothesis, given that the expected spot price $\bar{P}_s$ does not change during the life of the contract.

Normal Backwardation

The famous economist John Maynard Keynes felt that the expectations hypothesis did not correctly explain futures prices.[10] He argued that, on balance, hedgers will want to be short in futures, and therefore they will have to entice the speculators to be long in futures. Because there are risks associated with being long, Keynes hypothesized that the hedgers would have to entice the speculators by making the expected return from a long position greater than the riskfree rate. This requires the futures price to be less than the expected spot price:

$$P_f < \bar{P}_s.$$

Thus a speculator who bought a futures contract at a price P_f would expect to be able to sell it on (or near) the delivery date at a higher price $\bar{P}_s$. This relationship between the futures price and the expected spot price has been referred to as **normal backwardation** and implies that the price of a futures contract can be expected to rise during its life, as shown in Figure 21.4.

Futures

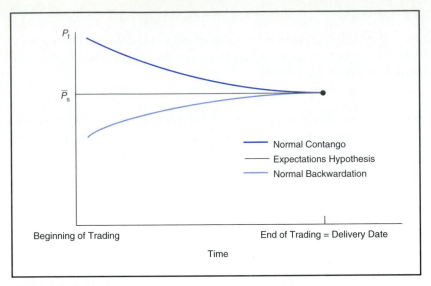

Figure 21.4
Price of a Futures Contract through Time When the Spot Price Expected at the Time of Delivery Does Not Change

Normal Contango

A contrary hypothesis holds that, on balance, hedgers will want to be long in futures and therefore they will have to entice speculators to be short in futures. Because there are risks associated with being short, it can be hypothesized that the hedgers will have to entice the speculators by making the expected return from a short position greater than the riskfree rate. This requires the futures price to be greater than the expected spot price:

$$P_f > \bar{P}_s.$$

Thus a speculator who short sold a futures contract at a price P_f would expect to be able to buy it back on (or near) the delivery date at a lower price, $\bar{P}_s$. This relationship between the futures price and the expected spot price has been referred to as **normal contango** and implies that the price of a futures contract can be expected to fall during its life, as shown in Figure 21.4.[11]

21.7   FUTURES PRICES AND CURRENT SPOT PRICES

The previous section discussed the relationship between the futures price associated with an asset and the expected spot price of the asset on the delivery date given in the futures contract. What about the relationship between the futures price and the current spot price of the asset? In general, they will be different, but is there some explanation for why these prices are different? Is there some

Commodity Futures: The Selling of an Asset Class

When institutional investors discuss investments in futures, we can safely assume that they are referring to *financial futures*—that is, futures contracts on, for example, stock market indices or Treasury bonds. Commodity futures, on the other hand, play only an insignificant role in institutional investors' portfolios.

Given the history of the futures markets, this situation might seem somewhat surprising. After all, financial futures are mere fledglings compared to commodity futures. The oldest futures exchange, the Chicago Board of Trade, was organized in 1848 for the sole purpose of trading futures contracts on agricultural commodities. The first financial futures contracts (a futures contract on foreign currencies) were established in 1972. The most popular financial futures contracts today, S&P 500 futures, were not created until 1981.

The dollar volume of trading in financial futures contracts now far exceeds the trading volume in commodity futures. Traditional users of commodity futures contracts have not become less enamored with those products. Rather, directly and indirectly institutional investors have helped create a gigantic market for financial futures.

The question then is not why institutional investors have become extensively involved in financial futures. The application of financial futures to the activities of institutional investors, in terms of both hedging and speculating, are obvious. More intriguing is why institutional investors have not entered the commodity futures market in any substantial way.

Institutional investors, particularly pension funds, in recent years have expanded the range of asset types (or classes) in which they invest. Whereas once they restricted themselves to domestic common stocks, high-grade bonds, and cash equivalents, institutional investors now own foreign securities, junk bonds, real estate, and oil and gas wells, to mention just a few. With some notable exceptions, however, institutional investors have been unwilling to add commodity futures to their asset class toolboxes.

Financial services providers have recognized the tremendous profit potential if institutional investors could be enticed to invest in commodities. If those investors chose to place just 2% to 3% of their immense wealth in commodities, the accompanying fees to brokers and money managers would easily run into the hundreds of millions of dollars.

How to convince institutional investors to trade in commodities? One potential means is to help publicize the risk-reward opportunities historically offered by investments in commodities. Institutional investors have generally shown a reluctance to become involved in investments lacking a quantifiable track record. By developing an index of a diversified investment in commodity futures, institutional investors would have performance data that could be compared against the results of investments in other asset classes. Furthermore, institutional investors would be able to construct simulated past portfolios that included commodity futures, thus emphasizing the diversification benefits of this asset class.

Beyond the industrywide benefit of stimulating institutional investor interest in commodity futures, a unique benefit accrues to the creator of an investable commodity futures index. If that index were to become widely accepted, the creator would have a considerable advantage in designing and trading products based on that index. That advantage could translate into significant revenue.

In 1991 Goldman Sachs, the large New York brokerage firm, with considerable fanfare introduced its own commodity futures index. Other organizations had previously developed such indices. Goldman Sachs, however, directly targeted institutional investors by designing its index to be more truly reflective of the commodity futures investment opportunities available to large investors. Furthermore, Goldman Sachs developed detailed simulated performance data for the index extending back to 1970.

The Goldman Sachs Commodities Index (GSCI) is composed of "near" futures commodity contract prices for which active liquid markets exist. ("Near" refers to the contract in a given commodity with the shortest time remaining until delivery.) This liquidity requirement allows large investors to replicate the index by buying its individual components. Weights in the index are based on world production of the respective commodities. Thus the most economically important commodities receive the most weight in the index.

Currently 18 commodities constitute the index, which is dominated by various energy, livestock, and grain futures (with weights of roughly 50%, 25%, and 15%, respectively). Historically the composition of the index has changed over time as new commodity futures contracts were created or met the GSCI liquidity requirements. In the 1970s the livestock and grain futures made up most of the index. Energy-related futures did not begin trading until 1983 and were not added to the index until 1987.

The reported historical performance of the GSCI has been impressive in terms of both return and risk. Ibbotson Associates reports the following returns, standard deviations, and correlations for the GSCI and comparative asset classes over the period of 1970 through the first quarter of 1992:

	Annual Return	Annual Standard Deviation	Correlation with GSCI
GSCI	14.8%	18.3	1.00
U.S. stocks	11.5	16.2	−.42
Foreign stocks	13.1	17.6	−.27
U.S. long-term bonds	9.0	11.5	−.32
U.S. Treasury bills	7.5	0.8	−.20
U.S. inflation	6.0	1.4	.26

The GSCI has produced returns exceeding those of U.S. and foreign stocks while offering only slightly more variability. Also impressive has been the GSCI's negative correlation with other asset classes and its positive correlation with inflation. The conclusions one draws from this data are that commodities offer equitylike returns, are excellent portfolio diversifiers, and are a good inflation hedge.

How Goldman Sachs has calculated the GSCI returns has generated some controversy. Those returns have three components: the spot return, the

Treasury-bill return, and the roll yield. The first two components are straightforward. The spot yield is how much the price of the underlying commodity changes. The Treasury-bill yield is the interest earned if the investor were to post as collateral the full dollar value (that is, the notional principal) of the investment in the commodities at the time of the futures contract purchase.

The roll yield is more complicated. It represents the change in the futures price over the life of the contract. If futures are priced according to normal backwardation (discussed in this chapter), then futures prices are expected to rise toward the spot price of the commodity over time. Therefore the process of "rolling" over expiring futures will be profitable on average.

Which is the correct explanation of the relationship between futures and expected spot prices: the expectations hypothesis, normal backwardation, or normal contango? As historically about one-third of the GSCI's return has come from roll yield, this question is more than academic. Goldman Sachs argues that the markets for commodities that are normally consumed as they are produced (such as energy or livestock) are typically subject to backwardation. Only if this will be the case in the future can a positive roll yield for the GSCI (and the resulting high GSCI total returns) be expected to persist.

Equally problematic is whether institutional investors can be expected to increase their investments in commodities. Current indications are that institutions are beginning to dip their toes in commodity futures through accounts called *managed futures*. In these accounts money managers actively take long and short positions in commodity and financial futures. The accounts gain only if their managers are adept at anticipating the direction of various futures price changes. Over $2 billion is now invested in managed futures accounts. Are these investments the harbingers of increased institutional activity or a mere passing fancy? The jury is still out.

model that can be used to forecast how the size of the difference will change over time? This section attempts to answer these questions.[12]

21.7.1   Introducing the Problem

Consider the owner of a circa 1910 Honus Wagner baseball card who is getting ready to sell the card. The owner knows that the current market price of the card is $100,000 because there are very few (reputedly fewer than five) of these cards available. (One actually sold for $451,000 in 1990.) Furthermore, an investor has offered to buy it but wants to pay for it a year from now. The buyer is willing to take delivery of the card then and wants to sign the contract for sale today. More specifically, he or she would like to sign a futures contract with the owner in which the delivery date is one year from now.

21.7.2   No Costs or Benefits of Ownership

What price should the owner ask for in the futures contract? Assume that there is no risk that either party will default on the contract, and that there are no benefits (such as from showing the card) or costs (such as insurance) associated with owning the card. Given that the current one-year interest rate is 4%, the owner could sell the card today on the spot market for $100,000, put the proceeds in the bank to earn 4%, and have $104,000 in one year. Hence the owner would not be willing to sign the futures contract for any futures price that is less than $104,000. The buyer, on the other hand, is unwilling to pay more than $104,000 because he or she could pay $100,000 now and get the card immediately but forgo $4,000 of interest that would have been earned had the $100,000 been left in the bank where it earned 4%. Since the seller wants to receive at least $104,000 and the buyer will pay no more than $104,000, they will settle at a futures price of $104,000.

To generalize, let P_s denote the current spot price of the asset (in this case, $100,000) and I the dollar amount of interest corresponding to the period of time from the present to the delivery date (in this case, $4,000). If P_f denotes the futures price, then:

$$P_f = P_s + I. \qquad (21.2)$$

This equation shows that the futures price will be greater than the spot price by the amount of the interest that the owner forgoes by holding onto the asset, provided that there are no costs or benefits associated with ownership.

21.7.3   Benefits from Ownership

To add a complication to the model, imagine that a baseball card exhibition will be held in 12 months, just before the delivery date. The exhibitor is willing to pay the card owner $1,000 in order to have the card displayed at the exhibition. How will this benefit of ownership affect the futures price?

As mentioned earlier, if the owner sells the card now, then he or she will receive $100,000 immediately, which could be invested right away and be worth $104,000 in 12 months. Alternatively, the owner could hold on to the card and receive the $1,000 exhibitor fee as well as the futures price. Hence the futures price must be at least $103,000 in order for the owner to be as well off financially by selling the card by means of a futures contract as by selling it immediately in the spot market. On the other side, the buyer will accept a futures price of no more than $103,000. This is because he or she could buy the card on the spot market for $100,000, thereby forgoing $4,000 of interest but receiving the $1,000 exhibitor fee. Consequently, the futures price will be $103,000, as this is the only price that is agreeable to both buyer and seller.

What if the exhibition were to be held in six months instead of one year? In that case the owner of the card would receive the $1,000 exhibitor fee in six months and would be able to invest it risklessly at 2% for the remaining six months until the delivery date. Thus the $1,000 in six months is equivalent to $1,020 in 12 months, and the futures price would be $102,980 ($= $100,000 + $4,000 - $1,020$).

Let B denote the value of the benefits of ownership (sometimes known as the convenience yield of the asset) as of the delivery date (in this case, $1,020). When such benefits are present, the futures price can be calculated as:

$$P_{\mathrm{f}} = P_s + I - B. \qquad (21.3)$$

This equation shows that the futures price can be greater or less than the spot price, depending on whether the net amount of interest forgone less benefits received is positive or negative and provided that there are no costs associated with ownership of the asset.

21.7.4   Costs of Ownership

What if the owner of the baseball card decides that it must be insured at an annual cost of $100? How will this affect the futures price? The easiest way to think of such costs of ownership as insurance and storage is to view them as the opposite of benefits of ownership. Because the benefits of ownership result in cash inflows to the owner, the costs of ownership result in cash outflows. Hence the previously calculated futures price of $102,980 would have to be increased by the $100 cost of insurance to $103,080. If C denotes the costs of ownership (in this example, $100), then the futures price will be:

$$P_{\mathrm{f}} = P_s + I - B + C. \qquad (21.4)$$

The total value of interest less benefits received plus cost of ownership, $I - B + C$, is known as the **cost of carry** associated with the futures contract. Note that the futures price can be greater or less than the spot price, depending upon whether the cost of carry is positive or negative.

It has now been shown how the futures price will be related to the current spot price. But is this compatible with the earlier discussion of the relationship between the futures price and the expected future spot price? It is. By adjusting production and consumption over time, producers and consumers of a good can bring about an appropriate relationship between the current price and the price expected in the future. The price of a futures contract will reflect both this relationship and that implied by the current price plus the cost of carry.

<table>
<tr><td>**21.8**</td><td>**FINANCIAL FUTURES**</td></tr>
</table>

Until the 1970s, futures contracts were limited to those on agricultural goods and natural resources. Since then, financial futures based on foreign currencies, fixed-income securities, and market indices have been introduced on major exchanges. Indeed, in terms of trading volume, they are now far more important than both the underlying assets and traditional futures contracts. Unlike other types of futures that permit delivery any time during a given month, most financial futures have a specific delivery date. (The exceptions involve some fixed-income futures.)

21.8.1 Foreign Currency Futures

Anyone who has crossed a national border knows that there is an active spot market for foreign currency, and that the rate at which one currency can be exchanged for another varies over time. At any particular point in time, however, all such rates must be in conformance or else a riskless profit-making situation may arise. For example, it is usually possible to exchange U.S. dollars for British pounds, then exchange the British pounds for French francs, and, finally, exchange the French francs for U.S. dollars. If all three exchange rates were not in line, an investor might end up with more dollars at the end of this chain of transactions than at the beginning. Such an opportunity would attract large amounts of money, placing pressure on exchange rates and rapidly restoring balance. Although transaction costs and certain exchange restrictions might limit the ability of people to exploit such imbalances among exchange rates, they would nevertheless force the rates into being closely aligned.

The familiar market in foreign currency, operated by banks, travel agents, and others, is in effect a spot market, because both the agreement on terms and the actual exchange of currencies occur at the same time. There are also markets for agreements involving the future delivery of foreign currency.

The largest such market is operated by banks and specialized brokers that maintain close communications with each other throughout the world. Corporations, institutions, and some individuals deal in this market via large banks. Substantial amounts of money are involved, and every agreement is negotiated separately. Typical rates are quoted daily in the financial press, as shown in Figure 21.5. This network of large institutions is generally termed the *market for forward exchange* because there is no marking to market. Furthermore, because the contracts are not standardized, no organized secondary market for them exists. However, there is a market that deals in standardized futures contracts for foreign currency.[13] Procedures are similar to those used for commodity futures.

CURRENCY TRADING

EXCHANGE RATES

Monday, December 13, 1993

The New York foreign exchange selling rates below apply to trading among banks in amounts of $1 million and more, as quoted at 3 p.m. Eastern time by Bankers Trust Co., Telerate and other sources. Retail transactions provide fewer units of foreign currency per dollar.

Country	U.S. $ equiv. Mon.	Fri.	Currency per U.S. $ Mon.	Fri.
Argentina (Peso)	1.01	1.01	.99	.99
Australia (Dollar)	.6715	.6715	1.4892	1.4892
Austria (Schilling)	.08329	.08384	12.01	11.93
Bahrain (Dinar)	2.6515	2.6522	.3772	.3771
Belgium (Franc)	.02796	.02815	35.76	35.52
Brazil (Cruzeiro real)	.0039259	.0039790	254.72	251.32
Britain (Pound)	1.4900	1.4955	.6711	.6687
30-Day Forward	1.4866	1.4924	.6727	.6701
90-Day Forward	1.4825	1.4880	.6745	.6720
180-Day Forward	1.4775	1.4826	.6768	.6745
Canada (Dollar)	.7533	.7524	1.3275	1.3291
30-Day Forward	.7524	.7519	1.3291	1.3300
90-Day Forward	.7520	.7511	1.3297	1.3314
180-Day Forward	.7510	.7500	1.3315	1.3333
Czech. Rep. (Koruna)				
Commercial rate	.0343761	.0342936	29.0900	29.1600
Chile (Peso)	.002439	.002421	410.03	413.00
China (Renminbi)	.172697	.172697	5.7905	5.7905
Colombia (Peso)	.001473	.001470	678.73	680.05
Denmark (Krone)	.1494	.1507	6.6956	6.6339
Ecuador (Sucre)				
Floating rate	.000515	.000520	1940.01	1923.00
Finland (Markka)	.17374	.17522	5.7556	5.7070
France (Franc)	.17116	.17219	5.8425	5.8075
30-Day Forward	.17058	.17166	5.8623	5.8253
90-Day Forward	.16978	.17082	5.8901	5.8542
180-Day Forward	.16883	.16987	5.9230	5.8870
Germany (Mark)	.5857	.5896	1.7074	1.6960
30-Day Forward	.5839	.5880	1.7125	1.7006
90-Day Forward	.5817	.5856	1.7192	1.7077
180-Day Forward	.5790	.5829	1.7272	1.7156
Greece (Drachma)	.004084	.004126	244.85	242.35
Hong Kong (Dollar)	.12948	.12948	7.7231	7.7230
Hungary (Forint)	.0101999	.0101802	98.0400	98.2300
India (Rupee)	.03212	.03212	31.13	31.13
Indonesia (Rupiah)	.0004755	.0004757	2103.01	2102.03
Ireland (Punt)	1.4136	1.4231	.7074	.7027
Israel (Shekel)	.3376	.3448	2.9625	2.9000
Italy (Lira)	.0005917	.0005986	1690.13	1670.56

Country	U.S. $ equiv. Mon.	Fri.	Currency per U.S. $ Mon.	Fri.
Japan (Yen)	.009172	.009166	109.03	109.10
30-Day Forward	.009180	.009173	108.94	109.02
90-Day Forward	.009200	.009195	108.69	108.76
180-Day Forward	.009242	.009236	108.20	108.27
Jordan (Dinar)	1.4577	1.4556	.6860	.6870
Kuwait (Dinar)	3.3495	3.3462	.2986	.2989
Lebanon (Pound)	.000583	.000583	1714.00	1716.00
Malaysia (Ringgit)	.3926	.3918	2.5474	2.5520
Malta (Lira)	2.5674	2.5445	.3895	.3930
Mexico (Peso)				
Floating rate	.3212335	.3222169	3.1130	3.1035
Netherland (Guilder)	.5229	.5265	1.9125	1.8992
New Zealand (Dollar)	.5537	.5555	1.8060	1.8002
Norway (Krone)	.1348	.1357	7.4161	7.3674
Pakistan (Rupee)	.0334	.0334	29.96	29.95
Peru (New Sol)	.4781	.4748	2.09	2.11
Philippines (Peso)	.03643	.03659	27.45	27.33
Poland (Zloty)	.00004993	.00004993	20028.00	20028.00
Portugal (Escudo)	.005714	.005772	175.01	173.25
Saudi Arabia (Riyal)	.26661	.26665	3.7508	3.7503
Singapore (Dollar)	.6272	.6258	1.5945	1.5980
Slovak Rep. (Koruna)	.0305250	.0303767	32.7600	32.9200
South Africa (Rand)				
Commercial rate	.2969	.2979	3.3683	3.3570
Financial rate	.2264	.2269	4.4175	4.4075
South Korea (Won)	.0012358	.0012356	809.20	809.30
Spain (Peseta)	.007136	.007210	140.14	138.70
Sweden (Krona)	.1187	.1199	8.4218	8.3384
Switzerland (Franc)	.6828	.6873	1.4645	1.4550
30-Day Forward	.6821	.6867	1.4661	1.4563
90-Day Forward	.6812	.6858	1.4679	1.4581
180-Day Forward	.6810	.6857	1.4685	1.4583
Taiwan (Dollar)	.037265	.037636	26.83	26.57
Thailand (Baht)	.03937	.03932	25.40	25.43
Turkey (Lira)	.0000721	.0000722	13865.00	13850.00
United Arab (Dirham)	.2723	.2723	3.6725	3.6725
Uruguay (New Peso)				
Financial	.229463	.225937	4.36	4.43
Venezuela (Bolivar)				
Floating rate	.00966	.00976	103.50	102.49
SDR	1.38994	1.38904	.71946	.71992
ECU	1.12990	1.13690	....	....

Special Drawing Rights (SDR) are based on exchange rates for the U.S., German, British, French and Japanese currencies. Source: International Monetary Fund.

European Currency Unit (ECU) is based on a basket of community currencies.

Figure 21.5

Quotations for Foreign Exchange

For example, one of the currency futures contracts traded on the International Monetary Market (IMM) of the Chicago Mercantile Exchange requires the seller to deliver 12,500,000 Japanese yen to the buyer on a specific date for a number of U.S. dollars agreed upon in advance. Only the price of the transaction (expressed in both dollars per yen and yen per dollar) is negotiated by the parties involved; all other terms are standard. Clearing procedures allow positions to be covered by reversing trades, and few contracts result in the actual delivery of foreign currency. As shown in Figure 21.1, prices and volumes for such contracts are quoted daily in the financial press along with those for other futures.

Markets for foreign currency futures attract both hedgers and speculators. Hedgers wish to reduce or possibly eliminate the risk associated with planned future transfers of funds from one country to another.

An Example

For example, an American importer might know on December 13, 1993, that he or she will have to make a payment of 50 million yen to a Japanese exporter in June 1994. The current exchange rate is $.009172 per yen (or, equivalently, 109.03 yen per dollar), so the anticipated dollar size of the payment is $458,600 (= $.009172 × 50,000,000). The risk the importer faces by simply waiting until June to make this payment is that the exchange rate will change in an unfavorable manner—perhaps rising to $.01 per yen, in which case the dollar cost to the importer will have risen to $500,000 (= $.01 × 50,000,000). The importer can hedge this risk by purchasing four June futures contracts for yen. Figure 21.1 indicates that the settlement price on December 13, 1993, for these contracts was $.009240, meaning that the dollar cost of one contract is $462,000 (= $.009240 × 50,000,000). Thus the importer can remove the risk of the yen's appreciating by more than $.000068 against the dollar before the payment date by purchasing the four yen futures contracts.

Speculators are attracted to the foreign currency futures market when they believe that the current price of the futures contract is substantially different from what they expect the spot rate to be on the delivery date.

For example, a speculator might believe that the price of the June futures contract for Japanese yen is too high. Perhaps a speculator might believe that when June comes around, the exchange rate will be $.009 per yen (or, equivalently, 111.11 yen per dollar). By selling (that is, short selling) a June futures contract for yen, the speculator will be selling yen for $.009240, the settlement price on December 13, 1993. At the time delivery has to be made, the speculator believes that yen can be bought on the spot market for $.009, thereby allowing a profit to be made on the difference between the selling and buying prices.[14] Specifically, the speculator expects to be able to make a profit of $3,000 [= ($.009240 − $.009) × 12,500,000)] per futures contract.

Pricing

Futures contracts involving foreign currencies are priced according to the notion of **interest-rate parity,** which is merely a special application of the model of futures pricing given in Equation (21.4).

Imagine that it is December 1993 and you are planning to invest some money for one year. You could simply invest in a one-year U.S. riskfree security and then receive the principal and interest a year later in the form of U.S. dollars. Alternatively, you could exchange the dollars for German marks and use the marks to buy a one-year German riskfree security. In addition, you would short sell the requisite number of one-year German mark futures contracts so that a year later, when you receive the principal and interest in the form of German marks, you would know exactly how many U.S. dollars you would receive for them.

Both of these strategies—investing in U.S. riskfree securities or investing in German riskfree securities—have no risk associated with them in that you know exactly how many U.S. dollars they will yield after one year. If the German strategy had a higher return per dollar invested, Americans would not buy the U.S.

riskfree securities because they could earn the same amount for a smaller investment by buying the German riskfree securities. Similarly, if the U.S. strategy had a higher return per dollar invested, Germans would not buy the German riskfree securities because they could earn the same amount for a smaller investment by buying U.S. dollars in the spot market, purchasing U.S. riskfree securities, and buying a one-year German mark futures contract. As a consequence, in equilibrium the two strategies must have the same cost if they have the same dollar payoffs.

Consider what would happen per dollar invested. The strategy of investing $1 in a U.S. riskfree security that has a return of R_{US} will provide a cash inflow of $\$1(1 + R_{US})$ after one year. The strategy of investing $1 in a German riskfree security that has a return of R_G, where the current spot rate of exchange is P_s and the futures price is P_f, will provide a dollar cash inflow of $(\$1/P_s)(1 + R_G)P_f$ after one year. (Here both P_s and P_f are stated in dollars per mark.) Given that these two strategies cost the same ($1), their payoffs must be equal:

$$\$1(1 + R_{US}) = \left(\frac{\$1}{P_s}\right)(1 + R_G)P_f. \tag{21.5}$$

Hence the futures price of the mark can be determined by rewriting Equation (21.5) as the interest-rate parity equation:

$$P_f = P_s\left(\frac{1 + R_{US}}{1 + R_G}\right). \tag{21.6}$$

Thus if the current spot rate of exchange for the German mark is $.60, and the U.S. and German one-year riskfree rates are 4% and 5%, respectively, then the one-year futures price of the mark will be $.5943 [= $.60 × (1.04/1.05)].

In relation to Equation (21.4), the cost of carry is $-\$.0057$ ($= \$.5943 - \$.60$). In the case of foreign currency, the costs of ownership C are zero. However, the net benefits of ownership $I - B$ amount to the $-\$.0057$ cost of carry. More generally, the cost of carry, denoted *carry*, will equal:

$$\text{Carry} = P_s\left(\frac{R_{US} - R_G}{1 + R_G}\right) \tag{21.7}$$

for foreign currency futures, where R_G now denotes the riskfree rate in the foreign currency under consideration. From Equation (21.7) it can be seen that because carry $= I - B$, it follows that:

$$I = \frac{P_s R_{US}}{1 + R_G} \tag{21.8a}$$

$$B = \frac{P_s R_G}{1 + R_G}. \tag{21.8b}$$

Hence in the example I, the amount of interest forgone by the owner by selling marks in the futures market instead of the spot market, equals $.0229 ($= $.60 × .04/1.05$), whereas B, the benefit of owning marks instead of selling them, equals $.0286 ($= $.60 × .05/1.05$). Consequently, the cost of carry equals $-\$.0057$ ($= \$.0229 - \$.0286$), as shown earlier.

Equation (21.4) indicates that the futures price will be less than the current spot price when the cost of carry is negative. This will occur when the U.S. risk-free rate is less than the foreign riskfree rate because the numerator on the right-hand side of Equation (21.7) will be negative whereas the denominator is positive in such a situation. Conversely, the futures price will be greater than the current spot price when the cost of carry is positive, which will occur when the U.S. riskfree rate is greater than the foreign riskfree rate. Hence the reason why futures prices are different from spot prices is that riskfree interest rates between countries are different.

21.8.2 Interest-Rate Futures

Futures involving fixed-income securities are often referred to as interest-rate futures because their prices are greatly influenced by the current and forecast interest rates. More specifically, their pricing can be related to the term structure of interest rates, which in turn is related to the concept of forward rates.[15]

An Example

Just how the pricing of interest-rate futures is related to the concept of forward rates can be illustrated with an example. Consider the futures market for 90-day Treasury bills. As Figure 21.1 indicates, on December 13, 1993, any purchaser of a futures contract calling for delivery in June 1994 of $1,000,000 face value of 90-day Treasury bills (maturing in September 1994) would have paid a settlement price of 96.48. More precisely, the seller of the contract was obligated to deliver Treasury bills to the buyer in June 1994 for an amount that would make the interest rate on the Treasury bills, stated on an annualized discount basis, equal to 3.52% per year.[16] Thus on December 13, 1993, the forward rate on 90-day Treasury bills to be delivered in June 1994 was 3.52%.

As with commodity futures, neither the buyers nor the sellers of such contracts must maintain their positions until the delivery date. Reversing trades can be made at any time, and relatively few contracts result in actual delivery.

Figure 21.1 shows that on December 13, 1993, the structure of 90-day forward rates was upward sloping, ranging from 3.24% for March 1994 delivery to 3.80% for September 1994 delivery. Under the unbiased expectations hypothesis (discussed in Chapter 5), these forward rates can be interpreted to represent what investors, on average, think that spot rates will be in the future. Specifically, the 3.52% forward rate on 90-day Treasury bills to be delivered in June 1994 can be taken as an indication that on December 13, 1993, investors, on average, expect the interest rate on 90-day Treasury bills to be equal to 3.52% in June 1994. Because the interest rate that is available on December 13, 1993, on 90-day Treasury bills for immediate delivery is approximately 3.06%, it can be seen that investors, on average, expect interest rates to rise in the near future.

Actively traded interest rate futures involve underlying securities ranging from short term (such as 90-day Treasury bills) to intermediate term (such as 10-year Treasury notes) to long term (such as 20-year Treasury bonds). Prices are generally stated in terms of percentages of par values for the corresponding securities. Yields-to-maturity (or discounts) associated with the settlement prices are also given.[17]

Pricing

In general, pricing of interest rate futures contracts involves applying the cost of carry model given in Equation (21.4). As an example, consider a 90-day Treasury bill futures contract that calls for delivery in six months. Note that nine-month Treasury bills will be equivalent to 90-day Treasury bills after six months have passed. Hence they could be delivered as the underlying assets in 90-day Treasury bill futures contracts where the delivery date is six months from now. What futures price is fair for these contracts?

Assume that the current market price of a nine-month Treasury bill is $95.24, providing a yield of 5% (= $4.76/$95.24) over the nine months. (This yield and those that follow are not annualized.) If an owner sold this security now, he or she would be able to risklessly earn 3% on the proceeds over the next six months. This means that the owner should not short sell a futures contract calling for delivery in six months of a 90-day Treasury bill where the price to be received is less than $98.10 (= $95.24 × 1.03). For example, if the price of the futures contract was $97, then the owner would be making only 1.85% on his or her initial investment of $95.24 over the subsequent six months. This is less than the 3% that could be earned by selling the nine-month Treasury bill now and investing in a six-month Treasury bill.

Conversely, the buyer should not agree to a price that is more than $98.10. This is because the buyer could buy the nine-month Treasury bill in the spot market today for $95.24 and receive $100 in nine months, or the buyer could risklessly invest the $95.24 for six months at 3% and then use the $98.10 proceeds to pay the futures price for a 90-day Treasury bill that pays $100 at maturity. If the futures price were greater than $98.10 (for example, $99), then the buyer would have to invest more than $95.24 today [for example, $96.12 (= $99/1.03) would have to be invested today] so that the principal plus 3% interest for six months would be sufficient to pay the futures price $99 after six months. In such a situation, nobody would choose to be long in the futures contract, because he or she would be better off buying a nine-month Treasury bill in the spot market for $95.24 instead of investing more at 3% for six months in order to be able to pay the futures price upon delivery of the Treasury bill. Consequently, the futures price must be $98.10, because this is the only price that is acceptable to both parties to the futures contract.

Generalizing, the futures price P_f must equal the spot price P_s plus the forgone interest I, just as shown in Equation (21.2), because the benefits B and costs C of ownership are zero with such assets. Equivalently, letting R denote the riskfree interest rate that exists on Treasuries that mature on the delivery date, the futures price is:

$$P_f = P_s(1 + R). \qquad (21.9)$$

Notice that the futures price will be greater than the spot price as long as the riskfree rate R is positive. Similarly, note that the cost of carry equals:

$$Carry = P_s R \qquad (21.10)$$

because both B and C are equal to zero. In this example, carry = $2.86 (= $95.24 × .03). Note that the difference between the futures price of $98.10 and the spot price of $95.24 also equals $2.86.

21.8.3 Market Index Futures

Figure 21.1 shows a set of quotations for futures contracts on two market indices. Each of these contracts involves the payment of *cash* on the delivery date of an amount equal to a *multiplier* times the difference between (1) the value of the index at the close of the last trading day of the contract and (2) the purchase price of the futures contract. If the index is above the futures price, those with short positions pay those with long positions. If the index is below the futures price, those with long positions pay those with short positions.

In practice, a clearinghouse is used, and all contracts are marked to market every day. In a sense, the delivery day differs from other days in only one respect—all open positions are marked to market for the last time and then closed.

Cash settlement provides results similar to those associated with the delivery of all the securities in the index. It avoids the effort and transaction costs associated with (1) the purchase of securities by people who have taken short futures positions; (2) the delivery of these securities to people who have taken long futures positions; and (3) the subsequent sale of the securities by those who receive them.

Major Contracts

Four major stock market index futures were available in 1993, with the most popular one in terms of both trading volume and open interest based on the Standard & Poor's 500 (S&P 500). This contract, along with one on the Nikkei 225 (a major Japanese index), are traded on the Index and Option Market Division of the Chicago Mercantile Exchange (CME). The two other stock index futures involve the New York Stock Exchange Composite Stock Index [traded at the New York Futures Exchange (NYFE)] and the CME's Standard & Poor's Mid-Cap 400. (There are also index futures contracts on the Major Market Index, which, when multiplied by five, closely resembles the Dow Jones Industrial Average; it is traded on the Chicago Board of Trade.)[18]

For all contracts but the Nikkei 225 futures, the multiplier is $500; for the Nikkei 225, it is $5. Thus the purchase of an S&P 500 contract when the index is 400 would cost $200,000 (= $500 × 400). The subsequent sale of this contract when the index is 420 would result in proceeds of $210,000 (= $500 × 420) and a profit of $10,000 (= $210,000 − $200,000).

Trading Volume

The volume of trading in futures contracts is very large. To assess its relative size, the number of contracts can be multiplied by the total dollar value represented by one contract. As shown in Figure 21.1, the estimated volume on December 13, 1993, for S&P 500 futures was 66,732 contracts. At a value of 466.50 for the lowest priced S&P 500 contract, the total dollar value is in excess of $15 billion (= 66,732 × 466.50 × $500). In comparison, the average daily dollar value of all trades of shares on the New York Stock Exchange during 1993 was $9.0 billion per day—a figure that is much less than the dollar size of the S&P futures on December 13, 1993. This is not unusual. On many days the dollar value involved in trades of S&P 500 futures exceeds that all of trades of individual stocks.

Hedging

What accounts for the popularity of market index futures in general and the S&P 500 in particular? Simply stated, they provide relatively inexpensive and highly liquid positions similar to those obtained with diversified stock portfolios.

For example, instead of purchasing 500 stocks in anticipation of a market advance, one can invest an equivalent amount of money in Treasury bills and take a long position in S&P 500 futures. Alternatively, instead of trying to take short positions in 500 stocks in anticipation of a market decline, one can take a short position in S&P 500 futures, using Treasury bills as margin.

Another important use of market index futures involves allowing broker-dealers to hedge the market risk that is associated with the temporary positions they often take in the course of their business.[19] This hedging ultimately benefits investors by providing them with greater liquidity than they would have otherwise.

For example, consider an investor who wants to sell a large block of stock. In this situation a broker-dealer might agree to purchase the stock immediately at an agreed-upon price, and then spend time "lining up" buyers. In the interim, however, economic news might cause the market to fall, and with it the price of the stock. This would cause the broker-dealer to experience a loss, because the broker-dealer owns the stock during the period between purchasing it from the investor and lining up the ultimate buyers. One traditional way that broker-dealers protect themselves (at least partially) from this risk is to pay the investor a relatively low price for the stock. However, the broker-dealer can now hedge this risk (at least partially) by short selling S&P 500 futures at the time the stock is bought from the investor and reversing this position when the ultimate buyers are found.

Conversely, when an investor wants to buy a large block of stock, a broker-dealer might agree to provide it at a certain price and then go about the task of lining up sellers. In the interim, however, economic news might cause the market to rise, and with it the price of the stock. This would cause the broker-dealer to experience a loss, because the price that will have to be paid to the sellers might end up being greater than the price agreed to with the investor. Traditionally, broker-dealers protect themselves from such risk by charging the investor a relatively high price for the stock. However, a broker-dealer can now hedge this risk (at least partially) by going long in S&P 500 futures at the time the investor agrees to buy the stock and then reversing this position when the stock is ultimately bought.

Given competition among broker-dealers, the existence of S&P 500 futures will lead them to provide higher bid prices and lower asked prices. This reduced bid-ask spread means that the existence of S&P 500 futures has provided the associated spot market for stocks with greater liquidity.

It should be pointed out that the use of S&P 500 futures in such situations does not remove all risk from the position of the broker-dealer. All that it removes is market risk, because these futures contracts involve a broad market index, not an individual stock. Thus it is possible for the broker-dealer to experience a loss even if an appropriate position has been taken in futures. Specifically, the individual stock with which the broker-dealer is involved may move up or down in price while the S&P 500 is stable, or the S&P 500 may move up or down while the individual stock is stable. In either case, the broker-dealer who has hedged with S&P 500 futures may still experience a loss. The possibility of this happening will be substantial when the broker-dealer has little diversification, with the greatest possibility associated with a one-stock portfolio.

Index Arbitrage

When stock index futures were first proposed, a number of people predicted that at long last there would be an indicator of investors' expectations about the future course of the stock market. It was said that the market price of such a futures contract would indicate the consensus opinion of investors concerning the future level of the associated index. In times of optimism, the futures price might be much higher than the current level of the market, whereas in times of pessimism, the futures price might be much lower.

Such predictions have since been found to be quite off the mark. This is because the price of a futures contract on an asset will not diverge by more than the cost of carry from the spot price of the asset. Should a relatively large divergence occur, clever investors known as *arbitrageurs* can be expected to make trades designed to capture riskless (that is, "arbitrage") profits.

What effect does the presence of these arbitrageurs have on the pricing of stock index futures? Their actions will force the price of a stock index futures contract to stay close to an "appropriate" relationship with the current level of the associated index. To find out just what is meant by appropriate, consider a hypothetical example. Today is a day in June when the Standard & Poor's 500 is at 100 and a December Standard & Poor's 500 futures contract is selling for 110. The following investment strategies will be compared:

1. Purchase the stocks in the S&P 500, hold them until December, and then sell them on the delivery date of the December S&P 500 contract.
2. Purchase a December S&P 500 futures contract along with Treasury bills that mature in December. Hold the futures contract until the delivery date in December.

Strategy 1 would cost $100 (in "index terms") at the outset. In return, it would provide the investor with (1) an amount of money equal to the value of the S&P 500 on the delivery date, and (2) dividends on those stocks that went ex-dividend prior to the delivery date. That is, by denoting the level the S&P 500 will have on the delivery date by P_d and assuming that the dividend yield over the six-month time period from June to December is 3%, the investor following strategy 1 will receive in December a net cash inflow that is equal to P_d + $3 [that is, P_d + (.03 × $100)].[20]

Assume that $100 is invested in Treasury bills in strategy 2. Because Treasury bills can be used as margin on futures, the total cost of strategy 2 is $100, which is the same as the cost of strategy 1. In return, strategy 2 would provide the investor with (1) an amount of money equal to the difference between the value of the S&P 500 and $110 on the delivery date, and (2) the face value of the Treasury bills on the delivery date. That is, by assuming that the six-month yield on the Treasury bills is 5%, the investor following strategy 2 will receive in December a net cash inflow that is equal to P_d − $5 [that is, $(P_d$ − $110) + (1.05 × $100)].

By design, both strategies require the same initial outlay. Furthermore, both strategies are subject to precisely the same uncertainty: the unknown level of the

S&P 500 on the future delivery date, P_d. However, the December net cash inflows are not equal, indicating that an opportunity exists for **index arbitrage.**[21]

In this example, the way index arbitrage would work is for an investor to go "long" strategy 1 and "short" strategy 2. Why? Because strategy 1 has a higher payoff than strategy 2 (note that $P_d + \$3 > P_d - \$5$). Going long strategy 1 means that the investor is to do exactly what was indicated earlier—purchase the stocks in the S&P 500 and hold them until the December delivery date. Going short strategy 2 means to do exactly the opposite of what was indicated earlier. Specifically, the investor is to short (that is, sell) a December S&P 500 futures contract and sell Treasury bills that mature in December. (It is assumed that the investor has these in his or her current portfolio.) The net cash outflow of going long strategy 1 and short strategy 2 is zero—$100 is spent buying the stocks in going long strategy 1, which is obtained by selling $100 worth of December Treasury bills when the investor goes short strategy 2. The margin necessary for being short the futures contract is met by having purchased the underlying stocks. Thus no additional cash needs to be committed in order to engage in index arbitrage—all that is necessary is for the investor to own Treasury bills that mature in December.

Having gone long strategy 1 and short strategy 2, consider the investor's position on the delivery date in December. First of all, the investor "bought" the individual stocks in the S&P 500 at $100 and "sold" them at $110 by being short the S&P 500 futures contract. Thus the investor has made $10 from being long the individual stocks and short the futures on the index. Second, the investor will have received dividends totaling $3 ($= .03 \times \$100$) from owning the stocks from June to December. Third, the investor will have given up $5 ($= .05 \times \$100$) in interest that would have been earned on the December Treasury bills. This is because the investor sold $100 of these Treasury bills in June in order to get the requisite cash to buy the individual stocks. Overall, the investor has increased the dollar return that would have been made on the Treasury bills by $8 ($= \$10 + \$3 - \$5$). Furthermore, this increase is certain, meaning that it will be received regardless of what happens to the level of the S&P 500. Thus by going long strategy 1 and short strategy 2 the investor will not have increased the risk of his or her portfolio but will have increased the dollar return.

Earlier it was mentioned that an investor going long strategy 1 would receive cash of $P_d + \$3$ in December, whereas an investor going long strategy 2 would receive cash of $P_d - \$5$. It can now be seen that going long strategy 1 and short strategy 2 will provide a net dollar return of $8 [that is, $(P_d + \$3) - (P_d - \$5)$], just as was shown in the previous paragraph. However, if enough investors do this, the opportunity for making the $8 profit will disappear. This is because (1) going long the individual stocks will push the prices of these stocks up, thereby raising the current level of the S&P 500 from 100, and (2) going short the S&P 500 futures will push the price of the futures down from 110. These two adjustments will continue until it is no longer profitable to go long strategy 1 and short strategy 2.

What if the price of the S&P 500 December futures contract was $90 instead of $110? The net cash inflow from being long strategy 1 is still equal to $P_d + \$3$. However, the net cash inflow from being long strategy 2 will be different. In particular, purchasing Treasury bills and the futures contract will provide the investor with $P_d + \$15$ [that is, $(P_d - \$90) + (1.05 \times \$100)$]. Because these two inflows are not equal, again there is an opportunity for index arbitrage. However, it would involve the investor going short strategy 1 and long strategy 2. Why? Because strategy 1 now has a lower payoff than strategy 2 (note that $P_d + \$3 < P_d + \$15$). By doing this, the investor will, without risk, earn $12 [that is, $(P_d + \$15) - (P_d + \$3)$]. Furthermore, being short the individual stocks and long the futures will push the current level of the S&P 500 down from 100 and the price of the futures up from 90.

In equilibrium, because these two strategies cost the same to implement, prices will adjust so that their net cash inflows are equal. Letting y denote the dividend yield on the stocks in the index, P_f the current price of the futures contract on the index, and P_s the current spot price of the index (that is, P_s denotes the current level of the index), the net cash inflow from strategy 1 is:

$$P_d + yP_s.$$

Letting R denote the interest rate on Treasury bills, the net cash inflow from strategy 2 is:

$$(P_d - P_f) + [(1 + R) \times P_s].$$

Setting these two inflows equal to each other results in:

$$P_d + yP_s = (P_d - P_f) + [(1 + R) \times P_s]. \tag{21.11}$$

Simplifying this equation results in:

$$P_f - P_s = (R - y)P_s \tag{21.12}$$

or

$$P_f = P_s + RP_s - yP_s. \tag{21.13}$$

Equation (21.12) indicates that the difference between the price of the futures contract and the current level of the index should depend only on (1) the current level of the index P_s, and (2) the difference between the interest rate on Treasury bills and the dividend yield on the index $R - y$. As the delivery date nears, the difference between the interest rate and the dividend yield diminishes, converging to zero on the delivery date. Thus as the delivery date approaches, the futures price P_f should converge to the current spot price P_s.

Equation (21.13) shows that index futures are priced according to the cost of carry model given earlier in Equation (21.4), where the costs of ownership C are zero. Here the interest forgone by ownership I is equal to RP_s, whereas the benefit of ownership B is the dividend yield yP_s. Hence the cost of carry is:

$$\text{Carry} = RP_s - yP_s \tag{21.14}$$

which will be positive as long as the riskfree interest rate R is greater than the dividend yield on the index y—a situation that exists nearly all the time.

In the example the interest rate was 5%, the dividend yield was 3%, and the current level of the S&P 500 was 100. This means that the difference between the S&P 500 December futures contract and the current level of the S&P 500 should be 2 $[= (.05 - .03) \times 100]$. Equivalently, the equilibrium price of the futures contract when the S&P 500 is 100 would be 102 because the cost of carry is 2. Note that when three of the six months have passed, the interest rate and the dividend yield will be 2.5% ($= 5\%/2$) and 1.5% ($= 3\%/2$), respectively. Thus the difference should be about 1 $[= (.025 - 015) \times 100]$, assuming that the S&P 500 is still at 100 at that time.

In practice, the situation is not this simple for a number of reasons. Positions in futures, stocks, and Treasury bills involve transaction costs.[22] This means that arbitrage will not take place unless the difference diverges far enough from the amount shown in Equation (21.12) to warrant incurring such costs. The futures price, and hence the difference, can be expected to move within a band around the "theoretical value," with the width of the band determined by the costs of those who can engage in transactions most efficiently.

To add to the complexity, both the dividend yield and the relevant interest rate on Treasury bills are subject to some uncertainty. Neither the amounts of dividends to be declared nor their timing can be specified completely in advance. Furthermore, because futures positions must be marked to market daily, the amount of cash required for strategy 2 may have to be varied via additional borrowing (if short this strategy) or lending (if long this strategy). Also on occasion market prices may be reported with a substantial time lag, making the current level and the futures price of the index appear to be out of line when they actually are not. Thus an investor may enter into the transactions necessary for index arbitrage when actual prices are in equilibrium, thereby incurring useless transaction costs. Nevertheless, index arbitrage is still actively pursued, most notably by brokerage firms, as shown in Figure 21.6.

PROGRAM TRADING

NEW YORK — Program trading in the week ended Dec. 10 accounted for 7.1%, or an average 20.1 million daily shares, of New York Stock Exchange volume.

Brokerage firms executed an additional 15.1 million daily shares of program trading away from the Big Board, mostly on foreign markets. Program trading is the simultaneous purchase or sale of at least 15 different stocks with a total value of $1 million or more.

Of the program total on the Big Board, 22.5% involved stock-index arbitrage, up from 19% the prior week. In this strategy, traders dart between stocks and stock-index options and futures to capture fleeting price differences.

Some 51.7% of program trading was executed by firms for their customers, while 35.3% was for their own accounts or principal trading. An additional 13% was designated as customer facilitation, where firms use principal positions to facilitate customer trades.

Of the five most-active firms, Nomura Securities executed most of its program trading for its own accounts, while Morgan Stanley, Bear Stearns, First Boston and Salomon Brothers did most of their program trading for their customers.

NYSE PROGRAM TRADING
Volume (in millions of shares) for the week ending December 10, 1993

Top 15 Firms	Index Arbitrage	Derivative-Related*	Other Strategies	Total
Morgan Stanley	....	0.5	12.0	12.5
CS First Boston	....	0.4	12.1	12.5
Salomon Bros.	0.4	0.3	10.9	11.6
Bear Stearns	....	0.6	6.9	7.5
Nomura Securities	4.2	....	2.6	6.8
Cooper Neff	....	4.5	0.7	5.2
Susquehanna	4.1	....	0.5	4.6
Nikko Securities	....	....	4.4	4.4
UBS Securities	3.3	....	1.1	4.4
Daiwa Securities	2.1	....	1.7	3.8
Lehman Brothers	....	1.1	2.6	3.7
W&D Securities	0.3	....	3.4	3.7
Goldman Sachs	....	0.2	2.9	3.1
Thomas Williams	2.6	....	0.1	2.7
Merrill Lynch	....	....	2.7	2.7
OVERALL TOTAL	22.6	8.2	69.7	100.5

*Other derivative-related strategies besides index arbitrage
Source: New York Stock Exchange

Figure 21.6
Index Arbitrage as a Form of Program Trading

Source: Reprinted by permission of *The Wall Street Journal,* ©Dow Jones & Company, Inc., December 17, 1993, p. C16. All rights reserved worldwide.

Stock index futures are also used extensively by other professional money managers. As a result, prices of such contracts are likely to track their underlying indices very closely, taking into account both dividends and current interest rates. It is unlikely that a private investor will be able to exploit "mispricing" of such a contract by engaging in index arbitrage. Nevertheless, stock index futures can provide inexpensive ways to take positions in the stock market or to hedge portions of the risk associated with other positions. Furthermore, their use can lower transaction costs by reducing the size of the bid-ask spread in individual securities, thereby benefiting investors who may never take direct positions in futures contracts.

21.9   FUTURES VERSUS OPTIONS

People occasionally make the mistake of confusing a futures contract with an options contract.[23] With an options contract there is the possibility that both parties involved will have nothing to do at the end of the life of the contract. In particular, if the option is "out of the money" on the expiration date, then the options contract will be worthless and can be thrown away. However, with a futures contract, both parties involved must do something at the end of the life of the contract. The parties are obligated to complete the transaction, either by a reversing trade or by actual delivery.

Figure 21.7 contrasts the situation faced by the buyer and the seller of a call option with the situation faced by the buyer and the seller of a futures contract. Specifically, terminal values for buyers and sellers are shown at the last possible moment—the expiration date for the option and the delivery date for the futures contract.

Figure 21.7
Terminal Values of Positions in Calls and Futures

Transportable Alpha

Years ago trustees of the $1 billion General Mills pension fund adopted a disciplined approach to allocating assets among various broad categories. This was accomplished by establishing specific long-run allocation targets: 60% to common stocks and 40% to fixed-income securities. The trustees believe that this *policy asset allocation* provides an optimal balance of expected return and risk, given their collective tolerance for possible adverse outcomes. The trustees expect the fund's staff, which handles the fund's day-to-day investment operations, to stick closely to this policy asset allocation. In turn, the staff follows a procedure of reducing exposure to the asset category that has appreciated in relative value and increasing exposure to the asset category that has depreciated in relative value.

To manage the pension fund's assets, the staff had retained what the trustees considered to be a superior group of domestic common stock managers. Over a ten-year period, those managers, in aggregate, had outperformed the S&P 500 by 1.5% annually (after all fees and expenses)—an exceptional amount by the standards of the investment management business. The trustees and staff expected such superior performance to continue in the future.

More recently the trustees found themselves facing a dilemma: The trustees would have liked to have assigned more than 60% of the fund's assets to the common stock managers. However, the trustees were also committed to the discipline of their asset allocation process. Could the trustees have their proverbial cake and eat it too? The answer was "Yes," through a concept called *transportable alpha*.

Consider three strategies through which General Mills could have maintained its policy asset allocation, yet taken advantage of its common stock managers' skills. Each strategy involves allocating more than 60% of the pension fund's assets to the common stock managers, while simultaneously reducing the pension fund's common stock exposure and increasing its fixed-income exposure in order to comply with the fund's asset allocation targets.

1. *Long-short strategy.* The managers, in aggregate, purchase long positions in stocks as they typically would with their assigned assets. However, they also short sell stocks (see Chapter 2) equal in value to the pension fund's overweighting of domestic equity assets. The cash generated by these short sales is used to buy fixed-income securities that are held as margin, but nevertheless provide returns through interest income and price changes. The particular long-short transactions result from the managers' investment research, which identifies under- and overpriced securities.

2. *Futures strategy.* The managers purchase long stock positions with their assigned assets. At the same time the pension fund's staff sells futures contracts on a stock market index and buys futures contracts on Treasury bonds in sufficient amounts to compensate for the over- and underweighting of common stocks and fixed-income securities.

3. *Swap strategy.* The managers purchase long stock positions with their assigned assets. Through a financial intermediary (such as a bank or a broker) the pension fund "swaps" (exchanges) with another institutional investor the return on a common stock index in order to receive the return on a fixed-income index. These swaps (see Chapter 24) are based on dollar amounts equal to the over and underweightings of the common stocks and fixed-income securities.

In general, these strategies can be characterized as allowing the pension fund to earn (1) the total return generated by a 40% allocation to fixed-income securities, (2) the total return produced by a 60% allocation to common stocks (that is, the normal plus abnormal returns of the common stock managers), and (3) the abnormal returns earned by the common stock managers associated with the allocation in excess of 60% to common stocks. The common stock managers' abnormal returns (known as *alphas*) are effectively "transported" to the fixed-income asset category.

In the final analysis, General Mills chose to implement the second strategy. The pension fund's staff believed that listed futures contracts provided the cheapest and administratively least cumbersome means of carrying out its alpha transport program. Nevertheless, the ability to customize the other strategies to specific situations may make those strategies attractive at times to certain institutional investors.

These strategies highlight fundamental changes in the financial markets that began in the 1980s and have rapidly gathered momentum in the 1990s. Through the development of derivative financial instruments (options, futures, and swaps) and the technological advancements in communications and computing power, financial markets have become highly integrated and fungible. Investors are increasingly able to exploit perceived profit opportunities and simultaneously maintain desired risk positions.

Pacific Investment Management Company (PIMCO) provides another example of the transportable alpha concept. PIMCO is one of the largest fixed-income managers in the world, with assets under management exceeding $60 billion. Over the years, the firm has produced an enviable track record, earning positive risk-adjusted returns under a variety of fixed-income investment assignments.

Since 1986, PIMCO has transported its fixed-income management skills to the U.S. stock market through a product called StocksPlus. PIMCO's process is simple. The firm purchases S&P 500 futures contracts equal to a specified *notional* principal. (A notional principal is the market exposure of the futures contracts—that is, the number of contracts purchased times the contracts' price times the contract multiplier.) At the same time PIMCO sets aside cash reserves equal to the notional principal. The cash reserves serve as collateral for the futures contracts.

As the text discusses, futures prices are set by investors predicated on the assumption that they can hold a combination of futures contracts and the riskfree asset. PIMCO uses its investment skills to create a short-term fixed-income portfolio that has substantially outperformed 90-day Treasury bills with little incremental risk. As a result, the firm's combination of S&P 500 futures contracts and short-term fixed-income investments has consistently exceeded the returns on the S&P 500.

PIMCO uses a variety of cash management strategies to add value relative to a portfolio of 90-day Treasury bills. The firm takes advantage of the most consistently upward portion of the yield curve—that is, maturities between zero days and one year. As the StocksPlus strategy needs liquidity from only a small portion of its fixed-income portfolio to meet margin requirements, PIMCO extends roughly one-half of its portfolio to maturities past 90 days. Further, the firm accepts some credit risk by purchasing non-government securities such as commercial paper. PIMCO also takes advantage of certain securities that offer little credit risk, but relatively high yields. At times these securities have included short-term tranches of collateralized mortgage obligations, floating-rate notes, and foreign government short-term securities (with currency risk fully hedged).

Transportable alpha involves investors capturing inefficiencies in certain markets, while maintaining desired exposure to markets beyond those in which the superior performance is earned. Transportable alpha is not a free lunch. Investors must pay commissions on their trades in stocks, options, futures, and swaps either directly or through bid-ask spreads. Real-world frictions such as collateral requirements and even custodial accounting difficulties still complicate the smooth implementation of the alpha transport strategies. Further, investors must take active management risk in order to earn their alphas. For example, General Mills's common stock managers, in aggregate, may underperform the stock market, or PIMCO's short-term portfolio may underperform 90-day Treasury bills. However, institutional investors applying the transportable alpha concept believe that their active management investment strategies possess sufficiently positive expected returns that more than compensate for the additional risk assumed.

As shown in panel (a), no matter what the price of the underlying stock, an option buyer cannot lose and an option seller cannot gain on the expiration date. Option buyers compensate sellers for putting themselves in this position by paying them a premium when the contract is signed.

The situation is quite different with a futures contract. As shown in panel (b), the buyer may gain or lose, depending on the price of the asset in the delivery month. Whatever the buyer gains or loses, an exactly offsetting loss or gain will be registered by the seller. The higher the contract price (that is, the price of the futures contract when the buyer purchased it from the seller), the greater the likelihood that the buyer will lose and the seller will gain. The lower the contract price, the greater the likelihood that the seller will lose and the buyer will gain.

21.10   SYNTHETIC FUTURES

For some assets, futures contracts are unavailable but both put and call options are available. In such cases, an investor can create a **synthetic futures contract.**

The clearest example involves European options on common stocks. As shown in the previous chapter, the *purchase* of a European call option and the *sale* of a European put option at the same exercise price and with the same expiration date will provide a value at expiration that will be related, dollar for dollar, to the stock price at that time. This is shown in Figure 21.8.

Panel (a) shows the payoff associated with the purchase of a call at an exercise price E, whereas panel (b) shows the payoff associated with the sale of a put at the same exercise price. The results obtained by taking *both* positions are shown by the solid line in panel (c).

Depending on the prices (that is, premiums) of the call and the put, this strategy may initially either require a net outflow of cash or provide a net inflow. For comparability with the purchase of a futures contract, this cash flow may be offset with borrowing or lending as required to bring the net investment to zero. The dashed line in panel (c) shows a case in which the call option costs more than is provided by the sale of the put option. The difference is borrowed, requiring the loan repayment shown in the figure. The dashed line thus indicates the net end-of-period payoffs for a strategy requiring no initial outlay. Because these payoffs are equivalent to the payoffs from a futures contract with a contract price equal to F, a synthetic futures contract has been created.

In practice, the equivalence is not perfect. Most listed options are American, not European, raising the possibility that the buyer of the put will exercise it prior to maturity. Moreover, the synthetic future is not marked to market on a daily basis. Despite these differences, the existence of well-functioning markets for call and put options will enable investors to create arrangements similar to futures on the underlying asset synthetically.

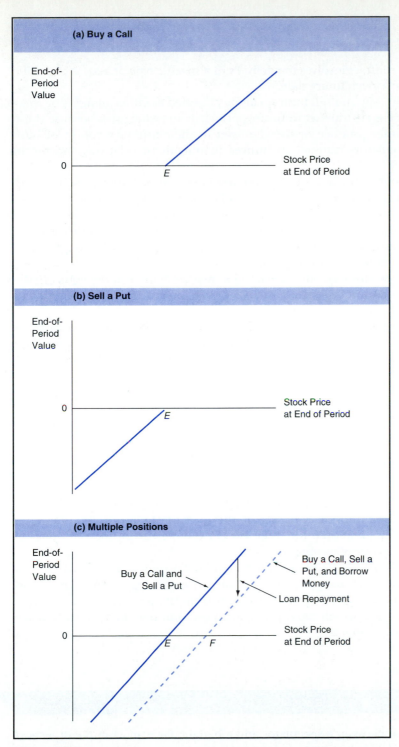

Figure 21.8
Creating a Synthetic Futures Contract

1. A futures contract involves the delivery of a specific type of asset at a specific location at a given future date.
2. People who buy and sell futures can be classified as either hedgers or speculators. Hedgers transact in futures primarily to reduce risk because these people either produce or use the asset in their ordinary course of business. Speculators transact in futures in pursuit of relatively short-term profits.
3. Futures are bought and sold on organized exchanges. Futures are standardized in terms of the type of asset, time of delivery, and place of delivery.
4. Each futures exchange has an associated clearinghouse that becomes the "seller's buyer" and the "buyer's seller" as soon as the trade is concluded.
5. A futures investor is required to deposit initial margin in order to guarantee fulfillment of his or her obligations.
6. A futures investor's account is marked to market daily, with the equity in the investor's account adjusted to reflect the change in the futures contract's settlement price.
7. A futures investor must maintain his or her account's equity equal to or greater than a certain percentage of the amount deposited as initial margin. If this requirement is not met, the investor will be requested to deposit variation margin in the account.
8. The basis for futures is the difference between the current spot price of the asset and the corresponding futures price.
9. There are three possible relationships between the current futures price and the expected spot price: the expectations hypothesis (futures price equal to expected spot price), normal backwardation (futures price less than expected spot price), and normal contango (futures price greater than expected spot price).
10. The current futures price should equal the current spot price plus the cost of carry. The cost of carry equals (1) the amount of interest that the owner forgoes by holding onto the asset less (2) the benefits of owning the asset plus (3) the costs of owning the asset.
11. If the price of a futures contract becomes too far removed from the current spot price of the asset plus the cost of carry, arbitrageurs will enter into transactions that generate riskless profits from the perceived price discrepancy. Their actions will cause prices to adjust until the opportunity to make such profits disappears.

QUESTIONS AND PROBLEMS

1. Distinguish between a speculator and a hedger. Give an example of a short hedger and a long hedger.
2. Using the latest *Wall Street Journal,* for the near futures contracts in corn, orange juice, and gasoline, calculate the percentage change in the settle-

ment price from the previous day. Find the open interest in these contracts. Into how many units of the commodities do these open-interest figures translate?

3. How do organized futures exchanges ensure that the obligations incurred as various parties enter into futures contracts are ultimately satisfied?

4. What is the purpose of initial and maintenance margins? How does marking to market affect the amount of funds held in the futures investor's margin account?

5. Chicken Wolf sells ten June 5,000–bushel corn futures at $2 per bushel. Chicken deposits $5,000 in performance margin. If the price of corn rises to $2.20 per bushel, how much equity is in Chicken's margin account? What if corn falls to $1.80 per bushel?

6. Zack Wheat has just bought four September 5,000–bushel corn futures contracts at $1.75 per bushel. The initial margin requirement is 3%. The maintenance margin requirement is 80% of the initial margin requirement.
   a. How many dollars in initial margin must Zack put up?
   b. If the September price of corn rises to $1.85, how much equity is in Zack's commodity account?
   c. If the September price of corn falls to $1.70, how much equity is in Zack's commodity account? Will Zack receive a margin call?

7. How does a futures contract differ from a forward contract?

8. Do exchange-imposed price limits protect futures traders from losses that would result in the absence of such limits? Explain.

9. Corky Withrow is long a stock market futures contract and short a diversified portfolio of stocks. Would Corky prefer the basis to widen or to narrow? Why?

10. A publication used by farmers such as Mordecai Brown provides diagrams of the typical annual patterns of cash prices for a number of seasonal commodities. Should Mordecai expect that the price of a futures contract will follow the same pattern? Why?

11. In the market for a particular agricultural or natural resource commodity, what kind of market forces might lead to normal backwardation or normal contango?

12. Consider a futures contract on mangoes that calls for the delivery of 2,000 pounds of the fruit three months from now. The spot price of mangoes is $2 per pound. It costs $.10 per pound to store mangoes for three months. What should be the price of this futures contract?

13. Byrd Lynn owns a famous Renoir painting that has a current market value of $5,000,000. It costs Byrd $200,000 annually to insure the painting, payable at the start of the year. Byrd is able to loan the painting to a local art gallery for $300,000 per year, paid at the end of the year. Byrd is considering selling the painting under a futures contract arrangement that calls for delivery one year from today. If the one-year riskfree rate is 5%, what is the fair value of the futures contract?

14. Tuck Turner is planning a trip in six months to Germany, where Tuck plans to purchase a BMW for 80,000 deutsche mark (DM). Using a recent *Wall*

Street Journal, calculate how much the purchase would cost in U.S. dollars at the current exchange rate. Given the recent settlement price of a six-month DM futures contract, how much would Tuck have to pay to hedge the cost of the BMW purchase?

15. Assume that the exchange rate between British pounds and U.S. dollars is currently $1.80 per pound. If the six-month riskfree rate is 3% in the United States and 3.5% in Great Britain, what should the six-month futures price of U.S. dollars in British pounds be? Why is the futures exchange rate greater or less than the current spot exchange rate?

16. The one-year futures price of the Utopian currency darmas is $2.03 per darma. The interest forgone by selling darmas in the futures market instead of the spot market is $.0591. The benefit of owning darmas instead of selling them is $.0788. If the U.S. one-year riskfree rate is 3%, according to interest rate parity, what should be the Utopian one-year riskfree rate?

17. What should be the price of a three-month 90-day Treasury bill futures contract if the spot price of a six-month Treasury-bill is currently $98 and the three-month riskfree rate is 1%?

18. Estel Crabtree believes that the spread between long-term and short-term interest rates is going to narrow in the next few months but does not know in which direction interest rates in general will move. What financial futures position would permit Estel to profit from this forecast if it is correct?

19. Sleeper Sullivan bought five S&P 500 December futures contracts at 310. If the S&P 500 index rises to 318, what is Sleeper's dollar profit?

20. Why does hedging a common stock portfolio using stock index futures work best if the portfolio being hedged is very similar to the underlying stock index of the futures contract?

21. Assume that the S&P 500 currently has a value of 200 (in "index" terms). The dividend yield on the underlying stocks in the index is expected to be 4% over the next six months. New-issue six-month Treasury bills now sell for a six-month yield of 6%.

    a. What is the theoretical value of a six-month futures contract on the S&P 500?

    b. What potential problems are inherent in this calculation?

22. In December 19X1 Granny Hamner bought a January 19X2 gold futures contract on the New York Commodity Exchange for $487.50 per ounce. Simultaneously, Granny sold an October 19X3 contract for $614.80. At the time, yields on Treasury notes with 1.75 years to maturity were 10.50%. Will this transaction be profitable for Granny? What factors are relevant to making this calculation?

23. In each of the following situations, discuss how Hippo Vaughn might use stock index futures to protect a well-diversified stock portfolio:

    a. Hippo expects to receive a sizable bonus check next month and would like to invest in stocks, believing that current stock market prices are extremely attractive (but realizing they may not remain so for long).

b. Hippo expects the stock market to decline dramatically very soon and realizes that selling a stock portfolio quickly would result in significant transaction costs.

c. Hippo has a large, unrealized gain and for tax purposes would like to defer the gain until the next tax year, which is several weeks away.

24. Does the fair value of a stock index futures contract depend on investors' expectations about the future value of the underlying stock index? Why?

25. Swats Swacina, a futures investor who has lost considerable sums in futures investments, said, "Even though I don't directly borrow to invest in futures, the performance of my investments acts as if I were highly leveraged." Is Swats correct? Why?

26. (Appendix Question) Distinguish between futures contracts and options on futures contracts.

27. (Appendix Question) Pinky Swander buys a call option on a March 5,000–bushel soybean futures contract. The call costs $.50 per bushel and has an exercise price of $5.25 per bushel. If Pinky exercises the option in February at a price of $5.55 per bushel, what is Pinky's return on investment in the option?

CFA EXAM QUESTIONS

28. Robert Chen, CFA, is reviewing the characteristics of derivative securities and their use in portfolios.

a. Chen is considering the addition of either a short position in stock index futures or a long position in stock index options to an existing well-diversified portfolio of equity securities. **Contrast** the way in which each of these two alternatives would affect the risk and return of the resulting combined portfolios.

b. Four factors affect the value of a futures contract on a stock index. Three of these factors are: the current price of the stock index, the time remaining until the contract maturity (delivery) date, and the dividends on the stock index. **Identify** the fourth factor and **explain** how and why changes in this factor affect the value of the futures contract.

c. Six factors affect the value of call options on stocks. Three of these factors are: the current price of the stock, the time remaining until the option expires, and the dividend on the stock. **Identify** the other three factors and **explain** how and why changes in each of these three factors affect the value of call options.

29. The foundation's grant-making and investment policy issues have been finalized. Receipt of the expected $45 million Franklin cash gift will not occur for 90 days, yet the committee believes current stock and bond prices are unusually attractive and wishes to take advantage of this perceived opportunity.

a. Briefly describe two strategies which utilize derivative financial instruments and could be implemented to take advantage of the committee's market expectations.

b. Evaluate whether or not it is appropriate for the foundation to undertake a derivatives-based hedge to bridge the expected 90-day time gap, considering both positive and negative factors.

APPENDIX

FUTURES OPTIONS

The previous chapter described options, while this chapter has described futures. Interestingly, there are contracts currently in existence that are known as **futures options** (or options on futures). As might be expected, these contracts are, in a sense, combinations of futures and options contracts. In particular, a futures option is an option in which the underlying asset is a specific futures contract, with the expiration date on the option being shortly after the delivery date on the futures contract.[24] Figure 21.9 provides a set of quotations on some of the more frequently traded ones. As the figure shows, there are both put and call options on futures. Thus an investor can be either a buyer or a writer of either a put or a call option on a futures contract.[25]

CALL OPTIONS ON FUTURES CONTRACTS

If a call option on a futures contract is exercised, then the writer must deliver the appropriate futures contract to the buyer—that is, the writer must assume a short position in the futures contract while the buyer assumes the long position. For example, consider the buyer of a call option on May corn futures where the exercise price is 300 (that is, $3) per bushel. Because the futures contract is for 5,000 bushels, the total exercise price is $15,000 ($= 5,000 \times \$3$). If the buyer purchased this option at the settle price on December 13, 1993, which is given in Figure 21.9, then the buyer would have paid the writer a premium of 9½ (that is, $.095) per bushel, or $475 ($= 5,000 \times \$.095$) in total.

Now if the buyer subsequently decides to exercise this option, then the writer of this option must deliver a May corn futures contract to the buyer. Furthermore, this futures contract will be fully marked to market at the time it is delivered. In the example, assume that the option is exercised in February when May corn futures are selling for $4.00 per bushel. What happens in February is that the call writer must provide the call buyer with a May corn futures contract that has a delivery price of $3 which has been marked to market. This can be accomplished in two steps. First, the writer must purchase a May corn futures

FUTURES OPTIONS PRICES

Monday, December 13, 1993.

AGRICULTURAL

CORN (CBT)
5,000 bu.; cents per bu.

Strike	Calls—Settle			Puts—Settle		
Price	Mar	May	Jly	Mar	May	Jly
280	14¼	18½	21	3	5⅜	8
290	6⅛	13¼	16¼	7⅜	10	13¼
300	4¾	9½	12	13½	15¾	18¾
310	2⅝	6¼	9¼	21¼	....	25½
320	1½	4¼	6¾	....	....	33
330	1	3	5	39¼	....	....

Est vol 6,000 Fri 4,258 calls 1,793 puts
Op int Fri 69,990 calls 47,194 puts

SOYBEANS (CBT)
5,000 bu.; cents per bu.

Strike	Calls—Settle			Puts—Settle		
Price	Jan	Mar	May	Jan	Mar	May
625	50¼	59	62½	⅛	3¾	...
650	24¾	37½	43¾	⅛	5¾	8½
675	5	22¾	29½	4¾	15	20
700	⅜	13¼	20	24¾	30¾	35½
725	⅛	7¾	13¾	49¾	50¼	53¾
750	⅛	4¾	9½	74¾	72¼	....

Est vol 12,000 Fri 5,906 calls 2,599 puts
Op int Fri 90,710 calls 57,592 puts

OIL

CRUDE OIL (NYM)
1,000 bbls.; $ per bbl.

Strike	Calls—Settle			Puts—Settle		
Price	Feb	Mar	Apr	Feb	Mar	Apr
1300	1.16	....	....	.13	.20	.23
1400	.81	1.58	1.88	.20	.27	.38
1500	.54	1.24	1.14	.30	.36	....
1550	.34	.93	....	.45	.51	.63
1600	.19	.64	.67	....	.70	....
1650	.12	.46	....	....	.91	1.16

Est vol 21,196 Fri 14,916 calls 12,680 puts
Op int Fri 147,148 calls 168,948 puts

METALS

COPPER (CMX)
25,000 lbs.; cents per lb.

Strike	Calls—Settle			Puts—Settle		
Price	Feb	Mar	May	Feb	Mar	May
76	4.90	5.15	6.15	0.40	0.75	1.25
78	3.20	3.65	4.60	0.75	1.20	1.85
80	2.10	2.50	3.50	1.60	2.00	2.70
82	1.20	1.60	2.60	2.50	3.00	3.80
84	0.80	1.05	1.90	3.95	4.45	5.00
86	0.35	0.70	1.35	5.60	6.10	6.45

Est vol 1,300 Fri 1,723 calls 120 puts
Op int Fri 15,460 calls 6,055 puts

GOLD (CMX)
100 troy ounces; $ per troy ounce

Strike	Calls—Settle			Puts—Settle		
Price	Feb	Mar	Apr	Feb	Mar	Apr
370	20.00	23.40	24.80	1.40	3.30	4.80
380	12.60	16.20	18.10	4.00	6.00	8.00
390	7.00	10.60	13.00	8.40	10.20	12.70
400	4.00	7.00	9.50	15.40	16.50	19.00
410	2.20	4.70	7.00	23.60	24.00	26.40
420	1.20	3.00	5.20	32.50	32.40	34.60

Est vol 9,500 Mon 2,738 calls 1,093 puts
Op int Mon 90,153 calls 31,474 puts

SILVER (CMX)
5,000 troy ounces; cts per troy ounce

Strike	Calls—Settle			Puts—Settle		
Price	Feb	Mar	May	Feb	Mar	May
475	46.0	52.7	62.0	5.0	11.2	17.7
500	29.0	37.0	48.2	12.6	20.5	28.7
525	17.2	25.0	37.0	25.7	33.5	42.2
550	10.0	17.5	29.0	43.0	49.8	59.0
575	5.8	12.0	22.6	63.5	68.5	77.2
600	3.2	8.2	17.5	86.0	89.7	96.0

Est vol 5,300 Fri 3,152 calls 1,279 puts
Op int Fri 40,114 calls 19,259 puts

INDEX

S&P 500 STOCK INDEX (CME)
$500 times premium

Strike	Calls—Settle			Puts—Settle		
Price	Dec	Jan	Feb	Dec	Jan	Feb
455	11.75	14.75	....	0.25	2.30	4.35
460	7.00	10.70	13.00	0.50	3.25	5.55
465	2.90	7.20	9.65	1.40	4.70	7.15
470	0.55	4.30	6.70	4.05	6.80	....
475	0.10	2.15	4.30	8.60	9.60	....
480	0.05	0.90	2.55	13.55	....	....

Est vol 9,089 Fri 3,724 calls 6,281 puts
Op int Fri 65,414 calls 163,417 puts

GSCI (CME)
$250 times GSCI nearby index

Strike	Calls—Settle			Puts—Settle		
Price	Jan	Feb	Mar	Jan	Feb	Mar
165	....	....	....	....	....	....
166	....	....	....	2.20	....	....
167	....	....	....	....	....	....
168	....	....	....	3.10	....	....
169	....	....	....	....	....	....
170	1.60	....	....	....	....	....

Est vol 0 Fri 0 calls 0 puts
Op int Fri 2,279 calls 2,327 puts

INTEREST RATE

T-BONDS (CBT)
$100,000; points and 64ths of 100%

Strike	Calls—Settle			Puts—Settle		
Price	Jan	Feb	Mar	Jan	Feb	Mar
113	2-13	....	....	0-03	0-29	....
114	1-19	....	2-22	0-09	0-47	1-12
115	0-36	1-19	....	0-26	1-09	....
116	0-10	0-55	1-19	0-62	1-45	2-09
117	0-03	0-34	....	1-57	2-24	....
118	0-01	0-19	0-40	2-55	....	3-29

Est. vol. 95,000;
Fri vol. 61,771 calls; 59,867 puts
Op. int. Fri 286,794 calls; 266,700 puts

EURODOLLAR (CME)
$ million; pts. of 100%

Strike	Calls—Settle			Puts—Settle		
Price	Dec	Mar	Jun	Dec	Mar	Jun
9600	0.62	0.48	0.28	.0004	0.03	0.17
9625	0.37	0.27	0.14	.0004	0.07	0.28
9650	0.12	0.10	0.06	.0004	0.15	0.44
9675	.0004	0.02	0.02	0.13	0.32	0.65
9700	.0004	.0004	.0004	0.38	0.55	0.89
9725	.0004	.0004	.0004	0.63	0.80	1.14

Est. vol. 36,786;
Fri vol. 32,110 calls; 75,109 puts
Op. int. Fri 760,038 calls; 1,121,411 puts

TREASURY BILLS (CME)
$1 million; pts. of 100%

Strike	Calls—Settle			Puts—Settle		
Price	Mar	Jun	Sep	Mar	Jun	Sep
9625	0.53	0.34	....	0.02	0.11	....
9650	0.30	0.18	0.18	0.04	0.19	....
9675	0.12	0.08	....	0.11	0.35	....
9700	0.03	0.03	....	0.27	0.54	....
9725	....	....	....	....	....	....
9750	....	....	....	....	....	....

Est vol 15 Fri 0 calls 17 puts
Op int Fri 340 calls 705 puts

CURRENCY

JAPANESE YEN (CME)
12,500,000 yen; cents per 100 yen

Strike	Calls—Settle			Puts—Settle		
Price	Jan	Feb	Mar	Jan	Feb	Mar
9100	1.45	1.93	2.35	0.45	0.94	1.36
9150	1.13	1.65	....	0.63	1.15	1.57
9200	0.85	1.38	1.80	0.85	1.38	1.80
9250	0.63	1.15	1.57	1.13	1.65	2.07
9300	0.46	0.95	1.36	1.46	1.94	2.35
9350	0.32	0.77	1.18	....	2.26	....

Est vol 4,453 Fri 2,670 calls 3,942 puts
Op int Fri 29,729 calls 45,921 puts

DEUTSCHEMARK (CME)
125,000 marks; cents per mark

Strike	Calls—Settle			Puts—Settle		
Price	Jan	Feb	Mar	Jan	Feb	Mar
5700	1.38	....	1.94	0.22	0.53	0.79
5750	1.03	1.36	....	0.37	0.71	0.99
5800	0.73	1.08	1.37	0.57	0.93	1.21
5850	0.49	0.85	1.12	0.83	1.19	1.46
5900	0.32	0.66	0.91	1.16	1.49	1.74
5950	0.20	0.50	0.74	1.53	1.83	....

Est vol 21,686 Fri 7,378 calls 9,073 puts
Op int Fri 164,483 calls 53,210 puts

Figure 21.9
Quotations for Futures Options (Excerpts)

contract and deliver it to the call buyer. Because the cost of the futures will be $4 per bushel (the current market price of May corn futures), this is costless to the call writer. Second, the futures contract that has been delivered must be marked to market, which is done by having the call writer pay the call buyer an amount of cash equal to $1 (= $4 − $3) per bushel, or $5,000 (= 5,000 × $1) in aggregate. Thus the call writer has lost $4,525 (= $5,000 − $475) while the call buyer has made an equivalent amount.

Whereas this example has shown what happens when the call is exercised, it should be noted that most futures options are not exercised. Instead, just as with most options and futures, buyers and writers of futures options typically make reversing trades before the expiration date.

If a put option on a futures contract is exercised, then the writer must accept delivery of the appropriate futures contract from the buyer—that is, the writer must assume a long position in the futures contract while the buyer assumes the short position. For example, consider the buyer of a put option on May corn where the exercise price is 300, meaning $3 per bushel or $15,000 in total because the futures contract is for 5,000 bushels. If the buyer purchased this put at the settlement price on December 13, 1993, that is given in Figure 21.9, then the buyer would have paid the writer a premium of 15¾ per bushel, or $787.50 (= 5,000 × $.1575) in total.

Now if the buyer subsequently decides to exercise this option, then the writer of this option must accept delivery of a May corn futures contract from the buyer. Furthermore, this futures contract must be fully marked to market at the time it is delivered. In the example, assume that the option is exercised in April when May corn futures are selling for $2 per bushel. What happens in April is that the put buyer will become the seller of a May corn futures contract where the purchase price is $2 per bushel. That is, when this contract is marked to market, the put writer must pay the put buyer an amount of cash equal to $1 (= $3 − $2) per bushel, or $5,000 (= 5,000 × $1) in aggregate. Thus the put writer has lost $4,212.50 (= $5,000 − $787.50) whereas the put buyer has made an equivalent amount.

Again, it should be kept in mind that most put options on futures are not exercised. Instead, these option buyers and writers typically enter reversing trades sometime before the expiration date.

In summary, the positions of futures options buyers and writers in the futures contracts upon exercise by the buyer are as follows:

	Buyer	**Seller**
Call	Long	Short
Put	Short	Long

As mentioned earlier, neither a writer nor a buyer needs to maintain his or her position. Both are free to enter into offsetting trades at any time, even after the buyer has exercised the option (but then the offsetting trade would be made in the futures market).

At this point it is worthwhile to think about the distinctions between futures and futures options. In doing so, consider an investor who is contemplating *buying* a futures contract. If this contract is purchased, the investor can potentially make or lose a great deal of money. In particular, if the price of the asset rises substantially, then so will the price of the futures, and the investor will have made a sizable profit. In contrast, if the price of the asset drops substantially, then the investor will have lost a sizable amount of money.

In comparison, if the investor had bought a futures call option on the asset, then the investor would also make a sizable profit if the price of the asset rose substantially. Unlike with futures, however, if the price of the asset dropped, then the investor need not worry about incurring a sizable loss. Instead, only the premium (the price paid to buy the futures option) would be lost. This does not mean that purchasing a futures call option is "better" than purchasing a futures contract. Why? Because the protection on the downside that an investor gets from buying a futures call option is paid for in the form of the premium. This premium would not be present if the investor had bought a futures contract instead.

Consider next an investor who is contemplating *selling* a futures contract. In doing so, the investor can potentially make a great deal of money if the price of the asset declines substantially. However, if the price of the asset rises substantially, then the investor will have lost a sizable amount of money.

In comparison, the investor could buy a futures put option on the asset. If this was done, the investor would make a sizable profit if the price of the asset declined substantially. Unlike futures, however, if the price of the asset rose, then the investor need not worry about incurring a sizable loss. Instead only the premium would be lost. Again, this does not mean that purchasing a futures put option is "better" than selling a futures contract.

A.4   COMPARISON WITH OPTIONS

Having established that futures options can exist if futures already exist, one may wonder why futures options exist if options already exist. For example, there are futures options and options on Japanese yen (as well as futures on Japanese yen). The commonly given reason why futures options exist in such a situation is that it is easier to make or take delivery of a futures contract on the asset as required by the futures options contract than to make or take delivery in the asset itself as required by the options contract. That is, the deliverable asset in the case of the Japanese yen futures option contract is a futures contract in Japanese yen, which is more easily delivered than Japanese yen, as required for the options contract.

In addition, there is sometimes more timely price information on the deliverable asset for the futures option contract (namely, price information on the futures contract) than on the deliverable asset for the options contract (namely, price information in the spot market).

For these reasons (although they are not compelling for certain contracts), futures, futures options, and options can exist simultaneously with the same underlying asset.

ENDNOTES

[1] The term *commodity futures* is often used to refer to futures on agricultural goods and natural resources. The term *financial futures* is typically used in reference to futures on financial instruments such as Treasury bonds, foreign currencies, and stock market indices.

[2] The **spot market** involves the immediate exchange of an asset for cash. The purchase price of the asset is known as its **spot price.**

[3] For a relatively complete description of the terms for many exchange-traded futures contracts, see the *Commodity Trading Manual* (Chicago Board of Trade, 1989); and Malcolm J. Robertson, *Directory of World Futures and Options* (Englewood Cliffs, NJ: Prentice Hall, 1990). These two books also contain descriptions of various futures exchanges.

[4] Since Black Monday and Terrible Tuesday (October 19–20, 1987), a number of people have advocated an increase in the size of the initial margin deposit for certain futures contracts (particularly stock index futures, which will be discussed later). The levels of initial and maintenance margins are set by each exchange, with brokers being allowed to set them higher. Typically, higher amounts of margin are required on futures contracts that have greater price volatility since the clearinghouse faces larger potential losses on such contracts.

[5] Actually, only brokerage firms belong to a clearinghouse, and it is *their* accounts that are settled by the clearinghouse at the end of every day. Each brokerage firm acts in turn as a clearinghouse for its own clients. For more information on clearing procedures, see Chapter 6 of the *Commodity Trading Manual.*

[6] Merrill Lynch, Pierce, Fenner & Smith, Inc., *Speculating on Inflation: Futures Trading in Interest Rates, Foreign Currencies and Precious Metals,* July 1979.

[7] Typically, the basis narrows over time until it equals zero on the delivery date. For more on the relationship between spot and futures prices as reflected in the basis, see the *Commodity Trading Manual,* Chapter 8. It should be noted that sometimes basis is defined as the futures price less the current spot price—the reverse of what is shown in Equation (21.1).

[8] The futures contracts consisted of agricultural goods and natural resources. See Zvi Bodie and Victor Rosansky, "Risk and Return in Commodity Futures," *Financial Analysts Journal,* 36, no. 3 (May/June 1980): 27–39. Similar conclusions were reached when the period from 1978 to 1981 was examined. See Cheng F. Lee, Raymond M. Leuthold, and Jean E. Cordier, "The Stock Market and the Commodity Futures Market: Diversification and Arbitrage Potential," *Financial Analysts Journal,* 41, no. 4 (July/August 1985): 53–60.

[9] These first two points do not mean that the current spot price will not change as time passes. For futures involving a seasonal commodity (such as wheat), the spot price will sometimes be greater than and sometimes be less than the futures price during the life of the contract. Furthermore, sometimes a futures contract involving a more distant delivery date will sell for more than one with a nearer delivery date, whereas at other times it will sell for less.

[10] J. M. Keynes, *Treatise on Money,* vol. 2 (London: Macmillan, 1930), 142–144.

[11] There are other hypotheses regarding the relationship between futures prices and expected spot prices. See, for example, Paul H. Cootner, "Speculation and Hedging," Stanford University, *Food Research Institute Studies,* Supplement, 1967.

[12] This section and the next one borrow from Kenneth R. French, "Pricing Financial Futures Contracts: An Introduction," *Journal of Applied Corporate Finance,* 1, no. 4 (Winter 1989): 59–66. It ignores the apparently minor effect that daily marking to market has on the futures price that is stated in futures contracts (see p. 65 and footnotes 5 and 6 in French's paper).

[13] The prices of foreign currency forward and futures contracts appear to be quite similar. See Bradford Cornell and Marc Reinganum, "Forward and Futures Prices: Evidence from the Foreign Exchange Market," *Journal of Finance,* 36, no. 5 (December 1981): 1035–1045. Their findings are challenged by Michael A. Polakoff and Paul C. Grier, "A Comparison of Foreign Exchange Forward and Futures Prices," *Journal of Banking and Finance,* 15, no. 6 (December 1991): 1057–1079, but supported by Carolyn W. Chang and Jack S. K. Chang, "Forward and Futures Prices: Evidence From the Foreign Exchange Markets," *Journal of Finance,* 45, no. 4 (September 1990): 1333–1336. See Kenneth R. French, "A Comparison of Futures and Forward Prices," *Journal of Financial Economics,* 12, no. 3 (November 1983): 311–342 for a discussion of the difficulties encountered when testing to see whether the prices of forward and futures contracts are similar.

[14] Actually the typical speculator will plan to realize this profit by entering a reversing trade instead of buying yen on the spot market and then making delivery. Similarly, the previously mentioned hedging importer will typically plan to enter a reversing trade.

[15] See Chapter 5 for a discussion of term structure and forward rates.

[16] The use of annualized discount-based yields introduces some errors into the analysis that are ignored here. See French, "Pricing Financial Futures Contracts," p. 62.

[17] For some interest-rate futures there is flexibility in just what the seller has to deliver, known as the *quality option.* Sometimes there is also some flexibility regarding when an intention to deliver must be announced, known as the *wild card option.*

[18] The NYFE is a subsidiary of the New York Stock Exchange. There are other market index futures available besides these four, such as the Value Line Average Stock Index (traded on the Kansas City Board of Trade).

[19] Similarly, interest-rate futures are often used by financial institutions to hedge interest-rate risk to which they may be exposed—that is, when a large movement in interest rates would cause a large loss, these institutions will seek protection by either buying or selling interest-rate futures.

[20] The 3% dividend yield is actually the accumulated December value of the dividends divided by the purchase price of the stocks. Hence the dividends might be received in three months and amount to 2.93% of the purchase price of the index. Putting them in a riskfree asset that returns 2.47% for the last three months results in a yield of 3%, or $3, in December.

[21] Index arbitrage is one of two major forms of program trading. The other form, known as portfolio insurance, was discussed in the previous chapter. For a discussion and example of how futures can be used to procure portfolio insurance, see Stephen R. King and Eli M. Remolona, "The Pricing and Hedging of Market Index Deposits," *Federal Reserve Bank of New York Quarterly Review,* 12, no. 2 (Summer 1987): 9–20; or Thomas J. O'Brien, *How Option Replicating Portfolio Insurance Works: Expanded Details,* Monograph Series in Finance and Economics no. 1988–4, New York University Salomon Center, Leonard N. Stern School of Business.

[22] People involved in index arbitrage need to be able to quickly make a large number of transactions in individual stocks. In order to do this, they often have their computers send in their orders through the SuperDOT system (discussed in Chapter 3). For a discussion of some of the complications involved in successfully executing index arbitrage strategies, see David M. Modest, "On the Pricing of Stock Index Futures," *Journal of Portfolio Management,* 10, no. 4 (Summer 1984): 51–57.

[23] Adding to the confusion is the existence of a contract known as a futures option, which is an option that has a futures contract instead of a stock as its underlying asset. Futures options are discussed in more detail in the Appendix.

[24] The near-simultaneous quarterly expiration of (1) options on individual stocks and market indices, (2) futures on market indices, and (3) options on market index futures has been referred to as the **triple witching hour.** When it occurs, the stock market is allegedly roiled, particularly in the latter part of the day. See Hans R. Stoll and Robert E. Whaley, "Program Trading and Expiration Day Effects," *Financial Analysts Journal,* 43, no. 2 (March/April 1987): 16–28; Arnold Kling, "How the Stock Market Can Learn to Live with Index Futures and Options," *Financial Analysts Journal,* 43, no. 5 (September/October 1987): 33–39; and G. J. Santoni, "Has Programmed Trading Made Stock Prices More Volatile?" *Federal Reserve Bank of St. Louis Review,* 69, no. 5 (May 1987): 18–29.

[25] For more on futures options, see Chapter 12 of the *Commodity Trading Manual.* For a computer program that can be used to determine the "true" value of these complex contracts, see Chapter 8 of Stuart M. Turnbull, *Option Valuation* (Holt, Rinehart and Winston of Canada, 1987).

KEY TERMS

futures
speculators
hedgers
spot market
spot price
short hedger
long hedger
reversing trade
settle
open interest
locals
performance margin
marking to market
variation margin

Commodity Futures Trading Commission
basis
basis risk
expectations hypothesis
normal backwardation
normal contango
cost of carry
interest-rate parity
index arbitrage
synthetic futures contract
futures options
triple witching hour

REFERENCES

1. Many books either are devoted exclusively to futures or have futures as one of their primary subjects. Most cover everything discussed in this chapter in more detail and with a more complete list of citations. Here are a few:

Stephen Figlewski, *Hedging with Financial Futures for Institutional Investors* (Cambridge, MA: Ballinger, 1986).

Edward W. Schwarz, Joanne M. Hill, and Thomas Schneeweis, *Financial Futures* (Homewood, IL: Richard D. Irwin, 1986).

Commodity Trading Manual (Chicago: Chicago Board of Trade, 1989).

Darrell Duffie, *Futures Markets* (Englewood Cliffs, NJ: Prentice Hall, 1989).

Daniel R. Siegel and Diane F. Siegel, *Futures Markets* (Hinsdale, IL: Dryden Press, 1990).

Don M. Chance, *An Introduction to Options & Futures* (Fort Worth, TX: Dryden Press, 1991).

Alan L. Tucker, *Financial Futures, Options, & Swaps* (St. Paul, MN: West, 1991).

David A. Dubofsky, *Options and Financial Futures* (New York: McGraw-Hill, 1992).

John C. Hull, *Options, Futures, and Other Derivative Securities* (Englewood Cliffs, NJ: Prentice Hall, 1993).

Hans R. Stoll and Robert E. Whaley, *Futures and Options* (Cincinnati, OH: South-Western, 1993).

Robert T. Daigler, *Financial Futures and Markets: Concepts and Strategies* (New York: HarperCollins, 1994).

Robert W. Kolb, *Understanding Futures Markets* (Miami, FL: Kolb, 1994).

2. For a discussion of the market structure of futures exchanges, see:

Sanford J. Grossman and Merton H. Miller, "Liquidity and Market Structure," *Journal of Finance,* 43, no. 3 (July 1988): 617–633.

Michael J. Fishman and Francis A. Longstaff, "Dual Trading in Futures Markets," *Journal of Finance,* 47, no. 2 (June 1992): 643–671.

3. For a more complete discussion of margin and marking to market, see:

Robert W. Kolb, Gerald D. Gay, and William C. Hunter, "Liquidity Requirements for Financial Futures Investments," *Financial Analysts Journal,* 41, no. 3 (May/June 1985): 60–68.

Don M. Chance, *The Effect of Margins on the Volatility of Stock and Derivative Markets: A Review of the Evidence,* Monograph Series in Finance and Economics no. 1990–2, New York University Salomon Center, Leonard N. Stern School of Business.

Ann Kremer, "Clarifying Marking to Market," *Journal of Financial Education,* 20 (November 1991): 17–25.

4. The concepts of spreads and basis are discussed in:

Martin L. Leibowitz, *The Analysis of Value and Volatility in Financial Futures,* Monograph Series in Finance and Economics no. 1981–3, New York University Salomon Center, Leonard N. Stern School of Business.

5. Foreign currency markets are discussed in:

J. Orlin Grabbe, *International Financial Markets* (New York: Elsevier Science, 1991), Part II.

6. Interest-rate futures were shown to be useful in immunizing bond portfolios by:

Robert W. Kolb and Gerald D. Gay, "Immunizing Bond Portfolios with Interest Rate Futures," *Financial Management,* 11, no. 2 (Summer 1982): 81–89.

Jess B. Yawitz and William J. Marshall, "The Use of Futures in Immunized Portfolios," *Journal of Portfolio Management,* 11, no. 2 (Spring 1985): 51–58.

7. Using futures to hedge bond portfolios is discussed in:

Richard Bookstaber and David P. Jacob, "The Composite Hedge: Controlling the Credit Risk of High-Yield Bonds," *Financial Analysts Journal,* 42, no. 2 (March/April 1986): 25–35.

Robin Grieves, "Hedging Corporate Bond Portfolios," *Journal of Portfolio Management,* 12, no. 4 (Summer 1986): 23–25.

8. Stock index futures and their relationship to the market crash in October 1987 have been heavily researched. Some of the papers are:

Paula A. Tosini, "Stock Index Futures and Stock Market Activity in October 1987," *Financial Analysts Journal,* 44, no. 1 (January/February 1988): 28–37.

F. J. Gould, "Stock Index Futures: The Arbitrage Cycle and Portfolio Insurance," *Financial Analysts Journal,* 44, no. 1 (January/February 1988): 48–62.

Lawrence Harris, "The October 1987 S&P 500 Stock-Futures Basis," *Journal of Finance,* 44, no. 1 (March 1989): 77–99.

Marshall E. Blume, A. Craig MacKinlay, and Bruce Terker, "Order Imbalances and Stock Price Movements on October 19 and 20, 1987," *Journal of Finance,* 44, no. 4 (September 1989): 827–848.

Lawrence Harris, "S&P 500 Cash Stock Price Volatilities," *Journal of Finance,* 44, no. 5 (December 1989): 1155–1175.

Hans R. Stoll and Robert E. Whaley, "The Dynamics of Stock Index and Stock Index Futures Returns," *Journal of Financial and Quantitative Analysis,* 25, no. 4 (December 1990): 441–468.

Kolak Chan, K. C. Chan, and G. Andrew Karolyi, "Intraday Volatility in the Stock Index and Stock Index Futures Markets," *Review of Financial Studies,* 4, no. 4 (1991): 657–684.

Avanidhar Subrahmanyam, "A Theory of Trading in Stock Index Futures," *Review of Financial Studies,* 4, no. 1 (1991): 17–51.

Kolak Chan, "A Further Analysis of the Lead-Lag Relationship Between the Cash Market and Stock Index Futures Market," *Review of Financial Studies,* 5, no. 1 (1992): 123–152.

9. Papers on index arbitrage and program trading include:

A. Craig MacKinlay and Krishna Ramaswamy, "Index-Futures Arbitrage and the Behavior of Stock Index Futures Prices," *Review of Financial Studies,* 1, no. 2 (Summer 1988): 137–158.

Michael J. Brennan and Eduardo S. Schwartz, "Arbitrage in Stock Index Futures," *Journal of Business,* 63, no. 1, part 2 (January 1990): S7–S31.

Hans R. Stoll and Robert E. Whaley, "Program Trading and Individual Stock Returns: Ingredients of the Triple-Witching Brew," *Journal of Business,* 63, no. 1, part 2 (January 1990): S165–S192.

Gary L. Gastineau, "A Short History of Program Trading," *Financial Analysts Journal,* 47, no. 5 (September/October 1991): 4–7.

10. Forward and futures prices were shown to be equal when interest rates are constant over time in:

John C. Cox, Jonathan E. Ingersoll, and Stephen A. Ross, "The Relation Between Forward Prices and Futures Prices," *Journal of Financial Economics,* 9, no. 4 (December 1981): 321–346.

11. The performance of commodity funds, which are investment companies that speculate in futures, has not been attractive, according to:

Edwin J. Elton, Martin J. Gruber, and Joel C. Rentzler, "Professionally Managed, Publicly Traded Commodity Funds," *Journal of Business,* 60, no. 2 (April 1987): 175–199.

12. The relationships among futures, options, and futures options are discussed in:

Clifford W. Smith, Jr., Charles W. Smithson, and D. Sykes Wilford, "Managing Financial Risk," *Journal of Applied Corporate Finance,* 1, no. 4 (Winter 1989): 27–48.

Clifford W. Smith, Jr., Charles W. Smithson, and D. Sykes Wilford, *Managing Financial Risk* (New York: Harper & Row, 1990).

13. The seminal paper on the pricing of futures options is:

Fischer Black, "The Pricing of Commodity Contracts," *Journal of Financial Economics,* 3, nos. 1/2 (January/March 1976): 167–179.

14. For a thought-provoking book that covers futures markets, among other subjects, see:

Merton H. Miller, *Financial Innovations and Market Volatility* (Cambridge, MA: Blackwell, 1991).

Investment Companies

Investment companies are a type of financial intermediary. They obtain money from investors and use it to purchase financial assets such as stocks and bonds. In return, the investors receive certain rights regarding the financial assets that the investment company has bought and any earnings that it may generate. In the simplest and most common situation, the investment company has only one type of investor—stockholders. These stockholders own the investment company directly, and thus own indirectly the financial assets that the company itself owns.

For an individual there are two advantages to investing in such companies instead of investing directly in the financial assets that these companies own. Specifically, the advantages arise from (1) economies of scale and (2) professional management. In describing these benefits, consider an individual with moderate financial resources who wishes to invest in the stock market.

In terms of economies of scale, the individual could buy stocks in odd lots and thus have a diversified portfolio. However, the brokerage commissions on odd lot transactions are relatively high. Alternatively, the individual could purchase round lots, but would only be able to afford a few different securities. Unfortunately the individual would then be giving up the benefits of owning a well-diversified portfolio. In order to receive the benefits of both diversification and substantially reduced brokerage commissions, the individual could invest in the shares of an investment company. This is because economies of scale make it possible for an investment company to provide diversification at a lower cost per dollar of investment than would be incurred by a small individual investor.

In terms of professional management, the individual investing directly in the stock market would have to go through all the details of investing, including making all buying and selling decisions as well as keeping records of all transactions for tax purposes. In doing so, the individual would have to be continually on the lookout for mispriced securities in an attempt to find undervalued ones for purchase, while selling any that were found to be overvalued. Simultaneously, the individual would have to keep track of the overall risk level of the portfolio so that it did not deviate from some desired level. However, by purchasing shares of an investment company, the individual can turn over all of these details to a professional money manager.

Many of these managers hope to identify areas of mispricing in the market, exploit them, and share the resultant abnormal gains with investors by charging them for a portion of the gains. However, it appears that most of them cannot find mispriced situations frequently enough to recoup more than the additional costs they have incurred, costs that take the form of increased operating expenses and transaction costs owing to the continual buying and selling of securities. Nevertheless, other potential advantages to be gained from investing in an investment company may still outweigh any disadvantages, particularly for smaller investors.

Investment companies differ in many ways, and classification is difficult. Common practice will be followed here, where the term *investment company* will be restricted to those financial intermediaries that do not obtain money from "depositors." Thus the traditional operations of savings and loan companies and banks, for example, will be excluded. However, the process of deregulation is rapidly breaking down barriers that previously prevented financial intermediaries from competing with traditional investment companies. The future will likely find many different types of organizations offering investment company services.

22.1 NET ASSET VALUE

An important concept in understanding how investment companies operate is **net asset value.** Given that an investment company has assets consisting of various securities, it is generally quite easy to determine the market value of all the assets held by the investment company at the end of each business day. For example, an investment company that holds various common stocks traded on exchanges and Nasdaq could easily find out what the closing prices of those stocks were at the end of the day and then simply multiply these prices by the number of shares that it owns. After adding up these figures, the investment company would subtract any liabilities that it had outstanding. Dividing the resulting difference by the number of outstanding shares of the investment company produces its net asset value.

Equivalently, an investment company's net asset value at the end of day t, NAV_t, can be determined by using the following equation:

$$NAV_t = \frac{MVA_t - LIAB_t}{NSO_t} \qquad (22.1)$$

where MVA_t, $LIAB_t$, and NSO_t denote the market value of the investment company's assets, the dollar amount of the investment company's liabilities, and the number of shares the investment company has outstanding, respectively, as of the end of day t.

As an example, consider an investment company with 4,000,000 shares outstanding whose assets consisted of common stocks with an aggregate market value of $102,000,000 and whose liabilities amounted to $2,000,000 as of November 15. This company would report a net asset value on that date of $25 [= ($102,000,000 − $2,000,000)/4,000,000] per share. This amount will change every day, as the values of either MVA_t, $LIAB_t$, or NSO_t (or of some combination of the three) will typically change daily.

Investors should note that calculating NAV_t can be difficult if some of the assets do not trade frequently. In such situations, estimates of their fair market value must be used. Referring to the previous example, what if on November 16 there were 3,800,000 shares outstanding, the liabilities were $2,200,000, but the common stocks had not been traded on any market since November 15? In this situation MVA_t is often calculated by using the last bid prices for the stocks on November 16, which in this example is assumed to result in a value for MVA_t of $101,000,000.[1] Hence the net asset value on November 16 is $26 [= ($101,000,000 − $2,200,000)/3,800,000].

MAJOR TYPES OF INVESTMENT COMPANIES

The Investment Company Act of 1940 classifies investment companies as follows[2]:

1. Unit investment trusts
2. Managed investment companies
    a. Closed-end investment companies
    b. Open-end investment companies

These types of investment companies are discussed next.

22.2.1 Unit Investment Trusts

A **unit investment trust** is an investment company that owns a fixed set of securities for the life of the company[3]—that is, the investment company rarely alters the composition of its portfolio over the life of the company.

Formation

To form a unit investment trust, a sponsor (often a brokerage firm) purchases a specific set of securities and deposits them with a trustee (such as a bank). Then a number of shares known as redeemable trust certificates are sold to the public. These certificates provide their owners with proportional interests in the securities that were previously deposited with the trustee. All income received by the trustee on these securities is subsequently paid out to the certificate holders, as are any repayments of principal. Changes in the original set of securities (that is, selling some of them and buying different ones) are made only under exceptional circumstances. Because there is no active management of a unit investment trust, the annual fees charged by the sponsor are correspondingly low (perhaps equal to .15% of the net asset value per year).

Most unit investment trusts hold fixed-income securities and expire after the last one has matured (or, possibly, sold). Lifespans range from six months for unit investment trusts of money market instruments to over 20 years for trusts of bond market instruments. Unit investment trusts usually specialize in certain types of securities. Some trusts include only federal government bonds, others only corporate bonds, others only municipal bonds, and so on.

Not surprisingly, the sponsor of a unit investment trust will seek compensation for the effort and risk involved in setting up the trust. This is accomplished by setting a selling price for the shares that exceeds the cost of the underlying assets. For example, a brokerage firm might purchase $10,000,000 worth of bonds, place them in a unit investment trust, and issue 10,000 shares. Each share might be offered to the public for $1,035. When all the shares have been sold, the sponsor will have received $10,350,000 (= $1,035 × 10,000). This is enough to cover the $10,000,000 cost of the bonds, leaving $350,000 for selling expenses and profit. Markups (or load charges) of this sort range from less than 1% for short-term trusts to 3.5% for long-term trusts.

Secondary Market

Typically an investor who purchases shares of a unit investment trust is not required to hold the shares for the entire life of the trust. Instead the shares usually can be sold back to the trust at net asset value, calculated on the basis of bid prices for the assets in the portfolio—that is, the market value of the securities in the portfolio is determined, using dealers' bid quotations. Because unit investment trusts have no liabilities, this amount is divided by the number of shares outstanding to obtain the net asset value per share. Having determined the per share price, the trustee may sell one or more securities to raise the required cash for the repurchase.

Alternatively, it is possible that a secondary market is maintained by the sponsor of the trust. In this situation investors can sell their shares back to the sponsor. Afterwards other investors (including those who did not participate in the initial sale) can purchase these shares. Typically the sponsor's selling price in the secondary market is equal to the net asset value of the securities in the portfolio (based on the dealers' asked prices) plus a markup charge equal to that in effect at the time the trust was created.

22.2.2 Managed Companies

Whereas a unit investment trust has no board of directors and no portfolio manager, **managed investment companies** have both. Because they are organized as corporations or trusts (a few are limited partnerships), a managed investment company will have a board of directors or trustees that is elected by its shareholders. In turn, the board will commonly hire a firm—the management company— to manage the company's assets for an annual fee that is typically based on the total market value of the assets.

These management companies may be independent firms, investment advisors, firms associated with brokers, or insurance companies. Often the management company is the business entity (for example, a subsidiary of a brokerage firm) that started and promoted the investment company. A management company may have contracts to manage a number of investment companies, each of which is a separate organization with its own board of directors or trustees.

Annual management fees (also known as advisory fees) usually range from .50% to 1% of the average market value of the investment company's total assets, with the percentage sliding downward as the dollar value of the assets increases. Some funds provide "incentive compensation," where the better the fund's investment performance, the higher the fee paid to the management company.

In addition to the fee paid by an investment company to its management company, there are administrative expenses that cover record keeping and services to shareholders. (Sometimes these are imbedded in the management fee.) Such annual expenses usually range from .20% to .40% of the average market value of total assets.

Lastly there are other operating expenses that the investment company incurs annually for such things as state and local taxes, legal and auditing expenses, and directors' fees. These annual expenses usually range from .10% to .30%. The combination of management fees, administrative expenses, and other operating expenses results in total annual operating expenses typically ranging from .80% to 1.70% of the average total assets.[4] This figure is referred to as a fund's **operating expense ratio.** It averages .85% for funds that invest primarily in bonds and 1.25% for funds that invest primarily in stocks.[5]

Closed-End Investment Companies

Unlike unit investment trusts, **closed-end investment companies** (or closed-end funds) do not stand ready to purchase their own shares whenever one of their owners decides to sell them. Instead their shares are traded either on an organized exchange or in the over-the-counter market. Thus an investor who wants to buy or sell shares of a closed-end fund would simply place an order with a broker, just as if the investor wanted to buy or sell shares of IBM.

Most closed-end funds have unlimited lives. Dividends and interest received by a closed-end fund from the securities in its portfolio are paid out to its shareholders, as are any net realized capital gains. However, most funds allow (and encourage) the reinvestment of such payments. The fund keeps the money and sends the investor additional shares based on the lower of net asset value or market price per share at that time. For example, consider a closed-end fund whose shares are selling for $20 that has just declared a dividend of $1 per share. If its net asset value were $15 per share, a holder of 30 shares would have a choice of receiving either $30 (= 30 × $1) or two shares (= $30/$15). However, if the shares were selling for $10, then the choice would be between $30 and three shares.

Being a corporation, a closed-end fund can issue new shares not only through reinvestment plans but also with public stock offerings. However, this is done infrequently, and the fund's capitalization is "closed" most of the time. Furthermore, the fund's capitalization will have little or no interest-bearing debt in it because of certain restrictions imposed by the Investment Company Act of 1940.

In general, a closed-end fund's shares are initially offered to the public at a price that is nearly 10% above its net asset value due to investment banking fees charged to the fund. This suggests that the shares are overpriced because most funds' shares sell for a price below their net asset value in the aftermarket. Evidence indicates that there are no unusual movements in the price of a typical fund on the offering day, but that in the 100 days thereafter its price declines relative to the market to the point where it sells for roughly 10% below its net asset value. This is in sharp contrast to the price behavior of nonfund initial public offerings around the same time period. These stocks experience a substantial price jump on the offering day of nearly 7% and no notable price movements thereafter. Left unanswered is why an investor would want to be involved in the initial public offering of a closed-end fund.[6]

Most closed-end funds can repurchase their own shares in the open market, although this is seldom done. Whenever a fund's market price falls substantially below its net asset value, a repurchase will increase the fund's net asset value per share. For example, if the net asset value were $20 per share at a time when the fund's shares could be purchased in the open market (say, on the New York Stock Exchange) for $16 per share, the managers of the fund could sell $20 worth of securities from the fund's portfolio, buy back one of the fund's outstanding shares, and have $4 left over. If the $4 were used to buy securities for the fund, the net asset value per share would increase, with the size of the increase depending on the number of remaining shares, in addition to the number of shares repurchased and their repurchase price.

Quotations

The market prices of the shares of closed-end funds are published daily in the financial press, provided that the funds are listed on an exchange or traded actively in the over-the-counter market. However, their net asset values are only published weekly, based on closing market prices for securities in their portfolios as of the previous Friday. Figure 22.1 provides an example. The first column indicates where a fund's shares are traded (N = NYSE, A = AMEX, O = Nasdaq, C = Chicago Stock Exchange, T = Toronto Stock Exchange, z = does not trade on an exchange). Both the net asset value and the last price at which the fund's shares traded on the day in question are shown next, followed by the percentage of net asset value that the difference between the two figures represents.

If this percentage is positive (meaning that the stock price is greater than the net asset value), then the fund's shares are said to be selling at a *premium*. Conversely, if this difference is negative (meaning that the stock price is less than the net asset value), then the fund's shares are said to be selling at a *discount*. For example, Figure 22.1(b) indicates that the France Growth Fund was selling at a 5.3% discount while the Korea Fund was selling for an 18.5% premium. (These two investment companies are known as "country funds," as they specialize in French and Korean stocks, respectively.) Most closed-end funds that invest in stocks (other than a few country funds) sell at a discount.[7]

Finally, the last column in the figure shows the rate of return over the past 12 months for funds investing primarily in stocks, and the past 12–month yield for funds investing primarily in fixed-income securities.

(a) CLOSED-END BOND FUNDS

Fund Name	Stock Exch	NAV	Market Price	Prem /Disc	12 Mo Yield 3/31/94
U.S. Gov't. Bond Funds					
ACM Govt Inc	N	9.62	11	+ 14.3	11.1
ACM Govt Oppty	N	8.30	8⅜	+ 0.9	10.1
ACM Govt Secs	N	9.30	10⅜	+ 11.6	11.1
ACM Govt Spec	N	7.94	8⅝	+ 8.6	11.0
Amer Govt Income -ac	N	6.83	8	+ 17.1	13.6
Amer Govt Port -ac	N	8.45	10⅛	+ 19.8	11.9
Dean Witter Govt -a	N	8.88	8	− 9.9	9.7
Excelsior Income -c	N	18.29	16⅛	− 11.8	7.0
Kemper Int Govt	N	8.27	7⅝	− 7.8	9.3
MFS Govt Mkts	N	7.32	6¼	− 14.6	7.1
Putnam Int Govt	N	8.55	7⅝	− 10.8	7.4
U.S. Mortgage Bond Funds					
2002 Target Term -c	N	13.76	12	− 12.8	9.0
Amer Adj Rate 95 -ac	N	9.40	9½	+ 1.1	5.1
Amer Adj Rate 96 -ac	N	9.16	9⅜	+ 2.3	5.7
Amer Adj Rate 97 -ac	N	9.05	9	− 0.6	6.6
Amer Adj Rate 98 -ac	N	9.05	8⅞	− 1.9	6.8
Amer Adj Rate 99 -ac	N	9.01	8¾	− 2.9	6.9
Amer Govt Term -ac	N	8.79	9⅜	+ 6.7	8.4
Amer Oppty Inc -ac	N	7.99	10⅛	+ 26.7	16.5
Amer Sel Port -ac	N	12.66	11⅝	− 8.2	N/A
Amer Str Inc II -ac	N	13.48	13⅞	+ 2.9	9.5
Amer Str Inc III -ac	N	13.02	13¾	+ 5.6	8.5
Amer Str Income -ac	N	14.20	14⅞	+ 4.8	9.1
BlckRk 1998 Term -c	N	9.34	9	− 3.6	7.9
BlckRk 1999 Term -c	N	8.79	8⅝	− 1.9	8.6
BlckRk 2001 Term -c	N	8.55	8⅛	− 5.0	8.9
BlckRk Adv Term -c	N	9.81	9	− 8.3	9.1
BlckRk Income -c	N	7.84	7⅜	− 5.9	11.4
BlckRk Inv 09 -c	A	12.80	11⅜	− 11.1	N/A
BlckRk Inv Q Tm -c	N	8.81	7⅞	− 10.6	10.2
BlckRk Str Tm -c	N	8.66	8⅜	− 3.3	10.0
BlckRk Tgt Tm -c	N	9.60	9⅛	− 4.9	8.8
Heritage US Govt -c	N	13.37	12⅞	− 3.7	N/A
Hyperion 1997 Tm -c	N	8.30	7¾	− 6.6	8.5
Hyperion 1999 Tm -c	N	7.79	7	− 10.1	9.2
Hyperion 2002 Tm -c	N	8.28	7⅜	− 10.9	10.4
Hyperion 2005 -c	N	9.05	8⅛	− 10.2	9.5
Hyperion Tot Rtn -c	N	10.08	10	− 0.8	11.1
Inc Opp 1999	N	8.81	8	− 9.2	7.2
Investment Grade Bond Funds					
1838 Bd-Deb	N	21.19	20½	− 3.3	8.2
All-American Tm -c	N	N/A	12¾	N/A	9.6
Amer Cap Bond -b	N	18.16	18⅛	− 0.2	8.6
Bunker Hill	N	15.39	15⅛	− 1.7	9.2
CNA Income -c	N	9.80	11	+ 12.2	10.6
Circle Income -c	O	11.66	11⅜	− 2.4	8.2
Current Inc Shs	N	13.29	11¾	− 11.6	8.2
Fortis Secs	N	9.60	9½	− 1.0	10.8
Ft Dearborn Inc	N	15.78	14⅞	− 5.7	7.8
Hatteras Income	N	16.11	17¼	+ 7.1	8.7
INA Investments	N	18.65	16½	− 11.5	8.7
Independence Sq	O	17.69	16¼	− 8.1	8.4
InterCap Income -a	N	17.70	18⅝	+ 5.2	8.8
Montgomery St	N	19.30	18	− 6.7	8.4
Op Fd Multi-Gov	N	8.16	7⅝	− 6.6	9.4
Pac Amer Income -c	N	15.43	14⅝	− 5.2	8.1
Pioneer Int Shs	N	13.47	13⅜	− 0.7	8.5
Transam Income	N	23.96	23⅝	− 1.4	8.3
Vestaur Secs -c	N	14.42	13½	− 6.4	8.0
Loan Participation Funds					
Eaton Vance Pr	z	10.00	N/A	N/A	N/A
Merrill Sen Fl	z	10.02	N/A	N/A	N/A
Pilgrim Pr Rate -a	N	9.97	9½	− 4.7	6.4
Prime Income	z	10.00	N/A	N/A	N/A
VanKamp Prime	z	10.05	N/A	N/A	N/A
High Yield Bond Funds					
CIGNA High Inc	N	7.23	8¼	+ 14.1	12.5
CIM High Yld	N	7.71	8	+ 3.8	10.4
Colonial Intmdt	N	6.65	6⅝	− 0.4	11.3
Corp Hi Yld	N	13.78	13¾	− 0.2	N/A
Corp Hi Yld II	N	13.48	13⅞	+ 2.9	N/A
Franklin Univ -c	N	8.98	8⅝	− 4.0	10.0
High Inc Adv -a	N	6.07	5⅞	− 3.2	11.0
High Inc Adv II -a	N	6.80	6⅜	− 6.3	11.0
High Inc Adv III -a	N	7.27	7⅛	− 2.0	12.1
Other Taxable Bond Funds					
ACM Mgd $	N	11.37	12⅝	+ 11.0	N/A
ACM Mgd Income	N	8.25	9¾	+ 18.2	12.1
AIM Strategic -a	A	9.60	8⅝	− 10.2	5.3
Alliance Wld $	N	12.41	15⅜	+ 23.9	10.4
Alliance Wld $ 2	N	12.56	13¾	+ 6.5	10.4
Amer Cap Inc	N	7.85	7⅛	− 9.2	10.7
Colonial Intrmkt	N	11.15	11⅛	− 0.2	9.4
Duff&Ph Util Cor	N	13.45	13⅛	− 2.4	10.3
First Boston Inc	N	8.67	7¾	− 10.6	10.7
First Boston Str	N	10.04	9	− 10.4	10.8
Franklin Mul-Inc -c	N	9.92	9⅝	− 3.0	8.5
Franklin Pr Mat -c	N	9.61	8½	− 11.6	6.5
Global Partners -a	N	12.16	12¾	+ 4.9	N/A
Highlander Inc -c	A	13.80	15	+ 8.7	N/A
J Hancock Income	N	15.97	15½	− 2.9	8.4
J Hancock Invest	N	20.89	21¼	+ 1.7	7.7
Kemper Multi Mkt	N	10.65	10	− 6.1	10.3
World Income Funds					
ACM Mgd MultiMkt	N	9.37	8¼	− 12.0	9.6
Alliance Wld $ 2	N	12.56	13¾	+ 6.5	N/A
Americas Inc Tr -ac	N	11.46	13	+ 13.4	N/A
BlckRk North Am -c	N	10.58	10⅜	− 1.9	10.7
Dreyfus Str Govt -a	N	10.36	9⅝	− 7.1	9.5
Emer Mkts Float	N	13.49	15	+ 11.2	N/A
Emer Mkts Inc	N	14.86	15⅝	+ 5.1	9.6
Emer Mkts Inc II	N	12.48	13⅞	+ 11.2	N/A
First Aust Prime	A	9.84	10¼	+ 4.2	9.5
First Commonwlth	N	12.69	11¼	− 11.3	8.8
National Muni Bond Funds					
ACM Muni Secs	N	12.48	12⅝	+ 1.2	N/A
Amer Muni Income -ac	N	12.36	12½	+ 1.1	N/A
Amer Muni Tm II -ac	N	10.62	10¼	− 3.5	6.2
Amer Muni Tm III -ac	N	9.78	9¾	− 0.3	5.8
Amer Muni Tm Tr -ac	N	10.92	10⅝	− 2.7	6.5
Apex Muni	N	10.12	10	− 1.2	8.1
BlckRk Ins 2008	N	14.61	14⅛	− 3.3	6.4
BlckRk Ins Muni	N	10.21	9¾	− 4.5	6.4
BlckRk Inv Q Mun	N	13.00	12¼	− 5.8	6.7
BlckRk Target	N	10.39	9¾	− 6.2	6.2
Colonial Hi Inc	N	8.26	8	− 3.1	8.3

f-NAV as of 3/31 was 23.72. g-Info for 3/31: 87.68 85 1/2 -2.49.
h-Actual div. date was 3/31.
Source-Lipper Analytical Services Inc.

Figure 22.1

Listing of Closed-End Funds (Excerpts)

Source: Reprinted by permission of *Barron's*, ©Dow Jones & Company, Inc., April 11, 1994, pp. MW73–MW74. All rights reserved worldwide.

(b) CLOSED-END STOCK FUNDS

Friday, April 8, 1994

General Equity Funds

Fund Name	Stock Exch	NAV	Market Price	Prem /Disc	12 Mo Yield 3/31/94
Adams Express	N	18.96	17⅛	− 9.7	− 8.1
Baker Fentress	N	20.49	16⅝	− 18.9	9.8
Bergstrom Cap -g	A	88.17	87	− 1.3	− 16.6
Blue Chip Value	N	7.45	7	− 6.0	− 4.8
Central Secs	A	17.37	15⅞	− 8.6	24.8
Charles Allmon	N	10.35	9⅞	− 4.6	6.2
Engex	A	12.25	9⅜	− 23.5	− 1.3
Equus II	A	20.18	15¼	− 24.4	65.5
Gabelli Equity	N	10.68	11⅛	+ 4.2	16.6
General American	N	23.59	20⅝	− 12.6	− 4.6
Inefficient Mkt	A	12.47	10	− 19.8	3.0
Jundt Growth	N	15.24	14	− 8.1	13.9
Liberty All-Star	N	9.94	10½	+ 5.6	9.5
Morgan Gr. Sm Cap	N	11.69	10⅛	− 13.4	4.8
NAIC Growth -c	O	10.81	9¾	− 9.8	0.9
Royce Value	N	13.30	12¾	− 4.1	9.7
Salomon SBF	N	14.29	12¼	− 14.3	8.0
Source Capital	N	40.39	41½	+ 2.7	− 5.8
Spectra	O	18.12	16	− 11.7	22.9
Tri-Continental	N	26.68	22¼	− 16.6	− 2.1
Z-Seven	O	16.64	16¼	− 2.3	− 1.8
Zweig -a	N	10.84	12⅞	+ 18.8	8.1

Specialized Equity Funds

Fund Name	Stock Exch	NAV	Market Price	Prem /Disc	12 Mo Yield 3/31/94
ASA Limited -cv	N	47.96	41¾	− 12.9	6.1
Alliance Gl Env	N	11.17	9¼	− 17.2	− 1.3
Anchor Gold&Curr	C	6.25	6⅜	+ 2.0	37.8
BGR Prec Metals -c	T	17.76	14½	− 18.4	N/A
C&S Realty	A	8.99	10	+ 11.2	11.0
C&S Total Rtn	N	14.04	14⅜	+ 2.4	N/A
Central Canada -c	A	N/A	5⅝	N/A	38.7
Counsellors Tand	N	15.18	12¾	− 16.0	− 11.9
Delaware Gr Div	N	13.91	13⅞	− 0.3	2.3
Delaware Grp Gl	N	13.54	14½	+ 7.1	N/A
Dover Reg Fincl	O	N/A	N/A	N/A	N/A
Duff&Ph Util Inc	N	8.13	8½	+ 4.6	− 12.8
Emer Mkts Infra	N	12.65	12	− 5.1	N/A
Emer Mkts Tel	N	20.43	21⅞	+ 7.1	53.9
First Financial	N	12.68	12⅛	− 4.4	25.3
Global Health	N	12.29	10¼	− 16.6	7.2
Global Privat	N	13.73	13⅝	− 0.8	N/A
H&Q Health Inv	N	17.19	16⅜	− 4.7	2.4
H&Q Life Sci Inv	N	11.24	10½	− 6.6	− 2.0
Hampton Utility -c	A	14.69	13⅞	− 5.5	− 1.7
New Age Media	N	N/A	10⅝	N/A	N/A
Patriot Glob Dvd -a	N	12.52	13	+ 3.8	0.4
Patriot Pr Dvdll	N	10.78	10¼	− 4.9	− 5.3
Patriot Pref Dvd -a	N	12.35	12⅝	+ 2.2	N/A
Patriot Prem Dvd	N	8.70	9⅛	+ 4.9	0.2
Patriot Sel Dvd -a	N	13.98	14⅛	+ 1.0	− 12.2
Petroleum & Res	N	28.57	27½	− 3.7	4.9
Pilgrim Reg Bk	N	11.69	10	− 14.5	− 14.0

Convertible Sec's. Funds

Fund Name	Stock Exch	NAV	Market Price	Prem /Disc	12 Mo Yield 3/31/94
Amer Cap Conv	N	23.86	20½	− 14.1	2.4
Bancroft Conv	A	23.01	21⅛	− 8.2	9.0
Castle Conv	A	25.90	23¼	− 10.2	3.0
Ellsworth Conv	A	9.85	8¾	− 11.2	5.3
Lincoln Conv -c	N	N/A	18¼	N/A	19.7
Putnam Hi Inc Cv	N	9.57	9¾	+ 1.9	7.6
TCW Conv Secs	N	8.30	9¼	+ 11.4	7.4

Dual-Purpose Funds

Fund Name	Stock Exch	NAV	Market Price	Prem /Disc	12 Mo Yield 3/31/94
Conv Hold Cap	N	12.57	9⅜	− 25.4	3.4
Conv Hold Inc	N	9.62	10¾	+ 11.7	1.7
Gemini II Fund	N	21.14	17⅜	− 17.8	0.4
Gemini II Fund	N	9.50	11⅜	+ 19.7	0.3
Quest Value Cap	N	26.58	22	− 17.2	− 4.7
Quest Value Inc	N	11.65	12¼	+ 5.2	1.3

World Equity Funds

Fund Name	Stock Exch	NAV	Market Price	Prem /Disc	12 Mo Yield 3/31/94
Americas All Sea	O	5.16	4	− 22.5	− 1.5
Argentina	N	14.03	13⅞	− 1.1	35.2
Asia Pacific	N	16.56	18⅞	+ 14.0	54.9
Asia Tigers	N	12.13	11¾	− 3.1	N/A
Austria	N	10.57	10	− 5.4	22.4
Brazil -c	N	25.74	24⅜	− 5.3	68.4
Brazilian Equity -c	N	18.82	20	+ 6.3	91.2
Cdn Genl Inv -cy	T	42.41	32½	− 23.4	11.9
Chile	N	41.88	45⅛	+ 7.7	46.7
China	N	15.71	17¼	+ 9.8	25.2
Clemente Global -c	N	11.74	9⅞	− 15.9	20.3
Emerging Mexico -c	N	18.10	17⅞	− 1.2	31.8
Emerging Tigers	N	14.02	13¾	− 1.9	N/A
Europe	N	12.93	12⅛	− 6.2	19.3
European Warrant -c	N	13.62	13¾	+ 1.0	74.6
Fidelity Em Asia	N	13.85	15	+ 8.3	N/A
First Australia	A	12.52	11¼	− 10.1	29.4
First Iberian	A	9.21	8⅛	− 11.8	23.5
First Israel	N	13.41	15¼	+ 13.7	27.6
First Philippine	N	21.81	17¾	− 18.6	61.0
France Growth	N	11.75	11⅛	− 5.3	3.3
GT Devel Mkts	N	13.03	12⅛	− 6.9	N/A
GT Gr Europe	N	15.02	14	− 6.8	40.7
Germany Fund	N	12.97	11¾	− 9.4	8.1
Germany, Emer	N	9.78	8½	− 13.1	15.3
Germany, Future	N	17.57	15	− 14.6	21.9
Germany, New	N	14.68	12⅜	− 15.7	17.3
Global Small Cap	A	N/A	12⅞	N/A	N/A
Greater China	N	17.35	18⅝	+ 7.3	41.3
Growth Fd Spain	N	12.25	10¼	− 16.3	17.1
Herzfeld Caribb	O	5.00	N/A	N/A	N/A
India Fund	N	13.87	12⅛	− 12.6	N/A
India Growth -d	N	21.99	21¾	− 1.1	57.1
Indonesia	N	10.15	13	+ 28.1	30.0
Irish Inv	N	10.08	9¼	− 8.2	20.3
Italy	N	11.27	11¾	+ 4.3	25.7
Jakarta Growth	N	8.91	9¾	+ 9.4	40.1
Japan Equity	N	14.24	15⅞	+ 11.5	38.5
Japan OTC Equity	N	11.00	12⅞	+ 17.0	25.6
Jardine Fl China -c	N	16.40	18	+ 9.8	24.0
Jardine Fl India -c	N	14.22	14½	+ 2.0	N/A
Korea	N	17.19	20⅜	+ 18.5	55.3
Korea Equity	N	9.96	10⅞	+ 9.2	N/A
Korean Inv	N	12.57	13½	+ 7.4	18.7
Latin Amer Disc	N	22.80	22⅜	− 1.9	64.9
Latin Amer Eq	N	21.79	24½	+ 12.4	72.7
Latin Amer Inv	N	24.97	24¼	− 2.9	38.8
Malaysia	N	19.75	20⅜	+ 3.2	38.5
Mexico -c	N	30.25	30	− 0.8	38.5
Mexico Eqty&Inc -c	N	19.18	20⅛	+ 4.9	35.8
Morgan St Africa	N	12.01	10⅝	− 11.5	N/A
Morgan St Em	N	24.14	24¾	+ 2.5	54.4
Morgan St India	N	14.05	13⅞	− 1.2	N/A

Figure 22.1 (continued)

Open-End Investment Companies

An investment company that stands ready at all times to purchase its own shares at or near their net asset value is termed an **open-end investment company** (or open-end fund). Most of these companies, commonly known as **mutual funds,** also continuously offer new shares to the public for a price at or near their net asset values. Hence their capitalization is "open," with the number of shares outstanding changing on a daily basis.

There are two methods utilized by mutual funds to sell their shares to the public—direct marketing and the use of a sales force. With direct marketing the mutual fund sells shares directly to investors without the use of a sales organization. In such a situation the open-end companies, known as **no-load funds,** sell their shares at a price equal to their net asset value. The other method of selling shares involves the use of a sales force that is paid a commission based on the number of shares it sells. This sales force often involves brokers, financial planners, and employees of insurance companies. The open-end companies that use this method are known as **load funds,** because the commission involves adding a percentage **load charge** to the net asset value.

The percentage load charge by law cannot exceed 8.5% of the amount invested. For example, a selling organization receiving $1,000 to be invested in a fund might retain as much as $85, leaving $915 to purchase the fund's shares at the current net asset value per share. Although this is usually described as a load charge of 8.5%, it is actually equal to 9.3% (= $85/$915) of the amount ultimately invested. Load charges of this magnitude are levied by many funds for small purchases, but typically they are reduced for larger purchases. It should also be noted that some funds have loads of less than 3.5% for purchases of all sizes, and are hence dubbed **low-load funds.**[8]

When mutual fund shareholders want to sell their shares, they usually receive an amount equal to the fund's net asset value times the number of shares sold. However, a few funds charge a **redemption fee,** which usually is no more than 1% of the fund's net asset value and typically is not levied if the investor has owned the shares for more than 60 days. Hence its basic purpose is to discourage investors from selling their shares right after buying them. By discouraging such in-and-out trading the fund avoids the transaction costs associated with having to sell securities frequently in order to satisfy some investors' desires to sell their mutual fund shares rapidly.

In addition, mutual funds may charge a **distribution fee** annually. This *12b-1 fee* (named for an SEC ruling involving a section of the Investment Company Act of 1940) is legally not allowed to exceed 1% of the average market value of the total assets. It pays for advertising, promoting, and selling the fund to prospective purchasers. Sometimes it is coupled with a load charge that is paid when shares are initially purchased. One alleged benefit of the 12b-1 fee to the current owners of the fund is that the subsequent increased size of the portfolio will bring with it certain economies of scale.

Some mutual funds have different classes of stock. In such a situation an investor can choose the class that he or she wants to purchase. For example, class *A* stock might involve a 5% load charge but no annual 12b-1 fee, whereas class *B* stock might not have a load charge. Instead this class might have a 12b-1 fee of .5% per year plus a **contingent deferred sales charge** (paid when the investor sells shares) that starts at 5% if the investor sells his or her shares within a year of purchase and declines thereafter by 1% a year for each year that the stock is held, reaching zero after the fifth year. In addition, the class B shares might be set up so that they convert to class A shares after five years (when the contingent deferred sales charge has declined to zero). This feature allows investors who initially bought class B shares to avoid 12b-1 fees after five years. There might also be class C stock where the investor pays an annual 12b-1 fee of 1% for as long as the shares are held.

In summary, there are many different methods that mutual funds use to get the cash needed to pay for sales commissions and other selling costs. Some methods (such as the class C stock) are more attractive to investors who plan to hold their investment only for the short-term. Others (such as the class A stock) are more attractive to investors who plan to hold their investment for the long term.

As will be discussed later, the investment performance of no-load funds as a whole does not differ in any notable way from that of load funds. This is not surprising. The load charge (roughly 30% to 50% of which goes to the individual who sold the shares, with the selling organization keeping the rest) represents the cost of advertising, education, and persuasion. Mail-order firms often sell items for less than stores charge. Salespeople who work in stores and those who sell mutual funds provide a service and require compensation. Buyers who consider such services worth less than their cost can and should avoid paying for them.

Quotations

Figure 22.2 shows a portion of the quotations for mutual funds provided in the *Wall Street Journal* following each business day. Funds that are listed under a name in boldface type have a common management company that is associated with that name. For example, note all the funds listed under AARP Invst. (AARP Invst stands for *AARP Investment Program from Scudder,* an investment program sponsored by the American Association of Retired People that involves mutual funds run by the management company of Scudder, Stevens & Clark.) After the name of the mutual fund comes a three-letter acronym that indicates the fund's investment objective. For example, the GRO after the AARP's CaGr (short for capital growth) indicates that this fund is a growth fund. The net asset value, based on closing prices for the fund's securities on the day in question, is shown second. This is followed by the "offer" price—the net asset value plus the load charge applicable to the smallest possible purchase. For no-load funds, this column contains the letters NL. The fourth column displays the change in net asset value from the close of the previous trading day, and the fifth column indicates the fund's rate of return for the year so far.

The remaining columns in Figure 22.2 display different information each day of the week. On Monday (as shown here) there are two columns that show the fund's maximum initial load charge (if any) and operating expense ratio. On the other four days of the week there are three columns instead of two. These three columns indicate the rate of return for various time periods, ranging from the previous four weeks to the previous five years, and an indication of the fund's pentile relative to other funds with the same investment objective (top 20% = A, next 20% = B, middle 20% = C, next 20% = D, bottom 20% =

Friday, December 10, 1993

Ranges for investment companies, with daily price data supplied by the National Association of Securities Dealers and performance and cost calculations by Lipper Analytical Services Inc. The NASD requires a mutual fund to have at least 1,000 shareholders or net assets of $25 million before being listed. Detailed explanatory notes appear elsewhere on this page.

Fund	Inv. Obj.	NAV	Offer Price	NAV Chg.	% Ret YTD	Max Initl Chrg.	Total Exp Ratio R
AAL Mutual:							
Bond p	BND	10.56	11.09	-0.03	+8.9	4.750	1.030 ..
CaGr p	GRO	15.18	15.94	-0.02	+5.0	4.750	1.200 ..
MuBd p	GLM	11.32	11.88	-0.01	+10.6	4.750	1.000 ..
SmCoStk p	SML	10.56	11.09	-0.01	NS	4.750	NA ..
AARP Invst:							
CaGr	GRO	36.48	NL	-0.04	+13.7	0.000	1.130 ..
GiniA	BND	15.78	NL	-0.03	+5.7	0.000	0.720 ..
Gthinc	G&I	32.86	NL	-0.01	+13.9	0.000	0.910 ..
HQ Bd	BND	17.01	NL	-0.01	+11.5	0.000	1.130 ..
TxFBd	ISM	18.94	NL	-0.01	+12.4	0.000	0.740 ..
ABT Funds:							
Emrg p	CAP	14.32	15.03	-0.06	+13.9	4.750	1.440 ..
FL HI	MFL	10.72	11.25	-0.01	+13.6k	4.750	0.000 ..
FL TF	MFL	11.55	12.13	...	+11.9	4.750	0.580 ..
Gthin p	G&I	10.94	11.49	-0.05	+3.5	4.750	1.230 ..
Utilin p	SEC	13.32	13.98	+0.01	+7.6	4.750	1.170 ..
Acc Mortg	BND	12.34	NL		+7.0	0.000	0.840 ..
Acc Shr Int	BST	12.40	NL	-0.01	+5.6	0.000	0.830 ..
AHA Funds:							
Balan	S&B	13.12	NL	-0.02	+10.4	0.000	0.380 ..
Full	BND	10.90	NL	-0.03	+11.8	0.000	0.420 ..
Lim	S&B	10.48	NL	-0.01	+5.3	0.000	0.290 ..
AIM Funds:							
AdlGv p	BST	9.85	9.95	...	+4.1	1.000	0.140 ..
Agrsv p	SML	23.46	24.83	-0.08	+26.7	5.500	1.250 ..
Chart p	G&I	9.20	9.74	-0.01	+8.8	5.500	1.170 ..
Const p	CAP	17.10	18.10	-0.02	+14.6	5.500	1.200 ..
BalA p	S&B	16.15	16.96	-0.06	+15.4	4.750	2.120 ..
GoScA p	BND	10.21	10.72	-0.02	+6.8k	4.750	0.980 ..
GrthA p	GRO	12.55	13.28	-0.04	+2.2	5.500	1.170 ..
HYIcIA p	BHI	10.06	10.56	+0.01	+7.8k	4.750	1.150 ..
IncoA p	BND	8.68	9.11	-0.03	+15.5k	4.750	0.990 ..
IntlE p	ITL	12.58	13.31	+0.07	+40.4	5.500	1.800 ..
LimvA p	BST	10.15	10.25	-0.01	+4.2	1.000	0.480 ..
MuniA p	GLM	8.70	9.13	-0.02	+11.1k	4.750	0.900 ..
SumIt	GRO	10.27	NA	+0.01	+6.5	8.500	0.760 ..
TeCf p	SSM	11.29	11.85	-0.01	+11.6	4.750	0.250 ..
TF Int	IDM	11.02	11.13	+0.01	+8.6	1.000	0.380 ..
UtliA p	SEC	14.11	14.93	+0.01	+10.3k	5.500	1.170 ..
UtliB p	SEC	14.10	14.10	...	NS	0.000	NA ..
ValuA p	GRO	21.02	22.24	+0.01	+15.2	5.500	1.160 ..
Valu3 p	GRO	21.02	21.02	+0.01	NA	0.000	NA ..
Weing p	GRO	17.50	18.52	+0.01	+1.0	5.500	1.100 ..
AMCORE Vintage Fds:							
Equity	GRO	10.37	10.83	-0.02	+4.5	4.250	NA ..
FxIncome	BIN	10.36	10.76	-0.02	+9.0	3.750	NA ..
IntdtTF	IDM	10.48	10.89	...	NS	3.750	NA ..
AMF Funds:							
AdIMtg	BST	10.00	NL		+4.5	0.000	0.440 ..
IntMtg	BND	9.93	NL	-0.02	+7.1	0.000	0.430 ..
IntlLiq	BST	10.85	NL	-0.01	+5.6	0.000	0.500 ..
MtgSc	BND	11.08	NL	-0.02	+6.3	0.000	0.530 ..
ARK Funds:							
CapGr p		10.72	NL	+0.04	NA	0.000	NA ..
Gr&Inc p		10.51	NL		NA	0.000	NA ..
Income p		10.08	NL	-0.01	NA	0.000	NA ..
ASM Fd	G&I	10.22	NL	+0.03	+4.8	0.000	NA ..
Acornin	ITL	15.18	15.18	+0.04	+42.0	0.000	NA ..
AcornF	SML	71.13	71.13	-0.16	+29.5	0.000	0.670 ..
AdsnCa p	G&I	22.19	22.88	+0.03	+11.8	3.000	2.130 ..
AdvCapl Bal p	S&B	10.57	10.57	-0.02	+4.8	0.000	1.130 ..
AdvCaplRet p	BND	10.69	10.69	-0.04	+14.4	0.000	NA ..
Advest Advant:							
Govt p	BND	10.50	10.50	-0.09	+20.0k	0.000	1.390 ..
Gwth p	GRO	17.81	17.81	...	+9.3	0.000	2.150 ..
HY Bd p	BHI	9.89	9.89	-0.02	+18.1k	0.000	1.500 ..
Inco p	S&B	13.31	13.31	-0.01	+13.6	0.000	2.020 ..
MuBdNal	GLM	10.22	10.22	-0.02	NS	0.000	NA ..
Spcl p	SML	20.83	20.83	+0.05	+19.7	0.000	2.840 ..
Aetna Funds:							
Aetna	S&B	10.08	NL		+8.6	0.000	0.070 ..
Bond	BND	10.42	NL	-0.02	+10.1	0.000	0.050 ..
Grwincm	G&I	10.96	NL	+5.1		0.000	0.330 ..
IntlGr	ITL	11.23	NL	+0.04	+26.5	0.000	0.500 ..
Alger Funds:							
Growth f	GRO	22.47	22.47	+0.05	+17.2	0.000	2.320 ..
IncGr r	G&I	14.06	14.06	+0.03	+6.2	0.000	3.090 ..
MidCpGr	GRO	12.46	12.46	+0.04	NS	0.000	NA ..
SmCap f	SML	25.43	25.43	-0.10	+8.5	0.000	2.170 ..
Alliance Cap:							
Allan p	GRO	7.53	7.86	...	+13.0	4.250	0.810 ..
Balan p	S&B	14.37	15.01	-0.02	+8.7	4.250	1.400 ..
BalB t	S&B	15.84	15.84	-0.03	+9.9	0.000	2.150 ..
Canad p	ITL	5.59	5.92	-0.01	+15.7	4.250	1.390 ..
CoBdA p	BND	15.51	15.82	+0.30	NE	4.250	1.390 ..
CoBdB	BND	15.15	15.15	-0.06	NS	0.000	2.100 ..
CpBdC	BND	15.15	15.15	-0.06	NS	0.000	NA ..
Count p	G&I	17.62	18.40	-0.10	+5.9	4.250	1.620 ..
GlbSA p	WOR	11.32	11.62		+16.9	4.250	2.340 ..
GovtA p	BND	8.58	8.96	-0.03	+9.8k	4.250	1.180 ..
GovtB p	BND	8.58	8.58	-0.03	+9.0k	0.000	1.810 ..
GovtC	BND	8.58	8.58	-0.02	NS	0.000	NA ..
GwthA p	GRO	25.51	26.64	-0.06	+26.9	4.250	1.400 ..
GwthB t	GRO	21.88	21.88	-0.05	+26.2	0.000	2.150 ..
Grinc p	G&I	2.58	2.69	...	+9.0	4.250	1.900 ..
GrincB	G&I	2.57	2.57	...	+8.4	0.000	1.900 ..
ICalTA p	ISM	13.81	14.42	-0.03	+12.0k	4.250	0.780 ..
InsMuA p	ISM	10.40	10.86	-0.01	+12.4k	4.250	0.810 ..
InsMuB	ISM	10.40	10.40	-0.01	+11.3k	0.000	NA ..
InsMuC	ISM	10.40	10.40	-0.01	NS	0.000	NA ..
IntlA p	ITL	16.85	17.60	+0.10	+25.5	4.250	1.820 ..
MrfgA p	BND	9.28	9.69	-0.02	+9.6k	4.250	1.180 ..
MrfgB p	BND	9.29	9.29	-0.01	+9.0k	0.000	1.870 ..
MrfgC	BND	9.28	9.28	-0.02	NS	0.000	NA ..
MrfgTrA p	BST	9.94	10.38	-0.01	+6.1k	4.250	1.440 ..
MrfgTrB p	BST	9.95	9.95	...	+5.4k	0.000	2.130 ..
MrfgTrC	BST	9.95	9.95	...	NS	0.000	NA ..
MltfG	SEC	10.37	10.47	-0.01	+8.2k	1.000	2.330 ..
Mltln t	WBD	1.88	1.88	...	+3.2k	0.000	1.810 ..
MMSA p	WBD	8.93	9.35	-0.01	+10.4k	4.250	2.530 ..
MMSB t	WBD	8.93	8.93	-0.01	+9.7k	0.000	3.240 ..
MuCA A p	MCA	10.81	11.29	-0.01	+11.7k	4.250	0.590 ..
MuCA B	MCA	10.81	10.81	-0.01	+10.9k	0.000	NA ..
MuCA C	MCA	10.81	10.81	-0.01	NS	0.000	NA ..
MuFLC	MFL	10.25	10.25	-0.02	NS	0.000	NA ..
MuNJC	MNJ	10.24	10.24	-0.02	NS	0.000	NA ..
MuNYA p	DNY	10.11	10.56	-0.01	+11.4k	4.250	0.700 ..
MuNYB	DNY	10.11	10.11	-0.01	+10.4k	0.000	NA ..
MuNYC	DNY	10.11	10.11	-0.01	NS	0.000	NA ..
NtImUA p	GLM	10.87	11.35	-0.02	+12.5k	4.250	0.830 ..
NtImUB p	GLM	10.87	10.87	-0.02	+11.8k	0.000	NA ..
NtImUC p	GLM	10.87	10.87	-0.02	NS	0.000	NA ..
NEur p	ITL	12.02	12.56	...	+30.8	4.250	2.250 ..
NAGVA	WBD	10.38	10.38	-0.04	+17.4k	4.250	2.450 ..
NAGVB p	WBD	10.38	10.38	-0.02	+16.6k	0.000	3.130 ..
NAGvC	WBD	10.37	10.37	-0.02	NS	0.000	NA ..
PrGrthA	GRO	11.88	12.41	-0.03	+8.8	4.250	NA ..
PrGrthB p	GRO	11.82	11.82	-0.02	+8.3	0.000	NA ..
QusrA p	SML	23.43	24.47	-0.04	+14.2	4.250	1.620 ..
ST Mia p	WBD	9.24	9.65	+0.01	+7.6k	4.250	1.100 ..
ST Mib t	WBD	9.24	9.24	+0.01	+6.9k	0.000	1.810 ..
Tech p	SEC	33.43	34.91	-0.16	+18.5	4.250	1.610 ..
Wlcln p	WBD	1.90	1.90	...	+3.8k	0.000	1.590 ..
AmenaIncome	EQI	13.30	NL	+0.05	+10.0	0.000	1.580 ..
Ambassador Fds:							
BalncdF	S&B	10.21	10.21	-0.02	+6.0	0.000	NA ..
BondF	BND	10.14	10.14	-0.02	+11.5	0.000	0.760 ..
CoreGrF	GRO	16.64	16.64	-0.03	-4.7	0.000	NA ..
CrGri	GRO	16.64	NL	-0.03	-4.7	0.000	NA ..
GrwthF	GRO	13.63	13.63	-0.02	+13.3	0.000	0.960 ..
Grwthi	GRO	13.63	13.63	-0.02	+13.3	0.000	NA ..
IdxStkF	GRO	12.01	12.01	...	+9.1	0.000	0.250 ..
IntBdF	BST	10.45	10.45	-0.02	+1.8	0.000	0.770 ..
IntBdI	BST	10.45	NL	-0.01	+8.1	0.000	NA ..
IntlStkF	ITL	13.26	13.26	+0.06	+26.1	0.000	1.020 ..
IntlStki	ITL	13.26	13.26	+0.06	+26.1	0.000	NA ..
SmCoGF	SML	13.87	13.87	-0.09	+7.9	0.000	0.960 ..
TxFBdI	STM	10.69	NL	-0.01	+6.7	0.000	NA ..
Amer AAdvant:							
Balan	S&B	13.19	13.19	-0.02	+14.3	0.000	0.350 ..
Equity	G&I	14.65	14.65	...	+14.7	0.000	0.360 ..
IntlEq	ITL	12.32	12.32	+0.06	+36.9	0.000	1.170 ..
LtdTr	BST	10.16	10.16	-0.01	+6.7	0.000	0.270 ..
Amer Capital:							
CrnstA p	G&I	18.10	19.20	...	+7.4	5.750	0.870 ..
CoBdA p	BND	7.24	7.60	-0.01	+12.6	4.750	1.050 ..
EmGrA p	SML	26.72	28.35	-0.05	+20.0	5.750	1.040 ..
EmGrB p	SML	26.33	26.33	-0.05	+19.2	0.000	NA ..
EntA p	GRO	13.19	13.99	+0.02	+8.5	5.750	0.990 ..
EntB p	GRO	13.11	13.11	+0.02	+7.7	0.000	1.900 ..
EqIncA p	EQI	5.71	6.06	...	+14.4	5.750	1.010 ..
EqIncB t	EQI	5.70	5.70	...	+13.3	0.000	1.870 ..
Exch	GRO	107.96	NL	...	+9.2	0.000	NA ..
FMgA p	BST	12.71	12.42	-0.01	+2.9	2.250	0.910 ..
FMgB p	BST	12.42	12.43	-0.01	+2.2	0.000	1.620 ..
GIEqA p	WOR	11.28	12.19	+0.06	+16.9	5.750	2.930 ..
GIEqB p	WOR	11.14	11.14	+0.06	+16.0	0.000	3.880 ..
GIGvA p	WBD	9.37	9.84	+0.01	+15.2	4.750	1.520 ..
GIGvB p	WBD	9.41	NL	+0.01	+14.6	0.000	2.190 ..
Grinc p	G&I	14.31	15.18	...	+14.3	5.750	1.150 ..
GvScA p	BND	10.82	11.36	-0.02	+8.4	4.750	0.970 ..
GvScB p	BND	10.83	10.83	-0.02	+7.6	0.000	1.740 ..
GvScC p	BND	10.81	10.81	-0.03	NS	0.000	NA ..
GvTIA p	BIN	9.12	9.57	-0.01	+6.7	4.750	NA ..
GvTIB p	BIN	9.12	9.12	-0.01	+5.9	0.000	NA ..
GvTIC p	BIN	9.12	9.12	-0.01	NS	0.000	NA ..
GvT97 p	BND	13.45	13.87	-0.01	+6.7	3.000	1.620 ..
HarbA p	S&B	16.06	17.04	...	+11.9	5.750	0.990 ..
HarbB p	S&B	15.97	15.97	...	+11.0	0.000	1.880 ..
HYIdA p	BHI	6.67	7.00	...	+18.0	4.750	1.090 ..
HYIdB	BHI	6.68	6.68	...	+17.1	0.000	1.900 ..
MunBA p	GLM	10.51	11.03	...	+10.6	4.750	0.900 ..
PaceA p	GRO	13.42	14.24	+0.01	+9.6	5.750	1.060 ..
PaceB p	GRO	13.27	13.27	...	+8.4	0.000	1.980 ..
TxE IA p	ISM	11.67	12.25	...	+8.4	4.750	1.200 ..
TxE IB p	ISM	11.66	11.66	-0.01	+7.5	0.000	NA ..
TXMSA p	SSM	10.35	10.87	...	+11.8	4.750	0.930 ..
TEHYA p	HYM	11.29	11.85	-0.01	+9.5	4.750	1.070 ..
TEHYB p	HYM	11.29	11.29	...	+8.6	0.000	NA ..
American Funds:							
A Bal p	S&B	13.09	13.89	-0.02	+10.5	5.750	0.740 ..
Amcp p	GRO	12.62	13.39	-0.01	+9.2	5.750	0.730 ..
AMutl p	G&I	21.57	22.89	-0.01	+13.2	5.750	0.600 ..
Bond p	BND	14.83	15.57	-0.04	+13.9	4.750	0.730 ..
CaplB p	EQI	33.97	36.04	-0.07	+13.3	5.750	0.810 ..
CapW p	WBD	16.68	17.51	...	+16.4	4.750	1.380 ..
CapWGr	WOR	17.47x	18.54	-0.08	NS	5.750	NA ..
Eupac p	ITL	21.47x	22.78	-0.19	+31.7	5.750	1.100 ..
Fdinv p	G&I	17.95	19.05	+0.04	+16.9	5.750	0.650 ..
Govt p	BND	14.42	15.14	-0.05	+10.3	4.750	0.830 ..
Gwth p	GRO	27.36	29.03	+0.03	+12.4	5.750	0.770 ..
Hi T p	BHI	15.48	16.25	...	+16.5	4.750	0.940 ..
Inco p	EQI	14.72	15.62	-0.01	+13.3	5.750	0.620 ..
IntBd p	BIN	14.39	15.11	-0.03	+9.0	4.750	0.820 ..
ICA p	G&I	19.33	20.51	+0.01	+10.2	5.750	0.580 ..
LtdTEBd	IDM	14.62	15.35	+0.01	NS	4.750	NA ..
NEco p	GRO	33.75	35.81	+0.05	+27.9	5.750	0.890 ..
N Per p	WOR	14.61x	15.50	-0.47	+2.6	5.750	0.850 ..
SmCo p	WOR	24.06	25.53	-0.01	+27.0	5.750	1.210 ..
TxEx p	GLM	12.47	13.09	-0.01	+11.3	4.750	0.710 ..
TECA p	MCA	16.32	17.13	-0.02	+12.3	4.750	0.710 ..
TEMd p	SSM	16.66	16.66	...	+10.0	4.750	0.830 ..
TEVA p	SSM	16.80	17.20	...	+10.8	4.750	0.710 ..
Wsh p	G&I	18.03	19.13	...	+12.6	5.750	0.700 ..
A GthFd	GRO	10.40	11.03	+0.07	+23.7	5.750	1.440 ..
A Heritg	CAP	1.56	NL	-0.01	+38.1	0.000	2.100 ..
Amer Nati Funds:							
Grth	GRO	4.78	5.07	-0.02	+6.8	5.750	1.070 ..
Inco	S&B	23.51	24.94	-0.02	+8.7	5.750	1.180 ..
Triflex	S&B	16.29	17.28	-0.06	+5.0	5.750	1.150 ..
API Gr fp	CAP	13.00	NL	+0.01	+14.6	0.000	2.050 ..
Am Perform:							
Bond	BND	10.92	11.38	-0.04	+9.9	4.000	1.060 ..
Equity	GRO	12.85	13.39	-0.05	+8.4	4.000	1.160 ..
IntBd	BIN	10.91	11.25	-0.02	+7.8	3.000	1.070 ..
AmSouth Funds:							
Balance	S&B	12.10x	12.67	-0.04	+13.4	4.500	0.840 ..
Bond	BND	11.72x	11.57	-0.08	+3.0	4.500	0.780 ..
Equity	CAP	14.94x	15.64	-0.02	+14.6	4.500	0.950 ..
Gvtin	BND	9.84x	10.14	-0.07	NA	3.000	NA ..
LtdMat	BST	10.76x	11.09	-0.06	+6.9	3.000	0.690 ..
RegEq	CAP	17.31x	18.13	-0.06	+14.4	4.500	0.800 ..
AmUtlFd	SEC	22.53	23.53	+0.03	+10.3	0.000	1.210 ..
Amwny	GRO	8.16	8.41	-0.01	+7.8	3.000	1.010 ..
AnalyT	EQI	12.51	12.51	+0.02	+6.6	0.000	1.020 ..
AnchrCa	GRO	22.74	22.74	+0.02	-2.8	0.000	1.080 ..
Aquila Funds:							
AZ TF	SSM	11.00	11.46	-0.01	+10.4	4.000	0.650 ..
CO TF	SSM	11.39	11.39	-0.01	+10.7	4.000	0.450 ..
HI TF	SSM	12.35		...	+9.8	4.000	0.490 ..
KY TF	SSM	11.41	10.93	-0.01	+10.1	4.000	0.420 ..
Nrgnst TF	SSM	10.30	10.73	-0.01	+12.9	4.000	0.000 ..
OR TF	SSM	10.94	11.38	...	+9.7	4.000	0.660 ..
A+F LqCap	...	10.00	NL		NA	0.000	NA ..
Arch Funds:							
Bal	S&B	10.27	10.75	-0.01	NS	4.500	NA ..
Em Gr	SML	13.43	14.06	-0.03	+3.4	4.500	0.300 ..
GovCorp	BND	10.70	11.20	-0.03	+9.4	4.500	0.930 ..
GroInc	G&I	14.85	15.55	...	+9.3	4.500	0.630 ..
MoTF	SSM	11.87	12.43	-0.01	+11.3	4.500	0.630 ..
US Gov	BND	11.29	11.78	-0.04	+9.0	4.500	0.950 ..
Amstng	GRO	8.80	NL	-0.06	+14.3	0.000	1.900 ..
AtlantaGr p	SEC	11.57	12.02	...	+4.0	3.750	2.530 ..
Atlas Funds:							
CaMuni	MCA	11.56	11.92	-0.01	+13.1	3.000	0.540

Figure 22.2

Listing of Mutual Funds (Excerpt)

Source: Reprinted by permission of *The Wall Street Journal*, ©Dow Jones & Company, Inc., December 13, 1993, p. C21. All rights reserved worldwide.

E), based on the longest time period shown in that day's issue. Just how a mutual fund's rate of return is calculated will be shown shortly.

Figure 22.3 shows the weekly quotations that appear for a special type of mutual fund known as a money market fund. These funds invest in short-term, fixed-income securities, such as Treasury bills, commercial paper, and bank certificates of deposit. A special type of money market fund that invests primarily in short-term

MONEY MARKET MUTUAL FUNDS

The following quotations, collected by the National Association of Securities Dealers Inc., represent the average of annualized yields and dollar-weighted portfolio maturities ending Wednesday, December 15, 1993. Yields don't include capital gains or losses.

Fund	Avg. Mat.	7Day Yld.	Assets
AALMny	52	1.84	70
AARP HQ	50	2.16	261
AIM MM C	32	2.25	259
AIM MMA	32	2.29	80
AccUSGov	54	2.76	26
ActAsGv	69	2.60	530
ActAsMnv	71	2.84	3739
Aetna MM	50	3.27	111
AlexBwn	51	2.62	1301
AixBTr	52	2.58	580
AlgerMM	54	3.12	146
AlliaCpRs	73	2.47	2279
AllaGvR	80	2.31	1908
AlliMny	80	2.44	1767
AmAAdTr	52	2.91	161
AmAAdMM	34	3.15	3208
AmCRes	27	2.21	336
AmPerCsh	47	2.67	182
AmPerTrs	58	2.41	152
AmSouth Pr	59	2.61	482
AmSouth US	52	2.45	254
AmbMMF	46	2.74	281
AmbTreas F	56	2.57	266
AmbTreasl	56	2.57	96
AmbMMI	46	2.74	265
Amcore Gv	38	2.63	121
AmAAdMilage	34	2.90	40
ArchUSTr	47	2.48	1
ArchFd	46	2.50	45
ArkMnyMkt	81	3.22	178
ArkUSGovt	40	3.02	61
ArkUSTrsy	83	2.81	116
AMF St Lq	13	2.66	57
AutCsh	60	2.81	1120
AutGvt	46	2.61	3373
AuGvSvc	48	2.67	489
AutTreasC	51	2.56	295
BB&T UST Tr	47	2.49	77
BHY Hmltn	51	2.93	301
BT InstCash	38	3.09	2044
BT Inst Trsy	53	2.86	169
BT InvCash	38	2.60	96
BT InvTrsy	53	2.36	929
Babson	54	2.35	42
BartCsR	50	2.57	81
BayTreasInv	75	2.54	36
BayFdMM	81	2.69	168
BedfdGv	65	2.33	189
BdfdMM	67	2.45	814
BenchmrkCA Mu	75	2.18	48
BenchmrkDivAst	55	2.96	3270
BenchmrkGovSel	45	3.01	377

Fund	Avg. Mat.	7Day Yld.	Assets
HTInsgtGv	23	2.50	446
HanvCsh	63	2.69	788
HanvGov	78	2.76	554
HanvUSTr	50	2.51	918
HanvTreas	63	2.52	980
Harbor	67	2.65	51
HelmsTresOnA	86	3.10	199
HrtgCsh	31	2.48	960
HiMrkDv	67	2.63	411
HiMrkUS	54	2.43	206
HiMrkUST	74	2.46	202
HilrdGovt	51	2.47	236
HmestdDiv	68	2.65	25

TAX EXEMPTS

Fund	Avg. Mat.	7Day Yld.	Assets
AARPHTe	54	1.22	133
AIMTx	63	1.66	41
AT OhioTx	52	1.71	309
ActAsCal	53	1.49	268
ActAstTx	55	1.68	1485
AlxB TF	47	1.53	350
AllMunCal	69	1.42	175
AllMuCT	75	1.29	59
AllMuNY	75	1.54	125
AlllaMun	82	1.44	1139
AmSouth TxEx	40	1.60	64
AmbTxFrF	64	1.87	73
AmbTxFrI	64	1.87	180
ArchFd	53	1.29	9
ArkTaxFree	76	1.97	50
AtlasCA	52	1.88	48
BT InvNY	80	1.67	103
BT InvTxFr	81	1.87	142
BdfdTxFr	57	1.63	261
BedfordNY	39	1.52	56
BenCAMu	53	1.74	249
BenCaTF	43	1.56	369
BenNaTF	50	1.59	114
Benchmrk TE	55	1.87	1181
BlltTF	61	1.84	64
BosCoCA A	51	2.03	15
BosCoMAB	50	1.57	33
BosCoTF A	45	1.67	21
BosCoMA A	50	1.49	68

Figure 22.3
Listing of Money Market Mutual Funds (Excerpt)

municipals is also shown in the lower right-hand part of the figure. Next to the name of such a fund are shown the average maturity of its holdings, the annual yield based on what was earned over the last seven days, and the aggregate market value of its assets. Not shown, but an important factor in selecting a money market fund, is the degree of safety (that is, default risk) associated with the assets held by each fund.

An Example

In order to highlight the differences in purchasing shares of closed-end funds, no-load funds, and load funds, consider the following example. An investor has $1,000 to use in purchasing shares of a fund and is considering the following funds, all of which have the same net asset value (NAV) of $10 per share.

Closed-end fund *E* is selling for a market price that equals its NAV, whereas closed-end fund *D* is selling at a 20% discount, or $8 (= $10 × .80). The broker charges a commission equal to 2% of the market price for each share purchased. Mutual fund N is a no-load fund, whereas mutual fund L charges an 8½% load. How many shares does the investor end up with in each case?

Closed-end fund E: cost per share = $10 + $.20 commission = $10.20
number of shares = $1,000/$10.20 = 98.04

Closed-end fund D: cost per share = $8 + $.16 commission = $8.16
number of shares = $1,000/$8.16 = 122.55

Mutual fund N: cost per share = $10
number of shares = $1,000/$10 = 100

Mutual Fund L: cost per share = $10 + $.93 load = $10.93
(note: 8.5% × $10.93 = $.93)
number of shares = $1,000/$10.93 = 91.50

Thus the largest number of shares would be received when buying the shares of discounted closed-end fund D, while the fewest shares would be received when buying the shares of load fund L.

22.3   INVESTMENT POLICIES

Different investment companies have different investment objectives (also termed investment styles). Some companies are designed as substitutes for their shareholders' entire portfolio; others expect their shareholders to own other securities. Some restrict their domain or selection methods severely; others give their managers wide latitude. Many engage in highly active management, with substantial portfolio changes designed to exploit perceived superior investment predictions. However, others are more passive, concentrating instead on tailoring a portfolio to serve the interests of a particular clientele.

Although categorization is difficult, broad classes of investment objectives are often defined. As mentioned earlier, money market funds hold short-term (typically less than one year) fixed-income instruments, such as bank certificates of deposit, commercial paper, and Treasury bills. These open-end funds make it possible for small investors to move in and out of the short-term market. The fund manager will extract an annual fee for this service, usually between .25% and 1% of the average value of total assets. There are usually no load charges, and investors may add or remove money from their accounts at almost any time. Dividends are usually declared daily. Arrangements with a cooperating bank often make it possible to write a check on an account, where the bank obtains the amount involved by redeeming "shares" in the fund when the check clears.

Bond funds invest in fixed-income securities. Some go further, specifying that only particular types will be purchased. There are corporate bond funds, U.S. government bond funds, GNMA (or Ginnie Mae) funds, convertible bond funds, and so on. Some are organized as open-end investment companies, others as closed-end investment companies.

Real Estate Investment Trusts

Real estate provides attractive investment opportunities for most institutional investors. Notwithstanding its 1980s boom-and-bust cycle, real estate offers long-lived assets with steady cash flows and a huge, diversified market. The returns on real estate exhibit relatively low correlations with those of stocks and bonds, and a positive correlation with inflation.

Insurance firms, particularly life insurance companies, have long maintained large real estate holdings. Most of their investments consist of "direct deals," where the investor has sole ownership of the properties, perhaps assisted in certain functions by various third parties. Pension funds, both public and private, entered into real estate primarily in the late 1970s and early 1980s. (Cynics will note that this entry coincided with the peak of the real estate pricing cycle.) Although some pension funds engaged in direct deals, most invested through *commingled funds*. These commingled funds are essentially partnerships with other investors. A management firm organizes the partnership and serves as the advisor and manager of the partnership's properties.

The earliest commingled real estate funds (CRFs) were open-end in that participants were permitted to enter and depart at prices based on the appraised value of the CRFs' assets, as determined by the funds' managers. Closed-end funds appeared later and quickly proved more popular. Those CRFs were created with a finite life and an initial subscription amount. Once the fund was formed, no new participants were accepted, nor were existing participants able to liquidate their holdings.

Institutional investors placed billions of dollars in CRFs and smaller amounts in direct deals. CRFs seemed particularly efficient investment vehicles as real estate prices continued to rise. However, as real estate prices began to tumble in the late 1980s, the primary weakness of the CRF structure became readily apparent—very limited or nonexistent liquidity.

Institutional investors found that they could not move out of their real estate investments. Directly owned properties were difficult to sell in a declining market. Closed-end CRFs, of course, never promised that liquidity would be available to participants until the end of the funds' lives. Moreover, secondary markets in participation interests have been frustratingly slow to develop.

Most disappointing were the open-end CRFs. Investors were required to queue up for withdrawals. Few new participants were entering, and the funds' managers were not required to sell properties to meet withdrawal requests unless such sales were in the best interests of the remaining investors. Perhaps more troubling were the prices at which the lucky investors were allowed to withdraw. As appraised property prices tend to lag market prices, in a downward market outgoing investors benefited at the expense of the remaining investors.

The liquidity and valuation problems faced by institutional real estate investors in the late 1980s begged the question: Was there a way that these investors might own real estate through a liquid vehicle with market-determined prices? The answer may lie with an instrument known as *real estate investment trusts* (REITs).

REITs have existed for over 30 years. They are essentially (although not legally) closed-end investment companies that invest in real estate instead of financial assets. Similar to true investment companies, as long as 95% of their income is distributed to shareholders, it is free from taxation. Further, at least 75% of their assets and income must be derived from real estate equity or mortgages. REITs must also have at least 100 shareholders. Their portfolios must be diversified, and no more than 30% of their income may come from selling properties held for less than four years. (This last requirement is designed to prevent REITs from becoming vehicles for real estate speculation.)

REITs engage in a common financial intermediation process known as *securitization*. (Mortgage participation pools—see Chapter 14—are another example.) A REIT manager converts (securitizes) properties into financial assets by purchasing properties (typically 35 to 40) for the REIT. In order to finance the purchases the REIT manager issues freely tradable ownership shares. Returns to REIT investors come from rental income, which is passed on to shareholders, and from property value changes, which are reflected in REIT prices.

REITs offer investors several benefits over direct investments or CRFs. Most importantly, as their shares can be traded on the open market (both through exchanges and over the counter), they provide liquidity and market-determined prices.

Further, REIT boards of directors must have a majority composed of independent outsiders, and REIT shareholders can remove directors if they are dissatisfied with their funds' results. In addition, REIT managers may enter into profit-sharing arrangements with REIT shareholders. As a result, the interests of REIT managers may be better aligned with those of shareholders than is the case under the CRF structure.

Like investment companies that own financial assets, REITs come in many different varieties. Some invest in real estate mortgages; others make equity investments. Most own specific types of properties, such as apartments or retail facilities, in specific geographic areas. Some employ leverage to boost expected returns, whereas others avoid debt financing. Some are traded publicly, whereas others have their shares exchanged on a privately arranged basis.

One important difference between investment companies specializing in financial assets and REITs is that most REITs today are really operating companies. The managers of financial asset investment companies generally do not participate in the operation of the firms whose securities they own. REIT managers, on the other hand, often have extensive real estate management capabilities and oversee the acquisition, property management, and disposition of a portfolio of real estate properties.

Although REITs offer institutional investors many advantages, the key question is whether the REIT market will offer sufficient trading volume to attract large investors. Currently, publicly traded REITs have a total market capitalization of only about $30 billion, with only one REIT worth more than $1 billion. (By comparison, the market capitalization of several U.S. companies is greater than that of the entire REIT market.) Thus even though REIT shares are freely tradable, a large investor may displace the market for a particular REIT's shares if the investor attempts to make a sizable transaction. Trading in REITs has historically not been large enough to accommodate a substantial influx of institutional investors. Instead, the REIT market has been geared toward retail investors.

Nevertheless, if demand increases, ultimately more REIT offerings will occur. Property development firms will package more properties into REITs to finance growth. Some CRFs may convert to a REIT format. Insurance companies and pension funds may create REITs to dispose of unwanted properties. Interestingly, a growing list of mutual funds has been established to invest solely in REITs, thereby producing a situation in which financial investment companies invest in real estate "investment companies." The 1990s could turn out to be the decade of the REITs.

As indicated earlier, the predominant type of unit investment trust in the United States is the bond unit investment trust. Some purchase only government issues, others purchase only corporate issues, and still others specialize to an even greater extent. Municipal bond unit investment trusts often make it easier for those in high tax brackets to obtain diversification and liquidity while taking advantage of the exemption of such securities from personal income taxation. Bond unit investment trusts typically hold securities with different coupon payment schedules and pay roughly equal-size dividends every month.

A few open-end investment companies and some unit investment trusts are restricted to holdings of preferred stocks. Others include both bonds and preferred stocks in their portfolios.

Many open-end companies consider themselves managers for the bulk of the investment assets of their clients. Those that hold both equity and fixed-income securities particularly fit this description. CDA/Wiesenberger Investment Companies Service refers to such companies as balanced funds, provided that at least 25% of their portfolios are invested in bonds. These funds seek to "minimize investment risks without unduly sacrificing possibilities for long-term growth and current income."[9] Somewhat similar to balanced funds are flexible income funds. These funds seek to "provide a liberal current income."[10] Whereas balanced funds typically hold relatively constant mixes of bonds, preferred stock, convertible bonds, and common stocks flexible income funds often alter the proportions periodically in attempts to "time the market." Similar to these flexible funds are asset allocation funds, which also attempt to time the market but, in doing so, focus on total return instead of current income.

A diversified common stock fund invests most of its assets in common stocks, although some short-term money market instruments may be held to accommodate irregular cash flows or to engage in market timing. In 1993 CDA/Wiesenberger classified the majority of diversified common stock funds as having one of three types of objectives: (1) capital gain, (2) growth, or (3) growth and income.[11] Two factors appear to be involved in this classification: the relative importance of dividend income versus capital gains and the overall level of risk taken. The classifications "are arranged in descending order of emphasis on capital appreciation and, consequently, in ascending order of the importance placed on current income and relative price stability."[12] Because high-dividend portfolios are generally less risky than portfolios with low dividends, relatively few major conflicts arise, although two rather different criteria are involved. It should also be mentioned that there is another class, equity income funds, that CDA/Wiesenberger describes as seeking to generate a stream of current income by investing in stocks with sizable dividend yields.

Borderline cases remain: "The difference between a capital gain fund and a growth fund is a matter of degree, and in some cases there is little distinction. Similarly, there is no sharp line of demarcation between a growth fund and a growth-income fund."[13] Classification is difficult because the official statement of investment objectives in a fund's prospectus is often fuzzy.

A few specialized investment companies concentrate on the securities of firms in a particular *industry* or *sector*. For example, there are chemical funds, aerospace funds, technology funds, and gold funds. Others deal in securities of a particular type; examples include funds that hold restricted (that is, "letter") stock, funds that invest in over-the-counter stocks, and funds that invest in the stocks of smaller companies. Still others provide a convenient means for holding the securities of firms in a particular *country*, such as the previously mentioned France and Korea funds. There are also investment companies that, by design, invest more widely internationally, purchasing stocks and bonds from a variety of different countries. (From a U.S. viewpoint, international funds are those investing in non-U.S. securities, whereas global funds invest in both U.S. and non-U.S. securities.)[14]

Although municipal bond unit investment trusts have been available for many years, open-end municipal bond funds were first offered in 1976. Some municipal bond funds hold long-term issues from many states. Others specialize in the long-term issues of governmental units in one state ("single-state" funds) in order to provide an investment vehicle for residents of that state who wish to avoid paying state taxes (as well as federal taxes) on the income. Still others buy short-term municipal securities (as noted in Figure 22.3), with some specializing in the short-term issues of governmental units in one state.

An index fund attempts to provide results similar or identical to those computed for a specified market index. For example, the *Vanguard Index 500 Trust,* a no-load open-end investment company, provides a vehicle for small investors who wish to obtain results matching those of Standard & Poor's 500-stock index, less operating expenses. Similarly, a number of banks have established commingled index funds, and corporations and other organizations have set up index funds for their own employee retirement trust funds.

Table 22.1 provides an indication of the number of mutual funds pursuing various kinds of investment objectives, along with the amount of assets under their control. In total there were nearly 4,000 mutual funds in existence at year-end 1992. At that time these funds had nearly $1.6 trillion invested in a variety of financial assets.

TABLE 22.1
MUTUAL FUND CLASSIFICATIONS AS OF YEAR-END 1992

Classification	Number of Funds	Total Assets (in billions)
A. Classification by assets:		
Equity	1,354	$475.4
Bond and income	1,630	580.9
Taxable money market	585	448.7
Tax-exempt money market	279	94.9
Total	3,848	$1,599.9
B. Classification by investment objectives:		
Aggressive growth	233	$83.4
Growth	429	133.2
Growth and Income	345	168.3
Precious metals	32	2.1
International	138	22.9
Global—equity	98	23.0
Income—equity	79	42.5
Flexible portfolio	59	14.8
Balanced	99	31.9
Income—mixed	106	34.7
Income—bond	156	39.8
U.S. government income	257	120.1
Ginnie Mae	77	57.5
Global bond	87	31.6
Corporate bond	71	20.0
High-yield bond	89	34.3
Long-term municipal bond	216	110.8
State municipal bond—long-term	413	85.4
Taxable money market	585	448.7
Tax-exempt money market	279	94.9
Total	3,848	$1,599.9

Source: Adapted from *1993 Mutual Fund Fact Book* (Washington, DC: Investment Company Institute, 1993): pp. 33, 100–101, 104. Used with permission of the Investment Company Institute.

CHAPTER 22

22.4.1   Taxation

The U.S. Internal Revenue Code allows an investment company to avoid corporate income taxation. A unit investment trust, a closed-end investment company, or an open-end investment company can qualify under Subchapter M of the code as a regulated investment company by meeting the following standards:

1. It is a domestic corporation.
2. It is registered according to the Investment Company Act of 1940.
3. At least 90% of its gross income comes from investing in financial assets.
4. No more than 30% of its gross income can come from selling securities that are held for less than three months.
5. At the end of each quarter at least 50% of its funds must be invested in a diversified manner, meaning that:
   a. Within this 50% portion of the portfolio, no single issuer's securities may account for more than 5% of the fund's assets.
   b. Within this 50% portion, the fund may not own more than 10% of the voting shares of any single issuer. (The other 50% portion is unrestricted so as to encourage funds to invest in small companies.)

By meeting these standards, and by paying at least 90% of its net income to its stockholders, the investment company will not have to pay any taxes. Instead, its stockholders must pay taxes on the income that they receive. Most investment companies choose to distribute their net income by making two kinds of cash payments to their shareholders—one for income (from dividends and interest that the fund has received) and one for net realized capital gains. These two payments are then taxed at the shareholder level as ordinary income and capital gains, respectively.

22.4.2   Accumulation Plans

Whereas an investor can purchase shares in a fund and receive all distributions in cash, this is only one of many possible arrangements. Mutual funds offer several types of plans to satisfy investors' desires for different patterns of contributions and withdrawals over time. Accumulation plans are designed for those who do not want to receive any income or capital gains distributions in cash over some period of time. The simplest procedure involves automatic reinvestment of these distributions, where the shareholder elects to receive additional shares in the fund instead of cash. As with other plans, this often involves fractional shares, but since accounts are maintained via computerized records, this poses no problem.

Voluntary accumulation plans allow an investor to add to an account as desired, subject only to some minimum amount that must be invested each time. Alternatively, a fixed dollar amount may be invested at periodic intervals—in some cases via automatic bank transfers.

Contractual accumulation plans call for a fixed amount to be contributed at regular intervals (usually monthly) over a relatively long period (often five or more years). Sales charges may or may not be lower than those applicable to a voluntary accumulation plan. The investor is not legally bound to make all the payments, but because a large proportion of early contributions typically goes toward sales charges, commitment to a contractual plan should not be considered if cancellation is at all likely.

The Investment Company Amendments Act of 1970 placed limits on the load charges for contractual plans. Specifically, no more than 50% of the first year's contribution may be allocated to sales charges (that is, at least half must be invested in fund shares). Moreover, if a 50% "front-end" load charge is assessed in the first year, cancellation of the plan within 18 months entitles the investor to a partial refund, reducing the effective charge to 15% of the amount initially contributed.

A few funds offer insurance with their contractual accumulation plans. This insurance provides the remaining contributions if the investor dies or is disabled before all of the contracted payments have been made. The premium for such insurance is, in effect, added to the sales charge.[15]

22.4.3   Retirement Plans

Accumulation of funds for retirement may be accomplished via an individual retirement account (IRA) or a Keogh plan. In 1993 anyone could contribute up to $2,000 of his or her earned income to an IRA, and if the income earner's spouse has no earned income, a total of $2,250 could be contributed to two IRAs. No taxes are paid on the earnings of such funds until the investor begins making withdrawals. Furthermore, under certain circumstances the investor can deduct the amount contributed from gross income when personal income taxes are being calculated.[16]

Self-employed individuals can contribute 25% of their net annual earnings from self-employment (up to a maximum of $30,000 annually) to a Keogh plan account, with such contributions also deductible from gross income for tax purposes. Either type of account is maintained by a custodian, often a bank. Contributions and any cash received from investments are invested in accordance with the investor's desires. Funds may be withdrawn beginning at age 59½, and withdrawals must begin by age 70½.

22.4.4   Exchange Privileges

It is increasingly common to find several investment companies operating as a "family of funds." An investor may purchase shares in more than one of the funds under common management and also may exchange shares of one fund for another. For a family of load funds, sales charges for such exchanges are typically lower than those applicable to similar transactions involving funds managed by different companies. In some cases, exchanges within a family of load funds may be made without charge.

In this situation the investor is given the opportunity to make timing decisions, switching shares from one fund to another one that he or she believes is underpriced at that time. For example, consider an investor who owns shares of a gold fund that is in a family that includes a technology fund. If the investor feels that technology stocks are, in general, quite underpriced, then the investor could exchange the gold fund shares for technology fund shares. Usually sponsors of families of funds reserve the right to either limit the amount of transfers that an investor can make between funds in order to avoid blatant abuses of the switching privileges or levy a fee for such transfers.

22.4.5 Withdrawal Plans

Many mutual funds offer voluntary withdrawal plans. The investor instructs the fund to pay out either a fixed amount or a specified percentage of the account's value periodically (for example, monthly), decreasing the number of shares that the investor owns in the process.

22.5   MUTUAL FUND PERFORMANCE

Mutual funds are required to compute and publicize their net asset values daily. Because their income and their capital gain distributions are also publicized, they are ideal candidates for studies of the performance of professionally managed portfolios. Thus it is hardly surprising that mutual funds have frequently been the subject of extensive study.

22.5.1 Calculating Returns

In studies of performance, the rate of return on a mutual fund for period t is calculated by adding the change in net asset value to the amount of income and the capital gains distributions made during the period, denoted by I_t and G_t, respectively, and dividing this total by the net asset value at the beginning of the period:

$$r_t = \frac{(\text{NAV}_t - \text{NAV}_{t-1}) + I_t + G_t}{\text{NAV}_{t-1}}. \tag{22.2}$$

For example, a mutual fund that had a net asset value of $10 at the beginning of month t, made income and capital gain distributions of, respectively, $.05 and $.04 per share during the month, and then ended the month with a net asset value of $10.03 would have a monthly return of:

$$r_t = \frac{(\$10.03 - \$10.00) + \$.05 + \$.04}{\$10.00}$$

$$= 1.20\%.$$

It should be noted that returns calculated in this manner can be used to evaluate the performance of the portfolio manager of a mutual fund because this indicates the results of the manager's investment decisions. However, it does not necessarily indicate the return earned by the shareholders in the fund, as there may have been a load charge involved. In the example, perhaps the investor paid $10.50 at the beginning of the month for one share of this fund, with $.50 being a front-end load. If this were the case, the investor's return for this month is calculated using Equation (22.2), where NAV_{t-1} is $10.50, not $10.00:

$$r_t = \frac{(\$10.03 - \$10.50) + \$.05 + \$.04}{\$10.50}$$

$$= -3.62\%.$$

Thus the return for the investor who bought one share at the beginning of the month and paid a $.50 per share load charge at that time would be -3.62%. However, the portfolio manager was only given $10.00 per share to invest, because the load charge was paid to certain people who were responsible for getting the investor to buy the share. Accordingly, the portfolio manager should be evaluated on the basis of the return provided on the $10.00, which in this example was 1.20%.

Recently data on professionally managed pension funds and bank commingled funds have become available. The performance of the managers of such funds appears to be similar to that of mutual fund managers: They do reasonably well tailoring portfolios to meet clients' objectives, but few seem to be able to consistently "beat the market." Although the following sections deal only with U.S. mutual funds, many of the results apply to other investment companies, both in the United States and in other countries. A more detailed discussion of certain risk-adjusted measures of performance and their application to mutual funds is deferred to Chapter 25.

22.5.2 Risk Control

One of the functions that a mutual fund can perform for its investors is the maintenance of a particular risk posture. Formal statements of objectives provide some idea of a fund's intended posture, but often the wording is vague. Nevertheless, there appears to be a general relationship between portfolio risk and stated objectives.

Figure 22.4 summarizes information on the standard deviations of monthly excess returns over a ten-year period for funds with similar objectives, using classifications assigned by CDA/Wiesenberger at the beginning of the period. In particular, the monthly returns for each one of 123 mutual funds were calculated using Equation (22.2). Then, using these 120 monthly returns, the standard deviation was calculated for each one of the funds. Each rectangular horizontal bar in the figure plots the range of values of the standard deviations for funds having the same objective, with the average standard deviation being shown by a square near the middle of the bar. Generally, the lower the amount of promised risk, the lower the amount of actual risk. (A similar-looking figure resulted when beta was used.) However, the overlapping of some of the bars indicates that some funds with more conservative objectives experienced more volatility than others with less conservative objectives.

22.5.3 Diversification

An important task for any investment manager is the provision of an appropriate degree of portfolio diversification. The correct amount depends on the proportion of clients' funds managed and on the likelihood that superior abnormal returns can be obtained by sacrificing diversification. As most mutual funds are

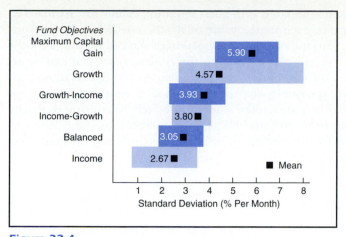

Figure 22.4

Risk versus Fund Objectives: 123 Mutual Funds, 1960–1969

Source: John G. McDonald, "Objectives and Performance of Mutual Funds, 1960–1969," *Journal of Financial and Quantitative Analysis*, 9, no. 3 (June 1974): p. 316.

intended to be a major component of a shareholder's portfolio, it is reasonable to expect them to be substantially diversified.

Figure 22.5 shows that many are. Excess returns (that is, returns above or below the riskfree rate) were calculated quarterly over a five-year period for 100

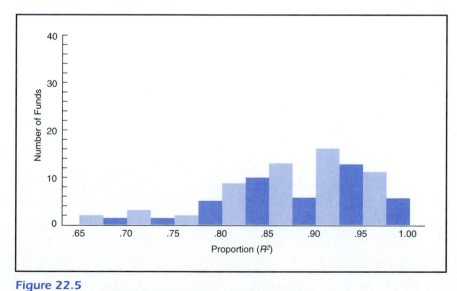

Figure 22.5

Proportion of Variation in Quarterly Returns Attributable to Market Fluctuations: 100 Mutual Funds, 1970–1974

Source: Merrill Lynch, Pierce, Fenner & Smith, Inc., *Investment Performance Analysis, Comparative Survey, 1970–1974*. Reprinted by permission.

common stock funds and compared with corresponding values for Standard & Poor's 500-stock index. For each fund a value of R^2, the coefficient of determination, was computed. This indicates the proportion of the variation in a fund's excess returns (that is, returns above or below the riskfree rate) that can be attributed to variations in excess returns on the index. As the figure shows, approximately 90% of the quarter-by-quarter variation in a typical fund's excess returns was associated with swings in the value of the S&P 500 during this period, with values ranging from 66% to 98%. Lower correlations have been observed for funds that invest internationally or in sectors (such as gold funds that invest in gold-mining stocks).[17]

22.5.4 Average Return

Some organizations have established two kinds of indices based on the net asset values of mutual funds that have similar investment objectives. One kind of index is based on nearly all of the U.S.-based mutual funds, whereas the second kind is based on a much smaller sample. As shown in Figure 22.6, this comparison is done every week (and, more extensively, every quarter) in *Barron's*, where mutual fund indices that have been prepared by Lipper Analytical Services are published. Note that the first three parts of the figure (General Equity Funds, Other Equity Funds, and Other Funds) present broad-based indices, whereas the last part (Lipper Indexes) presents narrower-based indices. Just above the last part are a set of stock market indices made up of U.S. and foreign stocks. Unfortunately, with the exception of the American Stock Exchange (ASE) Index, all of the U.S. indices are presented without giving any consideration to the dividends paid on the underlying stocks. Because the mutual fund indices do consider dividends, they are not directly comparable to the stock market indices.

Many studies have compared the performance of investment companies that have invested primarily in common stocks with the performance of a **benchmark portfolio** that generally consisted of a combination of (1) a market index, such as Standard & Poor's 500-stock index, and (2) a riskfree asset, such as Treasury bills. Each particular combination was chosen so that the benchmark portfolio had a risk level that was equal to that of the investment company. Thus an investment company that had a beta of .80 would be compared with a benchmark portfolio that had 80% invested in the market index and 20% in the riskfree asset.[18]

One way of determining whether or not a mutual fund has had superior performance is to subtract the average return on the benchmark portfolio from the average return of the mutual fund. This amount is known as the fund's **ex post alpha,** denoted α_p:

$$\alpha_p = ar_p - ar_{bp} \tag{22.3}$$

where ar_p is the average return on portfolio p and ar_{bp} is the average return on the benchmark portfolio associated with portfolio p. Note that if $\alpha_p > 0$, then the portfolio will have performed well because it will have had positive risk-adjusted returns. Conversely, if $\alpha_p < 0$, then the portfolio will have had inferior returns.

LIPPER MUTUAL FUND PERFORMANCE AVERAGES

Weekly Summary Report: April 7, 1994
Cumulative Performances With Dividends Reinvested

NAV Mil. $	No. Funds		10/11/90-4/07/94		7/12/90-4/07/94		4/08/93-4/07/94		12/31/93-4/07/94		3/31/94-4/07/94
General Equity Funds:											
40,067.3	155	Capital Appreciation	+ 94.25%	+	49.13%	+	12.84%	−	1.75%	+	1.73%
173,318.0	476	Growth Funds	+ 80.46%	+	41.94%	+	8.73%	−	1.73%	+	1.75%
27,936.4	81	Mid Cap Funds	+ 123.13%	+	64.94%	+	16.77%	−	1.14%	+	2.14%
29,763.0	218	Small Company Growth	+ 127.15%	+	62.54%	+	16.89%	−	1.01%	+	2.06%
174,989.4	362	Growth and Income	+ 72.41%	+	42.20%	+	6.64%	−	1.86%	+	1.39%
17,873.1	40	S&P 500 Objective	+ 67.01%	+	36.49%	+	4.37%	−	2.79%	+	1.18%
60,740.8	100	Equity Income	+ 67.21%	+	41.68%	+	4.68%	−	2.78%	+	1.00%
524,688.0	1432	Gen. Equity Funds Avg.	+ 86.24%	+	46.32%	+	9.86%	−	1.72%	+	1.66%
Other Equity Funds:											
4,409.5	16	Health/Biotechnology	+ 79.52%	+	51.00%	+	23.90%	−	2.89%	+	1.61%
2,235.5	29	Natural Resources	+ 21.50%	+	13.27%	+	4.98%	−	2.79%	+	0.81%
280.5	11	Environmental	+ 18.20%	−	8.41%	+	1.03%	−	3.76%	+	0.75%
4,035.6	25	Science & Technol.	+ 163.20%	+	78.14%	+	28.92%	+	4.47%	+	3.07%
2,385.5	26	Specialty/Misc.	+ 112.12%	+	60.45%	+	16.16%	−	1.65%	+	1.24%
27,248.1	73	Utility Funds	+ 52.13%	+	45.13%	−	2.60%	−	6.81%	+	0.05%
1,903.0	14	Financial Services	+ 187.43%	+	114.61%	+	1.72%	−	1.95%	+	1.06%
970.4	11	Real Estate	+ 88.67%	+	51.89%	+	8.29%	+	1.27%	+	0.94%
5,774.7	34	Gold Oriented Funds	+ 35.81%	+	28.57%	+	37.27%	−	7.24%	−	2.67%
32,039.9	97	Global Funds	+ 53.47%	+	30.14%	+	19.73%	−	2.13%	+	0.23%
4,833.4	15	Global Small Co. Funds	+ 84.76%	+	48.83%	+	27.45%	−	0.14%	+	0.23%
45,275.2	165	International Funds	+ 44.56%	+	23.24%	+	22.45%	−	1.05%	+	0.00%
5,298.6	33	European Region Fds	+ 23.54%	+	5.29%	+	21.64%	+	3.06%	−	0.03%
11,322.9	41	Pacific Region Funds	+ 67.27%	+	38.00%	+	29.82%	−	10.98%	+	0.63%
6,177.8	19	Emerging Markets Funds	+ 96.27%	+	54.48%	+	40.25%	−	10.30%	−	2.29%
953.7	7	Japanese Funds	+ 9.15%	−	12.03%	+	16.94%	+	17.69%	+	0.35%
2,246.2	10	Latin American Funds	N/A%		N/A%	+	41.04%	−	7.21%	−	4.68%
142.3	2	Canadian Funds	+ 36.80%	+	25.63%	+	16.19%	−	2.60%	+	0.35%
114,064.7	423	World Equity Funds Avg.	+ 45.42%	+	24.99%	+	24.93%	−	2.74%	−	0.31%
682,220.8	2060	All Equity Funds Avg.	+ 79.95%	+	43.52%	+	12.74%	−	2.06%	+	1.18%
Other Funds:											
23,562.8	114	Flexible Portfolio	+ 60.98%	+	42.35%	+	5.73%	−	2.20%	+	0.76%
8,339.7	25	Global Flex Port.	+ 46.48%	+	34.52%	+	12.39%	−	3.18%	+	0.31%
47,075.6	155	Balanced Funds	+ 60.74%	+	41.75%	+	4.92%	−	2.53%	+	0.77%
976.5	9	Balanced Target	+ 64.82%	+	44.84%	+	4.46%	−	3.65%	+	0.41%
3,705.8	26	Conv. Securities	+ 82.02%	+	55.76%	+	8.78%	−	1.43%	+	0.43%
13,666.3	21	Income Funds	+ 56.71%	+	45.53%	+	3.71%	−	2.80%	+	0.26%
34,508.7	156	World Income Funds	+ 25.86%	+	33.97%	+	3.74%	−	4.26%	−	0.28%
344,469.3	1135	Fixed Income Funds	+ 43.85%	+	41.01%	+	2.31%	−	2.67%	−	0.46%
1,158,525.5	3701	Long-Term Average	+ 66.57%	+	42.59%	+	8.51%	−	2.37%	+	0.57%
		Long-Term Median	+ 58.70%	+	39.20%	+	5.20%	−	2.40%	+	0.40%
		Funds with % Change	1635		1589		2869		3530		3604

Securities Market Indexes

Value	U.S. Equities:										
3693.26	Dow Jones Ind. Avg. xd		+	56.16	+	24.36	+	8.74	−	1.62	+	1.58
450.88	S&P 500 xd		+	52.60	+	23.38	+	2.05	−	3.34	+	1.15
527.43	S&P 400 xd		+	52.06	+	21.70	+	5.07	−	2.38	+	1.18
250.22	NYSE Composite xd		+	54.27	+	25.54	+	2.62	−	3.42	+	1.28
441.76	ASE Index		+	50.41	+	21.96	+	6.13	−	7.42	−	0.31
255.95	Russell 2000 Index xd		+	113.26	+	51.07	+	14.86	−	1.02	+	1.95
Value	**International Equities:**										
2,201.41	DAX Index		+	54.12	+	14.88	+	32.96	−	2.88	+	3.20
3,129.00	FT S-E 100 Index		+	48.84	+	32.00	+	10.89	−	8.47	+	1.38
1,989.09	Nikkei 225 Average xd		−	11.93	−	38.94	−	0.38	+	14.20	+	4.08

xd–Price only index. Calculated without reinvestment of dividends. The Nikkei index value is divided by 10 due to space limitation. Source: Lipper Analytical Services Inc., Summit, New Jersey 07901

Figure 22.6
Mutual Fund Indices

LIPPER MUTUAL FUND PERFORMANCE REPORTS

Weekly Summary Report: April 7, 1994

NAV Mil. $	No. Funds		10/11/90-4/07/94	7/12/90-4/07/94	4/08/93-4/07/94	12/31/93-4/07/94	3/31/94-4/07/94
Value		**Lipper Indexes:**					
425.22	30	Capital Apprec Index	+ 87.39%	+ 48.69%	+ 14.67%	− 1.26%	+ 2.10%
756.55	30	Growth Fund Index	+ 84.66%	+ 45.60%	+ 11.07%	− 1.28%	+ 2.17%
434.04	30	Small Co Growth Index	+ 115.13%	+ 57.32%	+ 17.31%	− 1.58%	+ 1.96%
1,138.06	30	Growth & Income Index	+ 75.11%	+ 45.80%	+ 7.72%	− 1.98%	+ 1.41%
766.57	30	Equity Income Index	+ 66.52%	+ 45.87%	+ 5.10%	− 2.44%	+ 1.04%
333.12	10	Sci & Tech Index	+ 142.09%	+ 68.37%	+ 26.12%	+ 0.90%	+ 2.63%
399.92	30	Global Fund Index	+ 50.47%	+ 25.41%	+ 21.93%	− 1.79%	+ 0.37%
466.45	30	International Index	+ 47.58%	+ 26.22%	+ 25.54%	− 1.92%	− 0.29%
199.48	10	Gold Fund Index	+ 40.77%	+ 32.30%	+ 38.55%	− 8.43%	− 2.69%
845.50	30	Balanced Fund Index	+ 61.36%	+ 42.30%	+ 5.18%	− 2.09%	+ 0.88%
191.71	10	Conv Secur Index	+ 69.87%	+ 47.25%	+ 6.04%	− 7.06%	+ 0.50%

Source: Lipper Analytical Services Inc., Summit, New Jersey 07901

Figure 22.6 (continued)

Figure 22.7(a) shows the distribution of ex post alpha values for 70 mutual funds, based on monthly returns from 1955 through 1964. The average value was .09% per year, suggesting that the typical fund provided approximately the same return as a market-based passive fund with a constant beta equal to the fund's average beta. Of the 70 funds, 40 had positive ex post alphas and 30 had negative ex post alphas.

Different time periods give slightly different results. Figure 22.7(b) shows the distribution of ex post alphas based on monthly returns for 125 funds from 1960 through 1969. The average alpha was .05% per month (or about .60% per year) and slightly over half (53%) of the funds had positive ex post alphas.

Figure 22.7(c) provides a third example. It shows returns for 100 funds based on quarterly returns from 1970 through 1974. The average ex post alpha was − .50% per quarter (or approximately −2.00% per year), and only 20 of the funds had positive alphas.

Although not shown in the figure, two more recent studies of mutual funds that invest in common stocks reached similar conclusions. In the first study, annual returns for 143 mutual funds from 1965 through 1984 were examined. The average ex post alpha was − .88% per year, and only 44 of the funds had positive alphas. The second study, using monthly returns from April 1979 through March 1989, found the average ex post alpha value to be equal to − .062% per month (or − .74% per year), with only 115 out of 257 funds having positive alphas.[19]

These results collectively suggest that the average mutual fund has not significantly outperformed an equal-risk passive alternative over any extended period.[20] This is not too surprising. After all, the market's performance is itself an average of the performance of all investors. If, on average, mutual funds had "beaten" the market, then some other group of investors would have "lost" to the market. With the substantial amount of professional management in today's stock market, it is difficult to think of a likely group of victims.

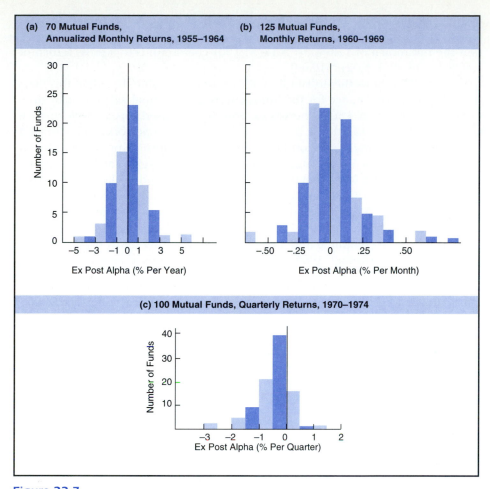

Figure 22.7

Mutual Fund Performance: Ex Post Alpha Values

Source: (a) Adapted from Norman E. Mains, "Risk, the Pricing of Capital Assets, and the Evaluation of Investment Portfolios: Comment," *Journal of Business*, 50, no. 3 (July 1977): pp. 378–80 ©The University of Chicago, 1977. (b) United States Securities and Exchange Commission, *Institutional Investor Study Report*, March 10, 1971 (Washington, DC: U.S. Government Printing Office). (c) Merrill Lynch, Pierce, Fenner & Smith, Inc., *Investment Performance Analysis, Comparative Study, 1970–1974*.

22.5.5 Expenses

Funds typically incur two kinds of expenses. Management fees, administrative expenses, and other operating expenses are direct and generally reported. However transaction costs are only partly measurable in that brokerage commissions are reported, but implicit costs such as bid-ask spreads and the price impacts of trading are often not even estimated.

By adding operating expenses and explicit transaction costs to a fund's rate of return, it is possible to obtain an estimate of its gross performance (that is, its performance based on the assumption that such expenses were nonexistent). This is done by adding to the numerator of Equation (22.2) the per share values of such expenses. In the example shown earlier, perhaps the fund had paid expenses of this nature totaling $.02 per share during month t. In such a situation the net return of 1.20% ($= $.12/$10.00$) corresponds to a gross return of 1.40% [$= ($.12 + $.02)/$10.00$].

Figure 22.8 shows the distribution of ex post alpha values based on this measure of gross performance for the funds covered in the analysis previously summarized in Figure 22.7(a). Whereas ex post alphas based on *net* performance averaged .09% per year, the ex post alphas based on *gross* performance averaged 1.07% per year. Moreover, 50 of the 70 funds had positive ex post alphas based on gross performance. This suggests that portfolio managers might have some skill, but not enough to recoup the operating expenses and brokerage costs that are incurred in hiring them and carrying out their buy and sell orders.

A study by the Securities and Exchange Commission attempted to estimate the relationship between several factors and portfolio performance.[21] Ex post alpha values were computed and analyzed for 132 mutual funds using monthly returns from 1965 through 1969. The following observations were made:

1. Larger funds performed no better, other things being equal, than smaller funds, where size is measured by the dollar value of the fund's total assets.

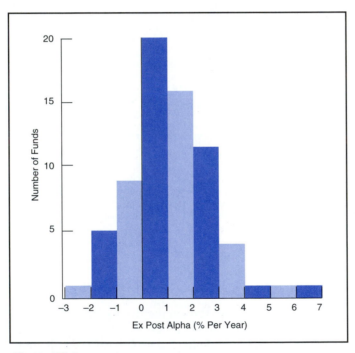

Figure 22.8

Mutual Fund Performance: Ex Post Alpha Values Based on Gross Returns

Source: Adapted from Norman E. Mains, "Risk, the Pricing of Capital Assets, and the Evaluation of Investment Portfolios: Comment," *Journal of Business*, 50, no. 3 (July 1977): pp. 378–380 ©The University of Chicago, 1977.

2. Funds with load charges performed no better, other things being equal, than those with no load charges. Because of the load charge, investors in load funds consequently did worse than those in no-load funds.
3. Funds with higher **portfolio turnover rates** had lower levels of performance. (A fund's portfolio turnover rate is the ratio of the smaller of purchases or sales during a time period divided by the average total asset value during the period, and hence is a measure of how much trading was done during that period.)

More recently another study confirmed some of these results.[22] Examining the returns from 1965 through 1984, 143 mutual funds were divided into two groups based on whether or not they had a load charge. The average ex post alpha value of the load funds was -1.6%; for no-load funds it was $-.8\%$. This suggests that funds with load charges do not on average earn sufficiently higher returns to justify investors' buying their shares.

The 143 funds were also divided into five groups based on the size of their operating expense ratios. Then the average ex post alpha value was calculated for each group. Going from the highest to the lowest expense group, these values were equal to -3.9%, -1.7%, $-.7\%$, -1.2%, and $-.6\%$. Note that with one exception there is a perfect ordering between performance and expenses—lower expenses are associated with better (but still negative) performance.

The mutual funds were again divided into five groups, but this time the division was based on the size of their turnover ratios. Again the average ex post alpha value was calculated for each group. Going from the highest to the lowest turnover group, these values were equal to -2.2%, -1.9%, -2.2%, -1.1%, and $-.6\%$. Like the expense ratio results, there is a perfect ordering (again with one exception) between performance and turnover—lower turnover is associated with better performance.

One reasonable explanation for these observations is that in an efficient market, higher expense ratios and more frequent revisions will cause a fund to incur more costs, but without being able to consistently earn gains from the purchase of underpriced securities as an offset. Furthermore, whereas revisions in a fund's portfolio may be desirable so as to maintain a desired risk level or dividend yield, the evidence indicates that revisions intended to exploit supposed market inefficiencies generally prove unproductive because of the associated transaction costs.

22.5.6 Market Timing

To achieve superior portfolio performance, an investor must either select securities that outperform others of comparable risk or switch from risk class to risk class at appropriate times. The latter strategy is often called market timing or asset allocation (discussed more fully in Chapter 24). The idea is to hold a high-beta portfolio prior to market rises and a low-beta portfolio prior to market declines. This is typically done by altering the relative proportions that the fund has invested in stocks, bonds, and cash equivalents. Typically the more a fund has invested in stocks, the higher its beta.

In a study of the performance of 57 mutual funds over the period from 1953 through 1962, only one was found with a record suggesting any significant ability to time the market.[23] A later study of the performance of 116 funds from February 1968 through June 1980 found that only three funds had significant timing ability over the entire period, with only one fund having a record indicating significant market timing ability in both the first half and the second half of the period.[24] Furthermore, a recent study of 257 funds from April 1979 through March 1989 indicates that the average fund had negative timing ability.[25] This suggests that the average fund might have been better off if its timing activities had been the exact opposite of what was actually done.

Such results are not surprising. If many funds were consistently successful at market timing, they would have shown up in the previously mentioned tests for superior overall performance unless they were consistently engaging in inferior security selection that offset their superior timing ability. However, such a situation seems highly improbable. More likely, investment managers find it as difficult to time the market as to select underpriced securities. Such is the lot of an investor in a highly efficient market.

22.5.7 Bond Mutual Funds

All of the results reported so far focus on mutual funds that have at least a large part of their assets invested in common stocks. This leaves open the question of bond mutual funds: Is their performance similar to that of stock funds? One study looked at a sample of 41 bond funds over the period from 1979 through 1988.[26]

Using a variety of models to produce benchmark returns, the average ex post alpha value ranged from $-.023\%$ to $-.069\%$ per month. Furthermore, regardless of the model, at least two-thirds of the funds had negative alphas. Expanding the sample to cover 223 bond funds over the period of 1987 to 1991 produced similar results. It was determined that there was an inverse relationship between the size of a fund's expense ratio and its performance—that is, higher expenses tended to be associated with worse performance. In summary it appears that the results regarding stock funds are also applicable to bond funds.

22.5.8 Persistence of Performance

Even if the average mutual fund displays no ability at selecting underpriced securities or timing the market, it is still possible that a few of the funds do have such abilities. If so, they should continually generate higher returns and rank at or near the top of their peer groups over consecutive nonoverlapping evaluation periods.

Persistence of Returns

One study carefully examined the quarterly excess returns of 165 mutual funds from 1974 through 1988 in order to see whether funds with relatively high returns in one period tended to have relatively high returns in the next period.[27] These funds had invested primarily in common stocks with objectives of either growth, growth and income, or aggressive growth.

In the study each fund was placed in one of eight groups based on its excess return over the first quarter of 1974. Then the excess return of each group was measured for the second quarter of 1974 by averaging the excess returns of the funds in that group. The process was then repeated, except that funds were assigned to one of eight groups based on their quarterly excess returns for the second quarter of 1974, and then the average fund excess return for each group was calculated for the third quarter of 1974. This process was repeated through the fourth quarter of 1988, resulting in a set of quarterly excess returns for each group ranging from the second quarter of 1974 through the fourth quarter of 1988. At this point average excess quarterly returns for these eight groups were calculated over the entire period.

The top line of Table 22.2 displays the results. Mutual funds that were in the bottom one-eighth (group 1) had an average quarterly excess return of 1.42% in the quarter after they were ranked in the bottom. Conversely, mutual funds that ranked in the top one-eighth (group 8) had an average quarterly excess return of 2.67% in the quarter after their top ranking. Glancing at the other averages indicates that mutual funds that did better in one quarter were likely to do better in the next quarter.

The evidence presented in the next three lines of the table is even stronger. Consider the second line. Here funds were assigned to one of eight groups based on their excess returns over the previous two quarters, and then their excess returns were recorded over the next quarter. Note again how it appears that mutual funds that did better over two quarters were more likely to do better in the next quarter. The last two lines were similarly constructed, except that the assignment of the funds to groups was based on their excess returns over the previous four and eight months, respectively.

Of particular interest is the extreme difference in the sizes of the average excess returns in groups 1 and 8. For formation periods of at least four quarters, the difference is more than 2% per quarter, with the largest difference for four quarters. This suggests that an investor should be concerned with short-term relative

TABLE 22.2

CONSECUTIVE-PERIOD RETURNS FOR MUTUAL FUNDS, 1974–1988

Formation Period (# of Quarters)	Subsequent Average Excess Quarterly Rate of Return							
	Group Number (#1 = Worst; #8 = Best)							
	1	2	3	4	5	6	7	8
One	1.42%	1.66%	1.84%	1.91%	2.11%	2.45%	2.41%	2.67%
Two	1.33	1.73	1.81	1.99	2.07	1.99	2.33	3.24
Four	.99	1.68	1.40	1.82	1.90	2.32	2.94	3.47
Eight	.69	1.05	1.40	1.76	1.59	2.24	2.11	2.80

Source: Adapted from Darryll Hendricks, Jayendu Patel, and Richard Zeckhauser, "Hot Hands in Mutual Funds: Short-Run Persistence of Relative Performance, 1974–1988," *Journal of Finance*, 48, no. 1 (March 1993): Table III, pp. 108–109.

performance, avoiding mutual funds that are in the bottom octile, while seeking those that are in the top octile (or two), based on the funds' returns over the past four quarters. Similar results were obtained when various risk-adjusted measures of performance, such as ex post alphas, were used. However, it is important to remember that these results are based on averages, and that individual funds can differ significantly from these averages. In other words, there are no assurances that top performing funds will continue to do so.

Persistence of Rankings

Another study looked at the performance rankings of broad-based equity funds in consecutive time periods.[28] For each year beginning in 1976 each mutual fund in a sample of 258 was labeled either "winner" or "loser" based on whether its return was in the top or bottom half. This continued through 1988, by which time the sample had grown to 728 funds. Then fund labels were compared to see what labels the winners and losers received in adjacent years. The results are shown in Table 22.3.

If there is persistence in performance, then substantially more than half the winners in year t should be winners in year $t + 1$ (and substantially less than half should be losers). Similarly, substantially more than half of the losers should remain losers in the next year. The table shows that this is what happened. Over 55% of the winners remained winners and losers remained losers. Even more dramatic results were obtained as adjacent two-year and three-year periods were examined, when about 60% of the winners remained winners in the next period. As for losers, over two-year periods about 60% of them remained losers and over three years over 70% of them remained losers. These results were confirmed when using subgroups of funds and risk-adjusted measures of performance. However, it should again be noted that about 40% of the three-year winners turned into losers over the next three years, indicating that there is plenty of uncertainty about good performance continuing into the future.

Instead of looking at above-average funds, another study looked at only the best performing funds.[29] Specifically, for each year beginning in 1982 the top 20 funds were identified based on their annual returns that year. Then their rank was determined for the next year based on their annual return then, and the process was repeated through 1992. The average rank of the top 20 funds in the

TABLE 22.3
CONSECUTIVE-PERIOD RANKINGS FOR MUTUAL FUNDS, 1976–1987

| | Subsequent Period | | | | | |
| | One-Year | | Two-Year | | Three-Year | |
	Winners	Losers	Winners	Losers	Winners	Losers
Initial Period:						
Winners	55.3%	44.7%	59.9%	40.1%	61.2%	38.8%
Losers	44.9	55.1	40.3	59.7	22.9	77.1

Source: Adapted from William N. Goetzmann and Roger G. Ibbotson, "Do Winners Repeat?" *Journal of Portfolio Management*, 20, no. 2 (Winter 1994): Exhibits 1, 8, and 11, pp. 11, 13, and 17.

year after being so honored was 284th out of 681, which is only slightly above the median. Furthermore, the top 20 funds based on their returns over the 1972–1982 period had ten-year average returns over the subsequent decade that resulted in their having a slightly above-median average rank of 142nd out of 309. Lastly, the equity funds on the *Forbes* Honor Role (prepared since 1974 and analyzed through 1992, and similar to the top 20) had average annual returns in the year after being so honored of 13.0%, whereas the average equity fund had an average return of 12.8%.

The results from these three studies indicate that there is a mild degree of persistence of performance among mutual funds.[30] Investors still face a good deal of risk if they purchase a fund that recently was a top performer. Clearly, past performance is not a strong predictor (let alone a guarantee) of future performance.

22.6   EVALUATING MUTUAL FUNDS

Along with the rapid growth in money invested in mutual funds in recent years has come a corresponding increase in the number and diversity of mutual funds offered to investors. Not surprisingly then, various organizations have created businesses devoted to evaluating mutual funds. One of the most prominent of these organizations is Morningstar, Inc., located in Chicago. Besides providing a wealth of information on a given fund, it also provides an in-depth analysis of past returns.

The best way to understand the breadth of Morningstar's mutual fund evaluations is to consider an analysis of a specific fund. An example involving the Fidelity Magellan Fund, an equity fund, is shown in Figure 22.9 and explained next. Where different, a description of the analysis is also given for a fixed-income fund.

22.6.1 Performance/Risk Analysis

In the left column of Figure 22.9 is a section with the heading *Performance/Risk*. Displayed here are the average returns earned by the fund over various time periods ending February 28, 1994, and ranging from the past three months to the past 15 years. These returns are calculated net of operating expenses and 12b-1 fees, although load charges are ignored. Thus the average returns reflect what an investor would have earned after having bought the fund's shares. Next to each average return is an indication of how it compares with the average return on the S&P 500 over the same time period. For fixed-income funds the S&P 500 is replaced by the Lehman Brothers Aggregate Bond Index.

In the third and fourth columns from the left are the percentile ranks of the fund's average return relative to all mutual funds and relative to those categorized as having a similar stated investment objective. Here a rank of 1 places a

Performance/Risk 02/28/94

	Total Return %	+/− S&P 500	% Rank All	% Rank Obj	Growth of $10,000
3 Mo	6.27	4.46	17	22	10,627
6 Mo	3.95	1.82	30	52	10,395
1 Yr	22.77	14.45	14	11	12,277
3 Yr Avg	18.63	7.02	12	16	16,695
5 Yr Avg	18.59	4.95	6	11	23,459
10 Yr Avg	19.69	4.21	2	2	60,323
15 Yr Avg	26.16	10.52	1	1	326,290

	Risk % Rank All	Risk % Rank Obj	Return 1.00=Equity Average	Risk Average	Morningstar Risk-Adj Rating
3 Yr	61	13	1.37	0.65	★★★★
5 Yr	63	13	1.54	0.75	★★★★★
10 Yr	58	26	1.92	0.84	★★★★★

Average Historical Rating: 5.0★s over 183 months

Historical Profile

Return	**High**
Risk	**Below Avg**
Rating	★★★★★
	Highest

Alpha	6.4
Beta	1.01
R^2	84
Std Dev	11.13
Mean	17.81
Sharpe Ratio	1.27

Investment Style

	Stock Portfolio Avg	Relative S&P 500
Price/Earnings Ratio	23.9	1.14
Price/Book Ratio	3.6	0.98
5 Yr Earnings Gr %	10.9	1.17
Return on Assets %	7.4	1.02
Debt % Total Cap	32.0	1.09
Med Mkt Cap ($mil)	2854	0.22

Style: Value Blend Growth
Size: Large Med Small

Figure 22.9

Performance and Risk Analysis of the Magellan Fund (Excerpts)

Source: Excerpts from *Morningstar Mutual Funds*. A comprehensive publication covering 1,310 mutual funds. Morning Star, Inc. 225 W. Wacker Dr., Chicago IL. 60606. 312-696-6000. March 18, 1994, p. 154.

fund at the top and a rank of 100 places a fund at the bottom. The fifth column shows to what amount a $10,000 dollar investment in the fund would have grown over the applicable time period (ignoring taxes and load charges).

Over the three months ending February 28, 1994, Magellan had a return of 6.27%, which was 4.46% better than the S&P 500. This return caused the fund to be ranked at about the 20th percentile against both all funds (17th percentile) and those funds having a similar objective (22nd percentile). Furthermore, over the past 15 years it can be seen that the Magellan Fund did substantially better than the S&P 500, placing it in the first percentile overall and in its category. Note how a $10,000 investment in the Magellan Fund that was made on February 28, 1979, would have grown to $326,290 on February 28, 1994, 15 years later.

22.6.2 Ratings

In the lower part of the *Performance/Risk* section of Figure 22.9 are two columns under *Risk % Rank*, as well as individual columns for *Return, Risk, Average,* and *Morningstar Risk-Adj Rating*. In order to understand these columns the two columns labeled *Return* and *Risk Average* need to be explained first. Here it is easiest to focus on the three-year row, as the other two rows are straightforward extensions of it. First, the average return for Magellan and all other portfolios having similar objectives are determined for the past three years. Here the actual net return is adjusted for any load charges that the fund levies on investors. Second, the average three-year returns for all of the similar funds are averaged. Third, Magellan's average return is divided by this overall average. Hence a return measure of greater than 1 means that the fund did better than average, whereas a return measure of less than 1 indicates that the fund did worse than average. In Magellan's case the return measure of 1.37 indicates that its average return was 37% better than the overall average.

For the *Risk Average* entry, the appropriate monthly Treasury bill return is subtracted from each of the previous 36 monthly net returns to calculate the fund's excess returns. Then only the negative excess returns are summed and the absolute value is divided by 36 to provide a measure of the fund's downside risk. (This risk measure is similar to the risk measure known as *mean shortfall*, which was discussed in Chapter 7's *Institutional Issues* section.)

For example, imagine that this risk measure is calculated over six months instead of 36 months, and that the following returns are observed:

Month	Fund Return	T-bill Return	Fund Return less T-bill Return
1	4.0%	.5%	3.5%
2	−2.0	.5	−2.5
3	.4	.6	−.2
4	5.0	.6	4.4
5	−3.0	.6	−3.6
6	1.0	.7	.3

The three negative excess returns of −2.5%, −.2%, and −3.6% sum to −6.3%. Dividing this sum by 6, the total number of months, results in a downside risk measure of 1.05 (= 6.3/6).

Downside risk measures are calculated by Morningstar for all similar funds, and an overall average for these funds is determined. Then the fund's downside risk measure is divided by this overall measure; the resulting number is Morningstar's measure of the fund's relative risk. In the case of Magellan, it is .65, indicating that it had 35% less downside risk than the average similar fund over the three-year period.

Under the heading *Risk % Rank* the percentile rankings are found for the fund's downside risk measure against all funds (*All*) and the set of similar funds (*Obj*). Here a percentile rank of 1 indicates that the fund had the least risk, whereas a rank of 100 indicates that the fund had the most risk. In the case of Magellan, its ranks of 61 and 13 over three years indicate that it had more risk than 61% of all the other funds and 13% of the other funds having a comparable objective.

Morningstar's rating system has five categories, as follows:

Stars	Percentile	Return Category	Risk Category
*****	1–10	Highest or High	Lowest or Low
****	11–32.5	Above Average	Below Average
***	33.5–67.5	Average	Average
**	68.5–90	Below Average	Above Average
*	91–100	Lowest or Low	Highest or High

Hence the percentile rank, based on the set of funds with similar objectives, determines how many stars the fund is given and the category in which it is placed.[31]

The *Morningstar Risk-Adj Rating* is determined by subtracting the fund's downside risk measure from its return measure. In the case of Magellan, its three-year risk-adjusted measure is .72 (= 1.37 − .65). This measure is also determined for all the other funds having similar objectives, and then percentile ranks are determined. In the case of Magellan, it ranked somewhere between 11 and 32.5, causing it to receive a four-star rating.

22.6.3 Historical Profile

Summary performance measures are contained in the *Historical Profile* box in the center of Figure 22.9. Consider the return measure first. Here the previously described return measures for three, five, and ten years are averaged using weights of 20%, 30%, and 50% to arrive at a weighted-average return. After doing this for each of the other funds that have similar objectives, the fund is given a percentile rank and then a rating, as indicated before. In the case of Magellan, its percentile rank was somewhere between 1 and 10, giving it a *high* ranking. Similar weighted-average calculations are done for the fund's downside risk measure and risk-adjusted measure, resulting in Magellan's receiving a *below average* risk rating and a five-star *highest* risk-adjusted rating.

At the bottom of the Performance/Risk section is an indication of the *Average Historical Rating* that is based on the *Rating* in the Historical Profile section for all of the months that Morningstar has rated the fund. In the case of Magellan, its average overall rating over the past 183 months is five stars—the highest rating category.

22.6.4 MPT Statistics

In the upper right part of Figure 22.9 is the section that Morningstar refers to as *MPT Statistics,* for Modern Portfolio Theory. The top part provides values for *Alpha, Beta,* and R^2. They correspond to the statistics related to a portfolio's ex post characteristic line, which is a regression model like the market model that was discussed in Chapter 8.[32] The only difference between the two is that the ex post characteristic line uses excess returns instead of returns. Hence Morningstar regresses the previous 36 monthly excess returns on the mutual fund (that is, the fund's net returns less the corresponding Treasury bill rates) on the previous 36 monthly excess returns on the S&P 500 (that is, the index's returns less the corresponding Treasury bill rates). As a result the fund's ex post alpha (*Alpha*) and beta (*Beta*) are estimated. Similarly, R^2 is the coefficient of determination (multiplied by 100) that is determined when the 36 excess returns of the fund are compared with those of the S&P 500.

It can be seen that Magellan had a beta of 1.01, similar to that of the S&P 500. Its ex post alpha of 6.4% indicates that it did much better than the market on a beta-adjusted basis over the last 36 months. The R^2 of 84 means that roughly 84% of the variation in the excess returns of the fund could be attributed to variations in the excess returns on the S&P 500.

The second part of this section provides values for *Std Dev, Mean,* and *Sharpe Ratio*. These three values are also based on the previous 36 monthly rates of return on the fund. *Std Dev* and *Mean* are the standard deviation and the average return (annualized) for the portfolio, which for Magellan are 11.13% and

17.81%, respectively. The *Sharpe Ratio,* discussed more fully in Chapter 25, gives a risk-adjusted measure of performance. Here Morningstar takes the fund's excess return over the previous 12 months and divides it by the fund's standard deviation over the previous 36 months. Hence it is the ratio of return to risk, which for Magellan equals 1.27.

22.6.5 Investment Style

This section appears in the lower center part of Figure 22.9. On the left are six descriptive measures of the average stock held by the fund using the most recently available data. For example, the average *Price/Earnings Ratio* of the stocks held in the Magellan Fund was 23.9 as of February 28, 1994. This number is divided by the average price-earnings ratio of the stocks in the S&P 500, indicating a value of 1.14, or 14% greater than the average ratio in the index. Similarly, the average *Price/Book Ratio* of the stocks held by Magellan was 3.6, or 2% less than the average price-book ratio of the stocks held in the S&P 500. Both of these ratios are weighted averages, where the weight for each security is based on the relative proportion of the fund that is invested in the security. With the exception of the fourth measure, the other measures are also weighted averages of measures of the securities in the fund:

1. *5-Year Earnings-Growth Rate* (%). This measures the average of the securities' five-year earnings-growth rate. Stocks with negative earnings are not included in calculating the average.
2. *Return on Assets* (%). This measures the average of the securities' ratios of earnings after taxes to total assets.
3. *Debt as a Percent of Total Capitalization.* This measures the average of the securities' ratios of long-term debt to total assets.
4. *Median Market Capitalization* (in million dollars). This measures the stock market capitalization of the median security.

The values of these measures are also divided by their respective values for the S&P 500, thereby allowing a quick comparison of how the securities in the fund stack up against the securities in this index.

In the case of a fund that invests in fixed-income securities, all six of these measures are replaced by measures such as average maturity, credit quality, and coupon rate. As mentioned, the Lehman Brothers Aggregate Bond Index replaces the S&P 500 as a standard for comparison.

Also in this part of Figure 22.9 is a 3×3 matrix, which Morningstar calls a *style box.* The two extreme columns represent the investment styles of value and growth, with the middle column representing a mixture of the two. A fund's style is determined by summing the fund's price-earnings ratio and price-book ratio, where both are expressed relative to the S&P 500. Note that this sum for the S&P 500 itself is 2.00 (since each ratio is, by definition, equal to 1.00). Morningstar has decided that if the sum for a fund is less than 1.75, then the fund follows a *value style.* This is because the fund has invested in stocks that collectively have relatively low valuation ratios and hence are viewed as value stocks. On the other hand, if the sum is greater than 2.25, then the fund is deemed to follow a *growth style* because it has invested in stocks with relatively high valuation ratios. Sums between 1.75 and 2.25 indicate that the fund follows a *blended style*, investing in stocks that in aggregate have no distinct style.

In the case of Magellan, its sum is 2.12 (= 1.14 + .98), indicating that it follows a blended style. As the value of this sum for the S&P 500 itself is 2.00, the Magellan Fund tends to purchase stocks that have price-earnings and price-book ratios that on average are only slightly higher than the valuation ratios of stocks in the S&P 500.

The three rows of the style box are based on the size of the stocks held by the fund, where size is measured by the Median Market Capitalization figure for the fund. If this figure is less than $1 billion, the fund is deemed to be *small*, and if it is greater than $5 billion, then the fund is deemed to be *large*. A figure between $1 billion and $5 billion—as is the case with Magellan, as the median size of its holdings is $2.854 billion—results in the fund's being categorized as *medium*.

In Chapter 17 it was mentioned that stocks can be classified along the two dimensions of value-growth and size. Now it can be seen that investment companies can be similarly classified. Morningstar does this by use of the style box, thereby allowing investors to quickly understand a fund's investment strategy. Nine combinations of the three levels of value-growth and size are possible. Morningstar indicates its classification of a fund by darkening one of the nine sections of the style box. In the case of Magellan the center box is darkened, indicating that its investment strategy involves purchases of both value and growth stocks without concentrating on either large or small ones.

In the case of fixed-income funds, the columns of the style box are based on the average maturity (soon to be changed to duration) of the securities in the fund, and hence the style box focuses on the fund's interest rate sensitivity. The column headings are *Short Term* (if the average maturity is less than four years), *Intermediate Term* (if the average is between four and ten years), and *Long Term* (if the average is greater than ten years). The rows are based on the average credit quality of the securities in the fund, and hence measure default risk. The row headings are *High* (if the average bond rating is at least AA), *Average* (if the average is between BBB and AA), and *Low* (if the average is less than BBB).

22.6.6 Caveats

Morningstar's performance measures are useful in giving an investor a quick reading of how a mutual fund has performed in the past relative to other funds. However, several things should be kept in mind.

1. Comparisons are made with the S&P 500 for all equity funds, but this index may not be appropriate for certain funds. For example, a fund that invests primarily in securities listed on Nasdaq might more appropriately be compared with an over-the-counter index.
2. As will be discussed in Chapter 24, portfolio managers can attempt to earn abnormal returns by trying to (1) buy underpriced securities and then profit from their subsequent abnormal price appreciation, or (2) shift funds out of the stock market just before it goes down and then back

into the stock market just before it rises, or (3) do both. Morningstar's performance measures do not indicate which approach the fund is using in its quest for abnormal returns.

3. The use of peer group comparisons to evaluate performance has several serious conceptual and practical shortcomings. For example, the set of similar funds may not be entirely appropriate (even though they may be the best match that Morningstar can provide), causing the ratings to be misleading. One fund may be restricted to buying just NYSE-listed common stock whereas another is free to purchase stocks that are listed on the NYSE, AMEX, or Nasdaq. Furthermore, similar funds may differ considerably in the amount of risk that they take on. Finally, *survivorship bias* (the tendency for poorly performing funds to go out of business and hence leave the peer group) hampers comparisons with similar funds.

22.7 CLOSED-END FUND PREMIUMS AND DISCOUNTS

Several studies have shown that the performance of diversified closed-end investment company managers in the United States is similar to that of open-end investment company managers.[33] When returns are measured by changes in net asset values (plus all distributions), closed-end investment companies appear to be neither better nor worse than open-end ones. Again, there is little evidence that portfolio managers can, on average, either select underpriced securities or time the market successfully.

22.7.1 Pricing of Shares

However, there is more to be said about closed-end funds. An investor can purchase an open-end fund's shares for their net asset value (plus any required load charge) and sell them later at the subsequent net asset value. Except for any load charges and 12b-1 fees, the performance of the *management* of such a fund, based on net asset values, corresponds exactly to the returns provided to the *shareholders.* This is not the case for closed-end investment companies, because investors buy and sell shares of investment companies at prices determined on the open (secondary) market. Whereas some companies have share prices that are above their net asset values (such shares are said to sell at a premium), many have share prices below their net asset values (such shares are said to sell at a discount).

This has resulted in several "puzzles" concerning the typical pricing of closed-end fund shares. Two of the most prominent are as follows. First, as mentioned earlier, the shares sell at a premium of roughly 10% of their net asset value when initially sold and then fall to a discount of roughly 10% of their net asset value shortly thereafter. Why would investors buy such shares when they are initially offered for sale, knowing that their price is going to fall substantially afterward? Second, the size of this discount fluctuates widely over time.[34] Figure 22.10 shows the price behavior of a sample of 18 closed-end funds. Note how the average fund sells at a discount that ranged from roughly 1.5% to 9% over the previous four quarters. What causes these fluctuations?

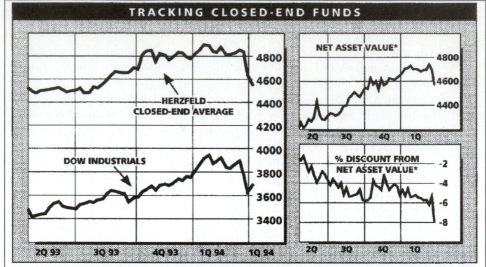

Figure 22.10
Closed-End Fund Performance
Source: Reprinted by permission of *Barron's,* ©Dow Jones & Company, Inc., April 11, 1994, p. MW73. All rights reserved worldwide.

22.7.2 Investing in Fund Shares

The fact that the share price of a closed-end investment company differs from its net asset value, with the magnitude of the difference varying over time, introduces an added source of risk and potential return to investors. By purchasing shares at a discount, an investor may be able to earn more than just the change in the company's net asset value. Even if the company's discount remains constant, the effective dividend yield will be greater than that of an otherwise similar no-load, open-end investment company, because the purchase price will be less. If the discount is substantial when the shares are purchased, it may subsequently narrow and the return will be even greater.[35] On the other hand, if the discount increases, the investor's overall return may be less than that of an otherwise comparable open-end investment company.

Consider a closed-end fund that at the beginning of the year has a net asset value of $10 per share but is selling at a 10% discount for $9 per share. Over the year it receives cash dividends amounting to $.50 per share, which it distributes to its shareholders. Hence its dividend yield is 5.6% (= $.50/$9.00), which is larger than the 5% yield (= $.50/$10) that it would pay if it were an open-end fund. Furthermore, if its net asset value at year-end remains at $10 per share but its discount shrinks to 4% so that it is selling at $9.60 per share, then its annual return of 12.2% [= ($.60 + $.50)/$9] would be notably larger than the 5% return of its open-end counterpart. Of course, if its discount widened to 20% so that it was selling at $8 per share, then its annual return of −5.6% [= (−$1 + $.50)/$9] would be notably lower than the counterpart's 5% return.

CHAPTER 22

Some of the risk associated with varying discounts can be reduced by holding a portfolio of shares in several closed-end investment companies. Discounts on different companies move together, but not perfectly. For example, past data suggests that the standard deviation of the percentage change in the ratio of market price to net asset value for a *portfolio* of 10 to 12 closed-end investment companies is likely to be approximately half that of a typical investment in the shares of a *single* closed-end investment company.[36]

22.7.3 Open-Ending Closed-End Funds

Explaining the puzzling behavior of prices of closed-end investment companies is a challenge for anyone who believes that capital markets are highly efficient. For anyone not firmly committed to such a view, the purchase of shares of closed-end investment companies at prices sufficiently below net asset values may provide an opportunity for superior returns.[37] One way of realizing superior returns is for the closed-end investment company to convert to an open-end one.[38] By doing so, the discount on the shares would have to disappear because conversion would result in the investment company's offering its shareholders the right to redeem their shares for their net asset value.

22.8 SUMMARY

1. Investment companies are financial intermediaries that obtain money from investors and use it to purchase financial assets.
2. Investment companies offer investors the advantages of economies of scale and professional management.
3. The net asset value of an investment company is the difference between the market value of its assets and its liabilities divided by the number of outstanding shares.
4. The operating expense ratio of an investment company represents the annual percentage of total assets that are spent in operating the fund. Typically these expenses consist of fees paid to the management company as well as administrative and other operating expenses.
5. The three major types of investment companies are unit investment trusts, closed-end investment companies, and open-end investment companies.
6. Unit investment trusts typically make a set of initial investments in fixed-income securities, and then hold those securities until they mature.
7. Closed-end investment companies issue an initial number of shares to capitalize the fund. After that, new shares are rarely issued (or repurchased). Closed-end investment company shares trade on organized exchanges or on the over-the-counter market at prices determined by the market.
8. Open-end investment companies have a variable capitalization, standing ready to issue new shares or repurchase existing shares at prices based on their net asset values.
9. Different investment companies follow different investment policies. These policies determine such characteristics as the asset classes in which the in

vestment companies invest, the degree of active management (if any), and the emphasis on income as opposed to capital appreciation.

10. Owing to data availability, mutual funds have been the subject of many performance studies. The results show that, on average, mutual funds consistently maintain risk postures in line with their stated investment policies. However, the typical fund has not been able to produce superior rates of return consistently.

11. There is some evidence that the superior results of top performing mutual funds persist over time. However, this evidence is not strong, indicating that many top performers subsequently become either mediocre or below average performers.

12. Closed-end investment companies typically sell at premiums to their net asset values at their initial offerings. Later they typically sell at discounts to their net asset values, which vary over time. Explaining why investors buy initial public offerings of closed-end investment companies and why the discounts of these companies vary over time are puzzles for efficient market proponents.

QUESTIONS AND PROBLEMS

1. The Neptune Value Fund has sold 150,000 shares to investors. Currently the fund has accrued investment management fee obligations of $50,000. The fund's portfolio is shown below. Calculate the fund's net asset value.

Stock	Shares	Price/Share
A	50,000	$ 10
B	20,000	7
C	35,000	30
D	10,000	100

2. Using a recent *Wall Street Journal,* find the NAV for the following funds:
   a. The Magellan Fund (Fidelity Investments)
   b. The Wellington Fund (Vanguard Group)
   c. The Quasar Fund (Alliance Capital)
   What is the percentage change in each fund's NAV over the previous day? Calculate each fund's load as a percentage of its NAV.

3. Wildfire Schulter, a veteran mutual fund investor, argued: "I can compute the monthly rate of return on a mutual fund by calculating the percentage change in the fund's NAV from the beginning to the end of the month (assuming no distributions to shareholders)." Is Wildfire correct? Why?

4. The X Fund, a closed-end investment company, has a portfolio of assets worth $500 million. It has liabilities of $2 million. It also has 40 million shares outstanding.
   a. What is the fund's NAV?
   b. If the fund trades at an 8% discount from its NAV, what is the market price of the fund's shares?

5. Discuss the advantages and disadvantages of unit investment trusts compared with managed investment companies.

6. Distinguish between closed-end and open-end investment companies.

7. Why do some mutual funds have load charges whereas others do not? Why are investors willing to pay load charges?

8. Assume that you placed a $1,000 investment with a mutual fund that charged an 8.5% load. Management and other fees charged by the fund total 1.10% per annum. Ignoring other costs, over five years, what annual return would the fund have to produce to equal the value that your initial investment would have earned in a savings account paying 5% interest? (Assume annual compounding of income and no taxes.)

9. In recent years so-called families of funds that offer a wide range of investment policies through narrowly focused mutual funds have become popular. Discuss why these funds have achieved such popularity.

10. There are literally thousands of mutual funds available for purchase. Describe what criteria you might use in selecting from among these many funds.

11. At the beginning of the year, the Saturn Fund's NAV was $18.50. At the end of the year its NAV was $16.90. At year-end the fund paid out $1.25 in income and capital gains. What was the return to an investor in the Saturn Fund during the year?

12. Over the last three years, the Pluto Fund produced the following per share financial results. Calculate the annual returns on an investment in the Pluto Fund over this period.

	Year 1	Year 2	Year 3
NAV at Beginning of Year	$13.89	$14.40	$15.95
NAV at End of Year	14.40	15.95	15.20
Income Distribution	0.29	0.33	0.36
Capital Gains Distribution	0.12	0.25	0.05

13. Analysis of mutual fund performance has been extensive. What does the evidence indicate about the ability of mutual fund managers, as a group, to produce positive abnormal returns consistently?

14. Lip Pike is attempting to select a superior-performing mutual fund. Based on the evidence presented in the text, discuss how much importance Lip should attach to the past performance of mutual funds in making decisions.

15. What is the purpose of Rule 12b-1? Does it seem designed to serve the interests of existing shareholder? Explain.

16. Why do the stated percentage load charges of mutual funds not fully reflect the percentage costs of these sales fees?

17. Distinguish between a common stock fund and a balanced fund. In particular, compare their expected return and risk characteristics.

18. If most investment managers appear unable to "beat the market" on a risk-adjusted basis, should an investor still consider investing in investment companies? Why?

19. Consider three individuals: a young, well-educated woman just beginning a career with high expected future earnings; a middle-aged man with a young family who has a secure job but modest expected future earnings growth; a widow in her seventies, living comfortably but not richly off a pension. Referring to Table 22.1, prescribe and explain an investment strategy for these

persons involving investments in the various funds listed. (Feel free to introduce other assumptions regarding such things as the individuals' risk tolerances and consumption preferences.)

20. Assuming that certain conditions are satisfied, an investment company does not have to pay federal tax on the income it earns. Why?

21. Why do the market prices of closed-end investment company shares represent a "mystery" to proponents of market efficiency?

ENDNOTES

[1] As mentioned in Chapter 3, dealers in securities generally quote both bid and asked prices. The bid price is the amount the dealer will pay for a security; the asked price is the amount an investor must pay to purchase the security from the dealer.

[2] Another classification covers certain companies that issue "face-amount certificates" promising specific payments. This type of company is rare and will not be discussed here.

[3] In a number of other countries (such as the United Kingdom), a unit trust is an open-end investment company.

[4] Many investment companies require their management companies to cover all expenses over a specified amount, effectively limiting total expenses. All of these fees are discussed extensively in Chapter 10 of John Bogle, *Bogle on Mutual Funds* (Burr Ridge, IL: Richard D. Irwin, 1994).

[5] CDA/Wiesenberger Investment Companies Service, *Investment Companies Yearbook 1993* (Rockville, MD: CDA Investment Technologies, 1993), p. 19.

[6] Closed-end funds that have received permission from foreign governments to invest in their securities do not show the type of price behavior described here, and hence may be initially attractive to investors. See John W. Peavey III, "Returns on Initial Public Offerings of Closed-End Funds," *Review of Financial Studies,* 3, no. 4 (1990): 695–708. For more information about closed-end investment companies, see Albert J. Fredman and George Cole Scott, "Analyzing and Finding Data on Closed-End Funds," *AAII Journal,* 13, no. 8 (September 1991): 15–19, and "Guidelines for Handling Closed-End Fund Transactions," *AAII Journal,* 14, no. 5 (June 1992): 18–22.

[7] **Real estate investment trusts** (REITs), although not classified as investment companies for legal purposes, are similar to closed-end funds in that they serve as a conduit for earnings on investments in real estate or loans secured by real estate, passing earnings on to their shareholders and avoiding corporate taxation. They are discussed in this chapter's Institutional Issues section.

[8] Investing in a **wrap account** is similar to investing in a mutual fund. This type of account is sponsored by a brokerage firm and involves brokers helping investors identify suitable money managers (or mutual funds) that will manage some of the investors' wealth. All of the fees for financial planning, investment management, and securities trading are "wrapped up" into one annual fee that typically amounts to 3% of assets. See John Bogle, *Bogle on Mutual Funds,* p. 54, for a discussion of the analogy between wrap accounts and mutual funds. Also see Endnote 5 in Chapter 2.

[9] CDA/Wiesenberger, *Investment Companies Yearbook 1993,* p. 23.

[10] CDA/Wiesenberger, *Investment Companies Yearbook 1993,* p. 24. Option-income funds are a type of income fund that invests primarily in high-dividend-paying common stocks while also writing call options on these stocks. (Call options were discussed in Chapter 20.) Equity income and fixed-income funds are other types of income funds that invest in common stocks and fixed-income securities, respectively.

[11] Sometimes the capital gain category is referred to as "maximum capital gain" or "aggressive growth." A fourth category ("specialized") consists of funds that, by design, are not highly diversified. One interesting kind of fund (typically organized as a limited partnership) is a hedge fund, where the manager will often engage in short selling and margin purchases of securities.

[12] CDA/Wiesenberger, *Investment Companies Yearbook 1993,* p. 22.

[13] Ibid.

[14] For more information about mutual funds that specialize in investing in foreign stocks, see Ken Gregory, "Traveling Overseas Via No-Load Mutual Funds," *AAII Journal,* 13, no. 9 (October 1991): 22–25.

[15] Very similar to this kind of investment is the *variable annuity,* which combines an investment in a special type of mutual fund (similar to the ones sold to the general public but limited to annuity investors) with a life insurance policy. This policy pays a stated amount to a named beneficiary in the event of the investor's death. Taxes on the earnings in the "mutual fund" are deferred until withdrawal, but a 10% tax on earnings will be levied if withdrawal begins before the investor is 59½. The annual expenses of a variable annuity are higher than those of a mutual fund by .5% to 1.75% because of the cost of the life insurance component. See Albert J. Fredman and Russ Wiles, "An Introduction to Investing in Variable Annuities," *AAII Journal,* 15, no. 8 (September 1993): 9–12; and Bogle, *Bogle on Mutual Funds,* pp. 223–226.

[16] For example, the contribution to an IRA will be deductible provided that (1) the investor is not covered by an employer-sponsored retirement plan and does not have a Keogh plan; or (2) the investor is single and earns less than $25,000; or (3) the investor is married and their combined incomes are less than $40,000. IRAs and Keogh plans are discussed more fully in Chapter 13. Also see Richard R. Simonds, "Mutual Fund Strategies for IRA Investors," *Journal of Portfolio Management,* 12, no. 2 (Winter 1986): 40–43.

[17] See Bogle, *Bogle on Mutual Funds,* Chapter 4.

[18] Benchmarks can be calculated in many different ways. For example, the benchmark may be based on the investment company's standard deviation relative to that of a market index, such as the S&P 500. Thus if the investment company's standard deviation has been 60% of the index's standard deviation, then the mix would consist of 60% invested in the index and 40% invested in the riskfree asset. The results from evaluating mutual fund performance using this type of benchmark are very similar to the results when beta-based benchmarks are used. See, for example, Hany A. Shawky, "An Update on Mutual Funds: Better Grades," *Journal of Portfolio Management,* 8, no. 2 (Winter 1982): 29–34. As mentioned earlier, portfolio performance evaluation is discussed in detail in Chapter 25.

[19] Edwin J. Elton, Martin J. Gruber, Sanjiv Das, and Matthew Hlavka, "Efficiency with Costly Information: A Reinterpretation of Evidence from Managed Portfolios," *Review of Financial Studies,* 6, no. 1 (1993): 1–22; and Ravi Shukla and Charles Trzcinka, "Performance Measurement of Managed Portfolios," *Financial Markets, Institutions and Instruments,* 1, no. 4 (1992).

[20] Similar conclusions can be drawn regarding pension and endowment funds. See Eugene F. Fama, "Efficient Capital Markets: II," *Journal of Finance,* 46, no. 5 (December 1991): 1575–1617, particularly pp. 1605–1607, and the Lakonishok, Schleifer, and Vishny study cited in Endnote 30.

[21] *Institutional Investor Study Report of the Securities and Exchange Commission* (Washington, D.C.: U.S. Government Printing Office, 1971), vol. 2, pp. 328–332.

[22] Elton, Gruber, Das and Hlavka, "Efficiency with Costly Information." The results reported here (and in endnote 19) are based on ex post alpha values arising from the use of three indices, one of which is the S&P 500, in establishing a benchmark.

[23] Jack L. Treynor and Kay Mazuy, "Can Mutual Funds Outguess the Market?" *Harvard Business Review,* 44, no. 4 (July–August 1966): 131–136.

[24] Roy D. Henriksson, "Market Timing and Mutual Fund Performance: An Empirical Investigation," *Journal of Business,* 57, no. 1, pt. 1 (January 1984): 73–96. Similar results suggesting that mutual fund managers have no special ability to time the market is provided by Stanley J. Kon, "The Market-Timing Performance of Mutual Fund Managers," *Journal of Business,* 56, no. 3 (July 1983): 323–347; and Eric C. Chang and Wilbur G. Lewellen, "Market Timing and Mutual Fund Investment Performance," *Journal of Business,* 57, no. 1, pt. 1 (January 1984): 57–72. Contrary evidence is provided by Cheng F. Lee and Shafiqur Rahman, "New Evidence on Timing and Security Selection Skill of Mutual Fund Managers," *Journal of Portfolio Management,* 17, no. 2 (Winter 1991): 80–83.

[25] Shukla and Trzcinka, "Performance Measurement of Managed Portfolios."

[26] Christopher R. Blake, Edwin J. Elton, and Martin J. Gruber, "The Performance of Bond Mutual Funds," *Journal of Business,* 66, no. 3 (July 1993): 371–403.

[27] Darryll Hendricks, Jayendu Patel, and Richard Zeckhauser, "Hot Hands in Mutual Funds: Short-Run Persistence of Relative Performance, 1974–1988," *Journal of Finance,* 48, no. 1 (March 1993): 93–130.

[28] William N. Goetzmann and Roger G. Ibbotson, "Do Winners Repeat?" *Journal of Portfolio Management,* 20, no. 2 (Winter 1994): 9–18. For a discussion of rankings in general, see John Markese, "Mutual Fund Rankings: What Accounts for Differences?" *AAII Journal,* 15, no. 4 (April 1993): 31–33.

[29] John Bogle, *Bogle on Mutual Funds,* Chapter 4. Also see John C. Bogle, "Selecting Equity Mutual Funds," *Journal of Portfolio Management,* 18, no. 2 (Winter 1992): 94–100.

[30] Persistence of performance was also observed in the study of bond mutual funds cited in Endnote 26, and in a study of pension funds. See Josef Lakonishok, Andrei Shleifer, and Robert W. Vishny, "The Structure and Performance of the Money Management Industry," *Brookings Papers on Economic Activity: Microeconomics 1992,* pp. 339–379. It should be noted that all of these studies finding persistence have been challenged by others on methodological grounds.

[31] Similar ratings are provided in *The Individual Investor's Guide to No-Load Mutual Funds* (Chicago: American Association of Individual Investors, 1994).

[32] The ex post characteristic line is discussed more fully in Chapter 25.

[33] See, for example, William F. Sharpe and Howard B. Sosin, "Closed-End Investment Companies in the United States: Risk and Return," *Proceedings, 1974 Meeting of the European Finance Association,* ed. B. Jacquillat (Amsterdam: North-Holland Publishing, 1975): 37–63; Antonio Vives, "Analysis of Forecasting Ability of Closed-End Fund's Management" (unpublished working paper, Carnegie-Mellon University, September 1975), and "Discounts and Premiums on Closed-End Funds: A Theoretical and Empirical Analysis" (unpublished Ph.D. thesis, Carnegie-Mellon University, 1975).

[34] These puzzles are presented and investigated in Charles M. C. Lee, Andrei Shleifer, and Richard H. Thaler, "Investor Sentiment and the Closed-End Fund Puzzle," *Journal of Finance,* 46, no. 1 (March 1991): 75–109. In the June 1991 issue of *Journal of Finance* there is a contentious debate about their findings.

[35] There is some evidence that discounts narrow during "down markets" and widen during "up markets." See R. Malcolm Richards, Donald R. Fraser, and John C. Groth, "Premiums, Discounts, and the Volatility of Closed-End Mutual Funds," *Financial Review* (Fall 1979): 26–33; and "The Attractions of Closed-End Bond Funds," *Journal of Portfolio Management,* 8, no. 2 (Winter 1982): 56–61.

[36] Sharpe and Sosin, "Closed-End Investment Companies in the United States."

[37] Burton G. Malkiel advocated such an investment strategy in the 1973, 1975, and 1981 editions of *A Random Walk Down Wall Street* (New York: W. W. Norton), but not in the 1985 and 1990 editions. The basis for his initial advocacy can be found in two studies: Burton Malkiel, "The Valuation of Closed-End Investment Company Shares," *Journal of Finance,* 32, no. 3 (June 1977): 847–859; and Rex Thompson, "The Information Content of Discounts and Premiums on Closed-End Fund Shares," *Journal of Financial Economics,* 6, no. 2/3 (June/September 1978): 151–186.

[38] For an analysis of the "open-ending" of closed-end investment companies, see Gregory A. Brauer, "'Open-Ending' Closed-End Funds," *Journal of Financial Economics,* 13, no. 4 (December 1984): 491–507.

KEY TERMS

investment companies	load funds
net asset value	load charge
unit investment trust	low-load funds
managed investment companies	wrap account
operating expense ratio	redemption fee
closed-end investment companies	distribution fee
real estate investment trusts	contingent deferred sales charge
open-end investment company	benchmark portfolio
mutual funds	ex post alpha
no-load funds	portfolio turnover rates

REFERENCES

1. Good reference sources for information on investment companies are:

   William J. Baumol, Stephen M. Goldfeld, Lilli A. Gordon, and Michael F. Koehn, *The Economics of Mutual Fund Markets: Competition Versus Regulation* (Boston: Kluwer Academic Publishers, 1990).

   Investment Companies Yearbook 1993 (to order, write: CDA Investment Technologies, Inc., 1355 Piccard Drive, Rockville, MD 20850).

   1993 Mutual Fund Fact Book (to order, write: Investment Company Institute, P.O. Box 66140, Washington, DC 20035–6140).

   John C. Bogle, *Bogle on Mutual Funds* (Burr Ridge, IL: Richard D. Irwin, 1994).

   The Individual Investor's Guide to No-Load Mutual Funds (to order, write: American Association of Individual Investors, 625 North Michigan Avenue, Research Department, Chicago, IL 60611).

   Morningstar Mutual Funds (to order this biweekly publication, write: Morningstar, Inc., 225 West Wacker Drive, Chicago, IL 60606).

2. Although annual management fees of investment companies are usually a given percentage of the market value of the assets under management, performance-based fees are allowed. In addition to the January/February 1987 issue of the *Financial Analysts Journal,* which is devoted to this topic, see:

Laura T. Starks, "Performance Incentive Fees: An Agency Theoretic Approach," *Journal of Financial and Quantitative Analysis,* 22, no. 1 (March 1987): 17–32.

Mark Grinblatt and Sheridan Titman, "How Clients Can Win the Gaming Game," *Journal of Portfolio Management,* 13, no. 4 (Summer 1987): 14–23.

Joseph H. Golec, "Do Mutual Fund Managers Who Use Incentive Compensation Outperform Those Who Don't?" *Financial Analysts Journal,* 44, no. 6 (November/December 1988): 75–78.

Mark Grinblatt and Sheridan Titman, "Adverse Risk Incentives and the Design of Performance-Based Contracts," *Management Science,* 35, no. 7 (July 1989): 807–822.

Jeffery V. Bailey, "Some Thoughts on Performance-Based Fees," *Financial Analysts Journal,* 46, no. 4 (July/August 1990): 31–40.

Philip Halpern and Isabelle I. Fowler, "Investment Management Fees and Determinants of Pricing Structure in the Industry," *Journal of Portfolio Management,* 17, no. 2 (Winter 1991): 74–79.

3. The imposition of 12b-1 distribution fees by mutual funds has been contentious. See:

Stephen P. Ferris and Don M. Chance, "The Effect of 12b-1 Plans on Mutual Fund Expense Ratios: A Note," *Journal of Finance,* 42, no. 4 (September 1987): 1077–1082.

Charles Trzcinka and Robert Zweig, *An Economic Analysis of the Cost and Benefits of S.E.C. Rule 12b-1,* Monograph Series in Finance and Economics 1990–1, New York University Salomon Center, Leonard N. Stern School of Business.

4. Closed-end investment companies known as "country funds" have been examined by:

Catherine Bonser-Neal, Greggory Brauer, Robert Neal, and Simon Wheatley, "International Investment Restrictions and Closed-End Country Fund Prices," *Journal of Finance,* 45, no. 2 (June 1990): 523–547.

Gordon Johnson, Thomas Schneeweis, and William Dinning, "Closed-End Country Funds: Exchange Rate and Investment Risk," *Financial Analysts Journal,* 49, no. 6 (November/December 1993): 74–82.

5. Real estate investment trusts (REITs) are discussed in:

William L. Burns and Donald R. Epley, "The Performance of Portfolios of REITS + Stocks," *Journal of Portfolio Management,* 8, no. 3 (Spring 1982): 37–42.

Robert H. Zerbst and Barbara R. Cambon, "Real Estate: Historical Returns and Risks," *Journal of Portfolio Management,* 10, no. 3 (Spring 1984): 5–20.

Paul M. Firstenburg, Stephen A. Ross, and Randall C. Zisler, "Real Estate: The Whole Story," *Journal of Portfolio Management,* 14, no. 3 (Spring 1988): 22–34.

Stephen E. Roulac, "How to Value Real Estate Securities," *Journal of Portfolio Management,* 14, no. 3 (Spring 1988): 35–39.

Steven D. Kapplin and Arthur L. Schwartz, Jr., "Investing in REITS: Are They All They're Cracked Up to Be?" *AAII Journal,* 13, no. 5 (May 1991): 7–11.

6. For evidence on the performance of funds outside the United States, see:

John G. McDonald, "French Mutual Fund Performance: Evaluation of Internationally Diversified Portfolios," *Journal of Finance,* 28, no. 5 (December 1973): 1161–1180.

Juan A. Palacios, "The Stock Market in Spain: Tests of Efficiency and Capital Market Theory," in *International Capital Markets,* eds. Edwin J. Elton and Martin J. Gruber (Amsterdam: North-Holland Publishing, 1975): 114–149.

Andre L. Farber, "Performance of Internationally Diversified Mutual Funds," in *International Capital Markets,* eds. Edwin J. Elton and Martin J. Gruber (Amsterdam: North-Holland Publishing, 1975): 298–309.

Michael A. Firth, "The Investment Performance of Unit Trusts in the Period 1965–75," *Journal of Money, Credit and Banking,* 9, no. 4 (November 1977): 597–604.

James R. F. Guy, "The Performance of the British Investment Trust Industry," *Journal of Finance,* 33, no. 2 (May 1978): 443–455.

———,"An Examination of the Effects of International Diversification from the British Viewpoint on Both Hypothetical and Real Portfolios," *Journal of Finance,* 33, no. 5 (December 1978): 1425–1438.

R. S. Woodward, "The Performance of U.K. Investment Trusts as Internationally Diversified Portfolios Over the Period 1968 to 1977," *Journal of Banking and Finance,* 7, no. 3 (September 1983): 417–426.

Jess H. Chua and Richard S. Woodward, *Gains from Market Timing,* Monograph Series in Finance and Economics 1986–2, New York University Salomon Center, Leonard N. Stern School of Business.

Robert E. Cumby and Jack D. Glen, "Evaluating the Performance of International Mutual Funds," *Journal of Finance,* 45, no. 2 (June 1990): 497–521.

Cheol S. Eun, Richard Kolodny, and Bruce G. Resnick, "U.S.-Based International Mutual Funds: A Performance Evaluation," *Journal of Portfolio Management,* 17, no. 3 (Spring 1991): 88–94.

A. Black, P. Fraser, and D. Power, "UK Unit Trust Performance 1980–1989: A Passive Time-Varying Approach," *Journal of Banking and Finance,* 16, no. 5 (September 1992): 1015–1033.

7. Studies of mutual fund performance are discussed and cited in:

Gordon J. Alexander and Jack Clark Francis, *Portfolio Analysis* (Englewood Cliffs, NJ: Prentice Hall, 1986), Chapter 13.

Mark Grinblatt and Sheridan Titman, "Mutual Fund Performance: An Analysis of Quarterly Portfolio Holdings," *Journal of Business,* 62, no. 3 (July 1989): 393–416.

Edwin J. Elton and Martin J. Gruber, *Modern Portfolio Theory and Investment Analysis* (New York: John Wiley & Sons, 1991), Chapter 22.

Ravi Shukla and Charles Trzcinka, "Performance Measurement of Managed Portfolios," *Financial Markets, Institutions & Instruments,* 1, no. 4 (1992).

Edwin J. Elton, Martin J. Gruber, Sanjiv Das, and Matthew Hlavka, "Efficiency with Costly Information: A Reinterpretation of Evidence from Managed Portfolios," *Review of Financial Studies,* 6, no. 1 (1993): 1–22.

Richard A. Ippolito, "On Studies of Mutual Fund Performance," *Financial Analysts Journal,* 49, no. 1 (January/February 1993): 42–50.

Christopher R. Blake, Edwin J. Elton, and Martin J. Gruber, "The Performance of Bond Mutual Funds," *Journal of Business,* 66, no. 3 (July 1993): 371–403.

8. The finding of inferior performance by mutual funds is contested in:

Bruce N. Lehmann and David M. Modest, "Mutual Fund Performance Evaluation: A Comparison of Benchmarks and Benchmark Comparisons," *Journal of Finance,* 42, no. 2 (June 1987): 233–265.

Richard A. Ippolito, "Efficiency with Costly Information: A Study of Mutual Fund Performance," *Quarterly Journal of Economics,* 104, no.1 (February 1989): 1–23.

Mark Grinblatt and Sheridan Titman, "Mutual Fund Performance: An Analysis of Quarterly Portfolio Holdings," *Journal of Business,* 62, no. 3 (July 1989): 393–415.

Cheng-few Lee and Shafiqur Rahman, "Market Timing, Selectivity, and Mutual Fund Performance: An Empirical Investigation," *Journal of Business,* 63, no. 2 (April 1990): 261–278.

Cheng F. Lee and Shafiqur Rahman, "New Evidence on Timing and Security Selection Skill of Mutual Fund Managers," *Journal of Portfolio Management,* 17, no. 2 (Winter 1991): 80–83.

9. The persistence of performance of mutual funds is examined in:

John C. Bogle, "Selecting Equity Mutual Funds," *Journal of Portfolio Management,* 18, no. 2 (Winter 1992): 94–100.

Mark Grinblatt and Sheridan Titman, "The Persistence of Mutual Fund Performance," *Journal of Finance,* 47, no. 5 (December 1992): 1977–1984.

Darryll Hendricks, Jayendu Patel, and Richard Zeckhauser, "Hot Hands in Mutual Funds: Short-Run Persistence of Relative Performance, 1974–1988," *Journal of Finance,* 48, no. 1 (March 1993): 93–130.

William N. Goetzmann and Roger G. Ibbotson, "Do Winners Repeat?" *Journal of Portfolio Management,* 20, no. 2 (Winter 1994): 9–18.

John Bogle, *Bogle on Mutual Funds* (Burr Ridge, IL: Richard D. Irwin, 1994), Chapter 4.

10. *Survivorship bias* refers to the problems incurred in mutual fund studies due to the fact that unskilled portfolio managers are usually fired while the skilled ones stay around. These problems are examined in:

Stephen J. Brown, William Goetzmann, Roger G. Ibbotson, and Stephen A. Ross, "Survivorship Bias in Performance Studies," *Review of Financial Studies,* 5, no. 4 (1992): 553–580.

11. For a discussion and extensive set of references regarding closed-end funds, see, along with the citations given in the chapter, the following papers:

Rex Thompson, "The Information Content of Discounts and Premiums on Closed-End Fund Shares," *Journal of Financial Economics,* 6, no. 2/3 (June/September 1978): 151–186.

Greggory A. Brauer, "'Closed-End Fund Shares' Abnormal Returns and the Information Content of Discounts and Premiums," *Journal of Finance,* 43, no. 1 (March 1988): 113–127.

Kathleen Weiss, "The Post-Offering Price Performance of Closed-End Funds," *Financial Management,* 18, no. 3 (Autumn 1989): 57–67.

Charles M. C. Lee, Andrei Shleifer, and Richard H. Thaler, "Anomalies: Closed-End Mutual Funds," *Journal of Economic Perspectives,* 4, no. 4 (Fall 1990): 153–164.

John W. Peavey III, "Returns on Initial Public Offerings of Closed-End Funds," *Review of Financial Studies,* 3, no. 4 (1990): 695–708.

Charles M. C. Lee, Andrei Shleifer, and Richard H. Thaler, "Investor Sentiment and the Closed-End Fund Puzzle," *Journal of Finance,* 46, no. 1 (March 1991): 75–109.

Albert J. Fredman and George Cole Scott, "An Investor's Guide to Closed-End Fund Discounts," *AAII Journal,* 13, no. 5 (May 1991): 12–16.

James Brickley, Steven Manaster, and James Schallheim, "The Tax-Timing Option and Discounts on Closed-End Investment Companies," *Journal of Business,* 64, no. 3 (July 1991): 287–312.

J. Bradford DeLong and Andrei Shleifer, "Closed-End Fund Discounts," *Journal of Portfolio Management,* 18, no. 2 (Winter 1992): 46–53.

Nai-fu Chen, Raymond Kan, and Merton H. Miller, "Are the Discounts on Closed-End Funds a Sentiment Index?" and "A Rejoinder," *Journal of Finance,* 48, no. 2 (June 1993): 795–800 and 809–810.

Navin Chopra, Charles M. C. Lee, Andrei Shleifer, and Richard H. Thaler, "Yes, Discounts on Closed-End Funds Are a Sentiment Index," and "Summing Up," *Journal of Finance,* 48, no. 2 (June 1993): 801–808 and 811–812.

12. Open-ending of closed-end investment companies is discussed in:

Greggory A. Brauer, "'Open-Ending' Closed-End Funds," *Journal of Financial Economics,* 13, no. 4 (December 1984): 491–507.

James A. Brickley and James S. Schallheim, "Lifting the Lid on Closed-End Investment Companies: A Case of Abnormal Returns," *Journal of Financial and Quantitative Analysis,* 20, no. 1 (March 1985): 107–117.

Financial Analysis

In a broad sense, financial analysis involves determining the levels of risk and expected return of individual financial assets as well as groups of financial assets. For example, financial analysis involves both individual common stocks, such as IBM; groups of common stocks, such as the computer industry; or, on an even larger basis, the stock market itself. In this case, financial analysis would result in a decision of how to split the investor's money between the stock, bond, and money markets, as well as a decision of whether to buy or sell computer stocks in general and IBM in particular.

An alternative definition of financial analysis is more pragmatic: the *Financial Analyst's Handbook*[1] defines the term **financial analyst** as synonymous with security analyst or investment analyst—"one who analyzes securities and makes recommendations thereon."[2] Using this definition, financial analysis can be viewed as the activity of providing inputs to the portfolio management process. This chapter (as well as Chapters 18 and 19) takes such a view in discussing the financial analysis of common stocks. Chapter 24 subsequently discusses how financial analysis can be used by **portfolio managers,** also known as investment managers.

In the United States, those who belong to a local society of financial analysts automatically belong to a national organization known as the Association for Investment Management and Research (AIMR). Among other things, membership brings with it a subscription to the *Financial Analysts Journal,* a major source of information on basic research done by other analysts and by members of the academic community. In 1993 there were over 24,000 members in the AIMR.

In 1962 the Institute of Chartered Financial Analysts (ICFA) was formed by the Financial Analysts Federation (the precursor to the AIMR) to award the professional designation of Chartered Financial Analyst (CFA). In 1993 over 19,000 analysts held the CFA designation. The CFA program is designed to establish a common set of investment knowledge and ethical standards for the various types of investment professionals. The ICFA attempts to accomplish the first objective by requiring that prospective CFAs pass a series of three exams and attain several years of investment experience. It attempts to achieve the second objective by disseminating and enforcing a set of professional conduct guidelines. (The CFA program is discussed further in this chapter's *Institutional Issues* section.)

Societies of financial analysts have been formed around the world. For example, the European Federation of Financial Analysts draws its membership from ten European countries. Other societies are located in countries such as Canada, Australia, Japan, and Brazil.

There are two primary reasons for engaging in financial analysis. The first is to try to determine certain characteristics of securities. The second is to attempt to identify mispriced securities.[3] These reasons are discussed next.

23.2.1   Determining Security Characteristics

According to modern portfolio theory, a financial analyst will want to estimate a security's future sensitivity to major factors and unique risk because these are needed to determine the risk (measured by standard deviation) of a portfolio. Perhaps the analyst will also want to estimate the dividend yield of a security over the next year in order to determine its suitability for portfolios in which dividend yield is relevant. Careful analysis of such matters as a company's dividend policy and likely future cash flows may lead to better estimates than can be obtained by simply extrapolating last year's dividend yield.

In many cases it is desirable to know something about the sources of a security's risk and return. If a portfolio is being managed for a person who is in the oil business, one might want to minimize the sensitivity of the portfolio's

The Chartered Financial Analyst Program

The investment profession encompasses a wide range of activities. Investment bankers, brokers, portfolio managers, traders, security analysts, salespeople, consultants, and pension fund administrators all fall under the rubric of investment professionals. These individuals, and the organizations for which they work, directly or indirectly affect the financial well-being of millions of people.

The Chartered Financial Analyst (CFA) program was born of a need to bring a common set of investment management concepts and standards of professional conduct to the diverse membership of the investment industry. From its modest beginnings in 1963, when 268 professionals were effectively "grandfathered" as chartered members, the CFA program has grown to a worldwide organization, with approximately 19,000 CFA charters awarded and more than 18,000 candidates currently enrolled. Although the CFA charter is far from a prerequisite for employment in the investment industry, many organizations are encouraging or even requiring new employees to participate in the CFA program.

From its inception, the Institute of Chartered Financial Analysts (ICFA), which administers the CFA program, has pursued three explicit objectives:

1. To compile a comprehensive set of currently accepted concepts and techniques relevant to the investment decision-making process (the CFA "Body of Knowledge").
2. To establish a uniform set of ethical standards to guide the activities of investment professionals.
3. To ensure that CFA charterholders have demonstrated satisfactory understanding of the Body of Knowledge and that they adhere to the established ethical standards.

Of course, like any other professional certification organization, the ICFA has multiple motives for promoting the CFA designation. By setting difficult hurdles for prospective members to clear, the CFA certification process enhances the monetary value of the charter to existing holders. Further, by demonstrating a responsible and comprehensive education and ethics program, the ICFA helps the investment industry ward off onerous government regulation and provides the industry with wider latitude to police itself.

To enroll in the CFA program, an individual must hold a bachelor's degree (or equivalent work experience), provide three acceptable character references, and pay the required registration fee. Once accepted into the program, to earn the CFA designation a candidate must pass three exams, possess three years of investment-related work experience, be a member of (or have applied to) a constituent financial analyst society, demonstrate a high level of professional conduct, and abide by the Code of Ethics and Standards of Practice of the Association for Investment Management and Research.

The CFA course of study and examinations are the cornerstone of the CFA certification process. Candidates must pass three six-hour exams. The ICFA administers these exams once a year in June at 140 locations, primarily in the United States and Canada. As candidates may take only one exam per year, a minimum of three years is required to complete the examination sequence.

The ICFA specifies a set of review materials and assigned readings for candidates to use in preparation for the exams. The study program has evolved over the years as new concepts have been introduced into the exams. The ICFA estimates that candidates average 200 hours per exam in individual study time. Many candidates also participate in independently sponsored study groups.

The CFA examinations are designed in a progressive format. The exam levels become increasingly comprehensive, building on previous levels. The CFA curriculum underwent a major change in 1993, which is being phased in over three years. When it is fully implemented in 1995, the exams will be divided into four major subject areas and several subtopics within each major subject:

1. Ethical and professional standards
   a. Applicable laws and regulations
   b. Professional standards of practice
   c. Ethical conduct and professional obligations
   d. International ethical and professional considerations

2. Tools for Inputs for Investment Valuation and Management
   a. Quantitative methods and statistics
   b. Macroeconomics
   c. Microeconomics
   d. Financial statements and accounting
3. Investment (Asset) Evaluation
   a. Overview of the valuation process
   b. Applying economic analysis in investment valuation
   c. Applying industry analysis in investment valuation
   d. Applying company analysis in investment valuation
   e. Equity securities
   f. Fixed-income securities
   g. Other investments
   h. Derivative securities
4. Portfolio Management
   a. Capital market theory
   b. Portfolio policies
   c. Expectational factors
   d. Asset allocation
   e. Fixed-income portfolio management
   f. Equity portfolio management
   g. Real estate portfolio management
   h. Specialized asset portfolio management
   i. Implementing the investment process
   j. Performance measurement

The CFA exams are rigorous and difficult. A high number of the candidates fail at least one exam, although exams can be retaken. In 1993, a total of 12,809 candidates sat for the exams. Only 55%, 56%, and 76% of the candidates taking the first, second, and third exams, respectively, passed.

The CFA program experienced tremendous growth in the 1980s. The number of candidates sitting for the exams has increased over sevenfold since 1980. Given this past success, where does the CFA program go from here?

Clearly, the ICFA desires to continue to enhance the prestige and uniqueness of its CFA certification. In recent years, however, the ICFA has also begun to strongly emphasize the continuing education aspect of its mission. Technological obsolescence is a serious problem in the rapidly changing investment industry. (For example, organized financial futures markets—see Chapter 21—did not even exist in 1980.) Many professionals who received the CFA designation just a decade ago might find it difficult to pass an exam now. Current charterholders are encouraged (although not yet required) to participate in a self-administered continuing education program.

The ICFA also sees a role for itself globally. With the investment industry becoming increasingly international in scope, the ICFA has moved to administer its program abroad. (Twenty percent of the current CFA candidates reside outside of the United States.) It has also begun to join forces with analyst societies in other countries to develop means of jointly recognizing one another's certification programs.[4]

return to changes in oil prices. This is because it is likely that if oil prices are in a decline, then the person's income from the oil business will also be in a decline. If the portfolio were sensitive to oil prices (which would be the case if it contained a substantial investment in oil stocks), then it too would be in a decline in value, thereby reinforcing the deterioration of the person's financial position.[5]

23.2.2 Attempting to Identify Mispriced Securities

The search for mispriced securities typically involves the use of **fundamental analysis.** In essence, this process entails identifying situations in which the financial analyst's estimates of such things as a firm's future earnings and dividends:

1. differ substantially from consensus (that is, average) estimates of others;
2. are viewed as being closer to the correct values than the consensus estimates; and
3. are not yet currently reflected in the market price of the firm's securities.

Two rather different approaches may be taken in the search for mispriced securities using fundamental analysis. The first approach involves valuation, where an attempt is made to determine the appropriate "intrinsic" or "true" value for a security. After making this determination, the intrinsic value is compared with the security's current market price. If the market price is substantially greater than the intrinsic value, the security is said to be overpriced or overvalued. If the market price is substantially less than the intrinsic value, the security is said to be underpriced or undervalued.

Instead of comparing price with value, the analyst sometimes estimates a security's expected return over a specified period, given its current market price and intrinsic value. This estimate is then compared with the "appropriate" return for securities with similar attributes.

Determining a security's intrinsic value may be done in great detail, using estimates of all major factors that influence security returns (for example, gross domestic product of the economy, industry sales, firm sales and expenses, and capitalization rates). Alternatively, a shortcut may be taken where, for example, an estimate of earnings per share may be multiplied by a "justified" or "normal" price-earnings ratio to determine the intrinsic value of a share of common stock. (To avoid complications arising when seeking the intrinsic value of a stock that has negative earnings per share, some analysts estimate sales per share and multiply this figure by a "normal" price-sales ratio.)

A second approach involves estimating only one or two financial variables and then comparing these estimates directly with consensus estimates. For example, next year's earnings per share for a stock may be estimated. If the analyst's estimate substantially exceeds the consensus of other analysts' estimates, the stock may be considered an attractive investment. This is because the analyst expects the actual earnings to provide a pleasant surprise for the market when announced. In turn, there will be an increase in the stock's price at that time, resulting in the investor's receiving a greater-than-normal return. Conversely, when an analyst's estimate of earnings per share is substantially below that of the other analysts, then the analyst expects that the market will receive an unpleasant surprise. The resulting decrease in the stock's price will lead to a smaller-than-normal return.

At an aggregate level, an analyst may be more optimistic about the economy than the consensus of other analysts. This would suggest that a larger-than-normal investment in stocks be taken, offset perhaps by a smaller-than-normal investment in fixed-income securities. Conversely, a relatively pessimistic view would suggest a smaller-than-normal investment in stocks, offset perhaps by a larger-than-normal investment in fixed-income securities.

Alternatively, the analyst might agree with the consensus view on both the economy and the individual characteristics of specific securities but feel that the consensus view of the prospects for a certain group of securities in a particular industry is in error. In such a case, a larger-than-normal investment may be made in stocks from an industry having prospects about which the analyst feels relatively optimistic. Conversely, a smaller-than-normal investment would be made in stocks from an industry about which the analyst feels relatively pessimistic.

The use of fundamental analysis to identify mispriced common stocks and fixed-income securities was discussed in previous chapters. This chapter will introduce the method of technical analysis and compare it to fundamental analysis.

23.2.3   Beating the Market

Many books and articles have been written that allegedly show how financial analysis can be used to "beat the market," meaning that they purport to show how to make abnormally high returns by investing in the stock market. In order to evaluate such systems, an understanding of what "the market" is and how to measure its performance is in order.

Market Indices

What did the market do yesterday? How much would an unmanaged common stock portfolio have returned last year? Such questions are often answered by examining the performance of a **market index.** Figure 23.1 displays many indices that are commonly referenced. These indices differ from one another with respect to (1) the securities included in the index and (2) the method employed in calculating the value of the index.

In order to understand how some of the most popular indices are computed, consider a simple example where the market index is based on two stocks, referred to as A and B. At the end of day 0, their closing prices are, respectively, $10 and $20 per share. Furthermore, at this time A has 1,500 shares outstanding and B has 2,000 shares outstanding.

There are three weighting methods that are most often used in computing a market index. The first method, involving **price weighting,** begins by summing the prices of the stocks that are included in the index, and ends by dividing this sum by a constant (the "divisor") in order to calculate an average price. If the index includes only stocks A and B and was started on day 0, the divisor would be equal to the number of stocks in the average, 2. Thus on day 0 the average price would be 15 [= (10 + 20)/2], and this would denote the level of the index. The divisor is adjusted thereafter whenever there is a stock split in order to avoid giving misleading indications of the "market's" direction.[6]

For example, assume that on day 1, B splits 2-for-1 and closes at $11 per share, while A closes at $13. In this situation, it is clear that the "market" has risen because both stocks have a higher price than on day 0 after adjusting B for the split. If nothing were done in computing the index, its value on day 1 would be 12 [= (13 + 11)/2], a drop of 20% [= (12 − 15)/15] from day 0 that falsely suggests that the market went down on day 1. In reality, the index went up to 17.5 {= [13 + (11 × 2)]/2}, a gain of 16.67% [= (17.5 − 15)/15].

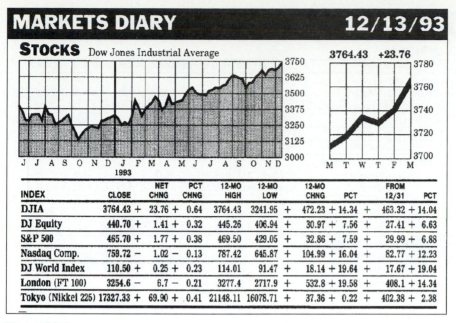

MARKETS DIARY 12/13/93

STOCKS Dow Jones Industrial Average

3764.43 +23.76

INDEX	CLOSE	NET CHNG	PCT CHNG	12-MO HIGH	12-MO LOW	12-MO CHNG	PCT	FROM 12/31	PCT
DJIA	3764.43 +	23.76 +	0.64	3764.43	3241.95 +	472.23 + 14.34 +		463.32 + 14.04	
DJ Equity	440.70 +	1.41 +	0.32	445.26	406.94 +	30.97 + 7.56 +		27.41 + 6.63	
S&P 500	465.70 +	1.77 +	0.38	469.50	429.05 +	32.86 + 7.59 +		29.99 + 6.88	
Nasdaq Comp.	759.72 −	1.02 −	0.13	787.42	645.87 +	104.99 + 16.04 +		82.77 + 12.23	
DJ World Index	110.50 +	0.25 +	0.23	114.01	91.47 +	18.14 + 19.64 +		17.67 + 19.04	
London (FT 100)	3254.6 −	6.7 −	0.21	3277.4	2717.9 +	532.8 + 19.58 +		408.1 + 14.34	
Tokyo (Nikkei 225)	17327.33 +	69.90 +	.41	21148.11	16078.71 +	37.36 + 0.22 +		402.38 + 2.38	

Figure 23.1
Stock Market Indices Published Daily in The Wall Street Journal
Source: Reprinted by permission of *The Wall Street Journal,* © Dow Jones & Company, Inc., December 14, 1993, pp. C1–C2. All rights reserved worldwide.

A stock split is accounted for in a price-weighted index by adjusting the divisor whenever a split takes place. In the example, the divisor is adjusted by examining the index on day 1, the day of the split. More specifically, the following equation would be solved for the unknown divisor *d:*

$$\frac{13 + 11}{d} = 17.5. \tag{23.1}$$

The value of *d* that solves this equation is 1.37. The new divisor will continue in use after day 1 until there is another split, when it will again be recalculated.

If it is desired to have the index begin at a given level, such as 100 on day 0, then updating it is straightforward. First the percentage change in average price is calculated. In the example, this was determined to be 16.67%. Second this percentage is multiplied by the previous day's index value in order to determine the change in the index. Continuing with the example, the index level on day 0 was 100, so the change from day 0 to day 1 would be 16.67 (= 16.67% × 100), resulting in a level on day 1 of 116.67.[7]

The *Dow Jones Industrial Average,* one of the most widely followed indices, is this type of index. It involves the prices of 30 stocks that generally represent large-size firms. Other Dow Jones Averages, for example one involving 20 transportation stocks and another involving 15 utility stocks, are similarly calculated. Furthermore, Dow Jones calculates stock market indices for each of several countries as well as an Asia/Pacific index and two World Indices, one with and one without the United States. Levels of several of these Dow Jones Averages are

MAJOR INDEXES

HIGH	LOW (†365 DAY)		CLOSE	NET CHG	% CHG	†365 DAY CHG	% CHG	FROM 12/31	% CHG
DOW JONES AVERAGES									
3764.43	3241.95	30 Industrials	3764.43 +	23.76 +	0.64	+ 472.23	+ 14.34	+ 463.32	+ 14.04
1771.95	1396.83	20 Transportation	1771.95 +	8.12 +	0.46	+ 375.12	+ 26.86	+ 322.74	+ 22.27
256.46	217.14	15 Utilities	x225.28 +	0.52 +	0.23	+ 7.08	+ 3.24	+ 4.26	+ 1.93
1382.17	1180.97	65 Composite	x1382.17 +	7.19 +	0.52	+ 195.37	+ 16.46	+ 177.62	+ 14.75
445.26	406.94	Equity Mkt. Index	440.70 +	1.41 +	0.32	+ 30.97	+ 7.56	+ 27.41	+ 6.63
NEW YORK STOCK EXCHANGE									
260.48	236.21	Composite	257.59 +	0.66 +	0.26	+ 19.43	+ 8.16	+ 17.38	+ 7.24
313.74	287.65	Industrials	313.41 +	0.93 +	0.30	+ 19.76	+ 6.73	+ 19.02	+ 6.46
246.95	206.60	Utilities	228.93 +	0.82 +	0.36	+ 22.33	+ 10.81	+ 19.27	+ 9.19
269.17	207.00	Transportation	269.17 +	1.90 +	0.71	+ 61.22	+ 29.44	+ 54.45	+ 25.36
233.33	194.56	Finance	215.41 −	0.15 −	0.07	+ 20.68	+ 10.62	+ 14.58	+ 7.26
STANDARD & POOR'S INDEXES									
469.50	429.05	500 Index	465.70 +	1.77 +	0.38	+ 32.86	+ 7.59	+ 29.99	+ 6.88
540.25	496.48	Industrials	538.47 +	1.90 +	0.35	+ 31.76	+ 6.27	+ 31.01	+ 6.11
425.73	355.88	Transportation	425.73 +	2.61 +	0.62	+ 69.32	+ 19.45	+ 61.98	+ 17.04
189.49	156.46	Utilities	173.80 +	1.14 +	0.66	+ 17.34	+ 11.08	+ 15.34	+ 9.68
48.40	39.45	Financials	44.25 +	0.10 +	0.23	+ 4.80	+ 12.17	+ 3.36	+ 8.22
177.84	155.07	400 MidCap	174.48 +	0.06 +	0.03	+ 18.32	+ 11.73	+ 13.92	+ 8.67
NASDAQ									
787.42	645.87	Composite	759.72 −	1.02 −	0.13	+ 104.99	+ 16.04	+ 82.77	+ 12.23
809.72	660.17	Industrials	786.21 −	1.15 −	0.15	+ 83.54	+ 11.89	+ 61.27	+ 8.45
956.91	772.63	Insurance	908.20 −	1.60 −	0.18	+ 132.07	+ 17.02	+ 104.29	+ 12.97
725.65	516.16	Banks	683.65 −	3.24 −	0.47	+ 166.40	+ 32.17	+ 150.72	+ 28.28
348.22	285.44	Nat. Mkt. Comp.	335.65 −	0.46 −	0.14	+ 45.04	+ 15.50	+ 35.09	+ 11.67
323.59	263.79	Nat. Mkt. Indus.	314.44 −	0.48 −	0.15	+ 32.09	+ 11.37	+ 23.04	+ 7.91
OTHERS									
484.28	389.30	Amex	464.77 −	1.51 −	0.32	+ 72.21	+ 18.39	+ 65.54	+ 16.42
293.73	259.55	Value-Line(geom.)	290.24 +	0.41 +	0.14	+ 29.25	+ 11.21	+ 23.56	+ 8.83
260.17	212.72	Russell 2000	252.23 −	0.58 −	0.23	+ 37.30	+ 17.35	+ 31.22	+ 14.13
4701.68	4219.27	Wilshire 5000	4622.61 +	8.26 +	0.18	+ 385.42	+ 9.10	+ 332.87	+ 7.76

†-Based on comparable trading day in preceding year.

Figure 23.1 (continued)

reported in almost every daily newspaper. Historical data on the Averages, including quarterly dividends and earnings figures, are published from time to time in *Barron's* and other periodicals.[8]

A second weighting method is known as **value weighting** or capitalization weighting. With this method, the prices of the stocks in the index are multiplied by their respective number of shares outstanding and then added up in order to arrive at a figure equal to the aggregate market value for that day. This figure is then divided by the corresponding figure for the day the index was started, with the resulting value being multiplied by an arbitrarily determined beginning index value.

Continuing with the example, assume that the start-up day for the index is day 0, and that the index will be assigned a beginning value of 100. First note that the aggregate market value on day 0 is equal to $55,000 [= ($10 × 1,500)

+ ($20 × 2,000)]. Next note that the aggregate market value on day 1 is equal to $63,500 [= ($13 × 1,500) + ($11 × 4,000)]. Dividing $63,500 by $55,000 and then multiplying the result by 100 gives the index value for day 1 of 115.45 [= ($63,500/$55,000) × 100]. Thus the market would be reported as having risen by 15.45% [= (115.45 − 100)/100] from day 0 to day 1.

The *Standard & Poor's 500,* widely used by institutional investors, is a value-weighted average of 500 large-sized stocks. Standard & Poor's also computes value-weighted indices for industrial, transportation, utility, and financial stocks. Industry indices are also calculated. Values for all indices, along with quarterly data on dividends, earnings, and sales, may be found in Standard & Poor's *Analysts' Handbook* (annual), *Trade and Securities Statistics* (annual), and *Analysts' Handbook Supplement* (monthly).

More comprehensive value-weighted indices for U.S. stocks are computed by other organizations. The New York Stock Exchange publishes a composite index of all stocks listed on that exchange, as well as four subindices (industrials, utilities, transportation, and finance). The American Stock Exchange computes an index of its stocks. The National Association of Securities Dealers (NASD), using its automated quotation service (Nasdaq), computes indices based on the market value of approximately 5,000 over-the-counter stocks. In addition to this composite index, NASD calculates indices for six categories representing industrials, banks, insurance, other finance, transportation, and utilities. NASD also publishes four indices that are based on just those stocks in their National Market System (the previously mentioned NASD indices are based on both NMS and non-NMS stocks). The broadest value-weighted index is calculated by Wilshire Associates. Their index, known as the *Wilshire 5000 Equity Index,* is based on all stocks listed on the New York and American Stock Exchanges plus those "actively traded over-the-counter."[9] Levels of all these indices are published weekly in *Barron's,* with the *Wall Street Journal* providing daily values for several of them.

The third method of weighting is known as **equal weighting.** This index is computed daily by multiplying the level of the index on the previous day by the arithmetic mean of the daily **price relatives** (today's price divided by yesterday's price) of the relevant stocks in the index. For example, the value of the index consisting of *A* and *B* on day 1 would be calculated by first determining the price relatives to be equal to 1.3 (= 13/10) for *A* and 1.1 [= (11 × 2)/20] for *B*. Note how an adjustment was made in calculating the price relative for *B* due to its stock split. All that was required was to multiply the postsplit price of 11 by 2, the split ratio.

Once the price relatives have been determined, then their arithmetic mean would be calculated as:

$$(1.3 + 1.1)/2 = 1.20.$$

If the value of the index on day 0 was 100, then the value on day 1 would be reported as 120 (= 100 × 1.20), an increase of 20% (= 1.20 − 1). (When the index is created, its value on that day can be set at any arbitrary starting value, such as 100.) The Value Line Composite (Arithmetic) Index, based on 1,635 stocks, is prepared in this manner.

Value Line also prepares a popular index that does not involve price weighting, value weighting, or equal weighting. This index is computed daily by multiplying the previous day's index by the *geometric mean* of the daily price relatives of the relevant stocks in the index.[10] It is referred to as the Value Line Composite (Geometric) Index, and is based on the same 1,635 stocks in the arithmetic index.

Using the example, the geometric index for day 1 is calculated in the following manner. First, the geometric mean of the daily price relatives of stocks A and B is calculated:

$$(1.3 \times 1.1)^{1/2} = 1.1958.$$

Second, given that the value of the index on the previous day (day 0) was 100, then the value on day 1 would be reported as 119.58 ($= 100 \times 1.1958$). Note that this represents an increase of 19.58% ($= 1.1958 - 1$).

In summary, four types of indices have been presented. Investors often use these indices interchangeably when they refer to how "the market" has done. However, the indices can give notably different answers. In the example shown here, the market was calculated to have risen by either 16.67%, 15.45%, 20%, or 19.58%, depending on the index used. In practice, most professional money managers use a value-weighted index such as the S&P 500 as the barometer of the stock market because such an index, by weighting larger companies more heavily than smaller companies, represents the performance of the average dollar invested in the corresponding part of the market.

Conveying Advice on Beating the Market

It is interesting to ponder whether or not advice on how to beat the market will remain useful after becoming public. It seems logical that any such prescription that has been in print for long is not likely to allow the investor to continue to beat the market consistently. Just because someone asserts that an approach has worked in the past does not mean that it, in fact, has worked. Moreover, even if it did work in the past, as more and more investors apply it, prices will be driven to levels at which the approach will not work in the future. Any system designed to beat the market, once known to more than a few people, carries the seeds of its own destruction.

There are two reasons for not including advice on "guaranteed" ways to beat the market in this book. First, to do so would make a successful system public and hence unsuccessful. Second, the authors know of no such system. Some apparent anomalies and possible inefficiencies have been described previously. But any book that purports to open the door to the *certainty* of making abnormally high returns for those who follow its advice should be regarded with the greatest skepticism.

This does not mean that financial analysis is useless. Although individuals should be skeptical when others tell them how to use financial analysis to *beat* the market, individuals can try to *understand* the market with the use of financial analysis.

23.2.4 Financial Analysis and Market Efficiency

The concept of an efficient market (discussed in Chapter 4) may appear to be based on a paradox. Financial analysts carefully evaluate the prospects for companies, industries, and the economy in the search for mispriced securities. If an undervalued security is found, then it will be purchased. However, the act of purchasing the security will tend to push its price upward toward its intrinsic value, thereby making it no longer undervalued. That is, financial analysis tends to result in security prices that reflect intrinsic values, and hence it tends to make markets efficient. But if this is the case, why would anyone perform financial analysis in an attempt to identify mispriced securities?

There are two responses to this question. First, there are costs associated with performing financial analysis. This means that financial analysis may not be conducted on all securities all the time. As a result, the prices of all securities will not reflect intrinsic values all the time. Pockets of opportunity may arise from time to time, thereby opening the possibility for added benefits from financial analysis. This suggests that people should engage in financial analysis only to the point at which the added benefits cover the added costs.[11] Ultimately, in a highly competitive market, prices would be close enough to intrinsic values to make it worthwhile for only the most skillful analysts to search for mispriced securities. Thus the market would be nearly, but not perfectly, efficient. Skilled investors will be able to earn abnormally high gross returns, but after the costs of gathering and processing information and then making the requisite trades are taken into consideration, they will end up with a net return that is not abnormal.[12]

The other response to the question focuses on the first reason given earlier for engaging in financial analysis: to determine relevant characteristics of securities. This reason is appropriate even in a perfectly efficient market. As investors differ in their circumstances (consider the person in the oil business, discussed earlier), portfolios should be tailored to accommodate such differences. Successful performance of this task generally requires estimation of certain characteristics of securities, thereby justifying the use of financial analysis.

23.2.5   Needed Skills

To understand and estimate the risk and return of individual securities as well as groups of securities (such as industries), financial markets and the principles of valuation must be understood. Much of the material required for such an understanding can be found in this book. However, even more is required. Future prospects must be estimated and interrelationships assessed. This requires the skills of an economist and an understanding of industrial organization. To process relevant historical data, some command of quantitative methods is needed, along with an understanding of the nuances of accounting.

This book cannot provide all the material one needs to become a successful financial analyst. Books on accounting, economics, industrial organization, and quantitative methods are required. Instead, some techniques used by financial analysts will be discussed, along with some of the pitfalls involved. In addition, sources of investment information will be presented.

23.3	EVALUATION INVESTMENT SYSTEMS

Many statements have been made in the past asserting that some mechanical investment system, using only available historical data and a set of objective analytical procedures, can provide results superior to those obtained with a passive investment system. (A **passive investment system** involves simply buying and holding a well-diversified portfolio of securities over a performance evaluation period. The return on a market index is often used to estimate the return on such a portfolio.) Some mechanical systems simply provide predictions of how "the market" will behave; others prescribe a complete set of instructions for investing in individual securities. Almost all of them present impressive statistics based on tests using data from some past evaluation period.

Consider as examples the following four statements:

1. "...Switch from bonds to stocks after the growth rate of the money supply has risen for two months; switch from stocks to bonds after the growth rate of the money supply has been below its most recent peak for 15 months. Historically, such a policy would have produced over twice the return obtained by simply holding stocks."
2. "...This simple formula predicted over 95% of the quarterly variation in Standard & Poor's 500–stock index over the period studied."
3. "...A portfolio of the 25 stocks with the greatest historical relative strength would have outperformed a portfolio of the 25 stocks with the lowest relative strength in 8 months out of 12."
4. "...This completely objective stock selection procedure, which can be performed without error on a microcomputer, would have outperformed 80% of the professionally managed portfolios during the period in question."

Statements such as these four have been made in the past and will undoubtedly continue to be made in the future. Advocates of such mechanical investment systems may sincerely believe that they have found the path to instant affluence. However, their proofs often rest on shaky ground. When evaluating any system, it is imperative that several possible errors be avoided.

23.3.1   Failure to Adjust for Risk

Any investment system that results in the selection of high-beta stocks is likely to produce above-average returns in bull markets and below-average returns in bear markets. Because the stock market over the long term has trended upward, on balance such a system will tend to produce above-average returns over the long run. Therefore, an evaluation of the performance of any investment system should involve not only measuring the resulting average return but also determining the amount of risk incurred. Then the average return from a passive investment system of similar risk can be computed for comparison. Techniques for making such comparisons will be presented in Chapter 25.

23.3.2   Failure to Consider Transaction Costs

Systems that rely on constant trading may produce *gross* returns that exceed those of a passive investment strategy of comparable risk. But this is not an accurate evaluation of a system's performance, because transaction costs should be considered in measuring returns. *Net* returns are calculated by adding transaction costs to the purchase price of an investment, and deducting them from the investment's selling price.

For example, if 100 shares of Widget are purchased at $19 per share with a transaction cost of $100, then the cost of the investment is $2,000 [= (100 × $19) + $100]. If Widget is subsequently sold for $23 per share, with another $100 transaction cost, then the proceeds from the sale are $2,200 [= (100 × $23) − $100]. As a result, the net return is 10% [= ($2,200 − $2,000)/$2,000], while the gross return is 21.05% [= ($2,300 − $1,900)/$1,900], a substantial difference.

23.3.3 Failure to Consider Dividends

When the performance of a mechanical system is compared with that of a passive investment system, dividends (and interest payments) are often ignored. This may seriously bias the results. For example, a system may be advocated that, in effect, selects low-yield stocks. The prices of such stocks should increase at a faster rate than those of high-yield stocks with the same amount of risk. This is because a stock's return consists of both dividends and capital appreciation. If two stocks have the same risk, they should have the same return, meaning that the stock with a smaller yield will have a larger capital appreciation. Thus if just capital appreciation is examined, a system that selects low-yield stocks would tend to show a more rapid rate of capital appreciation than a passive investment strategy involving a well-diversified portfolio consisting of both low- and high-yield stocks. Consequently, when yields of systems differ significantly from average yields, it is important to examine total returns, not just the rate of capital appreciation.

23.3.4 Nonoperational Systems

Although obvious, it still must be mentioned: to be useful, a system must not require knowledge about the future. For example, many systems require action after some time series of values (such as a stock's price) has reached a "peak" or "trough." But it is rarely apparent until well afterwards that in fact a peak or trough has been reached. Hence such a system is nonoperational.

A similar situation arises when an equation representing the system is estimated from the same set of data that is used to test the predictive accuracy of the equation. For example, a system might assume that there is a relationship between the money supply at time $t - 1$ and stock prices at time t. The general relationship might be:

$$\overline{SP}_t = a + bM_{t-1} \tag{23.2}$$

where $\overline{SP}_t$ is the predicted level of the S&P 500 at time t, M_{t-1} is the level of the money supply at time $t - 1$, and a and b are constants. In this system, the level of the S&P 500 one period from now can be predicted from the current level of the money supply.

To make such a system operational, specific numerical values for a and b are needed. These numbers might be estimated by examining monthly data over a ten-year period from 1985 through 1994, which means that these numbers would only be known after 1994. However, some people might test the predictive ability of the equation over the same ten-year period of 1985 to 1994 using these numbers. In doing so, they fail to realize that the system would not have been operational with these numbers for this test period because the numbers were determined after the test period. A true test of the predictive ability of this or any system must involve an estimation period that is earlier than the test period. That is, the test period must use out-of-sample data, as will be discussed shortly.

23.3.5 Spurious Fits

Using a set of data from a past period, it is not too difficult to discover a system that works quite well when tested on the same data.[13] In spite of the previously mentioned criticism that such a system would not have been operational during the test period, some investors might still be tempted to use it in the future if it worked well enough in retrospect. However, there is another criticism that can be made about such a system.

Imagine that Equation (23.2) did not appear to work well. If so, then the following equation could be tried:

$$\overline{SP}_t = a + bM_{t-1} + cM_{t-2} \tag{23.3}$$

where M_{t-2} is the level of the money supply at time $t - 2$ and c is a constant. If Equation (23.3) does not seem to work well, more variables and constants could be tried. Ultimately an equation could be found that appears to work quite well. However, this does not mean that it would be useful to the investor. If 100 seemingly irrelevant systems are tried with a set of data, due to the laws of probability one of them is likely to give results that are "statistically significant at the 1% level." This should not cause undue excitement because it would not have any notable predictive power in the future.

For example, stock prices in the United States have been shown to be correlated with both sunspot activity and with the length of skirts. However, these correlations are unlikely to demonstrate actual causal relationships. Instead, these correlations are likely to have been "spurious," meaning that they probably were coincidental. Without solid reasons to believe that a relationship is due to underlying forces, it would be unwise to predict its continuation in the future.

23.3.6 Comparisons with Easily Beaten Systems

Often an investment system is said to "explain" a large part of the variation in some stock index. Figure 23.2 shows the quarterly level of the S&P 500 over a ten-year period (the solid line), and the levels predicted by a system based on historic levels of the money supply (the dotted line). The two sets of values appear to be quite similar.

Impressive? Not very. An extremely simple set of predictions, shown by the dashed line is even better. This procedure predicts that each quarter's index will equal that of the preceding quarter:

$$\overline{SP}_t = SP_{t-1}. \tag{23.4}$$

Any system that is purported to be able to beat the market must predict percentage price changes (or returns), not price levels, because such changes (or returns) determine profits and losses. Thus a good test is the extent to which predicted changes conform to actual changes. Figure 23.3 shows the percentage price change predicted by the system analyzed in Figure 23.2, along with the corresponding actual change for each quarter. The relationship is, at best, tenuous.

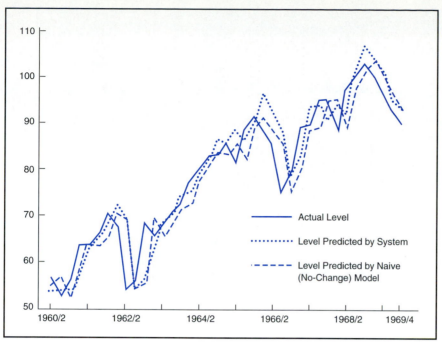

Figure 23.2
Actual and Predicted Levels, Standard & Poor's 500–Stock Index,
Second Quarter 1960 Through Fourth Quarter 1969
Source: Kenneth E. Homa and Dwight M. Jaffee, "The Supply of Money and Common Stock Prices,"
Journal of Finance, 26, no. 5 (December 1971): p. 1052.

23.3.7 Reliance on Misleading Visual Comparisons

Occasionally the proponent of a system will produce a graph that plots both the
level of an indicator intended to predict market moves and the levels of the market itself. Visual comparison of the two curves may suggest that the indicator does
indeed predict changes in the market. However, the eye cannot easily differentiate between a situation in which changes in a market "predictor" *lead* the market
and one in which the changes *lag* behind the market. This is a crucial distinction
because only a leading indicator can bring superior investment performance.

23.3.8 Ex Post Selection Bias

Many studies describe a stock selection system that outperformed standard stock
market indices. Some of these systems avoid the errors considered thus far, but
another error may be involved. To facilitate computer-based analysis, a standard
set of data might have been employed. For example, an investigator might use a
database prepared in 1994 with stock price data relating to the period from 1983
through 1993. The stocks included in the database may have been chosen because they existed and were important in 1994 (for example, they may have been
considered important because they were listed on the NYSE in 1994). Discover-
ing a superior investment system from analysis of this database is subject to the

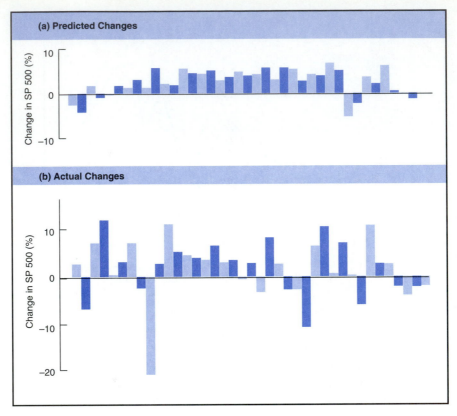

Figure 23.3

Predicted and Actual Quarterly Percentage Changes, Standard & Poor's
500–Stock Index, Second Quarter 1960 Through Fourth Quarter 1969

Source: Kenneth E. Homa and Dwight M. Jaffee, "The Supply of Money and Common Stock Prices,"
Journal of Finance, 26, no. 5 (December 1971): 1052.

criticism of *ex post* **selection bias** (or survivorship bias). That is, the system discovered in 1994 was based on an analysis of those stocks that were certain to be alive, well, and important in 1994. Accordingly, it should have done well over the period of 1983 to 1993. However, studies of this type implicitly commit an error described earlier—they require some information not available in advance. In particular, they require knowledge before 1994 of which stocks will be around in 1994.[14]

23.3.9 Failure to Use Out-of-Sample Data

Can any evidence concerning a system's ability to beat the market be persuasive? Probably not to those who believe absolutely in market efficiency. But there are appropriate tests that can be undertaken.

The search for a system should be conducted using one set of data, and the test of the system's predictive ability should be performed using an entirely different set of data. The latter set of data is sometimes known as **out-of-sample data** or a holdout sample. To be complete, such a test should involve the (simulated) management of a portfolio and be designed so that each investment decision is based solely on information available at the time the decision is made. Finally, the performance of the system should be measured in the way one would measure the performance of any investment manager (to be discussed in Chapter 25). This involves, among other things, attempting to determine the probability that the investment results were due to chance rather than skill.

Figure 23.4 shows the performance of one system using out-of-sample data. Values forecast by three predictive systems for quarterly percentage changes in the S&P 500 are shown, along with the subsequent actual changes. Each of the predictive systems worked extremely well with past data. The same cannot be said for their predictions using out-of-sample data. The next section describes some systems in more detail.

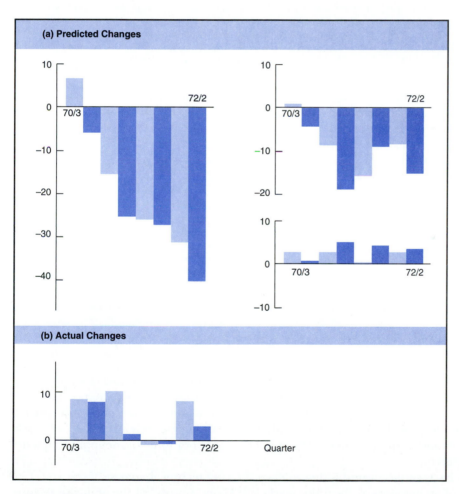

Figure 23.4
Predicted and Actual Quarterly Percentage Changes, Standard & Poor's
500–Stock Index, Third Quarter 1970 Through Second Quarter 1972
Source: James E. Pesando, "The Supply of Money and Common Stock Prices: Further Observations on the Econometric Evidence," *Journal of Finance,* 29, no. 3 (June 1974): p. 916.

One of the major divisions in the ranks of financial analysts is between those using fundamental analysis (known as fundamental analysts or fundamentalists) and those using **technical analysis** (known as technical analysts or technicians). The fundamentalist tends to look forward; the technician backward. The fundamentalist is concerned with such matters as future earnings and dividends, whereas the technician thinks little (if at all) about such matters.

> *Technical analysis is the study of the internal stock exchange information as such. The word "technical" implies a study of the market itself and not of those external factors which are reflected in the market. . . . [A]ll the relevant factors, whatever they may be, can be reduced to the volume of the stock exchange transactions and the level of share prices; or more generally, to the sum of the statistical information produced by the market.[15]*

The technician usually attempts to predict short-term price movements and thus makes recommendations concerning the *timing* of purchases and sales of either specific stocks or groups of stocks (such as industries) or stocks in general. It is sometimes said that fundamental analysis is designed to answer the question "What?" and technical analysis to answer the question "When?"

The concept of technical analysis is completely at odds with the notion of efficient markets:

> *The methodology of technical analysis . . . rests upon the assumption that history tends to repeat itself in the stock exchange. If a certain pattern of activity has in the past produced certain results nine times out of ten, one can assume a strong likelihood of the same outcome whenever this pattern appears in the future.* **It should be emphasized, however, that a large part of the methodology of technical analysis lacks a strictly logical explanation.[16]** *(Emphasis added.)*

Thus technicians assert that the study of past patterns of variables such as prices and volumes will allow the investor to accurately identify times when certain specific stocks (or groups of stocks, or the market in general) are either overpriced or underpriced. Most (but not all) technical analysts rely on charts of stock prices and trading volumes. The appendix describes some of the more frequently used ones.

Early studies found little evidence showing technical analysis to be useful in enabling investors to "beat the market."[17] Many "proofs" of the ability of technical analysis to "beat the market" were offered, but most committed at least one of the errors described earlier. However, several recent studies have indicated that technical analysis may be useful to investors.[18] The evidence presented in these studies can be divided into two groups based on the strategies involved.

The first group, consisting of momentum and contrarian strategies, simply examines the returns on stocks over a time period that just ended in order to identify candidates for purchase and sale. The second group, consisting of moving average and trading range breakout strategies, makes such an identification based on the relationship of a security's price over a relatively short time period that just ended to its price over a relatively longer time period.

23.4.1 Momentum and Contrarian Strategies

Consider ranking a group of stocks based on the size of their returns over some time period that just ended. *Momentum investors* seek out for purchase those stocks that have recently risen significantly in price on the belief that they will continue to rise due to an upward shift in their demand curves. Conversely, those stocks that have recently fallen significantly in price are sold on the belief that their demand curves have shifted downward.

Investors who call themselves *contrarians* do just the opposite of what most other investors are doing in the market: They buy stocks that others have shunned and think of as losers, and they sell stocks that others have feverishly pursued and think of as winners. They do so in the belief that investors tend to overreact to news. That is, stocks that have plunged in price because of some recent piece of bad news (such as recently announced weak earnings) are thought to have fallen too far in price. Hence such stocks are viewed as being ready for a price rebound as investors realize that they have overreacted to the bad news associated with the stock and subsequently drive the price upward toward the stock's fundamental value.

Similarly, stocks that have risen rapidly in price due to some recent piece of good news (such as recently announced strong earnings) are thought to have risen too far in price. Hence such stocks are viewed as being ready for a price drop as investors realize that they have overreacted to the good news associated with the stock and subsequently drive the price downward toward the stock's fundamental value. Researchers have tested strategies of this type. Their overall test design is discussed first, followed by the results.

The Test Design

Consider the following investment strategy:

1. Identify those stocks that have been listed on either the NYSE or AMEX (or just the NYSE). This focuses the technician's attention on established stocks.
2. Rank these stocks based on the size of their returns over a just-ending time period, referred to as the portfolio "formation period."
3. Assign some of those stocks that have the lowest average return in the formation period to the "loser" portfolio and some of those stocks that have the highest average return in this period to the "winner" portfolio.
4. Determine the returns on the winner and loser portfolios over a just-starting subsequent time period, referred to as the portfolio "test period."

5. Repeat the analysis all over again, starting with step 1, but moving forward one time period. Stop after several repetitions.
6. Determine the abnormal returns on the winner portfolio by subtracting the returns on a benchmark portfolio having a comparable level of risk (see section 5.4 of Chapter 22); calculate the average of these abnormal returns. Similarly, determine the average abnormal returns on the loser portfolio.

If a momentum strategy works, then the winner portfolio should have a positive average abnormal return and the loser portfolio a negative one. Furthermore, the difference in their abnormal returns should be significantly positive. Conversely, if a contrarian strategy works, then the loser portfolio should have a positive abnormal return and the winner portfolio a negative one, and the difference should be significantly negative.

However, if stocks are priced efficiently, then their past price behavior is useless in terms of its predictive value. Neither momentum nor contrarian strategies should "work" in that winner portfolios should perform no differently from loser portfolios. Both portfolios should have average abnormal returns of approximately zero. Even more important, *the difference in these returns should be approximately zero.*

Test Results

Table 23.1 presents the test results. In part A, portfolios were formed based on their returns during the past week. All stocks with an above-average return were put into a winner portfolio and those with a below-average return were put into a loser portfolio. Then the returns on these two portfolios were tracked for the next week. When this was done repeatedly week by week from 1962 through 1986, it was found that there were marked differences in the annualized average abnormal returns on the two portfolios. Specifically, the returns were nearly -25% for the winners and $+90\%$ for the losers, with a difference of -115%. *This difference (as well as the differences in the other parts of the table) was found to be statistically significantly different from zero.* Note that a similar but not as extreme observation is apparent in part B, where the time frame is one month instead of a week.[19] Overall, this evidence indicates that contrarian strategies hold promise. Interestingly, the correction for the overreaction is asymmetric in part A because the losers rebound by a much larger percentage than the winners fall. This suggests that contrarians should concentrate more on identifying losers than on winners if they are going to focus on weekly returns.

In part C of Table 23.1, portfolios were formed based on their returns over the past six months. The 10% of stocks with the highest returns were put in the winner portfolio whereas the 10% with the lowest returns were put in the loser portfolio. Tracking their returns over the next six months revealed significant differences. In complete contrast to parts A and B, now the winners have a much higher average abnormal return than the losers, suggesting that momentum strategies have promise. Stocks that shot up in price over six months continued to go up during the next six months, whereas those that plunged over six months continued their plunge. Although not quite as strong, similar results were observed when the top 10% and bottom 10% were identified based on a full year's returns, as shown in part D.[20]

TABLE 23.1
RETURNS FROM MOMENTUM AND CONTRARIAN STRATEGIES

Length of Portfolio Formation and Test Periods	Annualized Abnormal Returns		
	Winner Portfolio	Loser Portfolio	Winner Return less Loser Return
A. Weekly, 1962–1986:			
Top 50% and bottom 50% of NYSE and AMEX stocks	−24.9%	89.8%	−114.7%
B. Monthly, 1929–1982:			
Top 10% and bottom 10% of all NYSE and AMEX stocks	−11.6%	12.1%	−23.7%
C. Semiannually, 1962–1989:			
Top 10% and bottom 10% of all NYSE and AMEX stocks	8.7%	−3.5%	12.2%
D. Annually, 1929–1982:			
Top 10% and bottom 10% of all NYSE and AMEX stocks*	5.0%	−6.1%	11.1%
E. Three years, 1926–1982:			
Top 35 and bottom 35 NYSE stocks	−1.7%	6.5%	−8.2%
F. Five years, 1926–1982:			
Top 50 and bottom 50 NYSE stocks	−2.4%	7.2%	−9.6%

*Abnormal returns were measured over one month subsequent to the portfolio formation date.

Source: Adapted from:

A. Bruce N. Lehmann, "Fads, Martingales, and Market Efficiency," *Quarterly Journal of Economics*, 105, no. 1 (February 1990): p. 16.

B. Narasimhan Jegadeesh, "Evidence of Predictable Behavior of Security Returns," *Journal of Finance*, 45, no. 3 (July 1990): pp. 890–891.

C. Narasimhan Jegadeesh and Sheridan Titman, "Returns to Buying Winners and Selling Losers: Implications for Stock Market Efficiency," *Journal of Finance*, 48, no. 1 (March 1993): p. 79.

D. Narasimhan Jegadeesh, "Evidence of Predictable Behavior of Security Returns," *Journal of Finance*, 45, no. 3 (July 1990): pp. 890–891.

E. Werner F. M. De Bondt and Richard Thaler, "Does the Stock Market Overreact?" *Journal of Finance*, 40, no. 3 (July 1985): p. 799.

F. Werner F. M. De Bondt and Richard Thaler, "Further Evidence on Investor Overreaction and Stock Market Seasonality," *Journal of Finance*, 42, no. 3 (July 1987): p. 561.

Oddly, parts E and F show that the momentum strategy would not have worked if the winner and loser portfolios were formed based on three-year or five-year stock returns. (It should be noted that there are subtle differences in how the portfolios in parts E and F were formed.) Instead, the contrarian strategy appears to have worked once again. Note that the average annual abnormal return in part E on the loser portfolio was +6.5%. Conversely, the average annual abnormal return on the winner portfolio was −1.7%, resulting in a significant difference of 8.2%. Part F shows that similar results were obtained when portfolios were formed based on returns over the previous five years.[21] As in part A, the correction for the overreaction is asymmetric in that losers rebound by a much larger percentage than the winners fall.

In summary, there does appear to be some merit to the contrarian strategy for both very short (a week or month) and very long (three or five years) time periods.[22] Surprisingly, for intermediate periods such as six months and one year, an exact opposite strategy—momentum—seems to have merit. Unfortunately, both strategies involve a high degree of turnover, as portfolios are reconstituted frequently—particularly for the weekly contrarian strategy.[23] As the strategies would incur substantial transaction costs, it remains to be seen whether they are profitable after such costs are fully accounted for.

23.4.2   Moving Average and Trading Range Breakout Strategies

Consider the following investment strategy:

1. Calculate the average closing price of a given stock over the last 200 trading days.
2. Take today's closing price and divide it by the 200–day average to form a short-to-long price ratio.
3. If the ratio is greater than one, this is a buy signal that indicates that the stock is to be bought tomorrow. If the ratio is less than one, this is a sell signal that indicates that the stock is to be sold tomorrow.
4. Tomorrow after closing, repeat the above process.
5. At the end of a test period, calculate the average daily return during both the "buy" days and "sell" days.

If the stock market is efficient, the average return during the buy days should be approximately the same as the average return during the sell days. That is, *the difference in their returns should be approximately zero.* However, technical analysis might have merit if they are significantly different.

A study examined this strategy using daily data from 1897 to 1986, a total of over 25,000 trading days. However, the daily closing level of the Dow Jones Industrial Average (DJIA) was used instead of daily closing prices for individual stocks. As shown in part A of Table 23.2, this strategy resulted in markedly different returns on buy and sell days. In particular, the annualized average return on buy days was 10.7%, whereas the return on sell days was -6.1%. *The difference of 16.8% was statistically significantly different from zero (as were the differences in the other parts of the table).*

Because this strategy classifies every day as either a buy day or a sell day, thereby allowing a given stock to be bought on consecutive days, it is referred to as a variable-length moving average strategy. However, it can result in many trades over the course of a year, as an investor using it could be "whipsawed" into

---

TABLE 23.2

RETURNS FROM MOVING AVERAGE AND TRADING RANGE BREAKOUT STRATEGIES

	Annualized Average Returns		
	Buy Signal	Sell Signal	Buy Return less Sell Return
A. Moving average tests:			
Variable length	10.7%	-6.1%	16.8%
Fixed length	13.8	-4.8	18.6
B. Trading range breakout tests:	11.8%	-5.8%	17.6%

Source: Adapted from William Brock, Josef Lakonishok, and Blake LeBaron, "Simple Technical Trading Rules and the Stochastic Properties of Stock Returns," *Journal of Finance,* 47, no. 5 (December 1992): pp. 1739, 1741, 1742. Based on one–day short and 200–day long periods during 1897 to 1986 with no filter; annualized assuming that there are 260 trading days in a year and 26 ten–day trading periods in a year.

---

buying and selling repeatedly. In order to reduce the frequency of changing positions from buying to selling, or selling to buying, the strategy can be modified as follows to become a fixed-length moving average strategy. Buy signals are now generated only when the ratio *changes* from less than one to greater than one, and sell signals are generated only when the ratio *changes* from greater than one to less than one. Furthermore, when a buy signal is generated, the stock is bought the next day and then held for ten days. Similarly, when a sell signal is generated, the stock is sold and not bought for ten days. In either case, when the ten days are over, the investor starts looking again for a buy or sell signal. Whereas the variable-length strategy classified every day as either a buy or sell day, there can be days that are not classified as either buy or sell with the fixed-length strategy.

Part A of Table 23.2 shows that the fixed-length moving average strategy performed similarly to the variable length one. The annualized average return on buy days was 13.8% and on sell days was −4.8%, resulting in a significant difference of 18.6%. On average there were about 1.3 and 1.7 buy and sell signals per year, respectively.

The trading range breakout strategy is similar to the fixed-length moving average strategy. Here the high and low prices over the past 200 trading days are noted. A buy signal is generated on a given day only when that day's closing price is greater than the high, provided that the previous day's closing price was less than the high. Conversely, a sell signal arises when the closing price moves from being above the low on one day to being below the low on the next day. When a buy signal is generated, the stock is bought the next day and then held for ten days. Similarly, when a sell signal is generated, the stock is sold and not bought for ten days. In either case, when the ten days are over, the investor starts looking again for a buy or sell signal.

Part B of Table 23.2 shows that the trading range breakout strategy performed similarly to the two moving average strategies. The annualized average returns on buy days was 11.8% and on sell days was −5.8%, with a significant difference of 17.6%. On average there were about 5.2 and 2.0 buy and sell signals per year, respectively.

23.4.3 The Bottom Line

What is the bottom line? The four strategies reported in Tables 23.1 and 23.2 have been rigorously tested, avoiding the pitfalls mentioned earlier. Furthermore, although not reported, slight variations among the strategies had only a minor effect on their results. However, the usefulness of such technical strategies remains an open question subject to much debate. Despite appearing to be profitable, even after considering transaction costs, it is quite possible that a more complete consideration of these costs (including such things as the impact of bid-ask spreads) will reveal that they are incapable of generating abnormal profits. Hence evaluating investment systems will not always provide unambiguous answers on their potential usefulness. Furthermore, it has been speculated that the commonplace usage of computerized trading programs designed to implement technical strategies will ultimately eliminate any potential such strategies have for generating abnormal profits.[24] Nevertheless, the apparent success of these strategies offers a challenge to those who contend that the U.S. stock market is highly efficient.

23.5	FUNDAMENTAL ANALYSIS

The rest of this chapter is concerned with the principles of fundamental analysis of common stocks. Although technical analysis is used by many investors, fundamental analysis is far more prevalent. Furthermore, unlike technical analysis, it is an essential activity if capital markets are to be efficient.

23.5.1 Top-Down versus Bottom-Up Forecasting

Fundamental analysts forecast, among other things, future levels of the economy's gross domestic product, future sales and earnings for a number of industries, and future sales and earnings for an even larger number of firms. Eventually such forecasts are converted to estimates of expected returns of specific stocks and, perhaps, certain industries and the stock market itself. In some cases the conversion is made explicitly. For example, an estimate of next year's earnings per share for a firm may be multiplied by a projected price-earnings ratio in order to estimate the expected price of the firm's stock a year hence, thereby allowing a forecast of the expected return to be made. In other cases the conversion is implicit. For example, stocks with projected earnings exceeding consensus estimates may be placed on an "approved" list.

Some investment organizations that employ financial analysts follow a sequential **top-down forecasting approach.** With this approach, the financial analysts are first involved in making forecasts for the economy, then for industries, and finally for companies. The industry forecasts are based on the forecasts for the economy and, in turn, a company's forecasts are based on the forecasts for both its industry and the economy.

Other investment organizations begin with estimates of the prospects for companies and then build to estimates of the prospects for industries and ultimately the economy. Such **bottom-up forecasting** may unknowingly involve inconsistent assumptions. For example, one analyst may use one forecast of foreign exchange rates in projecting the foreign sales of company A, while another analyst may use a different forecast in projecting the foreign sales of company B. Top-down systems are less susceptible to this danger because all the analysts in the organization would use the same forecast of exchange rates.

In practice, a combination of the two approaches is often employed. For example, forecasts are made for the economy in a top-down manner. These forecasts then provide a setting within which financial analysts make bottom-up forecasts for individual companies. The sum of the individual forecasts should be consistent with the original economywide forecast.[25] If not, the process is repeated (perhaps with additional controls) to ensure consistency.

23.5.2 Probabilistic Forecasting

Explicit **probabilistic forecasting** often focuses on economywide forecasts, as uncertainty at this level is of the greatest importance in determining the risk and expected return of a well-diversified portfolio. A few alternative economic scenarios may be forecast, along with their respective probability of occurrence. Then accompanying projections are made of the prospects for industries, companies, and stock prices. Such an exercise provides an idea of the likely sensitivities of different stocks to surprises concerning the economy and hence is sometimes referred to as "what-if" analysis. By assigning probabilities to the different scenarios, risks may also be estimated.

23.5.3 Econometric Models

An **econometric model** is a statistical model that provides a means of forecasting the levels of certain variables, known as **endogenous variables.** In order to make these forecasts, the model relies on assumptions that have been made in regard to the levels of certain other variables supplied by the model user, known as **exogenous variables.** For example, the level of next year's car sales may be specified by an econometric model to be related to next year's level of gross domestic product and interest rates. The values of next year's gross domestic product and interest rates, the exogenous variables, must be provided in order to forecast next year's car sales, the endogenous variable.

An econometric model may be extremely complex or it may be a simple formula that can be implemented with a calculator. In either case, it should involve a blend of economics and statistics, where first economics is used to suggest the forms of relevant relationships and then statistical procedures are applied to historical data to estimate the exact nature of the relationships involved.

Some investment organizations use large-scale econometric models to translate predictions about such factors as the federal budget, expected consumer spending, and planned business investment into predictions of future levels of gross domestic product, inflation, and unemployment. Several firms and nonprofit organizations maintain such models, selling either the forecasts or the computer program itself to investment organizations, corporate planners, public agencies, and others.

The developers of such large-scale models usually provide several "standard" predictions, based on different sets of assumptions about the exogenous variables. Some also assign probabilities to the alternative predictions. In some cases, users can substitute their own assumptions and subsequently examine the resulting predictions.

Large-scale econometric models of this type employ many equations that describe many important relationships. Although estimates of the magnitudes of such relationships are obtained from historical data, these estimates may or may not enable the model to work well in the future. When predictions turn out to be poor, it is sometimes said that there has been a structural change in the underlying economic relationships. However, the failure may result from the influence of factors omitted from the model. Either situation necessitates changes in either the magnitudes of the estimates or the basic form of the econometric model, or both. Rare indeed is the user who does not "fine-tune" (or completely overhaul) such a model from time to time as further experience is accumulated.

23.5.4 Financial Statement Analysis

For some, the image of a typical financial analyst is that of a gnome, fully equipped with green eyeshade, poring over financial statements in a back room. While the physical description is rarely accurate, it is true that many analysts do study financial statements in an attempt to predict the future.

A company's financial statements can be regarded as the output of a model of the firm—a model designed by management, the company's accountants, and (indirectly) the tax authorities. Different companies use different models, meaning that they treat similar events in different ways. One reason this is possible is because generally accepted accounting principles (GAAP), as established by the Financial Accounting Standards Board (FASB), allow a certain degree of latitude in how to account for various events. Examples include the method of depreciating assets (straight line or accelerated) and the method of valuing inventory (FIFO or LIFO).

To fully understand a company and to compare it with others that use different accounting procedures, the financial analyst must be a financial detective, looking for clues in footnotes and the accompanying text that discuss how the financial statements were prepared. Those who take bottom-line figures such as earnings per share on faith may be more surprised by future developments than those who try to look behind the accounting veil.

The ultimate goal of fundamental analysis is to determine the values of the outstanding claims on a firm's income (claimants include the firm's bondholders and stockholders). The firm's income must first be projected, then the possible distributions of that income among the claimants must be considered, with relevant probabilities assessed.

In practice, shortcut procedures are often used. Many analysts focus on reported accounting figures, even though such numbers may not adequately reflect true economic values. In addition, simple measures are often used to assess complex relationships. For example, some analysts attempt to estimate the probability that short-term creditors will be paid in full and on time by examining the ratio of liquid assets to the amount of short-term debt. Similarly, the probability that interest will be paid to bondholders in a timely fashion is often estimated by examining the ratio of earnings before interest and taxes to the periodic amount of such interest payments. Often the prospects for a firm's common stock are estimated by examining the ratio of earnings after taxes to the book value of equity.

Ratio Analysis

The use of ratios such as these to facilitate predicting the future is widespread. Some ratios use items from the same financial statement (either a particular balance sheet or income statement), whereas others use items from two different statements. Still other ratios use items from two or more statements of the same type but from different years (for example, this year's balance sheet and last year's balance sheet), or incorporate data on market values.

Ratios may be used in several ways. Some analysts apply absolute standards, on the grounds that a substandard ratio indicates a potential weakness that merits further analysis. Other analysts compare a company's ratios to those of the "average" firm in the same industry in order to detect differences that may need further consideration. Others analyze trends in a company's ratios over time, hoping that these trends will help them predict future changes. Still others combine ratios with technical analysis in order to arrive at investment decisions.

Another use of ratios is illustrated in Figure 23.5. In this figure, each ratio is equal to the product of the two ratios on its right-hand side, with one exception. The exception is the turnover ratio (sales/assets), whose reciprocal (assets/sales) equals the sum of the reciprocals of the four ratios on its right-hand side. Given the interrelationships among the ratios, it can be seen that once the future values of these ratios are forecast, then an implied forecast for the price of the firm's stock can be computed. The difficulty with such an approach, however, is in accurately predicting the future values of the ratios.

Ratio analysis can be very sophisticated, but it can also be overly simplistic. Routine extrapolation of a present ratio (or its recent trend) may produce a poor estimate of its future value. (For example, there is no reason for a firm to maintain a constant ratio of inventory to sales.) Moreover, a series of simple projections may produce inconsistent financial statements. For example, projections of ratios imply predictions of the levels of various balance sheet items. However, it may be that when these levels are looked at altogether, the resulting balance sheet does not balance.

Spreadsheets

To project future financial statements, one should build a model that includes the relationships among the items on such statements and outside factors. Traditional ratio analysis does this, but somewhat crudely. A much better procedure uses personal computers and spreadsheet software.[26]

Basically, a spreadsheet is an arrangement of information in rows and columns. Each cell on a traditional (paper) spreadsheet typically contains a number or a label. Some of the numbers (for example, sales) are entered directly, whereas others (for example, earnings before interest and taxes) are computed from the numbers in other cells.

An electronic spreadsheet simulates a traditional spreadsheet on a computer screen. There are, however, notable differences. Most importantly, cells can contain formulas. For example, the cell for earnings before interest and taxes (EBIT) could contain the formula for calculating the value as well as the value produced by the formula. Normally, only the value would be displayed,

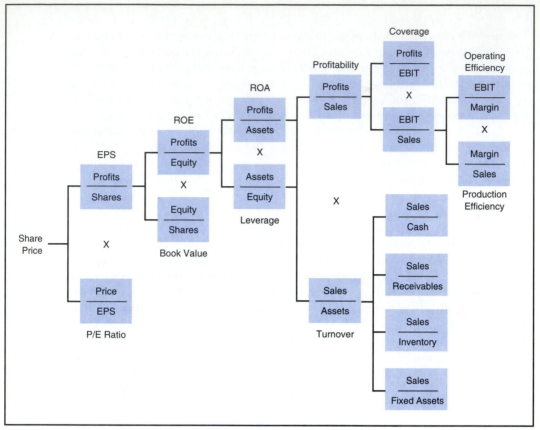

Figure 23.5
The Use of Predicted Ratios to Compute Predicted Price
Source: Samuel S. Stewart, Jr., "Corporate Forecasting," in Sumner N. Levine, ed., *Financial Analyst's Handbook I* (Homewood, IL: Dow Jones-Irwin, Inc. 1975), p. 912.

giving an outward appearance similar to that of a traditional spreadsheet. However, any change in the number in the cell for sales would immediately change the value of EBIT because the formula for EBIT would contain the value for sales as an input. This feature of electronic spreadsheets allows the user to rapidly explore the implications of changes in key assumptions (such as prices, quantities, and costs) on various balance sheet and income statement items. Accordingly, exploration of this sort is often known as *sensitivity analysis* or *what-if analysis*.

In summary, financial statement analysis can help an analyst understand a company's current situation, where it may be going, what factors affect it, and how these factors affect it. If others are doing such analysis and doing it well, it will be difficult to find mispriced securities in this manner. But it should be possible to more accurately identify firms likely to go bankrupt, firms with higher or lower betas, and firms with greater or lesser sensitivities to major factors. Increased understanding of such aspects may well provide ample rewards.

When a security analyst decides that a stock is mispriced and informs certain clients of this, some of the clients may act on the information. As they do so, the price of the security may be affected. As news of the analyst's recommendation spreads, more investors may act, and the price may react even more. At some point, the analyst's information will be "fully reflected" in the stock price.

If the analyst decides that a stock is underpriced and clients subsequently purchase it, the stock's price will tend to rise. Conversely, if the analyst decides that a stock is overpriced and clients subsequently sell it, the stock's price will tend to decline. If the analyst's views were well founded, no subsequent counter-reaction in the stock's price would be expected. Otherwise, the price is likely to return to its pre-recommendation level at some later time.

An interesting example of the impact of analysts' recommendations is provided by the behavior of prices of stocks mentioned in the "Heard on the Street" column of the *Wall Street Journal,* which periodically summarizes recent stock recommendations. An analyst's opinion is typically published in "Heard on the Street" after it is first given to clients. The analyst's view is thus "somewhat public" for several days before publication, but when the column appears the opinion becomes "very public" because it then reaches a substantially larger audience.

Panel (a) of Figure 23.6 summarizes the price reactions of 597 stocks that received positive opinions in "Heard on the Street" during 1970 and 1971. Panel (b) summarizes the reactions of 188 stocks that received negative opinions during the same time period. In each panel the vertical axis plots the average cumulative abnormal return—that is, the average return, adjusted for normal reactions to overall market moves. The two horizontal axes indicate trading days relative to the recommendation's date of publication, going from 20 days before to 20 days after publication.

As shown in the figure, the publication of such a recommendation typically affects the stock's price.[27] Specifically, the stocks recommended for purchase had, on average, an abnormal return of about 1% on the publication date, while the stocks recommended for sale had an abnormal return of roughly −2%. Furthermore, after making such adjustments, the prices of 70% of the 597 stocks recommended for purchase rose on the date of publication, and the prices of 90% of the 188 stocks recommended for sale fell on the date of publication.

The roughly horizontal lines after day 0 in both panels show that both types of recommendations appeared to contain information. This is because the horizontal lines indicate that there was no significant counterreaction in the 20 days after either a buy or sell recommendation was made.[28]

The upward moves in panel (a) prior to day 0 suggest that prior purchases of the stocks have been made by clients of the analysts. An alternative explanation is that analysts simply recommended purchases of stocks that had recently risen in price. Note, however, that panel (b) is quite different: there is no distinct pattern prior to the date of publication of a sell recommendation. This suggests that the analysts did not tend to recommend the sale of securities that had recently fallen in price.[29]

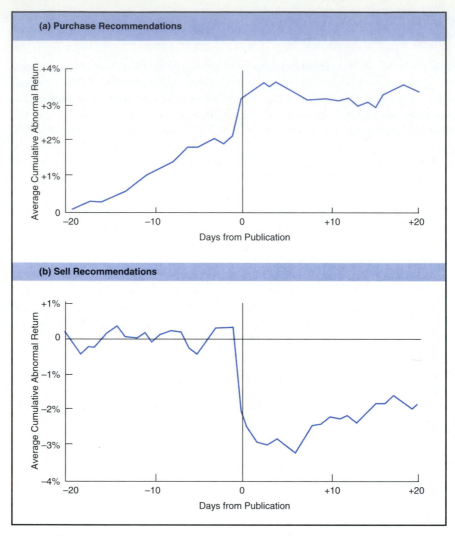

Figure 23.6
Effect on Stock Prices of Stock Recommendations in "Heard on the Street": 1970 and 1971

Source: Peter Lloyd-Davies and Michael Canes, "Stock Prices and the Publication of Second-Hand Information," *Journal of Business,* 51, no. 1 (January 1978): p. 52. ©1978, The University of Chicago.

23.7   ANALYST FOLLOWING AND STOCK RETURNS

An interesting issue involves the relationship between the amount of attention devoted by analysts to individual stocks and the price behavior of those stocks. Do stocks that are intensively followed have significantly different returns from those stocks that are relatively neglected by analysts? One study examined all stocks in the S&P 500 for the period from 1970 to 1979 in order to answer such a question. Table 23.3 summarizes the results.

TABLE 23.3
ANALYST FOLLOWING AND STOCK RETURNS

Amount of Following	All Stocks (1)	Small Firms (2)	Medium Firms (3)	Large Firms (4)
High	7.5%	5.0%	7.4%	8.4%
Moderate	11.8%	13.2%	11.0	10.2%
Low	15.4	15.8	13.9%	15.3
Low-high	7.9%	10.8%	6.5%	6.9%
Average return	11.0	13.5	10.7	9.8

Source: Adapted from Avner Arbel and Paul Strebel, "Pay Attention to Neglected Firms!" *Journal of Portfolio Management*, 9, no. 2 (Winter 1983): p. 39.

Column (1) shows that the stocks followed by the largest number of analysts had the lowest average returns. However, the stocks followed by the fewest analysts had the highest average returns, thereby suggesting the presence of a **neglected firm effect.**

It is possible that this effect is simply a reflection of the size effect, as the average return on small-sized firms has been shown to be larger than the average return on larger firms.[30] The reason for this possibility is that the number of analysts following a stock is generally related to the size of the underlying firm. However, columns (2), (3), and (4) show that this is not simply another manifestation of the size effect.[31] It can be seen that the neglected firm effect exists for all firm sizes. Furthermore, it is most pronounced for small firms—note that the difference between the high and low categories is largest in column (2).

What are the implications of the neglected firm effect? First, it could be that the higher average return associated with neglected firms is a reward for investing in securities that have less available information. Second, because the neglected firm effect exists across all sizes of firms, large institutional investors that are prohibited from investing in small firms can still take advantage of this effect, as it also exists for medium and large firms (although it is notably less significant). Finally, whether or not such a simple rule will be useful in the future is open to debate. Why? If investors increase their purchases of neglected firms, then such firms will no longer be neglected and hence will no longer provide abnormally high returns.

23.8   SOURCES OF INVESTMENT INFORMATION

Because information affects the values of investments, the serious financial analyst must be well informed. There is a staggering array of such "investment information," some of it published on paper ("hard copy") and some of it appearing in computer-readable form.

23.8.1 Publications

Space precludes a detailed listing here of publications relating to various industries. An excellent bibliography of such sources, compiled by the New York Society of Security Analysts, can be found in the *Financial Analyst's Handbook*.[32] Periodical literature of interest to the financial analyst is indexed by industries, products, and companies in the *Predicasts F&S Index*.

Every investor should read the *Wall Street Journal*. It provides extensive statistical data, financial news, and even a bit of humor. An alternative is the financial section of the *New York Times* or the *Investors Business Daily*. Most other daily newspapers contain financial information, but much less than the *Journal* or the *Times*. A weekly publication with a wealth of statistical data (particularly in the "Market Laboratory" section) is *Barron's*. Another weekly publication that contains reports prepared by security analysts at various brokerage firms is the *Wall Street Transcript*.

A useful source of daily stock price and volume figures is the *Daily Stock Price Record*, published by Standard & Poor's Corporation. Each issue covers one calendar quarter, and all values for a given stock are listed in a single column. Standard & Poor's also publishes forecasts of company earnings in the weekly *Earnings Forecaster*, and dividend information in the *Dividend Record*. Furthermore, some brokerage houses provide their major clients with copies of Standard & Poor's monthly *Stock Guide* and *Bond Guide*, which are illustrated in Figures 23.7 and 23.8.

Standard & Poor's *Corporation Records* are a major reference source for the financial history of and data on individual companies. They consist of six alphabetical volumes and are periodically updated. A second major reference source is provided by Moody's Investor Services, Inc. Their *Manuals* are published annually, with periodic updates, and cover various fields: *Bank & Finance, Industrial, International, Municipal & Government, OTC Industrial, OTC Unlisted, Public Utility,* and *Transportation* are the titles of various volumes. In addition, both Standard & Poor's and Moody's also provide a number of other publications to subscribers.

Historical data and analyses for approximately 1,700 stocks and most major industries can be found in the *Value Line Investment Survey*. Adjusted betas are also shown for the individual stocks in the *Survey*. The *Value Line Options* and *Convertibles* manuals, along with the *Survey*, offer estimates of the relative attractiveness of these investments.[33]

Publications of major security analysts' societies include the *Financial Analysts Journal* (United States); *Analyse Financière* (France); and the *Investment Analyst* (United Kingdom). Academic journals that include articles on various aspects of investing include the *Journal of Business*, the *Journal of Finance*, the *Journal of Financial and Quantitative Analysis*, the *Journal of Financial Economics*, and the *Review of Financial Studies*.

Anyone interested in the management of money for institutional or corporate investors (especially pension funds) should read the *Journal of Portfolio Management*, the *Journal of Fixed Income*, and the *Journal of Derivatives*, which publish the views of both practitioners and academicians. A biweekly periodical that covers current industry news and that is widely read by institutional investors and money managers is *Pensions and Investment Age*. *Institutional Investor*, a periodical

Figure 23.7

Standard & Poor's Stock Guide, April 1994

Source: Standard and Poor's, *Stock Guide* (New York: Standard & Poor's, April 1994): pp. 6–7.

Index	Cash Divs. Ea.Yr. Since	Latest Payment Period $	Date	Ex. Div.	Total $ So Far 1994	Ind. Rate	Paid 1993	Cash& Equiv.	Curr. Assets	Curr. Liab.	Balance Sheet Date	Lg Trm Debt Mil-$	Pfd.	Com.	End	1989	1990	1991	1992	1993	Last 12 Mos.	Period	1992	1993	Index
1	....	None Since Public				Nil		14.1	19.2	6.50	9-30-93	1.81	...	5964	Dc	...	...	pd0.15			9 Mo Sep	n/a	pꙨd0.44	1
2♦	1992	⁵¹Q0.075 2-22-94		2-4	0.075	0.30	⁵²0.30	Equity per shr $5.14			12-31-93	0.82	...	5806	Je	...	...	p0.74	0.76	1.13	1.03	6 Mo Dec	0.55	0.45	2
3♦	....	None Paid				Nil		0.02	15.4	12.3	9-30-93	4.42	...	5538	Dc	0.04	0.16	0.08	0.28	P0.48	0.48				3
4	1973	Q0.12 3-3-94		1-25	0.12	0.48	0.48	28.7	300	59.5	11-30-93	116	...	15909	My	1.56	1.60	0.93	0.63	0.02	0.53	9 Mo Feb△	d0.06	0.45	4
5	....	None Since Public				Nil		8.26	8.70	2.19	12-31-93	1.26	...	6246	Mr	...	d0.91	d1.46	d1.30		d1.34	9 Mo Dec	d0.89	d0.93	5
6	....	None Since Public				Nil		11.9	98.7	47.6	10-02-93	★290	...	7557	Dc	...	...	...	1.31	Pᵉˢ1.71	1.71				6
7♦	1926	Q0.19 5-15-94		4-11	0.36	0.76	0.66	379	3586	3095	12-31-93	307	...	819811	Dc	0.96	1.11	A△1.27	1.47	1.69	1.69				7
8	....	None Since Public				Nil		...	44.9	24.9	10-31-93	p21.2	...	★7140	Jl	...	...	...	...	p0.72	0.82	3 Mo Oct	p0.08	pꙨ0.18	8
9	....	None Since Public				Nil		72.0	233	168	9-30-93	134	...	19758	Dc	...	...	pd17.66	Ꙩd9.97	PΔd2.12	d2.12				9
10	....	None Since Public				Nil		0.72	4.58	1.31	12-31-93	8.90	...	±6466	Mr	d0.36	d1.06	d0.79	±d0.60		d0.35	9 Mo Dec	±d0.49	±d0.24	10
11	1949	g0.12½ 4-30-93		4-8	...	0.25		120	453	385	j12-31-92	383	1697	69267	Dc	0.70	d0.68	d1.12	d3.19	Pd1.71	jd1.71				11
12♦	1965	Q0.13 5-4-94		4-11	0.255	0.52	0.50	1.69	167	90.3	10-31-93	20.9	...	8800	Oc	1.12	Δ1.24	1.36	1.43	1.45	1.48	3 Mo Jan△	0.28	0.31	12
13	....	1.45 12-8-93			...	2.95	1.45	Book Value 53.04			j6-30-93	59440	363000	286000	Dc	5.93	5.02	5.22	5.51		j5.86	6 Mo Jun	2.89	3.24	13
14♦	1960	Q0.03 3-22-94		3-4	0.06	0.12	0.09	5.94	24.9	15.3	1-31-94	53.5	...	2994	Ap	0.48	0.51	0.34	0.34	Δ0.42	0.57	9 Mo Jan△	Δ0.15	0.30	14
15	....	None Since Public				Nil		0.55	51.3	17.4	p12-31-93	25.9	...	12136	Dc	...	...	...	p0.66	Ꙩ1.50	1.50				15
16♦	1989	Q0.03 5-3-94		3-30	†0.56	0.12	0.12	0.07	62.3	46.9	9-30-93	10.1	...	6820	Dc	0.29	0.35	0.15	0.28	P1.70	1.70				16
17♦	....	0.07 5-1-92		3-28	...	Nil		Equity per shr $6.69			9-30-93	20.7	...	4446	Dc	⁺1.02	1.50	0.23	Ꙩd4.29		d0.96	9 Mo Sep	Ꙩd3.78	d0.45	17
18♦	....	5%Stk 12-17-84		11-26	...	Nil		Equity per shr $6.38			9-30-93	19.9	...	9692	Dc	⁵⁴d2.20	⁵⁰d1.76	AΔd12.76	d0.26	P0.86	0.86				18
19	....	Terms&trad. basis should be checked in detail						Wrts expire 1-27-97				...	...	3992	Dc	...	...	...	...	...	...				19
20	....	None Since Public				Nil		10.6	17.1	4.88	12-31-93	0.95	...	6099	Sp	0.11	d0.05	0.21	0.24	0.20	0.18	3 Mo Dec	0.05	0.03	20
21♦	....	None Since Public				Nil		26.7	179	78.2	11-30-93	1.96	...	37667	Au	0.36	0.51	d0.21	0.37	0.63	0.75	3 Mo Nov	0.15	0.27	21
22	1993	0.10 4-19-94		3-25	0.20	0.40	†0.43	Equity per shr $27.47			9-30-93	...	★4000	49586	Sp	...	...	p0.21	p4.49	5.37	3 Mo Dec	p1.07	1.95	22
23♦	1985	S0.16 1-3-94		12-13	0.16	0.32	0.28	13.3	59.4	15.1	9-30-93	2.25	328	5031	Je	0.88	0.90	0.97	1.15	0.36	1.32	6 Mo Dec	d0.48	0.48	23
24	....	None Since Public				Nil		5.21	45.9	44.9	9-30-93	213	...	±15431	Dc	±d0.48	±d0.94	±d2.54	±d0.21	P±0.16	0.16				24
25	1987	0.091 4-15-94		3-25	⁹⁹1.007	1.10	0.994	Net Asset Val $9.95			3-25-94	...	...	48457	Dc	§10.66	§10.15	§10.59	§10.51		...				25
26	1988	0.066 4-15-94		3-25	0.26½	0.80	⁸¹2.009	Net Asset Val $8.53			3-25-94	...	...	12346	Jl	§9.59	§9.01	§9.02	§9.66	§9.92	...				26
27	1988	0.091 4-15-94		3-25	⁸²1.105	1.10	†1.044	Net Asset Val $9.65			3-25-94	...	...	67626	Dc	§10.60	§10.16	§10.55	§10.47		...				27
28	1988	0.77½ 4-15-94		3-25	⁵⁰0.77½	0.96	†0.886	Net Asset Val $8.24			3-25-94	...	...	31747	Dc	§9.13	§8.76	§9.15	§8.89		...				28
29	1993	M0.122 4-15-94		3-25	0.488	1.46	0.122	Net Asset Val $12.21			3-25-94	...	...	★25007	Dc	...	...	...	...	...	...				29
30	1988	0.09 4-15-94		3-25	0.41	1.08	⁴²2.65½	Net Asset Val $8.64			3-25-94	...	⁸⁹95	18508	Au	§9.40	§7.93	§8.39	§9.32		...				30
31	1990	0.06 4-15-94		3-25	0.24	0.72	0.73½	Net Asset Val $9.25			3-25-94	...	...	9974	Nv	...	§11.53	§11.22	§9.61						31
32	1993	0.075 4-15-94		3-25	0.30	0.90	⁵⁰0.563	Net Asset Val $13.22			3-25-94	...	2	10507	Oc	...	...	...	§14.66						32
33	1936	Q0.11 2-18-94		2-1	0.11	0.44	0.42	37.2	81.3	40.3	9-30-93	2.29	161	6176	Sp	Δ0.78	Δ0.44	d0.52	⁺0.53⁻	⁻0.77	0.81	3 Mo Dec	Δ0.13	Ꙩ0.17	33
34	....	0.08 12-3-90		11-5	...	Nil		0.75	31.2	8.07	12-31-93	21.7	...	4861	Je	Δ0.75	0.78	d0.60	0.13	Δd0.14	d0.24	6 Mo Dec	Δ0.02	d0.06	34
35	....	⁴⁷0.02 4-6-92		3-10	...	Nil		51.5	169	72.3	9-26-93	56.0	...	5407	Dc	3.00	1.05	d0.43	Ꙩd0.53	P1.15	1.15				35
36	1990	0.05 3-5-93		2-8	...	Nil	0.05	0.06	31.6	8.33	9-30-93	16.2	...	3338	Dc	Δd0.46	0.40	0.41	d0.16	Pd0.18	d0.18				36
37	1992	Q0.15 3-24-94		3-4	0.15	0.60	0.42	91.3	149	137	9-30-93	4.92	...	13045	Dc	1.01	1.26	1.41	1.53	PꙨ1.96	1.96				37
38	1976	0.09 1-3-94		12-10	0.09	Nil	0.36	49.7	497	385	9-30-93	402	...	17635	Dc	0.30	Δd0.06	d3.08	Δ0.64	PꙨ2.52	d2.52				38
39	....	None Since Public				Nil		34.1	51.0	16.3	9-30-93	1.59	...	16784	Dc	...	...	pd0.02	Ppo.32	0.32				39
40	....	0.06 6-15-87		5-26	...	Nil		0.74	43.4	25.0	12-25-93	8.77	...	5539	Je	0.33	d3.08	0.44	0.44	d2.60	d2.18	6 Mo Dec	d0.30	0.12	40
41	....	Wrrt 12-1-88		10-26	...	Nil		0.22	2.06	0.57	12-31-93	0.33	...	973	Dc	d0.19	d0.12	⁺0.15⁻	Nil	Ꙩ0.08	0.08				41
42♦	....	None Since Public				Nil		56.3	196	83.0	10-02-93	...	...	28602	Dc	1.07	1.33	1.59	1.08	P0.13	0.13				42
43	....	None Since Public				Nil		10.3	234	180	9-30-93	...	...	12784	Dc	...	...	Ꙩd1.69	P1.02	1.02				43
44♦	....	None Since Public				Nil		1.75	37.2	15.9	9-30-93	37.4	...	10476	Mr	0.58	0.39	0.22	0.60		0.70	9 Mo Dec	0.45	0.55	44
45♦	1992	Q0.06 4-11-94		3-25	0.24	0.48	0.36	5.31	69.4	38.2	1-02-94	...	...	15805	Sp	0.21	0.06	0.81	1.10	1.17	3 Mo Dec	0.25	0.32	45
46	1936	⁸⁰0.12 3-1-94		2-8	⁸⁰0.12	Ꙩ0.36	⁸⁸1.63	Net Asset Val $19.50			3-25-94	...	...	42496	Dc	§18.35	§16.82	§20.21	§20.48	§19.78	...				46
47♦	....	0.20 8-15-78		7-10	...	Nil		1.45	46.1	43.1	9-30-93	3.38	...	4167	Dc	0.44	0.46	0.45	Δ0.18	P0.36	0.36				47
48♦	....	None Since Public				Nil		173	267	37.8	12-31-93	11.9	...	52023	Mr	0.38	0.30	0.35	0.95		1.03	9 Mo Dec	0.70	0.78	48
49♦	....	None Since Public				Nil		16.3	143	54.9	10-31-93	0.81	...	27697	Oc	0.63	0.87	0.83	0.77	1.15	1.20	3 Mo Jan△	0.19	Ꙩ0.24⁻	49
50♦	....	None Since Public				Nil		23.4	112	89.3	9-30-93	138	...	15629	Dc	0.67	0.93	Ꙩd0.41	0.72	E0.25	0.17	9 Mo Sep	0.60	0.05	50
51	1984	Q0.04 3-11-94		2-18	0.04	0.16	0.16	20.5	165	80.7	9-30-93	0.80	...	12571	Dc	1.57	d0.67	±d1.63	±1.41	±d0.67	±0.97	P±1.64	1.64		51

♦Stock Splits & Divs By Line Reference Index ²4-for-3,'93. ³1-for-4 REVERSE,'93. ⁷2-for-1,'90,'92. ¹²2-for-1,'92. ¹⁴4-for-3,'89. ¹⁶3-for-2,'93. ¹⁷Adj to 5%,'90. ¹⁸1-for-4 REVERSE,'92. ²¹1-for-2 REVERSE,'89;3-for-2,'93. ²³Adj to 4%,Jun,'90:10%,'91:6-for-5,'92. ⁴²3-for-2,'90. ⁴⁴2-for-1,'92. ⁴⁵1-for-3 REVERSE,'93. ⁴⁷1-for-2 REVERSE,'92. ⁴⁸2-for-1,'92,'94. ⁴⁹2-for-1,'93. ⁵⁰2-for-1,'89.

Figure 23.7 (continued)

Standard & Poor's

Title-Industry Code & Co. Finances (in italics) / Exchange / Individual Issue Statistics / Interest Dates	Fixed Charge Coverage 1990	1991	1992	Year End	S&P Debt Rating	Date of Last Rating Change	Prior Rating	Eligible Bond Form	Cash & Equiv.	Curr. Assets	Curr. Liab.	Balance Sheet Date	Regular Price	Begins Thru	Sinking Fund Price	Begins Thru	Refund/Other Restriction Price	Begins Thru	L. Term Debt (Mil $)	Capitalization (Mil $)	Total Debt % Capital	Outstg (Mil $)	Underwriting Firm, Year	Price Range 1994 High	Low	Mo. End Price Sale(s) or Bid	Curr. Yield	Yield to Mat.
A I M Management Gr. ...62	n/a	n/a	2.45	Dc	BB				8.49			p6-30-93					★170.0		72.90	237.0				104	98⅜	98⅜	9.14	9.24
Sr¹Sec²Notes 9s 2003 ...mN15	Δ3.45	Δ3.32						Dc	104.50		59.50	(11-15-98)	300.0	(11-15-98)			²2108.50	11-14-96	110	M2 '93	237.0							
AAR Corp. ...3e		Δ2.12		My				R	28.70	304.0		11-30-93					116.0		304.0	38.5				117	107⅞	107⅞	8.85	8.17
Nts⁴ 9¼s 2001 ...mN		X		R	BBB				NC										65.0	G1 '89				97½	90½	90½	8.04	8.80
Nts 7⅛s 2003 ...aO15		X		R	BBB				NC										50.0	G1 '93								
Abbey Healthcare Group ...30a	0.73	0.76	4.04	Dc	B-			R	11.90	98.70	47.60	10-2-93		(11-1-98)			★290.0		171.0	58.5				103⅜	96⅜	96⅜	9.87	10.16
Sr²Sub Nts 9¾s 2002 ...mN	Δ25.19	Δ28.70	Δ35.69	Dc	B-		BBB		104.75			(11-1-98)																
Abbott Laboratories ...21a		X		Dc	AAA		BBB	BE	379.5	3586	3095	12-31-93					307.0		4625	23.8		D6 '93		95⅛	89⅜	89⅜	6.23	7.08
ACF Indus. ...56	0.33	2.55		Dc			AAA	Dc	No Recent Fin'ls								926.0		200	76.0		G1 '93						
Eq Tr Ctf 14½s '96 ...	4.86			R	B+		BBB		NC		100								1518			B1 '81		104	100⅜	102½	14.15	13.33
Eq Tr Ctf 11.60s 2000 ...Mn15	4.86			R	B+		BBB		NC		100								15.0			B1 '80		80	78	78	14.87	17.60
Acme Holdings Inc. ...25c	0.43	0.36	0.92	Dc	B				1.43			9-30-93	(6-1-96)				82.0		20.0	165.0				94	82	82	14.33	16.50
Sr Nts⁵ 8¼s 2000 ...Jd		X		Dc					107				49.80						49.80									
Act III Broadcasting ...12c	0.02	0.09	0.24	Dc	B				23.10		25.90	9-30-93	²2111.75	5-31-96			★183.0		78.0	138.0		C3 '93						
Sr²Sub Nts 9¾s 2003 ...jD15	n/a	n/a		R	B			R	103.61			(12-15-98)	16.10	(12-15-98)			²2108.625	12-15-96	83.20			D6 '93		103¼	94½	94½	10.19	10.54
Act III Theatres ...24b		X		Dc	B-	dd0.27	2.34		11.90	105.938	25.70	(2-1-98)	16.10	(2-1-98)			231.0		100	118.0		B1 '81		112⅜	107½	107½	11.05	10.54
Sr Sub Nts² 11⅛s 2003 ...Fa	3.00			R		d0.27			49.70	497.0	365.0	(2-1-02)	497.0				402.0		206.0			K3 '93						
Actava Group ...40d		5/91		Dc	B			R	101.035		100	3-14-95					²24.2		85.0	48.6		L4 77		101⅛	93½	e98	10.08	10.68
Sr Sub SF Deb⁶ 9¾s '97 ...Ms15		5/91		R			B+												847.0									
Sub SF Deb¹⁰ 10s '99 ...aO	1.25	5/91	1.81	R	B		B+	R	100		100	9-30-93	112.0	6-30-94			138.0		8.77	74.73		Exr. 73		102	97	97	10.31	10.74
Sub Deb⁹ 9⅞s '98 ...1A	1.25	0.25	1.81	Dc	B		B+		100										59.5			Exr. 73		102	86½	s93	10.22	11.59
Addington Resources, Inc. ...45a	1.25	1/93	1.81	Dc	BB-		BB+	R	23.40		89.30	9-30-93							281.0	49.8				104⅜	103⅜	104¼	11.52	8.43
Adelphia Communications ...12a	0.51	0.58	0.68	Mr	BB-			Mr	103.43	112.0		12-31-94		6-30-94			★1626		125	238.0		D6 '88						
Sr Deb 11⅞s 2004 ...mS15		Y		R	B			R	104.50		427.0	(9-15-99)	544.0	(9-15-99)			709.0		747.0					115⅜	107⅜	107½	11.05	10.67
Nts 12¼s 2002 ...Mn15	1.72	1.97	2.89	R	B			R	166	243.0		(5-15-97)	544.0	(5-15-97)					125			S1 '92		116⅜	108¼	108⅛	11.55	10.94
ADT Operations ...63		Y		Dc	BB			Dc	243.0			(8-1-98)							400	44.5		S1 '92						
Sr Nts¹³ 8½s 2000 ...lA		Y		R	BB-			R	NC										1704			M2 '93		103½	94⅜	94⅜	8.73	9.42
Sr²Sub Nts¹³ 9¼s 2003 ...lA		Y		R	BB-			R	103.75			(8-1-98)							250			M2 '93		103⅜	95⅜	95⅜	9.69	10.00
ADVANTA Corp ...25e	1.50	2.39	6.09	Dc	BBB-			Dc	NC			(1-15-97)	264.0	(6-15-97)			★494.0		350	52.0		M2 '93		100⅛	97¼	97¼	5.27	6.26
Nts 5¼s '96 ...mN15		X		BE				BE	194.0	264.0	136.0								662.0			C4 '93						
AES Corp. ...63	1.44	1.60	1.65	Dc	B+			Dc	103.25			(6-15-97)					1234		150	81.1		M5 '90		107	103⅜	103⅜	9.43	9.02
Sr Sub Nts² 9½s 2000 ...jD15	7.33	4.91	1.27	Dc				R	1420								1168		75.0	12.9								
Aetna Life & Casual. ...35d		X		BE	AA-	6-93	AA	BE	NC		100	(1-15-97)		(1-15-97)					9402									
Deb 6¾s 2013 ...mS15		X		R	AA-	6-93	AA	R	104								200		200			G1 '93		96⅜	87⅜	87⅜	7.70	8.02
Deb 8s 2017 ...jJ15		X		R	AA-			R	NC								200		200			M2 '87		105⅛	97⅜	97⅜	8.21	8.24
Deb 7¼s 2023 ...lA15		X		BE	AA-			BE	NC								200		100			G1 '93		101⅜	89⅜	89⅜	8.06	8.17
Nts 8¼s '96 ...Ms		X		R	AA-			R	NC								200		100			M6 '88		108⅜	103¼	103⅛	8.35	7.65
Nts 6⅞s 2003 ...lA15		X		BE	AA-			BE	NC								200		200			G1 '93		100⅜	92⅜	92½	6.92	7.56
Affinity Group. ...23e	0.18	0.47	0.47	Dc	B			Dc	11.70	26.70	77.60	9-30-93		(10-15-98)			★161.0	10-14-94	61.50	242.0		C3 '93		108⅜	102	102	11.27	11.15
Sr²Sub Nts 11¾s 2003 ...aO15		X		Dc	B				104.313			(10-15-98)	49.80	(10-15-98)			²2111.50	10-15-96	120									

Uniform Footnote Explanations-See Page 1. Other: ¹ Gtd by AIM Advisors Inc. ² (HRO)On Chge of Ctrl at 101 ³ Max $35M red w/proceeds of Pub Equity Off'g. ⁴ (HRO)For Trigger Event at 100.
⁵ Co must offer repurch at 101 on Chge of Ctrl. ⁶ Max $15.6M red w/proceeds of IPO ⁷ Max $33.3M red w/proceeds of Pub Eq Off'g. ⁸ Was Fuqua Inc. ⁹ Incl disc. ¹⁰ Was Nat'l Indus.
¹¹ Gtd by & data of ADT Ltd. ¹² Gtd by ADT Ltd ¹³ Max $36M red w/proceeds of Pub Eq Off'g ¹⁴ Fr 10-15-93.

Figure 23.8

Standard & Poor's Bond Guide, April 1994

Source: Standard and Poor's, *Bond Guide* (New York: Standard & Poor's, April 1994), p. 22.

full of feature stories on the investment industry, is published monthly. Individual investors will find the articles in the monthly issues of the *AAII Journal,* published by the Chicago-based American Association of Individual Investors, to be informative. Also of interest are *Business Week* (a weekly publication) and two bi-weeklies, *Forbes* and *Fortune.*

Data on mutual funds is published in a number of places. Morningstar provides extensive information in both hard copy and computer-readable forms. Other sources include publications put out by Lipper Analytical Services, William E. Donoghue, American Association of Individual Investors, Value Line, and CDA/Wiesenberger Financial Services.

Although a company's annual and quarterly reports provide useful information, the annual and quarterly business and financial reports (10–K and 10–Q, respectively) filed with the Securities and Exchange Commission usually include more details. Whereas the annual reports are audited, it should be noted that quarterly reports are unaudited.

A source of macroeconomic data such as monetary aggregates (like the money supply) and other monetary items is the *Federal Reserve Bulletin,* a monthly publication by the Board of Governors of the Federal Reserve System. The Department of the Treasury publishes quarterly the *Treasury Bulletin,* which contains data on government debt and interest rates. Data on national income and production is published monthly by the U.S. Department of Commerce in the *Survey of Current Business.* The Department of Commerce also publishes on a monthly basis the *Business Conditions Digest,* where various economic indicators can be found. (These indicators include **leading indicators** that have been found to signal future changes in the economy; **lagging indicators** that change after the economy has done so; and **coincident indicators** that change simultaneously with the economy.)

23.8.2 Computer-Readable Data

The rapid increase in the use of personal computers by those who invest money for others, as well as by those who invest for themselves, has led to a major expansion in the availability of computer-readable investment data.

Large amounts of financial and economic data, such as common stock prices, mutual fund information, and financial statements, are provided on computer tapes and disks that are made available to investors for a fee by Standard & Poor's Compustat Services, Value Line, Inc., and Morningstar. These databases are also available on a dial-up basis via time-shared computer services.

Dial-up services are also provided by *Compuserve, Dow Jones News/Retrieval, Interactive Data Corporation,* and others. Each service is designed so that users of microcomputers can "download" prices and other data into their own machines easily and inexpensively. Often the data is in spreadsheet format so that it is readily available for analysis using, for example, Lotus 1–2–3.

Databases containing prices, fundamental information, mutual fund data, and predictions made by brokerage houses and others are provided on compact discs by the Lotus Development Corporation, Standard & Poor's Corporation, Morningstar, and others.

1. Financial analysts are investment professionals who evaluate securities and then make investment recommendations. Those recommendations may be used by professional money managers (portfolio managers) or by certain clients of the analysts.

2. There are two primary reasons for engaging in financial analysis: to determine certain characteristics of securities and to attempt to identify mispriced securities.

3. To understand and estimate the risks and returns of individual securities as well as groups of securities, both financial markets and the principles of security valuation must be understood.

4. Market indices are portfolios of securities designed to represent the performance of an entire asset class (for example, stocks or bonds) or a specific segment of an asset class.

5. Market indices are typically computed on the basis of either price-weighting, value-weighting, or equal-weighting the component securities.

6. Many investors claim to have identified investment systems that can outperform a passive investment system. Frequently, however, the investors testing these systems commit fundamental errors that invalidate their results.

7. Technical analysis involves short-term predictions of security price movements based on past patterns of prices and trading volumes. Fundamental analysis concerns estimates of the basic determinants of security values, such as future sales, expenses, and earnings for firms.

8. Many financial analysts focus their research efforts on analyzing company financial statements. Such research permits an analyst to better understand a company's business operations, its plans for future growth, what factors affect its profitability, and how those factors affect its profitability.

QUESTIONS AND PROBLEMS

1. Using a recent *Wall Street Journal,* find the closing value of the Dow Jones Industrial Average. On the same date, find the closing prices of the DJIA's component stocks. (The names of those stocks are usually listed on page 3 of the *Journal*'s third section.) Calculate the value of the DJIA's divisor.

2. Consider a price-weighted market index composed of two securities, A and B, with prices of $16 and $30, respectively. The index divisor is currently 2.0. Calculate the value of the divisor when:
    a. Stock A issues a 5% stock dividend.
    b. Stock B undergoes a 3-for-1 stock split.
    c. Stock A undergoes a 4-for-1 stock split.

3. It is often argued that the S&P 500 is a better indicator than the Dow Jones Industrial Average of the performance of the entire U.S. stock market. Explain the reasoning behind this contention.

4. Assume that the market is composed of the following three securities:

Security	Current Price	Shares Outstanding
A	$20	20,000
B	35	40,000
C	30	40,000

   a. What is the aggregate value of the market?
   b. If security *C*'s price increases by 20%, what is the percentage change in the market's aggregate value?
   c. If security *B* splits 2-for-1, what is the percentage change in the market's aggregate value?

5. Consider three stocks, *X*, *Y*, and *Z*, with the following closing prices on two particular dates:

Stock	Date 1	Date 2
X	$16	$22
Y	5	4
Z	24	30

On date 1 there are 100 shares of stock *X*, 200 shares of stock *Y*, and 100 shares of stock *Z* outstanding.

   a. Construct a price-weighted market index using the three stocks, *X*, *Y*, and *Z*. What is the index's value on date 1?
   b. What is the price-weighted index's value on date 2?
   c. Assume that, on date 2, stock *X* splits 4-for-1. What is the price-weighted index's value on that date?
   d. Construct a value-weighted index using the three stocks. Assign the value-weighted index a value of 100 on date 1. What is the index's value on date 2?

6. According to Ferris Fain, "The success of a stock market index depends on its ability to measure the performance of stocks not included in the index." Explain what Ferris means.

7. Consider an equal-weighted market index composed of three securities. The market prices of those securities on three dates are shown below.

	Market Prices		
Security	Date 1	Date 2	Date 3
A	$50	$55	$60
B	30	28	30
C	70	75	73

a. What is the return on the index from date 1 to date 2?

b. What is the return on the index from date 2 to date 3?

8. Consider a market index based on three securities and their associated prices on three dates.

Security	Market Prices		
	Date 1	Date 2	Date 3
L	$20	$23	$30
M	27	30	31
N	40	35	29

If the index's value is 200 on date 1, calculate its value on date 2 and date 3 if the index return is computed on a geometric mean basis.

9. What types of stocks or industries will an equal-weighted market index emphasize relative to a value-weighted market index?

10. List and describe several possible uses of security market indices.

11. If security markets are highly efficient, what role is there for financial analysts?

12. Compare the price reaction to the purchase of stocks that have been identified with a system that previously has been able to "beat the market" with the reactions to (a) the accurate prediction of rainfall and (b) the accurate prediction of the locations of enemy submarines.

13. Listed below are several test results from studies of mechanical investment systems. For each test result, identify the primary research error committed, and comment as to why the error is applicable to the study.

a. A portfolio managed using a filter rule (that is, buying a stock after it has appreciated in price by $x\%$, holding the stock until its price has depreciated by $x\%$, then selling the stock) outperforms a broad market index when the filter is very small (that is, when x is small).

b. An investment system estimated over the 1970 to 1980 time period indicates that the system outperformed a broad market index in the latter half of the period.

c. A portfolio composed of stocks of highly cyclical industrial companies outperforms a broad market index.

d. Buying and selling U.S. stocks based on a measure of liberal and conservative voting patterns in Great Britain produces returns that outperform a broad U.S. market index.

e. The price performance of a portfolio of ipo (that is, initial public offering) high-technology stocks outperforms a broad market index.

14. Bibb Falk, a portfolio manager for a large pension fund, is fond of saying "Buy low, sell high." Why is the system suggested by Bibb not operational?

15. Despite the arguments and evidence of efficient markets proponents, many investors pay attention to technical analysis in some form. Speculate as to why these investors use this kind of investment research.

16. Distinguish between "top-down" and "bottom-up" approaches to financial forecasting. What are the primary advantages and disadvantages of each approach?

17. Last year both Hudson Homes and Baldwin Construction earned $1 million in net income. Both companies have assets of $10 million. However, Hudson generated a return on equity of 11.1% whereas Baldwin produced a return on equity of 20.0%. What can explain the differences in return on equity between the two companies?

18. Last fiscal year, Afton Machinery had the following financial statement data:

Sales/Assets	2.10
Profits/EBIT	0.65
EBIT/Sales	0.10
Assets/Equity	3.00

Calculate Afton's return on assets and return on equity.

19. Augusta Ironworks reported the following fiscal year-end financial data (stated in 000's).

Assets	$1,500
Liabilities	$900
Stockholders' equity	$600
Net income	$200
Dividends per share	$0.50
Stock price	$30.00
Shares outstanding	100

Given this information, calculate Augusta's:
a. Price-earnings ratio
b. Book value per share
c. Price-book ratio
d. Dividend yield
e. Payout ratio

20. Is it true that, when comparing the reported earnings of corporations, "a dollar is a dollar"?

21. (Appendix Question) Technical analysis is predicated on stock prices moving in repetitive patterns. What would one have to believe about the timing of the receipt of information by financial markets' participants in order to believe in the existence of such patterns?

22. (Appendix Question) The closing, high, and low prices for Fort McCoy Packaging stock over a ten-day interval are shown below. Construct a bar chart for Fort McCoy Packaging stock over this period of time.

Fort McCoy Packaging

Day	Closing Price	High	Low
1	20	21	19
2	20¼	20¼	18
3	21	22	20½
4	21⅛	22⅞	21⅛
5	21	23¼	20
6	21¾	22	20¾
7	22	23½	20⅛
8	20⅛	22	19¼
9	19⅛	21½	19
10	18¼	21⅞	17⅛

23. (Appendix Question) Calculate the relative strength of Fort McCoy Packaging stock versus the S&P 500 over the ten-day period referred to in Problem 22, given the following closing prices for the S&P 500:

	DAY									
	1	**2**	**3**	**4**	**5**	**6**	**7**	**8**	**9**	**10**
S&P 500 Closing Price	300	302	306	310	320	315	330	325	325	330

CFA Exam Question

24. The duPont formula defines the net return on shareholders' equity as a function of the following components:

- operating margin,
- asset turnover,
- interest burden,
- financial leverage, and
- income tax rate.

Using only the data in the table shown below:

a. Calculate each of the five components listed above for 1985 and 1989, and calculate the return on equity (ROE) for 1985 and 1989, using all of the five components. Show calculations.

b. Briefly discuss the impact of the changes in asset turnover and financial leverage on the change in ROE from 1985 to 1989.

	1985	1989
Income Statement Data		
Revenues	$542	$979
Operating Income	38	76
Depreciation and amortization	3	9
Interest Expense	3	0
Pretax income	32	67
Income taxes	13	37
Net income after tax	19	30
Balance Sheet Data		
Fixed assets	$ 41	$ 70
Total assets	245	291
Working capital	123	157
Total debt	16	0
Total shareholders' equity	159	220

APPENDIX

TECHNICAL ANALYSIS

As mentioned earlier, most (but not all) technical analysts rely on charts of stock prices and trading volumes. Virtually all employ colorful, and sometimes even mystical, terminology. For example, a significant price rise on relatively large trading volume might be described as an accumulation, where the stock is allegedly moving from "weak hands" to "strong hands." This is because a rising stock price on large trading volume is viewed as a situation where demand is stronger than supply. In contrast, a significant price decline on relatively large trading volume may be described as a distribution, where the stock is allegedly moving from "strong hands" to "weak hands." This is because a declining stock price on large trading volume is viewed as a situation where supply is stronger than demand. In both situations, relatively large trading volume might be considered a sign of a sustainable change in the stock's price, while relatively small trading volume indicates a transitory change.

What if there is a period when a stock's price does not move significantly? If the stock's price movements are within a narrow band, the stock is said to be in a consolidation phase. A price level that a stock has difficulty rising above is known as a *resistance level*, and a price level that a stock does not seem to fall below is known as a *support level*.

Such statements may sound meaningful, but an efficient market proponent would argue that they fail to pass the tests of simple logic. First, changes in a stock's price occur when the consensus opinion concerning its value changes. This means that large volume associated with a price change only reflects a substantial difference of opinion concerning the impact of new information on the stock's value; small volume reflects smaller differences of opinion. Second, if price or volume data could be used to predict future short-term price movements, investors would rush to exploit such information, moving prices rapidly enough to make the information useless. However, as shown in Tables 23.1 and 23.2, some evidence suggests that there may be some technical trading rules that have merit. Whether they will be useful after transaction costs are fully taken into account is difficult to determine. Even if they do pass muster with respect to transaction costs, it is uncertain whether they will be useful in the future.

Chartists (technicians who rely on chart formations) nonetheless believe that certain patterns carry great significance, although they often disagree among themselves on the significance of a pattern or even on the existence of a pattern. Before displaying some hypothetical examples of patterns, it should be noted that there are three basic types of charts used. They are known as bar charts, line charts, and point and figure charts.

For a *bar chart* the horizontal axis is a time line, with the vertical axis measuring a particular stock's price. More specifically, corresponding to a given day on the horizontal axis will be a vertical line, the top and bottom of which represent the high and low price for that stock on that day. Somewhere on this vertical line will be a small horizontal line representing the closing price for the day. As an example, consider the following hypothetical stock, whose trading background over the last five days is as follows:

Day	High Price	Low Price	Closing Price	Volume
t − 5	11	9	10	200
t − 4	12	9	11	300
t − 3	13	12	12	400
t − 2	11	10	11	200
t − 1	14	11	12	500

Panel (a) of Figure 23.9 presents a bar chart for this stock, whereas panel (b) indicates how such a bar chart of prices can be augmented by adding trading volume at the bottom.

Figure 23.10 (a) shows a bar chart exhibiting a pattern that is known as "head and shoulders." As time passed, the stock's price initially rose, hit a peak at *A*, and then fell to a bottom at *B*. Recovering from this fall, it went up to an even higher peak at *C*, but then fell again to a bottom at *D*. Next it rose to a peak at *E* that was not as high as the previous peak, *C*, and then started to fall. As soon as the price went down past its previous low, *D*, immediately a forecast was made that the stock was going to plunge much lower (if the stock had not reached a level equal to *D*, no such forecast would have been made).

Figure 23.10 (b) shows a bar chart pattern known as "inverted head and shoulders," which results in a forecast that the stock is going to quickly rise by a substantial amount.[34]

For a *line chart,* the axes are the same as with a bar chart. However, only closing prices are presented, and they are connected to each other successively with straight lines, as illustrated in panel (c) of Figure 23.9. Although it is not shown, line charts are also frequently augmented with volume data in a manner identical to bar charts.

Details of construction of *point and figure charts* vary, but the idea is to plot closing prices that form a trend in a single column, moving to the next column only when the trend is reversed. For example, closing prices might be rounded to the nearest dollar and the chart begun by plotting a beginning rounded price on a certain day. As long as the (rounded) price does not change, nothing is done. When a different price is recorded, it is plotted on the chart. A price higher than

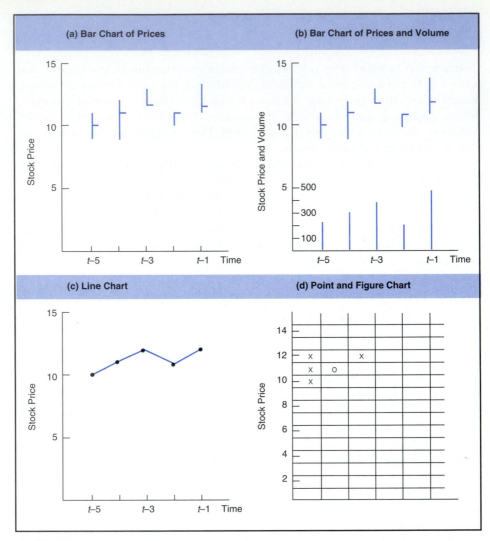

Figure 23.9
Types of Charts

the initial price is indicated with an *X*, with any gaps between the prices also marked with an *X*. A price below the initial price is marked with an *O* in a similar fashion. Then when a price that is different from the last one is recorded, it is plotted in the same column only if it is in the same direction.

For example, if the first different price is above the beginning price, this price is plotted above the beginning one. Then, if a price is recorded that is above the second one, it is plotted in the same column, but if it is below the second one, then it is plotted in a new column to the right of the first column. Continuing, as long as new prices are in the same direction, they are plotted in the same column. Whenever there is a reversal, a new column is started. Panel (d) of Figure 23.9 presents a point and figure chart for the same hypothetical stock used in the other panels.

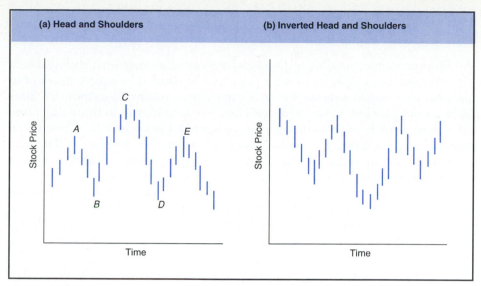

Figure 23.10
Bar Chart Patterns

Point and figure enthusiasts look for all sorts of patterns in their charts. As with all chartist techniques, the idea is to recognize a pattern early enough to profit from one's ability to foresee the future course of prices—a neat trick, if one can do it.

A.2   MOVING AVERAGES

Many other procedures are used by technicians. Some construct moving averages to try to detect "intermediate" and "long-term" trends. Here a set number of the most recent closing prices on a security are averaged each day. (For example, daily closing prices over the previous 200 days may be used.) This means that each day, the oldest price is replaced with the most recent price in the set of closing prices that will be averaged. Frequently a line chart of these moving averages is plotted, along with a line chart of daily closing prices. Each day the charts are updated and then examined for trends to see if there is a buy or sell signal present somewhere.

Alternatively, a long-term moving average may be compared with a short-term moving average (the distinction between the two averages is that the long-term average uses a substantially larger set of closing prices in its calculations than the short-term average). When the short-term average crosses the long-term average, a "signal" is said to have been given. The action recommended will depend on such things as whether the averages have been rising or falling, as well as the direction from which the short-term average crossed the long-term average (it may have been below and now is above, or it may have been above and now is below). A moving average trading rule was used to generate the returns shown in part A of Table 23.2.

Financial Analysis

Another procedure used by technicians involves measuring what they call relative strength. For example, a stock's price may be divided by a price index of its industry each day to indicate the stock's movement relative to its industry. Similarly, an industry index may be divided by a market index to indicate the industry's movement relative to the market, or a stock's price may be divided by a market index to indicate a stock's movement relative to the market. The idea here is to examine changes in these relative strength measures with the hope of finding a pattern that can be used to accurately predict the future.

The momentum trading rules used in preparing Table 23.1 were based on the notion of relative strength in its simplest form. Stock returns over a just-ended holding period were calculated and then portfolios of winners and losers were formed. When this was done using semiannual or annual returns, the momentum trading rules seemed to have merit.

Some procedures of technical analysts focus on relationships among different indexes. For example, the Dow Theory requires that a pattern in the Dow Jones Industrial Average be "confirmed" by a certain movement in the Dow Jones Railroad (now Transportation) Average before action be taken.[35] Another example involves computing the difference between the number of issues advancing and the number declining each day. A chart of the differences cumulated over time, known as the *advance-decline line,* may then be compared with a market index such as the Dow Jones Industrial Average.

Many technical procedures are based on the idea of contrary opinion. The idea here is to determine the consensus opinion and then do the opposite. Two examples that were discussed earlier involved (1) buying stocks that had recently dropped in price and selling stocks that had recently risen in price, and (2) buying stocks with low P/E ratios and selling stocks with high P/E ratios. For a third example, one might see whether the "odd-lotters" (those with trade orders involving less than 100 shares) are buying, and then sell any holdings of these stocks. If "the little investor is usually wrong," this will be a procedure that is usually right. However, the basic premise about the little investor has yet to be factually established.

The widespread availability of personal computers and "dial-up" services with data on stock prices and volumes has made it possible for individual investors to engage in technical analysis in the privacy of their own homes. Producers of software have been quick to provide programs to perform such analysis, complete with multicolored graphs. Nevertheless, the number of investors using fundamental analysis is much larger than the number using technical analysis.

[1] Sumner N. Levine, ed., *Financial Analyst's Handbook I* (Homewood, IL: Dow Jones-Irwin, 1975).

[2] William C. Norby, "Overview of Financial Analysis," in Levine, *Financial Analyst's Handbook I,* p. 3.

[3] Some would add a third reason for conducting financial analysis: monitoring the firm's management in order to prevent managers from consuming an excessive amount of perquisites and failing to make appropriate decisions to the detriment of the firm's shareholders. See Michael C. Jensen and William H. Meckling, "Theory of the Firm: Managerial Behavior, Agency Costs and Ownership Structure," *Journal of Financial Economics,* 3, no. 4 (October 1976): 305–360.

[4] To obtain more information about becoming a CFA, contact the Institute of Chartered Financial Analysts. Their mailing address is P.O. Box 3668, Charlottesville, VA 22903, and their telephone number is (804) 977–6600. A useful annual publication of the institute is *The CFA Candidate Study and Examination Program Review.*

[5] For a discussion regarding portfolio selection by an investor who has earned income (for example, from wages or from running a business), see Edward M. Miller, "Portfolio Selection in a Fluctuating Economy," *Financial Analysts Journal,* 34, no. 3 (May/June 1978): 77–83.

[6] The divisor is also adjusted whenever the composition of the index changes (meaning whenever one stock is substituted for another).

[7] This is equivalent to dividing the average price on day 1 (17.5) by the average price on the beginning date (15) and then multiplying the result by the index's level on the beginning day (100). Mathematically the formula is $I_t = I_0 \times AP_t / AP_0$ where AP_t denotes the average price on day t and I_t denotes the index level on day t.

[8] Some bond market indices are also calculated in this manner. For example, the *Dow Jones 20–Bond Index* is computed by averaging the prices of ten utility and ten industrial bonds. Bond indices using different procedures are published by Merrill Lynch, Salomon Brothers, Lehman Brothers, Standard & Poor's, and others. For more on bond indices, see Chapter 25 (Figure 25.9, for example) and John Markese, "The Complexities of Bond Market Indicators," *AAII Journal,* 14, no. 9 (October 1992): 34–36.

[9] The *Russell 1000, 2000,* and *3000* are also broad value-weighted indices, covering roughly the largest 1,000 stocks; the next 2,000; and the sum of the two. In terms of international indices, *Morgan Stanley Capital International Perspective* publishes value-weighted indices using various combinations of over 1,000 stocks from many different countries, resulting in a "world market index." These, and other international indices, are discussed in Chapter 26.

[10] In order to determine the geometric mean for N stocks, multiply their price relatives and then take the Nth root of the resulting product.

[11] If the added benefits exceeded the added costs, then it would be profitable to perform more financial analysis, because the incremental benefits from doing so would cover the associated costs. If, on the other hand, the added costs exceeded the added benefits, then it would be profitable to cut back on the amount of financial analysis, because costs would be reduced by an amount greater than benefits.

[12] For an interesting argument on why the existence of trading costs results in some investors' performing financial analysis in an efficient market, see Sanford J. Grossman,

"On the Efficiency of Competitive Stock Markets Where Traders Have Diverse Information," *Journal of Finance*, 31, no. 2 (May 1976): 573–585; Sanford J. Grossman and Joseph E. Stiglitz, "On the Impossibility of Informationally Efficient Markets," *American Economic Review*, 70, no. 3 (June 1980): 393–408; and Bradford Cornell and Richard Roll, "Strategies for Pairwise Competitions in Markets and Organizations," *Bell Journal of Economics*, 12, no. 1 (Spring 1981): 201–213.

[13] This is sometimes known as "data snooping." See Andrew W. Lo and A. Craig MacKinlay, "Data-Snooping Biases in Tests of Financial Pricing Models," *Review of Financial Studies*, 3, no. 3 (1990): 431–467; and Fischer Black, "Beta and Return," *Journal of Portfolio Management*, 20, no. 1 (Fall 1993): 8–18.

[14] For a discussion of how *ex post* selection bias influences studies of the performance of mutual funds, see Stephen J. Brown, William Goetzmann, Roger G. Ibbotson, and Stephen A. Ross, "Survivorship Bias in Performance Studies," *Review of Financial Studies*, 5, no. 4 (1992): 553–580.

[15] Felix Rosenfeld, ed., *The Evaluation of Ordinary Shares*, a summary of the proceedings of the Eighth Congress of the European Federation of Financial Analysts Societies (Paris: Dunod, 1975), p. 297.

[16] Rosenfeld, *The Evaluation of Ordinary Shares*, pp. 297–298. For an argument that technical analysis can be of value in an efficient market, see David P. Brown and Robert H. Jennings, "On Technical Analysis," *Review of Financial Analysis*, 2, no. 4 (1989): 527–551. Also see Jack L. Treynor and Robert Ferguson, "In Defense of Technical Analysis," *Journal of Finance*, 40, no. 3 (July 1985): 757–773; and Lawrence Blume, David Easley, and Maureen O'Hara, "Market Statistics and Technical Analysis: The Role of Volume," *Journal of Finance*, 49, no. 1 (March 1994): 153–181.

[17] See, for example, Eugene F. Fama, "Efficient Capital Markets: A Review of Theory and Empirical Work," *Journal of Finance*, 25, no. 2 (May 1970): 383–417.

[18] See, for example, Eugene F. Fama, "Efficient Capital Markets: II," *Journal of Finance*, 46, no. 5 (December 1991): 1575–1617.

[19] There are other studies that present evidence that is consistent with these results. See Barr Rosenberg, Kenneth Reid, and Ronald Lanstein, "Persuasive Evidence of Market Inefficiency," *Journal of Portfolio Management*, 11, no. 3 (Spring 1985): 9–16; John S. Howe, "Evidence on Stock Market Overreaction," *Financial Analysts Journal*, 42, no. 4 (July/August 1986): 74–77; and Andrew W. Lo and A. Craig MacKinlay, "When Are Contrarian Profits Due to Stock Market Overreaction?" *Review of Financial Studies*, 3, no. 2 (1990): 175–205.

[20] One explanation for these results that has been offered is that investors underreact to quarterly earnings announcements. See Chapter 19, particularly section 8.1, and Victor L. Bernard, Jacob K. Thomas, and Jeffery S. Abarbanell, "How Sophisticated Is the Market in Interpreting Earnings News?" *Journal of Applied Corporate Finance*, 6, no. 2 (Summer 1993): 54–63. Another related observation involving one-year formation periods concerns the Dow dividend strategy. This strategy requires buying the ten highest dividend-yielding stocks in the Dow Jones Industrial Average (DJIA) and holding them for one year, at which point the portfolio is revised accordingly for another year. From 1973 through 1992 this strategy outperformed the DJIA by 5.15% per year, on average. Interestingly, it turns out that the stocks purchased in any year had a return that was 5.99% less than the DJIA the previous year, on average. Thus the strategy actually involves buying last year's "losers" among the Dow Jones 30. See Dale L. Domian, David A. Louton, and Irene M. Seahawk, "The Dow Dividend Strategy: How it Works—and Why," *AAII Journal*, 16, no. 4 (May 1994): 7–10.

[21] A puzzling observation associated with part F was that 5% of the 7.2% abnormal return for the loser portfolio was earned during the Januaries that occurred during the test period. Conversely, −.8% of the −2.4% abnormal return for the winners was earned during Januaries. Hence the January anomaly (discussed in the appendix to Chapter 17) appears to somehow be intertwined with the long-term contrarian strategy.

[22] It should be noted that other studies have examined contrarian strategies and have been unable to confirm the usefulness of such strategies. In two of these studies it was argued that the benchmark portfolio returns were incorrectly determined. This means that the abnormal returns were not calculated correctly because by definition they are equal to the difference between the returns on the portfolio and its benchmark. In a third study, the alleged cause of the overreaction—security analysts underpredicting earnings on losers and overpredicting earnings on winners—was contested. A fourth study suggested that the size effect (discussed in the appendix to Chapter 17) was largely responsible for the results because losers tend to be smaller than winners. Lastly, a fifth study argued that incorrect prices were used when the costs of buying and selling stocks were determined in arriving at the results reflected in parts E and F of Table 23.1. However, these studies have, in turn, been contested in a sixth study. Specifically, after taking their objections into consideration it was found that losers outperform winners by 5% to 10% per year, with the difference being the largest when only small firms were classified into winners and losers. The six studies are, respectively, K. C. Chan, "On the Contrarian Investment Strategy," *Journal of Business,* 61, no. 2 (April 1988): 147–163; Ray Ball and S. P. Kothari, "Nonstationary Expected Returns: Implications for Tests of Market Efficiency and Serial Correlations in Returns," *Journal of Financial Economics,* 25, no. 1 (November 1989): 51–74; April Klein, "A Direct Test of the Cognitive Bias Theory of Share Price Reversals," *Journal of Accounting and Economics,* 13, no. 2 (July 1990): 155–166; Paul Zarowin, "Size, Seasonality, and Stock Market Overreaction," *Journal of Financial and Quantitative Analysis,* 25, no. 1 (March 1990): 113–125; Jennifer Conrad and Gautam Kaul, "Long-Term Overreaction or Biases in Computed Returns?" *Journal of Finance,* 48, no. 1 (March 1993): 39–63; and Navin Chopra, Josef Lakonishok, and Jay R. Ritter, "Measuring Abnormal Performance: Do Stocks Overreact?" *Journal of Financial Economics,* 31, no. 2 (April 1992): 235–268.

Adding to the puzzle is the behavior of Canadian stocks. For one-year test periods the results were similar to those in the United States in that a momentum strategy seemed to work (as in part D of Table 23.1). For three-year and five-year test periods, neither a momentum nor a contrarian strategy worked (unlike parts E and F of Table 23.1). See Lawrence Kryzanowski and Hao Zhang, "The Contrarian Investment Strategy Does Not Work in Canadian Markets," *Journal of Financial and Quantitative Analysis,* 27, no. 3 (September 1992): 383–395.

[23] Apparently significant returns can be earned from the weekly strategy if transaction costs are small (such as for large institutional investors). However, larger transaction costs result in negative net returns. See Bruce N. Lehmann, "Fads, Martingales, and Market Efficiency," *Quarterly Journal of Economics,* 105, no. 1 (February 1990): 1–28. For an argument that Lehmann has underestimated the size of transaction costs, see Jennifer Conrad, Mustafa N. Gultekin, and Gautam Kaul, "Profitability of Short-Term Contrarian Portfolio Strategies," unpublished paper, The University of Michigan, 1991.

[24] Lehmann, "Fads, Martingales, and Market Efficiency," p. 26.

[25] Input-output analysis is sometimes used to ensure consistency between various industries and the economy in aggregate. This type of analysis is based on the notion that the output of certain industries (for example, the steel industry) is the input for certain other industries (for example, the household appliance industry).

26 Lotus Development Corporation, Microsoft Corporation, and Borland International Corporation have been leading developers of such software. Their products, Lotus 1–2–3, Excel, and Quattro Pro, respectively, have been top sellers.

27 Similar observations have been made in regard to the recommendations made by major brokerage houses. See John C. Groth, Wilbur G. Lewellen, Gary G. Schlarbaum, and Ronald C. Lease, "An Analysis of Brokerage House Securities Recommendations," *Financial Analysts Journal,* 35, no. 1 (January/February 1979): 32–40; James H. Bjerring, Josef Lakonishok, and Theo Vermaelen, "Stock Prices and Financial Analysts' Recommendations," *Journal of Finance,* 38, no. 1 (March 1983): 187–204; and Philip Heitner, "Isn't It Time to Measure Analysts' Track Records?" *Financial Analysts Journal,* 47, no. 3 (May/June 1991): 5–6. For a comment on the first study, see the Letter to the Editor in the May/June 1980 issue by Clinton M. Bidwell, with a responding Letter to the Editor in the July/August 1980 issue by Wilbur G. Lewellen. Also see Endnote 1 in Chapter 24.

28 The "Dartboard" column, appearing monthly in the *Wall Street Journal,* contains one buy recommendation from each of four security analysts. In the two-day period after publication these stocks have an abnormal return of just over 4% and their trading volume is roughly double the normal amount. However, unlike the recommendations in the "Heard on the Street" column, over the next 25 trading days these stocks drop in price, losing about half their 4% gain. See Brad M. Barber and Douglas Loeffler, "The 'Dartboard' Column: Second-Hand Information and Price Pressure," *Journal of Financial and Quantitative Analysis,* 28, no. 2 (June 1993): 273–284.

29 Two more recent studies made similar observations. Both also noted unusually high returns for two days prior to a buy recommendation and unusually low returns for two days prior to a sell recommendation. According to one of the studies, trading volume was unusually high prior to both types of recommendations, leaving open the possibility that some investors traded on advance notice of the contents of the column. See Pu Liu, Stanley D. Smith, and Azmat A. Syed, "Stock Price Reactions to *The Wall Street Journal*'s Securities Recommendations," *Journal of Financial and Quantitative Analysis,* 25, no. 3 (September 1990): 399–410, and Messod D. Beneish, "Stock Prices and the Dissemination of Analysts' Recommendations," *Journal of Business,* 64, no. 3 (July 1991): 393–416. Interestingly, a former author of the "Heard on the Street" column, R. Foster Winans, was convicted of fraud and theft in 1985 for leaking the contents of his column to four brokers and subsequently sharing in the associated trading profits.

30 See the appendix to Chapter 17 for a discussion of the size effect.

31 The presence of the size effect can be seen by noting that the average return for small firms of 13.5% is much larger than the average return for medium and large firms of 10.7% and 9.8%, respectively.

32 See Levine, *Financial Analyst's Handbook I,* pp. 883–926.

33 Such estimates for common stocks might be useful in helping the investor "beat the market." See the appendix to Chapter 19.

34 For details on many kinds of patterns, see Alan R. Shaw, "Technical Analysis," in Levine, *Financial Analyst's Handbook I,* pp. 944–988; Chapter 8 in Jerome B. Cohen, Edward D. Zinbarg, and Arthur Zeikel, *Investment Analysis and Portfolio Management* (Homewood, IL: Richard D. Irwin, 1987); and Richard L. Evans, "Chart Basics Using Bars, Point & Figure and Candlesticks," *AAII Journal,* 15, no. 4 (April 1993): 24–28.

35 For more on the Dow Theory, see Richard L. Evans, "Dow's Theory and the Averages: Relevant . . . or Relics?" *AAII Journal,* 15, no. 1 (January 1993): 27–29.

financial analyst
portfolio managers
fundamental analysis
market index
price weighting
value weighting
equal weighting
price relatives
passive investment system
ex post selection bias
out-of-sample data
technical analysis

top-down forecasting
bottom-up forecasting
probabilistic forecasting
econometric model
endogenous variables
exogenous variables
neglected firm effect
leading indicators
lagging indicators
coincident indicators
chartists

REFERENCES

1. For a discussion of contrarian investment strategies, see the references in Endnotes 19 and 22 and:

David Dremen, *Contrarian Investment Strategies* (New York: Random House, 1979).

Werner F. M. De Bondt and Richard Thaler, "Does the Stock Market Overreact?" *Journal of Finance,* 40, no. 3 (July 1985): 793–805.

Werner F. M. De Bondt and Richard H. Thaler, "Further Evidence on Investor Overreaction and Stock Market Seasonality," *Journal of Finance,* 42, no. 3 (July 1987): 557–581.

Paul Zarowin, "Short-Run Market Overreaction: Size and Seasonality Effects," *Journal of Portfolio Management,* 15, no. 3 (Spring 1989): 26–29.

Paul Zarowin, "Does the Stock Market Overreact to Corporate Earnings Information?" *Journal of Finance,* 44, no. 5 (December 1989): 1385–1399.

Bruce N. Lehmann, "Fads, Martingales, and Market Efficiency," *Quarterly Journal of Economics,* 105, no. 1 (February 1990): 1–28.

Narasimhan Jegadeesh, "Evidence of Predictable Behavior of Security Returns," *Journal of Finance,* 45, no. 3 (July 1990): 881–898.

Jennifer Conrad, Mustafa N. Gultekin, and Gautam Kaul, "Profitability of Short-Term Contrarian Portfolio Strategies," unpublished paper, The University of Michigan, 1991.

Victor L. Bernard, Jacob K. Thomas, and Jeffery S. Abarbanell, "How Sophisticated Is the Market in Interpreting Earnings News?" *Journal of Applied Corporate Finance,* 6, no. 2 (Summer 1993): 54–63.

2. Closely related to the issue of contrarian investment strategies is the issue of how stock price levels in one period are related to stock price levels in a subsequent period. This issue, like the usefulness of contrarian strategies, has been open to debate. Two of the earliest papers and two recent ones that contradict them are:

Eugene F. Fama and Kenneth R. French, "Permanent and Temporary Components of Stock Prices," *Journal of Political Economy*, 96, no. 2 (April 1988): 246–273.

James M. Poterba and Lawrence H. Summers, "Mean Reversion in Stock Prices: Evidence and Implications," *Journal of Financial Economics*, 22, no. 1 (October 1988): 27–59.

Myung Jig Kim, Charles R. Nelson, and Richard Startz, "Mean Reversion in Stock Prices? A Reappraisal of the Empirical Evidence," *Review of Economic Studies*, 58, no. 3 (May 1991): 515–528.

Grant McQueen, "Long-Horizon Mean-Reverting Stock Prices Revisited," *Journal of Financial and Quantitative Analysis*, 27, no. 1 (March 1992): 1–18.

3. Momentum strategies are discussed in:

Narasimhan Jegadeesh and Sheridan Titman, "Returns to Buying Winners and Selling Losers: Implications for Stock Market Efficiency," *Journal of Finance*, 48, no. 1 (March 1993): 65–91.

4. Moving average and trading range breakout strategies are discussed in:

William Brock, Josef Lakonishok, and Blake LeBaron, "Simple Technical Trading Rules and the Stochastic Properties of Stock Returns," *Journal of Finance*, 47, no. 5 (December 1992): 1731–1764.

5. The reaction of stock prices to the publication of analysts' recommendations is discussed in:

John C. Groth, Wilbur G. Lewellen, Gary G. Schlarbaum, and Ronald C. Lease, "An Analysis of Brokerage House Securities Recommendations," *Financial Analysts Journal*, 35, no. 1 (January/February 1979): 32–40.

James H. Bjerring, Josef Lakonishok, and Theo Vermaelen, "Stock Prices and Financial Analysts' Recommendations," *Journal of Finance*, 38, no. 1 (March 1983): 187–204.

Philip Heitner, "Isn't It Time to Measure Analysts' Track Records?" *Financial Analysts Journal*, 47, no. 3 (May/June 1991): 5–6.

Brad M. Barber and Douglas Loeffler, "The 'Dartboard' Column: Second-Hand Information and Price Pressure," *Journal of Financial and Quantitative Analysis*, 28, no. 2 (June 1993): 273–284.

6. The reactions of stock prices to recommendations published in the "Heard on the Street" column in the *Wall Street Journal* are discussed in:

Peter Lloyd-Davies and Michael Canes, "Stock Prices and the Publication of Second-Hand Information," *Journal of Business*, 51, no. 1 (January 1978): 43–56.

Pu Liu, Stanley D. Smith, and Azmat A. Syed, "Stock Price Reactions to *The Wall Street Journal*'s Securities Recommendations," *Journal of Financial and Quantitative Analysis,* 25, no. 3 (September 1990): 399–410.

Messod Beneish, "Stock Prices and the Dissemination of Analysts' Recommendations," *Journal of Business,* 64, no. 3 (July 1991): 393–416.

The "Heard on the Street" column also sometimes discusses takeover rumors. For an analysis of the effects these rumors have on stock prices, see John Pound and Richard Zeckhauser, "Clearly Heard on the Street: The Effect of Takeover Rumors on Stock Prices," *Journal of Business,* 63, no. 3 (July 1990): 291–308.

7. For a discussion of the neglected firm effect, see:

Avner Arbel and Paul Strebel, "Pay Attention to Neglected Firms!" *Journal of Portfolio Management,* 9, no. 2 (Winter 1983): 37–42.

Avner Arbel, Steven Carvel, and Paul Strebel, "Giraffes, Institutions, and Neglected Firms," *Financial Analysts Journal,* 39, no. 3 (May/June 1983): 57–63.

8. Leading books on technical analysis, financial statement analysis, and fundamental analysis are, respectively:

Robert D. Edwards and John Magee, *Technical Analysis of Stock Trends* (Boston: John Magee, 1966).

George Foster, *Financial Statement Analysis* (Englewood Cliffs, NJ: Prentice Hall, 1986).

Sidney Cottle, Roger Murray, and Frank Block, *Graham and Dodd's Security Analysis* (New York: McGraw-Hill, 1988).

9. Information sources for investing are described in:

Maria Crawford Scott and John Bajkowski, "Sources of Information for the Simplified Approach to Valuation," *AAII Journal,* 16, no. 3 (April 1994): 29–32.

John Markese, "Picking Common Stocks: What Seems to Work, At Least Sometimes," *AAII Journal,* 16, no. 5 (June 1994): 24–27.

Investment Management

Investment management, also known as portfolio management, is the process by which money is managed. It may (1) be active or passive, (2) use explicit or implicit procedures, and (3) be relatively controlled or uncontrolled. The trend is toward highly controlled operations consistent with the notion that capital markets are relatively efficient. However, approaches vary, and many different investment styles can be found. This chapter will discuss investment management, and in doing so it will present various types of investment styles.

24.1 TRADITIONAL INVESTMENT MANAGEMENT ORGANIZATIONS

Few people or organizations like to be called "traditional." However, some investment management organizations follow procedures that have changed little from those that were popular decades ago and thus deserve the title. Figure 24.1 shows the major characteristics of a traditional investment management organization.

Projections concerning the economy and the money and capital markets are made by economists, technicians, fundamentalists, or other market experts within or outside the organization. The projected economic environment is communicated via briefings and written reports—usually in a rather implicit and qualitative manner—to the organization's **security analysts.** Each analyst is responsible for a group of securities, often those in one or more industries (in some organizations, analysts are called industry specialists). Often a group of analysts report to a senior analyst responsible for a sector of the economy or market.

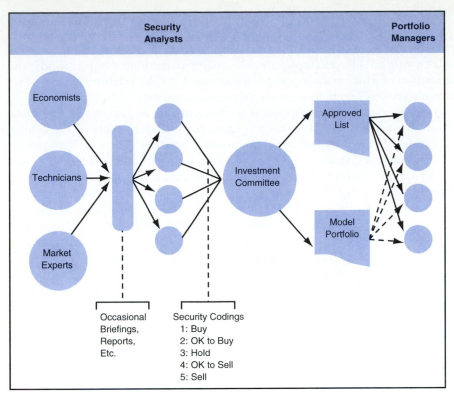

Figure 24.1
A Traditional Investment Management Organization

Within the figure:

Security Analysts

Portfolio Managers

Economists

Technicians

Market Experts

Investment Committee

Approved List

Model Portfolio

Occasional Briefings, Reports, Etc.

Security Codings
1: Buy
2: OK to Buy
3: Hold
4: OK to Sell
5: Sell

The analysts, often drawing heavily on reports of others (for example, "street analysts" in brokerage houses), make predictions about the securities for which they are responsible. In a sense, such predictions are conditional on the assumed economic and market environments, although the relationship is typically quite loose.

Analysts' predictions seldom specify an expected rate of return or the time over which predicted performance will take place. Instead, an analyst's feelings about a security may be summarized by assigning it one of five codes, where a 1 represents a buy and a 5 represents a sell, as indicated in Figure 24.1.[1] (Some organizations reverse the numbers, so that a 5 is a buy and a 1 is a sell; some European organizations favor five codes that are denoted $+$, $0+$, 0, $0-$, and $-$; some organizations have long-term lists as well as short-term lists.)

These security codings and various written reports constitute the information formally transmitted to an **investment committee,** which typically includes the senior management of the organization. In addition, analysts occasionally brief the investment committee on their feelings about various securities. The investment committee's primary formal output is often an **approved** (or authorized) **list,** which consists of the securities deemed worthy of accumulation in a given portfolio. The rules of the organization typically specify that any security on the list may be bought, whereas those not on the list should be either held or sold, barring special circumstances.

The presence or absence of a security on the approved list constitutes the major information transmitted explicitly from the investment committee to a **portfolio manager.** In some organizations, senior management supervises a "model portfolio" (for example, a bank's major commingled equity fund), the composition of which indicates to portfolio managers the relative intensity of senior management's feelings regarding different securities.

In many ways, this description is a caricature of an investment organization—even one run along traditional lines. Nevertheless, most of these attributes can be observed in practice in one form or another.

In recent years, specialty investment firms have gained considerable popularity. As opposed to traditional investment firms that invest in a broad spectrum of securities, these organizations concentrate their investment efforts on a particular asset class, such as stocks or bonds. They often specialize even further, focusing on a narrow segment of a particular asset class, such as the stocks of small start-up companies.

Although these specialty investment firms may follow many of the security analysis procedures of the traditional investment organizations, they usually employ few security analysts. Often the portfolio managers serve jointly as analysts. Furthermore, their decision-making processes are typically more streamlined, often avoiding investment committee structures entirely, thereby permitting portfolio managers considerable discretion to research securities and construct portfolios. Whether this less hierarchical approach to investing actually produces superior results is open to question.

24.2 INVESTMENT MANAGEMENT FUNCTIONS

In Chapter 1 a five-step procedure was outlined for making investment decisions. These steps can all be viewed as functions of investment management, and they must be undertaken for each client whose money is being managed. They are as follows:

1. *Set investment policy*—identify the client's investment objectives, particularly as regards his or her attitude toward the trade-off between expected return and risk.
2. *Perform security analysis*—scrutinize individual securities or groups of securities in order to identify mispriced situations.
3. *Construct a portfolio*—identify specific securities in which to invest, along with the proportion of investable wealth to be put into each security.
4. *Revise the portfolio*—determine which securities in the current portfolio are to be sold and which securities are to be purchased to replace them.
5. *Evaluate the performance of the portfolio*—determine the actual performance of a portfolio in terms of risk and return, and compare the performance with that of an appropriate "benchmark" portfolio.

The remainder of this chapter deals with how an investment management organization could perform the first four functions; the next chapter deals with the fifth function.

24.3 SETTING INVESTMENT POLICY

An investment manager who is in charge of a client's entire portfolio must be concerned with the client's risk-return preferences. Investors who use more than one manager can select one to help in this important phase, or they may employ the services of a consultant or financial planner. In any event, one of the key characteristics that differentiates clients from one another concerns their investment objectives. According to modern portfolio theory, these objectives are reflected in the client's attitude toward risk and expected return. As mentioned in Chapter 7, specifying indifference curves is one method of describing these objectives. However, determining a client's indifference curves is not a simple task. In practice, it is often done in an indirect and approximate fashion by estimating the client's level of **risk tolerance,** defined as the largest amount of risk that the client is willing to accept for a given increase in expected return.

24.3.1 Estimating Risk Tolerance

The starting point in making such an estimation is to provide the client with a set of risks and expected returns for different combinations of two hypothetical portfolios. For example, imagine that the client is told that the expected return on a stock portfolio is 12%, while the return on a riskfree portfolio consisting of Treasury bills is 7.5% (that is, $\bar{r}_S = 12\%$ and $r_F = 7.5\%$). Similarly, the client is told that the standard deviation on the stock portfolio is 15%, while the standard deviation on the riskfree portfolio is, by definition, 0.0% (that is, $\sigma_S = 15\%$ and $\sigma_F = 0.0\%$).[2] Additionally, the client is told that all combinations of these two portfolios lie on a straight line that connects them. (This is because the covariance between these two portfolios is 0.0, meaning that $\sigma_{SF} = 0.0$.) Some combinations of these two portfolios are shown in Table 24.1.

Note that the investor is being presented with the efficient set that arises when there is a set of stocks and a riskfree borrowing and lending rate. As shown in Chapter 9, this efficient set is linear, meaning that it is a straight line that emanates at the riskfree rate and goes through a tangency portfolio that consists of a certain combination of securities. (In this case those securities are common stocks.) Hence negative percentages in Treasury bills (shown at the bottom of Table 24.1) represent riskfree borrowing in order to purchase greater amounts of stocks.

At this point, the client is asked to identify the combination that appears to be most desirable, in terms of expected return and standard deviation. Note that asking the investor to identify the most desirable combination is equivalent to asking the investor to locate where one of his or her indifference curves is tangent to the linear efficient set, as this point will represent the most desirable portfolio.[3]

TABLE 24.1

COMBINATIONS OF STOCK AND RISKFREE TREASURY BILL PORTFOLIOS

Proportion In		Expected	Standard	Implied Level of
Stocks	Bills	Return	Deviation	Risk Tolerance
0%	100%	7.50%	0.0%	0
10	90	7.95	1.5	10
20	80	8.40	3.0	20
30	70	8.85	4.5	30
40	60	9.30	6.0	40
50	50	9.75	7.5	50
60	40	10.20	9.0	60
70	30	10.65	10.5	70
80	20	11.10	12.0	80
90	10	11.55	13.5	90
100	0	12.00	15.0	100
110	− 10	12.45	16.5	110
120	− 20	12.90	18.0	120
130	− 30	13.35	19.5	130
140	− 40	13.80	21.0	140
150	− 50	14.25	22.5	150
.	.	.	.	.
.	.	.	.	.
.	.	.	.	.

After the client has selected the best stock/Treasury bill mix, what can be said about his or her risk tolerance? One would, of course, like to identify all the indifference curves that represent a client's attitude toward risk and expected return. However, in practice a more modest goal is usually adopted—to obtain a reasonable representation of the shape of such curves in the region of risk and expected return within which the client's optimal choices will most likely fall.

The points in Figure 24.2 plot the alternative mixes presented to the client that were given in Table 24.1. Curve *FCS* shows the risk-return characteristics of all possible mixes, and point *C* identifies the attributes of the mix chosen by the client. Note that in this figure expected return is measured on the vertical axis and *variance* on the horizontal axis. Although the combinations available to the client plot on a straight line when standard deviation is measured on the horizontal axis, the combinations plot on a concave curve when variance is used (as in this figure).

Assuming that all the possible mixes had been presented to the client and point *C* had been chosen, it could be inferred that the slope of the client's indifference curve going through *C* is precisely equal to that of curve *FCS* at this point. As mentioned earlier, this follows from the observation that the portfolio on the efficient set that a client identifies as being the "best" corresponds to the one where the client's indifference curves are just tangent to the efficient set.

24.3.2 Constant Risk Tolerance

In principle, the choice of a mix provides information about the slope of an indifference curve at only one point. To go beyond this, an assumption must be made about the general shape of the client's indifference curves. An assumption

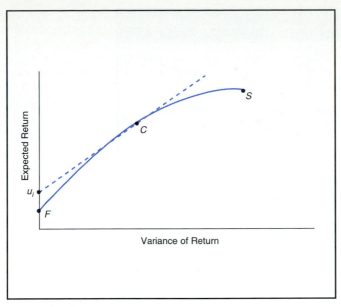

Figure 24.2
Inferring Client Risk Tolerance

commonly made is that the client has constant risk tolerance over a range of alternative portfolios in the neighborhood of the point originally chosen. Figure 24.3 shows the nature of this assumption. As indicated in panel (a), indifference curves in a diagram with *variance* on the horizontal axis are *linear* when it is assumed that the client has constant risk tolerance. This means that the equation for an indifference curve of such an investor is equivalent to the equation for a straight line where the variable on the horizontal axis is variance (σ_P^2) and the variable on the vertical axis is expected return ($\bar{r}_p$). Given that the equation of a straight line takes the form of $Y = a + bX$, where a is the vertical intercept and b is the slope, the equation for an indifference curve can be written as:

$$\bar{r}_p = a + b\sigma_P^2$$

or:

$$\bar{r}_p = u_i + \frac{1}{\tau}\sigma_P^2 \qquad (24.1)$$

where u_i is the vertical intercept for indifference curve i and the slope of the indifference curve is $1/\tau$.[4] Note how any two indifference curves for a client differ from one another by only the value of the vertical intercept. This is because the indifference curves are parallel, meaning that they have the same slope, $1/\tau$.

Figure 24.3(b) plots the same indifference curves in a more familiar manner—with *standard deviation* on the horizontal axis. Note that the curves have the conventional shape—they indicate that the investor requires more return to compensate for an additional unit of standard deviation as the risk of the

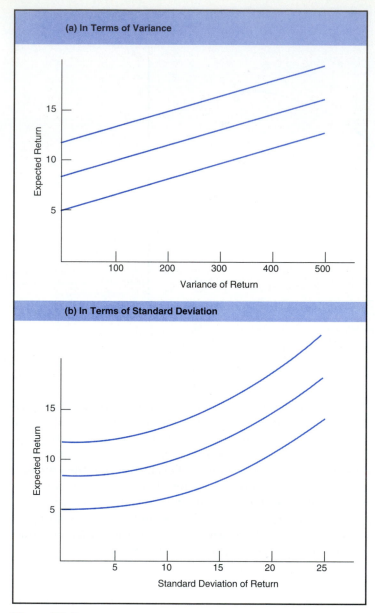

Figure 24.3
Constant Risk Tolerance

portfolio increases. That is, the curves are *convex* when standard deviation is measured on the horizontal axis.

In order to estimate the client's level of risk tolerance τ, it was mentioned that the slope of the indifference curves, $1/\tau$, would be set equal to the slope of the efficient set at the location of the portfolio that was selected, denoted portfolio C. Doing so results in the following formula for estimating τ:

$$\tau = \frac{2[(\bar{r}_C - r_F)\sigma_S^2]}{(\bar{r}_S - r_F)^2} \tag{24.2}$$

where $\bar{r}_C$ denotes the expected return of the portfolio that the client selected, $\bar{r}_S$ and r_F denote the expected return of the stock portfolio and riskfree rate, respectively, and σ_S^2 denotes the variance of the stock portfolio. (A detailed presentation of how this formula was derived is presented in the appendix.)

In the example, the client was given a choice between S, F, and various combinations of S and F where $\bar{r}_S = 12\%$, $r_F = 7.5\%$, and $\sigma_S^2 = 15^2 = 225$. Now, by using Equation (24.2), the level of risk tolerance τ inferred from the choice of portfolio C can be determined to equal:

$$\tau = \frac{2[(\bar{r}_C - 7.5)225]}{(12 - 7.5)^2} \tag{24.3}$$

$$= 22.22\bar{r}_C - 166.67.$$

Assuming the choice of a portfolio consisting of a 50% investment in stocks and a 50% investment in riskfree Treasury bills, the client in this example has chosen a portfolio C with an expected return of 9.75%. Accordingly, Equation (24.3) can be used to determine the value of τ for this client, resulting in an estimated level of τ equal to $50 = (22.22 \times 9.75) - 166.67$. This means that the client will accept up to an additional 50 units of variance in order to receive an extra 1% in expected return. Thus, the client's indifference curves are estimated to have the form of:

$$\bar{r}_P = u_i + \frac{1}{50}\sigma_P^2. \tag{24.4}$$

Table 24.1 shows the inferred level of risk tolerance τ if a different portfolio had been chosen by the client [these levels were determined by substituting the appropriate values for $\bar{r}_C$ into the right-hand side of Equation (24.3) and then solving for τ]. First, note that the level of risk tolerance is the same as the percentage invested in the stock portfolio associated with C. That is, Equation (24.3) can be rewritten as $\tau = 100X_S$, where X_S is the proportion invested in the stock portfolio associated with C. It can be shown that this will always be the case when $\bar{r}_S - r_F = 4.5\%$ and $\sigma_S = 15\%$. Other estimates would give different expressions for τ, but the relationship between X_S and τ would still be linear.

Second, note how the level of risk tolerance is lower if the selected portfolio is more conservative (that is, when the selected level of expected return and standard deviation is lower). Thus more conservative risk-averse clients will have lower levels of risk tolerance than less conservative risk-averse clients.

Having estimated the client's indifference curves, recall from Chapter 7 that the objective of investment management is to identify the portfolio that lies on the indifference curve furthest to the northwest because such a portfolio will offer the investor the level of expected return and risk that is preferable to all the other portfolios. This is equivalent to identifying the portfolio that lies on the indifference curve that has the highest vertical intercept, u_i. This can be seen graphically in Figures 24.3(a) and 24.3(b), where the indifference curves have been extended to the vertical axis.

24.3.3 Certainty Equivalent Return

The term u_i can be thought of as the **certainty equivalent return** for any portfolio that lies on indifference curve i.[5] Thus portfolio C in Figure 24.2 is as desirable for this particular client as a hypothetical portfolio with an expected return of u_i and no risk—that is, one providing a return of u_i with certainty. When viewed in this manner, the job of the portfolio manager is to identify the portfolio with the highest certainty equivalent return.

Equation (24.1) can be rewritten so that the certainty equivalent return u_i appears on the left-hand side. Doing so results in:

$$u_i = \bar{r}_P - \frac{1}{\tau}\sigma_P^2. \qquad (24.5)$$

This equation shows that the certainty equivalent return can be thought of as a risk-adjusted expected return because a risk penalty that depends on both the portfolio's variance and the client's risk tolerance must be subtracted from the portfolio's expected return in determining u_i.

In the example, the investor selected the portfolio with $\bar{r}_P = 9.75\%$ and $\sigma_P^2 = 56.25 \ (= 7.5^2)$. Thus the certainty equivalent return for this portfolio is $8.625\% \ [= 9.75 - (56.25/50)]$. Equivalently, the risk penalty for the portfolio that was selected was $1.125\% \ (= 56.25/50)$. If the certainty equivalent return for any other portfolio shown in Table 24.1 is calculated, it will have a lower value [for example, the 80/20 portfolio has a certainty equivalent return of 8.22% $[= 11.1 - (144/50)]$. Thus the goal of investment management can be thought of as identifying the portfolio that has the maximum value of $\bar{r}_P - (\sigma_P^2/\tau)$, because it will provide the client with the maximum certainty equivalent return.

24.4   SECURITY ANALYSIS AND PORTFOLIO CONSTRUCTION

24.4.1 Passive and Active Management

Within the investment industry, a distinction is often made between **passive management**—holding securities for relatively long periods with small and infrequent changes—and **active management.** Passive managers generally act as if the security markets are relatively efficient. Put somewhat differently, their decisions are consistent with the acceptance of consensus estimates of risk and return. The portfolios they hold may be surrogates for the market portfolio that are known as **index funds,** or they may be portfolios that are tailored to suit clients with preferences and circumstances that differ from those of the average investor.[6] In either case, passive portfolio managers do not try to outperform their designated benchmark.

For example, a passive manager might only have to choose the appropriate mixture of Treasury bills and an index fund that is a surrogate for the market portfolio. The best mixture would depend on the shape and location of the client's indifference curves. Figure 24.4 provides an illustration.

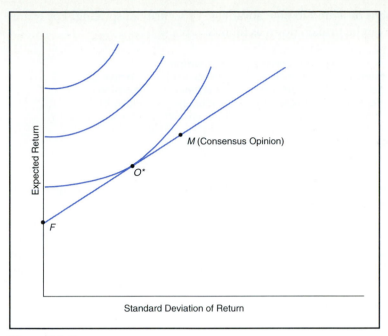

Figure 24.4
Passive Investment Management

Point *F* plots the riskfree return offered by Treasury bills, and point *M* plots the risk and expected return of the surrogate market portfolio, using consensus forecasts. Mixtures of the two investments plot along line *FM*. The client's attitude toward risk and return is shown by the set of indifference curves, and the optimal mixture lies at the point O* where an indifference curve is tangent to line *FM*. In this example, the best mixture uses both Treasury bills and the surrogate market portfolio. In other situations, the surrogate market portfolio might be "levered up" by borrowing (that is, money might be borrowed and added to the client's own investable funds, with the total being used to purchase the surrogate market portfolio).

When management is passive, the overall mixture is altered only when (1) the client's preferences change; or (2) the riskfree rate changes; or (3) the consensus forecast about the risk and return of the benchmark portfolio changes. The manager must continue to monitor the last two variables and keep in touch with the client concerning the first one. No additional activity is required.

Active managers believe that from time to time there are mispriced securities or groups of securities. They do not act as if they believe that security markets are efficient. Put somewhat differently, they use deviant predictions—that is, their forecasts of risks and expected returns differ from consensus opinions. Whereas some managers may be more bullish than average about a security, others may be more bearish. The former will hold "more-than-normal" proportions of the security, while the latter will hold "less-than-normal" proportions.

Assuming that there is no tailoring, it is useful to think of a portfolio as having two components: (1) a benchmark portfolio (actually, a surrogate for it);

and (2) deviations designed to take advantage of security mispricing. For example, a portfolio can be broken down as follows:

Name of Security (Col.1)	Proportion In Actual Portfolio (Col. 2)	Proportion In Market Portfolio (Col. 3)	Active Position (Col. 4)
S1	.30	.45	−.15
S2	.20	.25	−.05
S3	.50	.30	+.20
	1.00	1.00	.00

The second column shows the actual proportions in the actively managed portfolio. The third column indicates the percentages in a benchmark portfolio which in this case is represented by a surrogate market portfolio—the holdings that might be best for an average client in a perfectly efficient market. The **active positions** can be represented by the differences between the proportions in the actual and benchmark portfolios. Such differences arise because active managers disagree with the consensus forecast about expected returns or risks. When expressed as differences of this sort, the actual portfolio can be viewed as an investment in the benchmark portfolio with a series of *bets* being placed on certain securities (such as *S3*) and against certain other securities (such as *S1* and *S2*). Note how the bets are "balanced" in that the amount of the negative bets exactly counters the amount of the positive bets.

24.4.2 Security Selection, Asset Allocation, and Market Timing

Security Selection

In principle, the investment manager should make forecasts of expected returns, standard deviations, and covariances for all available securities. This will allow an efficient set to be generated, upon which the indifference curves of the client can be plotted. Having done this, the investment manager should invest in those securities that form the optimal portfolio (that is, the portfolio indicated by the point where an indifference curve is tangent to the efficient set) for the client in question. Such a one-stage **security selection** process is illustrated in Figure 24.5(a).

In practice, this is rarely (if ever) done. Excessive costs would be incurred to obtain detailed forecasts of the expected returns, standard deviations, and covariances for all the individual securities under consideration. Instead, the decision on which securities to purchase is made in two or more stages.

Figure 24.5(b) illustrates a two-stage procedure where the investment manager has decided to consider investing in common stocks and corporate bonds for a client. In this case, the expected returns, standard deviations, and covariances are forecast for all common stocks under consideration. Then based on just these common stocks, the efficient set is formed and the optimal stock portfolio identified. Next the same analysis is performed for all corporate bonds under consideration, resulting in the identification of the optimal bond portfolio. The security selection process used in each of these two **asset classes** can

The Active Versus Passive Debate

The debate between proponents of active and passive management has raged for over two decades, with little resolution in sight. At stake are billions of dollars in investment management fees, professional reputations, and, some would argue, even the efficient functioning of our capital markets.

As the text describes, passive management involves a long-term, buy-and-hold approach to investing. The investor selects an appropriate target and buys a portfolio designed to closely track the performance of that target. Once the portfolio is purchased, little additional trading occurs, beyond reinvesting income or minor rebalancings necessary to accurately track the target. Because the selected target is usually (although not necessarily) a broad, diversified market index (for example, the Wilshire 5000 for domestic common stocks), passive management is commonly referred to as "indexation," and the passive portfolios are called "index funds."

Active management involves a systematic effort to exceed the performance of a selected target. A wide array of active management investment approaches exists, far too many to summarize in this space. Nevertheless, all active management entails the search for mispriced securities, or mispriced groups of securities. Accurately identifying and adroitly purchasing or selling these mispriced securities provides the active investor with the potential to outperform the passive investor.

Passive management is a relative newcomer to the investment industry. Prior to the mid 1960s, it was axiomatic that investors should search for mispriced stocks. Some investment strategies had passive overtones, such as buying "solid, blue-chip" companies for the "long term." Nevertheless, even these strategies implied an attempt to outperform some nebulously specified market target. The concepts of broad diversification and passive management were, for practical purposes, nonexistent.

Attitudes changed in the 1960s with the popularization of Markowitz's portfolio selection concepts (see Chapter 8), the introduction of the efficient market hypothesis (see Chapter 4), the emphasis on "the market portfolio" derived from the Capital Asset Pricing Model (see Chapter 10), and various academic studies proclaiming the futility of active management. Many investors, especially large institutional investors, began to question the wisdom of actively managing all of their assets. The first domestic common stock index fund was introduced in 1971. By the end of the decade, roughly $100 million was being invested in index funds. Today, hundreds of billions of dollars are invested in domestic and international stock and bond index funds. Even individual investors have become enamored with index funds. Passively managed portfolios are some of the fastest growing products offered by many large mutual fund organizations.

Proponents of active management argue that capital markets are inefficient enough to justify the search for mispriced securities. They may disagree on the degree of the markets' inefficiencies. Technical analysts (see Chapter 23), for example, tend to view markets as dominated by emotionally driven and predictable investors, thereby creating numerous profit opportunities for the creative and disciplined investor. Conversely, managers who use highly quantitative investment tools often view profit opportunities as smaller and less persistent. Nevertheless, all active managers possess a fundamental belief in the existence of consistently exploitable security mispricings. As evidence they frequently point to the stellar track records of certain successful managers and various studies identifying market inefficiencies (see the appendix to Chapter 17 that discusses empirical regularities).

Some active management proponents also introduce into the active-passive debate what amounts to a moralistic appeal. They contend that investors have virtually an obligation to seek out mispriced securities, because their actions help remove these mispricings and thereby lead to a more efficient allocation of capital. Moreover, some proponents derisively contend that passive management implies settling for mediocre, or average, performance.

Proponents of passive management do not deny that exploitable profit opportunities exist or that some managers have established impressive performance results. Rather, they contend that the capital markets are efficient enough to prevent all but a few with inside information from consistently being able to earn abnormal profits. They point out that examples of past successes are more likely the result of luck rather than skill. If 1,000 people flip a coin ten times, the odds are that one of them will flip all heads. In the investment industry, this person is crowned a brilliant money manager.

Passive management proponents also argue that the expected returns from active management are actually less than those for passive management. The fees charged by active managers are typically much higher than those levied by passive managers. (The difference averages anywhere from 0.30% to 1.00% of the managers' assets under management.) Further, passively managed portfolios usually experience very small transaction costs, whereas, depending on the amount of trading involved, active management transaction costs can be quite high. Thus it is argued that passive managers will outperform active managers because of cost differences. Passive management thus entails settling for superior, as opposed to mediocre, results.

The active-passive debate will never be totally resolved. The random "noise" inherent in investment performance tends to drown out any systematic evidence of investment management skill on the part of active managers. Subjective issues therefore dominate the discussion, and as a result neither side can convince the other of the correctness of its viewpoint.

Despite the rapid growth in passively managed assets, most domestic and international stock and bond portfolios remain actively managed. Many large institutional investors, such as pension funds, have taken a middle ground on the matter, hiring both passive and active managers. In a crude way, this strategy may be a reasonable response to the unresolved active-passive debate. Clearly, all assets cannot be passively managed—who would be left to maintain security prices at "fair" value levels? On the other hand, investors with above-average investment skills are clearly in the minority of the group currently offering their services to investors.

be described as being myopic. That is, covariances between the individual common stocks and corporate bonds have not been considered in the identification of the two optimal portfolios.

Although this example has two asset classes—stocks and bonds—it should be noted that the number of asset classes can be relatively large. Other asset classes that are often used consist of money market securities ("cash"), foreign stocks, foreign bonds, and real estate.

Asset Allocation

The second stage of the process divides the client's funds among two asset class portfolios, and is known as **asset allocation**.[7] In this stage, forecasts of the expected return and standard deviation are needed for both the optimal stock portfolio and the optimal bond portfolio, along with the covariance between the two portfolios. This will allow the expected return and standard deviation to be determined for all combinations of these two portfolios. Finally, after generating the efficient set from these combinations, the indifference curves of the client can be used to determine which portfolio should be chosen.

Some people refer to two types of asset allocation. *Strategic asset allocation* refers to how a portfolio's funds would be divided, given the portfolio manager's long-term forecasts of expected returns, variances, and covariances, whereas *tac-*

Figure 24.5
Investment Styles

(a) Security Selection

Securities — Security Selection → Overall Portfolio

Overall Portfolio

(b) Security Selection and Asset Allocation

Securities — Security Selection → Asset-Class Portfolios — Asset Allocation → Overall Portfolio

Stock Portfolio

Bond Portfolio

Overall Portfolio

(c) Security Selection, Group Selection, and Asset Allocation

Securities — Security Selection → Group Portfolios — Group Selection → Asset Class Portfolios — Asset Allocation → Overall Portfolio

Group 1

Group 2

Group 3

Stock Portfolio

Long-Term Bond Portfolio

Intermediate-Term Bond Portfolio

Short-Term Bond Portfolio

Bond Portfolio

Overall Portfolio

(d) Market Timing

Securities — Passive Security Selection → Risky and Riskless Portfolios — Market Timing → Overall Portfolio

Market Portfolio of Risky Securities

Riskless Security

Overall Portfolio

tical asset allocation refers to how these funds are to be divided at any particular moment, given the investor's short-term forecasts. Hence the former reflects what the portfolio manager would do for the long term and the latter reflects what he or she would do under current market conditions.

For example, the first stage might have indicated that the investor should hold the proportions of stocks $S1$, $S2$, and $S3$ given earlier (that is, the optimal stock portfolio has proportions of .30, .20, and .50, respectively). Similarly, the first stage might have indicated that the investor should hold a proportion of .35 in bond $B1$ and .65 in bond $B2$. Then under tactical asset allocation, the second stage might indicate that the client's funds should be split so that 60% goes into stocks and 40% into bonds because of current market conditions (whereas under strategic asset allocation these percentages might have been 70% and 30%, respectively). This translates into individual investments of the following magnitudes:

Stocks:
$S1$ .60 × .30 = .18
$S2$ .60 × .20 = .12
$S3$ .60 × .50 = .30
Bonds:
$B1$ .40 × .35 = .14
$B2$ .40 × .65 = .26
____
1.00

The two-stage process just discussed can be extended by introducing groups (sometimes referred to as sectors). Figure 24.5(c) illustrates a three-stage process. In the first stage, known as security selection, the investment manager would exercise discretion in identifying groups of securities in each asset class. Then having identified the groups, the investment manager would determine the optimal portfolio for each one. For example, within the asset class of common stocks, it could be that the investment manager has identified all industrial stocks as the first group, all utility stocks as the second group, and all transportation stocks as the third group. Within the asset class of bonds, groups of long-term, intermediate-term, and short-term bonds have been identified. Then, the investment manager would proceed to identify six optimal portfolios, one for each group of securities.

In the second stage, known as **group selection** (or group rotation), the investment manager determines the appropriate combination of the groups within each asset class. For example, the manager may have decided that the appropriate combination is 70% industrials, 10% utilities, and 20% transportation stocks. Similarly, the manager may have decided that the appropriate combination of bonds is 100% in long-term, with nothing in either intermediate-term or short-term bonds. Thus in this stage the manager will determine the composition of an optimal stock portfolio and an optimal bond portfolio but will not know how much to allocate to each one.

The third and final stage makes this allocation and, as noted previously, is referred to as asset allocation. It is performed in a manner that is identical to the second stage of the two-stage procedure illustrated in Figure 24.5(b).

Active or passive management may be used in any stage. For example, *active bets* might be placed on individual securities, but with funds allocated across asset classes based on consensus long-term forecasts of expected returns for such classes. That is, the investment manager may decide to stick to a long-term mix of 75% stocks and 25% bonds. However, the choice of individual stocks and bonds in which to invest will change with time, based on the manager's forecasts.

Alternatively, passive portfolios of individual securities might be constructed, with deviant predictions of asset class returns used to allocate funds actively among the asset classes. For example, the investment manager may decide to always hold common stocks in the same relative proportions they have in the S&P 500, which is often used as a surrogate for the U.S. stock market portfolio. However, the proportion of funds invested in the S&P 500 will change at the start of every period, based on the overall prognosis for the stock and bond markets. Thus during one period the manager may have as much as 100% of the client's funds in stocks, on the strong belief that the stock market is going to rise rapidly in the near future. Conversely, during another period the manager may have as much as 100% of the client's funds in bonds on the strong belief that the stock market will soon crash dramatically.

Market Timing

Figure 24.5(d) portrays a manager following an investment style that is known as **market timing.** The only active decision concerns the appropriate allocation of funds between a surrogate market portfolio (usually consisting of either stocks or long-term bonds) and a riskfree asset, such as Treasury bills. An investment organization following this style changes its mixture of risky and riskfree assets based on its own forecasts of the risk and expected return of "the market" relative to the riskfree rate, even if there is no change in consensus forecasts or the client's attitude toward risk and return.

Investment organizations that engage in the type of management where active bets are placed on individual securities are said to have a *security selection style.* Those that engage in the type of management where active bets are placed on asset classes are said to have an *asset allocation style,* with market timing being one specific example. Lastly, investment organizations that place active bets on certain groups of securities are said to employ a *group rotation style.* Some organizations use relatively pure **investment styles,** meaning that they use basically just one of the three styles previously mentioned. Others employ various combinations, making it difficult to classify them into neat categories.

Although these styles have been described in terms of modern portfolio theory, it should be pointed out that other procedures could be used to implement them. For example, with modern portfolio theory an optimal stock portfolio [as in Figure 24.5(b)] is to be identified by use of forecast expected returns, standard deviations, and covariances in conjunction with indifference curves. Once it is identified, the portfolio manager will have determined the appropriate relative investments in individual common stocks. However, such an identification could be made using some other procedure. Often it is done on a much less formal and more qualitative basis.

24.4.3 International Investing

An interesting extension of the previous discussion of investment styles involves international investing. Consider security selection first. This style, when applied internationally, would involve determining the efficient set associated with a number of stocks found around the world. Alternatively, a security selection style could be combined with an asset allocation style. Here, for example, the portfolio manager could first determine the optimal portfolios associated with just Japanese stocks, just American stocks, and just German stocks. Then, using these optimal portfolios, the manager would decide how much to allocate to each one of the three countries.

Imagine that the optimal Japanese portfolio consisted of two stocks, J_1 and J_2, in proportions of 70% and 30%, respectively, and half of the portfolio's funds were to be devoted to Japanese stocks. As a result, 35% ($= .50 \times 70\%$) and 15% ($= .50 \times 30\%$) of the portfolio would be invested in J_1 and J_2, respectively. Similar calculations could be done for the sets of American and German stocks.

Analogous procedures to those previously described could be followed for the security selection, group rotation, asset allocation, and market timing styles in an international setting. However, the issue of foreign currency risk adds a confounding element to this comparison.[8]

24.5 PORTFOLIO REVISION

With the passage of time, a previously purchased portfolio that is currently held will often be viewed as suboptimal by the investment manager, meaning that the portfolio is no longer viewed as the best one for the client. This is because either the client's attitude toward risk and return is thought to have changed or, more likely, the manager's forecasts have changed. In response, the manager could identify a new optimal portfolio and then make the necessary revisions to the current portfolio so that subsequently the new optimal portfolio will be held. However, this is not as straightforward as it might seem at first because transaction costs will have to be paid when any revisions are made. Such costs must be compared with the perceived benefits associated with the revision in order to determine what course of action to take.

24.5.1 Cost-Benefit Analysis

Transaction costs were discussed in Chapter 3. They include brokerage commissions, price impacts, and bid-ask spreads. Because of these costs, a security would have to increase in value by a certain amount just to pay these costs and leave the investor neither better nor worse off. This necessary increase in value may exceed 1% for many securities and can range as high as 5% to 10% or more for others, particularly small-size stocks.

The existence of transaction costs greatly complicates the life of any investment manager, and the more active the manager, the greater the complications. The hoped-for advantage of any revision must be weighed against the cost of making that revision. That is, a revision can be viewed as bringing certain kinds of benefits—either it will increase the expected return of the portfolio, or it will reduce the standard deviation of the portfolio, or it will do both. To be weighed against these benefits are the transaction costs that will be incurred if the revision is made. As a result, some of the revisions in the holdings of individual securities that the manager may initially want to make will be dropped from consideration because of the transaction costs involved. The goal of the manager is to identify the set of individual revisions that collectively maximizes the improvement, after transaction costs, in the risk-return characteristics of the current portfolio.

In order to identify the appropriate set of individual revisions, sophisticated procedures (for example, quadratic programming) are required to compare the relevant costs and benefits. Fortunately, improvements in procedures and dramatic decreases in computing costs have made such approaches economically feasible for many investment managers.

In some situations investors may find it economically more attractive to revise their portfolios by transacting in entire asset classes instead of individual securities. Buying or selling futures contracts (see Chapter 21) on stock market indices or Treasury bonds is one such approach. A potentially more flexible strategy makes use of the swaps market.

24.5.2 Swaps

Consider a situation where a portfolio manager wants to make major changes in the proportions of funds that are invested in different asset classes. He or she recognizes that substantial transaction costs will be incurred if the traditional method of selling certain securities and replacing them with others is used to make these changes. Indeed, these costs can be so large that most of the changes, if conducted in this manner, should not be made. One relatively new method that has become very popular in allowing such changes to be made at relatively low transaction costs involves the use of swaps.[9]

While the unique features of swaps can become quite complicated, their general nature is quite simple. Such "plain-vanilla" swaps are contracts that typically involve two parties (in the language of swaps they are referred to as *counterparties*) exchanging sets of cash flows over a predetermined period of time.[10] Two types of swaps—equity and interest rate—are considered here.

Equity Swaps

With an **equity swap,** one counterparty agrees to pay a second counterparty a stream of variable-size cash payments that is based on the rate of return of an agreed-upon stock market index. In return, the second counterparty agrees to pay the first counterparty a stream of fixed-size cash payments that is based on current interest rates. Both sets of payments are to be made for a given time period and are based on a certain percentage (the percentage is variable for one counterparty and fixed for the other) of an underlying *notional principal.* Through an equity swap the first counterparty has, in essence, sold stocks and bought bonds while the second counterparty has sold bonds and bought stocks.

Both of them have effectively restructured their portfolios without having to pay any transaction costs, other than a relatively small fee to a **swap bank** (usually a commercial or investment bank) that set up the contract.

Consider the example that is shown in Figure 24.6(a). Ms. Bright, a pension fund manager, thinks that the stock market is going to move upward sharply in the next three years. In contrast, Mr. Gloom, who also runs a pension fund, thinks that the stock market is likely to move downward in the next three years. Ms. Bright is considering selling $100 million of bonds and investing the proceeds in common stocks whereas Mr. Gloom is thinking of selling $100 million of common stocks and using the proceeds to purchase bonds. However, both portfolio managers realize that such changes will involve the payment of substantial transaction costs. Consequently, both of them contact a swap bank.

The swap bank sets up the following contract for Ms. Bright and Mr. Gloom. Shortly after the end of each quarter Mr. Gloom is to pay Ms. Bright an amount that is equal to the rate of return on the S&P 500 for the quarter times the notional principal. At the same time, Ms. Bright is to pay Mr. Gloom an amount that is equal to 2% of the notional principal. Both Ms. Bright and Mr. Gloom agree that the notional principal will be equal to $100 million, and that the contract will last for three years. Each pay the swap bank a fee for setting up the contract.[11]

Imagine that the quarterly rates of return on the S&P 500 during the first year of the swap contract are equal to 3%, −4%, 1%, and 5%, as shown in Figure 24.6(b). While Ms. Bright must pay $2 million (= .02 × $100 million) to Mr. Gloom each quarter, in return Mr. Gloom must pay Ms. Bright the following amounts:

Figure 24.6
Equity Swap

a. The Contract:

b. The Cash Flows:

		Ms. Bright's Cash Flows*			Mr. Gloom's Cash Flows*		
Quarter	S&P 500 Return	Payment from Gloom	Payment to Gloom	Net	Payment from Bright	Payment to Bright	Net
First	3%	$3	$2	$1	$2	$3	− $1
Second	− 4	− 4	2	− 6	2	− 4	6
Third	1	1	2	− 1	2	1	1
Fourth	5	5	2	3	2	5	− 3

*All cash flows are in millions as the notional principal is $100 million.

First quarter:	.03 × $100 million =	$3 million
Second quarter:	− .04 × $100 million =	− 4 million
Third quarter:	.01 × $100 million =	1 million
Fourth quarter:	.05 × $100 million =	5 million

Hence it appears that in the first quarter Ms. Bright pays $2 million to Mr. Gloom and in return Mr. Gloom pays $3 million to Ms. Bright. However, the way the contract is structured, only the net amount is paid—in this case, Mr. Gloom will pay $1 million (= $3 million − $2 million) to Ms. Bright. In the second quarter it appears that Mr. Gloom must pay − $4 million to Ms. Bright. What the minus sign means is that Ms. Bright must pay Mr. Gloom $4 million plus the fixed payment of $2 million, for a total payment of $6 million. In the third period, Ms. Bright must pay Mr. Gloom $1 million (= $2 million − $1 million), and in the fourth quarter Mr. Gloom must pay Ms. Bright $3 million (= $5 million − $2 million). In summary, the net payments are:

First quarter:	Mr. Gloom pays $1 million to Ms. Bright
Second quarter:	Ms. Bright pays $6 million to Mr. Gloom
Third quarter:	Ms. Bright pays $1 million to Mr. Gloom
Fourth quarter:	Mr. Gloom pays $3 million to Ms. Bright

These amounts reflect what would have happened (roughly) if Mr. Gloom had sold stocks and bought bonds and Ms. Bright had sold bonds and bought stocks, and both incurred relatively low transaction costs. Consider the first quarter. If Mr. Gloom had sold the stocks and replaced them with 2% bonds, he would have earned $2 million. Instead, he kept the stocks and earned $3 million on them (remember that the S&P 500 went up 3%) but had to pay Ms. Bright a net amount of $1 million, leaving him with $2 million, the same amount.

There are many ways that equity swaps can be modified. For example, a foreign stock market index such as the Nikkei 225 could be used instead of the S&P 500. This would allow one counterparty to cheaply achieve the benefits of international diversification. Alternatively, the swap could involve two stock market indices, such as a large stock index like the S&P 500 and a small stock index like the Russell 2000. There are many other variations, limited only by investors' imaginations and their ability to periodically determine the value of the swaps.

Interest Rate Swaps

With an **interest rate swap,** one counterparty agrees to pay a second party a stream of cash payments whose size is reset regularly based on the current level of a highly visible interest rate. A popular one is the London Interbank Offered Rate (LIBOR), which is an interest rate set daily in London that applies to loans made among large international banks. In return, the second counterparty agrees to pay the first counterparty a stream of fixed-size cash payments that is based on the level of interest rates in existence at the time the contract is signed. Like equity swaps, both sets of payments are to be made for a certain number of years and are based on a certain percentage of an underlying notional principal. (The percentage is variable—or "floating"—for one counterparty and fixed for the other.) Through the interest rate swap the first counterparty has, in essence, sold short-term fixed-income securities and bought long-term bonds while the second counterparty has sold these bonds and bought the short-term fixed-income securities. Both of them have effectively restructured their portfolios without having to pay any transaction costs other than a relatively small fee to a swap bank that set up the contract.

Consider the example that is shown in Figure 24.7(a). Ms. Uppe, a fixed-income mutual fund manager, thinks that interest rates are going to move upward in the near future. In contrast, Mr. Downe, who also runs a fixed-income mutual fund, thinks that interest rates are likely to soon move downward. Consequently, Ms. Uppe is considering selling $100 million of long-term bonds and investing the proceeds in money market securities, whereas Mr. Downe is thinking of selling $100 million of money market securities and using the proceeds to purchase long-term bonds.[12] As with the case of an equity swap, both of them contact a swap bank to help them make such changes without the payment of substantial transaction costs.[13]

The swap bank sets up the following contract for the two of them. Shortly after the end of each quarter Mr. Downe is to pay Ms. Uppe an amount that is equal to the end-of-quarter three-month LIBOR times the notional principal. At the same time Ms. Uppe is to pay Mr. Downe an amount that is equal to 2% of the notional principal. Both Ms. Uppe and Mr. Downe agree that the notional principal will be equal to $100 million, and that the contract will last for five years. Each pays the swap bank a fee for setting up the contract.

Imagine that the three-month LIBOR at the beginning of each of the next four quarters equals, successively, 1.5%, 1.8%, 2.1%, and 2.4%. This means that the following amounts are to be paid by Mr. Downe to Ms. Uppe:

Figure 24.7
Interest Rate Swap

a. The Contract:

b. The Cash Flows:

		Ms. Uppe's Cash Flows*			Mr. Downe's Cash Flows*		
		Payment	Payment		Payment	Payment	
Quarter	LIBOR	from Downe	to Downe	Net	from Uppe	to Uppe	Net
First	1.5%	$1.5	$2	−$.5	$2	$1.5	$.5
Second	1.8	1.8	2	−.2	2	1.8	.2
Third	2.1	2.1	2	.1	2	2.1	−.1
Fourth	2.4	2.4	2	.4	2	2.4	−.4

*All cash flows are in millions as the notional principal is $100 million.

First quarter:	$.015 \times \$100$ million $= \$1.5$ million
Second quarter:	$.018 \times \$100$ million $= 1.8$ million
Third quarter:	$.021 \times \$100$ million $= 2.1$ million
Fourth quarter:	$.024 \times \$100$ million $= 2.4$ million

In return, Ms. Uppe must pay \$2 million ($= .02 \times \$100$ million) to Mr. Downe each quarter.

Since the payments from Ms. Uppe and Mr. Downe are netted against each other, the net payments are:

First quarter:	Ms. Uppe pays \$.5 million to Mr. Downe
Second quarter:	Ms. Uppe pays \$.2 million to Mr. Downe
Third quarter:	Mr. Downe pays \$.1 million to Ms. Uppe
Fourth quarter:	Mr. Downe pays \$.4 million to Ms. Uppe

These amounts reflect what would have happened (roughly) if Ms. Uppe had sold bonds and bought money market securities and Mr. Downe had sold money market securities and bought bonds, and both incurred relatively low transaction costs. Consider the first quarter. If Ms. Uppe had sold the bonds and replaced them with money market securities yielding roughly LIBOR, she would have earned \$1.5 million in interest. Instead, she kept the bonds and earned \$2 million on them but had to pay Mr. Downe a net amount of \$.5 million, leaving her with \$1.5 million, the same amount.

As with equity swaps, there are many variations on this plain-vanilla type of interest rate swap. For example, the notional principal could change over time. Or one variable-rate stream of cash flows based on one interest rate (such as LIBOR) could be swapped for a variable rate stream of cash flows based on another interest rate (such as Treasury bills). In addition, there can be caps or floors or collars on the size of the variable payments.

Swaps Market

The swaps market is an unregulated market in that no governmental agency has oversight responsibilities. As a consequence, there has been a high degree of innovation in the types of swap contracts that have been created.[14] Furthermore, there is privacy for all parties involved, as no reporting requirements exist other than those imposed by accountants. In addition, it means that anyone involved in a swap must be concerned with *counterparty risk.* That is, each counterparty to a swap must pay close attention to the creditworthiness of the other counterparty in order to reduce the risk that the other counterparty will default in making his or her required payments under the terms of the contract.

At the heart of the swaps market are swap banks. These "banks" facilitate the creation of swaps for their clients, and they will often take the other side of the contract if another counterparty is not available at the moment. In such situations they are acting as *swap dealers,* and they will use various kinds of techniques (such as taking positions in futures or contacting other swap banks) to hedge their exposure to financial risk. In such a situation no fee is typically charged to the counterparty. Instead, the terms of the swap are set in the swap dealer's favor, thereby allowing the dealer to make a profit after hedging his or her position.

What happens if at some point during the life of the swap one counterparty wants to get out of the contract? In such a situation the counterparty has a choice of contacting either the other counterparty or a swap bank. In the first case, it is possible that the swap contract can be cancelled if a mutually acceptable cash payment is made from one counterparty to the other. In the interest rate swap example, if interest rates have risen high enough (as in the third and fourth quarter), then Ms. Uppe will be in a favorable position because the swap's net cash flows will be going from Mr. Downe to her. Hence, regardless of who wants to get out of the swap, Ms. Uppe would want to be compensated for the loss of the anticipated future cash flows. This means that Mr. Downe would give her a lump sum payment when the contract is cancelled.

Similarly, if a swap bank is contacted, then either it will assume the counterparty's position in the contract or it will search for someone else to do so. (Note that the counterparty that wants to get out of the contract can conduct such a search without using a swap bank.) In the previous example, if Ms. Uppe wants to get out of the contract, then the swap bank will pay her a lump sum. Conversely, if Mr. Downe wants to get out, then he will have to pay a lump sum to the swap bank. In either case, the contract remains in force afterward for the other counterparty.

It is also possible that the swap bank will arrange for the party that wants to get out to agree to a second swap contract that effectively cancels the first one. For example, if after one year Ms. Uppe wants to get out of the contract where she "pays fixed and receives floating," then the swap bank could construct a four-year swap where she "pays floating and receives fixed" for the same amount of notional principal. With the first contract she pays 2% and receives LIBOR, and with the second contract she will pay LIBOR and receive 2.3%. Note that the fixed rate is higher with the second contract (2.3% > 2%) as interest rates have risen since the first contract was signed. Now Ms. Uppe both receives and pays LIBOR, so those two cash streams effectively cancel each other out. She also pays 2% and receives 2.3%, meaning that, on balance, she receives .3%, or $300,000 (= .003 × $100 million). Thus for the next four years she will receive $300,000 quarterly.

24.6   MANAGER-CLIENT RELATIONS

The larger the amount of money managed, the more communication there is likely to be between investment manager and client. Not surprisingly, corporate, union, and government officials responsible for pension funds spend a great deal of time with those who manage their money. Such officials also concern themselves with a number of questions: Who should manage the money, how should it be managed, and how should the managers be instructed and constrained?

Manager Structuring

Administrators of pension and endowment funds might be surprised to find themselves referred to as investment engineers. Yet these particular institutional investors (who are often called "plan sponsors") face the complex problem of efficiently allocating their assets among various investment managers so as to best achieve their stated investment objectives. The disciplined process through which this manager "structuring" problem can best be resolved is analogous to an engineer designing a building or a machine.

When plan sponsors choose to invest in a particular asset class, especially a well-defined and liquid one such as the U.S. common stock market, they typically choose a market index to characterize the expected return and risk opportunities of the asset class and to serve as a benchmark against which to evaluate the subsequent performance of their investments. In this context, the selected market index is called an *asset class target*. For example, a plan sponsor might specify the Standard & Poor's 500 and the Salomon Brothers Broad Bond Index as the asset class targets for its U.S. common stock and fixed-income investments, respectively. In a sense these market indices represent the portfolios that the plan sponsors would own if all of their investments in these asset classes were passively managed.

Plan sponsors rarely opt to conduct all of their investments in an asset class on a strictly passive basis. Instead, they typically hire a number of active investment managers (possibly in addition to using an index fund). In aggregate, these active managers are expected to exceed the performance of the asset class target on a risk-adjusted basis.

For various reasons most active investment managers pursue distinct investment styles, focusing their efforts in particular niches of the marketplace. For example, some common stock managers concentrate on small capitalization growth stocks, whereas some bond managers invest only in mortgage-backed securities.

Just as an investment manager will diversify within a portfolio to avoid unintended risks, a plan sponsor will diversify across investment managers. This manager diversification reduces the possibility that one manager's mistakes will seriously harm the plan sponsor's total portfolio. Further, it avoids the risk that the total portfolio will be excessively exposed to the results of a specific investment style. In particular, it is this "diversification of style" that underlies the plan sponsor's investment engineering problem.

The goal of efficient style diversification is to be *style neutral* relative to the asset class target. That is, in aggregate, the investment styles of a plan sponsor's managers should exhibit exposures to factors of risk and return (see Chapter 11) similar to those of the asset class target.

Suppose that a plan sponsor decision-maker, who had selected the S&P 500 as the asset class target for his or her U.S. common stock investments, were to hire only investment managers that invested in large capitalization, high-dividend-yield stocks. The aggregate of the managers' investment styles would display investment characteristics quite different from those of the S&P 500. For example, relative to the S&P 500, the aggregate manager style would heavily emphasize utility stocks, which pay high dividends, and deemphasize technology stocks, which pay small dividends or none.

In some periods, such as during an economic downturn, these large high-yield stocks would perform well relative to the S&P 500. In other periods, they might perform relatively poorly. This relative performance difference would occur regardless of whether the large capitalization, high-yield managers were good or bad stock pickers within their area of expertise. The aggregate style of these managers does not "fit" with the asset class target. Therefore the risk that the aggregate manager style will perform differently from the asset class target is known as *misfit risk*. Style diversification seeks to limit misfit risk.

Unfortunately, simply hiring many active managers with differing investment styles is not a cost-effective means of controlling misfit risk. Investment skill is a rare commodity. A plan sponsor decision-maker may not be able to identify what he or she believes to be skillful managers in sufficient quantity to provide a diverse group of investment styles. As the costs of active management are much higher than those of passive management, a strategy of hiring a large number of active managers with different investment styles within an asset category is likely to produce nothing more than an expensive index fund.

Plan sponsors would prefer to allocate their assets only to those managers who they believe can perform best relative to the managers' investment styles, without concern for how those investment styles in aggregate compare to the asset class target. How can plan sponsors accommodate this preference and at the same time control misfit risk? That is the essence of the investment engineering problem.

Consider a plan sponsor who has identified certain managers that he or she believes will be the strongest risk-adjusted performers. Upon examining the managers' aggregate investment style, the plan sponsor finds that it heavily emphasizes smaller companies and companies expected to produce high relative earnings growth. The plan sponsor has selected the S&P 500 as the asset class target, which tends to be dominated by large, mature companies. Thus considerable misfit risk exists.

The plan sponsor could reduce this misfit risk by also investing in a specially designed, passively managed portfolio. This portfolio, called a *completeness fund,* would hold long positions in securities underrepresented by the managers' aggregate investment style relative to the asset class target. Conversely, it would contain short positions in overrepresented securities. In our example, the completeness fund would purchase large capitalization, low-growth stocks and sell short smaller, high-growth stocks.

Properly constructed, the completeness fund will eliminate misfit risk and create a style-neutral total portfolio. If the active managers exceed the performance of their respective investment style benchmarks, then the total portfolio will outperform the asset class target.

Complicating the issue is the fact that the active managers' investment styles may have non-zero covariances with one another. If so, various allocations among them will produce different levels of misfit risk. Moreover, the plan sponsor may have more confidence in some managers than in others, and therefore wish to allocate more funds to the former than to the latter. These active manager allocation decisions directly affect the aggregate manager investment style and thus the composition of the completeness fund.

Determining desired allocations to the active managers and the composition of the resulting completeness fund requires a disciplined, quantitative approach. Further, the problem is dynamic, with the appropriate solution shifting over time as the investment characteristics of securities evolve and plan sponsors' estimates of the relative skills of their current and prospective managers change. The task of manager structuring is truly one of investment engineering.

Many of the aspects of manager-client relations can be characterized as responses to a difference of opinion concerning the manager's abilities to make "good bets." Often clients will divide their funds among two or more managers. This type of **split-funding** is used by most pension funds. Two reasons are given. First, it allows the employment of managers with different skills or different styles. Second, the impact of erroneous "bets" can be reduced by diversifying across different managers because the managers are the "bettors." However, if a client were to broadly diversify across managers without regard to the managers' investment abilities, the overall portfolio would likely produce results similar to those of the market portfolio. Thus excessive use of split-funding is like explicitly investing in a passive fund, but at considerably greater cost to the client, owing to the expenses associated with transaction costs and fees charged by the investment managers.

Whether or not split-funding is used, a client who feels that a manager is "betting" too much would like to simply reduce the size of the "bets." For example, the client might ask a manager to diverge only half as much as he or she normally would from passive proportions of individual securities. Thus, if the manager decides that the optimal proportion in stock $S1$ is 30% and the market proportion is 45%, this would mean that the manager would ultimately invest only a proportion equal to 37.5% $[=(30\% + 45\%)/2]$. However, there is no simple way to monitor compliance. In the example, the manager could buy 30% of $S1$ and state that he or she originally wanted to invest 45% in it but settled for 30%, even though truthfully he or she originally wanted 30%. Instead, a simpler approach is often employed: Limits are placed on the holdings in any single security.[15]

Institutional investors (for example, pension and endowment funds) often use more than one investment manager and provide each with a set of objectives and a set of constraints on allowed divergences from specified target positions.[16] Individual investors who employ investment managers tend to give such instructions implicitly, if at all. This may reflect less sophistication, a less formal relationship with the manager, or the fact that the management fee for a small account is not large enough to cover the cost of dealing with a series of client-specific objectives and constraints.

24.7   SUMMARY

1. Investment decisions are made through a five-step procedure: (1) set investment policy; (2) perform security analysis; (3) construct a portfolio; (4) revise the portfolio; and (5) evaluate the performance of the portfolio.
2. To set investment policy, an investor should specify his or her risk tolerance— that is, the maximum amount of additional risk that the investor will accept for a given increase in expected return.
3. One means of establishing an investor's risk tolerance is for the investor to identify the most desirable portfolio from a set of portfolios. Once this identification has been made, the slope of the investor's indifference curve, and hence the investor's attitude toward risk and expected return, can be established.
4. Passive management rests on the belief that markets are efficient and typically involves investing in an index fund. Active management, conversely, involves a belief that mispriced situations occur and can be identified with reasonable consistency.
5. There are many forms of active management. They can involve security selection, group selection, asset allocation, and market timing.
6. Portfolio revision involves both realizing that the currently held portfolio is not optimal and specifying another portfolio to hold with superior risk-return characteristics. The investor must balance the costs of moving to the new portfolio against the benefits of the revision.
7. Swaps often provide a low-cost method of restructuring a portfolio's funds across various asset classes.

1. Describe the functioning of a "traditional" investment management organization. Much of the decision-making in these organizations is "qualitative" in nature. What types of "quantitative" decision-making techniques might be introduced?

2. Technological changes have decreased the cost and increased the speed of information dissemination in security markets. Why might one suspect that firms following a "traditional" approach to investment management would find it increasingly difficult to generate "positive alphas" (that is, to identify and acquire underpriced securities) in this environment?

3. Consider Table 24.1. If your investment advisor presented you with this data, which stock/Treasury bill combination would you choose? Describe your thought process in making this choice.

4. Why is it difficult to specify the risk-return preferences of investment management clients? Why are these problems particularly acute in the case of institutional investor clients (for example, pension and endowment funds)?

5. Consider a portfolio whose asset mix can vary between stocks and Treasury bills. Given the historical returns on these two assets that is provided in Chapter 1, describe the distribution of possible portfolio returns as the proportion of the portfolio invested in stocks increases and that invested in Treasury bills decreases. What causes the distribution to change as the asset mix changes?

6. Explain the meaning of the slope of an investor's indifference curve at any particular point. For a "typical" risk-averse investor, describe how the investor's risk-return trade-off changes at different points along one of his or her indifference curves.

7. Assume that the expected return on stocks is 12%, the standard deviation of stocks is 18%, and the riskfree rate is 5%. Given this information, an investor selects a portfolio comprised of a 70% allocation to stocks and a 30% allocation to the riskfree asset. According to the derivation of risk tolerance found in Equation (24.2), what risk tolerance is indicated by this choice?

8. Buzz Arlett, a portfolio manager for an investment management firm, has estimated the following risk-return characteristics for the stock and bond markets.

	Expected Return	Standard Deviation
Stocks	18.0%	22.0%
Bonds	10.0	5.0

The correlation between stocks and bonds is estimated to be 0.50.

Using these estimates, Buzz ran a number of simulations, tracing out the implications of different bond/stock mixes for the financial situation of Zinn Beck, a client. After much thought, Zinn indicated that, of the mixes considered, the most desirable was the allocation of 60% to stocks and 40% to bonds. Given this information, calculate Zinn's risk tolerance. [Hint: To solve this problem algebraically, write Equation (24.5) using the 60/40 stock/bond allocation. Do the same for a 61/39 allocation. Finally, set these two formulas equal to each other and solve for the risk tolerance.] Is this answer likely to represent Zinn's risk tolerance over all possible stock/bond allocations?

9. Should an "overpriced" stock definitely be excluded from an investor's portfolio? Why?

10. Studies that simulate the value of an investment portfolio under alternative mixes of stocks and bonds invariably demonstrate that higher stock allocations produce higher returns, particularly as the holding period increases. If you as an investor have a time horizon that is reasonably long, say over ten years, and you have no current income needs, could you justify holding any bonds in your portfolio?

11. Assume a riskfree return of 7%, an expected stock return of 18%, and a standard deviation of 21%. Under these conditions, if Birdie Cree chooses a 40% stock, 60% riskfree portfolio, what is Birdie's risk tolerance? In words, describe what this value means.

12. Dee Cousineau can earn a riskfree return of 6%. Dee expects the stock market to return 15% and exhibit a standard deviation of 20%. If Dee chooses a portfolio of 60% stocks and 40% riskfree asset, calculate Dee's certainty equivalent return.

13. The portfolio manager's job can be defined as identifying the portfolio with the highest certainty equivalent return. Explain.

14. Despite its obvious simplicity and potential benefits, common stock passive management is a relatively "new" investment tool. Yet in the last 20 years, assets under passive management have grown from essentially zero to hundreds of billions of dollars. What are some possible reasons for the tremendous growth in passive management?

15. It is often argued (especially by active managers) that passive management implies settling for "mediocre" performance. Is this statement necessarily true? Why?

16. Gavvy Cravath, an astute investor, once commented, "With the stock market composed of about 6,000 actively traded securities, I view my portfolio as about 5,950 short positions and 50 long positions." Explain what Gavvy means.

17. Why is the "one-stage" approach to security selection theoretically superior to the "two-stage" approach? Why is the "two-stage" approach preferred by most investment managers?

18. Why should investment portfolios, even those that are passively managed, be periodically revised? What factors weigh against making such revisions?

19. A typical money management firm, particularly one specializing in stocks or bonds, invests in essentially the same portfolio for all of its clients, regardless of the clients' individual risk-return preferences. Speculate as to why money managers often operate in this manner. What can clients do to ensure that their portfolios reflect their own specific risk-return preferences?

20. Many investment management clients split their assets among a number of managers. Two rationales for this approach have been described as "diversification of judgment" and "diversification of style." Explain the meaning of these two terms.

CFA Exam Questions

21. Advisor 1: "Long-term asset allocation should be determined using an efficient frontier. Returns, risks (standard deviations), and correlations can be determined for each asset class from historical data. After calculating the efficient frontier for various allocations, you should select the asset mix on the efficient frontier that best meets your fund's risk tolerance."

    Advisor 2: "History gives no guide to the future. For example, everybody agrees that bond risk has increased above historical levels as a result of financial deregulation. A far better approach to long-term asset allocation is to use your best judgment about expected returns on the various asset classes, based on current market conditions. You should rely on your experience to determine the best asset mix and avoid being influenced by computer printouts."

    Advisor 1 Rebuttal: "Current market conditions are not likely to persist into the future and are not appropriate for long-term asset allocation decisions. Moreover, your use of judgment and experience can be influenced by biases and emotions and is not as rigorous a method as my efficient frontier approach."

    Evaluate the strengths and weaknesses of each of the two approaches presented above. Recommend and justify an alternative process for asset allocation that draws from the strengths of each approach and corrects their weaknesses.

22. Colinos Associates is an investment management firm utilizing a very rigorous and disciplined asset allocation methodology as a key element of its investment approach. Twice a year, three or four economic scenarios are developed, based on the judgment of Colinos' most senior people. Probabilities are then assigned to the scenarios; return forecasts for U.S. stocks, bonds, and cash equivalents (the only asset types used by the firm) are generated; and expected values are computed for each asset category. These expected values are then combined with historical standard deviations and covariances to produce forecasts of results from various combinations of the three asset classes.

    From this range of possible outcomes, senior staff selects what it regards as the best asset combinations, defined as those combinations promising the highest three-year returns with a 90% probability of achieving a pre-set minimum annual return requirement. These optimal allocations (sample output in the following table) are then presented to all clients for discussion and implementation. The process is repeated in roughly six months' time, when new allocations are developed.

Minimum Annual Required Return (90% Probability)	Anticipated 3–Year Compound Annual Return	Recommended Asset Allocation		
		Cash	Bonds	Stocks
− 6%	12.0%	10%	30%	60%
− 4	11.0	20	40	40
− 2	10.0	30	40	30
0	9.0	50	30	20
2	8.5	60	30	10
4	8.0	70	20	10
6	7.5	80	15	5

a. Discuss the strengths and weaknesses of Colinos' asset allocation approach.

b. Recommend and justify an alternative asset allocation approach for wealthy individuals.

APPENDIX

DETERMINING THE RISK TOLERANCE OF AN INVESTOR

The purpose of this appendix is to derive in some detail the formula for determining the risk tolerance τ of an investor. As mentioned earlier, the equation for an indifference curve of an investor having constant risk tolerance is of the form:

$$\overline{r}_P = u_i + \frac{1}{\tau}\sigma_P^2 \qquad (24.1)$$

where u_i and $1/\tau$ are the vertical intercept and slope for indifference curve i when variance is measured on the horizontal axis. As the equation shows, an indifference curve will be a straight line because u_i and $1/\tau$ are constants (thus the equation is of the general form $Y = a + bX$, which is a straight line). Furthermore, any two indifference curves for an investor will have the same slope $(1/\tau)$ but will have different vertical intercepts (u_i).

In order to estimate the investor's level of risk tolerance τ, it was mentioned that the slope of the indifference curve, $1/\tau$, would be set equal to the slope of the efficient set at the location of the portfolio that was selected, denoted portfolio C. This is because the indifference curve is tangent to the efficient set at this point, so the two must have the same slope. Thus the slope of the efficient set at point C must be determined in order to estimate τ.

Let X_s denote the proportion invested in the stock portfolio S and $(1 - X_s)$ denote the proportion invested in a riskfree Treasury bill portfolio F. Now the expected return of any portfolio consisting of S and F is simply:

$$\overline{r}_P = X_s \overline{r}_s + (1 - X_s) r_F \tag{24.6}$$

where $\overline{r}_s$ and r_F are the expected return of the stock portfolio and the riskfree rate, respectively. This equation can be solved for X_s, resulting in:

$$X_s = \frac{\overline{r}_P - r_F}{\overline{r}_S - r_F}. \tag{24.7}$$

The equation for the variance of portfolio P is equal to:

$$\sigma_P^2 = X_s^2 \sigma_S^2 + (1 - X_s)^2 \sigma_F^2 + 2X_s(1 - X_s)\sigma_{SF} \tag{24.8}$$

where σ_S^2 and σ_F^2 are the variances of the stock and riskfree portfolios, respectively, and σ_{SF} is the covariance between these two portfolios. However, because F is the riskfree portfolio, by definition, σ_F^2 and σ_{SF} are equal to zero. Thus, Equation (24.8) reduces to:

$$\sigma_P^2 = X_s^2 \sigma_S^2. \tag{24.9}$$

Next, the right-hand side of Equation (24.7) can be substituted for X_s in Equation (24.9), resulting in:

$$\sigma_P^2 = \frac{(\overline{r}_P - r_F)^2}{(\overline{r}_S - r_F)^2} \sigma_S^2. \tag{24.10}$$

This equation can be viewed as describing the functional relationship between the expected return and variance of any portfolio P that can be formed by combining the stock portfolio S and the riskfree portfolio F. That is, for a particular S and F, it gives the variance for a portfolio consisting of S and F with expected return $\overline{r}_P$. Equivalently, it represents the slope of the curved line in Figure 24.2 that connects S and F. Using calculus, the slope of this line can be shown to be equal to:[17]

$$\text{Slope} = \frac{(\overline{r}_S - r_F)^2}{2[(\overline{r}_P - r_F)\sigma_S^2]}. \tag{24.11}$$

The next step in estimating the slope of the client's indifference curves is to note that the portfolio on the curve connecting S and F that is of concern is the tangency portfolio C. Thus, the slope of the curve at C is determined by substituting $\overline{r}_C$ for $\overline{r}_P$ in Equation (24.11) and equating this value with the slope of the indifference curves, $1/\tau$. Doing this results in the following equation:

$$\frac{1}{\tau} = \frac{(\overline{r}_S - r_F)^2}{2[(\overline{r}_C - r_F)\sigma_S^2]}. \tag{24.12}$$

Finally, Equation (24.12) can be solved for τ:

$$\tau = \frac{2[(\overline{r}_C - r_F)\sigma_S^2]}{(\overline{r}_S - r_F)^2}. \tag{24.13}$$

Note that this is the same formula that was given earlier in Equation (24.2) for estimating τ, given the client's choice of portfolio C.[18]

After substituting $\bar{r}_c$ for $\bar{r}_P$, Equation (24.7) can be rewritten as:

$$(\bar{r}_S - \bar{r}_F)X_S = \bar{r}_C - r_F. \tag{24.14}$$

Thus, $(\bar{r}_S - r_F)X_S$ can be substituted for $\bar{r}_C - r_F$ in the numerator of Equation (24.13). Doing so and simplifying results in:

$$\tau = \frac{2[X_S\sigma_S^2]}{(\bar{r}_S - r_F)}. \tag{24.15}$$

In the example given earlier in the chapter, $\sigma_S = 15\%$ and $\bar{r}_S - r_F = 4.5\%$. Substituting these values into Equation (24.15) and simplifying results in:

$$\tau = \frac{2[X_S \times 15^2]}{4.5} \tag{24.16}$$

$$= 100X_S$$

as was previously mentioned and illustrated in Table 24.1.

ENDNOTES

[1] One study found that a firm's stock price tended to move upward when analysts upgraded its coding, and downward when analysts downgraded its coding. See Edwin J. Elton, Martin J. Gruber, and Seth Grossman, "Discrete Expectational Data and Portfolio Performance," *Journal of Finance*, 41, no. 3 (July 1986): 699–713, and Chapter 23.

[2] This example is taken from William F. Sharpe, *Asset Allocation Tools* (Redwood City, CA: Scientific Press, 1987), p. 38.

[3] If such a decision is made on behalf of the client (for example, by a trustee for one or more beneficiaries), the task is much more difficult, but a decision is still required.

[4] Normally risk tolerance τ is expressed as units of variance per unit of expected return. However, the reciprocal of risk tolerance $1/\tau$ appears in Equation (24.1). This is necessitated by having risk on the horizontal axis in Figure 24.3.

[5] The term u_i is also known as the expected utility of indifference curve i. It represents the level of satisfaction associated with all portfolios plotting on indifference curve i. For more about utility theory, indifference curves, and certainty equivalent returns, see Mark Kritzman, ". . . About Utility," *Financial Analysts Journal*, 48, no. 3 (May/June 1992): 17–20.

[6] An example of a tailored portfolio would be one consisting of stocks with high dividend yields. Such a portfolio might be purchased for a corporate investor because 80% of all dividends received by a corporate investor are exempt from corporate income tax.

[7] For evidence suggesting that asset allocation is the most important decision an investor has to make, see Gary P. Brinson, L. Randolph Hood, and Gilbert L. Beebower, "Determinants of Portfolio Performance," *Financial Analysts Journal*, 42, no. 4 (July/August 1986): 39–44; and Gary P. Brinson, Brian D. Singer, and Gilbert L. Beebower, "Determinants of Portfolio Performance II: An Update," *Financial Analysts Journal*, 47, no. 3 (May/June 1991): 40–48.

[8] An intriguing description of how to use equilibrium models (like the CAPM, discussed in Chapter 10) and portfolio optimizers (see the *Institutional Issues* section in Chapter 8 for more on portfolio optimizers) to make asset allocation decisions in a global setting is presented in Fischer Black and Robert Litterman, "Global Portfolio Optimization," *Financial Analysts Journal*, 48, no. 5 (September/October 1992): 28–43. Black and Litterman's model includes foreign currencies as one of the assets; see Chapter 26 for a discussion of foreign currencies and their risks.

[9] The discussion of swaps here should not be confused with the discussion of bond swaps in Chapter 16.

[10] For a discussion of many of the complicating features present in swaps, see Robert H. Litzenberger, "Swaps: Plain and Fanciful," *Journal of Finance*, 47, no. 3 (July 1992): 831–850. He reports that at that time the amount of outstanding interest rate and currency swaps was estimated to be about $3 trillion, with over ⅔ of them being of the "plain vanilla" variety, and that the first major swap took place in 1981.

[11] Swaps can be compared to a series of forward contracts (forward contracts were discussed in Chapter 5). In this case, Ms. Bright has a swap position equivalent to having long positions in a series of equity forward contracts, whereas Mr. Gloom has short positions in these contracts. Consider the swap contract's first quarterly payment. Imagine that instead of the swap contract Ms. Bright had taken a long position in a forward contract. In general, forward contracts involve the exchange of a stated amount of cash for a given asset at a specified future date. Here Ms. Bright has agreed to pay $2 million one quarter later for delivery of an asset that can be thought of as shares in an S&P 500 index fund (the number of shares will be determined on the delivery date, and will be equal to $100 million times the quarterly return on the S&P 500, divided by the fund's net asset value at the end of the quarter).

[12] By convention, the counterparty that makes the fixed payments (Ms. Uppe) is known as the *swap buyer*, and the counterparty that makes the variable payments (Mr. Downe) is known as the *swap seller*. Hence the swap buyer "pays fixed and receives floating," and the swap seller "pays floating and receives fixed."

[13] In this case, Ms. Uppe has a swap position equivalent to having long positions in a series of money market forward contracts, whereas Mr. Downe has short positions in these contracts. For example, the first quarterly payment is identical to what would happen if Ms. Uppe signed a forward contract agreeing to pay $2 million in exchange for the delivery of shares in a money market mutual fund (the number of shares will be determined on the delivery date, and will be equal to $100 million times the LIBOR, divided by the fund's net asset value at the end of the quarter). See Endnote 11.

[14] One interesting innovation is the *swaption*, a contract that combines an option (usually European) with an interest rate swap (or some other kind of swap). Call swaptions involve the right to "pay fixed and receive floating" and put swaptions involve the right to "pay floating and receive fixed." The notional principal, fixed rate, source of the floating rate, and swap life are all set when the swaption is created, as is the life of the swaption itself. If the owner of either type of swaption decides to exercise the option, then the writer (usually a swap bank) must become the other counterparty to the swap. In return for this right, the owner pays the writer a premium. Owners of calls will exercise their options if interest rates rise because then the fixed payment cash outflows will be less than the floating rate cash inflows. Conversely, put owners will exercise their options if interest rates fall. See David R. Smith, "A Simple Method for Pricing Interest Rate Swaptions," *Financial Analysts Journal*, 47, no. 3 (May/June 1991): 72–76.

[15] There are other kinds of limits frequently imposed on the manager, such as limits on the holdings of bonds versus stocks, or on the amount invested in a single industry.

[16] Sometimes these objectives and constraints are stated vaguely; in other cases they are specified precisely.

[17] Note that the slope of this line, $d\bar{r}_p/d\sigma_p^2$, is equal to $1/(d\sigma_p^2/d\bar{r}_p)$. Thus the slope can be determined by taking the derivative of σ_p^2 with respect to $\bar{r}_p$ in Equation (24.10) and then inverting the resulting expression.

[18] Risk tolerance, along with a procedure for estimating the value of τ, is presented in William F. Sharpe, *Asset Allocation Tools* (Redwood City, CA: Scientific Press, 1987): 33–39.

KEY TERMS

security analyst	security selection
investment committee	asset classes
approved list	asset allocation
portfolio manager	group selection
risk tolerance	market timing
certainty equivalent return	investment styles
passive management	equity swaps
active management	swap banks
index funds	interest rate swaps
active positions	split-funding

REFERENCES

1. Investment management is discussed in:

   William F. Sharpe, "Decentralized Investment Management," *Journal of Finance,* 36, no. 2 (May 1981): 217–234.

   Jeffery V. Bailey and Robert D. Arnott, "Cluster Analysis and Manager Selection," *Financial Analysts Journal,* 42, no. 6 (November/December 1986): 20–28.

   Richard A. Brealey, "Portfolio Theory versus Portfolio Practice," *Journal of Portfolio Management,* 16, no. 4 (Summer 1990): 6–10.

   William F. Sharpe, "The Arithmetic of Active Management," *Financial Analysts Journal,* 47, no. 1 (January/February 1991): 7–9.

   Robert H. Jeffery, "Do Clients Need So Many Portfolio Managers?" *Journal of Portfolio Management,* 18, no. 1 (Fall 1991): 13–19.

   C. B. Garcia and F. J. Gould, "Some Observations on Active Manager Performance and Passive Indexing," *Financial Analysts Journal,* 47, no. 6 (November/December 1991): 11–13.

2. Investment management for an individual investor is discussed in:

   Burton G. Malkiel, *A Random Walk Down Wall Street* (New York: W. W. Norton, 1990), particularly Chapter 11.

3. Assessment of investor risk tolerance is discussed in:

Gail Farrelly and Dean LeBaron, "Assessing Risk Tolerance Levels: A Prerequisite for Personalizing and Managing Portfolios," *Financial Analysts Journal,* 45, no. 1 (January/February 1989): 14–16.

W. V. Harlow and Keith C. Brown, "Understanding and Assessing Financial Risk Tolerance: A Biological Perspective," *Financial Analysts Journal,* 46, no. 6 (November/December 1990): 50–62.

William B. Riley, Jr., and K. Victor Chow, "Asset Allocation and Individual Risk Aversion," *Financial Analysts Journal,* 48, no. 6 (November/December 1992): 32–37.

4. An extensive discussion of risk tolerance is included in:

William F. Sharpe, *Asset Allocation Tools* (Redwood City, CA: Scientific Press, 1987), Chapter 2.

William F. Sharpe, "Integrated Asset Allocation," *Financial Analysts Journal,* 43, no. 5 (September/October 1987): 25–32.

5. Market timing, asset allocation, and investment styles are discussed in the previous article and in:

Keith P. Ambachtsheer, "Portfolio Theory and the Security Analyst," *Financial Analysts Journal,* 28, no. 6 (November/December 1972): 53–57.

Jack L. Treynor and Fischer Black, "How to Use Security Analysis to Improve Portfolio Selection," *Journal of Business,* 46, no. 1 (January 1973): 66–86.

William F. Sharpe, "Likely Gains From Market Timing," *Financial Analysts Journal,* 31, no. 2 (March/April 1975): 60–69.

———, "Major Investment Styles," *Journal of Portfolio Management,* 4, no. 2 (Winter 1978): 68–74.

Keith P. Ambachtsheer and James L. Farrell, Jr., "Can Active Management Add Value?" *Financial Analysts Journal,* 35, no. 6 (November/December 1979): 39–47.

Robert D. Arnott and James N. von Germeten, "Systematic Asset Allocation," *Financial Analysts Journal,* 39, no. 6 (November/December 1983): 31–38.

Jess H. Chua and Richard S. Woodard, *Gains From Market Timing,* Monograph Series in Finance and Economics #1986–2, New York University Salomon Center, Leonard N. Stern School of Business.

Richard A. Brealey, "How to Combine Active Management with Index Funds," *Journal of Portfolio Management,* 12, no. 2 (Winter 1986): 4–10.

André F. Perold and William F. Sharpe, "Dynamic Strategies for Asset Allocation," *Financial Analysts Journal,* 44, no. 1 (January/February 1988): 16–27.

William F. Sharpe, "Asset Allocation," in *Managing Investment Portfolio: A Dynamic Process,* eds. John L. Maginn and Donald L. Tuttle (Boston, MA: Warren, Gorham & Lamont, 1990), Chapter 7.

David E. Tierney and Kenneth Winston, "Defining and Using Dynamic Completeness Funds to Enhance Total Fund Efficiency," *Financial Analysts Journal,* 46, no. 4 (July/August 1990): 49–54.

Craig B. Wainscott, "The Stock-Bond Correlation and its Implications for Asset Allocation," *Financial Analysts Journal,* 46, no. 4 (July/August 1990): 55–60, 79.

John Markese, "All Eggs in One Basket, or A Basket for Each Egg?" *AAII Journal,* 12, no. 7 (August 1990): 31–33.

David E. Tierney and Kenneth Winston, "Using Generic Benchmarks to Present Manager Styles," *Journal of Portfolio Management,* 17, no. 4 (Summer 1991): 33–36.

P. R. Chandy and William Reichenstein, "Timing Strategies and the Risk of Missing Bull Markets," *AAII Journal,* 13, no. 7 (August 1991): 17–19.

William F. Sharpe, "Asset Allocation: Management Style and Performance Measurement," *Journal of Portfolio Management,* 18, no. 2 (Winter 1992): 7–19.

P. R. Chandy and William Reichenstein, "Stock Market Timing: A Modest Proposal," *AAII Journal,* 14, no. 4 (April 1992): 7–10.

Mark Hulbert, "Market Timing Strategies: Taxes are a Drag," *AAII Journal,* 14, no. 7 (August 1992): 18–20.

Maria Crawford Scott, "Asset Allocation Among the Three Major Categories," *AAII Journal,* 15, no. 4 (April 1993): 13–16.

Mark Hulbert, "Bond Market Timing: Even More Tough Than Timing the Stock Market," *AAII Journal,* 16, no. 3 (April 1994): 11–13.

Joseph B. Ludwig, "The Market Timing Approach: A Guide to the Various Strategies," *AAII Journal,* 16, no. 4 (May 1994): 11–14.

6. Investing in an international context is discussed in Chapter 26 (see the references listed there) and in:

Robert D. Arnott and Roy D. Henriksson, "A Disciplined Approach to Global Asset Allocation," *Financial Analysts Journal,* 45, no. 2 (March/April 1989): 17–28.

Bruno Solnik, *International Investments* (Reading, MA: Addison-Wesley, 1991), particularly Chapter 5.

Fischer Black and Robert Litterman, "Global Portfolio Optimization," *Financial Analysts Journal,* 48, no. 5 (September/October 1992): 28–43.

Carlo Capaul, Ian Rowley, and William F. Sharpe, "International Value and Growth Stock Returns," *Financial Analysts Journal,* 49, no. 1 (January/February 1993): 27–36.

7. For a discussion of portfolio revision procedures, see:

Gordon J. Alexander and Jack Clark Francis, *Portfolio Analysis* (Englewood Cliffs, NJ: Prentice Hall, 1986), 221–228.

William F. Sharpe, *Asset Allocation Tools* (Redwood City, CA: Scientific Press, 1987), 65–68.

8. Swaps are discussed in many of the textbooks on options and futures listed in the references for Chapters 20 and 21. Also see the following and their lists of references:

Clifford W. Smith, Jr., Charles W. Smithson, and D. Sykes Wilford, *Managing Financial Risk* (New York: Harper & Row, 1990), Chapters 9–12.

Robert H. Litzenberger, "Swaps: Plain and Fanciful," *Journal of Finance*, 47, no. 3 (July 1992): 831–850.

John F. Marshall and Vipul K. Bansal, *Financial Engineering* (Miami, FL: Kolb Publishing, 1993), Chapters 13, 23–24.

John F. Marshall and Kenneth R. Kapner, *The Swaps Market* (Miami, FL: Kolb Publishing, 1993).

Frank J. Fabozzi, Franco Modigliani, and Michael G. Ferri, *Foundations of Financial Markets and Institutions* (Englewood Cliffs, NJ: Prentice Hall, 1994), Chapter 29.

Robert W. Kolb, *Futures, Options, and Swaps* (Miami, FL: Kolb Publishing, 1994), Chapters 18–19.

Portfolio Performance Evaluation

An investor who has been paying someone to actively manage his or her portfolio has every right to insist on knowing what sort of performance was obtained. Such information can be used to alter either the constraints placed on the manager, the investment objectives given to the manager, or the amount of money allocated to the manager. Perhaps more importantly, by evaluating performance in specified ways, a client can forcefully communicate his or her interests to the investment manager and, in all likelihood, affect the way in which his or her portfolio is managed in the future. Moreover, an investment manager, by evaluating his or her own performance, can identify sources of strength or weakness. Thus although the previous chapter indicated that portfolio performance evaluation was the last stage of the investment management process, it can also be viewed as simply part of a continuing operation. More specifically, it can be viewed as a feedback and control mechanism that can make the investment management process more effective.

Superior performance in the past may have resulted from good luck, in which case such performance should not be expected to continue in the future. On the other hand, superior performance in the past may have resulted from the actions of a highly skilled investment manager. Conversely, inferior performance in the past may have been the result of bad luck, but it may also have resulted from excessive turnover, high management fees, or other costs associated with an unskilled investment manager. This suggests that the first task in performance evaluation is to try to determine whether past performance was superior or inferior. Once this task is done, the second task is to try to determine whether such performance was due to skill or luck. Unfortunately, there are difficulties associated with carrying out both of these tasks. Accordingly, this chapter will present not only certain methods that have been advocated and used for evaluating portfolio performance, but also a discussion of the difficulties encountered with their use.

25.1 MEASURES OF RETURN

Frequently portfolio performance is evaluated over a time interval of at least four years, with returns measured for a number of periods within the interval—typically monthly or quarterly. This provides a fairly adequate sample size for statistical evaluation (for example, if returns are measured quarterly for four years, there will be 16 observations). Sometimes, however, a shorter time interval must be used in order to avoid examining a portfolio's returns that were earned by a different investment manager. The examples to follow will involve 16 quarterly observations for tractability. In practice, one would prefer monthly observations if only four years were to be analyzed.

In the simplest situation where the client neither deposits nor withdraws money from the portfolio during a time period, calculation of the portfolio's periodic return is straightforward. All that is required is that the market value of the portfolio be known at two points in time—the beginning and the end of the period.

In general, the market value of a portfolio at a point in time is determined by adding the market values of all the securities held at that particular time. For example, the value of a common stock portfolio at the beginning of a period is calculated by (1) noting the market price per share of each stock held in the portfolio at that time; (2) multiplying each of these stock prices by the corresponding number of shares held; and (3) adding up the resulting products. The market value of the portfolio at the end of the period is calculated in the same way, only using end-of-period prices and shares.

With the beginning and ending portfolio values in hand, the return on the portfolio (r) can be calculated by subtracting the beginning value (V_b) from the ending value (V_e), and then dividing the difference by the beginning value:

$$r = \frac{V_e - V_b}{V_b} \tag{25.1}$$

For example, if a portfolio has a market value of $40 million at the beginning of a quarter and a market value of $46 million at the end of the quarter, then the return on this portfolio for the quarter would be 15% [= ($46 million − $40 million)/$40 million].

Measurement of portfolio returns is complicated by the fact that the client may either add to or withdraw money from the portfolio. This means that the percentage change in the market value of the portfolio during a period may not be an accurate measurement of the portfolio's return during that period.

For example, consider a portfolio that at the beginning of a quarter has a market value of $100 million. Just before the end of the quarter the client deposits $5 million with the investment manager, and subsequently at the end of the quarter the market value of the portfolio is $103 million. If the quarterly return was measured without consideration of the $5 million deposit, the reported return would be 3% [= ($103 million − $100 million)/$100 million]. However, this would be incorrect because $5 million of the ending $103 million market value did not result from the investment actions of the manager. Consideration of the deposit would suggest that a more accurate measure of the quarterly return would be −2% {= [($103 million − $5 million) − $100 million]/$100 million}.

Identification of exactly *when* any deposits or withdrawals occur is important in accurately measuring portfolio returns. If a deposit or withdrawal occurs just *before* the end of the period, then the return on the portfolio should be calculated by adjusting the ending market value of the portfolio. In the case of a deposit, the ending value should be reduced by the dollar amount (as was done in the previous example). In the case of a withdrawal, the ending value should be increased by the dollar amount.

If a deposit or withdrawal occurs just *after* the start of the period, then the return on the portfolio should be calculated by adjusting the beginning market value of the portfolio. In the case of a deposit, the beginning value should be increased by the dollar amount. In the case of a withdrawal, the beginning value should be decreased by the dollar amount. For example, if the $5 million deposit in the earlier example had been received just after the start of the quarter, the return for the quarter should be calculated as −1.90% {= [$103 million − ($100 million + $5 million)]/($100 million + $5 million)}.

25.1.1 Dollar-Weighted Returns

Difficulties are encountered, however, when deposits or withdrawals occur sometime *between* the beginning and end of the period. One method that has been used for calculating a portfolio's return in this situation results in the portfolio's **dollar-weighted return** (or internal rate of return). For example, if the $5 million deposit in the earlier example was made in the middle of the quarter, the dollar-weighted return would be calculated by solving the following equation for r:

$$\$100 \text{ million} = \frac{-\$5 \text{ million}}{(1 + r)} + \frac{\$103 \text{ million}}{(1 + r)^2}. \tag{25.2}$$

The solution to this equation, $r = -.98\%$, is a semiquarterly rate of return. It can be converted into a quarterly rate of return by adding 1 to it, squaring this value, and then subtracting 1 from the square, resulting in a quarterly return of −1.95% {= [1 + (−.0098)]² − 1}.[1]

25.1.2 Time-Weighted Returns

Alternatively, the **time-weighted return** on a portfolio can be calculated when there are cash flows occurring between the beginning and end of the period. This method involves using the market value of the portfolio just before each cash flow occurs. In the earlier example, assume that in the middle of the quarter the portfolio had a market value of $96 million, so that right after the $5 million deposit the market value was $101 million (= $96 million + $5 million). In this case, the return for the first half of the quarter would be -4% [$= (\$96$ million $- \$100$ million$)/\$100$ million], and the return for the second half of the quarter would be 1.98% [$= (\$103$ million $- \$101$ million$)/\$101$ million]. Next these two semiquarterly returns can be converted into a quarterly return by adding 1 to each return, multiplying the sums, and then subtracting 1 from the product. In the example, this procedure results in a quarterly return of -2.1% $\{= [(1 - .04) \times (1 + .0198)] - 1\}$.

25.1.3 Comparing Dollar-Weighted and Time-Weighted Returns

Which method is preferable for calculating the return on a portfolio? In the example given here, the dollar-weighted return was -1.95%, whereas the time-weighted return was -2.1%, suggesting that the difference between the two methods may not be very important. While this may be true in certain situations, examples can be given to show that such differences can be quite large, and that the time-weighted return method is preferable.

Consider a hypothetical portfolio that starts a quarter with a market value of $50 million. In the middle of the quarter, it has fallen to a market value of $25 million, at which point the client deposits $25 million with the investment manager. At the end of the quarter the portfolio has a market value of $100 million. The semiquarterly dollar-weighted return for this portfolio is equal to the value of r in the following equation:

$$\$50 \text{ million} = \frac{-\$25 \text{ million}}{(1 + r)} + \frac{\$100 \text{ million}}{(1 + r)^2}. \tag{25.3}$$

Solving this equation for r results in a value of 18.6%, which in turn equals a quarterly dollar-weighted return of 40.66% [$= (1.186)^2 - 1$]. However, its quarterly time-weighted return is 0% because its return for the first half of the quarter was -50% and its return for the second half of the quarter was 100% [note that $(1 - .5) \times (1 + 1) - 1 = 0\%$].

Comparing these two returns—40.66% and 0%—indicates that a sizable difference exists. However, the time-weighted return figure of 0% is more meaningful for performance evaluation than the dollar-weighted return figure of 40.66%. The reason for this can be seen by considering the return over the entire quarter on each dollar that was in the portfolio at the start of the quarter. Each dollar lost half of its value over the first half of the quarter, but then the remaining half-dollar doubled its value over the second half. Consequently, a dollar at the beginning was worth a dollar at the end, suggesting that a return of 0% on the portfolio is a more accurate measure of the investment manager's performance than the 40.66% figure.

In general, the dollar-weighted return method of measuring a portfolio's return for purposes of evaluation is regarded as inappropriate. The reason behind this view is that the return is strongly influenced by the size and timing of the cash flows (namely, deposits and withdrawals) over which the investment manager typically has no control. In the example, the dollar-weighted return was 40.66% because the client fortuitously made a big deposit just before the portfolio appreciated rapidly in value. Thus the 40.66% return figure results at least partly from the actions of the client, not of the manager.

25.1.4 Annualizing Returns

The previous discussion focused on calculating quarterly returns. Such returns may be added or multiplied to obtain an annual measure of return. For example, if the returns in the first, second, third, and fourth quarters of a given year are denoted r_1, r_2, r_3, and r_4, respectively, then the annual return can be calculated by adding the four figures:

$$\text{Annual return} = r_1 + r_2 + r_3 + r_4. \qquad (25.4)$$

Alternatively, the annual return could be calculated by adding 1 to each quarterly return, then multiplying the four figures, and finally subtracting 1 from the resulting product:

$$\text{Annual return} = [(1 + r_1)(1 + r_2)(1 + r_3)(1 + r_4)] - 1. \qquad (25.5)$$

This return is more accurate because it reflects the value that one dollar would have at the end of the year if it were invested at the beginning of the year and grew *with compounding* at the rate of r_1 for the first quarter, r_2 for the second quarter, r_3 for the third quarter, and r_4 for the fourth quarter. That is, it assumes reinvestment of both the dollar and any earnings at the end of each quarter.

25.2   MAKING RELEVANT COMPARISONS

The essential idea behind performance evaluation is to compare the returns obtained by the investment manager through active management with the returns that could have been obtained for the client if one or more appropriate alternative portfolios had been chosen for investment. The reason for this comparison is straightforward—performance should be evaluated on a relative basis, not on an absolute basis.

As an example, consider a client who is told that his or her portfolio, invested in a diversified common stocks portfolio of average risk, had a return of 20% last year. Does this suggest superior or inferior performance? If a broad stock market index (like the Wilshire 5000) went up by 10% last year, then the return on the portfolio suggests superior performance and is good news. However, if the index went up by 30% last year, then the return on the portfolio suggests inferior performance and is bad news. In order to infer whether the manager's performance is superior or inferior, the returns on "similar" portfolios that are either actively or passively managed are needed for comparison.

Such comparison portfolios are often referred to as **benchmark portfolios.** In selecting them, the client should be certain that they are relevant, feasible, and known in advance, meaning that they should represent alternative portfolios that could have been chosen for investment instead of the portfolio being evaluated. That is, the benchmark should reflect the objectives of the client. Hence, if the objective is to earn superior returns by investing in small stocks, then the S&P 500 would be an inappropriate benchmark. Instead, an index like the Russell 2000 would be more suitable. *Return* is a key aspect of performance, of course, but some way must be found to account for the portfolio's exposure to *risk*. The choice of benchmark portfolios may be restricted to portfolios perceived to have similar levels of risk, thereby permitting a direct comparison of returns.

Figure 25.1 illustrates such a comparison for a hypothetical common stock (or "equity") portfolio referred to as Fund 07632. In this figure, Fund 07632's performance for each year is represented by a diamond. The hypothetical comparison portfolios are other common stock portfolios that are represented by the box surrounding the diamond (hence such a representation is known as a *box plot* or a *floating bar chart*). The top and bottom lines of the box indicate the returns of the 5th and 95th percentile comparison portfolios, respectively. Similarly, the top and bottom dashed lines represent the 25th and 75th percentiles, respectively. The solid line in the middle represents the median (that is, the 50th percentile) portfolio. Note that this particular evaluation technique presumes that the comparison portfolios exhibit risk similar to Fund 07632 and that they represent feasible alternatives for Fund 07632's owner. Failing to meet these conditions (as is often the case in such peer group comparisons) will generally invalidate the performance evaluation.

Alternatively, risk may be explicitly measured so that a single measure of performance taking both return and risk into account can be employed. This will allow benchmark portfolios of varying degrees of risk to be compared with the portfolio being evaluated.

	Year 1	Year 2	Year 3	Year 4	Year 5	Year 6	Year 7
5th Percentile	51.8	9.0	36.4	34.9	17.2	46.9	35.0
25th Percentile	39.5	.2	27.5	25.5	10.2	37.4	26.6
Median	32.7	−5.0	21.9	21.4	7.1	33.1	21.2
75th Percentile	26.6	−9.8	17.0	16.7	4.5	28.1	16.5
95th Percentile	16.9	−16.9	5.5	9.3	−.2	19.9	10.4
Fund 07632	24.2	0.0	29.8	20.5	8.3	40.0	21.1
Percent Rank	82	25	17	56	39	16	50

Figure 25.1

Comparing Returns of Equity Portfolios

Source: Adapted from SEI, *Funds Evaluation Service.*

Custom Benchmark Portfolios

Investment management has become increasingly specialized in recent years. Managers have chosen not only to concentrate on specific asset classes (for example, stocks or bonds), but within those asset classes they have further focused their efforts on certain types of securities. This specialization has been particularly prevalent among domestic common stock managers. For example, some managers specialize in small, emerging growth company stocks. Others select only from certain industries, such as health care. These specializations have come to be known as "investment styles." Investment styles have significant ramifications for the evaluation of investment manager performance.

Investment management can be viewed as a fishing contest. Each angler has his or her own fishing hole (investment style). No one fishing hole is assumed to be any better than another, although from year to year the sizes and quantity of fish fluctuate independently in each hole. The anglers attempt to catch the largest fish from their fishing holes. How should institutional investor clients evaluate the proficiency of these anglers based on their catches? It would make little sense to directly compare the anglers' respective catches. If Angler *A*'s fishing hole was extremely well-stocked this year and Angler *B*'s was not, Angler *B* would be at a tremendous disadvantage. More appropriately, clients would like to compare what each angler caught against the opportunities available in their respective fishing holes. In other words, the clients should want to take into account the impact of managers' investment styles on their performance.

Investment styles tend to dominate the performance of investment managers within a particular asset class. For example, suppose that the domestic common stock market was split along two dimensions similar to those discussed in Chapter 17: market capitalization (share price times shares outstanding) and growth prospects. In 1991, for example, the best-performing group was large, high-growth stocks, which returned 45.0%. Conversely, small, low-growth stocks returned 19.0%, a difference of 26 percentage points. Differences between investment styles of similar magnitudes can

be found in other years. These differences are typically large enough so that no investment manager can hope to consistently overcome the performance effect of his or her investment style. Therefore to evaluate a manager's investment skill, how the manager has performed relative to his or her investment style should be considered explicitly.

One means of dealing with this issue is to develop a comparison portfolio that specifically represents the manager's investment style. This comparison portfolio is referred to as a *custom benchmark portfolio*. The custom benchmark contains the types of securities from which the manager typically selects. Further, these securities are weighted in the custom benchmark in a manner similar to weights typically assigned by the manager. Moreover, the custom benchmark displays portfolio characteristics (for example, price-earnings ratios, earnings growth rates, and market capitalizations) consistent with the manager's actual portfolio.

Consider a manager whose investment style entails investing in large-capitalization, high-dividend-yield stocks. In building portfolios, the manager follows certain rules, some explicitly, others implicitly. For example, the manager does not buy stocks with less than $500 million in market capitalization. All stocks in the manager's portfolio must display at least a 5% dividend yield. The manager assigns each stock an equal weight in the portfolio. Further, to avoid overconcentrations, no industry may constitute more than 10% of the portfolio's market value.

A custom benchmark can be designed to reflect these characteristics of the manager's investment style. The custom benchmark might be composed of 300 stocks, as opposed to the manager's portfolio, which might contain only 30 stocks. The manager, in effect, has searched through his or her fishing hole and selected the 30 stocks that he or she thinks will perform the best. An evaluation of the manager's performance will be based over time on how these 30 stocks perform relative to the 300 stocks.

This performance evaluation process takes advantage of a powerful paired-comparison test.

Given a group of stocks, can the manager consistently identify the best-performing issues? The question is simple and the results easy to interpret. No special risk-adjusted performance measures are required. If the custom benchmark has been properly constructed, it exhibits a risk level consistent with that exhibited on average by the manager.

The primary drawback of custom benchmarks is the effort required to design them. Each manager's investment style has unique aspects, and not all of them are as explicit as those of the large-capitalization, high-yield manager discussed above. Typically, identifying those unique aspects involves examining past portfolios and engaging in lengthy discussions with the manager.

Recently a number of analysts have adopted a method in which a benchmark made up of combinations of standard indices is constructed based on statistical analysis of a manager's past returns. The use of this procedure, known as *style analysis,* can in many cases provide some of the advantages of custom benchmark portfolios at a fraction of the cost, time, and effort. (For details on this approach, see the references listed at the end of the chapter.)

Custom benchmarks, whether derived via detailed analyses or using style analysis, can provide effective performance evaluations. Moreover, they have uses outside of performance evaluation. For example, as discussed in Chapter 24's *Institutional Issues* section, clients who hire more than one investment manager can use custom benchmarks to examine how various investment styles fit together into an aggregate portfolio. This type of analysis permits a client to better understand and control the investment risks present in the client's total portfolio.

25.3   RISK-ADJUSTED MEASURES OF PERFORMANCE

Having measured the periodic returns for a portfolio during a time interval (say, quarterly returns for a four-year time interval), the next step is to determine if these returns represent superior or inferior performance. In order to do this, an estimate of the portfolio's risk level during the time interval is needed. Two kinds of risk can be estimated—the portfolio's market (or systematic) risk, measured by its beta, and the portfolio's total risk, measured by its standard deviation.

It is important to analyze risk appropriately. The key issue here is determining the impact of the portfolio on the client's overall level of risk. If the client has many other assets, then the market risk of the portfolio provides the relevant measure of the portfolio's impact on the client's overall level of risk. If, however, the portfolio provides the client's sole support, then its total risk is the relevant measure of risk. Risk-adjusted performance evaluation is generally based on one of these two viewpoints, taking either market risk or total risk into consideration.

Assume that there are T time periods in the time interval (for example, $T = 16$ when there are four years of quarterly data) and let r_{pt} denote the return on the portfolio during period t. The average return on the portfolio, denoted ar_p, is simply:

$$ar_p = \frac{\displaystyle\sum_{t=1}^{T} r_{pt}}{T}.$$
(25.6)

Having calculated ar_p, the *ex post* (that is, "after the fact" or historical) standard deviation σ_p can be calculated as:

$$\sigma_p = \left[\frac{\displaystyle\sum_{t=1}^{T}(r_{pt} - ar_p)^2}{T-1}\right]^{1/2}.$$
(25.7)

This estimate of the portfolio's standard deviation can be used as an indication of the amount of total risk that the portfolio had during the time interval.[2] It can be compared directly with the standard deviations of other portfolios, as illustrated in Figure 25.2. (This figure is to be interpreted in the same manner as Figure 25.1.)

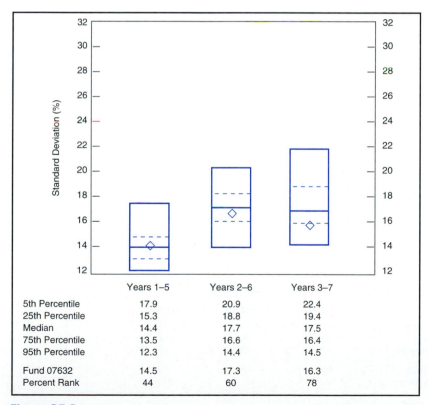

	Years 1–5	Years 2–6	Years 3–7
5th Percentile	17.9	20.9	22.4
25th Percentile	15.3	18.8	19.4
Median	14.4	17.7	17.5
75th Percentile	13.5	16.6	16.4
95th Percentile	12.3	14.4	14.5
Fund 07632	14.5	17.3	16.3
Percent Rank	44	60	78

Figure 25.2
Comparing Standard Deviations of Equity Portfolios
Source: Adapted from SEI, *Funds Evaluation Service.*

The returns of a portfolio may also be compared with those of a substitute for the market portfolio, such as Standard & Poor's 500, in order to determine the portfolio's *ex post* beta during the time interval. Denoting the *excess return* on the portfolio during period t as $er_{pt} = r_{pt} - r_{ft}$, the return on the S&P 500 (or some other market substitute) during period t as r_{Mt}, and the excess return on the S&P 500 during period t as $er_{Mt} = r_{Mt} - r_{ft}$, this beta can be estimated as follows:

$$\beta_p = \frac{\left(T \sum_{t=1}^{T} er_{Mt} er_{pt} \right) - \left(\sum_{t=1}^{T} er_{pt} \sum_{t=1}^{T} er_{Mt} \right)}{\left(T \sum_{t=1}^{T} er_{Mt}^2 \right) - \left(\sum_{t=1}^{T} er_{Mt} \right)^2}. \tag{25.8}$$

This estimate of the portfolio's beta can be used as an indication of the amount of market risk that the portfolio had during the time interval.[3] It can be compared directly with the betas of other portfolios, as illustrated in Figure 25.3. (This figure is to be interpreted in the same manner as Figures 25.1 and 25.2.)

Although a portfolio's return and a measure of its risk can be compared individually with those of other portfolios, as in Figures 25.1 through 25.3, it is often not clear how the portfolio performed on a risk-adjusted basis relative to these other portfolios. For the fund shown in the figures, the average percentile rank for the portfolio's return over years 3 through 7 is 36 [= (17 + 56 + 39 + 16 + 50)/5]. Over the same period, its standard deviation put it in the 78th

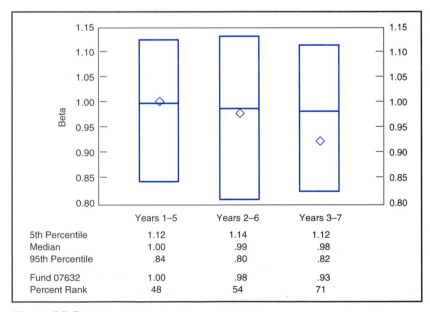

	Years 1–5	Years 2–6	Years 3–7
5th Percentile	1.12	1.14	1.12
Median	1.00	.99	.98
95th Percentile	.84	.80	.82
Fund 07632	1.00	.98	.93
Percent Rank	48	54	71

Figure 25.3
Comparing Betas of Equity Portfolios
Source: Adapted from SEI, *Funds Evaluation Service.*

percentile rank. Assuming that the client is concerned with total risk, how does he or she interpret these percentile ranks? In the case of the return, the portfolio was slightly above average. In terms of standard deviation, it was less risky than approximately three–quarters of the other portfolios. Overall, this suggests that the portfolio did better on a risk-adjusted basis than the others, but it does not give the client a clear and precise sense of how much better.

Such a sense can be conveyed by certain CAPM-based measures of portfolio performance. Each one of these measures provides an estimate of a portfolio's risk-adjusted performance, thereby allowing the client to see how the portfolio performed relative to other portfolios and relative to the market. They will be presented next.

25.3.1 Ex Post Characteristic Lines

Over a time interval, an *ex post* Security Market Line (SML) can be estimated by determining the average riskfree rate and market return:

$$ar_f = \frac{\sum_{t=1}^{T} r_{ft}}{T} \tag{25.9}$$

$$ar_M = \frac{\sum_{t=1}^{T} r_{Mt}}{T}. \tag{25.10}$$

Once these averages have been calculated, the *ex post* SML is simply the equation of the line going through the points $(0, ar_f)$ and $(1, ar_M)$:

$$ar_p^e = ar_f + (ar_M - ar_f)\beta_p. \tag{25.11}$$

Equivalently, the equilibrium average return during this interval of time for a portfolio with a beta of β_p would simply be equal to $ar_f + (ar_M - ar_f)\beta_p$. Accordingly, ar_p^e can be used as the benchmark return for a portfolio with a beta of β_p.

Panel (a) of Table 25.1 presents an example by using the quarterly returns for the S&P 500 over a 16–quarter time interval, along with corresponding returns on 90–day Treasury bills. Using Equations (25.9) and (25.10), the average riskfree return and market return were, respectively, 2.23% and 4.88%. Inserting these values into Equation (25.11), the *ex post* SML for this time interval was:

$$ar_p^e = 2.23\% + (4.88\% - 2.23\%)\beta_p \tag{25.12}$$
$$= 2.23\% + 2.65\%\beta_p.$$

Thus, after estimating a portfolio's *ex post* beta and entering this value on the right-hand side of Equation (25.12), a benchmark return for the portfolio can be determined. For example, a portfolio with a beta of .8 during the 16–quarter time interval would have a benchmark return of 4.35% $[= 2.23 + (2.65 \times .8)]$. Figure 25.4 presents a graph of the *ex post* SML given by Equation (25.12).

TABLE 25.1
THE EX POST CHARACTERISTIC LINE FOR THE FIRST FUND

(a) Data

Quarter	Treasury Bill Return	First Fund Return	First Fund Excess Return	S&P 500 Return	S&P 500 Excess Return
1	2.97%	−8.77%	−11.74%	−5.86%	−8.83%
2	3.06	−6.03	−9.09	−2.94	−6.00
3	2.85	14.14	11.29	13.77	10.92
4	1.88	24.96	23.08	14.82	12.94
5	1.90	3.71	1.81	11.91	10.01
6	2.00	10.65	8.65	11.55	9.55
7	2.22	−.22	−2.44	−.78	−3.00
8	2.11	.27	−1.84	.02	−2.09
9	2.16	−3.08	−5.24	−2.52	−4.68
10	2.34	−6.72	−9.06	−1.85	−4.19
11	2.44	8.58	6.14	8.73	6.29
12	2.40	1.15	−1.25	1.63	−.77
13	1.89	7.87	5.98	10.82	8.93
14	1.94	5.92	3.98	7.24	5.30
15	1.72	−3.10	−4.82	−2.78	−4.50
16	1.75	13.61	11.86	14.36	12.61

(b) Calculations[a]

Quarter		First Fund Excess Returns = Y (1)	S&P 500 Excess Returns = X (2)	Y^2 (3)	X^2 (4)	$Y \times X$ (5)
Year 1	1	−11.74%	−8.83%	137.83	77.93	103.66
	2	−9.09	−6.00	82.63	36.05	54.54
	3	11.29	10.92	127.46	119.26	123.29
	4	23.08	12.94	532.69	167.53	298.66
Year 2	1	1.81	10.01	3.28	100.11	18.12
	2	8.65	9.55	74.82	91.28	82.61
	3	−2.44	−3.00	5.95	8.97	7.32
	4	−1.84	−2.09	3.39	4.35	3.85
Year 3	1	−5.24	−4.68	27.46	21.94	24.52
	2	−9.06	−4.19	82.08	17.54	37.96
	3	6.14	6.29	37.70	39.53	38.62
	4	−1.25	−.77	1.56	.60	.96
Year 4	1	5.98	8.93	35.76	79.82	53.40
	2	3.98	5.30	15.84	28.07	21.09
	3	−4.82	−4.50	23.23	20.25	21.69
	4	11.86	12.61	140.66	158.93	149.56
Sum (Σ) =		27.31	42.49	1,332.34	972.16	1,039.85
		$= \Sigma Y$	$= \Sigma X$	$= \Sigma Y^2$	$= \Sigma X^2$	$= \Sigma XY$

As shown in Chapter 22, one measure of a portfolio's risk-adjusted performance is the difference between its average return (ar_p) and the return on its corresponding benchmark portfolio, denoted ar_{bp}. This difference is generally referred to as the portfolio's *ex post* **alpha** (or differential return), and is denoted α_p:

$$\alpha_p = ar_p - ar_{bp}. \tag{22.3}$$

TABLE 25.1 (continued)

THE EX POST CHARACTERISTIC LINE FOR THE FIRST FUND

1. Beta:

$$\frac{(T \times \Sigma XY) - (\Sigma Y \times \Sigma X)}{(T \times \Sigma X^2) - (\Sigma X)^2} = \frac{(16 \times 1{,}039.85) - (27.31 \times 42.49)}{(16 \times 972.16) - (42.49)^2} = 1.13$$

2. Alpha:

$$[\Sigma Y/T] - [Beta \times (\Sigma X/T)] = [27.31/16] - [1.13 \times (42.49/16)] = -1.29$$

3. Standard Deviation of Random Error Term:

$$\{[\Sigma Y^2 - (Alpha \times \Sigma Y) - (Beta \times (\Sigma XY)]/[T - 2]\}^{1/2}$$
$$= \{[1{,}332.34 - (-1.29 \times 42.49) - (1.13 \times 1{,}039.85)]/[16 - 2]\}^{1/2} = 3.75$$

4. Standard Error of Beta:

Standard Deviation of Random Error Term$/\{\Sigma X^2 - [(\Sigma X)^2/T]\}^{1/2}$
$$= 3.75/\{972.16 - [(42.49)^2/[16]]\}^{1/2} = .13$$

5. Standard Error of Alpha:

Standard Deviation of Random Error Term$/\{T - [(\Sigma X)^2/\Sigma X^2]\}^{1/2}$
$$= 3.75/\{16 - [(42.49)^2/972.16]\}^{1/2} = 1.00$$

6. Correlation Coefficient:

$$\frac{(T \times \Sigma XY) - (\Sigma Y \times \Sigma X)}{\{[(T \times \Sigma Y^2) - (\Sigma Y)^2 \times [(T \times \Sigma X^2) - (\Sigma X)^2]\}^{1/2}}$$

$$= \frac{(16 \times 1{,}039.85) - (27.31 \times 42.49)}{\{[(16 \times 1{,}332.34) - (27.31)^2] \times [(16 \times 972.16) - (42.49)^2]\}^{1/2}} = .92$$

7. Coefficient of Determination:

$$(Correlation\ Coefficient)^2 = (.92)^2 = .85$$

8. Coefficient of Nondetermination:

$$1 - Coefficient\ of\ Determination = 1 - .85 = .15$$

[a]All summations are to be carried out over t, where t goes from 1 to T (in this example, t = 1, . . ., 16).

A positive value of α_p for a portfolio would indicate that the portfolio had an average return greater than the benchmark return, suggesting that its performance was superior. On the other hand, a negative value of α_p would indicate that the portfolio had an average return less than the benchmark return, suggesting that its performance was inferior.

By substituting the right-hand side of Equation (25.11) for ar_p in Equation (22.3), it can be seen that a portfolio's *ex post* alpha based on the *ex post* SML is equal to:[4]

$$\alpha_p = ar_p - [ar_f + (ar_M - ar_f)\beta_p]. \tag{25.13}$$

After determining the values for α_p and β_p for a portfolio, the *ex post* **characteristic line** for the portfolio can be written as:

$$r_p - r_f = \alpha_p + \beta_p(r_M - r_f). \tag{25.14}$$

The characteristic line is similar to the market model except that the portfolio's returns and the market index's returns are expressed in excess of the risk free return. Graphically, the characteristic line formulation is the equation of a straight line where $(r_M - r_f)$ is measured on the horizontal axis and $(r_p - r_f)$ is measured on the vertical axis. Furthermore, the line has a vertical intercept of α_p and a slope of β_p.

As an example, consider the performance of the hypothetical portfolio "First Fund," indicated in panel (a) of Table 25.1, for the given 16–quarter time interval. During this interval, the First Fund had an average quarterly return of 3.93%. Using Equation (25.8), it can be shown that First Fund had a beta of 1.13. Having an average beta over the 16 quarters that is greater than the market portfolio's beta of one indicates that First Fund was relatively aggressive (if it were less than one, it would have been relatively defensive).

Given these values for its beta and average return, the location of First Fund in Figure 25.4 is represented by the point having coordinates (1.13, 3.93), denoted FF. The exact vertical distance from FF to the *ex post* SML can be calculated by using Equation (25.13):

$$\alpha_p = ar_p - [ar_f + (ar_M - ar_f)\beta_p]$$
$$= 3.93\% - [2.23\% + (4.88\% - 2.23\%)1.13]$$
$$= -1.29\%.$$

Because FF lies below the *ex post* SML, its *ex post* alpha is negative, and its performance would be viewed as inferior.[5] Using Equation (25.14), the *ex post* characteristic line for First Fund would be:

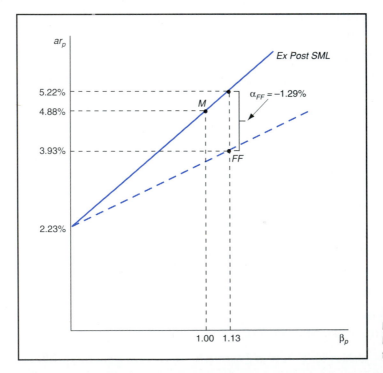

Figure 25.4
Performance
Evaluation Using
the Ex Post SML

$$r_p - r_f = -1.29\% + 1.13(r_M - r_f).$$

Figure 25.5 provides an illustration of this line.[6]

The method for determining a portfolio's *ex post* alpha, beta, and characteristic line suggests the use of a five-step procedure:

1. Determine the periodic rates of return for the portfolio and market index over the time interval, as well as the corresponding riskfree rates.
2. Determine the average market return and riskfree rate by using the formulas in Equations (25.9) and (25.10).
3. Determine the portfolio's *ex post* beta by using the formula in Equation (25.8).
4. Determine the portfolio's *ex post* alpha by using the formula given in Equation (25.13).
5. Insert these values for alpha and beta in Equation (25.14) in order to determine the portfolio's *ex post* characteristic line.

However, there is a simpler method for determining a portfolio's *ex post* alpha, beta, and characteristic line that also provides a number of other pieces of information relating to the portfolio's performance. This method involves the use of **simple linear regression,** and corresponds to the method presented in Chapters 8 and 17 for estimating the market model for an individual security.

With this method, the excess return on portfolio *p* in a given period *t* is viewed as having three components. The first component is the portfolio's alpha, the second component is a risk premium equal to the excess return on the market times the portfolio's beta, and the third component is a random error term.[7] These three components can be seen on the right-hand side of the following equation:

$$r_{pt} - r_{ft} = \alpha_p + \beta_p(r_{Mt} - r_{ft}) + \epsilon_{pt}. \tag{25.15}$$

Because α_p and β_p are assumed to be constant during the time interval, Equation (25.15) can be viewed as a regression equation. Accordingly, there are certain standard formulas for estimating α_p, β_p, and a number of other statistical parameters associated with the regression equation.

Panel (b) of Table 25.1 presents these formulas, with First Fund being used as an example. As can be seen, the formulas indicate that First Fund's *ex post* alpha and beta were equal to -1.29 and 1.13, respectively, over the 16–quarter time interval. These values are the same as those arising when Equations (25.8) and (25.13) were used earlier. Indeed, they will always result in the same values.

Figure 25.5 presents a scatter diagram of the excess returns on First Fund and the S&P 500. Based on Equation (25.15), the regression equation for First Fund is:

$$r_{FF} - r_f = -1.29\% + 1.13(r_M - r_f) + \epsilon_{FF} \tag{25.16}$$

where -1.29 and 1.13 are the estimated *ex post* alpha and beta for First Fund over the 16–quarter time interval. As mentioned earlier, also shown in the figure is the *ex post* characteristic line for First Fund, a line that is derived by the use of simple linear regression:

$$r_{FF} - r_f = -1.29\% + 1.13(r_M - r_f). \tag{25.17}$$

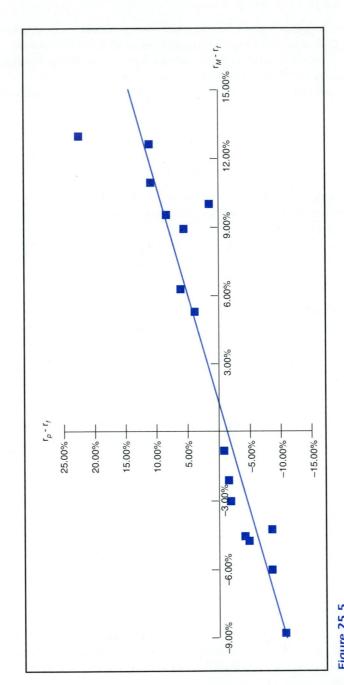

Figure 25.5
Ex Post Characteristic Line for First Fund

The vertical distance between each point in the scatter diagram and the regression line represents an estimate of the size of the random error term for the corresponding quarter. The exact distance can be found by rewriting Equation (25.16) as:

$$\epsilon_{FF} = (r_{FF} - r_f) - [-1.29\% + 1.13(r_M - r_f)]. \qquad (25.18)$$

For example, in the 11th quarter the excess return on First Fund and the S&P 500 were 6.14% and 6.29%, respectively. The value of ϵ_{FF} for that quarter can be calculated by using Equation (25.18) as follows:

$$\begin{aligned} \epsilon_{FF} &= (6.14\%) - [-1.29\% + 1.13(6.29\%)] \\ &= .32\%. \end{aligned}$$

The value of (ϵ_{FF}) can be calculated similarly for the other 15 quarters of the time interval. The standard deviation of the resulting set of 16 numbers is an estimate of the standard deviation of the random error term (also known as the residual standard deviation), and is shown in panel (b) of Table 25.1 to be equal to 3.75%. This number can be viewed as an estimate of the *ex post* unique (or unsystematic or nonmarket) risk of First Fund.

The regression line for First Fund that is shown in Figure 25.5 is the line of best fit for the scatter diagram. What is meant by "best fit"? Given that a straight line is defined by its intercept and slope, it means that there are no other values for alpha and beta that fit the scatter diagram any better than this one. In terms of simple linear regression, this means that there is no line that could be drawn such that the resulting standard deviation of the random error term is smaller than the one of best fit.

It should be pointed out that a portfolio's "true" *ex post* beta cannot be observed. All that can be done is to estimate its value. Thus, even if a portfolio's "true" beta remained the same forever, its estimated value, obtained in the manner illustrated in Table 25.1 and Figure 25.5, would still change from time to time because of errors (known as sampling errors) in estimating it. For example, if a different set of 16 quarters were examined where the first quarter was replaced by a more recent quarter, the resulting estimated beta for First Fund would almost certainly be different from 1.13.

The standard error of beta shown in Table 25.1 attempts to indicate the extent of such estimation errors. Given a number of necessary assumptions (for example, the "true" beta did not change during the 16–quarter estimation period), the chances are roughly two out of three that the "true" beta is within one standard error, plus or minus, of the estimated beta. Thus First Fund's "true" beta is likely to be between the values of 1.00 (= 1.13 − .13) and 1.26 (= 1.13 + .13). Similarly, the value under standard error of alpha provides an indication of the magnitude of the possible sampling error that has been made in estimating it.

The value under correlation coefficient provides an indication of how closely the excess returns on First Fund were associated with the excess returns on the S&P 500. As its range is between −1 and +1, the value for First Fund of .92 indicates a strong positive relationship between First Fund and the S&P 500. That is, larger excess returns for First Fund seem to have been closely associated with larger excess returns for the S&P 500.

The coefficient of determination represents the proportion of variation in the excess return on First Fund that is related to the variation in the excess return on the S&P 500. That is, it shows how much of the movement in First Fund's excess returns can be explained by movements in the excess returns on the S&P 500. With a value of .85, it can be seen that 85% of the movement in the excess return on First Fund over the 16 quarters can be attributed to movement in the excess return on the S&P 500.

Because the coefficient of nondetermination is one minus the coefficient of determination, it represents the proportion of movement in the excess return on First Fund that does not result from movement in the excess return on the S&P 500. Thus 15% of the movement in First Fund cannot be attributed to movement in the S&P 500.

Although Table 25.1 shows the formulas for calculating all these values, it should be pointed out that there are many different software packages that can quickly carry out these calculations. The only substantive effort involves gathering all the return data shown in panel (a) of Table 25.1 and then entering it into a computer.

25.3.2 The Reward-to-Volatility Ratio

Closely related to the *ex post* alpha measure of portfolio performance is a measure known as the **reward-to-volatility ratio**.[8] This measure, denoted $RVOL_p$, also uses the *ex post* Security Market Line to form a benchmark for performance evaluation, but in a somewhat different manner. The calculation of the reward-to-volatility ratio for a portfolio involves dividing its average excess return by its market risk as follows:

$$RVOL_p = \frac{ar_p - ar_f}{\beta_p}. \tag{25.19}$$

Here the beta of the portfolio can be determined using the formula in Equation (25.8).

Continuing with the example of First Fund, it was noted earlier that its average return for the 16–quarter time interval was 3.93%. Furthermore, it was noted that the average Treasury bill rate was 2.23%. Thus the average excess return for First Fund was 1.70% ($= 3.93\% - 2.23\%$) and, given a beta of 1.13, its reward-to-volatility ratio was 1.50% ($= 1.70\%/1.13$).

The reward-to-volatility ratio corresponds to the slope of a line originating at the average riskfree rate and going through the point (β_p, ar_p). This can be seen by noting that the slope of a line is easily determined if two points on the line are known—it is simply the vertical distance between the two points ("rise") divided by the horizontal distance between the two points ("run"). In this case, the vertical distance is $ar_p - ar_f$ and the horizontal distance is $\beta_p - 0$, so the slope is ($ar_p - ar_f$)/β_p and thus corresponds to the formula for $RVOL_p$ given in Equation (25.19). Note that the value being measured on the horizontal axis is β_p and the value being measured on the vertical axis is ar_p, suggesting that the line can be drawn on the same diagram as the *ex post* SML.

In the First Fund example, remember that the *ex post* SML for the 16–quarter time interval was shown by the solid line in Figure 25.4. Also appearing in this figure was the point denoted *FF,* corresponding to $(\beta_p, ar_p) = (1.13, 3.93\%)$ for First Fund. The dashed line in this figure originates from the point $(0, ar_f) = (0, 2.23\%)$, goes through *FF,* and has a slope of 1.50% $[= (3.93\% - 2.23\%)/1.13]$ that corresponds to the value noted earlier for RVOL_p.

The benchmark for comparison with this measure of performance is the slope of the *ex post* SML. Because this line goes through the points $(0, ar_f)$ and $(1, ar_M)$, its slope is simply $(ar_M - ar_f)/(1 - 0) = (ar_M - ar_f)$. If RVOL_p is greater than this value, the portfolio lies above the *ex post* SML, indicating that it has outperformed the market. Alternatively, if RVOL_p is less than this value, the portfolio lies below the *ex post* SML, indicating that it has not performed as well as the market.

In the case of First Fund, the benchmark is 2.65% $[= (ar_M - ar_f) = (4.88\% - 2.23\%)]$. Because RVOL_p for First Fund is less than the benchmark $(1.50\% < 2.65\%)$, according to this measure of portfolio performance, First Fund did not perform as well as the market.

In comparing the two measures of performance that are based on the *ex post* SML, α_p and RVOL_p, it should be noted that they will *always* give the same assessment of a portfolio's performance relative to the market portfolio. That is, if one measure indicates that the portfolio outperformed the market, so will the other. Similarly, if one measure indicates that the portfolio did not perform as well as the market, the other measure will show the same thing. This can be seen by noting that any portfolio with a positive *ex post* alpha (an indication of superior performance) lies *above* the *ex post* SML and thus must have a slope *greater* than the slope of the *ex post* SML (also an indication of superior performance). Similarly, any portfolio with a negative *ex post* alpha (an indication of inferior performance) lies *below* the *ex post* SML and thus must have a slope *less* than the slope of the *ex post* SML (also an indication of inferior performance).

However, it should also be noted that it is possible for the two measures to *rank* portfolios differently on the basis of performance simply because the calculations are different. For example, if Second Fund had a beta of 1.5 and an average return of 4.86%, its *ex post* alpha would be -1.34% $\{= 4.86\% - [2.23 + (4.88 - 2.23) \times 1.5]\}$. Thus its performance appears to be worse than that of First Fund because it has a smaller *ex post* alpha $(-1.34\% < -1.29\%)$. However, its reward-to-volatility ratio of 1.75% $[= (4.86\% - 2.23\%)/1.5]$ is larger than the reward-to-volatility of 1.50% for First Fund, suggesting that its performance was better than First Fund's.

25.3.3 The Reward-to-Variability Ratio

Both measures of risk-adjusted performance described so far, *ex post* alpha (that is, differential return) and the reward-to-volatility ratio, use benchmarks that are based on the *ex post* Security Market Line (SML). Accordingly, they measure returns relative to the market risk of the portfolio. In contrast, the **reward-to-variability ratio** is a measure of risk-adjusted performance that uses a benchmark based on the *ex post* Capital Market Line (CML).[9] This means that it measures returns relative to the total risk of the portfolio, where total risk is the standard deviation of portfolio returns.

In order to use the reward-to-variability ratio (RVAR_p), the location of the *ex post* CML must be determined. This line goes through two points on a graph where average return is measured on the vertical axis and standard deviation is measured on the horizontal axis. The first point is the vertical intercept of the line and corresponds to the average riskfree rate during the 16–quarter time interval. The second point corresponds to the location of the market portfolio, meaning that its coordinates are the average return and standard deviation of return for the market portfolio during the evaluation interval, or (σ_M, ar_M). Because the *ex post* CML goes through these two points, its slope can readily be calculated as the vertical distance between the two points divided by the horizontal distance between the two points, or $(ar_M - ar_f)/(\sigma_M - 0) = (ar_M - ar_f)/\sigma_M$. Given a vertical intercept of ar_f, the equation of this line is:

$$ar_p^e = ar_f + \frac{ar_M - ar_f}{\sigma_M}\sigma_p. \tag{25.20}$$

In the example shown in Table 25.1, the average return and standard deviation for the S&P 500, calculated using Equations (25.6) and (25.7), were 4.88% and 7.39%, respectively. As the average return on Treasury bills was 2.23%, the *ex post* CML during these 16 quarters was:

$$ar_p^e = 2.23\% + \frac{4.88\% - 2.23\%}{7.39\%}\sigma_p \tag{25.21}$$

$$= 2.23\% + .36\sigma_p.$$

Figure 25.6 presents a graph of this line.

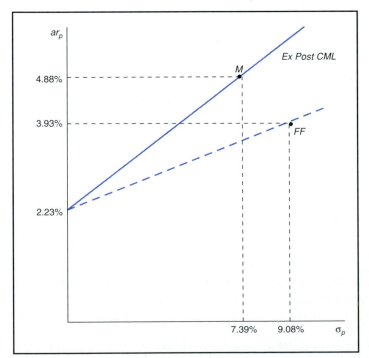

Figure 25.6
Performance Evaluation Using the Ex Post CML

Having determined the location of the *ex post* CML, the average return and standard deviation of the portfolio being evaluated can be determined next by using Equations (25.6) and (25.7). With these values in hand, the portfolio can be located on the same graph as the *ex post* CML. In the case of First Fund, its average return and standard deviation were 3.93% and 9.08%, respectively. Thus in Figure 25.6 its location corresponds to the point having coordinates (9.08%, 3.93%), which is denoted *FF*.

The calculation of the reward-to-variability ratio $RVAR_p$ is analogous to the calculation of the reward-to-volatility ratio $RVOL_p$ described earlier. Specifically, $RVOL_p$ involves dividing the portfolio's average excess return by its beta, while $RVAR_p$ involves dividing the portfolio's average excess return by its standard deviation:

$$RVAR_p = \frac{ar_p - ar_f}{\sigma_p}. \tag{25.22}$$

Note that $RVAR_p$ corresponds to the slope of a line originating at the average riskfree rate and going through a point having coordinates of (σ_p, ar_p). This can be seen by noting that the slope of this line is simply the vertical distance between the two points divided by the horizontal distance between the two points, or $(ar_p - ar_f)/(\sigma_p - 0) = (ar_p - ar_f)/\sigma_p$, which corresponds to the formula for $RVAR_p$ given in Equation (25.22). As the value being measured on the horizontal axis is σ_p and the value being measured on the vertical axis is ar_p, the line can be drawn on the same diagram as the *ex post* CML.

In the First Fund example, recall that the *ex post* CML was shown by the solid line in Figure 25.6. Also appearing in this figure was the point denoted *FF*, corresponding to $(\sigma_p, ar_p) = (9.08\%, 3.93\%)$ for First Fund. The dashed line in this figure originates from the point $(0, ar_f) = (0, 2.23\%)$ and goes through *FF*. The slope of this line is simply .19 $[= (3.93 - 2.23)/9.08]$.

Because the *ex post* CML represents various combinations of riskfree lending or borrowing with investing in the market portfolio, it can be used to provide a benchmark for the reward-to-variability ratio in a manner similar to the SML-based benchmark for the reward-to-volatility ratio. As noted earlier, the slope of the *ex post* CML is $(ar_M - ar_f)/\sigma_M$. If $RVAR_p$ is greater than this value, the portfolio lies above the *ex post* CML, indicating that it has outperformed the market. Alternatively, if $RVAR_p$ is less than this value, the portfolio lies below the *ex post* CML, indicating that it has not performed as well as the market.[10]

In the case of First Fund, the benchmark is .36 $[= (4.88 - 2.23)/7.39]$. Because $RVAR_p$ is less than the benchmark $(.19 < .36)$, First Fund did not perform as well as the market according to this risk-adjusted measure of portfolio performance.

25.3.4 Comparing the Risk-Adjusted Measures of Performance

The measures of performance that are based on the *ex post* SML, α_p and $RVOL_p$, can be compared with the measure of performance that is based on the *ex post* CML, $RVAR_p$. Focusing on $RVOL_p$ (the comparison also applies to α_p), it should be noted that in certain situations, $RVOL_p$ and $RVAR_p$ can give different assessments of a portfolio's performance relative to the market portfolio.

In particular, if $RVOL_p$ indicates that the portfolio outperformed the market, it is possible for $RVAR_p$ to indicate that the portfolio did not perform as well as the market. The reason for this is that the portfolio may have a relatively large amount of unique risk. Such risk would not be a factor in determining the value of $RVOL_p$ for the portfolio, as only *market risk* is in the denominator. However, such risk would be included in the denominator of $RVAR_p$ for the portfolio because this measure is based on *total risk* (that is, both market and unique risk). Thus a portfolio with a low amount of market risk could have a high amount of total risk, resulting in a relatively high $RVOL_p$ (due to the low amount of market risk) and a low $RVAR_p$ (due to the high amount of total risk). Accordingly, $RVOL_p$ could indicate that the portfolio outperformed the market, whereas at the same time $RVAR_p$ indicates that it did not perform as well as the market.[11]

As an example, consider Third Fund, which had an average return of 4.5%, a beta of .8, and a standard deviation of 18%. Accordingly, $RVOL_{TF} = 2.71\%$ $[= (4.5\% - 2.23\%)/.8]$, indicating that Third Fund outperformed the market portfolio because the benchmark is 2.65% $[= (4.88\% - 2.23\%)/1.0]$. However, $RVAR_{TF} = .12$ $[= (4.5\% - 2.23\%)/18\%]$, indicating that Third Fund did not perform as well as the market portfolio because the benchmark is .36 $[= (4.88\% - 2.23\%)/7.39\%]$. The reason for the difference can be seen by noting Third Fund's low beta relative to the market ($.8 < 1.0$) but high standard deviation relative to the market ($18\% > 7.39\%$). This suggests that Third Fund had a relatively high level of unique risk.

It also follows that it is possible for $RVOL_p$ and $RVAR_p$ to rank two or more portfolios differently on the basis of their performance. This is because these two measures of risk-adjusted performance utilize different types of risk.

Continuing with the example, recall that earlier it was shown that First Fund had an average return of 3.93%, a beta of 1.13, and a standard deviation of 9.08%. Thus, $RVOL_{FF} = 1.50\%$ $[= (3.93\% - 2.23\%)/1.13]$, which is less than $RVOL_{TF} = 2.65\%$, thereby indicating that First Fund ranked lower than Third Fund. However, $RVAR_{FF} = .13$ $[= (3.93\% - 2.23\%)/9.08\%]$, which is greater than $RVAR_{TF} = .12$, thereby indicating that First Fund ranked higher than Third Fund.

Did Third Fund do better or worse than the market on a risk-adjusted basis? And did Third Fund perform better or worse than First Fund? The answer to these two questions lies in identifying the appropriate measure of risk for the client. If the client has many other assets, then beta is the relevant measure of risk, and performance should be based on $RVOL_p$. To such a client, Third Fund should be viewed as a superior performer relative to both the market and First Fund. However, if the client has few other assets, then standard deviation is the relevant measure of risk, and performance should be based on $RVAR_p$. To such a client, Third Fund should be viewed as an inferior performer relative to both the market and First Fund.

25.4 MARKET TIMING

A market timer structures a portfolio to have a relatively high beta when he or she expects the market to rise and a relatively low beta when a market drop is anticipated. Why? Because, as noted earlier, the expected return on a portfolio is a linear function of its beta:

$$\overline{r}_p = \alpha_p + r_f + (\overline{r}_M - r_f)\beta_p. \qquad (25.23)$$

This means that the market timer will want to have a high-beta portfolio when he or she expects the market to have a higher return than the riskfree rate because such a portfolio will have a higher expected return than a low-beta portfolio. Conversely, the market timer will want to have a low-beta portfolio when he or she expects the market to have a lower return than the riskfree rate as it will have a higher expected return than a high-beta portfolio. Simply put, the market timer will want to:

1. Hold a high-beta portfolio when $\overline{r}_M > r_f$, and
2. Hold a low-beta portfolio when $\overline{r}_M < r_f$.

If the timer is accurate in his or her forecasts of the expected return on the market, then his or her portfolio will outperform a benchmark portfolio that has a constant beta equal to the average beta of the timer's portfolio.

For example, if the market timer set the portfolio beta at zero when $\overline{r}_M < r_f$ and at two when $\overline{r}_M > r_f$, the return on the portfolio would be higher than the return on a portfolio having a beta constantly equal to one, provided that the timer is accurate in forecasting $\overline{r}_M$. Unfortunately, if the market timer is inaccurate in his or her forecasts and consequently alters the portfolio's beta in ways unrelated to subsequent market moves, then the timer's portfolio will not perform as well as a constant beta portfolio. For example, if the timer sometimes sets the portfolio's beta equal to zero when the market is forecast to fall but actually rises, and at other times sets the beta equal to two when the market is forecast to rise but actually falls, then the portfolio will have an average return that is less than what a portfolio with a constant beta of one would have earned.

To "time the market," either the average beta of the risky securities held in the portfolio can be changed or the relative amounts invested in the riskfree asset and risky securities can be altered. For example, to increase the beta of a portfolio, bonds or low-beta stocks could be sold, with the proceeds used to purchase high-beta stocks. Alternatively, Treasury bills in the portfolio could be sold (or the amount of borrowing increased), with the resulting proceeds invested in stocks.

In Figure 25.7, the excess returns of two hypothetical portfolios are measured on the vertical axis while those of a market index are on the horizontal axis. Straight lines, fit via standard regression methods, reveal positive *ex post* alpha values in each case. However, the scatter diagrams tell a different story.

The scatter diagram for the portfolio shown in panel (a) seems to indicate that the relationship between the portfolio's excess returns and the market's excess returns was linear, because the points cluster close to the regression line. This suggests that the portfolio consisted of securities in a manner such that the beta of the portfolio was roughly the same at all times. Because the *ex post* alpha was positive, it appears that the investment manager successfully identified and invested in some underpriced securities.

The scatter diagram for the portfolio shown in panel (b) seems to indicate that the relationship between this portfolio's excess returns and the market's excess returns was not linear because the points in the middle lie below the regression line and those at the ends lie above the regression line. This suggests that

(a) Superior Stock Selection

(b) Superior Market Timing

Figure 25.7
Superior Fund Performance

the portfolio consisted of high-beta securities during periods when the market return was high and low-beta securities during periods when the market return was low. Upon examination, it appears that the portfolio has a positive *ex post* alpha because of successful market timing by the investment manager.

25.4.1 Quadratic Regression

To measure the ability of an investment manager to successfully time the market, something more complex than a straight line must be "fit" to scatter diagrams such as those shown in Figure 25.7. One procedure fits a curve, where statistical methods are used to estimate the parameters a, b, and c in the following *quadratic regression equation:*

$$r_{pt} - r_{ft} = a + b(r_{Mt} - r_{ft}) + c[(r_{Mt} - r_{ft})^2] + \epsilon_{pt} \qquad (25.24)$$

where ϵ_{pt} is the random error term.

The *ex post* characteristic *curve* shown in Figure 25.8(a) is simply the following quadratic function, where the values of a, b, and c for the portfolio have been estimated by standard regression methods:

$$r_{pt} - r_{ft} = a + b(r_{Mt} - r_{ft}) + c[(r_{Mt} - r_{ft})^2]. \qquad (25.25)$$

If the estimated value of c is positive [as it is for the portfolio depicted in Figure 25.8(a)], the slope of the curve would decrease as one moves to the left. This would indicate that the portfolio manager successfully timed the market. Note how this equation corresponds to the equation for the *ex post* characteristic line if c is approximately equal to zero. In such a situation, a and b would correspond to the portfolio's *ex post* alpha and beta, respectively.

Figure 25.8
Ex Post Characteristic Curve and Lines

25.4.2 Dummy Variable Regression

An alternative procedure fits two *ex post* characteristic lines to the scatter diagram, as shown in Figure 25.8(b). Periods when risky securities outperform risk-free securities (that is, when $r_{Mt} > r_{ft}$) can be termed *up markets*. Periods when risky securities do not perform as well as riskfree securities (that is, when $r_{Mt} < r_{ft}$) can be termed *down markets*. A successful market timer would select a high up-market beta and a low down-market beta. Graphically, the slope of the *ex post* characteristic line for positive excess market returns (up markets) is greater than the slope of the *ex post* characteristic line for negative excess market returns (down markets).

To estimate such a relationship, standard regression methods can be used to estimate the parameters *a, b,* and *c* in the following *dummy variable regression equation:*

$$r_{pt} - r_{ft} = a + b(r_{Mt} - r_{ft}) + c[D_t(r_{Mt} - r_{ft})] + \epsilon_{pt}. \tag{25.26}$$

Here, ϵ_{pt} is the random error term, and D_t is a "dummy variable" that is assigned a value of zero for any past time period t when $r_{Mt} < r_{ft}$ and a value of minus one for any past time period t when $r_{Mt} > r_{ft}$. To see how this works, consider the effective equations for different values of $r_{Mt} - r_{ft}$.

Value of $r_{Mt} - r_{ft}$	Equation
> 0	$r_{pt} - r_{ft} = a + b(r_{Mt} - r_{ft}) + \epsilon_{pt}$
$= 0$	$r_{pt} - r_{ft} = a + \epsilon_{pt}$
< 0	$r_{pt} - r_{ft} = a + (b - c)(r_{Mt} - r_{ft}) + \epsilon_{pt}$

Note that the parameter *b* corresponds to the portfolio's up-market beta, while $(b - c)$ corresponds to the portfolio's down-market beta. Thus the parameter *c* indicates the difference between the two betas and will be positive for the successful market timer.

For the portfolio shown in Figure 25.8(b), the *ex post* characteristic line on the right side of the graph corresponds to the equation:

$$r_{pt} - r_{ft} = a + b(r_{Mt} - r_{ft}) \qquad (25.27\text{a})$$

whereas the *ex post* characteristic line shown on the left side of the graph corresponds to the equation:

$$r_{pt} - r_{ft} = a + (b - c)(r_{Mt} - r_{ft}). \qquad (25.27\text{b})$$

In this example, the investment manager has successfully engaged in market timing, because the slope of the line on the right side (that is, b) is greater than the slope of the line on the left side (that is, $b - c$).

In either regression Equation (25.24) or (25.26), the value of the parameter a provides an estimate of the investment manager's ability to identify mispriced securities (that is, security selection ability), and the value of the parameter c provides an estimate of the manager's market timing ability. The difference between the two equations is that the quadratic equation indicates that the portfolio's beta fluctuated over many values, depending on the size of the market's excess returns. This can be seen graphically by noting that the slope of the quadratic curve is continually increasing when moving from left to right in Figure 25.8(a). On the other hand, the dummy variable equation indicates that the portfolio's beta fluctuates between just two values, depending on whether r_{Mt} is less than or greater than r_{ft}. This can be seen graphically by noting that the slope of the equation increases from one value (that is, $b - c$) to a second value (that is, b) when moving from left to right in Figure 25.8(b).

As an example, again consider First Fund. Table 25.2 presents the results from applying regression Equations (25.24) and (25.26) to this portfolio over the 16–quarter time interval, along with the *ex post* characteristic line results. The table does not provide any evidence of either selectivity or market timing ability by the portfolio manager. This can be seen by noting that the parameter a is negative whereas the parameter c is near zero.[12] Further evidence is provided regarding the lack of market timing ability by noting that the correlation coefficient is higher for the *ex post* characteristic line than for either of the other equations.

	TABLE 25.2		
	MARKET TIMING TEST RESULTS FOR FIRST FUND		
Parameter Being Estimated[a]	Ex Post Characteristic Line	Quadratic Equation	Dummy Variable Equation
a	− 1.29%	− 2.12%	− 1.33%
	(1.00)	(1.65)	(2.54)
b	1.13	1.03	1.13
	(.13)	(.20)	(.28)
c	—	.02	.02
	—	(.03)	(.78)
Correlation[b]	.92	.91	.91

[a]Standard errors are shown in parentheses below the respective parameters.
[b]The correlation coefficient for the quadratic and dummy variable equations has been adjusted for the number of independent variables.

The previously mentioned risk-adjusted measures of portfolio performance have been criticized on several grounds. Some of the major criticisms are described in this section.

25.5.1 Use of a Market Surrogate

All of the measures other than the reward-to-variability ratio require the identification of a market portfolio. This means that whatever surrogate is used, it can be criticized as being inadequate. Indeed, it has been shown that by making slight changes in the surrogate, the performance rankings of a set of portfolios can be completely reversed (that is, the top-ranked portfolio with one surrogate could be the bottom-ranked portfolio if a slightly different surrogate was used). However, it also has been noted that when commonly used NYSE-based surrogates are involved, such as the Dow Jones Industrial Average, the S&P 500, and an index comparable to the New York Stock Exchange Composite, the performance rankings of common stock portfolios appear to be quite similar.[13]

A related criticism of using a market index such as the S&P 500 to determine the benchmark portfolio's return is that it is nearly impossible for an investor to form a portfolio whose returns replicate those on such an index over time. This is because transaction costs will be encountered in initially forming the portfolio, in restructuring the portfolio when stocks are replaced in the index, and in purchasing more shares of the stocks when cash dividends are received.[14] Hence it has been argued that the returns on an index overstate the returns that a passive investor could earn, meaning that the returns on the benchmark portfolio are too high.[15]

25.5.2 Distinguishing Skill from Luck

A very long time interval is needed in order to be able to obtain a measure of performance that can distinguish skill from luck on the part of the investment manager. That is, it would be useful to know if an apparently successful manager was skilled or just lucky because skill can be expected to have a favorable impact on the portfolio's performance in the future, whereas luck cannot be expected to continue. Unfortunately, too many years' worth of data are generally needed to make such a determination.[16]

25.5.3 Measuring the Riskfree Rate

The use of Treasury bills for measuring the riskfree rate in determining benchmark portfolios based on either the *ex post* SML or CML can be criticized. Consider a benchmark portfolio that involves an investment in both Treasury bills and the market portfolio. Such a benchmark portfolio can be criticized for having too low a rate of return, making it easier for a portfolio to show superior performance. This is because Treasury bills may provide excessively low returns to compensate for their high degree of liquidity. If a higher riskfree rate (such as the commercial paper rate) is used, then any benchmark portfolio that lies between this riskfree rate and the market portfolio on either the *ex post* SML or CML will have a higher rate of return, and thus represent a higher but more appropriate standard.

Furthermore, consider a benchmark portfolio that involves levering a positive investment in the market portfolio by borrowing at the riskfree rate. Use of the Treasury bill rate can be criticized because realistic borrowing alternatives typically involve a higher rate, and are thus less attractive. Accordingly, benchmarks that involve borrowing at the Treasury bill rate have too high a rate of return, making it more difficult for a portfolio to show superior performance. If a higher riskfree borrowing rate (such as the call money rate plus a small premium) is used, then any benchmark portfolio involving riskfree borrowing will have a lower rate of return, and thus represent a lower but more appropriate standard.

In summary, measures of portfolio performance based on either the *ex post* SML or CML and utilizing Treasury bills to determine the riskfree rate are alleged to discriminate in favor of conservative portfolios and against aggressive ones.

25.5.4 Validity of the CAPM

The measures of portfolio performance that involve beta (namely, the *ex post* alpha and reward-to-volatility measures) are based on the CAPM, yet the CAPM may not be the correct asset pricing model. That is, perhaps assets are priced according to some other model. If so, the use of beta-based performance measures will be inappropriate.

Interestingly, a measure analogous to *ex post* alpha has been shown to be a meaningful gauge of performance if the Arbitrage Pricing Theory's (APT) model of asset pricing is believed to be more appropriate.[17] In such a situation, APT is used to estimate the benchmark portfolio's return ar_{bp} that is used in Equation (22.3) to calculate α_p.

It should also be noted that the reward-to-variability ratio is immune to this criticism because it uses standard deviation as a measure of risk and does not rely on the validity of the CAPM or the identification of a market portfolio or APT.

25.5.5 Performance Attribution

The previously mentioned risk-adjusted measures of performance concentrate on the question of *how* a portfolio did relative to both a benchmark and a set of other portfolios. The use of quadratic and dummy variable regression is an attempt to evaluate separately the manager's ability at selectivity and timing. However, the client might want to know more about *why* the portfolio had a certain return over a particular interval of time. **Performance attribution** using a *factor model* is one method that has been used to try to make such a determination. An example is presented in the appendix.

The performance of portfolios of bonds and other types of fixed-income securities is often evaluated by comparing their total returns (consisting of coupon payments plus capital gains or losses) with those of an index representing a comparable class of securities over some interval of time. Hence a portfolio that invested in investment-grade long-term corporate bonds would be compared with an investment-grade long-term corporate bond index, a portfolio invested in mortgage-backed securities would be compared with a mortgage-backed securities index, and a junk bond fund would be compared with a "high-yield" index.

25.6.1   Bond Indices

Bond indices typically represent either the average total return or the average price on a portfolio of bonds that have certain similar characteristics. Figure 25.9 presents various bond indices that are published daily in the *Wall Street Journal*.[18] The Lehman Brothers Long Treasury Bond Index is typical of many bond market indices. This index is a total return index, reflecting interest income and changes in prices from one day to the next of nearly all Treasury securities with maturities between 10 and 30 years. It is value weighted in that price changes and interest income for each bond in the index are weighted by the bond's issue size relative to the combined size of all the securities in the index. It was set at a level of 1,000 at year-end 1980, and each day since then it has changed by the average total return measured from the previous day. Note that the way this index is constructed makes it easy to determine the return on long-term Treasuries over any time period. For example, Figure 25.9 indicates that on December 13, 1993, the index was at 5536.02 and a year before it was at 4643.73. Thus the annual return was 19.2% [= (5536.02 − 4643.73)/4643.73].

There is a yield figure also presented for the Lehman Brothers Long Treasury Bond Index. In calculating this index, the annual interest payments for each bond are divided by its current market price, and then these interest yields are averaged by using value weighting. Hence it is an index of *current yields*.

The second index shown in Figure 25.9 is the Dow Jones 20 Bond Index, where the prices of 20 bonds (10 utilities and 10 industrials) are simply added together and then divided by 20. Similarly, the yield on this index is an average of the yields on the 20 bonds. In Figure 25.9 this index was at 111.11, indicating that the average bond was selling at an 11.11% premium on December 13, 1993, with a yield of 6.17%.

The third index is the Salomon Brothers mortgage-backed bond index. It is based on conventional mortgage pass-through securities as well as those issued by GNMA, FHLMC, FNMA, and FHA. Like the Lehman Brothers Long Treasury Bond Index, it is a total return index standardized to equal 100 at year-end 1979.

The fourth index is the *Bond Buyer* municipal bond index. It is based on a set of long-term investment-grade general obligation and revenue bonds whose prices and yields are averaged in a manner similar to those of the Dow Jones 20 Bond Index.

The fifth index is the Merrill Lynch corporate bond index. It is based on a set of corporate bonds, including industrial, utility, financial, and transportation

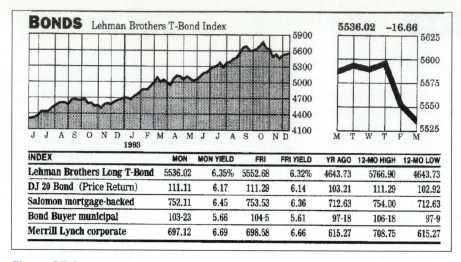

Figure 25.9

Bond Indices Published in the Wall Street Journal, December 14, 1993

Source: Reprinted by permission of *The Wall Street Journal* ©Dow Jones & Company, Inc., December 14, 1993, p. C1. All rights reserved worldwide.

bonds, of all maturities. It is a total return index, like the Lehman Brothers Long Treasury Bond Index, except that its base of 100 was set at year-end 1972.

25.6.2 Time-Series and Cross-Sectional Comparisons

Figure 25.10 illustrates two ways of evaluating the returns on a bond portfolio by comparing them with those on a bond index over a time interval. In part (a), a time-series comparison is made, where the bond portfolio's quarterly returns over time (for example, the last 16 quarters) during the time interval are graphed along with those of a comparable bond index.

In part (b), a cross-sectional comparison is made in a manner similar to the equity performance measures that were based on the *ex post* CML. Here the bond portfolio's average return and standard deviation are graphed and compared with a line that goes through the average riskfree rate and the average return and standard deviation of the bond index (instead of a common stock index), based on quarterly returns during the time interval.

A variation of this procedure involves estimating the bond portfolio's *ex post* alpha by using the *ex post* characteristic line approach described earlier. That is, a figure similar to Figure 25.5 would be prepared, but now the excess returns on a bond portfolio would be measured on the vertical axis and the excess returns on a bond index would be measured on the horizontal axis.[19] Often the returns on the Lehman Brothers government/corporate bond index, which is a value-weighted index of government and corporate investment-grade bonds that have more than one year remaining until maturity, is used as the market index. Others use the returns on a bond index that most closely fits with the investment objectives and policies of the portfolio under scrutiny. In either case, an *ex post* alpha would be calculated and used as a measure of portfolio performance.

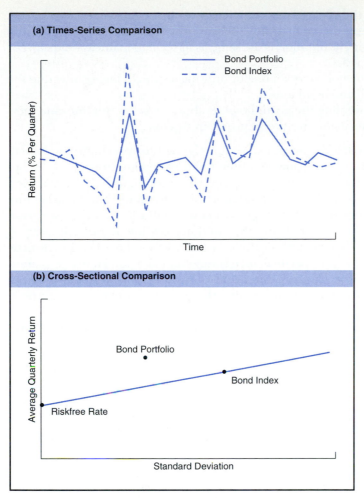

Figure 25.10
Bond Portfolio Performance Evaluation

25.6.3 Bond Market Line

A different approach involves the use of a *bond market line*.[20] Assume that the performance of a bond portfolio is to be evaluated over a given quarter (or year, as this approach can be used for a longer period). There are five steps to this approach:

1. Calculate the quarterly return for the portfolio, along with its average duration for the quarter (this could be calculated by averaging the portfolio's duration at the beginning and end of the quarter), and plot the portfolio on a graph that measures return on the vertical axis and duration on the horizontal axis. (Duration is discussed in Chapter 16.)
2. Calculate the return and average duration for a broadly representative bond index for the same quarter, and plot the index on the same graph.

3. Determine the 90-day Treasury bill rate at the beginning of the quarter, and plot it on the same graph (because the Treasury bill is a pure discount security, its duration is the same as its term-to-maturity—90 days, or roughly .25 years).
4. Construct the bond market line by drawing a straight line connecting the Treasury bill and bond index.
5. Determine whether the portfolio plots above or below this line, and measure its performance by its distance from this line.

With this approach the bond market line is used to determine the benchmark in evaluating the performance of the bond portfolio. If the portfolio lies above the bond market line, such as the one shown in Figure 25.11, it outperformed the benchmark (the benchmark portfolio lies on the bond market line directly below the portfolio) and its performance would be viewed as superior. Conversely, if the portfolio lies below the bond market line, it underperformed the benchmark (the benchmark portfolio lies on the bond market line directly above the portfolio) and its performance is viewed as inferior. Hence, Equation (22.3) is being used to calculate the bond portfolio's *ex post* alpha, with the bond market line being used to determine the return on the benchmark portfolio, ar_{bp}.[21]

Other bond portfolios and indices can also be shown on the graph to give more information on the relative performance of the portfolio being evaluated.

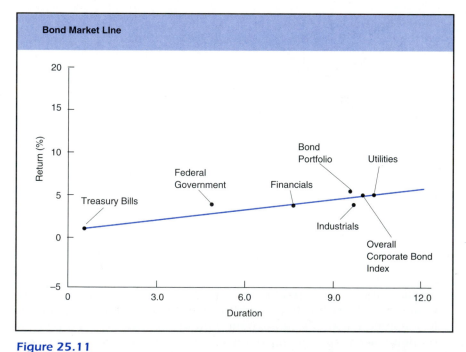

Figure 25.11
Bond Market Line
Source: Adapted from Wayne H. Wagner and Dennis A Tito, "Definitive New Measures of Bond Performance and Risk," *Pension World*, 13, no. 5 (May 1977): p. 12.

CHAPTER 25

In Figure 25.11, one federal government bond index and three corporate bond indices are shown, in addition to the overall bond index published by Merrill Lynch. Their *ex post* alphas can be compared to the bond portfolio's *ex post* alpha. Furthermore, the bond portfolio's *ex post* alpha can be used to determine its rank among a group of bond portfolios.

25.7 SUMMARY

1. Performance measurement is an integral part of the investment management process. It is a feedback and control mechanism that can make the investment management process more effective.
2. In evaluating performance, there are two major tasks: determine whether the performance is superior or inferior, and determine whether the performance is due to luck or skill.
3. Without intraperiod contributions or withdrawals, measurement of periodic portfolio returns is simple: the difference between ending and beginning portfolio values divided by beginning portfolio value.
4. Intraperiod cash flows complicate the calculation of periodic portfolio returns. Two methods have been developed to calculate returns when these cash flows occur: dollar-weighted and time-weighted returns.
5. The dollar-weighted return is influenced by the size and timing of cash flows, whereas the time-weighted return is not. As a result, the time-weighted return is generally the preferred method when evaluating portfolio performance.
6. The essential idea behind performance evaluation is to compare an actively managed portfolio's returns against the returns of an alternative benchmark portfolio. An appropriate benchmark should be relevant and feasible, and it should exhibit risk similar to that of the actively managed portfolio.
7. Risk-adjusted performance measures involve both a portfolio's *ex post* return and its *ex post* risk.
8. *Ex post* alpha (differential return) and the reward-to-volatility ratio compare a portfolio's excess return to the portfolio's systematic risk. The reward-to-variability ratio compares a portfolio's excess return to the portfolio's total risk.
9. Successful market timers will hold portfolios with relatively high betas during market rises and relatively low betas during market declines. Quadratic regression and dummy variable regression are two methods designed to measure market timing performance.
10. Risk-adjusted measures of performance have been criticized for using a market surrogate instead of the "true" market portfolio; being unable to statistically distinguish luck from skill except over very long periods of time; using an inappropriate riskfree rate; and relying on the validity of the CAPM.

1. Crungy Patrick owns a portfolio of three stocks. Crungy's holdings and the prices of the stocks at the end of Year 1 and Year 2 are shown below. Assuming no contributions, withdrawals, or dividends paid, what is the return on Crungy's portfolio in Year 2?

Stock	Shares Owned	Year 1 Price	Year 2 Price
A	100	$10	$15
B	300	5	4
C	250	12	14

2. Why do cash inflows and outflows between the beginning and end of a performance evaluation period complicate the measurement of portfolio returns?

3. At the beginning of the year, Lave Cross's portfolio was worth $39,000. At year-end, Lave received a gift of $4,000, which was invested in the portfolio. The portfolio's value at year-end was $42,000. What was the return on Lave's portfolio during the year?

4. New Lisbon Laundry's pension fund was worth $30 million at the end of Year 1. On the first day of Year 2 the firm made a $2 million contribution to the fund. At the end of Year 2, the pension fund was valued at $38 million. What was the return on the New Lisbon pension fund during Year 2?

5. At the beginning of the year, Con Daily's portfolio was worth $9,000. At the end of each of the next four quarters, Con received a gift of $500, which was invested in the portfolio. At the end of each quarter, Con's portfolio was worth, respectively, $9,800, $10,800, $11,200, and $12,000. What was the time-weighted rate of return on Con's portfolio during the year?

6. Dell Darling's portfolio is worth $12,000 at the beginning of a 30–day month. On day 10 of the month, Dell received a contribution to the portfolio of $800. At the end of the month, Dell's portfolio is worth $13,977.71. What was the dollar-weighted return on Dell's portfolio for the month?

7. Ginger Beaumont began the year with a portfolio valued at $10,000 and made a contribution to and a withdrawal from this portfolio over the next three months. Information regarding amounts and dates of these cash flows and the portfolio's market value at various dates is shown below.

Date	Contribution (+) or Withdrawal (−)	Portfolio Value
12/31	$ 0	$10,000
1/31	+956	9,000
2/28	−659	12,000
3/31	0	13,000

a. Calculate the dollar-weighted return for the three-month period. (Hint: Unless you have a suitable calculator, you will have to use trial and error to find the dollar-weighted return. To begin, the monthly dollar-weighted return is less than 10%.)

b. Calculate the time-weighted return for the three-month period.

c. Why is the time-weighted return for the quarter less than the dollar-weighted return in this particular problem?

8. Distinguish between time-weighted and dollar-weighted rates of return. Under what performance measurement circumstances might the dollar-weighted return be preferred to the time-weighted?

9. Oats DeMaestri's portfolio is valued at $22,000 at the beginning of a 31–day month. During the month, Oats withdrew $1,500 from the portfolio on day 12 and contributed $600 on day 21. At month-end, the portfolio was worth $21,769.60. What was Oats's dollar-weighted return for the month?

10. At the beginning of a 30–day month, Buttercup Dickerson owned a portfolio valued at $5,000. On day 10, Buttercup's portfolio was worth $7,300 after a $2,000 contribution had been made on that day. At the end of the month, the portfolio was worth $9,690.18. Calculate both the time-weighted and dollar-weighted returns on Buttercup's portfolio for the month. Why do the two returns differ so substantially?

11. Why does performance evaluation require an appropriate benchmark in order to be meaningful? How would you define the term *appropriate* in this context?

12. It is common practice for performance evaluation services to compare the returns on a common stock portfolio to a distribution of returns obtained from a large sample of other common stock portfolios. What potential problems are involved in this sort of analysis?

13. Pickles Dillhoefer owns a portfolio that over the last five years has produced a 16.8% annual return. During that time the portfolio produced a 1.10 beta. Further, the riskfree return and market return averaged 7.4% and 15.2% per year, respectively. What was the *ex post* alpha on Pickles's portfolio over this time period? Draw the *ex post* SML and the position of Pickles's portfolio.

14. The performance of the Venus Fund, a common stock mutual fund, compared with that of the S&P 500 over a ten-year period, is as follows:

	Venus Fund	S&P 500
Average quarterly excess return	0.6%	0.5%
Standard deviation of quarterly excess returns	9.9%	6.6%
Beta	1.10	1.00

Dazzy Vance is considering investing in either the Venus Fund or another mutual fund whose objective is to track the performance of the S&P 500. Which fund would you recommend that Dazzy select, assuming that your decision is based solely on past performance? Justify your answer using various measures of risk-adjusted performance.

15. Why is the reward-to-variability ratio a more appropriate measure of performance than the *ex post* alpha if the portfolio being assessed represents the entire wealth of the portfolio's owner?

16. Can the *ex post* alpha, the reward-to-volatility ratio, and the reward-to-variability ratio give conflicting answers to the question of whether a particular portfolio has outperformed a market index on a risk-adjusted basis? If so, which of these measures can conflict with the others, and why can this conflict occur?

17. Does a portfolio's *ex post* alpha measure gains and losses due to security selection, market timing, or both? Explain.

18. Assume that broad stock market indices, such as the S&P 500, are not good surrogates for the "true" market portfolio. What potential problems does this cause for performance evaluation using the *ex post* alpha measure?

19. You are given the following historical performance information on the capital markets and the Jupiter Fund, a common stock mutual fund.

Year	Jupiter Fund Beta	Return on Jupiter Fund	Return on Market Index	Return on Treasury Bills
1	0.90	−2.99%	−8.50%	6.58%
2	0.95	0.63	4.01	6.53
3	0.95	22.01	14.31	4.39
4	1.00	24.08	18.98	3.84
5	1.00	−22.46	−14.66	6.93
6	0.90	−25.12	−26.47	8.00
7	0.80	29.72	37.20	5.80
8	0.75	22.15	23.84	5.08
9	0.80	0.48	−7.18	5.12
10	0.85	6.85	6.56	7.18

a. Compute the Jupiter Fund's average beta over the ten-year period. What investment percentages in the market index and Treasury bills are required in order to produce a beta equal to the fund's average beta?

b. Compute the year-by-year returns that would have been earned on a portfolio invested in the market index and Treasury bills in the proportions calculated in part (a).

c. Compute the year-by-year returns that would have been earned on a portfolio invested in the market index and Treasury bills in the proportions needed to match Jupiter's beta year by year. (Note: These proportions will change yearly as the fund's beta changes yearly.)

d. One measure of a fund's market timing ability is the average difference between (1) what the fund would have earned annually by investing in the market index and Treasury bills so that the year-by-year beta equals the fund's actual year-by-year beta, and (2) what the fund would have earned annually by investing in the market index and Treasury bills so that the year-by-year beta equals the fund's average beta. Given your previous calculations, evaluate the market timing ability of Jupiter's manager.

e. One measure of a fund's security selection ability is the average difference between (1) the fund's annual returns and, (2) what the fund would have earned annually by investing in the market index and Treasury bills so that the year-by-year beta equals the fund's actual year-by-year beta. Calculate Jupiter's average return and then, using your previous calculations, evaluate the security selection ability of Jupiter's manager.

20. Consider the following annual returns produced by a MiniFund, a mutual fund investing in small stocks:

1971	16.50%	1976	57.38%	1981	13.88%	1986	6.85%
1972	4.43	1977	25.38	1982	28.01	1987	−9.30
1973	−30.90	1978	23.46	1983	39.67	1988	22.87
1974	−19.95	1979	43.46	1984	−6.67	1989	10.18
1975	52.82	1980	39.88	1985	24.66	1990	−21.56

Referring to Table 1.1, use the Treasury bill returns as the riskfree return and the common stock returns as the market return, and calculate the following risk-adjusted return measures for the small stock mutual fund:

a. *Ex post* alpha
b. Reward-to-volatility ratio
c. Reward-to-variability ratio.

Comment on the mutual fund's risk-adjusted performance. What problems are associated with using a large capitalization index such as the S&P 500 (the source of the common stock returns) as the benchmark in evaluating this small company mutual fund?

21. In an article in *Journal of Finance* (March 1983), Jess Chua and Richard Woodward investigated the investment skill of the legendary economist John Maynard Keynes. A portfolio managed by Keynes had the following returns:

	Keynes's Return	Market Return	Riskfree Return
1928	−3.4%	7.9%	4.2
1929	0.8	6.6	5.3
1930	−32.4	−20.3%	2.5
1931	−24.6	−25.0	3.6
1932	44.8	−5.8	1.6
1933	35.1	21.5	0.6
1934	33.1	−0.7	0.7
1935	44.3	5.3	0.6
1936	56.0	10.2	0.6
1937	8.5	−0.5	0.6
1938	−40.1	−16.1	0.6
1939	12.9	−7.2	1.3
1940	−15.6%	−12.9	1.0
1941	33.5	12.5	1.0
1942	−0.9	0.8	1.0
1943	53.9	15.6	1.0
1944	14.5	5.4	1.0
1945	14.6	0.8	1.0

Chua and Woodward concluded that Keynes demonstrated superior investment abilities. They did not, however, distinguish between his market timing and security selection skills. Using the quadratic regression and dummy variable techniques, evaluate Keynes's market timing skills. (Hint: Use of a regression package found in a standard personal computer spreadsheet program is highly recommended.)

22. Discuss the potential drawbacks of evaluating bond portfolio performance by using a bond market line.

23. (Appendix Question) What is the purpose of performance attribution? What types of problems can hinder performance attribution?

24. (Appendix Question) Assume that security returns are explained by a sector-factor model. Eugene Stephens has been asked to develop a performance attribution report analyzing the returns on portfolio A versus those of a market index for the latest year, and he has collected the following information:

	Portfolio A	Market Index	Sector-Factor Values
Return	12.50%	5.50%	—
Beta	1.10	1.00	−0.50
Size	1.30	6.00	−0.60
% Industrial	40%	80%	8.00
% Nonindustrial	60%	20%	16.00

Unfortunately, Eugene is confused by the subject of performance attribution. Carry out the analysis for him.

CFA EXAM QUESTION

25. As a corporate treasurer, you are responsible for evaluating prospective investment managers for your company's pension fund. You have interviewed three managers, examined their reported investment performances, and identified clear-cut differences in their investment approaches.

Manager A has developed a very appealing and apparently successful investment process based on extensive research and back-testing, but she has not yet managed money using this process.

Manager B has been investing relatively small amounts of money over only the past two years, producing what appears to be extraordinary investment performance. His process is based on exploiting what he believes to be a market inefficiency (or anomaly) to produce superior returns.

Manager C is a global investment counselor who emphasizes active selection of stocks and bonds across the major world markets. He has a long track record and uses a well-established and widely accepted process for selecting securities.

a. Discuss the usefulness of historical investment performance in evaluating investment managers.

b. For each of the three managers, identify and discuss the two most important factors that you would consider in assessing the manager's performance.

APPENDIX

PERFORMANCE ATTRIBUTION

With performance attribution, an attempt is made to ascertain why a portfolio had a given return over a particular time period. One procedure for making such a determination involves assuming that security returns are related to a number of prespecified factors as well as to *sector-factors*.[22] For example, there may be a beta factor, a size factor, and two sector-factors that indicate whether or not a stock is issued by an industrial company. With such a model, the returns for a set of stocks during a given time period are related to these factors and sector-factors in the following manner:

$$r_i = \beta_i F_1 + s_i F_2 + c_{i1} SF_1 + c_{i2} SF_2 + \epsilon_i. \tag{A.1}$$

Here each stock has four attributes—β_i, s_i, c_{i1}, and c_{i2}. The attributes β_i and s_i are, respectively, the beta and firm size of stock i in a given time period; and c_{i1} and c_{i2} are sector-factor attributes that have values of one and zero, respectively, if stock i is an industrial firm, and values of zero and one if stock i is not an industrial firm. (For example, it may be a utility or transportation company such as Northern States Power or Delta Air Lines.)

The factors and sector-factors F_1, F_2, SF_1, and SF_2 are parameters that can be estimated using a statistical technique known as multiple regression. For example, the annual returns for 500 firms for 1994 could be calculated. Then, the betas for each stock could be estimated using 16 quarters of returns ending with the last quarter of 1993 (by using the *ex post* characteristic line equation given earlier). The firm size for each stock could be measured by taking the market price per share as of December 31, 1993, multiplying it by the number of shares outstanding at that time, and then taking the logarithm of the product (expressed in billions). Lastly, each firm can be classified as either an industrial or nonindustrial, resulting in a zero or one value assigned to c_{i1} and c_{i2}. This will result in four columns of 500 numbers representing security attributes—one column with the betas for each stock, one column for the firm sizes of each stock, and two columns of zeros and ones corresponding to whether the firms are industrials or nonindustrials—upon which will be regressed the column of annual returns for the 500 stocks during 1994.

Suppose that the resulting regression produced estimated values for F_1, F_2, SF_1, and SF_2 of 1.20, $-.40$, 10.00, and 9.00, respectively. Thus Equation (A.1) for 1994 would be:

$$r_i = 1.20\beta_i - .40s_i + 10.00c_{i1} + 9.00c_{i2} + \epsilon_i. \tag{A.2}$$

As the estimated value of F_1 ($= 1.20$) is positive, the year of 1994 was one where high-beta stocks tended to outperform low-beta stocks. Furthermore, since the estimated value of F_2 ($= -.40$) is negative, the year 1994 was one where the stocks of small firms tended to outperform the stocks of large firms. With an estimated value for SF_1 that is greater than the estimated value of SF_2 ($10.00 > 9.00$), 1994 also appears to have been a year when industrials tended to outperform nonindustrials.

Equation (A.2) can be used to analyze the 1994 return on a stock. Consider, for example, a hypothetical industrial stock that had a return of 12.13%, a beta of .8, and a size of 4.00. (Its market value was $54.6 billion, so $s_i = $ natural logarithm of $54.6 = \ln 54.6 = 4.00$.) According to Equation (A.2), the "normal" return on such a stock is 9.36% [$= (1.20 \times .8) - (.40 \times 4.00 + (10.00 \times 1) + (9.00 \times 0)$]. Thus, for this stock, its "nonfactor return" (ϵ_i) for 1994 was 2.77% ($= 12.13\% - 9.36\%$), suggesting that this particular stock did relatively well in comparison with other stocks having comparable attributes.

Similar analysis can be conducted on a portfolio's return for 1994. Consider a hypothetical portfolio that had a return of 10.03% in 1994. Upon close examination, it has been determined that this portfolio had an average beta of 1.3 and an average size of 3.2 (that is, the average value of s_i for all the stocks held was 3.2). Furthermore, 67% of the stocks in the portfolio were industrials and 33% were nonindustrials. According to Equation (A.2), the normal return on such a portfolio is 9.95% [$= (1.20 \times 1.30) - (.40 \times 3.20) + (10.00 \times .67) + (9.00 \times .33)$]. As the nonfactor return on this portfolio was .08% ($= 10.03\% - 9.95\%$), this portfolio shows little evidence of successful security selection.

Such absolute performance evaluation with a factor model is interesting, but in many cases comparative performance is more relevant. A manager may do poorly in a bad market. But if he or she provides a higher return than would have been obtained otherwise, the client is clearly better off. With comparative performance, the overall return of a portfolio is compared with that of one or more other benchmark portfolios in order to determine the *differences* in the returns. Then the *sources* of the differences can be determined with **comparative performance attribution.**

Assume that the i in Equation (A.1) refers to the portfolio under evaluation. Letting j refer to the return on a benchmark portfolio to which it is to be compared, the difference in their returns for the year is simply $r_i - r_j$. Using Equation (23.28), this difference can be expressed as:

$$r_i - r_j = (\beta_i F_1 + s_i F_2 + c_{i1} SF_1 + c_{i2} SF_2 + \epsilon_i) \tag{A.3}$$
$$- (\beta_j F_1 + s_j F_2 + c_{j1} SF_1 + c_{j2} SF_2 + \epsilon_j).$$

Gathering similar terms, this equation can be rewritten as:

$$r_i - r_j = F_1(\beta_i - \beta_j) + F_2(s_i - s_j) \tag{A.4}$$
$$+ SF_1(c_{i1} - c_{j1}) + SF_2(c_{i2} - c_{j2}) + (\epsilon_i - \epsilon_j).$$

Each of the first four terms represents a differential effect equal to the product of (1) the difference in the attributes of the two portfolios and (2) the actual value of the related factor. The last term in the equation indicates the difference in the nonfactor returns of the two portfolios.

Table 25.3 provides an example where portfolio i is the one mentioned earlier that had a return in 1994 of 10.03%. It is being compared with a benchmark portfolio that had a return in 1994 of 11.21%. This benchmark portfolio had a beta of 1.50 and the average size of the firms whose stocks it held was 1.40. Furthermore, 80% of the portfolio's funds were invested in industrials, with the remaining 20% being invested in nonindustrials. Using Equation (A.2), the normal return on such a portfolio in 1994 was 11.04% $[= (1.20 \times 1.50) - (.40 \times 1.40) + (10.00 \times .80) + (9.00 \times .20)]$, indicating that the portfolio had a nonfactor return of .17% $(= 11.21\% - 11.04\%)$.

A direct comparison of the two portfolios reveals a difference in returns of -1.18% $(r_i - r_j = 10.03\% - 11.21\%)$. That is, portfolio i performed worse than the benchmark by 1.18%. Security selection played a small role because the nonfactor returns were both quite low (.08% for portfolio i and .17% for the benchmark). On balance, sector selection lowered returns for portfolio i relative to the benchmark slightly—the sum of the values in the last column for the two sector-factors was -0.13%. In portfolio i, industrials were underweighted relative to the benchmark, whereas nonindustrials were overweighted. A successful "sector picker" would have placed bets on (that is, overweighted) the sector with a relatively high factor value (industrials) and placed bets against (that is, underweighted) the sector with a relatively low factor value (nonindustrials), leading to a net positive "sector bet effect." In 1994 the investment manager for portfolio i was not a successful sector picker relative to the benchmark.

The major sources of the relatively lower performance of portfolio i were those associated with common factors. The manager had lower-beta stocks than those in the benchmark during a period when high-beta stocks tended to do

TABLE 25.3
COMPARATIVE PERFORMANCE ATTRIBUTION

	Attribute				
	Portfolio i (a)	Portfolio j (b)	Difference (c) = (a) − (b)	Factor (d)	Differential Effect (e) = (c) × (d)
a. Factors:					
Common factors					
Beta	1.30	1.50	−.20	1.20	−.24%
Size	3.20	1.40	1.80	−.40	−.72
Sector-factors					
Industrials	.67	.80	−.13	10.00	−1.30
Nonindustrials	.33	.20	.13	9.00	1.17
					−1.09

	Returns		
	Portfolio i (a)	Portfolio j (b)	Difference (c) = (a) − (b)
b. Returns:			
Factor return	9.95%	11.04%	−1.09%
Nonfactor return	.08	.17	−.09
Total return	10.03	11.21	−1.18

better than low-beta stocks. That is, the manager placed a bet against high-beta stocks in favor of low-beta stocks and lost. He or she also had invested in stocks that were larger than those in the benchmark during a period when larger stocks tended to do poorly. That is, the manager placed a bet against smaller firms in favor of larger firms and lost. Both differences lowered returns relative to the benchmark portfolio, with the "size bet" being more detrimental than the "beta bet."

ENDNOTES

[1] This procedure provides a quarterly return with "quarterly compounding." Alternatively, the semiquarterly return could be doubled, resulting in a quarterly return with "semiquarterly compounding" of -1.96% ($= -.98\% \times 2$).

[2] Sometimes the excess return for a portfolio, which is equal to its return minus the risk-free rate ($= r_{pt} - r_{ft}$), is used instead of r_{pt} in Equation (25.6) to determine the average excess return (denoted aer_p). Then, the summation in the numerator of Equation (25.7) is carried out using $[(r_{pt} - r_{ft}) - aer_p]^2$ instead of $(r_{pt} - ar_p)^2$. The resulting number is the standard deviation of excess returns, which is sometimes used as an estimate of the total risk of the portfolio. Typically, the two standard deviations are quite similar in numerical value.

[3] Equation (25.8) corresponds to the formula for estimating the slope term in a simple regression model where the independent variable is er_{Mt} and the dependent variable is er_{pt}. Sometimes returns are used in Equation (25.8), where er_{Mt} is replaced by r_{Mt} and er_{pt} is replaced by r_{pt}. In this situation, the beta corresponds to the slope term in the *market model* for the portfolio (as discussed in Chapter 8). Typically, the two betas are quite similar in numerical value.

[4] This measure of performance is sometimes known as the *Jensen coefficient* because it was developed by Michael C. Jensen in "The Performance of Mutual Funds in the Period 1945–1964," *Journal of Finance*, 23, no. 2 (May 1968): 389–416.

[5] Alternatively, if *FF*'s average return had been 6%, then its coordinates would have been (1.13, 6.00), placing it above the *ex post* SML. In this situation, *FF*'s *ex post* alpha would have been .78%, and its performance would have been viewed as superior.

[6] An alternative measure of performance involves dividing the *ex post* alpha by an estimate of the *ex post* unique (or unsystematic) risk of the portfolio. This measure, known as the *appraisal (or information) ratio*, would be equal to $-.34$ ($= -1.29/3.75$) for First Fund. Comparisons can be made with the value of the appraisal ratio for the market portfolio (its value is defined to be zero) and other portfolios. Note that a positive value indicates superior performance, and that the larger the value, the better the performance. See Jack L. Treynor and Fischer Black, "How to Use Security Analysis to Improve Portfolio Selection," *Journal of Business*, 46, no. 1 (January 1973): 66–86.

[7] The random error term can be viewed as a number that arises from a spin of a roulette wheel, where the numbers on the wheel are symmetrically distributed around zero. That is, the expected outcome from a spin of the roulette wheel is zero. The standard deviation associated with the wheel is denoted $\sigma_{\epsilon p}$.

[8] This measure of performance is sometimes known as the *Treynor ratio* because it was developed by Jack L. Treynor in "How to Rate Management of Investment Funds," *Harvard Business Review*, 43, no. 1 (January/February 1965): 63–75.

[9] This measure of performance is sometimes known as the *Sharpe ratio* because it was developed by William F. Sharpe in "Mutual Fund Performance," *Journal of Business,* 39, no. 1 (January 1966): 119–138. Chapter 22 mentioned that it is utilized by Morningstar, Inc. in its evaluation of mutual fund performance.

[10] There is a second measure of portfolio performance that is based on the *ex post* CML. This measure, called the *ex post total risk alpha,* is simply the vertical distance the portfolio lies above or below the *ex post* CML. It is similar to the measure referred to earlier as *ex post* alpha, except that it is based on a different risk measure (total risk instead of market risk) and uses a different benchmark (the *ex post* CML instead of the *ex post* SML).

[11] Because the market portfolio does not have any unique risk, it can be shown that if $RVOL_p$ indicates that a portfolio did not perform as well as the market, then $RVAR_p$ must also indicate that the portfolio did not perform as well as the market. This is because a portfolio with a relatively high amount of market risk will also have a relatively high amount of total risk.

[12] The size of parameter c (as well as the parameters a and b) should be judged relative to its standard error. In both of the equations shown here, it is quite small relative to both zero and the respective standard errors. Most standard statistical textbooks have an introductory discussion of the regression procedures that are utilized here. See, for example, Chapters 11 and 12 in James T. McClave and P. George Benson, *Statistics for Business and Economics,* 5th ed. (San Francisco: Dellen Publishing, 1991).

[13] See Richard Roll, "Ambiguity When Performance Is Measured by the Security Market Line," *Journal of Finance,* 33, no. 4 (September 1978): 1051–1069; David Peterson and Michael L. Rice, "A Note on Ambiguity in Portfolio Performance Measures," *Journal of Finance,* 35, no. 5 (December 1980): 1251–1256; and Heinz Zimmermann and Claudia Zogg-Wetter, "On Detecting Selection and Timing Ability: The Case of Stock Market Indexes," *Financial Analysts Journal,* 48, no. 1 (January/February 1992): 80–83.

[14] The problem is much more severe when the index is equal-weighted, because periodically part of the holdings of those stocks that had risen the most would have to be sold and the proceeds invested in additional shares of those stocks that had risen the least in order to keep equal weights in each stock.

[15] With the existence of index funds and index futures (discussed in Chapter 21), this criticism has lost much of its validity.

[16] See Dan W. French and Glenn V. Henderson, Jr., "How Well Does Performance Evaluation Perform?" *Journal of Portfolio Management,* 11, no. 2 (Winter 1985): 15–18.

[17] Under APT (discussed in Chapter 12), there is another measure of portfolio performance that has even more theoretical justification than the APT-based *ex post* alpha. This measure is analogous to the CAPM-based *appraisal ratio* mentioned in Endnote 6 and involves dividing the APT-based *ex post* alpha by the *ex post* standard deviation of the APT-based random error term.

[18] Many of these and other indices are published in *Barron's.* A discussion of various methods of preparing market indices is contained in Chapter 23. For more on bond indices, see John Markese, "The Complexities of Bond Market Indicators," *AAII Journal,* 14, no. 9 (October 1992): 34–36.

[19] As discussed in Chapter 22, this method is used by Morningstar, Inc. in evaluating bond mutual fund performance. It is also used by Christopher R. Blake, Edwin J. Elton, and Martin J. Gruber in "The Performance of Bond Mutual Funds," *Journal of Business,* 66, no. 3 (July 1993): 371–403. These authors also used multiple regression where the excess returns on more than one bond index were the explanatory variables.

[20] See Wayne H. Wagner and Dennis A. Tito, "Definitive New Measures of Bond Performance and Risk," *Pension World*, 13, no. 5 (May 1977): 10 – 12; and "Is Your Bond Manager Skillful?" *Pension World*, 13, no. 6 (June 1977): 9 – 13. Bond portfolio performance evaluation is also discussed in Peter O. Dietz and Jeannette R. Kirschman, "Evaluating Portfolio Performance," Chapter 14 in *Managing Investment Portfolios: A Dynamic Process*, eds. John L. Maginn and Donald L. Tuttle (Boston, MA: Warren, Gorham & Lamont, 1990).

[21] Using the bond market line as a benchmark in this manner is similar to using the SML as a benchmark in evaluating the performance of stock portfolios.

[22] For a discussion of factor models, see Chapter 11 and William F. Sharpe, "Factors in New York Stock Exchange Security Returns, 1931 – 1979," *Journal of Portfolio Management*, 8, no. 4 (Summer 1982): 5 – 18.

KEY TERMS

dollar-weighted return	simple linear regression
time-weighted return	reward-to-volatility ratio
benchmark portfolios	reward-to-variability ratio
ex post alpha	performance attribution
characteristic line	comparative performance attribution

REFERENCES

1. The use of portfolio benchmarks for performance evaluation is discussed in:

Richard Roll, "Performance Evaluation and Benchmark Errors (I)," *Journal of Portfolio Management*, 6, no. 4 (Summer 1980): 5 – 12.

————,"Performance Evaluation and Benchmark Errors (II)," *Journal of Portfolio Management*, 7, no. 2 (Winter 1981): 17 – 22.

Gary P. Brinson, Jeffrey J. Diermeier, and Gary G. Schlarbaum, "A Composite Portfolio Benchmark for Pension Plans," *Financial Analysts Journal*, 42, no. 2 (March/April 1986): 15 – 24.

Mark P. Kritzman, "How to Build a Normal Portfolio in Three Easy Steps," *Journal of Portfolio Management*, 13, no. 4 (Summer 1987): 21 – 23.

Jeffery V. Bailey, Thomas M. Richards, and David E. Tierney, "Benchmark Portfolios and the Manager/Plan Sponsor Relationship," *Journal of Corporate Finance*, 4, no. 4 (Winter 1988): 25 – 32.

Arjun Divecha and Richard C. Grinold, "Normal Portfolios: Issues for Sponsors, Managers, and Consultants," *Financial Analysts Journal*, 45, no. 2 (March/April 1989): 7 – 13.

Edward P. Rennie and Thomas J. Cowhey, "The Successful Use of Benchmark Portfolios: A Case Study," *Financial Analysts Journal*, 46, no. 5 (September/October 1990): 18 – 26.

Jeffery V. Bailey, "Are Manager Universes Acceptable Performance Benchmarks?" *Journal of Portfolio Management,* 18, no. 3 (Spring 1992): 9 – 13.

————,"Evaluating Benchmark Quality," *Financial Analysts Journal,* 48, no. 3 (May/June 1992): 33 – 39.

T. Daniel Coggin, Frank J. Fabozzi and Shafiqur Rahman, "The Investment Performance of U.S. Equity Pension Fund Managers: An Empirical Investigation," *Journal of Finance,* 48, no. 3 (July 1993): 1039 – 1055.

2. The three measures of risk-adjusted performance were initially developed in:

Jack L. Treynor, "How to Rate Management of Investment Funds," *Harvard Business Review,* 43, no. 1 (January/February 1965): 63 – 75.

William F. Sharpe, "Mutual Fund Performance," *Journal of Business,* 39, no. 1 (January 1966): 119 – 138.

Michael C. Jensen, "The Performance of Mutual Funds in the Period 1945 – 1964," *Journal of Finance,* 23, no. 2 (May 1968): 389 – 416.

————,"Risk, the Pricing of Capital Assets, and the Evaluation of Investment Portfolios," *Journal of Business,* 42, no. 2 (April 1969): 167 – 185.

3. More sophisticated measures of portfolio performance that also measure market timing ability were initially developed by:

Jack L. Treynor and Kay K. Mazuy, "Can Mutual Funds Outguess the Market?" *Harvard Business Review,* 44, no. 4 (July/August 1966): 131 – 136.

Robert C. Merton, "On Market Timing and Investment Performance I. An Equilibrium Theory of Value for Market Forecasts," *Journal of Business,* 54, no. 3 (July 1981): 363 – 406.

Roy D. Henriksson and Robert C. Merton, "On Market Timing and Investment Performance II. Statistical Procedures for Evaluating Forecasting Skill," *Journal of Business,* 54, no. 4 (October 1981): 513 – 533.

4. There have been many criticisms leveled at the various measures of portfolio performance that are presented in this chapter. One of the most formidable critiques was:

Richard Roll, "Ambiguity When Performance Is Measured by the Security Market Line," *Journal of Finance,* 33, no. 4 (September 1978): 1051 – 1069.

5. APT-based measures of portfolio performance have been developed by:

Gregory Connor and Robert Korajczyk, "Performance Measurement with the Arbitrage Pricing Theory: A New Framework for Analysis," *Journal of Financial Economics,* 15, no. 3 (March 1986): 373 – 394.

Bruce N. Lehmann and David M. Modest, "Mutual Fund Performance Evaluation: A Comparison of Benchmarks and Benchmark Comparisons," *Journal of Finance,* 42, no. 2 (June 1987): 233 – 265.

Nai-Fu Chen, Thomas E. Copeland, and David Mayers, "A Comparison of Single and Multifactor Portfolio Performance Methodologies," *Journal of Financial and Quantitative Analysis,* 22, no. 4 (December 1987): 401 – 417.

6. Some recent developments in measuring portfolio performance are discussed in:

Stanley J. Kon, "The Market-Timing Performance of Mutual Fund Managers," *Journal of Business,* 56, no. 3 (July 1983): 323 – 347.

Anat R. Admati and Stephen A. Ross, "Measuring Investment Performance in a Rational Expectations Equilibrium Model," *Journal of Business,* 58, no. 1 (January 1985): 1 – 26.

Philip H. Dybvig and Stephen A. Ross, "Differential Information and Performance Measurement Using a Security Market Line," *Journal of Finance,* 40, no. 2 (June 1985): 383 – 399.

————,"The Analytics of Performance Measurement Using a Security Market Line," *Journal of Finance,* 40, no. 2 (June 1985): 401 – 416.

Mark Kritzman, "How to Detect Skill in Management Performance," *Journal of Portfolio Management,* 12, no. 2 (Winter 1986): 16 – 20.

Ravi Jagannathan and Robert A. Korajczyk, "Assessing the Market Timing Performance of Managed Portfolios," *Journal of Business,* 59, no. 2, pt. 1 (April 1986): 217 – 235.

Anat R. Admati, Sudipto Bhattacharya, Paul Pfleiderer, and Stephen A. Ross, "On Timing and Selectivity," *Journal of Finance,* 41, no. 3 (July 1986): 715 – 730.

Gary P. Brinson, L. Randolph Hood, and Gilbert L. Beebower, "Determinants of Portfolio Performance," *Financial Analysts Journal,* 42, no. 4 (July/August 1986): 39 – 44.

William Breen, Ravi Jagannathan, and Aharon R. Ofer, "Correcting for Heteroscedasticity in Tests for Market Timing Ability," *Journal of Business,* 59, no. 4, pt. 1 (October 1986): 585 – 598.

Robert E. Cumby and David M. Modest, "Testing for Market Timing Ability: A Framework for Forecast Evaluation," *Journal of Financial Economics,* 19, no. 1 (September 1987): 169 – 189.

Larry J. Lockwood and K. Rao Kadiyala, "Measuring Investment Performance with a Stochastic Parameter Regression Model," *Journal of Banking and Finance,* 12, no. 3 (September 1988): 457 – 467.

Alex Kane and Gary Marks, "Performance Evaluation of Market Timers: Theory and Evidence," *Journal of Financial and Quantitative Analysis,* 23, no. 4 (December 1988): 425 – 435.

Mark Grinblatt and Sheridan Titman, "Portfolio Performance Evaluation: Old Issues and New Insights," *Review of Financial Studies,* 2, no. 3 (1989): 393 – 421.

Cheng-few Lee and Shafiqur Rahman, "Market Timing, Selectivity, and Mutual Fund Performance: An Empirical Investigation," *Journal of Business,* 63, no. 2 (April 1990): 261 – 278.

Michel Gendron and Christian Genest, "Performance Measurement Under Asymmetric Information and Investment Constraints," *Journal of Finance,* 45, no. 5 (December 1990): 1655 – 1661.

Cheng-few Lee and Shafiqur Rahman, "New Evidence on Timing and Security Selection Skill of Mutual Fund Managers," *Journal of Portfolio Management,* 17, no. 2 (Winter 1991): 80 – 83.

Gary P. Brinson, Brian D. Singer, and Gilbert L. Beebower, "Determinants of Portfolio Performance II: An Update," *Financial Analysts Journal,* 47, no. 3 (May/June 1991): 40 – 48.

Chris R. Hensel, D. Don Ezra, and John H. Ilkiw, "The Importance of the Asset Allocation Decision," *Financial Analysts Journal*, 47, no. 4 (July/August 1991): 65–72.

Eric J. Weigel, "The Performance of Tactical Asset Allocation," *Financial Analysts Journal*, 47, no. 5 (September/October 1991): 63–70.

G. L. Beebower and A. P. Varikooty, "Measuring Market Timing Strategies," *Financial Analysts Journal*, 47, no. 6 (November/December 1991): 78–84, 92.

L. R. Glosten and R. Jagannathan, "A Contingent Claim Approach to Performance Evaluation," *Journal of Empirical Finance*, 1, no. 2 (January 1994): 133–160.

7. An alternative approach to portfolio performance evaluation that is called style analysis is described in:

William F. Sharpe, "Determining a Fund's Effective Asset Mix," *Investment Management Review*, (December 1988): 59–69.

———,"Asset Allocation: Management Style and Performance Measurement," *Journal of Portfolio Management*, 18, no. 2 (Winter 1992): 7–19.

8. Some other major articles on portfolio performance evaluation are listed in:

Gordon J. Alexander and Jack Clark Francis, *Portfolio Analysis* (Englewood Cliffs, NJ: Prentice Hall, 1986), Chapter 13.

Ravi Shukla and Charles Trzcinka, "Performance Measurement of Managed Portfolios," *Financial Markets, Institutions & Instruments*, 1, no. 4 (1992).

9. Bond portfolio performance evaluation is discussed in:

Wayne H. Wagner and Dennis A. Tito, "Definitive New Measures of Bond Performance and Risk," *Pension World*, 13, no. 5 (May 1977): 10–12.

———,"Is Your Bond Manager Skillful?" *Pension World*, 13, no. 6 (June 1977): 9–13.

Peter O. Dietz, H. Russell Fogler, and Donald J. Hardy, "The Challenge of Analyzing Bond Portfolio Returns," *Journal of Portfolio Management*, 6, no. 3 (Spring 1980): 53–58.

Mark Kritzman, "Can Bond Managers Perform Consistently?" *Journal of Portfolio Management*, 9, no. 4 (Summer 1983): 54–56.

Robert N. Anthony, "How to Measure Fixed-Income Performance Correctly," *Journal of Portfolio Management*, 11, no. 2 (Winter 1985): 61–65.

Peter O. Dietz and Jeannette R. Kirschman, "Evaluation Portfolio Performance," Chapter 14 in *Managing Investment Portfolios: A Dynamic Process*, eds. John L. Maginn and Donald L. Tuttle (Boston: Warren, Gorham & Lamont, 1990).

Ronald N. Kahn, "Bond Performance Analysis: A Multi-Factor Approach," *Journal of Portfolio Management*, 18, no. 1 (Fall 1991): 40–47.

Christopher R. Blake, Edwin J. Elton, and Martin J. Gruber in "The Performance of Bond Mutual Funds," *Journal of Business*, 66, no. 3 (July 1993): 371–403.

10. Performance attribution was initially developed and then expanded in:

Eugene F. Fama, "Components of Investment Performance," *Journal of Finance,* 27, no. 3 (June 1972): 551 − 567.

H. Russell Fogler, "Common Stock Management in the 1990s," *Journal of Portfolio Management,* 16, no. 2 (Winter 1990): 26 − 35.

Ernest M. Ankrim, "Risk-Adjusted Performance Attribution," *Financial Analysts Journal,* 48, no. 2 (March/April 1991): 74 − 82.

Peter J. Higgs and Stephen Goode, "Target Active Returns and Attribution Analysis," *Financial Analysts Journal,* 49, no. 3 (May/June 1993): 77 − 80.

Extended Diversification

One of the major themes of modern portfolio theory concerns the merits of diversification: In an efficient capital market, sensible investment strategies will include holdings of many different assets. Previous chapters have considered traditional securities, such as stocks and bonds, and some less traditional ones, such as options and futures. However, an investor should also consider holding foreign securities and tangible assets.

This chapter will discuss these two aspects of diversification, and then turn to a less lofty subject: betting on sporting events. As indicated in previous chapters, active investment management can be considered a form of betting. Now this rather subtle form of wagering that is handled by security brokers and dealers will be compared and contrasted with the more explicit form handled by people at racetracks and by "bookmakers."

26.1 INTERNATIONAL INVESTMENT

If the world were under one political jurisdiction, with one currency and complete freedom of trade, then "the market portfolio" could be thought of as including all securities in the world, each in proportion to its market value. In such a situation, limiting one's investments to securities representing firms located in only one part of the world would most likely result in a relatively low rate of return per unit of risk. After all, few people would advocate that Californians own only securities issued by California firms. And in a world without political boundaries, few people would advocate that Americans own only securities issued by American firms.

Unfortunately, there are political boundaries, different currencies, and restrictions on trade and currency exchange. Such irritants diminish, but do not destroy, the advantages to be gained from international investment.

26.1.1 The Total Investable Capital Market Portfolio

Figure 26.1 provides a 1993 year-end estimate of the size of the total investable capital market portfolio in the world, which can be thought of as representing the set of investments that are available to U.S. portfolio managers. Many problems are encountered in the construction of such a portfolio. It is almost impossible to adequately represent *all* security markets, as undoubtedly certain classes of assets have been omitted (such as foreign real estate) and double counting is involved in that some firms own parts of other firms.[1]

The figure indicates that non-U.S. bond and equity markets amount to $17.8 trillion (= $7.2 + $.7 + $9.9), and comprise about one-half the value of the entire $33.7 trillion portfolio (there are three foreign categories—*Other Equity, Other Bonds,* and *Dollar Bonds;* the latter are foreign and Eurobonds denominated in U.S. dollars). Also of interest is the observation that fixed-income securities amount to $19.7 trillion (= $7.2 + $9.9 + $.7 + $1.6 + $.3), and make up nearly 60% of the portfolio's value.[2] About one-half of this total is non-U.S. fixed-income securities. Similarly, about 60% of the $12.6 trillion (= $5.3 + $7.2 + $.1) equity market consists of non-U.S. stocks.

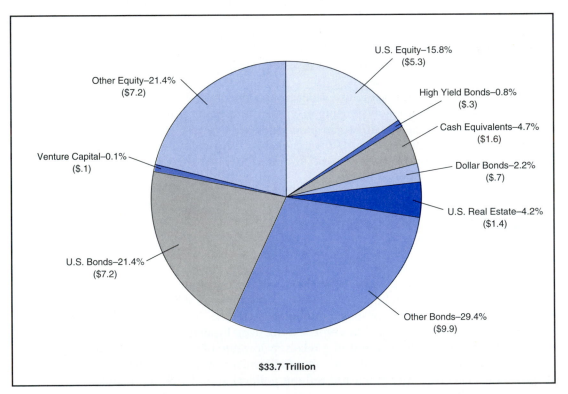

Figure 26.1

Total Investable Capital Market Portfolio, Year-end 1993*

*Preliminary, figures measured in trillions of U.S. dollars.

Source: Provided by Brinson Partners, Inc. (Chicago, 1994).

A more detailed breakdown of the stock market capitalization at the end of April 1994 in the countries followed by *Morgan Stanley Capital International Perspective* is provided in column (2) of Table 26.1. The largest market for common stocks is the United States, followed by Japan. In total, these two countries make up 64.2% of the total. A distant third is the United Kingdom, and then notably behind the United Kingdom come Germany and France. These five countries represent 81.4% of the total. It will be shown next how Morgan Stanley calculates international stock market indices involving these countries.

26.1.2 International Equity Indices

In most countries, there are indices of overall stock values and of the values of stocks within various industry or economic sectors. Such indices can be used for assessing "market moves" within the country and, more importantly, for comparative performance measurement. Important indices include the Financial Times-Stock

TABLE 26.1			
STOCK MARKET CAPITALIZATION, APRIL 1994			
	Market Capitalization		GDP
Country (1)	Dollars* (2)	Percentage (3)	Weight (4)
Austria	$18.1	.2%	1.0%
Belgium	49.9	.7	1.2
Denmark	30.0	.4	.8
Finland	20.4	.3	.8
France	280.3	3.7	7.5
Germany	295.4	3.9	10.8
Ireland	11.4	.2	.3
Italy	122.6	1.6	8.0
Netherlands	145.1	1.9	1.9
Norway	16.9	.2	.6
Spain	84.4	1.1	2.9
Sweden	72.1	1.0	1.4
Switzerland	207.2	2.7	1.4
U.K.	722.7	9.6	4.7
Total Europe	$2,076.3	27.5%	43.2%
Australia	$119.7	1.6	1.7%
Hong Kong	163.3	2.2	.6
Japan	2,142.5	28.4	20.1
Malaysia	105.2	1.4	.5
New Zealand	16.2	.2	.3
Singapore	50.0	.6	.3
Total Pacific	$2,597.0	34.4%	23.4%
Canada	$168.8	2.2	2.8%
U.S.	2,703.6	35.8	30.5
Total North America	$2,872.4	38.0%	33.4%
South Africa Gold Mines	$11.5	.1	0.0%
Total World	$7,557.2	100.0%	100.0%

*Measured in billions of U.S. dollars

Source: Adapted from *Morgan Stanley Capital International Perspective*, May 1994, p. 8.

Exchange 100 Index (often referred to as FT-SE, or the "footsie") for the London Stock Exchange; the Nikkei 225 Average for the Tokyo Stock Exchange; and the TSE 300 Composite Index for the Toronto Stock Exchange. As shown in Figure 26.2(a), these and other indices are published daily in the *Wall Street Journal*.[3]

On the international level, the indices produced by *Morgan Stanley Capital International Perspective* are also widely used for such purposes.[4] Each index is based on a value-weighted portfolio of stocks (using total shares outstanding) in a particular country. Nearly all of these stocks can be purchased by foreigners. Values for each of 22 national indices (plus an index of South African gold mining companies) are given in both the local currency and in U.S. dollars based on exchange rates at the time. Approximately 1,500 stocks are currently included, representing about 60% of the aggregate market value of the 22 covered equity markets.[5] The countries involved are listed in Table 26.1.

The individual country indices are combined into various regional indices. Furthermore, all of the country indices are also used to compute two "World" indices that involve different sets of weights. These weights are based on market capitalization (thus producing a value-weighted index) and gross domestic product (GDP), and are shown in columns (3) and (4) of Table 26.1. Compared with the market capitalization weights, the United States, Japan, and the United Kingdom have lower GDP weights but Germany, France, and Italy have notably larger ones.

(a) Foreign Stock Market Indices

EXCHANGE	12/13/93 CLOSE	NET CHG	PCT CHG
Tokyo Nikkei 225 Average	17327.33 +	69.90	+ 0.41
Tokyo Nikkei 300 Index	270.98 +	0.66	+ 0.24
Tokyo Topix Index	1462.14 +	5.43	+ 0.37
London FT 30-share	2453.3 −	6.3	− 0.26
London 100-share	3254.6 −	6.7	− 0.21
London Gold Mines	257.6 +	10.9	+ 4.42
Frankfurt DAX	2172.75 +	11.62	+ 0.54
Zurich Swiss Market	2876.9 +	15.7	+ 0.55
Paris CAC 40	2196.31 −	1.82	− 0.08
Milan Stock Index	1293 +	12	+ 0.94
Amsterdam ANP-CBS General	270.1 −	0.6	− 0.22
Stockholm Affarsvarlden	1357.8 +	7.2	+ 0.53
Brussels Bel-20 Index	1431.37 +	2.59	+ 0.18
Australia All Ordinaries	2094.5 +	9.6	+ 0.46
Hong Kong Hang Seng	10248.59 +	20.48	+ 0.20
Singapore Straits Times	2245.27 +	24.87	+ 1.12
Johannesburg J'burg Gold	2135 +	85	+ 4.15
Madrid General Index	308.46 +	0.41	+ 0.13
Mexico I.P.C.	2411.61 +	2.26	+ 0.09
Toronto 300 Composite	4293.38 +	13.08	+ 0.31
Euro, Aust, Far East MSCI-p	969.6 +	1.2	+ 0.12

p-Preliminary
na-Not available

(b) Morgan Stanley Indices

	Dec 10	Dec 9	% This Year
U.S.	432.6	432.9	+ 6.4
Britain	992.5	994.7	+ 17.8
Canada	443.1	443.7	+ 18.8
Japan	868.2	858.7	+ 12.7
France	657.9	660.8	+ 22.5
Germany	318.5	319.0	+ 39.5
Hong Kong	7211.3	7040.9	+ 83.8
Switzerland	359.1	358.9	+ 40.7
Australia	433.5	435.7	+ 29.0
World Index	593.8	591.8	+ 19.5

Figure 26.2

International Equity Indices on December 13, 1993

Source: Reprinted from *The Wall Street Journal*, ©Dow Jones & Company, Inc., December 14, 1993, p. C12. All rights reserved worldwide.

Morgan Stanley also calculates the "Europe, Australia, Far East" (EAFE) index, which is widely used by U.S. investors as a benchmark when evaluating the performance of international portfolio managers. The index excludes the United States, Canada, and South Africa and is currently based on the stock performance in the remaining 20 countries listed in Table 26.1 and shown at the bottom of panel (a) of Figure 26.2. Several of the Morgan Stanley individual country indices are published daily in the *Wall Street Journal,* as shown in panel (b) of Figure 26.2, with the World index at the bottom.

In recent years several countries have instituted organized stock exchanges or highly active over-the-counter stock markets. In general, these countries have in common a relatively low (compared to Western countries) level of per capita gross domestic product, improved political and economic stability, a currency convertible into Western countries' currencies (or at least some means for foreigners to repatriate income and capital gains), and most important, securities available for investment by foreigners. Such countries have what are referred to as **emerging markets.**

Investments in emerging market stocks have proven attractive to a number of institutional investors, who in many cases have invested directly in those securities, or when that is not possible, through country funds, (such as the Taiwan Fund; see Chapter 22). Because many emerging market economies are undergoing rapid growth, and because their stock markets are not highly developed and therefore are less efficient, there is considerable opportunity for relatively high returns from emerging market investments. However, there is also a relatively high level of risk involved.

Morgan Stanley Capital International defines 21 countries as emerging markets: India, Indonesia, South Korea, Malaysia, Pakistan, the Philippines, Sri Lanka, Taiwan, Thailand, Argentina, Brazil, Chile, Colombia, Mexico, Peru, Venezuela, Greece, Israel, Jordan, Portugal, and Turkey. They publish stock market indices for each of these countries as well as three regional stock market indices (Asia; Latin America; Europe and Middle East) and an overall emerging markets index.[6] Also popular are the International Financial Corporation (IFC) Emerging Market Indexes and the IFC Investable Indexes. The latter are based on stocks that can be held by foreigners, and hence are often the indices of choice for international investors.

26.1.3 Risk and Return from Foreign Investing

Investing in a foreign security involves all the risks associated with investing in a domestic security plus additional risks. The investor expects to receive cash flows in the future from the foreign security. However, these cash flows will be in a foreign currency and thus will be of relatively little use to the investor if they cannot be converted into the investor's domestic currency. The additional risks associated with foreign investing result from uncertainties associated with converting these foreign cash flows into domestic currency. They are known as **political risk** and **exchange** (or currency) **risk.**[7]

Political risk refers to uncertainty about the *ability* of an investor to convert the foreign currency into domestic currency. Specifically, a foreign government might restrict, tax, or completely prohibit the exchange of one currency for another. Because such policies change from time to time, the ability of an investor to repatriate foreign cash flows may be subject to some uncertainty.

There may even be a possibility of complete expropriation, making the political risk very large.

Exchange risk refers to uncertainty about the *rate* at which a foreign currency can be exchanged for the investor's domestic currency in the future. That is, at the time a foreign security is bought, the rate at which future foreign cash flows can be converted into domestic currency is uncertain, and it is this uncertainty that is known as exchange risk.

Hedging Exchange Risk

To an extent, exchange risk can be reduced by hedging in the forward (or futures) market for foreign currency. In the case of default-free fixed-income securities, it may be possible to completely eliminate such risk in this way. For example, assume that a one-year pure discount bond paying 1,000 British pounds at maturity can be purchased for 850 British pounds. Furthermore, assume that a forward contract can be signed where the investor will receive $1,300 for delivering 1,000 British pounds a year from now. In this situation, the rate of return *in British pounds* on this security is 17.65% [= (1,000 − 850)/850].

If the current (that is, spot) exchange rate were $1.35 per pound, then the cost of this bond to an American investor would be $1,147.50 (= 850 × $1.35). Thus the rate of return *in American dollars* on this British security would be 13.29% [= ($1,300 − $1,147.50)/$1,147.50]. Except for political risk, this is a certain return, as exchange risk has been completely removed by hedging with a forward contract.

Unfortunately, it is not possible to completely hedge the exchange risk associated with risky investments. Forward contracts can be made to cover expected cash flows, but if the actual cash flows are larger or smaller than expected, then some of the foreign currency may have to be exchanged at the spot rate prevailing at the time that the cash is received. Because future spot rates usually cannot be predicted with complete certainty, this will affect overall risk. As a practical matter, this "unhedgeable" risk is likely to be small. Nevertheless, the cost of hedging foreign investments may exceed the benefit (see the *Institutional Issues* section "Currency Risk: To Hedge or Not to Hedge").

Foreign and Domestic Returns

Changes in exchange rates can cause major differences between the returns obtained by domestic investors and the returns obtained by unhedged foreign investors.

Consider an American investor and a Swiss investor, both of whom purchase shares of a Swiss company whose stock is traded only in Switzerland. Let the price of the stock in Swiss francs be P_0 at the beginning of a period and P_1 at the end of the period. The **domestic return,** denoted r_d, is:

$$r_d = \frac{P_1 - P_0}{P_0}. \tag{26.1}$$

For example, if $P_0 = 10$ Swiss francs and $P_1 = 12$ Swiss francs, then $r_d = 20\%$ [= (12 − 10)/10].

For the Swiss investor, r_d is the stock's return. Not so for the U.S. investor. Assume that at the beginning of the period the price (in dollars) of one Swiss franc is $.50. Denoting this exchange rate (that is, the exchange rate at the beginning of the period) as X_0, the cost of a share to the American investor will be $X_0 P_0$. In the example, this cost will be $5 (= $.50 \times 10$).

Now assume that the exchange rate rises to $.55 per Swiss franc at the end of the period. Denoting this by X_1, the ending value of the stock for the American investor will be $X_1 P_1$. In the example, this value will be $6.60 (= $.55 \times 12$).

The **foreign return** (that is, the return to a foreign investor), denoted r_f, is:

$$r_f = \frac{X_1 P_1 - X_0 P_0}{X_0 P_0}. \tag{26.2}$$

In the example, the foreign investor (an American) would have earned a return of $r_f = 32\% \, [= (\$6.60 - \$5.00)/\$5.00]$ on an investment in the Swiss firm's stock.

In effect, the American made *two* investments: (1) an investment in a Swiss stock, and (2) an investment in the Swiss franc. Accordingly, the overall return to the American can be decomposed into a return on the investment in the Swiss stock and a return on the investment in the Swiss franc. This can be illustrated by considering an American who had purchased a Swiss franc at the beginning of the period. If the American subsequently sold the franc at the end of the period, the return on foreign currency, denoted r_c, would be:

$$r_c = \frac{X_1 - X_0}{X_0}. \tag{26.3}$$

In the example, $r_c = 10\% \, [= (\$.55 - \$.50)/\$.50]$.

From Equations (26.1), (26.2), and (26.3), it can be shown that:

$$1 + r_f = (1 + r_d)(1 + r_c) \tag{26.4}$$

which can be rewritten as:

$$r_f = r_d + r_c + r_d r_c. \tag{26.5}$$

In the example, Equation (26.5) reveals that $r_f = 32\% \, [= .20 + .10 + (.20 \times .10)]$.

The last term in this equation $(r_d r_c)$ will generally be smaller than the two preceding ones because it equals their product, and both are generally less than 1.0. Thus Equation (26.5) can be restated as an approximation:

$$r_f \cong r_d + r_c. \tag{26.6}$$

It can now be seen that the return on a foreign security (r_f) can be decomposed into two parts, representing the domestic return on the security (r_d) and the return on foreign currency (r_c). In the example, the precise value for r_f was shown earlier to be 32%. Use of the approximation indicates its value to be equal to 30% (= .20 + .10). Thus the approximation is in error by 2%, a relatively small amount.

Expected Returns

Equation (26.6) leads directly to the proposition that the expected return on a foreign security will approximately equal the expected domestic return plus the expected return on foreign currency:

$$\bar{r}_f \cong \bar{r}_d + \bar{r}_c. \qquad (26.7)$$

It might be tempting for an investor to purchase a foreign security that has a high expected return in its host country on the belief that this means that the security will have a high expected return to the foreign investor. However, Equation (26.7) reveals this type of logic to be flawed. Just because a foreign security has a high value for r_d does not mean that it has a high value for r_f, because r_c can be negative. This can be shown by considering the case of bonds.

The expected domestic returns of bonds in countries with high expected inflation rates will typically be high. However, a foreign investor in a country with a lower expected inflation rate should expect a *negative* return on foreign currency, as his or her currency can be expected to *appreciate* relative to that of the country with the higher expected inflation rate. Thus in evaluating the expected return on the foreign security, there is good news (a high expected domestic return r_d) and bad news (a negative expected return on foreign currency r_c). On balance, the expected foreign return r_f might not be as exceptional as first thought when just r_d was considered. Indeed, if markets were completely integrated, it would be reasonable to expect the values of r_d and r_c to sum to an amount r_f that is equal to the expected return on an equivalent bond in the investor's own country.

Columns (2) and (3) of Table 26.2(a) indicate what the average excess returns (that is, returns over the London Interbank Offered Rate, an estimate of the riskfree rate) were for the stocks and bonds of six countries as well as the United States for the 200–month period ending August 1991. These averages were measured from the perspective of a U.S. investor, and hence represent the historical average value of r_f. The table indicates that while the stock and bond averages for the six countries are very similar to the U.S. averages, there are some notable differences among individual countries. For both stocks and bonds, the Canadian market had an average return that was much lower than the U.S. average, while the U.K. and Japanese averages were notably higher.[8]

Foreign and Domestic Risks

Having seen in Equation (26.7) that the expected return on a foreign security consists of two components, it is appropriate that the risk of the foreign security be evaluated next. As before, consider an American investor and a Swiss investor who have purchased shares of a Swiss company. The domestic variance, denoted σ_d^2, is the risk that the Swiss investor faces with respect to the Swiss stock. Correspondingly, the foreign variance, denoted σ_f^2, is the risk that the American investor faces with respect to the Swiss stock. Based on Equation (26.6), it can be shown that the foreign variance consists of three components:

$$\sigma_f^2 = \sigma_d^2 + \sigma_c^2 + 2\rho_{dc}\sigma_d\sigma_c \qquad (26.8)$$

where σ_c^2 is the variance associated with the currency return to an American from investing in Swiss francs and later exchanging them for American dollars, and ρ_{dc} is the correlation coefficient between the return on the Swiss stock and the return on Swiss francs.

For example, assume that the domestic variance is 225 (meaning that the domestic standard deviation, σ_d, is $\sqrt{225}$ or 15%) and the currency variance is

TABLE 26.2

SECURITY RETURNS, JANUARY 1975–AUGUST 1991*

(a) Excess Returns and Standard Deviations:

Country (1)	Average Excess Returns		Standard Deviation	
	Stocks (2)	Bonds (3)	Stocks (4)	Bonds (5)
Australia	4.5%	− .8%	21.9%	5.5%
Canada	.9	− 1.5	18.3	7.8
France	4.8	− .1	22.2	4.5
Germany	4.7	.9	18.3	4.5
Japan	7.3	2.1	17.8	6.5
U.K.	8.6	1.2	24.7	9.9
U.S.	5.2	− .3	16.1	6.8
Average (ex. U.S.)	5.1%	.3%	20.5%	6.4%
Average	5.1	.2	19.9	6.5

(b) Correlations with U.S. Stocks and Bonds:**

Country (1)	U.S. Stocks with Foreign		U.S. Bonds with Foreign	
	Stocks (2)	Bonds (3)	Stocks (4)	Bonds (5)
Australia	.48	.24	− .05	.20
Canada	.74	.31	.18	.82
France	.50	.21	.20	.31
Germany	.43	.23	.17	.50
Japan	.41	.12	.11	.28
U.K.	.58	.23	.12	.28
Average	.52	.22	.12	.40

*Results are given from U.S. investor perspective and are in excess of the London Interbank Offered Rate (LIBOR).

**Correlation of U.S. stocks with U.S. bonds was .32.

Source: Adapted from Fischer Black and Robert Litterman, "Global Portfolio Optimization," *Financial Analysts Journal*, 48, no. 5 (September/October 1992): pp. 30–31.

25 (meaning that the currency standard deviation, σ_c, is $\sqrt{25}$ or 5%). If $\rho_{dc} = 0$, then Equation (26.8) indicates that the foreign variance is 250 (= 225 + 25). Accordingly, the foreign standard deviation is 15.8% (= $\sqrt{250}$), which is only slightly greater than the domestic standard deviation of 15%.

Equation (26.8) reveals that the smaller the correlation between returns on a foreign currency and returns on a foreign investment, the smaller will be the foreign variance.[9] One study that used data from seventeen countries over the period from January 1971 through December 1980 found an average correlation of .034, which is effectively zero.[10] Thus it appears that the correlation is sufficiently small that the foreign variance will typically be near, but not less than, the sum of the domestic and currency variances.[11] However, it should be remembered that this is an *average figure*, and that there can be individual situations where the correlation is not approximately zero (such as the United States and Canada).

Columns (3) and (4) of Table 26.2(a) provide the standard deviations of the excess returns for six foreign countries along with the United States from the perspective of a U.S. investor. Hence it provides estimates of the value of σ_f for the 200–month period ending in August 1991. The six-country average standard deviation for both stocks and bonds is similar to the respective U.S. values, with the United Kingdom having notably larger values for both stocks and bonds.

Table 26.3 provides evidence on the relative magnitudes of the three types of risk. Standard deviations of monthly values over the period from December 1970 through December 1980 are shown for domestic risk (corresponding to σ_d), currency risk (corresponding to σ_c), and foreign risk (corresponding to σ_f), where the latter two types of risk have been measured from the perspective of an American investor. The last column represents the ratio of foreign risk to domestic risk. Thus a ratio greater than one can be taken as an indication that the risk to an American investor is greater than the risk to a domestic investor. Indeed, with the exception of Hong Kong stocks, all the ratios are greater than one, suggesting that fluctuations in currency exchange rates increased the risk an American investor would have faced in buying foreign securities.

TABLE 26.3

RISKS FOR DOMESTIC AND U.S. INVESTORS BASED ON HISTORICAL VALUES, DECEMBER 1970–DECEMBER 1980

	(1) Domestic Risk	(2) Currency Risk	(3) Foreign Risk	(4) Foreign/ Domestic Risk
Stocks				
Australia	24.62%	9.15%	27.15%	1.10
Belgium	13.28	11.02	18.76	1.41
Canada	18.92	4.16	20.29	1.07
Denmark	15.41	10.28	17.65	1.15
France	22.00	10.24	25.81	1.17
Germany	13.87	11.87	18.39	1.33
Hong Kong	47.95	5.63	45.80	.96
Italy	24.21	8.58	26.15	1.08
Japan	16.39	10.42	19.55	1.19
Netherlands	16.37	10.97	18.91	1.16
Norway	28.61	8.89	29.92	1.05
Singapore	35.82	6.52	36.03	1.01
Spain	16.71	9.10	20.26	1.21
Sweden	15.05	8.89	18.06	1.20
Switzerland	16.80	14.67	21.40	1.27
U.K.	28.94	8.84	31.61	1.09
U.S.	16.00	.00	16.00	1.00
Bonds				
Canada	6.16	4.16	7.93	1.29
France	4.39	10.24	11.80	2.69
Germany	6.91	11.87	14.35	2.08
Japan	6.53	10.42	14.36	2.20
Netherlands	7.16	10.97	13.61	1.90
Switzerland	4.33	14.67	15.33	3.54
U.K.	12.30	8.84	16.29	1.32
U.S.	8.96	.00	8.96	1.00

Source: Adapted from Bruno Solnik and Bernard Noetzlin, "Optimal International Asset Allocation," *Journal of Portfolio Management,* 9, no. 1 (Fall 1982): p. 13.

The importance of currency risk can easily be exaggerated. Calculations such as those in Table 26.3 assume that investors purchase only domestic goods and services and thus convert all proceeds from foreign investments into their own currency before engaging in any spending for consumption purposes. But most people buy foreign goods and many buy foreign services as well (for example, as tourists). The cheaper another country's currency relative to one's own, the more attractive purchases of its goods and services will be. Other things being equal, it may make sense to invest more in countries whose products and scenery are admired, for the effective currency risk is likely to be smaller there than elsewhere.

26.1.4 Multinational Firms

Firms operating in many countries provide international diversification at the corporate level. One might expect that investment in the stocks of such **multinational firms** could serve as a good substitute for investment in stocks of foreign ("national") firms.

A number of studies have shown that this may not be the case. In one, returns on portfolios of stocks of multinational firms headquartered in each of nine countries were calculated for the period from April 1966 through June 1974. Then each portfolio's returns were compared with the returns on the market index for the country of its headquarters. The middle column in Table 26.4 shows the proportion of each portfolio's variance that can be attributed to movements in its corresponding "domestic" market index. Finally, each portfolio's returns were compared with the returns on market indices in all nine countries. The final column in Table 26.4 shows the proportion of each portfolio's variance that can be attributed to movements in its domestic market index as well as the foreign market indices.

TABLE 26.4

PROPORTIONS OF RETURNS ON STOCKS OF MULTINATIONAL FIRMS EXPLAINED BY STOCK MARKET INDICES

Headquarters Country of Multinational Firms	Proportion of Variance in Returns Explained by	
	Domestic Market Index	Domestic and Other Market Indices
Belgium	45%	58%
France	45	62
Germany	65	74
Italy	47	51
Netherlands	50	63
Sweden	42	50
Switzerland	52	75
U.K.	44	49
U.S.	29	31

Source: Adapted from Bertrand Jacquillat and Bruno Solnik, "Multinationals Are Poor Tools for Diversification," *Journal of Portfolio Management*, 4, no. 2 (Winter 1978): p. 10.

Currency Risk: To Hedge or Not to Hedge

Investors in securities denominated in currencies other than those of their home country incur a risk not borne by their domestic investor counterparts: currency risk. For investors in foreign assets, currency risk is the variability in portfolio returns caused by fluctuations in the rate at which foreign currencies can be converted into their home currency. Whether investors in foreign securities should attempt to minimize currency risk in their portfolios has become a topic of considerable controversy in recent years. Among institutional investors, the issue has taken on increased importance as these investors have expanded their foreign investments.

As the text describes, the return on an investor's foreign portfolio can be divided into two components: a domestic (also called local) return and a currency (also called foreign exchange) return. Likewise, foreign portfolio risk can be decomposed into domestic risk, currency risk, and any possible interaction between the two. Most studies indicate that currency risk can increase total portfolio risk by anywhere from 15% to 100% of the underlying domestic risk.

Investors have a choice of whether to bear currency risk. Through a variety of techniques, currency risk can be "hedged" and almost eliminated. The most popular means of hedging currency risk is to purchase units of the investor's home currency in the forward market equal to the value of the foreign investment. For example, consider a U.S. investor holding 1,000 shares of a Japanese company selling for 4,000 yen per share. He or she can purchase dollars for delivery six months from today at a rate of 125 yen per dollar. (The forward market is quite similar to the futures market—see Chapter 21. Both forward and futures contracts involve a promise to deliver something of value on a specified future date at a currently agreed-upon price. The forward market, however, does not involve a standardized contract traded on an organized exchange with a third-party clearinghouse that ensures that contracts are honored. Moreover, forward contracts, unlike futures contracts, are not "marked to market" daily.) By purchasing $32,000 for delivery six months from today to be paid for with 4 million yen, the investor insulates himself or herself from changes in the exchange rate between the yen and the dollar over the next six months.

Despite the availability of effective hedging tools, why do many investors in foreign securities choose not to hedge their currency risks and instead remain exposed to exchange rate fluctuations? Considered next are the primary arguments in support of and in opposition to currency risk hedging.

Proponents of hedging currency risk contend that a no-hedge policy violates one of the basic laws of modern portfolio theory: Only accept risks for which adequate compensation is expected to be earned. They view currencies as having zero expected returns. That is, in a world in which capital is free to flow across borders, there is no reason to expect the value of foreign currencies to move systematically in one direction relative to an investor's home currency. However, exchange rates do fluctuate, generating additional risk for an investor in foreign securities. Proponents view currency risk as uncompensated and believe that risk-averse investors should seek its minimization. Investors who do not hedge would seem to be passing up an opportunity to reduce portfolio risk while not diminishing portfolio returns. Proponents point out that the reduction in portfolio variability gained by hedging currency risk can be substantial.

Opponents of currency hedging generally concede that forgoing hedging means accepting additional uncompensated risks. (However, there is a school of thought that contends that currency risk should be systematically rewarded by the market.) Nevertheless, they believe that market "frictions" cause the costs of currency hedging to outweigh the risk reduction benefits. That is, significant expenses are likely to be incurred by an investor managing currency risk. Currency dealers must be compensated for facilitating hedging transactions. Custodian banks must be paid for record keeping. Investment managers charge fees for maintaining the hedge. Estimates of the total cost of hedging typically range from .25% to .50% per year of the value of the hedged assets, enough to convince opponents that currency risk hedging may not be cost-effective.

In addition, some hedging opponents have questioned the wisdom of hedging for an investor who spends a high percentage of his or her income on goods produced abroad. Suppose the value of foreign currencies declines relative to the investor's home currency (thereby negatively affecting the investor's foreign portfolio returns, other things being equal). The declining relative value of the foreign currencies also reduces the effective cost of foreign-produced goods to the investor. In a sense the investor's own consumption basket serves as a hedge against currency risk in his or her portfolio.

In the final analysis, an investor's optimal currency hedge will depend on a number of factors, including the following:

1. correlations between currencies,
2. correlations between domestic returns and currency returns,
3. the cost of hedging,
4. the portions of the investor's portfolio allocated to foreign securities,
5. the variability of foreign asset returns,
6. the variability of currency returns,
7. the investor's consumption basket,
8. the investor's level of risk aversion, and
9. the premium earned (if any) for holding foreign currencies.

These factors are difficult to quantify, making it hard to build a strong case for or against currency hedging. Moreover, as investors differ in both their financial circumstances and their beliefs about the characteristics of currencies and security markets, it is not surprising that everything from zero hedges to fully hedged positions is observed.

During the period covered in Table 26.4, the returns on multinational firms based in the United States had only 2% (= 31% − 29%) of their variance that could be attributed to foreign market indices. This suggests that U.S.-headquartered multinationals were a poor substitute for direct investment in foreign stocks by U.S. investors.[12] The situation was somewhat better for non-U.S. multinationals because the differences in the percentages shown in the two columns were greater than 2%. One possible explanation for this is that non-U.S. multinationals have more extensive foreign operations than U.S. multinationals.

26.1.5 International Listings

The common stocks of many firms are traded not only on the major stock exchange in their home country but also on an exchange in a foreign country. For this reason foreign investors no longer have to engage in foreign currency transactions when buying and selling the firm's stock. It is also possible that foreign investors can escape certain taxes and regulations to which they would be subject if the security were to be bought in the firm's home country. As mentioned in Chapter 3, there are two ways that such internationally listed foreign securities can be traded in the United States, They involve the use of ordinary shares and American Depository Receipts (ADRs).

The first way foreign securities may be traded in the United States is for the shares of the firm to be traded directly, just like the shares of a typical U.S. firm. Generally Canadian firms are traded in this manner in the U.S.—at year-end 1993, none of the 28 Canadian firms that had their stock listed on the NYSE involved ADRs. Stocks traded in this form are referred to as *ordinary shares* or simply *ordinaries.*

The second way foreign securities may be traded in the United States is with **American Depository Receipts** (ADRs).[13] ADRs are financial assets that are issued by U.S. banks and represent indirect ownership of a certain number of shares of a specific foreign firm that are held on deposit in a bank in the firm's home country. The advantage of ADRs over direct ownership is that the investor need not worry about the delivery of the stock certificates or converting dividend payments from a foreign currency into U.S. dollars. The depository bank automatically does the converting for the investor and also forwards all financial reports from the firm. The investor pays the bank a relatively small fee for these services. Typically non-Canadian firms utilize ADRs. For example, Mexican firms are traded in this manner in the United States—at year-end 1993, all 13 Mexican firms with their stock listed on the NYSE utilized ADRs.

Table 26.5 displays the extent of foreign stock listings in the United States at year-end 1993. As the table shows, over 500 foreign firms had stock issues listed on either the NYSE, AMEX, or Nasdaq, and nearly 40% of them were in the form of ADRs. Interestingly, the NYSE has nearly 70% of its foreign issuers utilizing ADRs, whereas for Nasdaq the percentage is about half of this amount, due in large part to the over 100 Canadian firms that are traded on Nasdaq without the use of ADRs.

One study that examined the diversification implications of investing in ADRs found that such securities were of notable benefit to U.S. investors.[14] Specifically, a sample of 45 ADRs was examined and compared with a sample of 45 U.S. securities over the period from 1973 to 1983. Using an index based on all NYSE-listed stocks, the betas of the ADRs had an average value of .26, which was much lower than the average beta of 1.01 for the U.S. securities. Furthermore, the correlation of the ADRs' returns with those of the NYSE market portfolio averaged .33, whereas U.S. securities had a notably higher average correlation of .53.

Given these two observations, it is not surprising that portfolios formed from U.S. securities and ADRs had much lower standard deviations than portfolios consisting of just U.S. securities. For example, portfolios consisting of 10 U.S. securities had an average monthly standard deviation of 5.50%, whereas a 10-security portfolio split evenly between U.S. securities and ADRs had an average monthly standard deviation of 4.41%. Thus in contrast to investing in multinationals, it seems that investing in ADRs brings significant benefits in terms of risk reduction.

TABLE 26.5
FOREIGN COMPANY LISTINGS IN THE UNITED STATES, YEAR-END 1993

	Number of Companies	ADR Issuers	
		Number	Percent
NYSE	159	108	67.9%
AMEX	74	8	10.8
Nasdaq	303	97	32.0
Total	536	213	39.7%

Source: *1994 NASDAQ Fact Book & Company Directory* (Washington, DC: National Association of Security Dealers, 1994): p. 28.

The SEC currently requires that foreign firms prepare their financial statements using U.S. generally accepted accounting principles (GAAP) if they want their shares or ADRs to be listed on a U.S. exchange or on Nasdaq. There are two consequences of this requirement. First, many foreign firms have their shares and ADRs traded in the part of the over-the-counter market that does not involve Nasdaq.[15] Second, many large and actively traded foreign firms have decided against listing their shares in the United States. This has caused U.S. exchanges to fear that certain foreign exchanges which do not have such reporting requirements (particularly London) will become the financial centers of the world in the future. In response to the complaints of the exchanges, the SEC argues that this requirement is necessary to protect U.S. investors and that it would be patently unfair to U.S. firms if they had to meet such requirements but their foreign competitors did not have to do so. One thing is certain—this conflict between the exchanges and the SEC will not go away.[16]

26.1.6 Correlations between Markets

If all economies were tied together completely, stock markets in different countries would move together, and little advantage could be gained through international diversification. However this is not the case. Table 26.2(b) shows the correlations of returns on stocks and bonds in six countries with the returns of stocks and bonds in the United States. There are three general observations to be made:

1. With the exception of Canada, the correlations of foreign stocks with U.S. stocks are less than .60; see column (2).[17] This, along with the results in panel (a), suggests that there are sizable potential diversification advantages to a U.S. stock investor of investing in the stocks of these five countries.

2. Similarly, the correlations of foreign bonds with U.S. bonds are .50 or less with the exception of Canadian bonds; see column (5).[18] Again, this observation, combined with the observations in panel (a), suggests that there are sizable potential diversification advantages to a U.S. bond investor of investing in the bonds of these five countries.

3. The correlations of foreign bonds with U.S. stocks—column (3)—and the correlations of foreign stocks with U.S. bonds—column (4)—are all less than roughly .30. Once again, there are sizable potential advantages to diversification—but now the advantages are in diversifying both across asset classes and across countries. That is, a U.S. stock investor would find it advantageous to buy foreign bonds, and a U.S. bond investor would find it advantageous to buy foreign stocks.

The bottom line is that international diversification is beneficial. Investors can either increase their expected return without increasing their risk or decrease their risk without decreasing their expected return by judiciously adding foreign securities to their portfolios.[19]

Investing in the PRC

by Ann Guenther Sherman
Hong Kong University of Science and Technology

Companies in the communist People's Republic of China (PRC) are very different from those of capitalist countries. Almost all large firms are State-Owned Enterprises (SOEs) and must return reported "profits" to the government each year. On the other hand, any losses can be covered by "loans" from the state-owned banks, which do not have to be repaid. Few incentives exist to promote efficiency and economic growth.

Recently, there have been moves toward a new system in the PRC. The government has put forth a new model that will allow an unprecedented degree of separation of ownership and control. Unless there is another major policy shift in the People's Republic, most large enterprises will eventually be privatized. Through privatization the government hopes to raise funds for new investment and to transform management by using markets both to allocate capital efficiently and to give companies the right incentives.

The privatization of SOEs offers foreign investors potentially lucrative opportunities to participate in the rapid growth of the PRC's economy. With those opportunities, however, comes considerable risk due to the uncertain standing of shareholders in the PRC's "socialist market system."

Several ways already exist for a PRC company to acquire capital. Joint ventures allow an SOE to raise funds through a subsidiary in order to take on a new project and are common. However, they are not methods for transforming existing SOEs, as they usually involve creating a new firm. Another popular method has been a "back door listing" on the Stock Exchange of Hong Kong (SEHK). PRC firms have been buying controlling interests in small, thinly traded shell companies already listed on this exchange. The PRC parent can then issue new shares or debt through the subsidiary in order to raise funds.

A third way in which a PRC company can raise funds is through an *A* or *B* share listing on one of the country's two stock exchanges, located in Shanghai and Shenzhen. Shanghai is a traditional business center for China, and Shenzhen is in Guangdong province, bordering Hong Kong. The southern part of the PRC, particularly Guangdong, has shown the most rapid economic development so far, due to the close proximity to Hong Kong and also perhaps to the great distance from Beijing (because it is easier to allow experimentation in remote provinces).

For a PRC company to be listed on any stock exchange (local or foreign), it must first become a stock company, which is defined as an enterprise with legal person status that divides its capital into equal shares. Currently, equity in a stock company must be divided into four categories: state shares (purchased with state assets by government departments), legal person shares (held by a PRC "legal person," or corporation), individual shares (purchased by a PRC citizen), and foreign investment shares (purchased by foreigners). The first three categories are collectively known as *A* shares, while the last category, shares held by foreign parties, are known as *B* shares. Because each type of share has a separate legal status, there is a potential for discrimination—state shares may be treated better than individual shares, or *A* shareholders may be favored over *B* shareholders. Prices, therefore, vary widely across the different share types.

Listing standards for *A* and *B* shares on the Shanghai and Shenzhen stock exchanges are noticeably lower than for reputable foreign stock exchanges. The company must be of "reasonable quality" and have good prospects for earnings growth, but responsibilities to shareholders are weak at best. For instance, *B* share firms have disclosed financial performance figures to analysts before revealing them to shareholders and failed to comply with disclosure obligations. Moreover, in direct contradiction to the plans outlined in prospectuses, a large portion of the funds raised so far have been used for property speculation. Nevertheless, *A* shares have been popular with PRC investors, who have high saving rates and very few investment choices. Not surprisingly, *B* shares have been much less successful, selling at a considerable discount to *A* shares and suffering from a lack of liquidity.

A more prestigious funding choice for eligible firms is an *H* share listing. *H* shares are shares that may be purchased and traded in a foreign currency only by non-PRC residents. In 1992, nine companies were selected by the PRC government to issue *H* shares listed on the SEHK, and six of them had completed their listings by December 1993, with the others expected to list in early 1994. In addition, a few PRC companies are currently traded as American Depository Receipts (ADRs) on the U.S. market (examples are Brillance Automotive and Shanghai Petrochemical). Another group of companies has been selected for the next set of Hong Kong listings, and firms are also seeking to list on the New York, Singapore, Taiwan, and Vancouver exchanges. All of these fall into the category of *H* shares, although the term "H share" has so far been thought to signify a Hong Kong listing (since most H shares so far have been listed in Hong Kong), while the U.S. listings have been known as ADRs.

Although the SEHK has worked hard to attract listings from the PRC, it has also been careful not to lose the reputation that it has worked so hard to build. It has attempted to develop criteria for *H* share listings that offer some protection to investors and do not significantly lower the standards of the exchange. These listing requirements include:

- Three years of audited accounts conducted according to either Hong Kong or international standards. (This requirement makes the listing of PRC companies a lengthy process, as those companies have never been audited to outside standards by an independent auditor.)
- Two independent nonexecutive (outside) directors.
- Minimum market capitalization of HK$50 million (about US$6 million).

- Dividends paid in Hong Kong currency and based on market exchange rates.
- At least 10% public ownership of *H* shares and 25% public ownership of total equity held as *A* and *H* shares.
- Retention of a sponsor or other professional advisor acceptable to the SEHK for at least three years. (The sponsor advises the firm as to its responsibilities to shareholders and makes sure that it fulfills all listing requirements.)
- Inclusion of certain provisions in the firm's articles of association. (These provisions are intended to replace the legal protections normally provided to investors in Hong Kong stock issues.)

In addition to these listing requirements, there are many other adjustments for PRC firms wanting to list in Hong Kong. One problem is that many SOEs have several operating units, and it is difficult to decide which should be included in the public company. For instance, PRC firms in the past have been responsible for providing housing, medical care, education, and pensions to workers and their families, all operations that do not generate revenues. Changing accounting standards is another major adjustment. For example, PRC accounting methods do not recognize "prudence concepts," such as making provisions for bad debts or writing off obsolete inventory. Finally, one of the biggest adjustments is in the attitude of managers toward stockholders. It is very difficult to convince PRC managers that they have duties to shareholders, such as an obligation to use funds in the way that they have promised to use them. The question of dividend policy has not arisen so far, since most of these firms are in a phase of rapid expansion, but it is a potential problem for the future. Most PRC managers today would consider it foolish to take their own (that is, the firm's) money and give it to strangers (that is, shareholders).

In addition to these sources of equity financing, a developing bond market exists in the PRC. There have been some major defaults already, and most bonds pay very high interest rates. Bonds of PRC companies would be considered "junk" in the United States, but PRC investors have few investment choices and are happy to get another option. There has also been a recent trend for listed PRC companies to issue convertible bonds in Europe or the United States, but foreign debt issues are unlikely to be a funding source for unlisted firms.

Finally, the PRC has two nationwide quotation systems, the Securities Trading Automated Quotations (STAQ) and the National Electronic Trading System (NETS), giving firms yet another potential funding alternative for the future, although currently only stocks already listed on one of the two exchanges can trade on the quotation systems. NETS promises to become a PRC version of the United States's Nasdaq, although 6 of its 13 stocks were suspended by the end of 1993 due to the lack of laws to guide trading.

26.2 ， TANGIBLE ASSETS

In the first half of the 1970s, marketable securities such as stocks and bonds provided returns that were relatively disappointing, especially after adjusting for inflation. And, as shown in Chapter 13, neither bonds nor stocks have served as good hedges against unanticipated inflation in recent years. Overall, tangible assets have been better hedges against inflation. One example, real estate, was shown in Chapter 13 to have been an attractive inflation hedge in recent years.[20] Other examples, such as collectible assets and precious metals (for instance, gold and silver), provide various degrees of protection against inflation.

26.2.1 Collectible Assets

Not surprisingly, periodic disenchantment with returns on marketable securities has led some investors to examine a host of tangible assets that are normally considered only by "collectors." Table 26.6 shows the average returns over three five-year periods for several different kinds of collectible assets (often referred to as simply *collectibles*).

TABLE 26.6		
ANNUAL RETURNS ON COLLECTIBLE ASSETS,		
FIVE-YEAR PERIODS ENDING JUNE 1		
1969–1974	**1974–1979**	**1979–1984**
Chinese ceramics 31.1%	−3.1%	15.7%
Coins 9.5	32.4	11.3
Diamonds 11.6	13.6	6.1
Old masters 7.3	17.3	1.5
U.S. stamps 14.1	24.9	9.8

Source: Based on data in R. S. Salomon, Jr., and Mallory J. Lennox, "Financial Assets—A Temporary Setback," *Stock Research Investment Policy,* Salomon Brothers, June 8, 1984.

Some of the returns shown in the table are quite high. However, none of the collectible assets provided consistently high results over all three periods. This is not surprising because if one (or more) had provided consistently high returns, many investors would have been attracted to it and bid its price up to a level where high returns would no longer have been possible. Indeed, more recent studies of prints and paintings have concluded that their risk and return characteristics make them relatively unattractive investments for risk-averse investors.[21]

In a sense, a collectible asset often provides income to the owner in the form of consumption. For example, an investor can admire a Roberto Clemente rookie baseball card, sit on a Chippendale chair, gaze upon a Georgia O'Keefe painting, play a Stradivarius violin, and drive a Stutz Bearcat automobile. Value received in this manner is not subject to income taxation and is thus likely to be especially attractive for those in high tax brackets. However, the value of such consumption depends strongly on one's preferences.

If markets are efficient, collectible assets will be priced so that those who enjoy them most will find it desirable to hold them in greater-than-market-value proportions, whereas those who enjoy them least will find it desirable to hold them in less-than-market-value proportions (or, in many cases, not at all).

Institutional funds and investment pools have been organized to own paintings, stamps, coins, and other collectible assets. These arrangements are subject to serious question if they involve locking such objects in vaults where they cannot be seen by those who derive pleasure from this sort of consumption. On the other hand, if the items are rented to others, the only loss may be that associated with the transfer of a portion of the consumption value to the government in the form of a tax on income.

Investors in collectibles should be aware of two especially notable types of risk. The first is that the bid-ask spread is often very large. Thus an investor must see a large price increase just to recoup the spread and break even. The second is that collectibles are subject to fads (this risk has been referred to as *stylistic risk*).[22] For example, Chinese ceramics may be actively sought by many investors today, leading to high prices, and big returns for earlier purchasers. However, they may fall out of favor later on, and plunge in value. Unlike financial assets, there is no such thing as fair value for collectibles that can act as a kind of anchor for the market price.

26.2.2 Gold

In the United States, private holdings of gold bullion were illegal before the 1970s. In other countries, investment in gold has long been a tradition. According to one estimate, at the end of 1984 gold represented over 6% of the world market wealth portfolio.[23]

Table 26.7 contrasts a U.S. investor's returns from gold with the returns from U.S. equities over the period from 1960 through 1984. Gold is clearly a risky investment, but in this period, at least, it also provided high average returns.

For any single investment, risk and return are only parts of the story. Correlations of an asset's return with the returns on other assets are also relevant. In the period covered in Table 26.7, gold price changes were slightly negatively

TABLE 26.7		
CHARACTERISTICS OF GOLD AND U.S. EQUITY RETURNS, 1960–1984		
	Average Annual Return	Standard Deviation of Annual Returns
U.S. equities	10.20%	16.89%
Gold	12.62	29.87
Correlation:		
Gold and U.S. equities	−.09	
Gold and inflation	.63	

Source: Adapted from Roger G. Ibbotson, Laurence B. Siegel, and Kathryn S. Love, "World Wealth: Market Values and Returns," *Journal of Portfolio Management*, 12, no. 1 (Fall 1985): 17, 21.

correlated with stock returns. Similar results have been obtained for other periods. Gold thus appears to be an effective diversifying asset for an equity investor.[24] Table 26.7 also shows that gold prices were highly correlated with the rate of inflation in the United States as measured by changes in the Consumer Price Index. This is consistent with gold's traditional role as a hedge against inflation, because higher inflation generally brings higher gold prices.

Investors interested in gold need not restrict themselves to bullion. Other possibilities range from stocks of gold mining companies to gold futures to gold coins and commemoratives. Furthermore, there are other types of precious metals, such as silver, that investors may want to consider.

26.3 SPORTS BETTING

Throughout the world, large amounts of money are wagered on the outcomes of sporting events. In the United States, betting on horse races is conducted legally at racetracks in many states and via legal off-track betting establishments in some states. In addition, illegal bookmakers in every state accept bets on horse races. Bets on other events—most notably professional football games—are made legally in Nevada and illegally with bookmakers almost everywhere.

There are some interesting parallels between sports betting and investing in securities. Both involve an initial outlay of cash and an outcome that, being uncertain, can be thought of as a random variable. For both betting and investing, an individual must have some sort of strategy in deciding where to put his or her money—after all, there are many sporting events as well as securities. Furthermore, these strategies can be thought of as being either fundamental or technical in nature. In the case of fundamental strategies, an investor or bettor looks at the underlying strength of the firm or team or horse that is being evaluated, whereas in the case of a technical strategy, only past performance is of concern. Both of these strategies are typically based on publicly available information. Thus the historical performance of investors and bettors can be examined in order to see if the respective financial markets and "sports markets" are semistrong-form efficient. To begin the discussion, a parallel will be made between a security dealer and a bookmaker.

Alternative Investments

Institutional investors have long acknowledged the wisdom of holding well-diversified portfolios. For many years, however, they focused their investments almost exclusively on U.S. common stocks, bonds, and short-term securities. The spectrum of investable asset categories extends well beyond these three (for example, see the discussion of the world capital market portfolio in this chapter). Thus for a considerable time institutional investors overlooked fertile opportunities to reduce their portfolios' risks and perhaps even enhance returns as well.

That myopia receded in the 1980s. Institutional investors began to take significant positions in international stocks and bonds. Furthermore, they made sizable commitments to a variety of asset categories commonly grouped under the rubric *alternative investments*.

Although there is no precise definition of the term, in practice institutional investors consider alternative investments to be virtually any type of asset not actively traded in the public markets. In terms of their relative importance in institutional investors' portfolios, the most prominent types of alternative investments are:

- *Venture capital,* which involves investments in young companies, ranging from start-up firms to developed businesses preparing to initially offer their stock in the public market.
- *Resource investments,* which involve primarily holdings of properties producing or expected to produce crude oil and natural gas. In recent years, timber properties have gained in relative importance as a resource investment.
- *Leveraged buy-outs,* which involve acquisitions of existing companies using large amounts of debt and little equity to finance the deal. Typically, these companies are restructured, with various divisions sold off to retire debt and other divisions consolidated or otherwise altered to improve efficiency for later reissuance of equity in the public market.
- *Real estate,* which involves investments in income-producing physical structures, including retail shopping centers, office buildings, apartments, and commercial warehouses.

Each type of alternative investment exhibits its own distinct risk and return characteristics. As a result, treating them as one monolithic category leads to faulty analysis. Yet each of these asset types has several similar features:

- Illiquidity
- Difficulty in determining current market values
- Limited historical return and risk data
- Extensive investment analysis required.

The primary distinguishing characteristic of alternative investments is their illiquidity. Institutional investors typically participate in alternative investments through a limited partnership structure (although sometimes direct investments are made with the issuing entity). In a limited partnership, a general partner (or partners) negotiates a deal with the issuing entity. The general partner then solicits limited partners to provide the financing for the deal. The general partners exercise complete control over the investment, while limited partners absorb the risk of failure and share any profits with the general partners.

With rare exceptions, limited partnerships are not registered with the Securities and Exchange Commission. Thus the limited partners cannot freely trade their ownership interests in the public market. Some secondary markets for limited partnership interests have begun to form, but their volume is extremely small. Essentially, institutional investors participating in alternative investments must be prepared to hold those investments until they expire.

For similar reasons, little pricing data is available for alternative investments. General partners periodically (at most quarterly, often annually) supply estimates of a partnership's current market value. Limited partners, however, have few practical means of independently verifying those prices.

Because of the relative newness of alternative investments and the paucity of market prices, virtually no historical return and risk data on these investments is available. Such questions as, "How can the standard deviation of my existing portfolio be expected to change if I place 10% of my funds in venture capital?" are essentially unanswerable.

Thus when making portfolio allocation decisions, institutional investors must rely on highly subjective estimates of alternative investments' expected returns, standard deviations, and correlations with other asset categories.

Finally, alternative investments require considerable analysis on the part of institutional investors. Information on potential investments is not readily available. Investors must carefully study partnership agreements, consider the management fees and other operating costs, and investigate the capabilities of the general partners. Unlike common stocks and bonds, investors cannot rely on the market to provide efficient pricing. Although these less efficient markets present many potential pitfalls, conversely they offer the opportunity for relatively high returns.

Each of the alternative investment categories described previously has seen dramatic highs and lows over the last 20 years. For all these categories, the high-water marks of performance were attained in the late 1970s and early 1980s, followed soon after by disappointing results. Venture capital returns declined in the poor market for small capi-

talization stocks in the mid and late 1980s. Real estate suffered staggering losses in the late 1980s. Oil and gas prices plummeted in the mid-1980s and have yet to rebound significantly. Leveraged buyout deals have fallen in terms of volume and profitability after the most obvious targets were purchased in the 1980s. Perhaps not coincidentally, these performance downturns occurred in a period of declining inflation, whereas the best performance took place during a period of relatively high inflation.

Despite this recent unimpressive track record, the diversification argument remains intact for alternative investments. Over the last two decades, returns on alternative investments have exhibited low or even negative correlations with those of the stock and bond markets. Given the historically high returns provided by these traditional investments, perhaps one should not be surprised or even dissatisfied with the recent results. At some point in the future, alternative investments will almost certainly again offer attractive returns relative to traditional investments and reward the patient, well-diversified investor.

A security dealer typically wishes to operate with, on average, a small inventory of securities so as to have relatively little exposure to loss through security price fluctuations. To do this, the dealer usually sets a bid price and an asked price that will bring roughly an equal number of orders for purchases and sales in a given time period (say, a week's time). The bid-ask spread represents the dealer's profit margin and part of the investor's transaction costs.

Similarly, in sports betting the bookmaker acts as dealer and wishes to have relatively little "inventory" (exposure to loss). Two major methods are employed to achieve this: *spread betting* and *odds betting*. The former is used for bets on games such as football and baseball and the latter for bets on contests such as horse races and presidential elections.

26.3.1 Spread Betting

In order to understand spread betting, consider a hypothetical professional football game between the San Francisco 49ers and the Minnesota Vikings. It is widely felt that the 49ers are likely to win. Thus the bookmaker establishes a spread, perhaps deciding that the 49ers are "favored by 7 points." This means that the final score will, in effect, be modified by subtracting 7 points from the 49ers score and then paying those who bet on the winner using that adjusted score.

People who bet on San Francisco believe that the San Francisco team will "cover the spread"; those who bet on Minnesota believe that Minnesota will cover the spread. If the final score is 28–20 in favor of San Francisco, then after adjusting for the spread the score is 21–20 in favor of San Francisco, and those betting on San Francisco will have won. However, if the final score is 24–20 in favor of San Francisco, then the adjusted score will be 17–20 in favor of Minnesota, and those betting on Minnesota will have won.[25]

The point spread serves as an equilibrating mechanism. Other things being equal, the greater the spread, the smaller will be the amount bet on San Francisco and the larger the amount bet on Minnesota. At some level the "books will be balanced," meaning that an equal amount has been bet on both teams. Given local prejudices, this may be accomplished by San Francisco bookmakers "laying off" excess money bet on the 49ers with Minnesota bookmakers who have excess money bet on the Vikings.

How does the bookmaker make a living? With a range that corresponds to the security dealer's bid-ask spread. Typically the bettor puts up $11 for a $10 bet, meaning that a winner will receive $10 (plus his or her initial $11 bet, if paid in advance) while a loser is out the initial $11 bet. If the books are balanced, the bookmaker will pay out $21 for every $22 taken in. For example, if there is one $11 bet on San Francisco and one $11 bet on Minnesota, the books are balanced. Then, whichever team wins, the bookmaker will pay out $21 of the $22 that was bet.

Although bookmakers generally set point spreads to balance their books, in an efficient market such spreads would provide good estimates of the expected differences in points scored. (It turns out that, by and large, the evidence is consistent with market efficiency.)

26.3.2 Odds Betting

A goal of all bookmakers is to be reasonably certain that after the contest is over, less money will be paid out than is received. Hence, if they are successful, the average return to bettors will be negative. To do this, terms must be set so that bets on underdogs are attractive. Spreads are one way; odds are another.

An example from horse racing will illustrate the procedure. Assume that Black Socks is favored to win the sixth race at Golden Gate Fields, while the other seven horses are considered inferior but of roughly equal speed. If the payoff per dollar bet were the same for all eight horses, most of the bets would be placed on the favorite. To spread the betting over the contenders, a larger amount must be paid per dollar bet if a long shot is bet on and subsequently wins.

Assume that the odds are set at 7-to-1 for each of the seven slow horses. This means that if $1 is bet on one of them and the horse wins, the bettor will receive $8 (the original $1 that was bet plus $7 in winnings). Assume also that the odds on Black Socks are set at 5-to-3, so that every $3 bet on the favorite will return $8 (the original $3 that was bet plus $5 in winnings) if the horse wins. Now imagine that the amounts bet, given these odds, are as shown in Table 26.8. The total pool or *handle* (that is, the total amount bet) is $1,000, but no matter which horse wins the race, only $800 will be paid out. The remaining $200 is for the track, the government, and the bookmaker and is known as the *take*. Note that the average return to the bettors is -20% ($= -\$200/\$1,000$) because of the take.

The numbers in Table 26.8 may seem contrived, but they represent the kind of situation achieved automatically by parimutuel betting. In this form of wagering (used at most horse racetracks), the actual odds for a horse are determined after all betting has finished by subtracting the take (typically about 20%) and the amount bet on the horse from the handle, then dividing this amount by the amount bet on that horse.[26] For example, in the case of Black Socks (horse number 1), the odds are 5-to-3 [$= (\$1,000 - \$200 - \$300)/\$300 = \$500/\$300$], as shown in the table. It should be noted that the "dealer" is always assured of receiving a fixed percentage (20%) for "transaction costs" with this procedure.

Thus betting on horses is a negative-sum game. Owing to transaction costs, the amount paid out is less than the amount paid in. Consequently, the expected return on the average bet will be negative. As it is difficult to justify such activity on the basis of hedging, a bettor either (1) believes that he or she is a superior predictor, or (2) is willing to pay in this manner for entertainment, or (3) prefers risk. Undoubtedly, all three aspects play a role in the sports betting market. One attribute that makes betting on sports entertaining is the suspension of the bettor's usual mind-set and the taking of risks with relatively small amounts of money. In such an environment and with limited exposure, even a conservative investor may take pleasure in acting like a riverboat gambler.

Evidence consistent with risk preference of this sort has been found in many analyses of the expected returns from bets on horses with different probabilities of winning races. Figure 26.3 summarizes a number of such studies. The horizontal axis indicates closing odds (on a logarithmic scale). Favorites plot at the left end of the scale and extreme long shots at the right end. The vertical axis indicates average returns. All are negative, but the returns on favorites are considerably better than those on long shots. "Investors" at the track are apparently willing to give up some expected return to get more risk—in this domain they appear to prefer risk.

TABLE 26.8
ODDS, AMOUNTS BET, AND PAYOUTS FOR A HORSE RACE

Horse	Amount Bet	Odds	Amount Paid Out If Horse Wins
#1 (favorite)	$ 300	5-to-3	$800
2	100	7-to-1	800
3	100	7-to-1	800
4	100	7-to-1	800
5	100	7-to-1	800
6	100	7-to-1	800
7	100	7-to-1	800
8	100	7-to-1	800
Total amount bet =	$1000		

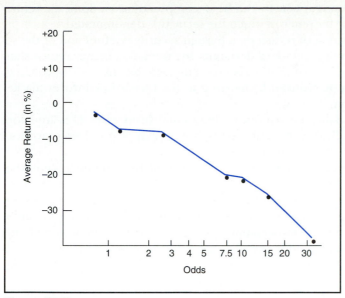

Figure 26.3

Average Return versus Odds in Horse Race Betting

Source: Wayne W. Snyder, "Horse Racing: Testing the Efficient Markets Model," *Journal of Finance,* 33, no. 4 (September 1978): p. 1113.

26.3.3 The Efficiency of Horse Race Betting

Investors in stocks can avail themselves of the results of financial analysis, both fundamental and technical. However, the high degree of efficiency of the stock market diminishes the value of such information for a single investor because much of it is already reflected in security prices.

A similar situation prevails in the market for horse race betting. Fundamental analyses of such factors as the abilities of horses and trainers and the effects of weather abound, as do technical analyses of trends, reversals, and other changes in "form." If the market is efficient, public information provided by such analysts (*handicappers*) will be reflected in prices (*closing odds*).

In one test that examined the bets placed at Belmont Race Track in New York State, the odds at the track appeared to reflect the information contained in published picks by 14 handicappers. However, this did not seem to be the case in the less professional (and higher-transaction-cost) off-track betting market—a fact that may give some solace to those who invest in small and little-followed stocks.[27]

26.4 **SUMMARY**

1. Investing in a foreign security involves all the risks associated with investing in a domestic security, plus political and exchange (currency) risks associated with converting foreign cash flows into domestic currency.

2. The return on a foreign security can be decomposed into a domestic return and a return on the currency in which the security is denominated.

3. The standard deviation of return on a foreign security is a function of the security's domestic return standard deviation, the foreign currency return standard deviation, and the correlation between the two returns.

4. Exchange risk can be reduced by hedging in the forward or futures market for foreign currency.

5. Investments in U.S.-headquartered multinational firms offer U.S. investors only limited diversification benefits. ADRs, however, appear to bring investors significant risk reduction benefits.

6. Overall, tangible assets have been better hedges against unanticipated inflation than stocks or bonds.

7. Sports betting and security investing exhibit interesting parallels. For example, both involve an initial outlay of cash and generally uncertain outcomes. Further, publicly available information appears to be quickly impounded into both betting spreads and odds as well as security prices.

QUESTIONS AND PROBLEMS

1. What types of political risks are relevant only for foreign investors? What types are relevant for both foreign and domestic investors? To what extent and in what manner would you expect the current prices of securities in a particular country to reflect these types of political risk?

2. Using a recent *Wall Street Journal,* find the exchange rate between German marks, British pounds, and U.S. dollars. Lyle Luttrell, a British citizen, is planning a trip to Germany and has budgeted expenses of 30 pounds per day. At current exchange rates, into how many dollars and marks does 30 pounds translate?

3. Why would an investor wish to hedge the currency risk in a portfolio of foreign securities? What considerations are relevant to making the decision whether to hedge?

4. How might a U.S. citizen or company use currency futures to hedge against exchange-rate risk?

5. Wickey McAvoy, a U.S. citizen, holds a portfolio of French common stocks. Last year the portfolio produced an 8% return, denominated in French francs. Over that year the franc appreciated 20% against the U.S. dollar. What was Wickey's return measure in U.S. dollars?

6. Tris Speaker bought a Japanese stock one year ago when it sold for 280 yen per share and the exchange rate was $0.008 per yen. The stock now sells for 350 yen and the exchange rate is $0.010 per yen. The stock paid no dividends over the year. What was Tris's rate of return on this stock? What would be the rate of return on the stock to a Japanese investor?

7. Why is international diversification attractive to an investor like Jigger Statz who already has a well-diversified domestic portfolio?

8. Ownie Carroll owns a portfolio composed of U.S. stocks and bonds. Interested in further diversifying the portfolio, Ownie decides to add investments in

Canadian common stocks. Ownie's broker, Slick Castleman, voices the opinion that the Canadian securities would not be particularly effective risk-reducing investments. Discuss the logic behind Slick's opinion.

9. Peek-A-Boo Veach, a U.S. citizen, estimates that a diversified portfolio of German common stocks has a standard deviation of 24%. Peek-A-Boo also estimates that the standard deviation of the U.S. and German currency return is 7%. Finally, Peek-A-Boo estimates the correlation between the dollar-mark currency return and the German stock market return to be 0.20. Given this information, what should Peek-A-Boo conclude is the standard deviation for a U.S. investor investing solely in the German stock market?

10. When a U.S. citizen like Smead Jolly is attempting to estimate the expected return and standard deviation for a foreign security, what factors, in addition to those recognized in domestic security analysis, should be considered?

11. Lin Storti, a U.S. citizen, is considering investing in both U.S. and Zanistan common stock index funds. Lin estimates the following market characteristics:

U.S. market expected return	20%
U.S. market standard deviation	18%
Zanistan market expected return	30%
Zanistan market standard deviation	30%
U.S.-Zanistan expected currency return	0%
U.S.-Zanistan currency return standard deviation	10%
Zanistan domestic return and U.S.-Zanistan currency return correlation	0.15

Further, Lin estimates that the U.S. and Zanistan markets are uncorrelated as is the U.S. market return (or the Zanistan market return) and the U.S.-Zanistan currency exchange rate. Given that Lin is planning to hold a portfolio 60% invested in the U.S. index fund and 40% invested in the Zanistan index fund, what is the expected return and standard deviation of Lin's portfolio?

12. Eva Lange wants the diversification benefits of international investments but does not want to own foreign securities directly. Would investing in domestically headquartered multinational corporations and ADRs be effective substitutes for Eva? Explain.

13. Discuss why mutual funds are a particularly cost-effective means for small investors to own foreign securities.

14. Is a low correlation between the price movements of two countries' market indices a sufficient condition to ensure that a portfolio containing securities of both countries dominates a portfolio containing only domestic securities?

15. What practical difficulties prevent collectible assets from playing a major role in most investors' portfolios?

16. Hal Chase, a neophyte sports gambler, was heard to remark, "The bookmakers took a terrible beating this week because 80% of the underdogs beat the point spread." Does this seem plausible? Why?

17. In the third race at Canterbury Downs, the handle is $25,000. The track's take is 15%. If $2,000 is bet on Harvest Harry to win, what are the parimutuel betting odds on the horse?

18. Picks of handicappers such as Dolph Luque generally do not add directly to the information reflected in the odds given at the track. Does this mean that Dolph and the other handicappers cannot pick winners? Does this mean that their picks are of no value? What aspects of security markets are comparable to the position of track handicappers?

CFA EXAM QUESTIONS

19. Robert Devlin and Neil Parish are portfolio managers at the Broward Investment Group. At their regular Monday strategy meeting, the topic of adding international bonds to one of their portfolios came up. The portfolio, an ERISA-qualified pension account for a U.S. client, was currently 90% invested in U.S. Treasury bonds, and 10% invested in 10–year Canadian government bonds. Devlin suggested buying a position in 10–year German government bonds, while Parish argued for a position in 10–year Australian government bonds.

    a. Briefly discuss the three major issues that Devlin and Parish should address in their analysis of the return prospects for German and Australian bonds relative to those of U.S. bonds.

Having made no changes to the original portfolio, Devlin and Parish hold a subsequent strategy meeting and decide to add positions in the government bonds of Japan, United Kingdom, France, Germany, and Australia.

    b. Identify and discuss two reasons for adding a broader mix of international bonds to the pension portfolio.

20. Advisor 1: "A currency cannot consistently appreciate or depreciate relative to an investor's local currency, since some local or global economic adjustment must eventually redress the currency change. Therefore, having currency exposure in a portfolio increases risk but does not increase long-term expected returns. Since you are not compensated for taking currency risk, you should always hedge a portfolio's currency exposure back to your local currency."

Advisor 2: "I completely disagree, except as to the implication that economic changes are related to currency changes. Because economic changes affect international stocks, bonds, and currencies, as well as domestic stocks and bonds in ways that often offset each other, currency exposure improves diversification in a portfolio. Portfolios should never hedge their currency exposures; otherwise, they would be less diversified."

Advisor 1 Rebuttal: "I have evidence which would appear to refute your claim of improved diversification resulting from currency exposure. My studies of hedged and unhedged international bond portfolios show very little difference between either their risks or returns over the past ten years."

Evaluate the strengths and weaknesses of each of the two approaches presented above. Recommend and justify an alternative currency strategy that draws from the strengths of each approach and corrects their weaknesses.

[1] For a discussion of the difficulties in measuring the size of the world portfolio along with an estimate of its size at year-end 1984, see Roger G. Ibbotson, Laurence B. Siegel, and Kathryn S. Love, "World Wealth: Market Values and Returns," *Journal of Portfolio Management,* 12, no. 1 (Fall 1985): 4–23.

[2] A more detailed study of bonds estimated their global value to be $11 trillion at the end of 1989. Of this total, $6.3 trillion was government debt, $2.4 trillion was local corporate debt, $1 trillion was "crossborder" debt (that is, foreign bonds and Eurobonds), and $1.3 trillion was "other domestic" debt. See Roger G. Ibbotson and Laurence B. Siegel, "The World Bond Market: Market Values, Yields, and Returns," *Journal of Fixed Income,* 1, no. 1 (June 1991): 90–99.

[3] It should be noted that the *Wall Street Journal* also publishes daily a set of Dow Jones stock market indices for 20 countries. These country indices are combined into four regional indices (Americas; Europe; Asia/Pacific; Asia/Pacific except Japan) and a World Stock Index that are also reported daily. For a discussion of European stock markets, see Gabriel Hawawini, *European Equity Markets: Price Behavior and Efficiency,* Monograph Series in Finance and Economics #1984-4/5, New York University Salomon Center, Leonard N. Stern School of Business. Also see Victor A. Canto, "Everything You Always Wanted to Know About the European Monetary System, the ECU and ERM, But Didn't Know Who to Ask," *Financial Analysts Journal,* 47, no. 6 (November/December 1991): 22–25.

[4] For a discussion of the Morgan Stanley indices, see Campbell R. Harvey, "The World Price of Covariance Risk," *Journal of Finance,* 46, no. 1 (March 1991): 111–157.

[5] For more on these and other indices, see Chapter 5 in Bruno Solnik, *International Investments* (Reading, MA: Addison-Wesley, 1991); and John Markese, "An Investor's Guide to the International Marketplace", *AAII Journal,* 14, no. 7 (August 1992): 29–32.

[6] For more on emerging markets, see Vihang Errunza, "Emerging Markets: A New Opportunity for Improving Global Portfolio Performance," *Financial Analysts Journal,* 39, no. 5 (September/October 1983): 51–58; Vihang Errunza and Etienne Losq, "How Risky are Emerging Markets? Myths and Perceptions Versus Theory and Evidence," *Journal of Portfolio Management,* 14, no. 1 (Fall 1987): 62–67; and Vihang Errunza and Prasad Padmanabhan, "Further Evidence on the Benefits of Portfolio Investments in Emerging Markets," *Financial Analysts Journal,* 44, no. 4 (July/August 1988): 76–78.

[7] The effects these types of risk have on asset pricing has been considered by a number of people. For a discussion and list of references, see Chapters 1 and 5 in Solnik, *International Investments.*

[8] In a study of monthly stock returns from February 1970 through May 1989 using the Morgan Stanley indices, it was found that the return on Japanese stocks was inexplicably high. See Harvey, "The World Price of Covariance Risk."

[9] The importance of accurately estimating the correlations between asset and currency returns in determining whether or not to hedge a portfolio is stressed in Victor S. Filatov and Peter Rappoport, "Is Complete Hedging Optimal for International Bond Portfolios?" *Financial Analysts Journal,* 48, no. 4 (July/August 1992): 37–47.

[10] Bruno Solnik and Eric Nemeth, "Asset Returns and Currency Fluctuations: A Time Series Analysis," paper presented at the second conference, Geld, Banken und Versicherungen, University of Karlsruhe, December 1982.

[11] Because standard deviation is the square root of variance, this means that the foreign standard deviation will typically be substantially less than the sum of the domestic and currency standard deviations.

[12] However, a study of U.S multinationals found that the percentage of a firm's sales that were overseas varied directly with a measure of how sensitive the firm's stock price was to an index of the dollar's value. That is, the greater the percentage, the larger the positive effect of dollar depreciations on the firm's profits and hence on its stock returns. Accordingly, investing in U.S. firms that have a large percentage of their sales overseas may be beneficial. See Philippe Jorion, "The Exchange-Rate Exposure of U.S. Multinationals," *Journal of Business,* 63, no. 3 (July 1990): 331–345; and "The Pricing of Exchange Rate Risk in the Stock Market," *Journal of Financial and Quantitative Analysis,* 26, no. 3 (September 1991): 363–376.

[13] The London Stock Exchange began trading many of these ADRs in August 1987, with prices quoted in U.S. dollars.

[14] Dennis T. Officer and J. Ronald Hoffmeister, "ADRs: A Substitute for the Real Thing?" *Journal of Portfolio Management,* 13, no. 2 (Winter 1987): 61–65. See also Leonard Rosenthal, "An Empirical Test of the Efficiency of the ADR Market," *Journal of Banking and Finance,* 7, no. 1 (March 1983): 17–29. ADRs are also briefly discussed in Chapter 3, where additional references are provided.

[15] An article published in 1993 stated that at that time there were 722 ADRs listed in the U.S. over-the-counter market. (Large bid-ask spreads are commonplace for these thinly traded ADRs, thereby limiting the ability to invest profitably in them.) In comparison, Table 26.5 shows that at year-end 1993, there were 536 foreign companies (with 213 of them being ADRs) that had their shares listed on a U.S. exchange. See Franklin R. Edwards, "Listing of Foreign Securities on U.S. Exchanges," *Journal of Applied Corporate Finance,* 5, no. 4 (Winter 1993): 28–36.

[16] Rule 144A (see Chapter 3), which permits the issuance of unregistered securities on a private placement basis, was intended in part to accommodate foreign issuers of stock that did not want to meet the SEC's financial reporting requirements.

[17] Over the period 1960–1980, another study found that stocks in Austria and Spain had slightly negative correlations with U.S. stocks whereas stocks in Norway had a correlation of .01. See Roger G. Ibbotson, Richard C. Carr, and Anthony W. Robinson, "International Bond and Equity Portfolios," *Financial Analysts Journal,* 38, no. 4 (July/August 1982): 61–83. Yet another study of 349 stocks in 11 countries revealed an average intercountry correlation coefficient of .234 for the period from January 1973 to December 1983. See D. Chinhyung Cho, Cheol S. Eun, and Lemma W. Senbet, "International Arbitrage Pricing Theory: An Empirical Investigation," *Journal of Finance,* 41, no. 2 (June 1986): 313–329. In addition, the correlations between emerging markets and the United States have historically been near zero; see the references given in Endnote 6. For a multiperiod approach that indicates the benefits from international diversification, particularly for highly risk-averse investors, see Robert R. Grauer and Nils H. Hakansson, "Gains from International Diversification: 1968–85 Returns on Portfolios of Stocks and Bonds," *Journal of Finance,* 42, no. 3 (July 1987): 721–739. Although the correlations between the U.S. and foreign stock markets is surely much less than one, the actual values are highly dependent on the time period studied.

[18] Similar results were found in another study involving the period of 1960 to 1980. A negative correlation between the bonds in Italy and the United States was observed. See Ibbotson, Carr, and Robinson, "International Bond and Equity Portfolios."

[19] Unfortunately, a recent study has found that the benefits from international diversification are lessened just when these benefits are most needed by investors. Specifically, the low correlations between market returns appear to increase when markets become more volatile. See Patrick Odier and Bruno Solnik, "Lessons for International Asset Allocation," *Financial Analysts Journal,* 49, no. 2 (March/April 1993): 63–77.

[20] Although not a tangible asset, commodity futures were shown in Chapter 21 to have also been an attractive inflation hedge.

[21] See James E. Pesando, "Art as an Investment: The Market for Modern Prints," *American Economic Review,* 83, no. 5 (December 1993): 1075–1089. See also William N. Goetzmann, "Accounting for Taste: Art and the Financial Markets Over Three Centuries," *American Economic Review,* 83, no. 5 (December 1993): 1370–1376.

[22] The term *stylistic risk* was coined by William N. Goetzmann in "Accounting for Taste," p. 1371.

[23] Ibbotson, Siegel, and Love, "World Wealth: Market Values and Returns," p. 9.

[24] For a view against investing in gold, see James B. Cloonan, "Goodbye Gold: It's Now Just Another Commodity," *AAII Journal,* 14, no. 9 (October 1992): 25–26.

[25] In the event of a tie in the adjusted score, the money that was bet is returned to both sides.

[26] This applies only to bets that a horse will win the race. More complex procedures are used for *place* (second or better) and *show* (third or better) in bets. In addition, the actual payoff is usually rounded down to the nearest multiple of, say, $.10 per $2 bet.

[27] Stephen Figlewski, "Subjective Information and Market Efficiency in a Betting Market," *Journal of Political Economy,* 87, no. 1 (February 1979): 75–88. It should be noted that there is some evidence that information is better reflected in the win pool than in the show and place pools. For details of a "system" designed to exploit such discrepancies, see Donald B. Hausch, William T. Ziemba, and Mark Rubenstein, "Efficiency of the Market for Racetrack Betting," *Management Science,* 27, no. 12 (December 1981): 1435–1452; and Peter Asch, Burton G. Malkiel, and Richard E. Quandt, "Market Efficiency in Racetrack Betting," *Journal of Business,* 57, no. 2 (April 1984): 165–175, and "Market Efficiency in Racetrack Betting: Further Evidence and a Correction," *Journal of Business,* 59, no. 1 (January 1986): 157–160.

KEY TERMS

emerging markets
political risk
exchange risk
domestic return

foreign return
multinational firms
American Depository Receipts

REFERENCES

1. Two books devoted to understanding international financial markets and investing are:

   J. Orlin Grabbe, *International Financial Markets* (New York: Elsevier Science, 1991).

   Bruno Solnik, *International Investments* (Reading, MA: Addison-Wesley, 1991).

2. Foreign stock market indices are studied in:

   Campbell R. Harvey, "The World Price of Covariance Risk," *Journal of Finance,* 46, no. 1 (March 1991): 111–157.

Richard Roll, "Industrial Structure and the Comparative Behavior of International Stock Market Indices," *Journal of Finance*, 47, no. 1 (March 1992): 3–41.

3. Investing internationally in bonds has been recently studied by:

Kenneth Cholerton, Pierre Pieraerts, and Bruno Solnik, "Why Invest in Foreign Currency Bonds?" *Journal of Portfolio Management*, 12, no. 4 (Summer 1986): 4–8.

Haim Levy and Zvi Lerman, "The Benefits of International Diversification of Bonds," *Financial Analysts Journal*, 44, no. 5 (September/October 1988): 56–64.

Paul Burik and Richard M. Ennis, "Foreign Bonds in Diversified Portfolios: A Limited Advantage," *Financial Analysts Journal*, 46, no. 2 (March/April 1990): 31–40.

Roger G. Ibbotson and Laurence B. Siegel, "The World Bond Market: Market Values, Yields, and Returns," *Journal of Fixed Income*, 1, no. 1 (June 1991): 90–99.

Victor S. Filatov, Kevin M. Murphy, Peter M. Rappoport, and Russell Church, "Foreign Bonds in Diversified Portfolios: A Significant Advantage," *Financial Analysts Journal*, 47, no. 4 (July/August 1991): 26–32.

Mark Fox, "Different Ways to Slice the Optimization Cake," *Financial Analysts Journal*, 47, no. 4 (July/August 1991): 32–36.

Richard M. Ennis and Paul Burik, "A Response from Burik and Ennis," *Financial Analysts Journal*, 47, no. 4 (July/August 1991): 37.

Fischer Black and Robert Litterman, "Asset Allocation: Combining Investors Views with Market Equilibrium," *Journal of Fixed Income*, 1, no. 2 (September 1991): 7–19.

Shmuel Hauser and Azriel Levy, "Effect of Exchange Rate and Interest Rate Risk on International Fixed-Income Portfolios," *Journal of Economics and Business*, 43, no. 4 (November 1991): 375–388.

Mark R. Eaker and Dwight M. Grant, "Currency Risk Management in International Fixed-Income Portfolios," *Journal of Fixed Income*, 1, no. 3 (December 1991): 31–37.

Steven Dym, "Global and Local Components of Foreign Bond Risk," *Financial Analysts Journal*, 48, no. 2 (March/April 1992): 83–91.

John Markese, "Foreign Bond Funds: What Are You Buying Into?" *AAII Journal*, 14, no. 10 (November 1992): 28–31.

Kent G. Becker, Joseph E. Finnerty, and Kenneth J. Kopecky, "Economic News and Intraday Volatility in International Bond Markets," *Financial Analysts Journal*, 49, no. 3 (May/June 1993): 81–86, 65.

Richard M. Levich and Lee R. Thomas, "The Merits of Active Currency Risk Management: Evidence from International Bond Portfolios," *Financial Analysts Journal*, 49, no. 5 (September/October 1993): 63–70.

4. Investing internationally in stocks has also been studied recently by:

Jeff Madura and Wallace Reiff, "A Hedge Strategy for International Portfolios," *Journal of Portfolio Management*, 12, no. 1 (Fall 1985): 70–74.

CHAPTER 26

Lee R. Thomas III, "Currency Risks in International Equity Portfolios," *Financial Analysts Journal*, 44, no. 2 (March/April 1988): 68–71.

Fischer Black, "Universal Hedging: Optimizing Currency Risk and Reward in International Equity Portfolios," *Financial Analysts Journal*, 45, no. 4 (July/August 1989): 16–22.

Warren Bailey and Rene M. Stulz, "Benefits of International Diversification: The Case of Pacific Basin Stock Markets," *Journal of Portfolio Management*, 16, no. 4 (Summer 1990): 57–61.

Mark R. Eaker and Dwight Grant, "Currency Hedging Strategies for Internationally Diversified Equity Portfolios," *Journal of Portfolio Management*, 17, no. 1 (Fall 1990): 30–32.

John E. Hunter and T. Daniel Coggin, "An Analysis of the Diversification Benefit from International Equity Investment," *Journal of Portfolio Management*, 17, no. 1 (Fall 1990): 33–36.

Martin L. Leibowitz and Stanley Kogelman, "Return Enhancement from 'Foreign' Assets: A New Approach to the Risk Return Trade-off," *Journal of Portfolio Management*, 17, no. 4 (Summer 1991): 5–13.

Mark Eaker, Dwight Grant, and Nelson Woodard, "International Diversification and Hedging: A Japanese and U.S. Perspective," *Journal of Economics and Business*, 43, no. 4 (November 1991): 363–374.

5. Many of the previously cited papers include a discussion of hedging foreign exchange risk. For a description, see:

Andre F. Perold and Evan C. Schulman, "The Free Lunch in Currency Hedging: Implications for Investment Policy and Performance Standards," *Financial Analysts Journal*, 44, no. 3 (May/June 1988): 45–50.

Fischer Black, "Equilibrium Exchange Rate Hedging," *Journal of Finance*, 45, no. 3 (July 1990): 899–907.

Stephen L. Nesbitt, "Currency Hedging Rules for Plan Sponsors," *Financial Analysts Journal*, 47, no. 2 (March/April 1991): 73–81.

Ira G. Kawaller, "Managing the Currency Risk of Non-Dollar Portfolios," *Financial Analysts Journal*, 47, no. 3 (May/June 1991): 62–64.

Evi Kaplanis and Stephen M. Schaefer, "Exchange Risk and International Diversification in Bond and Equity Portfolios," *Journal of Economics and Business*, 43, no. 4 (November 1991): 287–307.

Michael Adler and Bhaskar Prasad, "On Universal Currency Hedges," *Journal of Financial and Quantitative Analysis*, 27, no. 1 (March 1992): 19–38.

Mark Kritzman, ". . . About Currencies," *Financial Analysts Journal*, 48, no. 2 (March/April 1992): 27–30.

Mark Kritzman, "The Minimum-Risk Currency Hedge Ratio and Foreign Asset Exposure," *Financial Analysts Journal*, 49, no. 5 (September/October 1993): 77–79.

Ira G. Kawaller, "Foreign Exchange Hedge Management Tools: A Way to Enhance Performance," *Financial Analysts Journal*, 49, no. 5 (September/October 1993): 79–80.

Jack Glen and Philippe Jorion, "Currency Hedging for International Portfolios," *Journal of Finance,* 48, no. 5 (December 1993): 1865–1886.

John Markese, "How Currency Exchange Rates Can Affect Your International Returns," *AAII Journal,* 16, no. 2 (February 1994): 29–31.

6. International asset allocation has been studied by:

Philippe Jorion, "Asset Allocation with Hedged and Unhedged Foreign Stocks and Bonds," *Journal of Portfolio Management,* 15, no. 4 (Summer 1989): 49–54.

Fischer Black and Robert Litterman, "Global Portfolio Optimization," *Financial Analysts Journal,* 48, no. 5 (September/October 1992): 28–43.

Patrick Odier and Bruno Solnik, "Lessons for International Asset Allocation," *Financial Analysts Journal,* 49, no. 2 (March/April 1993): 63–77.

Bruno Solnik, "The Performance of International Asset Allocation Strategies Using Conditional Information," *Journal of Empirical Finance,* 1, no. 1 (June 1993): 33–55.

7. The evaluation of the performance of professionally managed portfolios that invest internationally has been the subject of:

Robert E. Cumby and Jack D. Glen, "Evaluating the Performance of International Mutual Funds," *Journal of Finance,* 45, no. 2 (June 1990): 497–521.

Cheol S. Eun, Richard Kolodny, and Bruce G. Resnick, "U.S.-Based International Mutual Funds: A Performance Evaluation," *Journal of Portfolio Management,* 17, no. 3 (Spring 1991): 88–94.

8. For an interesting paper that examines the market crash of October 1987 from a worldwide perspective, and three subsequent related papers, see:

Richard Roll, "The International Crash of October 1987," *Financial Analysts Journal,* 44, no. 5 (September/October 1988): 19–35.

Mervyn A. King and Sushil Wadhwani, "Transmission of Volatility Between Stock Markets," *Review of Financial Studies,* 3, no. 1 (1990): 5–33.

Yasushi Hamao, Ronald W. Masulis, and Victor Ng, "Correlations in Price Changes and Volatility Across International Stock Markets," *Review of Financial Studies,* 3, no. 2 (1990): 281–307.

C. Sherman Cheung and Clarence C. Y. Kwan, "A Note on the Transmission of Public Information Across International Stock Markets," *Journal of Banking and Finance,* 16, no. 4 (August 1992): 831–837.

9. In addition to the references provided in Endnote 6, emerging markets are also discussed in:

W. Scott Bauman, "Investment Research Analysis in an Emerging Market: Singapore and Malaysia," *Financial Analysts Journal,* 45, no. 12 (November/December 1989): 60–67.

Jarrod W. Wilcox, "Global Investing in Emerging Markets," *Financial Analysts Journal,* 48, no. 1 (January/February 1992): 15–19.

Warren Bailey and Joseph Lim, "Evaluating the Diversification Benefits of the New Country Funds," *Journal of Portfolio Management,* 18, no. 3 (Spring 1992): 74–80.

Arjun B. Divecha, Jamie Drach, and Dan Stefek, "Emerging Markets: A Quantitative Perspective," *Journal of Portfolio Management,* 18, no. 1 (Fall 1992): 41–50.

10. Discussions of international and global factor models can be found in:

Richard Grinold, Andrew Rudd, and Dan Stefek, "Global Factors: Fact or Fiction?" *Journal of Portfolio Management,* 15, no. 1 (Fall 1989): 79–88.

Martin Drummen and Heinz Zimmermann, "The Structure of European Stock Returns," *Financial Analysts Journal,* 48, no. 7 (July/August 1992): 15–26.

11. For some general thoughts on investing in collectibles and three studies of collectibles (stamps, prints, and paintings), see:

Burton G. Malkiel, *A Random Walk Down Wall Street* (New York: W. W. Norton, 1990): pp. 304–309.

William M. Taylor, "The Estimation of Quality-Adjusted Auction Returns with Varying Transaction Intervals," *Journal of Financial and Quantitative Analysis,* 27, no. 1 (March 1992): 131–142.

James E. Pesando, "Art as an Investment: The Market for Modern Prints," *American Economic Review,* 83, no. 5 (December 1993): 1075–1089.

William N. Goetzmann, "Accounting for Taste: Art and the Financial Markets Over Three Centuries," *American Economic Review,* 83, no. 5 (December 1993): 1370–1376.

12. In addition to the sports betting citations given in Endnote 27, here are a few more:

Colin Camerer, "Does the Basketball Market Believe in Hot Hands?" *American Economic Review,* 79, no. 5 (December 1989): 1257–1261.

Joseph Golec and Maurry Tamarkin, "The Degree of Inefficiency in the Football Betting Market," *Journal of Financial Economics,* 30, no. 2 (December 1991): 311–323.

William O. Brown and Raymond D. Sauer, "Does the Basketball Market Believe in the Hot Hand? Comment," *American Economic Review,* 83, no. 5 (December 1993): 1377–1386.

Linda M. Woodland and Bill M. Woodland, "Market Efficiency and the Favorite-Longshot Bias: The Baseball Betting Market," *Journal of Finance,* 49, no 1 (March 1994): 268–280.

GLOSSARY

Abnormal Return The return earned on a financial asset in excess of that required to compensate for the risk of the asset.

Account Executive A representative of a brokerage firm whose primary responsibility is servicing the accounts of individual investors.

Accounting Beta A relative measure of the sensitivity of a firm's accounting earnings to changes in the accounting earnings of the market portfolio.

Accounting Earnings (alternatively, **Reported Earnings**) A firm's revenues less its expenses. Equivalently, the change in the firm's book value of the equity plus dividends paid to shareholders.

Accrued Interest Interest earned, but not yet paid.

Active Management A form of investment management that involves buying and selling financial assets with the objective of earning positive abnormal returns.

Active Position The difference between the percentage of an investor's portfolio invested in a particular financial asset and the percentage of a benchmark portfolio invested in that same asset.

Actual Margin The equity in an investor's margin account expressed as a percentage of the account's total market value (for margin purchases) or total debt (for short sales).

Adjusted Beta An estimate of a security's future beta, derived initially from historical data, but modified by the assumption that the security's "true" beta has a tendency over time to move toward the market average of 1.0.

Adverse Selection A problem in pricing insurance in that those with above-average risk are more likely to purchase insurance than those with below-average risk.

Aggressive Stocks Stocks that have betas greater than one.

Alpha The difference between a security's expected return and its equilibrium expected return.

American Depository Receipts (ADRs) Financial assets issued by U.S. banks that represent indirect ownership of a certain number of shares of a specific foreign firm. These shares are held on deposit in a bank in the firm's home country.

American Option An option that can be exercised any time up until and including its expiration date.

Annual Percentage Rate (APR) With respect to a loan, the APR is the yield-to-maturity of the loan, computed using the most frequent time between payments as the compounding interval.

Anomaly An empirical regularity that is not predicted by any known asset pricing model.

Approved List A list of securities that an investment organization deems worthy of accumulation in a given portfolio. For an organization that uses an approved list, typically any security on the list may be purchased by the organization's portfolio managers without additional authorization.

Arbitrage The simultaneous purchase and sale of the same, or essentially similar, security in two different markets for advantageously different prices.

Arbitrage Portfolio A portfolio that requires no investment, has no sensitivity to any factor, and has a positive expected return. More strictly, a portfolio that provides inflows in some circumstances and requires no outflows under any circumstances.

Arbitrage Pricing Theory An equilibrium model of asset pricing that states that the expected return on a security is a linear function of the security's sensitivity to various common factors.

Arbitrageur A person who engages in arbitrage.

Asked (or Ask) Price The price at which a market-maker is willing to sell a specified quantity of a particular security.

Asset Allocation The process of determining the optimal division of an investor's portfolio among available asset classes.

Asset Class A broadly defined generic group of financial assets, such as stocks or bonds.

Asymmetric Information A situation in which one party has more information than another party.

At the Money Option An option whose exercise price is roughly equal to the market price of its underlying asset.

Attribute See Factor Loading.

Automated Bond System (ABS) A computer system established by the New York Stock Exchange to facilitate the trading of inactive bonds.

Average Tax Rate The amount of taxes paid expressed as a percentage of the total income subject to tax.

Bank Discount Basis A method of calculating the interest rate on a pure-discount fixed-income security that uses the principal of the security as the security's cost.

Bankers' Acceptance A type of money market instrument. It is a promissory note issued by a business debtor, with a stated maturity date, arising out of a business transaction. A bank, by endorsing the note, assumes the obligation. If this obligation becomes actively traded, it is referred to as a bankers' acceptance.

Basis The difference between the spot price of an asset and the futures price of the same asset.

Basis Point 1/100 of 1%.

Basis Risk The risk to a futures investor of the basis widening or narrowing.

Bearer Bond A bond that has attached coupons representing the right to receive interest payments. The owner submits each coupon on its specified date to receive payment. Ownership is transferred simply by the seller's endorsing the bond over to the buyer.

Benchmark Portfolio A portfolio against which the investment performance of an investor can be compared for the purpose of determining investment skill. A benchmark portfolio represents a relevant and feasible alternative to the investor's actual portfolio and, in particular, is similar in terms of risk exposure.

Best-Efforts Underwriting A security underwriting in which the members of the investment banking group serve as agents instead of dealers, agreeing only to obtain for the issuer the best price that the market will pay for the security.

Beta Coefficient (alternatively, **Market Beta**) A relative measure of the sensitivity of an asset's return to changes in the return on the market portfolio. Mathematically, the beta coefficient of a security is the security's covariance with the market portfolio divided by the variance of the market portfolio.

Bid-Ask Spread The difference between the price that a market-maker is willing to pay for a security and the price at which the market-maker is willing to sell the same security.

Bidder In the context of a corporate takeover, the firm making a tender offer to the target firm.

Bid Price The price at which a market-maker is willing to purchase a specified quantity of a particular security.

Block House A brokerage firm with the financial capacity and the trading expertise to deal in block trades.

Block Trade A large order (usually 10,000 shares or more) to buy or sell a security.

Bond Ratings An indicator of the creditworthiness of specific bond issues. These ratings are often interpreted as an indication of the relative likelihood of default on the part of the respective bond issuers.

Bond Swapping A form of active bond management that entails the replacement of bonds in a portfolio with other bonds so as to enhance the yield of the portfolio.

Book Value of the Equity The sum of the cumulative retained earnings and other balance sheet entries classified under stockholders' equity, such as common stock and capital contributed in excess of par value.

Book Value per Share A corporation's book value of the equity divided by the number of its common shares outstanding.

Bottom-Up Forecasting A sequential approach to security analysis that entails first making forecasts for individual companies, then for industries, and finally for the economy. Each level of forecasts is conditional on the previous level of forecasts made.

Broker An agent, or "middleman," who facilitates the buying and selling of securities for investors.

Call Market A security market in which trading is allowed only at certain specified times. At those times, persons interested in trading a particular security are physically brought together and a market clearing price is established.

Call Money Rate The interest rate paid by brokerage firms to banks on loans used to finance margin purchases by the brokerage firm's customers.

Call Option A contract that gives the buyer the right to buy a specific number of shares of a company from the option writer at a specific purchase price during a specific time period.

Call Premium The difference between the call price of a bond and the par value of the bond.

Call Price The price that an issuer must pay bondholders when an issue is retired prior to its stated maturity date.

Call Provision A provision in some bond indentures that permits an issuer to retire some or all of the bonds in a particular bond issue prior to the bonds' stated maturity date.

Capital Asset Pricing Model (CAPM) An equilibrium model of asset pricing that states that the expected return on a security is a positive linear function of the security's sensitivity to changes in the market portfolio's return.

Capital Consumption Adjustment As calculated by the U.S. Department of Commerce, a measure of the portion of corporate earnings attributable to understated depreciation owing to inflation. It is the estimated difference between aggregate depreciation of corporate fixed assets based on historic cost and aggregate depreciation based on replacement cost.

Capital Gain (or Loss) The difference between the current market value of an asset and the original cost of the asset, with the cost adjusted for any improvement or depreciation in the asset.

Capital Market Line The set of portfolios obtainable by combining the market portfolio with riskfree borrowing or lending. Assuming homogeneous expectations and perfect markets, the Capital Market Line represents the efficient set.

Capital Markets Financial markets in which financial assets with a term-to-maturity of typically more than one year are traded.

Capitalization of Income Method of Valuation An approach to valuing financial assets. It is based on the concept that the "true" or intrinsic value of a financial asset is equal to the discounted value of future cash flows generated by that asset.

Capitalization-Weighted Market Index See **Value-Weighted Market Index.**

Cash Account An account maintained by an investor with a brokerage firm in which deposits (cash and the proceeds from security sales) must fully cover withdrawals (cash and the costs of security purchases).

Cash Matching A form of immunization that involves the purchase of bonds that generate a stream of cash inflows identical in amount and timing to a set of expected cash outflows over a given period of time.

Certainty Equivalent Return For a particularly risky investment, the return on a risk-free investment that makes the investor indifferent between the risky and riskfree investments.

Certificate of Deposit A form of time deposit issued by banks and other financial institutions.

Certificate of Incorporation See **Charter.**

Characteristic Line A simple linear regression model expressing the relationship between the excess return on a security and the excess return on the market portfolio.

Charter (alternatively, **Certificate of Incorporation**) A document issued by a state to a corporation that specifies the rights and obligations of the corporation's stockholders.

Chartist A technical analyst who relies primarily on stock price and volume charts when evaluating securities.

Clearinghouse A cooperative venture among banks, brokerage firms, and other financial intermediaries that maintains records of transactions made by member firms during a trading day. At the end of the trading day, the clearinghouse calculates net amounts of securities and cash to be delivered among the members, permitting each member to settle once with the clearinghouse.

Close See **Closing Price.**

Closed-end Investment Company A managed investment company, with an unlimited life, that does not stand ready to purchase its own shares from its owners and rarely issues new shares beyond its initial offering.

Closing Price (alternatively, **Close**) The price at which the last trade of the day took place in a particular security.

Closing Purchase The purchase of an option contract by an investor that is designed to offset, and thereby cancel, the previous sale of the same option contract by the investor.

Closing Sale The sale of an option contract by an investor that is designed to offset, and thereby cancel, the previous purchase of the same option contract by the investor.

Coefficient of Determination (alternatively, **R-Squared**) In the context of a simple linear regression, the proportion of the variation in the dependent variable that is related to variation in (that is, "explained by") the independent variable.

Coefficient of Nondetermination In the context of a simple linear regression, the proportion of the variation in the dependent variable that is not related to variation in (that is, not "explained by") the independent variable. Equivalently, one minus the coefficient of determination.

Coincident Indicators Economic variables that have been found to change at the same time that the economy is changing.

Collateral Trust Bond A bond that is backed by other financial assets.

Commercial Paper A type of money market instrument. It represents unsecured promissory notes of large, financially sound corporations.

Commission The fee an investor pays to a brokerage firm for services rendered in the trading of securities.

Commission Broker A member of an organized security exchange who takes orders that the public has placed with brokerage firms and sees that these orders are executed on the exchange.

Commodity Fund An investment company that speculates in futures.

Commodity Futures Trading Commission (CFTC) A federal agency established by the Commodity Futures Trading Commission Act of 1974 that approves (or disapproves) the creation of new futures contracts and regulates the trading of existing futures contracts.

Common Factor A factor that affects the return on virtually all securities to a certain extent.

Common Stock Legal representation of an equity (or ownership) position in a corporation.

Comparative Performance Attribution Comparing the performance of a portfolio with that of one or more other portfolios (or market indices) in order to determine the sources of the differences in their returns.

Competitive Bidding With respect to selecting an underwriter, the process of an issuer's soliciting bids on the underwriting and choosing the underwriter offering the best overall terms.

Competitive Trader See **Floor Trader**.

Complete Market A market where there are enough unique securities so that for any given contingency an investor can construct a portfolio that will produce a payoff if that contingency occurs.

Composite Stock Price Tables Price information provided on all stocks traded on the national exchanges, the regional stock exchanges, the Nasdaq system, and the Instinet system.

Compounding The payment of interest on interest.

Computer-Assisted Order Routing and Execution System (CORES) A computer system for trading all but the 150 most active stocks on the Tokyo Stock Exchange.

Computer-Assisted Trading System (CATS) A computer system for trading stocks on the Toronto Stock Exchange that involves a computer file containing a publicly accessible limit order book.

Consolidated Quotations System A system that lists current bid-asked prices of specialists on the national and regional stock exchanges and of certain over-the-counter dealers.

Consolidated Tape A system that reports trades that occur on the national stock exchanges, the regional stock exchanges, the Nasdaq system, and the Instinet system.

Constant-Growth Model A type of dividend discount model in which dividends are assumed to exhibit a constant growth rate.

Consumer Price Index A cost-of-living index that is representative of the goods and services purchased by U.S. consumers.

Contingent Deferred Sales Charge A fee charged by a mutual fund to its shareholders if they sell their shares within a few years after initially purchasing them.

Contingent Immunization A form of bond management that entails both passive and active elements. Under contingent immunization, as long as favorable results are obtained, the bond portfolio is actively managed. However, if unfavorable results occur, then the portfolio is immediately immunized.

Continuous Market A security market in which trades may occur at any time during business hours.

Contrarian An investor who has opinions opposite those of most other investors, leading to actions such as buying recent losers and selling recent winners.

Convertible Bond A bond that may, at the holder's option, be exchanged for other securities, often common stock.

Convexity The tendency for bond prices to change asymmetrically relative to yield changes. Typically, for a given yield change, a bond will rise in price more if the yield change is negative than it will fall in price if the yield change is positive.

Corner Portfolio An efficient portfolio possessing the property that, if it is combined with any adjacent corner portfolio, the combination will produce another efficient portfolio.

Correlation Coefficient A statistical measure similar to covariance, in that it measures the degree of mutual variation between two random variables. The correlation coefficient rescales covariance to facilitate comparison among pairs of random variables. The correlation coefficient is bounded by the values -1 and $+1$.

Cost of Carry The differential between the futures and spot prices of a particular asset. It equals the interest forgone less the benefits plus the costs of ownership.

Cost-of-Living Index A collection of goods and services, and their associated prices, designed to reflect changes over time in the cost of making normal consumption expenditures.

Counterparty Risk The risk posed by the possibility that the person or organization with which an investor has entered into a financial arrangement may fail to make required payments.

Coupon Payments The periodic payment of interest on a bond.

Coupon Rate The annual dollar amount of coupon payments made by a bond expressed as a percentage of the bond's par value.

Coupon Stripping The process of separating and selling the individual cash flows of Treasury notes or bonds.

Covariance A statistical measure of the relationship between two random variables. It measures the extent of mutual variation between two random variables.

Covered Call Writing The process of writing a call option on an asset owned by the option writer.

Cross-Deductibility An arrangement among federal and state tax authorities that permits state taxes to be deductible expenses for federal tax purposes, and federal taxes to be deductible expenses for state tax purposes.

Crown Jewel Defense A strategy used by corporations to ward off hostile takeovers. The strategy entails the target company's selling off its most attractive assets to make itself less attractive to the acquiring firm.

Cumulative Dividends A common feature of preferred stock that requires that the issuing corporation pay all previously unpaid preferred stock dividends before any common stock dividends may be paid.

Cumulative Voting System In the context of a corporation, a method of voting in which a stockholder is permitted to give any one candidate for the board of directors a maximum number of votes equal to the number of shares owned by that shareholder times the number of directors being elected.

Currency Risk See **Exchange Risk.**

Current Yield The annual dollar amount of coupon payments made by a bond expressed as a percentage of the bond's current market price.

Customer's Agreement See **Hypothecation Agreement.**

Date of Record The date, established quarterly by a corporation's board of directors, on which the stockholders of record are determined for the purpose of paying a cash or stock dividend.

Day Order A trading order for which the broker will attempt to fill the order only during the day on which it was entered.

Day-of-the-Week Effect (alternatively, **Weekend Effect**) An empirical regularity whereby stock returns appear to be lower on Mondays than on other days of the week.

Dealer (alternatively, **Market-maker**) A person who facilitates the trading of financial assets by maintaining an inventory in particular securities. The dealer buys for and sells from this inventory, profiting from the difference in the buying and selling prices.

Dealer's Spread The bid-ask spread quoted by a security dealer.

Debenture A bond that is not secured by specific property.

Debit Balance The dollar amount borrowed from a broker as the result of a margin purchase.

Debt Refunding The issuance of new debt for the purpose of paying off currently maturing debt.

Dedicated Portfolio A portfolio of bonds that provides its owner with cash inflows that are matched against a specific stream of cash outflows.

Default Premium The difference between the promised and expected yield-to-maturity on a bond arising from the possibility that the bond issuer might default on the bond.

Defensive Stocks Stocks that have betas less than one.

Delisting The process of removing a security's eligibility for trading on an organized security exchange.

Delta See **Hedge Ratio.**

Demand Deposit A checking account at a financial institution.

Demand-to-Buy Schedule A description of the quantities of a security that an investor is prepared to purchase at alternative prices.

Demand-to-Hold Schedule A description of the quantities of a security that an investor desires to maintain in his or her portfolio at alternative prices.

Depository Trust Company A central computerized depository for securities registered in the names of member firms. Members' security certificates are immobilized and computerized records of ownership are maintained. This permits electronic transfer of the securities from one member to another as trades are conducted between the members' clients.

Differential Return A portfolio's *ex post* alpha where the CAPM is used to estimate the return on the benchmark portfolio.

Discount Broker An organization that offers a limited range of brokerage services and charges fees substantially below those of brokerage firms that provide a full range of services.

Discount Factor The present value of one dollar to be received from a security in a specified number of years.

Discount Rate The interest rate used in calculating the present value of future cash flows. The discount rate reflects not only the time value of money, but also the riskiness of the cash flows.

Discounting The process of calculating the present value of a given stream of cash flows.

Discretionary Order A trading order that permits the broker to set the specifications for the order.

Disintermediation A pattern of funds flow whereby investors withdraw funds from financial intermediaries, such as banks and savings and loans, because market interest rates exceed the maximum interest rates that these organizations are permitted to pay. The investors reinvest their funds in financial assets that pay interest rates not subject to ceilings.

Distribution Fee (or **12b-1 Fee**) An annual fee charged by a mutual fund to its shareholders to pay for advertising, promoting, and selling the fund to new investors.

Diversification The process of adding securities to a portfolio in order to reduce the portfolio's unique risk and, thereby, the portfolio's total risk.

Dividend Decision The process of determining the amount of dividends that a corporation will pay its shareholders.

Dividend Discount Model The term used for the capitalization of income method of valuation as applied to common stocks. All variants of dividend discount models assume that the intrinsic value of a share of common stock is equal to the discounted value of the dividends forecast to be paid on the stock.

Dividend Yield The current annualized dividend paid on a share of common stock, expressed as a percentage of the current market price of the corporation's common stock.

Dividends Cash payments made to stockholders by the corporation.

Dollar-Weighted Return A method of measuring the performance of a portfolio over a particular period of time. It is the discount rate that makes the present value of cash flows into and out of the portfolio, as well as the portfolio's ending value, equal to the portfolio's beginning value.

Domestic Return The return on an investment in a foreign financial asset, excluding the impact of exchange rate changes.

Double Auction Bidding among both buyers and sellers for a security that may occur when the specialist's bid-ask spread is large enough to permit sales at one or more prices within the spread.

Duration A measure of the average maturity of the stream of payments generated by a financial asset. Mathematically, duration is the weighted average of the lengths of time until the asset's remaining payments are made. The weights in this calculation are the proportion of the asset's total present value represented by the present value of the respective cash flows.

Earnings per Share A corporation's accounting earnings divided by the number of its common shares outstanding.

Earnings-Price Ratio The reciprocal of the price-earnings ratio.

Econometric Model A statistical model designed to explain and forecast certain economic phenomena.

Economic Earnings The change in the economic value of the firm plus dividends paid to shareholders.

Economic Value of the Firm The aggregate market value of all securities issued by the firm.

Efficient Market A market for securities in which every security's price equals its investment value at all times, implying that a specified set of information is fully and immediately reflected in market prices.

Efficient Portfolio A portfolio within the feasible set that offers investors both maximum expected return for varying levels of risk and minimum risk for varying levels of expected return.

Efficient Set (Frontier) The set of efficient portfolios.

Efficient Set Theorem The proposition that investors will choose their portfolios only from the set of efficient portfolios.

Emerging Markets Financial markets in countries that have a relatively low level of per capita gross domestic product, improved political and economic stability, a currency that is convertible into Western countries' currencies, and securities available for investment by foreigners.

Empirical Regularities Differences in returns on securities that occur with regularity from period to period.

Endogenous Variable In the context of an econometric model, an economic variable that represents the economic phenomena explained by the model.

Equal-Weighted Market Index A market index in which all the component securities contribute equally to the value of the index, regardless of the various attributes of those securities.

Equilibrium Expected Return The expected return on a security assuming that the security is correctly priced by the market. This

"fair" return is determined by an appropriate asset pricing model.

Equipment Obligation (alternatively, **Equipment Trust Certificate**) A bond that is backed by specific pieces of equipment that, if necessary, can be readily sold and delivered to a new owner.

Equipment Trust Certificate See **Equipment Obligation.**

Equity Premium The difference between the expected rate of return on common stocks and the riskfree return.

Equity Swap A contract between two counterparties where one pays the other a fixed stream of cash flows and in return receives a varying stream whose cash flows are regularly reset based on the performance of a given stock market index.

Equivalent Yield The annualized yield-to-maturity on a fixed-income security sold on a discount basis.

Eurobond A bond that is offered outside of the country of the borrower and usually outside of the country in whose currency the security is denominated.

Eurodollar Certificate of Deposit A certificate of deposit denominated in U.S. dollars and issued by banks domiciled outside of the United States.

Eurodollar Deposit A U.S. dollar-denominated time deposit held at a bank domiciled outside of the United States.

European Option An option that can be exercised only on its expiration date.

Ex Ante Before the fact; future.

Ex-Distribution Date The date on which ownership of stock is determined for purposes of paying stock dividends or issuing new shares due to stock splits. Owners purchasing shares before the ex-distribution date receive the new shares in question. Owners purchasing shares on or after the ex-distribution date are not entitled to the new shares.

Ex-Dividend Date The date on which ownership of stock is determined for purposes of paying dividends. Owners purchasing shares before the ex-dividend date receive the dividend in question. Owners purchasing shares on or after the ex-dividend date are not entitled to the dividend.

Ex Post After the fact; historical.

Ex Post Alpha A portfolio's alpha calculated on an *ex post* basis. Mathematically, over an evaluation interval, it is the difference between the average return on the portfolio and the average return on a benchmark portfolio.

Ex Post Selection Bias In the context of constructing a security valuation model, the use of securities that have performed well and the avoidance of securities that have performed poorly, thus making the model appear more effective than it truly is.

Ex-Rights Date The date on which ownership of stock is determined for purposes of granting rights to purchase new stock in a rights offering. Owners purchasing shares before the ex-rights date receive the rights in question. Owners purchasing shares on or after the ex-rights date are not entitled to the rights.

Excess Return The difference between the return on a security and the return on the riskfree asset.

Exchange Distribution or Acquisition A trade involving a large block of stock on an organized security exchange whereby a brokerage firm attempts to execute the order by finding enough offsetting orders from its customers.

Exchange Risk (alternatively, **Currency Risk**) The uncertainty in the return on a foreign financial asset owing to unpredictability regarding the rate at which the foreign currency can be exchanged into the investor's own currency.

Exercise Price (alternatively, **Striking Price**) In the case of a call option, the price at which an option buyer may purchase the underlying asset from the option writer. In the case of a put option, the price at which an option buyer may sell the underlying asset to the option writer.

Exogenous Variable In the context of an econometric model, an economic variable taken as given and used in the model to explain the model's endogenous variables.

Expectations Hypothesis A hypothesis that the futures price of an asset is equal to the expected spot price of the asset on the delivery date of the futures contract.

Expected Rate of Inflation That portion of inflation experienced over a given period of time that was anticipated by investors.

Expected Return The return on a security (or portfolio) that an investor anticipates receiving over a holding period.

Expected Return Vector A column of numbers that correspond to the expected returns for a set of securities.

Expected Value See **Mean.**

Expected Yield-to-Maturity The yield-to-maturity on a bond calculated as a weighted average of all possible yields that the bond might produce under different scenarios of default or late payments, where the weights are the probabilities of each scenario's occurring.

Expiration Date The date on which the right to buy or sell a security under an option contract ceases.

Face Value See **Principal.**

Factor (alternatively, **Index**) An aspect of the investment environment that influences the returns of financial assets. To the extent that a factor influences a significant number of financial assets, it is termed common or pervasive.

Factor Beta A relative measure of the mutual variation of a particular common factor with the return on the market portfolio. Mathematically, a factor beta is the covariance of the factor with the market portfolio, divided by the variance of the market portfolio.

Factor Loading (alternatively, **Attribute** or **Sensitivity**) A measure of the responsiveness of a security's returns to a particular common factor.

Factor Model (alternatively, **Index Model**) A return-generating process that attributes the return on a security to the security's sensitivity to the movements of various common factors.

Factor Risk That part of a security's total risk that is related to moves in various common factors and, hence, cannot be diversified away.

Factor Risk Premium The expected return over and above the riskfree rate on a portfolio that has unit sensitivity to a particular factor and zero sensitivity to all other factors.

Fail to Deliver A situation in which a seller's broker is unable to deliver the traded security to the buyer's broker on or before the required settlement date.

Fallen Angel A junk bond that was of investment grade when originally issued.

Feasible Set (alternatively, **Opportunity Set**) The set of all portfolios that can be formed from the group of securities being considered by an investor.

Federally Sponsored Agency A privately owned organization with government backing that issues securities and uses the proceeds to support the granting of various types of special-purpose loans.

Fill-or-Kill Order A trading order that is canceled if the broker is unable to execute it immediately.

Financial Analyst (alternatively, **Security Analyst** or **Investment Analyst**) An individual who analyzes financial assets in order to determine the investment characteristics of those assets and to identify mispricings among those assets.

Financial Asset See **Security.**

Financial Institution See **Financial Intermediary.**

Financial Intermediary (alternatively, **Financial Institution**) An organization that issues financial claims against itself and uses the proceeds of the issuance primarily to purchase financial assets issued by individuals, partnerships, corporations, government entities, and other financial intermediaries.

Financial Investment An investment in financial assets.

Financial Leverage The use of debt to fund a portion of an investment.

Financial Market (alternatively, **Security Market**) A mechanism designed to facilitate the exchange of financial assets by bringing buyers and sellers of securities together.

Firm Commitment An arrangement between underwriters and a security issuer whereby the underwriters agree to purchase, at the offering price, all of the issue not bought by the public.

Floating Rate (alternatively, **Variable Rate**) A rate of interest on a financial asset that may vary over the life of the asset, depending on changes in a specified indicator of current market interest rates.

Floor Broker A member of an organized security exchange who assists commission brokers when there are too many orders flowing into the market for the commission brokers to handle alone.

Floor Order Routing and Execution System (FORES) A computer system for trading the 150 most active stocks on the Tokyo Stock Exchange.

Floor Trader (alternatively, **Competitive Trader** or **Registered Competitive Marketmaker** or **Registered Trader**) A member of an organized security exchange who trades solely for his or her own account and is prohibited by exchange rules from handling public orders.

Foreign Return The return on an investment in a foreign financial asset, including the impact of exchange rate changes.

Forward Rate The interest rate that links the current spot interest rate over one holding period to the current spot interest rate over a longer holding period. Equivalently, the interest rate agreed to at a point in time where the associated loan will be made at a future date.

Fourth Market A secondary security market in which investors (typically, financial institutions) trade securities directly with one another, bypassing the brokers and dealers on organized security exchanges and the over-the-counter market.

Fundamental Analysis A form of security analysis that seeks to determine the intrinsic value of securities based on underlying economic factors. These intrinsic values are compared to current market prices to estimate current levels of mispricing.

Futures (Futures Contract) An agreement between two investors under which the seller promises to deliver a specific asset on a specific future date to the buyer for a predetermined price to be paid on the delivery date.

Futures Option (alternatively, **Options on Futures**) An option contract for which the deliverable asset is a specific futures contract.

General Obligation Bond A municipal bond that is backed by the full faith and credit of the issuing agency.

Generally Accepted Accounting Principles (GAAP) Accounting rules established by recognized U.S. authorities, such as the Financial Accounting Standards Board (FASB).

Geometric Mean Return The compounded per-period average rate of return on a financial asset over a specified time interval.

Good-till-Canceled Order See **Open Order**.

Greenmail An offer by the management of a corporation that is the target of an attempted hostile takeover to repurchase its shares from the hostile bidder at an above-market price.

Group In the context of a specific asset class, a collection of financial assets that have common distinguishing financial characteristics.

Group Selection A component of the security selection process involving the identification of desirable combinations of groups within an asset class.

Growth Stock A stock that has experienced or is expected to experience rapidly increasing earnings per share, and is often characterized as having low earnings-to-price and book-value-to-market-value ratios.

Guaranteed Bond A bond issued by one corporation but backed by another corporation.

Hedge Ratio (alternatively, **Delta**) The expected change in the value of an option per dollar change in the market price of the underlying asset.

Hedger An investor in futures contracts whose primary objective is to offset an otherwise risky position.

Historical Beta An estimate of a security's beta, derived solely from historical returns. Equivalently, the slope of the market model or the *ex post* characteristic line.

Holding Period The length of time over which an investor is assumed to invest a given sum of money.

Holding-Period Return The rate of return on an investment over a given holding period.

Holdout Sample See **Out-of-Sample Data**.

Holiday Effect The observation that average stock returns have been abnormally high on the trading day immediately before a federal holiday.

Homogeneous Expectations A situation in which all investors possess the same perceptions with regard to the expected returns, standard deviations, and covariances of securities.

Horizon Analysis A form of active bond management where a single holding period is selected for analysis and possible yield structures at the end of the period are considered. Bonds with the most attractive expected returns under the alternative yield structures are selected for the portfolio.

Hypothecation Agreement (alternatively, **Customer's Agreement**) A legal arrangement between a brokerage firm and an investor that permits the brokerage firm to pledge the investor's securities as collateral for bank loans, provided that the securities were purchased through the investor's margin account.

Idiosyncratic Risk See **Nonfactor Risk**.

Immunization A bond portfolio management technique that permits an investor to meet a promised stream of cash outflows with a high degree of certainty.

Implicit (or Implied) Volatility The risk of an asset derived from an options valuation model, assuming that an option on the asset is fairly priced by the market.

Implied Return See **Internal Rate of Return.**

In the Money Option In the case of a call option, an option whose exercise price is less than the current market price of its underlying asset. In the case of a put option, an option whose exercise price is greater than the current market price of its underlying asset.

Income Bond A bond for which the size of the interest payments varies, based on the income of the issuer.

Indenture A legal document formally describing the terms of the legal relationship between a bond issuer and bondholders.

Index See **Factor.**

Indexation A method of linking the payments associated with a bond to the price level in order to provide a certain real return on the bond.

Index Arbitrage An investment strategy that involves buying a stock index futures contract and selling the individual stocks in the index, or selling a stock index futures contract and buying the individual stocks in the index. The strategy is designed to take advantage of a mispricing between the stock index futures contract and the underlying stocks.

Index Fund A passively managed investment in a diversified portfolio of financial assets designed to mimic the investment performance of a specific market index.

Index Model See **Factor Model.**

Indifference Curve All combinations of portfolios, considered in terms of expected returns and risk, that provide an investor with an equal amount of satisfaction.

Individual Retirement Account A tax-advantaged means for people to set aside income (typically on an after-tax basis) and avoid taxes on the subsequent earnings until those earnings and the original funds are later withdrawn.

Industrial Development Bond (IDB) A form of revenue bond used to finance the purchase or construction of industrial facilities that are leased by the issuing municipality to firms on a favorable basis.

Inefficient Portfolio A portfolio that does not satisfy the criteria of an efficient portfolio and, hence, does not lie on the efficient set.

Inflation The rate of change in a price index over a certain period of time. Equivalently, the percentage change in the purchasing power of a unit of currency over a certain period of time.

Inflation Hedge An asset that preserves the value of its purchasing power over time despite changes in the price level.

Information Coefficient The correlation coefficient between a security analyst's predicted returns and subsequent actual returns that is used to measure the accuracy of the analyst's predictions.

Information Content of Dividends Hypothesis The proposition that dividend announcements contain inside information about a corporation's future prospects.

Initial Margin Requirement The minimum percentage of a margin purchase (or short sale) price that must come from the investor's own funds.

Initial Public Offering (ipo) (alternatively, **Unseasoned Offering**) The first offering of the shares of a company to the public.

Initial Wealth The value of an investor's portfolio at the beginning of a holding period.

Inside Quotes The highest bid price and the lowest asked price for a given stock offered by a group of dealers in a particular stock.

Insider Narrowly defined, a stockholder, officer, or director of a corporation who owns a "significant" proportion of a corporation's stock. More broadly defined, anyone who has access to information that is both "materially" related to the value of a corporation's securities and unavailable to the general public.

Instinet Acronym for Institutional Network. A computerized communications system that provides price quotations and order execution for fourth market participants.

Interest-Rate Parity An explanation for why spot and futures exchange rates differ. It asserts that such differences result from different interest rates in the two countries.

Interest-Rate Risk The uncertainty in the return on a fixed-income security caused by unanticipated fluctuations in the value of the asset owing to changes in interest rates.

Interest Rate Swap A contract between two counterparties where one pays the other a fixed stream of cash flows and in return receives a varying stream whose cash flows are regularly reset based on the level of a given interest rate.

Intermarket Spread Swap A type of bond swap where an investor moves out of one market segment and into another because the investor believes that one segment is significantly underpriced relative to the other.

Intermarket Trading System An electronic communications network that links the national and regional organized security exchanges and certain over-the-counter dealers. The network provides market-maker price quotes and allows participating brokers and dealers to route orders to market-makers offering the best prices.

Internal Rate of Return (alternatively, **Implied Return**) The discount rate that equates the sum of the present value of future cash flows expected to be received from a particular investment to the cost of that investment.

Intrinsic Value of an Option The value of an option if it were exercised immediately. Equivalently, the market price of the asset upon which a call option is written less the exercise price of the option (or the exercise price less the market price of the asset, in the case of a put option).

Inventory Valuation Adjustment As calculated by the U.S. Department of Commerce, a measure of the portion of corporate earnings attributable to changes in the value of inventories owing to inflation.

Investment The sacrifice of certain present value for (possibly uncertain) future value.

Investment Advisor An individual or organization that provides investment advice to investors.

Investment Analyst See **Financial Analyst**.

Investment Banker (alternatively, **Underwriter**) An organization that acts as an intermediary between issuers and the ultimate purchasers of securities in the primary security market.

Investment Banking The process of analyzing and selecting a means of procuring financing on behalf of an issuer of securities.

Investment Committee With a traditional investment organization, a group of senior management responsible for establishing the organization's broad investment strategy.

Investment Company A type of financial intermediary that obtains money from investors and uses that money to purchase financial assets. In return, the investors receive shares in the investment company, and thus indirectly own a proportion of the financial assets that the company itself owns.

Investment Environment The financial structure in which investors operate, consisting of the kinds of marketable securities available for purchase or sale and how and where these securities are bought and sold.

Investment-Grade Bonds Bonds that possess bond ratings that permit them to be purchased by the vast majority of institutional investors, particularly regulated financial institutions. Usually, investment grade bonds have a BBB (Standard & Poor's) or Baa (Moody's) or higher bond rating.

Investment Policy A component of the investment process that involves determining an investor's objectives, particularly as regards his or her attitude toward the trade-off between expected return and risk.

Investment Process The set of procedures by which an investor decides what marketable securities to invest in, how extensive those investments should be, and when the investments should be made.

Investment Style The method an investor uses to take active positions in certain types of securities.

Investment Value The present value of a security's future prospects as estimated by well-informed market participants.

January Effect An empirical regularity whereby stock returns appear to be higher in January than in other months of the year.

Junk Bonds See **Speculative-Grade Bonds.**

Keogh Plan A tax-advantaged means by which people who are self-employed (or otherwise have no access to an employer-sponsored retirement plan) can set aside income on a before-tax basis and invest tax-free until the original funds and subsequent earnings are later withdrawn.

Lagging Indicators Economic variables that have been found to follow movements in the economy.

Lambda The expected return premium (above the riskfree rate of interest) per unit of sensitivity to a particular common factor. Also, the sensitivity of the price of an option to changes in its volatility.

Leading Indicators Economic variables that have been found to signal future changes in the economy.

Letter Stock (alternatively, **Restricted Stock**) Stock that is unregistered and sold directly to the purchaser, rather than through a public offering. Such stock must be held at least two years and cannot be sold even at that time unless ample information on the company is available and the amount sold is a relatively small percentage of the total shares outstanding.

Leveraged Buy Out A situation in which a private investment group, using substantial amounts of debt financing, buys all of the shares of a publicly held firm, thereby gaining complete control of the firm.

Limit Order A trading order that specifies a limit price at which the broker is to execute the order. The trade will be executed only if the broker can meet or better the limit price.

Limit Order Book (alternatively, **Specialist's Book**) The records kept by the specialist identifying the unfilled limit, stop, and stop limit orders that brokers want to execute in a particular security.

Limit Price The price specified when a limit order is placed with a broker, defining the maximum purchase price or minimum selling price at which the order can be executed.

Limited Liability An aspect of the corporate form of organization that prevents common stockholders from losing more than their investment if the corporation should default on its obligations.

Liquidity (alternatively, **Marketability**) The ability of investors to convert securities to cash at a price similar to the price of the previous trade in the security, assuming that no significant new information has arrived since the previous trade. Equivalently, the ability to sell an asset quickly without having to make a substantial price concession.

Liquidity Preference (Premium) Theory An explanation of the term structure of interest rates. It holds that the term structure is a result of the preference of investors for short-term securities. Investors can be induced to hold longer-term securities only if they expect to receive a higher return.

Liquidity Premium The expected incremental return of longer-term securities over shorter-term securities that compensates investors for the greater interest rate risk entailed in holding longer-term securities.

Listed Security A security that is traded on an organized security exchange.

Load Charge A sales charge levied by a mutual fund when an investor buys its shares.

Load Fund A mutual fund that has a load charge.

Local (alternatively, **Scalper**) A member of an organized futures exchange who trades for his or her own account and has a very short holding period.

Long Hedger A hedger who offsets risk by buying futures contracts.

Low-Load Fund A mutual fund that has a small load charge, usually 3.5% or less.

Maintenance Margin Requirement The minimum actual margin that a brokerage firm will permit investors to keep in their margin accounts.

Majority Voting System (alternatively, **Straight Voting System**) In the context of a corporation, a method of voting in which a stockholder is permitted to give any one candidate for the board of directors a maximum number of votes equal to the number of shares owned by that shareholder.

Managed Investment Company An investment company with a portfolio that may be altered at the discretion of the company's portfolio manager.

Management Buy Out A situation in which the existing management of a publicly owned firm, perhaps joined by an outside investment group, buys all the shares of the existing stockholders, thereby gaining complete control of the firm.

Margin Account An account maintained by an investor with a brokerage firm in which securities may be purchased by borrowing a portion of the purchase price from the brokerage firm, or may be sold short by borrowing the securities from the brokerage firm.

Margin Call A demand upon an investor by a brokerage firm to increase the equity in the investor's margin account. The margin call is initiated when the investor's actual margin falls below the maintenance margin requirement.

Margin Purchase The purchase of securities financed by borrowing a portion of the purchase price from a brokerage firm.

Marginal Tax Rate The amount of taxes, expressed as a percentage, paid on each additional dollar of taxable income received.

Markdown The difference in prices between what an investor's broker receives and what the investor receives for a security sold in the over-the-counter market.

Marked (or Marking) to the Market The process of calculating, usually on a daily basis, the actual margin in an investor's account. Equivalently, the daily process of adjusting the equity in an investor's account to reflect the daily changes in the market value of the account's assets and liabilities.

Market Beta See **Beta Coefficient.**

Market Capitalization The aggregate market value of a security, equal to the market price per unit of the security multiplied by the total number of outstanding units of the security.

Market Discount Bond A bond that sells at a price below its par value in the secondary market.

Market Discount Function The set of discount factors on all default-free bonds across the spectrum of terms-to-maturity.

Market Index A collection of securities whose prices are averaged to reflect the overall investment performance of a particular market for financial assets.

Market-maker See **Dealer.**

Market Model A simple linear model that expresses the relationship between the return on a security and the return on a market index.

Market Order A trading order that instructs the broker to buy or sell a security immediately at the best obtainable price.

Market Portfolio A portfolio consisting of an investment in all securities. The proportion invested in each security equals the percentage of the total market capitalization represented by the security.

Market Risk (alternatively, **Systematic Risk**) The portion of a security's total risk that is related to moves in the market portfolio and, hence, cannot be diversified away.

Market Segmentation Theory An explanation of the term structure of interest rates. It holds that various investors and borrowers are restricted by law, preference, or custom to certain maturity ranges. Spot rates in each market segment are determined by supply and demand conditions there.

Market Timing A form of active management that entails shifting an investor's funds between a surrogate market portfolio and the riskfree asset, depending on the investor's perception of their relative near-term prospects.

Marketability See **Liquidity.**

Markup The difference in prices between what an investor pays and what the investor's broker pays for a security purchased in the over-the-counter market.

Maturity Date The date upon which a bond issuer promises to repay investors the principal of the bond.

May Day The date (May 1, 1975) that the New York Stock Exchange ended its fixed-commission rate requirement and permitted member firms to negotiate commission rates with customers.

Mean (alternatively, **Expected Value**) A measure of central tendency of the probability distribution of a random variable that equals the weighted average of all possible outcomes using their probabilities as weights.

Median The outcome of a random variable where there is an equal probability of observing a value greater or less than it.

Member Corporation See **Member Firm.**

Member Firm (alternatively, **Member Corporation** or **Member Organization**) A brokerage firm with one or more memberships in an organized security exchange.

Member Organization See **Member Firm.**

Merger A form of corporate takeover in which two firms combine their operations and become one firm. Mergers are usually negotiated by the management of the two merging corporations.

Mispriced Security A security that is trading at a price substantially different from its investment value.

Mode The outcome of a random variable that has the highest probability of occurring.

Money Market Deposit A short-term fixed income security.

Money Markets Financial markets in which financial assets with a term-to-maturity of typically one year or less are traded.

Moral Hazard A problem in pricing insurance where the likelihood of the insured event's occurring increases after insurance is purchased.

Mortgage Bond A bond that is secured by the pledge of specific property. In the event of default, bondholders are entitled to obtain the property in question and sell it to satisfy their claims on the issuer.

Multinational Firm A corporation that carries on a substantial portion of its business in countries other than the country in which it is domiciled.

Multiple-Growth Model A type of dividend discount model in which dividends are assumed to grow at different rates over specifically defined time periods.

Municipal Bond A bond issued by a state or local unit of government.

Mutual Fund See **Open-end Investment Company.**

Naked Call Writing The process of writing a call option on a stock that the option writer does not own.

Naked Put Writing The process of writing a put option on a stock when the writer does not have sufficient cash (or securities) in his or her brokerage account to purchase the stock.

Nasdaq International An early morning system for trading NYSE, AMEX, and Nasdaq securities through the use of a dealer network.

National Association of Securities Dealers (NASD) A self-regulatory agency that establishes rules and regulations and monitors the activities of brokers and dealers in the over-the-counter market.

National Association of Securities Dealers Automated Quotations (Nasdaq) An automated nationwide communications network operated by the NASD that connects dealers and brokers in the over-the-counter market. Nasdaq provides current market-maker bid-asked price quotes to market participants.

National Market System (Nasdaq/NMS) A segment of the over-the-counter market comprised of issues with relatively large trading volumes. More detailed trading information is provided on stocks included in Nasdaq/NMS than on other over-the-counter stocks.

Neglected Firm Effect An empirical observation that firms followed by relatively few security analysts have had abnormally high returns.

Net Asset Value The market value of an investment company's assets, less any liabilities, divided by the number of shares outstanding.

Net Present Value The present value of future cash flows expected to be received from a particular investment less the cost of that investment.

No-Growth Model See **Zero-Growth Model.**

No-Load Fund A mutual fund that does not have a load charge.

Nominal Return The percentage change in the value of a financial asset, where the beginning and ending values of the asset are not adjusted for inflation over the time of the investment.

Nonfactor Risk (alternatively, **Idiosyncratic Risk**) The portion of a security's total risk that is not related to moves in various common factors and, hence, can be diversified away.

Non-Market Risk See **Unique Risk.**

Nonsatiation A condition whereby investors are assumed to always prefer higher levels of terminal wealth to lower levels of terminal wealth.

Normal Backwardation A relationship between the futures price of an asset and the expected spot price of the asset on the delivery date of the contract. Normal backwardation states that the futures price will be less than the expected spot price.

Normal Contango A relationship between the futures price of an asset and the expected spot price of the asset on the delivery date of the contract. Normal contango states that the futures price will be greater than the expected spot price.

Normal Probability Distribution A symmetrical bell-shaped probability distribution, completely described by its mean and standard deviation.

Normative Economics A form of economic analysis that is prescriptive in nature, dealing with what "ought to be."

Odd Lot An amount of stock that is less than the standard unit of trading, generally from 1 to 99 shares.

Open See **Opening Price.**

Open-end Investment Company (alternatively, **Mutual Fund**) A managed investment company, with an unlimited life, that stands ready at all times to purchase its shares from its owners and usually will continuously offer new shares to the public.

Open Interest The number of a particular futures contract that are outstanding at a particular point in time.

Open Order (alternatively, **Good-till-Canceled Order**) A trading order that remains in effect until it is either filled or canceled by the investor.

Opening Price (alternatively, **Open**) The price at which the first trade of the day took place in a particular stock.

Operating Expense Ratio The percentage of an investment company's assets that were used to pay for management fees, administrative expenses, and other operating expenses in a given year.

Opportunity Set See **Feasible Set.**

Optimal Portfolio The feasible portfolio that offers an investor the maximum level of satisfaction. This portfolio represents the tangency between the efficient set and an indifference curve of the investor.

Option A contract between two investors in which one investor grants the other the right to buy (or sell) a specific asset at a specific price within a specific time period.

Options on Futures See **Futures Option.**

Order Book Officials The people who keep the limit order book in those option markets that involve market-makers instead of specialists.

Order Specification The investor's instructions to a broker regarding the particular characteristics of a trading order, including the name of the security's issuing firm, whether to buy or sell, order size, maximum time the order is to be outstanding, and the type of order to be used.

Ordinary Least Squares See **Simple Linear Regression.**

Organized Exchange A central physical location where trading of securities is done under a set of rules and regulations.

Original Issue Discount (OID) Bond A bond that was originally issued at a price below its par value.

Out of the Money Option In the case of a call option, an option whose exercise price is greater than the market price of its underlying asset. In the case of a put option, an option whose exercise price is less than the market price of its underlying asset.

Out-of-Sample Data (alternatively, **Holdout Sample**) In the context of constructing a security valuation model, information that is obtained from periods different from those used to estimate the valuation model. Out-of-sample data can be used to test the model's validity.

Over-the-counter Market (OTC Market) A secondary market for securities distinct from an organized security exchange.

Overmargined Account (alternatively, **Unrestricted Account**) A margin account in which the actual margin has risen above the initial margin requirement.

Overpriced Security (alternatively, **Overvalued Security**) A security whose expected return is less than its equilibrium expected return. Equivalently, a security with a negative alpha.

Oversubscription Privilege The opportunity given shareholders who have exercised their rights in a rights offering to buy shares that were not purchased in the offering.

Overvalued Security See **Overpriced Security.**

Pac-Man Defense A strategy used by corporations to ward off hostile takeovers. The targeted company reverses the takeover effort and seeks to acquire the firm making the initial takeover attempt.

Par Value The nominal value of shares of common stock as legally carried on the books of a corporation.

Par Value of Bond See **Principal.**

Participating Bond A bond that promises to pay a stated rate of interest to its owner, but may also pay additional interest if the issuer's earnings exceed a specified level.

Participation Certificate A bond that represents an ownership interest in a pool of fixed-income securities. The holders of the certificates receive the interest and principal payments on the pooled securities in proportion to their ownership of the pool.

Passive Investment System (alternatively, **Passive Management**) The process of buying and holding a well-diversified portfolio.

Passive Management See **Passive Investment System.**

Payout Ratio The percentage of a firm's earnings paid to shareholders in the form of cash dividends.

Pegging The process by which investment bankers attempt to stabilize the price of an underwritten security in the secondary market for a period of time after the initial offering date.

Perfect Markets Security markets in which no impediments to investing exist. These impediments include finite divisibility of securities, taxes, transaction costs, and costly information.

Performance Attribution The identification of sources of returns for a portfolio or security over a particular evaluation interval of time.

Performance Margin The initial margin that must be posted by a futures buyer or seller.

Pink Sheets Written published quotations on over-the-counter stocks that are not listed on Nasdaq.

Poison Pill Defense A strategy used by corporations to ward off hostile takeovers. The targeted company gives its shareholders certain rights that can be exercised only in the event of a hostile takeover, and that, once exercised, will be extremely onerous to the acquirer.

Political Risk The uncertainty in the return on a foreign financial asset owing to the possibility that the foreign government might take actions that are detrimental to the investor's financial interests.

Portfolio Construction (alternatively, **Security Selection**) A component of the investment process that involves identifying which assets to invest in and determining the proportion of funds to invest in each of the assets.

Portfolio Insurance An investment strategy designed to earn a minimum rate of return while allowing the investor to benefit substantially from the positive returns generated by an investment in a risky portfolio.

Portfolio Manager An individual who utilizes the information provided by financial analysts to construct a portfolio of financial assets.

Portfolio Performance Evaluation A component of the investment process involving periodic analysis of how a portfolio performed in terms of both returns earned and risk incurred.

Portfolio Revision A component of the investment process, involving periodically repeating the process of setting investment policy, conducting security analysis, and constructing a portfolio.

Portfolio Turnover Rate A measure of how much buying and selling occurs in a portfolio over a given period of time.

Positive Economics A form of economic analysis that is descriptive in nature, dealing with "what is."

Preemptive Rights When a corporation plans an issuance of new common shares, the right of existing shareholders to purchase the new shares in proportion to the number of shares that they currently own.

Preferred Stock A hybrid form of security that has characteristics of both common stocks and bonds.

Premium The price of an option contract.

Price-Earnings Ratio A corporation's current stock price divided by its earnings per share.

Price Impact The effect on the price of a security resulting from a trade in that security. Price impact is the result of several factors, including size of the trade, demand for immediate liquidity, and presumed information of the individual or organization placing the order.

Price-Relative The price of a security at the end of one period divided by its price at the end of the previous period.

Price-Weighted Market Index A market index in which the contribution of a security to the value of the index is a function of the security's current market price.

Primary Security Market The market in which securities are sold at the time of their initial issuance.

Principal (alternatively, **Face Value** or **Par Value of Bond**) The nominal value of a bond that is repaid to bondholders at the maturity date.

Private Placement The direct sale of a newly issued security to a small number of large institutional investors.

Probabilistic Forecasting A form of security analysis that begins with a series of economic scenarios, along with their respective probabilities of occurrence. Under each of these scenarios, accompanying projections are made as to the prospects for various industries, companies, and stock prices.

Probability Distribution A model describing the relative frequency of possible values that a random variable can assume.

Professional Money Manager An individual or organization that invests funds on behalf of others.

Program Trading The purchase or sale of a collection of securities as if the collection were one security. Program trades are prominently employed in portfolio insurance and index arbitrage strategies.

Promised Yield-to-Maturity The yield-to-maturity on a bond calculated assuming that all promised cash flows are received on a full and timely basis.

Prospectus The official selling circular that must be given to purchasers of new securities registered with the Securities and Exchange Commission. The prospectus provides various information about the issuer's business, its financial condition, and the nature of the security being offered.

Proxy The signing by a shareholder of a power of attorney, thereby authorizing a designated party to cast all of the shareholder's votes on any matter brought up at the corporation's annual meeting.

Proxy Fight An attempt by dissident shareholders to solicit proxies to vote against corporate incumbents.

Purchasing Group See **Syndicate**.

Purchasing-Power Risk The risk experienced by investors in financial assets owing to uncertainty concerning the impact of inflation on the real returns produced by those financial assets.

Pure-Discount Bond (alternatively, **Zero Coupon Bond**) A bond that promises to make only one payment to its owner.

Pure Factor Play See **Pure Factor Portfolio**.

Pure Factor Portfolio (alternatively, **Pure Factor Play**) A portfolio that possesses a unit sensitivity to one factor and no sensitivity to any other factor and has zero nonfactor risk.

Pure Yield Pickup Swap A type of bond swap where an investor exchanges one bond for another to obtain a higher yield over the long term, with little attention paid to the near-term outlook for the bond's respective market segments or the market as a whole.

Put-Call Parity The relationship between the market price of a put and a call that have the same exercise price, expiration date, and underlying stock.

Put Option A contract that gives the buyer the right to sell a specific number of shares of a company to the writer at a specific price within a specific time period.

R-Squared See **Coefficient of Determination**.

Random Error Term The difference between the actual value of a random variable and the predicted value based on some model.

Random Variable A variable that takes on alternative values according to chance.

Random Walk (or **Random Walk Model**) In general, a situation in which changes in the value of a random variable are independent and identically distributed. When applied to common stocks, it refers to a situation in which security price changes are independent and identically distributed, meaning that the size of a security's price change from one period to the next can be viewed as being determined by the spin of a roulette wheel.

Rate Anticipation Swap A type of bond swap where an investor exchanges bonds that are expected to perform relatively poorly for those that are expected to perform relatively well, given an anticipated movement in interest rates.

Rate of Return The percentage change in the value of an investment in a financial asset (or portfolio of financial assets) over a specified time period.

Real Estate Investment Trust (REIT) An investment fund, similar to an investment company, whose investment objective is to hold primarily real estate–related assets, either through mortgages, construction and development loans, or equity interests.

Real Investment An investment involving some kind of tangible asset, such as land, equipment, or buildings.

Real Return The percentage change in the value of an investment in a financial asset, where the beginning and ending values of the asset are adjusted for inflation over the time of the investment.

Realized Capital Gain (or Loss) A capital gain (or loss) on an asset that is recognized, for tax purposes, through the sale or exchange of the asset.

Red Herring A preliminary prospectus that provides much of the information in the final prospectus but is not an offer to sell the security, nor does it display an actual offering price.

Redemption Fee A fee levied by an investment company when an investor sells his or her shares back to the investment company within a few days of purchase.

Regional Brokerage Firm An organization offering brokerage services that specializes in trading the securities of companies located in a particular region of the country.

Regional Exchange An organized exchange that specializes in trading the securities of companies located in a particular region of the country.

Registered Bond A bond for which the owner is registered with the issuer. The bondholder receives coupon payments directly from the issuer. Ownership changes require notification of the issuer.

Registered Competitive Market-maker See **Floor Trader.**

Registered Representative See **Account Executive.**

Registered Trader See **Floor Trader.**

Registrar A designated agent of a corporation responsible for canceling and issuing shares of stock in the corporation as these shares are issued or traded.

Registration Statement A document filed with the Securities and Exchange Commission prior to initiating a public security offering.

Reinvestment-Rate Risk The uncertainty in the return on a fixed-income asset caused by unanticipated changes in the interest rate at which cash flows from the asset can be reinvested.

Replacement Cost Accounting The use of estimated replacement costs instead of historical book-value costs when calculating corporate earnings.

Repo Rate The rate of interest involved in a repurchase agreement.

Reported Earnings See **Accounting Earnings.**

Repurchase Agreement A type of money market instrument that involves the sale of a financial asset from one investor to another. The investor selling the asset simultaneously agrees to repurchase it from the purchaser on a stated future date at a predetermined price, which is higher than the original transaction price.

Repurchase Offer An offer by the management of a corporation to buy back some of its own stock.

Residual Standard Deviation See **Standard Deviation of the Random Error Term.**

Restricted Account A margin account in which the actual margin has fallen below the initial margin requirement but remains above the maintenance margin requirement.

Restricted Stock See **Letter Stock.**

Retention Ratio The percentage of a firm's earnings that are not paid to shareholders but instead are retained by the firm. Equivalently, one minus the payout ratio.

Return-Generating Process A statistical model that describes how the returns on a security are produced.

Return on Equity The earnings per share of a firm divided by the firm's book value per share.

Revenue Bond A municipal bond that is backed solely by the revenues from a designated project, authority, or agency, or by the proceeds from a specific tax.

Reverse Stock Split A form of stock split whereby the number of shares is reduced and the par value per share is increased.

Reversing Trade The purchase or sale of a futures (or options) contract designed to offset, and thereby cancel, the previous sale or purchase of the same contract.

Reward-to-Variability Ratio (Sharpe Ratio) An *ex post* risk-adjusted measure of portfolio performance where risk is defined as the standard deviation of the portfolio's returns. Mathematically, over an evaluation period, it is the excess return of a portfolio divided by the standard deviation of the portfolio's returns.

Reward-to-Volatility Ratio (Treynor Ratio) An *ex post* risk-adjusted measure of portfolio performance where risk is defined as the market risk of the portfolio. Mathematically, over an evaluation period, it is the excess return of a portfolio divided by the beta of the portfolio.

Right An option issued to existing shareholders that permits them to buy a specified number of new shares at a designated subscription price. For each shareholder this number is proportional to the number of existing shares currently owned by the shareholder.

Rights Offering The sale of new stock conducted by first offering the stock to existing shareholders in proportion to the number of shares owned by each shareholder.

Risk The uncertainty associated with the end-of-period value of an investment.

Risk-Adjusted Return The return on an asset or portfolio, modified to explicitly account for the risk to which the asset or portfolio is exposed.

Risk-Averse Investor An investor who prefers an investment with less risk over one with more risk, assuming that both investments offer the same expected return.

Risk-Neutral Investor An investor who has no preference between investments with varying levels of risk, assuming that the investments offer the same expected return.

Risk Premium The difference between the expected yield-to-maturity of a risky bond and the expected yield-to-maturity of a similar default-free bond.

Risk-Seeking Investor An investor who prefers an investment with more risk over one with less risk, assuming that both investments offer the same expected return.

Risk Structure The set of yields-to-maturity across bonds that possess different degrees of default risk but are similar with respect to other attributes.

Risk Tolerance The trade-off between risk and expected return demanded by a particular investor.

Riskfree Asset An asset whose return over a given holding period is certain and known at the beginning of the holding period.

Riskfree Borrowing The act of borrowing funds that are to be repaid with a known rate of interest.

Riskfree Lending (Investing) The act of investing in a riskfree asset.

Round Lot An amount of stock that is equal to a standard unit of trading, generally 100 shares or a multiple of 100 shares.

Savings Forgone consumption. Also, the difference between current income and current consumption.

Scalper See **Local.**

SEAQ Automated Execution Facility (SAEF) A small-order execution system, similar to the Small Order Execution System of Nasdaq, that is used on the London Stock Exchange.

Seat The designation of membership in an organized exchange. By holding a seat, the member has the privilege of being able to execute trades using the facilities provided by the exchange.

Secondary Distribution A means of selling a block of stock where the shares are sold away from an organized exchange after the close of trading in a manner similar to the sale of new issues of common stock.

Secondary Security Market The market in which securities are traded that have been issued at some previous point in time.

Sector-Factor A factor that affects the return on securities within a particular economic sector.

Sector-Factor Model A special kind of multiple-factor model in which the factors are particular industries or economic sectors.

Securities and Exchange Commission (SEC) A federal agency established by the Securities Exchange Act of 1934 that regulates the issuance of securities in the primary market and the trading of securities in the secondary market.

Securities Investor Protection Corporation (SIPC) A quasi-governmental agency that insures the accounts of brokerage firms against loss owing to any of the firms' failure.

Security (alternatively, **Financial Asset**) A legal representation of the right to receive prospective future benefits under stated conditions.

Security Analysis A component of the investment process that involves determining the prospective future benefits of a security, the conditions under which such benefits will be received, and the likelihood that such conditions will occur.

Security Analyst See **Financial Analyst.**

Security Market See **Financial Market.**

Security Market Line Derived from the Capital Asset Pricing Model, a linear relationship between the expected returns on securities and the risk of those securities, with risk expressed as the security's beta (or equivalently, the security's covariance with the market portfolio).

Security Selection See **Portfolio Construction.**

Selectivity An aspect of security analysis that entails forecasting the price movements of individual securities.

Self-Regulation A method of governmental regulation where the rules and standards of conduct in security markets are set by firms that operate in these markets, subject to the oversight of various federal agencies such as the SEC and CFTC.

Selling Group A group of investment banking organizations that, as part of a security underwriting, are responsible for selling the security.

Semistrong-Form Market Efficiency A level of market efficiency in which all relevant publicly available information is fully and immediately reflected in security prices.

Sensitivity See **Factor Loading.**

Separation Theorem A feature of the Capital Asset Pricing Model that states that the optimal combination of risky assets for an investor can be determined without any knowledge about the investor's preferences toward risk and return.

Serial Bond A bond issue with different portions of the issue maturing at different dates.

Settle (or Settlement) Price The representative price for a futures contract determined during the closing period of the futures exchange.

Settlement Date The date after a security has been traded on which the buyer must deliver cash to the seller and the seller must deliver the security to the buyer.

Shelf Registration Under Securities and Exchange Commission Rule 415, issuers may register securities in advance of their issuance and sell these securities up to a year later.

Short Hedger A hedger who offsets risk by selling futures contracts.

Short Interest Position The number of shares of a given company that have been sold short and, as of a given date, have loans remaining outstanding.

Short Sale The sale of a security that is not owned by an investor but rather is borrowed from a broker. The investor eventually repays the broker in kind by purchasing the same security in a subsequent transaction.

Simple Linear Regression (alternatively, **Ordinary Least Squares**) A statistical model of the relationship between two random variables in which one variable is hypothesized to be linearly related to the other. This relationship is depicted by a regression line, which is a straight line, "fitted" to pairs of values of the two variables, so that the sum of the squared random error terms is minimized.

Sinking Fund Periodic payments made by a bond issuer to reduce, in an orderly manner, the amount of outstanding principal on a bond issue over the life of the bond.

Size Effect (alternatively, **Small Firm Effect**) An empirical regularity whereby stock returns appear to differ consistently across the spectrum of market capitalization. Over extended periods of time, smaller capitalization stocks have outperformed larger capitalization stocks on a risk-adjusted basis.

Small Cap Issues Less active stocks that are listed on Nasdaq.

Small Firm Effect See **Size Effect.**

Small Order Execution System (SOES) A computer system associated with Nasdaq that provides for automatic order execution of as many as 1,000 shares.

Soft Dollars Brokerage commissions ostensibly paid for having a brokerage firm execute a trade and indirectly designated, in part, as payment for non-trade-related services rendered.

Special Offering or Bid A trade involving a large block of stock on an organized security exchange whereby a number of brokerage firms attempt to execute the order by soliciting offsetting orders from their customers.

Specialist A member of an organized exchange who has two primary functions. First, the specialist maintains an orderly market in assigned securities by acting as a dealer: buying and selling from his or her inventory of securities to offset temporary imbalances in the number of buy and sell orders. Second, the specialist facilitates the execution of limit, stop, and stop limit orders by acting as a broker. This is done by maintaining a limit order book and executing these orders as they are triggered.

Specialist Block Purchase or Sale The accommodation of a relatively small block trade by a specialist who buys or sells from his or her inventory at a price negotiated with the seller or buyer.

Specialist's Book See **Limit Order Book.**

Speculative-Grade Bonds (alternatively, **Junk Bonds**) Bonds that are not investment grade bonds. Usually, speculative bonds have a BB (Standard & Poor's) or Ba (Moody's) or lower rating.

Speculator An investor in futures contracts whose primary objective is to make a profit from buying and selling these contracts.

Split-Funding A situation in which an institutional investor divides its funds among two or more professional money managers.

Spot Market The market for an asset that involves the immediate exchange of the asset for cash.

Spot Price The purchase price of an asset in the spot market.

Spot Rate The annual yield-to-maturity on a pure-discount security.

Standard Deviation A measure of the dispersion of possible outcomes around the expected value of a random variable.

Standard Deviation of the Random Error Term (alternatively, **Residual Standard Deviation**) In the context of simple linear regression, a measure of the dispersion of possible outcomes of the random error term.

Standard Error of Alpha The standard deviation of a security's estimated alpha, as derived from the *ex post* characteristic line.

Standard Error of Beta The standard deviation of a security's estimated beta, as derived from the *ex post* characteristic line.

Standardized Unexpected Earnings The difference between a firm's actual earnings over a given period and an estimate of the firm's expected earnings, with this quantity divided by the standard deviation of the firm's previous earnings forecast errors.

Standby Agreement An arrangement between a security issuer and an underwriter as part of a rights offering. The underwriter agrees to purchase at a fixed price all securities not purchased by current stockholders.

State-Preference Method A method of valuing securities that is based on analyzing a security's payoffs in different states of the world (outcomes) and the probabilities of those states occurring.

Stochastic Process Risk In the context of immunization, the risk that the yield curve will shift in a way that prevents an immunized bond portfolio from producing its expected cash inflows.

Stock Dividend An accounting transaction that distributes stock to existing shareholders in proportion to the number of shares currently owned by the shareholders. A stock dividend entails a transfer from retained earnings to the capital stock account of a dollar amount that is equal to the market value of the distributed stock.

Stock Exchange Automated Quotations (SEAQ) A computer system, similar to Nasdaq, that is used to trade stocks on the London Stock Exchange.

Stock Split Similar to a stock dividend, an accounting transaction that increases the amount of stock held by existing shareholders in proportion to the number of shares currently owned by the shareholders. A stock split entails a reduction in the par value of the corporation's stock and the simultaneous exchange of a multiple number of new shares for each existing share.

Stop Limit Order A trading order that specifies both a stop price and a limit price. If the security's price reaches or passes the stop price, then a limit order is created at the limit price.

Stop Loss Order See **Stop Order.**

Stop Order (alternatively, **Stop Loss Order**) A trading order that specifies a stop price. If the security's price reaches or passes the stop price, then a market order is created.

Stop Price The price specified by an investor when a stop order or a stop limit order is placed that defines the price at which the market order or limit order for the security is to become effective.

Straddle An options strategy that involves buying (or writing) both a call and a put on the same asset, with the options having the same exercise price and expiration date.

Straight Voting System See **Majority Voting System.**

Street Name An arrangement between an investor and a brokerage firm where the investor maintains an account in which the investor's securities are registered in the name of the brokerage firm.

Striking Price See **Exercise Price.**

Strong-Form Market Efficiency A level of market efficiency in which all relevant information, both public and private, is fully and immediately reflected in security prices.

Subordinated Debenture A debenture whose claims, in the event of bankruptcy, are junior to other bonds issued by the firm.

Subscription Price The price at which holders of rights are permitted to purchase shares of stock in a rights offering.

Substitution Swap A type of bond swap where an investor exchanges one bond with a lower yield for another with a higher yield, yet both bonds have essentially the same financial characteristics.

Super Designated Order Turnaround (SuperDot) A set of special procedures established by the New York Stock Exchange to handle routine small trading orders. Through these procedures, participating member firms can route orders directly to the specialist for immediate execution.

Supply-to-Sell Schedule A description of the quantities of a security that an investor is prepared to sell at alternative prices.

Sustainable Earnings The amount of earnings that a firm could pay out each year, with the result that the firm's future earnings would neither increase nor decrease.

Swap Bank Typically a commercial or investment bank that sets up equity, interest rate, and other kinds of swaps between interested counterparties.

Syndicate (alternatively, **Purchasing Group**) A group of investment banking organizations that, as part of a security underwriting, are responsible for purchasing the security from the issuer and reselling it to the public.

Synthetic Futures (Synthetic Futures Contract) The creation of a position equivalent to either the purchase of a futures contract by buying a call option and writing a put option on the asset, or to the sale of a futures contract by buying a put option and writing a call option on the asset.

Synthetic Put A form of portfolio insurance that emulates the investment outcomes of a put option through the use of a dynamic asset allocation strategy.

Systematic Risk See **Market Risk.**

Takeover An action by an individual or a firm to acquire controlling interest in a corporation.

Target Firm A firm that is the subject of a takeover attempt.

Taxable Municipal Bond A municipal bond whose income is fully taxable by the federal government.

Tax-Exempt Bond A security whose income is not taxable by the federal government.

Technical Analysis A form of security analysis that attempts to forecast the movement in the prices of securities based primarily on historical price and volume trends in those securities.

Tender Offer A form of corporate takeover in which a firm or individual offers to buy some or all of the shares of a target firm at a stated price. This offer is publicly advertised, and material describing the bid is mailed to the target's stockholders.

Term Bond A bond issue where all of the bonds mature on the same date.

Term Structure The set of yields-to-maturity across bonds that possess different terms-to-maturity, but are similar with respect to other attributes.

Term-to-Maturity The time remaining until a bond's maturity date.

Terminal Wealth The value of an investor's portfolio at the end of a holding period. Equivalently, the investor's initial wealth multiplied by one plus the rate of return earned on the investor's portfolio over the holding period.

Third Market A secondary security market where exchange-listed securities are traded over the counter.

Time Deposit A savings account at a financial institution.

Time Value (Time Premium) The excess of the market price of an option over its intrinsic value.

Time-Weighted Return A method of measuring the performance of a portfolio over a particular period of time. Effectively, it is the return on one dollar invested in the portfolio at the beginning of the measurement period.

Timing An aspect of security analysis that entails forecasting the price movements of asset classes relative to one another.

Top-down Forecasting A sequential approach to security analysis that entails first making forecasts for the economy, then for industries, and finally for individual companies. Each level of forecasts is conditional on the previous level of forecasts made.

Total Risk The standard deviation of the return on a security or portfolio.

Trading Halt A temporary suspension in the trading of a security on an organized exchange.

Trading Post The physical location on the floor of an organized exchange where a specialist in a particular stock is located and where all orders involving the stock must be taken for execution.

Transfer Agent A designated agent of a corporation, usually a bank, that administers the transfer of shares of a corporation's stock between old and new owners.

Treasury Bill A pure-discount security issued by the U.S. Treasury with a maximum term-to-maturity of one year.

Treasury Bond A security issued by the U.S. Treasury with a term-to-maturity of over seven years. Interest is paid semiannually, and principal is returned at maturity.

Treasury Note A security issued by the U.S. Treasury with a term-to-maturity between one and seven years. Interest is paid semiannually, and principal is returned at maturity.

Treasury Stock Common stock that has been issued by a corporation and then later purchased by the corporation in the open market or through a tender offer. This stock does not include voting rights or rights to receive dividends and is equivalent economically to unissued stock.

Triple Witching Hour The date when options on individual stocks and market indices, futures on market indices, and options on market index futures expire simultaneously.

Trustee An organization, usually a bank, that serves as the representative of bondholders. The trustee acts to protect the interests of bondholders and facilitates communication between them and the issuer.

Turn-of-the-Month Effect The observation that average stock returns have been abnormally high during a four-day period beginning on the last trading day of the month.

Two-Dollar Broker See **Floor Broker.**

Unbiased Expectations Theory An explanation of the term structure of interest rates. It holds that a forward rate represents the average opinion of the expected future spot rate for the time period in question.

Undermargined Account A margin account in which the actual margin has fallen below the maintenance margin requirement.

Underpriced Security (alternatively, **Undervalued Security**) A security whose expected return is greater than its equilibrium expected return. Equivalently, a security with a positive expected alpha.

Undervalued Security See **Underpriced Security.**

Underwriter See **Investment Banker.**

Underwriting The process by which investment bankers bring new securities to the primary security market.

Unexpected Rate of Inflation That portion of inflation experienced over a given period of time that was not anticipated by investors.

Unique Risk (alternatively, **Non-Market Risk** or **Unsystematic Risk**) The portion of a security's total risk that is not related to moves in the market portfolio and, hence, can be diversified away.

Unit Investment Trust An unmanaged investment company with a finite life that raises an initial sum of capital from investors and uses the proceeds to purchase a fixed portfolio of securities (typically bonds).

Unrealized Capital Gain (or Loss) A capital gain (or loss) on an asset that has not yet been recognized for tax purposes through the sale or exchange of the asset.

Unrestricted Account See **Overmargined Account.**

Unseasoned Offering See **Initial Public Offering (IPO).**

Unsystematic Risk See **Unique Risk.**

Upstairs Dealer Market An adjunct to organized exchanges, where block houses that are member firms handle large block trades. The block houses act as both agents and principals, lining up trading partners to take the other side of the block orders.

Uptick A trade in a security made at a price higher than the price of the previous trade in that same security.

Value-Relative The holding period return for a security, plus one.

Value Stock Typically, a stock that has experienced relatively poor past price performance, or whose issuing company has experienced relatively poor past earnings results. It is often characterized as having high earnings-to-price and book-value-to-market-value ratios.

Value-Weighted Market Index (alternatively, **Capitalization-Weighted Market Index**) A market index in which the contribution of a security to the value of the index is a function of the security's market capitalization.

Variable Rate See **Floating Rate.**

Variance The squared value of the standard deviation.

Variance-Covariance Matrix A table that symmetrically arrays the covariances between a number of random variables. Variances of the random variables lie on the diagonal of the matrix, whereas covariances between the random variables lie above and below the diagonal.

Variation Margin The amount of cash that an investor must provide to meet a margin call on a futures contract.

Voting Bond A bond that gives its holder a voice in the management of the issuer.

Wash Sale The sale and subsequent purchase of a "substantially identical" security solely for the purpose of generating a tax-deductible capital loss.

Weak-Form Market Efficiency A level of market efficiency in which all previous security price and volume data are fully and immediately reflected in current security prices.

Weekend Effect See **Day-of-the-Week Effect.**

White Knight Another firm, favorably inclined toward a target firm's current management, that during the process of a hostile takeover of that corporation agrees to make a better offer to the corporation's stockholders.

Wrap Account A type of account at a brokerage firm that involves having a broker provide the investor with advice. All fees for financial planning, investment management, and securities trading are "wrapped" into one annual fee.

Yield The yield-to-maturity of a bond.

Yield Curve A visual representation of the term structure of interest rates.

Yield Spread The difference in the promised yields-to-maturity of two bonds.

Yield Structure The set of yields-to-maturity across bonds differing in terms of a number of attributes. These attributes include term-to-maturity, coupon rate, call provisions, tax status, marketability, and likelihood of default.

Yield-to-Call The yield-to-maturity of a callable bond calculated assuming that the bond is called at the earliest possible time.

Yield-to-Maturity For a particular fixed-income security, the single interest rate (with interest compounded at some specified interval) that, if paid by a bank on the amount invested in the security, would enable the investor to obtain all the payments made by that security. Equivalently, the discount rate that equates the present value of future promised cash flows from the security to the current market price of the security.

Zero Coupon Bond See **Pure-Discount Bond.**

Zero-Growth Model (alternatively, **No-Growth Model**) A type of dividend discount model in which dividends are assumed to maintain a constant value in perpetuity.

Zero-Plus Tick A trade in a security made at a price equal to that of the previous trade in that security but higher than that of the last trade made in the security at a different price.

Selected Solutions to End-of-Chapter Questions and Problems

Chapter 1

3. 18.2%
4. a. 30.0%
   b. −13.3%
   c. 4.0%
8. First period average return: 0.67%
   First period standard deviation: 0.45%
   Second period average return: 2.08%
   Second period standard deviation: 0.72%
9. Small stock average return: 16.05%
   Small stock standard deviation: 24.79%
   Common stock average return: 12.48%
   Common stock standard deviation: 17.05%

Chapter 2

2. Five round lots and one 11-share odd lot
5. Total assets: $15,000
   Total liabilities: $6,750
6. a. 62.5%
   b. 75.0%
   c. 57.1%
8. 40.0%
9. $9.23
10. $30,000
12. 17.1%
13. 74.0%, −26.0%

14. a. 56.0%
    b. −65.2%
    c. 36.7%, −30.0%
16. Total assets: $18,750
    Total liabilities: $12,500
17. a. 25.0%
    b. 72.6%
18. Actual margin: 39.5%
19. $53.57
21. −20.0%
22. a. −27.6%
    b. 43.6%
25. a. $5,400
    b. $5,500
26. Total assets: $12,750
    Total liabilities: $7,600

Chapter 3

19. Round trip transaction cost: 27.3%
    Return before transaction cost: 12.5%

Chapter 4

3. $30   100 shares
   $40   90 shares
   $50   80 shares

$60   70 shares
$70   60 shares

Chapter   5

1. 5.0%
2. −5.6%
3. a. 7.0%
   b. 9.0%
4. $939.26, $1,066.23
5. a. 10.0%
   b. 9.8%
7. One-year spot rate: 7.5%
   Two-year spot rate: 4.0%
   Three-year spot rate: 2.8%
8. Three-year discount factor: .810
   Four-year discount factor: .731
   Five-year discount factor: .650
10. Forward rate from year one to year two: 6.0%
    Forward rate from year two to year three:
    8.5%
    Forward rate from year three to year four:
    8.5%
11. One-year spot rate: 10.0%
    Two-year spot rate: 9.8%
    Three-year spot rate: 9.5%
    Four-year spot rate: 9.2%
12. $994.45
13. a. One-year discount rate: .909
       Two-year discount rate: .819
       Three-year discount rate: .749
    b. Forward rate from today to one year.
       10.0%
       Forward rate from year one to year two:
       11.0%
       Forward rate from year two to year three:
       9.4%
    c. $1,470.20
14. a. 6.1%
    b. 6.2%
15. a. $39,916.80
    b. $40,195.58
21. Yield on one-year pure-discount bond: 10.0%
    Yield on two-year pure-discount bond: 12.0%
22. 6.2%, $40,495.76
23. $923.36

Chapter   6

1. a. $0.0067
   b. $0.0040
   d. $0.0330
2. 7.1%
9. b. $14.98
10. Expected return: 21.6%
11. $2.03
13. 6.7%

14. 10.2 years
15. a. .234
    b. −30.5%
16. 16.3%

Chapter   7

11. 18.3%
12. 35.0%
13. Expected return: 8.5%
    Standard deviation: 10.1%
14. Expected return: 17.0%
    Standard deviation: 15.4%
17. Covariance: −52.1
    Correlation: −.98
18. Correlation (A,B): .53
    Correlation (A,C): .71
    Correlation (B,C): .21
19. 11.6%
20. Expected return: 5.3%
    Standard deviation: 4.7%
23. a. 34.1%
    b. 25.0%
    c. 9.2%
24. a. 8.8%
    b. 4.7%
    c. Weight in security A: .556
       Weight in security B: .444

Chapter   8

7. Minimum standard deviation: 9.2%
   Maximum standard deviation: 23.3%
9. 12.3%
15. 1.03%
17. 19.7%
18. Portfolio 1 standard deviation: 25.0%
    Portfolio 2 standard deviation: 22.1%
21. 0.80
22. a. 1,325
    b. 152

Chapter   9

4. a. 17.0%
   b. 14.0%
   c. 12.5%
5. Risky portfolio weight: 1.46
6. a. 26.0%
   b. 18.0%
   c. 14.0%
7. 11.0%
14. b. Expected return: 9.0%
       Standard deviation: 10.2%
    c. Expected return: 8.0%
       Standard deviation: 7.7%

Chapter 10

10. $\bar{r}_p = 5.0\% + .39\sigma_p$
12. 15.8%
18. 1.03
19. 25.2%
20. c. Security A expected return: 9.4%
    Security B expected return: 10.8%
21. b. $\beta_1 = 1.50$
    $\beta_2 = 0.60$
23. $\beta_A = 0.74$
    $\beta_B = 1.17$

Chapter 11

6. 82% factor related, 18% nonfactor related
7. a. 1,069.3
   b. 43.8
   c. 33.4%
8. a. 866.1
   b. 35.5
   c. 30.0%
9. 22.4%
10. Standard deviation of security A: 28.9%
    Standard deviation of security B: 26.3%
11. 22.5, 2.25, 0.225
13. 220, 20
15. Sensitivity to factor 1: 0.28
    Sensitivity to factor 2: 4.60
    Sensitivity to factor 3: 0.24
17. Expected return: 15.5%
    Standard deviation: 15.8%
19. Earnings yield factor value: .243%
    Book-price factor value: 4.286%
20. Security A standard deviation: 64.8%
    Security B standard deviation: 30.2%
    Covariance (A,B): 1,936.5

Chapter 12

5. Weight of security B: $-.10$
   Weight of security C: $-.10$
9. 26.0%
11. $r_f = 5.0\%$
13. 13.6%
14. a. $b_{p1} = 0.0$
       $b_{p2} = 0.5$
    b. $b_{p1} = 0.0$
       $b_{p2} = 1.0$
    c. 17.0%
    d. 7.0%
15. a. Weight of security A: $-.043$
       Weight of security B: $-.019$
       Weight of security C: .012
    b. 0.3%
20. a. $\beta_A = 0.65$
       $\beta_B = 1.02$

b. Security A expected return: 9.9%
   Security B expected return: 12.1%
21. $\beta_A = 2.08$
    $\beta_B = 1.56$

Chapter 13

3. Preferred stock after-tax return: 6.2%
   Corporate bond after-tax return: 6.5%
5. $14,122.00
8. a. 6.7%
   b. 8.3%
   c. 9.0%
9. Municipal bond tax-equivalent yield: 7.1%
10. Tax bill if:
    Gain is long-term: $23,203.00
    Gain is short-term: $23,528.50
    Gain is half short-term, half long-term:
    $23,203.00
11. $23,203.00
12. a. 6.1%
    b. 23.5%
    c. 29.6%
14. a. 20.0%
    b. 13.4%
    c. 7.4%
15. Arithmetic average inflation rate:
    1926–1933: -3.7%
    1934–1952: 3.9%
    1953–1965: 1.4%
    1966–1981: 7.1%
    1982–1993: 3.8%
16. a. $0.78
    b. $0.62
    c. $0.50
17. $20,286.85
18. 8.1%
20. Nominal value triples in 12.8 years
    Real value triples in 29.5 years

Chapter 14

1. 16.9%
2. a. 13.0%
   b. 13.6%
10. 12.8%
19. Corporate bond after-tax return: 6.3%
24. a. 14.9%
    b. 10.4%

Chapter 15

1. Bond's intrinsic value: $937.82
2. Bond's intrinsic value: $9,358.16
3. a. $9,366.03
   b. 12.0%

4. Change in five-year bond's price: -7.6%
Change in ten-year bond's price: -12.3%
6. 107 basis points
7. a. 9.0%
b. 12.5%
8. 12.9%
9. Actual yield with 15% reinvestment: 9.7%
Actual yield with 0% reinvestment: 8.0%
14. 7.6%

Chapter 16

1. $10,000.00, $8,770.68, $12,316.36
2. Price of bond A: $10,912.50
Price of bond B: $10,388.70
3. 5-year bond's price: $713.00
10-year bond's price: $508.30
20-year bond's price: $258.40
4. 4-year bond's price change: -11.7%
15-year bond's price change: -24.6%
5. -7.2%, 8.0%
6. Proportion of 5-year bond's price increase
due to change in present value of principal:
79.1%
Proportion of 20-year bond's price increase
due to change in present value of principal:
42.4%
7. 10% coupon bond's price increase: 14.1%
8% coupon bond's price increase: 14.7%
8. 2.8 years
9. 2.7 years
11. 3.4 years
14. $-.98\%$
21. Overall rate of return: 50.9%

Chapter 17

2. a. 750,001
b. 500,001
c. 1
8. a. 1,380,000, $34.78
b. 1,600,000, $30.00
c. 400,000, $120.00
9. a. 0.05
b. $0.476
c. $74.00
10. a. $6.00
b. $35,310.00
c. $34,050.70
d. $34,050.70
13. 0.67
14. 1.04
15. a. 1.18
b. -0.05
c. 1.45
d. 0.91

17. $308 million
18. a. 1.07
b. 1.39
20. 0.69

Chapter 18

1. $25.82
2. $1,978.10
3. 7.0%
4. a. $6.52
b. 8.0%
5. $80.00
6. $52.00
7. 12.0%
10. $106.83
11. $70.44
12. a. $35.00
b. $46.34
c. 3.13
13. $73.03
15. $44.00
16. 10.60
17. 27.8%
18. 14.53

Chapter 19

2. a. Purchase $400,000 of new equity
b. Sell $400,000 of existing equity
c. No action
7. $D_1 = \$13.0$ million
$D_2 = \$15.7$ million
$D_3 = \$15.3$ million
$D_4 = \$13.6$ million
$D_5 = \$14.4$ million
8. 0.60
18. $4.88
19. $SUE_6 = -0.03$
$SUE_7 = +1.14$
$SUE_8 = +0.77$
$SUE_9 = -0.91$

Chapter 20

5. $815.00
6. $1,130.00
11. $4.87
12. $3.28
13. $5.08
16. .41
17. .40
18. 216 contracts
19. a. 5.4%
b. 5.94

20. $3.13
21. $11.48
23. a. $2.19
27. a. $750.00
    b. $240.00
    c. $900.66

Chapter 21

5. $15,000.00, $0.00
6. a. $1,050.00
   b. $3,050.00
   c. $50.00
12. $4,200.00
13. $5,164,286.00
15. $1.79
16. 4.0%
17. $98.98
19. $20,000.00
21. a. 204
27. −40.0%

Chapter 22

1. $17.60
4. a. $12.45
   b. $11.45
8. 8.0%
11. −1.9%
12. Year 1: 6.6%
    Year 2: 14.8%
    Year 3: −2.1%

Chapter 23

2. a. 1.967
   b. 1.130
   c. 1.478
4. a. $3,000,000
   b. 8.0%
   c. 0%
5. a. 15.0
   b. 18.7

c. 18.7
d. 120.0
7. a. 3.5%
   b. 4.5%
8. 207.6, 215.3
18. ROA = 13.7%
    ROE = 41.1%
19. a. 15.0
    b. $6.00
    c. 5.0
    d. 1.7%
    e. 25.0%

Chapter 24

7. 64.8
8. 51.5
11. 32.1
12. 8.7%

Chapter 25

1. 12.7%
3. −2.6%
4. 18.8%
5. 10.5%
6. 9.4%
7. a. 26.0%
   b. 22.6%
9. 3.1%
10. 40.7%, 43.0%
13. 0.8%
14. 0.05, 0.55, 0.06
19. d. −0.51%
    e. 1.11%
20. 3.50, 8.24, 0.35

Chapter 26

5. 29.6%
6. 56.3%
9. 26.3%
11. 17.0%

INDEX

I

Margin accounts, 25–38
aggregation, 37–38
margin purchases, 26–29, 37–38
actual margin, 26–28
initial margin requirement, 26, 27
maintenance margin, 28
multiple, 37
rate of return, 28–29
short sales, 29–38
Marginal tax rate, 348–49, 352–53
combined state and federal, 360
tax-exempt bonds investment and, 355–56
Margin call, 28
Markdown, 55
Marked to the market, 27
Market(s)
aggregation, 37–38
beating the, 832–36
call, 44
capital, 9
central, 64–65
continuous, 44–45, 100
correlations between, 979
down, 941
efficient, 8, 105–7, 836–37
emerging, 969
foreign, 56–60
for forward exchange, 745–46
fourth, 56, 57–58
futures, 728–35
money, 248–49
order specifications, 22–25
over-the-counter, 54–55
perfect, 263
primary, 2, 73
secondary, 2, 44, 779
security. See Security markets
spot, 770n2
swaps, 901–2
third, 56
3.5, 86n15
up, 941
upstairs dealer, 52
Marketability, bond, 436
Market beta, 632–33
Market capitalization, 71, 967
Market consensus of stock's risk, 694–95
Market discount bonds, 409, 436
Market discount function, 117, 119, 123

Market index futures, 734–35, 751–57
Market indices, 275–76, 335, 832–36, 943
Market-makers, 54, 55, 669–70
Market model, 293, 527
capital asset pricing model and, 274–77
determining tangency portfolio composition with, 255
as example of one-factor model, 298
portfolio analysis and, 206–12, 226–27, 229n17
actual returns and, 211–12
beta, 211, 226
graphical representation of, 209–10
random error terms, 208–9, 210, 229n17
Market neutral strategies, 35–36
Market orders, 23
on NYSE, 48–49
Market portfolio, 264–67, 275, 332
standard deviation of, 269
Market segmentation theory of term structure, 132–33
Market (systematic) risk, 212, 214, 276–77, 445, 938
Market timing, 803–4, 893, 895, 938–42
dummy variable regression, 941–42
quadratic regression, 940–41
Market valuation of risky securities, 144–45
Market value, earnings and, 614–16
Market value per share, 625
Marking to market, 730–31
Markowitz, Harry M., 167–68, 169, 178, 193, 322, 891
Markowitz approach. See Portfolio selection problem
Markowitz model, 220–25
determining composition and location of efficient set, 220–24
determining composition of optimal portfolio, 224–25

Markup, 55
Married put, 687, 704–5
Match Plus, 58
Matrix bond pricing, 449
Maturity date, 384
Maturity (steady-state) stage, 591
Maturity strategy, 127, 128, 130
May Day, 67
Mean shortfall, 179
Mean value, 154–55
Mean-variance approach, 165n2
Mechanistic hypothesis, 653n10
Median of probability distribution, 154
Member firm of NYSE, 45, 85n2
Merger, 556n2
Merrill Lynch, Pierce, Fenner & Smith Inc., 21, 449, 528, 529
Merrill Lynch corporate bond index, 945–46
Microforecasting, 13
Miller, Merton, 611, 620
Mills, Robert H., 443
Misfit risk, 903
Mispriced securities, identification of, 830–32
Mode of probability distribution, 154
"Modern" expectations theory, 140n5
Modern portfolio theory (MPT), 167, 810–11
Modigliani, Franco, 611, 620
Momentum strategy, 845–48, 872
Monday effect, 549
Money market, 9, 248–49
Money market fund, 786–87, 788
Money market instruments, 388–91
bankers acceptances, 390
certificates of deposit (CDs), 385–86, 387, 390
commercial paper, 249, 388–89
Eurodollars, 390
interest rates on, 388, 389
repurchase agreements (repos), 390–91
Money supply announcements, 465

Rebalancing of portfolio, 479
Redemption fee, mutual fund, 784
Red herring, 75
Regional brokerage firm, 21
Regional exchanges, 53–54, 520
Registered market-maker, 54, 55
Registered note, 396
Registered representatives, 21
Registrar, 502
Registration statement, 75
Regression
    dummy variable, 941–42
    multiple, 300
    quadratic, 940–41
    simple, 296, 593
    simple linear, 525, 931
Regulation of security
        markets, 80–82
Reinvestment-rate risk, 233
Relationship investing, 507–8
Relative growth rates of firms'
        earnings, 629–32
Relative strength measures, 872
Relevant risk, 154
Reorganization, 416
Replicating portfolio, 682–83, 686
Repurchase agreements
        (repos), 390–91
Repurchase offer, 505
Repurchases, stock, 508–10, 612–13
Required returns, 594
Reserved stock, 506–10
Residual standard deviation, 525, 527, 528
Resistance level, 868
Resolution Funding
        Corporation, 403
Resource investments, 985
Restricted account, 28
Restricted stock, 511
Retail investors, 11
Retention ratio, 587
Retirement plans, 794
Return(s)
    abnormal, 636–38, 846, 847
    active, 207, 208
    annualizing, 921
    certainty equivalent, 888
    dollar-weighted, 919, 920
    domestic, 970–71
    expected. See Expected
        returns

expected holding-period, 159–62
factor model of security. See
        Factor models
from foreign investing, 969–75
on futures, 737–38
historical, 524
implied, 593, 594, 595
measures of, 918–21
mutual fund
    average returns, 798–801
    calculating, 795–96
    persistence of, 804–6
nominal and real, 366, 367–68
predicted versus actual, 597–98
realized, 435, 480
required, 594
risk and, 8
time-weighted, 919–20
Return-generating processes, 293–94. See also Factor
    models
Return on equity (ROE), 622
Revenue anticipation notes
    (RANs), 409
Revenue bonds, 408
Reverse stock split, 513
Reversing trades, 725, 732–33
Reward for waiting, 268
Reward per unit of risk borne, 268
Reward-to-variability ratio, 935–38, 944
Reward-to-volatility ratio, 934–35, 937–38
Rights, 515, 714–15
    preemptive, 515–16, 714
    voting, 32, 502
Rights offering, 75, 515
Risk
    active, 207, 208
    alternative risk measures, 178–79
    basis, 737
    call, 476
    counterparty, 703, 901
    currency, 969, 970, 976–77
    default, 476
    diversification and, 202, 212–17
        portfolio market risk and, 214, 215
        portfolio total risk and, 212–13, 215

portfolio unique risk and, 214–15
factor, 299, 302
failure to adjust for, 838
foreign and domestic, 972–75
from foreign investing, 969–75
interest-rate, 233
market (systematic), 212, 214, 276–77, 445, 938
misfit, 903
motivation for partitioning of, 277
nonfactor (idiosyncratic), 299–300, 302, 324
non-market, 276–77
political, 969–70
prepayment, on
        participation
        certificates, 403–4
price, 130, 140n8
purchasing-power, 370, 372
reinvestment-rate, 233
relative levels versus
        absolute levels, 447–50
relevant, 154
return and, 8
Safety Rank, 656n40
standard deviation as
        measure of, 177–83
stochastic process, 478
stock
    estimating, from historical
        prices, 693–94
    market consensus of, 694–95
    stylistic, 983
    total, 938
    unique (unsystematic), 212, 277, 938
Risk-adjusted measures of
        performance, 924–38
    comparing, 937–38
    criticisms of, 943–44
    ex post characteristics lines, 927–34, 940, 941, 942, 946
    reward-to-variability ratio, 935–38, 944
    reward-to-volatility ratio, 934–35, 937–38
Risk-averse investor, 170, 173–74, 196, 197
Risk control, mutual funds
        and, 796, 797
Riskfree asset
    defining, 233–34

White knight, 505
Wild card option, 771n17
Wilshire Associates, 835
Wilshire 5000 stock index,
    275–76, 835
"Window dressing," 552
Withdrawal plans for mutual
    funds, 795
Wrap accounts, 41n5, 818n8
Wunsch Auction System, Inc.,
    100

Y

Yankee bonds, 419
Yield
    current, 417
    dividend, 517
    equivalent, 396
Yield curves, 125–26
    downward-sloping, 131
    flat, 131–32
    multiple nonparallel shifts
        in nonhorizontal,
            476–78
    riding, 484–85
    upward-sloping, 127–28,
        132
Yield spreads, 433, 434,
    447–51
    determinants of, 450–51
    economic uncertainty and,
        447–50
Yield structure, 433
Yield-to-call, 140n1, 457n4
Yield-to-maturity
    annualized, 124
    on bond, 425n6, 466
    call provisions and, 434–36
    expected, 157–59, 442
    promised, 157–59, 431, 442
    realized return, 435
    on riskless securities,
        114–16
    on Treasury bonds, 397
    on yield curve, 125–26

Z

Zacks Investment Research,
    639, 655n33
    Icarus Service, 644
Zaraba, 59
Zero-beta capital asset pricing
    model, 283
Zero-beta security market line,
    284
Zero coupon bond, 118, 119
Zero coupon Treasury security
    receipts, 398–400
"Zero factor exposures" of
    arbitrage portfolio,
    324
Zero-growth model, 571–73,
    575, 583–84
Zero-plus tick, 29
Z-score, 453